RECORDS OF SOCIAL AND ECONOMIC HISTORY
NEW SERIES XI

THE EARLY RECORDS OF MEDIEVAL COVENTRY

EDITED AND INTRODUCED BY
PETER R. COSS.

WITH THE HUNDRED ROLLS OF 1280

EDITED AND INTRODUCED BY
TREVOR JOHN

LONDON · *Published for* THE BRITISH ACADEMY
by THE OXFORD UNIVERSITY PRESS

INTRODUCTORY NOTE

As one of the wealthiest towns of provincial England at the end of the fourteenth century, Coventry's social and economic history has a special claim on our attention. Little is known of its origins and early history which have been the subject of some controversy. Dr. Coss's edition of the surviving records, mainly charters, relating to the city in the twelfth and thirteenth centuries, together with the 1280 Hundred Roll (separately edited by Mr. Trevor John), will therefore make available vital source material for the study of medieval urban history. It takes its place as Volume XI of the New Series of Records of Social and Economic History.

D.C.COLEMAN

Chairman
Records of Social and Economic History Committee

CONTENTS

GENERAL INTRODUCTION I: LORDSHIP, GOVERNANCE AND GENERAL HISTORY		xv
GENERAL INTRODUCTION II: PHYSICAL GROWTH, ECONOMY AND SOCIETY		xxx
ILLUSTRATIONS		xliii
CHARTERS OF THE EARLS OF CHESTER:	INTRODUCTION	1
	1–21	
DOCUMENTS BEARING ON THE LORDSHIP AND GOVERNANCE OF COVENTRY:	INTRODUCTION	29
	22–34	
EXTRACTS FROM THE CROWN PLEAS OF THE WARWICKSHIRE EYRES:	INTRODUCTION	47
	35–39	
DEEDS FROM VARIOUS COLLECTIONS:	INTRODUCTION	63
BROADGATE	40–59	67
CHEYLESMORE LANE	60–81	76
PAULINE'S LANE [COW LANE]	82	84
PARK ST./LITTLE PARK ST.	83–133	85
PARK ST./MUCH PARK ST.	134–166	103
DEAD LANE	167–173	115
EARL ST.	174–258	118
GOSFORD ST. (INCLUDING GOSFORD, TOWARDS GOSFORD, OUTSIDE OR BEYOND GOSFORD)	259–354	151
EARL'S MILL LANE	355–359	184
TOWARDS ST. MICHAEL'S CHURCH BAYLEY LANE	360–375	186
TOWARDS HOLY TRINITY, LODELAWE'S LANE [HAY LANE]	376–378	192
SMITHFORD ST. (INCLUDING SMITHFORD, OUTSIDE OR BEYOND SMITHFORD)	379–406	194
SPON, SPON ST.	407–523	205
HILL AND RADFORD MILLS	524–526	247
HILL, HILL ST., TOWARDS HILL	527–552	250
WELL ST.	553–581	260
BISHOP ST.	582–599	272
ST. NICHOLAS ST. (INCLUDING TOWARDS THE CHURCH OF ST. NICHOLAS, TOWARDS RADFORD)	600–631	279
COOK ST., TOWARDS HARNALL	632–640	291
BETWEEN THE BRIDGES (ST. JOHN'S BRIDGES OR THE BURGES)	641–647	295

WEST ORCHARD	648–659	298
MARKET AREA	660–704	303
LOCATION UNCERTAIN	705–715	321
WHITEMORE, AND PARTS NEAR	716–731	326
FIELDS AND CROFTS	732–756	334
ACQUISITIONS OF ROBERT DE STOKE	757–766	345
DEEDS (ABSTRACTS) IN COMBE CARTULARY:	INTRODUCTION 767	352
COVENTRY HUNDRED ROLLS:	INTRODUCTION 768	365
INDEX I: PERSONS AND PLACES		395
INDEX II: SUBJECTS		442

ILLUSTRATIONS

MAPS

I	Coventry in the Thirteenth Century	xliv
II	The County of Coventry, 1841	xlv

PLATES

I	Document No. 29	xlvi
II	Document No. 30a	xlvii

The maps have been drawn by Mr Gary Haley, cartographer in the Faculty of Humanities, Newcastle upon Tyne Polytechnic. I am most grateful to him, and to the Coventry City archivist for permission to photograph documents and to utilize maps in his care.

ACKNOWLEDGEMENTS

The preparation of this volume has involved much work in record repositories over a number of years and I would like to express my gratitude to all those record office staff who have eased my path. I would especially like to thank Dr. Robert Bearman and Miss Mairi Macdonald of the Shakespeare Birthplace Trust, Mrs J. Hampartumian of Lichfield Joint Record Office, Dr. Edith Henderson of Harvard Law Library, Mr. Michael Farr and his staff at Warwick County Record Office, Miss Annette M. Kennett and her staff at the Chester City Record Office and Mr. David Smith Gloucestershire County Archivist. Of a different order of magnitude is my debt to the staff of Coventry City Record Office, in particular the current archivist Mr. David Rimmer, assistant archivist Mr. Michael Hinman and past archivist Mr. Alan Dibben, for considerable and sustained help over a long period. I would like to convey especial thanks to Mr. Rimmer for allowing me access whilst the record office in Hay Lane was undergoing alteration in the summer of 1977. I have also profited from the existence of calendars by other scholars, notably Dr. Bearman's calendar of the Gregory Hood Collection at Stratford-upon-Avon and Miss Diana Greenway's calendar of deeds in the Fuller Collection at the University of London Library. Dr. N. W. Alcock brought numerous deeds to my attention, some of which I would undoubtedly have missed, and for this I am most grateful.

Scholars who have given help and advice particularly during the latter stages of the work include Dr. Paul Brand, Dr. Richard Britnell, Dr. Michael Clanchy, Dr. David Crook, Mr. Kevin Down, Dr. Susan Reynolds and Dr. Simon Lloyd. My work on the Coventry charters of the earls of Chester was greatly aided by a number of scholars: Professor Geoffrey Barraclough who brought several documents to my attention and made many useful observations, Professor R. H. C. Davis who kindly loaned his work on the witnesses to the charters of Earl Ranulf II and gave considerable encouragement, Mrs. Eileen Gooder who kept a watchful eye on my Latin syntax, and Dr. Brian Harris who was generous not only with his transcripts but also his hospitality during my brief stay at Chester.

Two fellow students of medieval Coventry have acted with characteristic generosity. In addition to bringing additional material to my attention Dr. Arthur Gooder has given freely and selflessly of his views on a host of issues during the course of our correspondence. Mrs. Joan C. Lancaster Lewis has been swift to share her work on the Gregory Hood Cartulary and on the Coventry Priory Register which she is currently editing. To both of them I am extremely grateful. I would also like to register my sincere thanks to Mr. Trevor John who, in addition to agreeing to contribute his edition of the Coventry Hundred Rolls for this volume, most generously provided his transcript and index at an early stage which considerably aided the dating of the urban deeds.

My other debts are perennial ones. Professor Rodney Hilton has once again given much guidance during the preparation of the volume in addition to reading and commenting on the typescript during the final stage. The burden of typing and retyping has fallen again on my mother, and the indexes once again on my wife.

For permission to publish documents I am grateful to the trustees of the Berkeley Muniments, to Queen's College Oxford, to the University of London Library and to Harvard Law Library. Deeds from the Middleton Collection, housed at the University of Nottingham, are published by courtesy of Lord Middleton. Small grants from the British Academy have provided essential microfilm and financed several short stays in London, whilst a grant from the Social Science Research Council provided twelve months leave of absence from Newcastle upon Tyne Polytechnic without which the production of the volume would have been considerably delayed.

ABBREVIATED REFERENCES

Annales Cestriensis	*Annales Cestriensis* ed. R. C. Christie, Lancashire and Cheshire Record Society vol. xiv, 1886
Barraclough 'Some Charters of the Earls of Chester'	'Some Charters of the Earls of Chester' in *A Medieval Miscellany for Doris Mary Stenton*, Pipe Roll Society vol. lxxxvi, 1962
Book of Fees	*Liber Feodorum. The book of fees commonly called Testa de Nevill* 3 vols. 1920–31
Book of Seals	*Sir Christopher Hatton's Book of Seals* ed. L. C. Loyd and D. M. Stenton (Oxford, 1950)
B.I.H.R.	*Bulletin of the Institute of Historical Research*
C.A.D.	*A descriptive catalogue of ancient deeds preserved in the Public Record Office*
C.Ch.R.	*Calendar of Charter Rolls*
C.C.R.	*Calendar of Close Rolls*
C.L.R.	*Calendar of Liberate Rolls*
C.I.P.M.	*Calendar of Inquisitions Post Mortem*
C.P.R.	*Calendar of Patent Rolls*
Cal. Papal Letters	*Calendar of Entries in the Papal Registers, relating to Great Britain and Ireland: Letters*
Chartulary of St. Werburgh	*Chartulary of St. Werburgh*, ed. J. Tait, Chetham Society New Series vols. 79, 82
City of Coventry: Archaeology and Development	*City of Coventry: Archaeology and Development* by Margaret Rylatt with historical background by E. and A. Gooder (Coventry, 1977)
Coventry Priory Register	P.R.O. E164/21
Derbyshire Charters	*Descriptive Catalogue of Derbyshire Charters*, ed. I. H. Jeayes, (London, 1906)
D.N.B.	*Dictionary of National Biography*
Early Cheshire Charters	*Facsimiles of Early Cheshire Charters*, ed. G. Barraclough, (Oxford, 1957)
Excerpt. e Rot. Fin.	*Excerpta e Rotulis Finium*, Record Commission 1835–6
Eyre Rolls 1221	*Rolls of the Justices in Eyre for Gloucestershire, Warwickshire and Staffordshire 1221–1222*, ed. D. M. Stenton, Selden Society, 1940
Eyre Rolls 1232, 1247 etc.	Warwickshire Eyre Rolls P.R.O. JI 951–961
Farrer, *H.K.F.*	W. Farrer, *Honors and Knights' Fees* vol. II (London, 1924)
F.F. Warwicks	*Warwickshire Feet of Fines* vols. I & II, ed. Ethel Stokes *et al.* Dugdale Society Main Series vols. XI, XV (1932, 1939)
Feudal Aids	*Inquisitions and Assessments relating to Feudal Aids*
G.E.C.	*Complete Peerage*, ed. G. E. Cokayne, revised by V. Gibbs and others, 1910–1957
Handbook of British Chronology	*Handbook of British Chronology*, ed. Sir Maurice Powicke and E. B. Fryde, 2nd edn. 1961

Lancashire Pipe Rolls	*Lancashire Pipe Rolls*, ed. W. Farrer (Liverpool, 1902)
Langley Cartulary	*The Langley Cartulary*, ed. P. R. Coss, Dugdale Society Main Series vol. XXXII (1980)
Lincs. Final Concords	*Lincolnshire Final Concords*, vol. I, ed. W. O. Massingberd, (London, 1896); vol. II, ed. C. W. Foster (Lincoln Record Society, 1920)
Magnum Registrum Album	*Magnum Registrum Album*, ed. H. E. Savage, William Salt Archaeological Society vol. xlviii, 1924
Monasticon	Sir William Dugdale, *Monasticon Anglicanum*, new edn. by Caley, Ellis and Bandinel, 1817–1830
Ormerod, *Cheshire*	G. Ormerod, *The History of the County Palatine and City of Chester*, 3 vols., 2nd edn. by T. Helsby, 1882
Pipe Rolls (followed by regnal year)	*The Great Rolls of the Pipe*, published by the Pipe Roll Society
Registrum Antiquissimum	*Registrum Antiquissimum of the Cathedral Church of Lincoln*, vols. I, II, ed. C. W. Foster, Lincoln Record Society vols. 27–28
Rot. Lit. Claus.	*Rotuli litterarum clausarum in turri Londinensi asservati*, ed. T. Duffus Hardy, 2 vols., Record Commission 1833–4
Rot. Cur. Regis	*Rotuli curiae regis*, ed. Sir Francis Palgrave, 2 vols., Record Commission 1835
Stenton, *Documents Illustrative of the Danelaw*	*Documents Illustrative of the Social and Economic History of the Danelaw*, ed. F. M. Stenton, British Academy Records of Social and Economic History, (London, 1920)
Tout, *Chapters*	T. F. Tout, *Chapters in the Administrative History of Medieval England*, 6 vols. (Manchester, 1920–1933)
V.C.H. Warwicks, Stafford, Derby, Cheshire, Northants	*The Victoria History of the Counties of England*, (London, 1900–)
V.C.H. Coventry	*Victoria County History of Warwickshire vol. VIII: The City of Coventry and Borough of Warwick*, ed. W. B. Stephens, (London, 1969)
Record Repositories:	
C.R.O.	Coventry City Record Office
W.R.O.	Warwick County Record Office
L.R.O.	Leicestershire Record Office
P.R.O.	Public Record Office, London
S.B.T.	Shakespeare Birthplace Trust, Stratford-upon-Avon
B.L.	British Library, British Museum London

METHOD OF EDITING

The charters of the earls of Chester and the documents bearing on the governance of Coventry (Nos. 1–34) have been rendered in full as has the survey of 1280 (No. 768). The remainder of the volume has been calendared, except where documents are not in common form. Every effort has been made, however, to include the maximum information. In only two circumstances has [etc.] been employed, viz. freely [etc.] for *libere quiete bene et in pace* and variants, and for all secular services [etc.] for *pro omni servicio seculari exactione vel demanda* and variants. All details of properties and their locations have been included, with original readings italicized in brackets to avoid any possible ambiguity. The original readings of all streets and place names have been included with two exceptions. The form of Coventry is given only in cases where this deviates from the standard *Coventre* and *Covintre* or contractions thereof. In the Combe abstracts the form *Cumba* (or *Cumb'*) is invariable and has not been rendered. Messuage translates *messuagium* unless otherwise stated. Where surnames and descriptions of occupation are in Latin, these have been translated with the original rendering italicized in brackets. Again there are a few exceptions, *viz* clerk, coroner and bailiff (unless qualified in some manner other than 'bailiff of Coventry'). English and French forms of names have been left in the original.

Where a clause is unusual, of particular interest or doubtful in meaning it has been rendered in full in italics. Individual words or phrases have been italicized and bracketed following their translation where appropriate to avoid any possible ambiguity. Insertions in the text, for example to complete the sense, have been inserted in square brackets. Round brackets have been employed in other circumstances. Where the text is rendered wholly or partially in the original the following principles have been adopted. The use of i and j has been modernized, as has that of u and v wherever possible; c and t have been rendered as in the original text. The ampersand has been replaced by *et*. The several symbols employed for the thorn have been rendered þ. The use of capitals has been standardized in line with modern convention, except in the case of titles and positions e.g. Hugh Earl of Chester, Robert abbot of Alcester, which have been rendered as in the original. A modest degree of punctuation has been introduced. Abbreviations have been expanded wherever possible, but no attempt has been made to expand the suspended form of place-names.

In general only medieval endorsements have been noted, and these only where they convey information additional to the text. With the exception of the original charters among Nos. 1–34 seals have not been described. Their survival or otherwise, however, has been noted.

INTRODUCTION

I. LORDSHIP, GOVERNANCE AND GENERAL HISTORY

A monastery was founded at Coventry c.1043 on the slopes of a small hill overlooking the River Sherbourne.[1] In 1086 it lay at the heart of a group of estates once in the hands of various members of the Leofric family. Those of the late Countess Godiva were now held of the king at farm. They included a manor of five hides with extensive woodland at Coventry itself, but there is no mention of an urban community. Recently, however, Professor R. H. C. Davis has postulated the existence of an eleventh-century town which he believes was omitted, like a number of others, from the Domesday Survey.[2] There is no direct evidence of this and the suggestion has not yet received archaeological support.[3] There is, however, some indirect evidence. By 1102 at the latest, and perhaps as early as 1095, Bishop Robert de Limesey had removed his see from Chester to Coventry.[4] He obtained papal permission for the move and custody of the abbey from the crown. Henceforth the bishops were to be titular abbots and a prior the active head of the community. According to William of Malmesbury Robert made the move in order to appropriate the wealth of the monastery and he proceeds to chronicle the bishop's subsequent depredations. It may well be that the move had at least as much to do with the turbulent state of Cheshire. In either case, given the strong Norman preference for locating episcopal sees in towns rather than villages, it seems hardly likely that Robert could have contemplated this move unless Coventry were already a town of some importance, or, at the very least, an embryonic urban community which could be fostered and developed.

But fostered by whom? The date of origin and the extent of ecclesiastical jurisdiction within Coventry have occasioned much debate in recent years.[5] It has generally

[1] For the evidence of the date and for some discussion of the monastery's endowment and early estates see Joan C. Lancaster Lewis (née Lancaster), 'The Coventry Forged Charters: A Reconsideration' *B.I.H.R.* xxvii (1954), pp. 115, 130–133, and the same author's *Godiva of Coventry* (Coventry, 1967) chs. iv–v.

[2] R. H. C. Davis, *The Early History of Coventry*, Dugdale Society Occasional Papers No. 24, (Oxford, 1976), pp. 16–19.

[3] Excavation at Broadgate in 1974 revealed no evidence of pre-conquest domestic occupation. There were, however, problems associated with the particular site. See *City of Coventry: Archaeology and Development* pp. 30–31. It may well be, of course, that this is not the correct location. See below p. xxx.

[4] For the details of what follows see Davis, *op. cit.* pp. 16–17, Lancaster Lewis 'Coventry Forged Charters' pp. 134–135 and P. Heath, 'The Medieval Church' in *V.C.H. Stafford* iii (London, 1970), pp. 7–8. Sources from Coventry (13th century) and Lichfield (14th century) indicate that Robert took possession of the abbey following the death of Abbot Leofwine in 1095. The Annals of Winton, on the other hand, say that he acquired the abbey from Henry I in 1100. Papal approval was granted in April 1102.

[5] For divergent views on the lordship and governance of early Coventry see the following: J. C. Lancaster Lewis, 'The Coventry Forged Charters: A Reconsideration', pp. 113–139, and *Historic Towns: Coventry* (London, 1974), pp. 1–6; A. A. Dibben, *Coventry City Charters*, (*Coventry Papers No. 2*, 1969), espec. pp. 16–17; P. R. Coss, 'Coventry before Incorporation: A Reinterpretation' *Midland History* ii, 1974, pp. 137–151; R. H. C. Davis, 'An Unknown Coventry Charter', *English Historical Review*, vol. lxxxvi, No. 340, (1971) pp. 539–545, and *The Early History of Coventry, passim*; A. and E. Gooder, 'Coventry before 1355: Unity or Division?' *Midland History* vol. vi, (1981), pp. 1–38. *Medieval Coventry – A City Divided?* (Coventry and Warwickshire Pamphlets No. 11, 1981), based on a symposium held at Coventry in 1979, contains a summary of the foregoing views.

been agreed, however, that the monastic lordship, whether envisaged as half of Coventry held in barony or as a soke within the earl of Chester's seigneury, was created by means of the priory's forged foundation charters and from within the lands formerly bestowed on the earls. Both propositions may be unfounded; indeed it is possible that the forged charters have been allowed to loom too large in the debate on Coventry's early history. Assuming the existence of a small urban community in the eleventh century, it does not necessarily follow that this was conveyed, *in toto* or even in part, to the earl of Chester. It is sometimes overlooked that the date when the earls came to Coventry is itself unknown. James Tait suggested that Godiva's lands may have been given to Earl Hugh I in recompense for his support of William Rufus in the rebellion of 1088. The evidence he adduced for this was unsound, but his instinct may well have been correct.[6] There is, in fact, stronger evidence which has been overlooked to indicate that Godiva's lands were indeed acquired at some point by Earl Hugh. One of them, Atherstone near Nuneaton, was to pass into the hands of the monks of Bec, conveyed according to a confirmation charter of Henry II by Hugh earl of Chester. Hugh, moreover, had strong associations with this house. In 1092 the abbot, Anselm, came to Chester on the earl's invitation to supervise the transformation of its church of secular canons into a Benedictine abbey.[7] The first monks of St. Werburgh's appear, therefore, to have been derived from Bec. Godiva's lands, then, must surely have passed to the earls of Chester some time before the death of Hugh I in 1101. It does not follow from this, however, that this earl held sole lordship over a small urban community. Indeed there is nothing other than probability to argue for the existence of the earl's burgesses before the time of Earl Ranulf I, 1120–1129 (11).

There are, however, some indications of the existence of an ecclesiastical lordship during the first half of the twelfth century. One clue may lie in the charter of Henry II to Bishop Walter Durdent in 1155.[8] This confirmed his liberties and customs *infra burgum et extra* (an undoubted reference to Coventry) with seignorial rights and a court (*hallemote*) in all his lands, as fully as his church held them in the time of Edward the Confessor and Earl Leofric and as the charter of Henry I testifies that Bishop Robert substantiated his claim in the king's court at Portsmouth. This, as Mrs. Lancaster Lewis has argued, was most probably Robert de Limesey, although it might conceivably have been Robert Peche.[9] Always supposing the allusion to be genuine, the events at Portsmouth may well have been occasioned by the advent of the earls of Chester. It would be dangerous to place too much reliance on this last point, however, for Durdent's quarrel lay not with the earl of Chester, as we shall see, but with Prior Lawrence. There are signs here of an attempt to accommodate the forgeries, and there can be little doubt that the charter is referring to monastic lands.

[6] 'An Alleged Charter of William the Conqueror', in *Essays in History presented to R. L. Poole*, ed. H. W. C. Davis (Oxford, 1927), p. 162. The argument here rests on the identification of 'Kerile' with Keresley, north of Coventry. According to a source quoted by Dugdale, Abbot Leofwine was said to have received this from Earl Hugh in exchange for Eyton-on-Dee (*Monasticon* iii, p. 182). In fact there is no evidence other than the forged foundation charters to suggest that the monks ever held Eyton-on-Dee, whilst Keresley, undocumented before the mid-twelfth century, did not come into the monastery's sphere of interest until the Montalt grant of 1249.

[7] *Monasticon* vi, p. 1068; *V. C. H. Cheshire* iii, ed. B. E. Harris (Oxford, 1980), p. 133. For Atherstone see also M. Chibnall, *Select Documents of the English Lands of the Abbey of Bec* (Camden Soc. 3rd ser. lxxiii) esp. p. 26.

[8] *Magnum Registrum Album* No. 18; Davis, 'An Unknown Coventry Charter' p. 542 n.2.

[9] 'Coventry Forged Charters' pp. 135–136; The years when Henry I is known to have been at Portsmouth are 1107, 1111 and 1116 in the time of Limesey, and 1123 in the time of Peche (see *Regesta Regum Anglo-Normannorum* ii, 1100–1135, ed. Charles Johnson and H. A. Cronne, Oxford, 1956).

A second clue lies in Innocent II's confirmation of the provision Bishop Roger de Clinton made for the monks of Coventry out of the priory's lands, in April 1139.[10] These included half the rental (*dimidium census*) of Coventry together with the church of Holy Trinity there. There are two possible interpretations of this. Either the bishop was retaining half of the income from Coventry himself, and allowing the remainder to the monks, or the church enjoyed half of the entire Coventry rents. On the face of it the former is the more likely, although it is just possible that the bishop and the earl had earlier agreed a division of the rents.[11] If the bishop had, indeed, retained half the monastic rent it must soon have been returned for there is no evidence of Coventry rents in the hands of the bishop later in the century.[12] In either case these rents seem likely to have been extensive and compact. The inclusion of the church with them is indicative. Holy Trinity may have originated between 1101 and 1113, although the evidence is once again ambiguous, but it must surely have been founded for the use of the priory's tenants.[13] It did after all become the parish church serving the northern part of the town, in contrast to the earl's old chapel of St. Michael which served the south. (below p. xxii). With tenants came courts. In short, an ecclesiastical lordship surely existed in Coventry during the first half of the twelfth century.

How had this arisen? Coventry may have passed from the crown to the earls of Chester as a single lordship, as has been generally believed since the priory's foundation charters were proven to be forgeries. In this case the church may have continued to hold some rents, and perhaps successfully retained them following a claim made before the king at Portsmouth. It is possible, however, that a small town which had been growing up in very close proximity to the abbey since its foundation was subsequently regarded as belonging to the monastery.[14] If this were indeed the case the earl's introduction of burgage tenure on the erstwhile Domesday manor was secondary to the original urban nucleus immediately to his north.

The role of the forged foundation charters remains to be considered. It now seems beyond doubt that these belong to the reign of Stephen.[15] It does not follow, however, that the priory's jurisdiction postdates them. Forgeries can be made equally in the interests of preserving liberties as in creating them, as a much later set of priory forgeries clearly shows (below pp. 2–3). If, indeed, the charters were produced towards the end of Stephen's reign and after hostilities in this area, as seems most likely, then it might well be argued that they were intended to forestall any further encroachment along the lines Ranulf II had indulged in. Since he appears to have deprived

[10] *Magnum Registrum Album* No. 454. The full text is given in W. Holtzmann, *Papsturkunden in England* vol. ii (Berlin, 1935), pp. 157–158.

[11] For what it is worth the rent rolls from the two 'halves' at a later date were not dissimilar. At Michaelmas 1233 William Rufus accounted to the Treasurer, Peter des Rivaux, for £22 6s. 1½d. rent of assize from the 'Earl's half', together with £13 5s. 1d. from pleas, perquisites, and the sale of cider (P.R.O. SC 6 Bundle 1,117 No. 13). The fixed rent due to the priory in 1195 had amounted to £15 for ¾ of a year (below note 12).

[12] When the estates of the bishopric and the priory were both in the king's hands through the forfeiture of Bishop Hugh de Nonant, the custodian accounted for them separately at Michaelmas 1195. Coventry rents figure only for the priory (*Pipe Roll 7 Richard I* pp. 57–58).

[13] Continental bede-rolls designate the abbey as the church of St. Mary in 1101 but as Holy Trinity and St. Mary in 1113 and 1122 (Sir Alfred Clapham, 'Three Bede Rolls'. *Archaeological Journal* vol. cvi supplement, 1952, pp. 43–53). The most obvious interpretation of this is that the abbey had been rededicated, but if so it did not persist. The new *titulus* may reflect the appearance of a new church alongside St. Mary's earlier in the 12th century (Lancaster Lewis, 'Coventry Forged Charters' pp. 137–138; Davis, 'An Unknown Coventry Charter' p. 542.

In the case of the other estates reserved to the use of the priory by Roger de Clinton, their churches and tithes had been assigned as prebends for the canons of Lichfield.

[14] For a possible location of the earliest settlement see below p. xxx.

[15] See 'An Unknown Coventry Charter' pp. 543–544 and the references given there.

the monastery of the chapels in his fee, he may equally have treated the monks' tenants as his own. It is possible that he granted a charter to the entire burgess community to emphasize this, and it may also be reflected in his charter granting Coventry to Robert Marmion (1, 11). However, the central purpose of the foundation charters was not to protect the church's position in Coventry vis-à-vis the earl, let alone to create it, but rather to secure freedom from episcopal control.[16] Indeed, Professor Davis has pointed out that the earlier copies of 'Leofric's' foundation charter do not include half of Coventry in the endowment, which is found rather in 'the Confessor's' confirmation.[17] If the main thrust of the charters had been to secure half of the town then the textural discrepancy, curious at best, becomes inexplicable.

In fact, freedom from episcopal authority is the main theme and it runs throughout.[18] To understand this it is necessary to consider further the behaviour of Bishop Roger de Clinton. His interests were centred on Lichfield whose chapter he reorganized during the 1130s, creating new prebendaries for the canons from the churches belonging to Coventry priory.[19] He acquired papal confirmation of his arrangements, and this was repeated by Lucius II in 1144.[20] As a result Coventry Priory, and its prior, were placed in a very subservient position. Thus Roger's death on crusade in April 1148 must have seemed to Prior Lawrence a heaven-sent opportunity. There followed the first recorded canonical election of a bishop in this see, and the first in a long series of disputes between the chapters of Coventry and Lichfield.[21] The man elected was Walter Durdent, prior of Christ Church Canterbury, and in reality probably Archbishop Theobald's nominee. According to an early 13th-century source emanating from Coventry Priory the Lichfield canons disputed his election forcing Prior Lawrence to journey to Rome to have their appeal quashed.[22] His consecration was in fact delayed until October 1149. It has often been said that Durdent, himself a Benedictine, is likely to have been sympathetic towards the monks and may, indeed, have winked at their forged charters. In fact, the same Coventry source says that Walter brought many evils to the monks and that he and Lawrence were called to Rome, where they were reconciled in the presence of the pope. The result was an agreement, on 14 February 1152, which overturned that of 1139.[23] It was reaffirmed that the monks should remain under the bishop's obedience, but it was declared unlawful for any future bishop to abstract the possessions bestowed on the monks by Earl Leofric. Anything contrary to this in the privileges of Innocent II and Lucius II was declared invalid. Stephen's charter to Prior Lawrence and the monks granting the lands and tenures they held in the time of King Edward and King William would seem to follow this, for it includes four estates said to have been recently recovered by the precept of Eugenius III.[24] The latter refers to Earl Leofric, the royal charter to King Edward. Undoubtedly they follow hard upon the forged foundation charters which were at the heart of the contention between Walter and Lawrence. In 1155 both men acquired confirmations

[16] For discussion of the chartes and details of their contents see Lancaster Lewis, 'Coventry Forged Charters' *passim*, and Davis, 'An Unknown Coventry Charter' pp. 539–541.

[17] *loc.cit.* 'Leofric's' text was later brought into line.

[18] This is not to deny that the recent behaviour of the earl of Chester may have been a subsidiary consideration. The doctored writ of William I which purports to grant exemption from castle work was probably aimed at the earl (Tait, 'An Alleged Charter of William I' pp. 164–166).

[19] Heath *op. cit.* p. 141.

[20] *Magnum Registrum Album* No. 455.

[21] For a judicious account of these elections which tests the relative reliability of the Coventry and Lichfield sources see Heath *op. cit.* pp. 8–14.

[22] *Monasticon VI*, iii p. 1242.

[23] *ibid.*, *Magnum Registrum Album* No. 262.

[24] The text is printed in *Regesta Regum Anglo-Normanorum* iii, ed. H. A. Cronne and R. H. C. Davis (Oxford, 1968), No. 246, where it is assigned to 1145–53.

from Henry II as they continued jockeying for position.[25] Meanwhile Lawrence had acquired a deathbed restoration from Ranulf II of St. Michael's and its appurtenant chapels in the Coventry area. In the end he had succeeded in recovering for his church the control of its own estates, including rent and authority in Coventry, even if he failed to secure full freedom from episcopal control. The forged foundation charters, belonging most probably to 1148–1152, undoubtedly played a major part in this. It does not seem likely that they created a lordship, or even a soke, where none had existed before.

Towards the end of the life of the redoubtable Prior Lawrence the 'Earl's half' and the 'Prior's half' of Coventry emerge into the light of day. The Pipe Roll of 1175 records that the earl of Chester's men of Coventry and the prior's men of the same town each paid 10 marks separately for concealing the lands of the king's enemies. In 1180 the 'Earl's part' (*pars*) of the town paid 10 marks because it denied what it subsequently recognized, and the 'Earl's part' and the 'Prior's part' appear again three years later.[26] Problems arise, however, when we try to understand precisely how the town was administered. The Pipe Roll of 1184 records a fine paid by the township (*villata*) of Coventry for a judicial misdemeanour. Professor Davis believes that this refers to action by the portmoot established by Ranulf II, the 'Prior's half' being in the nature of a soke whose sokemoot coexisted with the portmoot functioning for the entire town.[27] The logic of the forged foundation charters, however, is that the 'Prior's half' was held of the crown in chief and this was certainly accepted as the case in 1280. Ranulf III's charter of c.1199–1204, which presumably superseded the charter presented for royal confirmation in 1182, was granted to 'his burgesses of Coventry'. It is hard to see how this can have applied to any but his own tenants.

The two jurisdictions are revealed a little more clearly in the 13th century. The presenting jury at the Warwickshire eyre held in the summer of 1232 was elected by the prior's bailiff William son of Simon and the earl's bailiff Richard de Aula. They each chose five men, drawn undoubtedly from their respective bailiwicks, who were then sworn with themselves as the jury. The twelve were all prominent townsmen and it could well be that their position on the jury reflects their ordinary status in the town courts. Working backwards from 1232 through the deeds of the previous 30 years we can begin to grasp something of the local administration. Richard de Aula figures prominently as the first witness in deeds relating to property in the 'Earl's half' a position which must surely reflect his role as bailiff, even though no designation is given. On one occasion Richard's clerk appears (420). Figuring in the same way, and for the most part a little earlier, is Richard of Worcester (*de Wigornia*). Both men belong to families which, judging from the charters, had been associated over a long period of time with both this and the previous earl. Worcester may have been succeeded by Richard de Aula c.1220 but one need not necessarily envisage a single bailiff operating solely for years at a time. The administration may

25 The charter to Prior Lawrence, in essence a reaffirmation of Stephen's, is unprinted. The text may be found in: P.R.O. Chart. Roll 22 EIII m5; B.L. Add. MS. 32100 fo.57v; *Gregory Leger Book*, S.B.T. DR 10/1406 fo.28. For the charter to Durdent see above note 8. R. W. Eyton, *Court, Household and Itinerary of King Henry II* (London, 1878), shows that both should be assigned to 1155.

The four manors specified in Stephen's charter included two, Chadshunt and Itchington, which the pope had specifically confirmed to the bishop in 1152. That the precept referred to by Stephen was an earlier instrument of Eugenius III is unlikely. In all probability the prior was attempting to interpret the 1152 agreement in his favour, taking his stand on the later clauses which forbade future bishops from taking the possessions bestowed on the monks by their founder and invalidated the arrangements confirmed by Innocent II. The later history of these manors shows Chadshunt and Itchington to have remained with the bishop, Southam and Ufton to have remained with the priory (*V.C.H. Warwicks.* v, p. 31; vi, pp. 122, 221, 245).

26 *Pipe Rolls 21 Henry II* p. 9; *26 Henry II* p. 102; *29 Henry II* p. 38.

27 *The Early History of Coventry* pp. 12–14; *Pipe Roll 30 Henry II* pp. 47–8.

already have been more complex than this. Other prominent witnesses, such as Hugh son of Martin, Vincent, and Gerard the Vintner, were similarly associated with the earl and may also have enjoyed some ministerial function. Ranulf III's charter confirmed the role of his bailiff as an officer of the portmoot and we surely see him in operation here. There is nothing to suggest that he is an elected official; moreover his position in the charter as against that of the *justicia* (and whom he may well have been intended to by-pass or eclipse) suggests otherwise. Whether or not the elected *justicia* of the royal confirmation of 1182 actually functioned is impossible to say without the aid of court rolls. However, it is important not to exaggerate the degree of communal organization among the burgesses at this date or their degree of independence from the earl's administration. The account of the royal custodian in 1233 shows that they did not have the borough at farm.[28] The exercise of power by the earls of Chester in this region has been misunderstood. There are many indications that their lordship was an active one. They were in a very real sense lords of the soil. Land and rents both within the town and in the surrounding area were granted to their officials and supporters. Access to the woodlands and assarting from the wastes were strictly controlled.[29] Legal records reveal the activities of the earl's stewards in relation to both free and villein land.[30] Other comital courts functioned in addition to the portmoot. Between c.1210 and c.1215 a Coventry lady abjured her right to a tenement 'before the court of the earl' (29). Whether or no this is the portmoot, and it may well have been, it is certainly an indication of the earl's authority. Property transactions in surrounding vills were also brought to a court some of whose personnel were very similar to those of the court recording transactions within the city.[31] How heavily the earl's lordship was felt by the burgesses it is difficult to say. He certainly appears to have taken regular aids from them, although this would seem to have been recouped from their own tenants (534). There was also a seignorial monopoly in the sale of cider.[32] References to the castle bakehouse and the earl's mill may be indicative too.[33]

The prior's administration is also revealed, but less clearly, for there are comparatively few deeds for the northern part of the town at this date. William the reeve who appears in the early 1230s is probably synonymous with William son of Simon of 1232. Another reeve during the 1230s was John son of William Humphrey. Judging by his position in the witness lists John's father, William son of Humphrey, was an earlier reeve and so probably was Matthew son of Roger. Others who carry the surnames of later ministers are already prominent in the deeds suggesting they exercised official functions. William de Hecham who makes a fleeting appearance as bailiff of the lord prior c.1215–c.1225 may perhaps have been a figure of wider significance (706). The early deeds, then, are supportive of a territorial division between the lords. The operation of a separate priory court is put on a more solid foundation by two transactions during the early–mid 1240s with the rising local lawyer Richard son of Richard Ernis. By the first of these Richard surrendered to the priory all his land and rents within Coventry and its immediate vicinity. By the second transaction he received property at Sowe, to be held by the same liberty as he had held in chief of their fee within the vill of Coventry except that he need no longer make suit to their fortnightly court as all others do save when he is required for the afforcement of their court (30 a & b).

[28] See above note 11.

[29] See for example below pp. 9–10.

[30] Four are known by name viz. William the Marshal, Nicholas son of Alan, Walter de Coventry and Walter d'Eyvill.

[31] For example at nearby Stoke. One Stoke deed is, in fact, witnessed by Simon the earl's clerk (Fuller II/16/3).

[32] See above note 11.

[33] See below p. 31.

The problem of the interlocking of these courts remains. Was there a court of the entire community? One interesting possibility which has been canvassed is that the entire town was represented at a twice-yearly court leet of the earls of Chester.[34] It was undoubtedly at a later Michaelmas leet that the assize of bread and ale was published with some local trading regulations in October 1278. These included matters relating to public health such as ensuring an uncontaminated water supply (31). This belongs, however, to a time when both jurisdictions were in the prior's hands and the view of frankpledge which he enjoyed by right of both lordships could be held as a single occasion. Unfortunately it is not at all clear at which dates a single view may have been in the hands of the earl of Chester and his successors before 1249. In 1189 Bishop Hugh de Nonant had secured quittance from shire and hundred courts with the probable effect of replacing the sheriff's twice-yearly tourn with a private court for his tenants.[35] Whether or not the lands restored to the priory after his death retained such quittance is unknown but in 1227 the priory received a similar grant with specified freedom from view of frankpledge.[36] Almost certainly from 1227, if not before, both jurisdictions enjoyed their own court leets. And yet regulations affecting the entire borough community must have been as necessary now as later.

In 1280 it was stated that the prior had in addition to his frankpledge court other free courts of the entire town at 8 days reasonable summons. There are unmistakable signs in the early deeds that a court over and above the two jurisdictions existed in the time of Ranulf III. There are numerous occasions when we find both comital and priory officials, and other prominent townsmen of the two halves, witnessing together. Most often this is where property transactions concerning the market area are involved, but not exclusively so. Another occasion concerned the sale of land at the quarry towards the church of St. Nicholas (604). It would seem that transactions involving shared or valued resources should be registered at a more representative gathering.

This may have been an entirely separate occasion, court leet or otherwise, or it may have been made possible by the courts of the two jurisdictions sitting simultaneously. This same court may have dealt with market or trading offences although it is clear enough from the 1280 survey that both lords had enjoyed fines for the infringement of the assizes of bread and ale. Both enjoyed annual fairs (under royal grants of 1218 and 1227 respectively).[37] Similarly each lord must have dealt with the criminal offences of their own tenants for each had gallows, pillory and cucking-stool. Roger de Montalt had his own prison (36.19). Matters must have been more complicated where minor civil actions were brought across the jurisdictions, and with the development of a brisk traffic in urban realty many townsmen must have ceased to be the exclusive tenant of prior or earl. No doubt regular procedures were devised for dealing with all such matters.

Joint jurisdiction over the market area creates a major difficulty when attempting to plot the boundary between the two fees with reference to the ministerial and other regular witnesses in the deeds. During the late 1220s, or the early 1230s at the latest, this joint administration ceased and the market area came within the jurisdiction of the prior's court. It may well be that the crucial date was 1227 when the prior acquired his own view of frankpledge. It is probable, but difficult to be certain, that the market had always lain on monastic land. When West Orchard comes properly into view it, too, was within the 'Prior's half'. There is some ambiguity in the early deeds relating to the area of Hill. From the 1230s onwards, however, the boundary clearly corresponds at least in essentials to that indicated in the forged charter of

[34] A. and E. Gooder, 'Coventry Before 1355: Unity or Division?' pp. 8, 24.

[35] *Magnum Registrum Album* No. 22; *V.C.H. Stafford* vol. iii, p. 17.

[36] *C.Ch.R.* i, p. 6.

[37] *Rot. Lit. Claus.* i, p. 351, ii, p. 171.

Earl Hugh II (see below pp. 1–2) and to the parish bounds as recorded in later times.[38]

The jurisdictions of the two major lords, however, was not the only cause of complexity. There were many other private courts in Coventry. Those local landowners, ministers and associates of the earl with rents in the town would have been inclined to operate their own courts for their tenants. The burgesses themselves did likewise. In 1280 it was stated that in association with the town courts the burgesses held courts for their own free tenants. Their existence can be illustrated from the deeds. When during the 1280s Roger de Birdingbury surrendered a tenement to his tenant Alexander the Vintner he included escheats, courts, pannages and tolls. When Alexander subsequently leased part of this property it was for rent with suit of court as necessary (113, 115, 116). Similarly, in what appears to have been a general reorganization of his rents in 1301, Sir John de Langley leased several tenements for rents plus suit to his court of Coventry by reasonable summons when it needs to be held (*quando eam teneri contigerit*) (241, 332, 402). How these operated we have no means of knowing. Did Langley's Coventry tenants attend a court at nearby Shortley? What we can be sure of is that these matters would have been generally regulated. Sir Nicholas de Segrave leased a messuage in Cheylesmore Lane for 12d. *per annum* for all demands except suit of his court 'according to the custom of the vill of Coventry'. No doubt these private courts were on the wane when, during the second half of the century, they are revealed in the deeds. They are likely to have flourished more in the time of the earls of Chester.[39]

During the time between the death of Ranulf III in 1232 and the prior's purchase of the Montalt lordship in 1249 the courts and their bailiffs seem to have functioned for the most part much as before. The designation 'reeve' (and later 'bailiff') came to be used increasingly frequently, though by no means regularly. One major new development seems to have occurred, however, during the mid 1240s. The kalendar of the 1247 Warwickshire eyre roll gives Coventry's 12 jurors and the chief bailiff Robert de Corley. The normal procedure for electing a presenting jury at this date was for the bailiff to nominate two electors who then chose another ten to sit with them. One might have considered the chief bailiff to have been brought into being solely for the purposes of the eyre but for several important considerations. When we look closely at the jurors we find that the first and seventh names are those of Osbert Durdent and Richard de Fonte. It is clear enough from the deeds that they were the reeves of the two jurisdictions. Thus they were probably the two electors, their choice by the bailiff was automatic and the jury was constructed as in 1232. Robert de Corley did, however, have a function. He appears himself in a prominent position in deeds of both jurisdictions during the mid–late 1240s and must have been a chief bailiff in more than name. Further clues come from the rather unsavoury homicide case involving Robert de Feugers in the same 1247 eyre (36.11). Robert

38 For the parish bounds (of St. Michael as walked in 1675, and of Holy Trinity as walked in 1815) see Benjamin Poole, *Coventry and its Antiquities* (London, 1870) pp. 175–8, 206–8. It should be noted here that the boundary of parishes and of fees lies behind the tenements north of Smithford St. and not along the street as suggested by the *Atlas of Historic Towns: Coventry* map 3. It is probable that the parishes finally took form at about this time. The charters of the earls of Chester speak of St. Michael's and its appurtenant chapels in their fee and in the parish of the monks. As late as 1233 St. Michael's was still referred to as a chapel (*Magnum Registrum Album* No. 271). In 1238 we hear of the mother church of St. Michael and from then on it is invariably described as a church (*ibid.* Nos. 239–240; *Langley Cartulary* Nos. 304, 384; *Cal. Papal Letters* i, pp. 184, 198).

39 The situation was revealed in 1249 when Roger de Montalt expressly included in his grant to the priory the services of the burgesses of his knights and of all others in England (22a). No doubt such men would claim the court and the fine where their tenants were involved just as the Montalts were to do henceforth according to the final concord of 1250 (below p. 30). Presumably the numerous references in the deeds to the limiting of fines when tenants fell into their chief lord's mercy are indicative of the operation of at least erstwhile private courts.

offered the king 100s. for a special inquisition to determine his case and pledges were named; 14 in all. They are Robert de Corley, Martin Colbrand and the 12 members of the presenting jury. From deeds it is clear that Martin Colbrand was another official, very probably therefore Robert's under-bailiff. This is made more probable when we look more closely at the order in which the pledges are named. Osbert Durdent and Richard de Fonte are followed by Richard the Burgess and John Simund. Osbert and Richard de Fonte, as we have already seen, were the reeves. Richard the Burgess and John Simund are numbers 2 and 8 respectively in the list of jurors. In other words they are deputies to Osbert Durdent and Richard de Fonte. John Simund (*alias* John son of Simon), moreover, succeeded Richard de Fonte as reeve or bailiff of the 'Prior's half'. The elaborate nature of the local administration is beginning to be revealed. It would seem that by the mid-1240s there was perceived a need for a set of coordinating bailiffs. Curiously Robert de Corley and Martin Colbrand seem to be more closely associated with the Prior's jurisdiction. Robert was undoubtedly the son of Roger de Corley who figures in Prior's half deeds earlier in the century (541). One possibility is that the Montalt conveyance of 1249 formalized a situation that had existed on an *ad hoc* basis for several years, and that the prior therefore already held both jurisdictions.

The double change of lordship in 1232 and 1243 must have strengthened the hand of the priory, the more so as it coincided with a period of general recovery in the fortunes of the monastic house. The priors had long been overshadowed by the secular lordship of the earls of Chester and threatened by the power of their bishop. Earl and bishop, moreover, had a tendency to act in concert as they had surely done in the time of Bishop Hugh de Nonant. The latter's reversal of the efforts of Prior Lawrence was a bitter blow from which the priory took a long time to recover. Relations with the bishops remained fraught and dangerous until the 1240s and the prolonged and often bitter contention with the Lichfield chapter over episcopal election was very much bound up with this. It is hardly surprising that the monks twice attempted to secure the election of their prior and once of their precenter.[40] In December 1221 they found it necessary to secure papal confirmation of the possessions they held before Nonant's activities and a reaffirmation that the bishop should not interfere with their possessions nor deny their right to elect their own prior.[41] St. Michael's and its appurtenant chapels were persistently denied them, and the initiatives by both Prior Geoffrey and Prior Roger resulted in the latter's humiliation in 1241. Only the death of Bishop Hugh de Pattishall prevented appropriation from taking place.[42] Litigation over canonical elections, the chapels and other matters must have cost the priory dearly, although the low pecuniary state of the monastery by the mid-13th century has probably been exaggerated. The dispersal of the monks to St. Albans and elsewhere c.1242–3 probably represents a ploy to husband resources with litigation at the *Curia* pending, and should perhaps be seen as an expression of monkish solidarity.[43] In reality, the monks were climbing back. In Geoffrey and Roger they had priors of great pertinacity. In 1227, as we have seen, they purchased the right to an annual fair at Coventry and a series of liberties including freedom from view of frankpledge. The cost of these was to be met by taking aids from their knights and free tenants and from their Coventry burgesses.[44]

[40] Each time unsuccessfully. See *V.C.H. Stafford* iii, pp. 10–14.

[41] *Cal. Papal Letters* i, pp. 84–85.

[42] See below.

[43] Matthew Paris, *Chronica Majora* iv, 171–2; *V.C.H. Stafford* iii, p. 13. Dugdale's statement that during the time of Prior Roger some of the monks were received by the Augustinian canons of Darley undoubtedly refers to the events of this time (*Monasticon* iii, pp. 180–181). They appear to have maintained that their convent was in danger of being dispersed, so great were their burdens. It was a claim much reiterated during the next twenty years especially in requests for aids, although it is doubtful whether it should be taken quite literally.

[44] *Rot. Lit. Claus.* ii, pp. 171, 181.

An accommodation had evidently been reached with Ranulf III and their position in Coventry was reasonably secure. Indeed the priory was already acquiring additional property in and around the town.[45]

The end of the Chester earldom and the second change of lordship with the death of the young earl of Arundel in 1243 allowed initiative locally to pass to the priors. In 1248 and 1249 they achieved a double coup. Firstly, the arbitrators appointed by the new bishop Roger de Weseham not only resolved the problem of episcopal elections, at least for the time being, but also decided the issue of St. Michael's and its dependant chapels in favour of Coventry Priory.[46] Prior Roger, however, resigned in the early summer of 1249 and it was left to his successor William de Brightwalton to reach a formal agreement with Roger de Montalt. In the autumn of 1249, probably in preparation for his intended crusade, Roger and his wife Cecily resigned their lordship of Coventry into the hands of the priory but with important reservations.[47] These included the manor house with the enclosed park, the house of Greyfriars, the leper house at Spon and the services of the military tenants who held of them in the surrounding villages and hamlets. The priory was to have all tenements not held by these and the services of all the burgesses including those holding of the knights and others. The prior and monks were to pay £100 *per annum* as well as taking on the 10 marks annually which the earl of Chester had assigned to the nuns of Polesworth. Although Matthew Paris maintains that Roger de Montalt raised a great sum of money thereby it seems unlikely, given the high fee-farm, that the monks can have made a heavy down payment. The final concord concluded in October 1250 carried a consideration of £300 and the delay in ratifying the agreement may have been to allow the monks to raise the cash. Once again it seems to have been raised partly from their tenants. On September 21, 1249 the king requested the knights, burgesses and free tenants of the priory of Coventry to grant the prior an aid to relieve his church from debt.[48]

Despite the question of the impending crusade it is to be doubted whether this transaction was quite as impulsive as it might appear. The Montalt position was elaborately safeguarded including provisions for policing. The final concord specifically protected their courts. From the priory's point of view the agreement was perhaps something of a gamble. The stage seemed set for the creation of an ecclesiastical *banleuca*, despite the troublesome Montalt enclave, with the prior controlling a compact territory in and around the vill. Leet jurisdiction was now in the hands of the prior, and their role in the surrounding villages was greatly enhanced, as is revealed in the Hundred Rolls of 1279. It was at this time, moreover, that the priory fully appropriated the local churches. For full security St. Michael's and its dependant chapels were once again included in the Montalt grant. The leper house and chapel of Spon, although reserved in 1249, were separately conveyed in 1253 (23). By November 1260 at the latest the priory had fully appropriated St. Michael's with 10 dependant chapels, viz. Ansty, Shilton, Wyken, Stoke, Binley, Sowe, Stivichall, Exhall, Foleshill and Spon; the church of Holy Trinity with its chapels (i.e. Holy Cross, St. Nicholas, and those of Coundon and Willenhall); the chapel of St. John the Baptist with its hospital; and the churches of Corley and Alspath.[49]

45 See below p. 31.

46 See below p. 6.

47 For more detailed discussion of this document see below pp. 29–30.

48 *C.P.R. 1247–58* p. 48.

49 This appears from a letter of Bishop Roger Meuland (Dugdale, *Monasticon* iii, p. 181, quoting the lost register of this bishop m4). The text is preserved in rather corrupt form in a later confirmation in B.L. Add. MS. 32100, fo.86r–v, where the date is given as March 1260. The same MS. preserves an earlier letter from Bishop Roger Weseham of 1255 which indicates that churches additional to St. Michael's had already been appropriated (fo.85r–v) although it does not specify. For further details on St. Michael's and the creation of its vicarage in 1249 see below p. 6. For the vicarage of Holy Trinity and notice of its dependant chapels see: *Year Book 1346–7* (1) *Rolls Series*, pp. 67–69n.

The final concord included specific permission to exploit the woodlands and wastes around the town and it was here that one of the greatest advantages for the future actually lay. In 1249, however, the Montalts had attempted to protect the rights of their free tenants, and the fine is endorsed with the claims of several local lords. The prior's determination to approve from the wastes and then to lease at economic rents was to cause considerable problems, however. Royal commissioners were sent in 1258 to assign common to claimants and the residue to the prior and convent. Further commissions were sent in 1277 and 1284 indicating that there had been delays in implementation.[50] Agreements were subsequently reached between successive priors and a number of local lords and freeholders.[51] By the early fourteenth century the policy was reaching full maturity. A waste rental drawn up for Prior Henry lists a considerable acreage enclosed and leased to tenants at Coundon, Keresley, Exhall and Foleshill.[52] Meanwhile the priory was continuing to extend its purchases in and around the town including land to the immediate north at Whitemore. In the course of time this was to become Whitmore Park and a symbol of lordship to rival that of the Montalts at Cheylesmore.[53]

The transfer of the 'Earl's half' to the prior in 1249 seems to have made no immediate perceptible difference, however, to the way Coventry was administered. The Montalt bailiffs were simply replaced by bailiffs responsible to the prior and affairs continued to be regulated more-or-less as before. In the 'Prior's half' from the late 1240s well into the 1250s the administration was dominated by Robert de Feugers, Richard de Fonte, Anketill de Wikewane, Martin Colbrand and John Simond. All but the last occur as reeve at a date before 1257. Around Michaelmas 1257 John is described as bailiff, the first time a man was so designated in a deed relating to the prior's half. At around the same time, however, another deed is witnessed by Richard de Bokerville bailiff of the 'Earl's part' and William Lewin bailiff of the 'Prior's part'. The latter is followed by John Simond and Richard de Fonte. William Lewin is also found with Matthew Mowbray as bailiff about this time, and it seems likely that he performed a coordinating function probably across both parts of the town. He is described as bailiff in the eyre of 1262. The presenting jury, however, was almost certainly formed in the same way as those of 1232 and 1247. The six from each half are revealed on this occasion by taking the names alternately, the first and second names, viz. John son of Simon and Alexander of Gloucester (*de Glovernia*) being the bailiffs of the 'Prior's half' and the 'Earl's half' respectively.

In the 'Earl's half' Richard de Bokerville functioned as bailiff for much of the 1250s. Pagan Pake and Alexander of Gloucester were also prominent as were Walter the White and John Beer. During the years leading up to the eyre we find Walter

[50] *C.P.R. 1247–58* p. 659, *1272–81* p. 199, and *1281–92* p. 200. The Langleys were in the forefront of the opposition here. In 1253, on his return from Gascony, Walter de Langley complained that the woodlands were closed to him, whilst his father Geoffrey de Langley had to be prevented from making waste or sale in the woods by reason of the common he enjoyed. (*C.C.R. 1251–53* p. 449, *1253–54* p. 12). In 1258 Geoffrey agreed to renounce his general claim in return for specified parcels of land and a formal agreement was made by final concord in 1262. Once again a host of local lords and freeholders appended their claims on behalf of themselves and their tenants (*C.P.R. 1247–58* p. 617, *Langley Cartulary* Nos. 181, 244; *F.F. Warwicks.* i, No. 791). The agreement with Geoffrey had been concluded, however, after he and the prior had been much at law (*Eyre Rolls 1260* m2, and *1262* mm12d., 13, 14, 21). From this it is clear that the prior was already ditching and turning the commons to arable very close to the town. A number of priory servants, including Henry Baker and more especially Robert de Chilton, were cited in actions over the destruction of Geoffrey's piggery (*porcheria*).

[51] A particularly interesting series were concluded with John de Hastings and his Allesley tenants in 1300 and 1305 (C.R.O. Box IB Nos. 28 EI/1/9–12/14a and b; 33 EI/1–11/15).

[52] C.R.O. Ecclesiastical Records Box No. 1 Priory.

[53] See below pp. 2, 326.

the White and Alexander of Gloucester as bailiffs with Pake and Beer remaining prominent. The appearance of William Lewin here, too, once again indicates a coordinating role. The 1262 eyre roll, moreover, reveals for the first time something of the activities of town bailiffs beyond the registering of property transactions. We learn that a forger had been taken by the bailiffs of Coventry and imprisoned, whence he had escaped. The rather unpleasant misdemeanours of bailiff Walter the White and his deputy Ranulf de Kaus were presented in this eyre, whilst the current bailiff of the 'Earl's half' Alexander of Gloucester was charged with false imprisonment but found to have been maliciously accused. Coventry's administrative system was by now well developed and rich in personnel. It is extremely difficult to unravel either the precise functions of individual bailiffs or the succession to the various offices.

During the late 1250s/early 1260s two men were rising in the prior's administration who came to dominate Coventry's government, viz. Robert de Chilton and Henry Baker. Chilton had appeared by 1257, when he was probably already part of the administration, and he is found on a number of occasions in the late 1250s/early 1260s. In 1264 a Bishop St. deed was witnessed by William Lewin, Robert de Chilton and Henry Baker, bailiffs. Again, during the late 1260s we find these three described as bailiffs, and from then until the time of the Hundred Rolls of 1280 Chilton and Baker tend to dominate the 'Prior's half' deeds with the latter designated bailiff. On one occasion around 1280 they are preceded by John de Pontefract the prior's steward. Henry Baker's first appearance c.1258–1260 is as Henry Baker son of Henry Baker when he received land in Bishop St. by gift of the prior. Like Chilton he is found in association with William Lewin during the 1260s. Meanwhile, however, he was described as bailiff in a deed relating to Whitemore to the north of Coventry. This brings into play the further complication of the administration of the prior's property around Coventry including the rents and overlordship which passed to him as a result of the Montalt grant. The appearance of Chilton in the 1262 eyre roll suggests that he had some responsibility here too. These 3 appear in the 'Earl's half' also in the late 1250s and early 1260s being described occasionally as bailiffs. On one occasion c.1260–62 they are called bailiffs of Coventry (360). One is led to the conclusion that Lewin headed a staff of bailiffs whose responsibility transcended the two halves of Coventry, and encompassed the prior's rights in the territory and vills around the town, with perhaps an overseeing or coordinating role over bailiffs with more limited responsibility. Their role may have given rise to a short-lived experiment during the mid-1260s. With a paucity of deeds and the inevitable imprecision in dating, the evidence is fragile but it does look as though the prior was attempting to subsume the 'Earl's half' and its court into the greater whole. In these years we find the earlier 'Earl's half' bailiffs (Alexander de Gloucester and the disgraced Walter the White) had given way to a regime dominated as in the 'Prior's half', by Chilton and Baker together with Richard Ernis and John de Pontefract. This regime seems to have lasted only a short time for Nicholas de la Barre appears as bailiff in 1268, and on numerous occasions around that time, and Richard de Bokerville returns in 1269. Baker and company may have returned to an overseeing role. The witnesses to one deed of the late 1260s is headed by Richard de Bokerville, Richard Ernis bailiff, and then Henry Baker with the curious designation 'bailiff of the lord prior for the bishop's half'. Any suggestion that Bokerville and de la Barre were the elected representatives of the men of the Earl's half must be resisted, and indeed the former is on one occasion described as the bailiff of the lord prior.[54] None-the-less if the interpretation of the deeds is correct it does help us to understand the nature of the serious challenge to the prior's authority which occurred during the years 1267–68 and indicates that the opposition did achieve a measure of success. To this opposition let us now turn.

[54] C.R.O. IA C12–13/62.

In March 1268 a commission was despatched to inquire into the recent disturbance at Coventry which had occurred when the sheriff had attempted to publish and maintain the liberties recently granted to the prior and monks. These included coroners at Coventry, a gild merchant and freedom from distraint for their burgesses, merchants and men for any debt for which they were not sureties or principal debtors, and the grant had been made on February 7 1267. It had clearly resulted in resistance and this may well be reflected in the year's protection granted on July 20 1267 to Hugh le Breton of Coventry, a clerk associated with the Prior's administration.[55] The disturbance, however, probably followed the royal confirmation of Henry II's charter on January 30 1268 for which the burgesses of Coventry had paid £10 by the hand of two of their number, Peter Baron and Roger le Chamberlain. Clearly the burgesses had formed an association to resist the prior. The charter acquired from Walter de Coventry by which he confirmed common pasture over his lands to all the fellow burgesses of Coventry is clearly an early example of communal action and may well belong to this time (34). The resistance to the prior, then, would appear to have wider causes than a reaction to the grant of February 1267 alone, for the latter represents a stage in an attempt by the prior to consolidate his hold on Coventry and produce the logical outcome of the Montalt grant of 1249, viz. a totally united town under a single lordship. To do this he needed to circumvent the portmoot and to extend the authority of his ministers functioning across the entire town. It may well be, though, that the traditional view of the rising as one of the 'Earl's half' only has conceived the situation too narrowly. For one thing locals other than townsmen were involved, which may well reflect the prior's determination to appropriate the commons and wastes around the town, and Walter de Coventry's charter would also appear to reflect this development. Until recently, moreover, no real attention has been paid to the date of this grant. As Professor Davis has pointed out, the prior's new charter of February 1267 followed hard upon a brief period when Coventry figured strongly in national politics. The committee of 12 who drew up the Dictum of Kenilworth deliberated at Coventry in the autumn of 1266 and the king was with the royal forces at the siege of Kenilworth during the second half of the year. Professor Davis suggests that the prior may have rendered special services to the king and/or the townsmen may have shown Montfortian sympathies.[56] In fact both are likely to be true. Certainly several Coventrians can be shown to have figured among the rebels. On June 29 1266 Thomas son of William of Coventry was admitted to the king's peace under sureties 'provided that if he have incurred the penalty of disherison or ransom or other penalty for such trespass he shall bear it'. So too were 3 members of the Shepey family at the instance of Prince Edmund on June 24.[57] On February 17 1266 Robert de Coventry had been granted protection 'providing that the king has not given his lands to anyone and that he stand his trial', and it is probable that the letters of protection granted to other Coventrians in that year should be similarly understood.[58] There is no direct evidence of a strong movement among the *mediocres* of the town, but with the landowners in the area with few exceptions strongly Montfortian (and some of the townsmen too) there must, at the very least, have been tension in the town and the prior's position was probably a difficult one. In fact, the prior and convent were granted protection on April 13 1264 at a critical juncture in national politics, and on several occasions after the war protection was similarly granted – in May 1266 and January 1267.[59] On the latter occasion a royal sergeant was despatched to keep the priory 'for greater security'. Undoubtedly the tensions of the war years took some time to subside. The prior, however, felt this was the right time to consolidate

55 *C.P.R. 1266–72* p. 90.
56 *The Early History of Coventry* pp. 7–8.
57 *C.P.R. 1258–66* pp. 667.
58 *ibid.* pp. 555, 618, 630, 637, 640.
59 *ibid.* p. 311, 575, and *1266–72* p. 29.

his hold on the town relying – it would seem – on an élite of servitors, rentiers and their allies (below pp. xxxviii–xl). It was only to be expected that the charters of the earls of Chester would figure in the resulting challenge to the prior's authority, and indeed in any future challenges. The preservation of the portmoot was undoubtedly a major aim of this resistance. However, we should be wary of thinking too much in terms of a divided community rather than divided jurisdictions.

As a result the dual jurisdiction remained. Three men figure prominently as bailiffs in the 'Earl's half' during the 1270s, viz. Peter Barun, John de Lodelowe and Gerard de Alspath. Chilton and Baker continue to occur sometimes with the designation bailiff and sometimes in association with Barun, Lodelowe and Alspath. Once again, it is clear enough that all are servitors of the prior. Gerard de Alspath is once described as bailiff of the lord prior, whilst Henry Baker and John de Lodelawe occur together at Radford as the bailiffs of the lord prior. Chilton and Baker meanwhile continue to function in the 'Prior's half', with Alexander the Vintner in all probability exercising some official function with them.

For the time being, then, the prior had failed to achieve complete jurisdictional unity. The coroner, however, was established. The eyre roll of 1285 gives the names of Hugh le Hoser and Walter Bacon as the coroners since the last eyre (1272) the former being now dead. Walter's name is found as the first of 13 jurors named in the 1280 survey, reflecting no doubt his position as coroner. Hugh on the other hand, although living in the late 1270s, does not figure in the survey. He seems to have died c.1279. Since he goes back to at least 1272 he was in all probability Coventry's first coroner. He occurs as a witness to deeds from time to time especially during the 1270s although he is not officially designated as coroner except curiously on two occasions at Radford, where he appears with Henry Baker the bailiff.[60] Oddly Hugh is once described as bailiff (299). His successor Walter Bacon does witness specifically as coroner in the 1280s and on other occasions his position in the witness lists clearly reflects his role as coroner. During the time of his successor William the Parker it became the general practice for the coroner to be second witness after the bailiff. Meanwhile, however, another major shift had taken place within the administration and it seems virtually certain that the prior had achieved what he set out to do in the 1260s. By the time of the 1280 survey we are on the eve of a major change. As is well known the survey's account of Coventry's courts is somewhat lacking. There is no mention of the portmoot as such. This may result from an omission, or rather suppression, in the extant transcript which clearly emanates from the priory (see below p. 365). There is undoubtedly room for a further clause between the statement that the prior has a court of the whole town by 8 days summons and the statement that the burgesses have courts of their own free tenants associated with the aforementioned courts (*sic*). On the other hand the language itself may reflect a situation in process of change. It may well be indicative that neither the jury of 1280 nor that of the 1285 eyre seems to have been constructed like those for 1232, 1247 and 1262. What is undoubted is that from Easter 1284 at the latest a single bailiff functions as chief witness throughout the town with the coroner increasingly associated with him. Henry Baker is by then sole bailiff and continues to be for some 13 years, making his last appearance in the deeds gathered here on 20 October 1297. It seems likely that he and Robert de Chilton were acting jointly across the town for a few years prior to this. They were both bailiffs early in 1282, Chilton at Lady Day (687), Baker on Ash Wednesday.[60a] Chilton, moreover, had been bailiff in 1281, was described in the early 1280s as bailiff of the vill and occurs about this time with Walter Bakun as coroner (312, 656–7). The division of responsibilities during the later 1280s, however, was clear. Henry Baker was bailiff of Coventry, Robert de Chilton bailiff of the foreign of the lord prior (756).[61]

[60] C.R.O. IA C13/51, EC13/78. [60a] C.R.O. 2/137.

[61] This had perhaps been his major responsibility for some time. See above note 50.

The clear inference, then, is that from the early 1280s there was a single court in operation. From the evidence of the prior of Coventry's petition to the Council in 1336 it appears that this court was held fortnightly for all his tenants in Coventry. In addition he held a three-weekly court for his tenants outside the town and a daily pie-powder court for strangers passing through which he referred to as a portmoot.[62]

From the time of Henry Baker and Walter Bakun the sequence of bailiffs and coroners of Coventry can be clearly constructed from the deeds. Henry Baker's immediate successor was Anketill de Coleshill who is found on 27 January 1298 and who last appears on 26 June 1300. Roger Dayseye is found from 30 November 1300 and for the last time on 2 June 1303. Meanwhile Robert Baker (son of Henry) had made occasional appearances in June and October 1301, and February and March 1303. He is found continuously from September 1303 to 1310. The sequence of coroners can also be constructed. William the Parker (*alias* William de Nailestone)[63] probably succeeded Walter Bacon c.1290[64] and was certainly coroner in 1291. He last appears on June 29 1298. John Lewyn appears from 20 April 1299 to 19 September 1305. Alexander de Stonlee occurs from 10 January 1306, Anketill de Coleshill from 26 February 1307. There are a few occasions when the coroner witnesses alone. John Lewyn occurs without the bailiff on half a dozen occasions in 1300–1301 and once in 1304. Similarly William the Parker functioned alone 6 times during the years 1295–8. The reasons for this are obscure. On some of these occasions, they were joined by Robert de Stoke, the prior's steward (618, 162).

The logic of the Montalt grant would appear to have been achieved. Whether Coventry life was harmonious during the 1280s and 1290s we cannot know. The first decade of the 14th century, however, was to see another challenge to the authority of the prior. From 30 September 1300 a large body of the prior's tenants boycotted his Friday market and sold instead from their houses and stalls in Earl St. Writs were brought against 24 of them in April 1302, and against a larger group of 67 in January 1307. The latter cited the charter of Earl Ranulf and Henry II's confirmation charter as their authority. Both groups, however, lost their case and the prior was awarded damages (33). Although the defendants appear to have been precisely what the record says they are, viz. tenants with shops and stalls in Earl St.,[65] the movement must undoubtedly have had broader overtones. At the very least it is hardly symptomatic of a healthy relationship between the priory and its tenants. Relations seem to have been deteriorating with the Montalts, too, at this time. Despite the elaborate precautions agreed between Roger de Montalt and Prior William, conflict over the jurisdiction of their respective courts was almost bound to occur. One such occasion was in 1295.[66] More seriously in March 1303 a special commission of oyer and terminer was despatched on the prior's complaint that Roger de Montalt and an armed gang had broken his close at Newlands, hunted there and assaulted his servants.[67] The forces were taking shape which, in a relatively short interval, were to wrest the prior's lordship from him.

[62] On this point and for the 14th-century evidence of Coventry courts in general see A. and E. Gooder, 'Coventry before 1355' pp. 9–12.

[63] C.R.O. IA C25.

[64] *Priory Register* fo. 88v.

[65] See below p. 45.

[66] See below pp. 30–1.

[67] *C.P.R. 1301–1307* p. 188.

II. PHYSICAL GROWTH, ECONOMY AND SOCIETY*

The earliest deeds reveal Coventry as a thriving community with a broadly-based economy and a well-established street pattern. Most of the major streets can be shown to have existed early in the 13th century, although in a few cases (Much Park St, West Orchard) the street itself is documented well before its tenements. There are, however, a few clues to the earlier phases of Coventry's growth. Two arteries of communication dominated: Bishop St. which linked Coventry with Tamworth and Lichfield to the north, and which led directly to the monastic house and to Coventry market; and Earl St. which, with its extensions to Smithford and Gosford, provided the east-west axis of the town. Through Gosford lay the exit to Leicester and most probably that to London, too. The nomenclature of the two arterial roads is immediately striking, and is reinforced in the documents. Bishop St. is once called the bishop's great street (*magnum vicum episcopi*, 589), and Earl St. (after the death of the earl of Chester) the street of the earl of Arundel (*in vico comitis de Arundel*, 767.24). The outlying districts of Spon, Gosford, Hill and the area around the church of St. Nicholas were also thriving by 1200.

The last-mentioned poses something of a problem as to its origins. The unusually heavy early documentation here reveals a well-established economy, whilst the church is evidenced as early as 1183–84 where significantly it is a chapel appurtenant to the monks' church of Holy Trinity rather than to the earl's chapel of St. Michael as is the case with the majority of the chapels serving the vills and hamlets around the town (12). Clearly it had originated within the monks' sphere of influence. This area alone of the outlying districts is referred to as a suburb of Coventry (608). Two possibilities emerge. Either it represents a genuinely early suburb with a distinct community warranting its own chapel (and pointing incidentally to the antiquity of this part of the town); or, alternatively, it was as Dugdale suggested the original nucleus from which the town of Coventry developed. It is conceivable that the centre of gravity may have shifted southwards, closer to the monastic house and, perhaps, to the earl's castle. The name Bishop St. points unequivocally to a major development on this side of the town at a time when the bishops played a significant role in directing local affairs. Since the time of Hugh de Nonant is too recent, given the level of development indicated by the deeds, the time in question must be that of Robert de Limesey and his immediate successors, in the early twelfth century, before the rise of Prior Lawrence (above p. xv). It is possible that the market may once have lain in this area. In the settlement of 1355 the prior was allowed to retain his cattle and timber markets held as of old on Fridays in Bishop St. and Cook St.[1] There was a tendency for cattle markets to be held on the outskirts of towns, but it may well be that this remained on its original site when the main market moved to a more central location. Such a move could be that referred to rather cryptically in 1203 when the sheriff accounted for a fine of 3 marks which the prior and monks had paid for moving their Coventry market (*pro mercato suo de Coventr' remouendo*).[2] There is no evidence of a rival market held by the earls, and it is clear from the early deeds that the market area came under the jurisdiction of a joint court (above p. xxi). Some degree of seignorial cooperation is indicated. The site was well-positioned to take advantage of trade stimulated by both monastery and castle. In the 14th-century it was claimed that the market lay on the soil of the foundation,

[1] Davis, *The Early History of Coventry* p. 25.
[2] *Pipe Roll 4 John* p. 38.

---

*The following account is not intended to be exhaustive but rather to reveal some of the characteristics of the town and to illustrate the potentiality of the material.

although whether this was strictly true is not clear. After the death of Ranulf III the market appears clearly within the jurisdiction of the prior's court (above p. xxi) although rarely before the 1270s do the deeds refer to the market specifically as the prior's. The Hundred Rolls of 1280 reaffirm that the market lay in the 'Prior's half'. In the first decade of the 14th century a section of the townsmen were in conflict with the prior over the exclusivity of his market. Under colour of the earl's charter they claimed the right to sell from their shops and stalls even on Fridays during the market (33). Interestingly, sales and leases of shops and stalls are well-evidenced in Earl St. and its immediate vicinity but are hardly ever found in the 'Prior's half' outside of the market. In the event the townsmen lost their case, and it seems almost certain that it was they who had defied established custom. Something of the trading arrangements as they had persisted during the 13th century is thus revealed.

That the earls of Chester played a major part in Coventry's development, even if this was a secondary one, seems certain enough. Ranulf II's charter to his Coventry burgesses, as revealed in the royal confirmation of 1182 (11), contained clauses encouraging the influx of merchants and freeing newcomers from dues for a period of two years. These clauses are probably genuine enough and it is probably correct, too, to see their omission from his grandson's charter as an indication of Coventry's growth during the interval (15). Ranulf II's charter most likely belongs to the period 1141–6 and betokens a concern to develop his interests in the area at the height of his power, rather than a policy of reconstruction at the end of the hostilities (below p. 8). The pace of Coventry's growth from the mid-twelfth century cannot be gauged but there are indications that it was both sustained and enjoyed a degree of seignorial encouragement. Among the signs are the steady appearance of new mills in the area under licence from the earls and the continued controlled assarting in the time of Hugh II and Ranulf III.[3] Of great interest in this context are the charters of Liulf de Brinklow (8,9). Liulf had held the vill of Bisseley from Earl Ranulf II, a tenure which was twice confirmed by the young Hugh II. Bisseley was, in fact, one of those vills which either enjoyed a chapel appurtenant to St. Michael's in 1153 or in which it was envisaged there should soon be one (above p. xix). The vill was held, however, in burgage tenure, an indication surely of anticipated, if not actual, economic growth. In the course of time, though, the vill of Bisseley seems to have declined and the intended chapel was never built. In the 13th century the estate became known as the manor of Shortley. The precise location of the vill is unclear but Bisseley Mill lay on the Sherbourne south of Gosford. There may have been some economic setback of which we are ignorant. It seems more likely, however, that Bisseley failed due to the growth of Coventry itself and, more particularly, to the development of a suburb at and beyond Gosford. Events at Spon to the west of the town may have been similar. Here a chapel was probably already in existence in 1153. There may also have been a family equivalent to the Liulfsons. Liulf of Spon who died a little before 1213 held substantial property here in right of his wife (407). During the time of Hugh II, however, the chapel was given to maintain a leper house (768 p. 371). Although the vill of Spon persisted into the 13th century, as a community it had probably already declined.[4] By the time of the deeds, in addition to Spon fields, woods and pasture, we find 'the street towards Spon' or Spon St. flourishing. Again, it is conceivable that the pull of suburban development served to sap the older

[3] *Langley Cartulary* Nos. 179, 188, 189, 194, 213; and see below p. 9–10.

[4] For litigation between the descendants of Liulf de Spon see the following: *Curia Regis Rolls* vol. VII 1213–15 pp. 93–94, 289; *Eyre Rolls 1221* Nos. 595, 1469, 1516; *Curia Regis Rolls* vol. XIV 1230–32 pp. 53–54; *F.F. Warwicks* Nos. 174, 207, 496, 497, 500. Pasture in the vill of Spon is mentioned as late as 1260 (*Eyre Rolls 1260* m4d). The site of Spon with its chapel, lands and rents was granted by Roger de Montalt to the priory in 1253 (23). The chapel was thus appropriated and was held by a chaplain at farm in 1280 (768 p. 371). The hospital had by now ceased to function. In 1316 the manor of Spon was given by the prior to Master

community. It is also possible that Spon St. was not a spontaneous growth but an early and deliberate act of town planning on the part of the earls.

Despite its role in Coventry's early history the earl of Chester's castle remains somewhat elusive. Little is known for certain of its size and location, or indeed of its duration. The vast dimensions suggested in the *Atlas of Historic Towns* have been challenged and shown to be unlikely.[5] In fact all documentary references to the castle, or more precisely to its associated features, are confined to the area north of Earl St. The castle ditch occurs twice in later 13th-century deeds (*le Casteldich*, 223; *fossatum castelli*, 226). One of these locates a messuage between Earl St. to the south and the castle ditch, whilst the other refers to land in close proximity. The castle bakehouse was also in this area. It was conveyed by Elias Despenser to Walter son of Terry in the early 13th century with land adjacent, opposite the church of St. Michael (below p. 31). Bayley Lane must surely bear some relation to the direction of the perimeter of the castle bailey, and the street name is undoubtedly derived from it. The form *Baililone* and associated renderings was preceded by *le Bayli*, *le Baille* and *viam Balii* in the 1220s–1240s (767.6, .18, .22). Two of the earliest references in fact locate property within the bailey itself (*in Balliva*, 767.20; *in ballivo qui ducit ad ecclesiam sancti Michaelis*, (*Langley Cartulary* No. 275). The original chapel of St. Michael would also seem to have been within the castle. A convincing argument has been made that the northern ditch caused engineering problems when the church was enlarged and its tower constructed in the 14th century.[6] The derivation of Broadgate from the castle seems undoubted, even though Hugh II's 'boundary charter' with its reference to the broad gate of his castle (*latam portam castelli mei*) is a fabrication (below pp. 1–2).[7] The relationship of Earl St. itself to the castle remains unclear. But undoubtedly it was here, within and in close proximity to the castle that the hub of the 'Earl's half' of Coventry lay, centring on Earl St. and Broadgate, the road leading to the earl's park (Little Park St.) and the road to the manor house (Cheylesmore Lane). It was in this area that rents were generally at their highest.

How long the castle endured is also a problem. That it played a major role in the hostilities of Stephen's reign is clear enough (below p. 8). The castle and its constables still figure in Ranulf III's charter to his burgesses c.1199–1204 (15), although this could have resulted from repetition of a clause in an earlier charter. It is probable that the castle had given way to Cheylesmore manor house before the death of this earl, as it had certainly done by the time of Roger de Montalt. It is here that the Franciscans were given their site, and it is certain now that they were in Coventry before the death of the earl (35.17). Also under Ranulf's protection was the Coventry Jewry. In June 1226 he received a grant from the king to the effect that the Jews should remain and dwell unmolested both at Coventry and at Leicester.[8] Cases involving debts to Amtera the Jewess of Coventry and the resultant forfeiture of land there occur in 1218, 1220 and 1221.[9] On the other hand it seems unlikely that the Jewry outlived the earl, or if so it was not by much. Ranulf de

Nicholas Pihod of Coventry as a living with the chapel and all lands belonging until he could be provided with a suitable benefice. He was to maintain the houses and the chapel and administer the customary *elemosinas leprosis* (G.H. 498).

---

[5] By A. and E. Gooder in *City of Coventry: Archaeology and Development* pp. 12–13.

[6] *ibid.* p. 13. The authors, however, are envisaging a chapel within the perimeter of a late Saxon town. For the rebuilding of the church see *V. C. H. Coventry* p. 353.

[7] Perhaps the tenement of Herman Attecastelgate, a deceased tenant referred to in 1262 was located there (*Eyre Rolls 1262* m7d). A charter of Eustace fitz John constable of Chester belonging to 1144–1157 refers to the south gate (*portam australem*) which presumably is also to the castle (*Langley Cartulary* No. 214).

[8] *Rot. Lit. Claus.* ii, p. 123.

[9] J. M. Rigg, *Plea Rolls of the Exchequer of the Jews* i, 1218–1272, pp. 1, 29, 42; *Eyre Rolls 1221* No. 974.

Stivichall whose indebtedness is revealed in 1236 owed Benedict de Coventry, of Northampton, and a Jew of Warwick.[10] In future, local landowners in difficulties and, indeed, burgesses like Richard of Worcester (710) were likely to turn to Jews of Worcester and of course Warwick.

Yet another problem lies in the relation of the castle to the defensive work behind the tenements south of Earl St. known as the Red Ditch. That the latter bounded the castle seems improbable. It has recently been suggested that the northern ditch and the red ditch may have been linked to enclose, not an over-large castle, but a small Saxon town.[11] Whether there was a complete circuit, however, is as yet unproven. Excavation at the back of the tenements on the east side of Broadgate in 1975 revealed the north-west corner of a ditch, presumably the castle ditch, as it turned southwards.[12] The early documents unfortunately provide no evidence of a ditch proceeding along the line of Cheylesmore Lane to connect this with the red ditch to the south. Similarly on the eastern side the red ditch running north-south beyond Much Park St. is not only further out than the line of Bayley Lane but appears to be running away from it. Neither would it appear to connect with the apparently twelfth-century ditch discovered during excavation in Godiva St. (east of Earl's Mill Lane).[13] The red ditch proper, running from Greyfriars' Lane in the west to cross Much Park St. and turn north to Jordan Well, is in fact much evidenced in 13th century deeds and remained a prominent feature in the 15th and 16th centuries. It has been shown archaeologically to be a major defence work dating from the twelfth century.[14] Although it is nowhere called the castle ditch it is on one occasion referred to as the earl's ditch (767.33). The most likely explanation is that in origin it was a defensive work constructed during the hostilities of Stephen's reign. This, however, fails to solve all problems. The reference to the earl's ditch is an early but isolated occurrence. From the 1240s onwards references to the red ditch abound. Occasionally we find town ditch (*fossatum ville*) as an alternative or even the red ditch of the town (*rubeam fossam ville*, 149). On one occasion we find south of Earl St. the common ditch of the vill of Coventry (*communem fossatum ville de Coventr'*, 237). Perhaps the earl's ditch stimulated the construction of a more extensive circuit. There is no doubt that the east–west section of the red ditch extended laterally in both directions. In the 1250s we find a tenement stretching from Gosford St. (here probably Jordan Well) to the *Hyrsumdich* (279), and at the beginning of the 14th century there are references to the town ditch south of Gosford St. (333, 335, 336). The term *Hersomdich* is found again in the 1250s south of Earl St. as yet another alternative name for the red ditch, and re-appears near the bar in Cheylesmore Lane c.1270 (185, 66). Further west we find the Poddycroft ditch in 1266–72, later referred to as the town ditch and as the great ditch of the Poddycroft (386, 392, 76).

References to the town ditch are not confined, however, to the south side of Coventry. In the 1240s and 1250s a tenement was said to stretch from Hill St. to the red ditch (*ruffam foveam*, 535, 536). The location of this is by no means clear but we are probably dealing with a section not too far distant from that excavated in Upper Well St. in 1960.[15] If so the latter ditch may be a little earlier than the post-1250 pottery finds would suggest and would seem to preclude the troubled years of the mid-1260s as the date of construction. More surprisingly, the town ditch appears

[10] *C.C.R. 1234–1237* p. 348.

[11] A. and E. Gooder *loc. cit*, and 'Coventry before 1355' pp. 5, 29.

[12] *City of Coventry: Archaeology and Development* pp. 13, 30–31. The full report is still awaited.

[13] See L. E. Webster and J. Cherry, 'Medieval Britain in 1972' *Medieval Archaeology*, xviii (1973) p. 171; *City of Coventry: Archaeology and Development* p. 40.

[14] For details see S. M. Wright, 'Excavations in Much Park St., Coventry: The Development of a Medieval Street. Excavations 1970–74'. Trans. Birmingham and Warwicks Arch. Soc. vol. 92 (forthcoming).

[15] The report, by Philip Rahtz, is in 'The Walls of Coventry' by E. Gooder, C. Woodfield and R. E. Chaplin, *Trans. Birmingham Arch. Soc.* vol. 81, 1966, pp. 99–138.

in the late 1260s/early 1270s on the northern outskirts of the town towards the church of St. Nicholas (616). It would seem then, that by the mid-13th century at the latest, a ditch encircled much of the town.

Bars are sometimes found in association with the ditch, as in Cheylesmore Lane and at Bishop's Bar towards the church of St. Nicholas (66,616). There were others in Little Park St., Much Park St. and Earl St. close to Earl's Mill Lane (110, 152, 767.43). The earliest reference to bars belongs, however, to the very beginning of the 13th century, towards Hill, and there were other early bars in the region of St. Nicholas' church (527, 607). The ditches and bars, however, do not seem to have delimited Coventry. Spon St., Hill and *extra* Gosford [Far Gosford St.], all presumably outside the circuit of the ditches, seem to have been regarded for the most part as within Coventry. So, too, do fields like the Poddycroft, Shockersfield and Spitelcroft, and Gosford Green. Beyond these we find the term *territorium* employed, especially when speaking of outlying crofts. We find the territories of Spon, Harnall, Coundon and Radford in addition to that of Coventry. There is, however, some inconsistency. Altegeder Mills, for example, were sometimes described as within, sometimes without Coventry. As we have seen only the area immediately to the north of the town is ever described as a suburb (608). Presumably all land held in burgage tenure came to be regarded as within Coventry. It is significant, perhaps, that the manor of Shortley was surveyed with Coventry in 1280 and generally regarded as within the town. On the other hand villein tenements at Coventry were once said to be held of the earl of Chester.[16]

On the south side Coventry seems to have expanded from the heart of the 'Earl's half' during the course of the 13th century. Much Park St., although in existence from the beginning of the century, is hardly documented until the 1270s – apart, that is, from references to the White Cellar which lay at its head. During the next 20 years, however, there are numerous property transactions in the street and the increasing necessity of differentiating between the two park streets led to the triumph of Little and Much Park Sts. as the enduring designations (below p. 85). It cannot be without significance that the north end of Much Park St. should figure disproportionately among its earlier deeds, as the references to the white cellar and to the red ditch clearly show. Equally significant is the fact that Dead Lane, linking the two park streets, is also first documented from c.1270. The deeds refer, however, to earlier transactions as well as indicating that there were already houses there. It seems likely that this area of the town was being intensively developed from the middle of the 13th century only and, as far as Much Park St. is concerned, this is borne out by the archaeological record.[17] It is possible once again that we have a planned extension of the town; on this occasion most probably undertaken by the priory following the Montalt purchase in 1249.[18] Pauline's Lane [Cow Lane] is similarly documented from the 1280s. From Dead Lane curtilages extended to the park and its ditch, and by the 1290s curtilages at the south end of Little Park St. towards the park gate are in evidence. By the first decade of the following century land in this area had been built on. Similarly, on the Much Park St. side we find in 1292 a tenement in the lane leading from Great Park St. (*sic*) up to the park and next to the curtilage of Richard de Weston, and in 1298 a curtilage towards the mill – stones extending from the highway up to the park of Sir Robert de Montalt (152, 160). The latter, at least, would seem to refer to the eastward extension of Much Park St. parallel to the park. In short a progressive but probably planned extension of the town is indicated, where curtilages can be discerned preceding building in the more southerly section.

16 *Eyre Rolls 1232* m14.

17 S. M. Wright *op. cit.* A brief account of the results of the excavations in Much Park St. may be found in *City of Coventry: Archaeology and Development* pp. 31–34.

18 Comparison between the deeds and Hundred Rolls gives no support to the idea that tenants in this area were those said to be holding directly of the Montalts at Cheylesmore.

No doubt there had also been steady growth within the existing built-up area. Indeed, the erection of new building on existing tenements was sometimes allowed for in the leases. Within the market area the development of permanent features can be discerned. There had been an important forge at the beginning of the century and shops and stalls which were clearly fixtures (676, 660, 661, 680). During the 1270s we hear of built-up land (*terra edificata*) in the market place where fish is sold, and of selds adjoining the stone hall which once belonged to Richard the Vintner (683, 684). There were chief messuages here, too, including those of Thomas Scelet before the cross, and of Margery, widow of Walter de Banbury in the corn market (687, 688, 695, 696). Specialized locations for specific commodities are strongly evidenced before the end of the century.

Used with caution the deeds can reveal some of the features and, in particular, the occupational structure of various streets/districts of the town. It is necessary, however, to make a number of qualifications. Only a minority of names are of the occupational type. Furthermore a tendency to heritability of surnames is already apparent. Indeed, it could cause problems for contemporaries as the use of *dictus* in, for example, Henry called Baker and Alexander called the Vintner indicates. It may also be part explanation of the increasing tendency during the second half of the century, accelerating during the 1290s, to distinguish the occupations of parties to transactions. A deeper study of Coventry surnames will be required and for a variety of purposes. In the meantime, as long as undue reliance on quantification is resisted, they can be used to yield an impression of the occupational structure of individual streets which is likely to be broadly valid. It may be noted that where sub-tenants occur they do tend to reinforce the impression gained from parties, witnesses and neighbouring property owners. One also needs to be aware of, and to make allowance for, the existence of *rentiers* with broad interests across the town.

The industrial complexion of the western side of the town is revealed clearly. Around Smithford there is the evidence of smiths, and of wheelwrights, that we might expect, but it is the textile crafts which predominate. As early as c.1210–c.1220 Osbert the Dyer purchased the land where Edwin the Fuller used to live (379). We find combers and weavers, as well as dyers. In Spon St. it is the dyers and, even more strongly, the tanners who dominate the local scene. Some of these, such as Robert of Canley and, to a lesser extent perhaps, Robert in the Hurne, become substantial property owners during the latter part of the century. The same interests are apparent towards Hill. In the area of Hill Mill itself we find tenter yards (538, 540) and it seems probable that the mill was in fact a fulling mill.

In Well St., in addition to the tanners, there is evidence of butchers and members of associated crafts. Gilbert the Butcher and Hugh the Butcher are witnesses to a deed as early as c.1200–c.1210 (553). William the Cordwainer purchased land here during the following decade, and Elias the Skinner, Robert the Salter and Osbert the Oilseller were all among the early holders of property (555, 556, 564). Butchers and *bocmongers* are similarly found in the area of Hill. The deed by which Henry Oky the butcher purchased land in Well St. in 1293 is endorsed Hill Cross, viz. the junction of Well St. and Abbot's Lane. Excavation at the town wall in Well St. in 1960 revealed considerable animal remains from which was diagnosed the existence of a 14th century horner's workshop.[19] There are, of course, good reasons why all of the foregoing crafts should be located on the periphery of the town.

The area to the north of Bishop St. towards the church of St. Nicholas is revealed as a more diverse industrial location, with Bishop St. itself sharing many of its characteristics. The textile industry is in evidence from the beginning of the documentation and becomes stronger mid-century. Smiths and farriers, carpenters and turners are also in evidence. With quarries in the vicinity the appearance of Thomas the Mason does not surprise us (601). Peculiar to this area, however, seem to be

[19] 'The Walls of Coventry' pp. 131–138.

the coopers who figure throughout the period, ranging from Herbert and Guy in the early deeds to Walter of Ireland, cooper, at the end of the century (600, 601, 626). Parchment-makers are another feature of the area. Bakehouses are found in Bishop St. and Cook St., and bakers, cooks, and indeed several millers, are found among the property owners.

In Gosford St., and more particularly at and beyond Gosford itself, it is metal-workers who dominate the economy, at least during the first half of the 13th century. Locksmiths, indeed, seem to abound. We find also Richard le Carbuner early in the century and Gilbert le Brenetur in the 1280s (264, 307). Other crafts include masons and carpenters as well as textile workers. From mid-century merchants, including mercers, seem to become more prominent in property transactions and in witness lists. Though we may suspect that cloth production is becoming increasingly important it is becoming more difficult to see the craft complexion of the area from the deeds. Towards the end of the century some prominent individuals, like Richard le Northerne and Ingram de Arningworth, are identifying themselves as drapers (316, 322). Others simply as merchants.

When we move to the heart of the 'Earl's half' it is the variety of crafts which is immediately striking. A range of textiles, leather and luxury metal trades is evidenced. Both victuallers and merchants are prominent among property owners, with merchant and mercer at times seemingly interchangeable. When the occupations of parties are given later in the century the same broad range is reinforced. Some areas do appear to have been more specialized than others however. In Broadgate, for example, goldsmiths and saddlers tend to predominate.[20] They are also prominent in Cheylesmore Lane although the range of occupations is wider. It is here that we find Roger the Bear-ward (*ursarius*) at the beginning of the century and Philip the Crossbowman (*balistarius*, *le arblaster*) and Philip le Enginur at the end (60, 70, 73, 74). In Little Park St. which, like Earl St. itself, displays a host of luxury crafts we find William son of Geoffrey the Scabbard-maker (*vaginator*), Liulf the Cutler, William le Silksewer, Roger le Burser (= purse-maker), and Ralph the Stone-cutter (*incisor*) (84–86, 94, 98). In Earl St. there is a strong contingent of weavers in addition to dyers, mercers and tailors. Carters are also particularly noticeable. It may well be that within Earl St. there were specialized areas, with a concentration of metal and metal-related luxury trades particularly noticeable in the area of Much Park St. and Earl's Mill Lane. Here, during the last 30 years of the century we find men like Richard the Brooch-maker (*fermailer*, *firmacularius*, *le brocher*), Ralf le Mirourer, Clement le Mirourer, girdlers like Alured, Elias, Henry de Milcote, William son of John le Floutere, and Adam le Latoner and William le Glaswright (137, 145, 146, 158, 165, 242, 356, 358). Metal-working in Much Park St. has been reaffirmed by the archaeological record[21] and we find also sub-tenants like Philip the Smith, William the Smith, Thomas le Cotiler (= cutler) and Simon le Bokelere (147, 151, 166, 194). It is in this area, too, that we find the evidence of soap making for which Coventry, according to a famous 13th-century list of towns in verse, was particularly noted. In the vicinity of the White Cellar we encounter the daughters of Geoffrey the Soap-maker (*savenator*) in the late 1230s/early 1240s whilst at the end of the century we find Thomas of Grantham *le Savonner* in Dead Lane (132, 172).

To attempt to draw evidence of industrial organization from the deeds is hazardous. The implications of property accumulation later in the century, by drapers and tanners for example, for the organization of their respective industries can only be guessed at. Although we might well believe in a loss of independence by some craftsmen and an involvement in the processes of production by some of

[20] The 1974 excavation behind the tenements on the east side of Broadgate revealed the existence of a 14th-century tannery and of a cobbler's workshop (*City of Coventry: Archaeology and Development* p. 31).

[21] See S. M. Wright *op. cit.* where a thorough discussion of the Much Park St. excavations and their implications may be found.

the merchants and members of finishing crafts, it would be difficult to substantiate. The master craftsmen, independent or not, can surely be seen, however, among those men of purely localized interest, often with occupational names characteristic of their respective areas, who are found so often among the tenants and witnesses in the deeds; men of the type of the locksmiths of Gosford, the coopers of the area around the church of St. Nicholas, and the girdlers, mirrorers and the like of Much Park St. Many of them, no doubt, had houses facing the street with workshops and yards behind, as indicated by the few excavations there have been of domestic sites.[22] In the vicinity of Earl St. many of these will have been fronted by shops and stalls. Such is likely to have been the case with Thomas the Goldsmith whose chief houses were in Broadgate and Matthew de Ryton the saddler whose chief messuage was also there (48, 51). One thinks also of John the son of William Sley who held a cutler's shop (*cultellarium*) next to his father's messuage in Earl St. (193).

We ought not to conclude too readily, however, that these men followed a single occupation to the exclusion of all else. Brewing, for example, may well have been a secondary calling for many. The case of Richard the Brooch-maker is of some interest. Richard figures prominantly in the 1270s and 1280s, and there seems no reason to doubt his basic interest. After his death his young son, with the consent of his guardian and other friends, leased his entire tenement in Earl's Mill Lane and his chief messuage in Earl St., together with a kiln and certain named vessels worth 12s. 6d. The latter were clearly used in brewing (356, and compare 701 below). The buildings were to be maintained in as good a state of repair as the lessee received them, unless the accident of fire had intervened. An addition on the fold of the deed, but in the same hand, indicates that the grantor had demised a table and trestles also. Were these used for a temporary stall? Similarly, when in 1294 Nicholas le Marchal leased a messuage in the market area he excluded a shop in front of the messuage but included all the brewing equipment found there (701). William le Glaswright held an alehouse (*pandoxinium*) in Much Park St. (165).

To an extent perhaps we should envisage streets or areas as comprising distinct communities. This is clearly the case at Gosford, especially early-mid 13th century, and at Spon. Some individuals were closely identified with a particular locality. Amfrey the Merchant who flourished with his sons in the 1220s and 1230s is identified, when away from his locality, as Amfrey of Park St. (here Little Park St. 347); whilst Robert the Miller and Geoffrey le Lef were similarly described later in the century as of Park St. (here Much Park St. 149). On other occasions we learn where individuals lived, e.g. Henry son of William Pye lived towards the White Cellar (136), or where their chief messuage lay. Hamo the Weaver's, for example, lay in Earl St., Richard le Pursere's near Spon bridge, Geoffrey le Dubbere's in Smithford St. extending back to West Orchard (248, 405, 508). In the latter part of the century some of the wealthier men, included some of those describing themselves as merchants, lived in Earl St. and in the streets leading off towards the churches to the north. Richard the Brooch-maker's chief messuage, as we have seen, was in Earl St., as was that of Richard de Weston merchant where we are told, in the 1280s, he used to live (234). In Bayley Lane lay the stone house or hall of Walter le Buttere, the chief messuage of Adam Russel merchant, and the chief messuage or stone hall of the Wikewanes. One Peter of Paris is also said to have lived there (58, 360, 369, 370). There must be a strong probability that John de Lodelawe lived in Hay Lane since it once bore his name. Some of the more substantial residences were clearly already of stone, drawing no doubt from the quarries north of the town and at nearby Harnall.

In the 'Prior's half' there appear to have been major residences particularly in Well St. and West Orchard. The chief messuage of Richard de Fonte lay very close to the well known as the Throstlewell, from which no doubt he and his relatives

[22] See above notes 20, 21.

took their name. The merchant Thomas de Fakenham had a hall not far away on the west side of Well St. (560, 562). Robert de Feugers had once lived between the bridges in a house he leased to Geoffrey de Willenhall in 1223 (641). The great house where William de Frankton lived lay in the proximity of West Orchard, and it was here that Gerard de Alspath had his tiled stone house which he conveyed to John de Maxstoke in the 1270s (651, 664). The Chiltons, too, may have lived here, and all the indications are that it was a very attractive quarter (657, 658, 699).

With the Lodelawes, Fontes, Alspaths and Chiltons we are in the company of ministerial families with major property interests across the town, and it is to a consideration of these that we must now turn. As has been observed there were no really great property accumulators in Coventry.[23] On the other hand the Hundred Rolls of 1280 do reveal the existence of a more modest group with multiple burgages and/or numerous recorded tenants. What is immediately striking about this group is the preponderance of ministerial figures and the descendants of erstwhile ministers of both the earl of Chester and his successors and of the prior. They range from the current officials – the bailiffs Henry Baker and Robert de Chilton, and Walter Bacon the coroner – and families of recent office like the Lodelawes, Alspaths, Barons and Lewins, through Fonte, Gloucester, Mowbray, Colbrand and Pake to the family of Ranulf III's old bailiff Richard de Aula (represented here principally by Richard de Burton and his wife Petronilla).

Accumulation by some of these figures – for example, Richard de Fonte and John de Lodelawe (and in the latter case its dispersal too) – can be seen clearly in the surviving deeds. Two features are highlighted. Firstly, of course, it indicates the origins of urban accumulation in the period before 1280. And, secondly it indicates a relatively high level of stability among the property-owning élite. The indications are that this may have been truer still during the time of the earls of Chester. The families of many of those who witnessed the local charters of Hugh II and Ranulf III remained prominent through to the mid-13th century – the Smithfords, Vintners and Worcesters – or well beyond – the Fordwins, Martins and Aulas. Beyond these circles there are other prominent families in 1280, such as the Franktons, Haldanes and Herberts, whose position can be traced as far back as the deeds will take us.

The ultimate origin of the early ministerial families is more problematic. In some cases, perhaps, they owed their rise entirely to their service to the earls. The Aulas, for example, may well come into this bracket. One thinks also of those parkers and foresters whose position can be seen clearly in the time of Ranulf III. Service to the earls of Chester was to a high degree the key to prosperity and position in the Coventry area. Higher ranking officials – stewards like William the Marshal, Walter de Coventry, and Walter d'Eyvile – developed interests both within Coventry and in the vills close to the town. So, too, did the familiars of the earl, families like the Picots, Hartshills, Camvilles, Bushervilles, Despensers, Audleys and Segraves. Many, perhaps most, of the more modest local landowners originated in service to the earls: the Barbe d'Averils, descended from members of the earl's secretariat, the Liulfsons (of Brinklow), the Foleshills and perhaps also Liulf of Spon. It becomes difficult to draw a clear dividing line between those with entirely urban and those with wider local interests, and it is probably unnecessary to try. If we exclude those whose significance transcends the locality we are left with a rent and property-owning élite, the greatest of whose common bonds was a past or present relationship with the earls.

Occasionally the names of the earl's witnesses suggest an alternative origin. We find Geoffrey the Goldsmith, for example, and Gerard the Vintner. Gerard, in particular, bears comparison with the prior's great minister of later years, Henry Baker. When Gerard conveyed some of his property to his son, another Gerard,

23 R. H. Hilton, 'Some Problems of Urban Real Property in the Middle Ages', in *Socialism, Capitalism and Economic Growth: Essays Presented to Maurice Dobb* ed. C. H. Feinstein (1967) p. 334.

c.1200–1210 (524) this included, in addition to several lands (*terre*), all the stalls below his chief burgage (very probably in the market area) and the two mills of Radford and Hill with appurtenances which included crofts, moor and meadow. The investment of Henry Baker, himself the son of another Henry Baker, was equally wide (e.g. 51, 575, 616, 729) as was that of his colleague Robert de Chilton and of Martin Colbrand before them. In the case of both Gerard and Henry, the family if not the individual himself, rose initially through provisioning.

Some further clues to the nature of Coventry's élite in the period up to the Hundred Rolls lie in the fines for breaches of the assizes recorded in the eyre rolls. Those for breaches of the assize of wine are recorded in 1221, 1232, 1247 and 1262 (35.11, 36.14, 37.20; *Eyre Rolls 1221* No. 975). Anketill de Wikewane was fined on all four occasions. Other members of his family were also fined, viz. William de Wikewane of London in 1221, and Robert de Wikewane in 1247. Others include: John Fordwin and Richard de Bruges in 1221, Richard de Boskervile in 1232, William Lewin and Martin Colbrand in 1247 and Alexander de Ryton in 1262. We hear of Anketill again in this context when in July 1257 the local sheriff was ordered to pay him for the 3 tuns of wine taken on the king's arrival at Coventry. William le Vineter of Coventry was to receive a similar payment in 1266.[24] Another commodity which the royal purveyors were occasionally interested in acquiring from Coventry was oil. In 1236 the sheriff was ordered to buy 20 sexters of good oil at Coventry for table use, and in 1257 he was ordered to pay Alexander of Coventry 45s. for oil taken for the queen during Lent.[25] Unfortunately, we can only guess as to Alexander's identity. He may conceivably have been Alexander of Gloucester the bailiff, one of whose activities was that of corn merchant. Shortly before his death Alexander had acquired corn from Sir Nicholas de Segrave's manor of Itchington, apparently on credit (197). It is of some interest that Alexander's son and heir was unable to pay the 5 marks his father owed. The solution was a 12-year lease on 10s. rent due from a tenement in Earl St., to run from 30 November 1269. The family seems to have been in some difficulty for not long after Alexander's daughters and sons-in-law sold his messuage in Earl St. to a glove-maker, and bound themselves under ecclesiastical sanctions to abide by the sale (228, 229).[26] Another indication of a lack of capital among Coventry merchants comes from the case of Thomas de Fakenham. Thomas was dead by the time of the 1285 eyre when it is stated that he died bankrupt. He had acknowledged debts of 60 marks to Florentine merchants and of 100 marks to unnamed local men. Having failed to meet the days assigned for repayment his houses and goods were duly sold.[27] Too much should not be made of this for we know little of his circumstances. It is probably of significance, though, that a fairly prominent Coventry merchant, of some standing over a period of time, should have been unable to find sums like these. Certainly it is in stark contrast with the great sums the wool merchants of the 1330s and 1340s were dealing in and the losses they were able to sustain.[28]

The interests of Thomas de Fakenham may well have been on the textile side. He was involved, as we have seen, with Florentines and one of his executors was the wool merchant Roger le Chamberlain. In terms of breaches of the assizes, the eyre rolls are a little less forthcoming in relation to cloth (35.10, 36.2, 36.15, 37.21). The town compounded with a fine in 1232 and again in 1247, although in the later year three individuals were also named, viz. Nicholas Warin, William de Willenhall and Richard de Henley. Two others appear in 1262. One was Anketill de Wikewane

[24] *C.L.R. 1251–60* p. 390, and *1260–67* p. 232.
[25] *ibid.* 1226–40 p. 245, *1251–60 p. 358.*
[26] For other examples of the use of such sanctions see 429, 613.
[27] *Eyre Rolls 1285* m5. For alienations by him at around this time see 141, 212.
[28] R. A. Pelham, 'The Early Wool Trade in Warwickshire and the Rise of the Merchant Middle Class', *Trans. Birmingham Arch. Soc.* vol. lxiii, 1944, p. 41–62.

once again, the other William le Poleter (or *Peleter*) whose name suggests he may have specialized in furs. Undeniably, there is less coincidence here with administrators and *rentiers* than there is in the case of the vintners. On the whole the evidence suggests that the élite of early and mid-13th century Coventry comprised an interlocking group of administrators, property owners and provisioners, with perhaps an admixture of non-victualling merchants and craftsmen such as goldsmiths.

It may well be that by the second half of the 13th century this group was ceasing to accurately reflect the wealth of the town, and it is tempting to see the resultant tension reflected in the challenge to the prior's lordship in 1267–8 and the apparent failure of his prospective gild merchant (above p. xxvii). Roger le Chamberlain, one of the two men who purchased a confirmation of Henry II's charter of 1182 with which to combat the prior, was among the native exporters of wool in 1275.[29] Among those who were admitted to the king's peace in 1266 had been three members of the Shepey family which was later to provide several of Coventry's greatest wool merchants (above p. xxvii). Similarly when we examine the names of the defendants who had challenged the prior's Friday market at the beginning of the 14th century we find among them some prominent wool merchants, and members of families which produced others of the second quarter of the century. There are 4 Meringtons, 3 Shepeys and 2 Tuwes. Hugh de Merington, Ralf de Tuwe, Robert de Stone, Ralf le Hunte and Henry atte Muyre were among the 13 Coventry wool merchants summoned to attend the York Council of 1322. It has been pointed out that Coventry men are in evidence as sellers of wool at Leicester in 1254 and that Hamo Totyng of Coventry shipped wool from London in 1303.[30] On the other hand Roger le Chamberlain was the only Coventrian among the licensees of 1275, and we have no guarantee that wool export, either directly or as intermediary for the Italians, was the main or the only interest of particular families over a long period of time. Many of them, no doubt, were capable of adapting to changing circumstances. The further we move back from the great days of the staple and the budding merchant oligarchs, the greater is the danger that we may make too much of the wool factor.

The role of cloth production is also, to a degree, problematic. Coventry was one of the towns which fined for breach of the assize of cloth in 1202, although it is also clear that it was not then in the first rank of cloth-producers.[31] On the other hand, as we have seen from the evidence for particular localities, the deeds do suggest that the cloth industry was growing during the course of the century. This growth was probably sustained.[32] By the latter part of the century the drapers appear to have been becoming an increasingly self confident group. Coventry's first chantry was founded by William de Copston, draper (714). Of course mercers had long been prominent, but the meaning of mercery was notoriously flexible. One is reminded of the list of merchandise which the prior specified as being sold in the shops and stalls of Earl St. to the detriment of his market. He began with cloth, and added cendal and silk in addition to girdles. A similar range is indicated by the names of the defendants to the 1307 writ. They include a number of girdlers and saddlers, and probably also some provisioners.[33] Continental imports must surely have figured in the merchandise sold in Coventry. Merchants from Amiens were there in 1216, much to the king's consternation for he feared their merchandise might fall into the

[29] *C.P.R. 1272–81* p. 24.

[30] Pelham *op. cit.* pp. 41–42.

[31] *Pipe Roll 4 John* p. xx. Coventry paid £5 whereas Leicester, for example, paid £10.

[32] Mrs. Lancaster Lewis has calculated that between a quarter and a third of those appearing in the surviving Coventry records of the 14th and early 15th centuries were involved in some aspects of the wool or cloth trades (*V.C.H. Coventry* pp. 154–5).

[33] A year book report substitutes spices for girdles, probably in error (33n). The defendants to the 1302 writ are described as mercers. In neither list do names corresponding to those of the drapers of Gosford St. occur.

hands of his enemies.[34] One of their number was William Godric', who may well be equatable with the William son of Godric who conveyed land in the market place to William de Frankton during the first decade of the century (660). Flemish merchants were certainly resident. Hugh de Arraz was married to the daughter of Geoffrey the Goldsmith (380). Richard de Bruges, juror and infringer of the assize of wine, conceivably had the same origins (35.1, *Eyre Rolls 1221* No. 975). Coventry men may not only have handled imported wine but have been importers themselves. A ship laden with the wines of Jordan de Coventre was held by the bailiffs of Winchelsea in 1236. In the event the cargo was directed to London, but it was probably not in this instance intended for Coventry.[35] It is necessary to bear in mind that Coventry was not only a manufacturing centre but also a centre of consumption of some importance.

That Coventry society underwent considerable change during the second half of the 13th century is evident enough. One major shift is reflected in the Hundred Rolls of 1280. Conspicuous by their absence now are many of those external interests which are seen so clearly in the earlier deeds. The statement that the lady of Ansty holds by the service of providing a candle to burn in the earl of Chester's stable is evocative of a world that had gone (768 p. 390). The prominence of external religious houses among the property holders, illustrated so clearly by the Combe abstracts (767), had also passed. Some of these interests passed to the priory (28), some passed through several hands, others became shorn of their urban dimension or cannot now be traced. One factor in this must have been the demise of the earldom of Chester which served to break the cohesion of local society. The phenomenon is by no means peculiar to Coventry, however, and deeper social changes were most assuredly at work. Another factor must have been the nature of the rents themselves. There is abundant evidence in the deeds that the original unit of tenure, in both parts of Coventry, was the land (*terra*) at a ground rent or rent of assize of 12d. In the course of time, in a buoyant and inflationary economy, the gap between this and the economic rent became increasingly wide. Of course, the operation of courts also yielded an income, but only direct involvement, vigilance and the real presence of an active bailiff could ensure the continued profitability of an urban interest. It is surely no accident that those landowners who retained rents late in the century were those with a very strong local interest – pre-eminently the Langleys, but also the Segraves and, as successors to the Foleshills, the du Bois. It was not only external families who could find their incomes waning. The Worcesters (*de Wigornia*) found themselves in difficulty. They are visible, as witnesses to the charters of the earls of Chester, as far back as the 1150s. A century later Richard de Wigornia the younger, described as a burgess of Coventry, divested himself of his property to Sir Gilbert de Segrave. In addition to a solar, stone cellar and forinsec chamber, which may have constituted the family home, and some shops, Richard sold rents amounting to 30s. 2d. from 15 tenants across the southern half of Coventry. The traditional nature of the rents is revealed when they are broken down. Two are of 13d., the remainder are 1s. or multiples thereof. As we have seen Gilbert acquitted him of his debts, of 25 marks and 70s., to the Jews (710).

It is at this time that the designation 'burgess of Coventry' begins to be found in the deeds, as does 'merchant of Coventry' and other similar distinctions. We find Robert de Chilton described as 'burgess of Coventry' for example, in the late 1250s/ early 1260s, John de Lodelawe and Reginald de Catesby likewise in the late 1260s/ early 1270s (292, 470, 666). Social distinctions appear to have been getting sharper, Coventry society more intra-mural.

[34] *Rot. Lit. Claus.* i, p. 173. The Picards were famous for woad, but it may not have been what they were handling on this occasion.

[35] The following year Jordan was handling the wine of Arnold of Périgord (*C.L.R. 1226–40* p. 256; *C.C.R. 1234–37* p. 485).

The evidence suggests an increasing tendency towards property accumulation on the part of some merchants and craftsmen during the last thirty years of the 13th century and if this is not particularly apparent in the Hundred Rolls of 1280 it is necessary to remember that the survey merely stops the clock at a particular point in time. Another characteristic of the defendants in the market cases is that many of them were, in fact, newcomers to Coventry. Neither the Meringtons nor the Tuwes, for example, were present until the 1290s. Hugh de Merington probably came to Coventry *via* marriage, as did another merchant defendant Richard de la Muyre (222, 643). John de Rydeware and John de Langley, both prominent merchants, were newcomers too, as was William Grantpe himself, the leading defendant in 1309–10 who came to Coventry with his father during the 1280s (233). We should be wary, though, of postulating a natural antipathy between the newcomers and the old guard. In fact they are found acting together in joint purchases and leases, itself a seemingly new development of the 1280s and 1290s. Henry Baker and Adam Russel the merchant were acting together in the 1280s (143–144, 213–215), whilst Richard de la Muyre and John de Langley jointly undertook leases of the Poddycroft and Shockersfield in the 1290s, an association which John continued with Richard's heir during the following decade (735–7). A most interesting example of such joint ventures was the leasing of Shortley mills which John and Richard undertook together with the ministerial figures Robert de Chilton and William le Parker in 1289 (750). Langley and de la Muyre were lessees of much arable land both in Coventry and neighbouring vills, as was John de Rydeware.[36] In fact, the penetration of surrounding communities by Coventry burgesses greatly accelerated during the last 30 years of the century. Once again, though, it was figures like Chilton and Baker who were leading the way.

Whether social cohesion was reinforced by any form of social organization remains obscure. There appears to have been no gild merchant. One would dearly like to know the nature of the *convivium* from which Robert de Feugers was returning with his wife one night when the unfortunate incident occurred which was to lead to the death of a young groom (36.11). Certainly the leading townsmen appear to have closed ranks to protect him. Some mechanism had no doubt evolved for the settling of disputes between them, as the intervention of 'friends' seems to indicate (231, 691). They could also combine to direct the affairs of a minor within their ranks (356). This is not to say, of course, that there were no rivalries. Richard de Bruges was undoubtedly an enemy of Alexander of Gloucester, as perhaps Richard of Henley had also been (37.23).

These men belong, of course, to the higher échelons of Coventry society which of necessity figure disproportionately in the foregoing account. The total resident population was probably not far short of 5,000 by 1280 (below p. 366). The question arises, however, as to whether a flourishing centre like Coventry had a significant short-term population of non-residents or itinerants. It is worth noting in conclusion that the eyre rolls indicate that a problem of this nature may have emerged as the century progressed. Whereas in the earlier rolls crimes are imputed to non-residents but rarely, in the later rolls the incidence is much stronger. In 1232 two individuals are described as unknowns (*ignoti*), one of whom turned out to be a burglar and a 'slayer of men', whilst in 1247 one of a group of thieves was described as a vagrant or itinerant (*itinerans*). When we moved forward to 1262, however, not only do we find a number of crimes recorded where the perpetrators were described as strangers or itinerants, but there is also a strong sense of the traditional means of social control proving unable to cope (35.4, 35.15, 36.16, 37.3, 37.7, 37.11–.16). By 1285 the word *vagabondus* had begun to be employed, no less than 13 persons (11 men and 2 women) being so described (38.6–38.8, 38.13). We may be dealing with a change in perception as much as the actuality of crime, of course, but nevertheless it is another significant symptom of social change.

36 C.R.O. 26 EI/8 a & b, 25 EI/11; *Langley Cartulary* No. 233; below 753, 754.

ILLUSTRATIONS

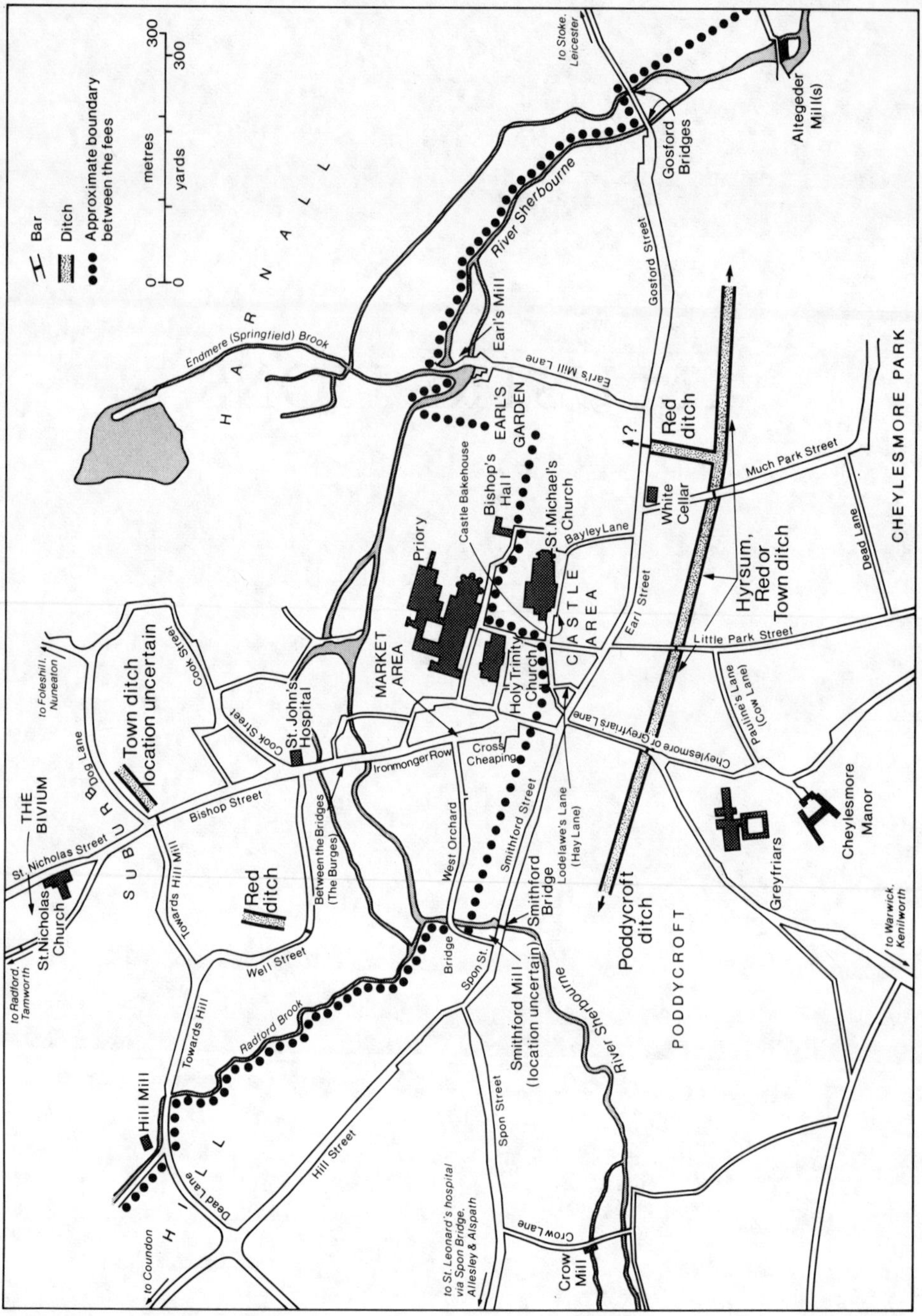

MAP I COVENTRY IN THE THIRTEENTH CENTURY. The street pattern is based necessarily on Samuel Bradford's map of 1748–9 and John Speed's plan of 1610. Only those streets and features which are evidenced in the thirteenth century are named. For additional street names given in the priory rental of 1410–11 see the map in the Atlas of Historic Towns. The monastic buildings are given as of their greatest (conjectured) extent and the churches of Holy Trinity and St. Michael likewise, as rebuilt in the later middle ages.

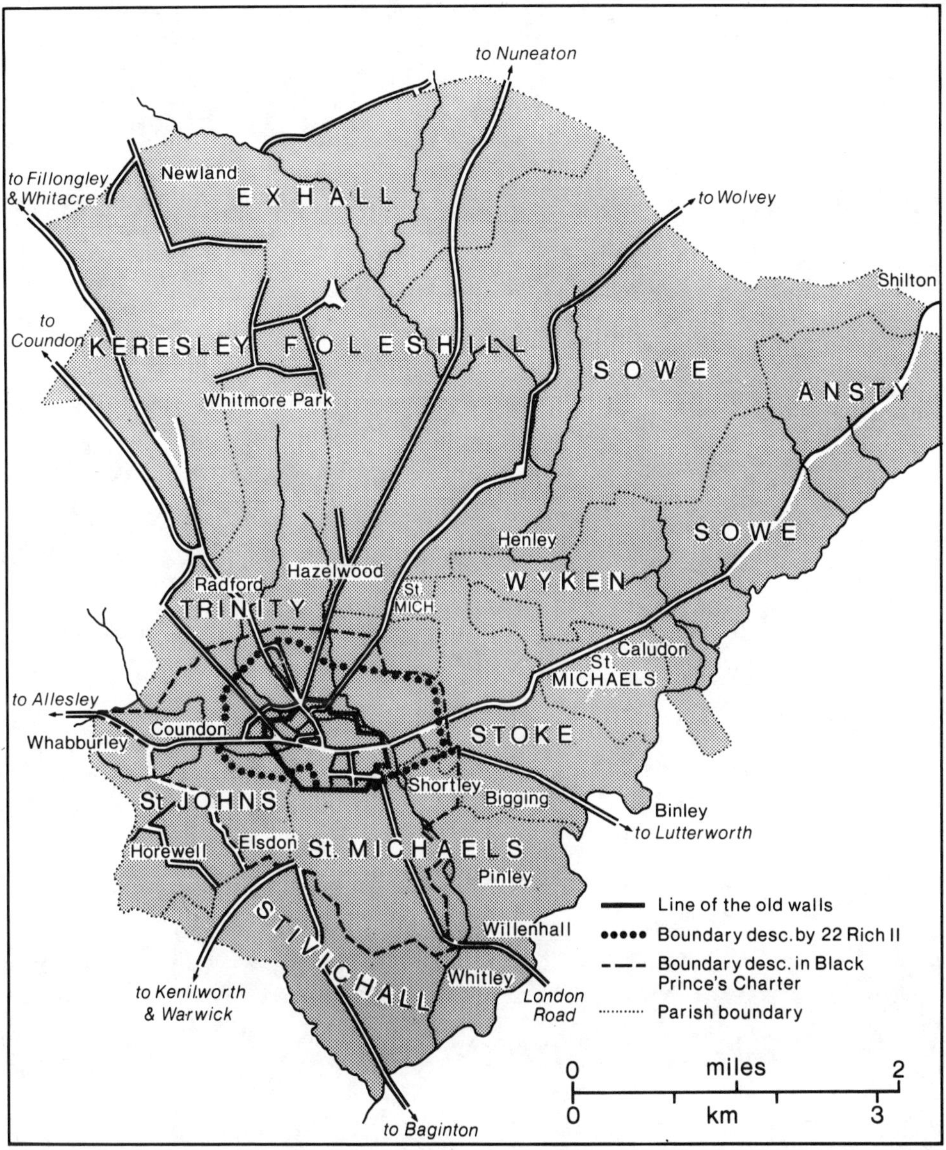

MAP II THE COUNTY OF COVENTRY, 1841 (From the plan exhibited in the action of the Corporation against Lythall and others.)

PLATE I

DOCUMENT NO. 29

DOCUMENT NO.

CHARTERS OF THE EARLS OF CHESTER

The authority of the earls of Chester was such as to command the respect of succeeding generations, and for this reason alone their few surviving charters, whether in copies or originals, need to be treated with extreme caution. Most especially is this true where the recipient was Coventry cathedral priory. Ten of these charters were submitted by the prior for royal confirmation in October 1348. Two of them, only, reappear in the early-15th century Priory Register together with one other charter (No. 6) which was not included in the *Inspeximus*. It is surprising that until very recently these charters should have been treated unreservedly as genuine, since they make their appearance precisely when the priory was fighting a losing battle to preserve its hard-won lordship over Coventry. The most famous of them is the so-called 'boundary charter' by which Earl Hugh II guarantees the integrity of the monks' fee against the action of his own ministers and tenants, forbids them from hindering the prior's Coventry market, and recites the boundary between their respective fees. The witness list, although plausible enough, is rather meagre, and the address is unusual in form. Serious doubts about its authenticity begin to arise, however, when the tenants mentioned in the body of the charter are examined in relation to the local deeds. The seven are the names of tenants who undoubtedly flourished in the time of Earl Ranulf III. William de Rependon occurs regularly as a witness from c.1210–early 1230s. He was a frankpledge head in 1232 (35.14). William son of Richard Fordwin *alias* William Fordwin occurs in 1204 and 1221 (*F.F. Warwicks* No. 150; *Eyre Rolls 1221* No. 360) and is found regularly in the deeds during the first quarter of the 13th century. W(illiam) Hacon occurs in 1209 (*F.F. Warwicks* No. 167) and in deeds from c.1215–c.1226. His son Roger is found from the 1230s. Gerard the Vintner figures from c.1200–c.1215. His son Gerard was often associated with him and, in fact, received Hill and Radford Mills from his father during the first decade of the century (below 524). Robert the Scot received a formal grant of his assart at *Ailwardesich'* from Ranulf III between c.1200 and 1213 (*Langley Cartulary* No. 179). He was dead by 1221 (*Eyre Rolls 1221* No. 963). Among the witnesses to Robert's charter was Anketill Lokard who was still living in 1221 but dead by 1230 (*F.F. Warwicks* No. 275; below 534). Finally R(obert) Beaufiz was dead by Michaelmas 1259 but apparently still living when the Montalt lordship was conveyed to the prior in 1249 (below 719, 721). By contrast only 3 of the 7 names are found before the death of Earl Hugh in 1181. Gerard the Vintner who witnessed for this earl (Nos. 9, 10, 13) may be the elder of the two men mentioned above. An Anketill Lokard witnessed in 1177–81 and may be equatable with Asket' Loc' who appears c.1162 (Nos. 9, 10). William son of Richard Fordwin witnessed with his father in 1177–81 (who was then known himself as Richard son of Fordwin) as he was to do on occasions during the first decade of the 13th century. His father Richard had not long died by 1221 (*Eyre Rolls 1221* No. 398). It is rather unlikely that William was a tenant in his own right before the death of Earl Hugh. Even allowing for longevity and for sons bearing their fathers' forenames it is hardly possible that seven tenants so-named were present in the time of Earl Hugh. All flourished, however, in the time of Ranulf III, the second decade of the 13th century being the time they most likely coincide.

The 'boundary charter' is, therefore, spurious. But when was it fabricated? The named tenants clearly held land at the locations specified and they are reasonably consistent in time with one another. Moreover, the section of the suggested boundary running across the town from east to west broadly corresponds to that revealed by the deeds, at least from the 1230s onwards.[1] It would be possible to argue, therefore,

[1] See above p. xxi–ii.

that the forged 'boundary charter' emanates from the 13th century, perhaps from the change of lordship in 1232/3, although it is strange that it should contain a mixture of tenants, living and dead. There are strong indications, however, that it was produced at a date closer to 1348, possibly utilizing an earlier statement of the bounds. If we move outside of the town to the tenants named in the area to the north, what is immediately striking is that the property of all three of them later passed into the hands of the priory – *Ailwardesich* in stages from the 1250s, the Beaufiz land in 1296, and the Lokard estate not until 1313–20 (below pp. 326–31). These acquisitions were, in fact, major stages in the creation of the priors' park at Whitemore whose origins go back to c.1260 and for which the prior received a retrospective licence in 1332.[2] The effect of the 'boundary charter' is to suggest that these acquisitions were made within the prior's original fee and not within the lands held from 1249 of the Montalts and in the 1330s of Queen Isabella. If this had been the case (and it is in fact contradicted by the Whitemore deeds below) then the prior's park would have been less vulnerable to attack from the queen and her allies. In 1334, at her instigation, an inquiry was commissioned into the priory's acquisitions since the Statute of Mortmain, the prior's exercise of view of frankpledge and his enclosure of the foreign woods 'wherein Isabella should have firewood, charcoal and palings'.[3] In his petition to the Council in 1336 the prior complained that his park was in effect in process of being destroyed by the actions of Isabella's ministers and the townsmen.[4] This attack was only one of the many actions being taken against him.[5] A later petition records how an inquiry was held by the queen's ministers at which townsmen testified as to the ancient bounds as they had existed in the time of the earls of Chester. The result was a new and much-reduced 'Prior's half' in operation from 1337 and corresponding, as far as can be ascertained, to the prior's soke as agreed under the settlement of 1355. One major effect of this must have been to deprive the prior of his jurisdiction over the Coventry market which the 'boundary charter' insists was on the soil of the foundation.[6] The 'boundary charter' then was fabricated in order to reassert the boundary between the jurisdictions as it had been in the mid-thirteenth century, to preserve the prior's jurisdiction over the market area, and to help protect his park. These issues point unmistakably to the years 1337–1348. The forgery may well reflect a realization that the battle to preserve the priory's lordship over the whole of Coventry was all but lost, and that the issue would soon be how much could be preserved. If this is so the charter is most likely to have originated during the 3–4 years between the charter of Incorporation on January 20 1345 and the date of the *Inspeximus* (October 24 1348).

Three other charters seem to be forgeries of around the same date (Nos. 17–19). The grantor is Ranulf III and the terms are as follows. No. 17 conveys 280 acres of woodland and waste in Exhall and Keresley in exchange for one of the two carts journeying daily in his woods which Ranulf had confirmed to the monks (No. 16). The land is located, and the charter concludes with permission to cultivate and enclose. No. 18 recites the bounds in rather different terms (and with more emphasis on natural features) so that future generations should be left in no doubt, whilst No. 19 is a quitclaim in the same together with a grant of view of frankpledge, escheats and all liberties and free customs. A striking feature is the near identity of the 3 witness lists, suggesting that if genuine they must have been issued in swift succession. It is also noticeable that they contain no witness who is not present in

[2] See above p. xxv.

[3] *C.P.R. 1330–34* p. 574.

[4] *Rotuli Parliamentorum Anglie Hactenus Inediti*: *MCCLXXIX-MCCCLXIII*, ed. H. G. Richardson and G. O. Sayles (Camden Soc. 3rd. series, vol. li, 1935) pp. 240–66.

[5] For what follows see, in particular, A. & E. Gooder, 'Coventry before 1355: Unity or Division?' *Midland History* vol. vi, 1981, espec. pp. 19–21 which effectively utilizes the petitions preserved by Humphrey Burton for the first time, and to which I am much indebted.

[6] See above p. xxx–xxxi.

the other 3 charters of Ranulf III to the church of Coventry (Nos. 13, 14, 16). The addresses, too, are suspicious. Those for Nos. 18 and 19 cannot be authentic as they stand. Like the boundary charter these three are clearly intended to bind not only the earl's heirs but also his local ministers and tenants, and this can be seen in the addresses, the prohibition clause of No. 17 and the malediction of No. 19. The language of No. 18 is also reminiscent of the 'boundary charter', both in its description of the bounds and its concern for the doubts of future generations. It is when we put the content of these charters in the context of the priory's activities since the Montalt grant of 1249 and of the challenge to its lordship during the 1330s that their full effect is apparent. The priory's attack on the woodlands and wastes was at its most intense in the area to the north of Coventry as Prior Henry's waste rental indicates.[7] His park at Newlands seems to have been a bone of contention with the later Montalts as early as 1303 whilst the prior complained of an attack on his manor here, too, in 1336.[8] Like enclosure of the commons, view of frankpledge was one of the central issues between the queen and the prior in their contention of 1330s, and Newlands persisted as an island within the queen's leet jurisdiction in the vills and hamlets surrounding Coventry.[9] The manner in which these charters settle all the issues in favour of the prior argues strongly against them. It is the anachronistic licence to approve which is most telling against No. 17, diplomatically the least unacceptable of the three. The re-stating of the bounds in No. 18 is curious, suggesting perhaps that No. 17 was felt to be inadequate. The specification of the perch by which the land was to be measured may also indicate this. It may also suggest that the forgeries were made in more than one stage, No. 17 lying at the beginning of the sequence.

The two charters of Ranulf II are more problematic. One of them (No. 2) is a restoration of the chapel of St. Michael with all appurtenant chapels, established or to be established, and parochial rights in 14 named vills, and is made to Prior Lawrence and the monks. There are confirmations by Hugh II (No. 5), by Ranulf III in a charter dated 30 July 1192 (No. 13), and by Bishop Gerard Pucelle in an extant charter (No. 12) of 1183–4. Two other charters are closely associated. Another charter of Hugh II (No. 6) again confirms his father's gift of St. Michael's but in terms different from No. 5, whilst a further charter of Ranulf III (No. 14) addressed to the bishop of Chester, the archdeacon of Coventry and the clergy of the diocese is concerned specifically with the disposition of tithes. These six charters are best considered as a group. The authenticity of two of them seems beyond doubt. Pucelle's charter is an original bearing his seal which there is no reason to dispute. Ranulf III's charter of 1192 although surviving only in the *Inspeximus* was referred to in 1238 when Bishop Alexander de Stavensby resolved his dispute with the prior and monks of Coventry over its custody, an immediate indication that the rights contained therein were a matter of contention.[10] The authenticity of the remaining four charters is open to at least some initial suspicion. There is a *prima facie* case against Ranulf II's charter (No. 2) and his son's confirmation of it (No. 5) on two grounds. Firstly, the existence of another charter of Earl Hugh (No. 6), from the Priory Register not the *Inspeximus*, granting St. Michael's only with appurtenances opens the way to doubt. It is granted not to Prior Lawrence but to the abbey and monks and confirms a charter of his father's in terms that indicate this was not No. 2. Secondly, it appears from the account at Michaelmas 1182 of the custodian of the

[7] See above p. xxv.

[8] *C.P.R. 1301–7* p. 188; Richardson and Sayles *loc. cit.*

[9] *ibid.* Dr. Gooder kindly drew my attention to some copies (or drafts) of a bill of complaint to the justices of *oyer and terminer* made by the prior against Isabella's steward in the mid–late 1330s (C.R.O. E2). They concern *inter alia* an attack on the prior's manorial rights at Newlands.

[10] The charter was to be entrusted to the abbot and convent of Combe, both parties having access (*Magnum Registrum Album* No. 500).

young Ranulf III's estates during the early years of his minority that 69s. 6d. was allocated annually to the clerks of the earl's chapel at Coventry. It would appear that, despite the charters, the monks were not then the recipients of the tithes. Since the sum reappears on the two following years it would seem that Pucelle's charter, at least in this respect, had no immediate effect.[11] Either, then, Nos. 2 and 5 are not genuine or, if they are genuine, a number of anomalies need to be explained. Supposing them to have been forgeries No. 2 would have to have been forged by or for Prior Lawrence himself, the undoubted instigator of the forged foundation charters, taking advantage perhaps of Hugh II's minority, or by his successor for presentation to Bishop Gerard Pucelle during the minority of Ranulf III. No. 5, on the other hand, since it is not referred to by Pucelle, would be more likely to have been forged when both were presented to Ranulf III in 1190. The fact that it would have involved two stages is the first argument against forgery. A second is that it would have involved a complex web of deceit. Not only would Bishop Pucelle and Ranulf III have been hoodwinked but also Bishop Richard Peche whose own charter is referred to by Pucelle (unless, of course, this too were a fabrication). More importantly, No. 2 is a very plausible instrument. Ranulf II made other deathbed restitutions, as well he might,[12] and the witnesses are consistent with this. Finally, a charter addressed to Prior Lawrence and the monks accords well with the date (1153), for he was the recipient of charters from Stephen, probably in 1152/3, and Henry II in 1155.[13]

How, then, do we account for the rival charter of Hugh II (No. 6)? It was granted to the abbey and monks, reflecting the situation as it had been in the time of Bishop Roger de Clinton and before the rise of the formidable Prior Lawrence. It may well be that its existence reflects, also, a rival claim to presentation to the chapel on the part of the bishop. By returning to the conditions of Ranulf II's original grant it would effectively by-pass Prior Lawrence. Although, like No. 2, it could conceivably be a forgery, on internal evidence the presumption must again be in favour of its authenticity. The witnesses are consistent and it contains the circumstantial evidence of the burial at Coventry of Hugh's brother Richard (who is otherwise unrecorded). If it does, indeed, represent a rival claim the instigator must have been Bishop Richard Peche; oddly, for he is one of the few 12th-century bishops with whom the monks are not known to have been on bad terms. On the other hand it may not be insignificant that the surviving confirmation is from Pucelle and that we do not know the terms of Peche's charter to the monks. Although Prior Lawrence had managed to acquire at least a measure of freedom from episcopal control there may well have continued to be a degree of strain in the relations between the bishop and the monastic house. In other words, Pucelle's charter would seem to be a recognition that the priory had won through. In short, we cannot be sure who had presented to the chapel between 1153 and 1183, but it is clear that the right was soon to be exercised by the bishop, though in close association with the earl. In fact, there may well have been a three-way contest for the valuable assets contained in Ranulf II's charter (No. 2), with Earl Hugh retaining the tithe in favour of his clerks and perhaps a major say in who was presented to the living. His confirmation charter (No. 5) omits the clause dealing with parochial rights[14] and in all probability we have here the explanation of the omission of any reference to this charter in Pucelle's confirmation. It is likely that Hugh II had declined to honour his father's deathbed

[11] *Pipe Rolls 28 Henry II* p. 149, *29 Henry II* p. 74, and *30 Henry II* p. 149.

[12] See below No. 2n, and also No. 4.

[13] See above 11.

[14] There is, of course, the possibility that this clause was omitted by error from the charter roll. It is also missing, however, from the transcript in B.L. Add. MS. 32100 (fos. 60–60v) which appears to have derived from the original *Inspeximus* rather than the charter roll. A marginal note reads: 'My brother Hales hath this under the great seal of king'.

grant, hence the allocation of the tithe to earl's clerks during the minority of his own son.

The position achieved by Prior Lawrence and cemented with Bishop Gerard de Pucelle was, of course, short-lived and the advent of Bishop Hugh de Nonant more than tipped the balance against the monks. At the end of July 1192 he submitted Nos. 2 and 5 to Ranulf III for confirmation. Ranulf made his own grant solemnly in the abbey church placing his charter with a gold ring attached on the altar, an old-fashioned form of investiture. Although this charter is undoubtedly genuine one of the clauses as it stands does present something of a problem. The grant was said to have been made to the prior and his successors of the church of Coventry at the entreaty of Bishop Hugh. But strictly speaking there was no prior in 1192. Indeed the circumstances would better fit 1190, i.e. between the resignation of Prior Moses in 1189 and the expulsion of the monks at the end of the following year. However, a scribal error seems unlikely. Both the charter roll and a transcript which seems to have been taken from the original *Inspeximus* (B.L. Add. MS. 32100 fos. 60v–61r) give the year as 3 Richard I. The charter makes no specific mention of the monks and perhaps Hugh's secular canons are to be understood here as successors to the prior. The latter was in any case, under a royal grant of 1188, an episcopal nominee.[15] Alternatively the phrase mentioning the prior and his successors may well be a later insertion to bring the charter into line with those of the earl's predecessors, or, less likely, the clause may itself be a later interpolation. Whatever the case, there may well be a connection between the hazards inherent in transferring these rights and the solemnity of the occasion.

A further charter (No. 14) now placed the tithes from the earl's Coventry estates firmly in the hands of the secular clergy.[16] Ralf, the earl's chaplain, is specifically mentioned here as the parson of St. Michael's. He may well be identical with the R. de Coventry, clerk, whom Hugh de Nonant was later said to have appointed after he had expelled the monks.[17] Relations between earl and bishop were probably quite close during these years, and the return of the monks and the death of Bishop Hugh in 1198 did not alter the situation with relation to the chapel of St. Michael. His successor, Geoffrey Muschamp (1198–1208), was said to have given the chapel to Ranulf de Mainwaring, clerk, at the earl's request.[18] The monks subsequently appealed to both Honorius III and Gregory IX and in each case commissions were established to decide on their claim. The dispute over the custody of charter No. 13 must be seen in this context. The issue of the chapels, then, was a constant sore and was raised again in the time of Bishop Hugh de Pattishall. On this occasion the prior was forced to drop his action and submit to the bishop (1 June 1241) who made the following arrangement: the monks were to be paid 30 marks annually by the vicar of St. Michael's and were in turn to pay 20 marks of this to the old incumbent Ranulf de Mainwaring. In terms that were doubtless intended to be humiliating to the monks of Coventry the church of Lichfield was given precisely

15 In 1186 or 1187 Pope Urban III, at the instance of Hugh de Nonant, quashed the election of priors which concession an earlier prior had obtained (*Magnum Registrum Album* No. 438). The prior in question was of course Lawrence. According to Honorius III in 1221 the election of the priors had been regulated in the agreement between Lawrence and Walter Durdent before Eugenius III (*Cal. Papal Letters* i, p. 85). The royal grants of the priory to Bishop Hugh in 1188 and 1189 included the right to institute the prior (*Magnum Registrum Album* Nos. 168, 591), and in 1189 Prior Moses surrendered the priory to him and promised never to return (*Rot. Cur. Regis* i, p. 66). Of the various accounts dealing with the events leading up to the expulsion the most judicious are by D. Knowles, *The Monastic Order in England* (Cambridge 1940), pp. 322–3, and by P. Heath in *V.C.H. Stafford* vol. III (Oxford, 1970), p. 24.

16 Even then he appears not to have abandoned all interests in the matter as the charter to William the Marshal of Olney indicates (see below p. 9).

17 *Magnum Registrum Album* No. 271.

18 *ibid.* No. 362.

19 *ibid.* Nos. 238–9, 271.

the same.[19] The bishop and his successors were to appoint and institute the vicars, and formal appropriation of the living by the bishop was approved by papal indult dated 18 June.[20] This, however, was not to be the end of the matter. The issue was finally resolved, after the prior had invoked the grand assize, by the award of mutually agreed arbitrators on 29 June 1248. On the authority of Bishop Roger de Weseham the prior and convent were to have St. Michael's with its chapels and apply its revenue to their use as their documents showed it belonged to them rather than to the bishop. A vicarage was to be established, to the value of 24 marks, and the rights of the present incumbents of the chapels were to be safeguarded.[21] Detailed arrangements for the vicarage were made in April of the following year by which time Richard de Sallowe had been appointed in succession to Ralph de Leicester.[22] St. Michael's and its appurtenant chapels had been, in effect, appropriated, a position that was formalized by Bishop Roger Meuland in 1260.[23] At some cost the priory had finally achieved the degree of control over Coventry's churches adumbrated by Ranulf II's charter and still probably uncertain at the time of Bishop Pucelle in 1183–4.

The other charter of Ranulf II (No. 3) is more doubtful. It purports to be a grant to the abbey and monks of Coventry of 2 carts journeying twice daily in his woods to take what is necessary for building repairs, for fuel and for hedging. It was confirmed by Ranulf III (No. 16). The address with its *nominatim ballivis et forestariis* is rather unusual but may be explained by the nature of the grant. The witness list, however, although headed by some ministers and close associates of Ranulf II, contains some odd features. Gilbert son of Picot is not otherwise known to witness for Ranulf II and seems much out of place here. A regular witness for the next earl, he was still living c.1190 and possibly a little later.[24] And then there is William Barbe d'Averil. William was the son of Ralf Barbe d'Averil, chaplain, and became the head of Hugh II's secretariat.[25] They seem to appear in reverse order here. Alternatively William could be William the chaplain, Barba Aprilis, who had witnessed for Earl Ranulf I and was the father of Ralf.[26] This would suggest a date early in Ranulf II's time. On the other hand Lamfram priest of Stoke witnessed a writ of Hugh II to Gilbert Foliot, bishop of London (1163–1187), where he is found with Gilbert son of Picot and Ralf and William Barba Aprilis.[27] Richard Hairun is not otherwise known in the pedigree of the Hairuns of Church Lawford.[28] No clear date emerges. Gilbert son of Picot might conceivably be accommodated, albeit with difficulty, if the date were 1153 but the circumstances are clearly not those of No. 2, and the witnesses bear no resemblance. Moreover, one would have expected Prior Lawrence to have been the recipient of such a charter at this date. Relations between the earl and Coventry priory had not been easy at the height of Ranulf's power in the area and the absence of Ivo the constable is also indicative of a date before the hostilities. A genuine charter would be more likely to belong to 1129–c.1140. The content of the charter once again reaffirms the impression that it is spurious. It is

20 *Cal. Papal Letters* i, p. 198.

21 *Magnum Registrum Album* Nos. 240, 345. The bishop was to be recompensed with the churches of Ryton and Bubbenhall, and the church of Lichfield was to receive its 30 marks in future from the priory's church of Southam.

22 *ibid.* No. 704.

23 See above p. xxiv. Incidentally, at this point the appurtenant chapels were named as Ansty, Shilton, Wyken, Stoke, Binley, Sowe, Stivichall, Foleshill, Exhall and Spon. There is no evidence that chapels had ever been built at Whitley, Pinley, Keresley, Whoberley and Bisseley named in Ranulf II's deathbed grant.

24 No. 13n.

25 Tait, *Chartulary of St. Werburgh* i, p. xlviii; Barraclough, 'Some Charters' p. 32.

26 Farrer *H.K.F.* p. 53 n4; *Genealogist* vol. 5 (1888) p. 68 No. 15. I owe this reference to Professor Barraclough.

27 Jeayes, *Derbyshire Charters* No. 1945.

28 *V.C.H. Warwicks* vol. vi, p. 147.

true enough that the earls, Hugh II and Ranulf III in particular, carefully controlled assarting in the area, as the latter's gifts to the hospital of St. John, for example, show (No. 20). Access to the woods for estovers on the other hand seems to be distinctively a problem of the early 13th century. It is damaging that there is no charter of confirmation from Hugh II. It seems very probable then, that Ranulf III was presented with a forgery for confirmation in 1204–1208. Indeed, repairs must have been a pressing problem just at this time, for Hugh de Nonant is reported to have destroyed the conventual buildings.[29] Hugh had himself launched a building programme and it is possible that the charter, which like No. 6 makes no mention of the prior, may have been forged for him. If so it was taken up and used to good effect by the restored monks.

Like the priory charters Ranulf II's charter to the burgesses of Coventry has hitherto been accepted as authentic without serious critical scrutiny. And yet it ought not to be accepted without at least some reservations. It survives not as an original charter but is embodied in a royal confirmation belonging to Jan.–March 1182 (No. 11). The disappearance of the original charter has always been difficult to account for, and the argument that a second charter by Ranulf III made the first superfluous is not wholly satisfactory. Moreover, there is no allusion to this charter after 1182.[30] Neither is there any trace of a confirmation charter from Hugh II. A royal confirmation, moreover, might have been expected from the minority of Hugh II, rather than that of his son. The date at which this charter first appears is suspicious from another point of view. The immediate effect of the royal confirmation would have been to severely limit the financial exactions of the custodian Philip de Kyme. The terms of the charter were, indeed, generous to the burgesses. They were confirmed in their burgage tenure as in the time of the earl's father (Ranulf I), and granted the laws and customs of the citizens of Lincoln. The earl forbade his constables taking burgesses into the castle to plead and created a portmoot for pleas between them and himself where they would be fined a maximum of 12d. for any misdemeanour. Moreover they were authorized to choose one of themselves as *justicia* who should know the laws and customs and keep them with the counsel of the earl, rendering him his rights. They need not supply him without security, incoming merchants were to be encouraged and to be justiciable at the portmoot and those who came to build were to be free of dues for two years. The right to elect their own justice was quite extraordinary. Such a privilege was granted to only three other borough communities in the twelfth century. They were London (1131) and the royal boroughs of Colchester (1189) and Northampton (1200). Furthermore only one of these can have preceded Ranulf's grant. In all three cases the chief function of their justice was to keep the Crown pleas.[31] Coventry's *justicia*, however, was clearly intended to be an authority on local law and presumably to function as president of the court. It was a privilege by no means mirrored in any other urban charters granted by the 12th-century earls of Chester. When Ranulf III granted his own charter to his burgesses of Coventry (No. 15) he made no specific reference to his grandfather's grant, and although he repeated the majority of its clauses, his charter was no slavish repetition of the earlier text. Indeed, the new charter would seem to suggest a seignorial tightening up. The clause freeing newcomers from dues is now dropped, as is freedom from maintaining the earl without security. More particularly, in place of the limitation of fines to 12d. maximum we now have a clause granting reasonable amercement by the lord's bailiff and the burgesses of the court. Although the elected *justicia* is allowed to remain it is the role of the earl's bailiff which is stressed; indeed his position is affirmed specifically as an officer of

29 *The Chronicle of Richard of Devizes* in *Chronicles of the reigns of Stephen, Henry II and Richard I*, ed. Richard Howlett (Rolls Series, 4 vols. 1884-89), iii, p. 440.

30 The charter which was proffered during the market case of 1309–10 was almost certainly that of Ranulf III (below No. 33).

31 See *British Borough Charters 1042–1216* ed. A. Ballard, (1913), lxxxvii.

the court. Occurrences of lords of boroughs abrogating clauses in the charters of their predecessors are not unknown[32] but it is difficult to see how Ranulf III could have overriden privileges hallowed by such long custom as a charter of Ranulf II would imply. There are, then, grounds enough for some suspicion. There are, on the other hand, a number of points in its favour. Tait in establishing the grantor as Ranulf II, rather than his grandson as had once been supposed, pointed to the appearance of the fuller form *portmannemot* as against the later *portimot* of Ranulf III's charter.[33] The grant of the laws and customs of Lincoln would suggest a date after the earl's success in acquiring that city in the winter of 1140–41. Between then and his arrest in 1146 Coventry figured strongly in his thinking.[34] Ranulf's grant of the constableship of Chester to Eustace fitz John was made at Coventry between 1144 and 1146 and was witnessed by Ivo the constable of Coventry who was clearly an official of some importance and authority.[35] This would seem to be reflected in the earl's Coventry charter. Ranulf, then, was much concerned to protect and consolidate his interest in Coventry during this period, and perhaps also to develop the area. For this reason his charter, which would seem in all probability to belong to 1141–1146, offered a substantial series of inducements. Even so, to place so much power in the hands of an elected official would seem uncharacteristic to say the least of this particular earl.

On balance, then, it would seem unlikely that Henry II was presented with a complete fabrication but there remains a strong possibility that this rather involved charter contains at least one, and perhaps several interpolated clauses. In such circumstances it would hardly be surprising that Ranulf II's original has not survived.

Of the charters to laymen the most extraordinary is Ranulf II's grant of Coventry to Robert Marmion (No. 1). This charter was brought to light by Professor R. H. C. Davis who has examined its context in detail and argued persuasively for a date of 1145/46.[36] Coventry was the scene of some fierce fighting between Robert Marmion II and Ranulf earl of Chester in the 1140s. In or before 1144 Marmion fortified Coventry priory presumably in order to lay siege to Ranulf's castle. In September 1144 he was killed during a foray against the earl who had appeared in force presumably to relieve the castle.[37] Arrested in August 1146 the earl purchased his freedom by surrendering his castles. After his release he attempted to recover Coventry but was unsuccessful.[38] Only the most extreme of circumstances can have induced Ranulf to part with the town. Such circumstances, Professor Davis shows, can only have been present between Ranulf's reconciliation with the king at Stamford (late 1145 or early 1146) and his arrest at Northampton on 28 August 1146. The charter probably represents one of a series of sacrifices intended to placate Stephen's adherents.[39] It does, however, display some curious features and these have given

[32] See, for example, the cases of Brecon and Tenby in *Boroughs of Medieval Wales* ed. R. A. Griffiths (Cardiff, 1978), pp. 53, 306.

[33] James Tait, 'The Earliest Municipal Charters of Coventry', *English Historical Review* vol. xliii, 1928, pp. 383–385.

[34] See, in particular, H. A. Cronne, 'Ranulf de Gernons, earl of Chester 1129–1153', *Trans. Royal Hist. Soc.* 4th ser. xx (1937) pp. 127–128.

[35] Barraclough, '*Some Charters of the Earls of Chester*', p. 28. Ivo also witnessed a grant by Earl Ranulf II to Robert de Barrow of the terms by which he was to hold his newly-constructed mill at Coventry (*Langley Cartulary* No. 189). The date is after the elevation of William de Roumare to the earldom of Lincoln in 1141 (*Handbook of British Chronology*, p. 436) and probably before the earl's arrest in 1146.

[36] 'An Unknown Coventry Charter', *English Historical Review* No. cccxl, 1971, pp. 533–545.

[37] *Chronicles of the reigns of Stephen, Henry II and Richard I*, ed. Richard Howlett (Rolls Series, 4 vols., 1884–89), i, p. 47.

[38] *Gesta Stephani*, ed. K. R. Potter (London, 1955), p. 132.

[39] *Op. cit.* pp. 530–539.

rise to doubts over its authenticity.[40] Apart from the rather bald grant of *Coventreiam* without qualification it contains some linguistic peculiarities, chief among them *jubeo* where one would expect *precipio* and *constanter* for *in perpetuum*. The script is a rather plain one and not that of any other known charter of Ranulf II. The seal, moreover, belongs to the late 13th or early 14th centuries and was probably affixed when nine words were added in a later hand, over an erasure. None the less the script is unmistakably of the 12th century, and it is extremely difficult to envisage a later context in which the charter might have been forged.[41] The only real alternative to its authenticity must be that it was fabricated by either Robert Marmion II or Robert Marmion III to bolster a claim to Coventry. No further Marmion interest in Coventry is evidenced after the death of Ranulf II. One way or another the charter is a curiosity emanating from the conditions of the civil war.

The two extant charters of Earl Hugh to Liulf de Brinklow appear to be genuine (Nos. 8, 9). The relationship between them, however, is not immediately apparent. The earlier (No. 8) belonging clearly to the earl's minority confirms the grantee's land within and without Coventry together with the vill of Bisseley, all of which he is to hold in burgage tenure. The additional grant of seignorial rights creates in effect an urban or suburban soke. An odd feature is the appearance of an unnamed prior of Coventry among the witnesses. The later charter (No. 9) belongs to the beginning of the earl's majority. Oddly it is this and not the former which is witnessed by his mother, the countess. The annual rent has now risen from 6s. 8d. to 14s. 6d. but the charter does contain an important additional grant of pannage. Seignorial rights are no longer mentioned. It may be that the earlier charter was felt to lack sufficient authority, particularly as it appears to have been issued early in the minority when the earl was a child of tender years.

A number of other grants, to the Liulfsons and others, are to be found in the *Langley Cartulary* (Nos. 179, 188, 189, 194, 213, 215, 223). Beyond these the texts of few charters to local lay figures have survived. Robert Halstead published the texts of three charters of Ranulf III in 1685, two to William the Marshal and one to Richard son of Robert.[42] The texts are rather unreliable due to indifferent transcription and to the editor's tendency to include insertions of his own out of genealogical interest. The substance of the grants, however, seems genuine. William the Marshal received a grant of 40 acres between Coventry and his land of Asthill (*Esthull*) with pannage and permission to either assart or hold the land as it is with its wood (*cum nemore*). The second grant was of permission to give the tithes from his demesne at Asthill and from all the lands and assarts which he held of the earl at Asthill to a chaplain to serve in his chapel there, rendering 1lb. incense annually to the church (*sic*) of St. Michael, Coventry. Both grants are before the fall of Normandy in 1204. Ranulf's plain title is employed, and below the former grant Halstead depicts the seal with a lion on a heater shield as in Ranulf's charter to the burgesses of c.1199–1204 (No. 15). William the Marshal was one of the earl's local stewards in the area and was undoubtedly functioning in the 1190s.[43] Dugdale noticed another grant to him of land at Caludon, but unfortunately the full text of this has not

[40] By Joan C. Lancaster Lewis in *Medieval Coventry – A City Divided?* (Coventry, 1981), pp. 33–35, and by Professor Barraclough in a letter to the present editor.

[41] The charter was employed to some advantage by Arthur Gregory in the 16th century but it seems most unlikely that it can have been fabricated by him. (See the appendix by R. Bearman to Professor Davis's essay, *loc. cit.* pp. 545–47). Professor Davis has made the interesting suggestion that the charter was refurbished in the 1330s as an attempt to check Queen Isabella's claims, based as these were on the rights of the earls of Chester (here transferred to Marmion).

[42] R. Halstead, *Succinct Genealogies of the Noble and Ancient Houses of Alno (and others)*, (London, 1685), pp. 451–452.

[43] *Pipe Roll Society* vol. 14. p. 45, *Rolls of the Kings Court, Richard I*, [Trinity term 1194]; *Eyre Rolls 1232* m18. William was dead by Michaelmas 1209 (*F.F. Warwicks* No. 174).

survived.[44] The grant to Richard son of Robert included a virgate of land with an appurtenant messuage and meadow at Olney (*Olneya*) which Geoffrey son of Osbert held and ½ virgate of land which pertains to the earl's mill (location unspecified). The date is c.1204. Richard was the brother or brother-in-law of William the Marshal (below No. 528), and Halstead's texts call both men *de Sutton* or *Suttonia*.

The late 16th-century cartulary of Arthur Gregory includes a transcript, without witnesses, of a charter of Ranulf III earl of Chester to Robert the Marshal of 40 acres of land at Stivichall, 35 of them said to be of assart (*de exarto*). Robert was permitted to enclose the land by view of the earl's foresters.[45]

A grant by Hugh II to Geoffrey his homager of 12d. land (*duodecim numeratos terre*) and 2 assarts at Coventry was noticed by Ormerod. This time we have the witnesses but not the text. The date is between his marriage to Bertrada (1169) who heads the witnesses and the earl's arrest in 1173.[46] The rent of 12d. reappears in Ranulf III's grant to Robert the Scot of a messuage in Coventry and his 17 acres of assart at *Alwardsica* (*Langley Cartulary* No. 179).

Many of the earl's ministers and associates must have received gifts of rents in and around Coventry, like those to Henry de Audley which were confirmed by the king in 1227 (below 347n). The later history of these can be traced. Like the local rents of another of the earl's stewards Walter d'Eyvill[47] they were eventually to find their way into the hands of Robert de Stoke (below 757–760, 764–766).

[44] Bodleian Dugdale MS. 18 fo. 6.

[45] *Et preterea concessi ei clausuram de nemore meo omnibus predictis acris rationabiliter per visum forestariorum meorum.* (*Shakespeare Birthplace Trust*, DR 10/1409 fo. 139).

[46] G. Ormerod, *Cheshire* I, p. 31. The seal is depicted. The original had belonged to Mr. Thomas Sharp of Coventry.

[47] *Eyre Rolls 1232* m14.

1 1145–1146

Charter of Ranulf II, earl of Chester, granting Coventry to Robert Marmion III.

Ran(ulfus) comes Cest' constab(ulario) suo et dapifero et omnibus baronibus suis et hominibus atque amicis clericis ac laicis francis et anglis tam presentibus quam futuris salutem. Notum sit vobis omnibus me dedisse Rob(er)to Marmion Coventreia(m) in feudo et hereditate sibi suisque heredibus tenendam constanter de me ac de meis heredibus cum omnibus pertinentiis in burgo et in villa in bosco et in plano in aquis et molendinis et in omnibus rebus. Quare volo et jubeo quatinus sic bene et quiete ac libere et honorifice et in pace et eisdem libertatibus teneat quibus tenebam quamdiu erat in meo dominio et eisdem conventionibus que prescripte sunt inter me et ipsum videlicet hac conventione [quod mihi serviat contra omnes homines et o(mne)s mulieres].[1] His etiam testantibus et cartam confirmantibus Hugo(n)e Wac Ric(ardo) de Ca(m)villa Sim(one) fil(io) Will(elm)i Hugo(n)e de Cuill(i) Will(elm)o de Redza(m)i Will(elm)o fil(io) Rad(ulfi) Rob(er)to Potario.

G.H. 256

Seal: equestrian in white wax, not original (late 13th/early 14th century).

[1] These words are written in a later hand over an erasure.

The above charter is reprinted, with the kind permission of the author, from R. H. C. Davis, 'An unknown Coventry charter', *English Historical Review* No. CCCXL. July 1971, pp. 533–545.

2 1153

Charter of Ranulf II, earl of Chester, returning to Prior Lawrence and the convent of Coventry the chapel of St. Michael which is sited in his fee at Coventry and all other chapels established or to be established within and without the vill in his fee and their parish, with all parochial rights in tithes, oblations and other benefits.

Ran(ulfus) Comes Cestr' omnibus hominibus suis francis et anglis et universis fidelibus tam presentibus quam futuris salutem. Notum sit vobis me recognovisse et reddidisse Deo et sancte Marie et Laurencio Priori et conventui monachorum Coventr' monasterii jus omni quod ad eos pertinere et eos habuisse multorum clericorum et laicorum assercione et testimonio michi certificatum est scilicet capellam sancti Michaelis que est in feudo meo sita apud Coventreia(m) omnesque alias capellas infra villam et extra in meo feudo et in eorum parochia constitutas vel constituendas cum omni jure parochiali in decimis et oblacionibus ceterisque beneficiis tam vivis quam mortuis videlicet de Anesty Sulftona Wica Bileneya Witeleia Pynneleia Stoca Stivechala Eccleshale Folkeshulla Keresleia Watburleia Spanna Bisseleia. Hec predicta beneficia cum omnibus suis pertinentiis Coventren(si) monasterio sicut matrici ecclesie plenarie reddidi et recognovi pro salute anime mee et patris et matris mee parentum et antecessorum meorum libere quiete et honorifice imperpetuum possidenda. Testibus Rodberto abbate de Alencest(r)ia Rogero capellano Comitis Willelmo presbitero Walkelino Maminot Rodberto Banastr' Warino de Vernoun Rodberto Basset Willelmo de Greseleia Yvone filio Ansketilli Rodberto de Buschervill' Hanr(ico)[1] filio Siwardi Ardarn' Ansketillo Lundoniens' Swyft de Cov'

[1] sic.

Nigello Morino de Ecclesh' Viel' de Folkeshull' Siwardo de Folkeshull' et multis aliis.

P.R.O. C53/135 mm5, 4.

[1] sic.
Another copy is in Coventry Priory Register fo. 76r.

This restitution was undoubtedly made towards the end of the earl's life. He died at Gresley on 16 December 1153 (*Handbook of British Chronology* p. 420; Cronne 'Ranulf de Gernons' p. 134), and had probably recovered Coventry only six months before (Davis, 'An Unknown Coventry Charter' p. 536). He made other restitutions, to Chester Abbey and to the church of Lincoln (Tait, *Chartulary of St. Werburgh* i, No. 349; C. W. Foster, *Registrum Antiquissimum* i, pp. 94, 96–7, ii, p. 7). Several of the witnesses also indicate a date late in the earl's life. Robert Banastre and Roger the chaplain witnessed in July 1149 but not earlier (*Lancashire Pipe Rolls*, p. 296). William de Gresley and Robert de Bushervill witnessed Ranulf's deathbed grant to Chester Abbey (Tait, *loc. cit.*).

3

Supposed charter of Ranulf II, earl of Chester, granting to the abbey and the monks of Coventry 2 carts journeying twice daily, excepting feast days, in his woods to take what is necessary for building repairs, for fuel and for the remaking of hedges, by view of his foresters.

Ran(ulfus) Comes Cestr' constabular(io) suo dapifero justiciar(iis) vic(ecomitibus) baronibus et omnibus hominibus suis francis et anglicis tam presentibus quam futuris et nominatim ballivis et forestariis suis de Coventr' salutem. Sciatis me dedisse et concessisse Deo et abbacie sancte Marie de Coventr' et monachis ibidem Deo servientibus pro amore Dei et salute anime mee et meorum antecessorum in puram et perpetuam elemosinam duas bigas errantes in bosco meo cotidie bis exceptis festivis diebus ad capiend(um) ibi de bosco meo quod eis necessarium fuerit ad edificia sua reparanda et ad focum suum et ad sepes illorum reficiend(as) per visum forestariorum meorum. Quare prohibeo omnibus hominibus meis et nominatim ballivis et forestariis meis de Cov' quod nullus eorum presumat hanc elemosinam disturbare vel impedire et qui hoc fecerint maledictionem Dei et mei habeant. Testibus Ricardo Pincerna Serlone Venatore Galfrido Dispensatore Ivone filio Ansketilli Hugone de Hardredeshull' Gileberto filio Picot Swyft de Coventr' Ada filio Godrici Hugone de Warrewic Nicholao de Foro Willelmo Barbedaveril Rad(ulf)o capellano Johanne clerico Ricardo Hairun Lanframo clerico et multis aliis.

P.R.O. C53/135 m4.

4

1153–1157

Charter of Hugh II, earl of Chester, and countess Matilda his mother giving Stivichall with the mill next to the park to Walter bishop of Chester and his church for the absolution of Earl Ranulf, the redemption of his soul, and for the injuries which he inflicted on the aforesaid church and bishop.

Hugo comes Cestre et Matill' comitissa mater ejus constab(ulario) dap(ifero) justic(iariis) baronibus [et] omnibus hominibus suis salutem. Vos scire volumus nos dedisse et concessisse in perpetuam elemosinam Walterio[1] episcopo Cestrensi et omnibus successoribus suis et ejus matri ecclesie pro comitis Ran(ulfi) domini nostri absolutione et pro a(n)i(m)e ipsius et antecessorum nostrorum et nostrarum animarum redemptione et nominatim pro damnis que Ran(ulfus) comes predicte ecclesie et episcopo intulit Stivinghale cum molendino quod est juxta parcum et cum terra

Duillet et cum terra parcarii et cum omnibus pertinentiis ipsius ville, ut teneat eam ab omni servitio seculari solam et liberam et quietam in bosco in plano in molendinis in aquis in paschuis[2] in pratis in panagiis et cum omnibus utilitatibus ad illam villam pertinentibus excepto parco et vivarii piscibus. Et volumus et precipimus ut ep(is)c(opus) teneat villam illam cum omnibus predictis ita libere et quiete sicut aliquis ep(is)c(opus) tenet liberius et quietius ecclesie sue possessiones. Test(ibus) Eustach(io) Constabulario Roberto Dapifero Willelmo Malbanc Willelmo Pat(r)ic Roberto Banast(re) Tom(a) de Verd(un) Alured de Co(m)br(ai) Hugone Austricario.

G.H. 575.

Seal: circular, brown, equestrian. It is damaged around the outer edges and no legend is extant.

[1] sic. [2] sic.

Ranulf II died 16 December 1153 leaving his son aged only 6. Hugh II had livery of his inheritance c. 29 September 1162. (*Handbook of British Chronology* p. 420). This grant in association with his mother was during his minority. The latest possible date is 1157 when Eustace fitz John died (*D.N.B.* vii, pp. 183–4). The purpose of the grant suggests a date close to 1153. Walter Durdent was consecrated bishop of Coventry on 2 October 1149 and died 7 December 1159 (*Handbook of British Chronology* p. 233). He had conveyed his Stivichall estate to Roger Durdent, knight (G.H. 576).

For a grant by Eustace fitz John of property near the south gate in Coventry see *Langley Cartulary* No. 214. This can be dated between 1144–46 when Eustace became constable of Chester (G. Barraclough, 'Some Charters of the Earls of Chester' pp. 25–29) and his death in 1157.

5 1162–1173

Charter of Hugh II, earl of Chester, confirming to Prior Lawrence and the monks of Coventry the chapel of St. Michael sited in his fee at Coventry which Ranulf his father acknowledged to be their right and returned to them and all other chapels established and to be established within and without the vill of Coventry, in his fee and their parish.

Hugo Comes Cestr' omnibus hominibus suis francis et anglicis et omnibus Christi fidelibus tam presentibus quam futuris salutem. Notum sit vobis quod ego pro salute mea et heredum meorum et pro salute anime patris mei et omnium antecessorum meorum concedo et confirmo Laur(encio) priori et monachis de Coventr' capellam sancti Michaelis in meo feodo apud Cov' sitam quam Ran(ulfus) pater meus ad jus Coventr' monasterii pertinere recognovit et reddidit et carta sua confirmavit omnesque alias capellas infra villam Cov' et extra in meo feodo et eorum parochia constitutas vel constituendas scilicet Anesty Sulfton' Wicham Stocham Biln' Pinnel' Witel' Stivesch' Ecclesh' Folkesh Keresl Watburl' Spannam Bissel. Hec vero beneficia Coventren(si) monasterio sicut matrici ecclesie concedo et confirmo in perpetuam elemosinam libere quiete integre et honorifice possidenda ita quod nullus heredum vel successorum meorum aliquid jus super donacionem predicte capelle sancti Michaelis adversus prefatos monachos de Cov' aliquo modo vel aliquo tempore possit vel debeat vendicare. Testibus Edm(undo) archid(iacono) Willelmo Maubanch' Roberto Banastr' Willelmo de Ruel[ent] Ivone de Allesp' Rad(ulfo) de Busch' Turaldo Sewale hominibus Com(itis) Sim(one) Johanne hominibus Prioris Cov' et multis aliis.

P.R.O. C53/135 m4.

This charter is between Hugh's livery of his inheritance on c.29 September 1162 and his deprivation in the summer of 1174, and is most unlikely to be after William de Rhuddlan was taken prisoner with the earl at Dol in August 1173 (Barraclough, 'Some Charters' p. 37). Hugh was restored to his lands on 13 January 1177 (*D.N.B.* vol. X, p. 164). Meanwhile, William Malbank had died in 1176 (G. Barraclough, *Early Cheshire Charters* p. 13). Prior Lawrence died on 29 January 1179 (D. Knowles and C. N. L. Brooke, *The Heads of Religious Houses 940–1216*, Cambridge, 1972, pp. 40–41), by which year Edmund who occurs 1161–65 had ceased to be archdeacon of Coventry (C. R. Cheney, *From Becket to Langton*, Manchester 1956, p. 187; R. W. Eyton, *Court, Household and Itinerary of King Henry II*, London, 1878, p. 226n).

Robert Banastre had witnessed for Ranulf II in 1149 and 1153 (*Lancashire Pipe Rolls*, p. 296; above No. 2). Ivo de Alspath fl. c.1155 (*V.C.H. Warwickshire*, vol. iv, ed. L. F. Salzman, London, 1947, p. 151; F. M. Stenton, *Documents Illustrative of the Danelaw* No. 331). He conveyed land at Alspath to the priory of Monks Kirby in recompense for his deeds committed on their land during the civil war (*Calendar of the Gregory Hood Deeds*, ed. R. Bearman, *The Shakespeare Birthplace Trust*, No. 524) and the chapel of Alspath to Coventry Priory (below No. 12). Turald and Torol' (below No. 9) are probably one and the same. William Malbank had witnessed early in Hugh's minority (above No. 4). The date is, therefore, likely to be closer to 1162 than 1173.

6

1162–1173

Charter of Hugh II, earl of Chester, confirming to the abbey and monks of Coventry, for the souls of himself, his father and his brother Richard whose body is buried in the abbey, the gift which his father made to them of the chapel of St. Michael of Coventry which is in his fee.

Universis sancte matris ecclesie filiis Hugo Comes Cestr' salutem. Sciatis me concessisse et hac presenti carta mea confirmasse Deo et abbacie sancte Marie de Coventr' et monachis ibidem Deo servientibus pro salute anime mee et patris mei et Ricardi fratris mei cujus corpus in predicta abbacia sepelitur donacionem illam quam pater meus Ranulphus Comes Cestr' eis fecit et carta sua confirmavit scilicet capellam sancti Michaelis de Coventr' cum omnibus pertinenciis suis que sita est in feodo meo libere et quiete imperpetuum possidend(am) sicut carta patris mei eis testatur. Et ut concessio rata et firma permaneat eam p(rese)nt(is) scripti auc(torita)te et sigilli[1] mei testimonio confirmavi. Testibus Edmundo arch(idiaco)no Coventr' Johanne Priore de Trentham Ricardo avunculo meo filio Comitis Glouc' Rogero Malfylastr' Hervi[2] de Missin' Rad(ulf)o Vide[3] Rogero de Liv[et] et Willelmo de Ruelent[4] Willelmo filio Ricardi Thurstano clerico et multis aliis.

Coventry Priory Register fo. 76r.

[1] sigillo [2] sic. [3] sic, for vicecomite? [4] Deruelent

This charter was printed by G. Ormerod from the version contained in Dodsworth Liber L (Bodleian Dodsworth MS. 65) fo. 24 (Ormerod, *Cheshire*, vol. 1, p. 25), which seems to have come from Bodleian Dugdale MS. 12 (fo. 238) and ultimately from the Coventry Priory Register. The Dugdale/Ormerod version contains only the first 4 witnesses and reads *sicut carta mea eis testatur* in place of *sicut carta patris mei eis testatur*. Richard the earl's uncle and son of Robert, earl of Gloucester died in 1175 (G.E.C., vol. v, p. 686). The charter is, therefore, before the earl's deprivation in 1174 and again almost certainly before William de Rhuddlan was taken prisoner with Earl Hugh in August 1173 (above No. 5n). Richard son of the earl of Gloucester, Roger de Malfillastre and Hervi de Missi are 3 of the 6 witnesses on behalf of the earl in a charter of c.1170 (F. M. Stenton, *The First Century of English Feudalism*, pp. 258–59). Another is Ralf the sheriff who may be the man transcribed as Ralf

Vide here. Richard the earl's uncle, Roger Malfillastre, Roger Livet, William de Rhuddlan and Ralf the sheriff all witnessed the earl's charter to Richard de Davenport of the same period (Barraclough 'Some Charters' No. 10). This charter may, therefore, be later than No. 5 but is still probably well before 1173/4.

7

Supposed letter of Hugh II, earl of Chester, prohibiting his ministers and tenants from interfering in the fee or demesne of the prior and monks of Coventry and from hindering the market on the soil of the church's foundation, with recital of the boundary between the fees.

Hug(o) Comes Cestr' omnibus hominibus suis et precipue sen(escallo) ballivis forestar(iis) ministris et tenentibus suis de Coventre tam presentibus quam futuris salutem. Quia pium est sanctam ecclesiam cum suis juribus et ministris contra mundi malignos incursus protegere et tueri vobis omnibus et singulis ex parte Dei et mei firmiter prohibeo ne quis vestrum religiosos viros priorem et monachos matricis ecclesie mee de Cov' de ten(ur)a sua quam nunc possident vel in futur(um) poterunt possidere inquietet jacturam seu injuriam faciat. Set sint omnia eorum terre et ten(ementa) cum libertatibus eis spectantibus ita libera quieta et soluta ab omni exactione calumpnia et impedimento mei heredum assign(atorum) seu ministrorum nostrorum sicut ipsorum fundator(es) et feoffator(es) ipsa liberius et quietius tenuerunt et eos inde plenius et liberius feoffaverunt. Prohibeo etiam vobis ne quis vestrum infra eorum feud(um) vel dominium seu m(er)catu(m) quod in solo fund(ationis)[1] ecclesie sue est statutum contra eorum voluntatem se intromittat vel homines ad idem m(er)catu(m) cum m(er)cimoniis suis vel alios quoscumque venire volentes impediat vel molestet quovismodo. Et ne quis post(er)or(um) ambigat qui sunt termini et bunde inter feuda scire vos volo quod terminus divisionis feudorum includendo semper feud(um) et dominium ipsorum religiosorum meumque excludendo incipit ad cimit(er)iu(m) capelle sancti Michaelis in Cov' dirigens se directe juxta lata(m) porta(m) mei castelli inter ten(ementa) Willelmi de Repyndon' et Willelmi filii Ricardi Forthwyn tenentium eorumdem religiosorum ex parte aquilonari et feudum meum ex parte australi descendens in rivum aque de Smythesford' et inde ascendendo per rivulum ad molendina Gerardi le Vineter de Hull' et Radeford' usque in Cundealm' et sic div(er)tendo se inter terram Roberti Scott de Ailwardesich' juxta Blakemore terras et ten(ementa) R. Beaufiz et Anketill(i) Locard ex parte una et boscum meum de Haselwode ex parte altera et sic per rivulum de Enedem(er)e usque ad altam viam ducentem per med(ium) Harenhal' juxta terit(orium) de Stoca usque gibetum et inde descendendo per terram de Bissel in rivum aque de Goseford' et sic per eundem et fossat(um) juxta terram W. Hakun usque ad clausu(m) prioratus monachorum et ibi terminatur. In hujus rei t(estimonium) huic l(itte)re sigillum meum apposui. Hiis testibus Eadmundo archid(iacono) Cov' Rad(ulf)o Meynilwar' G(ilberto) filio Pigot Willelmo de Aula Nicholao filio Liulfi et fratribus ejus Willelmo clerico et aliis.

P.R.O. C53/135 m5.

[1] For this reading see A. and E. Gooder, 'Coventry before 1355: Unity or Division' *Midland History*, vol. VI, 1981, pp. 6, 29.

8 1153–c.1155

Charter of Hugh II, earl of Chester, granting to Liulf de Brinklow the entire land within and without the vill of Coventry which he held of Earl Ranulf the grantor's father together with the vill of Bisseley and its mill which he held in the time of the grantor's father all of which he is to hold in free burgage for ½ mark of silver per annum. Grant also of seignorial rights.

Hugo Comes Cest(r)ie const(abulario) dap(ifero) baronibus ministris famulis hominibus suis omnibus francis et anglicis tam clericis quam laicis salutem. Vos scire volo me concessisse et reddidisse Liulfo de Brinchalauo et suis heredibus totam terram et tenuram suam infra villam Covintre et extra sicut pater meus Comes Ran(ulfus) ei concessit et carta sua confirmavit scilicet totum burgagium suum in domibus et mansuris infra burgum et extra, et ad incrementum feudi sui villam de Bisseleia cum uno molendino quod ibi est et cum omnibus aliis ejusdem ville pertinentiis et omnes alias tenuras quas t(em)p(o)r(e) p(at)ris m(e)i tenuit. Hec omnia predicta ipse Liulf et heredes sui teneant et habeant de me et heredibus meis in libero burgagio reddendo singulis annis pro omnibus serviciis dimidiam marcam argenti. Volo autem et precipio quod bene libere honorifice teneant i(n)perpetuum feudum et hereditatem cum saca et soca cum teloneo et team et infanganfel et cum omnibus aliis libertatibus. T(estibus) Ran(ulfo) vicecomite Rog(ero) capellano Rog(ero) de Bealca(m)po Ivo[1] filio Haschat' Hug(one) filio Haschat' Willelmo de Burvilla Willelmo filio Nig(elli) P(r)iore de Covintre Rad(ulfo) capellano Nig(ello) Willelmo filio Rog(eri) de Aula Willelmo de Wigornia Rob(erto) de Stoca Rob(erto) de Baru Haschat' de Lundoniis et alii multi[2] apud Covintre.

G.H. 257

Seal (detached): white, defaced.

[1] sic. [2] sic.

Unlike other confirmation charters issued during Hugh II's minority, this was not witnessed by his mother Countess Matilda. There can be no doubt of the date however; indeed it would seem to belong to the beginning of the minority. Ranulf the sheriff fl. c.1151 and witnessed 4 charters of Ranulf II (*P.R.O. Lists and Indexes* No. 9, p. 17A; J. Tait, *Chartulary of St. Werburgh*, i, No. 9; F. M. Stenton, *First Century of English Feudalism*, App. Nos. 23, 48; *Registrum Antiquissimum*, ii, No. 316). Yvo son of Ansketell, Roger the chaplain and Ralf the chaplain likewise witnessed for Ranulf II (Tait *op. cit.* Nos. 20, 352; *Monasticon*, iv, p. 313; *Lancashire Pipe Rolls*, p. 296; Farrer, *Honors and Knights Fees* 1923–5, vol. ii, p. 53; G. Barraclough, 'Some Charters of the Earls of Chester' No. 4; Nos. 2 and 3 above), whilst Robert de Barrow had received a grant from him in the Coventry area (*Langley Cartulary* No. 189, and above No. 3n). With the countess, Roger and Ralph witnessed Hugh's confirmation charter to Greenfield Priory c. 1155 (F. M. Stenton, *Documents Illustrative of the Danelaw*, Nos. 150, 151), and Roger, with the countess, a charter to Chester Abbey (Tait *op. cit.* No. 22). Roger also witnessed, with Hugh, Matilda's gift of Repton Church to the priory of Calke probably c.1153 (*Monasticon*, vi.i, p. 598; *V.C.H. Derby* ii, ed. W. Page, London, 1907, pp. 58–59).

9 c.1162

Charter of Hugh II, earl of Chester, granting to Liulf de Brinklow the entire land within and without the vill of Coventry and the vill and mill of Bisseley all of which Earl Ranulf the grantor's father gave him and which he is to hold in free burgage with quittance of pannage for 200 pigs.

Hugo Comes Cest' omnibus hominibus suis francis et anglicis clericis et laicis tam presentibus quam futuris salutem. Notum sit vobis me concessisse et reddidisse et ac carta mea confirmasse Liulfo de Brincolao et suis heredibus totam terram et tenuram quam Comes Rannulfus pater meus eis dedit et concessit in feudo et hereditate infra villam de Coventreia et extra, et ad incrementum feudi sui concedo eis et confirmo villam de Bisseleia quam pater meus predictus eis dedit et concessit et molendinum quod ibi est cum omnibus ejusdem ville pertinentiis in terris et in aquis pratis et pascuis in viis et semitis in bosco et plano ita quiete et libere sicut pater meus melius et liberius eis dedit et concessit et carta sua confirmavit. Hanc totam terram et tenuram predictus Liulfus et sui heredes mea confirmatione et concessu teneant et habeant et i(n)perpetuum possideant de me et meis heredibus in libero burgagio reddendo singulis annis pro omnibus serviciis quatuordecim solidos et sex denarios. Insuper dedi ei et heredibus suis quietationem de pannagio de ducentis porcis. Et pro hac mea concessione et donatione et confirmatione ipse Liulfus dedit mihi quadraginta et septem marcas. His testibus Matillide Comitissa Cest(r)ie matre mea Willelmo Pat(r)ico Willelmo de Solers Ricardo de Luvetot Willelmo de Ruelent Ricardo de Beumeis Jurd(ano) Rasur Rad(ulfo) capell(ano) Willelmo filio ejus Bertramo Cam(erario) Thorol' Willemo Sauenn' Asket' Loc' Willelmo de Aula Nigello de Covent' Gerard(o) Vinet(er) Willelmo filio Sunnul' Ricardo filio suo Petro filio Ade de Norhant' Adam[3] le Blunt de Norhamt'.

B.L. Harley 83 F.32

Large red equestrian seal, incomplete. Counter-seal on reverse: SIGILLUM WILELMI BARBEDA[VR]IL

[1] sic.

Countess Matilda seems to have functioned as Hugh's first witness, for the most part at least, during his minority. Five of the above, however, were regular witnesses for the adult earl: Richard de Luvetot who with William de Ruelent (= Rhuddlan) was among those taken prisoner with the earl, following his rebellion, at Dol in August 1173 (G. Barraclough, 'Some Charters of the Earls of Chester' pp. 37–38), William Patrick who died in 1184 (G. Barraclough, *Early Cheshire Charters*, p. 6), Bertram the Chamberlain and Ralph and William Barbe d'Averil. Bertram, who witnessed for the earl from the 1160s and who married the daughter of William Fleming of Great Meols c.1180, was still alive and in office in 1208 and possibly even later (Barraclough, *Early Cheshire Charters*, p. 39, and 'Some Charters of the Earls of Chester', p. 37). William Barbe d'Averil son of Ralph the chaplain, became the head of Hugh II's secretariat (Tait *op. cit.*, p. xlviii). The fact that he is here called William the son of Ralph may perhaps indicate a date early in his career. William de Ruelent witnessed for the earl in 1162–73 (Barraclough, 'Some Charters of the Earls of Chester' No. 10, and No. 5 above).

Hugh II's confirmation of his mother's grant of Repton church to the canons of Calke, which has been assigned to c.1162, has 6 witnesses in common with the above in addition to Matilda herself, who in each case witnesses first. (I. H. Jeayes, *Derbyshire Charters*, No. 535). They are: Ralph the chaplain and William the clerk, William Patrick, Richard Luvetot, Bertram the Chamberlain and Jordan Rasur. A date close to 1162 would seem therefore to be preferred.

10 1177–1181

Charter of Hugh II, earl of Chester, giving to Nicholas fitz Liulf in free burgage the entire land which his father held of the grantor on the day he was alive and dead.

Hugo Comes Cestr' constab(ulario) dapifero et omnibus baronibus suis et omnibus ballivis suis et omnibus hominibus suis Francis et Anglis presentibus et futuris salutem. Sciatis me dedisse concessisse et presenti carta mea confirmasse in feodo et hereditate et in libero burgag(io) Nicholao filio Liulphi et heredibus suis de [me et de] heredibus meis totas terras et tenuras quas Liulphus pater suus tenuit de me et heredibus meis anno et die quo ipse Liulfus[1] fuit vivus et mortuus etc.[2] Test(ibus) Ricardo de [ ][3] Waltero le Brett Gilberto filio Picott Willelmo Wastett Henrico Munsell' Rogero Luvetot Frumbaldo Willelmo filio Ricardi Roberto filio Gilberti Pigott Anketillo Locard Johanne Clerico Payone Camerario Ep(iscop)i Lamberto Willelmo de Verdun Eugenulfo de Coventr' Ricardo de Smiteford Gerardo Vinet(er) Rad(ulf)o le Turner Willelmo Clerico Comitis Henrico de Oxendona Ernisio de Coventr' Willelmo de Aula Odone Nigro Martino le Brut' Rogero de Aula et Ricardo fratre [suo] Ricardo filio Fordwini et Willelmo filio suo et multis aliis.

[1] sic. [2] sic. [3] blank in MS.

This charter is among transcripts of charters of the earls of Chester in Dodsworth Manuscript 31 in the Bodleian Library, fos. 94–94v.

The date is between Hugh II's reinstatement in 1177 and his death on 30 June 1181 (*Handbook of British Chronology*, p. 420). Liulf de Brinklow (above Nos. 8–9) was also known as Liulf or Lidolf of Coventry. He discharged a debt of £100 to the crown in 1158–60 (*The Great Rolls of the Pipe 1155–58* ed. J. Hunter, 1844, p. 184; *Pipe Rolls* 5 H. II p. 26 and 6 H. II p. 35) and was no doubt the *Luulf* who received 2 messuages in Coventry from Eustace fitz John before 1157 (*Langley Cartulary* No. 214 and above No. 4n). A Liulf of Coventry was again in debt to the crown for license to concord in 1179 and paid by instalments from 1179 to 1182 (*Pipe Rolls 25 H. II* p. 114, *26 H. II* p. 100, *27 H. II* p. 75, and *28 H. II* p. 94). If this is Liulf de Brinklow, however, the account should have appeared for the last time in his name at Michaelmas 1181, in view of the above charter. He may in fact have been dead by November 1179 (below 765.5). There is a possibility that the indebted Liulf of 1179–82 may be equatable with Liulf de Spon who occurs from 1196 (see below No. 407n).

Nicholas fitz Liulf, the grantee, accounted for 13 marks which he owed the earl of Chester in 1184 (*Pipe Roll 30 H. II* p. 23), perhaps in relief. Of the witnesses Walter le Bret of Wolfhamcote and Wyken, fl. 1181–5 and a little before (*Langley Cartulary* Nos. 507, 565–66) whilst Frembald, like Gilbert son of Picot a regular witness for Hugh II, died in 1183–4 (G. Barraclough, 'Some Charters of the Earls of Chester', p. 35). Many of the others were to witness for Ranulf III (see below No. 14).

11 Marlborough (Jan–March 1182)

Charter of Henry II confirming to the burgesses of Coventry the liberties and free customs which Ranulf II, earl of Chester, granted to them.

H(enricus) Dei gratia Rex Angl(ie) et Dux Norman(nie) et Aquit(annie) et Comes Andeg(avie) archiepiscopis episcopis abbatibus comitibus baronibus justic(iariis) vicec(omitibus) et omnibus ministris et fidelibus suis totius Angl(ie) salutem. Sciatis me concessisse et presenti carta mea confirmasse burgensibus de Covintr' omnes libertates et liberas consuetudines quas Rann(ulphus) Comes Cestr' rationabiliter eis concessit et carta sua confirmavit, scilicet ut ipsi burgenses bene et in pace et honorifice in libero burgagio teneant sicut umquam in tempore patris prefati Comitis vel aliorum antecessorum suorum melius et firmius tenuerunt, et habeant omnes leges et consuetudines quas cives Lincoll' meliores et liberiores habent. Et ne constabularii predicti Comitis eos aliqua causa in castellum ad placitum ducant, sed portmannemot suum libere habeant in quo omnia placita ad ipsum Comitem et ad illos pertinentia juste tractentur. Quemlibet autem ex semetipsis pro Comite eligant qui sub Comite super eos justicia sit et qui leges et consuetudines suas sciat et eos consilio comitis in omnibus rationabiliter omni causa remota custodiat et ipsi Comiti jura sua fideliter faciat. Et si forte aliquis in forisfactu(m) Comitis inciderit per xij den(arios) quietus sit. Si vero xij nu(m)mos testimonio vicinorum suorum dare non poterit eorundem consideratione ita admensuretur quod persolvere valeat. Et preterea cum aliis quietationibus quod nec ipsi burgenses prefato Comiti nec suis aliquid in corredio vel in alio acco(m)modent nisi ea conditione quod de redditione catalli sui tuti sint. Quoscumque autem mercatores secum ad ville emendationem adduxerint pacem h(abe)ant et nullus eis injuriam faciat vel injuste eos in causam mittat. Si vero aliquis extraneus mercator aliquod inconveniens in villa fecerit in portmannemot coram justicia supradicta sine causa illam emendet; et illi qui in villam venturi sunt ex illo die quo in villa edificare ceperint per biennium de omnibus quieti sint. Quare volo et firmiter precipio quod prenominati burgenses de Covintr' omnes predictas libertates et liberas consuetudines habeant et teneant bene et in pace libere et honorifice sicut carta sepedicti Comitis Rann(ulphi) rationabiliter testatur. Testibus Rann(ulpho) de Glanvill' Rogero le Bigot Roberto filio Bernard(i) Ricardo de Luci Patrich(io) de Chaurc' Rann(ulpho) de Geddeng', apud Merlebergam.

C.R.O. B2

Seal missing.

The identity of the grantor of the original charter as Ranulf II, not Ranulf III as had been supposed, and the date were established by James Tait in 1928 ('The Earliest Municipal Charters of Coventry', *English Historical Review*, vol. xliii, pp. 383–85). Henry II was at Marlborough in January 1182 and abroad from March. At Michaelmas 1182 men of Coventry (*homines de Covintre*) accounted at the Exchequer for 20 marks 'for having the king's confirmation of their liberties' (*Pipe Roll* 28 Henry II, p. 96). The charter has been printed several times but not altogether accurately. For these see A. A. Dibben, *Coventry City Charters* (Coventry Papers No. 2, Coventry, 1969) pp. 7–8, and in addition to the references given there *Archaeological Journal*, vol. 15, 1858, pp. 243–44. It was confirmed by Henry III on January 30 1268 (*C.Ch.R.*, vol. ii, p. 88; where it is rendered more accurately).

12 Jan. 1183–Jan. 1184

Charter of Gerard Pucelle, bishop of Coventry, taking the monks of Coventry under his protection and confirming their present and future possessions, including the site of their church and the chapels belonging to it, the chapel of St. Michael in the fee of the earl of Chester with tithes, oblations and appurtenant chapels granted by Ranulf II and confirmed by Richard bishop of Coventry, the chapel of Alspath, the church of Ryton on Dunsmore with the chapel of Bubbenhall, the grove on Dunsmore called *Stude* with the chapel built there, and the wood and church at Packwood.

G(erardus) divina permissione Covent' ep(is)c(opus) universis sancte matris ecclesie filiis ad quos presentes littere pervenerint salutem in eo qui salus est omnium. Licet ex off(ici)o cure pastoral(is) nobis injuncto teneamur religiosas personas et loca divini obsequii usibus deputata paterna affectione fovere et a malignanciu(m) improbitate tueri propensiori t(ame)n karitate et diligentiori sollicitudine inducimus providere ut monasterium Covent' et monachi ibidem D(e)o famulantes perpetua pace gaudeant et stabilitate. In(de) est quod ad omnium notitiam volumus pervenire nos idem monasterium et ordine(m) monasticu(m) cum omnibus ad illud spectantibus sub protectione D(e)i et nostra suscepisse et eidem monasterio ac monachis in eo divino mancipatis servicio q(ue)cumque inp(re)sentiar(um) juste possident aut inpost(erum) justis mod(is) poter(un)t D(e)o adjuvante adipisci presenti scripto confirmasse. Ex quibus q(ue)da(m) propriis duximus exp(r)imenda vocabul(is): Primo ipsum locum in quo ecclesia Cove[n]t' sita est cum omnibus suis pertinenciis et cum capell(is) ad eandem ecclesiam spectantibus, videlicet cum capella sancte Trinitatis et capella sancte Crucis infra cimit(er)ium sitis et capella sancti Nichol(ai) et capella sancti Johannis cum hospitali et capella de Wilenhala et capella de Cornleia ad jus prescripti monasterii pertinentibus; Et insuper capella(m) sancti Michaelis in feudo Comitis Cest' sita(m) quam Rann(ulfus) Comes ad jus Covent' ecclesie pertinere recognovit et carta sua confirmav(it) et cum omni jure parrochiali in decimis et oblacionibus et omnibus aliis b(e)n(e)ficiis et pertinentibus capell(is), videlicet capell(is) de Anesti Sulft' Wicha Witeleia Pinel' Stoch' Bilneia Stiveschale Ecclesal' Folchesal' Kareslea Watburlea Spanne Bissel et capell(a) sancte Marie in cimit(er)io Cov' ecclesie sita prescripto monasterio libere et quiete reddidit possidenda(m) sicut et carta prefati com(itis) et carta concessionis ac confirmacionis pie memorie R(icardi)[1] Cov' ep(iscop)i s(upe)r hoc confecte testantur quas et vidimus et coram nobis legi fecimus et propriis manibus contrectavimus; Item capell(am) de

Allespad' cum omnibus pertinenciis suis quam p(re)taxati monachi Cov' sicut tam prefati[2] Ivonis quam memorati ep(iscop)i[1] carte testantur rationabiliter adepti sunt libere et pacifice tenenda(m); It(em) ecclesia(m) de Rutuna cum capell(a) de Bubbenul; Ad h(ec) lucu(m) q(u)enda(m) s(upe)r Dunnesmora qui d(icitu)r Stude cum suis adjacenciis et ecclesia ibidem constructa ex dono et confirmatione Rogeri Heirun; Sed et nemus de Pacw(o)da cum ecclesia illic constructa. Volumus igitur et ea qua fungimur auctoritate precipimus ut monasteriu(m) Cov' et fratres ejusdem loci prelibatas possessiones libere integre et pacifice possideant inperpetuum sic(ut) eis r(ati)onabiliter collate et confirmate esse noscuntur. Volumus etiam ut elemosinaria prefati monast(eri)i omnes decimas de dominiis manerior(um) ejusdem monasterii plene et integre cum decima de Hedcota ad refectionem paup(eru)m percipiat sicut hactenus percipere consuevit. Liceat etiam priori et conventui co(m)monito prius arch(idiacono) Covent' in capella sancte Trinitatis presbit(eru)m idoneu(m) pon(er)e qui ibid(em) divina ministret. Preterea inhibemus ne in cimit(er)iis de Anesti Sulft' Wica Alleslea que te(m)pore hostilitatis ad refugiu(m) paup(eru)m rogatu R(annulfi) comitis Cest' et Turstan(i) Banast(re) et concessione R(ogeri)[3] Cov' ep(iscop)i et permissione Cov' capituli facta et dedicata noscuntur fuisse aliq(uo)d corpus sepeliatur sed omnia corpora cum consuetis b(e)n(e)ficiis ad matre(m) ecclesia(m) Coventr' deferantur sic(ut) carte memorati ep(iscop)i Rog(eri)[3] et predictorum comitis Cest' et Thurstani Banast(re) testantur. Volumus etiam ut hii qui in ep(iscop)atu Cov' decesserint et ap(ud) Cov' sepultura(m) elegerint absque omni contradictione ibidem sepeliantur et divise si quas fecerint monasterio libere relinquantur salvo jure parrochiali quod eccl(es)iis a quibus migrant debetur. Ut aut(em) alciori pace et pleniori gaudeant tranquillitate hanc n(ost)re protectionis et confirmacionis pagina(m) sigilli nostri appositione duximus roboranda(m) statuentes et sub int(er)minatione anatematis prohibentes ne quis eand(em) pagina(m) contra r(ati)onem infringere vel eidem temere contraire presumat. Test(es) hii Mag(ister) Adam Mag(ister) Rog(erus) Mag(ister) Gauf(ridus) de Lent' Albinus can(onicus) de D(er)bi Rodb(ertus) Monac(hus) de Cant' Mag(ister) Thom(as) Rad(ulfus) Senescald(us) Ada(m) Pincerna Rob(ertus) Ivo Rogerus Clientes domini ep(iscop)i Rog(erus) Cam(er)arius[4] et alii.[5]

G.H. 258

Seal: Green, oval with the full figure of the bishop granting benediction. The legend is partly lost – Si . . . ENTRENSIS EPISCOP . . . The reverse shows the bishop enthroned and has the legend – MAGISTER GERARDUS PUCELLA.

[1] Richard Peche, 1161–1182 [2] sic. [3] Roger de Clinton 1129–1148 [4] cam(er)ario [5] aliis

Gerard Pucelle was elected bishop of Coventry in January 1183 and consecrated on September 25. He died on January 13 1184. (see *Handbook of British Chronology*, p. 233, for Gerard and his predecescsors).

13 July 30th 1192

Charter of Ranulf III, earl of Chester, acknowledging the right of the mother church of Coventry in the chapel of St. Michael sited in his fee in the vill of Coventry and in all chapels established or to be established in his fee. He has made this gift publicly and solemnly in the church of Coventry, and placing his charter upon the altar has invested the church with the gift by a gold ring.

Ran(ulfus) Comes Cestr' omnibus hominibus suis francis et anglicis et universis fidelibus tam presentibus quam futuris salutem. Notum vobis facio me recognovisse jus matris mee ecclesie Coventr' quod habuerat et habere debebat in capella sancti Michaelis que sita est in feudo meo in villa de Coventr' et in omnibus capellis tam constitutis quam constituendis in feudo meo et in omnibus aliis pertinentiis ad prefatam capellam pertinentibus infra villam et extra tam in terris quam in decimis et oblationibus et pro vivis et pro mortuis factis et in omni jure parochiali. Hanc autem recognitionem feci inductus testimonio multorum et ex inspectione carte avi mei Ran(ulfi) Comitis et nichilominus carte patris mei Hug(onis) Com(itis) qui capellam predictam sancti Michaelis ecclesie Coventr' in perpetuam elemosinam concesserant et sigillis suis firmaverant imperpetuum. Sciant igitur tam presentes quam futuri quod ego ad preces venerabilis patris mei Hugonis ejusdem ecclesie episcopi concessi in puram et perpetuam elemosinam Priori et ejus successoribus ecclesie Cov' sepedictam capellam sancti Michaelis cum omnibus capellis ad eam pertinentibus et cum omni jure parochiali scilicet cum capella de Stokes et capella de Wike et capella de Stivechal' et capella de Ekeleshal et capella de Folkeshull' et capella de Billeneia et capella de Spanna et capella de Anesti et capella de Sulfton' et cum omni jure parochiali omnium villarum ad easdem capellas pertinencium scilicet Witeleia et Pinneleia et Keresleia et Wadburleia et Bisseleia et si que sunt alie vel ad majorem capellam sancti Michaelis vel ad minores predictas pertinentes vel si que alie constituentur infra terminos earundem capellarum. Hanc ergo donacionem et concessionem meam feci publice et solempniter in ecclesia Coventr' tercio anno regni regis Ricardi mense Julii in festo sanctorum Abdon et Sennes et cartam meam super altare ponens anulo aureo de donacione ista ecclesiam Coventr' investivi et imperpetuum confirmavi. Hiis testibus Magistro Roberto de Salop' Magistro Ricardo Thesaurario de Lichefeld Willelmo de Clavill' Thesaurario Cestr' Ada Noel Thoma Noel Rad(ulfo) de Maisnill' Warin' Petro Ruald Hugone de Nova Villa Willelmo de Hardredeshull' Rogero de Camvill' Willelmo de Aula Garard Vinetar Ricardo filio Fordwin' et multis aliis.

P.R.O. C53/135 m4

14 1190–1194

Charter of Ranulf III, earl of Chester, granting the tithe from his entire lands, tenements and rents of Coventry to [the churches of] St. Mary, St. Michael, St. Chad and St. Giles, and to Ralf his chaplain and his successors in the chapel of St. Michael and in all the chapels pertaining to it.

Ran(ulfus) Dux Brit' Comes Cestr' et Rich' Episcopo Cestr' et archid(iacono) Covintr' et omni clero ejusdem episcopatus ac omnibus hominibus suis francis et anglicis salutem. Sciatis me dedisse et concessisse pro me et heredibus meis decimam omnium terrarum tenementorum et reddituum meorum Covintr' Deo sancte Marie sancto Michaeli ac sancto Cedde acque sancto Egid(io) et Rad(ulf)o meo capellano et ejus successoribus personis in capella sancti Michaelis Covintr' et omnibus capellis eidem pertinentibus in perpetuam elemosinam pro salute anime mee et antecessorum meorum. Quare precipio sub pena anathematis omnibus ministris meis et ministris heredum meorum ut dictam decimam terminis statutis singulis annis imperpetuum fideliter prosolvant, et etiam decimam omnium que ad mei commodum per annum renovari poterunt scilicet de boscis pratis pasturis et aquis vel de aliis rebus quibuscumque. Testibus Gileberto filio Picot Bertramo Camerario Willelmo de Verdoun Martino filio Briton' Ricardo de Wygorn' Nicholao filio Liulphi Willelmo de Aula Vincencio Ada clerico et aliis quamplurimis apud Covintr'.

P.R.O. C53/135 m5

Ranulf III styled himself Earl of Richmond and Duke of Brittany following his marriage to Constance of Brittany on 3 February 1189 until his divorce from her in 1199 (B. E. Harris, 'Ranulf III, Earl of Chester', *Journal of the Chester Arch. Soc.*, 1975, pp. 101–2; *G.E.C.*, vol. III, p. 168). Gilbert son of Picot who had been a regular witness for Hugh II was still living in 1189/90 (*Pipe Roll 2 Richard I*, p. 30). The latest possible date is the early part of 1194. By Easter Bishop Hugh de Nonant had forfeited his manors to the king (*Pipe Roll 6 Richard I*, p. 44). Some time between May and Michaelmas, Ranulf III left for Normandy where he remained until 1199.

(James W. Alexander, *Ranulf of Chester*, Athens, Georgia, 1984, p. 7). However the charter is likely to be earlier than this, and probably not far distant from No. 13. Bishop Hugh had achieved the expulsion of the monks from Coventry by the end of 1190 (Knowles, *The Monastic Order*, p. 323). The charter's main purpose was to place the disposal of the tithes firmly in the hands of the secular clergy. A second effect was to include, for the first time, tithe from woodlands around Coventry. The king seems to have laid claim to dispose of extra-parochial tithe in general, including those from forests (see Norma Adams, 'The Judicial Conflict over Tithes', *English Historical Review*, vol. ccv, 1937, pp. 1–22), and Ranulf would appear to be doing the same here.

15 c.1199–1204

Charter of Ranulf III, earl of Chester, to his burgesses of Coventry.

Rannul(fus) Comes Cestrie omnibus baronibus et constabulariis et ballivis et ministris et hominibus et amicis suis francis et anglis tam presentibus quam futuris salutem. Sciatis me burgensibus meis de Covintr' concessisse et dedisse et hac carta mea confirmasse omnia que in presenti carta scripta sunt, videlicet ut bene et honorifice et quiete et in libero burgagio teneant predicti burgenses et heredes sui de me et de heredibus meis sicut unquam in tempore patris mei vel aliorum antecessorum meorum melius et firmius et liberius tenuerunt. Omnes autem liberas et bonas leges illis concedo quas burgenses Lincolnie meliores et liberiores habent. Prohibeo et defendo constabulariis meis ne eos aliqua ca(usa) in castellum ad placitum ducant sed portimot suum libere habeant in quo omnia placita ad me et ad illos pertinentia juste tractentur. Quemlibet autem ex semetipsis pro me eligant qui sub me super eos justicia sit qui leges et consuetudines sciat et eos meo consilio in omnibus rationabiliter omni causa remota custodiat et mihi jura mea fideliter faciat. Si forte aliquis in mi(sericordi)am meam inciderit m(erc)iatus sit rationabiliter per ballivum meum et fideles burgenses curie. Quoscumque autem m(er)catores secum ad ville emendationem addux(er)in(t)[1] precipio (ut)[2] pacem habeant et nullus eis injuriam facia(t)[3] vel injuste eos in ca(usa)m mittat. Si vero aliquis extraneus m(er)cator aliquod inconveniens in villa fecerit in portimot coram justic(ia) supradicta sine c(aus)a illud dirigat. His testibus Rogero Constabulario Cestrie Roberto Senescall(o) de Mohaut Radulfo de Meisnilwarin Petro Rouaat Symon Thuschet Thoma[4] dispensario Joello de Lovini Willelmo marescallo Joello Bereng' Phiiippo de Horrebi Rogero de Camville Rogero de Busservile Willelmo Picot Willelmo de Hardredes hull' Warino de Vernun et multis apud Covintr'.

C.R.O. B1.

The seal is green and depicts a lion rampart on a heater shield. Virtually nothing remains of the legend.

[1] The document shows signs of wear and there is superscript in places. This word ends with a sign rather like an ampersand but ultra violet reveals an impression of the final '*t*' slightly to the left of it.

[2] The document reads *in*, but grammar and the ultra violet lamp suggest *ut* as the original reading. Neither this word nor the preceding *precipio* are in the royal confirmation of the charter of Ranulf II which must have served as the model.

[3] The document now reads *faciau*.

[4] Thomas.

This charter has been printed in full only once, and somewhat inaccurately, in *Archaeological Journal*, xv, 1958. It was subsequently printed without the witnesses by W. Cunningham (*The Growth of English Industry and Commerce during the Early and Middle Ages*, 5th edn. 1922, p. 616). In 1921 James Tait suggested 1200–1208 as the date (*English Historical Review*, xxxvi, p. 53), but he later considered it to be slightly earlier (see A. A. Dibben, *Coventry City Charters*, 1969, p. 8, citing correspondence), presumably because he had revised the beginnings of Philip de Orreby's justiciarship to c.1202 and Philip is not so designated here. He seems, however, to have been mistaken in this view (see below No. 16n). Parameters are provided by Robert de Montalt's stewardship of Chester from c.1199 to May 1204 (*Cheshire Sheaf*, No. 7804, 1940, p. 40, and *ibid* No. 9394, 1951, p. 7), though the former date seems a little less secure than has been suggested. It is strengthened in the present context, however, by the earl's plain style, earl of Chester, which although it too cannot be entirely relied upon, strongly suggests a date after Ranulf's separation from Constance of Brittany in 1199, and this is reaffirmed by the use of the lion seal in preference to the seal which bore the legend duke of Brittany and earl of Richmond (*Ormerod, Cheshire*, i, pp. 33, 41; Tait, *loc. cit.*). 1204 as *terminus ad quem* is reinforced by the presence of Joel de Lovigny and Pierre Ruaut who withdrew to France after King John's loss of Normandy (G. Barraclough, 'Some Charters of the Earls of Chester', p. 39).

16 1204–1208

Charter of Ranulf III, earl of Chester, confirming to the abbey and monks of Coventry 2 carts journeying twice daily, excepting feast days, in his woods to take what is necessary for building repairs, for fuel and for the remaking of hedges, by view of his foresters, just as the charter of Ranulf, his grandfather, witnesses.

Ranulphus Comes Cestr' constabulario suo dapifero justic(iariis) vic(ecomitibus) baronibus et omnibus hominibus suis tam presentibus quam futuris et nominatim ballivis et forestariis suis de Covintr' salutem. Sciatis me concessisse et hac carta mea confirmasse Deo et abbacie sancte Marie de Covintr' et monachis ibidem Deo servientibus pro amore Dei et salute anime mee et antecessorum meorum in puram et perpetuam elemosinam duas bigas errantes in bosco meo cotidie bis exceptis festivis diebus ad capiend(um) ibidem de bosco meo quod eis necessarium fuerit ad edificia sua reparanda et ad focum suum et ad sepes illorum reficiend(as) per visum forestariorum meorum sicut carta Comitis Ran(ulphi) avi mei quam ipsi habent testatur. Quare prohibeo omnibus hominibus meis et nominatim ballivis meis et forestar(iis) de Coventr' quod nullus eorum presumat hanc elemosinam disturbare vel impedire. Et qui hoc fecerint maledictionem Dei et mei habeant. Testibus Rogero de Camvilla Willelmo de Warenum[1] Philippo de Oreby tunc Justic(iario) Thoma Dispens(atore) Johanne de Preaus Willelmo de Erdern' Waltero filio Terry sen(escallo) Thoma clerico Com(itis) Nicholao filio Liulfi Mil(on)e Barbedaveril Hugone filio Martini Galfrido Aurifabro et multis aliis.

P.R.O. C53/135 m4.

[1] sic.

Another copy is in Coventry Priory Register fo. 76v.

Ranulf's plain title suggests a date between his divorce from Constance in 1199 and his creation earl of Lincoln on 23 May 1217 (*Handbook of British Chronology*, p. 436). However, the charter can be pinned down with some confidence. Walter son of Terry *alias* Walter de Coventry who came to hold the stewardship of Ranulf's lands outside the earldom of Chester was in office, as regards Lincolnshire at least, from 1199 (Farrer, *H.K.F.* ii, pp. 156–7). Thomas the earl's clerk fl. c.1200–c.1208 (J. Tait, *op. cit.*, p. xlix). He witnessed 2 charters of the earl to the city of Chester in 1199 (W. F. Irving, 'The Dates of the City Charters', *Cheshire Sheaf No. 9390*, 1951, p. 5 correcting 1200–1202 given by R. H. Morris, *Chester in the Plantagenet and Tudor Reigns*, Chester, 1893, pp. 481–3), one of which he wrote, and another charter before 1208 (Tait, *op. cit.* No. 18). In a charter to Poulton Abbey between c.1202 and the fall of Normandy in 1204 he is described as (the earl's) chancellor (*Dieulacres Cartu-*

lary, ed. G. Wrottesley, in *Staffs. Hist. Collections*, *N.S.* vol. ix, 1888, No. 80). William de Warenne is probably he who died c.1208 (*Pipe Roll 10 John* p. 42). A William de Ardern was also said to be dead by 1208 (*Book of Seals*, p. 33). The date Philip de Orreby succeeded Ralph Mainwaring as justiciar has been revised backwards and forwards over the years. It now seems that Tait (*Cheshire Sheaf No. 7804*, June 1940, pp. 39–40) was premature in taking Philip's justiciarship back to 1202. Professor Barraclough, pointing to several charters of 1205 in which Philip was not so designated, argues for 1206 at the earliest. (One of these had been cited by Farrer, *H.K.F.* ii, p. 135). However, lack of consistency in designation must remain a problem. The absence of *Francis et Anglis* in the address also points to a date after the fall of Normandy in 1204.

17

Supposed charter of Ranulf III, earl of Chester, granting to the church of St. Mary and the monks of Coventry in free alms 280 acres of woodland and waste in Exhall and Foleshill in exchange for one of the two carts journeying in his woods of Coventry which had been granted by Ranulf his grandfather.

Ran(ulfus) Comes Cestr' omnibus hominibus et nominatim sen(escallo) ballivis et forestar(iis) suis de Coventr' presentes inspecturis salutem. Sciatis me dedisse et concessisse et hac presenti carta mea confirmasse Deo et ecclesie sancte Marie de Coventr' et monachis ibidem Deo servientibus et eorum successoribus pro amore Dei et salute anime mee et antecessorum meorum in liberam puram et perpetuam elemosinam quandam porcionem bosci et vasti mei in Eccleshal' et Keresl' ad estimacionem ducentarum et octoginta acrarum terre in escambium unius bige de duabus bigis errantibus in bosco meo de Coventr' eidem ecclesie et monachis et eorum successoribus per Ran(ulfum) avum meum et me concessis prout per cartas nostras inde eis factas plenius apparet. Et jacet dicta porcio bosci et vasti immediate inter ten(ementa) Willelmi de Turvill' et Nicholai le Clerc de Eccleshal' in Smercote et Eccleshal' ex parte una et viam que ducit de Coventr' per Keresl' versus Estel' ex parte altera; habend(am) et tenend(am) predictam porcionem bosci et vasti cum vestura arborum super crescentium et omnibus aliis suis pertinentiis per distinctas vias et bundas ibidem factas memoratis ecclesie et monachis ac eorum successoribus ita libere et integre sicut ego eam liberius melius et quietius umquam tenui. Et bene liceat eisdem monachis et eorum successoribus dictam porcionem bosci et vasti pro utilitate sua quando voluerint absque calumpnia reclam(acione) seu perturbacione mei seu heredum aut tenentium meorum frussire excolere includere et asportare ac in seperali solo absque omni exaccione et demanda liberam tenere imperpetuum. Quare omnibus her(edibus) sen(escallis) ballivis forestar(iis) hominibus et tenentibus meis firmiter prohibeo quod nullus eorum hanc meam elemosinam infringere contraire vel perturbare presumat quominus mea devota et sana voluntas in aliquo quod absit impleatur. Testibus hiis Thoma Dispens(atore) Willelmo de Hardredeshull' Philippo de Orreby tunc Justic(iario) Willelmo de Erdern' Waltero filio Terri tunc sen(escallo) Milone Barba Aprilis Thoma clerico Comit(is) et multis aliis.

P.R.O. C53/135 m4

Another copy is in Coventry Priory Register fo. 76v.

18

Supposed charter of Ranulf III, earl of Chester, reciting the bounds of the 280 acres of woodland and waste, to be measured by the 25 foot perch, which he has granted in free alms to the church of St. Mary and the monks of Coventry.

Ran(ulfus) Comes Cestr' baronibus justic(iariis) vic(ecomitibus) constabul(ariis) et dapifer(is) suis nominatim sen(escallo) ball(ivis) et forestar(iis) suis de Coventr' salutem. Ne posteris vertatur in dubium qui sint termini et divise infra quos continentur ducent(e) et octoginta acre bosci et vasti per perticam xxv pedum mensurand(e) quas ego dedi et concessi in liberam puram et perpetuam elemosinam Deo et ecclesie sancte Marie de Covintr' et monachis ibidem Deo servientibus et eorum successoribus pro escambio unius bige de duabus bigis in bosco meo de Covintr' cotidie errantibus de quibus bigis ipsi monachi habent penes se cartam Ran(ulfi) avi mei et meam, scire vos volo quod dicte acre jacent ex parte una infra a rivulo current(e) de Smerscote juxta ecclesiam de Eccleshal' et inde div(er)tendo se per circuitum juxta mansum I. del Ruydyng usque ad concavum et combustum stipitem et inde usque ad viam ducentem de Coventr' per Karesl' versus Estel' et sic per ipsam viam directe usque ad gravam N. de Cornl'. In hujus rei testimonium huic littere sigillum meum apposui. Hiis testibus Thoma Dispensator(e) Willelmo de Warrena Willelmo de Hardredeshull' Willelmo de Erdern' Milone Barba Aprilis Philippo de Orreby tunc Justic(iario) Waltero filio Terri tunc sen(escallo) Thoma clerico meo et multis aliis.

P.R.O. C53/135 m4

19

Supposed release and quitclaim by Ranulf III, earl of Chester, to the prior and monks of Coventry of all right in 280 acres of woodland and waste with view of frankpledge, escheats, and all liberties, free customs, easements and appurtenances, which he has granted to them in free alms.

Ran(ulfus) Comes Cestr' omnibus hominibus et tenentibus suis et nominatim sen(escallo) ballivis forestar(iis) ministris et tenentibus suis de Coventr' salutem. Sciatis me pro me heredibus et assignatis meis concessisse et omnino de me et ipsis imperpetuum relaxasse remisisse et quietumclamasse priori matricis ecclesie mee Coventr' et monachis ibidem Deo servientibus et eorum successoribus totum jus et clamium quod ego umquam plenius et liberius habui vel antecessores mei habuerunt in toto d(o)m(ini)o ducentarum et octoginta acrarum bosci et vasti et in pratis pasc(uis) pasturis aquis moris et haiis eidem pertinentibus una cum lib(er)tat(e) visuum[1] francipleg(ii) eschaetis ac aliis lib(er)tat(ibus) lib(er)is consuetud(inibus) commoditat(ibus) et pertin(entiis) quibuscumque eidem dominio et rebus pertinent(ibus), quas quidem acras ego eisdem Priori et monachis ac eorum successoribus pro escambio unius bige errantis cotidie in bosco meo de Coventr' in liberam puram et perpetuam elemosinam nuper concessi imperpetuum libere possidend(as) prout per cartam meam inde eis factam plenius apparet ita quod nec ego nec heredes vel assignati mei umquam in predicto d(o)m(ini)o cum libertatibus et ceteris suis pertinentiis predictis quicquid juris aut clamii de cetero exigere seu vendicare potero vel poterunt in futurum. Q(uicu)m(que) vero hanc meam elemosinam predictis Priori et monachis ut premittitur caritative et gratis concessam in aliqua sui parte infringere presumpserit Dei malediccione pro diploide perpetualiter induatur. In hujus rei testimonium huic littere mee sigillum meum apposui. Hiis testibus Thoma Dispens(atore) Willelmo de Erderne Philippo de Orreby tunc Justic(iario) Waltero Terry tunc sen(escallo) Willelmo de Aula Milone Barba April(is) et aliis.

P.R.O. C53/135 m4

[1] MS. reads visibus.

20

Abstracts of charters of Ranulf III, earl of Chester, granting to the Hospital of St. John the Baptist parcels of 12 and 7 acres of assarted land outside Coventry.

a. Omnibus sancte mat(r)is ecclesie filiis presentibus et futuris Ranulphus Comes Cestr' salutem. Noverit universitas vestra me divine caritat(is) intuitu pro anima mea et patris mei et matris mee et antecessorum meorum et heredum dedisse et concessisse et hac presenti carta mea confirmasse Deo et beate Marie et domui hospi(ta)l(i) sancti Johannis Baptiste de Co' et fratribus ibidem Deo servientibus duodecim acras terre de exarto meo extra Co', scilicet inter boscum meum qui vo(catur) Bernet et terram quam Stephanus filius Herb(er)ti tenuit ex una parte et inter terram quam Walterus Deivill' tenuit et terram quam Willelmus Kynne tenuit ex altera parte; habend(as) et tenend(as) predict(is) domui et fratribus imperpetuum libere quiete honorifice bene et in pace infra villam et extra in bosco et in plano et in al(iis) loc(is), reddendo michi et heredibus meis annuatim de predict(is) domo et fratribus quatuor s(olidos) ad iiij[or] anni terminos etc. ut patet in carta.

b. Omnibus sancte matris ecclesie filiis presentibus et futuris Ranulphus Comes Cestr' salutem. Noverit universitas vestra me divine carit(atis) intuitu pro ani(m)a mea et patris mei et matris mee et antecessorum meorum et heredum dedisse et concessisse et hac presenti carta mea confirmasse Deo et beate Marie et domui hospi(ta)l(i) sancti Johannis Baptiste de Co' et fratribus ibidem Deo servientibus septem acras terre de exarto meo extra Co', scilicet int(er) boscum meum qui vocatur Bernyt et exartum illud quod ill(is) p(r)ius contuli ex una parte et inter viam que tendit versus Bulkynton' et rubeam viam que ducit ad Harestan' ex altera, reddendo michi annuatim duos solid(os) et iiij[or] d(enarios) ad iiij[or] terminos etc.

Coventry Priory Register fo. 173r.

The rent, as the register makes clear, came to be paid to the priory, presumably as a result of the Montalt grant. For the history of the hospital see *V.C.H. Warwickshire* vol. ii, ed. W. Page, London, 1908, pp. 109–111.

21 1217–c.1222

Charter of Ranulf III, earl of Chester, granting to the nuns of Polesworth 10 marks annually to be taken from his rent at Coventry.

Omnibus sancte matris ecclesie filiis ad quos presentes litere pervenerint R. Comes Cestr' et Lincoln' salutem in Domino. Noverit universitas vestra nos pro amore Dei et intuitu pietatis donasse Deo et beate virgini Edithe de Pollesworth' et monialibus ibidem Deo servientibus pro anima nostra et pro animabus antecessorum et successorum nostrorum necnon et pro anima R. Marmiun patris R. Marmiun et antecessorum et successorum suorum decem marcas annuatim percipiendas de redditu nostro apud Coventr' per manum ballivorum nostrorum ad duos terminos medietatem ad festum sancti Michaelis et medietatem ad Pascha donec eis in certo loco redditum decem marcarum in puram et perpetuam elemosinam assignaverimus salvis duabus marcis annuis monachis de Barbareio quas predicte moniales eis de prenominato redditu ad pascha annuatim persolvent. Hujus autem elemosine nostre donacionem nos et heredes nostri predictis monialibus imperpetuum warentizabimus. Et ut hec nostra donacio perpetue firmitatis robur optineat eam presentis scripti testimonio et sigilli nostri apposicione communivimus. Hiis testibus Domino Coventr' Episcopo Philippo de Orreby Justic(iario) Cestr' Henrico de Aldithel' Waltero de Coventr' Willelmo de Vernon' Magistro Nicholao de Weston' Jocio capellano domini Comitis Johanne de Ardern' Ricardo Phiton' Hamone de Torvill' Magistro Gilberto de Weston' Stephano de Segrave et multis aliis.

P.R.O. C54/147 m39d.

Ranulf was created earl of Lincoln on 23 May 1217 (*Handbook of British Chronology*, p. 436). Philip de Orreby resigned as justiciar of Chester at Easter 1229 and was succeeded by William de Vernon (*Annales Cestriensis*, pp. 54–7). The latest possible date for this charter is February 1227 by which time Walter de Coventry's heir was in wardship (*Book of Fees*, p. 362). However, Walter is not in evidence after the autumn of 1221, and almost certainly died soon after.

DOCUMENTS BEARING ON THE LORDSHIP AND GOVERNANCE OF COVENTRY

The importance of the following documents is discussed in the general introduction (pt. I). Three of the items, however, warrant some further comment. The Montalt grant (No. 22) raises a number of problems. It is unusual in form being couched in the third rather than the first person. It was undoubtedly drawn up at Coventry Priory. Despite the loss of the Montalt seal, however, there seems no valid reason to doubt that it is an authentic 13th-century document. Difficulties begin to arise when we compare it with the version preserved in the *Priory Register*. The latter is couched in the first person in the usual manner and is the version submitted by the prior to the Council in 1336 in his dispute with Queen Isabella, and again for royal confirmation in the *Inspeximus* of 1348. All 3 copies are clearly based on a common original.[1] This may have been the counterpart of No. 22 despite the difference in form. It is possible, however, that the prior submitted a normalized version of his rather unusual original both in 1336 and in 1348. The 3 copies differ collectively from this not only in the person used but also occasionally in words and word order (e.g. *carta* is submitted for *scripto* in l.3, and *et sic* for *sicque* in l.93 whereas in ll.14–15 *in eadem warenna* follows from *tamen* and not from *liberis cursibus*) and in name forms (e.g. *Caloudon* for *Kaleudon*, *Audelegh* for *Audethel* and *Coventr'* for *Covintr'* throughout). Moreover, if the halves of the indenture were in different forms, No. 22 would make sense only as the prior's copy. In fact, of course, it was the prior who held and submitted the other version. There are, however, no substantive differences between the 2 versions.

A second problem lies in the dating. The agreement between the Montalts and Prior William is also embodied in a final concord dated 3 weeks from Michaelmas 34 Henry III, i.e. 20 October 1250 (*F.F. Warwicks* No. 689). In 1336 the prior submitted 3 documents in support of his case: a version of the original agreement, the final concord and a letter of the Montalts ordering their free tenants of the manor of Coventry to be responsive to their new lord.[2] The letter to the tenants is dated 14 November 1249. Unless the letter is not genuine the original agreement must have been in the autumn of 1249, that is virtually twelve months before the fine. The only other contemporary evidence comes from the *Chronica Majora* of Matthew Paris, under 1250. In that year, he says, Roger de Montalt, having taken the cross, demised at fee farm to the prior and convent his part in the woods and rents at Coventry, in return for a great sum of money to provide for him in his journey to the Holy Land.[3] Matthew Paris cites this case as his prime example of English nobles alienating their estates to take part in the crusading enterprise of which he clearly disapproved. The autumn of 1249 is, however, quite conceivable as the date of the original agreement. Although he had seen military action in the king's service Roger de Montalt does not appear to have been a *familiaris* and is therefore unlikely to have taken the cross in response to Henry's doing so on 6 March 1250. Roger's action betokens not only the taking of the cross but active and serious preparation for a spring expedition much more in keeping with the atmosphere of late 1249 than late 1250. Montalt is likely to have been the initiator, the prior nothing loathe to

[1] There is yet a fourth copy in the *Gregory Cartulary* (S.B.T. DR 10/1409 fos. 400–402) which is derived from a badly damaged and indecipherable priory cartulary (DR 10/1406).

[2] See *Rotuli Parliamentorum Anglie Hactenus Inediti* ed. H. G. Richardson and G. O. Sayles, *Camden Society* 3rd. Series vol. LI pp. 240–266 where the documents are printed in full together with the rest of the proceedings.

[3] *Chronica Majora*, v, ed. H. R. Luard, *Rolls Series*, p. 98.

comply. The fine carried a consideration of £300, though how far this represented the great sum of money Matthew Paris refers to is not clear. In the event Roger is most unlikely to have gone on crusade.[4]

There are, however, certain differences between the charter and the final concord. One is a form of words. In the original agreement the Montalts conveyed their right in the entire manor of Coventry with certain listed exceptions. In the fine, by contrast, they convey £60 of land and rent with appurtenances in Coventry, that is to say all the lands and tenements they held in the vill. Again, there are the listed exceptions and the fine goes on to reaffirm that the residue (*residuum*) of the entire manor of Coventry should remain with the priory. The difference reflects the greater tendency to quantify often found in final concords which warrant charters. The form of words became of crucial importance, however, in the 1330s when Queen Isabella sought to wrest the prior's lordship of Coventry from him. The Montalts, her counsel argued, had not conveyed the manor of Coventry but only £60 of land therein. These were merely parcel of her manor therefore, and the prior had no jurisdiction over the other tenants.[5] As part of his evidence the prior had submitted the letter of Roger de Montalt to his tenants which like the agreement refers to the entire manor of Coventry. It is its role here which prevents us from accepting the letter unreservedly. Virtually any body of rights could be called a manor, however, and we ought not to follow the logic of the queen's argument that there could be only one manor of Coventry.

Two other differences between the original agreement and the final concord are of some importance. The latter included specific permission to exploit the considerable woodland and wastes around Coventry which was not mentioned before. It was to be of immense value to the priory not only economically but in terms of the consolidation of lordship. The second difference is in the matter of courts. Whereas the former agreement contained elaborate police measures for the protection of the Montalt interest, the final concord was concerned in a more balanced fashion to safeguard the courts and judicial profits of both parties: *Et si ita contigerit quod aliquis hominum vel tenencium ipsius Rogeri et Cecilie vel heredum ipsius Cecilie deliquerit versus predictum priorem vel successores suos vel homines suos, predicti Rogerus et Cecilia et heredes ipsius Cecilie habebunt inde curiam suam et misericordiam, si inciderit in misericordia, et prior et successores sui et homines sui versus quos deliquerint habebunt racionabiles emendas. Et si aliquis hominum vel tenencium ipsius prioris vel successorum suorum forisfecerit versus predictum Rogerum et Ceciliam et heredes ipsius Cecilie vel homines suos idem prior et successores sui habebunt inde curiam suam, sicut superius.* It is not entirely clear whether the Montalt tenants referred to here are additional to the military tenants. They certainly had tenants at Cheylesmore, or within the park, in 1280 (see below No. 768) and this is strongly suggested by the inquisition post mortem of Robert de Montalt in 1275. The 'manor of Coventry' was then said to comprise, in addition to the military tenants, the chief messuage of Cheylesmore with the park, park mill and all that was in the park close (*molendino in parco et omnibus infra clausum parci*) worth 5 marks *per annum*, £36 9s. 7d. rent of assize and pleas and perquisites of the court worth ½ mark *per annum*. The whole was valued at £40 2. 11d.[6]

Despite the elaborate precautions agreed between Roger de Montalt and Prior William jurisdictional conflict was bound to occur, long before the Montalt interest passed to Queen Isabella. One such occasion was in 1295 when John le Govere brought a plea of debt against Robert de Shepey in the hundred court. The prior's bailiff claimed jurisdiction, but so did Robert de Stoke, described as the Montalt bailiff for the courts for military tenants. Adam des Okes for the prior claimed that

[4] The foregoing account is based on information supplied by Dr. Simon Lloyd, to whom I am most grateful.

[5] Richardson and Sayles *loc. cit.*

[6] P.R.O. C133 File 10/6; *C.I.P.M.*, vol. ii, No. 128.

the defendant did not hold by military service but in free burgage 'as the whole vill of Coventry is held'.[7]

The additional grants to the priory recorded baldly in the *Inspeximus* refer to acquisitions by the monastic house during the first half of the 13th century. Most of them can be otherwise verified. 28a and c correspond to Nos. 525 and 526 below. The grant by Roger le Gardiner (28b) seems to be confirmed by the quitclaim from his widow (639) in the early 1240s. 28d, e and f can be amplified. Comparatively little material relating to the monastic estates before the early 15th century has survived. Both the major cartulary possessed by Thomas Sharp in the 19th century and the folios abstracted for him from Bodleian MS. Douce 139 have been lost. Their contents had been listed meanwhile in *Monasticon*. However, a manuscript compiled by William Reader (Bodleian MS. Top. Warwicks C.8) contains notes and abstracts from sections of the lost texts. The gifts from Walter son of Terry *alias* Walter de Coventry were fully documented. The sequence relating to *the Beeches* begins with two grants to Walter son of Terry, one from Ranulf III of 13 acres in Foleshill (*Folkeshull*) which Roger de Bech' held, the other from William Butler of Exhall (*Pincerna de Eccleshale*) of 4 acres in Foleshill with the messuage, orchard (*pomerio*) and other appurtenances in the same close (*in eodem clauso*) which Gilbert del Bech' held. The former is before the loss of Normandy in 1204 since it was witnessed by Peter Ruald, the latter before 1213 for among the witnesses is Liulph of Spon. The earl's grant is also witnessed by his steward Nicholas son of Alan. A grant from Walter son of Terry to Henry son of Ralf de Sulfton of his land at *Beches* held of Ranulph and William Butler follows, and a quitclaim by the latter to the priory witnessed in the sheriff's court at Warwick and by the sheriff Philip des Ascens (*recte* Philip des Ascellis, sheriff 1240–46) among others. There are two grants to the priory from Walter de Coventry himself. 28d (below), of the service of Henry de Sowa and Richard de Asewey, is witnessed by Philip de Orrebi, justiciar of Chester, Wa(l)t(er) de Dayvill, Hugh Despenser, William de Hard[red]eshull, Viellus de Folk[eshull] and Richard de Aula. The other, of the 2½ marks rent for the land which was of Richard del Bech' and the land Richard Aswey once held with his entire offspring (*cum tota sequela*), is witnessed by Richard de Coventr' knight and Benedict, the grantor's sons. They were probably made shortly before Walter died, in the early 1220s (above No. 21n). The bakehouse conveyed by Walter (28f) was in fact the castle bakehouse. The Reader MS. notices the grant by Elias Despenser to Walter son of Terry of Co(ventry) of the bakehouse called the castle bakehouse (*furnu(m) castelli*) with land adjacent opposite the church of St. Michael, witnessed by Roger de Busch(er)vill and others (unnamed), and a grant to him by Alice daughter of Richard de Smytheforde. She is most probably the wife (later widow) of Elias (Nos. 411, 412). Walter's grant to the priory is baldly noticed (with the first witness only, Viellus de Folkeshull) as is another from Walter son of Richard de Co(ventre).

The two remaining grants are not so clear cut. The grantor of 28g must be either the Walter d'Eyvile who appears as a bailiff or steward of Ranulf III or, more probably, he who figures as a military tenant of the Montalts in 1249. The whole of the d'Eyvile interest in the Coventry area soon passed, however, from the hands of the heavily indebted Roger d'Eyvile to Sir Thomas de Ardern and ultimately to Robert de Stoke (757–761). Roger's alienation included his interest at Biggin, which interest is confirmed in a minor alienation by him (C.R.O. 2/155). Certainly in 1279 the prior is recorded having 8 unfree tenants at Biggin, said to be held directly of the Montalts, with the Ardern interest confined to Stoke. An intermediate grant of the d'Eyvile interest in the 1280s does not include Biggin, and it may be that these rents were in contention after 1249. As it stands, however, Walter d'Eyvile's quitclaim, with its specific inclusion of view of frankpledge, looks a little suspect. The

[7] P.R.O. C.P. 40/113 m50; quoted by R. C. Palmer, *The County Courts of Medieval England 1150–1350*, (Princeton, 1982), p. 106.

Despenser grant, 28h, has not been verified. Some at least of the Despenser rents in Coventry went elsewhere (411–416).

The charter of Walter de Coventry granting common pasture to the co-burgesses of Coventry (No. 34) is difficult to date with assurance. No William de Arthingworth occurs in the Coventry deeds before 1280, nor indeed in the survey of that year. On the other hand William de Arthingworth, sometimes described as draper or merchant, appears in the early-mid 1280s and remains prominent for 20 years. The charter, however, appears to be earlier than this and no grantor of that name is known after 1272. The witnesses fail to act as a certain guide. Henry was the usual Christian name of the eponymous Rugby family for much of the 12th and 13th centuries. Two Henrys appear to figure successively during the mid 13th century.[8] Several freeholders of Pinley by the name of William also occur, whilst Gilbert de Foleshill is otherwise unknown. Here the heads of the eponymous family were known as Vitalis or Viellus, the last of whom was dead by 1272.[9] Of the candidates for grantor the less likely is Walter de Coventry the earl of Chester's steward who died c.1221 (see above No. 21). An extant charter (1217–c.1221) of his granting 8 marks of silver for the monks of Combe to purchase a rent has a different seal *viz.* white and oval, bearing three wheat sheaves.[10] The probable grantor is his grandson Sir Walter whose homage and service the Montalts retained in 1249 (below No. 22). In evidence from the mid 1230s Walter was not long dead when his sons quarrelled over the inheritance in 1272.[11]

The charter was undoubtedly highly prized by the late medieval corporation. A deeds register belonging to the city which contains leases from the reign of Richard II onwards has the text of the charter on the fly leaf with the following statement: *hier is the dede essowr' comyne regest(er)yd & h(i)t lythe with the charter in a longe boxe.*[12] It looks as though it represents an early example of communal action by the burgesses. The reference to land newly brought into cultivation strongly suggests that it results from the priory's attack on the woodlands and waste around Coventry which followed from the Montalt purchase in 1249. It is tempting to connect it with either the royal commission of 1258 or with the first rising against the prior in 1267–8. The interests of the Coventry family were centred in Lincolnshire by this time,[13] and the role of William de Arthingworth would seem to have been that of go-between.

8 *V.C.H. Warwicks*, vi, pp. 36, 204.
9 *Eyre Rolls 1272* m13d.
10 G.H. 197.
11 *Lincs. Final Concords* ii, p. 272; *Lincs. Notes and Queries* ix, p. 115.
12 C.R.O. A2. It is also found in Humphrey Burton's book of 1635 (C.R.O. A34 fo. 113b).
13 See above note 4; *Book of Fees*, pp. 1057, 1058.

22a Autumn 1249

Notification that Sir Roger de Montalt and Cecily his wife have granted to Prior William and the convent of Coventry the entire manor of Coventry with the advowson of the church of St. Michael and of its dependent chapels, and with the warren, but excepting free hunting in the warren whenever they are in residence, the manor-house at Cheylesmore with the enclosed park, the dwelling of the Grey-friars exclosed next to the park, the homages and services, with the reliefs and escheats, of the military tenants of the manor and their heirs, the leper house at Spon and sufficient wood for various specified purposes. In return the prior and convent and their successors will pay £100 per annum, and 10 marks per annum to the nuns of Polesworth.

Noverint universi ad quos presens scriptum pervenerit quod Dominus Rogerus de Monte Alto pro se et Cecilia uxore sua ac heredibus suis dedit concessit et presenti scripto confirmavit nobis Willelmo et conventui de Covintr' ac successoribus nostris totum jus et clamium quod habuit vel habere potuit aut poterit in toto manerio de Covintr' ac in omnibus rebus et locis ad idem manerium infra et extra qualiter-cumque et ubicumque spectantibus videlicet in boscis planis viis semitis pascuis pratis acquis excepto tamen vivario dicti Rogeri sibi Cecilie ac heredibus eorum quod scilicet est infra parcum suum que videlicet ad dictum Rogerum et Ceciliam uxorem suam ac heredes eorum aliquo tempore vel aliqua ratione spectabant aut spectare poterunt unacum advocatione ecclesie sancti Michaeelis omniumque capellarum ad eandem pertinentium cum omnibus pertinentiis suis ac etiam unacum warenna quam Dominus Rex Angl' dictis Rogero Cecil(ie) ac heredibus suis dudum concessit, salvis tamen eisdem R(ogero) Cecilie ac heredibus eorum liberis cursibus in eadem warenna cum personaliter advenerint et moram fecerint in manerio predicto quod videlicet manerium dictus Rogerus pro se et Cecilia uxore sua ac heredibus suis nobis et successoribus nostris adeo libere possidendum cum omnibus pertinentiis suis concessit sicut unquam ipsi aut aliqui antecessorum suorum illud tenuer[u]nt aut possederunt, exceptis tamen et salvis dictis R(ogero) Cecilie ac heredibus eorum manso suo apud Cheilesmor' cum parco incluso et habitatione fratrum minorum juxta eundem parcum sita et inclusa ac eisdem fratribus assignata, salvis dictis Rogero et Cecilie ac heredibus suic homagiis et serviciis Domini Gilberti de Segrave in Kaleudon'. Willelmi de Olneya in Asthull' et Olneya. Vitalis de Folkeshull' in Folk' Walteri Deivill' in Whitel'. Stok' et Covintr' Roberti de Stok' in Stok'. Milonis Gerebold in Whitel' Hugonis de Log' in Sowe et heredum omnium predictorum cum releviis escaetis et omnibus aliis ad terras et tenementa ipsorum pertinentibus, exceptis etiam et salvis dictis R(ogero) Cecilie ac heredibus eorum homagiis et serviciis Hugonis Dispensatoris in Luhteburg' Radulfi de Bracebrug' in Kynesbur' Willelmi le Botiler in Eccleshal' et Folkeshull'. heredum Roberti Tuschet in Keresl'. Comitis Warwic et Wydonis filii Roberti. Jacobi de Audethel' in Folkeshull' et Eccleshal'. Walteri de Langel' in Wick. Thome le Yreis in Anesty. Thome de Neuvill. Walteri de Covintr' in Stok' Gilberti de Preston Johannis le Pouere in Takkel' Alexandri Doville in Takkel et heredum omnium predictorum cum releviis escaetis et omnibus aliis homagiis et serviciis militaribus et non militaribus ad terras et tenementa omnium predictorum pertinentibus, salvis etiam dictis R(ogero) Cecilie ac heredibus suis homagiis et serviciis militaribus cum releviis et escaetis et aliis pertinentiis omnium aliorum ubicumque fuerint in Angl' ad dictum manerium de Covintr' spectantibus salvis tamen nobis et successoribus nostris omnibus serviciis omnium burgagiorum cum pertinenciis omnium scilicet predictorum militum et omnium aliorum ubicumque fuerint in Angl' si que habent in dicto manerio de Covintr', salvis etiam nobis et successoribus nostris omnibus aliis tenementis cum pertinenciis ad idem manerium pertinentibus que non sunt de feudo militari ubicumque fuerint, exceptis semper et salvis domino R(ogero) Cecil(ie) et heredibus suis predictis homagiis et serviciis cum pertinenciis omnium prenominatorum ut dictum est absque omni impedimento nostro vel successorum nostrorum salvis etiam dictis R(ogero) Cecil(ie) et heredibus suis libere tenencium suorum libertatibus quos habere debent et habere consuever[u]nt de jure in bosco et manerio de Covintr' cum pertinentiis sine impedimento nostro vel successorum nostrorum, excepta et salva dictis R(ogero) Cecil(ie) et heredibus suis domo lep(ro)sorum de Span(n)a cum pertinenciis salvis etiam dictis R(ogero) Cecil(ie) et heredibus suis lignis focalibus ad focum suum et ad carbonem faciend(um) sufficient(er) sine wasto quociens apud Covintr' personaliter venerint et ibidem moram fecerint et palis ad claudendum parcum suum cum n(e)cc(ess)e fuerit et hoc per visum et lib(er)at(i)o(ne)m forestariorum nostrorum et successorum nostrorum sine impedimento aliquo. Quod si forte aliqui malefactores qui de nostra et successorum nostrorum fuerint potestate dampnum fecerint in dicto parco et inventi fuerint nos et successores nostri capiemus de ipsis festinas emendas ad opus dictorum R(ogeri) et heredum suorum secundum quantitatem forisf(ac)ti. Preterea si aliqui qui non fuerint de potestate nostra vel successorum nostrorum forisfecerint in eodem parco et se in fugam v(er)teri(n)t homines nostri et successorum cum clamore debito ipsos insequentur et capient si f(ier)i possit et liberabunt eos ballivis dictorum R(ogeri) Cecil(ie) et heredum suorum. Item si aliqui de hominibus nostris vel successorum nostrorum forisfecerint alicui de hominibus dictorum R(ogeri) Cecil(ie) ac heredum suorum nos et successores nostri capiemus de eis similiter festinas emendas ad opus eorundem R(ogeri) Cecil(ie) et heredum suorum. Item quocienscumque dicti R(ogerus) Cecil(ia) et heredes sui n(e)cc(ess)e habuerint distringere feoda sua infra comitatum Warwic' nos et successores nostri prestabimus eisdem auxilium per ballivos et homines nostros ad distringend(um) dicta feoda quociens ad hoc fuerimus interpellati. Item dicti R(ogerus) Cecil(ia) et heredes sui lib(er)e facient mutuationes et capturas suas in villa de Covintr' usque ad terminum quadgraginta dierum completum. Item si homines de Cestr' vel de aliis locis forisfecerint dictis R(ogero) Cecil(ie) et heredibus suis iidem et heredes sui liberam habebunt p(o)t(es)tatem distringendi eos in villa de Covintr' per ballivos suos et heredum suorum simul cum ballivis nostris et successorum nostrorum secundum leges et consuetudines ipsius ville. Preterea fratres hospital(is) sancti Johannis de Covintr' habebunt de bosco de Covintr' qualibus septimana unam carecatam bosci per visum et liberationem forestar(iorum) nostrorum. Dictus vero Rogerus pro se et Cecil(ia) uxor sua et heredibus suis warantizabit in perpetuum nobis et successoribus nostris dictum manerium cum suis pertinenciis omnibus ut dictum est contra omnes homines et feminas. Pro hac autem donacione et concessione solvemus nos et successores nostri dictis R(ogero) et heredibus eorum annuatim in perpetuum centum libras sterlingorum ad quatuor terminos anni scilicet infra oct(abas) sancti Andr(ee) viginti quinque libras infra oct(abas) sancte Marie in Marcio viginti quinque libras infra oct(abas) sancti Johannis Baptiste viginti quinque libras et infra oct(abas) sancti Michaelis viginti quinque libras, et preterea singulis annis monialibus de Pollesworth decem marcas ad duos terminos scilicet ad Pascha quinque marcas et ad festum sancti Michaelis quinque marcas quas videlicet decem marcas nos et successores nostri solvemus dictis R(ogero) Cecil(ie) et heredibus suis ad eosdem terminos annuatim in perpetuum sicque per manus ipsorum R(ogeri) Cecil(ie) ac heredum suorum fiet solutio annua monialibus an(te)dictis. Fiet autem ista solutio scilicet tam centum librarum quam decem marcarum predictarum in domo dictorum R(ogeri) et Cecil(ie) ac heredum suorum apud Cheilesmor' a nobis et successoribus nostris eisdem R(ogero) Cecil(ie) et heredibus suis vel attornatis eorundem litteras ipsorum patentes super hoc def(er)entibus, quod si nos vel successores nostri cessaverimus a solucione dictarum centum librarum et decem marcarum in aliquo termino predicto ut dictum est scilicet infra octab(as) predictas dabimus dictis R(ogero) Cecil(ie) et heredibus eorum infra octo dies dictas octabas proximo sequentes decem libras nomine debiti quas si tunc non solverimus liceat dictis R(ogero) Cecil(ie) et heredibus suis nos et successores nostros distringere infra dictum manerium de Covintr' tam pro eisdem decem libris quam pro firma principali. Liceat etiam vicecomiti Warewic' qui pro tempore fuerit nos et successores nostros per terras et catalla distringere in comitatu Warewic' extra Covintr' usque ad plenariam solutionem tam dictarum decem librarum quam firme principalis. Quicquid autem dicti R(ogerus) Cecil(ia) et heredes sui occasione dicte pecunie non solute expenderint nos et successores nostri plenarie refundemus eisdem per visum fidedignorum et legalium virorum sine omni dilacione impedimento dolo et fraude. Nos vero prior predictus de consensu conventus nostri pro nobis et successoribus nostris subiecimus nos jurisdictioni domini Episcopi Covintr' qui pro tempore fuerit ad compellendum nos ad plenariam et fidelem observationem omnium predictorum sub pena exco(mmunication)is et interdicti. In quorum omnium robur et testimonium huic scripto inter dictos R(ogerum) Cecil(iam) et heredes eorum et nos per modum cyrographi diviso tam sigilla dictorum Rogeri et Cecilie uxoris sue predicte quam sigillum nostrum unacum signo capituli nostri alternatim sunt appensa. Testibus Henrico de Hasting', Gilb(erto) de Segrave, Galfr(ido) de Langel', Willelmo de Burmi(n)gh(am), Fulcone de Orreby, Roberto de Hondesacre tunc sen(escallo), Roberto de Grendon', Willelmo Trussell', Hugone de Loges, Galfr(ido) de C(r)aft, Vital(e) de Folk' et aliis.

Indented P.R.O.A 4464

One seal extant (presumably monastic): oval, black, remnants of robed figure in centre.

22b 14 November 1249

Letters patent of Roger de Montalt and Cecily his wife ordering the free tenants of the manor of Coventry to be responsive to Prior William and the convent of Coventry and their successors.

Rogerus de Monte Alto et Cecilia uxor ejusdem omnibus libere tenentibus suis de manerio de Coventr' et aliis salutem. Mandamus vobis quatinus de cetero sitis intendentes et respondentes Willelmo priori Coventr' et ejusdem loci conventui ac successoribus eorundem in omnibus que ad manerium de Coventr' pertinent infra et extra secundum quod in instrumentis inter nos confectis plenius continetur. In cujus rei testimonium hiis litteris patentibus sigilla nostra appendimus. Valete. Dat' apud Coventr' die Dominica prox(ima) post festum sancti Martini anno regni regis Henrici filii regis Johannis xxxiiij^{to}.

P.R.O. C53/135 m3

23 13 June 1253

Charter of Roger de Montalt, steward of Chester, giving to Prior William and the convent of Coventry the site of Spon in Coventry with its chapel, lands and rents, notwithstanding the retention of the advowson made by chirograph in the royal court.

Sciant presentes et futuri quod ego Rogerus de Monte Alto Senescallus Cestr' dedi concessi et hac presenti carta mea confirmavi in liberam puram et perpetuam elemosinam Deo et ecclesie beate Marie de Coventr' Willelmo priori et ejusdem loci conventui ac eorundem successoribus ibidem servientibus situ(m) de Spanna in Coventr' cum capella cum terris cum redditibus cum possessionibus et cum omnibus aliis suis pertinentibus, habendum et tenendum predictis priori et conventui de Coventr' et eorundem successoribus libere quiete et honorifice et pacifice cum omnibus suis libertatibus et liberis consuetudinibus sicut aliqua elemosina liberius aut quietius dari poterit vel teneri non obstante retentione facta mihi et heredibus meis de advocatione predicte Spanne cum suis pertinenciis per cirographum in curia domini regis factum inter me et Ceciliam uxorem meam ex parte una et predictos priorem et conventum ex altera. Et ego predictus Rogerus et heredes mei predictis priori et monachis et eorundem successoribus predictis situm de Spanna[et] capellam cum omnibus pertinentiis suis predictis contra omnes homines et feminas warantizabimus imperpetuum ita tamen quod si aliquod servicium debeatur domino regi vel alicui alii vel eciam aliquis redditus de predictis situ Spanne capella terris redditibus possessionibus vel eorum pertinentibus predicti prior et conventus et eorum successores versus quoscumque satisfacient. In hujus rei testimonium presenti scripto impressionem sigilli mei apposui. Hiis testibus domino Fulcone de Orreby domino Willelmo de Burmyngham domino Johanne de Bukechum' domino Roberto de Hondesacr' militibus domino Ricardo decano de Poywyk Ricardo Fuckeram, Willelmo Clement clerico et aliis. Acta apud Stafford die Veneris proximo post festum sancti Barnabe Apostolis anno domini millesimo cc^{mo} liij^{o} et anno regni regis Henrici filii regis Johannis xxx$^{vij o}$.

P.R.O. C53/135 m3

24 June 1249–June 1260

Charter of Roger de Montalt, steward of Chester, giving to Prior William and the convent of Coventry all the homages and rent from the lands and fees which he had of the gift of the abbot and convent of Basingwerk in the vill of Coventry and without.

Omnibus Christi fidelibus ad quos presens scriptum pervenerit Rogerus de Monte Alto Senescallus Cestr' salutem in Domino. Noveritis me dedisse concessisse et presenti carta mea confirmasse in liberam puram et perpetuam elemosinam Deo et ecclesie beate Marie de Coventr' Willelmo priori et monachis ibidem Deo servientibus omnia homagia et totum redditum de terris et feodis que habui vel aliquo modo habere potui de dono et confirmacione abbatis et conventus de Basyngwerk in villa de Coventr' et extra cum wardis escaetis releviis et omnibus aliis suis pertinenciis sine aliquo retenemento ad opus meum vel heredum meorum, habend(a) et tenend(a) omnia predicta cum omnibus eorum pertinenciis eisdem monachis et eorum successoribus ac ecclesie sue de Coventr' de me et heredibus meis in puram et perpetuam elemosinam ut predictum est libere quiete bene et in pace cum omnibus libertatibus et liberis consuetudinibus ad predictum feodum spectantibus. Et ego predictus Rogerus et heredes mei predictis monachis et eorum successoribus ac ecclesie sue de Coventre totum predictum redditum cum omnibus suis pertinentiis sicut predictum est contra omnes homines et feminas warantizabimus acquietabimus et defendemus imperpetuum. Remisi eciam et quietum clamavi de me et heredibus meis eisdem monachis et eorum successoribus ac ecclesie sue de Coventr' totum jus et clamium quod habui vel habere potui in panagiis assisis annuis hospiciis et omnibus aliis rebus ad predictas terras et feoda pertinentibus imperpetuum. Et ut hec mea donacio concessio et predictis carte confirmacio perpetue firmitatis robur optineat huic scripto sigillum meum apposui. Hiis testibus domino Johanne Restuychim milite Willelmo Clement clerico Roberto de Parys Ricardo de Bukervill Viello de Folkeshull' Hugone de Stoke Ricardo Erneys Johanne Sym' Ricardo de Fonte de Coventre et aliis.

P.R.O. C53/135 m3

Prior William de Brightwalton's election received royal confirmation on June 17 1249 (*C.C.R. 1247–51*, p. 173). Roger de Montalt died on June 18 1260 (*G.E.C.* vol. IX, p. 13).

25 1260–1270

Release, remise and quitclaim by Cecily, widow of Roger de Montalt, to Prior William and the convent of Coventry of all right in the chapel and site of Spon, the lands, tenements, rents and services in Coventry which were once the abbot of Basingwerk's, and in the entire manor of Coventry with the exceptions reserved in the muniments between the prior and convent on the one hand and she and her husband on the other. Moreover she has granted licence for them to approve from the wastes, woods, meadows, pastures and all lands within the aforesaid manor.

Notum sit omnibus presentes litteras visuris vel audituris quod ego Cecilia que fui uxor domini Rogeri de Monte Alto in plena viduitate et libera potestate mea relaxavi remisi et omnino de me et heredibus meis quietumclamavi fratri Willelmo priori ecclesie cath(edralis) Coventr' et ejusdem loci conventui et eorum succ(essoribus) totum jus et clamium quod habui vel aliquo modo habere potero in capella et situ de Spanna cum suis pertinentiis et in terris ten(ementis) reddit(ibus) et servic(iis) que quondam fuerunt abbatis de Basingwerk in Coventr' cum omnibus pertinenciis suis ac eciam in toto manerio de Coventr' et omnibus libertatibus liberis consuetudinibus servic(iis) et omnibus rebus ad idem manerium qualitercumque spectantibus imperpetuum salvis tamen mihi et heredibus meis et meis assignatis forp(r)isis que in muniment(ibus) inter dictos priorem et conventum et eorum successores ex parte una et dominum Rogerum me et heredes meos ex parte altera confectis expressis vocab(u)lis reservantur. Concessi eciam pro me et heredibus meis eisdem priori et conventui et ipsorum successoribus plenam lic(enciam) et facultatem quod ipsi libere se possint app(ro)wiar(e) de vast(is) boscis pratis pascuis pastur(is) ac aliis terris quibuscumque infra manerium predictum includendo assartando excolendo arentando et commodum suum ubicumque viderint expedire faciendo ex(cep)tis in rebus et loc(is) in muniment(ibus) predictis reservat(is) et salva eciam co(mmun)ar(iis) rationabili pastura ad tot averia cu(m) quot terras suas arabiles convenient(es) excolere et wayniar(e) poterunt et qui ratione ipsarum terrarum tam de jure quam consuet(udine) communiam habere debent et solebant. In cujus rei testimonium huic littere sigillum meum apposui.

P.R.O. C53/135 m3

Roger de Montalt died on 28 June 1260 (see above no. 24n). Cecily had been succeeded by their son, Robert de Montalt, before 1271. (Farrer, *H.K.F.* vol. ii, p. 10).

26 28 August 1289

Remise, release and quitclaim by Roger de Montalt, steward of Chester, to Prior Thomas and the convent of Coventry of 40s. of the annual rent in which they are bound for certain lands and tenements in the vill of Coventry and outside just as the final concord between Roger de Montalt and Cecily his wife and Prior William witnesses.

Sciant presentes et futuri quod ego Rogerus de Monte Alto senescallus Cestr' concessi remisi relaxavi et penitus quietum clamavi pro me et heredibus meis fratri Thome priori de Coventr' et ejusdem loci conventui et ecclesie sue de Coventr' xls. annui redditus de quodam redditu in quo iidem prior et conventus mihi et antecessoribus meis tenebantur pro quibusdam terris et tenementis in villa de Coventr' et extra sicut finalis concordia facta inter Rogerum de Monte Alto avum meum et Ceciliam uxorem ejus ex una parte et fratrem Willelmum quondam priorem ex altera testatur, habend(os) et tenend(os) predicto priori et successoribus ejus et ecclesie sue predicte libere quiete bene et in pace in liberam puram et perpetuam elemosinam. Ita quod nec ego nec heredes mei nec aliquis nomine nostro in predictis xls. aliquid juris vel clamii exigere poterimus seu clamare set imperpetuum simus exclusi. In cujus rei testimonium presenti scripto sigillum meum apposui. Hiis testibus dominis Johanne de Hastinges Johanne Paniel Willelmo de Beyvile militibus Petro Breton' Alexandro le Vineter Roberto de Stoke Willelmo de Capeles Henrico Pistor(e) Roberto de Chilton' Thoma le Moubrey Petro Barun Anketello de Coleshul et aliis. Dat' apud Coventr' die Dominica proxima post festum sancti Bartholomei apostoli anno domini m° cc° octogesimo nono.

P.R.O. C53/135 m3

Royal licence for this grant was acquired on 18 August 1289 (*C.P.R. 1281–92* p. 320). The remise of 40s. rent was made in return for certain tenements which Roger then granted to the Franciscans to enlarge their precincts.

27 c. February 1286

Charter of Roger de Montalt, lord of Cheylesmore, granting to the church of the blessed Mary and to Prior Thomas and the monks of Coventry that as far as concerns him they may lawfully enter the Earl's Mill in Coventry, which is of his fee, the statute of Mortmain notwithstanding.

Sciant presentes et futuri quod ego Rogerus de Monte Alto d(omi)n(u)s de Cheylesmor' concessi et hac presenti carta mea confirmavi Deo et ecclesie beate Mar(ie) Coventr' fratri Thom(e) priori et ejusdem loci conventui et eorum successoribus quod quantum in me est possint licite et libere ingredi molendinum de Erlesmuln' in Coventr' quod est de meo feodo cum prato mora stagno et omnibus pertinenciis suis et ea omnia perpetuo possidere sine reclamacione mea et heredum meorum non obstante statuto domini regis de mortua manu edito salvis redditibus et serviciis inde debitis et consuetis. Et ut hec mea concessio perpetuo rata permaneat hoc presens scriptum sigillo meo signavi. Hiis testibus domino Rad(ulf)o de Monte Alto Magistro Gydone de Tyllebrok' Galfrido le Hyreys Petro le Bretoun Roberto de Stok' Ricardo de Burton' Petro Baroun Simone Ernys Willelmo Selet clerico et aliis.

Seal extant Fuller I/2/13

Endorsed: Carta Roger de Montealto de molendino quod vocatur Urlesmiln'.

The mill was acquired through Adam son of Thomas Olyver and the mortmain licence issued on 10 February 1286. (*Coventry Priory Register* fo. 155r).

28

Additional grants to Coventry Priory recorded in the royal inspeximus of January 23, 1348.

a. The gift and assignment which Master Richard called the Vintner (*dictus vinetarius*) of Coventry made by his deed (*scriptum*) to God, the church of the blessed Mary and the prior and convent of Coventry, of the 2 mills of Radford and Hill (*molendinis de Radeford et Hull'*), the fishpond of Radford (*vivario de Radeford*) and the moor of the same Richard next to Whitemore (*juxta Wytemor*) as it extends in length and in width according to the metes and bounds made there, and also of the meadow of Hill (*Hull'*) below the mill-pond (*subtus stagnum*).

b. The gift, grant and confirmation which Roger le Gardiner of Coventry made by his charter to God, the church of the blessed Mary and the monks of Coventry in free, pure and perpetual alms, of the entire garden (*gardino*) of the same Roger in Coventry which is called the Earl's garden (*quod dicitus comitis*) with all appurtenances, which William Deyvallo at one time (*aliquando*) held with the entire land attached (*annexa*) to the same garden which Thurstan father-in-law ([pater] uxoris) of the same Roger similarly held of the said lord earl.

c. The release, remise and quitclaim which Robert and Richard, heirs of Robert de Retham and Richard Lorymer, made by their deed (*scriptum*) to the aforesaid prior and convent of all right and claim in the mill, mill-pond and meadow of Hill (*Hull'*) with appurtenances, and also in 50s. rent which the said prior and convent used to render annually.

d. The gift, grant and confirmation which Walter son of Terry (*Terici*) of Coventry made by his charter to God, the blessed Mary, the altar of St. Katherine and the monks of Coventry in pure and perpetual alms of the entire service of Henry de Souua from the land which he held of the grantor at *Beches* namely 2½ marks, and moreover of the entire land with all appurtenances which Richard de Assewey held of the grantor at *Beches* with the same Richard and his entire offspring (*sequela*).

e. The grant and confirmation which Ranu(lf) earl of Chester and Lincoln (*Cestr' et Linc'*) made by his deed (*scriptum*) to God and the aforesaid church and monks of the entire land and the entire service which Walter de Coventr' gave to them at *Beches* in pure and perpetual alms, namely the entire service from the land which Richard son of Richard de Assewey held at *Beches* with the same Richard and his entire offspring (*sequela*) for maintaining the altar of St. Katherine (*ad sustinend(um) servicium pro fidelibus ad altare sancte Katerine virginis*).

f. The gift, grant, confirmation and warranty which the aforesaid Walter made by his charter to the prior, the church and the aforesaid monks in free, pure and perpetual alms of his bakehouse (*furno*) in Coventry which is between the land which was of Swanus (*Suani*) Parker and the land which was of Richard son of Fordwayn with a certain messuage pertaining to the same bakehouse and adjacent to it on the north in Earl St. (*et adjacenti versus aquilonem in vico Comitis*) with all other appurtenances.

g. The release, remise and quitclaim which Walter de Deyville knight made to the prior, the aforesaid church and monks and their successors of his entire right and claim in the hamlet (*villula*) of Biggin (*Bugginton*) and in the lands, meadows, pastures, groves, moors and waters pertaining to the same, and in view of frankpledge and all other liberties, free customs, profits and whatsoever appurtenances together with the villein-services and the works of all the inhabitants of the same hamlet and of all their offspring (*una cum villenag(iis) et operibus omnium h(ab)itator(um) ejusdem villule et tocius sequele eorum*).

h. The gift, grant, confirmation and warranty which Nigel son of Elias Despenser (*Dispensatoris*) of Coventry made by his charter to the then prior of Coventry and the aforesaid monks of all the lands, goods (*rebus*), rents, possessions and liberties which he had or could have within and without the vill of Coventry, namely in pleas (*pl(ac)itis*), fealties, pannages, tolls, reliefs, escheats, suits of courts and all else which may pertain or accrue to him or his heirs in any way.

P.R.O. C53/135 mm3,2

29 c.1210–c.1215

Quitclaim by Basilia daughter of Ailrich to Robert son of Matilda of land in Coventry of the fee of William de Willenhale, which she has abjured before the court of the lord earl.

Sciant presentes et futuri quod ego Basilia filia Ailrich quietum clamavi Roberto filio Matild(is) terram illam in Covi(n)tr' que est de feudo Willelmi de Wilnhale s(cilicet) inter terram quam Walterus Tixtor tenuit et terram quam Ricardus de Aula tenuit; habendam et tenendam sibi et heredibus suis inperpetuum sine omni calu(m)pnia mei et heredum meorum. Et hoc abjuravi coram curia domini Com(itis). Pro hac vero quieta clamatione et abjuratione dedit m(ich)i predictus Robertus sex solidos argenti et Annes[1] uxor ejus dedit m(ich)i unum peplum. His test(es) Nich(-olaus) filius Liulfi Milo Barba Ap(r)ilis Ricardus de Wigorn' Matheus frater ejus Vincentius Petrus de Kent Willelmus de Wilnhale Walt(erus) Loremarius Robertus Gen(er) Odonis et Alexander Aurifab(er) Willelmus Fordwi(n) et multis aliis.

C.R.O. IA/EC12/21

Seal extant.

[1] sic.

30a Early–Mid 1240s

Charter of Richard son of Richard Ernis of Coventry giving to the church of the blessed Mary and the prior and monks of Coventry, in free alms, all the lands and tenures which he held in chief of their fee within and without the vill of Coventry together with a croft called Swancroft.

Sciant presentes et futuri quod ego Ricardus filius Ricardi Ernis' de Covintr' pro salute anime mee antecessorum et successorum meorum dedi concessi et hac presenti carta mea confirmavi ecclesie beate Marie de Covintr' dominis meis priori et monachis ibidem Deo servientibus in liberam puram et perpetuam elemosinam omnes terras et omnes tenuras quas tenui aliq(ua)n(do) in capite de feodo dictorum dominorum prioris et conventus in villa de Covintr' et extra in t(er)ritorio ejusdem ville quas scilicet habui vel habere potui tam in dominicis redditibus et serviciis quam in omnibus aliis terre escaetis et insuper unum croftum quod vocatur Swanecroft; habend(as) et tenend(as) dictis priori et monachis et successoribus eorundem adeo libere et quiete sicut aliqua elemosina liberius et quietius haberi poterit et teneri sine omni clamio et contradictione mei vel heredum meorum inperpetuum. Et ego Ricardus et heredes mei dictis priori et conventui omnes terras et tenuras predictas cum pertinentiis et crofto ut dictum est contra omnes homines et feminas inperpetuum warantizabimus. Et ut hec mea donatio concessio et confirmatio rate sint et stabiles inperpetuum presenti scripto sigillum meum apposui. Hiis testibus Willelmo de Wilnhal' Anketillo de Wikewan' Ricardo Lewin' Ricardo de Fonte Osberto clerico Ada clerico Ricardo de Blokevill' Ricardo Burgensi Rogero Textore Sym(one) Joilin' Galfrido de Sireford et aliis.

Seal extant C.R.O. IA/EC13/102

30b Early–Mid 1240s

Charter of Prior Roger and the convent of Coventry giving to Richard son of Richard Ernis of Coventry 1½ virgates in the vill of Sowe to be held by the same liberty as he used to hold his land of them in the vill of Coventry except that he need not make suit to their fortnightly court of Coventry as all others do save when required for the afforcement of the court.

Omnibus presens scriptum visuris vel audituris frater R(ogerus) Covi(n)trii ecclesie prior humil(is) et ejusdem loci conventus salutem in domino. Noverit universitas vestra nos dedisse concessisse et hac presenti carta nostra confirmasse Ricardo filio Ricardi Ernis' de Covintr' quandam virgatam terre et dimid(iam) in villa de Sowe scilicet illam dimidiam virgatam terre quam Rad(ulfus) le Kolt tenuit cum uno mesuagio et aliam dimidiam virgatam terre quam Reginaldus Knarri tenuit cum uno mesuagio et aliam virgatam dimidiam terre quam Robertus Gustard tenuit sine mesuag(io), habend(as) et tenend(as) de nobis et successoribus nostris dicto Ricardo et heredibus suis vel suis assignatis exceptis aliis domibus religionis libere quiete et honorifice in bosco et plano pratis pascuis et pasturis viis et semitis et omnibus aliis aisiamentis ad dictam terram pertinentibus infra villam de Sowe et extra; habend(as) et tenend(as) per eandem libertatem per quam ten(er)e consuevit terram suam aliq(ua)n(do) in villa de Covintr' quam de nobis tenuit in capite de feodo nostro excepto quod non teneatur seq(u)i curiam nostram de Covi(n)tr' de q(u)indena in q(u)indena(m) sicut ceteri faciu(n)t sed cum necesse fuerit p(ro)pt(er) afforciamentu(m) curie. Concessimus etiam dicto Ricardo et heredibus suis vel hiis qui in dictis mesuagiis manebunt housbote et haibote de bosco nostro de Sowe. Volumus etiam quod quicumque dicta mesuagia de eisdem tenuerint quieti sint de pa(n)nagio porcorum suorum de propria nut(r)itura sua, reddendo inde annuatim nobis et successoribus nostris ipse et heredes sui vel ejus asignati unam lib(r)am cymini vel duos denarios argenti ad quatuor terminos anni secundum usum ville de Covintr'. Et nos dicti prior et conventus et successores nostri warantizabimus dicto Ricardo et heredibus suis vel ejus assignatis totam dictam terram cum pertinentiis ut predictum est contra omnes homines et feminas. In cujus rei testimonium presenti scripto signum capituli nostri apposuimus. Hiis testibus Willelmo de Wilnhal' Anketillo de Wikewan' Ricardo Lefwin' Ricardo de Fonte Osberto clerico Ada clerico Ricardo Burg(e)nsi Simone Joilin' Galfrido de Syreford Reginaldo de Sowe et aliis.

Seal missing C.R.O. 2/63

31

Assize regulating the sale of bread and ale and other matters, made at Coventry, 8 October 1278.

Assisa facta in villa de Coventr' die sabbati proxima ante festum sancti Dyonisii anno regis Edwardi vj° coram xij videlicet:

Dummodo quarta frumenti scilicet de medio blado venditur pro iij s(olidis) tunc panis wast(elli) bene coctus pond(eret) xlviij solidos et iiij panes ad d(enarium).

Panis vero de kokeit' de eodem bultello et blado pond(eret) plusquam wast(ellum) ij s(olidos).

Et de eodem blado minoris pretii pond(eret) plusquam wast(ellum) v solidos.

Panis vero de Simenell(o) ponder(et) minus quam wastell(um) ij solidos.

Panis vero de quadrante de pane integro pond(eret) kokeit' et dimidiam.

Panis vero de treyt pond(eret) d(uplicite)r wastell(um).

Panis vero de quolibet blado pond(eret) ij kokeit'.

Quilibet pistor signum suum habeat super panem suam[1] ut possit sciri cujus est.

Prohibitum est ne aliquis pistor furnat panem ad vendendum extraneis nisi fuerit de assisa predicta.

Prohibitum est ne aliquis pistor furnat panem ad obolum dummodo bladum fuerit infra dimidiam marcam.

Prohibitum est etiam quod nullus pistor vendat panem ad furnum suum regratar(iis) nisi in foro.

Item dummodo quarta frumenti venditur pro iij s(olidis) avene pro xx d(enariis) ordei[2] pro iij s(olidis) lagena cervisie nove de cupa vendetur ad obolum et de bona scala ad iij qua[dran]t(es).

Item preceptum est quod si Wardi invenerint cervisiam non valentem iij q(uadr)a(ntes) ponent eam ex officio suo ad obolum.

Item preceptum [est] quod nulla braciatrix vendat cervisiam sine signo nisi inf(ir)mis et viatoribus.

Item preceptum est quod si pistores et braciatrices fregerint dictam assisam primo sint in misericordia secundo amittent catalla coram ipsis inventa et tertio habeant judicium scilicet collistrigium et tribuchet.

Item provisum est quod omne genus regratitudinis prohibeatur usque ad horam tertiam a festo sancti Michaelis usque ad Pascham et a Pascha usque ad dictum festum usque ad horam primam.

Item provisum est quod nullus eat ad exitus viarum ad emendam[3] aliquam mercand(isam) et si inveniatur habeat ad[4] judicium collistrigii.
Item provisum est quod si aliquis mercator veniat in villam cum salmone vel alio pisce quod ipse cindat propria manu ita quod nullus regratar(ius) se intromittat.
Item provisum est quod nullus ponat stallum suum ultra noctem sed mane et quod nullus habeat nisi unum stallum.
Item provisum est quod nullus carnifex occidat taurum nisi primo beytiat illum canibus.
Item provisum est quod nulla caro s(upe)rseminata vendatur ad stallagium nisi dicat qualis sit.
Item provisum est quod nulla caro subito mortua vendatur et si inveniatur venditor trahat eam ad exitus viarum et nichilominus in misericordia domini.
Item provisum est quod nullus tinctor ponat pastum suum in aqua.
Item provisum est quod nullus blobestator lavat blobbas ad communem aquam ubi pistores et braciatrices hauriunt aquam et si faciant in misericordia domini et perdant bona.

B.L. Lansdowne MS. 564 fo. 109

[1] sic. [2] ordeu(m) [3] sic. [4] sic.

Dr. Arthur Gooder has pointed out that the assize of bread is based on the statute of 51 Henry III 6 of which an exemplification once existed in Coventry and was made 'at the request of the Bakers of the Towne of Coventry' (20th unnumbered folio at the front of Humphrey Burton's Book C.R.O., A34).

Lansdowne 564 is a composite volume the bulk of which is taken up by two registers of writs. It contains other local material, however, and was perhaps the possession of the lawyer Adam des Okes of Whitley (C. Palmer, *The County Courts of Medieval England 1150–1350*, p. 106).

32 March 1268

Commision to the Treasurer, Master Thomas de Wymondham, to inquire into the recent disturbance at Coventry which had arisen when the sheriff had attempted to publish and maintain the liberties recently granted to the prior and monks of Coventry, namely to have their own coroners in the town and a gild merchant for their men, which were being resisted.

Rex dilecto et fideli suo magistro Thome de Wymundh(am) thesaurario suo salutem. Quum nuper cons(uetudines) quiet(ancias) et libertates a progenitoribus nostris regibus Angl(ie) priori et conventui ecclesie Con(v)entr' per cartas suas quas inspeximus concessimus[1] concessas confirmav(er)imus eisdem et eciam quasdam libertates de novo sibi concesserimus inter quas concessimus eis quod ipsi de hominibus suis ville predicte de Conv(en)ter[2] coronatores habeant infra villam ipsam qui de omnibus que ad officium coronatoris pertinent coram justic(iariis) nostris itinerantibus in comitatu predicto illo respondeant et quod homines ipsorum prioris et conventus habeant in eadem villa gildam mercatoriam cum omnibus libertatibus et liberis consuetudinibus ad dictam gildam pertinentibus, ac quidam de villa predicta ut audivimus ipsos priorem et convent(um) ad eorum dampnum impedieri(n)t quominus coronatores sui dicte ville visum cujusdam hominis in eadem villa interfecti aut homines sui ejusdem ville gildam predictam habere potueru(n)t juxta concessionem nostram predictam, per quod ad queri(monia)m dictorum prioris et conventus vicecomiti nostro Warr' precepimus quod ad villam predictam accederit ad dictas libertates puplicandas et conservandas quidam de villa predicta ut audivimus vi armata una cum aliis de partibus illis Gilbertum clericum dicti vicecomitis ad hoc ubi transmissum ceperunt inprisonaverunt et brevia nostra et rotulos nostros fregerunt et conculcaverunt et homines dictorum p(rioris) et c(onventus) verberaverunt et maletractaverunt in contemptum nostri et contra pacem nostram, et quia super premissis plenius volumus certiorari et justiciam fieri assig(navimus) vos ad inquir(endum) etc qui dictas transgressiones fecerunt et qualiter et qua r(ati)one. Et ideo vobis mandamus etc. Et inquis(itio) etc. In cujus etc. Et mand(atum) est vicecomiti Warr' quod tot etc. Et quod attach(iet) ita quod habeat corpora etc.

(P.R.O. C66/86 m26d; *C.P.R. 1266–72* pp. 278–9)

[1] sic. [2] sic.

The commision is undated, but entries on the dorse of the preceding and following membranes bear the dates 9 March and 10 March respectively. On March 27 the king despatched William de Waffre to Coventry to act in the capacity of coroner and deal with the body of John de Malemote recently killed there. (*C.P.R. 1266–72* p. 29). For the text of a schedule attached to the roll in which it is recorded that Robert Walerand knows what the prior and convent owe for these concessions, see R. H. C. Davis, *The Early History of Coventry*, p. 21. On 17 February they paid £20 into the Wardrobe for confirmation of a charter (*C.C.R. 1264–68* p. 294).

33

Record of a plea brought in the Court of Common Pleas by the Prior of Coventry against named tenants in Coventry for trading elsewhere than in his market on Fridays from 30 September 1300 up to the day of the writ (20 January 1307). On 3 February 1310 the court finally found for the plaintiff, who was awarded £60 damages. The defendants were forbidden to trade outside the market on Fridays in the future.

Adhuc de Crastino Purificationis beate Marie [3 February 1309].

Willelmus Graunpe de Coventre senior Walterus de Meryton' Henricus de Middelton' Ricardus de Rothewell' Ricardus de Stoke Ricardus Lovel Ricardus de Leyc' Petrus de M(er)iton' Willelmus Graunpe (Rogerus de Tuwe)[1] Johannes de Lyndeseye Martinus Coittyng[2] Ph(ilipp)us de Barsham Robertus Clement Adam Russel Willelmus de Burbache Willelmus Oldman Johannes filius Johannis le Vynet(er) Laur(entius) de Schepeye Willelmus de Mildenhale Johannes de Mildenhale Willelmus de Crok Robertus de Rydeware Thomas le Cumbere Ricardus de Draycote Thomas de Northfeld Hugo de Meryton' Hugo de Lychesfeld Robertus de Derby Henricus de M(er)iton' Henricus de la Mire Johannes de Langeleye Simon Graunpe Robertus le Fyshere Thomas de Glouc' Willelmus Betun Willelmus le Wallere Galfridus le Wallere Gilbertus de Hegham Willelmus le Parker Johannes de Norton' Galfridus de Bannebury Robertus[3] de Hegham Hugo de Shepeye Rad(ulf)us de Tuwe Johannes le Longe Willelmus le Flout(er)e Walterus le Gurdelere Willelmus le Latouner Laur(entius) Graunpe Rogerus del Grene Robertus de Wygynton' Galfridus le Leef' Guido del Grene et Willelmus le Hore in m(isericord)ia pro pluribus defaltis etc.

Iidem Willelmus et alii et Willelmus de Wolritheston' Johannes Mynot Willelmus le S(er)jaunt' (et)[1] Adam le Sadelere sum(monitum) fuerunt ad respondend(um) priori de Coventre de placito quare cum predictus prior habere debeat et ipse et predecessores sui priores de Coventre a temp(or)e quo non extat memoria semper hactenus habere consueverint liberum mercatum suum singulis septimanis per diem veneris in quodam loco qui vocatur Priorshalf in villa de Coventr', ita quod m(er)cimonia et alia bona quecumque venalia alibi in eadem villa quam in loco predicto per diem predictum vendicioni exponi seu vendi non debent nec hactenus consueverunt, predicti Willelmus et alii simul cum Henrico de Barsham Galfrido le Chaloner Thoma de Stoke Ricardo de Manliv(er) Simone de Ruiton' Rogero le Brocher Thoma le Sadelere et Willelmo Crowe m(er)cimonia et alia bona sua venalia in domibus et in seldis suis in villa predicta extra dictum locum constructis jam de novo per diem predictum vendicioni exponunt et vendunt ad grave dampnum ipsius prioris etc. Et unde idem prior dicit quod cum ipse habere debeat et ipse et predecessores sui priores de Coventre a tempore quo non extat memoria semper hactenus habere consueverint liberum mercatum suum singulis septimanis per diem veneris in predicto loco de Priorshalf sicut predictum est etc. predicti Willelmus et alii simul etc. die veneris proxima post festum sancti Michaelis Archangeli anno regni domini E(dwardi) regis patris domini r(egis) nunc vicesimo octavo et singulis aliis diebus veneris usque diem impetrationis brevis etc. scilicet vicesimum diem Januar(ii) anno regni ejusdem r(egis) patris etc. tricesimo quinto m(er)cimonia et alia bona sua scilicet pannos sindonem sericum et cinctoria et alias mercandisas suas in domibus et seldis suis in quodam loco qui vocatur Erlestrete in eadem villa extra predictum locum de Priorshalf etc. de novo vendicioni exposueru(n)t per quod idem prior amisit proficuum suum allocationis stallor(um) etc. in predicto loco de Priorshalf etc.[4] Unde dicit quod deter(ioratum) est et dampnum habet ad valenciam ducentarum librarum. Et inde producit sectam etc.

Et Willelmus et alii per attornatos suos veniunt et defendunt vim et injuriam quando etc. Et bene cog(noscunt) quod predictus prior habet liberum mercatum suum in predicto loco qui vocatur Priorshalf in villa predicta et quod predecessores sui mercatum ibidem habuerunt ab antiquo set dicunt quod cum idem prior asserit ipsos Willelmum et alios mercimonia sua predicta jam de novo etc vendere et vendicioni exponere per predictum diem veneris in predicto loco de Erlestrete in domibus et seldis suis bene concedunt quod ipsi vendunt hujusmodi mercimonia sua ibidem sicut eis bene licet pro voluntate sua set non de novo etc. quia dicunt quod Ranulphus quondam comes Cestr' fuit dominus illius partis ville de Coventre que vocatur Erlestrete qui per cartam suam concessit hominibus suis loci illius quod essent burgens(es) et uti possent et gaudere eisdem libertatibus in omnibus quibus burgenses Lincoln' usi fuerunt et gavisi et proferunt quandam cartam sub nomine ipsius comitis que hoc testatur; proferunt eciam quandam cartam sub nomine H(enrici) regis patris R(egis) Ricardi que testatur quod idem H(enricus) rex predictam concessionem confirmavit prout carta predicti comitis rationabiliter testatur. Dicunt eciam quod idem comes tempore suo habuit feriam in eodem loco singulis annis die veneris proxima ante festum sancte Trinitatis et per octo dies proximo sequentes et similiter pilloriu(m) et tumerellu(m) ad faciend(um) jud(iciu)m de transgressoribus de assi(s)a panis et c(er)visie fracta et eciam heredes ejusdem comitis hoc idem optinuerunt quousque Rogerus de Monte Alto et Cecilia uxor ejus una heredum predicti comitis tempore domini H(enrici) regis avi domini r(egis) nunc predictam partem de Erlestrete cuidam priori de Coventre predecessori predicti prioris nunc ad feodi firmam dimiserunt, unde dicunt quod ipsi et antecessores sui ac eorum feoffatores ac eorundem antecessores tenentes tenementa que ipsi nunc tenent in predicto loco de Erlestrete a tempore quo non extat memoria ac eciam tempore predicti comitis et antecessorum suorum semper hucusque in domibus et seldis suis in ipso loco constructis omnimoda mercimonia sua venalia quecumque habuerunt vendiderunt et vendicioni exponere consueverunt per diem veneris quo predictus prior habet mercatum suum. Et predicti Willelmus et alii ques(iti) si ipsi aut aliquis alius mercatum per diem veneris in loco predicto de Erlestrete habeant seu habere clamant dicunt revera quod non set secundum consuetudinem predictam ab antiquo usitatam mercimonia sua in domibus et seldis suis vendunt et vendicioni exponunt prout ipsi et antecessores sui ut predictum est facere consueverunt ita quod iidem Willelmus et alii de novo nullam injuriam predicto priori fecerunt in hac parte etc. Et iidem Willelmus et alii quesiti per justic(iarios) si ipsi porrexerunt predictas cartas pro titulo an pro evidencia facti sui predicti et si se tenere velint ad cartas illas pro titulo etc. an ad consuetudinem predictam, dicunt quod ipsi protulerunt cartas predictas ad evidenciam etc.

Et prior dicit quod predicti Willelmus et alii et eorum antecessores et alii tenentes predicta ten(ementa) que ipsi modo tenent in predicto loco de Erlstrete non consueverunt (a tempore quo non extat memoria)[5] vendere seu vendicioni exponere mercimonia vel alia bona sua venalia in domibus et seldis suis in eodem loco per diem veneris quo idem prior mercatum suum tenet etc. quousque iidem Willelmus et alii hujusmodi mercimonia et alia bona sua venalia de novo in domibus et seldis suis extra mercatum predictum inceperunt vendere et vendicioni exponere etc. sicut idem prior quer(itur). Et hoc petit quod inquir(atur) per patriam. Et Willelmus et alii similiter. Ideo prec(eptum) est vicecomiti quod venire faciat hic a die Pasche in unum mensem per justic(iarios) xij etc. per quos etc. Et qui nec etc. Quia tam etc. ad quem diem veniunt partes per attornatos suos. Et vicecomes non mis(it) breve. Ideo sicut prius preceptum est vicecomiti quod venire faciat hic a die sancti Michaelis in tres septimanas nisi W(illelmus) de Bereford prius etc. xij etc. per quos etc. Et qui nec etc. Quia tam etc.

Postea continuato processu usque in crastino Purificationis beate Marie anno domini r(egis) nunc tercio venit predictus prior in propria persona etc. et predicti Willelmus Graumpe et alii per attornatum suum et similiter juratores de consensu partium electi. Qui dicunt super sacramentum suum quod predicti Willelmus et alii in brevi nominati et ceteri omnes manentes in predicto vico de Erlestrete in predicta villa de Coventre et eorum antecessores et alii prius tenentes (tenementa) que ipsi modo tenent in vico predicto semper hucusque vendiderunt et vendere consueverunt omnimoda mercimonia sua venalia in predicto mercato ipsius prioris de Prioreshalf per dies veneris quibus idem prior habet mercatum suum predictum et ea ibidem vendicioni exponere et non alibi in predicta villa de Coventre quousque jam octo annis elapsis quod predicti Willelmus Graumpe et alii in domibus et seldis suis in predicto vico de Erlestrete m(er)ces[6] suas de novo vendere inceperunt et vendicioni exponere sicut idem prior queritur ad dampnum ipsius prioris sexaginta librarum. Et ideo cons(ideratum) est quod predictus prior recuperet versus eos dampna sua predicta et quod predicti Willelmus et alii decetero mercimonia sua venalia per dies veneris quibus idem prior habet mercatum suum predictum alibi in predicta villa de Coventre quam in predicto mercato (suo)[5] non vendant seu vendicioni exponant etc. Et predicti Willelmus et alii in m(isericord)ia etc. (Dampna lx li. unde C(lericis) xm)[7].

PRO CP40/174 m151d

1 interlined 2 sic. 3 Robtm̄ 4 The year book account speaks of the loss of *estallage*, *cotage* and *terrage*. 5 interlined 6 sic. 7 at foot of roll

Details of some of the pleading in this case are to be found in the year book for 2 Edward II (*Year Books of Edward II* vol. ii, ed. F. W. Maitland, *Selden Society* vol. 19, 1904, pp. 71–74) where a bald translation of the record is appended, omitting the names of the defendants. This, however, was not the only case brought by the prior against townsmen for trading outside his Friday market. An earlier writ of 9 April 1302 named 24 who, together with one Hamo, had likewise traded from 30 September 1300 from selds and stalls newly-constructed before their doors (*coram hostiis suis*) in Earl St. The defendants are described as *mercenarii* and as residents (*inhabitantes*) of Earl St. The roll is badly damaged and some of the names are defective, though where the forenames are missing they can be supplied from their recital later in the roll. The 24 are: Richard le Mercer, John de Crok, William de Braundeston', John de Idelestr, William de [ ], [Henry] le Hosyere, Thomas Ballard, William de Bury, Robert de Stone, Henry Bagod, Richard de [ ], [Hugh] le Hosyere, Nicholas de Shepeye, Walter Box, Roger Box, John Russel, John de Rydew[are], [Richard . . .]toner, Thomas de Evesham, Hugh de Meriton', Henry Pane, Adam le Brocher, Simon L[ ], [Ralf] le Hunte. Only one of these names, that of Hugh de Merington, is found among the 67 given above. In content the record is broadly similar to that of the later plea. Both parties take their stand on long usage, the prior referring back to the time of his predecessors, William and Thomas. The defendants make no reference, however, to the earl of Chester. The commodities mentioned by name are cloth, cendal and silk. The verdict was given at Warwick before William de Bereford on 27 April 1304 and communicated to the Bench. The prior was awarded the £40 damages he claimed and the defendants were forbidden to trade outside his Friday market in future. [PRO CP40/144 m74d] What appear to be details of the pleading in this case are to be found in B.L. Add. MS. 31826 fos. 179r and 182r. I am extremely grateful to Dr. P. A. Brand for bringing these records to my attention.

34 Probably 1258–1268

Charter of Walter de Coventry giving to all the fellow burgesses of Coventry common pasture for all their animals in all his lands both newly approved and otherwise as they had hitherto.

Notum sit omnibus tam presentibus quam futuris quod ego Walterus de Coventre dedi et per cartam meam confirmavi omnibus comburgensibus de Coventre comuniam pasture pro omnibus animalibus suis in omnibus terris meis tam de novo appruatis quam alubi sicut actenus habuerunt; habend(am) et tenend(am) sibi et heredibus suis in feodo et hereditate imperpetuum. In cujus rei testimonium huic presenti carte mee ob reverenciam Willelmi de Arthingworthe sigillum meum apposui. Hiis testibus Henrico de Rokeby Gilberto de Folkesshul et Willelmo de Pinleya et multis aliis.

G.H. 265

Seal: circular, green, equestrian. Legend: SIGILL(UM) WALTERI DE COVINTREIA.
Endorsed: gyffu(n) þe comu(ns) in þe Was[ ][1] of Coventr'

[1] The remainder of this word is indecipherable.

EXTRACTS FROM THE CROWN PLEAS OF THE WARWICKSHIRE EYRES

The following extracts comprise the Coventry cases from the Crown pleas side of the Warwickshire eyres of 1232, 1247, 1262 and 1285, together with those held before the justices of oyer and terminer in 1306. For the corresponding cases from the earliest surviving Warwickshire eyre, that of 1221, see *Rolls of the Justices in Eyre for Gloucestershire, Warwickshire and Staffordshire, 1221–22*, ed. D. M. Stenton (*Selden Society*, 1940). Detailed discussion of the rolls themselves, and of the dates of the eyres, has been rendered unnecessary by the timely publication of Dr. David Crook's *Records of the General Eyre* (P.R.O. Handbooks No. 20, 1982). For the procedure and the content of the Crown pleas in general see the introductions by C. A. F. Meekings to *Crown Pleas of the Wiltshire Eyre, 1249* (Wiltshire Archaeological and Natural History Society, 1961) and the *1235 Surrey Eyre* (Surrey Record Society, 1979).

Except in two cases of exceptional interest (36.11, 37.17) the pleas are given in translation only, although care has been taken to avoid significant loss. The standard terminology of the rolls is easily accessible through the various Selden Society volumes. However, original readings have been bracketed where necessary in the interests of precision. Two additional editorial conventions have been adopted here: (   )^{i} denotes interlineation; (   )^{c} denotes cancellation. The cases have been taken from the following rolls at the Public Record Office:

1232	–	Just 1/951 A
1247	–	Just 1/952
1262	–	Just 1/954
1285	–	Just 1/961
1306	–	Just 1/966

35

Extracts from the Crown Pleas of the Warwickshire Eyre, held 22 June–8 July 1232.

35.1

Bailiffs and Presenting Jury

Vill of Coventry through 12 m23

[1]Prior's bailiff (*Baill(ivu)s (Prioris)*^{i}): William son of Simon, sworn

Earl's bailiff (*Baill(ivu)s (Com(itis))*^{i}): Richard de Aula, sworn

[1]Richard de Aula	sworn
William Crude	sworn
Osbert Duredent	sworn
Adam le Vineter	sworn
Richard le Burgeys	sworn
William le Buttere	sworn
William son of Simon	sworn
Matthew son of Roger	sworn
Richard de Bruges	sworn
Simon le Pestur	sworn
William le Paumer	sworn
Robert de Feug(er)es	sworn

[1] The bailiffs are given to the right of the vill, and the jury is given in a descending column to the right of the bailiffs.

Of the vill of Coventry (*Conventre*) m7d.

35.2

Henry le Drivere killed Robert de Berkeswell with a certain knife and fled. And the township did not make pursuit after the fugitive nor raise the hue and cry, so it is in mercy. And Henry was not in frankpledge but of the mainpast of the prior of Coventry, and so he is in mercy. No chattels. And let Henry be exacted and outlawed, because he is suspected.

35.3

Matthew Seliman killed Ivo le Tanur with a certain knife and fled, and the township did not make pursuit after him nor raise the hue and cry and so it is in mercy. And Matthew was in the frankpledge of Roger le Gardin(er) of Coventry, and so it is in mercy. And he is suspected; let him be exacted and outlawed. No chattels.

35.4

A certain unknown man (*ignotus*), grievously wounded in the belly, came to the hospital of St. John of Coventry and died there on the morrow and was buried in view of the coroner and the serjeant of the lord king. And so to judgement, and [it is] to be known that the hospital is in the hand of the prior of Coventry. And the jurors say that they knew this through the statement of a certain woman who was appointed to wash and treat the dead (*per narracionem cujusdam f(em)i(n)e que constituta est ad lavand(um) et insuendum mortuos*).

35.5

Agnes daughter of Anketill was crushed by a certain mill-wheel so that she died. No-one is suspected. Judgement: misadventure. Price of the wheel: 2s., (for which Adam le Vinet(er) and Richard the Goldsmith (*aurifab'*) of Coventry were responsible and are)[1] in mercy because they did not have them before the justices. Afterwards they were handed over to Robert de Notingeh(am) clerk.

[1] This line is cancelled and *stati(m) redd'* written above.

35.6

A certain infant of one year fell from the arms of Sarah (*sarre*) its mother, so that it died. No-one is suspected. Judgement: misadventure. And Sarah, its mother, was attached and comes and is not suspected, and so nothing.

35.7

Geoffrey[1] de Bruges who appealled Richard son of Richard de Hundelan' and Alan the clerk [and] William son of Richard the clerk of breach of the peace etc. and crime (?*f(ac)to*) etc., and Richard son of Roger and Richard de Hundelan' of incitement (*precepto*), has not followed up his appeal and so let him and his pledges for prosecuting, namely William[1] Ilpus and Alexander[1] the Red (*Ruffus*) of Coventry, be taken into custody. And the appellees do not come, and Richard son of Richard was attached by Peter[2] de Lutrewurth and Hugh son of Roger de Allespache. (And Richard son of Roger was attached)[3] and comes but because it is attested that they are accorded, so Richard son of Roger [is] in mercy by pledge. And the others were not attached because they were not found, and so should they be found let them be taken into custody because they are accorded.

[1] *nich(il)* interlined [2] *alibi* interlined [3] cancelled with *nich(il)* interlined

35.8

Christine daughter of William Hentetu who appealled Walter son of Thomas of rape has not followed up her appeal and has sworn to prosecute. And so nothing.

35.9

Evildoers killed Reginald the Miller (*molendinarium*). It is not known who they were. No-one is suspected except those same evildoers. And so nothing.

35.10

Concerning cloth sold contrary to the assize they say that they have made fine with the township by 6 marks.

35.11

Concerning wines sold contrary to the assize they say that Anketell the Vintner (*vinitarius*) and (Robert his brother)[1], Richard de Boskorvill' and Calle the boy (*Calle Garcio*)[2], William de Wykewan', Robert his boy (*Rob' Garcio suus*)[2], Richard the brother of Hugh de Allespath' who is dead [who was] his boy (*Garcio*) [were] sellers [contrary to the assize].

[1] *Rob' fr' ejus* underlined with *Garcio* written above *fr'*. [2] cancelled

35.12

Concerning evildoers in fishponds they say that Thomas le Fugelere of Coventry is suspected, and Thomas does not come but has withdrawn himself. And he was in the frankpledge of William le Sage in Coventry (*Covingtre*), and so it is in mercy. He is suspected; let him be exacted and outlawed.

35.13

Henry son of Robert the One-eyed (*monoculi*) fled to the church for suspicion of larceny and acknowledged the larceny and abjured the realm. And he was in the frank[pledge] of David de Fonte in Coventry, and so it is in mercy. His chattels: 3s. 4d., for which let the sheriff answer.

35.14

A certain Geoffrey le Hore was taken by the serjeants of the lord king upon Dunsmore (*Dun(n)esmore*) and David the reeve (*prepositus*) of the prior of Cov(entry)[1] replevied (*replegiavit*) him and committed him to the custody of a certain Simon Limgel' his serjeant (*servienti suo*), and he escaped from their custody. And to judgement. And Geoffrey fled to the church and abjured the realm and acknowledged larceny. And Geoffrey [was] in the frank[pledge] of William de Repingdon' in Coventry, and so it is in mercy. Geoffrey's chattels: 4s. 4d. And it is attested that Geoffrey was in the prior's prison and in the part which appertains to him (*in prisona prioris et in p(ar)te q(uam) eum conti(n)git*), and so to judgement concerning the escape.

[1] The membrane is torn here.

35.15

A certain unknown man (*ignotus*) came to Coventry and made himself the messenger (*fecit se nu(n)tiu(m)*) of Luke the chaplain later treasurer[1] of the lord king and became weak (*fecit se infirmum*) and died at Coventry. And later it was attested that he was a thief and a burglar and a slayer of men and that he was present when 2 men of Coventry were killed. And the township did not present this suit (*loquela*) at the county court and the same unknown man was buried in view of the coroner, and so [it is] in mercy.

[1] For Luke 'the king's treasurer' or controller of the Wardrobe (1224–27) see Tout, *Chapters* i, pp. 195–6; vi, p. 27.

35.16

Amercements	
Of the township of Coventry	m21
From the township of Coventry from their fine for transgression and for the drapers (*pro transgr' et pro draper'*)	6m.
From the frankpledge of Roger le Gardiner of Coventry for the flight of Matthew Seliman	½m.
From Hugh son of Roger de Alspath because he did not have Richard son of Richard whereas he was pledge	½m.
From Anketinus the Vintner (*vinetar'*) for wine sold contrary to the assize	1m.
From Richard de Boskervill' for the same	½m.
From William de Wikewan' of London (*Lond'*) for the same	1m.
From the frankpledge of William le Sage in Coventry for the flight of Thomas le Fugheler'	½m.
From the frankpledge of David de Fonte for the flight of Henry son of Robert	½m.
From the sheriff from the chattels of the same Henry	3s.4d.
From the sheriff from the chattels of Geoffrey le Hore who abjured the realm	4s.4d.
From Ralf son of Ralf the coroner for transgression	1m.
sum:	12m.12d

35.17

Deodands m21

To the fabric of the church of Coventry, ½m. to be rendered to the warden (*Custodi*).

To the hospital (*Hospic'*) of Coventry, 5s. by Robert Wauton'.
To the Franciscans (*fratribus minoribus*) of Coventry, 1m. by R(obert) de Lexington'.

36

Extracts from the Crown Pleas of the Warwickshire Eyre, held 8 April to 9 May 1247.

36.1

Chief Bailiff and Presenting Jury m46

Township (*villata*) of Coventry, Robert de Corlegh chief bailiff (*cap' Ball(ivu)s*), sworn.

Osbert Durdent, sworn; Robert de Recha(m), sworn; Ran(ulf) de Franketon', sworn; Richard Burgeys, sworn; Thomas de Souleye, sworn; Nicholas Forhtwyne, sworn; John Beer, sworn; Richard de Fonte, sworn; Peter Martin, sworn; Pagan Pake, sworn; John Simund, sworn; Robert Hamund, sworn.

The Township of Coventry comes by Twelve. mm43–43d.

36.2

William son of Geoffrey fell into a certain pit in the courtyard (*in quodam puteo in Cur'*) of Thomas Dowel and drowned. And Felice daughter of Geoffrey, the first finder, comes and is not suspected; nor is anyone else. Judgement: misadventure. And the township of Coventry buried him without view of the coroner, so it is in mercy. Afterwards the aforesaid township came and made fine by 100s. for itself for the 12 jurors and for the drapers, excepting the vintners (*Post' venit predicta vill' et finem fecit pro se et pro xij Jur' et pro Drapar' exc(ept)is vinetar' per Cs.*).

36.3

Benedict de Herdeberg' struck Nicholas Scot on the head with a certain stick in a certain alder grove near the vill of Coventry (*in quodam Alneto prope villam de Coventre*), so that on the morrow he died. And Benedict immediately fled and is suspected, so let him be exacted and outlawed. His chattels: 13s. for which let the sheriff answer. He was not in frankpledge because he is a free man (*liber homo*). And the township of Coventry did not take him nor make pursuit, so it is in mercy.

36.4

Richard de Rothwell was crushed to death by a certain beam (*lingnum*) which fell on him. No-one is suspected. Judgement: misadventure. Price of beam: 8d., for which let the sheriff answer.

36.5

Alice daughter of Robert Oselot fell into a certain cauldron full of boiling meal (*in quodam plumbo pleno grut' bullientis*) and was scalded, so that a fortnight later she died. No-one is suspected thereof. Judgement: misadventure. Price of cauldron: 2s. for which [let] the sheriff [answer].

36.6

William de la Sarcerin of Coventry appealled Peter son of Robert and Thomas his brother in the county court of the death of Alexander de la Sarcerin his brother. And Peter and Thomas were outlawed in the county court by the suit of the same William. They had no chattels nor were they in frankpledge because they are free men (*liberi homines*). And the jurors concealed this appeal, so they are in mercy and also for false presentment.

36.7

John son of Henry Lungemore wounded Simon son of Simon with a certain knife in the arm from which he afterwards died. And John immediately fled. And he is suspected, so let him be exacted and outlawed. He had no chattels. Nor was he in frankpledge because he is a clerk. And the township of Coventry did not take him, and so it is in mercy.

36.8

Edward son of Bateman a boy of 5 years was scalded by a certain bronze jar (*olla(m) eneam*) full of hot water which fell on him, so that 8 days later he died. No-one is suspected thereof. Judgement: misadventure. Price of the jar: 2s., for which let the sheriff answer.

36.9

William de Sallawe killed Simon son of Geoffrey Sot in the vill of Coventry by night. And immediately he fled, and he is suspected so let him be exacted and outlawed. (He had no)[i] chattels but he had land where from the king's year and waste: 2½ marks, for which let the sheriff answer. No Englishry. Judgement: murder, upon Coventry. And Humphrey le Rumong(er), attached because he was present when the aforesaid Simon was killed, comes. And the jurors attest that he is not guilty thereof. But because he did not take the aforesaid William let him be taken into custody. Afterwards the aforesaid Humphrey came and made fine by ½ mark, by pledge of Osbert Duredent.

36.10

Geoffrey Hildelay carrying a certain sack full of woad (*Wayd'*) fell on the pavement (*super pavim(en)tu(m)*) in Coventry so that his neck broke. And Peter Ingeram, the first finder, comes and is not suspected; nor is anyone else. Judgement: misadventure. Price of the woad: 7s. 7d., for which let the sheriff answer.

36.11

Robertus de Feuegers rettatus de morte Walteri filii Pain venit et ponit se super patriam de bono et malo. Et offert domino Regi C. solidos pro habenda inde bona inquis(itione). Et recipiuntur per plegium Roberti de Corleg' de Coventr' Martini Colebraund de eadem Osberti Duredent Ricardi de Fonte Ricardi Burgeys Johannis Simund' Roberti Hamund Nicholai Fordwyn Ranu(lfi) de Franketon Pagani Pake Petri Martin Johannis Beer Thome de Suleg' et Roberti [de] Rogeha de Coventre. Juratores dicunt super sacramentum quod Robertus de Feug(er)s veniens de quodam convivio in Coventre litigavit cum uxore sua, ita quod ipse tenuit quendam knipulum in manu sua. Et quidam garcifer Walterus filius Pain nomine superveniens timebat quod ipse voluit percutere uxorem suam knipulo illo venit et posuit se inter ipsos Robertum et uxorem suam, ita quod ipse jactavit brachium suum super predictum knipulum predicto Roberto invito et ignorante ita quod lesit se in brachio per predictum knipulum unde post tres septimanas post obiit. Et super mand(avit) dominus Rex per breve suum Justiciariis etc. quod si per inquis(itionem) quam fieri dec(er)et in itinere suo de morte hominis invenire(n)t quod predictus Walterus qui vulneratus fuit per cultellum Roberti de Feugers per infortunium in brachio quo vulnere postea mortuus est ut dic(unt) non fuit per feloniam ipsius Roberti vulneratus fuit. Ita . . .[1]

Robert de Feuegers accused of the death of Walter son of Pain comes and puts himself on the country for good and ill. And he offers 100s. to the lord king to have a proper inquisition. And they are received by the pledge of Robert de Corleg' of Coventry, Martin Colebraund of the same, Osbert Duredent, Richard de Fonte, Richard Burgeys, John Simund', Robert Hamund, Nicholas Fordwyn, Ranu(lf) de Franketon, Pagan Pake, Peter Martin, John Beer, Thomas de Suleg' and Robert de Rogeha of Coventry. The jurors say on oath that Robert de Feug(er)s coming from a certain banquet in Coventry quarrelled with his wife so that he held a certain knife in his hand. And a certain groom, Walter son of Pain by name, arriving on the scene and fearing that Robert intended to strike his wife with the knife, placed himself between them so that without Robert's will or knowledge he flung his arm upon the aforesaid knife injuring himself in the arm from which injury he died 3 weeks later. And on this the lord king ordered by writ to his justices etc., that if they should find by inquisition of homicide which ought to be made in their eyre that the aforesaid Walter, who was wounded in the arm by misadventure through the knife of Robert de Feugers from which wound he later died was not wounded by felony of the same Robert as they [the jurors] say, so . . .[1]

[1] foot of m43. The case is not continued on dorse.

36.12

. . . feuer[1] of Coventry appealled Richard le Clerk of Smercote that when he was in the peace of the lord king at the bar in Bishop St. (*in vico Episcopi scilicet ad Barram*) on St. Bartholomew's day in the 29th year he assaulted him, maltreated him, gave him a certain wound on the thumb and took 5s. from him in robbery. And that he did this wickedly and in felony against the peace etc. he offers to prove by his body as the court shall adjudge.

And Richard comes and denies felony, wounding and robbery and whatsoever is against the peace etc. And he asks that it be allowed him that the appellor names in his appeal neither the hour at which this is reported to have been done nor the hand in which the wound was made, and that he appealled him in the county court of wounding and now of wounding and robbery. And because this is found to be so it is adjudged that the aforesaid Richard ought not to be put to law through his appeal, but Matthew should be in mercy for false appeal. And in order that the peace of the lord king be preserved let the truth be inquired into by the country.

The same Matthew appealled Bateman (*Batemanu(m)*) de Hurst, Syward Morin, Nicholas juxta Brok', Robert de Birchemore and Roger Long (*Longu(m)*) of abetment (*de vi*) etc. And they all come and put themselves on the country for good and ill. The jurors say on oath that the aforesaid Richard le Clerk beat the same Matthew just as he appealled him, but stole nothing from him in robbery. And that the aforesaid Bateman and all the others were in abetment. So, let them all be taken into custody. Afterwards the aforesaid Siward, Nicholas and Richard [le clerk][1] came and made fine by 1 mark by pledge of Roger Shirlok and Elias the Reeve (*preposito*).

[1] The membrane is torn along the top left.

36.13

Alina the widow of Matthew le Yrreys[1] and Matilda and Margery her sisters accused of the death of the aforesaid Matthew come and put themselves on the country for good and ill. And the jurors of Knightlow (*Knyttelaw*) and the 12 of Hemlingford (*Humili(n)ford*) and the 12 jurors of Coventry say on oath that they are not guilty of the aforesaid death, so they are quit thereof. And it is attested by the 12 jurors of Coventry that William de Anesleye imputed this crime (*crimen*) to them from hatred (*de odio et atia*), so he is in mercy.

[1] *leyrreys*

36.14

Concerning wines sold contrary to the assize they say that Anketinus (de)[i] Wykewan, Walter de Panes, William Lewyn, Martin Colbraund and Robert de Wykewan sold wine contrary to the assize in Coventry, so they are in mercy.

36.15

Concerning cloth they say that Nicholas Warin, William de Wilenhal, Richard de Henle sold cloth contrary to the assize, so they are in mercy.

36.16

Concerning those indicted they say that Nicholas de Spalinges, (John de Totenhal, (Batteman)[i] Haldan' de Wytele)[c], Richard (son of Richard)[i] Pyhod, William le Goser (and Ralf his son)[i], John Stok', William le Taillur, Durantus Halleward, Peter le Parcher and Margery de Spaldinges, accused of many larcenies withdrew themselves and are suspected concerning oxen, cows and other stolen things, so let them all be exacted and outlawed except the aforesaid Margery. And let the aforesaid Margery be exacted and outlawed.[1] And the aforesaid Nicholas, John and Richard, William le Toser[2], Ralf his son, John le[3] Stok, Durantus, Peter and Margery had no chattels. And Nicholas was of the mainpast of Richard de Bruges in Coventry, so he is in mercy. And John was of the mainpast of Christine widow of Haldanus de Wytele, so she is in mercy. And Richard was of the mainpast of Richard Piod his father, so he is in mercy. And William and Ralf his son were of the mainpast of William de Kanel', so he is in mercy. And John Stok was not of any mainpast because he was a vagrant (*quia itin(er)ans*). And Durantus was of the mainpast of William Segrun, so he is in mercy. And Peter was of the mainpast of Richard de Norfouk, so he is in mercy. Chattels of the aforesaid Haldanus[4]: 3s., for which let the sheriff answer.

And he was of the mainpast of Adam son of Henry de Wytele, so he is in mercy. Chattels of the aforesaid William le Taillur: 12d., for which let the sheriff answer. And he was of the mainpast of Richard Meau, so [he is] in mercy. Afterwards John de Totenhal' came and he is not suspected, [he is] quit.

[1] sic for waived [2] sic [3] sic [4] presum. Batteman Haldanus.

36.17

Petronilla widow of John the Marshal (*mariscallus*) of Coventry appealled Roger the Weaver (*Tixtorem*) of Coventry in the county court of breach of the king's peace, battery etc. And she does not come now, so let her be taken and her pledges for prosecuting namely John Blakwyn of Coventry and Walter Marshal of the same [are] in mercy. And Roger does not come nor was he attached because he was not found. And the jurors concealed this appeal, so they are in mercy.

36.18

Afterwards the aforesaid Bateman Haldain came and made fine that he may be able to return to the peace etc. and stand to right etc. by 20s. by pledge of John de Wytele [and] Robert de Wytele.

The Coventry section ends here.

36.19

The jurors[1] present that William Grom and many others were taken at Coventry. And they were [imprisoned][2] in the prison of Roger de Montalt (*in prisona Rogeri de Monte Alto*) at Coventry. And they escaped from that prison. So, to judgement concerning the escape. And the aforesaid William fled to the church of St. Michael in Coventry where he acknowledged larceny and abjured the realm before the coroner. He had no chattels. And it is not known what became of the others. m41

[1] Of Knightlow hundred. [2] . . . *ti* The membrane is torn on the right.

37

Extracts from the Crown Pleas of the Warwickshire Eyre, held 5 June–20 July 1262

37.1

Bailiff and Presenting Jury m65

Borough (*Burg'*) of Coventry. William Lewyn bailiff, sworn.

John son of Symon, sworn; Geoffrey Bretun, sworn; William Tholy, sworn; Alexander de Gloucestr', sworn; Thomas Haldeyn, sworn; John Hapertachs, sworn; Henry Baker (*Pistor*), sworn; Robert Hamund', sworn; Peter Martin, sworn; Pagan Pake, sworn; Adam le Traue(n)t(er), sworn; William de Thurlauestu(n), sworn.

The Township of Coventry comes by Twelve mm58d.–59

37.2

Richard Labanc killed William de Esseby in Coventry and immediately fled and is suspected. And it is attested by the 12 that he was later taken at Northampton and there he became an approver and was hanged. His chattels: 4s., for which let the sheriff answer. The first finder has died and is not suspected. No Englishry. Judgement: murder, upon the township of Coventry.

37.3

Amicia widow of Reginald le Sopere appealled John Hally of Coventry in the county court of the death of her husband. And similarly she appealled of the death of her husband Richard le Burser and Alexander Huldeshut, who were outlawed in the county court. And Amicia comes now. And Richard had chattels: 2s. 3d., for which let the sheriff answer. And the aforesaid John and Alexander had no chattels nor were they in tithing but were received into the township of Coventry outside of tithing, so it is in mercy.

37.4

Geoffrey de Bygginge of Stoke (*Stok'*) and Mabel le Hucstere mutually quarrelled and the aforesaid Geoffrey threw her on the ground so that she burst internally (*interius rumpebatur*) and on the fourth day after she died, and he immediately fled and is suspected, so let him be exacted and outlawed. His chattels: 20d., for which let the sheriff answer. No-one else is suspected thereon. And he was received into the township of Coventry, so it is in mercy.

37.5

Roger le Seynturer struck Roger Stirthup on the head with a certain piece of firewood (*Astella*) in the house (*domo*) of a certain Emma in Coventry, so that on the eighteenth day after he died therefrom. And Roger immediately fled and is suspected of the aforesaid death. So let him be exacted and outlawed. His chattels: 18d., for which let the sheriff answer. And because the aforesaid Roger remained in the same vill after that deed, so the township of Coventry [is] in mercy.

37.6

Bartholomew de Frokeby placed himself in the church of the blessed Mary in Coventry and acknowledged that he was a thief concerning many larcenies and he abjured the realm before the coroner; and it is not known concerning his chattels nor his tithing.

37.7

Robert le Lokkere of Lawford (*Lalleford*) struck Geoffrey Kay of Coventry on the head, so that on the third day after he died therefrom; and Robert fled and is suspected, so let him be exacted and outlawed. He had no chattels nor was he in tithing because he was a stranger (*quia extraneus*).

37.8

John de Corle in Coventry struck William le Parber[1] on the head with a certain axe, so that within a fortnight after he died; and immediately after the deed he placed himself in the church of the blessed Mary of Coventry and acknowledged the deed and abjured the realm before the coroner. His chattels: 6s. 2d., for which let the sheriff answer. And William le Clerk of Coventry taken for the aforesaid death comes and says that he is a clerk and cannot answer here. And on this comes William the dean of Stanley (*Staunl'*) proctor of the bishop of Lichfield and Coventry (*Lych' et Coventre*) and claims him as a clerk. And the 12 jurors say on oath that he is guilty and as such he is handed over to him.

[1] sic

37.9

William son of William le Pipere of Brackley (*Brakkele*) placed himself in the church of the blessed Mary of Coventry and acknowledged that he was a thief concerning many larcenies and abjured the realm before the coroner.

37.10

Regin(ald) de Hales and his fellows, unknown evildoers (*socii sui ignoti malefactores*) fell upon John le Ropere of Coventry and Emma his wife outside the wood of Wem (*Wem(m)e*) in the county of Stafford (*Staff'*) and beat and wounded the same John, so that on the 8th day after he died therefrom in his house (*domum*) at Coventry. Regin(ald) is suspected thereof, so let him be exacted and outlawed. It is not known concerning his chattels nor his tithing because [they are] strangers (*quia extranei*).

37.11

Walter de Dunhamlyde [was] taken at Coventry with false money by the bailiffs of Coventry (*per ballivos de Coventre*) and imprisoned in the same place; and from their prison (*prisona eorum*) he escaped and placed himself in the church of the blessed Michael of Coventry and in the same place acknowledged that he was a thief and a forger and abjured the realm before the coroner. And judgement upon the aforesaid township for the escape. And afterwards it was attested by the 12 that William Maunsel, then sheriff, took 100s. from the same township for this escape, so let him answer for these. Chattels of the aforesaid Walter: 12d., for which let the sheriff answer. He was not in tithing because he was a vagrant (*quia Itinerans*).

37.12

William le Fossur of Stretton of the county of Oxford (*Oxon'*) placed himself in the church of St. John of Coventry and acknowledged that he was a thief concerning many larcenies and abjured the realm before the coroner. It is not known concerning his chattels nor tithing because he was a stranger (*quia extraneus*).

37.13

William de Kynardeby, tailor (*Cissor*), placed himself in the church of St. John of Coventry and acknowledged that he was a thief concerning many larcenies and abjured the realm before the coroner. He had no chattels nor is it known concerning his tithing because he was a vagrant (*Itinerans*).

37.14

Henry le Ceynturer of Coventry killed Cecily his wife and fled and is suspected, so let him be exacted and outlawed. His chattels: 6d., for which let the sheriff answer. He was not in tithing but was received into the township of Coventry which does not now have him here, so it is in mercy.

37.15

Adam son of Godwine de Wattell' placed himself in the church of the blessed Mary of Coventry. And Margery de Coventry [did] similarly, and they acknowledged themselves to be thieves concerning many larcenies and abjured the realm before the coroner. It is not known concerning their chattels nor the tithing of the same Adam because he was a stranger (*quia extraneus*).

37.16

Roger Scarie struck Henry Rypun on the head with a certain stick, so that he died the same night. And Roger Scarie immediately fled and is suspected thereof, so let him be exacted and outlawed. His chattels: 14d., for which let the sheriff answer. He was not in tithing but was dwelling (*manens*) in the vill of Coventry. And the 12 jurors concealed his chattels, so they are in mercy.

37.17

Juratores presentant quod Hugo Russell captus fuit cum quodam equo quem Ran(ulfus) de Kaus et Walterus le Blunt ballivi de Coventre dicebant ipsum furasse et ipsum incippaverunt et in cippo detinuerunt per octo dies, ita quod pedes ejus putrefacti fuerunt per inprisonamentum illud et postea a tibiis ceciderunt unde postea obiit. Et Walterus venit et bene defendit quod nunquam predictum Hug(onem) cepit nec inprisonavit nec per ipsum nec per assensum suum imprisonatus fuit, et de hoc ponit se super patriam de bono et malo. Et xij juratores simul cum xij de Knyttelowe dicunt super sacramentum suum quod predictus Ran(ulfus) cepit predictum Hug(onem) et per preceptum predicti Walteri ipsum incippavit ut predictum est, ita quod per inprisonamentum illud et per frig(orem) quod in cippo illo recepit pedes ejus inflati fuerunt et postea putrefacti fuerunt et de tibiis ceciderunt sicut predictum est. Et dicunt quod postea vix(it) per quartam partem anni et postea obiit. Et quia predictus Walterus inventus est in habitu clericali ideo committitur gayol(e). Et dicunt quod predictus Ran(ulfus) subtraxit se pro predicta morte et inde malecreditur, ideo exigatur et utlagetur. Catalla ejus nulla.

The jurors present that Hugh Russell was taken with a certain horse which Ranulf de Kaus and Walter le Blunt, bailiffs of Coventry, said he stole, and they put him in the stocks and held him there for 8 days so that his feet rotted through that imprisonment and later fell from his legs from which he afterwards died. And Walter comes and denies that he ever took the aforesaid Hugh or imprisoned him, or that he was imprisoned with his assent and concerning this puts himself on the country for good and ill. And the 12 jurors together with the 12 of Knightlow say on oath that the aforesaid Ranulf took the aforesaid Hugh and on the order of the aforesaid Walter put him in the stocks as aforesaid, so that through this imprisonment and through the cold which he suffered in the stocks his feet became swollen and later rotted and fell from his legs as aforesaid. And they say that afterwards he lived for a quarter of a year and then died. And because the aforesaid Walter was found in clerical habit let him be committed to gaol. And they say that the aforesaid Ran(ulf) withdrew himself on account of the aforesaid death and is suspected thereof, so let him be exacted and outlawed. He had no chattels.

37.18

Cecily daughter of Robert de Berewik' placed herself in the church of Coventry and acknowledged that she was a thief concerning many larcenies and abjured the realm before the coroner. She had no chattels.

37.19

Hugh son of Gilbert de Balisall' fell into the pond (*stagno*) of the monks of Coventry and drowned. The first finder comes and is not suspected. And Peter Barun of Coventry taken for the aforesaid death comes and says that he is a clerk and ought not to answer here. And on this comes William dean of Stanley (*Staunl'*) proctor of the bishop of Chester (*Cestr'*) and claims him as a clerk, but so that it may be known in what condition he ought to be handed over to him, let the truth be inquired into by the country. And the 12 jurors and the 4 neighbouring vills say that the aforesaid Peter threw (*projecit*) the aforesaid Hugh into the pond so that he fell [upon] a certain pointed stake (*palum acutum*), from which on the third day after he died. So, as such he is handed over to the aforesaid proctor.

37.20

Concerning wines sold they say that Anketill de Wykewane and Alexander de Ruyton' in Coventry sold wine contrary to the assize, so they are in mercy.

37.21

Concerning cloth sold they say that William le Poleter [and] Anketill de Wykewane sold cloth contrary to the assize, so they are in mercy.

37.22

The jurors present that Richard de Bruges, bailiff (*ballivus*), took 2s. from Henry le Cartesadelere for removing him from a certain assize, so he is in mercy.

37.23

Alexander de Glovern(ia) of Coventry was taken for the death of Richard de Henle whom he is reputed to have imprisoned (*imprisonasse debuit*); he comes and denies the imprisonment, death and everything, and for good and ill puts himself on the country. And Symon Skatheloc of Coventry and Thomas his brother taken for burglary and robbery come and deny the robbery etc. And the 12 jurors together with the jurors of Knightlow (*Knyttel'*) say on oath that in nothing are they guilty, so they are quit thereof. And Alexander offers the king ½ mark for inquiring by what abetment this was imputed to him, and it is received. And the aforesaid jurors say etc. that [it was] by the abetment of Richard de Bruges, and the same is present and cannot deny this so let him be committed to gaol.

38

Extracts from the Crown Pleas of the Warwickshire Eyre held 14 January–9 February 1285.

38.1

Bailiff and Presenting Jury m15

Township of Coventry[1]. William de Stodley bailiff, sworn.

John son of Nicholas, sworn; Henry Dobedy, sworn[2]; Richard de Weston, sworn; Thomas le Moubray, sworn; Robert the Miller (*Molendinar'*), sworn[2]; William le Parker, sworn; Roger the Fishmonger (*Piscator*), sworn; Henry de P[ar]lur, sworn; Robert in le Hurne, sworn; Adam Russell, sworn; Stephen de Hales, sworn; Hugh le Bretun, sworn.

[1] An incorrect jury headed by William de Stodl' is given earlier on the membrane and replaced by the above at the end of the list of juries. William is given as bailiff for the township of Stoneleigh, Brinklow and Kenilworth.

[2] These two are bracketed as electors.

The Township of Coventry comes by 12 Jurors. m11d.

38.2

These were the coroners since the last eyre, namely: Hugh le Hosiere who has died and Walter Bacon who is present and answers.

38.3

The jurors present that William de Keules struck Adam Laweles at night in the head with a certain axe, so that he immediately died therefrom. And William de Keules immediately fled and placed himself in the great (*majorem*) church of Coventry and in the same place acknowledged the deed and abjured the realm before the coroner. His chattels: 12d., for which let the sheriff answer. It is not known concerning tithing because he was a stranger (*quia extraneus*). And because the township of Coventry falsely valued the aforesaid chattels before the coroner, so [it is] in mercy.

38.4

Agnes le Wolf struck Matilda de Folkeshull with a certain scythe (*falce*) in the arm, so that on the morrow she died therefrom. And the aforesaid Agnes immediately fled and is suspected. So let her be exacted and waived. She had no chattels.

38.5

Bodinus le Pestur wounded Thomas Skathelok in the head with a certain stick, so that on the morrow he died therefrom. And Bodinus immediately fled and is suspected. So let him be exacted and outlawed. His chattels: 14s. 6d., for which let the sheriff answer. Afterwards it was attested through the coroners' rolls that Is(abella) widow of the aforesaid Thomas appealled in the county court Vincent le Pestur of Coventry, Ralf the Baker (*Pistorem*) and Geoffrey his brother, and Henry the clerk of *Roxhalle* of the death of the aforesaid Thomas her husband and did not pursue her appeal in the county court until etc. So let her be taken, and her pledges for prosecuting [are] in mercy namely Simon Skathelok and Walter le Marescal of the same. And the jurors say that they are accorded, so [they are] in mercy.

38.6

Robert Qhitloue[1] and William le Fann(er)e shot (*sagittaverunt*) John le Parker and so wounded him that he died immediately therefrom. And the aforesaid Robert and William fled and are suspected. So let them be exacted and outlawed. It is not known concerning chattels nor tithing because they are vagabonds (*quia vagabondi*). And because the township of Coventry did not make pursuit after them, so [it is] in mercy.

[1] Variously given as *Whytloue*, *Qwytloue* in the other rolls of this eyre.

38.7

Ralf of Dry Marston (*Drie Merston'*) struck Robert Gifford on the head with a certain stick at night, so that on the morrow he died therefrom. And the aforesaid Robert immediately fled and is suspected. So, let him be exacted and outlawed. It is not known concerning chattels nor tithing because he is a vagabond (*quia vagabondus*).

38.8

William de Salop' burgled the house (*domum*) of Christine Wry at night and immediately after the deed he placed himself in the church of Spon (*Spo(n)ne*) and acknowledged the deed and abjured the realm before the coroner. It is not known concerning chattels nor tithing because he was a vagabond (*quia vagabondus*).

38.9

Henry son of Richard le Moun(er) wounded Alice his wife in the breast with a certain sword so that immediately she died therefrom. And the aforesaid Henry immediately fled and is suspected. So let him be exacted and outlawed. His chattels: 5s. 8d., for which let the sheriff answer. And the 12 jurors falsely valued the aforesaid chattels, so [they are] in mercy etc.

38.10

William Dunte the miller (*molend'*) struck Nicholas de Wroxhalle in the head with a certain axe, so that immediately he died therefrom. William immediately fled and is suspected. So, let him be exacted and outlawed. He had no chattels. The first finder has died. And the jurors attest that he had no tithing.

38.11

Concerning the escape of thieves they say that Richard the Smith (*Faber*) and

Thomas de Cestria of the county of Northampton (*Norhampton*) escaped from Coventry prison (*prisona de Coventre*). So, let the township of Coventry answer concerning the escape etc. And the aforesaid Richard and Thomas are suspected. So, let them be exacted and outlawed. They had no chattels etc. Afterwards it was attested that the aforesaid Thomas had been taken and hanged. So nothing at present concerning the outlawry in respect of the aforesaid Thomas (nor concerning the escape)[i] but let Richard be outlawed etc.

38.12

Reginald Abot[1] of Sowe struck William Gopil on the head with a certain stick so that on the morrow he died therefrom. And the aforesaid Reginald immediately fled and is suspected. So let him be exacted and outlawed. He [had] no chattels.

[1] *Regin' Abot* deleted and *obiit* written above.

38.13

Concerning those indicted they say that Alice de Caldecote, William le Saltere and Dulcea his wife, Richard Dale, William de Norff', John Brun, Richard de Melcote, Richard le Cokere, Nicholas Byle have withdrawn themselves for many larcenies. So let them be exacted, and the men outlawed and the women waived. They had no chattels. It is not known concerning tithing because they are vagabonds (*quia vagabond'*) etc.

39

Extracts from the Warwickshire Crown Pleas held under commission of oyer and terminer, 1–9 May 1306.

39.1

Presenting Jury m14d

Vill of Coventry

Peter Baroun	sworn	Thomas de Lilleburn'	sworn
Henry de Merington'	sworn	Roger de Pakewode	sworn
John le Gover	sworn	Lawrence de Shepeye	sworn
Anketinus de Coleshill'	sworn	John de Wynton'	sworn
Adam Russel	sworn	William le Walker	sworn
Richard le Espicer	sworn	Henry Oky	sworn

39.2 m1d

The jurors present that Craddock le Taborrer of Coventry around the feast of St. Martin in the 25th year [11 Nov. 1297] killed Geoffrey de Riggeley in the vill of Coventry (*Coventree*), and that immediately after the deed he was taken and led to the royal prison at Warwick[1] and that there he was hanged. He had no chattels. And that Roger le Shephird of Coventry on the feast of St. Dunstan in the 27th year [19 May 1299] etc. killed Hugh[2] le Sker once the servant (*servient'*) of Richard de Loges, and that immediately he was taken and led to the royal prison at Warwick and [that] before the justices assigned to deliver the gaol etc. through an inquisition on which the aforesaid Roger put himself it was ascertained that he killed the aforesaid Hugh in self-defence and not by felony or malice aforethought so that he was remitted to prison in expectation of the king's grace etc., and that the lord king afterwards pardoned him his liability for the aforesaid death. So nothing from the same Roger for the present.

[1] *Warr'* and throughout the roll. [2] *occidit hugonem* repeated

39.3

The jurors present that Adam de Aula of Coventry on Sunday before the feast of the Exaltation of the Holy Cross etc. in the 27th year etc. [13 Sept. 1299] killed Alice de Norhamton' by night in the aforesaid vill of Coventry (*Coventree*). And that William le Keu of Basingwerk (*Basyng Werk'*) around the feast of the Annunication of the blessed Mary in the year aforesaid [25 March 1299] killed Robert le Fleccher of Sherwood (*Shyrewode*). And that John de Brinkelowe on Wednesday after the feast of St. Vincent in the 28th year etc. [26 Jan. 1300] killed Alice de Draicote [and] William son of the same Alice by night at Coventry. And that the aforesaid Adam de Aula and the others fled immediately after the aforesaid deeds. And the sheriff is ordered to take them if etc. And the sheriff attests that they are not found etc. So let them be exacted and outlawed. Chattels of the aforesaid Adam de Aula of Coventry (*Coventree*): 2s. 1d., for which let the township of Coventry (*Coventree*) answer (*respondeb'*). And the others had no chattels. Afterwards a certain Nicholas Crompe came and said that William le Keu of Basingwerk (*Basyng Werk*) is an Hospitaller and is overseas (*est hospitelar' et in partibus transmarinis*) and proffered a certain royal charter which attests that the lord king at the instance of his beloved and faithful Henry de Laci, earl of Lincoln (*Linc'*), pardoned the aforesaid William le Keu of Basingwerk (*Basyngwerk*) his liability for[1] the death of Robert le Fleccher of Sherwood (*Shyrewode*) and also his outlawry should it have been proclaimed for this cause; so that he should stand trial in the royal court, however, if anyone wishes to accuse him; charter given at Bothwell (*Bothevill'*) 11 September 29 Edward I [1301]. So nothing from the aforesaid William le Keu for the present nor from the outlawry etc.

[1] *per* for *pro*

39.4

The same jurors present that Roger de Burton' on Tuesday after the feast of the Nativity of St. John the Baptist in the 28th year etc. [28 June 1300] killed William de Shothewell' in the vill of Coventry, and that immediately he was taken and led to the royal prison at Warwick in the time of Philip de Gayton' then sheriff. So the sheriff is ordered to summon the aforesaid Philip to answer etc. how the aforesaid Roger left his custody.

39.5

The same jurors present that Richard son of Aleyn le Wodewarde of Stivichall (*Styvychehale*) [and] John the Carter (*Carectar'*) of Asthill (*Asthull'*) on Sunday after the feast of Sts. Tiburtius and Valerianus in the 29th year etc. [16 April 1301] killed Matthew de Routon' in the vill of Coventry. And that John de Aubenay on the aforesaid day and year killed John son of the aforesaid Matthew de Routon' in the same place. And that the aforesaid Richard and the others fled after the aforesaid felonies. And the sheriff is ordered to take them if etc. And the sheriff attests that they are not found. So let them be exacted and outlawed. Afterwards John de Aubeney comes, and asked how he wishes to clear himself of the aforesaid murder of John son of Matthew says that he is a clerk and that he ought not to answer here thereon. And on this comes the prior of St. Sepulchre, Warwick (*sancti sepulcri Warr'*) taking the place of the bishop of Worcester (*Wygorn'*) by his letters patent and claims him as a clerk. But so that it should be known how he is to be handed over to him let the truth of the matter be inquired by the country. The jurors say on oath that the aforesaid John de Aubeney is not guilty of the death of the aforesaid John son of Matthew de Routon'. So as such let him be handed over to the aforesaid bishop without need of purgation. And nothing from outlawry against him etc. And they say that he never did withdraw himself for the aforesaid death. So nothing from his chattels.

39.6

The same present that Ralf Persy of Repton (*Repyngdon'*) on Sunday the feast of St. Osberg in the 30th year etc. [23 Jan. 1302] killed Henry de Hales by night in the vill of Coventry (*Coventree*). And that John Hervy of Allesley (*Allesleye*) on Thursday before the feast of St. Michael in the 28th year etc. [27 Sept. 1300] killed Adam Weccheharm in the same vill of Coventry (*Coventree*) by night. And that Thomas Hager of Coventry and John de Essex' on Christmas eve in the 30th year etc. [24 Dec. 1301] killed Roger Burgoygne. And that the same Thomas was immediately taken and led to Warwick and there imprisoned in the time of John de Dene then sheriff. And that the aforesaid Ralf Persy and John Hervy fled immediately after committing the aforesaid felonies. And the sheriff is ordered to take them if etc. And the sheriff attests that they are not found. So, let them be exacted and outlawed.

They had no chattels. Afterwards the aforesaid John Hervy of Allesley (*Alleslie*) came and proffered a royal charter which attests that for the good service which the same John gave the king in Scotland (*in partibus Scot'*) the lord king has pardoned him his liability for the death of the aforesaid Adam Wet'hewe and for other trespasses against the peace of the same king in his realm of which he is accused, and granted his firm protection to him, so that he should stand trial, however, etc. if anyone etc., witnessed by the king himself at Linlithgow (*Linlyscu*) 18 January in the 30th year etc. And it is solemnly proclaimed if anyone etc. concerning the aforesaid death. And no-one comes. So he goes quit according to the tenor of the aforesaid charter etc. Afterwards it was attested by the jurors of Knightlow (*Knytheslawe*) that he had chattels to the value of 6s. 5½d., for which let the township of *Assheley*[1] answer for the flight of the same John as aforesaid. And nothing from the outlawry made against him. And the sheriff is ordered to summon the aforesaid John de Deyne to answer etc. how the aforesaid Thomas left his custody.

[1] sic

39.7 m2

The jurors present that William Fraunceys of Coventry on Thursday after the feast of St. Michael in the 28th year etc. [6 Oct. 1300] killed Alice his wife in the aforesaid vill of Coventry (*Coventree*). And that he immediately fled to the church of St. Michael in the same vill and there before John Lewyn, the coroner, he abjured the realm. And the same is ascertained through the rolls of the same coroner. He had no chattels.

39.8

Moreover, they present that John the Shoemaker (*sutor*) of Coventry on Monday after the feast of St. Edward (? *Ed'i*) in the 30th year etc. [8 Jan. 1302] killed Roger le Bours(er) in the same [vill]. And that he immediately fled and afterwards returned, and was taken and led to the royal prison at Warwick. And before R(alf) de Beaufey (*Bella fago*) and his fellows, justices[1] assigned to deliver the gaol there he was hanged. His chattels: 2s. 1d., for which let the township of Coventry answer when etc.

[1] followed by *suis*

39.9

The jurors present that William Oky of Coventry on Monday after the feast of St. Thomas the Martyr in the 31st year etc. [31 Dec. 1302] killed John le Palm(er) of Coventry in the same vill of Coventry. And that Richard de Shaynston' on Saturday after the feast of All Saints in the 32nd year etc. [7 Nov. 1304] killed William de Stretton' at Coventry by night. And that William de Wolricheston' on Monday the feast of St. Chad in the aforesaid year [2 March 1304] killed John de Stretton' by night. And that Nicholas son of Robert le Fissher of Coventry and Walter the Miller (*molendinar'*) called (*dictus*) le Glover in the 30th year etc. [1301/2] killed Robert de Glouc' at Coventry by night. And that Walter de Allesley on Friday before the Conversion of St. Paul in the 32nd year etc. [23 Jan. 1304] killed Hugh le Taillour by night at Coventry (*Coventree*). And William de Pacwode tailor (*cissor*) and John de Allespath' on Sunday after the feast of St. Matthew the Apostle in the 33rd year etc. [26 Sept. 1305] killed William de Brugges by night at Coventry. And that the aforesaid William Oky and the others fled immediately after committing the aforesaid felonies. And the sheriff is ordered to take them if etc. And the sheriff attests that they are not found etc. So, let them be exacted and outlawed. Chattels of the aforesaid William de Wollericheston' 16d., for which let the township of Coventry answer when etc. And the others had no chattels.

Delivery of Warwick Gaol before the justices of oyer and terminer 20 June 1307. m10

39.10

Thomas Jacob of Clifton is indicted at Coventry before Robert the Bailiff (*Balli(v)o*) and (*before*)[i] the coroner of Coventry for the death of Henry de Denecastel' of Coventry killed at Coventry etc. Taken, he comes and, asked how he wishes to clear himself of the aforesaid death, denies the death and all felony etc. And he denies that he is in any way guilty thereof. And for good and ill he puts himself on the country. The jurors say on oath that Thomas Jacob is guilty of the aforesaid death. So he etc. He [has] no chattels.

DEEDS FROM VARIOUS COLLECTIONS

The majority of the deeds which follow are from the great collection preserved in the archives of Coventry Corporation. A succinct account of their provenance was provided by J. C. Jeaffreson in his report to the Historical Manuscripts Commission in 1899:

> 'From the time of Edward III to the period of the Reformation Coventry was remarkable for the wealth and importance of its Guilds and the number of its Chantries. By two grants made in the reigns of Henry VIII and Edward VI, negotiated for the advantage of the municipality by Sir Thomas White, the greater part of the lands, rents, and other property of these Guilds and Chantries passed into the hands of the Corporation of the City, and together with the lands and rents there passed also a large proportion of the records that related to them. Moreover, on the suppresion of the ancient Priory . . . many of the writings belonging to them, of like character as evidence of more property, were transferred to the Mayor and Citizens of Coventry, instead of being carried away with the main body of the archives to the Court of Augmentations.'[1]

Of the broad validity of Jeaffreson's statement there can be no doubt. On 22 July 1542 the mayor, bailiffs, and commonalty received the grant of considerable rents from property once belonging to the Cathedral priory.[2] Property of the gilds and chantries followed on 18 September 1552.[3] Deeds relating to the gilds and religious institutions clearly provide the hard core of the collections, though they are unlikely to account for its entirety. Among additional items appear to be the muniments of the Stoke family whose property passed to the city during the second half of the sixteenth century.[4]

As they stand the early deeds are not easy to use. The original fonds appear to have been broken up by the time H. T. Riley completed his first report for the Historical Manuscripts Commission in 1870.[5] J. C. Jeaffreson later arranged the dated ones according to regnal years. They are now in bundles within large cardboard boxes. Three of these hold the deeds calendared here, *viz*:

Box 1A contains bundles with *circa* dates ascribed.

Box 1B contains the earliest dated leases, and dated deeds of the reign of Edward I.

Box 2 contains bundles of undated deeds without *circa* dates.

When the *circa* dates of Box 1A were added is not known, but they are sometimes seriously in error. Bundles are dated 11th–12th centuries, early 12th century, mid 12th century and so on. In fact, there appear to be no deeds in the collection before the first decade of the 13th century. In the calendar which follows the deeds of Box 1A are located by abbreviations denoting the bundles (e.g. 1A/MC12/32), those from Box 1B by reference to the regnal year (e.g. 1B/24E1/11), and those from Box 2 by their continuous numbering (e.g. 2/78). Those abstracted by Jeaffreson for his partial calendar[6] are indicated 1A/C followed by his number.

The Coventry deeds from two modern private collections – the Fuller Collection now deposited with the University of London Library, and a collection in Harvard Law Library – appear to have been derived ultimately from the Coventry Corpor-

1 *Fifteenth Report, Appendix, Part X* p. 102.

2 *Letters and Papers, Foreign and Domestic, of the reign of Henry VIII*, vol. XVII, ed. J. Gairdner and R. H. Brodie, (London, 1900), p. 321.

3 Jeaffreson, *op. cit.*, p. 124.

4 *V.C.H. Coventry*, pp. 97–98.

5 *First Report, Appendix*, p. 101.

6 J. C. Jeaffreson, *Coventry Charters and Muniments*, (Coventry, 1896).

ation archives, for some of them carry a stamp bearing the city's arms. Full references have been given for the deeds drawn from these collections.

It may be noted that some haemorrhaging from the Corporation deeds has taken place since the time of Jeaffreson's calendar in 1896 for a number of items mentioned by him are no longer in the collection (C55, C58). A few deeds seem to have been misplaced more recently and are no longer in the early boxes (see below Nos. 52, 73, 290, 292, 761n). In these cases their contents have been reconstructed from abstracts taken during the preliminary sifting for the present calendar in 1978, in one case (No. 52) with the aid of Dr N. W. Alcock who encountered the deed more recently than the present editor.

There are, in addition, several other significant collections of Coventry deeds. Warwick County Record Office contains the deeds of Holy Trinity parish church, once kept in a box marked 'Holy Trinity Feoffees'. Classified at Warwick as DR 564 they are indicated simply by W.R.O. and their individual numbers. A number of deeds abstracted from this collection were calendared by Mary Dormer Harris as *Documents in Trinity Vestry*. They are classified separately at Warwick as DR 429. This has been retained here to avoid confusion. The Gregory-Hood Deeds deposited at the Shakespeare Birthplace Trust, Stratford-upon-Avon (DR 10) are the muniments of the lords of Stivichall. They are complimented by the deeds in the *Langley Cartulary* and by those in the Middleton Collection now deposited with the University of Nottingham. The latter have been indicated by *Middleton*, the main Gregory-Hood collection by G.H. Deeds in the *Langley Cartulary* have not been recalendared here but their existence has been noted in introducing the deeds for each of the Coventry streets. Two other collections containing Coventry material result from estates in close proximity to the town, *viz.* those of Queen's College Oxford at Keresley, and those of the lords of Caludon. The former are now deposited at the Bodleian Library, Oxford and are denoted here by Q.C., whilst the latter remain at Berkeley Castle and are indicated by *Berkeley*.

The majority of the Coventry deeds surviving in the Public Record Office belong to Exchequer Series A (classification E 40) derived largely from private collections. Deeds relating to the forfeited property of the Catesby family seem to be heavily represented here.[7] Others belong to Series B (classification E326) indicating that they came into the hands of the Crown on the dissolution of religious houses. In addition to these there are further deeds without seals bound into volumes of *Cartae Miscellaneae* which similarly emanate from the Court of Augmentations (classification E315). Property of Stoneleigh abbey figures among these. There is also a single deed from the Chancery Series C (classification C146) and a handful from Exchequer Series D (E210) including several more from the muniments of Stoneleigh Abbey. Deeds from the Public Record Office are located by series and number, except in the case of those from the *Cartae Miscellaneae* where the full classification is given.

The intention has been to include all extant Coventry deeds before the close of the reign of Edward I. All obvious sources have been tapped and the editor has included all items which have come within his purview. However, given the scattered nature of the archives others may yet appear. It is hoped that the apparatus provided by the volume will allow any additional items to be placed in context. Two further qualifications are necessary. Firstly, all of the main collections referred to above contain deeds for the settlements near to Coventry. Considerations of space have made it impossible to include these. An exception has been made, however, for the property of the Stoke family, partly because of the position of these deeds within the Coventry collection but more particularly because they illustrate the type of rent complex which existed in the area in the time of the later earls of Chester. Secondly, it may well prove possible to locate many of the properties more precisely when the entire chronological range of deeds included in these collections has been closely

[7] *Ex inf.* Dr. N. W. Alcock, who is currently undertaking a study of the Catesby deeds.

studied. The ordering and dating of the early deeds is a necessary first step. Meanwhile the deeds have been grouped according to street or location with a brief introductory statement for each of the groups.

Method of Dating

The majority of the deeds, particularly those prior to the 1290s, are undated. Close dating immeasurably enhances the value of deeds as evidence. On the other hand, *circa* dates assigned on the basis of a single appearance of, say, two or three parties or witnesses can be very misleading. In order to bring the maximum available evidence to bear on the dating the following method has been employed. An index has been constructed from a variety of sources external to the deeds themselves. These include the Warwickshire Eyre Rolls for 1221, 1232, 1247, 1260, 1262, 1272 and 1285 (all but the first of these unpublished), and the published *Curia Regis Rolls*, *Pipe Rolls* and *Warwickshire Feet of Fines*. Using this index, a separate index of the 1280 *Hundred Rolls* and material from the few dated leases, all appearances of each party and witness have been noted on a sheet attached to every deed. Of particular value have been the juries of presentment from the Crown pleas of the eyres and the appearance of bailiffs both there and in the deeds. However, the town's administration during the period was complex and by no means static. Hence no simple sequence of bailiffs could be constructed and the evidence for dating from this quarter, although instructive, has had to be treated with some caution. Similarly, two much emphasis should not be placed on simple non-appearance in the *Hundred Rolls*. We have no assurance that the survey records all tenants; besides which it is clear from the deeds that individuals may be recorded under more than one name (e.g. under both trade-name and toponymic).

Circa dates provided by the above means have then been reinforced and supplemented by material generated internally from the deeds and by placing the deeds for individual streets in a chronological order. The few charters of the earls of Chester have been used to help provide a *terminus a quo* in default of a base line. It becomes clear that virtually none of the deeds belong to the period before c.1200–1210. For certain periods the material is fuller than for others and the dating consequently more precise. Similarly, some streets are better served than others. Spon St. and Gosford St., in particular, pose greater problems where there is an unusual preponderance of witnesses with very localized interests and where deeds seem to have been taken less regularly to the town's courts.

In the end, although a small margin of error must inevitably remain, the resultant dating rests on a solid foundation and can be used with some confidence. Throughout care has been taken to avoid dating more narrowly than the evidence strictly warrants, even to the extent of erring on the side of caution.

For practical reasons the bulky index from external data cannot be entirely reproduced here. The Crown pleas (but not the civil pleas) of the eyres with their presenting juries are included in the volume, as are the charters of the earls of Chester and the *Hundred Rolls* of 1280. Again, for reasons of space cross-referencing in footnotes has been avoided. Footnoting has been reserved for personages external to Coventry who are rarely found in the deeds. In addition to the data to be found within the volume, however, the following references to deaths have been particularly useful for dating purposes and should be noted:

Liulf of Spon	by 27 Jan. 1214 (*Curia Regis Rolls*, vol. VII, pp. 93–4).
William of Spon	by 13 Oct. 1221 (*Warwickshire Eyre Roll 1221* No. 595)
William Midnight	by 13 Oct. 1221 (*Warwickshire Eyre Roll* 1221 No. 393)

Richard son of Ernis	by 30 June 1224 (*Curia Regis Rolls* vol. XI, p. 342)
Leofwin or Lewin (son of Jordan)	by 25 Nov. 1226 (*F.F. Warwicks* No. 386)
Swanus or Sweyn the Parker *alias* Swanus son of Adam of Coventry	by 25 Nov. 1225 (*Curia Regis Rolls* vol. XII, p. 321)
Henry son of Edric or Edred	by 20 May 1229 (*Curia Regis Rolls* vol. XIII, p. 463)
Geoffrey the Goldsmith	by 9 June 1230 (*Curia Regis Rolls* vol. XIV, p. 18)
Matthew son of Gundreas	by 8 July 1232 (*Warwickshire Eyre Roll* 1232 m10d.)
Vincent the Parker	by 8 July 1232 (*ibid.* m17d.)
Adam son of Haldane *alias* Adam of Spon	by 3 Nov. 1232 (*Curia Regis Rolls* vol. XIV, pp. 453–4)
Walter de Alspath	by 15 June 1236 (*F.F. Warwicks* No. 522)
Nicholas fitz Nicholas of Withybrook	by 15 March 1243 (*Langley Cartulary* No. 216)
Ailmer the Dyer	by 29 Sept. 1255 (*ibid.* No. 365)
Henry Pye	by 8 June 1272 (*Warwickshire Eyre Roll 1272* m2)
Thomas de Fakenham	by 9 Feb. 1285 (*Warwickshire Eyre Roll* 1285 m5)

Dates by which some others were dead can be ascertained from the deeds themselves, e.g. Robert de Feugers by Michaelmas 1257 (No. 597), Alexander of Gloucester by 30 November 1269 (No. 197), Warin the Mercer by 30 Nov. 1272 (No. 295). Others, of course, were dead by the time of the *Hundred Rolls* of 1280.

BROADGATE*

*See also 162, 703 and 767.54.

40 c.1220–1225

Charter of Alice the wife of Hugh son of Martin giving to Richard Meu and his heirs a parcel (*unam p(ar)tic(u)lam*) of his land at Broadgate (*Latam portam*) next to the land of Adam Querdeliun, namely the seld (*seldam*) which Ralf the Stone-cutter (*incisor*) held of the grantor which contains in length towards Smithford (*Smitesford*) 12 feet and in width next to the street (*juxta vicum*) 10 feet; to be held in fee and inheritance to him and his heirs, of the grantor and her heirs freely [etc.], by rendering annually 4s. of silver at four terms of the year, namely 12d. at each of the feasts of St. Michael, St. Andrew, St. Mary in March and St. John the Baptist for all service and exaction. Clause for warranty. Richard gave a talent (*talentu(m)*) in recognition. Witnesses: Richard de Wigorn', Stephen his son, Swanus the Parker (*p(ar)car'*), Vincent his son, Geoffrey the Goldsmith (*aurifabro*), Adam Querdeliun, Eadward the Saddler (*sellar'*), Geoffrey the Cook (*coc'*), Robert the Saddler (*sellar'*), Walter Ketelb', Richard Burgeis, Adam the Scribe (*Scriptore*) and many others.

Seal missing C.R.O. IA/EC12/3

A grant by Hugh son of Martin to Richard Meu of land at Broadgate and at the above rent was noted by Jeaffreson (*Coventry Charters and Muniments* No. C55).

41 c. 1220–c.1225

Charter of Richard de Aula giving to Richard Meu and his heirs the entire land at Broadgate (*ad Latam portam*) in Coventry which Gerard the Black (*Niger*) once held with all appurtenances, namely the land which lies between the land the same Richard held and the road which leads from Broadgate towards Cheylesmore (*viam que tendit a lata porta versus Cheilesmora(m)*) and extends from the highway (*a magno vico*) up to the land Geoffrey the Goldsmith (*Aurifaber*) held, and contains in width towards the street (*vicum*) 11½ feet and in length 39 feet; to be held to him and his heirs, of the grantor and his heirs, in fee and inheritance freely [etc.] by rendering annually 6s. of silver at four terms of the year, namely 18d. at each of the feasts of St. Michael, St. Andrew, St. Mary in March and St. John the Baptist for all secular service [etc.]. Clause for warranty. Richard gave 2 marks of silver in recognition. Sealing clause. Witnesses: Richard de Wigorn', Hugh son of Martin, Richard Burg', Matthew son of Roger, William de Rependon', Hugh Cath', Vincent son of Swanus,

Walter Ketelb', Thomas the Goldsmith (aurifabro), William Liuet, Adam Querdeliun, Richard Hagemund and many others.

Seal extant C.R.O. IA/EC12/10

42 Mid 1240s

Charter of Richard son of Richard at Meu giving to Richard Scayl and his heirs or assigns or to whomsoever he will wish to give, bequeath, sell or assign, all his rents and lands with appurtenances which he held in the vill of Coventry and outside, namely the entire land at Broadgate (*apud latam portam*) with appurtenances which he held of Peter Martin by the service of 5s. and a pair of gloves or 1d. to Richard Burgeys, the land in Cheylesmore Lane (*in viculo de Cheylismor*) which he held of the fee of Philip son of Miles by the service of 12d., a certain curtilage and barn (*horreo*) of the Poddycroft (*de podicroft*) which he held of the fee of Elias Despenser (*dispensatoris*) by the service of 8d., 6d. rent from the heirs of Alexander the Red (*Ruffi*), another 6d. rent from Henry de Wihithawe, a shop at the abbey gate (*unam scoppam ad portam abacie*) which he held of the heirs of Nicholas de Wyþibroc by the service of 3s. between the land once of Robert the Cook (*Coci*) and the land of Matthew de Cymit(er)io, 12d. rent which Richard de Botelston rendered to the grantor from the curtilage once of Edith Scot which is of the fee of Nicholas de Causey by the service of 1d., the entire land in Hill St. (*Hullest(r)ete*) which Geoffrey Fretherich held which is of the fee of Nicholas Fordewin by the service of 20d., 1d. rent from Walter Picot and the entire land with appurtenances at *Dodemoneswelle*, another land (*aliam terram*) towards Coundon (*Cu(n)dulne*) next to the land of Roger Blanche which the grantor's father held of Robert the Vintner (*vinitario*) by the service of 4s., the land at Radford (*radefort*) which he held of the fee of Robert de Deyvile by the service of 20d. next to the land of Henry Beket, and another land (*aliam terram*) next to the royal highway (*regiam viam*) between the land of Geoffrey de Attleborgo and the land of Robert brother of the same; to be held to him, his heirs or assigns, freely [etc.] of the same lords as the grantor held *et per idem servicium prius nominatim de me et de heredibus meis*. Clause for warranty, by the service of a pair of gloves worth ½d. at Easter. Sealing clause. Witnesses: Osbert Durdent then bailiff, Richard Burgeys, William de Wilnhale, John Blacwin', Nicholas Fordewyn', Peter Martin, Richard Labanck, Robert Dile, Aylemer the Dyer (*Tinctore*), Roger de Stivechale, William Harp(uri)s, Geoffrey Page and others.

Seal missing C.R.O. IA/EC13/86

Endorsed: Carta Ric(ard)i Meu de ten' Ric(ardi) Facham ad latam portam et de aliis redditibus.

43 c.1230

Sale and quitclaim by Alice widow of Hugh son of Martin in her widowhood and free power, without any reservations by her and her heirs, to Hugh de Allispath' of the entire land at Broadgate in Earl St., Coventry (*In covintr' in vico comitis ad lata(m) portam*) which lies between the land William Bern held and the land John the Butcher (*carnifex*) held of that fee, a pair of gloves per annum from the land the aforesaid John held of the grantor, the land which lies between the land John the Butcher (*carnifex*) held and the land Nicholas Meau held of the same fee, 1lb. cumin which Robert the grantor's son used to render to her from the land Nicholas Meau held of the same fee, 12d. rent which Petronilla the grantor's daughter used to render from the land which Adam le Bursere held of the grantor, and all right and claim which she had in the aforesaid lands and rents with all liberties, issues and all kinds of appurtenances; to be held to him and his heirs or to whom he will wish to give or assign of the lord earl of Chester (*cestr'*) just as the grantor held of him and by the same service, namely 40d. per annum at four terms of the year according to the custom of the vill and 1lb. pepper at the feast of St. John the Baptist for all service and all demand. Moreover [she has granted] a ½ mark of silver rent from Henley Mill (*de molendino de henl'*) which she held of Roger son of Richard de Henl' and all right and claim which she had in that mill with all liberties, issues, profits (*eventibus*) and all appurtenances; to be held to him and his heirs or to whom he will wish to give or assign of the aforesaid Roger son of Richard de Henl' and his heirs just as the grantor held of him and by the same service, namely 3d. per annum for all service and demand at four terms of the year according to custom *firme solvende*. Clause for warranty. Hugh gave 13½ marks. Sealing clause. Witnesses: Richard de Aula, Richard son of Gerard the Vintner (*vinitar'*), William de Wilnhal', Geoffrey his brother, Richard Leuwin', John Ferthwin', Richard the Goldsmith (*aurifabro*), Adam the Vintner (*vinitar'*), William de Repindon', Walter de Allispath', Richard the Burgess (*burg(e)nsi*), Nicholas Meau and others.

Seal missing — Berkeley G341

44 — Late 1240s

Charter of Alice daughter of Geoffrey the Saddler (*sellarii*) in her widowhood and free power giving to Athelard the Painter (*pictori*) and Margery his wife and to William son of John the Painter (*pictoris*) and Christine his wife and their heirs the entire land with appurtenances which Geoffrey her father gave to her in free marriage, namely the land in Coventry at Broadgate (*apud latam portam*) between the land William the Glover (*Wantarius*) held and the land William Brond held, and besides this the entire curtilage at Cheylesmore (*apud Cheilesmora(m)*) which Walter the Saddler (*sellarius*) her late husband bought from Robert Tersi; to be held to them and their heirs, the tenement at Cheylesmore (*apud Cheilesmor'*) for ever and the tenement at Broadgate (*apud latam portam*) after the death of the grantor, freely and quietly, by rendering annually after her death from the tenement at Broadgate (*apud latam portam*) 26d. to William Brond and his heirs issuing from Christine his wife, and from the tenement at Cheylesmore (*apud Cheilesmor'*) 4d. to William de Sallowe and his heirs at four terms of the year according to the usage of Coventry. Athelard and William the painters (*pictores*) gave 3s. of silver for the grantor's support (*ad victu(m) meum*). Sealing clause. Witnesses: Richard de Fonte, Richard the Burgess (*Burgens'*), Nicholas Forthwine, Peter Martin, William Segri(m), Thomas the Goldsmith (*aurifabro*), William Brond, William the Glover (*Want'*), Hugh Ketelbern, Thomas le Furbur, Henry the Saddler (*sellario*), William the Saddler (*sellar'*), Hugh the Saddler (*sellar'*) and others.

Seal extant — C.R.O. IA/L12–13C/50

45 — 1250s

Charter of Walter called (*dictus*) Ketel and Hawisia his wife, daughter of Richard Amund of Coventry, giving to Henry le Sceler of Coventry a moiety of the entire land at Broadgate (*ad latam portam*) in Coventry which lies between the land Roger de Frodesham held on the one hand and the land Nigel Balle held on the other, namely the moiety which is nearer to the land of Nigel Balle in length and in width as it purports; to be held to him, his heirs or whatsoever assigns, of the grantors and the heirs of Hawisia freely [etc.], by rendering annually to the lords of the fee as the grantors' perpetual attorneys the rent due and accustomed, namely 11d. of silver at the four terms of the year fixed and usual in the vill of Coventry and 2 hens at Christmas, and to the grantors and the heirs of Hawisia a clove-gillyflower at Easter for all secular services, exactions, customs, whatsoever courts and their suits and all temporal demands pertaining to the grantors and the heirs of Hawisia. Clause for warranty. Henry gave 10s. of legal sterling beforehand. *Et ad illam donacionem concessionem et warrantizacionem firmiter tenendam et fideliter sine dolo observandam ego Walterus et Hawisia uxor mea fide nostra media nos obligavimus sub pena trium marcarum argenti subsidio terre solvendorum subicientis nos (con)jun(c)tim et divisim jur(is)d(ic)t(i)oni et coh(er)c(i)oni official(is) domini arch(i)diaconi Coventr' et decani ejusdem loci qui pro tempore fuerint quod ipsi ambo vel eorum alter possint vel possit nos vel nostrum alt(eru)m (com)pell(er)e de die in diem per s(ente)n(t)iam exco(mmunication)is et int(er)d(ict)i pulsatis campanis candelis accentis ad fidei nostre observacionem et etiam ad pene predicte solucionem si conting(er)it quod absit fidem nostram ledi et penam (com)mitti renu(n)ciando omni excepcioni cavillac(i)o(n)i defensioni et om(n)i jur(is) remedio tam canonici quam civil(i) et specialiter regie p(ro)hi(bi)-c(i)oni.* Sealing clause. Witnesses. Richard de Bok(er)vill' then bailiff, Pagan Pake, Thomas Haldeyn, John the Goldsmith (*aurifabro*), Henry le Cartesadeler', William de Thurlauston', Adam le T(r)auent(er), Richard Meu, Hugh the clerk and others.

Seal extant IA/L12–13C/53

46 1270s

Charter of Henry le Celer of Coventry giving to Richard his son, for his service, certain built-up land with appurtenances at Broadgate in Coventry (*quandam terram in Coventr' cum pertinentiis edificatam ad latam portam*) between the land of John de le Monkeshous once the land of Nigel Balle on the one hand and the land once of Roger de Froþesham on the other, which land he had by the gift, and confirmed by the charter, of Hawysia and Alice daughters of Richard Hamu(n)d, in length and in width as is manifest according to the metes and bounds made there; to be held to him, his heirs or whatsoever assigns of the grantor and his heirs freely [etc.], by rendering annually a clove-gillyflower at Easter, and to the lords of the fee, namely to Robert Herebert and his heirs 11d. at the four terms of the year fixed and usual in the vill of Coventry and 2 hens at Christmas for all secular service [etc.]. Warranty and sealing clauses. Witnesses: John de Lodelowe then bailiff, Robert de Chilton', Henry Baker (*pistor'*), Ralf the Baker (*pistor'*), John de Fillu(n)geley, Henry Carsadeler, Ranulf Chore, Thomas le Moubray, Henry the Marshal (*marescallo*) and many others.

Seal extant P.R.O.A 6981

47 Late 1250s–early 1260s

Charter of William de Canel' of Coventry giving to Sir Geoffrey de Langel and his heirs or to whomsoever he will wish to give or assign, his entire land with the houses sited there and all appurtenances at Broadgate (*ad latam portam*) in the vill of Coventry, which lies on the corner next to the lane which leads from the high street at Broadgate towards the church of St. Michael of Coventry (*ad Cornariu(m) juxta venell(um) qui ducit de alto vico ad lata(m) porta(m) versus ecclesiam sancti michaelis Coventr'*) and extends from the land of Simon de Bannebur' up to the land of Hugh de Sowe in length and in width as it purports with all appurtenances; to be held of the grantor and his heirs freely [etc.] by rendering annually to the chief lords of that fee 3s. 2d. at the four terms of the year usual in the vill of Coventry, namely 9½d. at each term, and 2 hens at Christmas to acquit the grantor and his heirs, and a rose at the Nativity of St. John the Baptist to the grantor and his heirs for all secular service [etc.]. Clause for warranty. Sir Geoffrey gave 6 marks of silver beforehand. Sealing clause. Witnesses: Alexander de Glov(er)nia then bailiff of Coventry,

Vital(is) de Folkishull', Richard Ernis, Reginald de Cockishal', Peter de Stokes, Geoffrey de Bilneya, Philip de Winchecombe of Coventry, Richard de Bokirvil', William Lewyne, William le Polet(er), Robert de Denecast(re) and many others.

Seal extant Middleton 3988

Langley Cartulary No. 283 is a corrupt version of this.

48 c.1260

Charter of Thomas the Goldsmith (*aurifaber*) of Coventry giving to Thomas Haldeyn of Coventry a certain part of his land behind his chief houses within Broadgate, Coventry (*retro capital(es) domos meas infra latam portam Covintr'*) which is between the land the grantor himself held and the land of William Bren, [and] on the other hand between the land Henry le Cartesadeler held and the land Hugh de Alispathe held in length and in width as the land purports according to the metes and bounds made there; to be held to him, his heirs or assigns, of the grantor and his heirs freely [etc.], by rendering annually 6d. of silver at the four terms of the year fixed in Coventry for all secular service [etc.]. Clause for warranty. Thomas gave 20s. beforehand. Witnesses: Walter the White (*albo*) then reeve (*p(re)po(s)ito*), John Beyr, Alexander de Glouc', Reginald the Red (*Ruffo*), Richard Haldeyn, Richard Wint(er)-keng, Henry le Cartesadeler, Henry le Seler, William Bern and others.

Seal missing C.R.O. 2/105

49 Late 1270s–early 1280s

Charter of Thomas Haldeyn son of Thomas Haldeyn of Coventry giving to Nicholas the Cook (*coquo*) son of Richard Harlaund of Wasperton (*Waspirton'*) and to Felicia his wife for 10s. of silver which he gave beforehand a messuage with appurtenances next to Broadgate (*juxta latam portam*) in the vill of Coventry between the land of Walter Bacun on the one hand and the land of the abbess of Polesworth (*Pollisworth'*) on the other; to be held to him, his heirs or assigns, or to whomsoever he will wish to give, bequeath, sell or assign, in sickness and in health, except to the Jews, of the grantor and his heirs after the death of Alice Haldeyn the widow of the grantor's father, by rendering annually a [ ][1] at Easter for all secular service [etc.] and the service to the lords of the fee according to the usage of Coventry. Warranty and sealing clauses. Witnesses: Robert de Chilton' then bailiff of Coventry, Henry Baker (*pistore*) of the same, Alexander the Vintner (*vinetar'*) of the same, Roger the Chamberlain (*camerar'*), Robert the Miller (*molendinar'*), John le Flouter of the same, Walter Bacun of the same, Thomas de Fakenham of the same [ ][1] Marechal and many others.

Seal extant P.R.O. A6887

[1] Lost, not revealed by ultra violet light.

50 Mid–late 1260s

Gift and quitclaim by Margery daughter of Ralf de Crophull' in her widowhood and lawful power to William Leuwin of all right and claim in a moiety of a messuage with appurtenances lying at Broadgate (*ad latam portam*) in Coventry which moiety John the Furbisher (*Furbar'*) held of the grantor; to be held to him and his heirs wheresoever and to whomsoever he will wish to assign freely [etc.], by making to the lords of the fee the service owed, namely 13d. of silver at four terms of the year according to the custom of the vill of Coventry for all secular service [etc.]. William gave ½ mark of silver beforehand. Sealing clause. Witnesses: Robert de Chilton', Henry Baker (*pistore*), Nicholas Fortwin, Peter Martin, Hugh Ketelbern, Roger the Miller (*molend'*), Walter Bacun, Adam le T(r)auent(er), Thomas the clerk and others.

Seal extant C.R.O. 2/86

51 c. early 1290s

Grant and quitclaim by Robert son of Jordan (*Jurdani*) Herbert, for himself and his heirs, to Henry called Baker (*dicto pistori*) of Coventry and Agnes his wife of 5s. 9d. annual rent in Coventry to be received annually at the four terms of the year usual and fixed in the same vill, namely 6d. from the chief messuage (*Capitali manso*) of Matthew de Ruyton' towards Broadgate (*versus latam portam*), 3s. 3d. from 2 selds (*duabus seldis*) which Richard le Taylur and Margery widow of Walter de Bannebury held in the Market-place (*in foro*) of Coventry between the land of Richard de Conedonere and the land of the aforesaid Margery, and 2s. from certain land which the same Henry held towards *Ouenotesforde* between the land of John de Teynton' on the one hand and the land which was once of Richard Pykedepere on the other; to be held with all rights, liberties, escheats and all other kinds of easements which will be able to accrue, to them, their heirs or assigns, well [etc.]. Exclusion clause. Henry and Agnes gave 40s. sterling beforehand. Sealing clause. Witnesses: Robert de Chilton', Thomas le Moubray, John Thole, Henry le Cnave, John de Teynton', William Maunsel, John de Macstoke, Richard de Conedonere, Roger the clerk and others.

Seal extant G.H. 296

Endorsed: Carta [ ]am portam quam Henricus le Clerk' tenet vi^d^ per annum et tres solidatos redditus de Ricardo le Frit[?] tenet et duos solidos in Harnhelle quam Thomas Pistor tenet.

52 2 March 1294

Grant by Richard Burgeis of Coventry to Matthew de Ruyton saddler (*sellario*) and Margery his wife of a messuage at Broadgate on the east between the land of John de Frankevile clerk and the land of Richard the Cook (*Coci*). Rent 18d. Witnesses: Henry Baker (*Pistore*) then bailiff in Coventry, William le Parker then coroner, Adam Russel', Richard de Weston, William Grantpe, Richard de St. James, Philip the Crossbowman (*Balistario*), William Maunsel', John de Catesby and others. Coventry, the feast of St. Chad (*Cedde*) 22 Edward I.

C.R.O. 1B/22 E1/9

Abstract only, see above p. 64.

53 30 January 1295

Charter of Henry le Marchal of Coventry and Matilda his wife giving to Symon de Coleshul in Coventry a certain part of their tenement which they had towards Broadgate (*versus latam portam*) in Coventry, which lies in width between the grantors' land on the one hand and the land of the aforesaid Symon on the other and extends in length from the royal highway (*a Regali via*) up to the grantors' curtilage just as the aforementioned part of the said tenement fully purports according to the metes and bounds made there, namely as long as Symon's land (*adeo longe quam terra Symonis tendit*); to be held with the buildings sited there and all appurtenances, to him, his heirs and assigns, well [etc.] of the lords of that fee by the service of 5s. 11d. of silver to be paid to the same lords annually at the four terms of the year usual and fixed in the vill of Coventry for all services [etc.]. Clause for warranty. Symon gave 4½ marks of silver beforehand. Witnesses: Henry Baker (*pistore*) then bailiff of Coventry, William le Parker then coroner, John Thole, William de Copston', Richard de St. James, Stephen le Marchal, Matthew de Ruyton', Jurdan le Seler, Roger the clerk and others. Coventry, Sunday after the feast of the Conversion of St. Paul 23 Edward I.

2 seals extant C.R.O. IB/23EI/8

54 1295–1297

Remise and quitclaim by Robert son of Henry le Marchal of Coventry, for himself and his heirs, to Symon de Coleshul in Coventry of all right and claim in that part of the tenement (*illa parte tenementi*) which was once of the said Henry the grantor's father towards Broadgate (*versus latam portam*) in Coventry which lies between the land of the same Symon on the one hand and the land of the aforesaid Henry the grantor's father on the other in length and in width as that part of the said tenement purports; to be held with appurtenances to him, his heirs or assigns, well [etc.] without any impediment by the grantor or his heirs. Exclusion and sealing clauses. Witnesses: Henry Baker (*pistore*) then bailiff of Coventry, William le Parker coroner, John Thole junior, William de Copston', Matthew de Ruyton', Richard de St. James, Thomas Haldeyn, Stephen le Marchal, Jordan le Seler and others. Coventry, the day [. . .][1].

Seal extant C.R.O. 2/174

[1] The document breaks off here.

55 6 March 1306

Charter of Robert le Mareschal of Coventry giving to Henry le Mareschal his brother 5s. annual rent with appurtenances in Coventry to be taken annually at the four terms of the year usual in Coventry from a certain seld (*selda*) at Broadgate (*ad latam portam in Coventr'*) where the grantor's forge (*fabrica*) is sited, which seld lies between the door of the chief messuage (*hostium Capitalis mesuagii*) of the same Henry on the one hand and the tenement of Simon le Pasteymakere on the other in width and in length as is fully manifest according to the metes and bounds made there. Robert grants moreover that in to whomsoever's hands the aforesaid seld will come it will remain burdened (*oneretur*) with the aforesaid rent; to be held to him, his heirs or assigns, freely and hereditarily of the chief lords of that fee by the services due and by right accustomed. Clause for distraint for arrears in the rent. Clause for warranty. Henry gave 40s. sterling beforehand. Sealing clause. Witnesses: Robert Baker (*Pistore*), Nicholas Crumpe, Richard le Mercer, Robert Facon, Richard de St. James, Stephen le Mareschal, Henry le Sower, John Dobedy and others. Coventry, Sunday after the feast of St. Chad (*Cedde*) the Bishop 34 Edward I.

Seal missing C.R.O. IB/34EI/11

56 12 September 1295

Gift, remise and quitclaim by Emma, widow of Richard Burgeis of Willenhall (*Wilnhale*), for herself and her heirs, to Matthew de Rwyton', his heirs and assigns, of all right in name of dower from the entire tenement which was once (*olim*) of Richard her husband at Broadgate, Coventry (*ad latam portam de Coventr'*), lying between the land of Richard the Cook (*Coci*) on the one hand and the land of John the monastery clerk (*clerici monasterii*) on the other. Exclusion and sealing clauses.

Witnesses: Henry Baker (*pistor'*) then bailiff, William le Parkere then coroner, Richard de St. James, Thomas Haldein, Henry le Mower, John de Catusbi, Roger the clerk and many others. Coventry, Monday after the Nativity of the blessed Mary 23 Edward I.

Seal extant C.R.O. IB/23EI/11

57 Whitsuntide 1296

Settlement at Whitsuntide 24 Edward I, through the intervention of common friends, of a dispute which had arisen between Margery widow of Walter de Bannebury on the one hand and Agnes widow of John de Macstok on the other concerning the dower of a certain tenement which Agnes deraigned against Margery by writ in the royal court, whereby Margery leased and granted for a term to Agnes 9s. annual rent to be taken from the entire tenement which Roger Mortimer held of the aforesaid Margery at Broadgate (*ad latam portam*) in Coventry and which lies between the land Robert Fackon held on the one hand and Greyfriars' Lane (*venellam ducent' ad fratres minores*) on the other; to be held to Agnes, her heirs and whatsoever assigns, of Margery and her heirs, freely [etc.] from the feast of the Nativity of St. John the Baptist in the aforesaid year for 2 years *extra extremo termino stdt' [?] anni*, with clause for distraint by Agnes for arrears in the aforesaid rent. Clause for warranty by Margery and her heirs. Mutual sealing clause [chirograph]. Witnesses: Henry Baker (*Pistor'*) then bailiff, William le P(ar)ker then coroner, Thomas le Mowbrey, Anketill de Coleshul', John Tole, John Mynot, Robert Baker (*Pistor'*), Richard de Cundoner' and others.

Indented
Seal missing C.R.O. IB/24EI/12

58 12 May 1301

Gift by Ida de Wykewane, in her widowhood and lawful power, for her entire life, to Thomas de Solihul baker in Coventry (*in Coventr' pistori*) of 2 cottages with the buildings sited there next to the road leading from Broadgate in Coventry towards the church of St. Michael (*juxta viam ducentem de lata porta in Coventr' versus ecclesiam sancti Michaelis*), which lie in width between the land of Master Richard de Aula on the one hand and the land of William de Aula and Avicia de Aula on the other and extend in length from the said road (*via*) up to the land of Henry de Hales dyer (*tinctoris*) according to the metes and bounds made there; to be held with all appurtenances to him or his assigns, of the grantor as long as she lives well [etc.]. The lessee and his assigns should maintain all the buildings in every way and render annually to the grantor or her assigns as long as she lives 5s. of silver at the four terms of the year usual in Coventry for all secular services [etc.]. Clause for warranty. Sealing clause [bipartite]. Witnesses: Roger Daieseie then bailiff of Coventry, William Colle, John the Goldsmith (*aurifabro*), John de Wedon', John le Govere, Richard Forthwyne, Roger the clerk and others. Coventry, Friday the morrow of the Ascension of the Lord 29 Edward I.

Indented P.R.O. E315/44/35

On 4 February 1308 Ida leased to John Minot for the term of her life the chief messuage (*capitale mansum*) of John de Wyckewane her husband for 16s. *per annum*. Located in the above street it comprised a stone hall (*aulam lapideam*) with a cellar and solar between the hall and the land of Robert de Burforde (P.R.O. B 1046).

59 18 April 1307

Charter of Richard le Mercer of Coventry giving to Robert le Chaundeler of Coventry and Beatrice his wife a messuage with appurtenances in Coventry which lies in Earl St. towards Broadgate (*in vico Comitis versus Latam Portam*) between the land Matthew de Ruyton' once held on the one hand and the land John de Staunford held on the other in width and extends in length from the royal highway (*a regia strata*) up to the land John de Ludboreu once held as is fully manifest according to the metes and bounds made there; to be held to them and the heirs issuing from their bodies of the grantor and his heirs freely [etc.] by rendering annually to the grantor, his heirs or assigns, 16s. of silver at the four terms of the year usual in Coventry for all services. Clause for warranty. Clause for reversion in default of heirs as above. Robert and Beatrice gave 40s. sterling in advance. Mutual sealing clause. Witnesses: Robert Baker (*Pistor'*), Peter Barun, John le Gouere, Richard le Spicer, Stephen le Mareschal, Robert Facon and others. Coventry, 18 April 35 Edward I.

Seal extant in both cases C.R.O. IB/35EI/4 and 35EI/6
(the 2 halves of an indenture)

Indented

35EI/6 is endorsed: sc(ri)ptu(m) po(s)itu(m) in custod' Walt(er)i Cok' ad vad' pro iijs ab eo mutuat'.

CHEYLESMORE LANE*

*See also 41, 42, 44, 57, 195, 430 and *Langley Cartulary* No. 482.

60

c.1210–c.1220

Charter of Robert de Retham giving to Hugh son of Martin and his heirs the messuage which Roger the Bear-ward (*ursarius*) held towards Cheylesmore (*versus Cheilesmora(m)*) and the croft which lies between the land Richard de Aula held and the land Richard de Hundelan' held in length and in width as the land purports with its appurtenances; to be held to him and his heirs, of the grantor and his heirs, in fee and inheritance freely [etc.], by rendering 18d. of silver annually at four terms of the year, namely 4½d. at each of the feasts of St. Michael, St. Andrew, St. Mary in March and St. John the Baptist for all secular service and demand. Clause for warranty. Hugh gave 4s. of silver in recognition. Witnesses: Richard de Wigorn', Richard de Aula, Robert the Vintner (*vinit'*), Vincent, Swanus the Parker (*parcar'*), Thomas de Wilnhal', Geoffrey and William his brothers, Stephen son of Herbert, Geoffrey the Goldsmith (*aurifabro*), Richard Meu, Matthew son of Gundr', Robert the Curly (*crispo*) and many others.

Seal extant

W.R.O. 209

61

c.1215–1225

Charter of Richard son of Richard the Lorimer (*Loremarii*) giving to Hugh son of Martin his entire part of a messuage which Roger the Bear-ward (*ursarius*) held towards Cheylesmore (*versus Cheilesmoram*) and a moiety of a croft which lies next to that part which Agnes the grantor's aunt (*mat(er)tera*) held with all appurtenances which pertain to the grantor or his heirs; to be held to him and his heirs, of the grantor and his heirs, in fee and inheritance freely [etc.] by rendering 6d. annually at four terms of the year, namely 1½d. at each of the feasts of St. Michael, St. Andrew, St. Mary in March and St. John the Baptist for all secular service and all demands. Clause for warranty. Hugh gave 4s. of silver in recognition. Witnesses: Richard de Wigorn', Stephen his son, Richard de Aula, Gerard the Vintner (*vinit'*), Geoffrey de Wilnhale, William his brother, Vincent, Stephen son of Herbert, Geoffrey the Goldsmith (*aurifabro*), Richard Meu, Matthew son of Gundr', Robert the Curly (*crispo*) and many others.

Seal extant

W.R.O. 211

62 c.1210–c.1220

Sale and quitclaim by Matilda (*Matill'*) widow of Ywein (*Yweini*) Surdi in her widowhood and free power, entirely and without any reservation, to Hugh son of Martin and his heirs of the entire part of the land of the aforesaid Ywein her husband which fell to her in reasonable dower in Coventry, in Cheylesmore Lane (*in vico versus Cheilesmora(m)*) by 7s. of silver which Hugh has given to her. Sealing clause, with interposition of faith. Witnesses: Richard de Wigorn', Vincent, Swanus the Parker (*Parcar'*), Matthew son of Gundr', Thomas de Wilnhal', Walter Alfled, Richard son of Richard the Lorimer (*Lorimar'*), Richard Meu, Adam Bursere, Gerard the Black (*nig(r)o*), Osbert the Baker (*fornatore*) Geoffrey the Goldsmith (*aurifabro*), Robert the Saddler (*sellario*), Robert the Goldsmith (*aurifabro*) and many others.

Seal extant W.R.O. 207

63 Early 1220s

Charter of Alice once the daughter of Gerard the Black (*Girardi Nigri*) giving to Osbert Duredent clerk her land in Cheylesmore Lane (*in vico versus Cheilismor*), namely that which lies between the land Alexander Russul clerk held and the street (*vicum*) which leads towards Poddycroft (*pudicroft*); to be held to him and his heirs or to whomsoever he will wish to give or assign, of the grantor and her heirs in fee and inheritance, freely [etc.] by rendering 16d. annually, namely 4d. at each of the feasts of St. John the Baptist, St. Michael, St. Andrew and St. Mary in March for all secular service and demand. Clause for warranty. Osbert gave 1 mark of silver in recognition. Sealing clause. Witnesses: Richard de Aula, Robert the Vintner (*vinetar'*), Hugh de Allispath, Hugh son of Martin, William Crude, Peter the Welshman (*Walensi*), Roger the Gardener (*Gardinar'*), William de Rependun', Nicholas Fortwin', Richard Burgeis, Richard Meu, Walter le Tipper and many others.

Seal missing W.R.O. 208

64 Early–mid 1240s

Remise and quitclaim by Richard son of Alexander le Rous the clerk to Peter son of Hugh Martin, his heirs or assigns, of the entire land with appurtenances which he held of the same Peter in Cheylesmore Lane (*in viculo de Cheilismor*) in Coventry, which lies between the land Robert le Cordiwaner held and the land Brouneta held of the same fee. Peter gave 14s. of silver. Sealing clause. Witnesses: Osbert Durdent, Richard Burgeys, Robert de Retham, Robert le Cordiwan(er), Nicholas Fortwin', Hugh Ketelbern', Hugh le Celer', Alan le Celer', John the clerk, William Harpuris, Roger Gourneys and others.

Seal extant W.R.O. 212

65 Mid 1240s

Gift and quitclaim by Henry de Bilifort to Peter son of Hugh son of Martin of 10d. annual rent in Coventry, towards Cheylesmore (*versus Cheilismor'*) from the land William de Cam(er)a held, which lies between the land which the same William held of the fee of Sir Thomas le Yreys, lord of Ansty (*Anesti*), and the land of the fee once of the lord earl; to be held to him, his heirs or assigns, as freely and quietly as the grantor held with appurtenances, of the same lords from whom the grantor held and by the same service, by rendering annually to Sir Roger de Montalt (*monte alto*) and his heirs 8d. of silver at the four terms of the year usual in Coventry for all secular service and charge. Sealing clause. Witnesses: Osbert Durdent, Robert de

Cornleya, Richard Burgeys, Nicholas Fortwin', Robert le Cordiwan(er), John Beer, William Segrim, Anketinus son of Roysia, Hugh Ketelbern', Robert Celeth and others.

Seal missing W.R.O. 213

66 c.1270

Remise and quitclaim by Thomas Durdent of Coventry, without any reservation by him or his heirs, to Matilda daughter of Peter Martin of Coventry of all right and claim in 8d. annual rent with appurtenances which the grantor used to receive from the land next to the bar in Cheylesmore Lane (*juxta Barram in veicl'o de Chelismor'*) which lies between the land which descended to Avicia daughter of the said Peter on the one hand and the ditch (*fossatum*) which is called *hursimisdich* on the other; to be held to her, her heirs or whatsoever assigns, freely [etc.]. Exclusion clause. Matilda gave 3s. of silver in recognition. Sealing clause. Witnesses: Nicholas de Barra then bailiff, Robert de Chilton', Peter the Welshman (*Walensi*), Geoffrey Breton', Hugh Ketelbern, Reginald the Red (*Ruffo*), Thomas Seled the clerk and others.

Seal missing W.R.O. 210

67 Late 1250s–early 1260s

Remise and quitclaim by Christine once the daughter of John the White weaver (*albi textor'*) of Coventry of all right and claim in the entire land (*totam predictam terram*) with appurtenances which Walter le Tippere held in Coventry in Cheylesmore Lane (*in vico de Cheylismor'*) in length and in width according to the metes and bounds made there as is contained in a certain document (*sedula*) between Henry le Cartsadelere of Coventry and Ranulph called (*dictum*) of Stivichall (*Stivichale*); to be held to the aforesaid Ranulph, his heirs or assigns, without any reservation by the grantor or her heirs, the entire messuage with appurtenances and with a curtilage as is contained in the charter between the said Henry and Ranulph freely [etc.] without contradiction or claim by the grantor or her heirs. Ranulph gave ½ mark of silver beforehand. Sealing clause. Witnesses: Walter the White (*Blundo*) of Coventry, Pagan Pake of the same, William Louwyne of Coventry, Henry Baker (*pistore*) of the same, Thomas Haldeyn, Thomas Selet, William le Poleter and others.

Seal fragment G.H. 286

68 c.1270

Charter of Walter son of Atherard the Painter (*atherardi pictoris*) of Coventry giving to John son of William the Painter (*pictoris*) in free marriage with Wymarkia daughter of Geoffrey the Girdler (*zonar'*) a certain parcel (*quandam particulam*) of his land in Coventry, in Cheylesmore Lane (*In vico de Cheylismor*) lying and extending in the shape of a shield (*ad modum scuti*) between the grantor's land on the one hand and the land of Robert de Etona on the other; to be held to them and the heirs issuing from the two of them, of the grantor and his heirs freely [etc.], by rendering annually a pair of white gloves worth ½d. or ½d. at Easter for all service [etc.]. Remainder to John and his other heirs should Wymarkia die (*fati munus implere*) without heirs of her body. Warranty and sealing clauses. Witnesses: Nicholas ad Barram then bailiff in Coventry, Henry le Cartesadeler', Henry le Seller, Robert le Seller, Reginald le Rus, Walter Liuet, William le Differ and others.

Seal extant C.R.O. IA/C7

Endorsed: de her's Wymark'
Frer' lane.

69 18 September 1303

Charter of John son of William the Painter (*Pictoris*) of Coventry giving to William de Metingham merchant of Coventry (*mercatori de Coventr'*) and Matilda his wife a curtilage with appurtenances in Coventry in Cheylesmore Lane (*in venella que vocatur Cheylesmorlane*) which lies between the land of Henry de Palintone on the one hand and the land of Adam de Schustok on the other in width and extends in length from the royal highway (*a regia strata*) up to the land of Geoffrey le Chalonere, Adam the Smith (*fabri*) and Henry de Palinton' as is fully manifest according to the metes and bounds made there; to be held to them, their heirs or assigns, of the chief lords of that fee freely [etc.], by rendering annually to the same lords the services due and by right accustomed, namely 4d. of silver at the four terms of the year usual in Coventry for all secular services [etc.]. Warranty and sealing clauses. Witnesses: Robert Baker (*Pistore*) then bailiff in Coventry, Roger Dayeseye, Alexander de Stonleye, William de Schepeye, Richard le Mercer, Henry de Palinton', John Dobedy clerk and others. Coventry, Wednesday after the feast of the Exaltation of the Holy Cross 31 Edward I.

Seal extant C.R.O. IB/31EI/5

Endorsed: F(re)relane

70 1280–1284

Grant and remise by Nicholas de Segrave to Philip le Enginur of Coventry of all right and claim in a certain messuage with appurtenances in Cheylesmore Lane (*in venela de Cheylesmor*) between the land John the Marshal (*marescallus*) held on the one hand and the land Philip de Winchecu(m)b' held on the other in length and in width according to the metes and bounds made there; to be held to him, his heirs or assigns, of the grantor and his heirs freely [etc.], by rendering 12d. annually at the four terms of the year usual in Coventry for all secular demands saving to the grantor and his heirs suits of courts (*sect' cur' mearum*) according to the custom of the vill of Coventry, and by making all the services due and accustomed. Sealing clause. Witnesses: Alexander the Vintner (*vinitar'*), Henry Baker (*Pistor'*), Thomas de Fakinham, Thomas de Moubray, Roger the Fishmonger (*Piscator'*), John Saunsum, Matthew de Ruyton', Henry del Parlur and others.

Seal extant C.R.O. IA/C13/55

Endorsed: quiet' clamanc' de ten' in le Frerelane.

71 c.1303–1307

Remise and quitclaim by Stephen son and heir of Philip le Gynur of Coventry in his full age (*in plena etate*) to Agnes widow of Henry Ballard of Coventry of all right and claim in the entire tenement once of Philip the grantor's father in Greyfriars' Lane (*in vico fr(atri)um minor(um)*) in the vill of Coventry lying between the land of Stephen le Mareschal on the one hand and the land of the prior of Coventry on the other in width and in length according to the metes and bounds made there; to be held with appurtenances to her, her heirs and assigns, of the lords of the fee freely, by the service owed. Warranty, exclusion and sealing clauses. Witnesses: Robert Baker (*Pistore*) then bailiff, John de Longgele, Peter Barun, Ralf de Tewe, Thomas Ballard, Henry de Lemynton', Roger de Tewe and many others.

Seal extant C.R.O. 2/131

Endorsed: frerelane.

This is presumably identical with the messuage which Agnes gave to Margery widow of Philip le Gynor of Coventry on 16 August 1307, located in Cheylesmore Lane (*in venella que vocatur Cheylesmorlane*) between the land of Stephen le Mareschal and the land of the prior and convent in width and in length from the lane to the land of John de Catesby. (C.R.O. 37 EIII [sic]/19).

72 1297–1300

Charter of Sir John de Segrave, knight, giving to John de Langele, merchant in Coventry (*in Coventr' mercatori*), a certain plot (*placiam*) of land which he had in Cheylesmore Lane (*in venella que vocatur Cheylesmorlone*) in Coventry with all the buildings sited there, which plot contains 18½ feet between the land of the oven (*terram furni*) of Thomas de Polesworthe merchant (*mercatoris*) on the one hand and the land of Ralf le Keu on the other, and 21 feet between the aforesaid lane on the one hand and the land of Robert Faccon on the other; to be held to him, his heirs or assigns, of the grantor and his heirs freely [etc.], by rendering annually 3s. of silver at the four terms of the year usual and fixed in the vill of Coventry *et faciendo sectam Curie nostre in villa de Coventr' per rationabilem summonitionem* for all secular services [etc.]. Warranty and sealing clauses. Witnesses: Anketill de Coleshul then bailiff of Coventry, John Leofwyne then coroner, Robert Baker (*Pistore*), Adam Russel, Nicholas Crumpe, Peter Barun, Matthew de Ruyton', Richard de la Muyre, Roger the clerk and others.

Seal extant G.H. 313

Endorsed: Carta de [duobus][1] shopis de Frerelone de Coventre.

[1] The reading is uncertain.

73 c.1290–1297

Charter of Ranulph de Brumerton of Ashow (*Ayssesho*) giving to Philip the Crossbowman (*Balistario*) of Coventry in free marriage with Margery daughter of Robert de Wyhtlakesforde of Ashow (*Ayssesho*) a messuage with appurtenances in Cheylesmore Lane (*in viculo qui dicitur Cheylesmorlone*) in Coventry, which lies between the land of Richard le Purser and the land of Stephen le Marchal in length and in width as is manifest according to the metes and bounds made there; to be held of the lord of the fee by the service owed. Clause for reversion to Philip's right heirs. Witnesses: Henry Baker (*Pistore*) then bailiff of Coventry, William le Parkur then coroner, Richard de St. James, Matthew de Ruyton', John Sampson, John de Rydeware, Richard de la Muyre, Richard le Mercer, John de Catesby and others. *Dat(um) apud Coventr' die* . . .[1]

Seal extant C.R.O. 2/125

[1] The document is incomplete. And see above p. 64.

74 Early 1290s

Charter of Henry the clerk (*clericus*) son of Robert in the Hurne of Coventry tanner (*tannator'*) giving to Stephen the Marshal (*marscallo*) in free marriage with Alice the grantor's sister certain pieces of land (*quasdam partes terre*) with appurtenances in the vill of Coventry, namely certain land with the buildings sited there in Cheylesmore Lane (*in Cheylesmorlane*) which lies between the land of Master Richard de Bourtone on the one hand and the land of Alice le Cartsadelere on the other in length and in width as is manifest according to the metes and bounds made there, by rendering annually to the lords of the fee 4d. at four terms of the year, and certain land with the buildings sited there in Cheylesmore Lane (*in Cheylesmorlane*) which lies between the land of Sir Walter, perpetual vicar of the church of St. Michael, on the one hand and the land Philip le Arblaster held on the other as is manifest according to the metes and bounds made there, by rendering annually to the lords of the fee a clove-gillyflower, and moreover certain land with the buildings sited there in Spon St. (*in vico de spon(n)a*) which lies between the land of Osbert de Crowelane on the one hand and the land Henry le Purser once held on the other as is manifest according to the metes and bounds made there, by rendering annually to the lords of the fee 1d. at four terms; to be held with all appurtenances to the aforesaid Stephen and Alice and the heirs begotten legitimately between them of the lords of the fee (*dominis feodalibus*) freely [etc.], by rendering annually to those lords the services due and accustomed for the aforesaid lands at the four terms of the year fixed and customary in the vill of Coventry. Should Stephen die without heirs begotten legitimately between him and Alice the entire aforesaid lands should remain to Alice as long as she lives without contradiction and then revert to the right heirs without obstacle or contradiction by anyone. Sealing clause. Witnesses: Henry Baker (*pistor'*) then bailiff, Robert de Chiltu(n), Robert Mau(n)cel, Henry Dobedi, William de Copston, Matthew de Rutun, Edward le Barkere, Symon Kiu, William Galewey clerk and others.

Seal extant C.R.O. 2/33

Endorsed: Carta henr' in le hurne dat' Stephano le marchal' cu(m) Alicia sorore sua de ten' in frerelone.

75 11 August 1296

Gift by Ida widow of William de Newenham to Henry de Paylinton' in Coventry for her entire life of a messuage with the buildings sited there and appurtenances in Cheylesmore Lane (*in viculo qui dicitur Chelesmorlone*) in Coventry between the chief messuage (*capitale mansum*) of the same Henry on the one hand and Pauline's Lane (*viculum qui dicitur Paulineslone*) on the other in length and in width as it purports according to the metes and bounds made there; to be held to him, his heirs or assigns, of the grantor as long as she lives well [etc.], by rendering annually to her, her assigns or attorneys, 4s. of silver at the four terms of the year usual and fixed in the vill of Coventry for all secular services [etc.]. Clause for warranty. Clause for distraint in Henry's chief messuage (*in capitali manso*) for non-payment of rent. Sealing clause [bipartite]. Witnesses: Henry Baker (*Pistore*) then bailiff of Coventry, William le Parker then coroner, Master Richard de Aula, William de Fennes, William de Copston', Richard de St. James, Stephen le Marchal, John Sampson, John le Govere and others. Coventry, Saturday the morrow of St. Lawrence the Martyr 24 Edward I.

Indented P.R.O.E315/42/58

76 30 March 1298

Charter of John son of John Dobedy of Coventry giving to Matthew de Ruyton', his heirs or assigns, a messuage with an adjacent curtilage and with all appurtenances and easements in Cheylesmore Lane (*in Cheylesmorlone*) in Coventry which Robert le Cordiwaner held and which lies between the land Master Richard de Aula and Petronilla his wife held on the one hand and the land the aforesaid Matthew held on the other in width and extends in length from the great ditch of the Poddycroft (*a magno fossato de Podycroft*) up to the land Simon Schathelok held as is fully manifest according to the metes and bounds made there; to be held of the chief lords of that fee freely [etc.], by rendering annually to the same chief lords the services due and by right accustomed, and to the grantor, his heirs or assigns, 8s. of silver at the four terms of the year usual and fixed in the vill of Coventry for all secular services and demands. Warranty and sealing clauses. Witnesses: Anketell de Colsul' then bailiff in Coventry, William le Parker' then coroner, Thomas le Moubray, John Pyhod, John de Langeleye, Richard le Brocher', William Grampe, Robert Grampe, Henry de Palynton' and others. Coventry, Wednesday after Palm Sunday 26 Edward I.

Seal extant C.R.O. IB/26EI/4

77 26 June 1300

Remise and quitclaim by Amicia widow of John Dobedy of Coventry to John her son of all right and claim in 2 cottages with their appurtenances which she had as her dower in Cheylesmore Lane (*In Cheylesmorlane*) in Coventry after the death of John the Goldsmith (*Aurifabro*) once her husband, and moreover in the curtilage with appurtenances which Richard le Spicer held of her; to be held to him, his heirs or assigns, of the chief lords of that fee by the services due and by right accustomed freely [etc.]. Exclusion and sealing clauses. Witnesses: Matthew de Ruyton', John Saunsum, John le Gover', Henry de Palinton', Adam de Schustok' and others. Coventry, Sunday after the feast of the Nativity of St. John the Baptist 28 Edward I.

Seal extant C.R.O. IB/28EI/5

78 6 August 1300

Charter of John son of John Dobedy of Coventry giving to Adam de Schustok' saddler (*selario*) of Coventry, his heirs or assigns, a certain piece (*placiam*) of his land with houses sited thereon and all appurtenances in Cheylesmore Lane (*in Cheylesmorlane*) in Coventry, namely that which lies between the land Simon le Pasteymaker held on the one hand and the grantor's land on the other in width and extends in length from the royal highway (*a regia strata*) up to the land Richard le Spicer held as is fully manifest according to the metes and bounds made there; to be held of the chief lords of that fee by the services due to the same and by right accustomed freely [etc.]. Clause for warranty. Adam gave 30s. of silver beforehand. Sealing clause. Witnesses: Matthew de Ruyton', William Maunsel, John Saunsum, John le Gover', Henry de Palinton', Roger the clerk and others. Coventry, Sunday after the feast of St. Peter's Chains 28 Edward I.

Seal missing C.R.O. IB/28EI/6

79 6 October 1303

Charter of John son of John Dobedy of Coventry, clerk, giving to Richard le Spicer of Coventry and Agnes his wife, their heirs or assigns, his entire tenement with appurtenances in Cheylesmore Lane (*in vico qui vocatur Cheylesmorlane*) in Coventry, namely that which is sited between the tenement which John Saunsum and Agnes his wife held of the grantor for the term of their life and the land of the same John and Agnes[1] on the one hand and the tenement of Richard le Mercer on the other in width, and extends in length from the royal highway (*a regia strata*) up to the land of Geoffrey le Chalonere as is fully manifest according to the metes and bounds made there; to be held of the chief lords of that fee freely [etc.], by rendering annually to the same lords the services due and by right accustomed, and to the grantor, his heirs or assigns, 3s. of silver at the four terms of the year usual in Coventry. Clause for warranty. Richard and Agnes gave 60s. sterling beforehand. Sealing clause. Witnesses: Robert Baker (*Pistore*) then bailiff in Coventry, Roger Dayeseye, John

Leuwyn, Alexander de Stonleye, Robert Fraunceys, John le Govere, John Saunsum and others. Coventry, Sunday after the feast of St. Michael 31 Edward I.

Seal extant C.R.O. IB/31EI/2

[1] followed by *terram que Johannis le Govere.*

80 6 October 1303

Grant, remise and quitclaim by Amicia widow of John Dobedy of Coventry, in her widowhood and lawful power, to Richard le Spicer of Coventry and Agnes his wife, their heirs or assigns, of all right and claim in name of dower or by any other means whatsoever through the death of John the Goldsmith (*Aurifabri*) the grantor's first husband and of John Dobedy her last husband in the entire tenement with appurtenances which the same Richard and Agnes had by the gift and enfeoffment of John the son of the aforesaid John Dobedy in Cheylesmore Lane (*in venella que vocatur Cheylesmorlane*) in Coventry on the day of the making of the present writing (*scripti*). Exclusion and sealing clauses. Witnesses: Robert Baker (*Pistore*) then bailiff in Coventry, Robert Fraunceys, Roger Dayeseye, John le Gover', John Saunsum, Richard de St. James, Henry de Palinton' and others. Coventry, Sunday after the feast of St. Michael 31 Edward I.

Seal missing C.R.O. IB/31EI/4

81 14 July 1305

Remise and quitclaim by John son and heir of John Dobedy of Coventry, for himself and his heirs, to Richard le Spycer of Coventry and Agnes his wife of 3s. annual rent with appurtenances in Coventry which they used to render annually to the grantor for a certain tenement which they held of him in Cheylesmore Lane (*in venella que vocatur Cheylesmorlane*) in Coventry and which they had of his gift as is fully contained in the charter to them thereon; to be held to them, their heirs or assigns, freely and hereditarily of the chief lords of that fee by the services due and by right accustomed. Exclusion and sealing clauses. Witnesses: Roger Dayeseye, Robert Fraunceys, Thomas Ballard, John le Govere, John Lewyn, Alexander de Stonleye, Alexander le Moubrey and others. Coventry, Wednesday after the feast of the Translation of St. Thomas the Martyr 33 Edward I.

Seal extant C.R.O. IB/33EI/16

PAULINE'S LANE* [COW LANE]

*See also 75, 126, 155.

82 1280s

Charter of John son of Walter the Goldsmith (*aurifabri*) of Coventry giving to Nicholas de Derbeya in free marriage with Isabella the grantor's sister a curtilage with appurtenances in the vill of Coventry in Pauline's Lane (*in venella que vocatur Paulyneslone*), namely that which is between the land Benedict le Fleut(er) held on the one hand and the land Henry Pope held on the other in length and in width as is manifest according to the metes and bounds made there; to be held to them and the heirs issuing from them of the grantor and his heirs freely [etc.] by rendering annually to the lords, namely to the heirs of Philip Barbe daveryl as the perpetual attorneys of the grantor and his heirs 8d. of silver at the four terms fixed and usual in the vill of Coventry, and to the grantor and his heirs a pair of white gloves worth 1d. or 1d. at Easter for all secular service [etc.]. Clause for warranty. Should Isabella die without heir begotten of her and the said Nicholas the curtilage will remain in the possession of Nicholas for his entire life and after his death revert to the grantor and his heirs. Sealing clause. Witnesses: Henry Baker (*pistor'*) then bailiff, Thomas Scelet, John the Goldsmith (*aurifabro*), John Sampson, John Tole, Adam le Trauent(er), Henry Pope, Benedict le Fleut(er), Hugh le Bretun and others.

Seal missing C.R.O. 1A/C13/41

PARK ST./LITTLE PARK ST.*

*The following deeds show clearly that the undifferentiated form Park Street (*in vico parci*) was used for either Little or Much Park Street continuously up to the 1270s. After this it became less usual, although even in the early fourteenth century the form still occurs. By close attention to parties, tenants and witnesses, however, it is possible to distinguish between them. The documentation for the street which became known as Little Park Street is stronger for the thirteenth century and is earlier, with ten extant deeds conveying property within it before 1250 and some of them going back to the first decades of the century. Moreover, a number of tenements in Little Park Street were also conveyed to Combe abbey at this time (see below 767). Much Park Street, on the other hand, which first appears in relation to the tenements close to the White Cellar is sparsely documented before the 1270s. During the second half of the century it seems to have become increasingly necessary to distinguish between the two streets. *In minori vico parci* (on one occasion *Lutleparkstreth*) had appeared by 1279, *in majori vico parci* by c. 1280. Their use, however, was neither entirely consistent nor invariable. Two deeds relating to the same property (in Much Park Street c.1280) describe it as *in minori vico parci* and *in majori vico parci* respectively (142, 143). Moreover, a rival and earlier form of differentiation was also in use. Upper or Higher (*superior*) Park Street, in use since the beginning of the century as the Combe abstracts indicate, was commonly employed for Little Park Street from the 1260s to the 1280s and contrasted with Lower (*inferior*) Park Street for Much Park Street which is found in the 1270s and 1280s. This usage would seem to have arisen from the fact that Little Park Street was on slightly higher ground and nearer the centre. Indeed, *in propinquiori vico parci* is found on one occasion for Little Park Street c.1280. *Overeparstrete* (no doubt for Upper or Little Park Street) is also found in a mid-thirteenth century deed in the Langley Cartulary (No. 377). Increasingly, though, it was Little Park Street that was coming to designate the street nearer Broadgate, and Much Park Street the street further from Broadgate.

Most of the references to Park Street in the Combe cartulary are to Little Park Street, Park Street and Upper Park Street being the forms employed (below 767.6, 767.10–.17, 767.32–.39). See also 195, 196 and *Langley Cartulary* Nos. 186, 252, 377.

83 c.1200–1214

Charter of Swanus son of Adam giving to Reginald de Stivechale and his heirs 2 messuages (*duo mesua*) in Park St. (*in vico de parc'*), namely those that are between the land Hugh Cath held and the land Christine (*Cristiana*) held; to be held to him and his heirs of the grantor and his heirs in fee and inheritance freely [etc.] by rendering annually 3s. of silver at four terms of the year, namely 9d. at each of the feasts of St. Michael, St. Andrew, St. Mary in March and St. John the Baptist for all secular service [etc.]. Clause for warranty. Reginald gave 3s. of silver in recognition. Witnesses: Miles Barba Ap(r)ilis, Liulf de Sponna, Richard de Wig(or)n', Ralf the Tailor (*talliatore*), Robert the Weaver (*textore*), Roger de Wikewan' and many others.

Seal missing W.R.O. 167

84 C.1210–1221

Charter of Philip son of Miles giving to William son of Geoffrey the Scabbard-maker (*vaginatoris*) and his heirs a messuage with appurtenances in Park St. (*in vico parci*), namely that which is between the land Matthew the Carter (*carectarius*) held and the land Richard le Huuere held; to be held to him and his heirs of the grantor and his heirs freely [etc.] by rendering annually for all secular service and exaction 2s. 6d. of silver at four terms of the year, namely 7½d. at each of the feasts of St. Michael, St. Andrew, St. Mary in March and the Nativity of St. John the Baptist, and 2 men in Autumn and 2 hens at Christmas. William gave 2s. 8d. Clause for warranty. Witnesses: William Midniht, Roger Pake, Christian the Smith (*fab(r)o*), Ralf the Miller (*molendinar'*), Aumfridus the Merchant (*m(er)catore*), Liulf the Cutler (*Cultellario*), William son of Alexander, Walter Wine, Nicholas Colle and many others.

Seal missing C.R.O. IA/C12/9

85 c.1215–c.1220

Charter of Richard son of Odo giving to William son of Richard Fordwin and his heirs his entire land in Park St. (*in vico parci*), namely the entire land which lies between the land Liulf the Cutler (*cultellari(us)*) held and the land Robert the son-in-law (*gener*) of Odo held in length and in width as the land purports with all appurtenances; to be held to him and his heirs, of the grantor and his heirs freely [etc.] by rendering annually 12d. at four terms, namely 3d. at each of the feasts of St. John the Baptist, St. Michael, St. Andrew and St. Mary in March, and at Easter a pair of gloves or ½d. for all secular service and demand. Clause for warranty. William gave 2½ marks of silver in recognition. Witnesses: Richard de Aula, Robert the Vintner (*vinit'*), Richard de Wigorn', Hugh son of Martin, Leofwin son of Jordan, Hamo his brother, William de Wilnhal', William de Rependon', William Crude, Matthew son of Gundr', Thomas de Wilnhal', Walter the Lorimer (*Lorimar'*), Robert the son-in-law (*g'no*) of Odo, Robert de Allespath' and many others.

Seal extant W.R.O. 165
Endorsed: vicus p(ar)ci minor'

86 c.1215–c.1225

Charter of Robert Cauvin giving to Hugh son of Robert son of Hereward the entire land in Park St. (*in vico parci*) which Hereward the grandfather (*avus*) and Robert the father of the same Hugh held in length and in width as the land purports with appurtenances; to be held to him and his heirs of the grantor and his heirs in fee and inheritance freely [etc.] by rendering annually for all secular service and demand 8d. at four terms of the year, namely 2d. at each of the feasts of St. Michael, St. Andrew, St. Mary in March and St. John the Baptist. Clause for warranty. Hugh gave a bezant (*bisantiu(m)*) in recognition. Witnesses: Richard de Wigorn', Matthew son of Gundr', William Crude, Geoffrey his son, Thomas de Wilnhal', Robert the son-in-law (*g(e)n(er)o*) of Odo, Robert de Alespath', William de Sallowe, Ralf the Stone-cutter (*Incisore*), Liulf the Cutler (*cutellar'*), Adam the Scribe (*scriptore*) and many others.

Seal missing G.H. 263

87 1220s–early 1230s

Sale and entire quitclaim by Agnes daughter of John le Loker, without any reservation or charge by her and her heirs, to Henry the Marshal (*marscallo*) and his heirs or to whomsoever he will wish to give or assign the land in Park St., Coventry (*in vico parci Cove(n)tria*) which lies between the land Hugh le Loker held and the land Matilda de Nova Bughincga held, entirely and fully in length and in width according to the metes and bounds made there with all appurtenances, and all right and claim in that land; to be held of the abbot and convent of Combe (*Cumba*) just as the grantor held it, and by the same service, namely by rendering annually to the said abbot and convent for all secular service and demand 12d. of silver at four terms of the year, namely 3d. at each of the feasts of St. Michael, St. Andrew, St. Mary in March and St. John the Baptist. Clause for warranty. Henry gave 1 mark of silver. Witnesses: Henry Cysun, Richard de Aula, William de Wilnhal', Richard de Brug', Richard the Goldsmith (*aurifabro*), Adam the Vintner (*vinitar'*), William de Repindon, William le Buttere, Thomas de Wilnhal', Walter de Allispath', William de Sallowe, Thomas le Geler and others.

P.R.O. E 315/39/24

88

1220s–early 1230s

Sale and quitclaim by Stephen de St. Edmund with the consent and goodwill of Agnes his wife to Henry the Marshal (*Marscallo*) and his heirs or to whomsoever he will wish to give or assign, of the entire land in Park St., Coventry, (*in vico parci de Coventr'*) which lies between the land Hugh le Loker held and the land Matilda de Nova Bughincar' held in length and in width according to the metes and bounds made there with all appurtenances, and of all right and claim in the said land; to be held to him, his heirs or assigns, of the abbot and convent of Combe (*Cumba*) just as the grantor held, by rendering annually to the said abbot and convent for all service and secular demand 12d. of silver at four terms of the year according to the custom *firme solvendo* in the vill of Coventry. Clause for warranty. Stephen gave 1 mark of silver. Sealing clause. Witnesses: Henry Cysing, Richard de Aula, William de Wilnhal, Richard de Brug(es), Richard the Goldsmith (*aurifabro*), Adam the Vintner (*vinitar'*), William de Repi(n)dona, William le Buttere, Thomas de Wilnhal', Walter de Allispath', William de Sallowe, Thomas le Geliner and others.

Seal missing

P.R.O. B1215

89

c.1230–1235

Sale and quitclaim by William Blod without any reservation by him or his heirs to Richard de Blukevill' and his heirs or to whom he will wish to assign of the entire land with appurtenances in Park St., Coventry (*in Covintr' in vico de p(ar)co*) which lies between the land Roger de Stoke held and the land Liulf son of Robert the clerk held; to be held to him of Thomas de Wilenhal' and his heirs, by rendering annually to them for all service and exaction 2s. of silver at four terms, namely 6d. at each of the feasts of St. Michael, St. Andrew, the Annunciation of the blessed Mary and the Nativity of St. John the Baptist. Clause for warranty. Richard gave 5 marks of silver beforehand. Sealing clause. Witnesses: Thomas de Wilenhal', Master John de Alespath', William the Butterer (*butar'*), William the Parker (*parcario*), John the Baker (*f(ur)nerio*), William de Sallowe, Roger de Stoke and others.

Seal extant

C.R.O. IA/C37

For John of Alspath see below 708.

90

1230s

Charter of Margery widow of Matthew son of Gundrias (*Gundrie*), in her widowhood and lawful power, giving to John her son 3s. rent with appurtenances in Coventry in Park St. (*in vico parci*), namely 18d. per annum from a certain parcel (*p(ar)ticula*) of land which Robert the Miller (*mol(e)ndinari(us)*) held which lies between the land Symon Amfrey held on the one hand and the land Geoffrey the Welshman (*Walensis*) held on the other and 18d. per annum from another parcel (*p(ar)ticula*) of land which Reginald Amfrey held which lies between the land Ralf the Miller (*molendinarius*) held on the one hand and the land Symon Amfrey held on the other; to be held to him and his heirs freely [etc.] by rendering annually a pair of white gloves at Easter worth ½d. and 12d. to Robert de Stokes and his heirs to whom the grantor used to render the same annually from the aforesaid tenement, namely at four terms of the year according to the usage of the township (*villate*) of Coventry. Warranty and sealing clauses. Witnesses: Thomas de Wilnhal', William his brother, Peter Martin, William de Sallowe, Ralf Sergant, Richard Burgeys, Anketill son of Rose, John the Painter (*pictore*), Geoffrey the Painter (*pictore*), Amfrey the Merchant (*m(er)catore*), John Beer, William Crude, Geoffrey his son and others.

Seal missing W.R.O. 168

91 Late 1230s–early 1240s

Sale and quitclaim by Matilda who was the daughter of Richard Grucoc, in her free power, to Nicholas Fordwin, his heirs or assigns, of her land in Park St. (*in vico parci*) which she held of him by the service of 12d. per annum, namely the land which lies between the land Petronella held on the one hand and the land the same Petronella held on the other in length and in width as the land purports; to be held to him, his heirs or assigns, without contradiction by the grantor or her heirs. Moreover, she has granted to the same Nicholas 13d. rent per annum which the said Petronella used to pay her from neighbouring land (*de terra p(ro)pinq(u)a*). Nicholas gave £5 (*quinque ll'*) of silver in recognition. Witnesses: Richard Leuin, John Forduin, Richard le Broker, Ralf the Serjeant (*serviente*), William de Sallauue, William the Parker (*parcario*), John le Forner, Thomas le Carpu(n)t', William the Butcher (*carnifice*), Henry the Miller (*mole(n)d'o*), Roger the man of Scanus (*homine Scani*) and many others.

Seal extant W.R.O. 166

Endorsed: de vico parci minor'.

92 c. Christmas 1247

Lease and grant for a term by Margery daughter of William de Sallowe to William her brother, his heirs or assigns, of a messuage with appurtenances in Coventry in Park St. (*in vico p(ar)ci*) which is between the land of Nicholas Warin on the one hand and the land of Richard de Blokevile on the other with a moiety of the grantor's curtilage which Loueas held in length and in width according to the metes and bounds made there, for 8 years from Christmas A.D. 1247; to be held to him, his heirs or assigns, of the grantor and her heirs freely [etc.] by rendering annually a pair of gloves worth ½d. or ½d. at Easter for all secular service [etc.]. Warranty and sealing clauses. Witnesses: Robert de Corleya, Richard Burgeys, Richard de Blokevile, Robert Pope, John le Forn(er), William Prett, Richard de Bathekintone, Henry the Miller (*molendinar'*), Reginald de Withibroc and others.

Seal extant C.R.O. IA/EC12/4

93 1260s

Charter of William Parser [of] Leicester (*leycestr'*) and Alice Meruin his wife, for themselves and their heirs, giving to Henry Lilleburne merchant of Coventry (*m(er)ca-*

tor(i) Covi(n)tr'), for 16s. of silver which he gave beforehand, the entire land in Coventry in Upper Park St. (*in sup(er)iori vico parci*) which lies between the land Richard de Bokirvil' held on the one hand and the land Nicholas de Bokirvil' held on the other in length and in width as is manifest according to the metes and bounds made there; to be held to him and his heirs or to whomsoever he will wish to give, bequeath, sell or assign, in sickness and in health, of the grantors and their heirs, freely [etc.] by rendering annually as the perpetual attorneys for them and their heirs the service due and accustomed, namely 2s. of silver at the four terms of the year usual and fixed in the vill of Coventry, and to them and their heirs a rose at the feast of St. John the Baptist for all secular service, custom, demand, suit of court and all other demands, plaints, petitions and escheats, and for all other rights and liberties. Warranty and sealing clauses. Witnesses: Pagan Pake, Richard de Bokirvil', Alexander de Glouc', Thomas Haldein, Peter the Welshman (*Walenc'*), Nicholas ad Barr' clerk, William Prest, Thomas de Fakinham, Richard le Fermiler and others.

2 seals extant C.R.O. IA/LC 12/25

94 c.24 June 1269

Agreement whereby William de Stiveschale, with the assent and goodwill of Matilda his wife, has leased and granted at farm to Roger le Burs(er) merchant of Coventry (*m(er)catore(m) de Coventr'*) his entire land with appurtenances in Coventry in Upper Park St. (*in sup(er)iori vico p(ar)ci*), namely that which lies between the land William le Mayden once held on the one hand and the land Henry le Mouner held on the other, and that land which lies between the land Richard son of Swanus once held on the one hand and the land which Richard le Harper' once held on the other in length and in width as is manifest according to the metes and bounds made there, for a term of 50 years from the feast of St. John the Baptist 53 Henry III; to be held to him, his heirs or assigns, of the grantor and his heirs freely [etc.] by rendering annually from the land which lies between the land of William le Mayden and the land of Henry le Moun(er) to the chief lord of the fee 2s. of silver at the four terms of the year fixed in the vill of Coventry, and 8d. to the heirs of Adam Hawen' from the land which lies between the land Richard son of Swanus [once held] and the land Henry le Harp(er)e once held, and to the grantor and his heirs a pair of gloves worth ½d. or ½d. at [Easter][1] for the one land and for the other land another pair of gloves of the same price [at the same term][1] for all secular services [etc.] Clause for warranty. Roger gave 3 marks of silver beforehand. Sealing clause. Witnesses: Richard de Blokerwill' then bailiff of the Earl's Half (*tunc ball(iv)o ex parte Comit'*), Thomas de Fakenham, Richard de Finham, Thomas de Barsam, Augustinus Godescop, Nicholas Mayden, Alexander Prest, William Peissable and many others.

Indented
Seal extant G.H. 284

[1] interlined

95 1270s

Charter of John son of Anketell son of Rose (*Royse*) giving to William Paysable of Coventry a certain curtilage of his in Coventry with appurtenances in Park St. (*in vico parci*) which lies between the grantor's land on the one hand and the land which John Bekoc once (*aliquando*) held on the other in length from the land of the said William up to the land of John Barbe de Averel, in length and in width as the land purports according to the metes and bounds made there; to be held to him, his heirs or whatsoever assigns, of the grantor and his heirs freely [etc.] by rendering annually a clove-gillyflower at Easter for all secular service [etc.] and especially for suits of court(s). Clause for warranty. William gave 10s. of silver beforehand. Sealing clause. Witnesses: John de Lodelawe, Peter Barun, Anq(us)tinus Godeskoup, Robert Kroun, Thomas Broun, Nicholas le [ ][1]im, Richard Brid', William the Carpenter (? *carentar'*), John le Grom and others.

Seal extant P.R.O.A 11518

[1] There is a hole here.

96 c.1270s

Remise and quitclaim by Margery le Loker in her widowhood, for herself and her heirs, to Richard son of Henry de Wytele of the entire land with appurtenances in Little Park St. Coventry (*in minori vico parci de Coventr'*) which lies between the land William le Butt(er) held on the one hand and the land Alan the Fishmonger (*piscator*) held on the other; to be held to him, his heirs or whatsoever assigns, freely [etc.] with exclusion clause. Clause for reversion to the grantor after Richard's death, and after the grantor's death to Richard's right heirs, without contradiction by anyone. The grantee, his heirs or assigns, should render annually to the lords of the fee 12d. of silver at the four terms of the year usual in Coventry for all secular services [etc.]. Sealing clause, for 20s. which Richard gave beforehand. Witnesses: Ralf de Witel', Adam des Okis, Adam Myle, William de Witel', Roger Gopile, Anketell the clerk and others.

Seal extant P.R.O. B 1081

97 1270s

Charter of Christine daughter of Thomas de Wylnhale in Coventry, in her pure widowhood, giving to Ralf de Totushale the grantor's son all the lands and rents which descended to her in name of inheritance in the vill of Coventry from (*ex parte*) Thomas de Wylnhale once her father; to be held to him, his heirs or assigns, or to whomsoever he will wish to give, sell, bequeath or assign freely [etc.] by rendering annually to the lord of that fee 8d. of silver at four terms of the year, namely 2d. at each of the feasts of St. Michael, St. Andrew the Apostle, St. Mary in March and St. John the Baptist for all secular service, suits of court(s), exactions and demands. Ralf gave 60s. of silver beforehand. Sealing clause. Witnesses: Henry Baker (*Pistor'*) then bailiff of Coventry, Robert de Chilton' of the same, John de Ludelawe, Viel de Bokervile, Thomas de Wiltesire, Nicholas de Bokervile, John Minot, Geoffrey Lonton, William the Deacon (*diacon'*) and many others.

Seal missing C.R.O. 1A/C13/28

98 Late 1270s–early 1280s.

Remise and quitclaim by Christine daughter of Alice de Wilnhale to Ralph son of John de Thotenhale of all right and claim in the chief messuage (*in Capitale mesuagio*) once of Vielis le Bokervile in Upper Park St., Coventry on the north side (*in sup(er)ior' vico parci coventr' a p(ar)te boriali*) with the lands, rents and other appurtenances within the vill of Coventry appertaining to the said messuage; to be held to him, his heirs or whatsoevr assigns, freely [etc.] with exclusion clause. Ralph gave ½ mark of silver beforehand. Sealing clause. Witnesses: Robert de Chilton' then bailiff, Peter Barun, Henry Ballard, Adam Russel, Augustinus Godescop, Hugh de Oxon', John le Butt(er)e, Osbert le Butt(er)e, William le Sulcsouere and others.

Seal extant C.R.O. 1A/C13/60

99 c. February 1279

Agreement whereby Ralph de Tote(n)hale has leased, granted and demised for a term to Richard de Stretone his entire hall (*Aulam*) with an adjacent curtilage within the walls (*infra muros*) in Little Park St., Coventry (*in minori vico p(ar)ci de Coventr'*) which lies between the land Henry de Lilleburne held on the one hand and the land Thomas Grimdel held on the other; to be held with appurtenances to him, his heirs or whatsoever assigns, of the grantor and his heirs freely [etc.] from the feast of the Purification of the blessed Mary 7 Edward I for a term of 5 years so that the aforesaid Richard ought to maintain the aforesaid hall with appurtenances in improvements and repairs (*in emendatione et rep(ar)atione*) at his own cost and it should remain in as good a state or better at the end of the term as when he received it, by rendering annually 6s. of silver at the four terms of the year usual in Coventry for all service. Warranty and sealing clauses. Witnesses: Gerard de Alispath' then bailiff in Coventry, Robert de Chilton', John le Butt(er), Osbert le Butt(er), William Paysable, Hugh Oxon', Anketell the clerk and others.

Indented
Seal extant C.R.O. IB/7EI

100 Late 1270s–early 1280s

Charter of Ralph de Totenhale son of John de Totenhal' giving to William le Sulcsowher' of Coventry and Margery his wife, their heirs or assigns, the entire land with the buildings built there and all appurtenances lying in Upper Park St. (*in sup(er)iori vico parci*) in the vill of Coventry between the land of John le Butt(er)e on the one hand and the land of Roger de Burthigbur' baker (*pistor'*) on the other in length and in width according to the metes and bounds made there; to be held with all appurtenances and easements to them, their heirs or whatsoever assigns, or to whomsoever they will wish to give, bequeath, sell or assign, in sickness and in health freely [etc.] by rendering annually 5s. 6d. of silver at the four terms of the year usual and fixed in Coventry for all secular services [etc.]. Warranty and sealing clauses. Witnesses: Robert de Chilton' then bailiff, Peter Baru(n), Geoffrey Lunton', Hugh de Oxon', Walter le Cumber', Henry Ballard, William Sley and others.

Seal missing C.R.O. IA/C13/3
Endorsed: mychep(ar)strete

101 Late 1270s–early 1280s

Charter of William son of Godfrey le M(er)cer of Coventry giving to William le Sulcsouher of the same and Margery his wife a certain messuage with appurtenances in the vill of Coventry which is in Upper Park St. (*in sup(er)iori vico parci*) between the grantor's land on the one hand and the land of Walter le Gurney on the other in length and in width as the messuage purports; to be held to them, their heirs or assigns, to whomsoever they will wish to give, sell, or assign, in sickness and in health freely [etc.] by rendering annually to the chief lords of the fee 6d. at the four terms of the year usual and fixed in Coventry, and to the grantor and his heirs a clove-gillyflower at Easter for all secular service [etc.]. Clause for warranty. William and Margery gave 20s. of silver beforehand. Sealing clause. Witnesses: Robert de Chilton' then bailiff of Coventry, Augustinus Godescop, William Paysable, Nicholas le Mayden, Hugh de Oxon', Alan the Fishmonger (*piscator'*) and others.

Seal missing C.R.O. 2/26

102 Late 1270s–early 1280s

Grant and quitclaim by William son of Godfrey le M(er)cer of Coventry, for himself and his heirs, to William le Sulcsouher' of Coventry and Margery his wife of his entire land in Upper Park St., Coventry (*in sup(er)iori vico parci Coventr'*) between the land of the said William and Margery on the one hand and the land of Henry the Miller (*molendinar'*) on the other in length and in width as is manifest according to the metes and bounds made there; to be held with all the grantor's right and all appurtenances to them, their heirs or assigns, to whomsoever they will wish to give, bequeath, sell or assign, in sickness and in health freely [etc.] with exclusion clause, by rendering annually to the lord prior of Coventry and his successors 6d. of silver at the four terms of the year usual and fixed in Coventry for all secular service [etc.]. William and Margery gave 2 marks of silver beforehand. Sealing clause. Witnesses: Robert de Chilton' then bailiff of Coventry, Peter Barun, Nicholas le Mayden, Augustinus Godescop, William Paysable, Hugh de Oxon', John le Butt(er)e and others. Henry Ballard, Osbert le Butt(er)e.[1]

Seal extant C.R.O. IA/EC13/63

[1] These names are added in the same hand.

103 Late 1270s–early 1280s.

Charter of Christine de Wilnhale, in her virginity and lawful power, giving to Geoffrey le Luff of Coventry a certain messuage with appurtenances in Upper Park St. (*in sup(er)iori vico parci*) of Coventry which is between the land William Colle once held on the one hand and the land Nicholas le Bokervile once held on the other in length and in width according to the metes and bounds made there *ab antiquo*, to be held to him, his heirs and assigns, to whomsoever he will wish to give, bequeath, sell or assign, in sickness and in health freely [etc.] by rendering annually to the chief lords of the fee 3¼d. of silver at the four terms of the year usual and fixed in Coventry for all secular service [etc.]. Clause for warranty. Geoffrey gave ½ mark of silver beforehand. Sealing clause. Witnesses: Robert de Chilton' then bailiff of Coventry, Richard de Esseby, Augustinus Godescop, Nicholas le Mayden, William Colle, William Paysable, Hugh de Oxon', Alan the Fishmonger (*piscatore*), William Bernard and others.

Seal extant C.R.O. 1A/C8

104 12 December 1295

Charter of Geoffrey le Lef of Coventry giving to William Colle of Coventry baker (*pistori*) a curtilage with appurtenances in Little Park St. (*in minori vico parci*) in Coventry towards the park gate (*versus portam parci*) which lies in width between the land of the same William on the one hand and the land which Geoffrey le Chaloner held on the other and extends in length from the aforesaid street up to the grantor's land as is fully manifest according to the metes and bounds there; to be held with all appurtenances to the aforesaid William, his heirs and assigns, well [etc.] of the lords of that fee by rendering annually to those lords the services due and by right accustomed, namely 3d. of silver at the four terms of the year usual and fixed in Coventry for all secular service [etc.]. Clause for warranty. William gave 1 mark of silver beforehand. Sealing clause. Witnesses: Henry Baker (*pistore*) then bailiff of Coventry, William le Parker then coroner, Henry Ballard, John de Langele, Richard de la Muyre, Reginald Ballard, John de Wedon', Richard Forthwyne, Nicholas le Mayden and others. Coventry, Monday before the feast of St. Lucia the Virgin 24 Edward I.

Seal extant C.R.O. IB/24 EI/13

Endorsed: Carte Walter de Wyly.

105 Late 1270s–early 1280s

Charter of Matthew Cat of *Sciton'* giving to Sir Henry de Bra(u)nteston' chaplain for his service, his entire land in the vill of Coventry in Little Park St., (*in propinquiori vico p(ar)ce*) which lies between the land of William de Stivechale on the one hand and the land of Thomas Simund on the other in length and in width according to the metes and bounds made there; to be held with appurtenances to him, his heirs or whatsoever assigns, in sickness and in health of the grantor and his heirs freely [etc.] by rendering annually a pair of gloves worth ½d. at Easter, and to Peter Baru(n) of Coventry and his heirs 12d. of silver at the four terms of the year fixed and customary in the vill of Coventry and 1 man for 1 day in Autumn and 2 hens at Christmas and to the abbot and convent of Combe (*Cumba*) and their successors 16d. of silver at the aforesaid terms, and to the heirs of Richard le Redeclerc ½d. at Easter for all secular service [etc.]. Henry gave 2 marks of silver beforehand. Warranty and sealing clauses. Witnesses: Robert de Chilton' of Coventry, Sir John le Tenterer of the same, Henry Baker (*pistor'*) of the same, Nicholas le Mayden of the same, William Paysable of the same, Osbert le Butter of the same, John le Butter of the same, Adam the Fishmonger (*piscator'*) of the same and many others.

Seal missing C.R.O. IA/C13/12

Endorsed: Carta inter Matheu(m) Cat et dominum Henr' de Braundeston' de quod' ten' in vico p(ar)ci minoris inde Petro Baroun et ejus heredibus xijd.

106 Late 1270s–early 1280s

Remise and quitclaim by John son of Nicholas le Bokerwil' of Coventry, for himself and his heirs, to Henry de Lilleburn' in Coventry of all right and claim in 2s. annual rent which he ought to pay to the grantor by right from a certain messuage with appurtenances in Upper Park St., Coventry (*in sup(er)ior' vico parci Coventr'*) which lies between the land Richard le Bokerwile once held on the one hand and the land Osbert le Butt(er)e once held on the other and extends in length from the royal highway (*a regia via*) up to the garden (*gardinu(m)*) of the said Richard; to be held to him, his heirs or whatsoever assigns, freely [etc.] with exclusion clause. Sealing clause for which Henry gave 15s. beforehand. Witnesses: Robert de Chilton' then bailiff, Henry Baker (*pistor'*), Henry Dobedy, Richard le Brocher, Peter de Chilton', Henry Ballard, Adam Russel, Richer de Weston and others.

Seal missing C.R.O. 1A/C13/18

107 Early 1280s

Charter of Robert le Comber of Coventry and Basilia his wife giving to Henry de Lylleburn' of Coventry, for 1 mark of silver which he gave beforehand, 2s. annual rent with appurtenances in the vill of Coventry which the grantor had by the gift and grant of John son of Nicholas de Blokevile, to be taken from certain land with appurtenances in Upper Park St. (*In sup(er)iori vico p(ar)ci*) which lies between the land Richard de Bokervile once held on the one hand and the land Osbert le Butt(er)e held on the other; to be held to him, his heirs or whatsoever assigns, freely [etc.] without any charge or reservation by the grantors or any of their heirs. Warranty and sealing clauses. Witnesses: Henry Baker (*pistor'*) then bailiff in Coventry, Robert de Chilton', Peter Barun, William de Eggisfeld', Richard le Brocher', Thomas de Fakynham, Thomas de Barsham, Henry Oysel, Osbert le Butt(er)e and others.

2 seals extant C.R.O. IA/EC13/92

108

Late 1280s

Charter of Basilia daughter of Nicholas de Bokervile of Coventry in her widowhood and lawful power giving to John son of Walter Sweteman, the comber (*le Combere*), a curtilage with appurtenances which she had in Little Park St., Coventry (*in minori vico parci de Coventr'*) between the land Geoffrey le Lef held on the one hand and the land Nicholas le Mayden held on the other in length and in width as the curtilage purports according to the metes and bounds made there, and 4s. 8d. annual rent which she had in the aforesaid street to be taken at the four terms of the year usual and fixed in the vill of Coventry, namely from the tenement which Henry de Lilleburne held next to the land of Ralf de Totenhale on the southern side 2s. per annum, from the tenement which John le Butt(er)e held next to the land of Osbert le Butt(er)e on the northern side 16d., and from the tenement which John Pope held between the land of the aforesaid John le Butt(er)e on both sides 16d., and all other rents, lands and tenements which she had in the vill of Coventry or will in any way be able to have by any right; to be held to him, his heirs or assigns, well [etc.] with all liberties and easements of the lords of the fee by the service due and accustomed, and by rendering annually to the grantor, her heirs or assigns, a clove-gillyflower at Easter for all secular service [etc.]. Clause for warranty. John gave 20s. sterling beforehand. Sealing clause. Witnesses: Henry Baker (*pistore*) then bailiff of Coventry, Richard de Weston', Adam Russel, John de Langeleye, Richard de la Muyre, Hugh de Oxonia, William le Selcsowere, Hugh Bocchi, Osbert le Butt(er)e and others.

Seal extant

C.R.O. IA/C51

109

c.1290–1297

Charter of John son and heir of Basilia de Bokervyle in Coventry giving to John son of Walter Sweteman the comber (*le Combere*) of Coventry a curtilage with appurtenances which was once of Basilia the grantor's mother in Little Park St., Coventry towards the park gate (*in minori vico parci in Coventr' versus porta(m) parci*) between the land Geoffrey le Lef held on the one hand and the land Nicholas le Mayden held on the other in length and in width as the curtilage fully purports according to the metes and bounds made there; to be held well [etc.] of the lords of that fee by rendering annually to those lords the service due and by right accustomed, namely 3½d. of silver at the four terms of the year usual and fixed in the vill of Coventry for all secular services [etc.]. Clause for warranty. John son of Walter gave 2s. of silver beforehand. Sealing clause. Witnesses: Henry Baker (*pistore*) then bailiff of Coventry, William le Parker then coroner, John de Langele, Richard de la Muyre, Geoffrey le Lef, Nicholas le Mayden, Hugh Bocchi, Hugh de Oxonia, Thomas Bernard and others.

Seal extant

C.R.O. IA/C12/18

110

1280s

Charter of Thomas Grundel of Coventry giving to John de Stivechale *le buttere* and Matilda his wife a certain part of his land in Little Park St. in Coventry outside the bar (*in minori vico parci in Coventre extra barram*) with the house sited there and all appurtenances, namely the land which lies in width between the land of Osbert le Butt(er)e on the one hand and the land of John de Brinkelowe on the other and extends from the royal highway (*a regali via*) up to the land of the lord prior and convent of Coventry just as the land purports according to the metes and bounds made there; to be held to them, their heirs or to whomsoever they will wish to give, bequeath, sell or assign in sickness and in health, of the grantor and his heirs freely [etc.] by rendering annually as the perpetual attorneys of the grantor and his heirs to the lord prior and convent of Coventry 12d. of silver at the four terms of the year usual and fixed in the same vill, and to the grantor and his heirs a rose-flower at the Nativity of St. John the Baptist for all secular services [etc.]. Clause for warranty. John and Matilda gave 8s. of silver beforehand. Sealing clause. Witnesses: Henry Baker (*pistor'*) then bailiff of Coventry, William Paysable, Hugh de Oxonia, William le Poleter, Alan the Fishmonger (*piscator'*), Hugh Bocchi, John le Butt(er)e, Osbert le But(er)e, Roger de Alesleye the clerk and others.

Seal extant C.R.O. 1A/C17

111 1280s

Charter of William called (*dictus*) Sley giving to Thomas Symu(n)d and Avicia his wife, for 1 mark of silver which they gave beforehand, a messuage with appurtenances in Upper Park St., Coventry (*in Coventr' in sup(er)iori vico p(ar)ci*), namely that which is between the land Matthew Cat held on the one hand and the land William Bernard held on the other in length and in width as is manifest according to the metes and bounds made there; to be held to them and their heirs or to whomsoever they will wish to give, sell, bequeath or assign in any way jointly or separately in sickness and in health of the grantor and his heirs freely [etc.] by rendering annually to the lords of the fee, namely to Peter Barun and his heirs as the perpetual attorneys of the grantor and his heirs 12d. of silver at the four terms of the year customary in the vill of Coventry and 1 man for 1 day in Autumn and 2 hens at Christmas, and to the grantor and his heirs a clove-gillyflower at Easter for all secular service [etc.]. Warranty and sealing clauses. Witnesses: Henry Baker (*pistore*) then bailiff of Coventry, Peter Barun, Augustinus Godiscoup, William Paysable, Ranulph de la Wyke, Adam le Blund, Hugh le Bretun and others.

Seal missing C.R.O. IA/EC13/89
Endorsed: Carta Willelmi Sly de uno mesuagio in vico parci minoris.

112 1280s

Charter of Master Richard de Burton' giving to Walter de Bannebur' and Margery his wife a messuage with appurtenances in Little Park St. (*in minori vico p(ar)ci de Coventr'*) and 4 marks, which messuage Alan the Fishmonger (*piscator*) once held of the lord prior of Coventry in length and in width according to the metes and bounds made there; to be held to them, their heirs or assigns, of the grantor and his heirs freely [etc.]. In exchange Walter and Margery gave a piece (*placeam*) of land with appurtenances which lies between the hall (*Aulam*) of the venerable father R(oger) by the grace of God bishop of Coventry and Lichfield (*Coventr' et lich'*) on the one hand and the land once of John de Wikewan on the other in length and in width according to the metes and bounds made there. Warranty and sealing clauses. Witnesses: Master Guy (*Gydone*) de Tillebrok', Master Robert de Leyc', Robert de Chilton', Henry Baker (*pistore*), Robert de Stoke, Adam le Werrour, Peter Baru(n), Richard de Esseby, Hugh le Breton' and others.

Seal missing W.R.O. 169
Endorsed: Hugo de grantham

113 1280s

Surrender, grant and quitclaim by Roger de Burþigburi to Alexander the Vintner (*vinetar'*) of Coventry of a certain tenement which the grantor held of him in Coventry, namely the messuage with appurtenances which is between the lane called Little

Park St. (*viculu(m) qui dicitur Lutleparkstreth*) on the one hand and the land of Richard le Coup(er)e in length on the other and which lies in width between the land once of Nicholas le Bocurvile on the one hand and the highway called Earl St. (*altam viam que dicitur strata Comitis*) on the other; to be held of the lord of the fee to him, his heirs or whatsoever assigns, with escheats, courts (*curiis*), pannages, tolls and all other liberties and free customs belonging to the said tenements *in omnibus et per omnia*, by the service due and by right accustomed. Exclusion clause. Alexander gave 20s. sterling beforehand. Sealing clause. Witnesses: Henry Baker (*Pistor'*) then bailiff, Walter Bacun then coroner, Robert de Chilton', Peter Barun, Richard de Weston', William le Selcsower', Henry de Parlur, Roger le Chamburleyn, Hugh de Oxneford', John Dobedi and many others.

Seal extant — C.R.O. 1A/C23

114 — 1298–1300

Gift and quitclaim by Milicenda widow of Richard the Cooper (*Cuvarii*) of Coventry with the consent and wish of William de Ecclessale her present husband, to Alexander son of Alexander le Vineter of Coventry for a certain sum of money which he gave beforehand of all right and claim in a certain house in Coventry next to Little Park St. (*juxta minore(m) vicu(m) parci*) with an adjacent curtilage and all other appurtenances once of Roger de Burthyngbury; to be held to him, his heirs or assigns, freely [etc.] with exclusion clause. Sealing clause, by the grantor and William her husband. Witnesses: Anketill de Colsull' then bailiff of Coventry, Robert Kelle, William le Parker, Reginald Ballard, Richard de Muyre, Richard de Weston', Peter Baron and others.

2 seals extant — C.R.O. IA/Misc.I/23

115 — c.29 September 1290

Agreement whereby Alexander called (*dictum*) Vineter of Coventry has leased, granted and demised at farm to Hugh le Taylur of the same the corner seld of his tenement at the head of Little Park St. (*selda(m) angulare(m) tenementi sui ad capud minoris vici parci*) in Coventry on the western side, with a solar (*solario*) pertaining to the said seld; to be held to him, his heirs or assigns, of the grantor and his heirs well [etc.] from the feast of St. Michael the Archangel 18 Edward I for a term of 6 years, by rendering annually 6s. of silver at four terms of the year usual and fixed in the vill of Coventry for all secular service [etc.] saving to the aforesaid Alexander and his heirs suit of court when necessary (*secta Curie si necesse fuerit*). Clause for warranty. Throughout the term Alexander and his heirs will maintain the aforesaid seld and solar against wind and rain. Mutual sealing clause [chirograph]. Witnesses: Henry Baker (*pistore*) then bailiff in Coventry, John Dobedy, John de Langeleye, William Grauntpe, Reginald Ballard, William le Selcsowere, John Stantilon, Richard de la Muyre, Roger the clerk and others.

Indented
Seal missing — C.R.O. IB/18EI/2

116 — c.24 June 1293

Agreement whereby Alexander called (*dictum*) Vineter of Coventry has leased, granted and demised at farm to Hugh le Taylur of the same and Matilda his wife the corner seld of his tenement at the head of Little Park St. (*selda(m) angulare(m) tenem(en)ti sui ad cap(u)d minoris vico*[1] *parci*) in Coventry on the western side, with a solar (*solario*) pertaining to the said seld; to be held to them, their heirs or assigns, of the grantor and his heirs well [etc.] from the feast of the Nativity of St. John the Baptist 21 Edward I for 20 years, by rendering annually 6s. of silver at the four terms of the year usual and fixed in the vill of Coventry namely 18d. at each term for all secular services [etc.] saving to the aforesaid Alexander and his heirs suit of court when necessary (*secta Curie si necesse fu(er)it*). Clause for warranty. Throughout the term Alexander and his heirs will maintain the aforesaid seld and solar against wind and rain. Hugh and Matilda gave 2s. of silver beforehand. Sealing clause [chirograph]. Witnesses: Henry Baker (*pistore*) then bailiff of Coventry, Robert de Chilton', John de Langeleye, Richard de la Muyre, Reginald Ballard, John le Butt(er)e, John Stantilon, Osbert le Butt(er)e, Roger the clerk and others.

Indented
Seal extant — C.R.O. IA/L12–13/51

[1] sic

117 — Mid–late 1280s

Charter of Richard son of Nicholas Forthwyne giving to Henry Baker (*pistor'*) of Coventry 4d. annual rent which John Holeweye used to render to the grantor at the four terms usual in Coventry from a certain tenement which the said John held in Little Park St. (*in minori vico parci*) between the land of William Paisable on the one hand and the land of John de Wedone on the other in length and in width as the tenement purports; to be held with all appurtenances to him, his heirs or assigns, well [etc.]. Clause for warranty. Henry gave 3s. of silver beforehand. Sealing clause. Witnesses: Robert de Chilton', Thomas le Moubray, John Cole, Adam Russel, Richard de la Muyre, John de Wedon', William Paysable, Hugh de Oxonia, Roger de Aleyleye the clerk and others.

Seal extant — C.R.O. IA/C12–C13/57
Endorsed: Carta de tenemento Henr' de Hetȝ in vico minori p(ar)ci quod h(ab)et Gilde Marie.

118 — Late 1280s

Remise and quitclaim by Osbert le Buttere of Coventry, for himself and his heirs, to John le Cu of Coventry and Matilda his wife of all right and claim in a piece of land (*una placia terre*) which the grantor bought from Roger son of Robert the Miller (*molendinarii*) in Little Park St. (*in minori vico parci*) in Coventry and which lies in width between the land Sir Geoffrey de Langeleye held on the one hand and the royal highway (*viam regalem*) on the other and extends in length from the land of the aforesaid Geoffrey up to the land John le Buttere *minor* held according to the metes and bounds made there; to be held with appurtenances to them, their heirs or assigns, well [etc.] without any reservation by the grantor or his heirs by rendering annually to the lords of the fee the services due and accustomed. Exclusion clause. John and Matilda gave 1 mark of silver beforehand. Sealing clause, with surrender of the charter which the grantor had from Roger son of Robert the Miller (*molendinar'*). Witnesses: Henry Baker (*pistore*) then bailiff in Coventry, Richard de Esseby, Richard de Weston', William le Selcsowere, Hugh de Oxonia, Matthew de Ruyton', John le Buttere, Richard del Muyre, Roger the clerk and others.

Seal missing — C.R.O. IA/EC13/62

119 — Late 1280s

Charter of Philip de Kereby chaplain giving to Geoffrey de Donechirche merchant a tenement in Little Park St. (*in minori vico parci*) in Coventry namely that which was once of William le Selcsowere and lies between the land of Alexander le Vineter on the one hand and the land of John le Buttere on the other in length and in width as the tenement fully purports according to the metes and bounds made there; to be held with the building sited there and all appurtenances to him, his heirs or assigns, well [etc.] of Ralph de Totenhale and his heirs by rendering annually to Ralph and his heirs 5s. 6d. of silver at the four terms of the year usual and fixed in the vill of Coventry for all secular services [etc.]. Clause for warranty. Geoffrey gave 18 marks sterling beforehand. Sealing clause. Witnesses: Henry Baker (*pistore*) then bailiff of Coventry, Adam Russel, John de Langeleye, Richard de Weston', John Dobedy, Symon Russel, Richard de la Muyre, Hugh de Oxonia, John le Buttere and others.

Seal extant Q.C. 2328

120 Late 1280s

Charter of Hugh Bocchi of Coventry giving to Walter son of Walter Tynel and Matilda his wife, the grantor's daughter, a certain part of his house and curtilage in Little Park St., Coventry (*in minori vico parci Coventr'*) between the grantor's land on the one hand and the land Henry Grundel held on the other which part of his house contains 8 feet in width next to the road (*juxta viam*) and 10 feet towards the curtilage and which part of the house and curtilage extends in length from the aforesaid street up to the land Sir Geoffrey de Langeleye once held according to the metes and bounds made there; to be held to them and the heirs legitimately begotten between them and to the heirs of their assigns, well [etc.] of the lord prior and convent of Coventry by the service of 6d. to be paid annually to the prior and convent at the four terms of the year usual and fixed in the vill of Coventry for all secular services [etc.]. Clause for warranty. Clause for reversion should they die without legitimately begotten heir, without any contradiction. Walter and Matilda gave ½ mark of silver beforehand. Sealing clause. Witnesses: Henry Baker (*pistore*) then bailiff in Coventry, John de Langeleye, Richard de la Muyre, Hugh de Oxonia, John le Butt(er)e, Osbert le Butt(er)e, William le Selcsowere, Nicholas le Mayden, Roger the clerk and others.

Seal missing C.R.O. IA/LC12/31

121 23 May 1296

Charter of Hugh Bocchi of Coventry giving to Walter son of Walter Tynel of Coventry and Matilda his wife, the grantor's daughter, for their services, his land with the buildings sited there and all appurtenances in Little Park St. (*in minori vico parci*) in Coventry, which lies in width between the land the grantor gave to Roger the clerk on the one hand and the land of Henry Grundel on the other, and extends in length from the aforesaid street up to the land of Sir Geoffrey de Langele as is manifest according to the metes and bounds made there; to be held to them, their heirs or whatsoever assigns, well [etc.] of the chief lords of that fee by rendering annually to those same lords the service due and by right accustomed, namely 16d. of silver at the four terms of the year usual and fixed in Coventry and 2 hens at Christmas and the service of 1 man working for 1 day in Autumn for all secular service [etc.]. Sealing clause. Witnesses: Henry Baker (*pistore*) then bailiff of Coventry, William le Parker then coroner, John de Langele, Richard de la Muyre, Henry the Painter (*pictore*), Hugh de Oxonia, Nicholas le Mayden, Thomas Bernard, Hugh le Taylur and others. Coventry, Wednesday after the feast of St. Dunstan the Bishop 24 Edward I.

Seal extant C.R.O. Acc. 87/2

122 23 May 1296

Grant, remise and quitclaim by Walter son of Walter Tynel of Coventry, for himself and his heirs, to Hugh Bocchi of Coventry, of a certain part of a certain house which the grantor held of the same Hugh in Little Park St. (*in minori vico parci*) in Coventry next to the land of Edelina la Botonere with a certain part of an adjacent curtilage according to the metes and bounds made there; to be held with appurtenances and easements and all right and claim to him, his heirs and whatsoever assigns, well [etc.] without any charge or impediment by the grantor or his heirs. Exclusion clause. In return Hugh gave to the grantor and confirmed by his charter the other entire part of his house (*totam aliam partem domus sui*) which is nearer to the land of Henry Grundel in the same street. Sealing clause. Witnesses: Henry Baker (*pistore*) then bailiff of Coventry, William le Parker then coroner, Hugh de Oxonia, Nicholas le Mayden, Thomas Bernard, Geoffrey de Donchirche, John Beyer and others. Coventry, Wednesday after the feast of St. Dunstan the Bishop 24 Edward I.

Seal extant C.R.O. IB/24 EI/6

123 7 January 1295

Charter of Mary widow of Robert le Quareur of Coventry in her widowhood and lawful power, giving to John de Macstoke baker in Coventry (*in Coventr' pistori*) and Alice his wife her moiety of a curtilage in Little Park St. (*in minori vico parci*) in Coventry between the land William Colle held on the one hand and the land Nicholas le Mayden held on the other in length and in width as the moiety of the said curtilage fully purports; to be held to them, their heirs or assigns, well [etc.] of the lords of that fee by the service of 2½d. of silver to be paid to those same lords annually at the four terms of the year usual and fixed in the vill of Coventry for all secular service [etc.]. Clause for warranty. John and Alice gave 6s. of silver beforehand. Sealing clause. Witnesses: Henry Baker (*pistore*) bailiff of Coventry, William le Parker coroner, Hugh de Oxonia, Hugh Bocchi, William Colle, John de Wedon', Nicholas le Mayden, Thomas Bernard, John le Buttere and others. Coventry, Friday the morrow of the Epiphany 23 Edward I.

Seal missing G.H. 303

124 18 March 1297

Charter of John Holoueye of Coventry miller (*molendinarius*) giving to John de Wedon' brewer in Coventry (*in Coventr' braciatori*) a certain piece (*placiam*) of land with appurtenances which the grantor had in Little Park St. (*in minori vico parci*) in Coventry which lies in width between the lands of Henry Baker (*Pistoris*) and Geoffrey le Lef on the eastern side and the lands of the aforesaid John de Wedon' and John de Atleberge and Christine Godescoup on the western side, and extends in length from the grantor's land up to the land of Richard son of William Reynald of Lawford (*Lalleforde*) as is manifest according to the metes and bounds made there; to be held to him, his heirs or assigns, well [etc.] of the lords of that fee by the service due and by right accustomed. Clause for warranty. John gave 8s. of silver beforehand. Sealing clause. Witnesses: Henry Baker (*Pistore*) then bailiff of Coventry, William le Parker then coroner, Master Richard de Aula, William Colle the Goldsmith (*aurifabro*), John de Langele, Richard de la Muyre, Hugh de Oxonia, Hugh the Tailor (*scissor'*) and others. Coventry, Monday after the feast of St. Gregory the Pope 25 Edward I.

Seal extant C.R.O. IB/25 EI/5

125 25 March 1297

Charter of William Colle baker (*pistor*) of Coventry giving to Emma daughter of John the Goldsmith (*aurifabri*), for her service, a curtilage with appurtenances which he once bought from Geoffrey le Leef in the vill of Coventry lying in Little Park St. towards the park gate (*in minori vico parci versus portam parci*) between the grantor's land on the one hand and the land which Geoffrey le Chaloner held on the other in width, and in length from the aforesaid street up to the grantor's land as is fully manifest according to the metes and bounds made there; to be held to her and the legitimately begotten heirs of her body well and in peace, with remainder to the said John the Goldsmith (*aurifabro*) the father of the aforesaid Emma and Alice his wife, their heirs or assigns, without contradiction or impediment by the grantor or his heirs, should Emma die without such heirs, rendering annually to the chief lords of that fee the services due and by right accustomed, namely 3¼d. of silver at the four terms of the year usual and fixed in the vill of Coventry for all secular service [etc.]. Warranty and sealing clauses. Witnesses: Henry Baker (*pistor'*) then bailiff of Coventry, William le Parker then coroner, John de Wedon', Richard Foþewyne, John le Gover', Robert de Dunstaple, Robert the clerk and others. Coventry, the feast of the Annunciation of the blessed Mary in March 25 Edward I.

Seal extant C.R.O. IB/25 EI/4

126 c.25 March 1299

Lease, grant and demise at farm by Alice daughter of Gilbert de Longedon' to William Baret of Coventry of a certain messuage with 4 adjacent cottages and appurtenances in Little Park St. (*in minori vico p(ar)ci*) in Coventry, which Hugh de Oxenford' held and which lies between the land Emma Wymund held on the one hand and Pauline's Lane (*venellam que vocatur Paulyles Lone*) on the other in width and extends in length from the royal highway (*a regia strata*) up to the land of William Maunsel as is fully manifest according to the metes and bounds made there; to be held to him, his heirs or assigns, of the grantor and her heirs freely [etc.] from the feast of the blessed Mary in March 27 Edward I for a term of 6 years by rendering annually 11s. of silver at the four terms of the year usual in the vill of Coventry for all secular service [etc.], on condition that if the aforesaid William, his heirs or assigns, should withhold the aforesaid rent for 3 weeks beyond any term the grantor, his heirs or assigns, will be allowed to eject the said William, his heirs or assigns, from the said messuage with appurtenances and to retain it in their possession without any contradiction or impediment. William, his heirs or assigns, will maintain the aforesaid messuage with adjacent cottages and appurtenances in as good a state as they received it or better. Clause for warranty. Mutual sealing clause [chirograph]. Witnesses: Anketell de Colshull' then bailiff, Matthew de Ruyton', Hugh le Tayllur, Geoffrey de Dunchurch', John Dobedy clerk and others.

Et si predictum mes(uagium) alicui vendi debiat seu dimici dictus Willelmus erit propinquior omnibus aliis p(er) duodecim denarios argenti.[1]

Indented
Seal extant W.R.O. 171

[1] Clause added in the same hand.

127 1298–1300

Charter of William Gamel of Coventry giving in free and perpetual alms to the window of the altar of the blessed Mary of the church of Holy Trinity, Coventry (*Coventreye*) 12d. annual rent to be taken at the four terms of the year usual in Coventry from a certain messuage which lies in Little Park St., Coventry (*in minori vico parci Coventr'*) in width between the land of John ad Cruce(m) on the one hand

and the land of William de Styvichale on the other according to the metes and bounds made there; to be held freely [etc.]. Clause for warranty. Clause for distraint by the wardens (*custodes*) of the window of the blessed Mary. Sealing clause. Witnesses: Sir Henry de Harunhale perpetual vicar of the same church, Anketell de Colushulle then bailiff of Coventry, John Lewyn then coroner, Robert Kelle, John the Glover (*Cirotecar'*), Robert Baker (*Pistore*), John Pyhod, John Abbot, John de Halys, Master Robert the Cook (*Coco*), John ad Cruce(m), John Saunsum, Richard Colebrond the clerk and others.

Seal extant W.R.O. 170

128 11 June 1301

Charter of Eadmund de Langel' lord of Shortley (*Sortel' Juxta Covintr'*) giving to John de Langel merchant of Coventry, a curtilage of the grantor's in the vill of Coventry in Little Park St. (*in vico p(ar)vi p(ar)ci*) with all appurtenances, namely that which lies in width between the land Hugh le Tayllur and William de Bury held on the one hand and the red ditch (*Rubeum fossatum*) on the other and extends in length from the land Hugh Bochi [held] up to the land of Ralf de Tewe as is manifest according to the metes and bounds made there; to be held to him, his heirs and assigns, of the grantor, his heirs and assigns, freely [etc.] by rendering annually 4s. at the four terms of the year fixed and customary in the vill of Coventry for all secular service [etc.]. Warranty and sealing clauses. Witnesses: Robert de Stok', John Lewyn coroner of Coventry, John de Rydewar', Matthew de Ruyton', William Grauntpe, Richard ad Muyr' and others. Shortley (*Sortel Juxta Covintr'*), Sunday the feast of St. Barnabas the Apostle 29 Edward I.

Seal extant C.R.O. IB/29 E1/3

129 18 September 1303

Charter of Joan de Rokeby in Coventry, in her pure virginity, giving to William de Borbache merchant of Coventry (*m(er)catori Coventr'*) a tenement with the buildings sited there in Little Park St. (*in minori vico p(ar)ci*) in Coventry lying in width between Dead Lane (*le Dedelone*) on the one hand and the tenement of the heirs of Geoffrey de Dunchurche on the other and extending in length from the said street up to the tenement of Hugh le Hosier according to the metes and bounds made and fixed there; to be held to him, his heirs or assigns, of the chief lords of that fee freely [etc.] by rendering annually to the aforesaid lords the service due and by right accustomed, namely 2½d. of silver at the four terms of the year usual in the vill of Coventry for all secular service [etc.]. Clause for warranty. William gave 2 marks of silver beforehand. Sealing clause. Witnesses: Robert called Baker (*dicto pistor'*) then bailiff of Coventry, Peter Barun, William de Schepeye, John de Longeleye, Henry de Wycho and many others. Coventry, Wednesday after the feast of the Exaltation of the Holy Cross A.D. 1303.

Seal extant G.II. 316

130 4 February 1304

Charter of Isabella widow of Master Robert de Wyssendene, in her pure widowhood, giving to John Bonde of Coventry 2 cottages with appurtenances which he had in Little Park St. (*in minori vico parci*) in Coventry which lie in width between the land of Roger Dayeseye on the one hand and the land of William de Stiveschale on the other and extend in length from the aforesaid street up to the land of William Gamel as is fully manifest according to the metes and bounds made there; to be held with the buildings sited there and all other appurtenances to him, his heirs or assigns, freely [etc.] of the chief lords of that fee by the services due and by right accustomed.

Warranty and sealing clauses. Witnesses: Robert Baker (*Pistore*) then bailiff in Coventry, Peter Barun, John de Langeleye, William de Schepeye, Robert de Rydewar', William de Stiveschale, John Dobedy and others. Coventry, Wednesday after the feast of the Purification of the blessed Virgin Mary 32 Edward I.

Seal missing C.R.O. IB/32 EI/7

131 14 August 1304

Charter of John Bonde of Coventry giving to Richard Huttyng of Coventry 2 cottages with appurtenances in Little Park St. (*in minori vico parci*) in Coventry which lie in width between the land of Roger Dayeseye on the one hand and the land of William de Styveschale on the other and extend in length from the aforesaid street up to the land of William Gamel as is fully manifest according to the metes and bounds made there; to be held to him, his heirs or assigns, freely [etc.] of the chief lords of that fee by the services due to the same and by right accustomed. Clause for warranty. Roger gave 4 marks sterling beforehand. Sealing clause. Witnesses: Robert Baker (*Pistore*) then bailiff in Coventry, John de Langeleye, Richard le Merc(er), William de Schepeye, Robert de Rydewar', Robert de Stone, Thomas Ballard, Robert le Fysscher', Henry Gryndel, William de Styveschale and others. Coventry, Friday after the feast of St. Lawrence 32 Edward I.

Seal extant C.R.O. IB/32 EI/11

132 15 June 1305

Grant, remise and quitclaim by John son of John de Atteleborwe of Coventry, for himself and his heirs, to John de Mildenhale merchant of Coventry and Agnes his wife of all right and claim in the entire messuage with appurtenances which lies in Little Park St., Coventry (*in minori vico Parci de Coventr'*) between the land of William de Schepeye on the one hand and the land of Geoffrey le Chalonere on the other in width and extends in length from the royal highway (*a regia via*) up to the land of John de Wedone as is fully manifest according to the metes and bounds made there; to be held with all appurtenances to them and to John's heirs and assigns, of the chief lords of that fee freely and hereditarily by the services which pertain to that messuage. Exclusion clause. John and Agnes gave 20s. sterling beforehand. Sealing clause. Witnesses: Robert Baker (*Pistore*), Roger Dayeseye, Peter Barun, Geoffrey le Chalon(er)e, William de Schepeye, Robert de Rydewar', Thomas de Grantham and others. Coventry, Tuesday after the feast of St. Barnabas the Apostle 33 Edward I.

Seal missing C.R.O. IB/33 EI/17

133 6 January 1306

Charter of Roger Daysye of Coventry clerk giving to Robert de London' chaplain and Joan the grantor's daughter the entire messuage which he had in Little Park St., Coventry (*in vico minoris parci de Coventr'*) lying between the land of Richard Huttyng' and William Gamul on the one hand and the land once of Hugh le Taylur on the other in width and extends from the royal highway (*a via Regia*) up to the park (*Parcu(m)*) of Robert de Montalt (*monte alto*) in length according to the metes and bounds made there; to be held with appurtenances to them and the heirs begotten legitimately of Joan's body, with reversion to the grantor or his heirs should she die without such heir, of the lords of the fee (*de dominis feodalibus*) by the services due and by right accustomed. Warranty and sealing clauses. Witnesses: Robert Baker (*Pistore*) then bailiff, Peter Barun, Thomas de Lilleburne, Thomas Ballard, Ralf de Twe, Adam Russel, William Pake, chaplain, and many others. Coventry, Thursday the feast of the Epiphany 34 Edward I.

Seal extant W.R.O. 172

PARK ST./MUCH PARK ST.

134 Late 1230s–1243

Charter of Nicholas son of Nicholas giving to Reginald the Merchant (*m(er)catori*) the land with appurtenances in Coventry at the White Cellar* against Park St. (*apud albu(m) Celariu(m) contra vicum parci*) which lies between the land Henry Baker (*furnarius*) held and the land which Hawise daughter of Geoffrey the Soap-maker (*savenatoris*) held, namely that which Mariota sister of the same Hawise sold to him and quitclaimed by her charter. Moreover, he has granted to Reginald for his service the farm and service which the aforesaid Hawise daughter of Geoffrey the Soap-maker (*savenatoris*) used to render to the grantor, namely 1½d. annually and ¼ of 1 hen and a ¼ of 1 man in Autumn; to be held to him, his heirs or assigns, except to a house of religion, in fee and inheritance of the grantor and his heirs, freely and quietly with appurtenances as of his tenement (*sic(ut) de tenemento meo*) by rendering annually 8d. at four terms of the year according to the usage of Coventry for all service and exaction. Clause for warranty. Reginald gave 32s. of silver in recognition. Sealing clause. Witnesses: Osbert Durdent then reeve (*p(re)posito*), Richard the Burgess (*burg'*), Geoffrey C(r)ude, John Forthwine, Herbert the Carter (*carettario*), John Bukkesbert, Stephen Vache, William Pie, Richard de Henleye, Henry Baker (*furnar'*), Warin le M(er)cer, Sephare[1] son of Ralf the Baker (*furnar'*), Ralf Crouleboys.

Seal missing C.R.O. 2/102

[1] sic

*This and the following 12 deeds concern the property close to the White Cellar or in one case a moiety of the cellar itself. This prominent landmark lay at the head of Much Park Street, on the eastern corner with Earl Street. Both Park Street and the White Cellar were in existence by the early 13th century when Combe abbey acquired 2 messuages next to the cellar (767.12, 767.36). For other deeds featuring the White Cellar see 178, 210–213, 280–281, 767.12, 767.36. For other deeds featuring Much Park Street see also 210–214, 217, 228, 229, 247 and *Langley Cartulary* No. 258.

135 Late 1230s–1243

Charter of Nicholas son of Nicholas giving to Reginald the merchant (*Mercatori*) of Coventry the land with appurtenances in the same vill at the White Cellar against Park St. (*apud albu(m) Celariu(m) contra vicu(m) parci*) which lies between the land

Henry the Baker (*furnari(us)*) held and the land Hawise daughter of Geoffrey the Soap-maker (*savenatoris*) held, namely the land with appurtenances which Mariota sister of the same Hawise sold to the grantor and quitclaimed by her charter. Moreover, he has granted to the same Reginald for his service the farm and service which the aforesaid Hawise used to render to the grantor, namely 1½d. annually, and ½d. annually which she has quitclaimed to the grantor and which she used to receive from the land which she gave to Segilia her daughter, and besides ¼ of a hen and ¼ of the service of 1 man for 1 day in Autumn; to be held to him, his heirs or assigns, except to a house of religion, in fee and inheritance of the grantor and his heirs freely [etc.] with appurtenances as of his tenement (*sicut de tenemento suo*) by rendering annually for all service and exaction 8d. of silver at four terms of the year according to the usage of Coventry. Clause for warranty. Reginald gave 32s. of silver in recognition. Sealing clause. Witnesses: Osbert the clerk, Richard the Burgess (*Burg'*), Geoffrey Crude, John Forthwine, Herbert the Carter (*carett'*), Stephen Vache, William Pie, Richard de Henlegh', Henry Baker (*furn'*) and others.

Seal missing C.R.O. IA/C12/1

136 Late 1250s–early 1260s

Letters of Henry son of William Pye of Coventry establishing Margery daughter of Henry le Norris of Coventry, her heirs and assigns, as perpetual attorneys for him and his heirs for paying to the lords of the fee the farm appertaining to them from all the lands with appurtenances which he gave to the same Henry le Nores and confirmed by his charters in the vill of Coventry, to be paid *per annum* at the terms named in those charters; with clause for exclusion saving to the grantor, his heirs or assigns, 3 clove-gillyflowers which the same Henry was accustomed to render annually from the aforesaid lands with appurtenances, namely the land in Park St. (*in vico parci*), the land in Earl's Mill Lane (*in vic(u)lo ducent' versus molend(inum) d(omi)ni Cov(i)ntr'*) and the house in which he dwelt towards the White Cellar (*de domo quo mansit v(ersus) alb(um) Celar'*) with all appurtenances, rights and escheats. Sealing clause. Witnesses: Alexander de Glouc', Robert de Denecastell', John le Flecher, William de Alisl', Godfrey the Merchant (*mercator*)[1], William Payn, Richer de Weston', Warin le M(er)c(er), Robert de Nortfolc and others.

Seal missing P.R.O. A 4442

[1] sic

137 Shortly after Whitsun 1272

Charter of William son of Richard le Garden(er) of Coventry giving to Alexander the Vintner (*vinitar'*) of Coventry and Isabella his wife a moiety of a messuage with appurtenances in Coventry in Park St. (*in vico p(ar)ci*) which he recovered by writ of entry against Ralf le Mirourer before Gilbert de P(re)stone and his fellows at Warwick (*Warewik'*), namely the moiety which is nearer to the land of Rosa Hors in length and in width just as the said moiety extends; to be held to them, and the heirs of Alexander freely [etc.] by rendering annually to the lord of that fee the service due and accustomed, namely that pertaining to the said moiety for all secular service [etc.]. Sealing clause. Alexander gave 20s. beforehand. Witnesses: John de Lodelawe, William Utting, Richard de Esseby, Peter Baru(n), Robert de Chiltu(n), Henry Baker (*pistor'*), Walter Bacu(n), Thomas de Fakenha(m), Hugh le Bretu(n) and others.

Seal extant C.R.O. IA/C13/25

Endorsed: De Tenement' juxta albu(m) Celar'.

William le Gardener who was said to be of full age recovered seisin against Ralf le Mirourer during the 1272 eyre (JI/955 m17).

138 Shortly after Whitsun 1272

Charter of William son of Richard le Gardener of Coventry giving to Hugh le Bretun of Coventry and Margery his wife a moiety of the messuage with appurtenances in Park St., Coventry (*In Coventr' in vico parci*) which the grantor recovered by writ of entry before the justices of the lord king in eyre at Warwick (*Warrewyke*) 56 Henry III, namely the moiety which is nearer to the land Thomas de Fakenham held in length and in width just as the moiety of the messuage purports according to the metes and bounds made there; to be held to them, their heirs or whatsoever assigns, of the lords of that fee freely [etc.] by rendering annually to those same lords a moiety of the service due and accustomed from the same messuage with appurtenances, namely 6d. of silver at four terms of the year according to the usage of Coventry for all secular service [etc.]. Sealing clause. Witnesses: John de Lodelawe then bailiff, William Huttyng, Richard de Esseby, Peter Barun, Geoffrey le Bretun, Ranulph de Franketun', Adam Colbrond, Henry Dodeby, Robert le Hunte, Richard the Weaver (*Textore*), Henry de Denecastr', Thomas de Fakenham, Ancketell de Coleshull clerk and others.

Seal missing C.R.O. IA/Misc.I/32

139 Shortly after Whitsun 1272

Remise and quitclaim by Hugh le Bretun of Coventry to Thomas de Fakinham of Coventry for 20s. of silver which he gave beforehand of a moiety of a messuage with appurtenances in Park St., Coventry (*In Coventr' In vico p(ar)ci*) lying next to the land of the same Thomas, namely the moiety of a messuage which the grantor had by the gift of William le Gardiner in length and in width as is manifest according to the metes and bounds made there; to be held with all right and claim therein to him, his heirs or whatsoever assigns, of the lords of the fee by the service due and accustomed freely [etc.], without any reservation by the grantor or his heirs. Exclusion clause. Sealing clause, with surrender of the charter of William le Gardin(er) for fuller security. Witnesses: Peter Barun then bailiff, Pagan Pake, Richard le Brocher, Thomas de Barsam, William de Eggisfeld, Bony, Adam Russel, Henry de Axeholm, William Crumpe, Walter de Winchelse and others.

Seal extant C.R.O. IA/C57

140 Shortly after Whitsun 1272

Remise and quitclaim by Alexander son of Adam the Vintner (*vinitar'*) of Coventry to Thomas de Fakynham of Coventry for 20s. of silver which he gave beforehand of a moiety of a messuage with appurtenances in Coventry in Park St. (*in vico parci*) lying next to the land which Rosa Hors held, namely that which the grantor bought from William son of Richard le Gardiner in length and in width as is manifest according to the metes and bounds made there; to be held with all right and claim therein to him, his heirs or whatsoever assigns, of the lords of the fee by the service due and by right accustomed freely [etc.] without reservation by the grantor or his heirs. Exclusion clause. Sealing clause, with surrender of the grantor's charter of enfeoffment. Witnesses: Peter Barun then bailiff, Richard le Brocher', Thomas de Barsam, William de Eggisfeld, Bogo le Mercer, Adam Russel', Henry de Axeholm, William Cru(m)pe, Walter de Winchelse and others.

Seal extant C.R.O. 2/170

141 Early 1280s

Remise and quitclaim by Thomas de Fackinham, for himself and his heirs, to Robert de Clother of all right and claim in the entire messuage with appurtenances in Little Park St., Coventry (*in minori vico p(ar)ci de Coventr'*) which lies between the land Rosa

Hors once held on the one hand and the land Agnes Bakun' once held on the other in length and in width according to what is manifest and according to the metes and bounds made there; to be held to him, his heirs or whatsoever assigns, freely [etc.] by rendering annually to the lords of the fee the rent due and accustomed. Exclusion clause. Robert gave 3 marks of silver beforehand. Sealing clause. Witnesses: Robert de Chiltun' then bailiff, Alexander the Vintner (*vinitar'*), William Bakun then coroner, Thomas le Moubray, John Thole, Richer de Westun, Richard de Esscheby, Adam Russel, Thomas de Barsham, Ralph the Huntsman (*venator'*) and others.

Seal extant C.R.O. IA/LC12/30
Endorsed: Carte de Albo Celario.

142 Early 1280s

Remise and quitclaim by Robert de Clother to Henry Baker (*pistor'*) and Adam Russel of Coventry of all right and claim in the entire messuage with all appurtenances in Much Park St., Coventry (*in majori vico parci de Coventr'*) which lies between the land Rosa Hors held on the one hand and the land Agnes Bakun held on the other in length and in width as the land purports and according to the metes and bounds made there; to be held to them, their heirs or whatsoever assigns, freely [etc.] by rendering annually to the lords of that fee the rent due and accustomed. Exclusion and sealing clauses. Witnesses: Alexander the Vintner (*vinitario*), Robert de Chiltun, Thomas le Moubray, John Pyhod, Richard de Esscheby, Richer de Westun, Richard de Westun, Thomas de Barsham, Anketell de Colishul' the clerk and others.

Seal extant C.R.O. 2/110

143 Early–mid 1280s

Remise and quitclaim by Robert de Clother to Henry Baker (*pistor'*) and Adam Russel of Coventry of all right and claim in the entire land with the houses sited there and all appurtenances in Much Park St., Coventry (*in majori vico parci de Coventr'*) which lies between the White Cellar (*Album Celariu(m)*) on the one hand and the land Thomas de Fackinham held on the other in length and in width as the land purports; to be held to them, their heirs or assigns, freely [etc.] by rendering annually to the lords of that fee the rent due and accustomed, namely to Agnes Bakun 10s. of silver at the four terms of the year usual in Coventry for all secular service [etc.]. Exclusion and sealing clauses. Witnesses: Alexander the Vintner (*vinitario*), Robert de Chiltun, Richard de Esscheby, Thomas de Barsham, Richer de Westun, Richard de Westun, Robert G(r)antpe, Ralf the Huntsman (*venator'*) and others.

Seal extant C.R.O. 2/139

144 c.1290

Charter of Adam Russel of Coventry merchant giving to Henry Baker (*pistori*) of Coventry and Agnes his wife the moiety which fell to him of the White Cellar and of a seld attached to the said Cellar in Much Park St., Coventry (*de Albo Celario et de una selda dicto Celario annexa in majori vico parci Coventr'*) next to the land once of Walter Bacun; to be held to them and their heirs or to whomsoever they will wish to give, bequeath, sell or assign, in sickness and in health, of the grantor and his heirs well [etc.] by rendering annually as the perpetual attorneys of the grantor and his heirs to the lords of the fee the services due and by right accustomed, and to the grantor and his heirs a clove-gillyflower at Christmas for all secular services [etc.]. Clause for warranty. Henry and Agnes gave 10 marks sterling beforehand. Sealing clause. Witnesses: Robert de Stoke, Robert de Chilton', Thomas le Moubray, John Thole, Richer de Weston', Thomas de Barsham, John de Langeleye, Richard de Weston', Roger the clerk and others.

Seal extant C.R.O. IA/EC13/81

145 c.1290–1297

Notification by Beatrice Haldeyn widow of Peter de Egesfeld in Coventry that she and her heirs are bound to Henry Oky of Coventry, Agnes his wife and their heirs, in 14s. of silver annual rent to be paid at the four terms of the year usual in the vill of Coventry from the entire tenement which she held of the same Henry and Agnes in Much Park St. (*in majori vico parci*) in Coventry, which tenement extends in length from the White Cellar (*de albo Celario*) up to her land as is manifest according to the metes and bounds made there; to be held to them and their heirs of the grantor and her heirs well [etc.] without any fraud (*fraude*) or reservation by the grantor or her heirs. *Et si contingat me vel heredes meos deficere in solutione dicti redditus ultra q(u)indenam post aliquem terminorum statutorum in Coventr' ex tunc volo et pro me et heredibus meis concedo quod predicti Henricus et Agnes et heredes eorum liberam potestatem habeant me et heredes meos et tenentes meos distringere in capitali manso meo in vico Comitis in Coventr' et in seldis ejusdem mansi si necesse fuerit sine aliquo impedimento et sine alicujus contradictione et dictrictiones retinere contra vadiu(m) et plegios quousque hoc quod aretro fuerit de dicto redditu plenarie p(er)solverimus. Preterea si contig(er)it me vel heredes meos cessare vel deficere in solutione dicti redditus per unum annu(m) ex tunc volo et pro me et heredibus meis concedo quod prefati Henricus et Agnes et heredes eorum plenam potestatem habeant tenementum eorum supradictum intrare et illud deinceps inperpetuum pacifice possidere sine aliquo obstaculo et sine aliquo impedimento mei vel heredum meorum.* Sealing clause. Witnesses: Henry Baker (*pistore*) then bailiff of Coventry, William le Parker then coroner, Adam Russel, Richard de Essceby, Ralf le Hunte, John de Rydeware, Henry de Barsham, Clement le Mirourer, Roger the clerk and others.

Seal extant C.R.O. 2/35

146 1298–1300

Charter of Nicholas Crumpe of Coventry giving to William son of John le Floutere of Coventry girdler (*zonario*) a shop (*Shoppam*) which he had in Much Park St., Coventry against the White Cellar (*in majori vico Parci in Coventr' contra Album Celariu(m)*) sited in width between the grantor's land on both sides and extending in length from the aforesaid street to the land Clement le Mirourer once held as the shop purports; to be held with appurtenances to him, his heirs or assigns, of the grantor and his heirs well [etc.] by rendering annually 10s. of silver at the four terms of the year usual in the vill of Coventry for all secular services [etc.]. Warranty and sealing clauses. Witnesses: Anketill de Coleshul then bailiff of Coventry, John Leofwyne then coroner, Adam Russel, Peter Barun, William Grauntpe, Thomas Symund, Ralf le Hunte, Hugh de Merynton', Roger the clerk and others.

Seal missing C.R.O. IA/C12/8

147 Early 1270s

Gift, remise and quitclaim by Philip Ba(r)bedaverul, for himself and his heirs, to Henry le Pestur of Coventry of 20d. annual rent which the grantor used to receive from the land Philip the Smith (*faber*) held in Park St. (*in vico de parco*) in the same vill, namely from the land which lies next to the land of the abbot and convent on the one hand and the town ditch (*Fossatum ville*) on the other together with all issues, escheats and other appurtenances pertaining to the aforesaid rent; to be held to him, his heirs or assigns, freely [etc.] with all liberties and free customs. Exclusion clause. Henry gave 1 mark of silver beforehand. Sealing clause. Witnesses: Peter Barun, Nicholas Attebarre, Robert le Mouner, Robert de Chiltone, William de Egisfeld, Bony, Thomas de Barssam, Richer de Westone, Richard de Esseby, Andrew le M(er)cer, Benedict le Fleuter and others.

Seal missing — C.R.O. 2/54

Endorsed: Carta Gilde marie quondam fuit Willelmi Mox de tenemento in vico majori p(ar)ci xxd. p(er) an.

148 — Late 1270s–early 1280s

Charter of Robert called the Miller of Coventry (*dictus molendinar' de Coventr'*) giving to Geoffrey le Lef of Coventry 8d. annual rent to be taken from the tenement of Hugh Wyne in Much Park St., Coventry (*in majori vico p(ar)ci de Coventr'*) which lies between the land of William le Walsse on the one hand and the land of Robert Box on the other; to be held to him, his heirs or whatsoever assigns, of the grantor and his heirs freely [etc.] by rendering annually a clove-gillyflower at Easter for all secular service [etc.]. Geoffrey gave 12s. of silver beforehand. Clause for distraint without contradiction by anyone for non-payment of rent. Warranty and sealing clauses. Witnesses: Robert de Chilton' then bailiff of Coventry, Peter Baru(n) of the same, Richard the Brooch-maker (*firmac(u)lario*) of the same, Richard de Asseby of the same, William Scot of the same, William Hod of the same, Rober(t) Box of the same and others.

Seal missing — Q.C. 2326

149 — Early 1280s

Charter of Geoffrey de Longeley knight giving to Robert de la Barre and Christine his wife 2 messuages in Coventry with appurtenances, namely those sited between the house of Jurdan le Aller on the one hand and the house of William Crumpe on the other in Park St. (*in vico de la parik*), the messuage which Boni le Mercer once held extending up to a certain place (*placeam*) pertaining to the messuage which Geoffrey le Wurkemon once held and the messuage which William Crumpe held extending to the said place and that place extending up to the red ditch of the vill (*rubeam fossam ville*) in length and in width according to the metes placed there; to be held to them, their heirs or assigns, or to whomsoever they will wish to give, sell or assign or *in extremis* bequeath, of the grantor, his heirs or assigns, freely [etc.] by rendering annually 6s. of lawful money at the four terms of the year as is the custom in Coventry, namely 18d. at each of the feasts of St. Michael, St. Andrew, St. Mary in March, and the Nativity of St. John the Baptist for all secular service, suit of court, custom and demand. Warranty and sealing clauses. Witnesses: Robert de Chiltyrne, Peter his son, Robert le Molener of Park St. (*de vico de la parik*), Jurdan le Aller, William Crumpe, Geoffrey le Luf of Park St. (*de vico de la parik*), William de Witeley and many others.

Seal missing — C.R.O. IA/MC12/38

150 1280s

Charter of William Utting of Coventry, for himself and his heirs, giving to William Godeslime and Ella (*Hele*)his wife the gift (*donationem*) which they had from William the grantor's father of a certain tenement in Much Park St., Coventry (*in majori vico parci de Coventr'*) which lies next to the land of Roger the clerk on the south side; to be held with the buildings sited there and all appurtenances to them, their heirs or assigns, of the grantor and his heirs well [etc.] by rendering annually 2s. 6d. of silver at the four terms of the year usual and fixed in the vill of Coventry for all secular service [etc.]. Warranty and sealing clauses. Witnesses: Henry Baker (*pistor'*) then bailiff in Coventry, Adam Russel, Richer de Weston', Peter de Egefeld, William Grauntpe, Thomas Symund, Roger the clerk and others.

Seal extant C.R.O. IA/C12/7

151 Late 1280s

Charter of John Scot of Coventry and Margery his wife giving to Henry de Wytinton' merchant and Agnes his wife a certain tenement in Lower Park St., Coventry (*in Inferiori vico parci de Coventre*) which the grantors had by enfeoffment of Adam Russel, which lies between the land of the same Adam on the one hand and the land of William the Smith (*fabri*) on the other and extends in length from the aforesaid royal highway (*a regali via predicta*) up to the land of Richer de Weston' as is fully manifest according to the metes and bounds made there; to be held with the buildings sited there and all appurtenances to them, their heirs or whatsoever assigns, of the grantors and their heirs, well [etc.] in fee and inheritance by rendering annually ½d. of silver at the feast of St. John the Baptist for all secular services [etc.]. Clause for warranty. Henry and Agnes gave 5 marks sterling beforehand. Sealing clause. Witnesses: Henry Baker (*pistor'*) then bailiff in Coventry, Thomas de Barsham, Richer de Weston', Peter de Egefeld, John de Langeleye, Robert the Miller (*molendinar'*), Geoffrey le Lef, Robert the Fishmonger (*piscator'*), Roger the clerk and others.

2 seals extant W.R.O. DR 429/4

152 28 September 1292

Charter of Roger son of Robert the Miller (*molendinarii*) of Coventry giving to Sir Nicholas lord of Segrave 2s. 0½d. annual rent from the grantor's rent in Great Park St. (*in magno vico parci*) in the vill of Coventry which he used to receive annually at four terms of the year namely 12d. from the tenement which Robert the Wheelwright (*Rotarius*) held, 12d. from the tenement which Nicholas ad Barram held next to the bar (*juxta Barram*) in the same street and from the tenement which Peter de Egesfeld held in the lane (*viculo*) which leads from Great Park St. (*a magno vico parci*) up to the park (*parcu(m)*) next to the curtilage of Richard de Westone ½d. annually at Easter; to be held to him, his heirs or assigns, freely [etc.] without any disturbance or contradiction by the grantor or his heirs. Warranty and sealing clauses. Witnesses: Peter le Bretun [and] Henry Baker (*pistore*) then bailiffs (*tunc ball(iv)is*), Robert de Chiltone, William de Nayleston' coroner of Coventry, Richard de Weston', Adam Russel, John de Langeleya, Henry Ballard, John Payn and others. Coventry, in Great Park St. (*in magno vico parci*), Sunday before the feast of St. Michael 20 Edward I.

Seal missing G.H. 298

153

20 July 1295

Charter of Alan Lyhtfot of Coventry giving to Thomas de Evesham and Emma his wife and to the heirs or assigns of the same Thomas a moiety of a tenement with appurtenances in Much Park St., Coventry (*in majori vico p(ar)ci Coventr'*) which the grantor had by the gift and enfeoffment of Geoffrey le Chalouner [and] which lies between the land of Geoffrey le Chalon(er) on the one hand and the land of Richard le Buttere on the other in length and in width as the moiety purports according to the metes and bounds made there; to be held of the chief lords of that fee freely [etc.] by making to those chief lords the service due and accustomed for all service [etc.]. Clause for warranty. Thomas and Emma gave 20 marks beforehand. Sealing clause. Witnesses: Henry Baker (*pistore*) then bailiff, William le P(ar)ker coroner, John de Longeleye, William Grantpe, Adam Russel, Geoffrey le Chalon(er), Ralf le Hunte, Richard le Buttere and others. Wednesday the feast of St. Margaret the Virgin A.D. 1295.

Seal extant

Q.C. 2329

154

2 October 1295

Charter of William del Blauncheval of Stoke and Isabella his wife giving to Robert de Stoke and Joan his wife, to the heirs of the same Robert, and to their assigns 11d. of silver annual rent to be taken at the four terms of the year usual in the vill of Coventry from the tenement which Robert the Fishmonger (*piscator*) held of the grantors in Much Park St. (*in majori vico parci*) in Coventry between the chief messuage (*Capitale mansum*) of the same Robert on the one hand and the land once of William Hod on the other; to be held well [etc.] of the lords of that fee by the services due and accustomed, saving to the grantors and their heirs all other profits (*expletiis*) and liberties issuing from the said tenement for ever. Warranty and sealing clauses. Witnesses: Alexander de Cruylefeld, Henry Baker (*pistore*) of Coventry, William le Parker then coroner, Adam Russel, Robert de Wylenhale, John Corbin of Stoke, Roger the clerk of Coventry and others. Coventry, Sunday after the feast of St. Michael 23 Edward I.

2 seals missing

C.R.O. IB/23 EI/9

155

14 February 1298

Agreement whereby John Corbin of Stoke and Joan his wife have granted and demised to Robert de Stokes and Joan his wife 12s. 6d. annual rent with appurtenances which the aforesaid John and Joan used to receive in the vill of Coventry at four terms of the year, together with a moiety of the pannage of pigs and a moiety of the toll of horses issuing from all the tenements which were once of Philip de Barbedaveryl in Coventry from the tenants written below: from Margery de Lodelowe 2s. 2d. *per annum*, from Roger de Allesley clerk 2s. 2d. *per annum* from a tenement in Much Park St. (*in vico parci majoris*), from Alexander de Assheby in Earl St. (*in vico Comitis*) 2d. *per annum*, from Henry Ballard from the tenement which Petronilla la Wyte holds 4d. *per annum*, from the tenement of Roger Daysye and Matilda widow of John Bras 16d. *per annum*, from the tenement of Henry de Barsham in Little Park St. (*in vico parci minoris*) 12d. *per annum*, from the tenement of John Wysmo(n) in Earl St. (*in vico Comitis*) 8d. *per annum*, from Nicholas de Derby in Pauline's St. (*in vico Paulini*) 8d. *per annum*, from Thomas Boydin from the tenement of William de Lymburg 3s. *per annum*, and from John de Coundulme from a certain field towards Radford (*campo versus Radeford*) 12d.; to be held freely [etc.] from the feast of the blessed Mary in March 26 Edward I for a term of 4 years. Clause for warranty. Should Robert and Joan be troubled in any way regarding the aforesaid rent or the pannage or toll or should part of the rent be unable to be levied, the aforesaid [John and] Joan grant for themselves and their heirs that Robert and Joan and their heirs should be able to retain the aforesaid rent with appurtenances without any reclaim or charge by the aforesaid John and Joan and their heirs until they shall be satisfied regarding both their damages and expenses. Mutual sealing clause. Witnesses: William Aubrey, Philip de Ansty, William le Parker', William de Arhyngworth', William le Taylour, John Payn chaplain, and others. Friday after the octaves of the Purification of the blessed Mary in the aforesaid year.

Indented
Seal missing C.R.O. IB/26 EI/7

156 c.1303–1310

Charter of Geoffrey le Leef of Coventry giving to Robert de Stoke 3s. annual rent to be taken from William le Cotiler and his heirs from the tenement which he holds in Coventry in Park St. of the fee of Barbe d'Averil (*in quodam loco qui vocatur Parkstrete de feodo barbe de Averil*); the entire aforesaid rent and service to be held to him and his heirs of the lords of the fee by the service due and accustomed. Warranty and sealing clauses. Witnesses: Robert Baker (*Pistore*) of Coventry, Henry de Barsham, Hugh de Meriton', Richard le Spicer, William le Wallere, Richard Utting, Richard de Walleshale, Gilbert de Eton', Adam le Bonde and others.

Seal missing C.R.O. 2/28

157 c.1300–c.1303

Charter of Geoffrey le Leef of Coventry giving to Robert de Stok' and his heirs 18d. annual rent with appurtenances to be taken from Richard de Weston' from a tenement which he held of the grantor in Park St., Coventry (*in vico p(ar)ci de Coventr'*); the rent and service with appurtenances to be held to him and his heirs of the lords of that fee by the services due and accustomed. Warranty and sealing clauses. Witnesses: Roger Daysie, John Lewyn, Robert de Chilton', William Aubrey, Sir John Payn, Robert de Wylenhale, Adam le Bonde and others.

Seal extant C.R.O. IA/Misc.I/6

158 20 October 1297

Charter of Geoffrey le Lef of Coventry giving to Adam le Latoner of Coventry 2s. annual rent with appurtenances which the grantor used to receive annually at the four terms of the year usual in Coventry from a certain messuage in Much Park St. (*in majori vico Parci*) in the same vill which lies between the grantor's land on the one hand and the land of Ralf le Hunte which was once of Robert Box on the other, which 2s. rent the grantor bought from John le Vineter; to be held with all appurtenances, liberties and easements to him, his heirs or whatsoever assigns, well [etc.] of the lords of that fee by the service due and accustomed. Clause for warranty. Adam gave to the grantor 20s. of silver beforehand. Sealing clause. Witnesses: Henry Baker (*Pistore*) then bailiff of Coventry, William called (*dicto*) Parker then coroner, Adam Russel, William G(r)antpe, Ralf le Hunte, John de Rydeware, Richard le Buttere, Elias (*Helya*) le Ceynturer, Roger the clerk and others. Coventry, Sunday after the feast of St. Luke the Evangelist 25 Edward I.

Seal extant C.R.O. IB/25 EI/2

159 1300–1303

Charter of Adam le Latoner of Coventry giving to Peter de Meryton' 2s. annual rent with appurtenances which he bought (*comparavi*) from Geoffrey le Lef' of Coventry to be taken from a certain messuage in Much Park St., Coventry (*in majori vico Parci in Coventr'*) which lies between the land of the aforesaid Geoffrey on the one hand and the land of Ralf le Hunte on the other; to be held to him, his heirs or assigns, well [etc.]. Clause for warranty. Peter gave 24s. sterling beforehand. Sealing clause. Witnesses: Roger Daieseie then bailiff in Coventry, Peter Barun, Adam Russel, Thomas Symund, William Grauntpe, John de Rydeware, Ralf le Hunte, Richard de Weston', Roger the clerk and others.

Seal extant C.R.O. 1A/C43

Endorsed: tradantur Willelmo de Leicestr'

160 29 June 1298

Charter of William de Copston' of Coventry giving to John de Whyteleye merchant and Margery his wife a certain curtilage with its appurtenances in Much Park St. (*in majori vico p(ar)ci*) in the vill of Coventry towards the mill stones (*versus le mulnestones*) which lies between the land Geoffrey le Lef once held on the one hand and the land Simon Russel once held on the other in width and extends in length from the royal highway (*a regia via*) up to the park (*parcum*) of Sir Robert de Montalt (*de monte alto*) as is fully manifest according to the metes and bounds made there; to be held to them, their heirs or assigns, freely [etc.] of the chief lords of that fee by the service due and by right accustomed. Clause for warranty. John and Margery gave 30s. sterling beforehand. Sealing clause. Witnesses: Anketell de Colsul then bailiff in Coventry, William de Naylleston' then coroner, John de Langeleye, Richard le Brocher', Richard de Weston', Adam Russel, William Grampe, Geoffrey le Lef and others. Coventry, Sunday after the feast of the Nativity of St. John the Baptist 26 Edward I.

Seal extant C.R.O. IB/26 EI/5

161 9 February 1300

Charter of Richard de Astleye giving to Richard le Butt(er)e of Coventry and Hawysia his wife a messuage with appurtenances in Much Park St., Coventry (*in vico p(ar)cii*[1] *majoris Coventr'*) which the grantor had by the gift of the same Richard; to be held to them freely [etc.] for their entire life and to the survivor, of the grantor and his heirs by the service of 7s. to be paid at the four terms of the year usual in Coventry annually for all services. Clause for reversion to the grantor, his heirs or assigns, with appurtenances and all improvements (*cum omni melioracione*) without impediment (*inpedimento*) or contradiction. Warranty and sealing clauses. Witnesses: Anketinus de Colleshull' then bailiff of Coventry, John Lewyne then coroner, William G(r)antpe, Robert de Schepeye, Thomas de Evesham, Geoffrey le Chalunner and others. Octaves of the Purification of the blessed Mary 28 Edward I.

Seal missing Q.C. 2327

[1] sic

162 1 August 1300

Charter of Robert Danet son of Ralph Danet of Leicester (*Leycestr'*) giving to Richard de la Muyre merchant in Coventry (*m(er)catori in Coventr'*) 5s. 4d. annual rent in Coventry, namely 12d. to be taken from the entire tenement in Much Park St. (*in majori vico parci*) between the land Peter de Egesfeld once held on the one hand and the land of William le Glasenwryth on the other, 2s. from the tenement which lies in Lodelowe's Lane (*Lodelowe lane*) between the land of Master Richard de Burton' on the one hand and the land of Reginald Ballard on the other, 12d. from the tenement which lies at Broadgate (*ad latam portam*) between the land of Matthew de Ruton' on the one hand and the land of Thomas Broun on the other, and 16d. from the entire tenement towards Potter's Row (*versus le Potter rowe*) which lies between the land once of William the Cook (*Coci*) of Caludon (*Calwedone*) on the one hand and the land of Richard Forthewyne. Moreover, he has granted to the aforesaid Richard his entire arable land with the appurtenant meadow and all [other] appurtenances which he had by hereditary right on behalf of Agnes his wife after the death of Henry de Rodynton' in Shokersfield and Poddycroft (*schocheresfeld et podicroft*); to be held to him, his heirs or whatsoever assigns, of the chief lords of that fee by the services due and by right accustomed freely [etc.]. Clause for warranty. Sealing clause, for 10 marks of silver which Richard gave beforehand. Witnesses: Robert de Stoke steward (*senescallo*) of the prior of Coventry, John Lewyn then coroner of Coventry, Anketell de Coleshulle, Henry Ballard, John de Langeleye, Reginald Ballard, William G(r)antpe, William de Toucestre, Geoffrey le Chaloner, Ralf le Hunte, Thomas de Northfeld, Nicholas de Schepeye, Richard de Boreford clerk and others. Coventry, Monday the feast of St. Peter 28 Edward I.

Seal extant C.R.O. IB/28 EI/8a

28 EI/8b is a charter of Robert Danet and Agnes his wife to Richard de la Muyre in identical terms to the above.

163 22 July 1300

Charter of Edmund de Langelee knight, lord of Shortley (*Schoertelee juxta Coventr'*), giving to John de Langelee of Coventry merchant his messuage in the vill of Coventry which lies in Much Park St. (*in majori vico parci*) between the land Richard le Aller once held on the one hand and the land Thomas de Coxale held on the other in width and extends in length from the royal highway (*a Regali via*) up to the garden (*gardinu(m)*) of William Grau(n)tpe as is manifest according to the metes and bounds made there; to be held with all appurtenances and easements to him, his heirs and assigns, freely [etc.] of the chief lords of that fee by the services due and by right accustomed. Clause for warranty. John gave the grantor 4 marks sterling beforehand. Sealing clause. Witnesses: Henry Ballard, Peter Barun, Richard de la Muyre, Adam Russel, Geoffrey le Chaluner, William Grau(n)tpe, John de Ridewar', and others. Coventry, Friday the feast of the blessed Mary Magdalen 28 Edward I.

Seal extant C.R.O. IB/28 EI/3

164 25 September 1306

Grant, remise and entire quitclaim by Eadmund de Langeleye knight to John de Langeleye merchant of Coventry of 6s. annual rent and all other services which he used to receive annually from a certain tenement with appurtenances in Coventry which lies between the tenement of Richard le Allere on the one hand and the tenement of Thomas de Coggeshale on the other in width and extends in length from Much Park St., Coventry (*a majori vico parci de Coventr'*) up to the land of William Grauntpe senior. Exclusion, warranty and sealing clauses. Witnesses: Nicholas Crumpe, John de Heyforde, Roger Dayeseye, John Dobedy, Robert de Rydewar',

William de Braundeston', William de Schepeye and many others. Coventry, Sunday after the feast of St. Matthew the Apostle and Evangelist 34 Edward I.

Seal extant C.R.O. IB/34 EI/4

165 21 February 1302

Charter of William le Glaswrihte of Coventry giving to Hugh de Meryton' in Coventry a certain piece (*placiam*) of his land in Much Park St. (*in majori vico Parci*) in Coventry, lying in width between the grantor's land on the one hand and the land of the aforesaid Hugh on the other and extending in length from the grantor's alehouse (*pandoxinio*) up to the ditch called the red ditch (*fossatu(m) quod vocatur le Rededych*) according to the metes and bounds made there; to be held with its easements as it is enclosed to him, his heirs or assigns, well [etc.] of the chief lords of that fee by the services due and by right accustomed. Clause for warranty. Hugh gave 6 marks sterling beforehand. Sealing clause. Witnesses: Roger Daieseie then bailiff of Coventry, Adam Russel, Peter Barun, Nicholas Crumpe, William Grauntpe, Thomas Symund, Ralf le Hunte, Thomas de Luesham, Roger the clerk and others. Coventry, Wednesday after the feast of St. Valentine the Martyr 30 Edward I.

Seal extant C.R.O. IB/30 EI/11

166 6 February 1306

Charter of William le Glasewrythe of Coventry giving to Henry de Merintone merchant of Coventry a certain messuage with appurtenances in Coventry lying in Much Park St. (*in majori vico Parci*) between the tenement of Hugh de Merintone on the one hand and the tenement of Simon le Bokelere on the other in width and extending in length from the royal highway (*a regia strata*) up to the ditch called the red ditch (*fossatum qui vocatur le Rededych*) as is fully manifest according to the metes and bounds made there; to be held to him, his heirs or assigns, of the chief lords of that fee by the services due and by right accustomed, freely and hereditarily. Clause for warranty. Henry gave £50 sterling beforehand. Sealing clause. Witnesses: Robert Baker (*Pistore*), William Graundpe, Hugh de M(er)inton', William de Schepeye, Peter Barun, William de Braundestone, Ralf le Hunte, Ralf de Tewe, Thomas Ballard, Henry de Barsham, John de Rydewar', Walter de M(er)inton', John Dobedy and others. Coventry, Sunday after the feast of the Purification of the blessed Mary 34 Edward I.

Seal missing C.R.O. IB/34 EI/2

DEAD LANE*

*See also 129, 353.

167 c.1270

Charter of Richard de Wynewik chaplain giving to Thomas the servant of the parson of Baginton (*servienti p(er)sone de Bathkynt'*) the entire lands with appurtenances which the grantor bought from Ralf Morcoc, Richard son of Roger Swaynesmon and John son of Claricia la Neulest(er) in the vill of Coventry, which lands are in Dead Lane (*in vic(u)lo qui appellatur dedelone*) opposite the house (*ex oppo(s)ito domus*) of Thomas Geliner in length and in width as the land purports; to be held to him, his heirs or assigns, of the grantor and his heirs freely [etc.] by rendering annually to the grantor, his heirs or assigns, a clove-gillyflower at Easter, and to Ralf Morcoc a gilly-flower at Easter, to Richard son of Roger Swaynesmon and his heirs ½d. at Easter, and to John son of Claricia and his heirs ½d. at Easter for all secular service [etc.]. Clause for warranty. Thomas gave 2 marks of silver beforehand. Sealing clause. Witnesses: Peter Baru(n)e, Nicholas de Barre, Robert the Miller (*molend'*), Augustinus Codiscoph, Thomas Geliner, John the Goldsmith (*aur(i)fab'*), Ralf Morcoc and many others.

Seal missing C.R.O. 2/60

168 c.1270

Charter of Thomas the servant of the parson of Baginton (*serviens persone de Bakinton'*) giving to Roger le Burs(er) and Alice his wife the entire land with appurtenances which he bought from Richard de Wynewyk lying in Dead Lane (*in vinculo qui vocatur Dedelane*) opposite the house (*ex opposito domus*) of Thomas le Geliner just as the charter which he has from the said Richard witnesses, in length and in width as is manifest according to the metes and bounds made there; to be held to them, their heirs or assigns, or to whomsoever and whensoever they will wish to give, sell or assign, in sickness and in health, of the grantor and his heirs freely [etc.] by rendering annually to the grantor and his heirs a clove-gillyflower at Easter, and to Ralf Morkoc and his heirs a clove-gillyflower, to Richard son of Roger Swanismon ½d., to Richard de Wynewyck a clove-gillyflower, and to John son of Claricia ½d. at Easter for all secular service [etc.]. Clause for warranty. Roger and Alice gave 20s. sterling of legal, new money beforehand. Sealing clause. Witnesses: Nicholas de la

Barre then bailiff, Thomas de Fakynham, Thomas de Barsam, Richard le Fermeiler, William Pain, Walter de Wynchelze, William Crumpe, Robert le Mouner, Robert le Cart(er), Peter de Arundel clerk and many others.

Seal extant C.R.O. 2/117

169 Early 1280s

Charter of Master Richard de Burton' and Petronilla his wife giving to Geoffrey le Lef' a curtilage with appurtenances which Ralf le Rasurer held in Dead Lane (*Le dedelone*) in Coventry beneath the Park (*sub p(ar)co*), which lies between the land the same Geoffrey held on the one hand and the land Matilda de Pinnelet held on the other in length and in width as the curtilage purports and according to the metes and bounds made there; to be held to him, his heirs or assigns, to whomsoever or whensoever (*q(ua)n(do)cumque*) he will wish to give, bequeath, sell or assign in sickness and in health of the grantors, their heirs or assigns, freely [etc.] by rendering annually 4d. of silver at the four terms of the year usual in the vill of Coventry for all secular service. Clause for warranty. Sealing clause for ½ mark cash (*denarior'*) which Geoffrey gave beforehand. Witnesses: Henry Baker (*pistor'*) then bailiff (*ball(iv)o tunc tempore*), Robert de Chilton', Thomas de Fackinham, William de Witele, William Haleward, Robert the Miller (*molendinar'*), William the Smith (*fabro*) and others.

2 seals missing W.R.O. DR 429/1
Endorsed: Hougo de grantha(m)

170 1280s

Charter of Geoffrey le Lef of Coventry giving to Richard le Hodere in Coventry a curtilage with appurtenances in Dead Lane (*in venella que vocatur le Dedelone*) in Coventry beneath the park (*sub parco*) which lies in width between the land Robert de Essceby once held on the one hand and the land Matilda Wale once held on the other and extends in length from the aforesaid lane up to the park ditch (*fossatum Parci*) according to the metes and bounds made there; to be held to him, his heirs or whatsoever assigns, well [etc.] of the chief lords of that fee by the services due and by right accustomed. Clause for warranty. Richard gave ½ mark of silver beforehand. Sealing clause. Witnesses: Henry Baker (*Pistore*) then bailiff of Coventry, Richer de Weston, Thomas Symund, Richard de Weston', William Grantpe, William de Wytele, Robert the Smith (*fabro*) and many others.

Seal extant W.R.O. DR 429/2
Endorsed: Hugo de grantha(m).

171 c.1290–1297

Charter of Geoffrey le Lef giving to Richard de Westone son of Richer de Weston' and Alice his wife, their heirs and assigns, a moiety of a curtilage once of Thomas le Hennemonger in Dead Lane, Coventry (*in le dedelone de Coventr'*) lying in width between the grantor's land on the one hand and the land of Thomas de Merston' baker (*pistoris*) on the other and extending in length from the royal highway of Dead Lane up to the ditch of Coventry Park (*a regali via del dedelone usque fossatum p(ar)ci de Coventr'*); to be held to them, their heirs or assigns, of the chief lords of that fee freely [etc.] by rendering annually to those same chief lords the service due and by right accustomed. Clause for warranty. Richard and Alice gave 6s. of silver beforehand. Sealing clause. Witnesses: Henry Baker (*pistore*) then bailiff, William le Parkere then coroner, Richer de Weston', William Grantpe, John de Mildenhale, Ralf le Hunte, Richard de Weston' and others.

Seal extant W.R.O. DR 429/3

172 16 March 1300

Charter of Richard de Dunnestable *le Hodere* living in Coventry (*manens in Coventr'*) giving to Thomas de Grantham soap-maker in Coventry (*in Coventr' le Savonner*) a curtilage in Dead Lane (*in venella que dicitur le Dedelone*) beneath Coventry Park (*subt(us) Parcu(m) de Coventr'*) lying in width between the land of Richard son of Richer de Weston' on the one hand and the land of Hugh le Hoser on the other and extending in length from the aforesaid lane (*venella*) up to the said park according to the metes and bounds made there; to be held with all appurtenances to him, his heirs or whatsoever assigns, well [etc.] of the chief lords of that fee by the services due and by right accustomed. Clause for warranty. Thomas gave a certain sum of money beforehand. Sealing clause. Witnesses: Anketell de Coleshul then bailiff of Coventry, Adam Russel, Peter Barun, Richard son of Richer, Hugh le Hoser, William de Wytele, Roger le Bruggewrithe, Robert the Smith (*Fabro*), Roger the clerk and others. Coventry, Wednesday after the feast of St. Gregory the Pope 28 Edward I.

Seal extant W.R.O. DR 429/7
Endorsed: Hugo de grantham

173 11 June 1300

Charter of Richard son of Richer de Weston' in Coventry giving to Thomas de Grantham in Coventry a curtilage with appurtenances in Dead Lane (*in venella que dicitur le Dedelone*) in Coventry towards the park (*Parcum*) of Sir Robert de Montalt (*monte alto*), namely that which lies between the land of the aforesaid Thomas on the one hand and the land of Thomas de Meryston' baker (*pistoris*) on the other and extends in length from the aforesaid lane (*venella*) up to the ditch (*fossatu(m)*) of the aforesaid park according to the metes and bounds made there; to be held to him, his heirs or whatsoever assigns, well [etc.] of the chief lords of the fee by the services due and by right accustomed. Clause for warranty. Thomas gave a certain sum of money beforehand. Sealing clause. Witnesses: Anketill de Coleshul then bailiff of Coventry, John Leofwyne then coroner, Adam Russel, William Grauntpe, Geoffrey de Donchirche, Richard de Weston' senior, Hugh le Hoser, William de Wytele, Roger the clerk and others. Coventry, Saturday the feast of St. Barnabas the Apostle 28 Edward I.

Seal extant W.R.O. DR 429/8
Endorsed: heugone de granham

EARL ST.*

*Earl St. here refers specifically to the section of the arterial road stretching from Broadgate eastwards to Earl's Mill Lane. However, the entire east-west axis of the town was in one sense 'the Earl's St.' as descriptions like 'Earl St. towards Broadgate' (59), 'Earl St. towards Smithford' (398, 400, 403, 404), 'Earl St. next to Smithford Bridge' (382), 'Earl St. outside Smithford Bar' (396), 'Earl St. towards Gosford' (259, 263, 295), and 'Earl St. at Gosford' (767.7) testify. Where such designations are given the deeds have been arranged under Broadgate, Smithford or Gosford as appropriate. A special problem attends deeds relating to the stretch of road between Much Park St. and Earl's Mill Lane which is variously described as Earl St. or Gosford St. Here, again, the deeds have been arranged according to the designation given. Occasionally, Earl St. is referred to as the high street (although it is not the only street to be so described) and not only when the property concerned lay in the section immediately to the east of Broadgate and later known as High St. See below 178, 257, 258.

For other references to Earl St. property see 59, 113, 155, 741; 767.6, .18, .19, .21, .24–.26, .43, .44, .50, .53, .57. See also *Langley Cartulary* Nos. 262, 263, 271, 276, 452.

174 c.1200–c.1215

Charter of Benjamin (*Bengeminus*) de Witelea giving to Walter the Brocher (*Brochero*) and his heirs, to be held of the grantor and his heirs in fee and inheritance, a third part of his land in Earl St. (*in vico Comitis*), namely the part nearer to Earl's Mill Lane (*vie que tendit versus molandinu(m) Comitis*) freely, quietly and honourably by rendering annually 4s. of silver at four terms of the year, namely 12d. at each of the feasts of St. Michael, St. Andrew, the Annunciation of St. Mary and the Nativity of St. John the Baptist for all secular service [etc.]. Walter gave 12d. to the grantor, and 12d. to Alice the grantor's wife. Witnesses: Nicholas son of Liulf, Miles Barba Ap(r)il(is), Nicholas de Smithesford', Roger the Chamberlain (*Camerario*), Richard de Wigornia, Stephen his son, Matthew son of Gundreas (*Gundree*), Geoffrey the Goldsmith (*aurifabro*), Ralf the scribe (*scriptore*), Richard de Lennis, Richard Botuluestan, John Joia, Roger Bagog', Elias (*Helia*) de Wicha, Robert de Pinelea, Geoffrey Gerebode, William de Montpedlers, Ralf his brother, Richard Want(er) and many others.

Seal extant G.H. 259

175 c.1210–c.1220

Charter of Geoffrey son of William the brother of Thedwus (*Thedwi*) giving to William son of Richard son of Fordwin the land in Earl St. (*in vico Comitis*) which

William the grantor's father held and the grantor afterwards held, namely the entire land which lies between the land Ywein son of Breton (*Bretonis*) held and the land which Thomas son of Richard de Turlaweston' the grantor's brother on his mother's side held in length and in width as the land purports; to be held to him and his heirs, of the grantor and his heirs, in fee and inheritance freely [etc.], by rendering annually 2d. of silver at four terms of the year, namely ½d. at each of the feasts of St. Michael, St. Andrew, St. Mary in March and St. John the Baptist for all secular service [etc.]. Clause for warranty. William gave 6 marks of silver and 10s. in recognition, and to Dusa (*Duse*) the grantor's wife a pair of leather boots and a ribbon (*unas botas de Cordubano et unam vittam de filo*). Witnesses: Richard de Wigorn', Matthew his brother, Richard de Aula, Robert the Vintner (*vinit'*), Leofwinus son of Jordan, Herbert his brother, Geoffrey de Wilnhal', William his brother, Hugh son of Martin, Vincent, Vincent his son, William Crude, Nicholas nephew (*nepote*) of Vincent, William de Lincoln', Ralf the Weaver (*textore*) and many others.

Seal extant W.R.O. 231

W.R.O. 232 is substantially as the above with the following differences: for Ywein son of Breton read Ywein son of Bretun; for Turlaweston' read Thurlaweston'; William gave 6 marks only in recognition; and the last 3 witnesses are absent. The seal is missing.

176 c.1215–c.1225

Charter of Nicholas son of Nicholas son of Liulf granting to William Crude and his heirs his land in Earl St. (*in vico Comitis*) which the grantee held of Nicholas the grantor's father, namely the land which lies between the land Nicholas the Carter (*caretarius*) held and Bayley Lane (*viam Balii*) in length and in width as the land purports; to be held to him and his heirs of the grantor and his heirs freely [etc.] and free from toll of horses and all custom (*solute a tolneto eq(u)oru(m) et omni consuetudine*), by rendering annually for all service and all demands 12d. of silver at four terms of the year, namely 3d. at each of the feasts of St. Michael, St. Andrew, St. Mary in March and St. John the Baptist. *Concessi etiam predicto Willelmo et heredibus suis in perpetuum h(abe)ndi duas vaccas in pastura mea pariter cum vaccis meis.* Clause for warranty. William gave 1 mark of silver in recognition. Witnesses: Richard de Aula, Richard de Wigorn', Viellus de Folkeshull', Richard de Hundelan', Swanus the Parker (*parcar'*), Hugh son of Martin, William Fordwin', Roger the Gardener (*Gardinario*), Adam Herre, Nicholas the Carter (*carectario*), William son of Helewis, Richard son of Richard son of Siward, Adam the clerk and many others.

Seal extant G.H. 267

177 Early 1230s

Gift and quitclaim by William de Barwe to God, the church of the blessed Mary and the monks of Stoneleigh (*stanleg'*) in pure and perpetual alms of 6d. rent in the vill of Coventry, namely from the land William son of Alexander held; so that the said monks should hold the aforesaid rent for ever together with the rent of 30d. which formerly was due to them [by the gift of Philip the grantor's brother][1] from the same land with all its appurtenances and liberties which pertained to the grantor or his heirs or in any way may be able to pertain from the said land as freely and quietly as any alms can be held. Sealing clause. Witnesses: Richard de Aula, Adam the Vintner (*vinitar'*), Richard the Goldsmith (*aurifabro*), Alexander Herlewin, Robert de Recham, William le Butter, Herbert Stok', Anketill son of Robert, Robert de Meleburn', Alexander de Crulfeld and many others.

Seal extant G.H. 270
Endorsed: in vico Comitis.

[1] Reading uncertain, some of the letters having peeled away.

178 Late 1230s–early 1240s

Charter of Herbert the Carter (*Karetarius*) of Coventry for the salvation of his soul, that of his wife and those of his ancestors and successors, giving to God, the church of St. Mary and the monks of Stoneleigh (*Stanleg'*) in free, pure and perpetual alms 12d. rent from the land and his messuage in Coventry, namely that which extends into the high street opposite the White Cellar (*de terra et mesuag' meo de coventr(e) illo scilicet quod se extendit in magnu(m) vicum ex opposito albi cellarii*) and is between the messuage of Randulph de Henel' and the messuage of Henry le Furner; to be held well [etc.] of the grantor and his heirs at the feast of All Saints. Clause for warranty. Clause for distraint for non-payment of rent. Witnesses: John son of Richard, William de Wilnehal', Osbert the clerk, William le Buttere, Anketyl' de Wykewan', Anketyl' son of Robert, Ralf the Miller (*molendinar'*), Robert de Retham and many others.

Seal missing P.R.O. A 10915
Endorsed: In vico Comitis

179 Late 1230s–early 1240s

Acknowledgement by Henry le Forner of Coventry that he is bound to render 8d. annually to the abbot and convent of Stoneleigh during the life of Petronilla, widow of Osbert Kempe. In return they will acquit him of the plea of dower which she has brought against him.

Noverint omnes ad quos presens scriptum pervenerit quod ego Henricus le Forner de Coventr' teneor reddere abbati et conventui de Stanl' tota vita Petronille que fuit uxor Osberti Kempe octo denar(ios) annuatim ad illos quatuor terminos quibus homines de Coventr' reddunt firmam suam de tenemento illo quod de eis teneo in Coventr' pro eo quod adquietaverunt me de placito illo de dote quo dicta Petronilla me implacitavit salva eis debita firma quam eis antea solvere consuevera(m). In cujus rei testimonium et securitatem hanc cartam eis fieri fecique sigilli mei impressione munivi. Hiis testibus Magistro Ricardo Vinetar(io) Osberto clerico Ricardo de Bouckeville Anketillo filio Roberti Roberto de Feugers Johanne de Stanl' Michaele de Hurst' et multis aliis.

P.R.O. E 315/41/146

180 1230s.

Charter of Henry the Dyer (*tinctor*) of Worcester (*Wigorn'*) with the permission and good will of Petronilla his wife giving to Robert Dale the land with appurtenances in Earl St. (*in vico Comitis*) in Coventry between the land Robert Gorsi held and the land Edith the widow of William the Carter (*carectarii*) held; to be held to him and his heirs, of the grantor and his heirs, freely and quietly with all appurtenances and liberties, by rendering annually 3s. of silver to be paid at four terms of the year according to the usage of Coventry for all service and exaction. Clause for warranty. Robert gave 3½ marks in recognition. Sealing clause. Witnesses: William de Wilnhal', Thomas his brother, Osbert the clerk, William the Butterer (*Buttario*),

Gilbert the Weaver (*textore*), Ralf the Serjeant (*serviente*), Richard de H[ ][1]e, Roger the Gardener (*Gardinario*), William Crude, Geoffrey his son, Osbert Kempe, Ralf the Miller (*molendinario*) and others.

Seal extant, fragmentary — Fuller II/16/1

[1] illegible.

181 — Late 1230s–1243

Sale and quitclaim by Osbert Kempe to Sir Nicholas son of Nicholas fitz Lithulph and his heirs of the entire land which he held in Earl St. (*in vico Comitis*) without any reservations by him or his heirs, namely the land which lies between the land William de Witele held on the one hand and the land John Hod held on the other according to the metes and bounds made there. Sir Nicholas gave 10 marks of silver beforehand. Witnesses: Osbert Duredent, Richard Herebert, Master Richard the Vintner (*Vinitar'*), John de Aula, Walter de Coventr', William de Aula, Richard de Blokevill, Richard Lewine, Nicholas Fordwin', John Fordwin', Ralf Croulebois, Reginald le M(er)cer and others.

Seal extant — C.R.O. IA/C13/27

182 — 1247–c.1250

Charter of Jurdan son of William Segrim giving to Edith his stepmother (*noverce*) the charter and gift which the said William the grantor's father made to her in name of dower from the stone messuage (*de mesuagio lapideo*) in Coventry in Earl St. (*in vico Comitis*) between the land Roger the clerk held and the land W. the Marshal (*Marescallus*) once held according to the metes and bounds made there; to be held to her all the days of her life freely [etc.] by the service of 4d. of silver at four terms of the year according to the usage of Coventry to be paid to the chief lord of the fee, and 8d. of silver to Robert de Stok' and his heirs similarly according to the usage of Coventry just as the charter which Edith has from the aforesaid W. the grantor's father purports. Clause for warranty. Edith gave 2 marks of silver. Sealing clause. Witnesses: Osbert the clerk, Robert de Cornlegh', Roger the clerk, Nicholas Forthwine, Robert de Denecastro, Robert Cordewan(er), Richard de St. Yvo, Ralf de Fillongel', Bertram Breton', John Sym', William Toly, Richard Scauerib, Hugh P(r)ude and others.

Seal missing — C.R.O. 2/82

183 — Late 1240s–early 1250s

Sale and quitclaim by Richard the Carpenter (*Carpu(n)tarius*) of *Gatham* to Michael le Oyler of Coventry of all right and claim in a messuage in the vill of Coventry with appurtenances which lies between the land of Nicholas Fortwin' on the one hand and the land of Robert Dale on the other; to be held to him, his heirs or assigns, as freely and quietly as the grantor at any time held, by rendering annually to the lords of that fee 2s. 6d. of silver at [four][1] terms of the year according to the custom of the vill of Coventry and a pair of gloves worth ½d. or a ½d. at Easter for all secular service [etc.]. Sealing clause. Witnesses: Anketinus de Vickewan', William de Folkishul', Peter Martin, Symon le Bocmonger', Robert Dale, William the Weaver (*textar'*) William de Gresel' and others.

Seal missing — W.R.O. 233

[1] There is a hole in the document.

184 Late 1250s–early 1260s

Sale, release and quitclaim by Michael Oliatte of Coventry to Nicholas Fortwyne of Coventry of all right and claim in the land with the buildings sited there and all appurtenances in Coventry, in Earl St. (*in vico Comit'*) between the land Richard the Weaver (*textor*) held on the one hand and the land Robert Dale once held on the other according to the metes and bounds made there; to be held to him, his heirs or assigns, freely [etc.] without contradiction, charge or demand by the grantor or his heirs. Nicholas gave 12s. of silver. Exclusion and sealing clauses. *Et ad majorem securitatem cart(as) et confirmat(iones) quas habui de dicta terra eidem Nicholao lib(er)avi.* Witnesses: Alexander de Glouc', Walter the White (*albo*) then bailiff, Pagan Pake, Nicholas ad Barr' clerk, John Beer, Roger the clerk, Peter Martin, Thomas Haldein, William de Therlauiston', William the White (*albo*) the weaver (*textor'*) Ralf le Butt(er)e, Roger the Dyer (*tintor'*) and others.

Seal extant W.R.O. 232.2

185 1250s

Charter of Richard son of Thomas Wint(er)king of Coventry giving to Stephen de Cleybrok weaver (*textori*) a moiety of his entire curtilage in Earl St., Coventry (*in vico Comitis de Coventr'*) which lies in width between the land Thomas de la Mine held on the one hand and the land William de Neuton' held on the other and extends in length from the aforesaid Earl St. (*a magno vico comitis predicto*) up to the ditch (*fossat(um)*) which is called *Hersomdich*, namely the moiety which is nearer to the land the aforesaid William de Neuton' held in length and in width as the said moiety purports according to the metes and bounds made there; to be held to him, his heirs or assigns, of the grantor and his heirs freely [etc.], by rendering annually 12d. of silver at the four terms of the year fixed in the vill of Coventry and ½d. at Easter for all secular service [etc.]. Clause for warranty. Stephen gave 1 mark of silver in recognition beforehand. *Et si contingat quod dictus Stephanus vel heredes sui vel ejus assignati pro aliquo delicto in m(isericord)ia mei vel heredum meorum cecid(er)int quieti eru(n)t per quatuor den(arios) sterlingor(um).* Sealing clause. Witnesses: Richard de Bok(er)vill' then bailiff, Pagan Pak', Alexander de Glov(er)nia, William the Weaver (*textor'*), Henry Dobedy, Thomas de la Mine, Hugh le Bretu(n) clerk and others.

Seal missing G.H. 283

186 1250s

Charter of Reginald the Merchant (*mercator*) of Coventry giving to Richard the Merchant (*mercatori*) of Coventry a certain part of his land in the vill of Coventry in Earl St. (*In vico Com(it)is*), namely the part with appurtenances which lies between the land of Richard de Wenga on the one hand and the land of Roger Haustin' on the other in length and in width according to how the land purports and according to the metes and bounds made there; to be held to him, his heirs or assigns, of the grantor and his heirs freely [etc.], by rendering annually 20s. of silver at four terms of the year according to the usage and custom of the vill of Coventry for all secular service [etc.]. Clause for warranty. Richard gave 1 mark of silver beforehand. Sealing clause. Witnesses: Richard de Blokevill', John Beyer, Pagan Pak', Walter the White (*Blundo*), Alexander de Glovernia, Godfrey le Mercer, Robert de Nortfolc, Benedict Floutar', William the Merchant (*m(er)cator'*), Warin the Merchant (*m(er)cator'*) and others.

Seal extant G.H. 281

Endorsed: Reginaldus m(er)c(er) filius Ormonis.

187 1250s

Charter of Richard de Walton' of Coventry giving to Sir Geoffrey de Langel a messuage with appurtenances in the vill of Coventry in Earl St. (*in vico Comitis*) between the house of William Sley on the one hand and the house which was of Stephen Vache on the other; to be held to him, his heirs or assigns, freely [etc.] without any reservation or reclaim by the grantor or his heirs, by rendering annually to the church of St. Michael of Coventry 6d. or 1lb. frankincense (*lib(er)i thuris*) at Christmas for all service and demand. Clause for warranty. Sir Geoffrey gave 1 mark of silver. Sealing clause. Witnesses: Anketill de Wikewan', Philip de Winchecumb', Pagan (*Pakano*) Pake, Walter the White (*blundo*) of Coventry, Alexander de Glov' of the same, William le Polet(er) of the same, Geoffrey de Wilenhal', William de Pinnel', Ranulf Caus and others.

Seal missing G.H. 275

188 1250s

Gift and quitclaim by Richard de Walton', son and heir of Richard de Walton' [his] father to Sir Geoffrey de Langel of all right and claim in a messuage with appurtenances in Coventry in Earl St. (*in vico Comitis*) between the house of William Sley on the one hand and the house which was of Stephen Vache on the other; to be held to Sir Geoffrey, his heirs and assigns, freely [etc.] just as the charter which the said Sir Geoffrey has from Richard the grantor's father testifies. Exclusion and sealing clauses. Witnesses: Anketill de Wykewan', Philip de Winchecumb', Pagan Pake of Coventry, Walter the White (*blundo*) of the same, Alexander de Gov' of the same, William le Polet(er) of the same, Geoffrey de Wilenhal', William le Pinneleg', John Beleteste of the same, Ranulf Caus and others.

Seal extant G.H. 276

189 c.1260

Gift and quitclaim by Matthew Tile of Coventry to Sir Geoffrey de Langel', chief lord of the fee, of the entire land and tenement [and] right and claim in the land and tenement which Richard de Walton' held of the grantor in the vill of Coventry; to be held to him, his heirs or assigns, in rents, escheats and all appurtenances which may or ought to fall to the grantor and his heirs. Exclusion clause. Geoffrey gave 5s. of silver beforehand. Sealing clause. Witnesses: Geoffrey de Wylenhal', Hugh de Stok', William de Pinnel', Anketill de Wikewin', John de Pont(e)f(r)acto, William le Blund, John Beer, Godfrey le M(er)c(er), Alexander de Glov' and others.

Seal missing G.H. 277

190 1250s

Charter of John the Weaver (*textor*) of Grove (*Grovia*) son of Symon del Phispot for himself and his heirs giving to Thomas Halden of Coventry his land (*unam terram meam*) in the vill of Coventry, in Earl St. (*in vico Comitis*) with all appurtenances namely the land which lies between the land of Henry le Cartesadeler towards the west on the one hand and the land of Henry de Rodinton' towards the east on the other as the land purports in length and in width and according to the metes and bounds made there; to be held to him, his heirs or assigns, of the grantor and his heirs freely [etc.], by rendering annually 10d. of silver at four terms of the year according to the usage and custom of the vill of Coventry and 2 hens for all secular service [etc.]. Clause for warranty. Thomas gave 30s. of silver fine (*in Gerismonia*).

Sealing clause. Witnesses: Richard de Blokevill', Pagan Pak', Walter the White (*blundo*), Reginald the Red (*Ruffo*), Alexander de Glov(er)nia, Symon le Bucmongere, John the Marshal (*marescall'*) of Daventry (*Davintr'*), William de Turlausto(n), Henry le Cartesadel(er), Thomas the Goldsmith (*aurifabr'*), Hugh the Lorimer (*Lorimar'*) and others.

Seal missing C.R.O. IA/EC12/15
Endorsed: de teneme(n)t' Haldein modo Pet(r)is Barun. Recipit illud Redditum.

191 Late 1250s–early 1260s
Sale and quitclaim by Thomas son of Osbert (*Osseb(er)ti*) of Coventry for himself and his heirs to Peter the Welshman (*Walenc'*) of Coventry, his heirs or assigns, of a certain curtilage with a certain barn (*orreo*) and free entrance and exit towards the highway (*mang(n)am viam*) pertaining to the said curtilage and barn namely that between the land of the said Peter on the one hand and the land of William de Bilnea on the other in the vill of Coventry in Earl St. (*in vico Comitis*); to be held of William de Bilneia and his heirs freely [etc.] by the service of 2s. of silver per annum at the four terms usual in Coventry for all secular service or demand. Exclusion and sealing clauses. Witnesses: Walter the White (*albo*) then reeve (*p(re)p(osi)to*), Roger the clerk, William le Polet(er), Hamo the Weaver (*textor'*), Hugh Breton', William Sley, Benedict le Fleut(er), Andrew the Merchant (*m(er)cator'*) and many others.

Seal missing C.R.O. IA/C21

192 Late 1250s–early 1260s
Charter of John le Furner of Coventry giving to Geoffrey Lonton a moiety of a certain messuage in Earl St. (*in vico Comitis*) which is opposite the hall (*ex opposito aule*) of Nicholas Liþulf and lies between the land of Robert Pope on the one hand and the land John Beer held on the other; to be held to him and his heirs or to whomsoever he will wish to give, sell or assign, of the grantor and his heirs, well and in peace, freely and quietly, by rendering annually 3s. of silver at the four terms of the year fixed in the vill of Coventry for all service [etc.]. Clause for warranty. Geoffrey gave a mark of silver beforehand. Sealing clause. Witnesses: Walter le Blund then bailiff, Roger the clerk, Peter Barun, Robert de Henl', Anketin(us) son of Roys, Robert Dale, John the Goldsmith (*aurifabro*), John Abbot, Robert Baret, Richard de Walton', Thomas de Henl', Hugh the clerk and others.

Seal missing Berkeley S324

193 Mid–late 1260s
Charter of William Sley of Coventry giving to John his son for his service a certain shop (*quandam shopam*) in Coventry with appurtenances where the said John used to have his cutler's shop (*tenere solebat cultellarium suum*) which lies in Earl St. next to the grantor's messuage (*in vico Comitis juxta mansum meum*) in length and in width according to the metes and bounds made there; to be held to him, his heirs or whatsoever assigns, of the grantor and his heirs freely [etc.], by rendering annually a clove-gillyflower at Easter for all secular service [etc.]. Warranty and sealing clauses. Witnesses: Robert de Chilton', Henry Baker (*pistore*) then bailiffs (*ball(iv)is*) in Coventry, Richard de Blokevile, Pagan Pake, Peter Barun, Nicholas ad Barram, Roger the Chamberlian (*Cam(er)ario*), Reginald de Catesby, Thomas the clerk and others.

Seal extant C.R.O. 2/159

194 Mid–late 1260s

Charter of Nicholas the Wheelwright (*Rotarius*) giving to Henry de Axiholem the entire land with appurtenances which he held in Earl St., Coventry (*in vico Comitis Coventr'*) which lies between the land Robert Dale once held on the west side and the land Roger le Harpour held on the east in length and in width according to the metes and bounds made there; to be held to him, his heirs or to whomsoever he will wish to give, sell or assign in sickness and in health of the grantor and his heirs freely [etc.], by rendering annually a pair of white gloves worth ½d. or ½d. at Easter and to the lords of the fee as the perpetual attorneys of the grantor and his heirs 2s. of silver at the four terms of the year usual in the vill of Coventry for all secular service [etc.]. Clause for warranty. Henry gave 11 marks of silver beforehand. Sealing clause. Witnesses: Richard Erneis, Robert de Chiltone, Pagan Pake, Nicholas ad Barram, William Uttyng, Richer de Weston', Thomas de Fakenham, Thomas de Barsham, Richard de Essebi, Benedict le Fleuter, William Crumpe, Thomas le Cotiler and others.

Seal extant C.R.O. IA/Misc. I/7

195 Mid–late 1260s

Gift and quitclaim by William le Polet(er) merchant (*mercator*) of Coventry without reservation or charge by himself or his heirs to John de Lodelawe of all right and claim in the entire land with buildings built there with all appurtenances which he had in Earl St., Coventry (*in vico Comit' Coventr'*) which was once of the tenement of Matthew son of Gundred' in length and in width as the land purports according to the metes and bounds made there, together with the entire land with appurtenances which the grantor bought from Robert Wythir in Park St., Coventry (*in vico Parci Coventr'*) which lies between Greyfriars' Lane (*viculum qui ducit versus fratres minor'*) and between the land Petronilla Cempe held in length and in width as is manifest according to the metes and bounds made there; to be held to him, his heirs or whatsoever assigns as freely and quietly as the grantor held of the lords of the fee by paying the same service, namely to Sir Nicholas de Segrave and his heirs ½ mark of silver at the four terms of the year usual and fixed in the vill of Coventry and to the heirs of Richard de Wygorn' 12d. of silver at the same terms for the aforesaid land in Earl St. (*in vico Comit'*), and to the lord prior of Coventry and his successors for the aforesaid land in Park St. (*In vico parci*) 12d. of silver at the aforesaid terms of the year and 2 hens at Christmas and the service of 1 man in Autumn for all service pertaining. John gave 30 marks of good, new and legal sterling. Exclusion and sealing clauses. Witnesses: Richard Ernis, Pagan Pake, Robert de Chilton', Nicholas ad Barram the clerk, Henry Baker (*pistor'*), Peter the Welshman (*Walenc'*), Bertram Bretun, Roger the Chamberlain (*Cam(er)ar'*), John Hingram', Hamo the Weaver (*textor'*), Augustine Godescop', John Rivel, John the Locksmith (*Locar'*) and many others.

Seal missing C.R.O. 2/29
Endorsed: Contra Par' de Coventr'

196 1270s

Sale, release and quitclaim by Christine once the daughter of Bateman (*Batemoni*) Haldeyn of Whitley (*Wyteley*) in her virginity and lawful power to John de Lodelawe of Coventry, his heirs and assigns, of all right and claim in the entire land with the buildings sited there and all appurtenances belonging to the said land in the vill of Coventry, in Earl St. (*in vico Comitis*), namely that which descended to her in name of inheritance from (*ex parte*) Alice de Wilnale once her mother and which lies in width between the land Nicholas le Bokervile held on the one hand and the royal highway (*viam regalem*) on the other and in length from the lane (*venella*) which is called *le Parkestret* [on the one hand] up to the land John Anketell held on the other; to be held as freely as the grantor held without demand, charge or contradiction by him or his heirs. Exclusion clause. John, his heirs and assigns, are to render annually to the lords of the fee, namely to the prior of Coventry and his successors, 8d. of silver at the four terms of the year fixed and usual in the vill of Coventry for all secular service [etc.]. John gave 10 marks of silver beforehand. Sealing clause. Witnesses: Henry Baker (*pistore*) then bailiff, Robert de Chilton', Geoffrey Luntoun, Richard le Brocher, Richard de Asseby, William de Egesfend, John Payn the clerk and others.

Seal missing C.R.O. IA/C13/26
Endorsed: Carta de alba aula
Contra Prior' de Coventr'

197

30 November 1269

Agreement made at the feast of St. Andrew the Apostle 1269 A.D. whereby John son and heir of Alexander de Glouc' once a burgess (*Burg'*) of Coventry in his free power has leased, demised and granted to Sir Nicholas de Segrave, knight, 10s. annual rent [in][1] the vill of Coventry for the 5 marks of silver which the said Alexander, his father, owed to Sir Nicholas for corn (*blad'*) purchased from him from Itchington (*Ikynton'*), to be taken at the four terms of the year usual and fixed in the vill of Coventry from a certain tenement in Earl St. (*in vico Comit'*) which is between the land Henry de Rodinton' held on the one hand and the land Robert the Carpenter (*Carp(e)ntar'*) held on the other; to be held to him, his heirs or assigns, for a term of 12 years freely [etc.], by rendering annually to the same John and his heirs a rose flower at the feast of St. John the Baptist, and to the lords of that fee as the perpetual attorneys of the said John and his heirs 2s. of silver at the four terms of the year usual and fixed in the vill of Coventry for all service. Should the said Sir Nicholas, his heirs or assigns, have expended any necessary costs in repairs or maintenance to the said tenement or in the houses sited there during the term through the default of the said John or his heirs, they will be recompensed for the entire costs by the view of upright and law-worthy men during the said term, or they may hold the said rent with all appurtenances beyond the aforesaid term without contradiction by anyone until the entire costs have been satisfied. Should the said Sir Nicholas, his heirs or assigns or anyone holding the said tenement of them, construct any new building (*novu(m) scit(um)*) upon the said tenement within the term they will be allowed to take it away entirely at the end of the term without contradiction by anyone, unless the said John and his heirs should wish to satisfy the entire costs expended by which it may remain. Should the said John or his heirs wish to sell the rent with all appurtenances within the said term or at the end of it or to lease it further, the said Sir Nicholas, his heirs or assigns, will have first refusal should they be willing to give as much as any other. Mutual sealing clause. Witnesses: Richard de Bok(er)vil', Pagan Pak', John de [Lodel]ow[e][1], Richer de Weston', Reginald de Catisby, Richard le Fermiler and others.

Indented
Seal extant G.H. 285

[1] There is a hole here. The document is in fact damaged in several places.

198

Late 1260s

Charter of Richard de St(re)tona giving to Richard le Fermiler of Coventry a certain part (*quamdam partem*) of his land with the buildings built there in the vill of Coventry in Earl St. (*in vico Com(i)t'*) between the land John le Furner once held on the one hand and the land Ralph the Red (*Ruffus*) of Pinley (*Pynel*) held on the other in length and in width as is manifest according to the metes and bounds made there; to be held to him and his heirs or to whomsoever he will wish to give, bequeath, sell or assign in sickness and in health freely [etc.], by rendering annually as the perpetual attorneys of the grantor or his heirs to the lords of the fee the service due and accustomed, namely 26d. at the four terms of the year usual and fixed in the vill of Coventry, and to the grantor and his heirs a pair of gloves at Easter worth 1d. or 1d. *ad volumptatem solventis* for all secular service [etc.]. Clause for warranty. Richard gave 10 marks of good, new and legal sterling beforehand. Sealing clause. Witnesses: Richard de Bok(er)vil', Robert de Chilton', Richard Ernis, Henry Baker (*pistor'*), Peter the Welshman (*Walenc'*), Thomas de Fak(en)ham, John de Lodelowe, William Hutting, Ralf the Red (*ruffo*) and others.

Seal missing C.R.O. 2/66

199 Late 1260s

Charter of brother Richard called abbot (*dictus abbas*) and the convent of Stoneleigh (*Stanl'*), for themselves and their successors, giving to William de Egisfeld merchant of Coventry (*mercatori Covi(n)tr'*) and Alice his wife, certain land in the vill of Coventry with the buildings built there in Earl St. (*in vico Comit'*) which Matilda Stok held of the grantors for the term of her life and which they had of the gift of Osbert Kempe, lying between the land William Wynt(er) once held on the one hand and the land John Hod once held on the other in length and in width as is manifest according to the metes and bounds made there; to be held with all appurtenances to them, their heirs or whatsoever assigns, of the grantors and their successors freely [etc.], by rendering annually 2s. 8d. of silver at the four terms of the year fixed in the vill of Coventry and a pair of white gloves at Easter worth ½d. or ½d. at the will of the payer for all secular service and custom, suits of court(s) and all other demands, plaints and petitions pertaining to them or their successors. Clause for warranty. William and Alice gave 20 marks of good, new and legal sterling beforehand. Sealing clause. Witnesses: Pagan Pak(e), Richard de Bok(er)vil', Peter the Welshman (*Walenc'*), Nicholas ad Barr' clerk, Robert the Miller (*molend'*), Thomas de Fakinh(am), Richard de Esseby, Richer de Weston', Richard le Fermiler' and others.

Seal missing P.R.O. D 9016

For Abbot Richard see below 386n.

200 Late 1260s or early 1270s

Charter of William the Chaplain (*Capell(anu)s*) son of William the Weaver (*Textor'*) of Coventry giving to Adam del Hay clerk a messuage with appurtenances in the vill of Coventry in Earl St. (*in vico Comit'*), namely that which lies between the land of Richard the Weaver (*Textor'*) on the one hand and the land of Adam the clerk on the other in length and in width as is manifest according to the metes and bounds made there; to be held to him, his heirs or assigns, and to whomsoever or whensoever he will wish to give, sell, assign or bequeath by will (*in testamento*) by hereditary right, of the grantor, his heirs or assigns, freely [etc.], by rendering annually to the chief lord of that fee 20d. at the four terms of the year usual and fixed in the vill of Coventry, and to the grantor, his heirs or assigns, a pair of gloves at Christmas worth ½d. for all services [etc.]. Adam gave 3 marks of good and legal sterling of new money (*nove monete*) beforehand for his great business (*ad meum magnum negocium*). Warranty and sealing clauses. Witnesses: Henry Dobedi, Pagan Pake, William the

White (*albo*) weaver (*Textor'*), Roger de Halles, William de Watford, Richard the Weaver (*Textor'*), Robert the Weaver (*Textor'*), William Hauþorn, Walter de Wygorn', William Swyn, Simon del P(ar)lur, Vincent the Goldsmith (*Wincent' Aurifabr'*), Richard the scribe (*Scriptor'*) and many others.

Seal extant C.R.O. IA/Misc.I/21

201 Late 1260s–early 1270s

Charter of Roger de Kesewych' of Coventry giving to William Crumpe of Coventry and Dyonisia his wife for 5 marks of silver which they gave beforehand his entire land with appurtenances in the vill of Coventry in Earl St. (*in vico Comitis*), namely that which lies between the land Robert de Northfolch' held on the one hand and the land the same William held on the other in length and in width as it purports according to the metes and bounds made there; to be held to them, their heirs or whatsoever assigns, and to whomsoever they will wish to give, sell, bequeath or in any way assign *divisim aut conjunctim* freely [etc.] by rendering annually to the lords of whom the grantor held for him and his heirs as their perpetual attorneys the rent due and accustomed, namely 2d. of silver at the four terms of the year fixed and customary in the vill of Coventry and a pair of gloves worth ½d. or ½d. at Easter *pro solvent' voluntate* for all secular service [etc.]. Warranty and sealing clauses. Witnesses: Robert de Chilton', Peter the Welshman (*Walens'*), John de Lodelawe, Richard de Asseby, Benedict le Fleut(er), Robert de Northfolch', Andrew le M(er)c(er), Richard le Brocher, William Scot, Thomas de Barsham, Henry Wandelard, Hugh le Bretun, Bony le Mercer and others.

Seal extant C.R.O. IA/EC13/73

202 Late 1270s–early 1280s

Remise and quitclaim by Nicholas de Kenelwrthe, for himself and his heirs, to William Crumpe of Coventry 12d. hitherto pertaining (*pertinent' hactenus*) to the grantor annually from the land lying between the land of the abbot of Combe (*Cumba*) on the one hand and the land of Roger de Kesewich on the other, with exclusion of future claims; by William, his heirs or assigns, rendering annually to the grantor and his heirs a clove-gillyflower at Christmas and to the lords of the fee 12d. of silver at the four terms of the year fixed in the vill of Coventry for all secular service, exaction, suit of court and demand. Clause for warranty. William gave 1 mark of silver beforehand. Sealing clause. Witnesses: Robert de Chilton' then bailiff, Pagan Pake, Thomas de Fakenham, Thomas de Barsham, Robert de Northfolk, Benedict le Fleut', Richard de Assebi and many others.

Seal missing C.R.O. IA/EC12/13

203 Late 1270s–early 1280s

Charter of Alice daughter of William Crumpe of Coventry in her virginity and lawful power giving to Henry de Muschote a messuage with appurtenances in Earl St., Coventry (*in vico Comitis de Coventr'*) which is between the land of William Crumpe the grantor's father on the one hand and the land of John Kidelomp on the other in length and in width according to the metes and bounds made there; to be held to him, his heirs and assigns, and to whomsoever he will wish to give, bequeath, sell or assign in sickness and in health freely [etc.], by rendering annually 8s. of silver at the four terms of the year usual and fixed in the vill of Coventry for all secular service [etc.]. Clause for warranty. Henry gave ½ mark of silver beforehand.

Sealing clause. Witnesses: Robert de Chilton' then bailiff of Coventry, Richard le Brocher, Adam Russel, Henry Ballard, Richard de Esseby, William Crumppe, John Kidelump, John Scot and others.

Seal extant C.R.O. 2/42

204 Early 1270s

Gift and quitclaim by Godfrey de Northfolchia for himself and his heirs to Adam Russel of all right and claim in a land (*una terra*) with buildings sited there in the vill of Coventry in Earl St. (*in vico Comitis*), namely in the land which lies between the land of the abbot and convent of Combe (*Cumba*) on the one hand and the land which Godfrey le Mercer held on the other and lies in length from the said Earl St. (*a dicto vico Comitis*) up to the land Richard de Assebi held with exclusion of future claims; to be held to him, his heirs or assigns, to whomsoever he will wish to give, bequeath, sell or assign, in sickness and in health, freely [etc.], by rendering annually as the perpetual attorneys of the grantor and his heirs to the lords of the fee the rent owed and accustomed, namely to Sir Geoffrey de Langeleye, his heirs or assigns, 2s. 6d. of silver at the four terms of the year fixed and usual in the vill of Coventry and 1 man throughout an entire day (*per unicum diem*) in Autumn and 1 hen at Christmas for all secular service, exaction, suit of court and demand. Adam gave 30 marks of silver beforehand. Sealing clause. Witnesses: Peter Barun then bailiff, Robert de Chilton', Henry Baker (*pistor'*), Thomas de Fakenham, Pagan Pake, Richer de Weston', Richard the Brooch-maker (*firmaclar'*), Thomas de Barsham, William de Eggisfeld, William Crumpe, Richard de Assebi, William Scot and others.

Seal extant P.R.O. A 4330

205 1 May 1274

Confirmation by Felice daughter of Godfrey de Kovintre burgess of Gloucester (*Burgens' Glouc'*) in her full power, to Adam Russel of Coventry (*Kovintre*) of the sale which she made to Adam of certain land in Coventry (*Kovintre*) as contained in her charter of enfeoffment, namely of the land which lies between the land of the abbot of Combe (*Chumbe*) on the one hand and the land of Godfrey le M(er)cer on the other. *Et si contingat me in aliquo tempore contra cartam meam et contra istam confirmacionem venisse vel placitum de dicta terra movisse tunc volo et concedo quod Ball(ivi) Glouc' qui pro tempore fuerint me distring(ant) de die in diem ad voluntatem dicti Ade quousque de placito inter nos moto cessaver(it) et quod dicti Ball(ivi) habeant pro qualibet dictriccione super me facta vel facienda occasione predicta dimid(iam) marc(am) argenti et nichilominus quod ep(is)c(opus) Wygorn' et sui offic(ialis) de die in diem per censuram ecclesiasticam me conpellant donec de dicto placito cessaver(it). Et ad hec omnia predicta fideliter observanda affidavi et sacramentum corp(or)ale prestiti, et ad majorem securitatem presenti scripto sigillum meum apposui.* Witnesses: Robert the clerk (*cler'*), Alexander de Bykenour' then bailiffs of Gloucester (*tunc Ball' Glouc'*), John the Cornishman (*cornubiens'*), Walter de Saundon', Walter de la Berwe, Roger F(er)agu, Walter de Assfeld, Roger Russel, William de Hupton' the serjeant of Gloucester (*tunc servient' Glouc'*) and others. Tuesday next before the feast of St. John ante portam latinam in the year of grace 1274.

Seal extant P.R.O. A 4329

206 Early 1270s

Charter of Adam Haldeyn of Coventry for himself and his heirs giving to John de Lodelawe 4d. annual rent to be taken from a seld (*selda*) which the prior of Kenilworth (*Kenelworth*) held and which lies between the land Geoffrey Luntoun held in the vill of Coventry in Earl St. (*in vico Comit'*) on the one hand and the lane (*venellam*) leading to the hall (*Aulam*) once of Master Walter le Buttor' with a meadow lying in Spon field (*in campo de Spaune*) between the grantor's lands on both sides and which abuts (*habuttat*) from the meadow of Roger Saretin towards Asthill (*Asthul*) in length and in width as is manifest according to the metes and bounds made there; to be held to him, his heirs or whatsoever assigns or to whomsoever he will wish to give, bequeath, sell or assign in sickness and in health of the grantor and his heirs freely [etc.] by rendering annually a clove-gillyflower at Easter for all secular service, exaction, claim, suit of court and demand. Clause for warranty. John gave 40s. of silver beforehand. Sealing clause. Witnesses: Peter Barun then (*tunc tempore*) bailiff, Robert de Chilton', Henry Baker (*pistor'*), Pagan Pake, John Minoth, Roger the Chamberlain (*camerar'*), Thomas Pavey and many others.

Seal extant C.R.O. 1A/C2
Endorsed: Carta de terra haldeyn ubi Christiana Pavey manebat.

207 1270s

Charter of John le Fleut(er) and Alice his wife with mutual consent giving to Peter the Welshman (*Walensi*) of Coventry for 2s. which he gave beforehand certain land with appurtenances in Coventry in the street called Earl St. (*in vico dicto Comitis*) namely that which lies between the grantor's land and the land of Geoffrey de Langeley on the one hand and the land of the said Peter on the other in length and in width as the land purports according to the metes and bounds made there, saving however to the grantors and their heirs access to their house and land as far as the gate (*aeysiamento vie ad domum et terram nostram usque ad portam predicti Petri*); to be held to him, his heirs or assigns, of the grantor and his heirs freely [etc.], by rendering annually 2s. of silver at the four terms of the year usual and fixed in the vill of Coventry for all secular service [etc.]. Warranty and sealing clauses. Witnesses: John de Lodelawe then bailiff, Robert de Chilton', Richard de Exeby, Richard le Fermailer, William Crompe, Gilbert de Longedon', William le Pelter, John le Cumbere, Walter the clerk and others.

2 seals missing C.R.O. 2/25

208 1270s

Charter of Brother William the prior and the convent of Kenilworth (*Kenillewrthe*) with the unanimous assent of their chapter giving to Roger le Burser and Alice his wife of Coventry the entire land with appurtenances in the vill of Coventry in Earl St. (*in vico Comit'*) which lies in width between the land Henry Sparewe once held on the one hand and the land Ranulph de Henle once held on the other and extends in length from the aforesaid Earl St. (*vico Comitis*) up to the land Richard de Esseby once held as the land purports according to the metes and bounds made there; to be held to them, their heirs or whatsoever assigns except to men of religion or to the Jews of the grantors and their successors freely [etc.], by rendering annually to them as the chief lords of the fee 4s. sterling at four terms of the year, namely 12d. at each of the feasts of St. Michael, St. Andrew the Apostle, the Annunciation of the blessed Mary and the Nativity of St. John the Baptist for all secular service and suits of court pertaining to them, saving however the rents and whatsoever services due and accustomed to others for which the aforesaid Roger and Alice, their heirs and assigns, will be answerable (*erunt responsur'*) in the future. Warranty and sealing clauses. Witnesses: Henry Baker (*pistor'*), John de Lodelowe then bailiffs (*ball'*),

Robert de Chiltron',[1] Thomas de Frakenham[1], Richard le Brocher, Thomas de Barsham, William de Egesfend, Richard de Esseby, William Cru(m)pe and many others.

Seal missing C.R.O. 2/113

[1] sic

209 1270s

Charter of Richard de Hessebi of Coventry giving to Roger le Burcer of the same vill a certain piece (*placiam*) of his land which is behind the curtilage (*retro curtilagium*) of the aforesaid Roger and is of the same width as the house of the said Roger sited at the end of the aforesaid curtilage (*et continet in latitudine sicut domus dicti Rogeri sita in extremitate predicti curtilagii*), namely the piece of land which lies between the land the same Richard held on the one hand and the land Thomas de Baresham held on the other in length and in width according to the metes and bounds made there; to be held to him, his heirs or assigns, or to whomsoever and whensoever he will wish to give, sell, bequeath or assign, in sickness and in health of the grantor and his heirs freely [etc.] by rendering annually a consound (*consolidam*) at the feast of the Nativity of St. John the Baptist for all secular service [etc.]. Clause for warranty. Roger gave 40s. of silver beforehand. Sealing clause. Witnesses: Robert de Chilton', Gerard de Alespaþe, Richard le Formailer, Thomas de Baresham, William Crompe, John Scot, Adam Ruscel, Adam le Blond, Richer de Weston' and many others.

Seal extant Fuller II/16/2

210 1270s

Charter of John son of Adam the clerk of Coventry, for himself and his heirs, giving to Thomas de Fakinham a certain tenement in the vill of Coventry in Earl St. (*in vico Comitis*) which is called the White Cellar (*album celariu(m)*) with the solar (*solario*) and all appurtenances which lies between the land Walter Bacun once held on the one hand and Earl St. (*magnum vicum Comitis*) on the other and between the land of the said Thomas and Lower Park St. (*inferiorem vicum parci*) in length and in width according to the metes and bounds made there, together with 5s. annual rent which the said Thomas used to render to the grantor from his inner cellar (*de interiore celario suo*) and from the land in Lower Park St, which lies between the aforesaid cellar and the land of the aforesaid Walter Bacun; to be held to him, his heirs or assigns, or to whomsoever he will wish to give, sell or bequeath except to men of religion or to the Jews of the grantor and his heirs freely [etc.], by rendering annually 10s. of silver and to the lords of the fee 3s. at the four terms of the year usual and fixed in the vill of Coventry for all secular service, suits of courts, customs and demands pertaining. Clause for warranty. Thomas gave 40s. of silver beforehand. Witnesses: John de Lodelawe then bailiff, Robert de Chilton', Henry Baker (*pistore*), Pagan Pake, Peter le Waleys, Richard le Firma(i)ler, William de Egesfeud, Richard de Esseby, Thomas de Barsam, Adam Russel, Henry de Haxholm, Boni le Mercer, Walter de Winchelse and many others.

Seal extant C.R.O. 2/55b

211 Late 1270s–early 1280s

Charter of John son of Adam the clerk of Coventry giving to Henry Baker (*pistori*) of Coventry 10s. of silver annual rent to be taken in the vill of Coventry in Earl St. (*in vico Comitis*) from the White Cellar (*albo Celario*)[1] and the rent he used to receive from Thomas de Fakenham of Coventry, which cellar lies between Park St. (*vicul' parci*) on the one hand and the land Alexander de Glovernia held on the other as it purports; to be held to him, his heirs and assigns, of the grantor and his heirs freely [etc.], by rendering annually a clove-gillyflower at Easter for all secular service [etc.]. Clause for warranty. Henry gave 5 marks of silver beforehand. Sealing clause. Witnesses: Alexander the Vintner (*vinetar'*), Robert de Chilton' then bailiff (*ballivo*), Thomas de Barsam, Henry Ballard, Richard de Esseby, William Crompe, Peter de Egesfend, Richard le Brocher junior, Richer de Weston and others.

Seal extant — C.R.O. IA/C90

[1] followed by *quod quid' Celar'*

212 — Early 1280s

Charter of Thomas de Fackinham giving to Robert de Clother the entire land with the houses sited there and all appurtenances which Alexander de Glov(er)nia once held in Earl St., Coventry (*in vico Comitis de Coventr'*) which lies between the land Henry le Noreys once held on the one hand and the cellar (*celarium*) which is called the White Cellar (*Album Celarium*) on the other in length and in width as the land purports according to the metes and bounds made there. Moreover he has granted to the same Robert a certain tenement which is called the White Cellar (*Album Celarium*) with the solar (*solario*) pertaining and all appurtenances in the aforesaid street which lies between the land Alexander de Glov(er)nia once held on the one hand and Much Park St. (*majorem vicum parci*) on the other and extends in length from the aforesaid Earl St. (*a vico Com' antedicto*) up to the land once of Agnes daughter of Walter Bakun' in length and in width as the land purports according to the metes and bounds made there; to be held to him, his heirs or assigns, or to whomsoever or whensoever he will wish to give, bequeath, sell or assign in sickness and in health of the grantor his heirs or assigns, freely [etc.] by rendering annually to the lords of the fee as the grantor's perpetual attorney the rent due and accustomed, namely 5s. to the heirs of Sir Geoffrey de Longeley for the land once of Alexander de Glov(er)nia and 3s. of silver to the heirs of Sir Robert de Montalt (*mont' alto*) at the four terms of the year usual in the vill of Coventry and[1] for the cellar with the aforesaid solar, and 10s. of silver to the grantor at the aforesaid terms for all secular services [etc.]. Clause for warranty. Robert gave 46 marks of silver beforehand. Sealing clause. Witnesses: Robert de Chiltun then bailiff, Alexander the Vintner (*vinitar'*), John Thole, Walter Bakun then coroner, Richer de Westun', Adam Russel, Richard de Esscheby, Richard de la Muyre, Ralf le Hunte, Henry Ballard, Thomas de Barsham and others.

Seal missing — C.R.O. 2/111

[1] sic

213 — 1280s

Remise and quitclaim by Robert de Clother to Henry Baker (*pistore*)[1] and Adam Russel of Coventry of all right and claim in the entire land with the houses sited there and all appurtenances which lies between the land Henry le Noreys once held in Earl St. (*in vico Comitis*) on the one hand and the cellar (*Celariu(m)*) which is called *Wyteceler* on the other in length and in width as the land purports according to the metes and bounds made there. Moreover he has remised and quitclaimed all right and claim in a certain tenement which is called the White Cellar (*album Celariu(m)*) with a solar (*Solario*) and with all its appurtenances in Earl St. (*in vico Comitis*) and which lies between the land Alexander de Glov(er)nia once held on the one hand and Much Park St. (*majorem vicum parci*) on the other and extends in length from the aforesaid Earl St. (*a vico Com' antedicto*) up to the land of Agnes Bakun daughter of

Walter Bakun in length and in width according to what is manifest according to the metes and bounds made there; to be held to them, their heirs or assigns, freely [etc.] by rendering annually to the lords of the fee the rent due, namely 5s. of silver to the heirs of Sir Geoffrey de Long' for the land once of Alexander de Glov(er)nia and to the heirs of Sir Robert de Montalt (*monte alto*) 3s. of silver, and to the aforesaid Henry Baker (*pistori*), his heirs or assigns, 10s. of silver at the four terms of the year usual in Coventry for all service. Exclusion and sealing clauses. Witnesses: Alexander the Vintner (*vinitario*), Robert de Chiltun, Thomas Moubray, John Pihod, Richer de Westun, Richard de Westun, Richard de Esscheby, Thomas de Barsham, Anketell the clerk and others.

Seal extant C.R.O. 2/55a

[1] sic

See also 144.

214 Late 1280s

Remise and quitclaim by Alice widow of Thomas de Fakenham merchant (*mercatoris*) to Henry Baker (*pistori*) of Coventry and Adam Russel of all right and claim by reason of dower in the entire tenement which was once of the aforesaid Thomas her husband in Earl St. (*in vico Comitis*) in Coventry between the land Richard le Brocher once held on the one hand and Much Park St. (*majorem vicum parci*) on the other; to be held to them, their heirs or assigns freely [etc.]. Exclusion clause. Henry and Adam gave 6 marks sterling beforehand. Sealing clause. Witnesses: Alexander le Vineter, Robert de Stoke, Robert de Chilton', Walter Bacun, Thomas le Moubray, John Tole, Richer de Weston', Richard de Essceby, Richard de Weston', Richard de la Muyre, John de Langeleye, Roger the clerk and others.

Seal missing C.R.O. 1A/C13/21

215 Late 1270s–early 1280s

Remise and quitclaim by Robert de Clother to Henry Baker (*pistore*)[1], Agnes his wife, Adam Russel and Alice his wife, of all right and claim in the entire land with the house sited there and all appurtenances in Earl St., Coventry (*in vico Comitis de Coventr'*) between the land Richard the Brooch-maker (*firmacularius*) held on the one hand and the land Thomas de Fakinham held on the other in length and in width according to what purports according to the metes and bounds made there; to be held with all the buildings sited there and all appurtenances to them and their heirs or whatsoever assigns freely [etc.], by rendering annually to the lords of that fee 7s. of silver at the four terms of the year usual in Coventry for all secular service [etc.]. Exclusion and sealing clauses. Witnesses: Robert de Chiltun, Alexander the Vintner (*vinitario*), Thomas le Moubray, John Pihod, John de Fillung', Richard de Esscheby, Richer de Westun', Richard de Westun, Thomas de Barsham, Anketell de Colishul clerk and others.

Seal extant C.R.O. 2/87

[1] sic

216 1280s

Remise and quitclaim by Margery widow of Ralf le Turnur of Gloucester (*Gloucestre*), for herself and her heirs to Henry Baker (*pistor'*) and Adam Russel', and Agnes and Alice their wives, of all right and claim in the entire land with the houses sited there and all appurtenances in Earl St., Coventry (*in vico Comitis Coventr'*) between the land Thomas de Fakenham once held on the one hand and the land Richard le Brochere once held on the other in length and in width as the land purports according to the metes and bounds made there; to be held to them, their heirs or whatsoever assigns, freely [etc.]. Exclusion and sealing clauses. Witnesses: Alexander the Vintner (*vinetar'*) of Coventry, Robert de Chilton', Richer de Weston', Thomas le Moubrey, John Tole, Anketell de Colishull, William called (*dicto*) Galewey the clerk and others.

Seal extant C.R.O. IA/C50

217 1270s

Charter of Margery le Noreys once the daughter of Henry le Noreys of Coventry, in her widowhood and lawful power, giving to Ralf le Torneur and Margery his wife her entire land which she had in name of the inheritance of her father Henry le Noreys, namely the land with the buildings built there which lies between the land Henry de Lilleburn' held of Robert de Northfolch in Earl St. (*in vico Comitis*) on the one hand and the land Thomas de Fakenham held on the other and extends in length from the said street up to the land Richard Hors once held, and the land with the buildings sited there which is between the land of Thomas de Fakenham in Park St. (*in vico parci*) on the one hand and the land Richard Hors once held on the other and which extends from the said street up to the town ditch (*fossatum ville*), and a garden (*Gardin(um)*) in Earl's Mill Lane (*in venella molendini Comit'*) which lies between the land William Payn once held on the one hand and the land of Nicholas Jori on the other and extends in length from the said lane (*venella*) up to the land of Nicholas de Canel; to be held to them, their heirs or assigns, or to whomsoever they will wish to give, sell, bequeath or assign of the grantor and his heirs freely [etc.], by rendering annually to the lords of the fee as the grantor's perpetual attorney the rent due and accustomed, and to the grantor and her heirs 10s. of silver at the four terms of the year fixed in the vill of Coventry for all secular service [etc.]. Clause for warranty. Ralf and Margery gave 20s. beforehand. Sealing clause. Witnesses: John de Lodelawe then (*tunc tempore*) bailiff, Robert de Chilton', Henry Baker (*pistor'*), Peter le Waleys, Pagan Pake, Richard Firmaclar', Thomas de Barsham, William Crumpe and many others.

Seal extant C.R.O. 2/47

218 Late 1270s

Charter of John called (*dictus*) Payn of Coventry priest (*presbit(er)*) giving to Henry Baker (*pistori*) and Agnes his wife of Coventry his entire land with all the buildings and the new chamber sited there (*cum omnibus edificiis et nova camera suprasitis*) and with all appurtenances in the vill of Coventry, in Earl St. (*in vico Comitis*), namely that which lies between the land Thomas Marye held on the one hand and the land which the grantor and Nicholas de Allyspath' held on the other in length and in width as is manifest from the aforesaid street up to the garden (*Gardinu(m)*) of the prior of Coventry according to the metes and bounds made there; to be held to them, their heirs and assigns, of the lords of that fee from whom the grantor held as freely and quietly and by the same warranty (*waranciam acquietanciam et defensionem*) and by the same service as is contained in the charter concerning the said land handed to the same Henry and Agnes by the grantor's hand. Sealing clause. Witnesses: Gerard de Allyspath' then bailiff of Coventry, Robert de Chilton', Hugh le Hoser, Peter the Welshman (*Walens'*), Richard le Brocher', William Utting, Rycher de Weston', William de Eggysfeld', Thomas de Fakynham, Adam Colbrond, Richard de Asseby, Thomas de Barsham, Robert the Miller (*molendinar'*), William Crumpe, Hugh le Bretun and others.

Seal extant G.H. 290

Endorsed: Carta de tenemento Robertus Marie ten' [in vico] comitis xiiid.

219 1270s

Charter of Roger once the son of John Habertas of Coventry giving to Henry called Baker (*dicto pistori*) of Coventry the entire land in the vill of Coventry in Earl St. (*in vico comitis*) with buildings sited there and all appurtenances which lies between the land Richard le Gardener held on behalf of his wife on the one hand and the red ditch (*rubeum fossatum*) on the other in length and in width as the land purports according to the metes and bounds made there; to be held to him, his heirs or whatsoever assigns, freely [etc.] by rendering annually for the grantor and his heirs to the lords of that fee 18d. at four terms of the year according to the usage and custom of the vill of Coventry (*Covent(re)e*) and to the grantor and his heirs a clove-gillyflower at Easter for all secular service [etc.]. Clause for warranty. Henry gave 40s. of good and legal sterling beforehand. Sealing clause. Witnesses: John de Lodeloue then bailiff, Robert de Chiltone, T[h]omas de Phabena(m), Richard le Brocher, T[h]omas de Barsam, William Schot, William de Egesford, Richer de Westone, William Hotting, John Bayn and many others.

Seal extant P.R.O. A 6990
Endorsed: Carta Roger filius Johannis Habertas de terra juxta Jordan Welle

This document is very faded and was revealed by ultra violet light.

220 1280s

Charter of Roger Hapirtas of Coventry giving to Henry Baker (*pistori*) of Coventry the entire land with the houses sited there and all appurtenances which he had in Earl St. (*in vico Comitis*) between the red ditch (*le Rededich*) on the one hand and the land once of Robert de Denecastel on the other in length and in width as is manifest; to be held to him, his heirs or whatsoever assigns, to whomsoever he will wish to give, bequeath, sell or assign, of the grantor and his heirs well [etc.], by rendering annually to the heirs of Roger de Montalt (*monte alto*) as the perpetual attorneys of the grantor and his heirs 18d. of silver at the four terms of the year usual in the vill of Coventry and to the grantor and his heirs a clove-gillyflower at Easter for all secular service [etc.]. Warranty and sealing clauses. Witnesses: Alexander the Vintner (*vinitar'*), Robert de Chilton', Adam Russel, Thomas de Barsham, Richer de Weston', Robert de Scepeie, Nicholas de Allespathe, Roger de Allesleye clerk and many others.

Seal missing P.R.O. A 8879
Endorsed: Carta Rogeri habertachs
Ten' jux(t)a Jordan Welle.

221 Early 1280s

Gift, grant and quitclaim by Henry son of Walter de Bannebur' in Coventry, for himself and his heirs, to Robert de Clocherio of Coventry clerk of his entire right and claim in the entire land with appurtenances in the vill of Coventry in Earl St. (*in vico Comitis*) which lies between the land William Spark held on the one hand and the land William Hod held on the other, with all right and claim in the entire land with appurtenances in the vill of Coventry in St. Nicholas St. (*in vico sancti Nicholai*) which lies between the land of Roger le Neue on the one hand and the land of Walter Marbatin on the other, with 2s. 6d. annual rent to be taken from the land and house of the aforesaid Walter Marbatin and with 2s. to be taken annually in Well St. (*in vico fontis*) [namely] 12d. from the land once of William Haune and 12d. from the land once of Adam Attegrene, in length and in width as is manifest according to the metes and bounds made there; to be held to him, his heirs or whatsoever assigns, freely [etc.] by rendering annually to the lords of that fee the rent due and accustomed, namely for the land in Earl St. (*in vico Comit'*) 2s. to the heirs of Margery de Retham at the four terms of the year fixed in the vill of Coventry, and for the land and tenement in St. Nicholas St. (*in vico sancti Nicholai*) 2s. to the lord prior of Coventry and his successors at the aforesaid terms for all secular service [etc.]. Exclusion and sealing clauses. Witnesses: Robert de Chilton' then bailiff, Henry Baker (*pistore*), Walter Bakun, Thomas Seleth, Richard Minut, Reginald the Baker (*pistor'*), John Piod, Richard Chouwe, John the Forester (*forestar'*) and others.

Seal missing P.R.O. A 10821

222 Early 1280s

Charter of Richard le Brocher of Coventry giving to Richard de la Muyre in free marriage with Alice his daughter and to the heirs begotten legitimately between them the entire land with the houses sited there and all appurtenances in the vill of Coventry which William le Sulcsouher' once held lying between the land of Ranulph de la Wikene on the one hand and the grantor's own land on the other in length and in width according to the metes and bounds made there; to be held to them and the heirs begotten legitimately between them freely [etc.] by rendering annually to the chief lords of the fee the rent due and accustomed, namely to the heirs of Robert de Mouhaut 2s. 6d. and to the lord prior of Coventry 3d. at the usual and fixed terms in Coventry for all secular service or demand. Clause for reversion in default of legitimately begotten heirs, without any reclaim by anyone. Warranty and sealing clauses. Witnesses: Robert de Chilton' then bailiff, Henry Baker (*Pistor'*), Thomas de Fakenham, Henry Ballard, Adam Russel and many others.

Seal extant C.R.O. 2/50

223 Early 1280s

Charter of Richard le Brochere of Coventry giving to John de Rydewale in free marriage with Margery his daughter the entire land with houses sited there and all appurtenances which he held in Earl St. (*in vico Comitis*), which lies in width between the land Richard de la Mure in Coventry held on the one hand and the land Thomas Forthwin' held on the other [and] extends in length from the royal highway (*a via regia*) up to the ditch (*fossatum*) which is called *le Casteldich*, and a certain curtilage with appurtenances which lies in width between the land William de Whiteleye held on the one hand and the land Richard de Wilnhale held on the other [and] extends in length from the royal highway (*a via Regia*) up to the ditch (*fossatum*) which is called *le Parkdich* in length and in width as the land purports according to the metes and bounds made there; to be held to them and their heirs of Margery's body legitimately begotten, of the grantor and his heirs freely [etc.], by rendering annually for the built-up land (*pro terra predicta edificata*) 3d. of silver to the lord prior of Coventry and 3s. of silver to the heirs of Sir Robert de Montalt (*monte alto*), and for the curtilage 6d. of silver to William de Whiteleye and his heirs at the four terms of the year fixed and customary in the vill of Coventry, and to the grantor and his heirs ½d. at Easter for all secular service [etc.]. Clause for warranty. Clause for reversion should Margery die without legitimate bodily heir. Sealing clause. Witnesses: Robert de Chilton' then bailiff, Henry Baker (*pistore*), Richer de Weston, Thomas de Fackenham, Adam Russel, Thomas de Barsham, Richard de la Mure, William the clerk and others.

Seal extant C.R.O. IA/C61

224 Mid–late 1280s

Charter of Rose le Furner in her widowhood and lawful power giving to Richard de la Muyre in Coventry a moiety of a messuage with appurtenances in Earl St. (*in vico Comitis*) in Coventry between the land Robert de Rydeware held on the one hand and the land of the aforesaid Richard on the other in length and in width as the aforesaid moiety purports according to the metes and bounds made there; to be held to him, his heirs or whatsoever assigns, or to whomsoever he will wish to give, bequeath or assign in sickness and in health of the grantor and his heirs well [etc.], by rendering annually as the perpetual attorneys of the grantor and her heirs to the lords of that fee the service due and accustomed as is contained more fully in the charter which Richard le Brocher had of the grantor, and to the grantor as long as she lives ½d. at Easter for all secular services [etc.], so that after her death the aforesaid rent of ½d. should cease. Clause for warranty. Richard gave ½ mark of silver beforehand. Sealing clause. Witnesses: Henry Baker (*pistor'*) then bailiff, Robert de Chilton', Henry Ballard, Adam Russell, William Crumpe, John de Rydeware, William Utting, Richard de Weston', Roger de Allesleye the clerk and many others.

Seal extant C.R.O. IA/EC13/69

225 25 February 1291

Grant, remise and quitclaim by Richard le Bouldere and Maria his wife daughter of Ranulph de Stivechale, for themselves and their heirs, to Richard de la Muyre merchant in Coventry (*in Coventr' mercatori*) and Alice his wife and their heirs or assigns, of all right and claim in a messuage with appurtenances which lies in Earl St. (*in vico Comitis*) in Coventry between the land of the aforesaid Richard and Alice on the one hand and the land Ranulph de Wyken once held on the other in length and in width as is manifest according to the metes and bounds made there; to be held to them, their heirs or assigns, well [etc.] without any reservation by the grantors or their heirs, by making annually to the lords of the fee the service due and accustomed. Exclusion clause. Richard and Alice gave 10s. sterling beforehand. Sealing clause. Witnesses: Robert de Stoke, Henry Baker (*pistore*) then bailiff in Coventry, William le Parker then coroner, Richard de Weston', John de Langeleye, John de Rydeware, John Dobedy, William le Selcsowere, Hugh de Oxonia and others. Coventry, 5 Kalends March 19 Edward I.

2 seals extant C.R.O. 1B/19EI/3

226 1293–1297

Grant, remise and quitclaim by Alice once the daughter of Ranulph de Stevechehale in her pure and lawful virginity, for herself and her heirs, to Richard de la Mure of Coventry and Alice his wife, their heirs and assigns, of all right and claim in the entire messuage with appurtenances in the vill of Coventry which lies in Earl St. (*in vico comitis*) between the land William de Beri once held on the west side and the land of the aforesaid Richard on the east side, and extends in length from the royal highway which is called Earl St. (*a via regia que vocatur via comitis*) towards the south up to the castle ditch (*fossatum castelli*) towards the north. Exclusion clause. Richard and Alice gave 40s. sterling beforehand. Sealing clause. Witnesses: Sir John le Bretun then warden of the city of London (*tunc custod' civitatis lond'*), Sir John de Bankewelle, John de Dunstapel, Thomas de Brauncestre, Geoffrey le Botuner, John le Botuner, John de Indg(r)ace, Henry le Baker then bailiff of Coventry, Robert de Chilton', William le Parker then coroner, John Tole junior, Robert de Schepeye, John de

Redwale, John de Langele, Richard de Weston', Guy le Brocher, Hugh de Stevechehale, Richard le Harpur and others.

Seal extant C.R.O. IA/C13/38

Sir John le Bretun was twice appointed warden of the city of London, once for a brief spell in 1289 and again in June 1293 until the mayoralty was restored in 1298 (*C.P.R. 1281–92* p. 312, and *1292–1301* p. 21). The above clearly belongs to the second spell. John de Dunstable was an alderman from 1293–1307 (A. B. Beaven, *Aldermen of London*, 1908–13, vol. i, p. 376).

227 c.1290–1297

Grant, remise and quitclaim by Richard called (*dictus*) de la Myre merchant in Coventry (*in Coventr' mercator*), for himself and his heirs, to William called (*dicto*) de Bury merchant (*mercatori*) of all right and claim in the land with the buildings sited there and its appurtenances in Earl St. (*in vico Comitis*) in Coventry which was once of Agnes widow of Ranulph de Wyken, which lies in width between the land of John Sley on the one hand and the grantor's land on the other and extends in length from the royal highway (*a regia via*) up to the small plot of land which the grantor has retained to himself and his heirs (*parva(m) placia(m) terre quam retinui michi et heredibus meis*) from the land once of Ranulph de Wyken, in length and in width as is manifest according to the metes and bounds made there; to be held to him, his heirs or whatsoever assigns well [etc.] without any impediment by the grantor or his heirs. Exclusion clause. William gave 10s. of silver beforehand. Sealing clause. Witnesses: Alexander le Vineter, Robert de Stoke, Henry Baker (*pistore*) then bailiff in Coventry, William le Parker then coroner, Thomas le Moubrai, Robert de Chilton', Adam Russel, John de Langeleye, Richard de Weston', Symon Russel, William de Touchestr', Peter de Egefeld, Roger the clerk and others.

Seal extant C.R.O. IA/C13/35

228 Early 1280s

Charter of Thomas son of Martin the Locksmith (*locarii*) of Coventry and Agnes his wife, daughter of Alexander de Glovernia, giving to John Stantilun of Coventry and Margery his wife a certain messuage with appurtenances in Earl St., Coventry (*in vico Comitis de Coventr'*) between the land Robert le Luttelwrite once held on the one hand and the land Geoffrey Lunton' held on the other with a certain curtilage in Lower Park St., Coventry (*in Inferior' vico parci Coventr'*) between the land William de Wilnhal' once held and the land John le Theyher' once held in length and in width as is manifest according to the metes and bounds made there; to be held to them, their heirs and assigns, to whomsoever they will wish to give, bequeath, sell or assign both in sickness and in health, freely [etc.], by rendering annually the service owed to the chief lords of the fee according to what is contained in the charter of old enfeoffment (*veteri feoffamenti*) of Alexander de Glovernia, and to the grantors and their heirs a rose at the feast of the Nativity of St. John the Baptist for all secular service [etc.]. Clause for warranty. John and Margery gave 40s. of silver beforehand. *Ut a(utem) hec omnia firma sint et stabilia et sine dolo inperpetuum observanda tactis sac(r)os(anc)tis et fide nostra media nos obligavimus et heredes nostros ad penam quadraginta solidorum fab(r)ice ecclesie beate Marie Lich' solvendorum sim(u)lque subicientes nos et heredes nostros choerc(iti)oni et jur(is)dict(i)oni domini archid(iaconi) Coventr' vel ejus offic(ialis) qui pro tempore fuerint suspend(e)ndos et etiam exco(mmun)icandos et pro exco(mmun)icatis denu(n)ciandos sine strepitu judiciali vel cause cognic(i)one si quod absit presentis carte nostre tenori verbo vel op(er)e consilio aut auxilio nequit(er) p(re)sumpserimus obviare, et quod idem judices videlicet archid(iaconus) vel ejus offic(ialis) qui pro tempore fuerint et quicumque alius judex ecc(lesia)sticus qui exinde int(er)posu(er)it et labores in verbis aut op(er)ibus aug(us)tias sustinu(er)int h(ab)eant sing(u)li eorum dimidiam marcam argenti si contra dicte carte nostre tenore(m) in lite vel in aliqua alia causa judiciali stet(er)imus cavillando.* Sealing clause. Witnesses: Robert de Chilton' then bailiff of Coventry, Henry Baker (*pistor'*), Roger the Chamberlain (*cam(er)ario*), Hugh de Oxon', Robert Kelle, William le Garden(er), Geoffrey Lunton', Peter Barun, William Sley and others.

2 seals extant C.R.O. IA/Misc.I/19

229 Early 1280s

Charter of John son of Brun the clerk (? *acuarii*) and Alice his wife, daughter of Alexander de Gloucestr', giving to John Stantilun of Coventry glove-maker (*cirotecario*) and Margery his wife a certain messuage with appurtenances in Earl St., Coventry (*in vico Comitis de Coventr'*) between the land Robert le Luttelewrite once held on the one hand and the land Geoffrey Lunton' once held on the other with a certain curtilage in Lower Park St., Coventry (*in Inferiori vico parci Coventr'*) between the land once of William de Wilnhale and the land once of John le Thayhere in length and in width as is manifest according to the metes and bounds made there; to be held to them, their heirs and assigns, to whomsoever they will wish to give, bequeath, sell or assign, both in sickness and in health freely [etc.], by rendering annually the service owed to the chief lords of that fee according to what is contained in the charter of old enfeoffment (*veteri feoffamenti*) of Alexander de Glovernia, and to the grantors and their heirs a rose at the feast of the Nativity of St. John the Baptist for all secular service [etc.]. Clause for warranty. John and Margery gave 40s. of silver beforehand. *Ut a(utem) hec omnia firma sint et stabilia et sine dolo inperpetuum observanda tactis sac(r)os(anc)tis et fide nostra obligavimus nos et heredes nostros choerc(iti)oni et jur(is)dict(i)ioni domini archid(iaconi) Coventre vel ejus offic(ialis) qui pro tempore fuerint suspendendos et etiam exco(mmun)icandos et pro exco(mmu)ic(a)tis denu(n)ciandos sine strepitu judiciali vel cause cognit(i)one sim(u)lque obligantes nos et heredes nostros ad penam quadraginta solidorum fab(r)ice ecclesie beate Marie Lich' solvendorum quod si absit presentis carte nostre tenori verbo vel opere consilio aut auxilio nequit(er) p(re)sumpserimus obviare, et quod iidem judices videlicet archid(iaconus) vel ejus offic(ialis) qui pro tempore fuerint et quicumque alius judex ecc(lesia)stic(us) qui exinde interposuerit et labores in verbis aut operibus aug(us)tias sustinu(er)int h(ab)eant sing(u)li eorum dimidiam marcam argenti si contra dicte carte nostre tenore(m) in lite vel in aliqua alia causa judiciali stet(er)imus cavillando.* Sealing clause. Witnesses: Robert de Chilton' then bailiff of Coventry, Henry Baker (*pistore*), Peter Barun, Roger the Chamberlain (*Cam(er)ario*), Hugh de Oxon', Robert Kelle, William le Garden(er), Geoffrey Lunton', William Sley and others.

Seal extant C.R.O. IA/C13/42

230 2 March 1284

Agreement between Henry Baker (*pistorem*) and Agnes his wife on the one hand and Thomas Marie and Edith his wife on the other on the feast of St. Chad (*Cedde*) the Bishop 12 Edward I, whereby Henry and Agnes gave to Thomas and Edith in name of exchange a messuage with appurtenances in Earl St., Coventry (*in vico Comitis Coventr'*) which was once of John Payn, namely that which is between the land of the aforesaid Thomas on the one hand and the land Roger Box held on the other according to the metes and bounds made there; to be held to them, and to the heirs or assigns of the same Edith freely [etc.], by rendering annually to the grantors, their heirs or assigns, 13s. of silver at the four terms of the year usual in Coventry for all secular service [etc.]. Clause for warranty. In return Thomas and Edith gave in name of exchange a messuage with appurtenances in Bishop St., Coventry (*In vico Episcopi Coventr'*) which is between the land of Walter Bakun' on the one hand and the land of Henry le Knave on the other according to the metes and bounds made there; to be held to Henry and Agnes, their heirs or assigns, freely [etc.], by rendering annually to the lords of that fee the rent due and accustomed namely 2s. of silver at the four terms of the year usual in Coventry for all secular service [etc.]. Clause for warranty. *Et si dictus Thomas decedente Editha predicta vel heredes ejus seu assignati jus vel clamium aliquod in mesuagio predicto in vico Episcopi sito exigere voluerint ex tunc ad plenam firmam annuatim viginti solidorum dicti Henr(icus) et Agn(es) et eorum hered(es) vel assignat(i) perpetuo teneantur de mesuagio predicto in vico Comitis prout more solito ante presentis scripti confectionem iidem Henricus et Agnes de eodem percipere consueverunt.* Sealing clause [chirograph]. Witnesses: Alexander the Vintner (*vinitario*), Robert de Chiltun', William Bakun, John Thole, Thomas le Moubray, Richard de Esscheby, Richard de Westun, Thomas de Barsham, Anketell the clerk and others.

Indented
2 seals extant C.R.O. 2/130

231 Easter 1284

Notification of the settlement by the intervention of friends of a controversy which had arisen between Hugh le Breton and Richard le Dubber over the houses, spouts, gutters and fences which Richard built in Earl St. and West Orchard to the nuisance of Hugh's free tenement.

Noverint universi hoc presens scriptum visuri vel audituri quod cum inter Hugonem le Breton de Coventr' ex parte una et Ricardum le Dubber' de eadem ex parte altera orta seu mota fuisset lis aut controversia super domibus stillicidiis gutter(iis) et sepibus dicti Ricardi in vicis Comit(is) et Westgardini Coventr' injuste et sine judic(i)o ad nocumentum liberi tenementi predicti Hugonis levat(is) sitis et edificat(is) ipsa lis seu controversia quibus amicis intervenientibus in festo Pasce anno domini m° cc° octogesimo quarto sub hac forma conquievit et inter partes sic convenit: videlicet quod predictus Hugo pro se et heredibus suis dicto Ricardo et heredibus suis domos et sepes predictos secundum quod tunc site fuerunt quoad fundamentum concessit tenendas et sustinendas inposterum planas et erectas, ita quod ulterius versus terram seu tenementum ipsius Hugonis aut heredum suorum jus aliquod vel aysiamentum seu proprietatem aliquam exigere non possunt vel clamare; et quia dictus Ricardus de libero tenemento dicti Hugonis plus quam debuit occupavit licitum sit eidem Hugoni et heredibus vel suis assignatis ad domos et sepes ipsius Ricardi et heredum suorum et eorum assignatorum ju(n)ctim edificare et arbores plantare proprietate hujusmodi edificarum et arborum penes dictum Hugonem et heredes suos vel ejus assignatos totaliter et integre permanent(e). Et cum a parte dicti Hugonis et heredum suorum vel assignatorum sic fuerit edificatum dictus Ricardus et heredes sui vel ejus assignati ipsa edificia a casu aque defendent et ipsum Hugonem et heredes suos et assignatos indempnes super hiis sustinebunt inperpetuum. Pro hac autem concessione et convencione tenenda dedit predictus Ricardus predicto Hugoni viginti solidos argenti. In cujus rei testimonium utraque pars predicta presenti scripto in modum cirograffi confecto sigillum suum alternatim apposuerunt. Hiis testibus Henrico Pistore tunc ballivo Coventr', Rober(to) de Chilton', Rober(to) de Stokes, Henrico Dobedy, Henrico de Parlur, Stephano de Hales, Ranulfo de Cundelme, Stephano Textore, Ricardo Chouhe, Petro de Cotesbech, Thoma le Mubray, Ricardo King, Anget(ino) de Coleshul et aliis.

Indented
Seal missing C.R.O. IB/12EI

232 c.30 November 1285
Agreement whereby William Hod of Coventry has leased and demised at farm to Richard de Leycestr' and Beatrice his wife a seld (*unam seldam*) in Earl St. (*in vico Comitis*) in Coventry, namely that which is between the land of Henry Baker (*Pistoris*) on the one hand and the land of the aforesaid William on the other in width and which extends in length from the royal highway (*a regali via*) up to the land of William Spart; to be held to them, their heirs or assigns, of the lessor and his heirs for a term of 22 years from the feast of St. Andrew the Apostle 14 Edward I. The lessees will maintain the seld in as good a state as they received it during the term, rendering 10s. of silver at the four terms of the year usual and fixed in the vill of Coventry for all service [etc.]. *Et si predicta selda infra dictum terminum vendi debeat vel ad longiorem terminum poni predicti Ricardus et Beatricia vel heredes eorum omnibus hominibus vel feminis ad illam habendam erunt propinquiores per duodecim denarios argenti.* Richard and Beatrice gave 40s. of silver beforehand. Mutual sealing clause [chirograph]. Witnesses: Henry Baker (*pistor'*) then bailiff, Adam Russel, William Spart, Richard de Esseby, Henry Ballard, Richard de Weston', John le Flout(er), Geoffrey le Chalon(er), Roger the clerk and others.

Indented.
Seal extant C.R.O. IB/14EI

233 1280–1285
Charter of William Pychard of Newton (*Neuton'*) giving to Robert Grantpe, William his son and Alice his daughter, the entire land with houses sited there and all appurtenances in Earl St., Coventry (*in vico Comit' Coventr'*) which lies between the land Robert de Nortfoilk held on the one hand and the land Roger le Burc(er) held on the other; to be held to them and to Robert's heirs or assigns freely [etc.] just as the grantor held, by rendering annually to the lords of the fee the rent due and accustomed, and to the grantor, his heirs and assigns, a pair of gloves worth ½d. or ½d. at Easter for all secular service [etc.]. Robert, William and Alice gave 10 marks of silver beforehand. Sealing clause. Witnesses: Henry Baker (*pistor'*) then bailiff, Alexander the Vintner (*vinitario*), Walter Bakun, Robert de Chiltun, Richard de Weston, Richard de Esseby, Peter de Egisfeild, Geoffrey le Chaloumer, Henry Ballard, Anketill de Colishul' and others.

Seal missing C.R.O. 2/4

234 1280s
Charter of Richard de Weston' merchant (*mercator*) giving to Sir Hugh le Cras chaplain his chief messuage in which he used to live in Earl St. (*capitale mansum meum in vico Comitis in quo manere solebam*), namely that which lies in width between the land of Henry Ballard on the one hand and the land of Edith Schatheloc on the other, and extends in length from the high street up to the land where the ox used to be (*ab alto vico usque ad terram que solebat esse bovi*) with the buildings sited there and all appurtenances together with all goods and chattels, movable and immovable, and all kinds of vessels and utensils found in the messuage (*cum omnibus bonis et catellis mobilibus et in mobilibus et omnimodis vasis et utensilibus in eodem manso inventis*); to be held to him, his heirs or assigns, of the lords of the fee (*dominis feodalibus*) from whom the grantor held with all appurtenances well [etc.], by rendering annually to those lords the service due and accustomed at the terms fixed in the vill of Coventry. Hugh gave £80 (*quatuor vengenti libras*) sterling beforehand. Sealing clause. Witnesses: Henry Baker (*Pistore*) then bailiff, Robert de Chiltona, Richer de Weston', Henry Ballard,

Thomas de Barsam, Adam Russel, William Otting, Roger the clerk, Peter de Egisfeld' and many others.

Seal extant Fuller II/16/9

235 Mid–late 1280s

Grant and demise at farm by Martin son of Walter de Burtoft and Giliana daughter of Richard ad Cimit(er)ium of Willenhall (*Wylenhale*) to Sarah (*Sarre*) widow of John Ryvel as long as she lives of the entire tenement which they had in Earl St. (*in vico Comitis*) in Coventry between the land of Robert de Wynchecumbe on the one hand and the land Geoffrey the Painter (*pictor*) once held on the other; to be held with the houses sited there and all appurtenances to her for life, of the grantors well [etc.], by rendering annually to them or their assigns 4d. of silver at the four terms of the year usual and fixed in the vill of Coventry for all secular service. Clause for warranty. Clause for reversion after Sarah's death. Sealing clause. Witnesses: Henry Baker (*pistor'*) then bailiff, Robert de Chilton', John Thole, John Dobedy, Henry del Parlur, Henry le Peyntur, Robert de Wynchecumbe, Richard de Coleshul, Matthew de Ruyton and others.

Indented
Seal missing C.R.O. 2/88

236 1280s

Charter of Geoffrey de Langeleye knight giving to William le Gardiner and Roeysia his wife, for their service, a seld (*seldam*) with an adjacent curtilage in Coventry, namely that which lies between the land Petronilla la Blunde held of the grantor on the one hand and the land William de Bokkeby held of the grantor near by (*proximo*) on the other; to be held to them and their assigns, for their life freely [etc.] with all liberties, by rendering annually 6s. of silver at the four terms of the year usual and fixed in Coventry, so that the grantees will maintain the aforesaid seld with the buildings standing there (*super astantibus*) and the curtilage in good condition during their life. Clause for reversion to the grantor and his heirs without contradiction by the heirs or assigns of the aforesaid William and Roesia. Clause for warranty. William and Roesia gave 4s. fine (*in gersumma*). Sealing clause. Witnesses: Henry Baker (*pistor'*) then bailiff, Peter Baron, Richard del Mure, Hugh de Oxonia, Ranulp(h) de la Wyke, Roger the clerk and many others.

Seal extant C.R.O. IA/L12–13C/46
Endorsed: Carta Edmundi de langele.

237 20 July 1289

Charter of Hugh de Vienna clerk with the consent of Sir Geoffrey de Langele knight giving to John de Langele merchant of Coventry (*mercatori de Coventr'*) and Felicia his wife the entire tenement which was of Nicholas Lythulf in the same vill and extends in length from the royal highway called Earl St. (*a regali via que dicitur strata Comitis*) up to the common ditch of the vill of Coventry (*com(m)une(m) fossatu(m) ville de Coventr'*) and lies in width between the tenements of Lady Alice de Langele, John le Floutere and Peter Baron on the one hand and the tenements which were of William de Allesleye and Peter de Paris on the other; to be held with all appurtenances to them and the heirs or assigns of the same John of the grantor for his entire life and after his death of Geoffrey de Langele by rendering annually to the grantor for his entire life and after his death to Sir Geoffrey, his heirs or assigns, 34s. 6d.

sterling at the four principal terms of the year equally for all services, suits of courts, and secular demands. John and Felicia gave 20s. sterling beforehand. Sealing clause. Witnesses: Robert de Chilton', Henry Baker (*pistore*) of Coventry then bailiff (*ballivo*), William le Parker, Richard de la Mure, Richard de Weston', Adam Russel, William Graunpe, William de Toucestr', John de Ridewale and others. Leicester (*Leycestr'*), 20 July 17 Edward I.

Seal extant C.R.O. IB/17EI/2
Endorsed: Cart Hug' de Viena de capit' [interlined] ten' Alicie de langeley in vico Comit'

238 28 August 1290
Inspeximus of the above by Geoffrey de Langeleye knight. Shortley (*Shorteleye*), Tuesday after the feast of St. Bartholomew the Apostle 18 Edward I.

Seal missing C.R.O. IB/18EI/1

239 c.1289
Grant by Hugh de Vienna clerk to John de Langeleya merchant in Coventry (*in Coventr' mercatori*) of the tenement which William le Gardiner once held of Sir Geoffrey de Langel' in Earl St. (*in vico Comitis*) in Coventry; to be held with the buildings sited there and all appurtenances to him, his heirs or assigns, of the grantor as long as the grantor lives well [etc.], by rendering annually 6s. of silver at the four terms of the year usual and fixed in the vill of Coventry for all secular service [etc.]. Clause for warranty. John gave ½ mark of silver beforehand. Sealing clause. Witnesses: John Basset, Henry Baker (*Pistore*) of Coventry, Robert de Chilton', Peter Baron, Henry Ballard, Richard de Weston', Gilbert de Langedon', Richard del Muyre, Roger the clerk and others.

Seal missing C.R.O. 2/138
Endorsed: Viene de Aula.

Sir Geoffrey de Langley created a life-tenancy at Shortley for Hugh in 1289 (*F.F. Warwicks*. No. 1068).

240 c.1291
Charter of Henry Ballard of Coventry and Agnes his wife giving to John de Langeleye of Coventry in free marriage with Alice their daughter 1 mark annual rent which they used to receive from a certain messuage in Coventry which Reginald Ballard and Felice his wife hold of the gift of the said Henry by fine made between them in the royal court, to be taken at 2 terms of the year namely a moiety at Michaelmas and the other moiety at Easter; to be held to them and the legitimately begotten heirs of their bodies with all appurtenances of the grantors and their heirs freely and quietly just as any maritagium is held (*sicut aliquod maritagium liberius teneri poterit*). Clause for warranty. Clause for reversion in default of legitimately begotten heirs, without any contradiction. Clause for distraint for arrears of the rent at any term. Sealing clause. Witnesses: Henry Baker (*pistore*) then bailiff of Coventry, Robert de Chylton', William le P(ar)ker, John Thole senior, Master Richard de Aula, Richard

le Dubbere, William de Copston', Richard de Weston', Geoffrey le Chalon(er), Richard de la Mure, John de Rydewale, Simon Russel and others.

1 seal extant, 1 missing C.R.O. 2/46
Endorsed: Carta de xiijs iiijd. redditus de ten' quod Johannes Delevyle tenet in vico Comit'.

The fine referred to is dated 9 February 1291 (*F.F. Warwicks.* No. 1088).

241 23 February 1301

Charter of John de Longeleye knight giving to John de Longeleye merchant in Coventry (*in Coventr' mercatori*) a seld (*seldam*) with appurtenances in Earl St. (*in vico Comitis*) in Coventry which lies between the tenement of William le Plout(er)e on the one hand and the tenement of the said John on the other in width and extends in length from the royal highway (*a regia strata*) up to the land of the same John as is fully manifest according to the metes and bounds made there; to be held to him, his heirs or assigns, of the chief lords of that fee freely [etc.] by making annually the service due and by right accustomed and by rendering to the grantor and his heirs or assigns, 5s. of silver at the four terms of the year usual in the vill of Coventry and by making suit to the grantor's court of Coventry by reasonable summons *quando eam teneri contigerit* for all secular services [etc.]. Warranty and sealing clauses. Witnesses: Roger Dayseye then bailiff in Coventry, John Leuwyne then coroner, Reginald Ballard, William de Schepeye, Thomas de Northfeld, Richard le Brochere, Robert de Rydewar', Peter Barun, John de Mildenhale, William de Branteston', John Dobedy clerk and others. Coventry, Thursday after the feast of St. Peter's Chair 29 Edward I.

Indented
Seal extant C.R.O. IB/29EI/I
Endorsed: Cart' domini Johannis de langley milit' de capit' mesuagio.

242 28 October 1293

Charter of Henry de Mulcote in Coventry girdler (*zonarius*) giving to Clement le Myrourer of Coventry a messuage with appurtenances in Earl St. (*in vico Comitis*) in Coventry between the land William Crumpe once held on the one hand and the land John Kydelomb held on the other in length and in width as is manifest according to the metes and bounds made there; to be held with the buildings sited there and all appurtenances to him, his heirs and assigns, well [etc.] of the lords of that fee by the service of 8s. of silver to be paid annually at the four terms of the year usual and fixed in the vill of Coventry for all secular services [etc.]. Clause for warranty. Clement gave 30s. sterling beforehand. Sealing clause. Witnesses: Henry Baker (*pistore*) then bailiff in Coventry, William le Parker then coroner, Adam Russel, Richard de Essceby, Richard de Weston', Peter de Egesfeld, Ralf le Hunte, William la Lef, Henry de Eyton and others. Coventry, the feast of the Apostles Simon and Jude 21 Edward I.

Seal extant C.R.O. 1B/21EI/4

243 22 April 1295

Charter of Alice widow of Roger le Pursere of Coventry in her widowhood and lawful power giving to Clement le Myrourer' of Coventry and Agnes his wife the messuage with appurtenances which she had in Earl St. (*in vico Comitis*) in Coventr' which lies in width between the land Henry de Wytinton' once held on the one hand

and the land Symon Russel once held on the other and extends in length from the royal highway (*a Regali via*) up to the land of Richard de Essceby as is fully manifest according to the metes and bounds made there; to be held with buildings sited there and all appurtenances to them and to the heirs of the said Clement and to his assigns well [etc.] of the lords of that fee by rendering annually the services due and by right accustomed. Clause for warranty. Clement and Agnes gave 30 marks sterling beforehand. Sealing clause. Witnesses: Henry Baker (*pistore*) then bailiff of Coventry, William le Parker then coroner, Richard de Essceby, Adam Russel, Richard de Weston', William Grantpe, Henry de Barsham, John de Rydeware, Roger the clerk and others. Coventry, Friday before the feast of St. George the Martyr 23 Edward I.

Seal extant C.R.O. IB/23EI/5

244 24 April 1295

Charter of Thomas son of Roger le Pursere of Coventry giving and quitclaiming for himself and his heirs, without any reservation by him or his heirs to Clement le Mirourer of Coventry and Agnes his wife and to the heirs and assigns of the said Clement all right and claim in the messuage with appurtenances once of the aforesaid Roger his father and Alice his mother in Earl St. (*in vico Comitis*) in Coventry between the land which Henry de Wytinton' once held on the one hand and the land which Symon Russel once held on the other and which extends in length from the royal highway (*a Regali via*) up to the land of Richard de Essceby as is fully manifest according to the metes and bounds made there, which messuage the aforesaid Clement and Agnes acquired (*co(m)paraverunt et habueru(n)t*) from the aforesaid Alice the grantor's mother by charter of enfeoffment; to be held to them and the heirs and assigns of the said Clement well [etc.] without any charge, reservation or impediment by the grantor or his heirs. Exclusion clause. Sealing clause. Witnesses: Henry Baker (*pistore*) then bailiff of Coventry, William le Park' then coroner, Adam Russel, Richard de Essceby, Nicholas Crumpe, Henry de Barsham, William Grantpe and others. Coventry, Sunday the morrow of St. George 23 Edward I.

Seal extant C.R.O. IB/23EI/4

245 c.1300–c.1310

Remise, surrender and quitclaim by Clement le Myrourer of Coventry for himself and his heirs to Nicholas son of William Crompe of the entire tenement which he had in Earl St. (*in vico Comitis*) in Coventry by the gift of the aforesaid William Crompe, which tenement William held by the law of England after the death of Dyonisia his wife, and of a shop (*schopa(m)*) in the same street which the grantor had by the gift of Henry le Graunger acknowledging the entire aforesaid tenement to be the right and inheritance of Nicholas descending to him after the death of Dyonisia le M(er)cer daughter of Reginald le M(er)cer whose heir he is; remising and quitclaiming to Nicholas, his heirs or assigns, all right and claim in the said tenements with appurtenances saving to the grantor, his heirs or assigns, that shop with appurtenances which the same Nicholas has granted to him and confirmed by his deed (*scriptum*), to be held to Nicholas, his heirs or assigns. Exclusion and sealing clauses. Witnesses: Peter son of Peter Baron, Thomas de Lylleburn', Roger Dayeseye, Robert le Pestour, Hugh de M(er)yton', Robert de Rydewar', Peter son of John de Rydewar', Hugh le Taylour and others.

Seal extant C.R.O. 2/49

246 25 July 1294

Charter of Hugh le Aguler of Coventry giving to Richard de Draycote girdler in Coventry (*in Coventr' zonario*) a messuage with appurtenances in Earl St. in Coventry towards Earl's Mill Lane (*in vico Comitis in Coventr' versus le Erlesmulnelone*) which lies in width between the land William Uttyng once held on the one hand and the land Matilda de Pakynton' once held on the other and extends in length from the royal highway (*a Regali via*) up to the land which Robert the Miller (*molendinarius*) once held as is fully manifest according to the metes and bounds made there; to be held with buildings sited there and all appurtenances to him, his heirs or assigns, well [etc.] of the chief lords of that fee by the service due and by right accustomed just as the grantor used to make. Clause for warranty. Richard gave 4 marks of silver beforehand. Sealing clause. Witnesses: Henry Baker (*pistore*) then bailiff of Coventry, William le Parker then coroner, Richer de Weston', Robert de Schepeye, John de Langele, Roger Box, Henry de Denecastel, Richard Utting, Alured the Girdler (*zonario*) and others. Coventry, Sunday the feast of St. James the Apostle 22 Edward I.

Seal extant C.R.O. IB/22EI/4

247 c.25 March 1296

Agreement whereby Nicholas Crumpe of Coventry has leased, granted and demised to William Grantpe junior (*minorem*) of the same the seld (*seldam suam*) which he had in Earl St., Coventry towards Much Park St. (*in vico Comitis in Coventr' versus majorem vicum parci*), namely the seld with appurtenances and easements which is nearer the corner seld towards the aforesaid park street (*que est propinquior angulari selde versus predictum vicum parci*); to be held to him, his heirs or assigns, of the grantor and his heirs well [etc.] for a term of 4 years from the feast of St. Mary in March 24 Edward I. Warranty and reversion clauses. Mutual sealing clause [chirograph]. Witnesses: Adam Russel, Henry Ballard, William Grantpe the elder (*majore*), Henry de Barsham, Ralf le Hunte, Geoffrey le Chaloner, Roger the clerk and others.

Indented
Seal extant C.R.O. IB/24EI/11

248 8 July 1296

Grant, remise and quitclaim by Richard Wetherhog of *Eton'* for himself and his heirs to Roger Dayeseie of Coventry clerk, his heirs or assigns, of all right and claim in the entire chief messuage (*Capitali manso*) with appurtenances which was once of Hamo the Weaver (*textoris*) in Earl St. (*in vico Comitis*) in Coventry between the land of Richard de Coleshul on the one hand and the land of Thomas de Lodelowe on the other as contained in the charter of enfeoffment thereon. Exclusion and sealing clauses. Witnesses: Henry Baker (*Pistore*) then bailiff of Coventry, William called (*dicto*) Park(er) then coroner, Henry the Painter (*Pictore*), John le G(l)overe, Thomas de Lodelowe, Henry le Mowere, Richard de Coleshul' and others. Saturday after the Translation of St. Thomas the Martyr 25 Edward I.

Seal missing W.G.O. DR 233.2

249 10 July 1296

Charter of Henry Brayn of Coventry son and heir of Henry Brayn and Alice le Wyte of Coventry giving to Henry in le Hurne of Coventry clerk 16d. annual rent with appurtenances in the vill of Coventry in Earl St. (*in vico Comitis*) which the grantor used to receive annually from a certain messuage which lies between the tenement of Walter Box on the one hand and the tenement of Gilbert de Hyam on the other at the usual terms in the vill of Coventry; to be held to him, his heirs or assigns, freely [etc.] of the lords of that fee by the services due and accustomed. Clause for warranty. The grantee gave 3s. of silver and 4d. beforehand. Sealing clause. Witnesses: William le Parker coroner, Nicholas Crompe, Roger Dayesie, Peter Baron, Richard de M(er)sten', John de Langeleye, Richard ate Mur', Bate[1] de Rutona, Robert le Comber', John le Gouer', William Loteman, William le Waller', Geoffrey le Waller', Thomas de Pollesworthe and many others. Coventry, Tuesday after the feast of the Translation of St. Thomas the Martyr 24 Edward I.

Seal missing C.R.O. IB/24EI/4

Endorsed: Carta de sexdecim denarat'[1] annui redditus de ten' in vico de Gosseford ultra mulnelone.

[1] sic

250 10 July 1296

Grant and demise by William de Aula in Coventry to Henry in le Hurne of Coventry clerk of all right in 3s. 9d. rent at Coundon (*Coundelme*) and 16d. from a certain messuage in Earl St. (*in vico Comitis*) in the vill of Coventry during the entire term which the grantor had through Henry Brayn *sicut in quadem scriptura inter nos (in)dentata litruereri potest evidenter*. Exclusion and sealing clauses. Witnesses: Matthew de Ruthon', Robert le Comber', John le Gouer', Richard de Merston', Adam de Wemme and many others. Coventry, Tuesday after the feast of the Translation of St. Thomas the Martyr 24 Edward I.

Indented

Seal extant C.R.O. IB/24EI/15

251 27 June 1299

Grant by Henry son of Nicholas de Allespathe in Coventry to Nicholas his father, for the grantee's entire life, of the grantor's messuage with the buildings sited there and appurtenances in Earl St. (*in vico Comitis*) in Coventry between the land of Roger Box on the one hand and the land of John de Erescote on the other and which extends in length from the aforesaid street up to the garden (*gardinum*) which is called *le Erlesorchard* according to the metes and bounds made there, so that the grantor and his heirs will maintain all the buildings of the said messuage against wind and rain at their own cost during the entire life of the said Nicholas the grantor's father; to be held to him for his entire life, of the grantor and his heirs well [etc.], by rendering annually 13s. of silver at the four terms of the year usual and fixed in the vill of Coventry for all secular services [etc.]. Clause for reversion without contradiction to the grantor or his heirs. Mutual sealing clause [bipartite]. Witnesses: Anketill de Coleshul then bailiff of Coventry, John Leofwyne then coroner, Adam Russel, Nicholas Crumpe, John de Rydeware, Henry de Barsham, Roger Box, Thomas Marie, Roger the clerk and others. Coventry, Saturday after the feasts of Sts. John and Paul 27 Edward I.

Seal missing G.H. 312

252 11 July 1300

Charter of William the Chaplain (*Capellanus*) son of Richer de Weston' in Coventry giving to Thomas son of Richard[1] the grantor's brother a piece (*placiam*) of land with buildings sited there which the aforesaid Richer his father gave to the grantor at the end of his chief messuage in Earl St. (*in extremitate Capitalis mansi sui in vico Comitis*) in Coventry next to the messuage of Robert de Stone, which piece (*placia*) contains 30 feet in length and 7 feet in width according to the metes and bounds made there; to be held to him, his heirs or whatsoever assigns, well [etc.] of the chief lords of that fee by the services due and by right accustomed. Sealing clause. Witnesses: John Leofwyne then coroner in Coventry, Robert called Baker (*dicto Pistore*), Adam Russel, Nicholas Crumpe, Peter Barun, John de Rydeware, Henry de Barsham, Thomas de Polesworthe, Roger the clerk and others. Monday after the Translation of St. Thomas the Martyr 28 Edward I.

Seal extant W.R.O. DR 234

[1] sic

253

c.29 September 1300

Agreement made on Sunday after the feast of St. Michael the Archangel 1300 A.D. between Sir Alexander de Esscheby chaplain in Coventry (*in Coventr' Capell(anu)m*) on the one hand and Richard de Todenham merchant (*mercatorem*) of the same on the other, whereby Alexander has granted and confirmed by charter to the aforesaid Richard and Alice his wife, their heirs and assigns, his entire right and claim in the messuage with appurtenances in Earl St. (*in vico Comitis*) in Coventry which Christine his stepmother (*noverca*) held in name of dower by the death of Richard de Esscheby, Alexander's father. In return Richard and Alice will give to Alexander 40 marks sterling at three terms, namely 10 marks on the aforesaid Sunday, another 10 marks at Christmas in the same year and 20 marks at the Easter following, so that the entire aforementioned money should be paid to the aforesaid Alexander or to his certain attorney at the said three terms without further delay when the aforesaid charter which is in the custody of Robert de Rydeware will be handed to the aforesaid Richard and Alice. Mutual sealing clause [bipartite] and pledge of faith. Witnesses: Sir Benedict de Harnhale chaplain, Adam Russel, Richard de Weston', Richard Utting, Robert de Rydeware, Robert de Stone, Roger the clerk and others.

Indented
2 seals missing P.R.O. A 4455

254

11 September 1302

Charter of Alice daughter of John le Buckmong(er)e of Coventry in her widowhood and lawful power giving to John Abbot of Coventry a moiety of a messuage with an adjacent curtilage and with appurtenances, which messuage lies entirely between the land of Robert de Stone on the one hand and the land of Thomas Ballard on the other, namely that moiety which lies nearer the land of Robert de Stone according to the metes and bounds there; to be held to him, his heirs or assigns, freely [etc.] of the chief lords of that fee, by the service and rent on his part (*pro parte sua*) due and by right accustomed and by rendering annually to the grantor, his heirs or assigns, 3s. of silver at the four terms of the year usual in Coventry. Clause for warranty. John gave 40s. of silver beforehand. Sealing clause. Witnesses: Roger Dayeseye then bailiff, John Lewyne then coroner, William de Schepeye, Robert de Stone, John Pyhod, John le Glov(er)e, Richard Colebrond and others. Coventry, Tuesday after the feast of the Nativity of the blessed Mary 30 Edward I.

Seal extant P.R.O. A 6378

255 1 October 1304

Grant, release and quitclaim by Alice daughter of John le Buchemongere of Coventry in her widowhood and lawful power for herself, her heirs or assigns, to John Abbot of Coventry of all right and claim in a messuage with appurtenances which lies in Earl St. (*in vico Comitis*) in Coventry in width between the land of Robert de Stone on the one hand and the land of Henry de Myddelton' on the other and extends in length from the aforesaid street up to the red ditch (*Le Rede dych'*) according to the metes and bounds made there, and also in 12d. annual rent to be taken at the four terms of the year usual in Coventry from a certain tenement with appurtenances which was once of Adam le Wyche in the same street next to the aforesaid messuage; to be held to John, his heirs or assigns, freely [etc.]. Exclusion clause. John gave 100s. of silver beforehand. Sealing clause. Witnesses: John Lewyne then coroner, Henry Oky, John Pyehod, John le Glov(er)e, Robert de Stone, Roger Box, Richard de Weston, Laurence de Schepeye, Richard Colebrond clerk and others. Coventry, Thursday after Michaelmas 32 Edward I.

Seal extant P.R.O. A 10689

256 8 September 1305

Charter of John Pat of Coventry and Alice his wife giving to William de Schepeye merchant (*mercatori*) of Coventry a third part of the messuage with appurtenances lying in Earl St. (*in vico Comitis*) in Coventry between the tenement Richard de la Muyre once held on the one hand and the tenement Reginald Ballard once held on the other, which third part descended to the aforesaid Alice by hereditary right after the death of William de Bury her father as daughter and one of the heirs; to be held with all appurtenances wheresoever in common with Edith and Agnes sisters of the same Alice and coparceners (*participibus*) of the aforesaid inheritance, to William and his heirs or assigns, freely and hereditarily of the chief lords of that fee by the services due and by right accustomed. Clause for warranty. William gave 20 marks sterling beforehand. Sealing clause. Witnesses: Robert Baker (*Pistore*) then bailiff of Coventry, William Graundpe, John de Langeleye, Thomas Ballard, Peter Barun, William de Braundestone, John de Mildenhale, Robert de Rydewar', John Dobedy clerk and others. Coventry, Wednesday the feast of the Nativity of the blessed Mary 33 Edward I.

2 seals extant C.R.O. IB/33EI/19

257 11 Devember 1306

Charter of William Gamel of Coventry giving to Richard de Walton' for a certain sum of money which Richard gave beforehand 2 shops (*Schoppas*) with appurtenances which lie in the high street (*in alto vico*) in Coventry between the tenement of William Patte on the one hand and the road (*viam*) which leads towards the grantor's chief messuage on the other in width, and extends from the aforesaid street up to the grantor's chief messuage in length as is manifest; to be held to him, his heirs or whatsoever assigns, freely [etc.] of the chief lords of that fee by the service due and by right accustomed. Warranty and sealing clauses. Witnesses: Robert le Baxtere then bailiff of Coventry, Alexander de Stonlee then coroner of the same, Richard le Typpere, Nicholas le Deystere, John de Halys, William de Galewey, John le Barker, Alexander de Colleshull, Richard Colebrond clerk and others. Coventry, Sunday after the feast of St. Nicholas the Bishop 35 Edward I.

Seal extant P.R.O. A 10493

258 26 February 1307

Charter of Richard de Walton of Coventry giving to William Gamel of Coventry, Alice his wife and their heirs or whatsoever assigns, 2 shops (*Schoppas*) with appurtenances which lie in the high street (*in alto vico*) in Coventry between the land of William Patte on the one hand and the road (*viam*) which leads towards the chief messuage (*capitale mesuag'*) of the said William Gamel on the other in width and extends in length from the aforesaid street up to the chief messuage of the said William Gamel as is fully manifest according to the metes and bounds made there; to be held freely [etc.] of the chief lords of that fee by the services due and by right accustomed. Exclusion clause. Walter and Alice gave a sum of money beforehand. Sealing clause. Witnesses: Robert le Baxtere then bailiff of Coventry, Anketinus de Colushull then coroner of the same, Alexander de Stonlee, Richard le Typpere, Alexander de Moubray, John Pyhod, Richard Colebrond the clerk and others. Coventry, Sunday next after the feast of St. Mathias the Apostle 35 Edward I.

Seal missing P.R.O. A 9262

GOSFORD ST.* (GOSFORD, TOWARDS GOSFORD, OUTSIDE OR BEYOND GOSFORD)

*See above p. 000. For other references see 249, 385, 454, 657, 686; 767.7, .42, .47. See also *Langley Cartulary* Nos. 231, 284, 339, 343, 352, 359, 400, 417, 424, 426, 470, 476.

259 c.1215–1225

Charter of William son of Hugh the Locksmith (*locar'*) of Coventry giving to Symon Pymme in free marriage with Alice his sister 2 shops (*duas scopas*) in the same vill in Earl St. towards Gosford (*in vico Com' versus Goseford*) between the land John Merwyne held on the one hand and the land Richard de Warewik held on the other with a certain croft next to Earl's Mill Lane (*juxta Erlesmolne lone*) between the Earl's meadow (*pratum Com'*) and the land Walter the White (*Blundus*) held; to be held to them and the heirs issuing from them freely [etc.] according to the metes and bounds made there, by rendering annually for the aforesaid shops 12d. of silver at four terms of the year according to the usage of Coventry and for the aforesaid croft with all appurtenances a pair of gloves worth ½d. or ½d. at Easter for all secular service and demand. Warranty and sealing clauses. Witnesses: Richard de Wigorn', John Merwine, William Crude, Walter Broch(er), Walter the White (*Blundo*), Richard Wymaneson', Roger de Kyrk', Roger Pake, Walter Lalle, Richard Syward, Robert Pottesmuth, William Hacon, Ranulf de Mora and others.

Seal extant C.R.O. IA/C59

260 c.1215–c.1225

Charter of Adam de Kinesbur' giving to Roger de Bubbenhull' a land outside Gosford (*unam terram extra Gosford*), namely half of his curtilage which is between the land Walter Alfled held and the land Ailwardus de Harnhale held just as it purports in length and in width; to be held to him and his heirs of the grantor and his heirs freely [etc.], by rendering annually 4d. of silver at four terms of the year for all service and all demand, namely 1d. at each of the feasts of St. Mary in March, St.[1] John the Baptist, St. Michael and St. Andrew. Clause for warranty. Roger gave 11½d. in recognition. Witnesses: Richard son of Wunman, William Hakun, Ranulf de Mora, Nicholas the Carpenter (*carpent'*), William the Mason (*cem(en)tar'*), Brunus the Locksmith (*loccar'*), Jordan the Locksmith (*loccar'*), Alan Broch(er), Adam the Locksmith (*Loccar'*), Alexander his brother and many others.

Seal extant C.R.O. IA/C16

[1] This is preceded by St. John, presumably to be deleted.

261 c.1215–1224

Charter of Philip son of Miles Barbeap(r)il' giving to Richard son of Wunman and his heirs 2 selions of the grantor's land at Altegeder Mill (*Altegedermulne*), namely those which are nearer (*proximiores*) to the garden (*orto*) of the said Richard and extend from the land Robert son of Pagan held up to the water [and] up to the grantor's bounds (*divisas nostras*), and his entire meadow at the same mill with appurtenances; to be held in fee and inheritance to him and his heirs of the grantor and his heirs freely [etc.], by rendering annually 2s. of silver at the four terms of the year, namely 6d. at each of the feasts of St. Mary in March, St. John the Baptist, St. Michael and St. Andrew for all service and demand. Clause for warranty. Richard gave 2 marks of silver in recognition. Witnesses: Richard de Wigorn', Stephen his son, Swanus the Parker (*parcar'*), William Crude, Adam Herre, William son of Helewis, Christian the Smith (*fabro*), Ralf the Miller (*molend'*), Amfridus, Richard de St. Botulf, Roger de Kirkeby, John M[eru][1]enne, Robert de Warewic' and many others.

Seal missing GH 264

[1] damaged

262 c.1215–1226

Charter of Walter son of Richard Wynma(n) giving to William Fordwin the entire land in Coventry towards Gosford (*versus Gosford*) which is between the land the monks of Combe (*Cumba*) held and the land Roger son of Robert Odein held, entirely and fully just as the land purports in length and in width from the street (*a vico*) up to the arable land with all appurtenances and with the entire service which the same Roger ought to make from the land which he held of the grantor namely 2d. rent and 2 hens at Christmas annually; to be held to him and his heirs, of the grantor and his heirs hereditarily, freely, quietly and honourably, by rendering annually 1lb. cumin at Christmas and a pair of gloves of a ½d. at Easter for all secular service and demand. Clause for warranty. *Et si forte predictus Willelmus vel heredes sui vel aliquis tenentiu(m) suorum de feodo illo cadant in m(isericord)ia mei vel heredum meorum quieti er(un)t per tres denarios.* William gave 40s. sterling in recognition. Witnesses: Richard de Wigorn', Richard de Aula, Robert the Vintner (*vinit'*), Leofwinus, Hamo his brother, William de Rependon', Peter the Welshman (*Walensi*), William Crude, Ralf the Weaver (*textore*), Walter Broch', Roger Pake, William Hakun and many others.

Seal extant W.R.O. 246

263 1230s

Charter of Nicholas son of William Fordwin giving to William son of Gladewinus a third part of his land (*cujusdam terre mee*) in Earl St. towards Gosford (*In vico Comitis versus Gosford*), namely the part which lies between the land Benedict Bucstan held of the grantor and the land John son of Robert de Biln' held of the grantor in length and in width just as that part purports with all appurtenances according to the metes and bounds made there; to be held to him and his heirs of the grantor and his heirs hereditarily, freely, quietly and honourably by rendering 2s. annually at four terms, namely 6d. at each of the feasts of St. Michael, St. Andrew, St. Mary in March and St. John the Baptist for all secular service and demand. Clause for warranty. William gave ½ mark in recognition. Witnesses: Richard the Burgess (*Burgense*), Walter le Broch', Roger de Kyrkeby, Reginald son of Tole, Roger Pake, John Broch', John the Mercer (*Merc'*), Martin the Locksmith (*Loccar'*), Alexander

Bucstan, William de Lond', Roger Hakun, Richard Wunman, Walter his son and others.

Seal extant W.R.O. 247

264 c.1215–c.1225

Charter of Walter Alfled giving to Henry de Gildenetre a land outside Gosford (*unam terram extra Gosford*) namely that which is between the land John the son of the clerk held of William Hakun and the land Richard le Carbuner held in length and in width as the land purports; to be held to him and his heirs, of the grantor and his heirs freely [etc.], by rendering 2s. of silver at four terms of the year for all service [etc.], namely 6d. at each of the feasts of St. Mary in March, St. John the Baptist, St. Michael and St. Andrew. Clause for warranty. Henry gave 14s. of silver in recognition. Witnesses: Richard son of Wunman, Walter his son, Robert de Warewic, William son of Hugh, Simon Pimme, William Hakun, William de Dunham, Ranulf de Mora, Brunus the Locksmith (*Loccar'*), Adam the Locksmith (*Loccar'*), Nicholas the Carpenter (*carpent'*), William the Mason (*cementar'*) and many others.

Seal extant C.R.O. 2/122

265 c.1240s

Charter of Henry de Guldintr' giving to Henry his son 13d. annual rent outside Gosford, Coventry (*extra Gosford de Covintr'*) which Philip son of Symon the Carter *Cartarii*) used to render to the grantor from the land which lies between the land William le Natt(er)e held on the one hand and the land Thomas son of Martin le Loker held on the other; to be held to him, his heirs or assigns, of the grantor and his heirs freely [etc.], by rendering annually 1d. of silver at four terms of the year according to the usage of Coventry for all secular service [etc.]. Clause for warranty. Henry gave 7s. of silver in recognition. Sealing clause. Witnesses: William Stoyle, Thomas Long (*Longo*), John M(er)ewin', William de London', Pagan Pake, Simon de Hoyland, William le Nat(er)e, William the Mason (*cem(en)tario*), Master Miles, Hugh le Hallere, Nicholas son of Jory and others.

Seal missing C.R.O. IA/LC12/27

266 c.1240s

Charter of Henry de Guldentre giving to John son of Symon and his heirs the land with appurtenances which Symon his father held of the grantor without charter, which is between the land of William le Natter and the land of Thomas the Locksmith (*Locar'*); to be held to him and his heirs of the grantor and his heirs with an increase of 4 feet at the end of his curtilage (*cum augm(en)to quatuor pedum terre in fine curtilagii sui*) according to the bounds made there freely and quietly with appurtenances by the service of 13d. per annum at four terms according to the usage of Coventry. Warranty and sealing clauses. Witnesses: William Natter, William the Mason (*cemetar'*), John the Locksmith (*locar'*), Symon de Hoyland', William Stoule, Hugh Aller, William de London', David the clerk and others.

Seal extant C.R.O. 2/2

267 c. late 1240s

Charter of Pagan Pake giving to Henry son of Henry de Guldinetr' a part (*unam partem*) of his land in Gosford St. (*in vico de Gosseford*) with a messuage and its appurtenances thereon (*supraposito*), namely that which lies between the land Richard Good Knight (*bonus miles*) held on the one hand and the land Pagan Pake held on the other; to be held to him, his heirs and assigns, of the grantor and his heirs freely [etc.] according to the metes and bounds made there, by rendering annually 3s. 6d. of silver at four terms of the year according to the custom of the vill of Coventry for all secular service and demand. Clause for warranty. Henry gave 1 mark of silver beforehand. Sealing clause. Witnesses: William le Stoile, John Merewin', Thomas son of Martin, Robert le Comb(er), Thomas the Locksmith (*locario*), William de Burebe'g, Robert Pimme, Ralf de Donham and others.

Seal extant C.R.O. IA/C35

268 c. late 1240s

Charter of Thomas son of Martin the Locksmith (*Locarii*) giving to Henry son of Henry de Guldinetr' his entire land outside Gosford (*extra Gosseford*) which the grantor held in chief of the lord prior of Coventry, namely that which lies between the land Philip son of Sym(on) le Caret(er) held on the one hand and the land of Henry de Guldinetr' on the other according to the metes and bounds made there; to be held to him and his heirs of the grantor and his heirs freely [etc.], by rendering annually 18d. of silver at four terms of the year according to the custom of the vill of Coventry for all secular service and demand. Clause for warranty. Henry gave 4s. of silver beforehand. Sealing clause. Witnesses: John Merewin', Thomas Long', William le Stoyle, William Brot', William de Lond', Martin the Locksmith (*loccar'*), William de Warewyc, Colin Jori and others.

Seal missing C.R.O. 2/133

269 1250s

Sale and quitclaim by Thomas son of Martin, for himself and his heirs, to Henry de Guldentr' of all right and claim in 3 selions of land which he held in Coventry outside Gosford (*extra Goseford*) in chief of the lord prior, which lie next to the land of the same Henry in the same place; to be held to him, his heirs or assigns, freely and quietly as the grantor held of the said prior of Coventry by the service of 12d. of silver at four terms of the year according to the usage of Coventry. Henry gave 4s. of silver. Sealing clause. Witnesses: John Sym' and Martin Colbrond then bailiffs (*ballivis*), Pagan Pake, William de Folkeshul, William le Natter, Hugh le Aller, Walter Outred and others.

Seal missing C.R.O. 2/90

270 Early 1270s

Charter of Henry de Gildenetr' clerk once the son of Henry de Gildenetr' of Coventry giving to Geoffrey de Nassinton' clerk 13d. annual rent which he used to receive from Hugh Pape from the land which lies between the land Henry the grantor's father held on the one hand and the land Ralf Bissop held on the other outside Gosford (*extra Gosford*) of the vill of Coventry; to be held to him, his heirs or whatsoever assigns, or to whomsoever he will wish to give, bequeath or assign of the grantor, his heirs or assigns, freely [etc.], by rendering annually a clove-gillyflower at Easter for all secular service pertaining. Clause for warranty. Geoffrey gave ½ mark of silver beforehand. Sealing clause. Witnesses: Peter Barun then (*tunc tempore*) bailiff, Pagan Pake, Walter Helewis, William Stoule, Ralf Bissop, Symon de Holand, Symon le Chaluner, Hugh Sigan, Walter le Butt(er)e and many others.

Seal extant C.R.O. IA/EC12/8

271 1220s

Charter of Brunus the Locksmith (*Loccarius*) giving to Ranulf de Grantham and his heirs a land outside Gosford (*unam terram extra Gosford*), namely the entire land *de la Roine* between 2 posts of the grantor's house (*que est in duobus postibus proprie domus mee*) up to the land which Adam the Locksmith (*Loccarius*) held of the grantor in length and in width as the land purports according to the metes and bounds made there; to be held of the grantor and his heirs freely [etc.], by rendering annually for all secular service and all demands 12d. of silver at four terms of the year, namely 3d. at each of the feasts of St. Michael, St. Andrew, St. Mary in March and St. John the Baptist. Clause for warranty. Ranulf gave 2 marks and 4s. of silver in recognition, and 2s. to Alice the grantor's wife. Witnesses: William son of Helewis, Hugh the Red (*rufo*), William the Locksmith (*Loccar'*), Henry de Gildenetre, Alexander the Cutler (*cutillario*), Peter Merc(er), Ralf Merc(er), Alexander the Locksmith (*loccar'*), Ivo the Locksmith (*loccar'*), Ranulf de Mora, William Hakun, William Patte and many others.

Seal extant C.R.O. IA/C33

272 Late 1230s–1243

Sale and quitclaim by Vincent Pottismud to Nicholas son of Nicholas and his heirs of all right and claim in the land which Richard son of Richard Syward held of the grantor in the vill of Coventry, in the land which Robert de Denecast(r)e held of the grantor, and in the land which William Pie held of the grantor, namely of the grantor and his heirs for ever. Nicholas gave 2s. of silver. Sealing clause. Witnesses: Osbert Durde(n)t, John Byher, Ralf the Miller (*molendinar'*), Richard Leuwine, Robert de Denecast(r)e, William Seg(r)im, Nicholas Fortwin', John Fortwin' and many others.

Seal extant G.H. 262

273 c.29 September 1245

Lease by William son of William le Paum(er) to Alexander de Ruton' of 4 messuages at Gosford (*apud Gosford*) with appurtenances which are between the land Ralf de Dunholm held and the land William de Burbache held in length from the street (*a vico*) up to the meadow of Pagan Pake; to be held to him, his heirs or assigns, of the grantor and his heirs freely [etc.] for a term of 12 years from Michaelmas 29 Henry III, by rendering annually to the lords of the fee the service owed, namely 12d. of silver at the four terms of the year fixed in Coventry (*Convintr'*), 2 men working for 1 day (*per unum diem Laborantes*) in Autumn and 2 hens at Christmas for all secular service and exaction. Clause for warranty *quod si dicta mesuagia corruant vel auxilio indigent infra terminum ego Willelmus vel heredes mei illud defectum adimplere tenemur sin autem solvemus eidem Alexandro vel heredibus suis vel assignatis universum custum suum appositum in rep(ar)acione et in sustentacione dictorum messuagiorum sine aliqua contradictione vel quod teneant de anno in annum dicta mesuagia quousque per visum bonorum hominum salvu(m) sit eis hoc quod apposuerint.* The lessee will be reimbursed for the cost of repairs at the end of the term. Alexander gave 30s. of silver beforehand. Sealing clause. Witnesses: Osbert the clerk, Robert de Cornleg', William de Pailinton', John son of Alan, William Toly, Pagan Pake, William Stoule, Thomas le Lungh, William Bront', Ralf de Dunholm, John the clerk, Richard the clerk son of William le Paum(er) and others.

Seal missing P.R.O. A10776

274 1240s

Sale and quitclaim by William son of William le Paum(er) without any reservation by him or his heirs to Robert de Denecast(r)e of the entire land with appurtenances which William le Paum(er) held and which lies between the land John Bockesberd held towards Gosford (*versus Goseford*) and the land William Stoule held, and of the land with appurtenances which lies [between the land][1] Master Miles (*Milo*) held and the land John Beyer held; to be held of the lords of that fee as freely and quietly as the grantor held and by the same service, namely 2s. annually to them for all service and exaction. Sealing clause. Witnesses: Miles (*Mile*), William Stoule, William de Loundres, Roger Hacoun, William Bronn, Walter Howtred, Simon le Hermon, William Brond, Pagan Pake and others.

Seal extant C.R.O. 2/12

[1] There is some damage here.

275 20 November 1246

Charter of Philip (*phelippus*) le Almer giving to Hugh Pope his entire land beyond Gosford (*ultra Gosseforde*) in the vill of Coventry, namely the land with appurtenances which lies between the land of Henry de Guldintre on the one hand and the land of William le Nater on the other; to be held to him and his heirs of the grantor and his heirs according to the metes and bounds made there freely [etc.], by rendering annually 13d. of silver at four terms of the year according [to the custom] of the vill of Coventry and a pair of gloves at Easter worth ½d. or ½d. for all secular service [etc.]. Warranty and sealing clauses. Witnesses: Robert de Cornil', Osbert (*Osseb(ert)o*) Durdent, William le Stoyl', Hugh le Alm(er), William de Lond', William le Nater, Ralf de Donham, Roger Hacun, John Gamil, Roger the clerk and others. Tuesday, St. Edmund's day A.D. 1246.

Seal extant C.R.O. IA/C64

276 1270s

Charter of Hugh Pope (*dictus Hugo Pope*) of Coventry with the assent and good will of Juliana his wife and his heirs giving to Ralph Bissop his entire land beyond Gosford (*ultra Gosford*) in the vill of Coventry, namely the land with appurtenances which lies between the land Henry de Gildenetr' once held on the one hand and the land of the said Ralph on the other in length and in width as it purports according to the metes and bounds made there; to be held to him, his heirs or assigns, of the grantor, his heirs or assigns, freely [etc.] by rendering annually to the lords of the fee as their perpetual attorneys 13d. of silver at the four terms of the year fixed and usual in the vill of Coventry, and to the grantor, his heirs or assigns, a pair of gloves at Easter worth a ½d. or ½d. for all secular services. Clause for warranty. Ralph gave a ½ mark of silver beforehand. *Et ad majorem securitatem observandam dicta Juliana uxor mea fide media se obligavit ne nomine dotis seu aliquo alio modo post decessum meum de dicta terra exigeret vel clamaret et tam ego quam dicta Juliana huic scripto sigilla nostra apposuimus.* Witnesses: John de Lodelawe then (*tunc tempore*) bailiff, Pagan Pake,

Thomas the Red (*Ruffus*), Roger the Chamberlain (*Cam(er)ar'*), William Stoule, Symon de Kateby, Geoffrey de Nassinton and many others.

2 seals extant C.R.O. IA/MC12/37

277 c.1240s

Charter of Ralf the Priest (*p(re)sbit(er)*) of Wyken (*Wyka*) giving to William le Poleter of Coventry the entire land with appurtenances in the same vill outside Gosford (*extra Goseford*) which Eadmund the Carter (*Carectar'*) once held of the grantor, which lies between the land Adam le Colyer held on the one hand and the land Matthew Tyle held on the other; to be held to him, his heirs or assigns, of the grantor and his assigns, freely [etc.] with 4 selions (*quatuor seylionibus ex parte Croft'*) which the same Eadmund held with all appurtenances by the service of 2s. of silver at four terms of the year according to the usage of Coventry. William gave 2s. of silver in recognition. Warranty and sealing clause. Witnesses: Master Miles (*Maylon'*), David de Mora, Nicholas the clerk, Richard the Mason (*Cementar'*), Walter Houtred, Henry de Goldentre, William Nat(er) and others.

Seal extant C.R.O. 2/9

278 c.1240s

Remise and quitclaim by Wymarca widow of Robert the Bearded (*cu(m)barba*), for herself and her heirs, to Reginald the Merchant (*mercatori*) and his heirs of all right and claim in her entire part of the house in which she used to live in Gosford St. (*domus in quam solitus*[1] *fui habitare in vico de Gosseforde*) in the vill of Coventry, namely that part of the house with appurtenances which is nearer to the house of the said Reginald on the western side; to be held to him and his heirs as freely and quietly as she held and from the same lords from whom she held, namely from Peter Falk' and his heirs and for the same service, namely 15d. annually at four terms of the year according to the usage of the vill of Coventry for all secular service [etc.]. Reginald gave 10s. of silver. Sealing clause. Witnesses: Robert de Cornil', Richard de Hul', William Pit', Henry Pit', Richard de Wenga, John Apirdas, William the Merchant (*mercatore*), Robert Hylwene, Robert de Novecast', Alexander de Glovernia, Henry Long', Peter the Welshman (*Walens'*), Roger the clerk and others.

Seal extant C.R.O. IA/EC12/20

[1] sic

279 1250s

Charter of Alexander Cok of Coventry son of Alexander Cok giving to Richer de Weston' the entire land with houses sited there and all appurtenances in Coventry, in Gosford St. (*in vico de Gosforde*), which lies between the land Robert Hawen' held on the one hand and the land John Hap(er)tas held on the other in length and in width as the land purports from Gosford St. (*a magno vico de gosford*) up to *Hyrsumdich* according to the metes and bounds made there; to be held to him, his heirs or whatsoever [assigns] of the grantor and his heirs freely [etc.], by rendering annually to the lords of that fee as the perpetual attorneys of the grantor or his heirs the rent due and accustomed, namely 12d. of silver at the four terms of the year fixed and customary in the vill of Coventry, and to the grantor and his heirs a pair of white gloves worth 1d. or 1d. at Easter for all secular service [etc.]. Clause for warranty. Richer gave 7 marks of silver in recognition. Sealing clause. Witnesses: Richard de Bok(er)vill' then bailiff, Pagan Pake, Alexander de Glov(er)nia, Walter le Blund,

John Beer, Nicholas ad Barram, John Hap(er)tas, Robert de Denecastr', William Payn, Godfrey le M(er)cer, Warin le M(er)cer, John le Bocmongere, Hugh le Bretun clerk and others.

Seal extant, fragmentary GH 282

280 1250s

Charter of Henry the Merchant (*m(er)cator*) of Titchmarsh (*Tichemers*) giving to Robert the Merchant (*m(er)catori*) of Welham the entire moiety of the land and tenement which he has of the gift of William Pye of Coventry, which lie between the land of Henry Noreys on the one hand and the White Cellar (*Album celariu(m)*) together with a moiety of the entire part which he has in the White Cellar (*Albo celario*) of the gift of the aforesaid William Pye and his heirs with appurtenances in Coventry; to be held to him and his heirs, or to whomsoever he will wish to give or assign, or to do with as he pleases (*aliud facere cum sibi placuerit*) freely [etc.] by rendering annually 3s. 6¾d. at four terms of the year to be paid according to the usage of Coventry for all secular service [etc.]. *Si autem ita contingat quod ego Henricus de Tichemers et heredes mei in aliquo termino redditus solvendi Capitalibus dominis feodi defecerimus ita quod predictus Robertus vel heredes sui aliquod dampnu(m) vel aliquam jacturam pro def(e)c(t)u nostri in redditu solvendo et ipsum et heredes suos adquietando incurrerint extunc autem bene liceat predicto Roberto vel heredibus suis vel aliis sicut predictum est predictum redditum feodi sine contradictione vel cavillacione mei vel heredum meorum capitalibus dominis feodi per manum propriam solvere sicut mihi et heredibus meis reddere solebat.* Clause for warranty. Roger gave 5 marks of silver in recognition. Sealing clause. Witnesses: Anketill de Wikewan', Roger the clerk (*Rog'm clicum*) of Coventry, Robert Cordewan', Nicholas ad Barra(m), William de Alesle, John Hap(er)tas, Robert Denecast(re), William Payn, Henry Nores, Walter de Lange't and others.

Seal missing C.R.O. IA/C13/29

281 c.1260

Charter of Henry son of William Pie giving to Alexander de Glovernia the entire land with appurtenances in the vill of Coventry in Gosford St. (*in vico de Goseforde*) between the land of Henry le Norreis on the one hand and the White Cellar (*album celarium*) on the other, together with the part of the White Cellar belonging to the said land; to be held according to the metes and bounds made there to him and his heirs or to whomsoever he will wish to give, sell, or assign of the grantor and his heirs well [etc.], by rendering annually to the chief lords of the fee 7s. at the four terms of the year usual and fixed in the vill of Coventry as the grantor's perpetual attorneys, namely to Sir Geoffrey de Langele 5s. at the aforesaid four terms, 15d. in each term, and to the heirs of Adam the clerk 2s. at the same terms namely 6d. at each term, and to the grantor and his heirs 1d. at the aforesaid terms and one pair of white gloves worth ½d. or ½d. at Easter for all services, suits of courts, customs and temporal demands. Clause for warranty. Alexander gave 2s. sterling in recognition. Sealing clause. Witnesses: Walter le Blunt, John le Beer, Roger the clerk, Pagan Pake, Godfrey the Mercer (*m(er)cero*), Henry le Norreis, John Hab(er)das, Robert de Denecastr, Nicholas de le Barre, William Pain, Reginald the Mercer (*m(er)cero*), Robert the Miller (*molendinar'*), Richard le Garden(er), Henry de Stannford' and many others.

Seal extant C.R.O. IA/C13

282 Late 1250s–early 1260s

Charter of Richard son of Thomas the Palmer (*palmeri*) of Coventry giving to John the younger (*juveni*) Hapirtas, 12d. rent of assize annually from the grantor's house with appurtenances, namely from the house with appurtenances which is between the land of John le Bucmong(er) on the one hand and the land which was once of Robert Hawen' on the other just as the house purports; to be held to him, his heirs or assigns, freely [etc.] and without any contradiction by the grantor or his heirs, with clause for distraint. Clause for warranty. John gave 10s. of silver fine (*in Gerismonia*). Sealing clause. Witnesses: Walter the White (*blundo*), Pagan Pak', Robert de Donecastr', Alexander de Glov(er)nia, Richard de St. Yvan, Godfrey the Merchant (*m(er)cator'*), Nicholas Jori, John Lalle, John le Bucmo(n)g(er) and others.

Seal missing P.R.O. A 9632

283 Early 1260s

Charter of William le Polet(er) of Coventry giving to John de Lodelowe the messuage in Coventry outside Gosford bridges (*extra pontes de Gosford*) which is between the land Matthew Tele held on the one hand and the land Gilbert son of Adam de Kenisbur' held on the other according to the metes and bounds made there with a certain croft above Gosford (*supra Gosford*) between the land Henry Louecot held on the one hand and the land Master Miles (*Milo*) held on the other in length and in width according to the metes and bounds made there; to be held to him, his heirs or assigns, freely [etc.], by rendering annually to the lords of the fee the due and accustomed services, namely 2s. of silver to the lord prior and convent of Coventry at the four terms of the year usual and fixed in the vill of Coventry, and 8d. of silver to the aforesaid Gilbert son of Adam de Kynisbur and his heirs at the aforesaid terms of the year as the perpetual attorneys of the grantor and his heirs, and to the grantor and his heirs a clove-gillyflower at Christmas for all service. Clause for warranty. Roger gave 5 marks of silver in recognition. Sealing clause. Witnesses: Anketill de Wikewan', Roger the clerk (*Rog'm clicum*) of Coventry, Robert Cordewan', Nicholas ad Barra(m), William de Alesle, John Hap(er)tas, Robert Denecast(re), William Payn, Henry Nores, Walter de Lange't and others.

Seal missing C.R.O. IA/C13/29

284 1270s

Release and quitclaim by Simon de Holand and Alice his wife of Coventry with their consent and good will and for themselves and their heirs to John de Lodelawe of Coventry, his heirs and assigns, of all right and claim in the entire land with the buildings sited there and all appurtenances in the vill of Coventry, in Gosford St. (*in vico de Gosforde*) which lies between the land Thomas the Red (*Ruffus*) held on the one hand and the land Pagan Pake held on the other in length and in width as the land purports according to the metes and bounds made there; to be held freely [etc.] without any demand, charge or contradiction by them or their heirs by rendering annually to the lords of that fee the rent due and accustomed, namely to the heirs of Pagan Pake of Coventry 3s. 6d. at four terms of the year according to the use and custom of the vill of Coventry, and a rose to the heirs of Henry le Guldentr' at the Nativity of St. John the Baptist for all secular service pertaining. Exclusion clause. John gave 20s. of good and legal sterling beforehand in their great need (*in nostro magno negocio*). Sealing clause. Witnesses: Henry Baker (*pistore*) then bailiff, Robert de Chilton', Richard le Brocher, William de Egesfend, Richer de Weston', Henry de Lilleborn', Henry Horsel, Simon de Sowe, Thomas Marie, Ralph Bussop, John Payn and many others.

2 seals extant C.R.O. IA/Misc.I/25

Endorsed: Carta Symo(n)is de holond de terra extra gosford de tenemento Nicholai Pake.

285 1260s

Charter of John son of Simon of Coventry giving to Ralf Bischop of Coventry a certain messuage in the vill of Coventry which lies outside Gosford (*extra Gosford*) between the land of Hugh Pope on the one hand and the land of Simon le Chalun(er) on the other in length and in width according to the metes and bounds made there; to be held to him, his heirs or assigns, of the grantor and his heirs freely [etc.], by rendering annually 12d. of silver at four terms of the year according to the custom of the vill of Coventry for all secular service [etc.]. Ralf gave 2s. of silver beforehand. Warranty and sealing clauses. Witnesses: Pagan Pak', William Brun of Foleshill (*folkesul'*), Walter Houtret, Simon le Chalun(er), Richard the Mason (*Cem(en)tar'*), William the Miller (*molend'*) and others.

Seal extant C.R.O. 2/146

286 Late 1260s

Letters of Brother William prior of the church of Coventry (*Coventr'*) with the assent of the convent giving to John de Pontefracto, his heirs and assigns, a certain part of his land in Gosford St., Coventry (*in Coventre in vico de Goseford*) namely that which lies between the land William de Dunholm once held on the one hand and the watercourse on the other with the moor which William le Stoule held, namely that which extends from the meadow of Peter Barun up to the land Philip Barbidaver(i)l once held between Gosford bridges (*inter pontes de Goseford*); to be held with all appurtenances to him, his heirs or assigns, in chief as their other burgesses hold in Coventry (*in capite sicut alii Burgenses nostri tenent in Coventr'*) of the grantors and their successors freely [etc.], by rendering annually 5s. of silver at the fixed terms in the vill of Coventry for all service pertaining to the aforesaid tenement. Sealing clause. Witnesses: Pagan Pake, Peter Barun, Nicholas a la Bare, Thomas de Fakenham, Roger the Chamberlain (*Camerario*), Robert Pymme, Reginald de Catesby, Walter Helewys and others.

Seal missing C.R.O. IA/EC13/94

287 Late 1260s

Charter of Adam Haldeyn of Coventry son of Richard Haldeyn of the same giving and quitclaiming to Henry son of Henry Baker (*pistoris*) of Coventry all right and claim in 2s. annual rent which the grantor was accustomed to receive annually by hereditary right from a certain furlong (*cultura*) which lies between the land Thomas le Long' used to hold on the one hand in width and the land Richard le Leper held on the other and which extends in length from Gosford St. (*a strata regia que d(icitu)r Gosford*) up to the land of the lord prior which is called *Bromyforlong'*; to be held to him, his heirs or assigns, or to whomsoever he will wish to bequeath or assign in sickness and in health, without clamour or claim, suit or action, by the grantor, his heirs or assigns, Henry gave 15s. sterling beforehand. Sealing clause. Witnesses: Richard de Bokevile, Robert de Chylton', Thomas de Facha(m), Alexander de

Ruton', Nicholas de la Bare, William Toly, Geoffrey Breton', John Tole, Hugh the clerk, Walter Bacun, Robert de Hynkel' priest (*pr(es)b(ite)ro*) and many others.

Seal extant G.H. 288

288 c.1270

Charter of Adam Haldeyn of Coventry, for himself and his heirs, giving to Thomas Symound of Coventry 12d. of silver rent of assize to be taken at the four terms of the year usual in Coventry from the house (*domo*) in Gosford St. (*in vico de Gosford*) which is between the land Thomas the Palmer (*Palmar'*) once held on the one hand and the land Thomas de Fakinham held on the other; to be held with all appurtenances to him, his heirs or assigns, of the grantor and his heirs freely [etc.] by rendering annually a rose at the feast of St. John the Baptist for all service. Clause for warranty. Thomas gave 11s. of silver beforehand. Sealing clause. Witnesses: Richard de Bok(er)vil', Thomas de Fakinh(am), William Hutting, Richer de Weston', William Payn, Richard de St. Yvo, Richard le Fermiler, Robert de Alisl', Warin le M(er)c(er) and others.

Seal extant P.R.O. A6068

289 c.1270

Charter of Adam Haldeyn of Coventry, for himself and his heirs, giving to Thomas Simund and Avicia his wife 12d. of silver rent of assize to be taken at the four terms of the year usual in the vill of Coventry from the house (*domo*) in Gosford St. (*in vico de Gosford*) which is between the land Thomas the Palmer (*Palmarius*) once held on the one hand and the land Thomas de Fakenham held on the other; to be held with all appurtenances to them and their heirs of the grantor and his heirs freely [etc.] or to whomsoever they will wish to give, sell, bequeath or assign in sickness and in health, by rendering annually a rose at the feast of St. John the Baptist for all secular service [etc.] and especially suits of courts. If they, their heirs or assigns, should fall into the grantor's mercy for any transgression, or that of his heirs or assigns, they will be quit for a ½d. of silver. Clause for warranty. Thomas and Avicia gave 11s. of silver beforehand. Sealing clause. Witnesses: Richard le Bokervile, Thomas de Fakenham, William Hutting, Richer de Westun, William Payn, Richard de St. Yvo, Richard le Fermiler, Robert de Allesle, Warin le Mercer and others.

Seal extant but damaged P.R.O. A11136

290 Late 1260s–early 1270s

Charter of Robert de Bylne giving to Reginald de Katisby the entire land with the buildings built there in which the grantor lived (*in qua mansi*) in Gosford St. (*in vico de Gosford*) in Coventry, which lies between the land Reginald de Pynel held and the land Pagan Pake held in length and in width as is manifest according to the metes and bounds made there; to be held by rendering annually to the heirs of Pagan Pake 2s. 6d. at 4 terms of the year, 3 hens and 1 cock at Christmas and the service of 1 man for 1 day in Autumn, and to the grantor and his heirs ½[d.] of silver at Easter. Clause for warranty. Reginald gave 3 marks of silver beforehand. Witnesses: Pagan Pake, Thomas de Fakanham, Richer de Weston, William Hutting, Walter Helewis,

Roger the Chamberlain (*Camerar'*), Reginald de Pinel, Ralf Biscop, William Filour and others.

Seal extant C.R.O. IA/LC12/29
Abstract only. See above p. 64.

291 Late 1260s–early 1270s
Charter of William son of Robert de Bylne of Coventry granting and confirming the charter and confirmation which the said Robert his father gave to the same [sic] Reginald concerning the entire tenement with appurtenances which he held in Gosford St. opposite Reginald's house (*in vico de Gosford ex oposito domus dicti Reginaldi*). Reginald gave 1 mark of silver beforehand. Warranty and sealing clauses. Witnesses: Pagan Pake, Thomas de Fakinham, Richard le Fermiler, Richer de Westona, William Hutting, Henry de Lilleburne, Roger the Chamberlain (*Cam(er)ar'*), Reginald de Pinel', William Stoule and others.

Seal extant C.R.O. IA/LC 12/24

292 Late 1260s–early 1270s
Charter of Reginald de Catisby burgess of Coventry giving to Symon his son, for his fidelity and service, a certain part of his land in the vill of Coventry in Gosford St. (*in vico de Gosford*) which the grantor bought (*comparavi*) from Robert de Bilney and which is between the land Reginald de Pynel held and the land Pagan Pak' held; to be held to him and the legitimate heirs of his body by rendering the service owed to the lords of the fee as the grantor's attorneys, and a gillyflower at Christmas to the grantor and his heirs. Warranty and reversion clauses. Witnesses: Pagan Pake, Thomas de Fakinham, Richard le Fermiler, Richer de Weston, William Hutting, Henry de Lilleburne, Roger the Chamberlain (*Cam(er)ar'*), Reginald de Pinel, Walter Herewis, William Stoule and others.

Seal extant C.R.O. IA/C46
Abstract only. See above p. 64.

293 Late 1260s–early 1270s
Charter of Philip Barbut Averel giving to Thomas Phortwine a messuage with a certain curtilage in the vill of Coventry, in Gosford Street between the bridges (*in vico qui vocatur goseworde stret inter pontes*), between the land of Master Miles (*Mile*) on the one hand and the river (*currentem Riveram*) on the other; to be held to him, his heirs or assigns, of the chief lord of that fee with all liberties, easements and appurtenances whatsoever which will be able to pertain in any way freely [etc.], by rendering annually to the chief lord and his heirs 1d. at four terms of the year according to the fixed customs of the vill for all secular service [etc.]. Clause for warranty. Thomas gave 2½ marks of sterling beforehand. Sealing clause. Witnesses: Richard le Brochare, William Otting, Robert the Miller (*molendinario*), William Crumpe, Payn Pake, Thomas de Fakunham, Richard de Weston' and others.

Seal extant C.R.O. IA/L12–13C/41
Endorsed: Ric' Blaunchend [?] de tenemento de Gosford.

294 29 September 1271
Agreement whereby Roger son of John Hapertahs of Coventry has leased and demised to Hugh de Stanford and Ralf de Burgo herychon' a messuage with appur-

tenances in Coventry in Gosford St. (*In vico de Gosford*), namely that between the land Warin le M(er)cer held on the one hand and the ditch called *le Rededich* on the other in length and in width according to the metes and bounds made there; to be held to them and their heirs and to whomsoever they will wish to give or in any way assign in sickness and in health of the grantor and his heirs freely for a term of 16 years from Michaelmas A.D. 1271, 55 Henry III, by rendering annually to the lords of the fee as the attorneys of Roger and his heirs 18d. at the four terms of the year fixed and usual in the vill of Coventry for all secular service. Any necessary costs expended by Hugh and Ralf, their heirs or assigns, in repairs or maintenance to the said messuage with appurtenances will be fully restored to them by the view of upright men at the end of the term, otherwise they will continue to hold by the aforesaid service until their entire costs have been met. Clause for warranty. Witnesses: Robert de Chilton', Henry Baker (*pistor'*), Alexander Lewin, Adam le T(r)anet(er), Hugh le Bretu(n), Henry Sweyn and others.

Seal extant P.R.O. A6989

295 30 November 1272

Charter of Alice daughter of Robert de Danecastr' widow of Warin le M(er)cer of Coventry in her widowhood and lawful power, at the feast of St. Andrew the Apostle A.D. 1272, giving to Henry de Lilleburn' 2s. annual rent which the grantor used to receive from William the Smith (*fabr'*) son of Philip the Smith (*fabr'*) of Coventry from a land in Earl St. towards Gosford (*de una terra in vico Comitis versus Gosford*) in the vill of Coventry between the land John the Brooch-maker (*Firmac(u)lar'*) once held on the one hand and the land Nicholas Jori held on the other; to be held to him, his heirs or assigns, to whomsoever he will wish to give, bequeath, sell or assign both in sickness and in health by rendering annually to Nicholas Jori and his heirs a pair of white gloves worth ½d. or ½d. at Easter, and to the grantor and her heirs a consound (*consolid'*) at the Nativity of St. John the Baptist for all secular service. Clause for warranty. Henry gave 16s. of silver beforehand. Sealing clause. Witnesses: Peter Baron then (*tunc tempore*) bailiff, Pagan Pake, Walter Helewis, Nicholas Jori, Alexander Bukston, Symon de Sepeya, Richard Burgeys and many others.

Seal extant C.R.O. 2/62

296 Late 1260s–early 1270s

Charter of Walter Helewis of Coventry giving to William Boydin of Stretton, for himself and his heirs, a part of his land with the building sited there in the vill of Coventry in Gosford Street (*in vico de Gosseford*), namely that which lies between the land of Walter once a carter (*Walt' quondam Caretar'*) on the one hand and the land of Roger de Cleybroc on the other in length and in width according to the metes and bounds made there; to be held to him, his heirs or to whomsoever he will wish to give, bequeath, sell or assign both in sickness and in health, of the grantor and his heirs freely [etc.], by rendering annually a pair of white gloves worth ½d. or ½d. *ad voluntatem soleventis* at Easter for all services pertaining. Clause for warranty. William gave 2 marks beforehand. Sealing clause. Witnesses: Robert de Chilton', Henry Baker (*Pistor'*) then bailiff, Pagan Pake, Henry de Lilleburn', Roger le Chaumburleyn, William Huttink, Simon de Sepeye and others.

Seal extant P.R.O. A6209

297 c.1280

Charter of William Boyden' of Stretton (*st(re)tton*) giving to Henry le Bouhestring(er)e of Coventry and Matilda his wife a certain messuage in Gosford Street, Coventry (*in vico de Gosforde de Coventr'*) which is between the land of Walter le Buttere on the one hand and the land of Ralph the Tailor (*cissoris*) on the other in length and in width as is manifest according to the metes and bounds made there; to be held with all its appurtenances to them and their heirs or to whomsoever they will wish to give, bequeath, sell or assign both in sickness and in health freely [etc.], by rendering annually 12d. at the four terms of the year usual and fixed in the vill of Coventry and a pair of gloves worth ½d. or ½d. at Easter for all secular service [etc.]. Clause for warranty. Henry and Matilda gave 20s. of silver beforehand. Sealing clause. Witnesses: Robert de Chilton' then bailiff of Coventry, Henry de Lilleburn', Richard le Northern', Symon de Seeppey, Robert de Allesl', Walter le Butt(er)e, Thomas de Bilneye smith (*fabr'*) and others.

Seal missing P.R.O. A11093

298 c.1290–1297

Charter of William Boydyn of Stretton giving to Ma[tilda][1] Bowestrengmakere a tenement in Gosford Street (*in vico de Gosforde*) in Coventry between the land Richard the Miller (*molendinar'*) bought from Walter le Buttere on the one hand and the land of William de Arningeworthe on the other in length and in width as is manifest according to the metes and bounds made there; to be held with buildings sited there and all appurtenances to her, her heirs or assigns, or to whomsoever she will wish to give, bequeath or assign, of the grantor and his heirs freely [etc.], by rendering annually a pair of gloves worth ½d. or ½d. at Easter for all secular [service][1], exaction and demand. Clause for warranty. Matilda gave (sex[ ])[1] beforehand. Sealing clause. [Witnesses:][1] Henry Baker (*pistore*) [then bailiff][1] of Coventry, William le Parker then coroner, Henry de Lilleburn, [ ][1], Richard le Norther[ne], Hugh Page, Richard Brid, William de Arningworthe, Roger the clerk and others.

Seal extant P.R.O. A4356

[1] The document is damaged and portions are lost.

299 1270s

Charter of Nicholas Jory of Coventry giving to Roger de Boudon' of Coventry the entire land with appurtenances in Coventry, in Gosford St. (*in vico de Gosford*) which lies between the land once of Emma de Wythybroc on the one hand and the land Ralph Pembyl held on the other in length and in width as it purports according to the metes and bounds made there; to be held to him, his heirs or whatsoever assigns, or to whomsoever he will wish to give, bequeath, sell or assign freely [etc.], by rendering annually ½d. of silver at Easter and to the sacrist of the church of the blessed Mary of Coventry 12d. of silver at the four terms of the year usual and fixed in the vill of Coventry for all secular services [etc.]. Clause for warranty. Roger gave 14s. of silver beforehand. Sealing clause. Witnesses: Hugh le Hoser then bailiff, Simon le Chalu(n)ner, Hugh de Burton', William Hobwyl, John le Ponter, William de Grendon' of Coventry, Walter the clerk and others.

Seal missing C.R.O. IA/EC13/82

300 1270s

Charter of Hawise once the daughter of Roger le Stemprer of Coventry, in her virginity and lawful power, giving to Richard the Brooch-maker (*fermacular'*), her entire part of a messuage which came to her by inheritance after the death of Roger her father, and which lies between the land of Roger Pimme on the one hand and the land of Hugh Page on the other in the vill of Coventry, in Gosford St. (*in vico de gosford*) in length and in width as it purports according to the metes and bounds made there; to be held with appurtenances to him, his heirs or whatsoever assigns, of the grantor and her heirs freely [etc.] without contradiction by the grantor or her heirs by rendering annually to the lords of that fee the due and accustomed service, namely to the lord abbot and convent of Combe (*Cumba*) and their successors 1d. of silver at the four terms of the year fixed in the vill of Coventry, and to the grantor and her heirs a clove-gillyflower at Easter for all secular service[etc.]. Clause for warranty. Richard gave 6s. of silver beforehand. Sealing clause. Witnesses: John de Lodelowe then bailiff, Robert de Chilton', Henry de Lillebourne, William de Keneyleworth', Henry Oysel, Thomas Marie, Henry the clerk and many others.

Seal missing C.R.O. IA/EC13/93

301 c.1280

Charter of Richard called (*dictus*) le Brochere in Coventry giving to Guy (*Gwydoni*) his son, for his service, the entire land with houses sited there and all appurtenances in Gosford St. (*in vico de Gosford*) in Coventry which lies between the land Alexander Page at one time held on the one hand and the land Roger Pymme held on the other in length and in width as is manifest according to the metes and bounds made there; to be held to him and his heirs or to whomsoever he will wish to give, bequeath, sell or assign both in sickness and in health of the grantor and his heirs freely [etc.], by rendering annually to the lords of that fee as the perpetual attorneys of the grantor and his heirs 2d. of silver at the four terms of the year fixed and accustomed in the vill of Coventry, namely to the abbot and convent of Combe (*Cumba*), and to Hawise daughter of Roger le Stemprer of Coventry and her heirs a clove-gillyflower at Easter, and to the grantor and his heirs 1d. of silver at the aforesaid terms customary in the vill of Coventry for all secular service [etc.]. Warranty and sealing clause. Witnesses: Robert de Chilton' then bailiff, Henry Baker (*Pistore*), Richer de Weston', Richard de Esseby, Adam Russel, Henry de Lillebourn', William the clerk and others.

Seal extant C.R.O. 2/120

302 c.25 March 1277

Agreement whereby Alice le Heyr and Geoffrey her son have leased, demised and granted to Ralf Biscop of Coventry, his heirs or assigns, 13d. annual rent which they used to receive by the hand of Ralf Byscop from a certain curtilage outside Gosford (*extra Goseford*) in Coventry between the land Henry de Guldentre held on the one hand and the land of Simon le Chalon(er) on the other; to be held to him, his heirs or whatsoever assigns, of the grantors freely [etc.] for a term of 8 years from the feast of the blessed Mary in March 5 Edward I, by rendering annually a clove-gillyflower at Easter for all secular service [etc.]. *Ita quod si dictum redditum dictorum tresdecim denariorum debeat vendi vel diutius ad terminum poni dictus Radulfus et heredes sui seu ejus assignati erunt omnibus aliis propinquiores. Concesserunt eciam dicti Galfridus et Alicia obligantes se jur(is)dictioni officialis archidiaconi Coventr' qui pro tempore fuerit quod de die in diem possint exco(mmun)ic(ationa)ri quamdiu contra tenorem scripti presentis vel aliquis pro eis presumpserint obviare.* Clause for warranty. Ralf gave 3s. of silver beforehand.

Witnesses: John de Lodelowe then bailiff, Henry de Lilleburne, William de Kenilworth, Simon Dras, Robert de Lichefeld, Hugh Page, Thomas Marye and others.

2 seals extant C.R.O. IB/5EI

303 Late 1270s

Charter of Beatrice widow of Richard le Mastlingbeter' giving to Maria her daughter [in free marriage][1], for her service, a certain messuage in Gosford St., Coventry (*in vico Goseforde de Coventr'*) between the land of William de Kenylworth on the one hand and the land of Henry de le Mor on the other with an adjacent curtilage and all appurtenances according to the metes and bounds made there; to be held to her and the heirs issuing from her freely [etc.], by rendering annually to the lords of that fee the service due and accustomed namely at the four fixed terms in Coventry, Should Maria die without heir of her body the entire aforesaid land will descend to Margery daughter of Alice the grantor's sister. Warranty and sealing clauses. Witnesses: Gerard de Allespath' then bailiff, Walter Holewis, William de Kenilleworth', Henry de Lilleburne, Hugh Page and others.

Seal extant C.R.O. 2/154

[1] interlined

304 Early 1280s

Charter of Robert de Lodelowe giving to Alexander the Vintner (*vinitario*) of Coventry a certain part (*quandam partem*) of his land with appurtenances in Coventry, namely a certain meadow next to Altegeder Mills (*juxta molendina que dicuntur Altegedermuilnys*) which lies in length between the grantor's land on the one hand and the meadow of the said Alexander which is called *Helewysemedwe* on the other and purports in width from the watercourse which comes from the bays (*provenit a Baiis*) of the said Alexander up to the arable land of John de Longeleye as the metes and bounds made there purport; to be held to him and his heirs, by (*faciend'*) a clove-gillyflower at Easter annually for all secular service [etc.]. Clause for warranty. Alexander gave 2 marks of silver beforehand. Sealing clause. Witnesses: Robert de Chiltun then bailiff, Henry Baker (*pistor'*), Walter Bakun, Peter Barun', Robert the Miller (*molendin'*), Richard de Esscheby, Geoffrey le Lef, Richard le Butt(er), William the Smith (*fabr'*), Richard le Northerenne, Anketell the clerk and others.

Seal extant C.R.O. IA/C38

305 Late 1280s

Charter of Robert de Lodelowe and Margery his wife giving to Alexander le Vinetar of Coventry and Alexander son of the same Alexander a certain part of their land in Coventry, namely a certain plot (*placeam*) of their land and of their meadow which lies in length from the highway beyond Gosford bridge which leads towards Stoke (*ab alta via ultra pontem de Gosford que ducit versus Stok'*) up to the meadow of the said Alexander which was once of John Wetot and lies in width between the watercourse from Gosford which runs below the bays of Altegeder Mill (*cursum aque de Gosford que currit subtus Bayas molendin' de altegedermulne*) on the one hand and the land of the said Robert which he holds of the inheritance of the said Margery his wife on the other, according to the metes and bounds made there; to be held to Alexander, Alexander his son and the heirs of Alexander junior of the grantors and their heirs entirely, freely and quietly, by rendering annually the said Alexander senior during his entire life, and Alexander junior and his heirs, 1d. at Easter for all secular service [etc.]. Clause for warranty. Alexander senior gave 20s. sterling beforehand. Sealing clause. Witnesses: Henry Baker (*pistor'*) then bailiff in Coventry, Walter Bakun then coroner, Robert de Chilton', Peter Barun, Richer de Weston', Richard de le Muyre, Henry de Lillebourn', Robert Graumpe, John de Lich' clerk and others.

2 seals extant C.R.O. 2/175

306 1280s

Charter of Robert de Lodelowe giving to Henry de Sowe of Coventry a croft with all appurtenances as it is enclosed in the territory of Coventry outside Gosford (*sicut includitur in teritorio de Covintr' extra Gosford*) which lies in width between the land of John le Poluut(er) on the one hand and the land of the same Henry on the other and extends from the furlong (*cultura*) of the lord prior of Coventry which is called *le Wonge* up to *le portweye* according to the metes and bounds made there; to be held to him, his heirs or whatsoever assigns, of the grantor and his heirs freely [etc.], by rendering annually to the grantor, his heirs or assigns, 2s. of silver at the four terms of the year usual and fixed in the vill of Coventry for all secular service [etc.]. Clause for warranty of the croft [here called *hermitescroft*]. Henry gave 20s. of silver beforehand. Sealing clause. Witnesses: Simon le Chaloner, William de Horsha(m), Richard le Northerene, Walter le Berch', Roger de Mora and others.

Seal extant C.R.O. IA/LC12–13/56

307 Early–mid 1280s

Charter of Robert de Lodelowe in Coventry giving to William de Arningworthe *le draper* certain land outside Gosford bridges (*quandam terram quam habui extra pontes de Gosforde*) in Coventry, namely the entire land with houses sited there and all appurtenances which lies in width between the lands Gilbert le Brenetur and Richard le Northerne held on the one hand and the land of Robert Uttred on the other and extends in length from the royal highway (*a regali via*) up to the land of John de Langeleye as is manifest according to the metes and bounds made there; to be held to him, his heirs or assigns, or to whomsoever he will wish to give, bequeath, sell or assign in whatsoever way in sickness and in health of the grantor and his heirs freely [etc.], by rendering annually as the perpetual attorney of the grantor and his heirs to Master Richard de Burton' and Petronilla his wife and their heirs 3s. of silver at the four terms of the year usual and fixed in the vill of Coventry, and to Henry Baker (*pistori*) of Coventry and Agnes his wife, their heirs or assigns, 2s. of silver at the same four terms, and to the grantor, his heirs or assigns, 3s. of silver at the same four terms for all secular services [etc.]. Clause for warranty. William gave 12 marks sterling beforehand. Sealing clause. Witnesses: Henry Baker (*pistor'*) then bailiff, Henry de Lilleburne, Richard le Northerne, Ralf Biscop, Robert Bonde, Robert Uttred, Hugh Page, Symon le Chaloner, Roger de Alesleye the clerk and many others.

Seal extant C.R.O. IA/EC12/9

Endorsed: Irrotulatur in Cur' domini Regis apud Coventre inter placita real' ibidem de anno r.r.h vj xxxij Rotulo xxxiij

308 c. 1290–1297

Charter of Margery widow of Robert de Loudeloue in Coventry in her widowhood giving to William de Arthingworth' merchant in Coventry (*mercatori in Coventr'*) the entire land which she had between Gosford bridges (*inter pontes de Gosseforde*) lying between the land of John Pope on the one hand and the royal highway (*viam Regiam*) on the other in width, and the land of Ralf Cook (*Coci*) on the one hand and the running water on the other in length according to the metes and bounds made there; to be held with all appurtenances to him, his heirs or assigns, of the lords of the fee (*de Dominis feodalibus*) freely [etc.] by rendering annually the services due and accustomed. Clause for warranty. William gave 10s. sterling beforehand. Sealing clause. Witnesses: Henry Baker (*Pistor'*), William le Park(er) then coroner, Adam Russel, Richard le Noreys, Henry de Lilleburne, Hugh Page, John Pope and many others.

Seal extant C.R.O. IA/Misc.I/27

309

c.1290–1297

Charter of Margery widow of Robert de Lodelowe, in her widowhood and lawful power, giving to Robert de Stoke and Joan his wife and the heirs of the same Robert 22d. annual rent with appurtenances in Coventry, 12d. to be received from Alan Lythfot, his heirs or assigns, from the tenement which was of Margery Sparwe and 10d. from Thomas Marie, his heirs or assigns, from a certain tenement in Gosford St. (*Gosforde strete*) between the land of the master of the hospital of St. John of Coventry on the one hand and the land of Robert Uthret on the other; to be held of the chief lords of that fee by the services due and accustomed freely [etc.]. Warranty and sealing clauses. Witnesses: Henry Baker (*pistor'*) then bailiff of Coventry, Henry Ballard, William le Parker, John de Longeleye, Adam Russel, Richard de la Mure, John de Ridiware, William de Artingwrthe, William the clerk and others.

Seal extant C.R.O. IA/C29

Endorsed: Coventr' xxij^{d} in Gosford strete
bars der[1] ante albu(m) celariu(m).

[1] The final letter appears to be an addition.

310

c.1280

Charter of Robert de Lodelawe, Thomas Haldeyn and Alice his wife giving to John le Hanapper in Coventry and Ysabella his wife a certain messuage with appurtenances outside Gosford (*extra Gosford*) in Coventry, which lies between the land of the said John and Ysabella on the one hand and the land of Bate[1] le Brenetour on the other in length and in width according to the metes and bounds made there; to be held to them, their heirs or to whatsoever assigns they will wish to give, sell, bequeath or assign in sickness and in health of the grantors and their heirs freely [etc.], by rendering annually 2 clove-gillyflowers at Easter, namely 1 to Robert de Lodelawe and his heirs and 1 to Thomas Haldeyn and Alice his wife and their heirs, and to the lord prior of Coventry 2s. of silver at the four terms of the year fixed and customary in the vill of Coventry for all secular service. Clause for warranty. John and Ysabella gave 8s. of silver and 6d. in recognition. Sealing clause. Witnesses: Robert de Chilton' then bailiff, Alan the Fishmonger (*piscatore*), Geoffrey de Bernagges, Hugh Sigan, Richard le Noreys, Ralph the Carter (*carectar'*), William de Forsham, Roger de Boudon', William le Lepere and others.

3 seals extant C.R.O. IA/C13/7

[1] sic

311

c.25 March 1280

Agreement whereby Robert de Lodelowe and Margery his wife have leased and granted for a term to Richard le Northrene certain land with the houses sited there and with a curtilage and all appurtenances in Gosford St. (*in vico de Gosford*) between the land Thomas de Fakinham held on the one hand and the land John de Pontefracte held on the other; to be held to him, his heirs or assigns, of the lessors, their heirs and assigns, for a term of 30 years from the feast of the blessed Mary in March 8 Edward I, by rendering annually 16d. of silver at the four terms of the year usual in Coventry. *Si contingat dictus Robertus infra terminum in fa(c)t(a) decedere quod absit et predicta Margeria dictam terram lucrari possit per placitu(m) ita quod dictus Ricardus seisinam termini sui amitat ex tunc concessit dictus Robertus quod idem Ricardus habeat tantam terram infra vill(am) Coventr' ad valorem predicte terre ex traditione heredum dicti Roberti ex eorum traditione sub forma predicta. Et si dictus Ricardus aliquod edificiu(m) de novo ibidem infra terminum apposuerit vel edificaverit in finem termini licebit eidem vel heredibus suis has portar(e); ins(uper) dictus Robertus faciat eidem Ricardo p(ro) suo dono ut(i)que in pace remaneat et predictus Ricardus dictos domos sumptibus suis propriis sustentar(e) debet.* Warranty and sealing clauses. Witnesses: Robert de Chiltun', Robert de Stoke, Peter de Chiltun, Henry de Lilleburn', Anketell de Coleshul' and others.

Indented
2 seals extant C.R.O. IA/Misc. I/28

312 c.24 June 1281

Agreement whereby Robert de Lodelowe has leased and demised to Richard le Northerne 15s. annual rent which he used to receive from William de Horsham from the land which the same William held for the term of his life; the aforesaid rent to be received at the four terms of the year usual in Coventry, to be held to him, his heirs or whatsoever assigns for the term of 2 years from the feast of the Nativity of St. John the Baptist 1281. Clause for warranty. Richard gave 20s. of silver beforehand. Sealing clause [chirograph]. Witnesses: Robert de Chilton' then bailiff, Ralf Bissop, William de Horsham, Hugh Fygon, Simon le Chaloner and others.

Indented
Seal extant C.R.O. IB/9EI/2

313 c.1280

Release and quitclaim by Robert de Lodelawe in Coventry, for himself and his heirs, to Richard le Noreys in Coventry of all right and claim in a house (*domo*) with adjacent curtilage and with appurtenances in the vill of Coventry in Gosford St. (*in vico de Gosforde*), which is sited between the land Ralph le Brocher held on the one hand and the land which the said Richard le Noreys and Thomas the Red (*Ruffus*) held on the other in length and in width as is manifest according to the metes and bounds made there; to be held to him, his heirs and assigns freely [etc.], by rendering annually to the lord of the fee namely Nicholas Pake, his heirs and assigns, 6d. of silver at the four terms of the year according to the usage and custom of the vill of Coventry for all service. Exclusion clause. Richard gave 20s. sterling beforehand. Sealing clause. Witnesses: Robert de Chilton', Thomas de Barsam, Richer de Weston', Robert Bond', Henry de Lilleborn', William de Toucestr', Ralf Bussop and many others.

Seal extant C.R.O. 2/112

314 c.1290–1297

Remise and quitclaim by Margery, widow of Robert de Lodelowe in Coventry, in her widowhood and lawful power to Richard le Northerne *draper*[1] of her third part which fell to her in name of dower from the moiety of a house (*domus*) which the same Richard bought from Robert her husband in Gosford St. (*in vico de Gosforde*) between his land on the one hand and the land Ralf de Belegrave held on the other; to be held to him, his heirs or assigns, well [etc.] by making to the lords of the fee the services due and accustomed. Exclusion and sealing clauses. Witnesses: Henry Baker (*pistor'*) then bailiff in Coventry, Henry de Lilleburne, Robert Bonde, Richard Brid, Hugh Page, Robert Grantpe, Roger the clerk and others.

Seal extant C.R.O. 1A/LC12/26

[1] sic

315 Late 1270s

Charter of William son of Robert de Bylneye and Felicia his wife with the consent and good will of Richard his brother giving to Ralf le Aller of Coventry and Matilda his wife the entire land with buildings sited there in Coventry, in Gosford Street (*in vico de Goseford*) between the land Hamond de Sowe once held on the one hand and the land William de Bromewich of Bentley (*Benteley*) held with Matilda his wife on the other extending from the aforesaid street up to the meadow once of Pagan Pake in length and in width according to the metes and bounds made there; to be held to them and their heirs or to whomsoever they will wish to give, bequeath or assign both in sickness and in health of the grantor and his heirs freely [etc.], by rendering annually to Nicholas Pake and his heirs the rent due and accustomed, namely 2s. 6d. of silver at the four terms of the year usual in Coventry and 3 hens and 1 cock at Christmas and 1 man for 1 day in Autumn, and to the grantor and his heirs a rose at the feast of the Nativity of St. John the Baptist for all secular services [etc.]. Clause for warranty. Ralf and Matilda gave 4 marks of silver beforehand. Sealing clause. Witnesses: Gerard de Alespath' then bailiff, Robert de Chilton', Henry de Lilleburne, Hugh Page, Roger Pymme, Ralf Biscop, Thomas Marie and others.

Seal extant C.R.O. 1A/EC13/62a

316 Late 1270s

Charter of Ralph le Aller of Coventry and Matilda his wife giving to Richard le Northerne of Coventry draper (*draper'*) a messuage with appurtenances in Gosford St. (*in vico de Gosforde*) in Coventry between the land Hadmu(n)d de Sowe once held on the one hand and the land William de Bromwich of Bentley (*Benitley*) with Matilda his wife [held] on the other, extending from the aforesaid street up to the meadow once of Pagan Pake in length and in width according to the metes and bounds made there; to be held to him, his heirs or to whomsoever he will wish to give, bequeath, sell or assign both in sickness and in health freely [etc.], by rendering annually to Nicholas Pake and his heirs the rent due and accustomed, namely 2s. 6d. of silver at the four terms of the year usual in Coventry and 3 hens and one cock at Christmas and one man for one day in Autumn for all secular services. Clause for warranty. Richard gave 5 marks of silver beforehand. Sealing clause. Witnesses: Gerard de Alesp[a]th then bailiff, Robert de Chilton', Henry de Lilleburne, Hugh Page, Roger Pymme, Ralph Biscop, Thomas Marie and others.

Seal extant C.R.O. IA/C13/45

317 Mid–late 1280s

Remise and quitclaim by Alice widow of Ralf Biscop of Coventry, in her widowhood and lawful power, to Richard le Northerne *draper*[1] her entire third part which fell to her by reason of dower of the land which the said Richard bought from the aforesaid Ralf her husband above Gosford (*supra Gosforde*) which lies between the land of the same Richard on the one hand and the land of Henry le Taylur on the other in length and in width as is manifest according to the metes and bounds made there; to be held to him, his heirs and assigns, well [etc.] by rendering annually to the lords of the fee the services due and accustomed. Exclusion clause. Richard gave 2s. of silver beforehand. Sealing clause. Witnesses: Henry Baker (*pistor'*) then bailiff of Coventry, Henry de Lilleburne, Hugh Page, Richard Brid, Robert Bonde, Robert Uttred, William de Arningworth, Symon le Chaloner, Roger the clerk and others.

Seal extant C.R.O. IA/C13/36

[1] sic

318 1280s

Charter of Nicholas de Coventr' chaplain (*Capellanus*) brother of Geoffrey de Nassinton' giving to Richard le Northurn' of Coventry, his heirs or assigns, 13d. annual rent which Geoffrey his brother bought from Henry de Guldentr'; to be held to him, his heirs or assigns, to whomsoever he will wish to give, bequeath or assign, of the grantor, his heirs or assigns freely [etc.], by rendering annually a clove-gillyflower at Easter for all secular services and demands. Clause for warranty. Richard gave 1 mark beforehand. Sealing clause. Witnesses: Henry Baker (*pistore*) then bailiff, Robert de Chilton', Hugh Page, William de Arnyngworth', Robert de Lodelawe and many others.

Seal extant C.R.O. 2/180

319 c.1280

Remise and quitclaim by Richard le Bosevile of Bourton on Dunsmore (*Boruton'*) and Edith his wife to Richard le Northerne of Coventry and Margaret his wife of all right and claim in the entire third part of a messuage with all appurtenances in Coventry in Gosford St. (*in vico de Gosforde*) which fell to her from the inheritance of Symon de Catesby once her husband. Exclusion clause. Should Richard le Bosevile die before his wife Edith, he binds his heirs to warrant the aforesaid third part of a messuage to Richard le Northerne and Margaret his wife and their heirs or assigns. Richard and Margaret gave 20s. of silver beforehand. Sealing clause. Witnesses: Robert de Chilton' then bailiff, Thomas de Barsham, Robert de Lodelowe, Symon de Scepeie, Hugh Page, Ralf Biscop, Henry de Lilleburne, Thomas de Burbathe, William del Parlur, Hugh Tochard, Roger the clerk and many others.

1 seal extant, 1 missing C.R.O. 2/169

320 1280s

Charter of Nicholas Pake of Coventry giving to Richard le Northurne of Coventry 3s. 6d. annual rent which the grantor used to receive from land lying in the vill of Coventry in Gosford St. (*in vico de Gosford*) between the land of Thomas le Rede on the one hand and the land Ralf de Belegrave held on the other; to be held to him, his heirs or assigns, to whomsoever he will wish to give, bequeath, sell or assign of the grantor, his heirs or assigns, freely [etc.] by rendering annually a clove-gillyflower at Easter for all secular services. Clause for warranty. Richard gave 3 marks of silver beforehand. Sealing clause. Witnesses: Henry Baker (*pistore*) then bailiff, Robert de Chilton', Henry de Lilleburn', Hugh Page, Simon de Scepeye, William de Arnynworth', Robert de Lodlawe and others.

Seal extant C.R.O. IA/Misc.I/24

321 Mid 1280s

Charter of Nicholas Pake of Coventry giving to Richard le Northerne of Coventry 3s. annual rent to be taken at the four terms of the year usual and fixed in the vill of Coventry from a certain tenement in Gosford St. (*in vico de Gosforde*) between the land Thomas le Rede held on the one hand and the land Ralf le Brocher held on the other in length and in width as is manifest; to be held with all liberties and easements (*utilitatibus*) which by any cause will be able to accrue to him, his heirs or whatsoever assigns, or to whomsoever he will wish to give, bequeath, sell or in any way grant both in sickness and health well [etc.], by rendering annually a rose at the feast of the Nativity of St. John the Baptist for all secular service. Clause for warranty. Richard gave 2 marks of silver beforehand. Sealing clause. Witnesses: Henry Baker (*pistor'*) then bailiff, Henry de Lilleburne, Richard Brid, Robert Bonde, Robert de Lodelowe, Hugh Page, Ralf Biscop, Robert Utred, Ralf le Brocher, Robert de Alesleye, Roger the clerk and many others.

Seal extant C.R.O. 2/7

322 c.1290–1297

Charter of Ingeram de Arningworthe *draper*[1] and Margery his wife giving to Richard le Northerne of Coventry *draper*[1] the third part which they had in name of Margery's dower through Robert de Lodelowe of a certain tenement which Henry de Sowe bought from the same Robert above Gosford (*supra Gosforde*) and which lies between the land of the same Richard le Northerne on the one hand and the land of Symon le Chaloner on the other; the aforesaid third part of the tenement, namely that which is nearer to the land of the said Richard to be held of the grantor as long as Margery lives well [etc.] to Richard le Northerne, his heirs or assigns, in length and in width just as the aforesaid part fully purports according to the metes and bounds made there with the buildings sited there and all appurtenances, by rendering a consound (*unam consolidam*) at Easter for all secular service [etc.]. Clause for warranty. Richard gave 2s. of silver in advance. Sealing clause. Witnesses: Henry Baker (*pistore*) then bailiff of Coventry, Henry de Lilleburne, Robert Granntpe, Hugh Page, William de Arningworthe, Symon de Arningeworthe, Hugh de Burton', Robert Uttred, Roger the clerk and others.

1 seal extant, 1 missing C.R.O. 2/162

[1] sic

323 8 April 1304

Grant, demise and quitclaim by Nicholas son of Ralph le Allere of Coventry, for himself and his heirs, to Margaret widow of Richard le Northerne of Coventry and to John son and heir of the same Richard of all right and claim in the entire tenement with appurtenances in Gosford St., Coventry (*in vico de Gosforde in Coventr'*) which lies between the tenement of William Pake on the one hand and the tenement of Alfred de Burbathe on the other in width and extends in length from the royal highway (*a regia strata*) up to the meadow of Pagan Pake as is fully manifest according to the metes and bounds made there; to be held to them, their heirs or assigns, freely [etc.] of the chief lords of that fee by the services to the same due and by right accustomed. Exclusion clause. Margaret and John gave 5 marks sterling beforehand. Sealing clause. Witnesses: Robert Baker (*pistore*) then bailiff in Coventry, William Graumpe, William de Schepeye, Adam Russel, John de Rydeware, William de Toucestr', Laurence de Schepeye, Nicholas de Alspade, Thomas de Lilleburne and others. Coventry, Wednesday after the feast of St. Ambrose the Bishop 32 Edward I.

Seal missing C.R.O. 1B/32 EI/5
Endorsed: vicus de Gosford infra pontes.

324 1280s

Charter of William called (*dictus*) Blabestere and Agnes his wife, daughter of Nicholas Drake, giving to Richard the Miller (*molendinar'*) ½d. annual rent or a pair of gloves worth ½d. at Easter to be taken from the heirs of Walter Helewys from a certain tenement which the said Walter once held in Gosford St. (*in vico de Gosforde*) between the land of Robert Grauntpe on the one hand and the land Henry de Eyton held for a term on the other; to be held with all rights and liberties which will accrue by any cause to him, his heirs and assigns, freely [etc.] without any service. Clause for warranty. Richard gave 12d. of silver beforehand. Sealing clause. Witnesses: Henry Baker (*pistor'*) then bailiff, Thomas le Moubrai, John de Fylongeleye, Robert Grauntpe, Richard le Northerne, Hugh Page, Thomas Symond, Robert Uttred, Roger the clerk and others.

1 seal extant, 1 missing C.R.O. IA/C13/39

325 Early–mid 1280s

Charter of Adam son of Walter le Blund of Coventry giving to Thomas Symond of Coventry 9d. annual rent to be taken annually from Robert Gamel, his heirs or assigns, at the four terms of the year usual in the vill of Coventry and a hen at Christmas from a certain tenement towards Gosford bridges (*versus pontes de Gosforde*) which lies between the land of the aforesaid Robert Gamel on the one hand and the land of Robert de Allesleye on the other; to be held to Thomas, his heirs or whatsoever assigns, of the grantor, his heirs or assigns, well [etc.] or to whomsoever he will wish to give, bequeath, sell or assign both in sickness and in health, by rendering annually a red consound (*unam consolidam rubeam*) at Whitsuntide for all secular service [etc.]. Clause for warranty. Thomas gave ½ mark of silver beforehand. Sealing clause. Witnesses: Henry Baker (*pistor'*) then bailiff, Robert the Miller (*molendinar*), Henry de Lilleburne, Henry de Sowa, Geoffrey le Lef, Hugh Page, Richard le Northerne, Ralph Biscop, Robert de Lodelowe, Robert de Allesleye, Roger the clerk and many others.

Seal extant P.R.O. A6879

326 Early 1290s

Charter of Christine Yori of Coventry daughter of Agnes Jori giving to Roger de Boudon' of Coventry the entire land with appurtenances in Gosford St. (*in vico de Gosford*) which lies between the land once of Emma de Wythibroc on the one hand and the land Ralph Pembel held on the other in length and in width according to the metes and bounds made there; to be held to him, his heirs or assigns, of the grantor and her heirs freely [etc.], by rendering annually ½d. at Easter and to the sacrist of the church of the blessed Mary of Coventry 12d. of silver at the four terms of the year fixed in the vill of Coventry for all secular services. Clause for warranty. Roger gave 2s. of silver beforehand. Sealing clause. Witnesses: Henry Baker (*pistore*) then bailiff, William le P(ar)ker, Robert Grauntpe, Henry the Carpenter (*carpentar'*), Himg(r)ammus le Drap(er), William de Arthinworth', Thomas le Chaluner and many others.

Seal extant C.R.O. 2/34

327 6 November 1302

Charter of Symon son of Roger de Boudon' in Coventry giving to Matilda his sister his messuage with appurtenances which he had outside Gosford bridges (*extra pontes de Gosford*) in Coventry which lies in width between the land of Richard Ballard on the one hand and the land of the aforesaid Matilda on the other and extends in length from the royal highway (*a Regali via*) towards the land of the lord prior of Coventry according to the metes and bounds made there; to be held with the buildings sited there and all appurtenances to her, her heirs or assigns, well [etc.] of the chief lords of that fee by the services due and by right accustomed. Clause for warranty. Matilda gave 20s. sterling beforehand. Sealing clause. Witnesses: Roger Daieseie then bailiff of Coventry, Adam Russel, John de Langele, John de Rydeware, William de Arthingworthe, William de Toucestr', Thomas le Chaloner, Richard Ballard, Roger the clerk and others. Coventry, Tuesday the feast of St. Leonard the Abbot 30 Edward I.

Seal extant C.R.O. 1B/30EI/8

328 Early–mid 1290s

Charter of William son and heir of John de Pountfreit giving to John Pope of Coventry and Beatrice his wife a tenement at Gosford (*apud Gosforde*) in the vill of Coventry between the land William Oysel held on the one hand and the watercourse from Gosford (*Gosforde*) on the other in length and in width as it fully purports with buildings sited there and all appurtenances. Moreover he has granted his entire meadow next to the water from Gosford (*juxta aquam de Gosforde*) which lies between the meadow once of Peter Baron on the one hand and the watercourse from Gosford (*Gosforde*) on the other in length and in width according to the metes and bounds made there; to be held to them, their heirs or assigns, of the grantor and his heirs well [etc.], by rendering annually as the perpetual attorneys of the grantor and his heirs to the infirmary of the monks of Coventry (*Infirmitorio monachorum de Coventr'*) 5s. of silver at the four terms of the year usual and fixed in the vill of Coventry, and to the grantor and his heirs a clove-gillyflower at Easter for all secular services [etc.]. Clause for warranty. John and Beatrice gave 3½ marks of silver beforehand. Sealing clause. Witnesses: Henry Baker (*pistore*) then bailiff in Coventry, Henry de Lilleburne, Richard Brid', Richard le Northerne, William de Touchestr', Hugh Page, Robert Grauntpe, William the Smith (*fabro*), Thomas le Rede, Robert Uttred, John Sley, Martin le Loker, Roger the clerk and others.

Seal missing C.R.O. IA/EC13/66
Endorsed: Carta de quod(am) tenemento et prato intra pontes de gosseford.

329 c.1290–1297

Release and quitclaim by Thomas son of William Atte'beh of Foleshill (*Folkeshul*), for himself, his heirs and assigns, to Henry the Carpenter (*Carpentar'*) of Coventry, Emma his wife, their heirs and assigns, of all right and claim in the messuage with appurtenances in the vill of Coventry in Gosford St. (*in vico de Goseford*) which he had by the gift of Walter le Butter of Coventry, which lies between the land the same Walter held on the one hand and the land William Hoysel held on the other and extends from the royal highway (*a regali via*) up to the meadow once of Pagan Pake of Coventry with the entire lane (*semita*) leading to the said messuage up to the aforesaid meadow of Pagan Pake as is manifest according to the metes and bounds there freely [etc.], by rendering annually to Alexander the Vintner (*Vinetar'*) of Coventry, his heirs or assigns, 2s. of silver at four terms of the year according to the use and custom of the vill of Coventry, and to William le Butter, his heirs and assigns, a rose flower at the feast of the Nativity of St. John the Baptist for all service pertaining; with exclusion clause. Henry and Emma gave 30s. of silver beforehand. Sealing clause. *Et ad majorem securitatem super hoc faciend' omnia feofamenta mea eisdem Henrico et Emma deliberavi.* Witnesses: Henry Baker (*pistore*) then bailiff, William the Parker (*Parcar'*), Henry de Lilleburn', Richard le Noreys, William de Fanigwrye, Robert Houtreyd, John Payn and others.

Seal extant P.R.O. A12045
Endorsed: tomas de bilneye.

330 4 April 1294
Charter of John le Hanaper of Coventry giving to John le Pursere of Beverley (*Beverleye*) in Coventry a tenement with appurtenances outside Gosford bridge (*extra pontes de Gosforde*) in Coventry which lies between the land of Geoffrey de Wlveye on the one hand and the land of William Tyle on the other in length and in width as is fully manifest according to the metes and bounds made there; to be held with the buildings sited there and all appurtenances to him, his heirs or assigns, well [etc.] of the chief lords of that fee by the services due and accustomed just as the grantor used to make. Clause for warranty. John gave 10s. of silver beforehand. Sealing clause. Witnesses: Henry Baker (*pistore*) then bailiff in Coventry, William le Parker then coroner, John Thole, Adam Russel, John de Langeleye, Robert de Schepeye, William de Toucestr', Richard le Northerne, William de Arningworthe and others. Coventry, Sunday the feast of St. Ambrose the Bishop 22 Edward I.

Seal extant C.R.O. 1B/22E1/3

331 13 November 1300
Charter of William de Toucestr' in Coventry giving to Richard de la Muyre in Coventry 6 selions of arable land in the field (*campo*) of Coventry outside Gosford (*extra Gosforde*), namely those which lie between the land of William Pake on the one hand and the land of the said Richard on the other in width and extend in length from the royal highway (*a regia via*) up to the land of Lady Alice de Langeleye as is fully manifest according to the metes and bounds made there; to be held with all appurtenances and whatsoever easements belonging thereto to Richard, his heirs or assigns, freely [etc.] of the chief lords of that fee by the services due and by right accustomed. Clause for warranty. Richard gave 40s. sterling beforehand. Sealing clause. Witnesses: Roger Dayeseye then bailiff, John Leuwyne then coroner, John de Langeleye, Adam Russel, Peter Barun, John de Rydewar', Robert Grampe, William de Arthingworth, John Dobedy clerk and others. Coventry, Sunday after the feast of St. Martin the Bishop 28 Edward I.

Seal extant C.R.O. 1B/28 E1/7
Endorsed: Carta Willelmi de Toucestr' de terra que f[uit H]enric' de lilleburn'

332 23 February 1301
Charter of John de Langele knight giving to William le Poter of Coventry a messuage with appurtenances in Gosford St., Coventry on the north side (*in vico de Gosford in*

Coventr' ex parte boreali) which lies in width between the land of Robert de Newenham on the one hand and the lands of William Brid and William de Rokeby on the other and extends in length from the aforesaid street up to the meadow which was once of Pagan Pake according to the metes and bounds made there; to be held with the buildings sited there and all appurtenances to him, his heirs or assigns, well [etc.] of the chief lords of that fee by making annually to them the services due and by right accustomed and by rendering annually to the grantor and his heirs 8s. of silver at the four terms of the year usual and fixed in Coventry and making suit to the grantor's court of Coventry by reasonable summons *quando eam teneri contigerit* for all secular services [etc.]. Clause for warranty. William gave 40s. sterling beforehand. Sealing clause. Witnesses: Roger Daieseie then bailiff of Coventry, John Leofwyne then coroner, Adam Russel, William Grauntpe, Peter Barun, William de Toucestr', Robert Grantpe, Robert de Newenham, Roger the clerk and others. Coventry, Thursday after the feast of St. Peter's Chair 29 Edward I.

Seal missing — Middleton D. 3991

333 — c.1303–1310

Charter of Sir John de Langeley lord of Pinley (*Pinneleye*) giving to William de Arþingworþe in Coventry a messuage in the vill of Coventry which lies between the messuage John de Langeleye merchant in Coventry (*mercator in Cove(n)tr'*) holds on the one hand and the messuage of William de Arþingworþe on the other, and one head abuts on Gosford highway and the other head on the town ditch (*et unum capud abuttat super regale de Gosford et aliud capud super le To(u)ndich*) in length and in width according to the metes made there; to be held with appurtenances to him, his heirs or assigns, of the chief lords of the fee freely [etc.] or to whomsoever he will wish to give, sell, bequeath or assign, by rendering annually to the grantor, his heirs or assigns, 8s. of silver at the four terms of the year usual in the vill of Coventry for all secular service [etc.]. Clause for warranty. William gave 4 marks beforehand. Sealing clause. Witnesses: Robert le Bacster in Coventry, Geoffrey le Chaluner in the same, Henry de Barsham in the same, Gilbert de Eton' in the same, Thomas de Lilleburne in the same and others.

Seal extant — Middleton D 3990

334 — c.25 March 1301

Charter of William de Eriscote and Edith his wife giving to Robert de Neunham of Coventry merchant (*mercatori*) a moiety of the land which Hugh Paie held for a term of years in Gosford St. (*in vico de Gosford*) in Coventry, namely the moiety which lies between the land the aforesaid Hugh held on the one hand and the land Henry the Carpenter (*Carpentar'*) held on the other in width [and] extends from the aforesaid street up to the meadow of William Pake chaplain (*capell(an)i*) in length; to be held with buildings sited there and all appurtenances to him and his assigns for his entire life of the grantors and their heirs after the death of William Eisel, or of their assigns freely [etc.], by rendering annually for a term of 46 years from the feast of the Annunciation of the blessed Mary 29 Edward I 6d. of silver at the four terms of the year usual in the vill of Coventry for all secular services and demands and after the aforesaid term 10s. of silver at the aforesaid four terms of the year for the life of the said Robert. Should Robert die within the term his heirs and assigns should hold by the aforesaid service of 6d. until the end of the term entirely and peacefully. Clause for warranty. Mutual sealing clause [bipartite]. Witnesses: John Leuwyn then coroner of Coventry, Peter Barun, William de Toucestr', Thomas de Lilleburn', William de Arthyngworth', Simon of the same, Gilbert Hichemon and others.

Indented
Seal missing L.R.O. DE/221/3/3/2

335 5 June 1302

Charter of Edmund de Langeleye knight, lord of Shortley (*Schorteleye*), giving to John de Langeleye merchant of Coventry (*mercator' Coventr'*) a messuage with appurtenances in the vill of Coventry lying in Gosford St. (*in vico de Goseford*) between the tenement of Sir John de Langeleye knight on the one hand and the tenement of Henry de Barsam on the other and which extends in length from the royal highway up to the town ditch of Coventry (*a regali via usque ad fossatum ville Coventr'*); to be held to him, his heirs or assigns, freely, [etc.] of the grantor, his heirs or assigns, by rendering annually 6s. sterling at the four terms of the year usual in the vill of Coventry (*Coventree*) for all secular service [etc.]. Warranty and sealing clauses. Witnesses: Roger Dayeseye then bailiff in Coventry, Peter Barun, William de Schepeye, Laurence de Schepey, Nicholas de Alspaye and many others. Coventry, Tuesday before Whitsuntide A.D. 1302.

Seal extant C.R.O. 1B/30EI/9
Endorsed: Carta de duobus cotagiis juxta tenement' Willelmi de Lauucham citra gosseford.

336 6 June 1302

Lease and demise by Eadmund de Langele knight, lord of Shortley (*Schorteleye*), to John de Langeleye of Coventry merchant (*mercatori*) of a messuage with appurtenances in the vill of Coventry lying in Gosford St. (*in vico de Goseforde*) between the tenement of Sir John de Langel' knight on the one hand and the tenement of Henry de Barsham on the other and which extends in length from the royal highway up to the town ditch of Coventry (*a regali via usque ad fossatum ville Coventr*) for the term of 60 years; to be held to him, his heirs or assigns freely [etc.], by rendering annually to the grantor and his heirs 6s. of silver at the four terms of the year usual in the vill of Coventry for all secular services and demands. Warranty and sealing clauses. Coventry, Wednesday after the feast of the Ascension of the Lord 30 Edward I. Witnesses: Roger Dayeseye then bailiff, Peter Barun, Nicholas Crumpe, William de Touecestr', William Grampe and others.

Seal extant C.R.O. 1B/30 EI/10

337 6 Junc 1302

Letters patent of Eadmund de Langeleye appointing his beloved in Christ Nicholas de Allispath of Coventry as his attorney for placing John de Langeleye merchant in Coventry (*in Coventr' mercatorem*) in full and peaceful seisin of a messuage with appurtenances in Gosford St., Coventry (*in vico de Goseforde de Coventr'*); to be held to him, his heirs or assigns, according to what is fully contained in the charter of enfeoffment completed thereon to the same John by the aforesaid Eadmund. Sealing clause. Coventry, Wednesday after the feast of the Ascension of the Lord 30 Edward I.

Seal missing C.R.O. 1B/30EI/4

338 27 August 1302

Charter of Ralf de Belgrave in Coventry giving to William de Schepeye merchant (*mercatori*) in Coventry 12d. annual rent to be taken from a messuage with appurtenances in Gosford St. (*in vico de Goseforde*) which lies between the land Richard le Noreys held on the one hand and the land of John Sleyth on the other; to be held with all liberties, escheats and all other appurtenances to William his heirs or whatsoever assigns freely [etc.] or to whomsoever and whensoever he will wish to give, bequeath, sell or assign in sickness and in health, of the grantor and his heirs, by rendering annually to the chief lords of that fee the service due and accustomed for all secular service and demand. Clause for warranty. William gave 10s. of silver beforehand. Sealing clause. Witnesses: Roger Daysie then bailiff, John Leuyn then coroner, William Graump(e) junior (*minor'*), Henry de Lylleborn' and Thomas his son, William le Potter', Laurence de Schepeye, William de Brauntestone and others. Coventry, Monday after [the feast of] St. Bartholomew 30 Edward I.

Seal missing C.R.O. 1B/30EI/6

339 1300–1303

Gift, remise and quitclaim by Nicholas son and heir of Ralf Aller to Sir John de Segrave of all right and claim in a messuage with appurtenances which lies between the land of William Pake on the one hand and the land of Awerad (*Aweradi*) de Borbage on the other in Gosford St., Coventry (*in vico de Goseford in Coventr'*) according to the metes and bounds made there; to be held to him, his heirs or assigns, well [etc.] without any reservation by the grantor or his heirs. Sealing clause. Witnesses: Roger Dayishee then bailiff of Coventry, William de Toucestr', Henry de Barsam, Peter Barun, Nicholas de Allespathe and others.

Seal extant C.R.O. 1A/EC13/98

340 1300–1303

Charter of Anketinus de Colshull' in Coventry giving to John de Paunthon' clerk 6d. annual rent which he used to receive from the tenement which John Dun holds between Gosford bridges (*inter pontes de Goseford*); to be held with appurtenances to him, his heirs or whatsoever assigns, freely [etc.] by making the services due and accustomed to the lords of that fee. Warranty and sealing clauses. Witnesses: Roger Daysie then bailiff of Coventry, John de Langel', William Graumpe, William de Schepeye, William de Toucestr', Roger de Pacwod', Thomas the clerk and others.

Seal missing C.R.O. 1A/C13/8

341 19 September 1306

Charter of William Oysel of Coventry giving to William de Erescote of Coventry and Edith his wife his entire tenement in Gosford St., Coventry (*in vico de Gosseforde de Coventr'*) lying between the land once of Henry the Carpenter (*carpentar'*) on the one hand and the land once of John Pope and the running water on the other in width and extending from the royal highway (*a via Regia*) up to the meadow of Henry Pake in length according to the metes and bounds made there; to be held to them, their heirs and assigns, of the lords of the fee by the services due and accustomed freely [etc.]. Warranty and sealing clauses. Witnesses: Robert Baker (*Pistor'*) then bailiff, Anketinus de Colsulle, Peter Barun, Adam Russel, Henry Pake, Thomas

Ballard, Richard de Weston' and many others. Coventry, Monday after the feast of the Invention of the Holy Cross 35 Edward I.

Seal extant P.R.O. A10460

342 c.1280

Charter of Thomas Haldeyn of Coventry and Alice his wife giving to Richard le Northenne half of the house with appurtenances which John de Lodelowe once [held] sited between the land of Robert de Lodelowe on the one hand and the land of Henry Ballard on the other in length and in width according to the metes and bounds made there; to be held with appurtenances to him, his heirs or assigns, of the grantors, their heirs or assigns, freely [etc.] to whomsoever they will wish to give, bequeath, sell or assign in sickness and in health by rendering annually to the lord of the fee the rent due and accustomed pertaining to that half, and to the grantors a clove-gillyflower at Easter for all secular service [etc.]. Clause for warranty. *Si vero contingat aliquem venire et aliq(uo)d jus vel clamium in dictam partem inpon(e)re de justo ego Thomas volo et concedo pro me et heredibus meis quod omnes custus intarii*[1] *quos in edificacione vel emendacione appo(s)iti fu(er)int dicto Ricardo et heredibus suis per visum fidedignorum plenarie restitua(n)tur vel quod escambiu(m) alibi de meo tenemento h(ab)ea(n)t quod p(os)sit un(de) equivalere illam partem antedictam sine aliqua contradictione alic(ujus) vel etiam uxoris mee post decessum meum si contingat quod h(ab)ea(n)t escambium sicut dictum est.* Sealing clause. Witnesses: Robert de Chiltone then bailiff, Richard le Brocher, Adam Russel, Richer de Weston', Henry de Lilleburn' and others.

Seal extant C.R.O. 2/126

[1] sic

343 Early 1290s

Charter of Thomas Haldeyn of Coventry and Alice his wife giving to Alexander called Vintner (*dicto vinetar'*) of Coventry their entire land in the field of Stoke near Gosford Green (*in campo de Stok' prope Gosefordegrene*) which was once of John de Lodelowe ancestor (*antecessoris*) of the aforesaid Alice; to be held to him, his heirs or whatsoever assigns, freely [etc.] with all appurtenances in meadows, pastures, roads, lanes, ditches and hedges without any reservation by the grantors or their heirs of the lords of that fee by the services due and accustomed. Clause for warranty. Alexander gave 10 marks of silver. Sealing clause. Witnesses: Henry Baker (*Pistor'*) then bailiff of Coventry, William le Parker then coroner, Robert de Chilton', Adam Russel, John de Ridewar', Roger le Chamburleyn, John de Langeley, Richard de Mur', William de Thoucestr', Henry de Lilleburn', Robert Grantpe and others.

2 seals extant C.R.O. IA/Misc.I/12

344 7 November 1296

Charter of Richard le Northerne of Coventry draper (*draparius*) giving to Richard de la Muyre merchant in Coventry (*in Coventr' mercatori*) and Alice his wife the land with appurtenances which he had towards Gosford Green (*versus Gosfordegrene*) in Coventry, which lies in width between the land Henry de Lilleburne held on the one hand and the land Henry de Sowe tailor (*scissor*) held on the other and extends in length from the royal highway (*a Regali via*) up to the land Lady Alice de Langele held as is manifest according to the metes and bounds made there; to be held with the buildings sited there and all appurtenances to them and the heirs of the same Richard and his assigns well [etc.] of the lords of that fee, by rendering annually to the same lords the services due and by right accustomed. Clause for warranty. Richard and Alice gave 10 marks sterling beforehand. Sealing clause. Witnesses: Henry Baker (*pistore*) then bailiff in Coventry, William called (*dicto*) Parker then coroner, Master Richard de Aula, Adam Russel, Richard de Weston', John de Langele, Geoffrey le Chaloner, Henry de Lilleburne, William de Toucestr', Robert Grantpe, Hugh Page, William de Arthyngworthe, Roger the clerk and others. Coventry, Wednesday after the feast of St. Leonard the Confessor 23 Edward I.

Seal missing C.R.O. 1B/23 EI/7

345 c.1290–1298

Gift by Richard le Northerne of Coventry to Richard de la Muyre merchant in Coventry (*in Coventr' mercatori*) for the entire life of Margery de Lodelowe her dower from the tenement of Henry de Sowe towards Gosford Green (*versus Gosfordegrene*) in Coventry on the southern side (*ex parte australi*) between the land of the same Richard de la Muyre on the one hand and the land of the said Henry de Sowe on the other in length and in width as it purports, which dower the said Richard le Northerne bought (*co(m)paravi*) from the aforesaid Margery in her widowhood; to be held to him, his heirs or assigns, well [etc.] during Margery's entire life of the lords of that fee by the services due and accustomed. Clause for warranty. Richard gave 3s. of silver beforehand. Sealing clause. Witnesses: William called (*dicto*) Parker then coroner of Coventry, Adam Russel, John de Langele, Ralf le Hunte, William de Touestr', William Grantpe, John de Rydeware and others.

Seal extant C.R.O. 2/15

346 1217–1221

Charter of Henry de Audley granting Altegeder Mill at Coventry to Richard son of Wunman of Coventry at a rent of 3 marks per annum.

Henricus de Aldithelega omnibus hominibus suis et amicis presentibus et futuris salutem. Notum sit vobis omnibus me dedisse et concessisse et hac presenti carta mea confirmasse Ricardo filio Wimon de Covent' et heredibus suis tenendum de me et de heredibus meis in feudo et hereditate molandinum meum apud Covent' quod vocatur altegedera mulna cum omnibus pertinenciis suis libere et quiete et honorifice reddendo annuatim mihi et heredibus meis ipse et heredes sui tres marcas argenti ad iiij terminos anni scilicet ad festum sancti Michaelis x solidos argenti et ad festum sancti Andree x solidos et ad festum sancte Marie in Marcio x solidos et ad Nativitatem sancti Johannis Baptiste x solidos pro omni seculari servicio mihi et heredibus meis pertinenti. Hiis testibus Waltero filio Therrici de Covent', Rogero de Buscherevill', Gilberto Capellano, Vihelo de Folkeshulla, Roberto Blundo, Ricardo de Hundelona, Swano filio Ade, Stephano filio H(er)eb(er)ti, Willelmo de Rependona, Willelmo Hacun, Rogero de Kirkebi, Johanne M(er)wine et multis aliis.

Seal missing C.R.O. 2/8

Henry de Audley was one of those who submitted their charters for royal confirmation in the spring of 1227. Among those he submitted were several grants from Ranulf, earl of Chester and Lincoln, during or shortly after he functioned for the earl as under-sheriff of Shropshire and Stafford (*C.Ch.R. 1226–1257* p. 36; *G.E.C.* vol. I, p. 337). They included Altegeder Mill. Walter de Coventry is not in evidence after 1221 (see above No. 21), by which time Roger de Busherville had been succeeded at Ansty by Henry (*Eyre Rolls 1221*, Nos. 718, 1504).

347 c.1220

Charter of Richard son of Wunman giving to William Falke and his heirs half his mill called Altegeder Mill (*Altegedere Mulne*) with all appurtenances within the mill-pond and without in lands and meadows, in fisheries and pastures from below the mill and from above and on both sides of the water (*desub molendino illo et desursum et ex utraque parte aque*) with all liberties pertaining to the aforesaid mill; to be held to him and his heirs of the grantor and his heirs hereditarily, freely [etc.], by rendering annually 21s. 6d. at four terms, namely 5s. 4½d. at each of the feasts of St. Mary in March, St. John the Baptist, St. Michael and St. Andrew for all secular service and all demand. Clause for warranty. William gave 3½ marks of silver in recognition, and to Walter the grantor's son ½ bezant. Witnesses: Viellus de Folkeshull', Nicholas son of Nicholas, Richard de Aula, Philip son of Miles, Peter the Welshman (*Walensi*), William Crude, Geoffrey his son, Amfr(idus) of Park St. (*de vico parci*), Reginald and Simon his sons, John Buckesb't, John M(er)uen' and others.

Seal extant C.R.O. 1A/MC12/40b

348 c.1220

Charter of Richard son of Wunman giving to Ralf the Miller (*molendinario*) and his heirs half his mill called Altegeder Mill [identical in form and content, including witnesses, to the above].

Seal extant C.R.O. 1A/MC12/40a

349 c.1220s

Charter of William de Bromlee giving to Ralf the Miller (*molendinar'*) half of his mill outside the vill of Coventry which is called Altegeder Mill (*altegedere mulne*) with all appurtenances within the mill-pond and without, in lands and meadows, fisheries and pastures, from above and from below the mill and on both sides of the water with all liberties pertaining to the aforesaid mill; to be held to him and his heirs of the grantor and his heirs, hereditarily, freely [etc.], by rendering annually for all secular service and demand 21s. 6d. at four terms of the year, namely 5s. 4½d. at each of the feasts of St. Mary in March, St. John the Baptist, St. Michael and St. Andrew. Clause for warranty. Ralf gave 10s. of silver in recognition. Witnesses: Vielus de Folkishul', Nicholas son of Nicholas, Richard de Aula, Robert the Vintner (*vinetar'*), Roger the Gardener (*gardinar'*), William Crude, Geoffrey his son, Aunfridus the Merchant (*Aunfr' mercator'*), Reginald and Simon his sons, John Buckisb(er)t, John Merwin' and many others.

Seal missing G.H. 266

350 1240s

Charter of Peter son of William Falke giving to Hugh Falke his kinsman (*consanguineo meo*) his entire part of Altegeder Mill (*molendini de Alteghedermulne*) with all appurtenances, liberties and easements in meadows, lands, pastures, waters and fisheries beneath and below the aforesaid mill ([?]*subter molendinum pred' et deorsum*) and in all liberties pertaining to the same mill; to be held to him, his heirs or to whomsoever he will wish to give, sell, bequeath or assign of the grantor and his heirs freely [etc.], by rendering annually to the grantor, his heirs or his attorneys, 2s. of silver at the four terms of the year fixed in Coventry, and to the lords of that fee the service owed *per annum*, namely 21s. 6d. at the same terms for all secular service [etc.]. Clause for warranty. Hugh gave 2 marks of silver in recognition. Sealing clause. Witnesses:

Osbert Durdent, Richard the Burgess (*Burgenci*), John Beer, Richard de Blokevill', Pagan Pake, Roger de Stivechale, Robert de Recham, William Pye, Reginald the Merchant (*mercatore*), Roger Spirie, John M(er)ewin', Nicholas Fordwin' and others.

Seal missing C.R.O. IA/C12/13

351 Mid 1240s

Charter of Peter son of William Falke granting to William Pye and his heirs that they may be his attorneys for receiving and paying his farm due (*firmam meam debitam quam debui reddere*) annually to the heirs of Nicholas de Widibrok', namely from Reginald the Merchant (*m(er)catore*) and his heirs 40d. to be received at four terms of the year according to the usage of Coventry, from Henry son of the said William Pye 3 men for 1 day in Autumn and 3 hens at Christmas and 24d. of silver at four terms of the year, and from the aforesaid William 1 hen at Christmas and 1 man for 1 day in Autumn. Sealing clause. Witnesses: Osbert Durdent, Richard Burgeys, Pagan Pake, Richard de Wengha, Reginald the Merchant (*mer)catore*), Robert Haune, Richard le Gardin(er) and others.

Seal extant G.H. 279

352 1260s

Grant by Henry de Bromleya and demise for the grantor's life to Henry de Sysiston' of his mill called Altegeder Mill (*altogedere mulne*) with appurtenances; to be held to him and his heirs by rendering annually 45s. in equal portions at the four terms of the year usual in Coventry, namely 11s. 3d. at each of the feasts of St. Michael, St. Andrew, St. Mary in March, and the Nativity of St. John the Baptist. Warranty and sealing clauses. Witnesses: Geoffrey de Wylenhal', Ralf de Wytel', Ranulph de Styvech', Robert de Chilton, Richard Ernis, Henry Baker (*pistore*), Hugh le Breton and others.

Indented
Seal extant C.R.O. IA/EC12/22

353 c.1280

Charter of Thomas Haldeyn of Coventry and Alice his wife giving to Henry de Dueston burgess of Bristol (*burgenc' BrustoWie*) their entire part of, and their right in, the two watermills called Altegeder Mills of the township of Coventry (*duorum molendinorum aquatic' qui vocantur altegideremulnes de villata de Coventr'*) with the meadow [and] the moor adjacent and with fisheries, lanes, roads and all appurtenances belonging to the said mills. Moreover they have granted their entire part of, and their right in, a meadow outside the vill of Coventry called *helewisewelle* which Richard le Masun of Coventry held and which lies between the meadow which Richard de St. Yvo once held on the one hand and the running water on the other as is manifest. Moreover they have granted their entire part of, and their right in, 1d. annual rent which Matilda de Pineley and her heirs used to render at Christmas from a house which she held in the vill of Coventry in the lane called Dead Lane (*in viculo quod d(icitu)r le Dedelon'*) sited between the land John le Butt(er) held on the one hand and the land Geoffrey le Lef held on the other as is manifest; to be held to him, his heirs or whatsoever assigns, of the grantors and their heirs freely [etc.], by rendering annually 45s. of silver to the lords of that fee, and to the grantors and their heirs a rose at the feast of the Nativity of St. John the Baptist for all secular service. Clause for warranty. Henry gave 10 marks of silver beforehand.

Sealing clause. Witnesses: Robert de Chilton', Henry Baker (*pistore*), Thomas de Fakenham, Richard the Brooch-maker (*fermaculario*), William de Egesfend, Geoffrey Lunton, Henry Brayn, John the Summoner (*Su(m)monitor'*), Peter Barun and others.

2 seals extant C.R.O. IA/Misc.I/11

354 16 August 1306

Charter of Alexander son and heir of Alexander le Vynet(er) of Coventry giving to Henry Bagod of Coventry merchant (*mercatori*) and Katherine (*katerine*) his wife his mills which are called Altegeder Mills (*Altegederemulnes*) in Coventry which the aforesaid Henry formerly held for the term of his life by the grantor's demise; to be held with mill-ponds, fishponds, fisheries, ditches, fences, hedges, meadows, pastures, roads, lanes, waters and with all other appurtenances wheresoever to them and the heirs of their bodies legitimately begotten, of the grantor and his heirs, freely and peacefully by rendering annually to the chief lords of that fee as their attorneys the services due and by right accustomed, and to the grantor and his heirs 40s. of silver at the four terms of the year usual in Coventry by equal portions. Clause for warranty. Successive remainders in default of such heirs to John Bagod brother of the aforesaid Henry and the heirs of his body legitimately begotten, to William Bagod brother of the aforesaid Henry and the heirs of his body legitimately begotten, to Felicia sister of the aforesaid Henry and the heirs of her body legitimately begotten, and to John de Bromleye and the heirs of his body legitimately begotten, with reversion to the grantor and his heirs. Mutual sealing clause. Witnesses: William Grauntpe, Geoffrey Grauntpe, Adam Russel, Henry his son, Ralf le Hunte, Peter Barun, Henry Pake, Robert de Chilton', William de Braundeston' and others. Coventry, Tuesday the morrow of the Assumption of the blessed Mary 34 Edward I.

Indented
Seal extant C.R.O. 1B/34EI/10

EARL'S MILL LANE*

*For other references to Earl's Mill Lane see 174, 217, 246.

355 c. late 1280s

Remise and quitclaim by Margery widow of Ralf le Turnur of Coventry in her pure and lawful widowhood, for herself and her heirs, to Peter Barun of Coventry of all right and claim in a curtilage in Earl's Mill Lane (*in vic(u)lo qui dicitur Erlesmilnelone*) lying between the land Richard le Brocher once held on the one hand and the land Robert Grauntpe once held on the other; to be held with all appurtenances to him, his heirs or whatsoever assigns, without reservation or impediment by the grantor or her heirs freely [etc.]. Exclusion clause. Moreover Margery has remised and released all actions and pleas (*causas actiones contentiones et omnia placita*) against Peter and his heirs. Sealing clause. Witnesses: Henry Baker (*pistor'*) then bailiff of Coventry, Adam Russel of the same, Thomas de Barsam of the same, Richard de Esseby of the same, Richer de Weston' of the same, Peter de Eggesfeld of the same, Geoffrey Lef of the same, Peter the clerk of the same and many others.

Seal missing C.R.O. IA/EC13/72

356 c.29 September 1291

Lease, grant and demise at farm by Guy son of Richard le Brocher of Coventry, with the consent of Henry Baker (*pistoris*) of Coventry, Adam Russel, Richard de la Muyre his guardian (*custodis mei*), John de Rydeware and his other friends (*aliorum amicorum meorum*), to John de Langeleye merchant (*mercatori*) of his entire tenement in Earl's Mill Lane (*Erlesmulnelone*) in Coventry with the buildings sited there and all appurtenances and his chief messuage (*capitale mansum meum*) in Earl St., Coventry (*in vico Comitis Coventr'*) with the buildings sited there and adjacent easements between the land of the same John on the one hand and the land of Sarah (*Sarre*) the grantor's sister on the other, and his kiln (*torrebulam meam*) and certain vessels (*quedam vasa*) here named worth 12s. 6d. namely *unum plumbum in fornace, unum maysfat, unum cappethron, unum gylfat, unum secur(em), et unum algeum quod appellatur Enedthron*; to be held to him, his heirs or assigns, freely [etc.] for a term of 6 years from Michaelmas 19 Edward I. During the term the lessee, his heirs or assigns, will maintain all buildings of the said tenement at their own cost in at least as good a state as they were at the beginning of the term *nisi fortuna incendii evenerit quod absit*, rendering 36s. of silver at the four terms of the year usual and fixed in the vill of Coventry for all secular service. Clause for warranty. Sealing clause [chirograph]. Witnesses: Henry Baker (*pistore*) then bailiff in Coventry, Robert de Chilton', William le Parker, Adam

Russel, Peter de Egesfeld, Richard de la Muyre, John de Rydeware, Symon Russel, William Grantpe and others.

Indented
Seal extant C.R.O. IB/19EI/2

The following is added on the fold in the same hand: Et predictus Gydo dimisit predicto Johanni unam mensa(m) cum trescellis ad dictum terminum.

357 16 August 1294

Letters of Guy son of Richard the Brocher of Coventry appointing John de Langeleye merchant in Coventry (*in Coventr' mercatorem*) as his lawful attorney for placing Richard de la Muyre merchant (*mercatorem*) and Alice his wife in seisin of the tenements which the aforesaid John held of him (Guy) in Earl's Mill Lane and Earl St., Coventry (*in Erlesmulnelone in Coventr' et in vico Comitis ejusdem ville*), to be held to them, their heirs and assigns, for a term of 10 years from Michaelmas 22 Edward I. Sealing clause. Coventry, the morrow of the Assumption of the blessed Mary the Virgin the year aforesaid.

Seal missing C.R.O. IB/22EI/11

358 22 September 1297

Charter of Henry son of Richard le Brocher of Coventry giving to John son of Sarah (*Sarre*) the grantor's sister a curtilage with appurtenances in Earl's Mill Lane (*Erlesmulnelone*) in Coventry between the land of Peter Baron and Nicholas Crumpe on the one hand and the land of Alured the Girdler (*zonarii*) on the other, which extends in length from Earl's Mill Lane (*Erlesmulne lone*) up to the land of Henry de la More and which contains in width 40 feet towards the land of the said Henry de la More and 24 feet towards Earl's Mill Lane (*Erlesmulnelone*); to be held to him, his heirs or whatsoever assigns, well [etc.] of the chief lords of that fee by the services due and accustomed. Warranty and sealing clauses. Witnesses: Henry Baker (*Pistore*) then bailiff of Coventry, William called (*dicto*) Parker then coroner, Adam Russel, John de Langele, Richard de la Muyre, William Grantpe, Roger Box, Thomas Marie, Roger the clerk and others. Coventry, Sunday the morrow of St. Matthew the Apostle 25 Edward I.

Seal extant C.R.O. IB/25EI/3

359 22 September 1297

Charter of Henry son of Richard le Brocher of Coventry giving to John son of Sarah (*Sarre*) the grantor's sister 12d. annual rent which Alured le Ceinturer used to render at the four terms of the year usual in Coventry from a curtilage he held of the grantor for a term of years in Earl's Mill Lane (*in venella que dicitur le Erlesmulnelone*) in Coventry which lies between the land of Nicholas Crumpe on the one hand and the land of the aforesaid Alured on the other in length and in width as is manifest together with the reversion of the said curtilage at the end of Alured's term; to be held to him, his heirs or assigns, well [etc.] of the lords of that fee by the services due and by right accustomed. Clause for warranty. Sealing clause. Witnesses: Henry Baker (*Pistore*) then bailiff of Coventry, William called (*dicto*) Park(er) then coroner, Adam Russel, John de Langele, Richard de la Muyre, William Grantpe, Henry de Barsham, Nicholas Crumpe, Roger Box and others. Coventry, Monday after the feast of St. Matthew the Apostle 25 Edward I.

Seal missing C.R.O.IB/25EI/8

TOWARDS ST. MICHAEL'S CHURCH, BAYLEY LANE*

*Exact locations are not always clear. It seems that we should include here not only the modern Bayley Lane running eastwards from the junction with Hay Lane but also the section running westwards from there to Broadgate (later Pepper Lane). This is undoubtedly the street referred to in 47, 58 above. 364, however, is endorsed as in Hay Lane, and some other properties (e.g. 360) may also lie there.

Bayley Lane is evidenced from c.1220 at the latest (above 176, *Langley Cartulary* Nos. 272, 270, 277). It is also given as *in balliva* (below 767.20), a usage which is echoed in the *Langley Cartulary* (*in ballivo qui ducit ad ecclesiam sancti Michaelis*, No. 275). For the relationship of this street to the castle see above p. xxxii. For other occurrences of Bayley Lane see 767.6, .18, .19, .20, .22, .23. Deeds relating to St. Michael's cemetery have also been included here. See also 761. For a tenement on the north side of St. Michael's church called *le Fouleslou* see *Langley Cartulary* Nos. 182, 202, 313.

360 c.1260–1262

Gift and quitclaim by Geoffrey once the brother and heir of Walter le Butt(er) of Coventry to John de Lodelawe of the entire stone house (*totam domum meam lapideam*) with all appurtenances in the street (*in vico*) towards the church of St. Michael which descended to him through the death of Walter his brother together with all lands and tenements which may accrue to him by hereditary right in any way; to be held to him and his heirs or to whomsoever he will wish to give, bequeath or assign by making to the lords of the fee the service due and accustomed. Exclusion clause. John gave £10 sterling beforehand. Sealing clause. Witnesses: William Leuwine, Robert de Chilton', Henry le Pestour' then bailiffs (*balli(vi)s*) of Coventry, John Sym', Anketill de Wekewane, Walter the White (*Blundo*), Ralf de Bannebur', Peter Baru(n), Richard de Brug' and others.

Seal missing C.R.O. 2/78

Endorsed: Carta Galfrid' fr(atr)is Walteri le butt(er)e de aula.

361 Late 1270s

Remise and quitclaim by Nicholas de Scheinto(n) son of William de Schenton' to Roger the Fishmonger (*piscator'*) of all right and claim in the entire land with all buildings and all appurtenances towards the church of St. Michael of Coventry, which lies between the land Thomas Pavy held on the one hand and the land Petronilla de Aula held on the other in length and in width as the land purports and according to the metes and bounds made there; to be held to him, his heirs or whatsoever assigns freely [etc.] by rendering annually to the lords of that fee the rent and service owed for all secular service [etc.]. Exclusion clause. Sealing clause, for 12s. of silver which Roger gave beforehand. Witnesses: Gerard de Allispath then bailiff in Coventry, Robert de Chilton', Hugh le Hos', John Thole, Robert Lond', Geoffrey Bretun, Henry Baker (*pistor'*), Hugh Bochy, Richard de Dunestaple, Anketell the clerk and others.

Seal missing C.R.O. IA/Misc.I/14

362 Early 1280s

Remise and quitclaim by Roger the Fishmonger (*piscator*) of Coventry for himself and his heirs to John de Wedone of all [right] and claim in the entire land with houses sited there and all other appurtenances towards the church of St. Michael which lies between the land Thomas Pavy once held on the one hand and the land Alice of Chester (*Cestrie*) held on the other in length and in width as the land purports according to the metes and bounds made there. Moreover he has remised and quitclaimed 6d. annual rent from the land which was given to Alice of Chester (*Cestrie*) next to the aforesaid land; to be held to him, his heirs or whatsoever assigns, or to whomsoever he will wish to give, bequeath, sell or assign in sickness and in health freely [etc.] by rendering annually to Master Richard de Burton' and Petronilla his wife and their heirs 4s. 6d. of silver at the four terms of the year usual in Coventry for all secular services [etc.]. Exclusion clause. Sealing clause, for 3 marks of silver which John gave beforehand. Witnesses: Henry Baker (*pistor'*), John Mynot, Thomas le Moubray, Thomas de Fakinham, John Thole, John the Miller (*molend'*), Anketell the clerk and others.

Seal extant C.R.O. 2/32

363 Early 1280s

Remise and quitclaim by William de Seinton', for himself and his heirs, to John de Wedone of all right and claim in certain land with the houses sited there and all appurtenances in the lane (*venela*) leading towards the church of St. Michael of Coventry, which lies between the land Thomas Pavy once held on the one hand and the land Alice daughter of William le Furn(er) held on the other in length and in width as the land purports according to the metes and bounds made there; to be held to him, his heirs or whatsoever assigns, or to whomsoever his term and his right in the aforesaid land with all appurtenances he will wish to give, sell, bequeath or assign in sickness and in health of the grantor, his heirs or assigns, freely [etc.] just as the grantor held and just as is fully contained in the chirograph made between the grantor and Nicholas de Scheinton' up to the end of the term by rendering annually to the lords of that fee the rent due and accustomed, namely 4s. 6d. of silver to Master Richard de Aula and Petronilla his wife at the four terms of the year usual in Coventry and to Nicholas de Stheinton' ½d. at Easter for all service. Moreover he has granted to the same John 6d. annual rent which Alice daughter of William le Furn(er) used to render from the land which was given to the same Alice opposite the said land. Exclusion clause. Sealing clause, for 6 marks of silver. Witnesses: Henry Baker (*pistore*), Thomas le Moubray, John Mynot, Roger Feribihinde(m), John the Miller (*molend'*), Anketell the clerk and others.

Seal extant C.R.O. IA/C13/4

364 Early 1280s

Remise and quitclaim by Symon Blythe of Elvaston (*? Elvistowe*), for himself and his heirs, to John de Wedon' of all right and claim in the entire land with the houses sited there and all appurtenances in the lane (*venela*) leading towards the church of St. Michael, which lies between the land Thomas Pavey held on the one hand and the land Alice la Furnere daughter of Margery (*m^a^rg'*) la Furnere held on the other together with all the goods, vessels and chattels there both movable and immovable (*symul cum omnibus bonis vasis et catall' mobilibus et inmobilibus ibidem cresscentibus et existentibus*); to be held to him, his heirs or whatsoever assigns, or to whomsoever he will wish to give, bequeath, sell or assign in sickness and in health freely [etc.]. Exclusion clause. John gave 4 marks of silver beforehand. Sealing clause. Witnesses: Robert de Chiltun then bailiff, Thomas le Moubray, William Lotemon, Edward the Tanner (*Ewardo tannatore*), Walter Bakun', John the Miller (*molendin'*), Anketull de Colishul clerk and others.

Seal extant C.R.O. IA/C13/61
Endorsed: vinell' voc' heylan' ducent' versus ecclesiam sancti Michaelis.

365 1280s

Charter of William de Copston of Coventry and Juliana his wife giving to John the Goldsmith (*aurifabro*) and Alice his wife the entire land with the houses sited there which Thomas Pavy once held in Coventry towards the church of St. Michael, which lies between the lane (*viculum*) which leads towards the monastery of St. Mary on the one hand and the land of John de Wedon' on the other in length and in width according to the metes and bounds made there *ab antiquo*; to be held with all appurtenances to them and the heirs begotten legitimately between them freely [etc.], by rendering annually to Master Richard de Aula of Coventry and Petronilla his wife and their heirs 2s. 2d. at the four terms of the year usual and fixed in the vill of Coventry, and to the grantors as long as they live 5s. annually at the aforesaid terms. After the death of the grantors Richard son of Robert de Estleye, his heirs or assigns, will have the aforesaid 5s. annual rent. Clause for warranty by the grantors during their lives and by Richard son of Robert de Estleye and his heirs thereafter. Remainder and reversion (*quiete remaneat et integre revertatur*) to Richard son of Robert de Estleye, his heirs or assigns, should John and Alice die without heir begotten legitimately between them. Sealing clause. Witnesses: Henry Baker (*Pistore*) then bailiff, Robert de Chilton', Thomas le Moubrey, John Tole, John Dobedy, Henry del Parlur, John Miniot, John de Wedon, John Colle, John Holeweye, Roger de Allesleye clerk and others.

2 seals missing C.R.O. IA/EC13/99

366

Another version of the above omitting the remainder and reversion clause. The witnesses are the same.

2 seals extant C.R.O. 1A/C13/1

367 Early–mid 1290s

Remise and quitclaim by John son of John Minot for himself and his heirs to Anketell de Coleshul of 5s. annual rent to be taken from the entire tenement which Peter de Parys once held in Bayley Lane (*en le Baililone*); to be held to him, his heirs or assigns, freely [etc.]. Exclusion and sealing clauses. Witnesses: Henry Baker (*pistore*) then bailiff, William de Toucestre, William de Galewey, John de Macstoke, Nicholas Crumpe, Richard the Tailor (*Cissore*), Richard de Cundouere, John Tole senior, Richard de Boreford the clerk and others.

Seal missing C.R.O. 2/27

368 c.1290–1297

Charter of John Mynot son of John Minot of Coventry giving to Anketell de Colishul 8s. annual rent to be taken from the entire tenement which Peter de P(ar)is once held towards the church of St. Michael which Symon Russel used to pay annually; to be held with all escheats and liberties of the chief lords of that fee to him, his heirs or assigns freely [etc.], by rendering annually to the same chief lords 9d. of silver at the terms usual in Coventry for all service and demand. Warranty and sealing clauses. Witnesses: Robert de Stoke, Henry Baker (*pistore*) then bailiff, William the Parker (*p(ar)cario*) then coroner, Thomas le Moubray, William Toucestre, Roger Daysie the clerk and others.

Seal extant C.R.O. IA/C13/31

369 c.1290–1297

Remise and quitclaim by Anketell de Colleshull to Simon Russel and Agnes his wife of 3d. annual rent which they used to render to the grantor from a certain tenement which they held of him in Bayley Lane (*en le Baylilone*) where Peter de Parys used to live (*quondam manere solebat*); to be held to them, their heirs or assigns of the grantor, his heirs or assigns, freely [etc.]. Exclusion and sealing clauses. Witnesses: Henry Baker (*pistore*) then bailiff, Robert de Chiltrene, William the Parker (*p(ar)cario*) then coroner, John de Langeleye, John de Rydeware, Richard de Asscheby, William Grantpe, William de Toucestr', Alan Lyhtfot and others.

Seal extant C.R.O. 2/108

370 24 June 1301

Charter of Adam Russel of Coventry giving to William his son, for his service, 2 cottages in Bayley Lane (*in venella que dicitur le Baylilone*) in Coventry which lie in width between the grantor's gate (*portam*) on the one hand and the land of Sir Alexander de Esscheby chaplain on the other, the cottage which is nearer to the land of the said Alexander extending in length from the aforesaid lane up to the grantor's solar at the end of his chief messuage (*et illud Cotagium quod est propinquius terre dicti Alexandri extendit se in longitudine de predicta venella usque ad solarium meum quod est ad finem capitalis mansi mei*) according to the metes and bounds made there; to be held with the buildings sited there to him, his heirs or assigns, freely [etc.] of the chief lords of that fee by the services due and by right accustomed. Warranty and sealing clauses. Witnesses: Roger Daieseie then bailiff of Coventry, Peter Barun, John de Langele, Nicholas Crumpe, Geoffrey le Chaloner, William G[ra]ntpe, Thomas Ballard, Ralf le Hunte, Roger the clerk and others. Coventry, Saturday the feast of the Nativity of St. John the Baptist 29 Edward I.

Seal extant P.R.O. A 4465

371

1297–1300

Charter of Henry le Latoner of Coventry giving to Robert de Melton merchant in Coventry (*in Coventr' mercatori*) his tenement with buildings sited there and its appurtenances which he had in Coventry against the church (*contra ecclesiam*) of St. Michael between the land John Holoneye the miller (*molendinar'*) holds of the grantor for the term of his life on the one hand and the land Symon Russel once held on the other in length, and in width as is manifest according to the metes and bounds made there; to be held to him, his heirs or whatsoever assigns well [etc.] of the chief lords of that fee by rendering annually to the same lords the service due and accustomed, namely 6s. of silver at the four terms of the year usual and fixed in the vill of Coventry, and to the grantor, his heirs or assigns, 6s. of silver at the same four terms for all secular services and demands. Clause for warranty. Robert gave a certain sum of money beforehand. Sealing clause. Witnesses: Anketill de Coleshul then bailiff in Coventry, Adam Russel, John de Langeleye, Matthew de Ruyton', Richard de la Muyre, John le Govere, Richard Forthwyne, John de Wedon', John the Goldsmith (*Aurifabro*) and others.

Seal extant — C.R.O. IA/L12–13C/49

372

c.24 June 1305

Lease, grant and demise by Henry le Latonere of Coventry to Richard atte Bekke of 2 selds (*seldas*) with an adjacent curtilage and other appurtenances in Bayley Lane (*in venella que vocatur le Baillilone*) in Coventry, namely those constructed at the front of his messuage next to the wood (*constructe sunt in anteriori parte mesuagii mei juxta boscum ejusdem mesuagii*) in length and in width as is fully manifest according to the metes and bounds made there; to be held to him, his heirs and assigns, of the grantor and his heirs freely and peacefully for a term of 10 years from the feast of the Nativity of St. John the Baptist 33 Edward I, by rendering annually 20s. of silver at the four terms of the year usual in Coventry for all services and demands. Clause for warranty, and for maintenance by the lessor (*et predictas seldas contra ventum et pluviam sustentabimus et reparabimus quocienscumque necesse fuerit*). *Et si predictus Ricardus vel heredes sui vel ejus assignati aliquod novum edificium vel aysiamentum ibidem fecerint tunc liceat eisdem illud edificium et aysiamentum in fine termini predicti p(ro)sternere et asportare sine aliqua contradictione mei vel heredum meorum nisi valorem illius edificii seu aysiamenti eisdem per visum proborum hominum et legalium voluerimus allocare. Et si predictus Ricardus vel heredes sui vel ejus assignati dictas seldas in aliquo deterioraverint tunc illud quod deterioraverint sumptibus suis propriis emendabunt.* Mutual sealing clause. Witnesses: Adam Russel, Ralf le Hunte, Hugh de Merinton', Henry de Barsham, Henry Bagod and others.

Seal extant — C.R.O. 33 EIII[1]/4

[1] sic

373

1297–1300

Charter of John son of John Mynot of Coventry giving to William de Braunteston' merchant in Coventry (*in Coventr' m(er)catori*) a curtilage with appurtenances which he had in the vill of Coventry lying in width between the cemetery (*Cimiteriu(m)*) of St. Michael on the one hand and the land of Henry le Latoner on the other and which extends in length from the lane (*venella*) which is called Bayley Lane (*le Baililone*) up to the land Walter de Bannebery butcher (*Carnifex*) once held according to the metes and bounds made there; to be held to him, his heirs or whatsoever assigns, of the grantor and his heirs well [etc.] by rendering annually a pair of gloves worth 1d. or 1d. at Easter for all secular services, suits of court and all kinds of demands. Clause for warranty. William gave a certain sum of money beforehand. Sealing clause. Witnesses: Anketill de Coleshul then bailiff of Coventry, Adam

Russel, Nicholas Crumpe, Peter Baron, John de Langele, Richard de la Muyre, Geoffrey le Chaloner, William de Schepeie, Roger the clerk and others.

Seal extant C.R.O. IA/EC12/5

374 25 March 1303

Remise and quitclaim by Anketinus de Colishul for himself and his heirs to John his son, his heirs or assigns, of all right and claim in 7s. 9d. annual rent which the grantor used to receive from the tenement once of Nicholas de Wykewane against the cemetery (*contra Cimiterium*) of St. Michael on the south side; to be held to him, his heirs or assigns, of the chief lords of that fee by the service due to the same and by right accustomed. Exclusion and sealing clause. Witnesses: Robert Baker (*Pistor'*) then bailiff, John Lewyn then coroner, Nicholas the Dyer (*Tinctor'*), Thomas the Tanner (*Tannator'*), Alexander Moubray, Thomas le Webbe and many others. Coventry, the day of the Annunciation of the blessed Mary in March A.D. 1303.

Seal extant C.R.O. IB/31EI/12

375 22 July 1307[?]

Lease and demise by Brother Henry the prior and the convent of Coventry to Geoffrey le Chalouner merchant (*mercatori*) of Coventry and Alice his wife and the heirs whom the said Geoffrey will beget from the aforesaid Alice the piece (*placeam*) of their land which lies in Coventry between the bishop's hall (*aulam Episcopi*) on the one hand and the land of William de Braundiston' on the other as is manifest according to the metes and bounds there, together with 5 acres of their waste next to the site of Spon (*vastri nostri juxta situm de Sponna*) which Master Richard de Fylu(n)gleye once held from them; to be held with appurtenances to them and their heirs legitimately issuing from them for their entire life of the grantors and their successors, by rendering annually 12d. for the said piece (*placea*) and 5s. sterling for the aforesaid 5 acres at the four terms usual in Coventry for all service pertaining to them, *ita videlicet quod dictus Galfridus predictas quinque acras redigat in culturam asp(or)tatis autem blad(is) ibid(em) crescentibus ibi co(m)m(un)icent qui de jur(e) ibi co(m)m(un)icare debent*. Reversion clause in default of heirs as specified *cum omni melioratione in eisdem facta*. Sealing clause. Witnesses: Robert le Pestour, Alexander de Stonleye, William Grau(n)pe, William de Brau(n)ston', Ralf le Hunte and others. Coventry, the feast of St. Mary Magdelen 35 Edward I.*

Seal extant C.R.O. IB/35EI/8

*For I Edward II?

Endorsed: Carta Galfrid' le chaloun(er) de Coventr'. totum istud redditum inh(ab)itabil' pro elarg' Cimit(er)ii sancti mich(aelis) sed Thom(as) heres dicti G. h(ab)et alia ten' propinquiora Aule Ep(iscop)i pro quibus redd' per annum xxxd.

For the site of the bishop's hall (outside the monks' cemetery and extending to the Earl's garden) on the land granted by Prior Geoffrey and the monks see *Magnum Registrum Album* No. 360. The house was later said to be dilapidated and was to be repaired and extended as part of the settlement of the controversy surrounding the bishop's Visitations in 1283 (*ibid.* No. 643).

TOWARDS HOLY TRINITY, LODELAWE'S LANE* [HAY LANE]

*See also 162, 761.

376 Late 1270s–early 1280s

Grant and quitclaim by Robert called (*dictus*) de Lodelawe of Coventry to Master Guy of a certain messuage of land (*mesuagium t(er)re*) in the vill of Coventry namely in the lane which leads from the high street towards the church of Holy Trinity (*in venella que se ducit ab alto vico versus ecclesiam sancte trinitatis*) which lies opposite the house (*ex oposito domu(m)*) once of John de Lodelawe towards the east between the land of the said Guy on the one hand and the land of Geoffrey Lontoun on the other; to be held to him, his heirs or assigns, freely [etc.] by rendering annually to the lords of the fee the service due at the terms of the year fixed in Coventry for all secular service [etc.]. Guy gave 2 marks of silver beforehand. Exclusion and sealing clauses. Witnesses: Robert de Chilton' then bailiff, John Tole, Geoffrey Lontoun, Henry the Painter (*pictor'*), William de P(ar)lur, Hugh de Oxonia, William le Selkesower' and others.

Seal missing C.R.O. 2/119

377 Late 1280s–early 1290s

Charter of Stephen le Marchal of Coventry son of John le Marchal giving to Reginald Ballard merchant (*mercatori*) and Felicia his wife certain land which he held in Lodelawe's Lane (*lodeloweslone*) in Coventry with the buildings sited there and all easements found in the same buildings, namely the land with appurtenances which lies in width between the land of Sir Hugh le Gras chaplain on the one hand and the land of William le Parker on the other and extends in length from Lodelawe's Lane (*a viculo qui dicitur Lodelowelone*) up to the land of the aforesaid Reginald and Felicia as is fully manifest according to the metes and bounds made there; to be held to them, their heirs and assigns, well [etc.] of the lords of that fee, by rendering annually to the same lords the service due and accustomed, namely to Walter le Parker and his heirs a clove-gillyflower at Easter and to Alexander le Vineter of Coventry and his heirs 2s. of silver at the four terms of the year usual and fixed in the vill of Coventry for all secular services [etc.]. Clause for warranty. Reginald and Felicia gave 7 marks of silver beforehand. Sealing clause. Witnesses: Henry Baker (*pistore*) then bailiff of Coventry, Richard de Weston', Henry Ballard, Adam Russel, John de Langeleye, John Dobedy, Richard de la Muyre, William Grauntpe, Geoffrey le Chaloner and others.

Seal missing G.H. 297

378 Late 1280s–early 1290s

Charter of Gilbert called (*dictus*) le Wyhte of Coventry giving to John ad Crucem his nephew (*nepoti*) for his service and for 1 mark of silver beforehand the entire messuage with appurtenances which he had in Coventry between the lane (*viculum*) which is called *Lodeloweslane* on the one hand and the land William de Copston' held on the other in length and in width as it purports; to be held with the buildings sited there to him, his heirs or assigns, well [etc.] by rendering annually to the heirs of John le Lorimer and Margery his wife a clove-gillyflower at Easter and to Peter de Haleforde and his heirs 12d. of silver at the four terms of the year usual and fixed in the vill of Coventry for all secular services [etc.]. Warranty and sealing clauses. Witnesses: Henry Baker (*pistore*) then bailiff in Coventry, John Thole, John Sampsum, John le Keu, Nicholas de Derby, John Dobedy, John de Wedon', John Stantilon, Roger the clerk and others.

Seal extant C.R.O. 2/64
Endorsed: de ten' in le haylane

SMITHFORD ST.* (SMITHFORD, OUTSIDE OR BEYOND SMITHFORD)

*See above p. 118. For other references see 454, 493.

379 c.1210–c.1220

Charter of Richard son of Gerard the Vintner (*vinit'*) giving to Osbert (*Oseberto*) the Dyer (*tinctori*) the land at Smithford where Edwin the Fuller used to live (*terram illam ad Smithesford ubi Edwinus fullo solebat manere*) as it purports in length and in width up to [ ][1] namely the land which is nearer to the land which the same Osbert held of Gerard the grantor's father; to be held to him and his heirs of the grantor and his heirs in fee and inheritance, freely, quietly and honourably by rendering annually 4s. of silver for all secular service. Clause for warranty. Osbert gave 20s. of silver in recognition. Witnesses: [ ][1], Vincent, Peter de Kent, Richard de Hundelon', Sw[anus the Parker][1], Hugh son of Martin, Richard de Wigorn', Stephen[his][1]son, [Matthew son of][1] Gundreas, William Crude, Elfred de Wicumba, H[ ][1]me and many others.

Seal missing C.R.O. 1A/EC12/7

[1] Badly damaged in places, leaving only a few letters.

380 c.1210–c.1220

Charter of Geoffrey the Goldsmith (*Aurifab'*) giving to Hugh de Arraz in free marriage with Alice his daughter 2s. rent from the land which Robert the Wheelwright (*Rotarius*) held of the grantor outside Smithford (*extra Smithesford*) which lies between the land Geoffrey son of David held and the land Walter the Smith (*fab'*) held; to be held to them and the heirs issuing from them of the grantor and his heirs freely [etc.] by rendering annually a pair of gloves worth ½d. at Easter for all secular services and demands. Warranty and sealing clauses. Witnesses: Hugh son of Martin, Swanus the Parker (*parcar'*), Richard Meu, William the Palmer (*palm'*), Richard de Wigorn', William Fordwin, Matthew son of Gundr', William Liuet, Richard Rafwine, Nigel son of Nigel and many others.

Seal extant G.H. 261

381 1220s

Charter of Lambert son of Osbert (*Oseberti*), *corveiser*, giving to Robert de Hamtona and his heirs from Matilda daughter of John de Redeford in fee and inheritance, of the grantor and his heirs, a moiety of his land in length and in width as it purports beyond Smithford (*ultra Smitheford*) namely the nearer part (*propinquiorem partem*) of the land which Matilda Bucstan held; to be held of the grantor and his heirs freely, quietly and honourably by rendering 12d. annually for all secular service and demand, namely 3d. at each of the feasts of St. Michael, St. Andrew, the Annunciation of St. Mary, and the Nativity of St. John the Baptist. Clause for warranty. Robert gave 16s. of silver. Witnesses: Richard de Hundel', Osbert the Dyer (*tinct'*), Nicholas de Smitesford, Ralf his brother, Richard son of Reuen, Hugh de Ludet', Adam de Grena, Richard son of Agnes, Walter the White (*albo*), Simon son of Roger, Adam son of Haldanus, Simon de Leircest', Robert the Wheelwright (? *rotat'*) and many others.

Seal extant C.R.O. 1A/EC12/1

382 Early–mid 1240s

Remise and quitclaim by Thomas de Souley of Coventry, without any reservation, charge or oppression (*gravamine*) by him or his heirs to Thomas de Henle of Coventry and Petronilla the grantor's daughter and the heirs issuing from them of the entire land with all appurtenances in Coventry in Earl St. next to Smithford bridge (*in vico Comit(is) juxta pontem de Smithisford*), between the watercourse of Smithford (*cursum aque de Smithisford*) and the land Adam the Vintner (*vinetar'*) held in width, and in length from the high street up to the land William de Heyham once held (*a magno vico et protendit se usque terram quam Willelmus de Heyham quondam tenuit*) as is manifest; to be held of the lords of the fee of whom the grantor held namely Sir Walter de Covi(n)tr' and his heirs by the service of 2s. of silver to be paid at four terms of the year according to the usage and custom of the vill of Coventry for all secular service [etc.]. Clause for reversion in default of bodily heirs. Sealing clause. Witnesses: Master Richard the Vintner (*vinetar'*), Anketill Wickewan', Pagan Pake, Richard de Fonte, Richard Labanc, Ralf the Miller (*molendinar'*), Roger the Dyer (*tintor'*), William de Folkishull', Adam the Vintner (*vinetar'*), John the Parchment-maker (*p(er)chamenar'*), Robert Wythir', Thomas de Stoke, Roger de Colishull' and others.

Seal extant P.R.O. A 4334

383 1250s

Sale and quitclaim by Alice daughter of Richard dil Dick of Coventry, for herself and her heirs, to Thomas Linot of Brackley (*Brackel*), his heirs or assigns, of all right and claim in the entire land (*totota [sic] terra*) which lies in Coventry in Smithford St. (*in vico Smithisford*) between the land of Thomas de Henle on the one hand and the land of John Coterel on the other with the houses and building(s) and other easements and with all appurtenances pertaining to the aforesaid land; to be held to him, his heirs or assigns, of the lords of the fee freely [etc.] by the service of 12d. *per annum* at the four terms of the year usual in the vill of Coventry for all secular service. Exclusion clause. Thomas gave 8 marks of silver beforehand. Sealing clause. Witnesses: Richard de Blokevill', Alexander de Gloucest', Thomas de Henle, William de Colishul', William Wilas, William the Weaver (*textor'*), Robert Withir, Roger de Colishul', Peter Walenc' and many others.

Seal extant C.R.O. 1A/EC13/96

384 1250s

Charter of Peter le Wales in his free and lawful power, for himself and his heirs, giving to Thomas Haldein of Coventry a certain part (*quandam partem*) of his land in Coventry in Earl St. (*in vico Comitis*) which lies in width between the land the same Thomas held on the one hand and the land John le Bucmang(er) held on the other and in length between the land Nicholas Fortwyne held and the great street leading towards Smithford (*magnum vicum ducent' versus Smithisford*); to be held to him, his heirs or whatsoever assigns except to men of religion or to the Jews, of the grantor and his heirs freely [etc.], by rendering annually 2s. of silver at four terms of the year according to the usage and custom of the vill of Coventry for all service pertaining. Clause for warranty. Thomas gave 10s. of silver beforehand. Sealing clause. Witnesses: Pagan Pake, Richard de Bokirvil, Alexander de Glouc', Walter the White (*albo*), Adam le T(r)auant(er), Reginald the Red (*Russo*), Henry the Saddler (*cellar'*), Vincent the Goldsmith (*aurifabro*), William de Thorlawiston and others.

Seal missing C.R.O. 2/150

385 Late 1260s

Charter of John de Lodelawe giving to Thomas son of Thomas Haldeyn and Alice the grantor's niece (*nepte*), the entire land with rent [and] all appurtenances which he bought from the same Thomas and which descended to Thomas hereditarily from Thomas Haldeyn his father in the vill of Coventry and outside with 6s. 6d. annual rent of assize, namely 2s. to be taken from the house (*domo*) which was once of Marior' the Doctor (*medic'*) outside Smithford bar (*extra Barram de Smithesford*), 18d. from the house of Robert de Cundulme in Spon St. (*In vico de Sponna*) and 3s. from the waste ground in the prior of Coventry's Market-place against the butchers' stalls on the western side (*de illa Wasta placea cum arreragiis in foro domini Prioris Coventr' contra stallagia carnificum ex parte occidentali*) with the house and adjacent croft with appurtenances which the grantor bought from William le Pulter(er) outside Gosford bridge (*extra pontem de Goseford*) next to the land once of Adam le Coliar'; to be held to him, his heirs or assigns, of the grantor, his heirs or assigns, freely [etc.], by rendering annually 20s. and 14d. of silver at the four terms of the year usual and fixed in the vill of Coventry, and the service of a moiety of a man for one day in Autumn, 5 hens at Christmas, 3 pairs of gloves each worth ½d. or a ½d. for each at Easter, a gillyflower at Christmas and a pair of gloves worth 1d. or 1d. at the feast of St. John the Baptist *ad voluntatem solventis* for all service. Warranty and sealing clauses. Witnesses: Richard de Bokervile, Richard Ernis then bailiff, Henry Baker (*pistor'*) then bailiff of the lord prior for the Bishop's Half (*tunc existente balli(v)o domini Prioris ex parte Episcopi*), Philip de Wynchecumbe, Robert de Chilton, Thomas de Fakenham, Henry the Saddler (Celar'), Richard le Brochar, Henry le Cartesadeler, Roger the Chamberlain (*Camer'*), Nicholas de Canneley clerk, Richard Fore and others.

Seal extant C.R.O. 1A/EC13/79

Endorsed: Carta feoffame(n)t' Alic' haldein ex dono Johann(is) de Lodelouue de teneme(n)t' ad latam portam.

386 1262–1272

Charter of Brother Richard, abbot, and the convent of Stoneleigh (*stanl'*) giving to Symon de Thurlauston' son of Henry Walt(er), for 3 marks of silver which he gave to them beforehand, 4s. rent in Coventry which William Wilace of Coventry used to pay annually from a certain tenement with appurtenances in Coventry which is between the land once of Stephen Scatheloc on the eastern side and the land once of William de Wylenhale on the western side, and which extends from the shops (*shoppis*) of the said William towards the street (*vicum*) on the northern side up to the Poddycroft ditch (*fossam de podicroft*); to be held to him, his heirs or whatsoever assigns, of the grantors and their successors freely [etc.] by rendering annually a root of ginger (*unam Radicem Gingib(er)is*) at Michaelmas for all secular service [etc.]. Warranty and sealing clauses. Witnesses: Robert de Chilton' then bailiff of Coventry, Henry le Seller, Symon Scatheloc, William the Weaver (*textor'*), John the Marshal (*marescallo*), William Wilace, Robert de Gri(m)misby, Vincent the Goldsmith (*aurifabr'*), Henry Dobedy and others.

Seal missing C.R.O. 1A/Misc.1/17

Richard was abbot from June 1262 until late in 1272 (*Stoneleigh Leger Book*, ed. R. H. Hilton, *Dugdale Soc.*, 1960, pp. 252–3).

387 1270s

Gift by Master Guy perpetual vicar of the church of St. Michael, Coventry to Alice de Stok of a certain messuage with buildings built there and an adjacent curtilage in the vill of Coventry, towards Smithford in the Earl's half (*ex parte comitis versus Smitheford*), which was once of Adam le Clerc and lies between the messuage of Michael (*micch'*) le P(ar)ber [*sic*] on the one hand and the messuage of Robert Mansel on the other; to be held with all appurtenances according to the metes and bounds made there to her, her heirs or assigns, of him and his heirs freely [etc.], by rendering annually a rose at the feast of St. John the Baptist, and 20d. to the chief lords at the four terms of the year fixed in the vill of Coventry for all secular services, customs, aids, tallages, reliefs, suits and demands. Clause for warranty. Alice gave 5 marks of silver beforehand. Sealing clause. Witnesses: John de Lodelawe and Henry Baker (*pistore*) then bailiffs (*tunc ballivis*), Robert de Chilterne, Peter Barun, Adam le T(r)ant(er), Richard le Brocher, Roger le Chambleyn and others.

Seal extant C.R.O. 2/91

388 c.1270s

Remise and quitclaim by Richard de Deyvile, for himself, his heirs or assigns, of all right and claim in 20d. annual rent which he used to receive from Alice de Stok' for certain tenements in Smithford St. (*pro quibusdam ten' in vico de Smithesford*) in the vill of Coventry to the aforesaid Alice, her heirs and whatsoever assigns. Exclusion and sealing clauses. Witnesses: Alexander le Vinet(er) of Coventry, Robert de Chilton', John Rivel of Coventry, Peter Baroun, Richard de Esseby, Roger le Chaunberleyn of Coventry, Robert Maunsel of the same and many others.

Seal missing C.R.O. 2/166

389 c.1270s

Grant by William le Poumfreit that henceforth Alice de Stoke and her heirs may be quit of the payment of 20d. rent which used to be paid annually for the lands, buildings, rent and all other tenements which she held of his fee in Smithford St. (*in vico de Smiseford*), by rendering annually, the aforesaid Alice her heirs and assigns, a rose flower at the feast of St. John the Baptist for all secular service [etc.]. Clause for warranty. Alice gave 11s. of silver beforehand. Sealing clause. Witnesses: Alexander le Wyneter' of Coventry, Robert de Chilton' of the same, John Rivel of the same, Peter Barun, Richard de Esseby, Roger le Chamburleyn, Robert Mancel, Stephen de Halis and others.

Seal extant C.R.O. 1A/Misc.1/9

390 c.1290–1297

Remise and quitclaim by Richard the Weaver (*Textor*) of Coventry, for himself and his heirs, to Alice de Stokes daughter of Robert de Stoke of all right and claim in the entire tenement with all appurtenances in Smithford St. (*in vico de Smethesforde*) which lies between the land Michael the Parker (*P(ar)carius*) held on the one hand and the land Robert Mauncel held on the other; to be held to her, her heirs or assigns, freely [etc.]. Exclusion and sealing clauses. Witnesses: Henry Baker (*Pistor'*) of Coventry then bailiff, William the Parker (*P(ar)cario*) then coroner, Thomas le Moubrei, Robert Mauncel, William de Copston', Richard le Dobb(er)e and Roger de Pacwod clerk and others.

Seal extant C.R.O. 1A/C13/32

391 11 December 1303

Lease and grant by Robert de Stoke to Alice de Stok' dwelling in Coventry (*manenti in Coventr'*) for her entire life of his messuage with appurtenances in Smithford St., Coventry (*in vico de Smythesford in Coventr'*) namely that which he had by the gift and enfeoffment of the same Alice; to be held with all appurtenances to her for life, of him and his heirs, freely and peacefully by the service of a rose at the feast of the Nativity of the blessed John the Baptist to be paid annually for all services. Warranty and reversion clauses. Mutual sealing clause. Witnesses: Robert Baker (*Pistore*) then bailiff in Coventry, William Maunsel, William de Copstone, Hugh de Copstone, Richard de Walyshale and others. Coventry, Wednesday after the feast of St. Nicholas 32 Edward I.

Indented
Seal extant C.R.O. 1B/32 E1/4

392 12 March 1307

Agreement whereby Robert de Stok' has given to Richard de Walyshale merchant of Coventry (*mercatorem Coventr'*) and Juliana his wife a messuage with appurtenances in Coventry which lies in Smithford St. (*in vico qui vocatur Smythesfordestret*) between the land of Master William Scelet on the one hand and the land of William Maunsel on the other in width, and extends in length from the royal highway up to the town ditch (*a regia strata usque ad fossatum ville*) as is fully manifest according to the metes and bounds found there; to be held to Richard and to his heirs issuing from the bodies of Richard and Juliana, of Robert and his heirs, freely and peacefully by rendering annually 13s. 4d. of silver at the four terms of the year usual in the vill of Coventry by equal portions for all services. Clause for warranty. In default of such heirs successive remainders to William de Walyshale brother of the aforesaid Richard and the heirs of his body, to Alan de Walyshale brother of the same William and the heirs of his body, to Margery de Walyshale sister of the same Alan and the heirs of her body, to Robert Greygos of Walsall (*Walyshale*) and the heirs of his body, and to Alice sister of the same Robert Greygos and the heirs of her body, with reversion to the aforesaid Robert de Stok' and his heirs. Clause for repossession in default of sufficient distress should distraint be necessary for arrears of rent during a whole year. Robert and Juliana gave 6 marks of silver beforehand. Mutual sealing clause. Witnesses: Robert Baker (*Pistore*), Nicholas Crumpe, Peter Baron, Robert de Ston', William de Schepeye, Richard de St. James, William Maunsel and others. Coventry, Sunday the feast of St. Gregory the Pope 35 Edward I. [Clause for warranty added below the body of the document].

Indented
Seal extant C.R.O. 1B/35E1/2

1B/35E1/3 is the counterpart of this. The seal is extant.

393 1270s

Gift and quitclaim by Luveday widow of Richard le Comber, for herself and her heirs, in her widowhood and lawful power to Gilbert Wry and Inga (*Inge*) his wife, their heirs or assigns, of the entire land with appurtenances in Coventry outside Smithford bar (*extra Le barre de Smithesford*) which Robert the Locksmith (*Locar'*) her father gave to her in free marriage with Richard le Comb(er) once her husband between the land Richard de St. Botulf held on the one hand and the land Richard le Dubb' held on the other. Exclusion clause. The grantees are to render annually to the lords of that tenement 4d. of silver at four terms of the year according to the usage of the vill of Coventry for all secular service. Gilbert and Inga gave 10s. of silver beforehand. Should Gilbert die before Inga she will possess the said land with appurtenances. Sealing clause. Witnesses: Henry Baker (*pistor'*) then bailiff, William the White (*alb'*) weaver (*tixtor'*), Hugh Schayl, William Aylm(er), Richard Schore, Adam Hert, Roger Neue, William le Palm(er), John de Cundulm', Adam the clerk and others.

Seal missing C.R.O. 1A/C11–12/19
Endorsed: Quieta clamancia de redditu ten' Thome In le Hurne jux(ta) Babbelake.

394 Late 1270s–early 1280s

Charter of Richard de Harnhale weaver (*textor*) and Inga Wry his wife giving to Robert in le Hurne of Coventry, tanner (*tannatori*) and Bela (*Bele*) his daughter a messuage with appurtenances in Coventry which was once of Richard le Comber outside Smithford bar (*extra Barram de Smythesford*) sited between the land of the aforesaid Robert on the one hand and the land Richard de Botulfston held on the other, in length and in width as is manifest according to the metes and bounds made there; to be held to them, their heirs or assigns, of the grantors and their heirs freely [etc.] by rendering annually to the lords of the fee, for the grantors and their heirs, the due and accustomed rent, namely 4d. of silver at the four terms of the year fixed and accustomed in the vill of Coventry, and to the grantors and their heirs a clove-gillyflower at Easter for all service. Clause for warranty. Robert gave 11s. of silver beforehand. Sealing clause. Witnesses: Robert de Chilton' then bailiff of Coventry, Henry Dobedy, Stephen de Halys, William le Palmere, Hugh Shayl, Robert de Kannel', William Lotemon, Symon de Kyldisby, William Rimild, John de Cundolm', John Aylem(er) clerk and others.

2 seals extant C.R.O. 2/151
Endorsed: Carta de redditu exeunte de ten' Thome in le Hurne juxta Babbelake.

395 Late 1270s–early 1280s

Charter of William de Cestr' and Aldith' Wry his wife giving to Robert in le Hurne of Coventry, tanner (*taunatori*), and Bela (*Bele*) his daughter a messuage with appurtenances in Coventry, outside Smithford bar (*extra Barram de Smythesford*) which was once of Richard le Comber, namely that which he had (*h(ab)u(i)t*) by gift and grant of Richard de Harnhale and Ynga (*Ynge*) Wry his wife according to the metes and bounds made there; to be held to them, their heirs and assigns, as freely [etc.] as in the charter of the aforesaid Richard de Harnhal and Ynga. Clause for warranty. Robert gave 7s. of silver beforehand. Witnesses: Robert de Chilton' then bailiff of Coventry, Henry Dobedy, Stephen de Halys, William le Palmere, Hugh Schayl, Robert de Kannel', William Lotemon, Symon de Kyldesby, William Rymild, John de Cundolm', John Aylem(er) clerk and others.

2 seal tags only C.R.O. 2/135

396 1280s

Charter of Guy de Tyllebrok' giving to Robert in le Huyrne tanner (*tannatori*) a messuage in Earl St., Coventry outside Smithford bar (*in vico Comitis Coventr' extra Barram de Smythsford*) with buildings and all appurtenances, namely that which William le Palmer' formerly held of the grantor and which lies between the land of the aforesaid Robert and the land of the heirs of Roger son of Peter; to be held to him, his heirs or assigns, of the grantor and his heirs, freely and quietly by rendering annually ½d. at Easter and to the chief lords 6d. owed annually as the attorneys of the grantor and his heirs for all secular service and demand. Clause for warranty. Robert gave 5 marks of silver. Sealing clause. Witnesses: Robert de Chilton', Henry Baker (*pistore*), Peter Barun, Richard le Burser, Geoffrey son of John, Hugh Schayl, Robert de Cannel', William Seleth and others.

Seal extant C.R.O. 1A/Misc. 1/4

397 Late 1270s

Charter of William Ottyng of Coventry giving to Henry le Whelwruyte of Stoneleigh (*stanley*) and Felicia his wife a messuage in Earl St., Coventry (*in vico Comitis de Coventr'*), which lies between the land of Stephen de Hales dyer (*tinctore*)[1] on the one hand and the land of William l[e][2] Hose on the other in length and in width according to the metes and bounds made there; to be held to them, their heirs or whatsoever assigns or to whomsoever they will wish to give, sell or assign in sickness and in health except to a house of religion or to Jews, of the grantor and his heirs, freely [etc.] by rendering annually 4s. of silver at the four terms of the year fixed and customary in the vill of Coventry for all secular service [etc.]. Clause for warranty. Henry and Felicia gave 4s. of silver beforehand. Sealing clause. Witnesses: Gerard de Alspathe then bailiff of the lord prior of Coventry, Stephen de Hales, Richard le Dubbere, Hugh Schayl, Walter the Tanner (*tannatore*), William de Watford, Richard the Weaver (*textore*), Roger de Hales, Robert Maunsel, Robert le Dobber and others.

Seal extant C.R.O. 2/5

Endorsed: Carta Willelmi Ottyng de uno messuagio vel 4s. redditus citra pontes de Smytheford.

[1] sic
[2] There is a hole here.

398 Early 1280s

Remise and quitclaim by William Otting, for himself and his heirs, to Henry de Axeholm and his heirs of 4s. annual rent in Earl St. towards Smithford (*in vico*

Comitis versus Smythesford) which he was accustomed to receive from the land with appurtenances which lies between the land once of William le Hose and the land of the said Henry; to be held to him, his heirs or assigns freely [etc.]. Exclusion clause. Sealing clause, for 40s. of silver which Henry gave beforehand. Witnesses: Robert de Chilton' then bailiff, Richard le Brocher, Thomas de Fakenham, Adam Russel, Richard de Esseby, Robert Grampe and others.

Seal missing C.R.O. 1A/Misc.1/2

399 Early 1280s

Remise and quitclaim by Maria daughter of Richard le Marichal in her virginity, for herself and her heirs, to Thomas Bisscop of Coventry son of Vincent Bisscop of all right and claim in the entire land with appurtenances which lies between the land of the aforesaid Thomas on the one hand and the land Eva Coc' held on the other and extends in length from the royal highway (*a Regia via*) up to the watercourse running towards Smithford Mill (*molend' de Smytheforde*) in length and in width as the land purports according to the metes and bounds made there; to be held to him, his heirs or assigns, or to whomsoever or whensoever he will wish to give, bequeath, sell or assign, in sickness and in health, freely [etc.]. Exclusion clause. Sealing clause, for 12s. of money (*solid' den'*) which the grantee gave beforehand. Witnesses: Robert de Chiltun, Henry Baker (*pistor'*) bailiff (*ball(iv)o tunc tempore*), William Aylm(er), Hugh Sach, Stephen de Halys, William le Palm(er), Richard Schore, Adam Hert, Roger le Neue, Anketell the clerk and others.

Seal missing W.R.O. 271

400 30 Mary 1295

Charter[1] of Simon de Waterwey in Coventry giving to Hugh de Schulfton' draper (*Drap(ar)io*) once the servant (*servient'*) of William de Copston' a certain part of his tenement in Earl St., Coventry towards Smithford (*in vico Comitis in Coventre versus Smythesforde*) with the buildings sited there, namely the part of the said tenement which lies in width between the land Pagan Pake once held on the one hand and the grantor's land on the other and which extends in length from the royal highway (*a Regali via*) up to the land of William le Parker as is fully manifest according to the metes and bounds made there; to be held with the buildings sited there and appurtenances to him, his heirs and assigns, well [etc.] of the lords of that fee by rendering annually to the same lords 12d. of silver at the four terms of the year usual and fixed in the vill of Coventry for all secular services [etc.]. Clause for warranty. Hugh gave 24s. of silver beforehand. Sealing clause. Witnesses: Henry Baker (*Pistore*) then bailiff of Coventry, William le Parkere then coroner, Thomas le Moubray, William de Copston', Richard de St. James, Matthew de Ruyton', Stephen le Marchall', Richard le Dubbere, Thomas Haldeyn and others. Coventry, Monday after the feast of St. Augustine Apostle of the English 23 Edward I.

C.R.O. 1B/23E1/6

[1] A parchment record, not the original.

401 c.1290–1297

Remise and quitclaim by Robert de Ghyldesboru clerk, for himself and his heirs, to Sir William Pake of Coventry chaplain (*Capellano*) of the entire land with appurtenances and easements which he held of the same William outside Smithford bridge (*extra pontem de Smythesforde*) in Coventry between the land Robert Croc held of Robert de Chylton' on the one hand and the land Stephen de Halys once held on the other in length and in width as is fully manifest according to the metes and bounds found on all sides; to be held with easement of water (*cum aisiam(en)to aque*) and all appurtenances to him, his heirs and assigns, well [etc.] without reservation by Robert or his heirs. Exclusion clause. William pardoned (*condonavit*) 9 marks sterling of arrears from the said land (*de arreragiis dicte terre*) and 20s. sterling beforehand. Sealing clause. Witnesses: Henry Baker (*pistore*) then bailiff in Coventry, Robert de Chilton', William le Parker then coroner, Richer de Weston', Henry de Lilleburne, Robert in Angulo, Richard le Dubbere, William de Copston', Roger the clerk and others. (*Dat' apud Coventr' . . .*)[1]

Seal extant C.R.O. 1A/L12–12C/55

[1] The clause goes no further.

402 23 February 1301

Charter of John de Langeleye, knight, giving to Hugh de Copston', merchant in Coventry (*in Coventr' mercatori*), the entire messuage with the houses sited there and all other appurtenances which he had in Smithford St. (*Smythesfordstrete*) in Coventry and which lies between the messuage of Henry de Pollesworth' on the one hand and the messuage of Roger de Cundulm' on the other in width and extends in length from the royal highway (*a regia strata*) up to the land of the master of the hospital of St. John of Coventry as is fully manifest according to the metes and bounds made there; to be held to him, his heirs or assigns, of the chief lords of that fee freely [etc.], by making annually to the same lords the service due and by right accustomed, and to the grantor, his heirs or assigns, 7s. of silver at the four terms of the year usual in the vill of Coventry, and by making suit of the grantor's court of Coventry by reasonable summons whenever it is held (*quando eam teneri contingerit*). Clause for warranty. Hugh gave 6 marks of silver beforehand. Sealing clause. Witnesses: Roger Dayseye then bailiff of Coventry, John Leuwyne then coroner, Matthew de Ruyton', William de Copston', Richard de St. James, Stephen le Mareschal, Robert Faccon, Adam de Schustok, Richard le Merc(er), Alexander le Schereman, John Dobedy clerk and others. Coventry, Thursday after the feast of St. Peter in Cathedra 29 Edward I.

Indented
Seal extant G.H. 314

403 c.30 November 1302

Agreement whereby Henry Normaund has leased, granted and demised for a term to Henry le Mowere of Coventry and Agnes his wife 2 messuages with houses sited there, with a curtilage and other appurtenances, which lie together in Earl St., Coventry towards Smithford (*in vico Comitis Coventr' versus Smytheforde*) of which one was once of William Oky and Petronilla his wife and the other is held in chief of the lord king, and they lie in width between the land of Walter le Wythe Webbe on the one hand and the land of Thomas le Rede on the other and extend in length from the aforesaid street up to the land of Master William Celet according to the metes and bounds made there; to be held to them and their heirs of the aforesaid Henry Normaund and his heirs freely and peacefully from the feast of St. Andrew the Apostle 31 Edward I for a term of 6 years, rendering annually 30s. of silver at the four terms of the year usual in Coventry and a pair of boots (*unum par botar'*) at the feast of St. Michael *Tali conditione quod ipsi predicti Henricus le Mower' et Agnes et eorum heredes edificia dictorum mes(uagiorum) in bono statu contra ventum et pluviam per totum tempus sustentabunt. Et si predictus Henricus Normaund predicta mes(uagia) longiori termino dimittere voluerit predicti Henricus le Mower' et Agnes uxor sua erunt propinquiores si dare velint sicut et alii homini*. Clause for warranty. Mutual sealing clause. Witnesses: Roger Dayesegh then bailiff, John Lewyne then coroner, William de Copuston', Richard de St. James, Stephen le Marchal and others.

Indented
Seal missing C.R.O. 1B/31E1/10

404 2 February 1303

Charter of Thomas called (*dictus*) Ballard merchant of Coventry (*mercator Coventr'*) giving to Agnes widow of Henry Ballard the grantor's father 4s. annual rent to be taken at the four terms of the year usual in the vill of Coventry from the tenement which Richard le Couureyour once held in Earl St., Coventry towards Smithford (*in vico Comitis Coventr' versus Smyþeforde*[1]) which lies between the grantor's tenement next to Smithford stream (*juxta Rivu(m) de Smyþeforde*[1]) and the tenement of William Haldeyn on the other and extends in length from the royal highway (*a Regali via*) up to the land of the aforesaid William Haldeyn according to the metes and bounds made there; to be held to Agnes, her heirs or assigns, of the grantor and his heirs freely [etc.]. Clause for warranty. Agnes gave 4 marks sterling beforehand. Sealing clause. Witnesses: Robert Baker (*Pistor'*) then bailiff of Coventry, Peter Barun of the same, William de Schepeye of the same, John de Langeleye of the same, Geoffrey le Schalonyr of the same and many others. Coventry, the feast of the Purification of the blessed Mary A.D. 1303.

Indented
Seal missing C.R.O. 1B/31 E1/9
Endorsed: Carta Thome Ballard de iiijs. redditus de ten' Johannis le Warde juxta Smytheforde vicus comitis.

[1] Smyyeforde

405 23 November 1305

Charter of Geoffrey le Dubbere of Coventry giving to Roger Box of Coventry merchant (*mercatori*) and Alice his wife 4s. annual rent with appurtenances to be taken at the four terms of the year usual in Coventry from the grantor's chief messuage in Smithford St., Coventry (*de capitali mesuagio meo in vico de Smythesforde in Coventr'*) which lies between the tenement of John Abbot on the one hand and the tenement of John le Barkere on the other in width and extends in length from the royal highway up to the lane called West Orchard (*a regia strata usque ad venellam que vocatur Le Westorchard*). *Volo eciam et concedo pro me et heredibus meis quod totum predictum mesuagium ad quorumcumque manus devenerit de predicto redditu quatuor solidorum imperpetuum oneretur*; to be held to them, their heirs or assigns, to be taken annually from the aforesaid messuage freely [etc.], of the chief lords of the fee by the services due and accustomed. Clause for distraint should the rent fall in arrears during any term. Clause for warranty. Roger and Alice gave 4 marks sterling beforehand. Sealing clause. Witnesses: Robert Baker (*Pistore*) then bailiff of Coventry, Stephen le Mareschal, Richard de St. James, Richard le Mercer, Robert de Stone, Hugh de Copestone, John Dobedy and others. Coventry, Tuesday the feast of St. Clement the Pope 34 Edward I.

Seal missing C.R.O. 1B/34 E1/9
Endorsed: de gilde Beate Marie iiijs. per annum.

406 3 May 1306

Charter of Geoffrey le Dobber of Coventry giving to Stephen the Marchal (*marescallo*) in Coventry 3s. annual rent to be taken annually from his chief messuage (*Capitali mesuagio meo*) which lies next to Smithford (*juxta Smethesforde*) in Coventry between the land of Sir Robert de Montalt (*monte alto*) which is called *le Mulnestede* on the one hand and the land once of Sir Benedict Coterel chaplain on the other in width and extends from the royal highway (*a Regia via*) up to West Orchard (*Le Westgardyn*) in length as is manifest according to the metes and bounds made there; to be held with appurtenances to him, his heirs or whatsoever assigns, freely [etc.] to be taken annually from the aforesaid messuage at the four terms of the year usual in the vill of Coventry by equal portions. Clause for warranty. Stephen gave 40s. sterling beforehand. Sealing clause. Witnesses: Robert called Baker (*dicto Pistore*) then bailiff, Alexander de Stannley then coroner, Richard de St. James, Richard le Espicer, Geoffrey le Waller, William le Waller, Richard le Mercer and others. Coventry, Tuesday the feast of the Invention of the Holy Cross 34 Edward I.

Seal extant W.R.O. 272

Endorsed: Cart' Will(elm)i fil' Galfr' le marchal de redd' in vico de Smythesford' de mesuag' quo(n)d' G. Dubber'.

SPON, SPON ST.*

*See above pp. xxxi–ii. For other references see 74, 206, 375, 385, 759, 761. See also *Langley Cartulary*, Nos. 205–6, 266, 281, 352, 357.

407 Late 1220s–early 1230s

Charter of Matilda daughter of Liulf de Spon giving to Stephen de Segrave the entire land which she held in the vill of Spon.

Sciant presentes et futuri quod ego Matill' filia Lyholf de Spanne dedi et concessi et hac presenti carta mea confirmavi Stephano de Segrave et heredibus suis totam terram quam habui in villa dc Spanne cum omnibus pertinentiis suis in villa et extra villam tenend(am) et habend(am) sibi et heredibus suis de capitali domino feodi faciendo inde ei servitium quod ad terram illam pertinet. Et sciendum quod nec ego nec aliquis heredum meorum umquam de cetero aliquod jus vel clamium in predicta terra habere poterimus. Pro hac autem donatione et concessione dedit mihi predictus Stephanus quatuor marcas argenti et in hujus rei testimonium presenti scripto sigillum meum apposui. Hiis testibus Johanne de Ripariis Willelmo filio Elye Willelmo de sancto Edmundo Waltero de Bissepesdon' Henrico Tylun Waltero de Kinton' Thoma Bluet et multis aliis.

Seal fragmentary G.H. 497

Liulf de Spon was dead by 1214 (*Curia Regis Rolls 1214*, pp. 93–94). The descent of his property which he seems to have held in right of his wife Amiria gave rise to considerable litigation. Matilda, one of 4 daughters, occurs with her husband Thomas de Rase in 1221 (*Eyre Rolls 1221*, Nos. 595, 1469). Stephen de Segrave's interest in the Coventry area stemmed from his association with the earl of Chester early in the reign of Henry III. He was one of the witnesses to Ranulf III's grant to the abbey of Polesworth in 1217–c.1222 (above 21). According to Dugdale Ranulf gave Stephen Caludon to hold by the service of a sore sparrowhawk (*Warwickshire*, p. 128). The above charter seems to belong to the late 1220s/early 1230s. Both William of St. Edmund and John de Ripariis were clearly associated with Stephen at this time. William accounted as under-sheriff of Warwickshire for him at Michaelmas 1229 and was succeeded by John in 1232 (*P.R.O. Lists and Indexes No 9*, p. 144). The former was a justice in eyre during the 1230s. He sat with Segrave in Hampshire in 1232 and was a justice in Warwicks., Leics., Bucks. and Beds. in 1236 (D. Crook, *Records of the General Eyre*, H.M.S.O. 1982, pp. 88, 95–6). Walter de

Kinton received land at Tamworth between 1229 and 1242, whilst Walter de Bishopston who occurs in 1221 received land at Drayton probably during the 1230s. (*Langley Cartulary*, No. 309, *Eyre Rolls 1221*, No. 711, *V.C.H. Warwicks.* iii, p. 266).

408

c.1200–1214

Charter of Richard de Aula giving to William the Black (*Nigro*) to be held to him, his heirs and whomsoever he will wish to give, sell or bequeath, of the grantor and his heirs, the moor which is between the wood of Liulf [de] Spon (*boscum liulfe spone*) and *Aishaga*, and between the watercourse on the one hand and the land William Gupill' held on the other freely [etc.], by rendering annually to the grantor, his heirs and assigns, 2s. for all service at four terms of the year according to the usage of Coventry, namely 6d. at each of the feasts of St. Michael, St. Andrew, the Annunciation of the blessed Mary and St. John the Baptist. Clause for warranty. Richard gave 20s. fine (*in gersuma*). Sealing clause. Witnesses: Liulf de Sponna, Viellus (*Vihelo*) de Folkesille, William Gupill', Vincent, Peter de Kent, Nicholas de Smerhesforde, Richard de Hundeslane, Richard de Wigornia and Stephen his son, Swanus son of Adam, Hugh son of Martin, Hugh son of Odo, Leuewin and Herbert and Hamo brothers and many others.

Seal extant C.R.O. 2/17

409

c.1200–1214

Charter of Richard de Aul(a) giving to William the Black (*Nigro*) the entire land which he held of the grantor and which is of the fee of the monks of Stoneleigh (*Stanlet*), to be held with appurtenances to him, his heirs or assigns or to whomsoever he will wish to give or assign, of the grantor and his heirs well and in peace by rendering annually 4s. of silver at Michaelmas for all secular service [etc.]. Moreover he has granted to the said William the land which pertains to Crow Mill (*ad molendinum de Crowemulne*); to be held [as above], by rendering annually 4s. of silver at Michaelmas for all secular service [and] exaction pertaining. Clause for warranty. William gave 20s. beforehand. Sealing clause. Witnesses: Liulf de Sponna and William his son, Viellus (*Wihelo*) de Folkesul, Vincent (*Wint'*) son of Gopil, Nicholas de Smeþeford, Peter de Keint, Richard de Hundelone and others.

Seal extant C.R.O. 2/19

410

c.1225–1232

Charter of Richard de Aula giving to Adam the Miller (*molendinar'*) a messuage in Coventry in Spon St. (*in vico de Spon(n)a*) which Robert Pi(m)me held, namely that with appurtenances which extends in width from the land Adam de la Grene held up to the land William de Whatburl' held, and in length from the highway (*ab alta via*) up to the water; to be held to him and his heirs of the grantor and his heirs, as freely as the aforesaid Robert Pi(m)me held it according to the metes and bounds made there, by rendering annually for all service 2s. of silver at four terms of the year, namely 6d. at each of the feasts of St. Michael, St. Andrew, St. Mary in March and St. John the Baptist and the work of 1 man for 3 days in Autumn and 2 hens at Christmas, saving the forinsec service pertaining to that messuage. Clause for warranty. Adam gave 18s. of silver in recognition. Sealing clause. Witnesses: Adam son of Haldanus, Richard his son, Adam de la Grene, Robert Skirewith, Richard his son, Alexander the Purse-maker (*bursario*), Osbert de Dereby, Alexander son of

Herlewin, David the Carter (*carectario*), Symon de Leicestr', Symon the Doctor (*medico*), William Bukston' and many others.

Seal extant G.H. 268

411 c.1215–1226

Charter of Elias Despenser (*Helyas dispensator*) with the consent of Alice his wife giving to William Fordwin 3s. 2d. rent in Coventry, namely 12d. from the land which Gerard de Alespathe held of the grantor in Spon St. (*in vico versus Sponna(m)*), 12d. from the land which Glademon the Tanner (*tannator*) held of the grantor, and 14d. from the land which Reginald de Schenton' held of the grantor in the Poddycroft (*Pudicroft*) with all appurtenances, issues and services which pertain or may pertain to the grantor or his heirs from the aforesaid lands; to be held to him and his heirs of the grantor and his heirs freely [etc.] by rendering annually 4d. of silver for all secular service and demand, namely 2d. from the lands the aforesaid Gerard and Glademon held and 2d. from the land Reginald de Schenton' held, namely 1d. at each of the feasts of St. John the Baptist, St. Michael, St. Andrew and St. Mary in March. Clause for warranty. William gave 2 marks of silver in recognition. Witnesses: Richard de Aula, Robert the Vintner (*vinit'*), Richard de Wigorn', Richard de Hundelan', William de Rependon', Leofwinus, Herbert his brother, Geoffrey de Wilnhal', William his brother, Adam the Vintner (*vinit'*), Osbert the Dyer (*tinctore*), William Crude, Ralf the Weaver (*textore*) and many others.

Seal extant W.R.O. 48

412 Mid–late 1230s

Gift, remise and quitclaim by Alice widow of Elias Despenser (*helie disp(e)nsatoris*) in her widowhood and free power, to the abbot and monks of Stoneleigh (*stanl'*) of all right and claim by reason of *maritagium*, dower or any other means in 12d. rent in Coventry which they owed from the lands which Guy Long (*Guido long(us)*), Hugh the Dyer (*tinctor*), Stephen Scathelok, Nicholas Love, Alexander Harlewin [and] Cecily widow of Jordan le Yhicher held; so that the aforesaid monks should hold the rent with appurtenances and liberties well [etc.], in free and perpetual alms, any right of reclaim by the grantor and her heirs being precluded. Sealing clause. Witnesses: William de Wilnale, Richard Burgeys, John de Aula, Adam the Vintner (*vinetario*), Anketill de Wigewan, Adam de la Grene, Alexander Harlewin', Michael de Hurst, Alexander Hulle, Herbert Stoc, Anketill son of Robert, Robert de Recham and many others.

P.R.O. E 315/46/96

Elias Despenser was dead by July 1233 (*F.F. Warwicks.* 494).

413 Mid–late 1230s

Gift, remise and quitclaim by Alice widow of Elias Despenser (*helye dispensatoris*) in her widowhood and free power, from herself and her heirs, to the abbot and monks of Stoneleigh (*Stanl'*) of 12d. rent in Coventry (*coventr'*) which they owed (*solebant et debebant*) from the lands which Guy Long (*Guido longus*), Hugh the Dyer (*tinctor*), Stephen Scathelok, Nicholas Luve, Alexander [Har][1]lewyn [and] Cecily [widow of Jordan][1] le Yhicher held; to be held in perpetual alms with all [appurtenances][1] and liberties, any right of reclaim by the grantor and his heirs being precluded. The abbot and convent gave [ ][2]s. of silver. Clause for warranty. Witnesses: William de

[Wil][1]nale, Richard Burgeys, John de Aula, Adam the Vintner (*vinetar'*), Anketill de Wygewan', Herbert Stoc, Anketill son of Robert, Robert de Retham, Adam de la Grene, Alexander Harlewyn, Michael de Hurst, Alexander de Hull' and many others.

Seal missing P.R.O. D 7703

[1] Damage here; gaps supplied from E315/46/96.
[2] The sum is lost.

414 Mid–late 1230s

Gift, remise and quitclaim by Nigel son of Elias Despenser (*Elie Dispe(n)satoris*) of Coventry to the abbot and monks of Stoneleigh (*Stanl'*) of 12d. rent in Coventry which they owed (*[sol]ebant et debebant*) to him and his mother from the lands which Guy Long (*Guido long(us)*), Hugh the Dyer (*tinctor*), Stephen Scathelok, Nicholas Love, Alexander Harlewyn [and] Cecily widow of Jordan le Yhicher held; to be held in perpetual alms with all its appurtenances and liberties whatsoever (*in omnibus rebus et locis*), any right of reclaim by the grantor and his heirs being precluded. The abbot and monks gave 10s. of silver. Clause for warranty. *Et sciendum quod si tenentes tocius dicti tenementi vel aliquis ipsorum destricti vel vexati fuerint pro aliquo redditu quem ego et heredes mei domino comiti de Covintr' et heredibus suis debemus ipsos omnino adquietabimus et indempnes cons(er)vabimus et hoc pro me et heredibus meis affidavi sub pena xxijd. dictis monachis ad quemlibet quatuor terminorum anni scilicet Natale, festum beate Marie in Marcio, festum sancti Johannis, festum sancti Michaelis insimul cum predicto redditu solvend(orum) si ipsos et tenentes ipsorum singulis terminis non adquietaverimus subicie(n)do me et heredes meos juri(s)dicc(i)oni official(is) et decani Covintr' ut co(m)pellant nos qualitercumque voluerint omnia predicta obs(er)vare renu(n)ciando etiam omni juris remedio tam in foro civili quam ecclesiastico.* Witnesses: William de Wilnale, Richard Burgeys, John de Aula, Adam the Vintner (*vinetar'*), Anketill de Wigewan', Adam de la Grene, Alexander Harlewin, Michael de Hurst, Alexander de Hulle, Herbert Stoc, Anketill son of Robert, Robert de Recham and many others.

P.R.O. E 315/39/39

415 Mid–late 1230s

Charter of Nigel son of Elias Despenser (*Elye dispensatoris*) giving to the abbey and the monks of Stoneleigh (*Stanl'*) the gift (*donat(i)o(ne)m*) in Coventry which Walter de Norton' made to them, namely of 2s. rent for ever from the messuage with appurtenances which Walter the Goldsmith (*aurifaber*) held hereditarily of him; to be held as freely, entirely and quietly as the charter which they have thereon witnesses. Sealing clause. Witnesses: Master Richard the Vintner (*vinitar'*), William de Wilinhal', Osbert the clerk, Anketill son of Rob(ert), Roger the Dyer (*tinctore*), John de Sta(n)l and others.

Seal extant G.H. 269

416 Mid–late 1230s

Charter of Nigel son of Elias Despenser (*Elye dispensatoris*) of Coventry granting to God, the church of St. Mary and the monks of Stoneleigh (*Stanl*) the gift which Walter del Enese of Norton' gave (*det(u)lit*) to them in Coventry of the messuage with appurtenances which Walter the Goldsmith (*aurifaber*) held, namely that which is between the messuage of William de Wylnhal' and the messuage of Stephen Scathelok; to be held freely [etc.] just as Walter's charter which they have thereon more fully witnesses. Sealing clause. Witnesses: Master Richard the Vintner (*vinitario*), William de Wylnhal', Anketill son of Robert, Roger the Dyer (*tinctore*), John de Stanl', Simon his son, Alexander de Hulle, Richard son of Moys and others.

Seal missing P.R.O. D 3687

417 Late 1230s–early 1240s

Charter of William son of Herbert [of] Coventry giving to God, the church of the blessed Mary and the monks of Stoneleigh (*Stanl'*) 12d. rent in Coventry from the tenement with appurtenances in Spon St. (*Sponnestret*) which Hugh le Burser held of the grantor and which is between the land Symon son of Symon the Doctor (*medicus*) held and the land Symon son of Richard held; to be held of the grantor and his heirs freely [etc.], by rendering annually a root of ginger (*unam radicem Gingib(er)is*) at Christmas for all service [etc.]. Clause for distraint. The rent is to be rendered at four terms as it used to be. The monks gave 9s. of silver. Clause for warranty. Witnesses: Master Richard the Vintner (*vinetario*), Osbert the clerk, Adam the Vintner (*vinetario*), Anketill son of Robert, Roger the Dyer (*tinctore*), Richard son of Moys' of Fletchamstead (*flichamstude*), Jordan (*Jurd'*) de Fl(i)chamstude and many others.

P.R.O. E315/49/191

418 c.1230s

Charter of William son of Herbert giving to Thomas the Weaver (*textori*) and Emma his wife, their heirs or assigns, a certain part of his land in Spon St. (*in vico sponne*) with appurtenances, that namely which lies between the land Adam the Vintner (*vinitarius*) held and the land Ralf son of Mansellus the Dyer (*tinctoris*) held and is marked by the hedge in the middle of the grantor's land (*m(er)cat se usque ad sepem in medio terre Mee suprascitam*) in length and in width as is manifest according to the metes and bounds made there; to be held to them, their heirs or assigns, of the grantor and his heirs freely [etc.], by rendering annually 2d. of silver at the four terms of the year fixed in Coventry for all secular service [etc.]. Clause for warranty. Thomas and Emma gave 10s. of silver in recognition. Sealing clause. Witnesses: Roger son of Peter, Adam the Vintner (*vinitario*), Ailmer the Dyer (*tinctore*), Geoffrey de Atleburgo, William Mauclerc, Robert de Cumdulme, Hugh Fortwine, Simon the Doctor (*medico*), Nicholas de Cauci, Thomas le Tanur, Thomas Wade, Richard Skirewith, Vincent the Shoemaker (*sutore*) and others.

Seal extant C.R.O. 1A/C12/4

419 c.1220–1225

Charter of John son of Osbert de Flichamestude giving to Richard son of Peter the grantor's uncle (*avunculo meo*) and his heirs a land in Spon St. (*unam terram In vico de Sponn'*) with appurtenances namely the entire messuage which lies between the land Richard son of Rauwin (*Rauwuni*) held and the land Ralf le Fuelere held, and 26d. rent, namely from the land which Walter the White (*Albus*) held 14d., and from the land which lies between the land Walter the White (*Albus*) held and the land Hugh Bucstan held 12d., and from the land Mansel held 6d., and from the land which lies between the land Mansel held and the land Roger Bucstan held 12d.; to be held to him and his heirs, of the grantor and his heirs freely [etc.], by rendering annually for all secular service [etc.] 2s. of silver at four terms, namely 6d. at each of the feasts of St. Michael, St. Andrew, St. Mary in March and St. John the Baptist. The grantee and his heirs will acquit the service to the chief lords. Clause for warranty. Richard gave 10s. of silver in recognition. Witnesses: Thomas de Finham, Swanus the Parker (*p(ar)car'*), Vincent his son, Simon de Leicestr', Robert de Kanel', Richard son of Agnes, Robert de Oldenhal, Simon the Doctor (*medico*), Simon de Warewic, William son of Herbert Bucstan, Robert the Carter (*carettar'*), Richard son of Rawin', Vincent son of Roger de Assesho and many others.

Seal missing — C.R.O. 1A/C12/3

420 — 1220s or early 1230s

Charter of Herbert Bucstan giving to Roger son of Richard son of Peter in free marriage with Alice his daughter the entire quarter (*totam quartam partem*) of his land which lies between the land Alexander *Linpulator*, brother of the hospital of St. Leonard, held on the one hand and the land Hugh Bucstan held on the other; to be held to him and the heirs issuing from him and the aforesaid Alice, of the grantor and his heirs quietly, peacefully and honourably, by rendering annually 4d. at four terms of the year namely 1d. at each of the feasts of St. Michael, St. Andrew, St. Mary in March, and the Nativity of St. John the Baptist, a hen at Christmas [and] one man in Autumn. Sealing clause. Witnesses: Richard de Aula, Robert his clerk, Simon son of Roger the Tanner (*tannatoris*), Richard his brother, Mansellus the Dyer (*tinctore*), Geoffrey the Palmer (*palmario*), Simon de Leicest' and many others.

Seal missing — C.R.O. 2/176

421 — Late 1230s–early 1240s

Sale and quitclaim by Agnes daughter of Peter the Weaver and Elena sisters (*Ego Angneta filia petri tixtoris et ego Elena sorores*), in their free power, to Roger son of Richard son of Peter, his heirs or to whom he will wish to assign, of all right and claim in the land which they held in Spon St. (*in vico de sponna*) of Roger's fee, namely the land which lies between the land Stephen son of Walter held and the land Henry son of Reginald Buston held; to be held freely [etc.]. Clause for warranty. Roger gave 18s. of silver. Sealing clause. Witnesses: Robert de Fug(ers), Richard Labbanc, Roger de F(ro)desham, Adam the Vintner (*vinet'*), Alexander Harlewin, Nicholas nephew (*nepote*) of Vincent, William son of Herbert, Simon son of Roger, Simon his son, Adam de la Grene, Stephen son of Walter, Mancel the Dyer (*tin(c)tore*), Geoffrey de Attleb', Ailmer the Dyer (*tin(c)tore*), William Buston and others.

2 seals extant — Fuller II/17/3

422 — Late 1250s–early 1260s

Charter of William Roke of Coventry giving to Roger son of Peter of Coventry a certain part of the land which he bought from Richard Caucey in Spon St. (*in vico Sponnet'*), namely that which lies between the land ( )[1] held on the one hand and the land ( )[1] held on the other; to be held to him, his heirs or assigns or to whomsoever he will wish to give or assign, by rendering annually a clove-gillyflower at Easter for all secular service and demand. Clause for warranty. Roger gave ½ mark beforehand. Sealing clause. Witnesses: William Leuyn then bailiff, William Mauclerc, Robert de Codu(m), Robert Mansel, Richard Lotemon, William de Canneley, Richard the clerk and many others.

Seal missing — C.R.O. 2/67

[1] blank, names omitted

423 Late 1250s–early 1260s

Charter of William son of Richard de Henl' of Coventry giving to Roger son of Roger son of Peter 12d. annual rent which the same Roger used to pay to him from certain land in the vill of Coventry, in Spon St. (*in vico sponne*) which lies between the land William Palm(er) held on the one hand and the land Adam de Allys[l][1]eg' held on the other; to be held to him, his heirs and assigns, of the grantor and his heirs freely [etc.], by rendering annually to the lord of that fee, namely to the heirs of Richard Schyrewhit as the perpetual attorneys of the grantor and his heirs 1d. of silver at Michaelmas, and to the grantor and his heirs a clove-gillyflower at Easter for all secular service. Clause for warranty. Roger gave 4s. of silver beforehand. Sealing clause. Witnesses: Walter le Blund then bailiff, Symon the Doctor (*medico*), Ranulph de Franketon', Robert de Cundolm', Richard Lutemon, Hugh de Kannel', Hugh le Bretun the clerk and others.

Seal extant C.R.O. 1A/L12–13C/45

[1] There is a tear here.

424 1280s

Charter of Christine daughter of Roger son of Roger son of Peter of Coventry, in her pure virginity, giving to Robert de Cannel of Coventry all the lands, rents, tenements and buildings which descended to her after the death of Roger her father, and which she had in Coventry, namely a messuage with buildings sited there in Spon St., Coventry (*in vico Spanne de Coventr'*) between the land Eadward the Tanner (*Tannator*) held on the one hand and the land John the Smith (*Faber*) of Weddington (*Wetinton*) held on the other, a messuage in the same street between the land Robert Remount held on the one hand and the land Robert Maggus (*mag̃go*) held on the other, a messuage in the same street between the land of Robert the Tanner (*Tannator'*) on the one hand and the land William Rouk held on the other, 18d. rent from the land Robert Maunsel and William his son held in the same street between the land of Jurdan de Flechamstud on the one hand and the land of Symon the Tanner (*Tannatoris*) on the other, 12d. annual rent, 2 hens at Christmas and the service of 1 man for 1 day in Autumn from the land of Walter Loteman between the land Robert Rimilt held on the one hand and the land Richard le Bourser held on the other, 14d. annual rent from the land of John de Kendal' in the same street between the land of William de Parlur on the one hand and the land of Thomas Champiun on the other, 12d. annual rent from the land of Thomas le Champiun in the same street between the land of John de Kendal' on the one hand and the land of Richard le Burser on the other, 4d. annual rent from the land of William le Proude in Cook Street (*in vico Coci*) between the land of the hospital of St. John the Baptist on the one hand and the land of Robert Herbert on the other, ½d. of silver from the land of John Ingram outside the bar towards the church of St. Nicholas (*extra Barram versus ecclesiam sancti Nicholai*) between the land of Sir John le Bel on the one hand and the land of Jurdan le Seler on the other; to be held to him, his heirs or assigns, freely [etc.] with all appurtenances, liberties and easements pertaining to all and each of the aforesaid, by rendering annually ½d. of silver at Easter and to the lords of the fee the service due and accustomed for all secular service [etc.]. Robert gave 16 marks of silver beforehand. Warranty and sealing clauses. Witnesses: Henry Baker (*Pistor'*) then bailiff of Coventry, Robert de Chilton' of the same, Geoffrey son of John of the same, Richard le Burser of the same, Robert the Tanner (*Tannator'*) of the same, Gilbert Coruwenne of the same, Walter Lotemon of the same, Peter the clerk of the same and others.

Seal extant C.R.O. 2/116b

Endorsed: Carta de tenemento quondam Willelmi le Waller. Cristiana filia Petri Roberto de Canley de ij ten(ementis) in le Sponnestrete & de diversis redditibus.

425 1280s

Demise and quitclaim by Christine daughter of Roger son of Roger son of Peter of Coventry, in her pure virginity, to Robert de Kannele of Coventry, of all right and claim in ½d. annual rent which she used to receive from the aforesaid Robert for the lands, rents, tenements and buildings which she sold him in Coventry; to be held with all appurtenances to him, his heirs or whatsoever assigns, freely [etc.]. Exclusion clause. Robert gave ½ mark of silver beforehand. Sealing clause. Witnesses: Henry Baker (*Pistor'*) then bailiff of Coventry, Robert de Chilton of the same, Geoffrey son of John of the same, Richard le Burser of the same, Robert the Tanner (*tannatore*) of the same, Gilbert Curuwenne of the same, Walter Luteman of the same, Peter the clerk of the same and others.

Seal extant C.R.O. 2/116a

426 Early 1230s

Charter of Alice daughter of William de Spon(n)a giving to Simon de Lymeseye a toft below the thorn-bush (*unum toftum sub spina*) which William Horsepurs' held and an acre of land with appurtenances in the territory of Spon (*In territorio de spon(n)a*); to be held to him, his heirs or assigns except to a house of religion, of the grantor and her heirs freely [etc.], by rendering annually for all secular service and demand pertaining to the grantor and her heirs 2s. of silver at four terms of the year, namely 6d. at each of the feasts of St. Michael, St. Andrew, St. Mary in March and St. John the Baptist. Clause for warranty. Simon gave 2s. of silver. Sealing clause. Witnesses: Richard de Aula, Philip de Winchecumb', Hugh de Allispath', Mansellus the Dyer (*tinctore*), Richard the Black (*Nig(r)o*), Adam de la Grene, Richard son of Adam, William Gupil, Simon the Doctor (*medico*), Alexander Harlewin' and others.

Seal extant C.R.O. 1A/C30

427 Early 1230s

Sale and quitclaim by Ailwin the Preacher (*predicator*) to Philip de Winchecumb', or to whom he will wish to give or assign, of a certain part of his land with appurtenances towards Spon in Coventry (*versus Sponnam In Covintr'*) which lies between the land the same Philip held and the land Mabel la Custeresse held, entirely and fully in length and in width as is manifest; to be held to him, his heirs or assigns, freely and quit of all exaction, well and in peace without any hindrance and charge by the grantor or his heirs just as the grantor held and by the same service, namely by rendering annually to the heirs of Vincent le Parker 16d. of silver for all secular service and demand according to the custom *firme solvende* in Coventry. Clause for warranty. Philip gave 3s. of silver. Sealing clause. Witnesses: Richard de Aula, Master Richard the Vintner (*Vinitar'*), William de Wilnhal', John Vincent, Nicholas de Smithisford, Simon de Leicestr', Simon the Doctor (*medico*), Alexander the Pursemaker (*bursario*), William Bucstan, Richard son of Adam de la Grene, Thomas de Novo Castro the clerk and others.

Seal extant C.R.O. 2/23

428 Late 1230s–early 1240s

Charter of John le Flecher with the consent of Alice his wife giving to Philip de Winchcombe and his heirs common for all his cattle in the pasture of Spon and free entrance and exit for cattle and for wagons through the middle of the pasture by the road leading from Cheylesmore to Spon bridge.

Sciant presentes et futuri quod ego Johannes le Flecher consensu et assensu Alicie uxoris mee dedi et concessi et hac presenti carta mea confirmavi Philippo de Winchecumba et heredibus suis in pastura mea de Sponna co(m)muniu(m) omnibus averiis suis inperpetuum omnibus diebus per annum et liberum introitum et exitum cum omnibus averiis suis et cum quadrigis suis plenarie ad fennia[1] sua et aratra sua adducenda et omnia aisiamenta sua in predicta pastura et sine aliqua calumpnia vel impedimento mei vel heredum meorum videlicet per viam que ducit de Cheylismora usque ad pontem de Sponna per mediam pasturam predictam. Pro hac autem donacione et concessione predictus Philippus et heredes sui michi et heredibus meis annuatim persolvent ad Pentecosten unum par cirotecarum de precio unius oboli pro omni servicio seculari et exaccione ad me vel ad heredes meos inde pertinente. Et ego Johannes et heredes mei predicto Philippo et heredibus suis predictum co(m)muniu(m) pasture mee cum omnibus libertatibus ut predictum est contra omnes gentes warantizabimus inperpetuum. Et ut hec autem mea donacio et concessio perpetua gaudeat firmitate presens scriptum sigilli mei impressione corroboravi. Hiis testibus Magistro Ricardo Vinitario Osberto clerico tunc preposito Ricardo Burgeys Johanne Beyer Roberto de Feug(er)s Ricardo Haldein Adam[2] de Lagrene Alexandro Bursario et aliis.

Seal extant C.R.O. 1A/C3

[1] sic [2] sic

429 10 April 1256

Agreement between Philip de Winchcombe and John le Fletcher whereby Philip has withdrawn his writ for common pasture in the fields of Spon on condition that the pasture will remain intact and that it will not be ploughed or sown by John, his heirs or assigns, in the future. Should John, his heirs or assigns, break this agreement they will be fined according to the assessment of good and lawful men. Moreover, John has renounced all further action in this matter and bound himself, his heirs and assigns, to keep the agreement under ecclesiastical sanction. He has also withdrawn his writ against Philip for a messuage towards Spon. All past disputes between them are now at an end and should any arise in the future the guilty party will be fined under the arbitration of the vicar of St. Michael's and the chaplain of Spon.

Anno ab incarnatione domini millesimo ducentesimo quinquagesimo sexto in crastino Palmarum conventum est inter Philippum de Winchecumb' ex parte una et Johannem le Flecher ex parte altera ita videlicet quod predictus Philippus retraxit breve domini regis super predictum Johannem perquisitum pro quadam com(m)uni pastura in campis de Sponna sub tali scilicet forma quod predictus Johannes vel heredes vel assignati sui in co(mmun)i pastura pretacta ulterius non arabunt nec etiam se(m)i(n)abunt sed secundum metas et divisas ibidem factas illa co(m)munis pastura predicta jacebit et permanebit intacta. Si tamen a casu contingat vel etiam voluntarie quod predictus Johannes vel heredes vel assignati sui ulterius in predicta pastura arent vel seminent vel etiam divisas sive metas aliquas ibidem positas removeant predicto Philippo vel ejus heredibus vel assignatis emendam facient per visum bonorum et legalium virorum ex consensu p(ar)tiu(m) eligendorum sub pena dimidie marce no(m)i(n)e peccunie solvende si virorum el(ec)torum visui vel etiam si viros aliquos honestos pro parte sua eligere[1] aliquo modo contradicere presumant. Et ad omnia predicta fideliter observanda renunciavit predictus Johannes pro se et heredibus vel assignatis suis omni exceptioni cavillationi et defensioni et omni juris remedio tam canonici quam civil(i) et specialiter regie prohibitioni. Subjecit se etiam predictus Johannes pro se et heredibus vel assignatis jur(is)dic(tion)i offic(ialis) domini archidiaconi Coventr' s(i)v(e) precentoris ejusdem loci quicumque fuerit pro tempore quod ipsos sine cause (con)gnit(i)one de die in diem per sentenciam excommunicationis vel aliam penam quam p(ar)s dicti Philippi duxerit eligendam possit ad observacionem convencionis (con)pellere una cum dampnis et expensis si p(ar)s dicti Philippi aliquas fecerit r(ati)one (con)venc(i)o(n)is non observate. Ex alia parte predictus Johannes retraxit breve domini regis super dictum Philippum perquisitum pro quodam mesuagio versus Spo(n)nam sub tali forma quod omnes discordie et etiam convenciones inter predictos Philippum et Johannem p(re)h(ab)ite a dictis die et anno in posterum relaxentur et (com)pescantur. Si tamen contingat quod absit quod alique rixe sive etiam (con)tenciones in dictis vel factis vel etiam in terris tenementis vel edificiis inter predictos Philippum et Johannem et eorum heredes vel assignatos dehinc evenerint quicumque eorum erga alium deliquerit et per juramentum fidelium probari possit per visum domini vicarii sancti Michaelis et capellani de Spo(n)na quicumque fuerint pro tempore alii emendabit sub pena dimidie marce qui dictorum vicarii et capellani arbitrio consentire voluerit. Et ad hoc omnia fideliter observanda uterque predictorum Philippi et Johannis fide media se obligavit et etiam huic presenti scripto in modum cyrographi confecto alternatim sigillum suum apposuit. Hiis testibus Anketino de Wikewane Symone Medico Henrico Burgeys Ada de la Grene Ricardo Nigro Alexandro de Crulefeld Ernard(o) de Aula Thoma de Horewell Hugone clerico istius cyrographi (com)positore et aliis.

Chirograph
Seal extant C.R.O. 1A/C76

[1] sic

430 Mid–late 1260s

Charter of Philip de Winchecumb' giving to God, to the church of the blessed Mary and to Prior William and the convent of Coventry and their successors, for the salvation of his soul, that of Alice his wife, and those of his ancestors and successors, in free, pure and perpetual alms, his entire messuage at Spon (*ad Spannam*) in Coventry with buildings, garden, dovecote and curtilage (*cum edificiis. Gardino. Columbar'. Curtilag'*), his croft above the garden called *Scatherscroft*, the other croft called *Cristescroft*; which extends from the aforesaid croft up to Dead Lane (*Dedelone*). Moreover he has granted 8 selions in the field of Spon (*in campo de Spa(n)na*) which lie between the land of Haldeyn and the land of Roger le Chamberleyn, and 5 selions in the same field between the land of Roger de Sakerston' and Ranulph de Cundelme, together with his enclosed meadow in the same field (*cum prato incluso meo in eodem campo*) and the meadow he bought from William Payn with the attached plot (*placia annexa*) which the grantor had from the prior of Coventry. And moreover he has granted his oven (*furnum*) which he bought from Richard de Wygorn' in Cheylesmore Lane (*Cheilesmore Lone*) with buildings, rents and all appurtenances; to be held in free, pure and perpetual alms saving the service of the chief lords, namely 12d. to the prior of Coventry for the aforesaid oven (*pro furno predicto*), 6d. to Margery de Recham and her heirs for the houses opposite the oven (*pro domibus ex opposito furni*), ½d. rent to John de Wikewan' for warranty of the same houses, and 18d. to William de Herdebur' and his heirs for Payn's meadow (*pro predicto prato payn*). Warranty and sealing clauses. Witnesses: John de Pontefr', Robert de Chilton', Richard Ernys, Henry Baker (*pistor'*), Pagan Pake, Thomas Selet, Peter Barun, Richard de Bokervil', Guy the clerk and others.

Seal extant (fragment) C.R.O. 1A/C62

431 Early 1270s

Notification by Richard called le Burser of Coventry that he and his wife and their heirs are bound to pay 30s. annual rent to the prior and convent of Coventry for

Philip de Winchcombe's property in Spon St. 10s. of the rent is to be remitted as long as Christine, Philip's widow, survives and Richard is to arrange her dower. The grantees should not sell, pledge or alienate until the prior and convent have received warning, and should they wish to do so the prior and convent will have first option.

Noverint universi presens scriptum visuri vel audituri quod ego Ricardus dictus le Burs(er) de Coventr' teneor perpetuo pro me Alicia uxore mea et heredibus meis Priori et conventui Coventr' et eorum successoribus in triginta solid(os) annui redditus pro mesuagio cum edificiis gardino columbar(i) curtilagio duobus croftis tresdecim selyonibus terre in camp(o) de Spo(n)na et prato incluso in eodem camp(o) cum pertinentiis que fuerunt quondam Philippi de Wynchecumb' in Coventr' in vico de Sponna solvend(os) eisdem ad quatuor anni terminos consuetos in villa de Coventr' scilicet in quolibet termino septem solidos et sex denarios. Ita quod licebit eisdem priori et conventui et eorum successoribus libere distringere omnes terras nostras et omnia tenementa nostra ubicumque fuerint infra villam et extra quociens in aliquo termino solucionis dicti redditus defecerimus usque ad plenam ejusdem redditus solucionem sine cujusque contradictione. Cessante tamen solucione decem solid(orum) de triginta solid(is) predictis ad totam vitam Christiane uxoris predicti Philippi si ipsum supervixerit et dotem suam de predictis dir(ati)onaverit. Ita quod post ejus decessum totus redditus triginta solidorum predictorum ad dictos Priorem et conventum et eorum successores libere et integre revertatur. Ita etiam quod nec nos nec heredes nostri possimus dictum mesuagium cum edificiis gardino columbar(i) curtilagio croftis selyonibus terre et prato incluso cum pertinentiis alicui vendere invadiare vel alienare donec super hoc dicti prior et conventus et eorum successores prius sint premuniti. Et si forte predictam vendere vel invadiare voluerimus quod iidem prior et conventus et eorum successores ad ea habenda omnibus aliis sint propinquiores secundum quod in carta super hiis confecta plenius ac melius continetur. In hujus autem rei testimonium presenti scripto sigillum meum apposui. Hiis testibus Petro Walens' Petro filio ejus Henrico Pistore Roberto de Chilton' Petro filio ejus Johanne de Lodelawe Roberto de Cloch' Ada Attegrene Galfrido filio Johannis Gilberto Corewenne Willelmo le Rok Willelmo de Kannel' Hugone le Bretun et aliis.

Seal extant C.R.O. 2/30

432 1230s

Grant and quitclaim by Alice sister (*sor(or)*) of David de Flichamestude to Alice wife of David de Flichamestude of a messuage in Coventry, namely the land which David held in Spon St. (*in vico sponne*) in length and in width as it purports; to be held to her for her entire life of the grantor and her heirs for the same service as David gave during his life, and to the grantor or her heirs a pair of gloves worth ½d. or ½d. at Easter for all secular service and demand. Clause for warranty. Alice gave 3s. of silver in recognition. Sealing clause. Witnesses: Simon de Leicestre, Simon de Varevic, Ralf his son, Geoffrey Paumer, John (*Joanne*) de Flicamestude, Mathias (*Mathee*) de Flicamestude, Jordan son of Simon, Nicholas (*Nicolao*) son of Luve, William (*Vilelmo*) son of Richard, Adam de la Grene and many others.

Seal extant W.R.O. 46

433 1230s

Demise, grant and quitclaim by Alice sister of David to Alice daughter of David de Flicha(m)cestude of a messuage in the vill of Coventry, namely that which David the grantor's brother held in Spon St. (*in vico de sp(a)nna*) and which fell to her by inheritance (*hereditarie pertinebat*) in length and in width as the land purports; to be held to her and her heirs of the grantor and her heirs for the same service as David held, and to the grantor or her heirs a pair of gloves annually at Easter for all secular service and demand. Clause for warranty after the death of Alice her step-mother (*Nov(er)ce sue*). Alice daughter of David gave 4s. of silver beforehand. Sealing clause. Witnesses: Simon de Leicestre, Simon de Varevic, Ralf his son, Geoffrey Paumer, John (*Joanne*) de Flica(m)estude, Mathias (*Mathee*) de Flicha(m)estude, Jordan son of Simon, Nicholas (*Niciolao*) son of Luve, William (*Vilelmo*) son of Richard, Adam de la Grene and many others.

Seal extant W.R.O. 47

434 Late 1230s–early 1240s

Charter of Alice daughter of David de Flichamstude giving to Luke son of Stephen de Berkeleswelle a messuage with appurtenances in Coventry in Spon St. (*in vico sponne*), namely that which lies between the land Robert de Dereby held on the one hand and the land Matilda the wife of Walter held on the other in name of dower; to be held to him, his heirs or assigns, of the grantor and her heirs freely [etc.] in length and in width according to the metes and bounds made there, by rendering annually to William Som(er) or his heirs 3s. of silver and to William de Paylinton' 2d. of silver according to the usage of Coventry, and to the lords of the fee 2 parts of the service of 2 men during 1 day in Autumn and 2 parts of the price of 2 hens at Christmas, and to the grantor or her heirs a pair of gloves worth ½d. or ½d. at Easter. Clause for warranty. Luke gave 7s. of silver in recognition. Sealing clause. Witnesses: Adam le Vinet(er), Richard Labannc, Roger son of Richard son of Peter, William son of Herbert, Simon the Doctor (*medico*), Richard Scyrewit, Hugh le Borser, William de Kannele, Adam de la Grene, John le Flecher, Robert Bocston, Osbert son of Jurd(an) and others.

Seal extant W.R.O. 53

435 c. late 1240s

Sale and quitclaim by Luke son of Stephen de Berkeleswelle to William Somer of all right and claim in a messuage with appurtenances in Coventry which lies between the land Robert de Dereby held on the one hand in Spon St. (*in vico spanne*) and the land Matilda the wife of Walter held on the other with the rent of 3s.; to be held to him, his heirs or assigns, freely [etc.] in length and in width according to the metes and bounds made there, by rendering annually to William de Paylinton' and his heirs 2d. of silver at four terms of the year according to the usage of Coventry, and to the lords of that fee 2 parts of the service of 2 men during 1 day in Autumn and 2 parts of the price of 2 hens at Christmas for all secular service, exaction or demand. William gave ½ mark of silver. Sealing clause. Witnesses: Anketill de Wikewane, Philip de Winchecu(m)be, John le Flecher, Richard Labaunc, William son of Herbert, Simon the Doctor (*Medico*), Richard Sckyrewyt, Hugh le Borser, William de Kannele, Osbert son of Jurd(an), William son of Ailm(er), Reginald de Withibroc and others.

Seal missing W.R.O. 52

436 c.1230s

Charter of Eduia daughter of Robert de Hampton' in her free power giving to Mansellus the Dyer (*tinctori*) a half (*dimidietatem*) of the land in Spon St. (*in vico de*

Sponn') which lies between the land the same Mansellus held and the land Roger Bucstan held, namely the half which is nearer to the land of the aforesaid Roger Bucstan with all appurtenances; to be held to him and his heirs of the grantor and her heirs hereditarily, freely, quietly and honourably, by rendering annually 6½d. for all secular service and demand, namely 1½d. at each of the feasts of St. Michael, St. Andrew, St. Mary in March and St. John the Baptist, and ½d. at Easter. Clause for warranty. Mansellus gave ½ mark of silver in recognition. Witnesses: Peter the Welshman (*Walensi*), Robert the Weaver (*textore*), Roger Bucstan, Geoffrey de Atleb(ur)g, Geoffrey the Palmer (*Palm'*), Robert the Locksmith (*Loccar'*), Thomas Wade, Robert the Plumber (*plumbar'*), Henry son of Elias (*Helye*) and many others.

Seal missing W.R.O. 50

437 1230s

Charter of Mansellus the Dyer (*tinctor*) giving to William Som(er) in free marriage with Beatrice his daughter 3s. rent in Spon St. (*sponnistrata*), namely those which Alice Harnwis used to render annually from the land which she held of the grantor between the land Robert de Derby held on the one hand and the land William Bucston held on the other; to be held to them and the heirs issuing from them of the grantor and his heirs freely [etc.] just as the grantor held, by rendering a pair of gloves worth ½d. or ½d. at Easter for all secular service. Clause for warranty. *Et si contingat quod dicti Willelmus et Beatricia et heredes sui pro aliquo del(ic)to in m(iser-icord)ia mea vel heredum meorum i(n)ciderint pro uno Clavo girofri sint quieti*. Sealing clause. Witnesses: Simon the Doctor (*medico*), William Herbert, William Bucston, Roger son of Peter, Geoffrey de Atleburgo, Ailmer the Dyer (*tinctore*), William de Wilinhale, Gilbert Fra(n)ceys, Adam de la Grene, Hugh the Merchant (*m(er)catore*), Alexander the Purse-maker (*Burc(er)*) and others.

Seal missing W.R.O. 51

438 Late 1230s–early 1240s

Charter of Elizabeth widow of John de Walton' in her lawful widowhood giving to God, the blessed Mary, St. Edmund and the nuns of Catesby (*Cattesby*), for the salvation of her soul, that of John de Walton' her late husband and those of her ancestors, in pure and perpetual alms, ½ mark rent with appurtenances which she used to receive from William le Gupill' outside Coventry (*extra Covintr'*) with homages, reliefs, escheats and all else which may accrue to her or her heirs from the aforesaid rent; to be held to the nuns and their successors, of the grantor and her heirs, freely [etc.]. Warranty and sealing clauses. Witnesses: Master Simon de Walton', Sir Henry de Ladbrok', Philip de Winchecumb', Robert de Canele, Richard Gubiu(n), Henry de Abbetot, Adam de Rudmarleg' and others.

Seal missing P.R.O. B 189
Endorsed: Termin(um) solucionis reddit(us) istius carte est ad Pach' d(omi)ni.

Simon de Walton was purchasing property in Warwickshire from the 1230s. (See P. R. Coss, 'Sir Geoffrey de Langley and the Crisis of the Knightly Class', *Past and Present*, No. 68, 1975, p. 12). Henry de Ladbroke had succeeded his father John by 1242 and was dead by 1257 (*V.C.H. Warwicks*, vi, p. 144).

439 Late 1230s–early 1240s

Sale and quitclaim by John son of William But to Nicholas son of Nigel (*Nigilli*) and his heirs or to whom he will wish to assign, of all right and claim in the land which the grantor held in Spon St. (*sponnistrata*) which lies between the land Benedict Bucston held on the one hand and the land Richard de Botildston' held on the other. Nicholas gave 8s. of silver. Warranty and sealing clauses. Witnesses: Robert de Hastinges, Osbert the clerk then reeve (*p(re)po(s)ito*), Richard Burgeys, Roger Bucston', Adam the Vintner (*vintario*), Roger son of Peter, Simon the Doctor (*medico*), Ailmer the Dyer (*tinctore*), Robert de Cu(n)dulme, Richard de Botildston', Geoffrey de Atlebur', John the White (*albo*) the clerk and others.

Seal missing W.R.O. 57

440 Late 1230s–early 1240s

Charter of William the Chaplain (*Capellanus*) son of Roger le Waffrer of Coventry giving to Thomas son of Thomas the Mason (*cementarii*) of Coventry in free marriage with Matilda daughter of Elias (*helye*) le Waffrer the grantor's niece (*nepte*) his land in Coventry in Spon St. (*in vico sponne*) which he held of Thomas Wade and which lies between the land the same Thomas held on the one hand and the land Geoffrey son of David held on the other with appurtenances in length and in width according to the metes and bounds made there; to be held to him and to their heirs issuing from the two of them freely [etc.] just as the grantor held, of the same lord and by the same service, namely of Thomas Wade by the service of 18d. of silver to be paid annually to Thomas and his heirs at four terms of the year according to the usage of Coventry. Sealing clause. Witnesses: Osbert the clerk then reeve (*preposito*), Richard Burgeys, Robert de Feug(er)s, Richard son of Roger Herbert, William the Palmer (*Palm(er)o*), Alexander his brother, William de Wilnhale, John Blagwin, Henry son of Herbert, Symon de Leycestre, Roger son of Richard son of Peter, William son of William Bugstan and others.

Seal extant C.R.O. 1A/C14

441 1240s

Charter of Thomas son of Martin le Loker granting to Osbert son of Jordan the Miller (*molendinarii*) the entire land with appurtenances in Spon St., Coventry (*in vico Spo(n)ne de Covintr'*) which lies between the land Ralf Abboth held and the land Gilbert le Franceys held in length and in width according to the metes and bounds made there; to be held to him and his heirs or to whom he will wish to assign of the grantor and his heirs freely [etc.], by rendering annually 2s. of silver at four terms of the year according to the usage of Coventry for all secular service [etc.]. Clause for warranty. Osbert gave 10s. of silver in recognition. Sealing clause. Witnesses: Osbert Durdent, John le Flecher', Alexander the Purse-maker (*Bursario*), Adam de la Grene, Simon the Doctor (*medico*), William de Kannele, William son of Herbert, Roger son of Peter, Gilbert the Frenchman (*fra(n)cisco*), Ailmer the Dyer (*tinctore*), Nicholas de Wico, Henry de Pinnele, Simon son of Simon the Doctor (*medici*) and others.

Seal extant W.R.O. 55

442 1250s

Charter of Nicholas de Wyþ giving to Osbert son of Jordan the Miller (*molendin'*) and his heirs a certain part of his land with appurtenances in Coventry, in Spon St. in Crow Mill Lane (*in vico Spanne In Croumulnelane*), which lies between the land the aforesaid Osbert held on the one hand and the land Richard le Ledbetere and Simon de Warewyke held on the other in length and in width as the land purports according to the metes and bounds made there; to be held to him, his heirs or assigns, of the grantor and his heirs, freely [etc.], by rendering 12d. of silver annually to the lords of the fee at 4 terms of the year according to the usage of Coventry and to the grantor and his heirs a pair of gloves worth a ½d. or ½d. at Easter for all services and demands. Clause for warranty. Nicholas gave 7s. of silver for entry. Sealing clause. Witnesses: John Flech(er), Simon the Doctor (*medico*), William Herbert, Hugh the Purse-maker (*bursario*), William de Canneley, Richard le Wed', Robert Bucston, Henry Burgeys, Robert the clerk of Coundon (*Cundolm*) and others.

Seal missing C.R.O. 2/153

443 Early 1270s

Charter of Osbert son of Jordan the Miller (*molendinar'*) of Coventry giving to Simon King of the same a certain piece of a curtilage (*placeam cortilag'*) in Crow Lane (*in Crowelane*) which came to him by inheritance (*cecidit in hereditar'*) after the death of his father between the land once of Nicholas de Wrþ on the one hand and Crow Lane (*Crowe lane*) on the other and which abuts on the small meadow of Petronilla de Aula (*abbutat se ad parvam homẽ petronull' de aula*) in length and in width with all appurtenances as is manifest, with another piece (*un^a^ placea*) which he bought from Nicholas de Wrþ between the aforesaid land and the land Simon de Warwick once held in Crow Lane (*in Crowelane*) and which abuts on Crow Lane (*Crowelan'*) in length and in width as manifest with all appurtenances, and with a third piece (*tercia place*) which he bought from Nicholas de Wrþ which lies between the land once of Reginald le Roumongere and the land of Richard le Plomin(er) and extends from the royal highway (*a regia via*) up to the watercourse coming from Crow Mill (*Crowemulne*) in length and in width as is manifest with all appurtenances; to be held to him, his heirs or assigns, or to whomsoever he will wish to give, bequeath, sell or assign in sickness and in health of the grantor and his heirs freely [etc.] by rendering a clove-gillyflower at Easter, to Petronilla de Aula as the grantor's attorney 13d. at four terms of the year according to the usage of the vill of Coventry, and the service owed and accustomed to the lords of that fee as the attorney of the grantor and his heirs, namely to the hospital of St. Leonard of Coventry 2s. at four terms of the year namely 6d. at each of the feasts of St. Michael, St. Andrew, the blessed Mary in March and the Nativity of St. John the Baptist for all secular service [etc.]. Simon gave 2 marks beforehand. Warranty and sealing clauses. Witnesses: Peter Baron then bailiff, Richard the Purse-maker (*bursar'*), Gilbert Chorvenne, William Roke, Richard Ledbet(er), Henry the Purse-maker (*bursar'*), William the Palmer (*p'alm'*), Richard Lotemon, Robert Reymund, Adam at Grene and others.

Seal missing C.R.O. 2/77

444 Early 1270s

Charter of Osbert son of Jordan the Miller (*molendinar'*) of Coventry giving to Symon Kyng of Coventry a certain curtilage which he bought from Nicholas de le Wiþ in Spon St. (*In vico de Sponne*) which lies between the land once of Reginald le Rowmonger on the one hand and the land of Richard le Pluminer on the other and which extends from the royal highway (*a Regali via*) up to the watercourse from Crow Mill (*Croumolne*) in length and in width according to the metes and bounds made there; to be held to him, his heirs and assigns, of the grantor, his heirs or assigns freely [etc.], by rendering annually a clove-gillyflower at Easter and to the lords of that fee namely the hospital of St. Leonard of Coventry 2s. to be taken at four terms of the year according to the usage of Coventry, 6d. at each of the feasts of St. Michael, St. Andrew, St. Mary in March and St. John the Baptist for all secular service [etc.]. Clause for warranty. Symon give 2 marks of silver beforehand. Sealing clause. Witnesses: Peter Baron then bailiff, Richard the Purse-maker (*Bursar'*), Gilbert Chorewenne, William Rok, Richard le Ledbetter, Henry the Purse-maker (*Bursar'*), William Phalmer', Richard Loteman, Robert Reymond, Adam ate Grene and others.

Seal extant C.R.O. 1A/C36

445 c.1280

Demise and quitclaim by Adam son of Nicholas de Wyþ to Simon King, his heirs or whatsoever assigns, of all right and claim without reservation in the tenement in Spon St., Coventry (*in vico de Sponn' de Coventr'*) between the land once of Richard Ledbeter and the land once of Reginald le Roumong(er), with exclusion clause. Simon gave 2s. of silver beforehand. Sealing clause. Witnesses: Robert de Chilton' then bailiff, Gilbert Corvenne, Geoffrey son of John, Robert Reymund, Robert de Kanneley, William Palm(er), Robert in Angulo, Adam the Smith (*fab*), William son of Reginald and many others.

Seal extant but detached C.R.O. 2/3

446 3 May 1294

Charter of Symon le King of Coventry giving to Gilbert Reymund of the same a piece of a curtilage in Spon St. (*unam placiam curtilag' in vico de Sponna*), namely that which lies next to the land Simon le King once held on the one hand and the land Robert Porstein held on the other and begins from the land John de Cornel' held on the one hand and extends up to the fish-pond (*stangnam vivari*) of the aforesaid Simon and up to *Cruowemulneham* in length and in width as it purports according to the metes and bounds made there; to be held to him, his heirs or assigns, of the grantor, his heirs or assigns, freely [etc.] by rendering annually to the lord of the fee a clove-gillyflower at Michaelmas for all secular services, suits of courts, exactions or demands belonging to the aforesaid piece (*placiam curtilagii*). Clause for warranty. Gilbert gave 7s. of silver beforehand. Sealing clause. Witnesses: Henry Baker (*Pistor'*) then bailiff, Geoffrey son of John, Gilbert de Heyham, William Loteman, Robert en le Hurne, William le Wallere, Hugh de Cantub' and others. Monday the Invention of the Holy Cross 22 Edward I.

Seal missing C.R.O. 1B/22 EI/I

447 1270s

Charter of Osbert son of Jordan the Miller (*molendinar'*) of Coventry giving to Osbert his son for his service a certain messuage with the houses sited there and with appurtenances in the vill of Coventry in Spon St. (*In vico sponn'*) lying between the land of Geoffrey son of John on the one hand and the land which Simon King holds of the aforesaid Osbert on the other in length and in width according to the metes and bounds made there; to be held to him, his heirs or assigns, of the grantor and his heirs freely [etc.], by rendering annually to the lords of that tenement 2s. at four terms of the year according to the usage of Coventry and to the grantor 1d. on Easter day for all secular service [etc.]. Warranty and sealing clauses. Witnesses:

John de Lodelawe then bailiff, William Roke, William Rimild, Richard Lotemo(n), Gilbert Choruenne, William de Cannel', Adam the clerk and others.

Seal missing W.R.O. 56

448 1 March 1294

Charter of Osbert de Crowelone of Coventry giving to John ate Cros and Matilda his wife a piece of his curtilage in Spon St. (*unam placiam terre Curtilagii mei in vico de sponne strete*), which piece lies between the land of Stephen le Marechal on the one hand and the grantor's own land on the other according to the metes and bounds made there; to be held with appurtenances to them, their heirs or assigns, of the chief lords of the fee freely [etc.] by rendering to Master Ralph de Bannebur' chief lord and his heirs 8d. of silver at the four terms of the year fixed according to the usage of Coventry for all secular service [etc.]. Clause for warranty. John and Matilda gave 6s. of silver beforehand. Sealing clause. Witnesses: Henry Baker (*pistor'*) then bailiff of Coventry, William P(ar)ser then coroner, Geoffrey son of John, Gilbert Corevan, Gilbert de Heiham, Robert in le Hurne, William Pat, Thomas the clerk and others. *Confectio hujus tituli die Lune proxima ante festum sancti Cedde anno regni regis Edwardi vicesimo secundo.*

Seal missing W.R.O. 59

449 27 February 1295

Charter of Osbert de Crowelone of Coventry giving to John ate Cros of Coventry, Matilda his wife, Agnes their daughter and their heirs, his entire tenement with the houses sited there and with all appurtenances which he had in Coventry in Spon St. (*in vico de sponne*), which tenement lies between the land of Geoffrey son of John on the one hand and the land of the said John on the other and extends from the royal highway (*a Regia via*) up to the land of Gilbert Corewan in length and in width according to the metes and bounds made there; to be held to them of Master Ralf de Bannebur' the chief lord of the fee freely [etc.], by rendering the service due and by right accustomed, namely 16d. of silver at four terms of the year according to the usage of Coventry for all secular service [etc.]. Clause for warranty. The grantees gave 15s. of silver beforehand. Sealing clause. Witnesses: Henry Baker (*pistor'*) then (*tunc temporis*) bailiff of Coventry, William le Parker then coroner of Coventry, William Pat, John Tole, Geoffrey Corewan, Geoffrey son of John, Gilbert de Heiham, Richard Kay, William Waller, Geoffrey his brother, Richard Kyng, Thomas the clerk and others. Coventry, Sunday before the feast of St. Chad (*Cedde*) 23 Edward I.

Seal extant W.R.O. 60

450 27 February 1295

Remise, release and quitclaim by Osbert de Crowelone of Coventry to John ate Cros of Coventry, Matilda his wife, Agnes their daughter and their heirs, of all right and claim in the entire tenement which he had in Spon St., Coventry (*in vico de Sponne de Coventr'*) and which he has sold to the said John, which tenement lies between the land of Geoffrey son of John on the one hand and the land of Stephen le Marechal on the other in length and in width according to the metes and bounds made there; to be held to them with all appurtenances freely [etc.]. Exclusion and sealing clauses. Witnesses: Henry Baker (*pistor'*) then (*tunc temporis*) bailiff, William Pat, Gilbert Corewan, Gilbert de Heyham, Richard le Bourcer, Richard Kay, Adam le Feu(er)e,

William le Waller', Geoffrey his brother, Thomas the clerk and others. Coventry, Sunday after the feast of St. Chad (*cedde*) 23 Edward I.

Seal missing W.R.O. 63

451 c.late 1240s

Charter of Walter le Marescal of Warwick (*Warewyk*) with the consent of Agnes his wife giving to Hugh son of Richard son of Agnes a messuage with appurtenances in Coventry in Spon St. (*in vico spanne*) between the land Gilbert de Berkyswelle held on the one hand and the land Richard son of Thomas the Tanner (*tanatoris*) held on the other in length and in width as it purports with appurtenances; to be held to him, his heirs or to whomsoever he will wish to give, assign or sell freely [etc.], by rendering annually 12d. of silver at the four terms of the year fixed in the vill of Coventry, 2 hens at Christmas and the service of one man for one day in Autumn. Clause for warranty. Hugh gave 2 marks of silver. Sealing clause. Witnesses: Philip de Wynchec(um)be, John le Flecher, Richard Burgeys, William de Kannele, William Herbert, Richard Skyrewit, Humphrey (*Unfrido*) le Rumangur, Vincent de Ashesoue, Robert de Cundolm, Roger son of Richard son of Peter, Robert son of Maunsel', Hugh the Purse-maker (*bursario*) and many others.

Seal missing C.R.O. 1A/C11

Endorsed: Willelmus Herdwyk.

452 c.late 1240s

Gift and quitclaim by Agnes daughter of Haylward the Tanner (*Hayluuardi thanatoris*) to Hugh son of Richard son of Agnes, his heirs or assigns, of all right and claim in a messuage with appurtenances in Spon St. (*in vico spanne*) between the land Gilbert de Berkyswelle held on the one hand and the land Richard son of Thomas the Tanner (*thanatoris*) held on the other, *et concessi omnia pacta que Walterus le Marescal vir meus pepigit cum predicto Hugone. Et ego predicta Agnes predicto Hugoni et heredibus suis vel ejus assignatis mea fide certificavi quod post obitum viri mei nichil accipiam de illo mesuagio predicto cum pertinentiis nisi redditum qui pertinet ad predictum mesuagium.* Sealing clause. Witnesses: Philip de Wynchecumbe, John le Flecher, Richard Burgeys, Simon the Doctor (*medico*), William Herbert, William de Kannele, Vincent (*Wincent'*) de Assehoue, Robert the clerk of Coundon (*Cundolme*) and many others.

Seal missing C.R.O. 1A/C10

453 1250s

Charter of Godfrey son of Walter the Marshal (*Marescalli*) of Warwick (*Warewic*) giving to Hugh son of Richard son of Agnes or to whomsoever he will wish to give, sell, bequeath or assign, a messuage with appurtenances in the vill of Coventry in Spon St. (*in vico spanne*), namely that between the land Gilbert de Berchswell held on the one hand and the land Richard son of Thomas le Barker held on the other in length and in width as the land purports and according to the metes and bounds made there; to be held to him, his heirs or assigns, freely [etc.] by rendering annually a pair of gloves worth ½d. or ½d. at Easter, and to the lords of that fee 6d. of silver at the four terms of the year fixed in the vill of Coventry and one man for one day in Autumn and two hens at Christmas as the grantor's perpetual attorney for all secular service [etc.]. *Et si contingat quod ego vel aliquis meorum cadam in m(isericord)ia dicti Godefr(idi) vel aliquorum suorum pro aliquo delicto quieti erimus pro uno denario.* Clause for warranty. Hugh gave 15s. of silver to the grantor and 12d. to his wife *ad soculares.*

Sealing clause. Witnesses: Philip de Vinchcombe, John Fleccar', Roger son of Peter, William de Kannel', Vincent de Asso, Gilbert de Berchswell and others.

Seal extant C.R.O. 1A/EC12/18

454 1250s

Charter of Elyanora widow of William de Aula of Coventry in her widowhood and [lawful power][1] giving to Ralph the Clerk son of Richard Omnibon of *Bann[bury]*[1] her annual rent which Sir Walter de Coventr' her brother, son of Richard de Coventr', gave to her (*mihi donavit*) [in][1] Coventry, namely 8d. from the land William son of Richard held in Spon St. (*In vico Spo(n)ne*), 20d. from the land Gilbert le [ ][1] held in the same street, 18d. from the land Martin le Loker held in the same street, 2s. from the land Richard Hyrenol held in the same street, [ ][1]d. from the land Henry le Burser held in the same street, 8d. from the land Alexander Cok held in the same street, 6d. from the land William Scathelok held next to Smithford bar (*Juxta barram de smithesford*), 18d. from the land Walter de Hulle held within Smithford bar (*Infra barram de Smithesford*), 2s. from the land Thomas the Dyer (*tinctor*) held in the same street, 2s. from the land Walter the Skinner (*pellipar'*) held in West Orchard (*In [Was]*[1]*to Gardino*), and 8d. from the land William Stoule held in Earl St. towards Gosford (*in vico Comitis versus Gosford'*); to be held to him, his heirs or whatsoever assigns, of the grantor and her heirs freely [etc.] by rendering a clove-gillyflower annually at Easter, and to the chief lords 4d. of silver at the four terms of the year fixed and customary in the vill of Coventry for all secular services, exactions, customs, whatsoever courts and their suits and all kinds of temporal demands pertaining to her and her heirs therefrom. Warranty and sealing clauses. Witnesses: [ ][1] of Walter de Coventr', Vitalis de Folkyshul', Robert de Busservill', Richard de Bok(er)vill' then bailiff in Coventry, [Philip de W][1]inchecumbe, John le Flecher, Pagan Pake, Alexander de Glovernia, John le Specer, Henry le Norreys, [ ][1], Godfrey le Mercer, William de Kanneleya, Osbert the Miller (*molend*), Hugh le Bretun and others.

Seal missing P.R.O. D 5384

[1] The deed is torn causing some loss.

455 1250s

Gift and quitclaim by Margery, widow of William Herbert of Coventry, in her widowhood and free power to Adam de Kydremunest(er) and Emma his wife, their heirs or assigns, of all right and claim in the land in Spon St., Coventry (*in vico Spon(n)e de Coventr'*) which lies between the land William Somer held on the one hand and the land William the grantor's son held on the other; to be held of the lords of the fee by the service due and accustomed without any charge. Exclusion clause. Adam and Emma gave 12d. of silver beforehand. Sealing clause. Witnesses: Richard de Bok(er)vill' then bailiff, Roger son of Peter, Vincent (*Wincent'*) de Asseso, Richard Lotemon, Osbert the Miller (*molend'*), Hugh the Carpenter (*Carpentar'*), Hugh le Bretun the clerk and others.

Seal extant C.R.O. 2/106

456 Late 1250s–early 1260s

Remise and quitclaim by William son of William Herbert of Coventry to Adam de Kydremunester of 2d. annual rent which Adam used to pay from certain land in Spon St. (*in vico Spo(n)ne*) which lies between the land William Somer held on the one hand and the land the grantor held on the other, and of all right and claim therein; to be held to him, his heirs or assigns, freely [etc.] and without charge or reservation by the grantor or his heirs. Exclusion clause. Adam gave 12d. of silver beforehand. Sealing clause. Witnesses: Walter le Blund, Alexander de Glovernia then bailiffs (*tunc ballivis*), Roger son of Peter, William Somer, William Mauclerc, Robert de Cundolm', Hugh de Kannel', Richard Lutemon, Hugh Bretun and others.

Seal missing C.R.O. 2/96

457 1270s

Charter of Henry son of Thomas the Weaver (*tixtor'*) of Coventry giving to Beatrice daughter of Adam de Kid(er)minst(er) his sister and her heirs whomsoever, the entire land which he had in Spon St., Coventry (*in vico de sponne de Coventr'*) with the buildings sited there and other appurtenances, which lies in width between the land the aforesaid Beatrice held and the land William Somer held and extends in length from the aforesaid Spon St. (*vico de sponne*) up to the land Henry de Rodinton' held; to be held to her, her heirs or assigns or to whomsoever she will wish to give, bequeath, sell or assign freely [etc.], by rendering annually to the lords of the fee 12d. at the four terms of the year usual and fixed in the vill of Coventry and to the grantor and his heirs or assigns a clove-gillyflower at Easter for all secular service. Clause for warranty. Beatrice gave 1 mark beforehand. Sealing clause. Witnesses: John de Lodelowe, Henry Baker (*Pistor'*) then bailiffs (*tunc ball'*), Robert de Chilton', Geoffrey son of John, William Mauncel, Robert the Tanner (*tanur'*), Walter de Kildisby, Robert the clerk and many others.

Seal extant C.R.O. 1A/C49

C.R.O. IA/EC13/65 is a quitclaim by the grantor with an identical witness list.

458 1270s

Charter of Henry son of Thomas the Weaver (*textoris*) of Coventry giving to Beatrice daughter of Adam de Kidermu(n)str' his sister, for her service and for a tunic (*tunica*) and 12d. of silver which she gave the grantor beforehand, a moiety of the land in Spon St., Coventry (*in vico sponne de Covintr'*) with the building sited there and all appurtenances which lies in width between the land Alexander le Kyng once held on the one hand and the land Henry le P(re)chur held on the other and extends in length from the aforesaid street up to the land Henry de Rodinton' held, namely the moiety which is nearer to the land of the said Henry le P(re)chur according to the metes and bounds made there; to be held to Beatrice, her heirs and whatsoever assigns, of the grantor and his heirs freely [etc.], by rendering annually to the lords of that fee the service due and accustomed as much as pertains to the said moiety of land, and to the grantor and his heirs a clove-gillyflower at Easter for all secular service [etc.]. Warranty and sealing clauses. Witnesses: John de Lodelowe then bailiff, Robert de Chilton', Robert de Kannel', Richard le Burser, Geoffrey son of John, Robert Maunceil, William his son, Robert le Tannur, John de Kundellum', William de Katesb', Walter de Burmicham, Henry le P(re)chur, Hugh Bretun the clerk and many others.

Seal extant C.R.O. 1B/30E1/1c

459 1270s

Charter of Emma de Kydeminst(er) with the counsel and assent of Adam her husband giving to Beatrice her daughter, for her service, a moiety of the land which lies between the land Alexander Knit held on the one hand and the land Henry the Preacher (*predicator*) held on the other with the houses sited there and all appurtenances in length according to the metes and bounds made there; to be held to her, her heirs or assigns, of the grantors and their heirs freely [etc.], by rendering annually to the lords of that fee the service due and accustomed and to the grantors and their heirs a clove-gillyflower for all secular service [etc.]. Warranty and sealing clauses. Witnesses: Robert de Chilton', Henry Baker (*Pistor'*), Robert de Cannelet', William de Cannel and Richard le Purc(er), Richard Lotemon, Anketell the clerk, Robert Mansel' and others.

2 seals extant C.R.O. 2/92

460 1270s

Letters of Henry called (*dictus*) de Kyderm[i]nst(er) granting and affirming to Beatrice his sister the gift (*donacionem*) which Adam de Kyderminst(er) and Emma the grantor's mother gave and confirmed by charter to her, namely a moiety of the land with appurtenances which lies between the land Alexander le Knit held on the one hand and the land Henry the Preacher (*predicator*) held on the other; to be held to her, her heirs or assigns, of them, their heirs or assigns, by making the service due and accustomed to the lords of that fee and to Adam and Emma and their heirs a clove-gillyflower at Easter as contained in the charter of enfeoffment which she has from the aforesaid Adam de Kyderminst(er) and Emma his wife. Exclusion clause. Sealing clause. Witnesses: Richard le Burcer, Geoffrey son of John, Robert Mansel, Walter Grym(er), Robert de Cannel and others.

Seal extant C.R.O. 2/134

461 1270s

Agreement whereby Beatrice de Kidermu(n)st(er) has leased and demised at farm to Adam de Kidermu(n)st(er) and Emma his wife the entire land with the buildings sited there which Adam de Kidermu(n)st(er) her father and Emma her mother gave to her by charter of confirmation (*per cartam unam confirmationis*) which lies between the land of the aforesaid [Adam and Emma] on the one hand and the land of Henry le P(re)chour on the other; to be held with the houses sited there and all appurtenances to Adam and Emma as long as they shall live, of the lessor and her heirs freely [etc.], by making annually to the lords of that fee the service due and accustomed, namely 1d. at the four terms of the year usual in the vill of Coventry and to the lessor a clove-gillyflower at Easter for all service. Warranty and sealing clause. Witnesses: Walter de Burmig', Richard le Purc(er), Adam de la Grene, John de Coundel', Richard the clerk and many others.

Seal extant C.R.O. 1B/30E1/1b

462 14 October 1302

Charter of Richard le Brocher son of Jordan le Brocher of Coventry giving to Richard de Kiderm(u)nstr' chaplain (*capellano*) a certain part of his land with buildings thereon, which land Roger le Parcheminer once held in Spon St. (*in vico Spanne*), in Coventry in length and in width as is manifest according to the metes and bounds made there; to be held to him, his heirs or whatsoever assigns, freely [etc.] by rendering annually after the completion of a period of 16 years from the making of this charter (*post sexdecim annos proximo(s) sequentes a confectione hujus carte plenarie completos*) to the chief lords of the fee the due and accustomed services pertaining to such a portion (*ad tantam portionem*), and to the grantor, his heirs or assigns, 20s. of silver for all secular service [etc.]. Clause for warranty, the grantor, his heirs and assigns, maintaining the buildings at their own cost during the 16 years. Sealing clause. Witnesses: John Lewyn then coroner of Coventry, Roger Dayesheye then bailiff in the same place, Robert in le Hurne, Eadward le Barkere, William le Wallere, Geoffrey le Wallere, William Loteman and others. Spon St. (*in vico Spanne*) Coventry, Sunday after the feast of St. Michael in Monte Tumba.

Seal missing C.R.O. 1B/30 EI/Ia

463 9 April 1304

Grant, demise and quitclaim by Richard de Kidermu(n)str' to Richard le Brocher and Edith Hod his wife of all right and claim in the land and building which he had in Spon St., Coventry (*in vico Spanne Coventr'*) lying between the lands once of Henry de Rodington' and William Mauncel; to be held to them and their heirs begotten legitimately between them freely [etc.] of the chief lords of the fee by the annual services due and accustomed for all secular services [etc.]. In default of heirs as above the land with the building and appurtenances should pass (*convertatur*) to the heirs of the said Richard le Brocher. Sealing clause. Witnesses: Robert Baker (*Pistor'*) then bailiff of Coventry, John Lewyn then coroner in the same place, William le Waller', William Mauncel, Eadward the Tanner (*tannator'*) and others. Coventry, Thursday after the feast of St. Ambrose the Bishop 32 Edward I.

Seal missing C.R.O. 1B/32EI/1

464 Mid–late 1250s

Gift, remise and quitclaim by Hawise daughter of William le Caret(er) of Coventry, for herself and her heirs, to Hugh le Bretun of Coventry of the entire service which Robert Mancel and Petronilla his wife were accustomed to make to her from the land with all appurtenances in Spon St., Coventry (*in vico Spo(n)ne de Coventr'*) which lies between the land the same Robert held on the one hand and the land Nicholas le Causey held on the other, namely a pair of white gloves worth ½d. or ½d. annually at Easter *una cum donacione totius terre predicte et tenencium predictorum seu quorumque ipsam terram tenuerint*, and moreover with all right and claim therein in rents, escheats and all other rights and customs which to the grantor or to whatsoever heirs by any cause or right will be able to accrue; to be held to him, his heirs or whatsoever assigns, freely [etc.] without any charge or reservation by the grantor or her heirs. Exclusion clause. Hugh gave 12d. of silver beforehand. Witnesses: Richard de Bok(er)vill' then bailiff, Alexander de Glovernia, Robert de Chilton', William Mauclerc, Robert de Condolm', Roger son of Peter, Henry Burg', Adam le T(r)auent(er), Osbert the Miller (*molendinar'*), Hugh the Carpenter (*carpentar'*), Peter the Welshman (*Walens'*) clerk and others.

Seal extant C.R.O. 824/1

465 Late 1250s–early 1260s

Charter of Peter the Welshman (*Walens'*) of Coventry called (*dictus*) Barun giving to William the Weaver (*textori*) son of Geoffrey de Burebathe, the entire land with appurtenances in the vill of Coventry in Spon St. (*in Vico Spon(n)e*) which lies between the land the grantor held on the one hand and the land Matilda widow of Thomas the Girdler (*zonar'*) held on the other in length and in width as it purports according to the metes and bounds made there; to be held to him, his heirs or assigns, of the grantor and his heirs freely [etc.], by rendering annually 10d. of silver at the four terms of the year customary in the vill of Coventry, and to the heirs of Nicholas le Serjant a pair of white gloves worth ½d. or ½d. at Easter for all secular service [etc.]. Clause for warranty. William gave ½ mark of silver beforehand. Sealing clause. Witnesses: Alexander de Glovernia then bailiff, Geoffrey Bretun, William Som(er), John Blacwin', Henry de Sartrin, Symon the Doctor (*medico*), Osbert the Miller (*molendinar'*), Stephen de Cleybrok, Hugh the clerk and others.

Seal missing C.R.O. 1A/Misc.I/3

466 1250s

Charter of William son of Jordan le Wchewritte giving to Nicholas his son a certain messuage with a garden (*orto*) and appurtenances which descended to him by inheritance from Nicholas son of Luve in Coventry in Spon St. (*In vico spanne*), namely that between the land Robert de Derby held on the one hand and the land Robert Bucston held on the other, in length and in width as is manifest according to the metes and bounds made there; to be held to him, his heirs or assigns, of the grantor and his heirs, freely [etc.] by rendering 8d. of silver at four terms of the year according to the usage of Coventry for all secular services [etc.]. Clause for warranty. Nicholas gave 20s. of silver in recognition. Sealing clause. Witnesses: Philip de Wynchecumbe, John le Flecher, Alexander the Purse-maker (*Bursar'*), Adam de la Grene, Henry (*Hñri*) Burgeys, Robert Bucston, William de Cannelegh, Nigel le Sponsere, William Herbert', Robert de Derbi, Gilbert de Berkyswelle, Robert the clerk of Coundon (*Cundolm'*) and many others.

Seal missing P.R.O. D3275

467 1270s

Lease by Geoffrey son of John of Coventry to William le Wychewritte for the term of his life of a messuage in Coventry in Spon St. (*in vico de Sponna*) with an adjacent curtilage, namely that which lies between the land William le Paumer held and the lessor's land in width, and which extends from the royal highway (*a Regia strata*) up to the land Roger le Neue held in length as the land purports according to the metes and bounds made there; to be held freely [etc.] by rendering annually to the grantor and his heirs 12d. of silver at the four terms of the year fixed in the vill of Coventry for all secular service. Clause for reversion to the lessor at the end of the term. Sealing clause. Witnesses: Roger Corewenne, Gilbert his brother, William de Cannele, Reginald le Bourser, Simon King, Adam ad Grenam, William le Rooc, William le Paumer and others.

Seal extant C.R.O. 2/24

468 1270s

Gift and quitclaim by William le Wychewrite of Coventry with the counsel and good will of Muriel his wife, to Nicholas his son of all right in the entire land with the house sited there and with an adjacent curtilage and all appurtenances which lies in Spon St., Coventry (*in vico de Sponna de Covintr'*) between the land Geoffrey son of John held and the land William le Paumer held in width and which extends from the royal highway (*a Regia strata*) up to the land Roger le Neue held in length as is manifest according to the metes and bounds made there; to be held to him, his heirs or assigns, of the lords of that fee freely [etc.], by rendering annually the service owed and accustomed. Nicholas gave 8s. of silver beforehand. Sealing clause. Witnesses: John de Lodelawe then bailiff, Richard le Bourser, William le Roc, Simon le King, Adam ad Grenam, William le Paumer, Geoffrey son of John and others.

Seal extant C.R.O. 2/11

469 Late 1250s–early 1260s

Charter of Vincent de Assigho of Coventry giving to Alexander son of Wyht of Canley (*Canele*) half of his entire land with the buildings sited there and with appurtenances which he held in the vill of Coventry in Spon St. (*in vico de Spanna*) between the land Robert de Canel' once held on the one hand and the land Walter Paucus once held on the other in length from the high street (*a magno vico ibidem*) up to the watercourse which is called *Syreford*, namely that moiety of land on the eastern side near the land Gilbert de Berchswell held in length and in width as is manifest according to the metes and bounds made there; to be held to him, his heirs or to whomsoever he will wish to give, bequeath, sell or assign in sickness and in health (*?colu(m)pnitate*) freely [etc.], by rendering annually 8d. of silver at the four terms of the year usual and customary in the vill of Coventry for all secular service [etc.], suits of court(s) and for all demands, plaints and pleas which to the grantor or his heirs pertain or will be able to pertain. Clause for warranty. Alexander gave 14s. of new and legal sterling beforehand and a cape of bluet (*unam capam de bluet'*) in recognition. Sealing clause. Witnesses: Alexander de Glouc', Walter the White (*albo*) then bailiffs (*tunc Ball'*), Pagan Pake, John le Flecher, Philip de Wychecumbe, Henry the Burgess (*Burgens'*), William de Canel', Roger son of Peter, Hugh de Canel', Gilbert de Canel', Richard Lotemon and others.

Seal extant C.R.O. 1A/C12–13/58

470 Late 1250s–early 1260s

Gift by Robert de Chilton' burgess of Coventry (*Burgens Covi(n)tr'*) giving to Robert son of Alexander of Canley (*Canel'*) a certain part of his land in Coventry in Spon St. (*in vico de Sponn*[a]) which lies between the land William Waldthave held on the one hand and the land Hugh le Burs(er) once held on the other in length and in width as is manifest according to the metes and bounds made there; to be held to him, his heirs or to whomsoever he will wish to give, bequeath, sell or assign in sickness and in health (? *columitat'*) except to men of religion freely [etc.], by rendering annually 12d. of silver at four terms of the year according to the use and custom of the vill of Coventry for all service. Clause for warranty. Robert gave a ½ mark of silver beforehand. Sealing clause. Witnesses: Alexander de Glouc' then bailiff, Walter the White (*albo*), Nicholas ad Barr' clerk, Adam le T(r)auant(er), Thomas Halden, William Waldthave, Richard le Burs(er), Roger son of Roger son of Peter, Robert Mauncel, William de Canel' and others.

Seal extant C.R.O. 1A/C12/11

471 Early 1270s

Gift and quitclaim by Nicholas Forþidwine to Robert de Cannel', his heirs or assigns, of 6d. annual rent which he used to render from a tenement and messuage (*mansio*) which lies (*jacet*) between the land once of Gilbert le Roumong(er) on the one hand and the land of Robert Reymund on the other; to be held with appurtenances freely [etc.] as freely as the grantor or his ancestors (*antecessores*) held. Clause for exclusion, excepting 2d. of the aforesaid 6d. to be rendered to the heirs of Nigel Despenser

(*Dispensator'*) as the grantor's perpetual attorney. Robert gave 4s. of silver beforehand. Witnesses: Peter Barun then bailiff, Geoffrey son of John, Richard the Pursemaker (*bursar'*), William Rimild, Robert Reymund, Richard Lotemon, Walter the Tanner (*tanator'*) and others.

Seal missing C.R.O. 2/56
Endorsed: Carta de vijd. redditus de domo quondam hugoni de chaucomb.

472 1270s
Grant and quitclaim by Gerard de Allispath' to Robert de Kanneleye, his heirs or whatsoever assigns, of all right and claim in 12d. annual rent to be received from a certain tenement in the vill of Coventry in Spon St. (*in vico sponn'*) which is between the land Hugh de Kanneley once held on the one hand and the land which Roger the Smith (*fab faber*) of Whitacre (*Withacre*) once held on the other, by rendering annually to Thomas Haldeyn and his heirs a rose flower at the feast of St. John the Baptist; with exclusion clause. Robert gave a ½ mark of silver beforehand. Sealing clause. Witnesses: Robert de Chilt', Thomas de Fakinham, Geoffrey son of John, William Palm(er), Richard le Borc(er), Robert the Tanner (*tanat'*), Adam the clerk and others.

Seal extant C.R.O. 1A/C5

473 Late 1270s
Charter of Thomas Hayldeyn of Coventry with the assent of Alice his wife giving to Robert de Kanneley of Coventry, his heirs or whatsoever assigns, a certain curtilage (*quandam cortilag'*) with the houses sited there and appurtenances in the vill of Coventry in Spon St. (*in vico sponne*) between the land once of John the Smith (*fab'*) of Weddington (*Wet(i)nton'*) on the one hand and the land of Hugh de Kanneley on the other and extending from the aforesaid street up to the watercourse in length and in width according to the metes and bounds made there; to be held to him, his heirs or assigns, of them and their heirs freely [etc.], or to whomsoever they will wish to give, bequeath, sell or assign in health and in sickness by rendering annually to the lords of that tenement the due and accustomed service and to the grantors and their heirs 12d. at four terms of the year according to the usage of the vill of Coventry for all secular service. Robert gave 20s. sterling. Warranty and sealing clauses. Witnesses: Gerard de Allispath' then bailiff, Robert de Chilton', Roger the Chamberlain (*Cam(er)ari(o)*), Robert the Tanner (*tanator'*), William Maunsel, William Lotemon, Adam the clerk and others.

2 seals extant C.R.O. 1A/C6

474 Late 1270s
Charter of Agnes widow of Hugh le Burs(er) of Coventry, in her widowhood and lawful power, giving to Robert de Kannel' for 2s. of silver which he gave beforehand a certain parcel (*particulam*) of her land in the vill of Coventry in Spon St. (*in vico Spo(n)ne*) between the grantor's land on the one hand and the land of the same Robert on the other *et continet a dicto vico versus ortum longitudinem quadraginta et octo ped(um). In capite vero versus vicum continet latitudinem duorum ped(um) et dimid(ie). et In fine versus ortum continet latitudinem quatuor ped(um) secundum metas et divisas ibidem factas*; to be held to him, his heirs or to whatsoever assigns, of the grantor and her heirs freely [etc.], by rendering a clove-gillyflower at Easter for all secular service [etc.]. Warranty and sealing clause. Witnesses: Robert de Chilton' then bailiff in Coventry,

Robert Remund, Richard Lotemon, Robert Mansel, Hugh Shayl, John de Condolm', William Rymild and others.

Seal extant C.R.O. 1A/C13/24

475 Late 1270s

Remise and quitclaim by Adam son of Hugh le Purs(er)e to Robert de Kannel' of all right and claim in a certain parcel (*particula*) of land in Coventry in Spon St. (*in vico Spo(n)ne*) lying between the land of Agnes the grantor's mother and the land of the same Robert, which parcel of land the said Robert had of the gift and grant of the aforesaid Agnes; to be held to him, his heirs or whatsoever assigns, without any reservation by the grantor or his heirs. Sealing clause. Witnesses: Robert de Chilton' then bailiff, Robert Reymu(n)d, Richard Lotemon, Robert Mansel, Hugh Shayl, John de Condolm, William Rimild and others.

Seal missing C.R.O. 1A/C89

476 c.1280

Demise and quitclaim by Alice widow of Hugh de Kannel' of Coventry to Robert de Kannel' of Coventry, his heirs or assigns, of all right and claim in the entire land with buildings and appurtenances in Spon St., Coventry (*in vico de Sponne Coventr'*) between the land once of Gilbert de Berkiswelle and the land of the said Robert in length and in width according to the metes and bounds made there; with exclusion clause. Robert gave ½ mark of silver beforehand. Sealing clause. Witnesses: Robert de Chilton then bailiff, William Lotemon, Robert the Tanner (*tanator'*), Walter de Kildisbi, Adam the clerk and others.

Seal extant C.R.O. 2/22

477 c.1280

Gift and quitclaim by Agnes wife of Geoffrey le Furn(er) of Coventry to Robert de Kannele, his heirs and assigns, of all right and claim in the entire tenement once of Geoffrey her husband in Spon St. (*in vico de le sponne*) which tenement lies between the land of Henry Fressi(n)g on the one hand and the land of William Lotemon on the other; to be held to him, his heirs or whatsoever assigns freely [etc.] to whomsoever he will wish to give, bequeath or assign in health and in sickness. Clause for warranty. Robert gave 10s. of silver beforehand *Tali conventione quod si alic(ub)i kalang(ia) super evenerit ab aliquo vel ab aliqua quod ego predicta Agnes vel Galfridus filius meus predicto Roberto decem solidos persolvamus sine aliqua contradictione et ad hoc Galfridus meus filius fide media se obligavit.* Witnesses: Robert de Chilt(er)n', Richard le Bourser, Geoffrey son of John, Richard King', Symon King', Robert de Cotiswold, William Lotemon and many others.

Document cut for 3 seal tags C.R.O. 1A/Mid C12/33

478 c.1280

Gift and quitclaim by Walter son of Ernis (*Herni*) of Coventry to Robert de Cannel', his heirs or assigns, of all right and claim in the land with appurtenances which Herni[1] the grantor's father held in the vill of Coventry in Spon St. (*In vico Spon'*) between the land Robert the Tanner (*tanator*) once held on the one hand and the land Agnes wife of Hugh le Burs(er) once held on the other. Exclusion clause. Robert gave 2s. of silver beforehand. Sealing clause. Witnesses: Robert de Chilt' then bailiff, Robert the Tanner (*tanat'*), Robert Maunsel, John de Cundulm, Geoffrey son of John (*filii Johannes*), Simon King, Richard the Purse-maker (*bursar'*) and others.

Seal missing C.R.O. 1A/EC13/74

[1] sic

479 1280s

Charter of Henry Rachel of Fletchamstead (*Flighamstede*) giving to Robert de Cannele 2s. rent which Roger son of Peter used to render from a tenement in Spon St. (*in vico de Sponna*) next to the tenement of Edward on the one hand and the land of John de Weddinton on the other; to be held to him, his heirs or assigns, of the grantor, his heirs or assigns, freely [etc.] to whomsoever and whensoever he will wish to sell or assign in health and in sickness by rendering annually a clove-gillyflower at Christmas *si predictus Henricus et heredes sui ad domum predicti Roberti petere voluerint* for all secular services [etc.]. Clause for warranty. Robert gave 20s. of silver fine (*in garsuma*) in recognition beforehand. Sealing clause. Witnesses: Henry Baker (*Pistor'*) then bailiff, Geoffrey son of John, Robert en le Hurne, William Maunsel, Walter de Kildesby, William Loteman, Hugh the clerk and others.

Seal missing C.R.O. 1A/C13/47

Endorsed: de tenemento Willelmi le Waller'

480 Late 1280s–early 1290s

Gift and quitclaim by Geoffrey the Chaplain (*capellanus*) son of Geoffrey the Baker (*Pistoris*) of Coventry to Robert de Cannele and his heirs, of all right and claim in a piece of land (*unam placiam terre*) with the houses sited there in Spon St. (*in vico de Sponna*), lying next to the land William Bate held on the one hand and the land Master Guy (*Gidonis*) held on the other with all appurtenances. Exclusion clause. Robert gave 12d. of silver beforehand. Sealing clause. Witnesses: Henry Baker (*Pistor'*) then bailiff, William Loteman, William le Wallere, John de Bineld, Hugh the clerk and others.

Seal extant C.R.O. 2/165

481 Late 1280s–early 1290s

Gift and quitclaim by Nicholas the Smith (*Faber*) to Robert de Canle of a small easement (*parvum heysiamentum*) at the end of his curtilage next to the water running from Crow Mill (*de le Crwemuln'*), to be held to him, his heirs or assigns, of the grantor, his heirs or assigns, according to the metes and bounds made between them (*inter ipsos factas*). Exclusion clause. Robert gave 2s. of silver beforehand. Witnesses: Geoffrey son of John, Walter de Kyldesby, William Maunsel, Walter Leteman, Hugh de Chaucumbe, Gilbert de Heyham and others.

Seal missing C.R.O. 2/43

482 Late 1280s–early 1290s

Charter of Gilbert de Berkeswelle giving to Nicholas the Smith (*fabr'*) of Coventry, Alice his wife, and William his son a moiety of a messuage with appurtenances in Spon St. (*in vico de Spanna*) *cum medietate amborum parietum ad capita domus dicti mesuagii*, which moiety of the said messuage lies in width between the grantor's land on the one hand and the land of Robert de Kannele on the other, and extends in length from the royal highway (*a regali via*) up to the water running from Spon ford towards Smithford (*de vado Spanne versus Smythesforde*) according to the metes and bounds made there; to be held with the buildings sited there and all appurtenances to them, their heirs or assigns, well [etc.] of the lords of that fee of whom the grantor held and as freely and quietly as he held by rendering annually as the perpetual attorneys of the grantor and his heirs to the lord prior and the convent of Coventry 3d. of silver at the four terms of the year usual and fixed in the vill of Coventry, a hen at Christmas, and a moiety of the service of a man working for one day in Autumn, and to the heirs of Richard de Bokervile ¼d. (*unum quadrantem*) of silver at Easter for all secular services [etc.]. Clause for warranty. The grantees gave 26s. of silver beforehand. Sealing clause. Witnesses: Henry Baker (*Pistore*) then bailiff in Coventry, Robert de Chilton, Robert de Cannele, Geoffrey son of John, Robert in Angulo, William Loteman, Eadward the Tanner (*tannatore*), John Reymund, Roger the clerk and others.

Seal extant C.R.O. 2/101

483 Late 1280s–early 1290s

Gift and quitclaim by Nicholas the Smith (*faber*) of Coventry, with the assent of Alice his wife, from himself and his heirs, to William the Glover (*Cerotecar'*), of all right and claim in the entire messuage with the curtilage and all appurtenances pertaining to the said messuage lying between the land of William de Cannebet on the one hand and the land of John Bektot on the other; to be held to him, his heirs or assigns, or to whomsoever he will wish to give, sell or assign well [etc.] without any charge by him or his wife or contradiction by their heirs. Exclusion clause. William gave 2s. beforehand. Sealing clause. Witnesses: Henry Baker (*pistor'*) then bailiff (*ball(iv)o tunc tempore*), Richard le Burc(er), Gilbert Corewenne, Geoffrey son of John, William de Cannel' and many others.

2 seals missing S.B.T. Archer 2081

484 Late 1280s–early 1290s

Lease by William son of Nicholas the Smith (*fabri*) of Coventry to Nicholas the Smith (*fabro*) his father and Alice his mother as long as they shall live or to the survivor of his messuage in Spon St., Coventry (*in vico de Spanna in Covintr'*) between the land which was of Gilbert de Berkeswelle on the one hand and the land of Robert de Kanneleye on the other in length and in width as is fully manifest with the buildings sited there and all appurtenances; to be held to them of the grantor and his heirs well [etc.], by rendering 1d. of silver at Easter for all secular services. The grantor will acquit the due and accustomed services towards the lords of the fee and will maintain the property in roofing and all other necessary repairs (*de coop(er)tura et omnibus aliis emendationibus necessariis*) during the term. Reversion clause. Sealing clause. Witnesses: Henry Baker (*pistore*) then bailiff in Coventry, Robert de Chilton', Robert de Kanneleye, Geoffrey son of John, Robert in Angulo, William Loteman, Eadward the Tanner (*tannatore*), John Reymund, Roger the clerk and others.

Seal extant C.R.O. 1A/C13/30
Endorsed: Carta de domo Willelmi filii Nicholay le Smyt

485 20 September 1293

Charter of Roger de Cannele clerk giving to Robert de Cannele of Coventry and Clarice his wife a certain messuage in Coventry in Spon St. (*in le Sponne strete*), which lies between the land which was of William Lotemon on the one hand and the land which was of Nicholas the Smith (*Fabri*) on the other; to be held to them and the heirs of Robert or their assigns with all utensils, goods and chattels whatsoever existing there freely [etc.], by making annually to the chief lords of the fee the services due and accustomed for all secular services [etc.]. Warranty and sealing clauses. Witnesses: Henry Baker (*Pistore*) then bailiff of Coventry, Robert de Chilton, Henry Ballard, John de Longeleye, Robert in le Hurne, Nicholas the Smith (*Fabro*), Laurence the clerk and others. Coventry, Sunday after the Exaltation of the Holy Cross 21 Edward I.

Seal extant — C.R.O. 1B/21 EI/3

486 — Late 1280s–early 1290s

Charter of Robert de Cannele giving to Richard de Royewelle with Alice the grantor's daughter 14d. rent which John de Warewic held of him in Spon St. (*in vico de Sponne*); to be held to him, his heirs or assigns, of the grantor, his heirs or assigns, freely [etc.] by rendering annually to William le Parlour, his heirs or assigns, 1d. at Easter for all charges and demands. Clause for reversion if Alice should die without bodily heir. Sealing clause. Witnesses: William Loteman, Robert en le Hurne, Gilbert Corewenne, Geoffrey son of John, William Mauncel, William le Wallere, Hugh the clerk and others.

Seal extant — C.R.O. 1A/EC13/103

487 — 8 September 1293

Charter of Robert de Canneleye of Coventry giving to John his son clerk 20d. annual rent with appurtenances from the tenement which Adam le Webbe held in Spon St. (*in vico Sponne*), into the hands of whomsoever the tenement will come; to be held to him, his heirs or assigns freely [etc.]. Warranty and sealing clauses. Witnesses: Robert de Chylton', Robert en le Hurne, Edward le Barkere, William Lutemon, Geoffrey son of John, Roger de Pakwode clerk, Richard le Dubbere and others. Coventry, Tuesday the feast of the Nativity of the blessed Mary 21 Edward I.

Seal missing — C.R.O. 1B/21 EI/2

488 — 8 September 1293

Charter of Robert de Canneleye of Coventry giving to Agnes his daughter a messuage with appurtenances in Coventry in Spon St. (*in vico Sponne*) lying between the land which was of John de Thurlaston' on the one hand and the land which was of William Pat on the other; to be held to her, her heirs or assigns, of the lords of that fee by making annually the services due and accustomed for all secular service [etc.]. Warranty and sealing clauses. Witnesses: Henry Baker (*Pistore*) then bailiff of Coventry, Robert de Chylton', Robert en le Hurne, Edward le Barkere, William le Wallere, William Luteman, Roger de Pacwode clerk and others. Coventry, Tuesday the feast of the Nativity of the blessed Mary 21 Edward I.

Seal extant — C.R.O. 1B/21 EI/I

489 — Late 1270s

Charter of John de Cundulme in Coventry giving to Robert the Tanour certain land of his with a curtilage lying in Spon St. (*in vico sponne*) between the land of William le Paumer on the one hand and the land Richard le Comber once held on the other in length and in width as is manifest according to the metes and bounds made there; to be held to him, his heirs or assigns, freely [etc.] to whomsoever he will wish to give, sell or assign, by rendering annually to William le Rok and his heirs 16d. at the four terms of the year fixed and customary in the vill of Coventry, and to the grantor and his heirs a clove-gillyflower at Christmas for all secular services [etc.]. Clause for warranty. *Et si contingat quod illam terram warantizare non potero dabo ei tantam terram equevalentem per consideracionem bonorum virorum et fidedignorum.* Robert gave 1 mark sterling beforehand. Sealing clause. Witnesses: Gerard de Alespath then bailiff, Robert de Chilt(er)n', William Rok, William Paum(er), Robert de Cannele, William Rimild, Hugh Chail and others.

Seal extant C.R.O. 1A/C13/11
Endorsed: aula de bablake

490 c.1280

Charter of Robert de Lodelowe burgess of Coventry (*Burgens Coventr'*) giving to Robert del Hyrne of Coventry tanner (*tannatori*) 18d. annual rent in the vill of Coventry which the grantor used to receive from certain land which Robert de Condolme had in Spon St. (*in vico sponne*) between the land Geoffrey de Atlberg' held and the land Vincent Bissop held; to be held to him, his heirs or to whomsoever and whensoever he will wish to give, sell or in any way assign or bequeath, in sickness and in health freely [etc.], by rendering annually a rose flower at the Nativity of St. John the Baptist for all secular service [etc.]. Clause for warranty. Robert gave 1 mark of silver beforehand. Sealing clause. Witnesses: Master Guy vicar of the church of the blessed Michael, Gerard de Allespath, William le Palm(er), Robert de Cannele, Walter de Kyldesby, William Lotemon, John de Gloucestr' chaplain (*capellano*) and others.

Seal extant C.R.O. 2/136

491 6 May 1296

Grant and quitclaim by Stephen le Mareschal of Coventry to Robert in le Hurne of Coventry of the entire tenement which the same Robert gave him in free marriage with Alice his daughter, which tenement lies in Spon St. (*in vico de Sponne*), in Coventry between the land of the same Robert on the one hand and the land of John ad Crucem on the other in width and extends in length from the royal highway (*a Regali via*) up to the land of Robert Falkon according to the metes and bounds made there; to be held with all appurtenances to him, his heirs or assigns, of the lords of that fee well and in peace for ever. Exclusion clause. Sealing clause. Witnesses: William le Parker coroner, Nicholas Crompe, Peter Barun, Richard de Merstone, John de Longeleye, Robert le Combere, John le Gouere, William Lutteman, William le Waller', Geoffrey son of John, Geoffrey le Waller', Richard called King (*dicto Rege*) and many others. Coventry, Sunday after the feast of the Ascension of the Lord A.D. 1296.

Seal detached, tag missing C.R.O. 1B/24EI/14

492 29 March 1306

Lease and grant by Brother Henry, prior of the church of the blessed Mary and the convent of Coventry to Robert in le Hyrne of Coventry and Agnes his wife of an acre of land of their waste at Spon (*vasti nostri apud Spannem*) lying between the land of the aforesaid Robert on the one hand and their waste on the other; to be held to them and the heirs of their bodies begotten legitimately, freely [etc.] of the grantors and their successors and their church by the service of 2s. annually at the four terms of the year usual in Coventry to be paid in equal portions for all secular service and demand. Clause for reversion with all improvement (*cum omni melioratione*) in default of heirs as above. Mutual sealing clause. Witnesses: Robert called Baker (*dicto pistor'*) of Coventry then bailiff, Alexander de Stonley then coroner, William Grauntpe, Geoffrey le Chaloner, Ranulph de Cundulme, William le Waller' and others. Coventry, Tuesday after the feast of the Annunciation of the blessed Mary 34 Edward I.

Indented
Seal extant C.R.O. 1B/34EI/5

493 20 November–31 December 1303

Charter of Robert in le Huyrne *barker*' [sic] giving to Thomas his son clerk a messuage with appurtenances in Spon St. outside Smithford bar (*in vico de Sponna extra barram de Smythesforde*) with buildings and all appurtenances, namely that which lies between the land of Roger de Pacwode clerk on the one hand and the land of Henry (*Hanr'*) brother of the aforesaid Thomas on the other in width and extends in length from the royal highway (*a regia via*) up to the land of Robert Fakkon according to the metes and bounds made there; to be held to him, his heirs and assigns, of the chief lords of that fee by the services due and by right accustomed freely [etc.]. Warranty and sealing clauses. Witnesses: Robert Baker (*pistore*) of Coventry then bailiff, John Lewyn, Robert de Chilton', Alexander le Vyneter', Alexander le Moubray, William le Wallere, John Corewenne, Henry Gopyl, Roger de Pacwode clerk and others. Monday the feast of St. Scolastica the Virgin A.D. 1303 and 32 Edward I.

Seal extant C.R.O. 1B/32 EI/8

There is a dating problem here. The feast of St. Scholastica the Virgin was normally celebrated on 10 February. However February 1303 is 31 Edward I (and 32 E.I is 1304). But in neither year, 1303 or 1304, is 10 February on a Monday. Presumably St. Scholastica was celebrated in Coventry at a date between 20 November and 31 December.

494 6 May 1296

Remise and release by Margery de Lodelawe, widow of Robert de Lodelawe, to Henry de Coventr' clerk of 6d. rent with appurtenances which she received annually in name of dower through the death of Robert de Lodelawe once her husband from a tenement which was of Robert Fraunceys in Spon St. (*in vico de Sponna*) and which lies between the land Geoffrey de Attleberge once held on the one hand and the land Vincent Bissop held on the other; to be held to him, his heirs and assigns, of the chief lords of that fee well, in peace and for ever. Exclusion clause. Sealing clause. Witnesses: William Loteman, Richard de St. James, Richard dela Mure, John de Ridewale, Richard Condenere, Henry de Pailinton', Adam de Ruton' saddler (*selario*) and many others. Coventry, the feast of the Holy Trinity 24 Edward I.

Seal extant C.R.O. 1B/24EI/I

495 2 June 1303

Grant by Henry son of Robert in le Huyrne of Coventry to Robert son of William le Clerk of Coundon (*Coundelme*) dwelling (*manenti*) in Coventry and Edith his wife for their entire life and to the survivor a messuage with buildings sited there, with an adjacent curtilage, and with its appurtenances, which messuage lies in Spon St. (*in vico de Spon(n)a*) in width between the land of Robert the grantor's father on the one hand and the grantor's land on the other and extends in length from the aforesaid street up to the land of Robert Fackon according to the metes and bounds made there; to be held of the grantor, his heirs or assigns, freely [etc.] by rendering annually 8s. of silver at the four terms of the year usual in Coventry for all services and demands pertaining to the grantor, his heirs or assigns. The grantees will repair and maintain the buildings at their own cost and the messuage will revert after their deaths with all improvements, buildings constructed and appurtenances (*Ita quod ipsi predicti Robertus et Editha in tota vita eorum edificia dicti mesuagii sub suis propriis custibus reparabunt emendabunt et in omnibus sustentabunt ita quod remaneant in meliori statu in extremis diebus ipsorum quam fuerunt in principio confectionis hujus scripti. Et post decessum predictorum Roberti et Edithe totum illud mesuagium prenominatum cum omnibus melioracionibus et edificiis ibidem constructis et aliis pertinentiis suis mihi predicto Henrico et heredibus vel assignatis meis sine alicujus contradictione integre revertatur*). Clause for warranty *tali condictione quod ego predictus Henricus habebo penes me in tota vita mea totum fructum unius pomarii ibidem crescentis ad eligendum ad voluntatem meam.* Mutual sealing clause. Witnesses: Roger Dayesegh' then bailiff in Coventry, John Lewyne then coroner, Robert in le Huyrne, Thurstan le Wyttauere, William le Wallere, Geoffrey le Wallere, Richard Colebrond clerk and others. Coventry, Friday after the feast of Holy Trinity 31 Edward I.

Indented
2 seal tags only C.R.O. 1B/31EI/3

496 1270s

Remise and quitclaim by Hawise (*Hauysia*) daughter of William le Paum(er), in her pure widowhood and lawful power, to John de Kendale and Isabel his wife, their heirs and assigns, of all right and claim in a messuage with appurtenances in Coventry in Spon St. (*in vico qui vocatur Sponnestret*) lying between the land Symon Kyng held and the land Adam le Campyun held. Exclusion clause. John and Isabel gave ½ mark of silver beforehand. Witnesses: Robert de Chilt(er)ne then bailiff, John de Lodelowe, Richard Shore, Adam de la Grene, Hugh Shail, Robert Croulone, Richard Kyng, Richard Lotemon, Robert Reymund and others.

Seal extant C.R.O. 1A/C32

497 Late 1280s–early 1290s

Charter of Gilbert de Berkeswelle dwelling in Baginton (*manens in Bathekynton*) giving to John de Kendale saddler in Coventry (*in Coventr' sellario*) 12d. annual rent to be received at the four terms of the year usual and fixed in the vill of Coventry from a tenement in Spon St. (*in vico Spanne*) between the land lately of Robert Bucston on the one hand and the land of Robert de Derby on the other; to be held with appurtenances to him, his heirs or whatsoever assigns, and to whomsoever he will wish to give, bequeath, sell or assign in sickness and in health well [etc.]. Warranty and sealing clauses. Witnesses: Henry Baker (*pistore*) then bailiff in Coventry, Gilbert Corwenne, Geoffrey son of John, Richard Kyng, Richard Kay, Robert de Canneleye, William Loteman, Gilbert de Heyham, Roger the clerk and others.

Seal extant C.R.O. 1A/EC13/104

498 18 November 1306

Grant, release and quitclaim by John de Kendale of Coventry to Adam his son of all right and claim in a messuage with appurtenances which lies in Spon St. (*in vico de Sponna*) in Coventry between the tenement of Richard Cay on the one hand and the tenement of John Campion on the other in width and extends in length from the aforesaid street up to the running water as is fully manifest according to the metes and bounds made there; to be held to him, his heirs and whatsoever assigns, freely [etc.] of the chief lords of that fee by the services due and by right accustomed. Exclusion and sealing clauses. Witnesses: Robert Baker (*Pistor'*) then bailiff of Coventry, Alexander de Stonlee then coroner of the same, Richard Kyng, Roger atte Grene, Richard Cay, John Curwenne, Geoffrey le Wallere and others. Coventry, Friday after the feast of St. Edmund the Archbishop 34 Edward I *finient'*.

Seal missing C.R.O. 1B/34EI/3

499 29 September 1284

Agreement at Michaelmas 12 Edward I whereby Alice daughter of Isolda le Lethe of Coventry has leased and demised at farm to Isolda her mother for the term of her life the entire land with the houses sited there and all appurtenances which she formerly had of the gift of the same Isolda in Spon St. (*in vico de Spanna*) between the land once of William Bucston on the one hand and the land of Margery le Mire on the other; to be held to her of Alice well [etc.], by rendering annually to the chief lords of the fee the service due and accustomed and to Alice or her assigns 1d. at Michaelmas for all secular service [etc.]. Warranty and sealing clauses. Witnesses: Henry Baker (*pistor'*) then bailiff, Alexander the Vintner (*vynitar'*), Robert de Chilton', Andrew de Condulme, Richard le Purser, Geoffrey son of John, Gilbert Corwenne, Symon le King, William Lotemon, Robert de Cannele, Roger de Allesl' the clerk and others.

Indented
Seal missing C.R.O. 12 EI1[1]/I

[1] sic

500 Late 1280s–early 1290s

Charter of Robert de Esscheby senior and Margery called (*dicta*) la Leche his wife giving to Reginald son of Thomas de Calwdone and Margery daughter of Alice la Leche of Coventry in free marriage a messuage with appurtenances in Spon St. (*in vico de Sponna*) in Coventry, namely that which lies between the land Symon le Riche once held on the one hand and the land Richard de Luton' held on the other and extends in length from the highway (*a Regali via*) up to the watercourse running from Crow Mill (*Crowmulne*) as is manifest according to the metes and bounds made there; to be held to them and the heirs begotten from them, of the grantors, their heirs or assigns, freely [etc.], by rendering annually to the lords of that fee 12d. [at the four terms of the year][1] fixed in Coventry, 2 hens at Christmas and the service of 2 men for [1 day in Autumn for all][1] secular service [etc.]. Should Margery die [without heir of her body][1] Reginald will hold the said messuage with appurtenances for his entire life, with reversion after his death to the right heirs of Margery without any contradiction. Warranty and sealing clauses. Witnesses: Henry Baker (*pistor'*) then bailiff, Thomas le Moubrey, Geoffrey son of John, Hugh de Stivechale, Robert de Cannele, Thomas de Honitone, Robert in le Hurne, John Brewys, Robert Reymu(n)d, Adam the Smith (*fabro*), Walter Gymere, Gilbert Corewenne, Gilbert de Heyham, Symon called (*dicto*) King, William the clerk and others.

2 seals extant G.H. 305

[1] lost by damage

501 Late 1280s–early 1290s

Demise and quitclaim by Walter son of Robert Schort for the term of the grantor's life (to Simon Eins and his heirs)[1] of all right in the entire land with appurtenances which Richard the Plumber (*plu(m)bar'*) once held in Spon St., Coventry (*In vico sponn' Coventr'*) between the land of the said Simon on the one hand and the land of Richard Sportot on the other and extending up to the plum tree (*unu(m) p(r)unari(um)*); to be held freely [etc.], with exclusion clause. Simon gave 2s. of silver beforehand. Sealing clause. Witnesses: Henry Baker (*pistor*) then bailiff, Geoffrey son of John, Gilbert Corvenne, Robert de Kannel', William Lotemon, Robert de Codiswold, John Remund, Edward the Tanner (*tanator*), Robert the Tanner (*tanator*), Adam the clerk and others.

Seal extant C.R.O. C12/5

[1] interlined

502 Late 1280s–early 1290s

Remise and quitclaim by Matilda Bonde widow of William Bonde once the daughter of Thomas the Goldsmith (*Aurifabr'*) of Coventry in her widowhood, for herself and her heirs, to Thomas Haldeyn of Coventry and Alice his wife of all right and claim in 3d. annual rent which they used to render to her from a certain plot of land (*de quadam placea terre*) with appurtenances which lies between the land Peter de Egesfeld held on the one hand and the land Henry le Cartsadelere once held on the other; to be held to them, their heirs or assigns freely [etc.]. Exclusion clause. Sealing clause. Witnesses: Henry Baker (*pistore*) then bailiff in Coventry, Robert de Chiltun, William the Parker (*p(ar)kario*), John Tole, Roger the Chamberlain (*Cam(er)ario*), Stephen the Marshal (*marescallo*), Jordan le Sadelere, Robert Fackon, Henry le Mowere and others.

Seal extant C.R.O. 2/61

503 14 December 1291

Charter of Robert called (*dictus*) de Engeland of Sheldon (*Scheldon'*) merchant (*mercator*) giving to William Brown of Coleshill (*Collershull'*) the entire messuage with curtilage which he had by the gift of William de Catone *Cappemakyere* in Spon St. (*in vico de le Sponne*) in Coventry; to be held as it is manifest to him, his heirs or whatsoever assigns, freely [etc.] of the chief lords of the fee by the service owed and by right accustomed. Warranty and sealing clauses. Witnesses: Thomas de Laxton, William le Waller', John Corewune, John Ball' and Peter de Yelvertoft carpenter (*carpentar'*) of Coventry and others. Coventry, Friday after the feast of St. Luke the Evangelist 20 Edward I.

Seal missing C.R.O. 1B/20 EI/I

504 9 March 1293

Grant by Ranulph son of John Walt(er) of Stivichall (*Stivechale*), for himself and his heirs, to Juliana widow of Adam Haldeyn of Coventry as long as she shall live of the entire third part of a curtilage which fell to her by name of dower from the curtilage which the grantor bought from Richard le Pursere of Coventry towards Spon bridge (*pontem de Spanna*), which was once of Adam Haldeyn her husband and lies between the land Robert de Chilton' held of the same Adam on the one hand and the land John de Leyre held on the other; to be held to her as long as she shall live well [etc.] without impediment by the grantor or his heirs, with reversion to him, his heirs or assigns, after her death without any contradiction. Sealing clause. Witnesses: Henry Baker (*pistore*) bailiff of Coventry, Robert de Chilton', Geoffrey son of John, Gilbert Corwenne, Gilbert de Heyham, Richard Kyng, Richard Kay and others. Coventry, 7 Ides of March 21 Edward I.

Seal extant G.H. 299

505 16 November 1303

Charter of Ranulph son of John Walter of Stivichall (*Styvychale*) of Coventry giving to Peter le Carpunter of *Yelvertoft* a certain piece (*placeam*) of his land with appurtenances in Spon St. (*in vico de Sponna*) which contains 32 feet in width between the grantor's land on the one hand and the land once of Adam Haldeyn on the other and extends in length from the aforesaid street up to the meadow once of the aforesaid Adam Haldeyn according to the metes and bounds made there; to be held to him, his heirs or assigns, freely [etc.] of the chief lords of that fee namely of the lord prior of Coventry by the service and rent of 18d. annually to be paid at the four terms of the year usual in Coventry for all services and demands. Clause for warranty. Peter gave 20s. of silver beforehand. Sealing clause. Witnesses: Robert le Pestur then bailiff, John Lewyn then coroner, John Pyehod, Richard Kyng, Richard Colebrond clerk and others. Coventry, Saturday the feast of St. Edmund the Archbishop 31 Edward I.

Seal extant C.R.O. 1B/31EI/6a

506 (14 February 1295)[1]

Charter of William Galewey of Coventry giving to Isabel daughter of Felicea de H(e)dewyt the entire land with the buildings sited there and all appurtenances which lies in width between the land once of Adam Haldeyn on the one hand and the land once of Thomas le Prechur on the other and extends in length from the highway (*a Regia via*) up to the watercourse as is manifest according to the metes and bounds made there; to be held to the aforesaid Isabel, her heirs or assigns, freely [etc.] of the chief lords of that fee by the service and rent due and by right accustomed. Warranty and sealing clauses. Witnesses: Henry Baker (*Pistore*) then bailiff, Robert his son, William the Parker (*Parcar'*), Anketell de Colushulle, Andrew de Coundulme, Richard Kyng, Geoffrey son of John, Thomas le Moubray, Richard Colebrond and others. Coventry, Monday after the feast of St. Scolastica the Virgin 23 Edward I.

Seal extant C.R.O. 1B/23 EI/3

[1] But see 493n.

507 c.1290–1297

Charter of Agnes daughter of Claricia Stockes of Allesley (*Allesle*) giving to William de Galewey clerk her entire land in Coventry in Spon St. (*in vico de la Sponne*) with the houses sited there and all appurtenances, which lies between [the land] of Richard le Purser on the one hand and the land once of Thomas de Stafford preacher (*predicator'*) on the other in length and in width as it purports according to the metes and bounds there; to be held to him, his heirs or assigns, of the lords of that fee freely [etc.] or to whomsoever he will wish to give, bequeath, sell or assign in sickness and in health by rendering annually to those lords of the fee the due and accustomed rent for all secular service [etc.]. Clause for warranty. Sealing clause. Witnesses: Henry Baker (*pistor'*) then bailiff in Coventry, Richard de St. James, Roger Dayseye,

John Lewin, William le P(ar)ker then coroner, Anketell de Coleshul, Geoffrey son of John and others.

Seal extant C.R.O. 2/21

508 c.1290–1297

Charter of Richard le Pursere of Coventry giving to Emma widow of William Wymund of Coventry a messuage with appurtenances which he had at Spon bridge (*apud Pontem de Spanna*) in Coventry and which was once of Roger Cade, and which lies in width between the grantor's chief messuage (*Capitale mansum*) on the one hand and his garden (*gardinum*) on the other and extends in length from the road which leads from Spon St. towards Wood Mill (*via que ducit de Spannestrete versus le Wodemulne*) up to the same garden according to the metes and bounds made there; to be held with the buildings sited there and all appurtenances to her, her heirs or to whatsoever assigns she will wish to give, bequeath or assign in sickness or in health well [etc.] of the lords of that fee, by rendering annually to the same lords 19d. of silver at the four terms of the year usual and fixed in the vill of Coventry and to the lord prior and the convent of Coventry 3s. of silver at the same four terms for all secular services [etc.]. Warranty and sealing clauses. Witnesses: Henry Baker (*Pistore*) then bailiff of Coventry, William called (*dicto*) Park(er) then coroner, Robert Kelle, Matthew de Ruyton', Geoffrey son of John, Gilbert Corewenne, Richard Kyng, Roger ad Grenam, Richard Kay and others.

Seal extant C.R.O. 1B/31E1/6b
Endorsed: Camera prioris

509 20 April 1299

Charter of Agnes daughter of Roger the Fishmonger (*Piscatoris*) of Coventry in her lawful power giving to Emma widow of William Wymund of Coventry her entire land with the buildings sited there and its appurtenances in the vill of Coventry, lying in width between the land once of Alexander le Kyng on the one hand and the running water on the other and extending in length from the land of William Gamel up to the land once of the said Alexander as is fully manifest according to the metes and bounds made there; to be held to her, her heirs or whatsoever assigns, freely [etc.] of the chief lords of that fee by making annually to those same lords the services due and by right accustomed, and by rendering annually to the grantor, her heirs or assigns, 3s. of silver at the four terms of the year usual and fixed in the vill of Coventry for all secular services [etc.]. Clause for warranty. Emma gave 20s. of silver beforehand. Sealing clause. Witnesses: Anketill de Coleshul then bailiff in Coventry, John Lewyne then coroner, John Pyhod, Robert Kelle, Peter Baroun, John de Langele, Matthew de Ruyton', Richard de St. James, Roger the clerk and others. Coventry, Monday before the feast of St. Mark the Evangelist 27 Edward I.

Seal extant P.R.O. A 10730

510 c.1290–1297

Grant, remise and quitclaim by Susan (*Sussanna*) daughter and heir of Avicia le Kembestere of Lawford (*Lalleforde*) in her widowhood and lawful power, for herself and her heirs, to Henry le Ledbetere of Coventry and Mabel his wife, of all right and claim in a curtilage with appurtenances which was once of Avicia the grantor's mother in Spon St. (*in vico de Spanna*) in Coventry between the land of the aforesaid Henry and Mabel on the one hand and the land of William le Wallere on the other;

to be held to them, their heirs or whatsoever assigns, well [etc.] of the lords of that fee by the service due and by right accustomed without any charge or impediment by the grantor or her heirs. Exclusion clause. Henry and Mabel gave a certain sum of money beforehand. Sealing clause. Witnesses: Henry Baker (*Pistore*) then bailiff of Coventry, William called (*dicto*) Park(er) then coroner, Thomas le Moubray, Robert in le Huyrne, William Loteman, Eadward le Barkere, John Reymund, William le Wallere, Roger the clerk and others.

Seal extant W.R.O. 58
Endorsed: ledbeter' & sibuston'

511 c.1290–1297
Charter of William son of William Somer of Coventry giving to John de Claybroc weaver (*textori*) and Emma his wife a messuage in Spon St. (*in vico de Spanna*) in Coventry between the land Gilbert Corwenne held on the one hand and the land John Bissop held on the other with the buildings sited there and an adjacent curtilage and with all appurtenances in length and in width as is fully manifest, together with 3s. rent which the aforesaid John Bissop used to render to the grantor annually from the tenement he held of him in the same place between the aforesaid messuage on the one hand and the land which Adam the Wheelwright (*Rotarius*) once held on the other; to be held to them, their heirs or assigns, with all liberties and easements well [etc.] of the lords of the fee by the service due and accustomed, namely to Sir Geoffrey de Langel', his heirs or assigns, 8d. of silver annually at the four terms usual and fixed in the vill of Coventry, the service of 1 man working for one day in Autumn and 1 hen at Christmas for all secular services [etc.]. Clause for warranty. John and Emma gave 4 marks sterling beforehand. Sealing clause. Witnesses: Henry Baker (*pistore*) then bailiff in Coventry, William le Parker then coroner, Thomas le Moubray, John Thole, John his son, John son of Nicholas, Geoffrey son of John, Gilbert Corewenne, William Loteman and others.

Seal missing W.R.O. 54
Endorsed: Carta Vill(elm)i Somer de teneme(n)t' in vico de spon' & co(n)stat Johanni Atte cro3

512 c.1290–1297
Charter of Robert son of Richard le Teler of Coventry and Agnes his wife, daughter of William le Rok, giving to Thomas le Waydur servant (*servienti*) of Drugo (*Drugonis*) Malerbe a curtilage in Spon St. (*in vico de Spanna*) in Coventry, lying in width between the land of Robert de Canneleye tanner (*tannatoris*) on the one hand and the land Richard de Dustone held on the other and in length from the aforesaid street up to the land of Robert Maunsel as it fully purports, and 4d. annual rent which Richard de Duston used to render at the four terms usual in the vill of Coventry from a message next to the aforesaid curtilage; to be held to him, his heirs or assigns, well [etc.], of the lord prior and the convent of Coventry and their successors by the service of 4d. *per annum* to be paid at the four terms [as above] for all secular services [etc.]. Clause for warranty. Thomas gave 40s. sterling beforehand. Sealing clause. Witnesses: Henry Baker (*pistore*) then bailiff in Coventry, Robert de Chilton', William le Parker then coroner, Stephen de Hales, William de Copston', Robert in Angulo, Robert de Canneleye, William Lotemon, Roger the clerk and others.

2 seal tags, 1 seal extant C.R.O. 1A/C13/52

513 23 January 1298

Charter of Agnes once daughter and heir of Walter de Kyldesby tanner in Coventry (*in Coventr' Tannatoris*) in her virginity and lawful power giving to John de Thurlaweston' tanner in Coventry (*in Coventr' Tannatori*) her messuage with appurtenances in Spon St. (*in vico de Spanna*) in Coventry between the messuage of Robert in le Huyrne on the one hand and the messuage of Eadward le Barker' on the other in length and in width as it fully purports together with all her chattels and goods, movable and immovable, found in the aforesaid messuage both in houses and outside houses (*tam in domibus quam extra domos*); to be held with all buildings sited there and all appurtenances, to him, his heirs or whatsoever assigns, well [etc.] of the lords of that fee by rendering annually the service due and by right accustomed. Clause for warranty. John gave 100s. sterling beforehand. Sealing clause. Witnesses: William called (*dicto*) Parker then coroner in Coventry, Richard de St. James, Robert in le Huyrne, William Loteman, Geoffrey son of John, Eadward le Barkere, John Reymund, William le Wallere, Roger the clerk and others. Coventry, Thursday the morrow of St. Vincent the Martyr 26 Edward I.

Seal extant W.R.O. 61

514 6 May 1299

Charter of John de Chilton' giving to William de Copston' draper (*drap(er)io*) a certain parcel of his moor at Spon (*quamdam particulam more mee apud Sponnam*) next to the tenement of Sir Geoffrey de Copston chaplain (*capellani*) as is manifest according to the metes and bounds; to be held with all appurtenances to William or whatsoever assigns, of the chief lords of that fee freely [etc.] by making the services due and accustomed, for all services and demands. Warranty and sealing clauses. Witnesses: Anketell de Colsull' then bailiff, Matthew de Ruyton', Robert Faccon, Richard de St. James, Roger atte Grene, Richard Kay and others. Coventry, Wednesday the feast of St. John ante portam latinam 27 Edward I.

Seal missing C.R.O. 1B/27 EI/9
Endorsed: Carte more ex(tra) pontem de Spone(n)d.

515 6 May 1299

Grant and quitclaim by John de Chilton', for himself and his heirrs, to Geoffrey de Copston' chaplain (*capellano*) and his successors of all right or claim in a certain parcel of moor at Spon (*in quaddam particula more apud le Sponne*) in Coventry next to the tenement of the same Geoffrey, which parcel William de Copston' held of the grantor's gift and enfeoffment; to be held with appurtenances of the chief lords of that fee by the services due and accustomed freely [etc.]. Exclusion clause. Sealing clause. Witnesses: Anketell de Colsull' then bailiff in Coventry, Matthew de Ruyton', Richard de St. James, William de Copston', Richard Dobedy, John Dobedy clerk and others. Wednesday the feast of St. John ante portam latinam 27 Edward I.

Seal extant C.R.O. 1B/27 EI/3

516 15 August 1302

Charter of William son of John Bissop of Coventry giving to Richard Corewenne of Coventry (*Coventreia*) and Alice his wife his messuage with appurtenances in Spon St. (*in vico de Spanna*) in Coventry, namely that which lies in width between the land of William le Wallere on the one hand and the land of John ad Crucem on the other and extends in length from Spon St. (*de vico Spanne*) up to the curtilages of Hill St. (*Hullestret*) according to the metes and bounds made there; to be held with the buildings sited there and all appurtenances to them, their heirs or assigns, well [etc.] of the chief lords of that fee by the service due and by right accustomed. Clause for warranty. Richard and Alice gave a certain sum of money beforehand. Sealing clause. Witnesses: Roger Daieseie then bailiff in Coventr', Geoffrey son of John, Richard Kyng, Gilbert de Heyham, Roger atte Grene, William le Wallere, Geoffrey le Wallere, Adam the Smith (*fabro*), John Corewenne, John the Brewer (*Braciatore*), Richard Kay, Hugh de Chaucumbe, Roger the clerk and others. Coventry, Wednesday the feast of the Assumption of the blessed Virgin Mary 30 Edward I.

Seal extant W.R.O.62

517 10 January 1306

Charter of Felicia Caucy of Coventry, in her widowhood and lawful power, giving to Thomas de Duston' her son a moiety of a messuage with a curtilage adjacent and its appurtenances in Spon St. (*in vico de Sponna*) in the vill of Coventry, namely that moiety which lies between the land Robert Mauncel once held on the one hand and the land of Thurstan de Allesleye and Agnes his wife on the other in width and extends from the aforesaid street up to the land of Nicholas le Deystere in length according to the metes and bounds made there; to be held to him, his heirs or whatsoever assigns, freely [etc.] of the chief lords of that fee by the services due and accustomed, namely the service of 2d. to the lord prior of Coventry and to his church (*ecclesie sue*) to be paid annually for all secular services and demands. Warranty and sealing clauses. Witnesses: Robert Baker (*Pistore*) then bailiff of Coventry, Alexander de Stonlee then coroner of the same, William le Wallere, Geoffrey le Wallere, Thomas in le Huyrne, Gilbert de Heyham, Henry de Kynewoldesham and others. Coventry, Monday after the feast of the Epiphany of the Lord 34 Edward I.

Seal missing C.R.O. 1B/31 EI/13

518 c.25 March 1307

Gift by Felicia Cause and Thomas de Duston' her son to Thomas le Waydur of Coventry of a messuage with appurtenances in Spon St., Coventry (*in vico de Sponne de Coventr'*) lying next to the land of William Maunsel on the one hand in width and which extends from the royal highway (*a via Reg'*) up to the land of the said Thomas in length according to the metes and bounds made there; to be held to him for his entire life of the said Felicia and Thomas her son freely [etc.] from the feast of the Annunciation of the blessed Virgin Mary 35 Edward I by rendering 4d. annually for all services [etc.] for the term of 10 years and 6s. thereafter as long as he lives. Clause for warranty. Thomas gave 15s. beforehand. Mutual sealing clause. Witnesses: Robert Baker (*pistor'*) then bailiff, Alexander de Stonleie, Robert Franceis, William le Wallere, Richard le Especer, Roger de Pacwode and many others.

Indented
2 seals extant C.R.O. 1B/35EI/I

519 16 March 1306

Grant, remise and quitclaim by John Dolfyn of Coventry and Isolda his wife to Thomas le Waydour' of Coventry of all right and claim in a certain curtilage with appurtenances lying in Spon St. (*in vico de Sponna*) in Coventry between the land once of Robert de Canneleye on the one hand and the land of Felicia Cauceey on the other in width and which extends in length from the aforesaid street up to the land once of Robert Maunscel as is fully manifest according to the metes and bounds made there; to be held to him, his heirs or assigns, freely [etc.] of the chief lords of that fee by the services due and by right accustomed. Exclusion clause. Clause for warranty. Thomas gave 1 mark of silver beforehand. Sealing clause. Witnesses: Robert Baker (*Pistore*), Nicholas Crumpe, Anketell de Colleshull', William le Waller', Geoffrey le Wallere, Gilbert de Heyham, John Dobedy and others. Coventry, Wednesday after the feast of St. Gregory the Pope 34 Edward I.

2 seals extant C.R.O. 1B/34 EI/6

520 19 May 1303

Charter of Geoffrey son of John of Coventry giving to Henry Gopyl and Christine his wife, and to the heirs of Henry or his assigns, the entire tenement which he had in Spon St. (*in vico de Sponne*) in Coventry lying between the tenement of Richard Kay on the one hand and the tenement once of Roger Corwenne on the other in width and which extends in length from the royal highway (*a Regali via*) up to the garden (*gardinum*) of Roger le Neue according to the metes and bounds made there; to be held of the lords of that fee by the services due and by right accustomed. Clause for warranty. Henry and Christine gave 10 marks sterling beforehand. Sealing clause. Witnesses: Roger Dayeseye then bailiff of Coventry, John Lewyn then coroner of the same, Robert son of Henry Baker (*Pistor'*), William le Wallere, Geoffrey le Wallere, John Corwenne, Alexander son of Thomas le Moubray and many others. Sunday after the feast of the Ascension of the Lord 31 Edward I.

Seal extant C.R.O. 1B/31EI/7

521 13 March 1304

Charter of John Waldyeve son of Gerard Waldyeve of Meriden (*Allespath'*) giving to William le Waller' and his heirs for a certain sum of money given beforehand the entire rent which he had or which has accrued to him in Coventry after the death of his father to be received annually at the terms fixed in Coventry, namely 8s. from the tenement once of Eadward the Tanner (*tannator'*) in Spon St. (*in vico Spanne*) which lies next to the land of the same William le Waller', 4s. 8d. from the tenement once of Walter de Kyldesby lying next to the land of the said Eadward in the same street, 4s. from the tenement once of Robert in le Hurne lying next to the land of the said Walter in the same street, 2s. from the tenement once of Hugh Shayl in Hill St. (*in vico de Hulle*), 3s. 2d. from the tenement once of Roger de Coundulme lying in the same street, 6d. from the curtilage which Gerard the grantor's father granted to William de Copston' for his entire life, and 2s. from the tenement once of John the Smith (*fabri*) the son of Geoffrey the Smith (*fabri*) lying between the land of John Tole and the land of Ysabel Kempe. Moreover he has granted and quit-claimed, for himself and his heirs, to the said William le Waller' and his heirs the said curtilage with appurtenances after the death of William Copston' which he held for life, and whatsoever will be able to accrue in the future through the said rent or curtilage by whatsoever right; to be held to him, his heirs or whatsoever assigns, of the chief lords of the fee freely [etc.] by making annually the services due and by right accustomed for all secular services [etc.]. Warranty and sealing clauses. Witnesses: Robert Baker (*Pistor'*) then bailiff of Coventry, John Lewyn coroner in the same place, Geoffrey le Waller', William Loteman, Henry de Schorlaston',

William Mauncel, Henry the Plumber (*plumbar'*) and others. Coventry, Friday after the feast of St. Gregory 32 Edward I.

Seal missing C.R.O. 1B/32 EI/6

522 c.30 November 1304

Lease by Roger Gopyl of Whoberley (*Wadburleye*) and Beatrice his wife to Stephen son of Richard le Webbe of Coventry and Agnes his wife for their lives of a house (*domum*) with an adjacent curtilage with a kiln (*torello*) and appurtenances which lies in Spon St. (*in vico de Sponna*) in Coventry, in width between the land of the heirs of Geoffrey son of John on the one hand and the land of Roger de Ruyton' on the other and extends in length from the aforesaid street up to the running water according to the metes and bounds made there; to be held to them of the lessors and their heirs, by rendering for six years from the feast of St. Andrew the Apostle A.D. 1304 4s. of silver at the four terms of the year usual in Coventry and then 20s. of silver at the same terms. The lessees will maintain the property in all necessary repairs so that it should remain in as good a state at the end of the term as it was at the beginning of the agreement. Should the lessees die within the term of six years their heirs or assigns should hold until the end of the term by the aforesaid service of 4s. Clause for warranty under pain of 20s. for support of the Holy Land (*ad subsidium terre sancte*). Mutual sealing clause. Witnesses: Robert Baker (*pistore*) then bailiff, John Lewyne then coroner, Richard Kyng, Richard Kay, Roger le Despencere and others.

Indented
Seal extant C.R.O. 1A/C13/50

523 12 August 1306

Grant and demise by Brother Henry, prior of the church of the blessed Mary and the convent of Coventry to Robert le Keu of Coventry, Alice his wife and John their son as long as they shall live of a garden (*gardinum*) with appurtenances in Coventry which lies in Spon St. (*in vico de Sponna*) between the land once of John de Chilton' on the one hand and the land of Andrew de Cundulm' on the other, and 3 selions of arable land with appurtenances in the same vill lying in the field of Spon (*in campo de Sponna*) between the land of the aforesaid Andrew on the one hand and the land of Richard de St. James on the other which tenements were once of Simon de Kyngeslond, and 3 selions of arable land with appurtenances in the same field lying between the land of the aforesaid Andrew on the one hand and the land once of Roger Werkwod on the other, 2 headlands (*foreras*) with appurtenances in the same field of which one lies between the land of John Pyhod on both sides and the other lies between the land of the aforesaid John Pyhod on one side and the land once of the aforesaid Roger on the other, a piece (*peciam*) of land with adjacent meadow and other appurtenances in the same field which is called *Le Waterforlong* and lies between the land of the aforesaid John Pyhod on the one hand and the land of the aforesaid Andrew on the other, and a piece (*peciam*) of land with appurtenances in the same field which is called *Doddescroft* and lies between the land once of John le Flecchere on the one hand and the furlong (*culturam*) which is called *le Spitel Ruydyng* on the other; all the aforesaid tenements with all appurtenances to be held to them for their entire life and to the survivor, of the grantors and their successors, and their church, freely and peacefully, by rendering annually to the chief lords of that fee as the grantors' attorney the services due and by right accustomed, and to the grantors 12s. of silver at the four terms of the year usual in Coventry in equal portions. *Ita quod non licebit eisdem Roberto Alicie nec Johanni aliquid de arboribus in predictis tenementis crescentibus cindere vel prosternere sive excidere nisi ad clausuram dictorum tenementorum et hoc per visum Thesaurariorum nostrorum qui pro tempore fuerint*. Clause for reversion with all improvement (*cum omni melioratione*). Mutual sealing clause. Witnesses: Robert the Baker (*Pistore*), William Grauntpe, Alexander de Stonleye, John Pyhod, William de Braundeston', Adam Russel and others. Coventry, Friday after the feast of St. Laurence A.D. 1306.

Indented (chirograph)
Seal extant C.R.O. 1B/34 EI/I
Endorsed: Thes' Coventr'

HILL AND RADFORD MILLS

524 c.1200–c.1210

Charter of Gerard the Vintner of Coventry, in his free power concerning acquisitions, giving to Gerard his son all the selds beneath his chief burgage in Coventry, the mills of Radford and Hill, the entire land he held of Simon nephew of Nicholas fitz Liulf and the entire land he held of Vincent in Hill St. The grantor undertakes to do nothing whereby the above may be lessened, but should he marry he will give nothing further to the grantee.

Sciant presentes et futuri quod ego Gerardus Vinitor Coventr' in libera potestate mea de libera adquisicione mea dedi et concessi et hac presenti carta mea confirmavi Gerardo filio meo et heredi totas seldas illas que sunt s(u)b(ter) capitali burgagio meo in Coventr' scilicet in longitudine ab exterio[ri][1] ang(u)lo illius selde quam Willelmus Slepus tenuit de me usque ad terram que fuit Nicolai Salmonarii tenend(as) et habendas in capite de priore et conventu ecclesie beate Marie in Coventr' reddendo inde annuatim xd. argenti pro omni servicio seculari, et molendinu(m) de Radeford cum gardino et stagno et vivario et cum croftis et cum mora et cum omnibus pertin(entiis) suis quod tenui de predicta ecclesia et de Willelmo de Brinkelawe reddendo inde annuatim predicte ecclesie ij petras cere et Willelmo de Brinkelawe ijs. argenti et unam libra(m) cimini. Et preterea dedi illi et concessi molend(inum) de Hulla cum prato et cum omnibus pertin(entiis) suis quod tenui de Ricardo filio Ricardi Lorimarii et de Agneta mat(er)tera sua reddendo inde annuatim quinquaginta s(olidos) argenti et xvjd., et totam terram illam quam tenui de Simone nepote Nicol(ai) filii Lithulfi reddendo inde annuatim vjd. argenti et totam terram illam in vico de Hulla quam tenui de Vincentio reddendo inde annuatim vjd. argenti. Istos autem molendinos et terras prenominat(as) dedi et concessi illi et heredibus suis hereditarie ad tenend(os) et habend(os) de predicta ecclesia et de dominis predictis de quibus tenui adeo libere et quiete et honorifice sicuti umquam melius et liberius et firmius tenui et habui in p(o)t(es)tate mea et per eadem predicta servicia et ad eosdem terminos et cartas predictorum dominorum quas habui de predictis molendinis et terris insimul cum terris illi donavi, ita integre quod nec de predictis terris et molend(inis) facia(m) per quod ipse aliquid sit p(er)dens vel heredes sui vel aliquo modo deterioratus et quod si uxore(m) ducere(m) ei inde dec(etero) non facia(m) nec aliquid dabo. Et ut hec mea donacio futuris temporibus robur perpetue firmitatis optineat istas terras et molendinos prenominatos illi et heredibus suis sigilli mei impressione et hujus presentis carte mee confirmatione roboravi. Hiis testibus Nichol(ao) filio Liulphi Milone Barba Ap(r)il(is) et Philipp(o) filio ejus Ricardo de Aula Willelmo de Brinkelawe et filiis ejus Willelmo et Johanne Willelmo filio Umfrei et Johanne filio suo Ricardo filio Forthwini et Willelmo filio suo Hugone filio Martini Rogero filio Herb(ert)i Stephano fratre suo Matheo filio Rogeri Ricardo de Warewic' Petro de Kancia Leuwino Ricardo de Wigornia Willelmo de Repe(n)d' et multis aliis.

[1] Hole here.

This and the following two documents are taken from a roll headed *Carte de molend(in)is de hull' et Radeford* and comprising two oblong strips of parchment. There is stitching at the bottom of the second and narrower strip but the last five, ruled lines are not used. The three charters are complete. (C.R.O. Corporation Ecclesiastical Records Box No. I: Priory).

525 1254–1258

Notification by Master Richard called the Vintner of Coventry of his gift to the church of the blessed Mary of Coventry of his 2 mills of Radford and Hill, his fish-pond of Radford, his moor next to Whitemore and his meadow of Hill below the mill, with specification of the disbursements to be made by the pittancer from the resultant revenue namely to the infirmary, to the guest-house, to the sacrist, in alms for the poor on the grantor's anniversary, and to the warden of the altar of the blessed Mary. Moreover the weak and sick are to be provided for from the fish-pond on specified days as need dictates and abundance allows.

Omnibus Christi fidelibus presens scriptum visuris vel audituris Magister Ricardus dictus Vinitari(us) de Coventr' salutem in domino sempiternam. Noverit universitas vestra me dedisse et assignasse Deo et ecclesie beate Marie de Coventr' dominis meis priori et conv(entui) ejusdem loci pro salute anime mee et antecessorum meorum in liberam puram et perpetuam elemosinam duo molendina mea de Radeford videlicet et de Hulle vivariu(m) meu(m) de Radeford mora(m) mea(m) juxta Wytemor secundum quod se extendit in longitudine et latitudine secundum metas et divisas ibidem factas, ita tamen quod p(re)textu hujus mee donacionis de terra Alani Hodart nec de terra Simonis de Stapelton' nichil exigere possint seu vendicare, pratu(m) meu(m) de Hulle subt(us) stagnu(m); h(ab)end(a) et tene(n)d(a) dictis dominis meis ac ecclesie predicte libere quiete bene et in pace reddendo inde annuatim dominis feodi per manus pytanciar(ii) dictorum prioris et conv(entus) qui pro tempore fuerit pro molendino de Hulle quinquaginta solidos hered(ibus) Roberti de Recha(m) et Ricardi Lorimarii pro eodem molend(ino) et tres solidos pro decima molendinor(um) et h(er)ed(ibus) Gilb(er)ti de Seg(r)ave pro quadam particula terre in mora mea juxta Wytemor quatuor solidos, ita scilicet quod dictus pytanciar(ius) p(ro)curat(us) et executor special(is) hujus rei g(er)ende et exeg(e)nde solvat singulis annis infirmarie de Coventr' xxx^{ta} s(olidos) de predictis, hostilarie ejusdem loci xs., sacriste dicte ecclesie beate Marie vs., ac die aniv(er)sorii[1] mei pitancie conv(entus) Coventr' xs. ita quod expendantur eodem die in esculento[2] et poculento[2] elemosinar(um) eodem die xs. ad distribuc(i)o(ne)m in pane (pro)[3] salute animee mee pauperibus facienda(m), et custodi altaris beate Marie ad unum cereu(m) levandu(m) coram altari beate virginis et perpetuo sustine(n)d(um) xs. De vivario meo predicto sic ordinavi videlicet quod dictus prior et conv(entus) diebus subscriptis videlicet Natal(is) domini Pur(ificationis) Anunc(iationis) Palmar(um) Cene Pasch(e) Assencionis Pentecost(e) sancte Trinitatis Petri et Pauli Assumpcionis Nat(ivitatis) et Omn(ium) Sanctorum de piscaria dicti vivarii p(re)cipue respiciantur debiles vero et egroti cum n(e)cc(essi)ttas exegerit et h(abe)ndancia suffec(er)it de dicta piscar(ia) recreentur. Et ego dictus Magister Ricardus et heredes mei vel mei assign(ati) dictam donacionem et assignacionem dictis priori et conv(entui) et ecclesie eorundem contra omnes homines et feminas warantizabimus inperpetuum. Et ut hec mea donacio et assignacio futuris temporibus p(er)petue firmitatis robur optineant presens scriptum sigilli mei impressione roboravi. Hiis testibus Domino Ricardo de Emundevill' milite Domino Ricardo vicar(io) ecclesie sancti Michaelis Philippo de Winchecombe de Coventr' Willelmo de Allesleg' Henrico Pistore Johanne Aurifabro Pagano Pake Nicholao ad Barra(m) Petro Barun et aliis.

[1] sic [2] sic
[3] interlined

526 Late 1250s

Release, remise and quitclaim by Robert and Richard heirs of Robert de Recham and Richard the Lorimer (*Lorim'*), for themselves and their heirs, to the lord prior and convent of the church of the blessed Mary of Coventry, and to their successors and church, of all right and claim in the mill, mill-pond and meadow of Hill (*hulle*) with appurtenances, and also in 50s. rent *per annum* which they used to receive justly therefrom; with exclusion clause. Sealing clause. Witnesses: Walter Pihod, Philip de Winchecumb', William de Allesleg', Hugh Breton', Pagan Pake, John Godescop, John the Goldsmith (*aurifabro*), Henry Baker (*Pistore*), Adam the clerk and others.

HILL, HILL ST., TOWARDS HILL*

*Towards Hill or towards Hill Mill refers, for the most part at least, to the approach from the east, viz. the streets known in modern times as Abbot's Lane and Upper Well St. This stretch was also known as Well St., and the designations 'Well St. towards Hill Mill' and 'the street towards Hill Mill' (endorsed Well St.) both occur (545–547, 575, 576). Nos. 553, 554 (below) also seem to refer to this stretch, whilst 577 is endorsed as of Hill Cross. On one occasion Hill St. was itself used to designate the section to the east of Hill Mill (535, 536). For other references to Hill St. see 42, 516, 521.

527 c.1200–c.1210

Charter of Richard son of Fordwin giving to Richard son of Aki and his heirs to be held of the grantor and his heirs in fee and inheritance the land which is between the land Stephen son of Herbert held towards Hill (*versus hulle*) and the land Roger son of Lifwi held at the bar (*ad barram*) and in length as it extends up to the land Herbert the Vintner (*vinet'*) held freely [etc.] by rendering annually to the grantor and his heirs 6d. for all service and exaction. Clause for warranty. Richard son of Aki gave 3s. of silver. Witnesses: William son of Durant, William son of Humphrey, Matthew son of Roger, Richard son of Ernis, Richard de Warewich, John the Mercer (*m(er)cennario*), Ralf Waldri(n)g, Elufwinus son of Seiet, Alan the Tanner (*tan(ur)*), Richard Molle, Gilbert de Spaldinge, Robert the Smith (*fabro*), Richard Wole, Walter Forcer, Stephen son of Herbert, William Midnith and many others.

Seal missing W.R.O. 49

528 c.1220–1225

Charter of Walter de Daivill' giving to Richard de Aula of Coventry, for his homage and service, the entire furlong (*culturam*) upon Hill outside Coventry (*super Hulle extra Covintr'*) with all appurtenances which William the Marshal (*marescall'*) held and which he gave to Leticia daughter of Richard de Sutton' his niece (*nepti*) for her homage and service; to be held to him and his heirs of the grantor and his heirs in fee and inheritance freely [etc.], by rendering annually for all service [etc.] 12d. of silver, namely 3d. at each of the feasts of the Annunciation of the blessed Mary, the Nativity of St. John the Baptist, St. Michael and St. Andrew. Clause for warranty. Richard gave 11 marks of silver in recognition. Sealing clause. Witnesses: Henry de Busch(er)vill', Robert de Stivechal', Viellus de Folkeshull, Nicholas son of Nic(holas), Richard de Wigorn', Vincent, Swanus the Parker (*p(ar)car'*), Robert the

Vintner (*vinit'*), William de Wilnhal', William de Repend', Richard the Goldsmith (*aurifabro*), Robert de Stok', William Crude and others.

Seal extant — Harvard Law Library 2.012.7

Walter d'Eyvill was closely associated with the earl of Chester. He witnessed the Magna Carta of Cheshire in 1215/16 (Tait, *Chartulary of St. Werburgh* i, p. 106). In 1232 it was stated that he had functioned as a bailiff of the earl after the death of Walter de Coventry i.e. in the 1220s (*Eyre Rolls 1232*, m14). Henry de Busherville lord of Ansty occurs in 1221 and 1227. He married the daughter of William Picot (*Eyre Rolls 1221*, Nos. 718, 1504; *C.P.R. 1227* No. 316). For William the Marshal and Richard de Sutton see above pp. 9–10.

529 — Early 1220s

Charter of Walter de Davill giving to Richard Meu a third part of the land which Ralf de Radeford held with appurtenances and with free entrance and exit, which land lies between the land Henry Beket held and the land Robert the Vintner (*vinetar'*) held and between the land John Alewi held and the land Robert and Geoffrey held and the land Rimild held; to be held to him and his heirs of the grantor and his heirs in fee and inheritance freely [etc.] by rendering annually 20d. at four terms of the year for all secular service [etc.], namely 5d. at each of the feasts of St. Michael, St. Andrew, St. Mary in March and St. John the Baptist. Warranty and sealing clauses. Witnesses: Viellus (*Viel'*) de Folkishul', Richard de Aula, Hugh son of Martin, Richard Burgeis, Adam de Spo(n)na, Richard the Black (*Nig(r)o*), Warin de Cundeum', Hugh le Neue, Richard Grenec(ur)til, Henry Cesar, William Liuet, Nicholas Caucey and many others.

Seal missing — C.R.O. IA/C12/17

The exact location of this land is uncertain but it would seem to be either upon Hill or between there and Radford.

In 1232 Edith daughter of Ralf de Radford brought an assize of novel disseisin for the recovery of 3 acres in Coventry. The defendants argued that the land in question was of the villeinage of the earl of Chester. The jury upheld this and related that Walter de Coventry, whilst the earl's steward, had leased the land to Ralf for 2s. per annum. After Walter's death, Walter de Aivill the earl's bailiff had taken the land as villein land (*Eyre Rolls 1232*, m14). Henry Beket received 6 acres of land in Stoke from Walter d'Eyvill (C.R.O. 2/172).

530 — Early 1220s

Sale and quitclaim by Margery daughter of Hardekin, in her widowhood and free power, without any reservation by herself or her heirs, to Robert the Vintner (*vinetario*) of all right and claim in the lands which Hardekin her father held of Gerard the Vintner (*Girardo vine[t]*[1]*ario*) father of the aforesaid Robert of the fee of William Picot for 6d. which the aforesaid Robert gave to her. Warranty and sealing clauses. Witnesses: Richard de Aula, Hugh de Allispath', Walter de Allispath, Hugh son of Martin, [ ][1] Ketelbern, Nicholas Fortwin', Richard Burgeis, Richard Meu, William de Wilinhal', Geoffrey de Wilinhal', Richard [ ][1]n, John Fortwin' and many others.

Seal missing — C.R.O. IA/L11–12C/22

[1] The document is torn with some loss along the left.

Again this land would seem to be in the vicinity of Hill.

William Picot occurs in 1199/1200 and in 1221. He was dead by 1227 (*F.F. Warwicks.* Nos. 43, 55; *Eyre Rolls 1221*, Nos. 718, 1504; *C.P.R. 1227*, No. 316).

531 1220s

Charter of Matilda daughter of John de Wittenas in her widowhood and free power giving to Nicholas de Lichesfeld and his heirs a land (*unam terram*) in Coventry upon Hill (*super Hulle*) lying between the land Philip super Hulle held and the land Giliana Sephare the grantor's sister held, and 3½d. rent namely 1d. from Richard de Aula, 1d. from Robert Bretun, 1d. from Richard de Mubray and ½d. from Adam the Vintner (*vinitario*); to be held to him and his heirs of the grantor and her heirs hereditarily, freely [etc.], by rendering annually for all secular service and demand 4d. at four terms, namely 1d. at each of the feasts of St. Andrew, St. Mary in March, St. John the Baptist and St. Michael, and a pair of gloves of ½d. at Easter. Clause for warranty. Nicholas gave 2 marks of silver in recognition. Witnesses: Richard de Aula, Robert de Retha(m), Richard Burg', Peter the Welshman (*Walensi*), William Crude, Adam the Vintner (*vinit'*), Simon de Leicestr', Herbert Bucstan, Ralf son of Baldwin, Reginald de Warewic', Ralf Bissop, Geoffrey Chinch and many others.

Seal extant C.R.O. IA/C12/14a

532 1220s

Charter of Nicholas de Lechisfeld' giving to Reginald his son as long as he lives a land (*unam terram*) in Coventry upon Hill (*super Hulle*) lying between the land Philip super Hulle held and the land Juliana Sefare held, and 4½d. rent namely 1d. from Richard de Aula, 1d. from Robert Breton', 2d. from Richard Mu(m)brai, and ½d. from Adam the Vintner (*vinetario*); to be held to him of the grantor and his heirs freely [etc.], by rendering annually for all secular service and all demand 4d. at 4 terms of the year, namely 1d. at each of the feasts of St. Andrew, St. Mary in March, St. John the Baptist and St. Michael, and 2 pairs of gloves of 1d. at Easter. Clause for warranty. Remainder to Richard son of Roger son of Herbert and his heirs for the above service. Sealing clause. Witnesses: Richard de Aula, Hugh de Alysspad', Richard Burg', William Crude, Walter de Alysph', Adam the Vintner (*vinetar'*), Simon de Leycestr', Robert de Recham, Herbert Bucstan, Adam Biscop', Ralf son of Baldwin, Nicholas Vincent, Vincent the Parker (*p(ar)car'*), Gilbert the Parker (*p(ar)car'*) and others.

Seal extant C.R.O. IA/C12/14b

533 Early 1220s

Sale and quitclaim by Geoffrey Fretherich, without reservation by him or his heirs, to Nicholas Fordwin and his heirs of a land (*unam terram*) which the grantor held of him in Coventry upon Hill (*super Hulle*), namely that which lies between the land Richard Grencurtel held and the land Robert Guterich held entirely and fully just as the land purports in length and in width from the street (*a vico*) up to the water with all appurtenances, for 24s. of silver which Nicholas gave to the grantor. Exclusion and sealing clauses. Witnesses: Richard de Aula, Richard de Wigorn', Robert the Vintner (*vinit'*), Hugh son of Martin, Vincent, Richard de Brug', William

Crude, Richard Burg', Richard Grenecurtel, Hugh le Neue, Ralf son of Baldwin, Adam the clerk (*scriptore*) and many others.

Seal extant W.R.O. 443

This and No. 548 are the first in a series grouped in the Warwick Record Office as deeds of Skinner's field near Hill Mill.

534 1221–1230

Charter of Alice de Witemora widow of Anketill Loccard, in her widowhood and free power, giving to Geoffrey Penivader a moiety of her land at Hill (*dimidietatem terre mee super hullam*) which she held of William Fordwin, namely the moiety which is nearer to the land Michael the Dyer (*tinctor*) held in length and in width as it purports from the street (*a vico*) up to the arable land which William Fordwin held with appurtenances; to be held to him, and his heirs of the grantor and her heirs in fee and inheritance freely [etc.], by rendering annually 2s. of silver at four terms of the year, namely 6d. at each of the feasts of St. Michael, St. Andrew, St. Mary in March and St. John the Baptist. When the earl of Chester takes aid from his burgesses Geoffrey and his heirs will be quit for 2d. (*Et quando Dominus Comes Cestr' ceperit auxiliu(m) de Burg(e)nsibus suis predictus Galfridus et heredes sui quieti erunt per duos denarios*). Clause for warranty. Geoffrey gave 8s. of silver in recognition. Witnesses: William son of Humphrey (*Umfr'*), Geoffrey the Goldsmith (*aurifabro*), Hugh de Luddelowe, Robert Norreis, Richard Molle, Henry Holdeburt', William Hagene, Michael the Dyer (*tinctore*), William Palm(er), Nicholas Wiele, William de Luddelowe, William Tok', Alan the Tanner (*tann'*) and many others.

Seal extant P.R.O. A 11186

Anketill Loccard was living in 1221. By 1230 Alice had re-married (*F.F. Warwicks.* 275; *Curia Regis Rolls*, vol. xiv, 1230–1232, p. 18).

535 1240s

Charter of Henry son of Michael the Dyer (*Tinctoris*) of Coventry giving to Geoffrey Penifad(er), his heirs or to whom he will wish to give, bequeath or assign, the land in Hill St. (*in vico de Hulle*) which lies between the land William de Soleby held on the one hand and the land of the same Geoffrey on the other in length from the high street up to the red ditch (*a vico magno usque ad ruffam foveam*) in length and in width as is manifest and according to the metes and bounds made there; to be held to him, his heirs or assigns, of the grantor and his heirs freely [etc.], by rendering 25d. of silver at the four terms usual according to the custom of Coventry for all secular service and exaction. Clause for warranty. Geoffrey gave 8s. of silver in recognition. Sealing clause. Witnesses: John the Butcher (*mascecrario*), William Alwine, William le Paum(er), Robert de Corleg', William Haune, William Segrim, Nicholas Fordwin', Alexander de Ruton', John son of Alan, Richard the Tanner (*tannatore*), Nicholas de Smithisford, John the White (*albo*) the clerk.

Seal missing P.R.O. A 11187

536 Mid 1240s

Charter of Henry son of Michael the Dyer (*Tinctoris*) of Coventry (*Cowintr'*) giving to Geoffrey Penifader, his heirs or to whom he will wish to give, bequeath or assign, the land in Hill St. (*in vico de hulle*) which lies between the land William de Solebi held on the one hand and the land of the same Geoffrey on the other in length from the high street up to the red ditch (*a magno vico usque ad ruffa(m) fovea(m)*) and in width as it purports by the metes and bounds made there with all appurtenances; to be held of the grantor and his heirs freely [etc.], by rendering annually 1d. of silver at four terms of the year, and 2s. to the lords of the fee at the terms usual and customary in Coventry (*Cowintr'*) for all secular service. Clause for warranty. Geoffrey gave 3s. in recognition. Sealing clause. Witnesses: Richard de Fonte, John son of Simon, Adam the Vintner (*Vinitar'*), William Toli, Adam the clerk, Matthew Moub(ray), Samson de Font(e), Alexander de Ruton', John Aleyn, Vincent (*Wincent'*) Toki, Vincent (*Winc'*) Molle, Richard the Tanner (*tannator'*), John de Denestapel.

Seal missing P.R.O. A 11121

537 c.1250s

Charter of Geoffrey Penifader giving to Alice his daughter for her service the entire land with appurtenances at Hill Mill (*apud molendinum de Hulle*) in Coventry which lies between the land William de Solebi held and the land William de Huchinton' held and in length up to the red ditch (*rubeam fovea(m)*) according to the metes and bounds made there; to be held to her and her heirs of the grantor and his heirs freely [etc.], by rendering annually a pair of gloves worth 1d. at the Nativity of St. John the Baptist, and to the lords of that fee the service due annually, namely 2s. to the heirs of John Vincent at the four terms of the year fixed in Coventry, 2s. to Adam the Vintner (*Vinitario*) and the heirs of Matilda his wife at the same terms, and 1d. to Henry son of Michael at the same four terms for all secular service and demand. Warranty and sealing clauses. Witnesses: John de Dunstapel, John Simu(n)t, Richard de Hulle, William Haune, William Toli, John Alein, Vincent, William le Paumer' and others.

Seal missing P.R.O. A 4436

538 Early 1230s

Charter of Herbert son of Jordan giving to Peter his son the entire land towards Hill Mill (*versus molendinu(m) de hulle*) which he held of Nicholas Forthwin' with the tenter (*tentore*) and all appurtenances, namely that which lies between the land Geoffrey de Wilenhal' held and the land John Blacwin' held in length and in width according to the metes and bounds made there; to be held to him and his heirs, of the grantor and his heirs freely [etc.], by rendering annually 6d. of silver at four terms of the year according to the usage of the vill of Coventry, and a pair of gloves worth ½d. or ½d. at Whitsuntide for all service and exaction. Warranty and sealing clauses. Witnesses: William the reeve (*p(re)posito*), Richard son of Lefwin', David de Fonte, William le Cnave, Robert de Feugers, Geoffrey de Wilenhal', John Blacwin', William de Spalding, Robert son of Ham(o), Robert Bretun, Roger de Lodelowe, William the Palmer (*Palm'*), Richard Kiu, William le Norreis and others.

Seal missing C.R.O. 2/39

539 Late 1230s

Charter of Margaret daughter of Hugh de Ludelawe in her widowhood and free power giving to Geoffrey de Hamtona her entire land towards Hill Mill (*molend' de hille*) which Hugh the grantor's father gave to her in length and in width as the land purports according to the metes and bounds made there; to be held to him and his heirs or to whom he will wish to assign, of the grantor and his heirs in fee and inheritance freely [etc.], by rendering annually 4d. of silver at four terms of the year according to the usage of the vill of Coventry for all secular service [etc.]. Clause for warranty. Geoffrey gave 8s. of silver in recognition. Sealing clause. Witnesses: William the Palmer (*Palm'*), Robert de Feug(ers), Robert de Pailint(on), William de Pailinton', Richard de Mub(r)ai, William son of Toli, William Hagne, William le Noreis, Richard le Tanur', Henry Holeburn', Ernaldus de Londona, Alexander son of Ralf, Adam kinsman of (*gen(er)e*) Colborn' and many others.

Seal extant C.R.O. 2/164

540 Late 1230s–1243

Charter of Adam the Vintner (*vinetarius*) of Coventry giving to God and to the church of St. Mary and the monks of Stoneleigh (*Stanl'*) 12d. rent with appurtenances in Coventry, namely that which Walter son of Henry le Tannur was accustomed and bound [to render] to him from certain land with appurtenances in Hill St. (*in hullestret*) which lies between the land of Richard Shayl and the land Vincent held and where his tenter-yard stood as divided by fixed bounds (*ubi tentorium suum stetit sicut per certas divisas dividitur*), and which extends from the said street in length up to the channel of water (*ductum aque*); to be held in pure alms with appurtenances and liberties well [etc.] and quit from all service and secular exaction. The monks gave 10s. to the grantor, and 12d. to his wife. Clause for warranty. Witnesses: Nicholas de Wythibroc, Osbert the clerk, William le Bucher, Ralf the Miller (*molendinar'*), Richard Burgeys, John Hod, Anketill son of Robert, Roger the Dyer (*tinctore*), Nicholas Vincent and many others.

Seal extant P.R.O. B 8937

541 Early 1240s

Sale and quitclaim by Vincent son of Reginald Kempe to Robert son of Roger de Cornlegh', his heirs or to whomsoever he will wish to give, sell or assign, the 12d. rent which William le Knave used to render annually from the land which he held of the grantor in Coventry towards Hill (*Hulle*), namely from the land which is between the land Thomas the Dyer (*tinctor*) held and the quarry (*q(u)arera(m)*) which John le Knave held; to be held as freely and quietly as the grantor held in chief of the lord prior of Coventry and by the same service, namely 6d. of silver at four terms according to the usage of Coventry. Robert gave 2s. of silver. Sealing clause. Witnesses: Richard de Fonte, John Umfrid', Richard Herb(er)t, Robert de Feug(er)s, John Sym', Geoffrey Pathe, William Toli, William Palmer (*Palm'*), Richard Leofwin, Robert Ham', Jurdan Halyday, William de Paylinton' and others.

Seal extant C.R.O. IA/CI
Endorsed: Carta Vinc' Molle

542 Late 1250s–early 1260s

Charter of John son of John Vincent' of Coventry giving to Ranulph de Stivichale 6d. annual rent in Coventry which he used to receive from a certain part of his land in Hill St. (*in vico de Hulle*) which John le Bocmonger once held of the grantor, which lies between the land Nicholas de Cestre held on the one hand and the land Batemo(n) Coppinc held on the other and which extends from the watercourse up to the road (*iter*) which extends to Hill Mill (*molendin' de hulle*) in length and in width according to the metes and bounds made there; to be held to him, his heirs or assigns, with all appurtenances *et contingentiis aysiam(en)t(iis) et achettis et Increm(en)tis dicti Redd(itus) pertinentibus* of the grantor and his heirs freely [etc.] with all liberties and easements pertaining to the aforesaid tenement and rent within and without the vill of Coventry, by rendering annually a clove-gillyflower at Easter for all secular services, customs, actions, demands, suits of court pertaining to the aforesaid rent. Ranulph gave 2s. of silver beforehand. Warranty and sealing clauses. Witnesses: Walter the White (*Blundo*) of Coventry, Alexander de Glovernia, Robert the clerk, Pagan Pake, Peter Barun, Richard Schore, Hugh Schail, Robert de Coundulme, William Louwyn, Robert de Chilton', Henry Baker (*pistore*), Geoffrey the clerk, Hugh Breton' and others.

Seal missing G.H. 274

543 25 March 1268

Agreement made at the feast of St. Mary in March 1268 whereby Ranulf de Stivechal' has leased and demised at farm to Richard Schore of Coventry his entire land lying upon Hill (*super hulle*) with appurtenances, namely that which lies between the land Adam Hert held on the one hand and the land Richard le Koker held on the other in length from the royal highway (*a via regia*) up to the watercourse running from the mill-pond of Hill (*de stagno de hulle*); to be held to him, his heirs or assigns, of the grantor and his heirs for a term of 8 years from the said feast of St. Mary freely [etc.] with all liberties and easements pertaining, by rendering in the last four years of the said term from year to year 2s. of silver at the four terms of the year customary in the vill of Coventry for all secular service and demand. Clause for warranty. Ranulf gave 9s. of silver in recognition. Clause for reversion at the end of the term. Sealing clause [chirograph]. Witnesses: Nicholas de Barra then bailiff, Robert de Chilton', Richard Meu, Hugh Scail, Robert de Cundulm', Adam Hert, Gilbert Wry, John son of Ceve, Thomas the clerk and others.

Seal missing G.H. 283A

544 c.29 September 1287

Lease by Jolinus de Stivechale to John called (*dicto*) Abbot of Coventry at Michaelmas 15 Edward I of a certain curtilage with a certain annual rent in Coventry in Hill Street (*in quodam vico qui discitur Hulle Strete*), namely that which lies with appurtenances between the land of William le P(ar)ker on the one hand and the land formerly of Simon le Bogmonger' on the other in length and in width as is manifest, and the annual rent to be received from the land which the heirs of the aforesaid Simon le Bogmonger' hold by the service of 14d. and which lies next to the curtilage of the aforesaid John; to be held for a term of 10 years freely [etc.] by rendering, the aforesaid John, his heirs and assigns, to the aforesaid Jolinus, his heirs and assigns, a clove-gillyflower at Easter for all service and demand. Clause for warranty. John gave 7s. of silver of good and legal money. Sealing clause. Witnesses: Henry Baker (*pistor'*) then bailiff, Robert de Chilton', Adam Hert, William le P(ar)lur, Richard le Purser and others.

Seal missing G.H. 293

545 Late 1260s–early 1270s

Remise and quitclaim by Petronilla widow of Simon de Bannebur' in her widowhood and free power to William brother of Matilda de Aula of Coventry of all right and claim in a certain curtilage in the vill of Coventry with appurtenances which lies in the street towards Hill Mill (*in vico versus molendinum de Hulle*) between the land Henry

Dru once held on the one hand and the land Robert de Feug(e)rs held on the other; to be held to him, his heirs or whatsoever assigns, freely [etc.], by rendering annually as the perpetual attorneys of the grantor and her heirs to Robert de Cornley 16d. of silver at the four terms of the year fixed and customary in the vill of Coventry for all secular service [etc.]. Sealing clause. Witnesses: Henry Baker (*pistore*) then bailiff, Alexander de Ruiton', William Toli, William Wylas, Walter Bacun, Osbert the Miller (*molend'*) and others.

Seal extant C.R.O. IA/EC13/67

546 Late 1260s–early 1270s

Charter of Walter Bacun, with the counsel and assent of Joan his wife, giving to William brother of Matilda de Aula a certain curtilage with appurtenances which John son of Stephen le Truggere once held, namely that which lies in Coventry in the street towards Hill Mill (*in vico versus molendinu(m) de hulle*) in the Prior's half (*ex parte p(r)ioris*) between the land Henry Dru once held towards the east and the land Robert de Feug(er)s once held towards the west; to be held to him, his heirs or whatsoever assigns, of the grantor and his heirs freely [etc.], in length and in width according to the metes and bounds made there, by rendering annually 12d. of silver at four terms of the year according to the custom of the vill of Coventry for all secular service [etc.]. Clause for warranty. In return William quitclaimed certain land next to his garden (*Gardinum*) once of Gunnilda daughter of Guy the Smith (*Gunnild' filie Wydonis fabri*). Sealing clause. Witnesses: Henry Baker (*pistore*) then bailiff, Robert de Chilton', Alexander de Ruiton', William Toli, Robert de Lond', John Yngeram, John the White (*albo*), Roger the Miller (*molendinar'*), William Kelle, Thomas the clerk and others.

Seal missing G.H. 289

Endorsed: Carta terre jacentis in vico fontis versus molend(in)u(m) hulle [quam][1] Will(elmu)s frater Matild' de Aula.

[1] interlined

547 1270s

Charter of William brother of Matilda de Aula of Coventry giving to Richard son of William de Colsull' a certain curtilage with appurtenances in the vill of Coventry which John son of Stephen le T(ur)uggere once held, namely that which lies in the street towards Hill Mill (*in vico versus molendinu(m) de hulle*) in the Prior's half (*ex parte p(r)ioris*) between the land which Henry Dru at one time held towards the east and the land Robert le Feug(er)s once [held] towards the west, which curtilage the grantor had by the gift of Matilda his sister and by the confirmation of Walter Bacun the lord of the fee; to be held to him, his heirs or assigns, of the grantor and his heirs freely [etc.], in length and in width according to the metes and bounds made there, by rendering annually to the lords of that fee, namely Walter Bacun and his heirs as the perpetual attorneys of the grantor and his heirs, 12d. of silver at the four terms of the year fixed and customary in the vill of Coventry, and to the grantor, his heirs or assigns, a clove-gillyflower at Easter for all secular service [etc.]. Clause for warranty. Richard gave 7s. of silver in recognition beforehand. Sealing clause. Witnesses: Henry Baker (*pistore*) then bailiff, Robert de Chilton', Thomas Fakinha(m), Alexander de Ruiton', Walter Bacun, John de Wikewin', Henry the Painter (*pictore*), John le Loker, Thomas the clerk and others.

Seal extant G.H. 291

548 1280s

Charter of Richard de Colesul chaplain giving to Thomas le Mubray 3 selions with appurtenances next to Coventry (*juxta Coventr'*) which lie between the land of Martin Colbrond on the one hand and the land once of John Simon (*Simonis*) on the other in width, and in length from the royal highway which leads towards Radford up to the meadow of Hill Mill (*a Regia via que ducit versus Radeforde usque ad pratum de Hulne mulne*) in length and in width just as the said selions purport according to the metes and bounds made there; the said 3 selions with appurtenances of which Nicholas once the grantor's father enfeoffed John Simon (*Simone(m)*) by charter to be held to him, his heirs or assigns, of the grantor, his heirs and assigns freely [etc.], by rendering annually a pair of gloves worth ½d. or ½d. at Easter for all secular service [etc.]. Warranty and sealing clauses. Witnesses: Henry Baker (*Pistore*) then bailiff, Robert de Chilton', John Thole, Thomas Selet, Walter Bakun, John de Cleybroc and others.

Seal missing W.R.O. 444
Endorsed: Carta ab alta via versus hullemell'

549 c.29 September 1287

Agreement whereby Nicholas de St. Mark (*sancto marco*) with the assent and good will of Alice his wife leased and demised at farm to John Tole of Coventry certain land in Hill Field (*Hullefeld*) once of Alice ad Fontem which lies in width between the land of Thomas Marie on the one hand and the land which was once of Richard Gilbert on the other and extends in length from the royal highway (*a regali via*) which leads from Coventry towards Radford (*Radeforde*) up to Hill Meadow (*Hullemedewe*); to be held with appurtenances as is manifest to him, his heirs or assigns, of them and their heirs well [etc.] for a term of 40 years from Michaelmas, 15 Edward I; to be held by rendering 6s. of silver at 2 terms of the year namely 3s. at Easter and 3s. at Michaelmas for all secular service [etc.]. Clause for warranty. John gave 10s. sterling beforehand. Mutual sealing clause [chirograph]. Witnesses: Henry Baker (*pistor'*) then bailiff in Coventry, Robert de Chilton', Thomas le Moubray, Walter Banne, Robert Herbert, John de Cundulme, Thomas Marie, John Pyhod, Roger the clerk and others.

Indented
Seal extant C.R.O. IB/15 EI

550 5 September 1294

Charter of Hugh Schail of Coventry giving to Emma his daughter a certain curtilage with appurtenances in the vill of Coventry in Hill St. (*in vico de hulle*) which lies between the land of William le Parker coroner on the one hand and the land of the aforesaid Hugh on the other in length and in width as is manifest according to the metes and bounds made there; to be held to her and the heirs issuing from her body, of the grantor and his heirs, freely [etc.]. Clause for reversion should the grantee die without bodily heir. The grantee is to render annually to the chief lords of that fee ½d. of silver at Easter for all secular service [etc.]. Warranty and sealing clauses. Witnesses: Henry Baker (*Pistore*) of Coventry then bailiff, William Lotemon, Robert in Anglio[1], Richard le Dobber, Robert Fackon and others. Sunday before the Nativity of the blessed Virgin Mary 22 Edward I.

Seal extant C.R.O. IB/22EI/2b

[1] sic

551 1294–1297

Charter of Richard Shal son of Hugh of Coventry giving to Emma his sister a curtilage with all appurtenances in the vill of Coventry in Hill St. (*in vico de Hulle*) which lies between the land of William le P(ar)cher of Coventry on the one hand and the land which William de Caldicote once held on the other in length and in width as is manifest according to the metes and bounds there; to be held to her and the legitimately begotten heirs of her body, of the grantor and his heirs freely [etc.]. Clause for reversion should the grantee die without bodily heir. The grantee is to render annually to the chief lord of the fee ½d. at Easter for all secular service [etc.]. Warranty and sealing clauses. Witnesses: Henry Baker (*pistor'*), William Lotemon, William le P(ar)chur, Robert in Anglulo[1], Robert Faccon and many others.

Seal, fragment only C.R.O. IB/22EI/2a

[1] sic

552 c.1290–1297

Charter of William Seleth of Coventry clerk giving to John de Hales dyer in Coventry (*in Cov' Tinctori*) and Margaret his wife a curtilage in Hill St. (*in vico de Hulle*) in Coventry which lies in width between the lane (*venellam*) which leads from Dead Lane (*Dedelone*) towards Hill Mill (*molendinum de Hulle*) on the one hand and the land of William de Sowe on the other and extends in length from the land of William de Copston' up to the watercourse (*filum aque*) according to the metes and bounds made there; to be held with all appurtenances to them and the heirs or assigns of the same John, of the grantor and his heirs well [etc.], by rendering 2s. of silver at the four terms of the year usual and fixed in the vill of Coventry, and to John le Vineter of Coventry and his heirs ½d. of silver at Easter for all secular services [etc.] as perpetual attorneys of the grantor and his heirs. Clause for warranty. John and Margaret gave ½ mark beforehand. Sealing clause. Witnesses: Henry Baker (*Pistore*) then bailiff of Coventry, William le Parker then coroner, Thomas le Moubray, John Thole, John Pyhod, John Abbot, William de Copston', Roger le Neue, Roger the clerk and others.

Seal extant C.R.O. 1A/C/47

WELL ST.*

*See above p. 250. For other references to Well St. see 221, 589, 591, 592, 598, 599.

553 c.1200–c.1210

Charter of Richard son of Ernis giving to William Bacun and his heirs, to be held of the grantor and his heirs in fee and inheritance, the land which is between the land Herbert son of Jordan held and the land Roger son of Herbert held, freely [etc.] by rendering annually 12d. for all service [etc.]. Clause for warranty. William gave ½ mark of silver. Witnesses: William de Brinkel', Gerard Vineter and Gerard his son, Richard de Aula, Matthew son of Roger, Hugh son of Martin, Richard de Warewic, John M(er)cer, Walter Bulli, William the White smith (*blundo fabro*), Haldanus Careter, Gilbert the Butcher (*carnifice*), Hugh the Butcher (*carnif'*), Richard son of Aki, Nicholas son of Everard and many others.

Seal extant Harvard 2.012.6
Endorsed: in vic' fo(n)t'

554 c.1210–c.1220

Sale and quitclaim by Master Clement de Newerc without any reservation by him or his successors to William de Waure and his heirs of the entire land in Well St. (*In vico de fonte*) which he held of Roger de Cornleg' and which Mary Pepin held, entirely and fully with all appurtenances from the street up to the watercourse (*de vico usque ad filum aque*) and of all right in that land for 10 marks of silver which William gave; to be held hereditarily of the aforesaid Roger de Cornleg' and his heirs as freely as the vendor held and by the same service of 2s. *per annum* to be paid at four terms, namely 6d. at each of the feasts of St. Mary in March, St. John the Baptist, St. Michael and St. Andrew for all service and exaction. In like manner [he has sold] the land he held of Robert the Locksmith (*Loccario*) by the service of 1d., and entirely quitclaimed and handed over with the aforesaid land the charters and confirmations which he had concerning those lands. Warranty and sealing clauses. Witnesses: Roger de Camvill', Thomas de Estleg', William de Hardredeshull', Henry de Rokeby, Richard de Aula, Vincent, Hugh son of Martin, William de Wilnhal', William de Franketon, Simon de Sowe, Richard de Waure and many others.

Seal missing P.R.O. D 7694

Roger de Camville had succeeded by 1207 and was dead by 1230 (*V.C.H. Warwicks*, IV, p. 206). Thomas de Astley had married one of his sisters and co-heirs (*ibid.*, p. 211). William de Hartshill died in 1226 (*Excerpt. e Rot. Fin.* i, p. 149).

555 c.1210–c.1220

Sale and quitclaim by Hugh de Arraz, entirely and without any reservation by him or his heirs, to William the Cordwainer (*Corduanario*) of his entire land in Well St., Coventry (*in vico fontis de Coventr'*) with appurtenances which lies between the land Alan the Tanner (*Tanator*) held and the land Gilbert de Ruton' held, and of all right in the same land; to be held to him and his heirs hereditarily, in chief of the same lords from whom the grantor held as freely and by the same service. William gave 7s. of silver. Sealing clause. Witnesses: William son of Humphrey (*Umfr'*), John his son, Roger de Cornl', Hugh de Luddelowe, Richard Molle, Richard de Warewic', Samson his son, Leofwin son of Jordan, Alan the Tanner (*tanatore*), Adam son of Adam, Walter son of John, David the Vintner (*vinit'*) and many others.

Seal extant C.R.O. IA/C31

556 1220s

Charter of Walter the Deacon (*Diaconus*) son of Henry de Fonte giving to Richard [his] brother and his heirs the land in Well St. (*in vico fontis*) which Henry the grantor's father held of Richard son of Ernis which lies between the land Elias the Skinner (*heli(a)s pelliparius*) held and the land Richard the grantor's brother held of William Blandiman and 6d. rent from the aforesaid land which William Blandiman used to render to the grantor, and also 12d. which David de Fonte used to render to the grantor for the service of a pair of gloves; to be held of the grantor and his heirs freely [etc.] by rendering annually 6d. of silver at four terms of the year according to the custom of the vill of Coventry and a pair of gloves at Easter for all service and exaction. Clause for warranty. Richard gave 20s. of silver. Sealing clause. Witnesses: Sir H. the priest (*p(re)sb(ite)ro*), Matthew son of Roger, William de Wilnhal', Adam Cusin, Richard de Warewic, Sampson his son, Simon de Leicestr', Simon the Baker (*pistor'*), J. his son, J. Mos', Elias the Skinner (*helys pellipar'*), H. Dru, John his son and others.

Seal missing C.R.O. IA/EC13/105
Endorsed: De Waltero de fonte.

557 Mid–late 1230s

Sale and quitclaim by Symon son of Richard, from himself and his heirs, to Richard son of Henry de Fonte and his heirs, or to whomsoever he will wish to give or assign, of his entire land in Well St. (*in vico fontis*) with 10d. rent from the forge (*de fabrica*) of the Market-place (*de foro*) of the lord prior and of all right and claim in lands and rents in Coventry (*Coventreia*); to be held in chief of the lord prior of Coventry (*Coventreia*) to him, his heirs or assigns, as freely as any of the grantor's ancestors and by the same service, namely 14d. per annum for all service. Richard gave 22s. of silver. Warranty and sealing clauses. Witnesses: Ralf de Arrabi, John son of William Unfrey then reeve (*p(re)po(s)ito*), Richard son of Roger Herbert, Robert de Feugers, Osbert Durdent, Richard Burgeys, Philip de Winchecumbe, William de Wilnhale, Adam Cosin, Richard son of Leuwin', Symon de Daventre, John son of Simon, Samson son of Richard and others.

Seal extant C.R.O. 2/161

558 Late 1230s

Gift and quitclaim by William Blandimer of Coventry to Richard de Fonte and his heirs or to whomsoever he will wish to give, sell or assign, a certain messuage with its appurtenances and liberties in Well St. (*in vico fontis*), namely that which the aforesaid Richard formerly held of him in length and in width according to the metes and bounds; to be held in chief of the lord prior and the convent of Coventry as freely [etc.] as the grantor held and by the same service namely 6d. of silver annually to the said prior and convent for all secular service [etc.]. Exclusion and warranty clauses. Richard gave ½ mark of silver. Sealing clause. Witnesses: Matthew de Cimit(er)io, Symon de Leycestr', Samson' son of Richard, John son of Symon, John Parcam', John el Mos, Adam Cosin, Symon de Davintr' and others.

Seal extant C.R.O. 2/144
Endorsed: De Will' fil' albi fabri

559 Early 1240s

Charter of David de Fonte giving to Margery his sister and her heirs or to whomsoever she will wish to give, bequeath or assign a certain part of his land in Well St. Coventry (*in vico fontis de Coventr'*), namely a certain moor (*moram*) with appurtenances which lies between the land of Amicia le Bel on the one hand and the land of the same Amicia on the other in length and in width as is manifest and according to the metes and bounds made there; to be held of the grantor and his heirs freely [etc.] by rendering annually 12d. of silver at the four terms of the year fixed according to the custom of Coventry and a pair of gloves worth a ½d. or ½d. at Easter for all secular service [etc.]. Notification that the grantor has attorned Margery his sister, her heirs or assigns, to make the aforesaid service of 12d. to the lord prior and convent of Coventry for himself and his heirs, saving the service of the aforesaid gloves to himself and his heirs. Clause for warranty. Margery gave 15s. of silver in recognition. Sealing clause. Witnesses: Osbert the clerk (*clerico*), Richard de Fonte, Richard Burgeys, Robert de Feugers, Robert Haum(un)t, Richard Leuwin, William le Paum(er), John Fordwin', Robert de Corleg', William Toly and others.

Seal missing C.R.O. 2/143
Endorsed: hered' Willelmi Palm' teneatur solvere de ten' in qua Willelmus lust(ur)ley manet quond' Rogeri Oky in vico font'

560 Mid–late 1270s

Charter of John son and heir of Richard de Fonte in Coventry giving to Nicholas son of Geoffrey de St. Medard and Alice his wife in free marriage his entire chief messuage against the well (*totum Capital' mesuagium meum contra Fontem*) which he had in Well St., Coventry (*in vico Fontis de Coventr'*) with his entire arable land and appurtenant meadow which he had in the territory of the same vill without any reservation and with all appurtenances, liberties and easements within and without the vill pertaining to such a tenement (*tanto tenemento*), and also his stone house (*Domum meam Lapideam*) with all appurtenances outside the bar in St. Nicholas St., Coventry (*extra Barram in vico beati Nicholai Coventr'*), 2 houses in Bishop St. (*in vico Ep'li*) next to the houses once of Agnes Pyhod on the northern side, 16s. annual rent to be taken from the houses which William de Allisley used to hold of the grantor, 16d. annual rent to be taken from the houses which Robert de Fonte used to hold of the grantor next to the houses of the aforesaid John on the southern side in Cook St. (*in vico Cocy*), and 3s. 6d. annual rent to be taken from the houses which Thomas de Fakinham held of the grantor namely from the houses nearer to the hall (*Aulam*) of the said Thomas on the western side in Well St., Coventry (*in vico Fontis Coventreye*);

to be held to them and the heirs legitimately begotten from Alice, of the grantor and his heirs freely [etc.], with reversion to the aforesaid John or Richard his brother should Alice die without such heir without contradiction by anyone, by rendering annually to the lords of the fee the service due and accustomed, and to the grantor and his heirs 1d. at Easter for all secular service [etc.]. Warranty and sealing clauses. Witnesses: [Sir] Geoffrey de St. Medard, Sir Robert Luterel, knights, Sir Roger rector of the church of Clyne, Robert de Chiltun' in Coventry, Henry Baker (*pistor'*) of the same, John Thole of the same, Thomas de Fackinham, Thomas le Moubray, Anketell de Coventr' clerk and others.

Seal extant C.R.O. 2/158

Robert Luterel was under age when his father died between Nov. 1269 and Feb. 1270. He was in possession of his estates, however, by 1276 (*C.P.R. 1266–72* pp. 392, 407; *G.E.C.* vol. VIII, p. 286). According to the Peterborough Chronicle Geoffrey de St. Medard, of Thornhaugh, Northants., was predeceased by his son Geoffrey and died in 1280 leaving his grandson Nicholas as heir (see *V.C.H. Northants.* II, p. 530). However, a Geoffrey de St. Medard was returned as holding the family estates in 1284 (*Feudal Aids* IV, p. 443).

561 1270s

Grant and quitclaim by Matilda widow of John de Witeley in Coventry (*Cowentr'*), in her lawful power and widowhood, to Nicholas de St. Medard and Alice his wife and their heirs of all right and claim in all the lands and tenements which were once of John de Witeley, her husband, in name of her dower, in the vill and territory of Coventry (*Cowentria*), namely in the lands and tenements which Nicholas and Alice had of the gift of John son of Richard de Fonte. Nicholas and Alice gave 10s. of silver for her urgent business (*in meo urgenti Negocio*). Sealing clause. Witnesses: Sir Roger rector of the church of Cline, Robert de Chiltern' of Coventry then bailiff, Roger Abel of the same, Henry Baker (*pistore*) of the same, Thomas de Fakenham, Thomas le Mubray and others.

Seal extant C.R.O. IA/EC13/101

562 Late 1280s

Grant and demise by Robert son of Simon called Cook (*dicti Coci*) of Berkswell (*Berkeswell'*) chaplain to Master Thomas de Canelee and Richard his brother of the entire tenement which the grantor had in Coventry in Well St. (*in vico de fonte*) by the lease and grant of Nicholas de St. Medard and Alice his wife for a term of 40 years, which tenement is almost opposite the well (*ex opposito fere fontis*) which is called *Throstlewell'*, namely that which Alice widow of Richard de Fonte once held and which is situated between the land or messuage (*terr' seu mansionem*) which John de Fillongeleye once held on the one hand and the lands of John Abbot, Walter Bacun, Agnes Pyod, Nicholas and Richard Bangeleys on the other according to the metes and bounds in length and in width made there; the right and term which the grantor had in the said tenement to be held to them and the heirs or assigns of the same Richard of the grantors, their heirs or assigns, for 40 years from the time when the grantor received the land from the said Nicholas and Alice which was in 15 Edward I, by rendering annually to the aforesaid Nicholas and Alice and their heirs 6s. of silver at the four terms of the year usual in the vill of Coventry for all secular service, suit of court, exaction or demand. *Et ut predicti magister Thomas et Ricardus vel eorum alter teneant vel teneat de predicto Nicholao et Alicia modo quo ego tenui scriptum meum eisdem magistro Thome et Ricardo liberavi et tradidi.* Thomas and Richard gave 1 mark of silver beforehand. Warranty and sealing clauses. Witnesses: Robert de Chyltona, John Tole, Thomas Moubrey, John de Halys, John le Gaunter, William Kelle and others.

Seal extant C.R.O. IA/Misc.I/31

563 Early–mid 1290s

Charter of Nicholas son and heir of Sir Geoffrey de St. Medard and Alice his wife giving to Alexander son of Simon de Stonel' and Eleanor (*Elionore*) his wife for their service their entire chief messuage against the well (*totum capitale mesuagium nostrum contra fontem*) which they had in Well St., Coventry (*in vico fontis de Coventr'*) with their entire arable land and appurtenant meadow in the territory of the same vill and with all other appurtenances, liberties and easements within and without the vill without any reservation, and also their entire stone house (*domum nostram lapideam*) with appurtenances outside the bar in St. Nicholas St., Coventry (*extra Barram in vico beati Nicholai Coventr'*) and 2 houses in Bishop St. (*in vico Episcopi*) next to the houses once of Agnes Pyot on the northern side, 16s. annual rent to be taken from the houses which Robert de Fonte used to hold in Cook St. (*in vico Coci*) and 3s. 6d. annual rent to be taken from the houses which Thomas de Fakenham used to hold namely from the houses nearer to the hall (*Aule*) of the said Thomas on the western side in Well St., Coventry (*in vico fontis Coventr'*), all of which they had by the gift and enfeoffment of John son and heir of Richard de Fonte in Coventry; all the aforesaid houses, lands, rents and all else belonging to the aforesaid tenement in whatsoever way and wheresoever to be held to them, their heirs or assigns, well [etc.] by making to the chief lords of those fees the services due and accustomed. Warranty and sealing clauses. Witnesses: Sirs Robert Lut(er)el and William de Colevyl knights, Robert de Potton', William de Lyndon', John de Holt, Robert de Schyltren' in Coventry, Robert Baker (*Pistore*) of the same, John Thole, Angtell de Coventr' and others.

2 seals missing C.R.O. IA/Misc.II/45

Sir Robert Luterel was dead by 18 June 1297 (*C.I. P.M.* vol. III, No. 406). Sir William de Coleville, a scion of the Colevilles of Normanton and Muston Leics. was living in 1288 (*ibid.* vol. II, p. 688).

564 c.25 March 1239

Lease by Adam son of Andrew de Coventr' to Alexander de Ruton' and his heirs or to whomsoever he will wish to assign, of his entire land in Coventry in Well St. (*in vico fontis*), namely that which lies between the land Robert le Salter held and the land Osbert the Oil-seller (*olearius*) held in length and in width as the land purports with all appurtenances; to be held of the grantor and his heirs freely [etc.] from the feast of St. Mary in March A.D. 1239 *luna tunc currente per quinque* for a term of 12 years by the service of 4s. of silver per annum for all service and demand, to be paid by rendering to Henry Hede lord of the fee and his heirs 18d. at four terms of the year according to the usage of Coventry (*Coventreie*) as the grantor's attorneys, *et de residuo quatuor solidorum ipse et heredes vel assignati sui emendabunt et preparabunt domos super eandem terram positas et sepes et alios domos si eisdem placuerit desup(er) edificabunt per visum bonorum hominum. Et si ipse Alexander et heredes vel assignati ejus plus de proprio custo in emendacione et preparacione domorum et sepium et in edificacione super eandem terram quam residuum quatuor solidorum salvo redditu domino feodi per visum bonorum hominum posuerint ego et heredes mei eidem Alexandro et heredibus vel assignatis suis totum custum eorum ad terminum duodecim annorum predictorum integre completorum plene restituemus vel si restituere non poterimus predictam terram cum pertinentiis omnibus ipsi habebunt et tenebunt per predictum servicium donec inde custos suos omnes plenarie receperint. Et si ego vel heredes mei post complecionem duodecim annorum predictorum eandem terram alicui ulterius ad firmam tradere voluerimus vel in feodo assidere upse Alexander et heredes sui vel ejus assignati propinquiores erunt.* Warranty and sealing clauses. Witnesses: William the Palmer (*palmero*), Robert de Paillinton', John son of Alan, Vincent Toki, Richard Mobrey, Osbert the Oil-seller (*olear'*), [ ][1]le Blund, Matthew son of Roger the Smith (*fabri*), John son of Humphrey (*unfr'*), William Toli, John son of Simon, Samson de Fonte and others.

Seal missing C.R.O. IA/C63

[1] There is a hole here.

565 c.1240

Sale and quitclaim by Matilda widow of Henry son of Richard son of Odo, in her widowhood and lawful power, to Alexander de Ruton' of all right and claim in name of dower in the land and the rent from that land in Well St. (*in vico Fontis*) which lies between the land of Robert le Saltere on the one hand and the land of Osbert le Oiler on the other; to be held well and in peace. Alexander gave 12d. of silver. Sealing clause. Witnesses: William le Palmer, Richard de Fonte, John son of Simon, Samson, Robert le Feugers, William son of Toly, Richard le Mubrey junior (*juvene*), Robert de Cornlye, Matthew son of Roger the Smith (*Fab'*) and many others.

Seal extant C.R.O. IA/MC12/32

566 c.25 March 1248

Grant and quitclaim by William son of William the Palmer (*Palmarii*) to Alexander de Rutu(n) of all right and claim in certain land in Well St., Coventry next to the bar (*in vico fontis Coventr' juxta barra(m)*), namely the entire land with appurtenances which lies between the land William the Palmer (*Palmar'*) held on the one hand and the land Vincent Toki held on the other in length and in width as the land purports according to the metes and bounds made there; to be held to him, his heirs or assigns, of the lords of the fee freely [etc.] by the service of 2d. of silver at the four terms of the year usual in Coventry, to be paid annually for all service [from the feast][1] of St. Mary the Virgin in March A.D. 1248 for the term for which the grantor has taken it. *Quicquid vero dictus Alexander vel heredes sui vel assignati sui in emendacione domorum illius terre per visum proborum hominum infra dictum terminum posuerint ad finem dicti termini eis persolvatur per visum fidelium hominum vel licebit eis habere dictam terram cum pertinentiis suis quousque habeant suum custum.* Alexander gave 10s. of silver. Sealing clause. Witnesses: Robert de Feug(er)s, Richard de Fonte, John son of Simon, Vincent Toki, William Toli, Martin Colbrond, William le Cnave, Richard the serjeant (*servient[e]*), William the serjeant (*serviente*), William the Miller (*molendinar'*) and others.

Seal extant C.R.O. 1A/EC12/16

[1] There is a hole here.

567 Late 1240s–early 1250s

Charter of Alexander de Ruton' giving to Thomas Oky in free marriage with Rose his daughter and to the heirs issuing from them part of his land in Coventry in Well St. (*in vico Fontis*), namely that which lies between the land William le Paum(er) once held on the one hand and the land Vincent Molle held on the other in length and in width as the land purports according to the metes and bounds made there;

to be held freely [etc.] by rendering annually a pair of gloves worth ½d. at Easter, and to the lords of the fee 4s. of silver at the four terms of the year fixed in Coventry for all secular service [etc.]. Warranty and sealing clauses. Witnesses: Anketin(us) de Wykewan, Robert de Corley, Richard de Fonte, John son of Symon, Robert de Feugers, Adam the clerk (*Cler'*), Richard de Hulmulne, Henry the clerk (*Cler'*) and others.

Seal extant C.R.O. IA/MC12/39

568 Early 1270s

[Sale, release] and quitclaim by Alexander de Ruton' without any reservation, charge or demand by him or his heirs to Thomas de Fakinham merchant of Coventry (*mercatori Covi(n)tr'*) and Margery his wife of all right and claim in the entire tenement with appurtenances in Well St., Coventry (*in vico Fontis Covintr'*) which is between the land William le Paum(er) once held on the one hand and the land which Robert le Salt(er)e once held on the other in length and in width according to the metes and bounds made there, with a certain tenement in the same street which is between the land the grantor himself held on the one hand and the land Alan Cestrefeld once held on the other according to the metes and bounds made there and a curtilage upon Hill (*super hull'*) between the land William le Maydin once held on the one hand and the land which Richard Herbert once held on the other according to the metes and bounds made there; moreover he has sold and quitclaimed to the same Thomas and Margery a certain tenement in the same street which is between the land Reginald le Cart(er)e once held on the one hand and the land of the hospital of St. John of Coventry on the other according to the metes and bounds made there, and a land with appurtenances in the same street towards Hill (*versus hull'*) which William le Paum(e)r once held on both sides according to the metes and bounds made there; to be held to him, his heirs or assigns, as freely as the grantor held of the lords of the fee and by the same service, namely to the heirs of Richard de Fonte 3s. 6d. of silver at the four terms of the year usual and fixed in the vill of Coventry and a clove-gillyflower at Easter, to the hospital of St. John of Coventry 18d. of silver at the aforesaid terms of the year and to the heirs of Henry Alen a consound (*unam florem consolid' minor'*) at Easter for all service. Thomas and Margery gave 100s. of silver beforehand. Exclusion and sealing clauses. Witnesses: Henry Baker (*pistore*), Robert de Chilton', William Toly, Walter Bacon, Geoffrey[1] [ ]nt, Adam le T(r)uant(er), [ ][2] Fermiler and others.

Seal missing C.R.O. IA/MC12/38a

[1] The surname and the 2 following names are lost.

[2] The forename is lost.

569 Mid 1240s

Sale and quitclaim by Richard son of William Toki, without any reservation by him or his heirs, to Vincent Thoki of all right and claim in the land which fell to him by inheritance from the Lady Rose widow of Robert de Paylint(on) in Coventry in Well St. (*in vico fontis*), namely that which lies between the land Hugh son of Nicholas Wole held on the one hand and the land William Lewin held on the other; to be held to him, his heirs or assigns, freely [etc.] of the lords of the fee of whom the grantor held and by the same service, namely 13d. to be rendered at the four terms of the year fixed in the vill of Coventry and 2 capons at Christmas for all service and demand. Vincent gave 6s. of silver beforehand. Sealing clause. Witnesses: Robert de Cornl', Robert de Felg(er)s, Richard de Fonte, John Simon', William Toli,

Matthew Mubrey, Alexander de Rutun, John Aleyn, Richard the Tanner (*tannator'*), William son of William the Palmer (*palmar'*), John de Dunstapel and others.

Seal missing G.H. 272

570 Late 1240s–early 1250s

Grant and quitclaim by Osbert le Oyler to Alan his son and his heirs or to whomsoever he will wish to give, sell or assign of the entire land with appurtenances which the grantor held in Well St., Coventry (*in vico fontis de Coventr'*) on behalf of Agnes his wife, Alan's mother, between the land Andrew the Tanner (*tan[nator*]) [held][1] and the messuage of Alexander de Rutone, and of all right and claim without [any reservation][1] in the said land and aforenamed[2] messuage. Alan gave 1 mark of silver. Sealing clause. Witnesses: Richard de Fonte, Robert de Cornleg', Robert de Feug(er)s, John son of Simon, Sampson de Fonte, William Toly, John son of Alan, Henry H(er)ebert [Martin][1] Colbront, Vincent Toky and others.

Seal missing C.R.O. IA/EC12/17

[1] partly obscured by holes
[2] sic

571 1250s

Sale and quitclaim by John de Herburi, for himself and his heirs, to Matthew son of Richard le Moubray of Coventry (*Cowintr'*) and his heirs or to whomsoever he will wish to give or assign of all right and claim in a certain messuage in Well St., Coventry (*in quodam mansio in vico fontis de Cowintr'*) with all its appurtenances which lies between the land of Vincent (*Wincencii*) Toki on the one hand and the land once of Nicholas Vele on the other according to the metes and bounds made there, [and] also 5d. annual rent from the aforesaid messuage (*mesuagio*) which the grantor bought from Richard son of William Toki; to be held freely [etc.] by rendering annually the service due and accustomed to the lords of the fee. Matthew gave 3s. of silver. Sealing clause. Witnesses: Richard de Fonte, William Toly, Alexander de Ruton', John Alein, Alan de Cesterfeld, John de Donestapel, Henry Alein, William ad Barram and others.

Seal extant C.R.O. 2/100

572 Early 1260s

Charter of John (*[Johan]nes*) son of Simon de Warwyc' giving to [Robert land] with appurtenances in Well St., Coventry (*In Coventr' In vico fontis*) [ ] which is [between] and the land Simon the Miller (*molendinar'*) held on the other in length and in width [ ] and to the same Robert 4s. annual rent which the aforesaid Simon the Miller [(*mo*) held] of the grantor lying between the land Henry Dru once held on the one hand [ ]; to be held to him [and his heirs] of the grantor and his heirs freely [etc.], by rendering annually [ ]s. rent at the four terms of the year fixed in Coventry for all service [etc.]. Clause for warranty. Robert gave 2s. of silver beforehand. Sealing clause. Witnesses: John Simond, Robert de Chilton' then bailiffs (*ballivis*), [ ] de Ruton', Robert his son, Thomas Mubray, Hugh the clerk and others.

Seal missing P.R.O. A 4468

About 1/3 of the document is lost along the left.

573 1270s

Charter of Alice daughter of Anketill Locard, in her widowhood and lawful power, giving to Henry del Parlur and Mary his wife for ½ mark of silver which they gave beforehand the entire land with appurtenances in Well St. (*in vico fontis*) which lies between the land of Alexander de Ruton' on the one hand and the land Symon the Doctor (*medicus*) once held on the other in length and in width as is manifest according to the metes and bounds made there; to be held to them, their heirs or whatsoever assigns, freely [etc.] without any reservation by the grantor or her heirs, by making annually to the prior of Coventry and his successors the service due, namely 4d. of silver at the four terms of the year customary in the vill of Coventry for all secular services. Sealing clause. Witnesses: Henry Baker (*pistor'*) then bailiff in Coventry, Alexander de Ruton', William Toly, Thomas Mubray, Robert Undermayst(er), William Kelle and others.

Seal missing C.R.O. IA/EC13/68

574 c.1280

Charter of William de Offechirche, with the assent of Agnes his wife, giving to Henry de P(ar)lour of Coventry the entire land with the building sited there and all appurtenances in the vill of Coventry in Well St. (*in vico fontis*) which lies between the lands which John son of Simon de Warewyk', Sir Robert de Hinkel chaplains and Alexander the Vintner (*vinetar'*) held on the one hand towards the east and the lands John Minot, the master and brothers of the hospital of St. John the Baptist of Coventry and Thomas de Fakenham held on the other towards the west, and extends from the aforesaid Well St. (*vico fontis*) up to the lands of Richard Midnit and Nicholas le Mayden in length and in width according to the metes and bounds made there; to be held to him and his heirs and to whomsoever he will wish to give, sell, bequeath or in any way assign in sickness and in health of the grantor and his wife and her heirs freely [etc.] by rendering annually to the lords of the fee (*dominis feodalibus*) as the perpetual attorneys of the grantor and his wife and her heirs the rent due and accustomed, namely from the aforesaid messuage with a certain portion of the garden (*particula gardini*) extending to the length of the land of the aforesaid John son of Simon to the lord prior of Coventry and his successors 4d. of silver at the four terms of the year fixed and customary in the vill of Coventry, and from the entire residue of the garden extending from the land of the aforesaid John son of Simon up to the lands of the aforesaid Richard Midnut and Nicholas Mayden to the heirs of Richard de Fonte 8d. of silver at the aforesaid four terms, and to the grantor and Agnes his wife and her heirs a clove-gillyflower at Easter for all secular service [etc.]. Clause for warranty. Henry gave 2 marks of silver beforehand. Sealing clause. Witnesses: Henry Baker (*pistore*) then bailiff, Robert de Chilton', Richard le Brocher, Thomas de Fakenham, Alexander Moubrey, Adam Colbrond', Walter Durant, Symon King, Hugh le Breton', Symon Pat, William le P(ar)lour, and others.

2 seals extant C.R.O. 2/160

575 Early 1280s

Grant and quitclaim by William son of William de Pynnele, for himself and his heirs, to Henry Baker (*pistori*) of Coventry and Agnes his wife of a messuage in Well St., Coventry towards Hill Mill (*in vico fontis de Coventre versus Hullemulne*), namely that which lies between the land once of Adam Haune on the one hand and the land of John de Donnestapel on the other and extends from the royal highway (*a via regia*) up to the watercourse from Hill Mill (*filum aque que vadit de Hullemulle*) in length and in width as is manifest according to the metes and bounds made there;

to be held to them, their heirs or assigns, well [etc.] without any reservation by the grantor or his heirs, by rendering annually to the lords of the fee the service due and accustomed, namely 20d. of silver at the four terms of the year usual in the vill of Coventry for all secular service [etc.]. Exclusion clause. Henry and Agnes gave 16s. of silver beforehand. Sealing clause. Witnesses: Robert de Chilton', Walter Bacon, John Tole, Thomas de Moubray, John Pyhod, Richard Midniht, Henry le Cnave, Walter le Coupere, Roger de Allesleye clerk and many others.

Seal missing G.H. 294

576 1280s

Charter of Emma daughter of Henry Baker (*pistoris*) of Coventry, in her virginity and lawful power, giving to Walter Bacon of Coventry a messuage in Well St., Coventry towards Hill Mill (*in vico fontis de Coventr' versus Hullemulne*) which lies between the land of the aforesaid Walter on both sides, which messuage Walter Woderoue and Milisent Gangerel once held; to be held to him, his heirs or assigns, well [etc.] by rendering annually to the lords of the fee the service due and accustomed. Clause for warranty. In return Walter gave 2s. annual rent, namely 12d. to be taken from the land which was of Adam Haune and 12d. from the land which was of Vincent Kempe. Sealing clause. Witnesses: Henry Baker (*pistor'*) then bailiff, Alexander the Vintner (*vinitar'*), Robert de Chilton', John Tole, Thomas de Moubray, John Abbot, Ranulph Oky, William Kelle, Henry le Cnave, John Pihod, Roger de Allesleye and others.

Seal extant C.R.O. 2/81

577 27 September 1293

Charter of Thomas Kempe of Coventry giving to Henry Oky butcher (*Carnifici*) a tenement with appurtenances in Well St. (*in vico fontis*) in Coventry between the land of the same Henry on the one hand and the land once of Adam ad Grenam on the other, in length and in width as the tenement fully purports according to the metes and bounds made there; to be held with the building sited there and all appurtenances to him, his heirs and whatsoever assigns, freely [etc.] of the lords of that fee by the service of 6d. of silver to be paid to those same lords annually at the four terms of the year usual and fixed in the vill of Coventry for all secular service [etc.]. Clause for warranty. Henry gave 24s. of silver beforehand. Sealing clause. Witnesses: Henry Baker (*pistore*) then bailiff in Coventry, William le Parker then coroner, Thomas le Moubray, John Thole, John Pyhod, William Kelle, John Abbot, Thomas le Wodeward, Roger the clerk. Coventry, Sunday after the feast of St. Matthew the Apostle and Evangelist 21 Edward I.

Seal missing W.R.O. 1
Endorsed: Carta tn' apud hullecros

578 5 October 1298

Demise, release and quitclaim by William son of William Kelle of Coventry, for himself, his heirs or assigns, to Emma Wymund, widow of William Wymund, her heirs or assigns, of all right and claim in a piece (*placea*) of land with the houses sited there and other appurtenances in the vill of Coventry, which lies next to the well in Well St. (*juxta fontem in vico Fontis*) between the land once of William de Haweþornth on the one hand and the land of William Path on the other in width, and in length from the high street (*ab alta via*) up to the land of Angketinus de

Colushul according to the metes and bounds made there; to be held to her, her heirs or assigns, [of][1] the grantor, his heirs or assigns, freely [etc.]. Exclusion and sealing clauses. Witnesses: Angketinus de Colushul then bailiff of Coventry, John Pyhod, John de Halis, Henry de Halis, Henry Oky, Symon de Sulton', Alexander de Colushul and others. Coventry, Sunday after Michaelmas 26 Edward I.

Seal extant C.R.O. IB/26 EI/1

[1] The document reads pro.

579 1298–1300

Charter of William Kelle of Coventry giving to Emma Wymund, widow of William Wymund of Coventry, a piece (*placeam*) of land with an adjacent moor and the houses sited there and appurtenances in the vill of Coventry lying in Well St. next to the well (*in vico fontis juxta fontem*) between the land once of William de Haweþornh on the one hand and the land of William Path on the other in width, and in length from the high street (*ab alta via*) up to the land of Anketinus de Colushul according to the metes and bounds made there, [and] moreover 4d. annual rent which John le Blound used to render to the grantor from a moor which Angketinus de Colushul held; to be held to her, her heirs or whatsoever assigns, freely [etc.] or to whomsoever she will wish to give, sell or assign by rendering annually to the chief lords of that fee the service due and by right accustomed. Clause for warranty. Emma gave £10 sterling. Sealing clause. Witnesses: Angketinus de Colushul' then bailiff of Coventry, Robert Kelle, John de Halis, John le Gaunt(er), John Pihod, Nicholas the Dyer (*Tingtor'*), Henry Oky, Symon Losewit, Robert de Assebi, William Losewyth, William Path', John Path, Symon de Sulton' and others.

Seal extant C.R.O. 2/163

580 19 June 1304

Grant, release and quitclaim by William son of William Kelle of Coventry in his full age, for himself and his heirs, to Richard le Typp(er)e of Coventry and Emma his wife, their heirs or assigns, of all right and claim in a piece (*placea*) of land with the houses sited there and other appurtenances in the vill of Coventry which lies next to the well in Well St. (*juxta Fontem in vico Fontis*) between the land once of William de Hawethorn on the one hand and the land of William Path on the other in width, and in length from the high street (*ab alta via*) up to the land of Anketinus de Colleshull' according to the metes and bounds made there; to be held to them, their heirs or assigns, freely [etc.]. Exclusion clause. Richard and Emma gave 20s. of silver beforehand. Sealing clause. Witnesses: Robert the Baker (*Pistore*) then bailiff, John Lewyne then coroner, Robert Kelle, Alexander de Colleshull', Alexander de Stonlee, Alexander le Vinet(er), Richard Colebrond the clerk and others. Coventry, Friday after the feast of St. Botulph the Abbot 32 Edward I.

Seal extant C.R.O. IB/32EI/9

581 30 March 1301

Grant and demise for life by Adam son of Thomas le Moubray of Coventry to Ranulph de Solihull' tanner of Coventry (*de Coventr' tannator'*) and Alice his wife, daughter of Adam de Chetwode, and their first born son, 2 messuages with the houses sited there, the adjacent curtilages and all appurtenances, namely those messuages which lie together in Well St., Coventry (*in vico Fontis Coventrye*) in width between the land of Alexander de Collushulle on the one hand and the land of Agnes

Dreu on the other, and which extend in length from the aforesaid street up to the grantor's land with the small road (*p(ar)va via*) leading up to the watercourse running towards the priory of Coventry and containing 12 feet in width; to be held of the grantor, his heirs or assigns, to them as long as they live or to the survivor freely [etc.] by rendering annually 9s. of silver at the four terms of the year usual in Coventry for all services and demands. The grantees during their lives will maintain the buildings (*edificabunt sustentabunt edificia*) of the said messuages at their own cost in all repairs, so that after their deaths the messuages will entirely revert to the grantor, his heirs or assigns, with all improvements and appurtenances. Should Ranulph and Alice die without a son, after their deaths the messuages will revert to the grantor, his heirs or assigns. It will not be lawful for Alexander, his heirs or assigns, or anyone in his name, to cause injury (*ullam injuriam . . . facere*) to Ranulph and Alice and their first born son regarding the aforesaid messuages during their lives. Mutual sealing clause [bipartite]. Witnesses: Roger Dayuseye then bailiff, John Lewyne then coroner, Henry Oky, Robert le Clav(er)e, William Patte, Alexander de Colushulle, John Pyhod and others. Coventry, Thursday after the feast of the Annunciation of the blessed Mary 29 Edward I.

Indented
Seal extant C.R.O. IB/29 EI/2

BISHOP ST.*

*For other references to Bishop St. see 230, 560, 563, 722.

582 c.1215–c.1225

Charter of Jordan son of William the Carpenter (*Carpentarii*) giving to William the Miller (*molendinario*) and Matilda his wife a part of his land in Coventry in Bishop St. (*in vico Episcopi*) next to the land of the same William, namely the part which is nearer to the land the aforesaid William held and contains in width 7 feet next to the road (*juxta viam*) and is in length as the metes and bounds purport; to be held to them and the heirs issuing from them, of the grantor and his heirs, in fee and inheritance freely [etc.], by rendering annually for all secular service and demand 12d. at four terms, namely 3d. at each of the feasts of St. John the Baptist, St. Michael, St. Andrew and St. Mary in March. Clause for warranty. William gave 9s. 4d. of silver in recognition. Witnesses: Matthew son of Roger, Roger de Cornl', Herbert son of Jordan, David de Fonte, Geoffrey de Wilnhal', Henry the Carpenter (*carpent'*), Richard son of the Cook (*Coci*), James his son-in-law (*g(e)n(er)o suo*), Reginald the Parchment-maker (*parchamen'*), John his brother, Richard de Warewic', Sanson his son and many others.

Seal extant C.R.O. 2/115

583 Early 1250s

Charter of William the Miller (*molendinar'*) giving to Richard his son, his heirs or assigns, a part of his land with appurtenances in Coventry in Bishop St. (*in vico episcopi*) next to the land of the same William, namely the part which he bought from Jordan son of William the Carpenter (*Carpentar'*) and which contains in width 7 feet next to the road (*septem pedes juxta viam*) and is in length as the metes and bounds purport; to be held to him of the lords of that fee of whom the grantor held and by the same service, namely 12d. of silver at four terms of the year according to the usage of Coventry, and to the grantor, his heirs or assigns, a clove-gillyflower at Easter. Warranty and sealing clauses. Witnesses: Richard de Fonte, John Simund, Robert de Feugers, John the Parchment-maker (*parchamen'*), William le Cnave, Peter Bacoun, John le Blound, Henry Scauerib, Reginald de Wythibroc and others.

Seal missing C.R.O. IA/LC12/28

584 Late 1230s–early 1240s

Charter of Peter son of Herbert son of Jordan giving to Richard son of Henry de Fonte a certain part of his land in the vill of Coventry in Bishop St. (*in vico qui dicitur vicus episcopi*), which is 6 feet in width and extends in length from the land John the Parchment-maker (*p(er)gamenarius*) held up to the land of the aforesaid Richard according to the metes and bounds made there; so that the aforenamed land should be held for a common way (*pro com(m)uni via*); to be held to him and his heirs or to whomsoever he will wish to give, bequeath or assign of the grantor and his heirs freely [etc.], by rendering annually 2d. at four terms of the year, namely ½d. at each of the feasts of St. Mary in March, St. John the Baptist, St. Michael and St. Andrew. Clause for warranty. Richard gave 5s. of silver in recognition. Sealing clause. Witnesses: Richard Lewin', John son of Symon, David de Fonte, Sampson son of Richard, Robert de Feugers, Warin Ouving, William le Cnave, Geoffrey Page, Robert de Cornleye, John in Mosso, Adam Cosin, Richard the Serjeant (*serviente*) and others.

Seal extant C.R.O. IA/MC12/34b

585 Late 1230s–early 1240s

Charter of Amilia daughter of Herbert son of Jordan giving to Richard son of Henry de Fonte a certain part of her land in Bishop St., Coventry (*in vico episcopi de Conventre*), namely the land which lies near to the land which Sampson son of Richard held in length and in width as the land purports and according to the metes and bounds made there; to be held to him and his heirs or to whomsoever he will wish to give, bequeath or assign of the grantor and her heirs freely [etc.], by rendering annually 4d. at four terms of the year, namely 1d. at each of the feasts of St. Mary in March, St. John the Baptist, St. Michael and St. Andrew the Apostle. Clause for warranty. Richard gave 20s. of silver in recognition. Sealing clause. Witnesses: Richard Lewin', John son of Symon, David de Fonte, Sampson son of Richard, Robert de Feugers, Warin Ouving, William le Cnave, Geoffrey Page, Robert de Cornleya, John in Mosso, Adam Cosyn, Richard the Serjeant (*serviente*) and others.

Seal extant C.R.O. IA/C42

586 Late 1230s–early 1240s

Charter of John the Parchment-maker (*p(er)gamenarius*) giving to Richard son of Henry de Fonte a certain part of his land in Coventry in Bishop St. (*in vico qui dicitur vicus episcopi*), namely that which lies between the land Peter son of Jordan held on the one hand and the land the said Richard held on the other in length and in width as the land purports according to the metes and bounds made there; to be held to him and his heirs or to whomsoever he will wish to give, bequeath or assign of the grantor and his heirs freely [etc.], by rendering annually 3d. at four terms of the year, namely ¾d. (*tres quadrantes*) at each of the feasts of St. Mary in March, St. John the Baptist, St. Michael and St. Andrew the Apostle. Clause for warranty. Richard gave 1 mark of silver beforehand in recognition. Sealing clause. Witnesses: Richard Lewin', John son of Symon, David de Fonte, Sampson son of Richard, Robert de Feugers, Warin Ouvingh, William le Cnave, Geoffrey Page, Robert de Cornleya, John in Mosso, Adam Cosyn, Richard the Serjeant (*serviente*) and others.

Seal extant C.R.O. IA/MC12/34a

587 Late 1240s

Charter of Richard Pihod of Coventry giving to Walter Pihod his son certain land in Bishop St., Coventry (*in vico Episcopi Coventr'*) towards the church of St. Nicholas, namely the entire land with appurtenances which lies between the land Alan le Cuver held on the one hand and the land Reginald le Rus held on the other in length and in width as the land purports according to the metes and bounds made there; to be held to him, his heirs or assigns, freely [etc.] by rendering annually 20d. of silver to the lords of the fee at the four terms of the year usual in Coventry for all secular service and demand. Walter gave 11s. of silver. Sealing clause. Witnesses: Robert de Feugers, Richard de Fonte, John son of Simon, Martin Colbrond, Adam Hadolf, Richard Coppinc, Matthew the Smith (*Fabro*), Roger the Weaver (*textore*), Walter the Young (*juvene*) and others.

Seal extant C.R.O. 2/147

588 Late 1240s–early 1250s

Charter of John de Estleye giving to Robert son of Hugh Martin of Coventry 5s. 2d. rent with appurtenances in the vill of Coventry, namely 2d. from the land Henry le Notte held in Bishop St. (*Biscopestrete*) which lies between the land Warin Ouving once held on the one hand and the land Henry the Carpenter (*carpentar'*) once held on the other, 12d. from the land John le Teler held in Cook St. (*in vico coci*) which lies between the land William Warin held on the one hand and the land William de Hamton' once held on the other, 6d. from the land Beatrice de la Barre held which lies between the land William Redwy held on the one hand and the land David de Wilnhale held on the other, 2d. from the bake house (*furno*) which Geoffrey de Wilnhale once held in Cook St. (*in vico Coci*) which lies between the land David de Wilnhale held on the one hand and the land Beatrice de la Barra held on the other, 12d. outside the bar (*extra Barram*) towards the church of St. Nicholas from the land Richard Durant held which lies between the land Richard son of Gilbert held on the one hand and the land William le Serjaunt held on the other, and 6d. from the land towards the church of St. Nicholas which lies between the land Thomas Oky held on the one hand and the land Margery H(er)berd held on the other; to be held and to be received from the aforesaid lands to him, his heirs or assigns, freely [etc.] by rendering annually a pair of gloves worth ½d. or ½d. at Easter and to the lords of the fee 27d. of silver at the four terms of the year according to the usage of Coventry for all secular service [etc.]. Warranty and sealing clauses. Witnesses: Anketill de Wikewan' then reeve (*p(re)posito*), Richard de Fonte, John Simund, Robert de Feugers, Peter Martin, John le P(ar)chemin(er), Martin Colbrond, John le Espec(er), Ralph the Miller (*molendinar'*), William Warin, William Redwy, Henry Simund and others.

Seal extant W.R.O. 136

This and Nos. 594, 595 are grouped with some later deeds relating to the Crane Inn, which property adjoined Bishop St. gate.

589 c.Michaelmas 1257

Lease by William son of Robert le Redeknave of Coventry to Hawise widow of Robert de Feugers of the same of the entire land with all appurtenances in Bishop St., Coventry (*in vico episcopi de Coventr'*) which is between the land Roger son of William le Moun(er) held on the one hand and Well St. (*vicum fontis*) on the other, in length and in width as is manifest along the Bishop's great street (*per magnu(m) vicu(m) episcopi*) with a garden (*gardino*) and all other appurtenances; to be held to her, her heirs or assigns, of the lessor and his heirs freely [etc.] for a term of 5 years from Michaelmas 1257 A.D. by rendering annually to the lords of that fee as the attorney of the grantor and his heirs the service owed for all service, exaction or secular demand. *Et si contingat quod dicta Hawisia vel heredes vel assignati sui infra predictum terminum aliquod novum edificaverint in predicta terra preter quod inv(en)erunt bene liceat eisdem quicquid novum in ea edificatum fuerit in fine termini predicti asportare nisi ego Willelmus vel heredes mei eisdem omnes custus de novo edific(at)o ibidem facto appositos velimus restaurare per visum legalium virorum.* Hawise gave ½ mark of silver beforehand. Sealing clause. Witnesses: John Sym' then bailiff, Richard de Fonte, Robert de Chilt', Roger le Mouner, Peter Bacun, William Dru, Henry Dru, Bertram Poleyn, Hugh the clerk and others.

Seal missing C.R.O. IA/C66

590 Michaelmas 1257

Charter of William son of Robert le Redeknave of Coventry giving to Richard son of William the Weaver (*textoris*) of Coventry a certain part of his land with the house sited there and all other appurtenances in Bishop St., Coventry (*in vico episcopi de Coventr'*) which Hawise widow of Adam le Redeknave held of the grantor in name of dower, which is between the land the grantor himself held on the one hand and the land Roger son of William le Muner held on the other, in length and in width as is manifest according to the metes and bounds made there, and all right and claim in the said land which will accrue to her or her heirs in demesnes, rents, escheats and all else (*omnibus rebus aliis*); to be held to him, his heirs or whatsoever assigns, of the grantor and his heirs freely [etc.], by rendering annually a clove-gillyflower at Easter for all service, exaction or secular demand. Clause for warranty, saving however the aforesaid land with appurtenances to Hawise before noted (*in hoc scripto prenotates*)[1] as long as she lives with reversion to Richard and his heirs entirely and fully without contradiction by anyone. Exclusion clause. Richard gave 4s. of silver in recognition beforehand. Sealing clause. Dating clause (Michaelmas 41 Henry III). Witnesses: Richard de Bok(er)vill' then bailiff of the Earl's half (*ballivo ex parte comitis*), William Lewin then bailiff of the Prior's half (*ballivo ex parte prioris*), John Sym', Richard de Fonte, Roger the Miller (*molend'*) Alexander de Glov(er)nia, John le Blund, John Yngeram, Hugh le Bretu(n) clerk and others.

Seal extant C.R.O. IA/C67

[1] sic

591 1257–1262

Lease, grant and remise by Hawise widow of Adam le Redeknave of Coventry, for herself and her heirs, to William the Weaver (*textori*) and Sarra his wife of the entire land with appurtenances and the houses sited there in Bishop St. (*in vico episcopi*) in Coventry which she took (*cepi*) from William son of Robert le Redeknave for a term of 5 years as the charter from him witnesses, namely the land lying between the land Roger son of William le Mun(er) held on the one hand and Well St. (*vicu(m) fontis*) on the other; to be held to them, their heirs or assigns, freely [etc.] up to the end of her entire term, by rendering annually to the chief lords of that fee the rent due and by right accustomed without any charge or reservation by her or her heirs. *Ita tamen quod bene liceat michi quamdiu vixero infra predictum terminum si voluero dictam terram tenere et locare pro den(ariis) meis per idem precium quod aliquis alius pro ea dare voluerit et ad amplius. Et si contingat quod absit quod ego predicta Hawisia vel etiam aliquis heredum meorum post obitum meum contra istam concessionem et penitus remissionem venire seu dicto vel facto aliquid atte(m)ptare presu(m)psero vel presu(m)pserit, volo et firmiter concedo quod tenear vel teneatur nomine debiti dictis Willelmo et Sarre et eorum heredibus vel assignatis in una marca argenti quam michi pro ista traditione et concessione dederunt premanibus. Et ad hoc firmiter tenend(um) et observand(um) subicio me et heredes meos jur(is)dictio(n)i domini offic(ialis) arch(i)d(iaconi) Coventr' et decani ejusdem loci vel alterius eorum quicumque fuerint vel fuerit pro tempore quod possint vel possit nos compellere per s(ente)n(c)iam exco(mmun)icat(io)nis et int(er)d(ic)ti pulsatis campanis candelis accensis ad soluc(i)o(n)em marc(e) predicte si contingerit quod absit ipsam committi renu(n)ciando omni excepcioni cavillacioni defensioni et omni juris remedio tam civili quam canonici et specialiter regie prohibicioni. In cujus rei testimonium ne super premissis in posterum hesitare contingat huic presenti scripto sigillum meum apposui.* Witnesses: Henry Dobedy, William the Weaver (*textore*), William de Colsul, William de Folkyshul, Wilace, John the Dyer (*tinator'*), Hugh the clerk and others.

Seal missing C.R.O. 2/69

592 1257–1262

Charter of William son of Robert le Redeknave of Coventry giving to William the Weaver (*textori*) and Sarra his wife the entire land with the houses sited there and all appurtenances in Bishop St., Coventry (*in vico episcopi de Coventr'*) which lies between the land Hawise widow of Adam le Redeknave held in name of dower on the one hand and Well St. (*vicum fontis*) on the other in length and in width as is manifest according to the metes and bounds found there; to be held to them and their heirs and to whomsoever both or either of them will wish to give, sell, grant, bequeath or assign in any way whatsoever, of the grantor and his heirs freely [etc.] by rendering annually as the perpetual attorneys of the grantor and his heirs to the chief lords of the fee 12d. of silver at four terms of the year according to the usage of Coventry and 2 men in Autumn and 4 hens at Christmas, and to the grantor and his heirs a clove-gillyflower at Easter for all secular services, exactions, temporal demands whatsoever, whatsoever courts and their suits, and all rights and customs which by any cause or right will be able to accrue to the grantor or his heirs. Clause for warranty. William and Sarra gave 2 marks of silver beforehand. Sealing clause. Witnesses: John Symon', William Lewin, Robert de Chilton', Matthew le Mubray, John le Blu(n)t, Roger le Mun(er), Henry Dobedy, Roger de Hales, William the Weaver (*textor'*), Thomas Scelet, Hugh le Bretu(n) the clerk and others.

Seal extant C.R.O. 2/114

593 c.1258–c.1260

Charter of Prior W(illiam) and the convent of the church of Coventry (*Covi(n)tren'*) giving to Henry once the son of Henry Baker (*pistoris*) of Coventry and his heirs the entire land with appurtenances in Coventry in Bishop St. (*In vico qui dicitur Episcopi*), namely that which was once of Nicholas Spille which lies between the land John the White (*Blundus*) held on the one hand and the land the same John held on the other in length and in width as the land purports according to the metes and bounds made there; to be held to him and his heirs of the grantors and their church of Coventry freely [etc.] by rendering annually to them and their successors 12d. of silver at the four terms of the year usual in the vill of Coventry. Sealing clause (*signum Capituli nostri*). Witnesses: Anketill de Wikewan, William Lewin', John Sym', Robert de Chilton', William de Allesleg', Martin Colbrond, Hugh le Hoser and Thomas Selet clerks, John the White (*Blundo*), Peter Martin', Walter Bacun and others.

Seal extant C.R.O. IA/EC13/71

594 1264

Sworn agreement (*convencio facta et utrimque affidata*) whereby Richard son of William de Walesgrave has leased and demised for a term to Walter de Banebur' a certain house in Bishop St. (*in vico episcopi*) in Coventry with appurtenances, namely that which is between the land Hugh the clerk held on the one hand and the land Henry le Notte once held on the other; to be held to him, his heirs or whatsoever assigns, of Richard, his heirs or assigns, freely [etc.] from the feast of St. John the Baptist A.D. 1264 for a term of 12 years, in length and in width according to the metes and bounds made there, by rendering annually 7s. of silver at the four terms of the year usual in Coventry for all secular service [etc.], *ita tamen quod dictus Ricardus et heredes sui vel assignati dictam domum cum omnibus suis pertinentiis et cum omnibus edificiis ibidem inventis sustinebunt et coop(er)ient usque ad firnem termini predicti propriis sumptibus sin autem bene liceat dicto Waltero et heredibus vel ejus quibuscumque assignatis predictas domos cum pertinentiis de firma emendare et coop(er)ire rationabiliter per visum legalium virorum ne ipse et heredes sui vel sui assignati aliquod dampnum vel nocumentum incurrant termino perseverante. Preterea si dictus Walterus et heredes sui vel assignati sui infra terminum ibidem edificaverint vel de suo aliquid apposuerint liceat eisdem totum edificatum asportare in fine termini nisi dicti Ricardus et heredes sui vel assignati dictum edificatum velint emere vel eorum custum rationabiliter adquietare*. Clause for warranty. Mutual sealing clause [chirograph]. Witnesses: William Lewin, John Simu(n)d, Robert de Chilton' then bailiffs (*ball(iv)is*), Ranulf the chaplain, Walter Piehod, Henry Baker (*pistore*), Robert de Hepel', Hugh le Hoser clerk, Henry le Notte, Walter Bacu(n), William the clerk and others.

Indented
Seal missing W.R.O. 137

595 Late 1260s–early 1270s

Charter of Nicholas Forwine with the consent of Joan his wife giving to Richard his son a messuage in the vill of Coventry in Bishop St. (*in vico episcopi*) with all appurtenances which is between the land John son of Adam le Winiter held on the one hand and the land William le Forner held on the other in length and in width as is manifest according to the metes and bounds made there; to be held of the grantor and his heirs freely [etc.] by rendering annually ½d. at Easter and to the lords of that fee 16d. of silver at the four terms of the year fixed in the vill of Coventry for all secular service [etc.]. Warranty and sealing clauses. Witnesses: Robert de Chiltone, Geoffrey Breton, John Thole, Henry C[a][1]rsad', Henry Pope, Hugh Cetelber', Hugh the clerk and many others.

Seal extant W.R.O. 135

[1] There is a hole here.

596 Early 1280s

Charter of Alexander son of Adam the Vintner (*vinitarii*) of Coventry giving to Walter Godmo(n) of Keresley (*Kersleya*) a certain part of his land in Bishop St., Coventry (*in vico episcopi de Coventr'*), namely that which William Wilhar once held of the grantor and which lies between the land of Henry Baker (*pistoris*) on the one hand and the lane (*viculum*) which leads to the bakehouse (*furnu(m)*) of the same Alexander in width and extends in length from the royal highway (*a regia via*) up to the wall of the said bakehouse (*p(ar)iette(m) dicti furni*); *Concessi et eidem Waltero quod possit edificare quodd(am) solariu(m) ultra predictum viculu(m) salva tamen larga via ad carectam summatam intrand(am) et exiend(am) ad voluntatem ipsius Alexandri*; to be held to him and his heirs of the grantor, his heirs or assigns, by[1] 4s. of silver at the four terms of the year usual in Coventry. Clause for re-entry and retention in fee and by hereditary right, without reclaim by Walter or his heirs, should the rent be partly or wholly in arrears by ½ year. Clause for warranty. Mutual sealing clause. Witnesses: Robert de Chiltun' then bailiff, Walter Bakun then coroner, Henry Baker (*pistor'*), John Thole, Thomas le Moubray, John Pihod, Henry le Knave, Anketell the clerk and others.

Indented
Seal extant C.R.O. IA/EC13/70

[1] *per*, inserted after the text had been written

597 Early 1280s

Remise and quitclaim by Prior Thomas and the convent of the church of Coventry, for themselves and their successors, to Peter Baron of Coventry and his heirs of 19d. rent with appurtenances in Coventry of the rent which the same Peter was accustomed to render to them for his tenements in the Earl's half (*ex parte Comitis in Covintr'*). In return Peter has remised to them 19d. rent with appurtenances in the same vill, in Bishop St. in the Prior's half (*ex parte Prioris in vico Episcopi*) which rent the said Peter used to take from the tenements once of John Hereberd. Sealing clause (*sigillum nostrum comune*). Witnesses: Robert de Chilton' then bailiff, Walter Bakun then coroner, Henry Baker (*Pistor'*), Alexander the Vintner (*vinitar'*), Richard de Asseby, Adam Russel', Henry Ballard, Thomas de Moubray, John Tole, Roger the Fishmonger (*Piscatore*) and many others.

Seal missing C.R.O. IA/C13/49

598 1280s

Charter of Christine Rimild of Coventry widow of William Rimild in her lawful widowhood giving to Richard le Draper of Corley (*Corle*) the entire land in the vill of Coventry in Bishop St. (*in vico Episcopi*) between the land Roger the Miller (*molendinar'*) once held on the one hand and Well St. (*vic' fontis*) on the other in length and in width according to the metes and bounds made there; to be held to him and his assigns of the grantor, his heirs or assigns, freely [etc.] by rendering annually to the lord prior of Coventry 12d. at four terms fixed in Coventry, namely 3d. at each term, and to the chief lord of that fee a pair of gloves worth ½d. at Easter for all secular service [etc.]. Warranty and sealing clauses. Witnesses: Henry Baker (*pistore*) then bailiff, Robert de Chiltone, Alexander the Vintner (*vinitario*), John Pyhod, Thomas Mubrey, John Thole, John le Ganter and others.

Seal extant C.R.O. 253

599 1280s

Grant and quitclaim by Richard de Cornleye, for himself and his heirs, to John Abbot of Coventry of the entire land with the houses sited there and all appurtenances which he had of the gift of Christine Rimild in Bishop St. (*in vico Episcopi*) in Coventry between the land of the aforesaid John Abbot on the one hand and Well St. (*vicum fontis*) on the other in length and in width as is manifest; to be held to him, his heirs or assigns, well [etc.] by rendering annually to the chief lords of the fee the service due and accustomed. Exclusion clause. John gave 40s. of silver beforehand. Sealing clause. Witnesses: Henry Baker (*pistor'*) then bailiff, Walter Bacon, Thomas de Moubray, John Pihod, John son of Nicholas, John de Claybroc, John de Cornleye, Henry le Cnave, Hugh le Breton, Roger de Allesleya the clerk and many others.

Seal extant C.R.O. 2/132

ST. NICHOLAS ST., TOWARDS THE CHURCH OF ST. NICHOLAS, TOWARDS RADFORD*

*For other references to St. Nicholas St. see 221, 424, 560, 563, 588, and for St. Nicholas Field see 739.

600

c.1210–c.1220

Charter of Geoffrey de Wilnhal' giving to Hugh son of John de Witemor and his heirs a land in Coventry towards the church of St. Nicholas which the grantor bought from William the Miller (*molendinario*), namely the 2 houses which are nearer to the land Matthew the Smith (*faber*) held with the entire land pertaining to those houses in length and in width according to the metes and bounds made there; to be held to him and his heirs of the grantor and his heirs hereditarily, freely [etc.] by rendering annually 18d. of silver at four terms of the year, namely 4½d. at each of the feasts of St. Andrew, St. Mary in March, St. John the Baptist and St. Michael. Clause for warranty. Witnesses: William Fordwi(n), Hugh son of Martin, Matthew the Smith (*fabro*), Osbert the Baker (*fornatore*), Alan the clerk, Gerard son of Odein, Herbert the Cooper (*cuppar'*), William the Turner (*tornatore*), Robert the kinsman (*cognato*) of Ernis and many others.

Seal missing

C.R.O. 1A/C11–12/20

601

c.1215–1224

Charter of Richard son of Ernis giving to Geoffrey de Wilnhale a land towards the church of St. Nicholas, namely that which is between the land Matthew the Smith (*faber*) held and the land Robert Mustard held in length and in width as the land purports; to be held to him and his heirs of the grantor and his heirs in fee and inheritance freely [etc.] by rendering annually for all service and demand 12d. of silver at four terms of the year, namely 3d. at each of the feasts of St. Andrew, St. Mary in March, St. John the Baptist and St. Michael. Clause for warranty. Geoffrey gave 1 mark in recognition. Witnesses: Alan the clerk, Matthew the Smith (*fabro*), Herbert Cuppere, Nicholas son of Thured, Ingelard, Robert nephew of Ernis, Richard his son, Guy (*Widone*) Cuppere, Richard Wele, Gerard Odein, Robert Musterd, Thomas the Mason (*cem(en)tario*) and many others.

Seal missing

GH 271

602 c.1215–1224

Charter of Richard son of Ernis giving to Geoffrey de Wilnhal' a land towards the church of St. Nicholas, namely that which is between the land Matthew the Smith (*faber*) held and the land Robert Mustard held, in length and in width as the land purports; to be held to him and his heirs of the grantor and his heirs, in fee and inheritance freely [etc.], by rendering annually for all secular service [etc.] 8d. of silver at four terms of the year, namely 2d. at each of the feasts of St. John the Baptist, St. Michael, St. Andrew and St. Mary in March. Clause for warranty. Geoffrey gave 20s. of silver in recognition. Witnesses: Alan the clerk, Matthew the Smith (*fabro*), Herbert Cuppere, Nicholas son of Thured, Ingelard, Robert nephew of Ernis, Richard his son, William Cuppere, Richard Wele, Gerard Odein, Robert Mustard, Thomas the Mason (*cementario*) and many others.

Seal missing C.R.O. 2/168

603 c.1215–1221

Charter of Richard Colbrond giving to Henry the Carpenter (*carpentario*) a part of his curtilage behind the garden (*retro Gardinu(m)*) of Richard son of Ernis (*Hernisii*) which lies between the land William Fordwin held and the land Walter de Wilnhal' held, namely the part which is nearer to the land of the aforesaid William Fordwin, in length and in width as the metes and bounds made there purport; to be held to him and his heirs of the grantor and his heirs freely [etc.] by rendering annually for all secular service [etc.] 4d. at four terms of the year, namely 1d. at each of the feasts of St. Mary in March, St. John the Baptist, St. Michael and St. Andrew. Clause for warranty. Henry gave 10s. of silver in recognition. Witnesses: Richard the Goldsmith (*aurifabro*), Adam the Vintner (*vinit'*), Hugh de Luddelowe, David de Fonte, Herbert son of Jord', Adam Redecnave, William de Sponna, Ralf the Parchment-maker (*parchamen'*), Richard son of Oki, Richard son of Ernis, Nicholas Thured, Ingelard the Farrier (*ferrario*) and many others.

Seal extant P.R.O. A 11185

604 c.1215–1225

Sale and quitclaim by Robert son of Thured without any reservation, for himself and his heirs, to William de Franketun, of the entire land and service which he held in chief of the lord prior of Coventry at the quarry towards the church of St. Nicholas (*apud Quareriam versus ecclesiam sancti Nicholai*), namely that land which lies between the land Sternulf held and the land Nicholas son of Thured held in length and in width as the land purports from the street up to the water (*a vico usque ad aquam*) with all appurtenances; to be held to him and his heirs in chief of the aforesaid prior as freely [etc.] as the grantor held and by the same service, namely 12d. *per annum*. William gave a bezant (*unum bisantium*). Warranty and sealing clauses. Witnesses: Richard de Aula, Robert the Vintner (*Vinit'*), Hugh son of Martin, Matthew son of Roger, William son of Humphrey (*Umfr'*), John his son, William de Wilnhal', Geoffrey his brother, David de Fonte, Robert Bretun, Bertram his son, William son of Simon the Baker (*pistoris*), Roger the Miller (*molendin'*) and many others.

Seal extant P.R.O. A4665

605 c.1215–c.1225

Charter of Godfrey son of Ailwin giving to William son of Simon the Baker (*pistoris*) 16d. rent with all its appurtenances and issues (*exitibus*) from a croft which the grantor held of the lord prior of Coventry towards Radford (*Radeford*), namely all rent and service which he had from the lands Adam Wele and Richard de Waleton' held of him; to be held to him and his heirs of the grantor and his heirs in fee and inheritance freely [etc.], by rendering annually for all secular service and demand 4d. of silver at four terms of the year namely 1d. at each of the feasts of St. John the Baptist, St. Michael, St. Andrew and St. Mary in March. Clause for warranty. William gave 10s. of silver in recognition. Witnesses: Richard de Warewic', Samson his son, William son of Humphrey (*Umfr'*), Matthew de Vado, Henry the Skinner (*pellipar'*), Ingelard, Nicholas son of Thured, Herbert Cuppere, Gerard Odein, Alan the clerk and many others.

Seal extant — C.R.O. 1A/C15
Endorsed: Carta Godefr' de Radeford

606 — c.1215–c.1225

Charter of Richard Copping giving to Roger the Smith (*fabro*) a part of his land towards the church of St. Nicholas, namely that which is between the land the grantor held and the land the same Roger the Smith (*faber*) held, in length from the street (*a vico*) up to the land Nicholas son of William the Butcher (*carnific'*) held and in width according to the metes and bounds made there, with a kiln (*Turallo*) and all other appurtenances; to be held to him and his heirs of the grantor and his heirs freely [etc.], by rendering annually for all service and demand 8d. of silver at four terms of the year, namely 2d. at each of the feasts of St. Andrew, St. Mary in March, St. John the Baptist and St. Michael. Clause for warranty. Roger gave 28s. of silver, and to Alice the grantor's wife a peacock-blue cape with a rabbit-fur hood (*unum palli(um) de pounaz cum pennula de konins*). Sealing clause. Witnesses: Richard Oki, Richard his son, Richard de Mubrai, Richard his son, Richard Toki, Yngelard, Matthew the Smith (*fabro*), William de Franketon', Geoffrey de Wilnhal', Godfrey de Doggelan', Walter Bulli, William Tranur, Herbert Cuppere, Michael the Smith (*fabro*), Henry son of Edred and others.

Seal extant — C.R.O. 2/149

607 — c.1215–c.1225

Charter of Richard son of Robert Copping giving to Roger the Smith (*fabro*) his entire land in the *bivium* of Coventry (*in bivio de Convintr'*) towards the church of St. Nicholas just as the land extends in length from the land which the aforesaid Roger held of Richard son of Ernis (*Hernisii*) towards the bar (*versus Barram*) and in width from one street to the other (*ab uno vico usque ad alium*) with all appurtenances; to be held to him and his heirs or to whomsoever he will wish to give or assign in fee and inheritance of the grantor and his heirs freely [etc.], by rendering annually for all secular service and demand 8d. at four terms of the year, namely 2d. at each of the feasts of St. Andrew, St. Mary in March, St. John the Baptist and St. Michael. Clause for warranty. Roger gave 3½ marks of silver in recognition. Witnesses: Richard Oki, Richard his son, Richard de Mubrai, Richard his son, William son of Humphrey (*umfr'*) Ingelard, Matthew the Smith (*fabro*), Gilbert (*Geleb(er)to*) de Spalding', Richard his son, Robert Bretun'[1], Bertram his son, William Toki, Richard his brother, Roger the Weaver (*textore*) and many others.

Seal extant — C.R.O. 2/129

[1] This name is repeated.

608 Late 1220s–early 1230s

Charter of Richard Hoki giving to Thomas his brother 6d. rent in the suburb (*In suburbio*) of Coventry towards the church of St. Nicholas, namely from the land Richard Coppi[n]g held of the grantor; to be held to him and his heirs of the grantor and his heirs freely [etc.], by rendering annually a pair of gloves or ½d. at Easter for all secular service and exaction. Clause for warranty. Witnesses: Richard le Moubrai', Roger the Weaver (*textor'*), William son of Simon, John son of Simon, John P(er)cbemin(er), Roger the Smith (*fabro*) and many others.

Seal missing C.R.O. 2/98

609 Late 1240s–early 1250s

Sale and quitclaim by Richard son of Durant of Coventry from himself and his heirs to William le Foleur of Coventry, his heirs or assigns, of all right and claim in the entire land with appurtenances in Coventry outside the bar towards Radford (*extra Barram versus Radeford*) which lies between the land William le Serjaunt held on the one hand and the land Thomas Oky held on the other with 6d. rent which he used to render to the vendor from the same land; to be held to him, his heirs or assigns, of the lords of the fee freely [etc.], by rendering annually 12d. of silver at four terms of the year according to the usage of Coventry for all secular service [etc.]. William gave ½ mark of silver. Sealing clause. Witnesses: Richard de Fonte then reeve (*p(re)posito*), Richard Burgeys, Robert de Feugers, John Simund, John le P(ar)chemin(er), William Tholi, Henry Dryu, Alexander de Ruton', Martin Colbrond, William le Cnave, William de Haweþorn, William le P(ar)chemin(er), Reginald de Withibroc and others.

P.R.O. E 315/43/93

610 Early 1250s

Charter of Gerard Odeyn of Coventry giving to Robert de Ichenton' clerk and his heirs, or to whomsoever he will wish to assign, give or bequeath, a land towards the church of St. Nicholas (*unam terram versus ecclesiam sancti Nicholay*), namely the entire land between the land Robert Muttard held on the one hand and the land Robert the Scot (*scoticus*) held on the other in length and in width as the land purports with appurtenances; to be held of the grantor and his heirs freely [etc.], by rendering annually a clove-gillyflower at Easter and to the lords of the fee as the grantor's attorney 6d. of silver at four terms of the year, namely 1½d. at each of the feasts of St. Michael, St. Andrew, St. Mary in March and St. John the Baptist for all secular service [etc.]. Clause for warranty. Robert gave 12s. of silver beforehand. Sealing clause. Witnesses: Martin [ ][1] then reeve (p(re)po(s)ito), John Simu[n]d, Richard de Fonte, Robert Feuger', William de Burmingham, William Yrland, [ ][1], Adam the Weaver (*textore*), Thomas Hoki, Henry the Painter (*pictore*), William [ ][1] and others.

Seal missing P.R.O. A4269

[1] Names lost through damage; the document is torn along the bottom left hand corner.

611 Late 1250s

Charter of William son of Robert le Redecnave giving to William Lewyn a land in Coventry towards the church of St. Nicholas, namely that which is between the land Alan the clerk once held on the one hand and the land Roger the Weaver (*textor*) once held on the other; to be held to him, his heirs or assigns, of the grantor and his heirs freely [etc.] according to the metes and bounds made there, by rendering annually to the lords of that fee as the grantor's attorneys 2s. of silver at the four terms of the year fixed in Coventry, and to the grantor and his heirs a clove-gillyflower at Easter. Clause for warranty. William gave 20s. of silver beforehand. Sealing clause. Witnesses: John Simond then reeve (*p(re)posito*), Richard de Fonte, Robert de Chiltu(n), Martin Colbrond', Richard Sauerib, John Yngeram, Thomas the Dyer (*tinctore*), John the White (*albo*), Peter Bacun, Walter his son, Hugh the clerk and others.

Seal missing C.R.O. 1A/C12–13/61a

612 Late 1250s–early 1260s

Grant, remise and quitclaim by Richard son of William the Miller (*molendinar'*) of Coventry, by the counsel and assent of Alice his wife, without reservation by him or his heirs, to William Leuwin of all right and claim in 2s. annual rent with appurtenances from the land towards the church of St. Nicholas which the said William Leuwyn held of William son of Robert le Redeknave by making the service owed to the lords of the fee; to be held to him, his heirs or assigns, freely [etc.], by making the service owed to the lords of the fee as the grantor's perpetual attorneys. *Tali condicione adjecta quod si umquam dicta Alicia vel heredes sui per se vel per procuratorem suum aliquod clam(ium) inposuerint super predictum redditum omni juris remedio postposito teneantur dicto Willelmo et heredibus suis in viginti solidis sterlingorum nomine testamenti.* William gave 5s. of silver in recognition. Sealing clause. Witnesses: Matthew le Mubray, Robert de Chilton', John son of Simon, Martin Colbront, Thomas Oki, Thomas the clerk and others.

2 seals extant C.R.O. 1A/C12–13/61b

613 Late 1250s–early 1260s

Acknowledgement by William de Hybernia that he is bound to pay 4s. 8d. annually to Henry le Seller of Coventry and Margery his wife, their heirs and assigns, from certain land in St. Nicholas St., binding himself, his heirs and assigns, to a penalty of ½ mark for any default and submitting to ecclesiastical sanction to secure payment.

Omnibus Christi fidelibus hoc presens scriptum visuris vel audituris Willelmus de Hyb(er)nia salutem. Noverit universitas vestra me et heredes meos et assignatos meos teneri annuatim inperpetuum reddere Henrico le Seller de Coventr' et Margerie uxori sue et eorum heredibus vel assignatis quatuor solidis et octo denariis argenti ad quatuor terminos anni statutos et consuetos in villa de Coventr' de quadam terra cum pertinentiis in Coventr' in vico illo versus ecclesiam sancti Nicholai in quo Michaelis Faber manere solebat que scilicet terra jacet inter terram quam Ricardus le Blessede tenuit ex una parte et terram quam fratres hospitalis sancti Johannis Baptiste Coventr' tenuerunt ex altera parte. Et ad istum redditum ad terminos prefixos fideliter et sine dolo et sine dil(aci)one solvendum ego Willelmus pro me et heredibus meis et etiam assignatis fide media me obligavi sub pena dimidie marc(e) argenti quocienscumque in solucione alicujus termini predicti defecero vel defecerint dictis Henrico et Margerie et eorum heredibus persolvende, subiciendo me et heredes vel assignatos meos et omnia bona nostra mobilia et inmobilia jur(is)d(i)c(t)ioni et plene potestati domini prioris Coventr' et successorum ejus et ballivorum suorum et etiam officialis domini archidiaconi Coventr' et ejusdem loci decani quicumque fuerint pro tempore quod ipsi omnes vel eorum alter possint vel possit nos per omnia bona predicta et per s(en)t(e)n(cia)m exco(mmunication)is ad solucionem redditus predicti et pene predicte sine strepitu judiciali et cause (con)gnic(i)one una cum dampnis et expensis si quas predicti Henricus et Margeria et eorum heredes fecerint ratione predicte oblig(aci)onis non observate infra octo dies (con)pellere si (con)tingat quod absit illam committi renunciando super premissis omnibus cavillacionibus excep(ci)onibus dil(aci)onibus app(e)ll(aci)onibus regie prohibicioni constitucioni quid adriavi et omni jur(is) remedio nobis (con)petenti tam canonici quam civili. Et ne super premissis in posterum hesitare (con)tingat in hujus rei testimonium huic oblig(aci)oni patenti ego predictus Willelmus pro me et heredibus et etiam assignatis meis sigillum meum apposui. Hiis testibus Willelmo Lewin Matheo de Mubray tunc ball(iv)is Thoma Haldeyn Henrico le Cartesadeler' Thoma Oky Waltero le Coppere Hugone le Bretu(n) clerico et aliis.

Seal missing P.R.O. A 4279

614 Early 1260s

Sale and quitclaim by John de Draycote with the consent and goodwill of Susan (*Sussanne*) his wife, to Walter son of Adam Edolf of all right and claim which he had in the land in Coventry outside the bar (*extra barram*) towards the church of St. Nicholas which fell to him with the aforesaid Susan in name of dower from the aforesaid Adam Edolf once her husband; to be held to him, his heirs or assigns, freely [etc.]. Walter gave 18s. of silver beforehand. Sealing clause. Witnesses: John Simond then reeve (*p(re)posito*), Martin Colbrond, William Lewin, Ranulf de F(r)anket(un), Peter the Dyer (*tinctore*), Roger the Miller (*molendinar'*), Henry Baker (*pistore*), Walter the Dyer (*tinctor'*), Thomas the Weaver (*text'*), Hugh the clerk and others.

Seal missing C.R.O. 2/6
Endorsed: Refector'

615 Early 1260s

Charter of Walter son of Adam Edolf giving to John son of Master Ralf de Aidelintu(n) the entire land in Coventry with appurtenances outside the bar (*extra Barram*) towards the church of St. Nicholas, namely that which is between the land Nicholas Spille held on the one hand and the street (*vicum*) which is called Dog Lane (*doggelone*) on the other in length and in width from the great street (*a magno vico*) on the one hand up to the land David de Wilnhal' held on the other; to be held to him, his heirs or assigns, of the grantor and his heirs freely [etc.], by rendering annually a clove-gillyflower at Easter, and to the lords of that fee the service due, namely 10d. to Lady Rose (*Royse*) de Brugges and 14d. of silver to the Infirmary of the monks of the blessed Mary of Coventry at the four terms of the year fixed in Coventry as the grantor's attorneys for all exaction, secular service and demand. John gave 6½ marks of silver beforehand. Sealing clause. Witnesses: John Simond then reeve (*p(re)posito*), Martin Colbrond, Ranulf de Franketu(n), Henry Baker (*pistore*), Richard Sauerib, William Lewin, Richard de Pakint(on), William the Serjeant (*servi-ente*), Walter Pyhod, John de Cornl', Peter F(r)ewin, Thomas Torel, Hugh the clerk and others.

Seal extant C.R.O. 2/127

616 Late 1260s–early 1270s

Charter of Alexander de Ruiton' giving to Henry Baker (*pistori*) of Coventry and Agnes his wife the entire land with the adjacent quarry (*cum quarrer' adjacente et ad dictam terram pertinente*) lying between the land of Nicholas Fortwyn on the one hand and the land of Walter Bacun on the other with the door (*janua*) and free entrance and exit to the aforesaid land, a messuage which lies next to the bar (*juxta Barram*) towards the church of St. Nicholas between the town ditch (*fossatum ville*) on the one hand and the land of [the hospital of] St. John on the other, a land lying in Dog Lane (*doggelone*) between the land Robert Asser once (*aliquando*) held and the land Little (*p(ar)vus*) Haldeyn held, 18d. annual rent in the territory of Radford (*in t(er)itor(io) de Radeford'*) from the furlong (*cultura*) which is called *Bulketoniscroft* lying between the land of John son of Adam the clerk on the one hand and the highway (*altam viam*) on the other, 6d. annual rent from a certain furlong in Radford (*cultura in Radeford'*) between the land of the said John and the land of Robert de Chilton', 12d. annual rent in Dog Lane (*doggelone*) from the land Little (*p(ar)vu(us)*) Haldeyn held, and 16d. annual rent from the land once of Robert Asser with all liberties, escheats, easements and all appurtenances pertaining to the said land and rents; to be held to him, his heirs begotten of himself and Agnes or their assigns, of the grantor and his heirs freely [etc.] by rendering annually for the land at the quarry (*pro terra ad quarr' primo nominata*) 2s. of silver to the lords of that fee at four terms of the year according to the custom of the vill of Coventry, and to the grantor and his heirs a clove-gillyflower at Easter for all secular service [etc.]. Clause for warranty. Henry and Agnes gave 4 marks of silver beforehand. Sealing clause. Witnesses: Robert de Chilton', William Tholi, Geoffrey Breton', William de Alisley, Robert de Londr', John Yngera(m), Martin Colbront, Adam his son, William Leuine, Walter Bacun, Walter Dourant, Thomas Seled clerk and others.

Seal missing — C.R.O. IA/EC12/2

617 — 17 September 1293

Gift and quitclaim by Isabella and Joan daughters of Richard Chowhe, in their lawful power and virginity, to Henry called Baker (*dicto Pistor'*) of Coventry of all right and claim in 12d. annual rent from the house of Walter de Hib(er)n' outside Bishop's bar, Coventry (*extra Barram Episcopi Coventr'*) which is between the lane (*venellam*) which leads towards Hill Mill (*molendinum de hulle*) on the one hand and the land of John Tole on the other; to be held to him, his heirs or assigns, of the grantors. Exclusion clause. Henry gave 10s. of silver beforehand. Sealing clause. Witnesses: Robert de Stokes then steward (*Senesch(all)o*), Robert de Chilton', William le P(ar)kere, Thomas le Mowbrey, John Tole, John Pyhot, Walter le Coup(er)e, Richard Mynnyht and many others. Coventry, Thursday after the feast of the Exaltation of the Holy Cross 21 Edward I.

2 seals extant — G.H. 300

618 — 17 September 1293

Gift and quitclaim by William de Halys of Coventry, with the consent and good will of Agnes his wife, to Henry called Baker (*dicto Pistori*) of Coventry of all right and claim in 6d. annual rent from the house of Walter de Hibern' outside Bishop's bar, Coventry (*extra barra(m) Episcopi Coventr'*), which is between the lane (*venellam*) which leads towards Hill Mill (*molendinu(m) de hulle*) on the one hand and the land of John Tole on the other; to be held to him, his heirs or assigns, of the grantor. Exclusion clause. Henry gave 6s. of silver beforehand. Witnesses: Robert de Stoke then steward (*Senesch(all)o*), Robert de Cilton', William le P(ar)kere, Thomas le Mowbrey, John Tole, John Pyhot, Walter le Coup(er)e, Richard Mynnyht, and many others. Coventry, Thursday after the feast of the Exaltation of the Holy Cross 21 Edward I.

2 seals extant G.H. 301
Endorsed: de filiis Ricardi Chowhe
De placea sup(er) cornera(m) versus hull' mulne extra Barra(m) episcopi x^{viid} et terram Johannis Tole

619 10 September 1295

Charter of Master William de Coventr' giving to Henry called Baker (*dicto pistori*), the grantor's father, the entire tenement with the houses sited there in St. Nicholas St., Coventry (*in vico sancti Nicholai de Coventr'*) lying between the land of Roger le Neue on the one hand and the land of Walter le Coup(er)e on the other in length and in width according to the metes and bounds made there; to be held to Henry, his heirs or assigns, of the lords of the fee (*de dominis feodalibus*), by rendering to those same lords the services due and accustomed. Clause for warranty. Henry gave 10 marks of silver beforehand. Sealing clause. Witnesses: Robert de Stok', William le Parkere then coroner, Thomas le Mowbrei, John Thole, Walter le Coup(er)e, Robert Kelle, John de Halis and many others. Coventry, Saturday after the Nativity of the blessed Mary 23 Edward I.

Seal extant C.R.O. IB/23E1/2
Endorsed: Redd' domino Priori Coventr' ij solid' per annum

620 1290s

Charter of Henry Brayn giving to Robert called the son (*filio dicto*) of Henry Baker (*Pistoris*) of Coventry a certain part of his land in Coventry, namely that which lies between the cemetery of St. Nicholas (*Symit(er)iu(m) sancti Nicholai*) on the one hand and the land once of Robert de Chilterne on the other [1] and the road which leads to Whitemore (*et wiam que ducit versus Wytemor*) according to the metes and bounds made there; to be held with all appurtenances to him, his heirs or assigns, of the grantor and his heirs freely [etc.], by rendering to the chief lords of that fee the services due and by right accustomed for all secular services and demands. Clause for warranty. Robert gave 4 marks of silver beforehand. Sealing clause. Witnesses: William the Parker (*Parcar'*) then coroner, John Pyot, Robert Kelle, Thomas le Moubrey, Walter le Couper, Richard Midnit, Robert de Ascheby and many others.

Seal missing P.R.O. 4275

[1] Omission here?

621 Late 1260s–early 1270s

Charter of John Yngeram of Coventry giving to Ranulph his son his entire land in the vill of Coventry towards the church of St. Nicholas, which lies between the land Adam Cosin once held on the one hand and the land William de Burmingham and Bela his wife held on the other and extends from the royal highway (*a regia strata*) up to the land Roger the Weaver (*textor*) once held in length and in width as the land purports according to the metes and bounds made there; to be held to him, his heirs or whatsoever assigns of the grantor and his heirs freely [etc.], by rendering annually to the lords of that fee 3s. of silver at the four terms of the year fixed in the vill of Coventry, namely 12d. to the heirs of David de Wylenhal', 12d. to the hospital of St. John the Baptist and 12d. to Petronilla a sister of the same hospital and her successors, and to the grantor and his heirs a clove-gillyflower at Easter for all service [etc.]. Warranty and sealing clauses. Witnesses: John de Pontefracto then steward (*senescall'*) of the prior of Coventry, Henry Baker (*Pistor'*), Robert de Chilton', William de Allysleg', John the Goldsmith (*aurifabro*), Robert de Lond', Alexander de Ruton', William Toly, William de Burmi(n)gham and others.

Seal extant C.R.O. 1A/L12–13C/43

622 Late 1260s–early 1270s

Grant and quitclaim by Henry Sampson of Coventry, for himself and his heirs, to Isabella his sister and Alice her daughter, of a curtilage of his in Coventry on the eastern side of the church of St. Nicholas (*juxta ecclesiam sancti Nicholai ex parte orientali*), namely that which lies between the land John the Marshal (*marescallus*) held on the one hand and the land Robert de Clocher held on the other, and between the land of [W][1]alter the Weaver (*Tixtoris*) on the one hand and the highway which leads towards Whitemore (*altam viam qui ducit versus [W][1]etemor*) on the other with all appurtenances [as is manifest][1] according to the metes and bounds made there; to be held to them, their heirs or assigns or to whomsoever they will wish to give [sell, bequeath][1] or assign [of the lords][1] of the fee, namely of the heirs of John Fortwin freely [etc.], by rendering annually to the said lords 4d. of silver at the four fixed terms of the year in the vill of Coventry for all secular service [etc.]. Sealing clause. Witnesses: Henry Baker (*Pistor'*), Robert de Chilton', Alexander de Rutu(n), Henry le Seler, William Kille, William Toli, Walter Baku(n), Martin Colbrond, Roger the Miller (*molendinar'*) and others.

Seal missing P.R.O. A6374

[1] Lost through damage.

623 Late 1260s–early 1270s

Charter of Thomas Oky of Coventry giving to Edith daughter of Henry le Celir of Coventry all right in 2 messuages in the vill of Coventry in St. Nicholas St. (*in vico sancti Nicholai*) which the grantor bought from Henry son of Roger the Smith (*fabri*), lying between the land Margery Herbert once held on the one hand and the land Richard Copping once held on the other in length and in width as is manifest according to the metes and bounds made there; to be held to him, his heirs or assigns, freely [etc.] by rendering annually to the heirs of Richard Copping 2d. of silver at the four terms of the year usual in the vill of Coventry for all secular service and demand. Clause for warranty. Edith gave 20s. of silver beforehand. Sealing clause. Witnesses: Robert de Chilton', Henry Baker (*Pistor'*), Hugh the clerk, Walter Bacoun, John the White (*Albo*), Adam le Trauenter, Nicholas Forthwyne, Henry le Cartsadeler, Hugh Ketelbern and others.

Seal missing C.R.O. 1A/C13/53

624 1270s

Charter of Ralf Biscop of Coventry giving to John Pihod a moiety of his land in St. Nicholas St. outside Bishop's Bar, Coventry (*in vico sancti Nicholai extra Barram episcopi de Coventr'*), namely the moiety on the southern side (*versus Australem partem*) lying between the land which John Pihod held on the one hand and the moiety of the land which the grantor holds on the northern side (*versus Boream partem*); to be held to him, his heirs or to whomsoever he will wish to give, bequeath, sell or assign, according to the metes and bounds made there, freely [etc.] by rendering annually 21d. at the four terms of the year fixed in the vill of Coventry for all secular service [etc.]. John gave 14s. of silver beforehand. Warranty and sealing clauses. Witnesses: Henry Baker (*pistor'*) then bailiff (*ballivo tunc tempore*), Robert de Chilton', Hugh the clerk, Walter Bakun, Roger the Miller (*molendinario*), Martin Colbrond, Thomas Oky, John the Weaver (*textore*), Anketell the clerk and others.

Seal extant C.R.O. 1A/Misc.I/15

625 c. early 1290s

Charter of Robert de Wylenhale son of Vitalis de Wylenhale giving to Anketell de Colishul a certain curtilage with appurtenances in St. Nicholas St., Coventry (*in vico beati Nicholai de Coventr'*) which lies between the land John Patte held on the one hand and the land of the lord prior of Coventry on the other, in length and in width as is manifest according to the metes and bounds made there; to be held to him, his heirs or assigns, of the chief lords of that fee by the service due and by right accustomed. Warranty and sealing clauses. Witnesses: John Tole, John Pyhod, Henry Baker (*pistor'*), Walter le Coup(er)e, Thomas le Moubrey, John son of Nicholas, John Abbot, William Patte, Nicholas le Deyster, William the Goldsmith (*aurifabr'*), Adam Pollsing, Thomas the clerk and others.

Seal missing C.R.O. 2/104

626 21 September 1293

Charter of Walter called (*dictus*) de Irlond cooper in Coventry (*in Coventr' le Coppere*) giving to John son of Nicholas de Teynton' farrier (*ferrario*) a certain part of his land outside Bishop's Bar (*extra barram Episcopi*) in the vill of Coventry with the house sited there and its appurtenances, which part lies in width between the land of Thomas Seleth on the one hand and the grantor's land on the other and extends in length from the royal highway which leads from Bishop's Bar towards the church of St. Nicholas (*a Regali via que ducit de Barra Episcopi versus ecclesiam sancti Nicholai*) up to the grantor's land as is manifest according to the metes and bounds made there; to be held to him, his heirs and assigns, well [etc.] of the lords of that fee of whom the grantor held by the service of 15d. of silver to be paid to the same annually at the four terms of the year usual and fixed in the vill of Coventry for all secular services [etc.]. Clause for warranty. John gave 20s. sterling beforehand. Sealing clause. Witnesses: Henry Baker (*pistore*) then bailiff in Coventry, Robert de Chilton', William le Parker then coroner, Thomas le Moubray, Richard Mydnyht, Alan the Butcher (*carnifice*), Walter le Coup(er)e, Henry le Knave, Robert the clerk and others. Coventry, the feast of St. Matthew the Apostle 21 Edward I.

Seal extant P.R.O. A 4431

627 14 February 1296

Grant, remise and quitclaim by Roger le Neue of Coventry to Stephen his son of the land with appurtenances which he held by the law of England in the name of Alice once his wife, Stephen's mother, which lies outside Bishop's bar (*extra Barram Episcopi*) in Coventry between the land of Henry Baker (*pistoris*) on the one hand and the land of Thomas le Seler on the other and extends from the royal highway (*a Regali via*) leading from the said bar towards the church of St. Nicholas up to the other royal highway leading from the aforesaid bar towards Radford (*Radeforde*); to be held to him, his heirs and assigns, well [etc.] of the chief lords of that fee by the services due and accustomed, without any reservation by the grantor. Exclusion and sealing clauses. Witnesses: Henry Baker (*pistore*) then bailiff of Coventry, William le

Parker then coroner, Thomas le Moubray, John Thole, Richard Mydnyht, Alan the Butcher (*Carnifice*), Walter le Coup(er)e, Robert de Sowe, Walter le Webbe and others. Coventry, Tuesday the feast of St. Valentine the Martyr 24 Edward I.

Seal extant C.R.O. IB/24EI/3
Endorsed: vicus sancti Nicholai.

628 c.1290–1297

Gift and quitclaim by Robert Fyel son of Fyel de Coventr' to Hugh de Schulton' once the servant (*servient'*) of William de Copston' of all right and claim in the entire land with appurtenances which John Abbot once held next to the church of St. Nicholas of Coventry, which lies between the land of Henry Baker (*pistoris*) and the land of Richard le Marchal on the one side and the royal highway (*regiam viam*) leading to Hazelwood (*haselwode*) on the other in length and in width as is fully manifest according to the metes and bounds; to be held to him, his heirs or assigns, freely [etc.]. Exclusion and sealing clauses. Witnesses: Henry Baker (*pistore*) then bailiff of Coventry, William le P(ar)ker then coroner, William de Copston', John Minot, Richard Dobedy, John the clerk and others.

Seal missing G.H. 304

629 27 January 1298

Charter of Robert son and heir of Fiel le Flechewer' of Coventry, in his full age, giving to Hugh de Schulton' once the servant (*servienti*) of William de Copston' in Coventry 12d. annual rent which John Ingram used to render for a certain parcel (*p(ar)tic(u)la*) of land which he held of the grantor in St. Nicholas St. (*in vico sancti Nicholai*) in Coventry, which lies between the land John le Bel chaplain held on the one hand and the land Jurdan the Saddler (*selarius*) held on the other, as is manifest according to the metes and bounds made there; to be held to him, his heirs or assigns, freely [etc.]. Clause for warranty. Hugh gave 10s. sterling beforehand. Sealing clause. Witnesses: Anketell de Colsul then bailiff, William le Parker then coroner, William de Copston', Matthew de Ruyton', Thomas le Moubray, John Pyhod, Robert Kelle and others. Coventry, Monday after the feast of the Conversion of St. Paul the Apostle 26 Edward I.

Seal missing G.H. 311

630 13 December 1304

Charter of John le Cnave of Coventry giving to Richard de Daleby of Coventry butcher (*carnifici*) and Felicia his wife a curtilage with appurtenances which lies in the lane which leads from Bishop's bar, Coventry towards Hill Mill (*in venella que ducit de Barra Episcopi de Coventr' versus molendinum de Hulle*) in width between the land of Henry Baker (*Pistoris*) on the one hand and the land of Simon Losewyt on the other, and which extends in length from the aforesaid lane up to the land of the aforesaid Henry Baker (*Pistoris*) according to the metes and bounds made there; to be held to them, their heirs or assigns, freely [etc.] of the chief lords of that fee by the service and rent due and by right accustomed, namely 6d. annually to be paid to them at the four terms of the year usual in Coventry. Clause for warranty. Richard gave 10s. of silver beforehand. Sealing clause. Witnesses: Robert Baker (*Pistore*) then bailiff, John Lewyne then coroner, Henry Oky, Richard Midnit, John Pyehod, John Abbot, Robert Kelle and others. Coventry, Sunday after the feast of St. Nicholas the Bishop 33 Edward I.

P.R.O. E 315/44/108

631

25 April 1307

Charter of William son and heir of John de Teynton' of Coventry giving to Robert de Teynton' his brother, his heirs or assigns, all the lands and tenements which he had by hereditary right after the death of John de Teynton' his father in Coventry and in Harnall (*Harnhale juxta Coventr'*) namely his entire tenement with all appurtenances outside Bishop's Bar in St. Nicholas St. (*extra Barram Episcopi in Coventr' in vico sancti N(icholai)*) [which][1] lies between the tenement John Preest held on the one hand and the tenement (*tm̄*) of Master Robert de Keu and Alice his wife [on the other in][1] width, and extends from the aforesaid street up to the land Henry le Baxtere held in length, a small moor (*(u)nam parvam moram*) in the same vill which lies between the moor called *Penymor* on the one hand and the land of the aforesaid Master Robert le Keu and Alice his wife on the other, 9 selions of land with an adjacent meadow and appurtenances which lie in a certain furlong (*cultura*) which is called *Pykedeperefeld* in the same vill between the land of the aforesaid Master Robert le Keu and Alice his wife on the other, and the entire arable land in Harnall (*Harnhal juxta Coventr'*) with moors, meadows, hedges and ditches and all other appurtenances which lies between the land John Lewyne of Coventry once held on the one hand and the water running from *Ovenetfforde* towards Coventry on the other in width and extends from the royal highway (*a Regia via*) which leads from Coventry towards *Bulkyn(ton)* and from the land of John Godmo(n) up to the aforesaid running water, in length and in width as all the aforesaid tenements fully purport according to the metes and bounds made there; to be held with all appurtenances and liberties belonging wheresoever within and without the vills of Coventry and Harnall (*Harnhale*) namely in [ ][1], plains, [ ][1], waters, lanes, commons and pastures, to them, their heirs or whatsoever assigns [by hereditary] right of the chief lords of those fees by the services due and by right accustomed. Clause for warranty. Robert gave a sum of money beforehand. Sealing clause. Witnesses: Robert le Baxtere then bailiff of Coventry, Anketinus de Colushull' then coroner of the same, Alexander de Stonlee, Alexander de Moubray, Robert Kelle, John Pyhod, Alexander de Colleshull, John Abbot, Richard Colebron clerk and others. Coventry, Tuesday the feast of St. Mark the Evangelist.

Seal missing P.R.O. A 6382

[1] lost

COOK ST.* TOWARDS HARNALL

*For other references to Cook St. see 424, 560, 563, 588. See also *Langley Cartulary* No. 296.

632 Mid–late 1260s

Charter of Ralf the Miller (*molendinar'*) of Coventry giving to Adam Hawene, for his service and for 10s. of silver which he gave beforehand, 2s. annual rent with appurtenances which Robert de Cornleya and his heirs were accustomed to render annually to the grantor from certain land with appurtenances in the vill of Coventry in Cook St. (*in vico Coci*), namely from 3 messuages which are next to (*propinquiora*) the land which Nicholas the Miller (*molendinar'*) held on the one hand and the grantor's land on the other; to be held to him, his heirs or whatsoever assigns, of the grantor and his heirs, freely [etc.] by the service of a clove-gillyflower to be paid annually for all service and demand. *Et si contingat quod dictus Adam vel heredes sui aut ejus assignati in tribus mesuagiis predictis aut eorum duobus vel uno pro firma dominis capitalibus debita aut aliquo alio casu per defectun mei vel heredum meorum aut assignatorum namientur ex tunc volo et firmiter concedo quod idem Adam et heredes sui vel ejus assignati dom(um) meam lapideam ceteraque tenementa mea cum pertinentiis in villa de Coventr' ubicumque fuerint distringant sine contradictione mei vel heredum meorum aut assignatorum quorumque donec ipsorum namia deliberentur.* Warranty and sealing clauses. Witnesses: William Lewin, Robert de Chilton' and Henry Baker (*pistore*) then bailiffs (*ball(iv)is*), William Toly, Alexander de Ruton', Walter Bacun, Roger the Miller (*molendinar'*), John Blacwine, John Abbot, William de Okam, Hugh le Bretun clerk and others.

Seal missing G.H. 292

633 c. early 1290s

Charter of John de Cornleye giving to the window (*luminari*) of the blessed Mary the Virgin in the church of Holy Trinity, Coventry (*Coventreye*), for the salvation of his soul, the soul of Giliana his wife and those of their ancestors ½lb. of wax (*cere*) annual rent to be taken by the wardens (*procuratores*) of the said window at the feast of St. Thomas the Apostle from a certain tenement in Cook St. (*in vico Coci*) in Coventry, which lies between the land William de la Hul once held on the one hand and the land John in le Huyrne held on the other; to be held in pure and perpetual alms well [etc.] without any reservation by the grantor or his heirs; with exclusion clause. Sealing clause. Witnesses: Henry Baker (*pistore*), Robert de Chilton', John

Thole, Thomas le Moubray, Thomas Selet, John Pyhod, Richard de Midnyht, John le Gaunt(er), Robert Kelle and many others.

Seal extant W.R.O. 164

634 10 October 1294

Charter of Nicholas de Stivechale glover in Coventry (*in Coventr' cyrotecari(us)*) giving to Robert de Abyndon' of Coventry *le Tippere* and Juliana his wife a certain piece (*partem*) of land with the buildings sited there which they previously held of the grantor for a term in Cook St. (*in vico Coci*) in Coventry in width between the posts (*inter postes*) of the grantor's house towards the east on the one hand and the road (*viam*) which leads towards the house which was once of William de la Hul on the other and which extends in length from the aforesaid street up to the small plot (*parva(m) aream*) next to the land which Richard Chowhe once held according to the metes and bounds made there; to be held to them and the heirs of Robert and their assigns well [etc.] of the lords of that fee by the service of 4d. of silver to be paid to those same lords at the four terms of the year usual and fixed in the vill of Coventry for all secular service [etc.]. Clause for warranty. Robert and Juliana gave 2 marks of silver beforehand. Sealing clause. Witnesses: Henry Baker (*pistore*) then bailiff in Coventry, John le Gaunter, Robert Kelle, John Pyhod, John Abbot, Geoffrey le Dubbere, Symon Losewyt, John de Cornleye, William his son and others. Coventry, Sunday after the feast of St. Denis 22 Edward I.

Seal extant G.H. 302

635 4 February 1296

Charter of Nicholas de Stivechale glover in Coventry (*in Coventr' cyrotecarius*) giving to Richard de Norton' *le Tippere* a messuage with appurtenances in Cook St. (*in vico Cocy*) in Coventry, which lies in width between the land John Portman held on the one hand and the land of Robert le Typpere on the other and extends in length from the aforesaid street up to the land which Hawise de[1] Wymplestere once held as is manifest according to the metes and bounds made there; to be held with the buildings sited there and all appurtenances to him, his heirs or assigns, well [etc.] of the lords of that fee, by rendering annually to those same lords the service due and by right accustomed. Clause for warranty. Richard gave 18s. of silver beforehand. Sealing clause. Witnesses: Henry Baker (*pistore*) then bailiff of Coventry, William le Parker then coroner, John Thole, Thomas le Moubray, John Pyhod, Robert Kelle, John son of Nicholas, John Portman, William de Cornleye and others. Coventry, Sunday after the feast of St. Blasius the Bishop 24 Edward I.

Seal extant G.H. 308

[1] sic

636 20 June 1300

Charter of Robert Herbert of Coventry giving to John de Hales dyer in Coventry (*in Coventr' Tinctori*) and Margaret his wife a certain part of the land with appurtenances which he had next to the road which leads from Cook St., Coventry towards Harnall (*juxta viam que ducit de vico Coci in Coventreia versus Harnhale*) lying in width between the land of the hospital of St. John of Coventry and the land of John le Gaunter on the one hand and the land of the lord prior and convent of Coventry which is called *gardinerescroft* on the other, and extends in length from the aforesaid road up to the garden (*gardinum*) of the lord prior and convent of Coventry just as the land fully purports; to be held with all appurtenances and easements to them, their heirs or whatsoever assigns, well [etc.] of the chief lords of that fee, by rendering annually to those same lords 12d. of silver at the four terms of the year usual in the vill of Coventry for all secular services [etc.]. Clause for warranty. John and Margaret gave a certain sum of money beforehand. Sealing clause. Witnesses: Anketill de Coleshul then bailiff of Coventry, John Leofwyne then coroner, Robert called Baker (*dicto Pistore*), John Pyhod, Henry Oky, John le Gaunt(er), Master Robert the Cook (*Coco*), Robert Kelle, Roger the clerk and others. Coventry, Monday after the feast of Sts. Gervasius and Prothasius the Martyrs 28 Edward I.

Seal extant C.R.O. IB/28 EI/13
Endorsed: Pitanc'

637 26 June 1300

Grant, remise and quitclaim by Margery daughter of Robert Herbert of Coventry in her widowhood and lawful power, for herself and her heirs, to John de Hales dyer in Coventry (*in Coventr' Tinctori*) and Margaret his wife, of all right and claim in a certain part of the land which the aforesaid Robert the grantor's father gave and confirmed by his charter to the aforesaid John and Margaret, which lies next to the royal highway (*juxta Regalem viam*) leading from Coventry towards Harnall (*Harnhale*), between the land of the hospital of St. John of Coventry and the land of John le Gaunter on the one hand and the land of the lord prior and convent of Coventry which is called *gardinerescroft*; to be held with all appurtenances to them, their heirs or whatsoever assigns, well, in peace, freely and wholly without any charge, hindrance or impediment by her or her heirs. Exclusion and sealing clauses. Witnesses: Anketill de Coleshull then bailiff of Coventry, John Leofwyne then coroner, John Pyhod, Henry Oky, John le Gaunter, Robert Kelle, John Abbot, Nicholas the Dyer (*Tinctore*), Roger the clerk and others. Coventry, Sunday after the feast of the Nativity of St. John the Baptist 28 Edward I.

Seal extant C.R.O. IB/28 EI/4

638 29 August 1300

Charter of Robert Herbert of Coventry giving to John de Hales dyer in Coventry (*in Coventr' Tinctori*) and Margaret his wife a certain part of the land with appurtenances which he had next to the road which leads from Cook St., Coventry towards Harnall (*juxta via(m) que ducit de vico Coci in Coventr' versus Harnhale*), lying in width between the land of the hospital of St. John of Coventry and the land of John le Gaunter on the one hand and the land of the lord prior and convent of Coventry which is called *gardinerescroft* on the other and which extends in length from the aforesaid road up to the garden (*gardinum*) of the lord prior and convent of Coventry just as the land fully purports; to be held with all appurtenances and easements to them, their heirs or whatsoever assigns, well [etc.] of the chief lords of that fee, by rendering annually to the same lords the services due and by right accustomed, namely 12d. of silver at the four terms of the year usual in the vill of Coventry for all secular services [etc.]. Clause for warranty. John and Margaret gave a certain sum of money beforehand. Sealing clause. Witnesses: Anketill de Coleshul, John Pyhod, Henry Oky, Master Robert the Cook (*Coco*), John le Gaunt(er), Robert Kelle, John Abbot, Nicholas the Dyer (*Tinctore*), Roger the clerk and others. Coventry, Monday the feast of the Decollation of St. John the Baptist 28 Edward I.

Seal extant C.R.O. IB/28 EI/2

639 Early 1240s

Remise and quitclaim by Alice widow of Roger the Gardener (*Gardinar'*) of Coventry, in her widowhood and lawful power, to God, the church of the blessed Mary of Coventry, and the prior and monks there, of all right and claim in name of dower in the entire land in the territory of Harnall (*in t(er)ritorio de Harnhal'*) once of Roger her husband, and moreover all right in all rents in the vill of Coventry which the same Roger her husband sold (*aliquo tempore vendiderat*) to them; to be held to them freely [etc.]. The prior and monks gave 8s. of silver. Sealing clause. Witnesses: Osbert the clerk, Richard Burg', Anketill de Wikewan', Richard Lefwin', Richard de Fonte, Robert de Feug(er)s, John Sym', Henry Herb', Robert de Cornl', William Crispin, Peter son of Martin, Nicholas son of Warin and others.

Seal extant C.R.O. IA/C60

640 Late 1230s–early 1240s

Charter of Roger the Gardener (*Gardinar'*) of Coventry giving to God and the church of the blessed Mary of Coventry and the prior and monks there, in free, pure and perpetual alms, his entire land in the field (*campo*) of Harnall (*Harnhal'*) with appurtenances which at one time (*aliquando*) he held of them; to be held to the said prior and monks and their successors freely [etc.] in free, pure and perpetual alms without any charge or contradiction by the grantor or his heirs. Warranty and sealing clauses. Witnesses: Sir Nicholas de Withib(r)oc, Osbert the clerk, William de Wilnh', Adam the clerk, Philip de Winchecu(m)ba, Thomas Oky, Andrew de Stok', Richard Gubiun, John the Butler (*pi(n)cerna*) and others.

Seal extant C.R.O. IA/C12/16

BETWEEN THE BRIDGES [ST. JOHN'S BRIDGES OR THE BURGES]

641 c.24 June 1223

Lease by Robert de Feugers to Geoffrey de Willenhall for a term of ten years of the house in which he used to live between the bridges in Coventry.

Sciant presentes et futuri quod ego Rob(ertus) de Feug(er)s tradidi ad firmam Galfrido de Wilnhal' dom(um) meam inter pontes in Covintr' in qua manere consuevi, scilicet dom(um) illam propinquior aque cum pertinentiis suis; habendam et tenendam de me et de heredibus meis sibi et heredibus suis libere et quiete et honorifice a Nativitate sancti Johannis Baptiste tercia post translationem b(eat)i Thome m(arty)ris[1] usque ad decem annos sequentes completos pro quatuor marcis argenti quas ipse Galfridus mihi dedit, scilicet totam firmam decem annorum premanibus. Et ego Rob(ertus) et heredes mei warantizabimus predicto Galfrido et heredibus suis predictam domum cum pertinentiis suis per decem annos contra omnes homines et omnes feminas. Et totum servitium quod debetur capitalibus dominis de domo illa singulis annis adquietabimus. Completis vero decem annis predicta domus cum pertinentiis suis remanebit mihi et heredibus meis sola et quieta ab ipso Galfrido et ab omnibus suis sine omni contradictione. Hanc autem conventionem legaliter et sine dolo tenendam utrunque affidavimus. In cujus rei testimonium presenti scripto sigillum meum apposui. Hiis testibus Willelmo filio Umfr(idi) Johanne filio ejus Swano Parcar(io) Vincentio filio ejus Henrico filio Edredi Willelmo de Franketon' Thoma Tinctore Hamone filio Jord(ani) Rog(ero) de Cornl' Roberto Blundo Michael(e) Tinctore et aliis.

Seal extant W.R.O. 205

[1] 7 July 1220

642 Late 1240s

Charter of William le Turner'[1] giving to Ranulf de Franketu(n) a certain part of his land with a house sited there in Coventry opposite the croft of Nicholas Forthwine which is between the land Peter Martin held on the one hand and the land Richard Erneys exchanged (*excambiavit*) with the lord prior of Coventry on the other in length and in width according to the metes and bounds there; to be held to him, his heirs or assigns, of the grantor and his heirs freely [etc.] by rendering annually a clove-gillyflower at Easter for all secular service [etc.]. Clause for warranty. Ranulf gave 5s. of silver beforehand. Sealing clause. Witnesses: Robert de Feug(er)s, Martin Colbrond', Thomas Oki, Matthew the Smith (*fabro*), Roger the Weaver (*textor'*), Thomas de Bannebur', Michael the Smith (*fabro*), Hugh the clerk and others.

Seal missing P.R.O. A9795

Endorsed: Inter pont' Coventre
versus pont'

[1] Leturner'

643

c.1290–1297

Charter of Roger son of Adam Attegrene of Coventry giving to Hugh de Meryton merchant in Coventry (*in Coventr' mercatori*) in free marriage with Agnes his sister a moiety of a tenement between the bridges towards the hospital of St. John in Coventry (*inter pontes versus hospitale sancti Johannis in Coventr'*), namely that moiety which lies in width between the land of Henry Baker (*Pistoris*) on the one hand and the grantor's land on the other and extends in length from the royal highway (*a Regali via*) up to the running water as is manifest according to the metes and bounds made there; to be held with buildings sited there and all appurtenances to them and their legitimately begotten heirs, and to the assigns of the same heirs, freely [etc.] of the lords of that fee, by rendering annually the services due and by right accustomed. Clause for warranty. Clause for reversion to the grantor and his heirs should Hugh and Agnes die without legitimately begotten heir. Sealing clause. Witnesses: [Henry][1] Baker (*pistore*) then bailiff of Coventry, Willelmo le Parker then coroner, Thoma le [M][1]oubray, John Thole, Adam Russel, Richard [ ][1], Willelmo Grantpe, Ralf le Hunte, Henry de Barsham and others. Coventry (*Dat ap(u)d Coventr' die . . .*)[2]

No seal or tag — P.R.O. A4451

[1] The document is damaged and torn with some loss, and [2] also appears to be incomplete.

644

c.1290–1297

Grant, release and quitclaim by Emma daughter of Richard the Purse-maker (*Bursarii*) of Coventry, for herself and her heirs, to John called (*dicto*) Abbot son of Roger the Miller (*Molendinar'*) of Coventry of all right and claim in a seld which lies between the bridges in the Prior's half of Coventry (*una selda que jacet inter pontes ex parte domini Prioris Coventr'*) between the land John le Blound of Coventry held on the one hand and the land William the Usher (*hostiariu(us)*) once held on the other in width, and in length from the land of the said William up to the royal highway (*regiam viam*) with all appurtenances according to the metes and bounds made there; to be held to him, his heirs and whatsoever assigns, freely [etc.] of the chief lords of that fee [by] the services due and by right accustomed. Exclusion and warranty clauses. John gave a sum of money beforehand. Sealing clause. Witnesses: Henry Baker (*Pistor'*) then bailiff of Coventry, William le Parkere then coroner of the same, William Graumpe, John de Langeleye, Richard de le Muyr', John Pyhod, Henry Oky and others. Coventry, Wednesday after Michaelmas 22 Edward I.

Seal extant — P.R.O. A 4310

645

5 October 1301

Charter of John son of Roger the Miller (*Molendinar'*) giving to Richard his son a messuage with appurtenances in the vill of Coventry lying between the bridges in the Prior's half (*jacens infra pontes ex parte prioris*) between the land Anketinus de Collushull' holds[1] on the one hand and the land the brothers and sisters of the hospital of St. John of Coventry held[1] on the other in width and in length from the aforesaid land of the brothers and sisters up to the royal highway (*regiam viam*) according to the metes and bounds made there; to be held to him, his heirs or assigns, of the grantor and his heirs freely [etc.], by rendering annually a clove-gillyflower at Easter for all secular service [etc.]. Clause for warranty. Richard gave 40s. of silver beforehand. Sealing clause. Witnesses: Robert Baker (*Pistore*) then bailiff of Coventry, John Leuwyn then coroner of the same, John Pihod, Nicholas the Dyer (*Tynctor'*), John de Halis, William Galewey, Richard Colebrond the clerk and others. Coventry, Thursday after Michaelmas 29 Edward I.

Seal missing P.R.O. A 4443

[1] sic

646 13 October 1298

Charter of John de Wedon' of Coventry and Beatrice his wife giving to Simon Child baker (*Pistori*) of Coventry and Alice daughter of John de Wedon' a messuage with the buildings sited there next to the road which leads from Coventry priory towards the hospital of St. John (*juxta viam que ducit de prioratu Conventr' versus hospital' sancti Johannis ejusdem ville*), and which lies between the land of John Leofwyne on the one hand and the land Richard Oysel held on the other, namely in length and width as is fully manifest according to the metes and bounds there; to be held to them and their legitimately begotten heirs freely [etc.] of the lords of that fee, by rendering 6d. of silver annually at the four terms of the year usual, principal and fixed in the vill of Coventry for all secular service [etc.]. Clause for warranty. Clause for reversion to the grantor and his heirs should Simon and Alice die without legitimately begotten heir. Sealing clause. Witnesses: Anketill de Coleshulle then bailiff of Coventry, John the Goldsmith (*aurifabro*), John Gover, William Maunsel, Richard de St. James, Robert in le Hurn', William Wallar', Edward le Barker', Roger the clerk and others. Coventry, Monday after the feast of St. Denis the Martyr 26 Edward I.

Seal extant P.R.O. A 4328

647 Early 1270s

Charter of Ranulf de Franketon' of Coventry giving to Hugh le Bretun 2d. annual rent which Hugh used to render from a moiety of a barn (*horrei*) and a moiety of a croft with appurtenances in Coventry towards the dovecote of the monks of Coventry (*versus columbar' monachorum*) which moieties of barn and croft with adjacent meadow and appurtenances William de Franketon gave in free marriage with Alice the grantor's sister to Bertram Bretun father of the aforesaid Hugh as is fully contained in a charter made thereon; to be held to him, his heirs and assigns, freely [etc.]. Sealing clause. Witnesses: Robert de Chilton' then bailiff in Coventry, Henry Baker (*pistor'*) of the same, Walter Bacun of the same, Thomas Celet of the same, Adam Colebrond of the same, Hugh le Hoser of the same, Peter de Cotesbech clerk and others.

Seal extant P.R.O. A7615

WEST ORCHARD*

*For other references to West Orchard see 231, 405, 406, 454, 661–665, 669, 670, 700.

648

Late 1250s

Charter of William de Weston' of Coventry giving to Martin Colebront of Coventry a certain part of his curtilage in the vill of Coventry, namely in West Orchard (*in Wasto Gardino*) with appurtenances, which extends in length from the land Martin Colebront held of the grantor up to the outer ash tree (*exteriorem frenam*) and lies in width between the land Reginald the Miller (*molendinar'*) held on the one hand and the lane (*veicl(u)m*) leading towards the land Thomas le Furner once held on the other; to be held to him, his heirs or assigns, of the grantor, his heirs or assigns, freely [etc.], by rendering annually a clove-gillyflower at Christmas for all secular service [etc.]. Martin gave 3s. of silver in recognition. Warranty and sealing clauses. Witnesses: John son of Simon then reeve (*p(re)po(s)ito*), Richard de Fonte, Robert Haumu(n)d, Andrew de Cundulm', Geoffrey Breton', Bertram Breton', Roger de Macstok', Reginald the Miller (*molend'*), Walter Pihot, William Frewin, Peter Frewin and others.

Seal missing

P.R.O. A 9224

The seal tag bears the beginning of a charter, of which the grantor is William de Weston.

649

Late 1250s

Charter of William de Weston' selling to Martin Colebront a certain messuage with appurtenances in the vill of Coventry, namely that which is situated in West Orchard (*situm est in Wastogardino*) between the land Reginald Rappoc held on the one hand and the land Ramitte de Heyam held on the other as the land purports in length and in width according to the metes and bounds made there; to be held to him and his heirs, and to whomsoever he will wish to give, sell or assign, of the grantor and his heirs freely [etc.] by rendering annually 4d. of silver at four terms of the year according to the usage of the vill of Coventry for all secular services, suits of court, customs and demands pertaining to the said messuage. *Et si ita contingat quod dictus Martinus incurrat dampnum vel jacturam pro defectu mei vel heredum meorum vel assignatorum meorum in dicto tenemento bene licet dictus Martinus distringere totum illud tenementum quod cepi in villa de Coventr' cum uxore mea quousque satisfactum fuerit ei per visum proborum hominum. Ita tamen quod predictus Martinus et heredes sui et sui assignati et omnes tenentes sui erunt quieti de tolneto equorum in dicto mesuagio. Et si eorum aliquis in m(isericord)ia mea vel heredum meorum inciderit erit quietus pro uno denario imperpetuum.* Clause for warranty. Martin gave 22s. of silver beforehand. Sealing clause. Witnesses: John son of Simon then reeve (*tunc p(re)po(s)ito*), Richard de Fonte, Robert Haumu(n)d, William Lewin, William de Pailinton', John Blacwine, Geoffrey Breton', Hugh de Macstok', Ranulf de Franketon', William de Huehinton', Thomas Leoras, John Ingeram, Bertram Bretun and others.

Seal missing P.R.O. A 8700

650 Late 1250s

Remise, grant and quitclaim by Martin Colbront of Coventry without any reservation by him or his heirs to Gerard de Alispath' of all right and claim in a certain messuage with appurtenances in the vill of Coventry lying in West Orchard (*in Wasto Gardino*) between the land of Reg(inald) Rappoc on the one hand and the land Ramette[1] de Heyham once held on the other, in length and in width according to the metes and bounds made there; to be held to him, his heirs or assigns freely [etc.], by making to the lords of that fee the service of 4d. *per annum* at four terms of the year for all secular service [etc.]. Gerard gave 2½ marks of silver in recognition beforehand. Sealing clause. Witnesses: John son of Simon, William Leuwin, William de Alisley, Alexander de Glov(er)nia, Geoffrey Breton', John Yngera(m), Ralf the Baker (*pistore*), Thomas the clerk and others.

Seal missing P.R.O. A 10810

[1] sic

651 1270s

Gift by Gerard de Alespath' to John de Makestoke of his tiled stone house with the entire land on which it is built and free entrance and exit pertaining to it in West Orchard, Coventry (*domum meam de Lapide coop(er)ata(m) cum tota terra sub quam edifficat(am) et cum libero introitu et exitu ad illam pertin(ente) In vasto g(a)rdino de Coventr'*) which lies between the land Roger the Fishmonger (*piscator*) held on the one hand and the lane (*venelam*) leading from the royal highway (*a Regia via*) up to the aforesaid house in width and extends in length from the land of Robert Lond' up to the land of Master Robert Leycestr', in length and in width as is manifest and according to the metes and bounds made there; to be held of the grantor and his heirs to him, his heirs or assigns, or to whomsoever or whensoever he will wish to give, bequeath, sell or assign, both in sickness and in health freely [etc.], except to a house of religion or to the Jews (*Judaismo*), by rendering annually 4s. of silver at the four terms of the year usual in the vill of Coventry, namely 12d. at each of the feasts of St. Michael, St. Andrew, the blessed Mary in March and St. John the Baptist for all secular services [etc.]. Should the rent be wholly or partly in arrears by a year and a day the grantor and his heirs may be allowed to enter and possess the house without hindrance (*obstac(u)lo*) or contradiction by John, his heirs or assigns. Clause for warranty. Sealing clause [chirograph]. Witnesses: Henry Baker (*pisto(re)*) then bailiff (*ballivo tunc tempore*), Robert de Chiltun, Geoffrey Bretun, Thomas de Fakinham, John Thole, Martin the Baker (*pistor'*), Vincent the Baker (*pistor'*), Anketell the clerk and others.

Indented
Seal missing P.R.O. A8822

652

1270s

Gift and quitclaim by Alice widow of William Copping in her lawful power to Walter called (*dicto*) de Wyrecestr' of Coventry of all right and claim in a third part of the land in West Orchard (*le Westhotiard*) which Geoffrey Breton once held and which lies between the land the said Walter held on the one hand and the land John le Vineter held on the other, to be held to him, his heirs or assigns; with exclusion clause. William gave 12d. of silver beforehand. Sealing clause. Witnesses: Henry Baker (*pistore*) then bailiff, Robert de Chilton', Hugh Breton, John Coterel, John de Makescot, Henry de le Sartrin, Richard le Dobbere and others.

Seal missing

W.R.O. 304

653

1270s

Remise and quitclaim by Richard de Honslap, for himself and his heirs, to Richard le Dubbere of all right and claim in the entire land with the houses sited there and all appurtenances in West Orchard, Coventry (*in vasto g^a^rdino de Coventr'*) which lies between the land Hugh le Bretun' held on the one hand and the land the same Richard le Dubbere held on the other, in length and in width as the land purports and according to the metes and bounds made there; to be held to him, his heirs or assigns, or to whomsoever and whensoever he will wish to give, bequeath, sell or assign, by rendering (*faciend'*) to the lords of the fee the rent due and accustomed. Exclusion clause. Sealing clause, for 2 marks of silver which Richard gave beforehand. Witnesses: Robert de Chiltun' then bailiff, Henry Baker (*pistor'*), Stephen de Halis, William de Watford', Roger de Halis, Robert Mansel, Henry Dobedy, Anketell the clerk and others.

Seal extant

C.R.O. 2/141

654

Late 1270s

Charter of William Rymild of Coventry giving to Richard le Dubbere the entire land with the houses sited there and all appurtenances in West Orchard, Coventry (*In vasto g^a^rdino de Coventr'*) which lies between the land John Coterel held on the one hand and the land Henry de Honslap held on the other in length and in width as is manifest according to the metes and bounds made there; to be held to him, his heirs or whatsoever assigns, in sickness and in health, of the grantor and his heirs freely [etc.] by rendering annually to the lords of that fee as the grantor's perpetual attorneys 6d. at the four terms of the year usual in the vill of Coventry and a pair of white gloves at Easter, and to the grantor and his heirs a pair of gloves worth ½d. or ½d. at Easter for all secular service [etc.]. Warranty and sealing clauses. Witnesses: Robert de Chylton', Vincent the Goldsmith (*aur'*), Stephen de Halys, William de Watford', Roger de Halys, Henry Dobedy, Michael the Parker (*parcar'*), Anketell the clerk and others.

Seal extant

C.R.O. 2/152

655

Early 1280s

Demise and quitclaim by Christine widow of William Rimild of Coventry, for herself and her heirs, to Richard le Dobber of the same, his heirs or whatsoever assigns, of all right and claim without any reservation in the entire land with buildings and appurtenances in West Orchard (*in vasto gardino*) between the land of John Coterel on the one hand and the land of Henry de Hamselape on the other in length and in width according to the metes and bounds made there. Exclusion clause. Richard gave ½ mark of silver beforehand. Sealing clause. Witnesses: Robert de Chilton then bailiff, Stephen de Halis, Henry Dobedi, John Coterel, Hugh Breto(n) and many others.

Seal extant C.R.O. 2/75

656 Early 1280s

Grant, remise and quitclaim by Nicholas son of Robert Dale of Coventry to Richard le Dobbere of the same of all right and claim in a messuage with all appurtenances in the vill of Coventry *in le Westorcharde*, namely that which is sited between the tenement of John Coterel on the one hand and the tenement of Henry de Hamslape on the other, for 4s. of silver which Richard gave beforehand. Exclusion and sealing clauses. Witnesses: Robert de Chilton' then bailiff of that vill (*tunc ballivo illius ville*), Alexander the Vintner (*vinetar'*), Henry le Bakere, Sir Thomas de Hakenham[1], Sir Henry Dobedi, Stephen de Hales, William Cro(m)pe and others.

Seal missing C.R.O. 2/173

[1] sic

657 Early 1280s

Charter of Henry son of Thomas Oky of Coventry giving to Alexander called the Vintner (*dicto vinitario*) of Coventry a certain part of his land in the same vill, namely a certain place with a fish-pond (*placiam cum s(er)vario*) and all its appurtenances near the bridge of West Orchard (*p(ro)pe Ponte(m) de Westo Gardino*) which place (*placi*) was once of John Vincent, according to the metes and bounds made there. Moreover he has granted 2s. rent with appurtenances in the same vill in Gosford St. (*in vico de Gosford*) which Richard le Northern' used to render to the grantor from a tenement which he held of him near Gosford bridge (*propinquiori Ponti de Gosford*), which tenement is between the water running towards Altegeder Mills (*Altegeder-emulnes*) on the one hand and the land once of Thomas de Fakenham on the other; to be held to him, his heirs or whatsoever assigns, of the lords of those fees by the services due and by right accustomed, by rendering annually to the grantor and his heirs a clove-gillyflower at Easter for all service [etc.]. Warranty and sealing clauses. Witnesses: Robert de Chilton' then bailiff in Coventry, Walter Bakon then coroner, Thomas de[1] Moubray, John Tole, Alexander le Moubray, Peter Baron, Roger the Fishmonger (*Piscator'*), Thomas Selet, John de Fillungeleye, William Kelle, John Pyhod, Alan de Estleya and others.

Seal extant C.R.O. IA/L12–13C/48

[1] sic

658 Mid–late 1280s

Charter of Alexander called the Vintner (*dictus vinitarius*) of Coventry giving to Henry Oky of Coventry a certain part of his land in Coventry, namely a curtilage with a fish-pond (*servario*) and a garden with appurtenances which were once of Thomas de Fakinham in West Orchard next to the bridge (*in vasto g^a^rdino juxta Ponte(m)*); to be held to him, his heirs or assigns, of the grantor, his heirs or assigns, by rendering annually 5s. of silver at the four terms of the year usual in the vill of Coventry. Sealing clause. Witnesses: Henry Baker (*Pistor'*) then bailiff, Robert de Chilton', John Thole, Thomas le Mobray, Robert Kalle, William Kelle, William Bacun the clerk and others.

Seal extant C.R.O. 1A/C18

659 1298–1305

Remise and quitclaim by Alice Hod of Coventry, for herself and her heirs, to Thomas the Cellarer (*Celario*) and Margery his wife of all right and claim in the entire tenement in West Orchard, Coventry (*in vasto g^a^rdino Coventr'*) which lies between the land Roger the clerk held on the one hand and the lane (*venella(m)*) leading to the house once of John Hod on the other in length and in width as the tenement purports; to be held with all appurtenances together with all goods, vessels and chattels (*bonis vasis et catallis ibidem crescentibus et existentibus*) to them, their heirs or assigns freely [etc.], of the chief lords of that fee by the service due and by right accustomed. Exclusion and sealing clauses. Witnesses: John Lewin then coroner, Robert de Chiltun', Robert H(er)berd, John de Witele, William le Golsmith, Ralph ad Crucem and others.

Seal missing C.R.O. IA/C13/19

MARKET AREA*

*Included here are tenements and lanes (e.g. Ylpus Lane and Sleper's Lane) to the west of Cross Cheaping, north and south of West Orchard, in addition to Ironmonger Row and Smiths' Row. There is always the possibility that some references are to the prior's market-place in Bishop St. (e.g. 689, which should be compared with 595, and perhaps 557). See above p.xxx.
For other references to the market area see 51, 385. For additional references to Smiths' Row see *Langley Cartulary* Nos. 438, 494.

660 c.1200–c.1210

Charter of William son of Godric the Miller (*molandinarii*) giving to William de Franketona and his heirs, to be held of the grantor and his heirs in fee and inheritance, his land in the Market-place (*in foro*) which is between the land Robert de Felgeris held and the shops (*soppas*) which William Midnit held just as the land purports in length and in width freely [etc.] by rendering annually 6d. for all secular service [etc.]. Clause for warranty. William gave 33s. of silver. Witnesses: Gerard the Vintner (*vinet'*) and Gerard his son, Richard de Aula, Matthew son of Roger, William son of Humphrey (*hu(m)fredi*) and John and William his sons, William de Brinkel' and William and John his sons, Vincent, Peter de Kent, Stephen son of Herbert, Leuewin and Herbert and Hamo brothers, Richard de Warewic, Henry son of Edred, William Midnit and many others.

Seal extant P.R.O. A 11959
Endorsed: de domo Joh(ann)is Tole

661 c.1210–1221

Charter of William Midneit giving to William de Franketon' and his heirs all his selds in the Market-place at the head of West Orchard (*omnes seldas meas in foro ad caput Wasti Gardinii*) with the entire land pertaining to the same selds and with all appurtenances, namely all the land and selds which are sited between West Orchard St. (*vicum de Wasto Gardino*) and the land which the aforesaid William de Franketon held of William son of Godric; to be held of the grantor and his heirs in fee and inheritance freely [etc.], by rendering annually for all secular services [etc.] 12d. of silver at four terms of the year, namely 3d. at each of the feasts of St. Michael, St. Andrew, St. Mary in March and St. John the Baptist. Clause for warranty. William gave 13 marks of silver in recognition. Witnesses: Richard de Aula, Vincent, William son of Humphrey (*Umfr'*), John his son, Matthew son of Roger, Richard de Warewic', William son of Helewis, Thomas the Dyer (*tinctore*), Leofwine, Geoffrey de Wilnhal',

William his brother, William de Sponsa, Matthew the Smith (*fabro*), William de Folkeshul' and many others.

Seal extant P.R.O. A4656

662 c.1210–c.1221

Charter of William de Franketon' giving to William the Cordwainer (*Cordubanario*) a part of his land with appurtenances in Coventry which he held of William Midneith, namely the part which is at the corner of West Orchard (*ad cornu Westgardini*) in length and in width as the seld sited there (*selda suprasita*) purports; to be held to him and his heirs of the grantor and his heirs in fee and inheritance freely [etc.], by rendering annually for all service and all demands 4s. of silver at four terms of the year, namely 12d. at each of the feasts of St. Michael, St. Andrew, St. Mary in March and St. John the Baptist. Clause for warranty. William gave 20s. of silver in recognition. Witnesses: William son of Humphrey (*Umfr'*), Richard de Aula, Robert the Vintner (*Vinit'*), Hugh son of Martin, William de Wilnhale, Vincent, Ralf the Dyer (*tinctore*), Geoffrey de Wilnhale, Thomas the Dyer (*tinctore*), Henry son of Edred (*Edredi*), John son of Blacwin', Stephen son of Herbert, Matthew son of Roger and many others.

Seal extant P.R.O. A 4434

663 Late 1220s–1232

Charter of Matilda widow of Stephen son of Herbert, in her widowhood and free power, granting to Ranulf son of William de Franketon' the land in Coventry in the street of the lord prior (*in vico domini Prioris*), namely that which lies between the land David the Vintner (*Vinitar'*) held and the road which leads to West Orchard (*viam que tendit in Westgardinu(m)*) and contains 52 feet in length from the high street towards West Orchard (*a magno vico versus Westgardinu(m)*); to be held to him and his heirs of the grantor and her heirs hereditarily, freely and quietly and with all appurtenances, by rendering annually for all service [etc.] 3s. of silver at four terms of the year, namely 9d. at each of the feasts of St. Michael, St. Andrew, St. Mary in March and St. John the Baptist. Clause for warranty. Ranulf gave 3 marks of silver. Sealing clause. Witnesses: Richard de Aula, William son of Humphrey (*Umfredi*), John his son, Richard de Brug', David de Fonte, Geoffrey de Wilnhal', William his brother, David the Vintner (*vinitar'*), Richard the Goldsmith (*aurifabro*), Robert Breton', Bertram his son, William de Pailinton', John Blacwin' and others.

Seal extant P.R.O. A 6530

664 Late 1240s–early 1250s

Charter of Ranulf de Franketon' giving to Nicholas son of Warin a certain part of his land in Coventry, namely that which is between the land Bertram Bretun held on the one hand and the land the grantor held on the other, together with the land which extends in length from West Orchard (*a vasto gardino*) up to the great house (*magnam domum*) where the grantor's father used to live and in width from the land Bertram Bretun and the aforesaid Nicholas held up to the land the grantor held, as is manifest in length and in width according to the metes and bounds there; to be held to him, his heirs or assigns, except to a house of religion, of the grantor and his heirs freely [etc.], by rendering annually ½ mark of silver at the four terms of the year fixed in Coventry for all secular service [etc.]. Clause for warranty. Nicholas gave 4 marks of silver beforehand. Sealing clause. Witnesses: Robert de Corleya,

Anketinus de Wykewan, William de Wilnal', Richard de Fonte, Richard Labanc, John Blacwine, William de Pailinton', Robert de Feug(er)s, William Lewyn, Robert Haumond, Roger de Fredesham, Ralf de Atleb(er)ge, Henry of St. John the clerk and others.

Seal missing P.R.O. A 6425

665 1270s

Remise and quitclaim by Joan daughter of Nicholas Waryn of Coventry, in her free widowhood and lawful power, without reservation by her or her heirs, to Ranulf de Franketon' of all right and claim in the entire land in Coventry in the Prior's Market-place (*in foro domini prioris*) which Nicholas Waryn her father once held of the said Ranulf at the head of West Orchard (*ad capud vastigardini*) according to the metes and bounds made there; to be held to him, his heirs or assigns, freely [etc.] without any charge by her or her heirs. Sealing clause. Witnesses: Robert de Chilton', John de Ludelowe, Robert de London', John Tole, Thomas de Fakinham, John the Goldsmith (*Aurifabr'*), Thomas Selet clerk, Hugh the clerk, Walter Bacun, John de Maxthoke and others.

Seal extant P.R.O. A 12050

666 Late 1260s–early 1270s

Sale, remise and quitclaim by John de Lodelowe burgess of Coventry (*Burgens' Coventr'*) without any reservation by him or his heirs to Ranulph de Franketon', of all right and claim in 3s. annual rent, which rent the grantor bought from Richard de Bruges and which Ranulph used to render to the said Richard from lands he held of him as is more fully contained in Richard's charter to the grantor; to be held to Ranulph, his heirs or assigns, freely [etc.], by rendering annually to Agnes daughter of William de Heyham and her heirs 6d. of silver at the four terms of the year fixed and customary in the vill of Coventry and a pair of gloves worth ½d. or ½d. at Easter for all secular service [etc.]. Ranulph gave 1 mark of silver. Sealing clause. Witnesses: Henry Baker (*Pistor'*), Hugh the clerk, Nicholas de Kannel', Peter the Welshman (*valenc'*), John Tole, Robert de London', Walter Bacun, Ralph the Baker (*Pistor'*), John Coterel and others.

Seal missing P.R.O. A 10740

667 c.25 March 1295

Agreement whereby Mariota once the daughter of Ranulph de Frangketon has leased and demised at farm to Robert de Dunstaple and Margaret his wife a plot of land (*placeam terre*) with the houses sited there and all appurtenances in the vill of Coventry for a term of 10 years beginning at the feast of the blessed Mary in March 23 Edward I, which plot lies between the land of John Thole senior on the one hand and the land of the master, brothers and sisters of the hospital of St. John of Coventry on the other in width, and in length from the royal highway (*a regali via*) up to the land once of Walter Bacun as is manifest according to the metes and bounds made there; to be held to them, their heirs or assigns, freely [etc.] during the term, by rendering annually to the lord prior and the convent of Coventry 6d. of silver at the four terms of the year usual and fixed in Coventry for all secular service and demand. Clause for warranty during the term. *Et si ita sit quod predicta Mariota predictam placeam terre cum domibus suprasitis et aliis pertinentiis infra terminum prenotatum alicui vendere vel diutius ad terminum velit ponere predicti Robertus et Margareta propinquiores erunt omnibus aliis.*[1] *Preterea si ita sit quod predicti Robertus et Margareta aliquod novu(m) edificiu(m) infra terminum prenominatum super predictam placeam terre edificare vel construere fac(iant) tunc bene liceat predictis Roberto et Margarete totum illud edificiu(m) ad finem termini predicti secum asportare et ubicumque et quandocumque voluerint removere sine aliqua contradiccione vel impedimento predicte Mariote et heredum suorum nisi ita sit quod predicta Mariota vel heredes sui predictis Roberto et Margareta omnes cust(us) et expens(as) sic inpo(s)it(os) plenarie et rationabiliter velint allocare et aquietare.* Robert and Margaret gave 24s. of silver. Mutual sealing clause [chirograph]. Witnesses: Henry Baker (*Pistor'*), William le Parker', John Thole, John de Halis, Henry de Halis, William the Tailor (*Cissor'*), Robert the clerk and others.

Indented
Seal missing P.R.O. A 10838

[1] *omnibus* repeated after *aliis.*

668 1295–c.1297

Charter of Mariota de F(r)anketon' daughter of Ranulph of the same in Coventry giving to Robert de Donestaple and Margaret his wife, the grantor's sister, and their legitimately begotten heirs, a messuage with the houses sited there and all appurtenances in the vill of Coventry, namely that which lies between the land of John Tole senior on the one hand and the land of the master, brothers and sisters of the hospital of St. John of Coventry on the other in length and in width from the royal highway (*a regia via*) up to the land once of Walter Bacun as is manifest according to the metes and bounds made there; to be held to them and their heirs as aforesaid freely [etc.] so that if the aforesaid Robert should survive Margaret *quod absit* he may give, bequeath, sell or assign the aforesaid messuage with the houses sited there to whomsoever, wheresoever and whensoever he will wish without contradiction by the grantor or her heirs, and similarly if the aforesaid Margaret should survive Robert *quicumque in supradicto mesuagio cum domibus suprasitis melius et utilius decreverit faciend' liberam habeat potestatem*, by rendering annually to the lord prior and convent of Coventry 6d. of silver at the four terms of the year usual and accustomed in the vill of Coventry for all secular service [etc.]. Clause for warranty. Sealing clause. Witnesses: Henry Baker (*Pistor'*), William le Parker', John de Hales, John the Goldsmith (*aurifabro*), Robert Kelle and others.

Seal missing P.R.O. A 8910

669 Mid 1290s

Grant, remise and quitclaim by Petronilla daughter of Ranulf de Franketon' widow of Roger le T(r)anour of Canley (*Canneleye*), for herself and her heirs, to Henry Baker (*pistori*) of Coventry of 2s. annual rent which she used to receive from a tenement lying between the lane (*venellam*) which is called West Orchard (*le Westorecart*) on the one hand and the land of Robert the Cook (*Coci*) of Kenilworth (*Kenelworþe*) on the other where iron is sold (*ubi ferru(m) venditur*); to be held to him, his heirs or assigns, in peace freely [etc.]. Exclusion and sealing clauses. Witnesses: Robert the Cook (*Coc'*) of Kenilworth (*Kenelworþe*), John Leuin of Coventry, Roger Dayseie of the same, John the Cook (*Coc'*), John ad Crucem, Robert Frande[ ][1], Henry de Hynkeleie and many others.

Seal missing C.R.O. 2/73
Endorsed: Carta pet(r)onille uxoris quond' Rogeri le T(r)ann(ur) de Canneleie de duobus sold' annual' redit' super cornera(m) de le Westorchard ex parte australi.

[1] Remainder of this name is lost.

670 Early 1280s

Remise, grant and quitclaim by Richard Midnyht of Coventry, for himself and his heirs, to Henry Baker (*pistori*) of Coventry of 18d. annual rent which he used to receive from the heirs of Ranulph de Franketon' at the four terms of the year usual in Coventry from the entire messuage which Henry Baker (*pistor*) holds between West Orchard (*vicum Westgardini*) on the one hand and the land of John Tole on the other and which extends from the royal highway where iron is sold (*a regali via ubi venditur ferru(m)*) up to the bake-house (*pistrinu(m)*) of Robert de Chilton'; to be held with its appurtenances and all courts (? *curibus*), liberties, customs and escheats and all other profits issuing from the aforesaid rent in whatsoever way, to him, his heirs or whatsoever assigns, well [etc.]. Exclusion clause. In return Henry gave a curtilage next to the road (*viam*) which leads from Coventry towards Radford (*Radeforde*) as is contained in the charter of enfeoffment which he had from the aforesaid Henry. Sealing clause. Witnesses: Robert de Chilton', Walter Bacun, Thomas le Moubrai, John Tole, Walter de Banneburi, John Sampson, John de Macstoke, Henry de Hynkele, Roger de Alesleye clerk and many others.

Seal missing G.H. 295

Endorsed: Quieta clamatio Ricardi de midnyht de xviii denar' reddit' pro quibus idem Ricardus tenet unum curtilagium supra barra(m) Episcopi pro vi den' per annum Henr' pistor'

Carta de octodecim denarios annual' reddit' de tenemento sup(er) corneram de la Westorchard ex parte borial'

671 c.1210

Charter of Stephen son of Herbert giving to William son of Richard Fordwine and his heirs, to be held of the grantor and his heirs in fee and inheritance, the entire land in the Market-place (*in foro*) which is between the land Philip Want(er) held and the land Robert Surebacstere held as the land purports in length and in width and as it extends from the street up to the messuage which was the grantor's (*a vico usque ad mansum quod meum fuit*) freely [etc.] by rendering annually for all secular service [etc.] 2s. of silver at four terms of the year, namely 6d. at each of the feasts of St. Michael, St. Andrew, St. Mary in March and St. John the Baptist. Clause for warranty. William gave 5 marks in recognition, and to the grantor's wife a pair of leather boots (*unas botas de cordubano*). Witnesses: Gerard the Vintner (*vinit'*), Gerard his son, Richard de Aula, Richard de Wigorn', Stephen his son, Hugh son of Martin, Richard de Hu(n)delan', Vincent, Peter de Kant, Swanus the Parker (*p(ar)car'*), William de Rape(n)don', Matthew son of Gundr', Matthew son of Roger, Hugh son of Odo, Lefwin son of Jordan, Thomas the Dyer (*tinctore*), Geoffrey de Wil[n]hale, William his brother and many others.

Seal extant W.R.O. 178

Endorsed: de foro Coventr'

672 Late 1230s–early 1240s

Remise and quitclaim by Jordan son of Stephen son of Herbert for himself and his heirs to Nicholas son of William Forthwin and his heirs of 12d. annual rent from the 2s. rent in Coventry which the same Nicholas rendered to him from the land which he held of the grantor between the land Robert the Plumber (*Plumbarius*) held and the messuage where William de Paylinton' lived (*mansit*). Clause for warranty. Nicholas gave 5s. of silver. Witnesses: Richard Leuwin, John Blacwin', William de Paylinton', Peter Martin, Walter the Goldsmith (*aurifabro*), Roger de Frodisham,

Hugh Ketelbern', Nicholas the nephew of Vincent, Adam the Red (*Ruffo*) baker (*Pistore*) and others.

Seal extant W.R.O. 180

673 Late 1230s–early 1240s

Remise and quitclaim by Matilda widow of Stephen Herbert in her widowhood and free power to Nicholas son of William Fordwin' and his heirs of 12d. rent from the 2s. which the same Nicholas rendered to her in name of dower from the land which lies between the messuage (*mansum*) of William de Paylinton' and the land of Robert the Plumber (*Plumbarii*). Nicholas gave 5s. of silver. Sealing clause. Witnesses: Richard Lefwin', William de Paylinton', Roger de Frodissam, John Blacwin', Walter the Goldsmith (*aurifabro*), Peter Martin, Hugh Ketelbern', Adam the Red (*Ruffo*) baker (*pistore*) and others.

Seal missing W.R.O. 179

674 Early 1270s

Charter of Nicholas Fortwin of Coventry giving to Robert de Eton' and Yseult (*Yseud'*) his wife certain land in the vill of Coventry with appurtenances lying in the Market-place (*in foro*) of the lord prior of Coventry between the land Martin the Baker (*pistor*) held on the one hand and the land of the said Robert on the other in length and in width according to the metes and bounds made there; to be held to them, their heirs or whatsoever assigns, wheresoever or to whomsoever they will wish to give, sell, bequeath or assign in sickness and in health of the grantor and his heirs freely [etc.] by rendering annually 6s. of silver at the four terms of the year fixed and accustomed in the vill of Coventry for all secular service [etc.]. Warranty and sealing clauses. Witnesses: Henry Baker (*pistore*) then bailiff, Robert de Chilton', Geoffrey Breton', Robert de Londr', Ralf de Abbathia, Martin the Baker (*pistore*), Thomas the clerk and others.

Seal missing C.R.O. IA/C13/57

675 1270s

Charter of Robert de Eton' with the assent and goodwill of Yseult (*Iseude*) his wife giving to Felice his daughter, for her service, the land with the building sited there which he held of Nicholas Fordwin' in the Market-place of Coventry where bread is sold (*in foro Coventr' ubi venditur pan'*) which lies between the land the grantor himself held on the one hand and the land Pagan Pake held on the other, in length and in width as is manifest according to the metes and bounds made there; to be held to her, her heirs or whatsoever assigns of the grantor and his heirs freely [etc.] by rendering annually to the aforesaid Nicholas and his heirs as the perpetual attorneys of the grantor and his heirs 6s. of silver at the four terms of the year usual in the vill of Coventry, and to the grantor and his heirs a rose-flower at the feast of the Nativity of St. John the Baptist for all secular service [etc.]. Warranty and sealing clauses. Witnesses: Henry Baker (*pistor'*) then bailiff, Robert de Chilton', Robert de London', John the Goldsmith (*aurifabro*), John Tole, Thomas Scelet, Ralf the Baker (*pistore*), John Coterel, Hugh Bretu(n) and others.

Seal extant C.R.O. IA/C40

676 c.1205–c.1215

Sale and quitclaim by Roger son of Robert the Smith to William son of Humphrey of the forge in the Market-place which William the Smith of Frankton and his associates held, for 15s. of silver.

Sciant presentes et futuri quod ego Rogerus filius Roberti fabri vendidi et quietam clamavi fabricam meam in foro quam Willelmus faber de Franketona et socii ejus tenuerunt Willelmo filio hu(m)fredi et heredibus suis imperpetuum pro quindecim solidis argenti quos michi solvit et totum jus meum quod in predicta fabrica habui; huic predicto Willelmo et heredibus suis vendidi ut habeat eam et teneat libere et quiete et honorifice et ego prefatus Rogerus et heredes mei debemus warantizare hanc vendicionem et hanc quietam clamanciam huic predicto Willelmo filio hu(m)fredi et heredibus suis contra omnes homines et feminas. Hiis testibus Gerardo Vint(er) Willelmo de Brinkelawa Ricardo de Aula Matheo filio Rogeri Stephano filio H(er)b(er)ti Willelmo Midnith Hugone filio M(ar)tini Vincentio Petro de Kent Hugone filio Odonis Ricardo de Warewi[ck][1] Willelmo Palm(er) Waltero Pellip(ar)io Davido Vinet Davido de Fonte Radulfo Waldri(n)g Johanne Mercer Elufwino Seret et multis aliis.

Seal extant P.R.O. A 6441

[1] There is a small hole here.

677 Late 1220s–early 1230s

Charter of Peter son of Henry son of Edric giving to Roger the Smith (*fabro*) certain land in the Market-place, Coventry (*In foro de Coventr'*), namely that which lies between the land Ranulf son of William de F(r)anketon' held and the land William son of William son of B(r)odric held and the seld sited upon that land, entirely and fully as the land purports in length and in width according to the metes and bounds made there; to be held to him and his heirs of the grantor and his heirs in fee and inheritance freely [etc.], by rendering annually for all service and demand 2s. 6d. of silver at four terms of the year, namely 7½d. at each of the feasts of St. John the Baptist, St. Michael, St. Andrew and St. Mary in March, and at Easter a pair of gloves worth ½d. or ½d. Clause for warranty. Roger gave 2½ marks of silver in recognition. Sealing clause. Witnesses: Geoffrey de Wilnhal', Robert de Feug(ers), John Humphrey (*umfr'*), Richard le Mubray, Richard Thoki, Ingillard, Matthew the Smith (*fabro*), Roger the Weaver (*tellar'*), Richard Oki, Thomas his brother, William Fing', Ranulf de F(r)anketon', and others.

Seal missing C.R.O. 2/41

678 1230s

Charter of Roger the Smith (*fab'*) of Coventry giving to Thomas Hoki in free marriage with Edith his daughter a part of his land in the vill of Coventry namely in the Market-place (*in foro*) between the land Ranulf son of William de F(r)anketon' held and the land William son of William son of Brodric held and the seld sited upon that land, entirely and fully as the land purports in length and in width according to the metes and bounds made there with all appurtenances; to be held to him and his heirs issuing from Edith the grantor's daughter, of the grantor and his heirs freely [etc.], by rendering annually 8d. to the chief lord of that fee at the four terms usual in Coventry for all secular service [etc.]. Warranty and sealing clauses. Witnesses: Geoffrey de Wilnhale, Robert de Feug(ers), Richard le Moub(r)ay, Richard Thoki, Matthew the Smith (*fabro*), Roger the Weaver (*tellario*),

Richard Oki, William Fing, Ranulf de F(r)anketon', William son of Simon, Nicholas Wele, Simon the Baker (*pistori*),[1] Godfrey de Cu(n)delm' and many others.

Seal missing C.R.O. 2/14

[1] sic

679 Late 1240s–early 1250s

Charter of Matthew son of Roger the Smith (*fabri*) giving to Thomas Oky all right and claim in the entire land which his father gave to the same Thomas with Edith the grantor's sister, and in the land which the grantor's father gave to Henry the grantor's brother and in *le Thorayl'* with the land 5 feet in width leading to the *Thorayl'*, namely that which lies on the other side of the road (*ex alia parte itin(er)is*) between the land Richard Copping' held on the one hand and the land Margery widow of Roger Herbert held on the other, in length and in width according to the metes and bounds made there with all appurtenances; to be held to him, his heirs or assigns, of the grantor and his heirs well [etc.] without charge by the grantor or his heirs, by rendering annually 2s. of silver at four terms of the year according to the usage of the vill of Coventry, and a pair of gloves worth ½d. or ½d. at Easter for all service and demand. *Et si contingat quod predictus Thomas heredes sui vel aliquis suorum in m(isericord)ia mea ceciderunt pro uno denar' quieti sint.* Thomas gave ½ mark of silver in recognition. Warranty and sealing clauses. Witnesses: Richard de Fonte, John Simon', Robert de Feug(er)s, Richard Oky, Roger the Weaver (*textore*), Thomas de Bannebur', Martin Colbront, John the White (*albo*) clerk, Henry Herb(er)t and others.

Seal missing C.R.O. 2/94

680 Early 1250s

Charter of Simon le Bocmong(er)e giving to Richard de Fonte a stall (*stalagiu(m)*) in the Market-place (*in foro*) of Coventry, namely that which lies between the stall of Walter Trot on the one hand and the stall of Nicholas son of Ralf on the other; to be held to him, his heirs or assigns, or to whomsoever he will wish to bequeath or sell, give or assign, of the grantor or his heirs freely [etc.] according to the metes and bounds made there, by rendering annually to the high altar of the blessed Mary of Coventry 9d. of silver at four terms of the year according to the usage of Coventry, and to the grantor and his heirs a clove-gillyflower at Easter for all secular service. Richard gave 2 marks of silver in recognition. Warranty and sealing clauses. Witnesses: William de Willenhale, Adam the clerk, John Simund, Martin Colbrond, William Toly, Henry Driu, William de Pailinton', William de Allesleye and others.

Seal extant C.R.O. IA/C52

681 Late 1240s–early 1250s

Charter of David son of Geoffrey de Wilnhale of Coventry giving to Walter de Coundelme a certain part of his land with appurtenances in the Market-place (*in foro*) of Coventry which lies between the land Robert de Maxstoke held on the one hand and the land William de Wilnhale once held on the other; to be held to him, his heirs or assigns, except to a house of religion, freely [etc.], in length and in width according to the metes and bounds made there, by rendering annually 2s. of silver, and to the lords of the fee as the grantor's attorney 4s. at four terms of the year according to the usage of Coventry for all secular service [etc.]. Clause for warranty. Walter gave 8s. of silver. Sealing clause. Witnesses: Robert de Feug(er)s then reeve (*p(re)posito*), Richard de Fonte, John Simond, William de Paylinton', Robert

Hamund, William de Allesleye, Roger Starie, Reginald le Rous, Robert de Maxstoke, Walter the Marshal (*marescall'*), Geoffrey Bretoun, Reginald de Withibroc and others.

Seal extant G.H. 280

682 Late 1250s

Charter of Edith daughter of Geoffrey de Wilenhale, in her lawful and free widowhood, giving to Richard de Fonte 2s. free rent (*liberi redditus*) in the vill of Coventry which the same Richard used to render annually from the land he held in the lane (*venella*) which is called Ylpus Lane (*ylpus lone*) between the land Thomas de Southleye once held on the one hand and the land of Robert de Londoniis on the other; to be held with all its appurtenances and all her right in the 2s. rent or in the aforesaid tenement to him and his heirs, or to whomsoever he will wish to assign, of the grantor and her heirs well [etc.], by rendering annually 6d. of silver at the four terms of the year usual in the vill of Coventry, namely 1½d. in each term for all secular services [etc.]. Clause for warranty. Richard gave 8s. sterling in recognition beforehand. Witnesses: John Simon', William Lewine, Matthew Mumbrai, William Toli, John Ingeram, William de Alesleye, Robert Hamun, William de Pailingtune, Robert de Chiltone, Robert de Lond', John the Goldsmith (*aurifabro*), Thomas le Gras, Thomas de Henleye, Henry de Stanford, Geoffrey Bretun and many others.

Seal missing C.R.O. 2/59

Endorsed: Editha fil' Galfr' de Wylnehale de duobus solid' redditus in vico fontis.

Despite the endorsement Ylpus Lane was in the area of Ironmonger Row (*V.C.H. Coventry*, p. 29).

683 1270s

Charter of Robert de Chilton' burgess of Coventry (*Burg' de Coventr'*), for the salvation of his soul, the soul of his wife Matilda, and those of his sons, ancestors and successors, giving in pure and perpetual alms to God and the blessed Virgin Mary and especially to the chapel of the blessed Virgin of Coventry 6d. annual rent to be taken at the four terms of the year usual in the vill of Coventry from the built-up land in the Market-place (*terra illa edificata in foro*) of the lord prior of Coventry where fish is sold (*ubi venduntur pisces*), namely that which lies between the land William Hawene held on the one hand and the royal highway (*viam regiam*) on the other in length and in width as the land purports according to the metes and bounds made there; to be held of the grantor and his heirs quietly [etc.] and as freely as any alms are given and held. Warranty and sealing clauses. Witnesses: John de Lodelawe, Henry Baker (*Pistore*), Peter le Waleis, Walter Bacun, Ralf the Baker (*Pistore*), Robert de Londoniis, John Thole, John the Goldsmith (*aurifabro*), Thomas Seleth the clerk and others.

Seal missing C.R.O. IA/EC13/76

684 1270s

Charter of Peter son of Peter de Bassinges giving to John de Wykewane and Ida his wife 2 selds near to the seld (*duas seldas propinquiores selde*) of William de Alisley in Coventry adjoining the stone hall (*aule lapidee*) once of Master Richard Winitar on the western side (*versus Occidentalem partem*) according to the metes and bounds made there, and 6d. annual rent from the selds and the tenement adjoining on the other side (*ex altera parte adjacent'*) which were once of Master Richard Winitar' opposite the cross in the Market-place of Coventry (*oppo(s)ito Crucis in foro de Coventr'*); to be held to them, their heirs or assigns, of the grantor and his heirs, freely [etc.] by rendering annually 4d. for all secular service, exaction, suit of court and demand. Warranty and sealing clauses. Witnesses: Henry Baker (*pistor'*), Peter the Welshman (*Walense*), Martin Colbrond, Walter Bacun, Roger the Miller (*molendinar'*), Robert de Lond', John Thole, Geoffrey Bretun, Hugh Bretu(n), Thomas Seleth, Henry Dobedi, Roger de Hales and others.

Seal missing G.H. 307
Endorsed: Petrus de Bassing'
Decem denariatas de le pecok et le maores parlor

685 Late 1270s–early 1280s

Charter of Margery Pake widow of Pagan Pake, in her widowhood and lawful power, giving to William her son for his service certain tenements which descended to her by hereditary right in the vill of Coventry after the death of Master Richard the Vintner (*vinitar'*) her uncle (*avunc(u)li*), which tenements lie between the land of John son of Adam the clerk on the one hand and the western selds (*seldas occidentales*) on the other in length and in width just as the said tenements with their appurtenances purport according to the metes and bounds made there; to be held to him, his heirs or assigns, of the grantor and her heirs freely [etc.] by rendering annually to the grantor as long as she lives 30s. of silver at the four terms of the year usual and fixed in Coventry, namely 7s. 6d. at each term for all secular service [etc.] and to the lords of the fee (*dominis feodalibus*) the service due and accustomed, and to the grantor's heirs after her death a pair of gloves worth 1d. or 1d. at Easter for all secular service. Warranty and sealing clauses. Witnesses: Robert de Chilton' then bailiff of Coventry, Alexander the Vintner (*vinitario*), Henry Baker (*Pistore*), Henry Ballard, Peter Barun, Richard le Broch(er), Adam Russel, John the Vintner (*vinitar'*) son of Adam the clerk, John Piehod and others.

Seal extant C.R.O. 1A/C 54
Endorsed: par sirotecar' vel den(ar)ius reditus de Croschepyng.

686 c. late 1280s

Charter of John le Vineter and Margery Pake giving to Robert Frraunceys *le Parmunter* a tenement which they had in the Market-place (*in foro*) of the lord prior of Coventry between the land of John Minot on the one hand and the land of Richard Condonere and Geoffrey de Whytele on the other in length and in width as the tenement fully purports according to the metes and bounds made there; to be held with the buildings sited there and all appurtenances to him and his heirs of the grantors and their heirs freely [etc.] by rendering annually as the perpetual attorneys of the grantors and their heirs to the lord prior of Coventry 2s. 6d. of silver at the four terms of the year usual and fixed in the vill of Coventry, and to the grantors, their heirs or assigns, 6s. 6d. of silver at the same four terms for all secular services [etc.]. Warranty and sealing clauses. Witnesses: Henry Baker (*pistore*) then bailiff in Coventry, John Tole, Thomas le Moubray, Walter Banne, John de Macstoke, John le Keu, Nicholas de Derby, John Sannsum, Roger the clerk and many others.

2 seals extant C.R.O. IA/C13/9
Endorsed: Gosford [sic]

687 c.25 March 1282

Agreement whereby John Cokum of *Grantebrugg'* has granted to Thomas Scelet of Coventry reasonable easement to his kiln (*torreb(u)le*) in Coventry sited next to the lane (*viculum*) which leads towards the chief messuage (*capitale mansum*) of the same Thomas before the cross (*ante c(r)uce(m)*), which kiln (*torrebula*) the aforesaid John previously had by the gift of the said Thomas; to be held to Thomas as long as he lives freely, quietly and peacefully whilst he dwells (*manserit*) in the aforesaid chief messuage. *Concessit etiam predictus Johannes dicto Thome de fenis que in dicto mesuagio collegentur (? colleg*to*ent) ipso Thom(a) vivente medietate(m).* Also the aforesaid John has granted to the same Thomas a certain parcel (*p(ar)ticulam*) of his land from the messuage which Gilbert de Gri(m)misbi once held of the same Thomas in the Market-place of the prior of Coventry (*in foro prioris de Cowentr'*), which messuage John previously had by the gift and grant of the same Thomas; to be held to him and to Nicholas de Dereby his assign with easement to the aforesaid kiln from the feast of St. Mary in March 10 Edward I up to the end of his term of 28 years, saving always to the said John, his heirs or whatsoever assigns, *diebus et horis nocte(m)*[1] *habuerint dicte torreb(u)le et ejus asiame(n)tor(um) prioritate; partic(u)la etiam terre predicta cum toto aysame(n)to torreb(u)le predicte finito termino antedicto plene et integre dicto Johanni et heredibus suis vel ejus assignatis R[evertantur], infra quem terminum dictus Nicholaus et heredes vel assignati sui ad clayas et [ ]*[2] *torreb(u)le predicte juvabunt secundum quod in scripto inter ipsum Nichol(aum) et dictum Thom(am) confecto plenius continetur.* Mutual sealing clause [chirograph]. Witnesses: Robert de Chilton' then bailiff of Coventry, Henry Baker (*pistore*), John the Dyer (*tynctor'*), John Thole, Ralph the Baker (*pistor'*), Matthew de Ruton', John Samson, Hugh le Breton', William de P(ar)lur and others.

Seal missing C.R.O. IB/10EI

[1] sic

[2] There is a hole here.

688 c.1280

Charter of Thomas Celeth of Coventry giving to Philip the Cook (*Coco*) of *Graunte-bregge* and Matilda his wife the entire messuage with appurtenances in Coventry in the Market-place (*in foro*) of the prior before the cross (*ante crucem*) which Gilbert de Grimmisby once held, namely that which is between the grantor's land on the one hand and the lane leading to his chief messuage (*viculum qui ducit versus capitale mansum meum*) on the other together with the grantor's kiln (*torredula mea*) sited at the end of the said messuage with the entire easement of the same, just as they purport in length and in width according to the metes and bounds made there; to be held to them, their heirs or assigns, except to men of religion and Jews, of the grantor and his heirs freely [etc.] by rendering annually 13s. 4d. of silver at the four terms of the year fixed and customary in the vill of Coventry for all secular service [etc.]. Clause for warranty. Philip and Matilda gave 60s. of silver beforehand. Sealing clause. Witnesses: Robert de Chilton' then bailiff of Coventry, Henry Baker (*pistor'*), John the Dyer (*Tinctor'*), John Tole, Ralph the Baker (*pistor'*), Matthew de Ruthon', John Sampson, Hugh Bretun, William de P(ar)lur and others.

Seal extant W.R.O. 182

689 1280s

Charter of Richard Fortwyne giving to Ranulph de Stafford and Matilda his wife 12d. annual rent to be taken at the four terms of the year usual in the vill of Coventry from the grantor, his heirs or assigns, from a certain tenement which is in the Market-place (*in foro*) of the lord prior in Coventry, between the land William le

Furner once held on the one hand and the land John le Wineter held on the other as is manifest; to be held to them, their heirs or assigns, or to whomsoever and whensoever they will wish to give, bequeath, sell or assign of the grantor, his heirs or assigns, well [etc.] by rendering annually a rose at the feast of St. John the Baptist for all secular service [etc.]. Clause for warranty. Ranulph and Matilda gave 10s. of silver beforehand. Sealing clause. Witnesses: Henry Baker (*pistor'*) then bailiff, Robert de Chilton', John Tole, Alan de Poleswrthe, Thomas de Moubray, Roger the Fishmonger (*piscator'*), John le Vineter, Thomas Selet, John le Combere, Roger the clerk and many others.

Seal extant W.R.O. 181

690 1280s

Charter of Avicia le Taylur giving to Walter called (*dicto*) Banne a certain messuage in the vill of Coventry, namely that which is between the land Henry Baker (*pistor*) once held on the one hand and the land Henry the Tailor (*cissor*) held on the other as the messuage purports; to be held to him, his heirs or assigns, or to whomsoever or whensoever he will wish to give, sell, bequeath or assign, of the grantor, his heirs or assigns, freely [etc.] by rendering annually to Henry Baker (*pistor'*), his heirs or assigns, 2s. 6d. at the four terms of the year usual in the vill of Coventry for all secular service. Warranty and sealing clauses. Witnesses: Robert de Chiltoun', Alexander the Vintner (*vinitar'*), Thomas le Moubray, Walter Bakun, Nicholas de Derbi, John Saumsun, Anketell the clerk and many others.

Seal extant G.H. 306

691 20 November 1291

Notification of the settlement by the intervention of friends of a dispute over the wall of the house of Nicholas Maunsel, dyer, and Margery his wife in the Market-place of Coventry which Richard Oysel of Coventry and Alice his wife say is constructed nearer to their bakehouse than it ought to be.

Noverint universi hoc presens scriptum visuri vel audituri quod cum mota fuit contentio inter Ricardum Oysel de Coventr' et Aliciam uxorem suam ex parte una et Nicholaum Maunsel tinctorem et Margeriam uxorem ejus de eadem ex parte altera de pariete domus predictorum Nicholai et Margerie in foro de Coventr' juxta furnum eorundem Ricardi et Alicie quem quidem parietem dicti Ricardus et Alicia dicunt esse constructum propinquius furno eorum quam debuit, illa contentio communibus amicis intervenientibus quievit in hac forma: videlicet quod predicti Nicholaus et Margeria dabunt prefatis Ricardo et Alicie premanibus duos solidos argenti et ipsi prefati Ricardus et Alicia concedunt pro se et heredibus suis dictis Nicholao et Margerie quod predictus paries eorum in pace remanebit inperpetuum sicut modo constructus est sine aliquo impedimento predictorum Ricardi et Alicie aut heredum eorum vel assignatorum. Et si forte contingat quod absit quod prefati Ricardus et Alicia aut heredes eorum in posterum aliquo tempore istam concessionem supradictam contradicere voluerint vel impedire aliquo modo concedunt pro se et heredibus eorum quod dabunt fabrice magni monasterii de Coventr' de bonis suis dimidiam marcam argenti nomine pene et etiam fabrice magni monasterii de Lich' aliam dimidiam marcam nomine pene, ad quam solutionem plenarie faciendam si necesse fuerit compellantur per censuram ecclesiasticam scilicet per suspensionem et exco(mmun)icationem de die in diem per official(em) domini archid(iacon)i Coventr' qui pro tempore fuerit seu per decanum Coventr'. Et ut ista concessio firma et stabilis permaneat inperpetuum partes predicte huic scripto sigilla sua alternatim apposuerunt. Hiis testibus Henrico Pistor(e) tunc balli(v)o Roberto de Chiltone Thoma le Moubrai Johanne Thole Henrico de Hynkele Roberto Aleyn Hugone de Oxonia et aliis. Dat(um) apud Coventr' in festo sancti Eadmundi regis et martiris anno regni regis Eadwardi nonodecimo.

Indented
Seal missing P.R.O. A 10417

692 c.1290–1297

Grant, remise and quitclaim by Agnes widow of John de Macstok' in her free widowhood to Margery widow of Walter de Bannebury of Coventry of all right and claim to a third part of a messuage with appurtenances lying in the street where corn is sold (*in vico quo vendu(n)t bladu(m)*) between the land of Henry Baker (*Pistor'*) on the one hand and the land of Robert F(r)aunceys on the other, and extends in length from the royal highway (*a Regali via*) up to the land of Robert le Slepere, which third part the grantor claimed (*petii*) from the aforesaid Margery by royal writ; to be held to her, her heirs or assigns, of the grantor and her heirs freely [etc.]. Sealing clause. Witnesses: Henry Baker (*Pistor'*) then bailiff of Coventry, William Parkar' then coroner, Thomas le Mowbrey, John Tole, Anketell de Coleshul, John Mynot, Robert Baker (*Pistor'*), Richard de Cundoner', John Samson and others.

Seal extant C.R.O. 2/93

693 16 June 1298

Charter of Margery widow of Walter de Bannebury of Coventry, in her widowhood and full power, giving to Robert Frau(n)ceys of Coventry and Nichola his wife a certain tenement of hers in the vill of Coventry which lies in the high street where corn is sold (*in alto vico ubi venditur bladu(m)*) between the tenement of John de Wyteleye and the tenement of Richard de Cundou(er)e on the one hand and her chief messuage on the other, and in width as it extends by the metes made there; to be held with all the buildings sited there and all appurtenances and easements to them, their heirs or assigns, freely [etc.] of the chief lords of that fee by the services due and by right accustomed. Clause for warranty. Robert and Nichola gave 40s. sterling beforehand. Sealing clause. Witnesses: Anketinus de Collishul then bailiff of Coventry, John Lewyn, Peter Barun, Henry Oky, Robert Kell, John son of Nicholas, John le Keu, Richard de Conedou(er)e, Robert de Rothewell' and many others. Coventry, Monday after the feast of St. Barnabas the Apostle 26 Edward I.

Seal extant C.R.O. IB/26 EI/6

694 22 December 1298

Charter of Margery widow of Walter de Bannebury in Coventry, in her widowhood and lawful power, giving to Robert Fraunceis of Coventry and Nichola his wife a messuage with appurtenances in the vill of Coventry in the Market-place where corn is sold (*in foro ubi venditur bladu(m)*), namely that which she bought (*comparavi*) from Henry Baker (*Pistore*) which contains 11 feet between the tenement (*tenement'*) of John de Wyteleye and Richard de Conedonere on the one hand and the small piece of land (*parva(m) placia(m) terre*) which the said Robert and Nichola had by the grantor's gift on the other, and which extends 60 feet in length from the royal highway (*a Regali via*) up to the grantor's other land according to the metes and bounds made there; to be held with the buildings sited there and all its appurtenances and easements, to them, their heirs or whatsoever assigns, well [etc.] of the chief lords of that fee by rendering annually to those same lords the services due and accustomed, namely 5s. 6d. of silver at the four terms of the year usual in the vill of Coventry for all secular services and demands. Clause for warranty. Robert and Nichola gave 4 marks of silver beforehand. Sealing clause. Witnesses: Anketill de Coleshul then bailiff of Coventry, Master Richard de Bourton', John Leofwyne, Peter Baron, Henry Oky, Robert le Keu, Henry de Hynkele, John ad Crucem, Roger the clerk and others. Coventry, Monday the morrow of St. Thomas the Apostle 27 Edward I.

Seal extant C.R.O. IB/27 EI/5

695 25 April 1299

Charter of Margery widow of Walter de Bannebur' of Coventry, in her widowhood and full power, giving to Robert Fraunceys of Coventry and Nichola his wife a certain portion (*porc(i)o(ne)m*) of her curtilage adjacent to her chief messuage in the Corn-market (*in foro bladi*) in the vill of Coventry, which lies between the tenement of Robert le Sleper' on the one hand and the tenement of John de Chilton' on the other in width, and extends in length from the tenement which the aforesaid Robert Frau(n)ceys held of Henry Baker (*Pistor'*) up to the tenement of the aforesaid Robert le Sleper' and the tenement of William de Weston clerk; to be held with all its appurtenances, profits and easements of the grantor, her heirs or assigns, to them, their heirs or assigns, freely [etc.], by rendering annually 18d. of silver at the four terms of the year usual in the vill of Coventry for all secular services and demands. Warranty and sealing clauses. Witnesses: Anketynus de Collishul then bailiff of Coventry, John Lewyn then coroner of the same, Robert Baker (*Pistor'*), Matthew de Ruyton', Roger Dayiseye, William Maunsel, John ate Cros and others. Coventry, Saturday the feast of St. Mark the Evangelist 27 Edward I.

Seal extant C.R.O. IB/27 EI/4
Endorsed: Croschepyng'

696 13 May 1301

Release, remise and quitclaim by Margery widow of Walter de Bannebury of Coventry, in her widowhood and full power, for herself and her heirs, to Robert Frau(n)ceys of Coventry and Nichola his wife, their heirs or assigns, of 18d. annual rent which they used to render for a certain tenement which they hold of her gift in the vill of Coventry and which used to pertain (*adjac(er)e solebat*) to her chief messuage in the Market-place where corn is sold (*in foro ubi venditur bladu(m)*), which lies between the tenement of Robert le Sleper' on the one hand and the tenement of John de Chilton' on the other in width and extends from the tenement which the aforesaid Robert Frau(n)ceys holds of Henry Baker (*pistor'*) up to the tenement of the aforesaid Robert le Slepere and the tenement of William de Weston clerk in length; with exclusion clause, saving however 6d. annual rent to the use (*ad opus*) of the chapel of the blessed Mary of the conventual church of Coventry due therefrom and to be rendered annually for ever. Sealing clause. Witnesses: John Loeuwyn then coroner of Coventry, Robert Baker (*pistor'*), Master Robert the Cook (*Coco*), John le Keu, Robert de Rothewell', John ate Cros, Stephen the Marshal (*marescallo*) and others. Coventry, Saturday after the feast of the Ascension of the Lord 29 Edward I.

Seal extant C.R.O. IB/29 EI/5

697 1297–1300

Charter of Robert de Okov(er)e and Alice his wife giving to Hugh de Okov(er)e and Joan his niece (*nepte*), the grantor's daughter, a messuage with appurtenances in the vill of Coventry together with the houses standing thereon (*superastantibus*) as is fully contained in the charter which the aforesaid Hugh and Joan previously had from them, namely the messuage which Master Richard de Southam had of the gift of Alexander le Kyng in the same vill; to be held to them, their heirs or assigns, freely [etc.] with all liberties and easements pertaining of the chief lords of that fee by the services due and accustomed. Clause for warranty. Clause for reversion to the grantors and their heirs. Sealing clause. Witnesses: Anketill de Colshull' then bailiff, John Lewyn, Robert Kelle, John Pyod, John de Halys, John le Gover', John the Cook (*Coco*), John Sampsun, John ad Crucem, William Mauncel, Nicholas le Deyster, Thomas the clerk and others.

2 seals missing P.R.O. A 7659

698 c.1290–1297

Gift and quitclaim by Jordan le Celer of Coventry, for himself and his heirs, to Robert called (*dicto*) Fraunceis and Nichola his wife of all right and claim in the entire land with the houses sited there and all appurtenances which lies in Sleper's Lane (*Slepuslone*) between the land of John Thole senior on the one hand and the land once of Robert de London' on the other and extends in length from the land of the said John Thole up to the bakehouse (*furnu(m)*) of the lord prior of Coventry, in length and in width as is manifest according to the metes and bounds made there; to be held to them, their heirs or assigns, of the grantor and his heirs freely [etc.], by making annually to the lords of that fee the rent due and by right accustomed. Exclusion and sealing clauses. Witnesses: Henry Baker (*pistor'*) then bailiff, William le Parker then coroner, Stephen the Marshal (*marescallo*), Symon le King, Andrew de Cundulme, William le Parkur, William de Galewey clerk and others.

Seal extant C.R.O. 2/97

699 c.1290–1297

Gift and quitclaim by Ysabella daughter of Jordan le Celer of Coventry, in her lawful power and full estate, for herself and her heirs, to Robert called (*dicto*) Fraunceys and Nichola his (wife)[1] of all right and claim in the entire land with the houses sited there and all appurtenances which Alice Cosin her late mother held in length and in width as is manifest according to the metes and bounds made there with free entrance and exit; to be held to them, their heirs or assigns, by making to the lords of that fee the services due and by right accustomed. Exclusion and sealing clauses. Witnesses: Henry Baker (*Pistore*) then bailiff, William le Parker then coroner, Richard de Cundore, William de P(ar)lur, Ranulf de Stafford', William the Smith (*fabro*), William Galewey and others.

Seal extant Fuller II/16/5

[1] interlined

700 14 June 1301

Charter of John de Chiltone of Coventry granting to Robert Fraunceys of Coventry and Nichola his wife that henceforth his tenement which extends towards West Orchard and is on the north side of theirs will receive all the water dripping and falling from the gutters and roofs of their buildings and that he will provide and maintain sufficient free water on the soil of his tenement.

Sciant presentes et futuri quod ego Johannes de Chiltone de Coventr' concessi et per presens scriptum confirmavi pro me et heredibus meis Roberto Frau(n)ceys de Coventr' et Nich(ol)e uxori ejus et heredibus seu assignatis eorum quod tenementum meum jacens juxta tenementum predictorum Roberti et Nich(ol)e ex parte boreali quod tene(n)t in villa Coventr' de dono Margerie relicte Walteri de Bannebur' et extendens se de tenemento eorum predicto versus le Westorchard recipiet et receptabit totam aquam stillante(m) et cadente(m) et de cetero stillatura(m) et casura(m) inperpetuum de gutteris tectis et domiciliis omnium edific(at)orum predictorum Roberti et Nichole usque ad tenementum meum predictum quoquo modo attingentium absque omni contradictione vel calumpnia mei vel heredum meorum inperpetuum. Preterea ego predictus Johannes et heredes mei inveniemus et inperpetuum sustentabimus lib(er)am ac sufficiente(m) aq(uam) stilla(ntem) et aq(uam) cadenciam[1] super solu(m) meum tenementi mei predicti gutteris tectis et domiciliis omnium predictorum edific(at)orum, et eas predictis Roberto et Nich(ol)e et eorum heredibus seu assignatis eorum contra omnes mortales warantizabimus inperpetuum. In cujus rei testimonium presenti scripto sigillum meum apposui. Hiis testibus Roberto filio Henrici Pistor(is) Johanne Loeuwyn tunc coronatore Coventr' Alexandro de Stonlee Magistro Roberto Coquo Rogero de Pakwode Roberto de Rothewell Johanne ad Crucem et aliis. Coventr' die Mercurii proxima post festum sancti Barnabe apostoli anno regni regis Edwardi filii regis Henrici vicesimo nono.

Seal extant C.R.O. IB/29 EI/4

[1] sic

701 c.29 September 1304

Agreement whereby Nicholas le Marchal of Coventry has leased, granted and demised for a term to John atte Crosse of the same a messuage with the houses sited there and appurtenances except a certain shop standing at the front of the messuage (*ex(cep)ta q(u)adam schopa ante predictum mesuagium asstante*), which messuage with appurtenances lies between the land once of Robert de Loundr' on the one hand and the land once of Richard Fortwyne on the other and extends in length from the royal highway up to the post of the kiln (*a Regio vico usque ad postu(m) torellis*) once of Roger Sybely and Isabella Tredegold according to the metes and bounds made there. Moreover, he has leased to the aforesaid John all the brewer's vessels found there (*omnia vasa b(r)aciatori conveniencia illuc inventa silicet plu(m)bu(m) in fornace et cuva(m) que vocatur maysfat et ylfat et alveola et cetera vasa ibidem inventa*); the aforesaid messuage with the houses sited there with the aforesaid curtilage[1] and with the appurtenances except the aforesaid shop together with the vessels aforesaid to be held to John, his heirs or assigns, of the lessor and his heirs freely [etc.] from the feast of St. Michael 32 Edward I for a term of 6 years, by rendering annually during the first two years of the term a rose at the feast of the Nativity of St. John the Baptist and during the following 4 years 12s. of silver at the four terms of the year usual in Coventry for all services pertaining. Clause for warranty, *et maxime domos dicti mesuagii per totum terminum predictum contra ventum et pluviam s(er)vabunt sed predictus Johannes et heredes vel assignati sui predicta vasa per totum terminum inde(m)pne(m) s(er)vab(un)t. Et si predictus Johannes et heredes vel assignati sui aliq(ui)d ibidem edificaverint tunc predictus Nicholaus et heredes sui ad finem dicti termini cust(us) suos allocab(un)t.* John gave 24s. of silver beforehand. Mutual sealing clause [bipartite]. Witnesses: Robert Baker

(*Pistore*) then bailiff, John Lewyne then coroner, John Sa(m)psum, John le Keu, Robert de Chilton' and others.

Indented
Seal extant C.R.O. IB/32 EI/2

[1] sic

702 5 February 1301

Agreement whereby Margery, Juliana and Edith, daughters and heiresses of Richard Forthewyne of Hill (*hulle*) have, with one accord, leased, granted and demised to William de Allislee of Coventry and Matilda his wife a certain messuage in the vill of Coventry which lies in the Market-place towards Broadgate (*in alto foro versus lata(m) porta(m)*) between the tenement once of Henry le Cartsadelere on the one hand and the tenement of Roger de Cundulme on the other in length and in width as is fully manifest; to be held with all appurtenances to them, their heirs or assigns, of the grantors, their heirs or assigns, from the feast of the Annunciation of the blessed Mary 29 Edward I [25 March 1301] for a term of 7 years freely [etc.], by rendering annually 6s. of silver at the 4 customary terms of the year in the vill of Coventry for all services and demands. The lessees, their heirs or assigns, will maintain all the buildings of the said messuage in as good a state as they received them or better at their own cost. *Et si super vacua(m) t(er)ra(m) ejusdem mesuagii aliquid de novo edifice(n)t illud id(em) in fine dicti termini secum asportabunt nisi dicte Ma(r)g(er)ia Julian(a) et Edith(a) heredes seu assignati eorum eis inde satisfacere volu(er)int competenter.* Warranty and sealing clauses. Witnesses: John Loeuwyn', Robert Frau(n)ceys, Matthew de Ruyton', William Maunsel, Roger de Cundulme and others. Coventry, Sunday after the feast of the Purification of the blessed Mary in the year aforesaid.

Indented
2 seals extant W.R.O. 206

703 24 February 1306

Gift by Margery, Juliana and Edith, daughters of Richard Fortwyne of Hill (*Hulle*), in their virginity and lawful power and full age, to William de Allesleye of Coventry shoe-maker (*cordiwanar'*) and Matilda his wife for their life, for a certain sum of money which they gave beforehand, a messuage with appurtenances which lies in the Market-place in Coventry towards Broadgate (*in alto foro in Coventr' versus latam portam*) between the tenement Henry le Cartsadeler' held on the one hand and the tenement John de Coundelme held on the other in length and in width as is manifest; to be held to them and their assigns for the life of the same William and Matilda, of the grantors and their heirs freely [etc.] by rendering annually to the chief lords of that fee as the grantors' attorneys 18d. of silver at the four terms of the year usual in Coventry, and to the grantors, their heirs or assigns, 4s. 6d. for all services and demands. The grantees should maintain all the buildings of the said messuage in a good state during their entire life at their own cost and undertake all necessary repairs. Clause for warranty. Sealing clause [bipartite]. Witnesses: Robert Baker (*Pistore*) then bailiff, Alexander de Stonlee then coroner, William Mauncel, John le Gov(er)e, Robert Fraunceys, Richard le Spic(er)e, Richard Colebrond the clerk and others. Coventry, Thursday the feast of St. Mathias the Apostle 34 Edward I.

Indented
1 seal extant, 2 missing W.R.O. 183

704 c.1306–c.1307

Charter of Henry de Hinkele of Coventry giving to Robert de Stoke his entire tenement in the vill of Coventry lying in Smiths' Row (*le Smethis rouwe*) between the tenement of Nicholas le Deyestere on the one hand and the tenement once of John Tole on the other in length and in width as is manifest according to the metes and bounds made there; to be held with all profits and easements to him, his heirs or assigns, freely [etc.] of the chief lords of that fee by the services due and by right accustomed. Warranty and sealing clauses. Witnesses: Robert Baker (*Pistor'*) of Coventry, Alexander de Stonle in the same, Robert de Chilton' of the same, Anketell de Collushull' of the same, Alexander le Moubray of the same, Robert the Cook (*coq(u)o*) of the same, John de Wincestr' of the same, Alan Schauelok' of the same, William le Floutere of the same and others.

Seal extant C.R.O. IA/C13/37

LOCATION UNCERTAIN

705 c.1195–1200

Charter of Juliana daughter of Adam de Coventry giving to Stephen de Nerbone 2 messuages in Coventry at a rent of 2s. *per annum*. She has quitclaimed the 14s. arrears for which she impleaded him in the county court of Warwick. Stephen gave 1 mark of silver.

Sciant presentes et futuri quod ego Juliana filia Ade de Covintr' dedi et concessi et hac presenti mea carta confirmavi Steph(ano) de N(er)bune et heredibus suis duo masag(ia) in Covi(n)tr' cum pertinentiis suis, illa scilicet que sunt inter domu(m) Willelmi filii Su(n)nulf et inter domu(m) Roberti filii Assulf' usque ad palaciu(m) Willelmi de Nerbun tenenda et habenda de me et de heredibus meis illi et heredibus suis in perpetuum reddendo annuatim ij solidos pro omni seculari servicio pro omni debito et pro omni exactione ad me vel ad heredes meos pertinente ad hos terminos: ad festum sancti Michaelis vjd. ad festum sancti Andree vjd. ad festum sancte Marie Marcial(is) vjd. ad festum sancti Johannis Baptiste vjd. Pro hac vero conventione et concessione dedit mihi prefatus Steph(anus) de N(er)bune j marca(m) argenti. Et ego Juliana warantizabo illi et heredibus suis illa prefata masag(ia) cum pertinentiis contra omnes homines. Et quietum clamavi illu(m) de xiiij solid(is) un(de) inplacitavi illu(m) in comitatu de Warewic qui era(n)t aretro de firma mea septem annorum. Hiis testibus Willelmo filio Hugonis Hosb(er)to de Clinton' Roberto de Curli Johanne de Curli Hugone filio Willelmi Aubreo de N(er)bune Bertramo filio Steph(ani) Roberto filio Ade Henrico fratre ejus Gilib(erto) fratre ejus Ingenulf de Covi(n)tre Milone Barbe de Averil Thoma de Erdi(n)tone et multis aliis,

Seal missing G.H. 260

Stephen de Nerbone held the manor of Stivichall in fee of the bishop of Coventry. For the fortunes of his estate after his death see 'Sir Geoffrey de Langley and the Crisis of the Knightly Class in 13th-Century England' *Past and Present* No. 68, 1975, pp. 12–17.

The Curlis held an estate at Budbrooke, Warwicks. (*V.C.H.* iii, p. 66). Robert de Curli occurs in the Pipe Rolls from 1190 to 1199 inclusive, his son John from 1195–1197. John de Curli chose his Norman lands in 1204 and the Pipe Roll of 1205 records the payment by his brother William for the privilege of retaining the family's possessions in England (*Pipe Roll 7 John*, p. 32). Osbert de Clinton is more likely he who figures on the Pipe Rolls from 1195–1200 and who was in fact dead by Michaelmas 1200 rather than his son who was dead by 1221 (*V.C.H. Warwicks.* iv, p. 50; *F.F. Warwicks.* Nos. 73, 495). The elder Osbert married one of the daughters of William son of Hugh of Hatton. Stephen de Nerbone married the other. Their brother Hugh son of William occurs in 1202 and 1208, and was dead by 1221 (*V.C.H. Warwicks.* iv, p. 247; *F.F. Warwicks.* Nos. 128, 328).

706 c.1215–c.1225

Sale and quitclaim by Beterica widow of William Bochart, in her widowhood and free power, to William son of Symon the Baker (*pistoris*) of Coventry and his heirs of her entire land in Coventry with all appurtenances both in rents and in other liberties which was of Henry Steinolf her father; to be held freely [etc.] of the lord prior and convent of Coventry by rendering annually for all service 2s. of silver at four terms of the year, namely 6d. at each of the feasts of St. John the Baptist, St.

Michael, St. Andrew and St. Mary in March. Clause for warranty. William gave 1 mark of silver and a green cloak (*palliu(m) de viridi*). Sealing clause. Witnesses: William de Hecham then bailiff of the lord prior, Geoffrey de Wilenh(al), William le Cnave, David de Fonte, Richard Hoki, Thomas his son, Roger the Smith (*fabro*), Gerard Hoden, Thomas the Mason (*cemetar'*), Ingelard, Michael the Smith (*fabro*) and others.

Seal extant C.R.O. 1A/C48
Endorsed: Carta bet(r)ica ux' Willelmi mol(e)ndin'.

707 c.1215–c.1225

Sale and quitclaim by Roger son of Mary, entirely and without any reservation from him and his heirs to Richard de Burmingeha(m) and his heirs of 2d. rent with appurtenances in Coventry from the land which Gilbert le Warude held of him, namely that which is between the land Warin de Davintr' held and the land Thomas the Dyer (*Tinctor*) held; to be held in chief of the lord prior of Coventry. Richard gave 2s. of silver. Clause for warranty. Sealing clause. Witnesses: William son of Humphrey (*Umfrid'*), John his son, Alan the Tanner (*Tanator'*), Richard de Mubrai, Richard his son, Roger de Cornl', Simon de Leicestr', Thomas the Dyer (*Tinctor'*), Warin de Davintr', David de Fonte, William de F(r)anket', William de Wilnhal', Geoffrey his brother and many others.

Seal missing C.R.O. 2/177

708 1 August 1235

Charter of Master John de Alspath giving to his servant, Thomas de Haitel, his entire land next to the *quadrivium* between the earl's fee and the land of Roger de Alspath should he die before being able to return to Coventry from Rome. If he does return he will repossess without contradiction but Thomas and his heirs will ultimately succeed him.

Sciant presentes et futuri quod ego Magister Johannes de Allespath' anno domini millesimo ducentesimo tricesimo quinto in advinc(u)la beati Petri apud Covintr' m(en)tis et noti co(m)pos in ligia potestate pro salute mea et antecessorum meorum dedi et concessi et hac presenti carta mea confirmavi Thome de Haitel' servienti meo totam terram illam cum pertinentiis juxta quadriviu(m) que jacet inter feudum comitis et inter terram quam Rogerus de Allespath' quondam tenuit in longitudine et latitudine sicut terra proportat et carta domini Ricardi de Aula exinde confecta designat si contingat me in p(ar)tibus cismarinis vel ultra mare antequam ad Coventr' de Roma rev(er)tar d(e)bitum universe carnis exsolv(er)e; habendam et tenendam sibi et heredibus suis et cui illam assignare voluerit libere quiete et honorifice reddendo inde annuatim dicto Ricardo et heredibus suis viginti sex denar(ios) pro omni servicio exactione consuetudine et demanda ad quatuor terminos anni secundum usum Covintr', ita tamen quod si voluntas divina permittat me ad Covintr' reverti liceat mihi sine contradictione et impedimento quorumcumque in jus et poss(essi)o(ne)m predicte terre ingredi. Et ipse Thomas et heredes sui mihi deced(e)nti vel vita(m) mutanti in plenum jus succedant siv(e) rev(er)tar siv(e) non. Et ego Johannes predictam terram cum pertinentiis donacionem et concessionem dicto Thome et heredibus suis et cui eandem assignaverit contra omnes homines et feminas et heredes mei similiter warantizabimus. In cujus rei firmitate(m) et memoriam perpetuam hanc cartam propria manu scripsi et sigillo proprio licet proprii nominis circumscriptio in eo non ponatur co(m)munivi. Hiis testibus Ricardo de Aula Magistro Ricardo filio Gerardi Anketillo de Wikewane Asketillo Pistore Roberto de P(ar)is' Thoma de Wilenhal' Ricardo de Blukevill' Willelmo But' Anketillo filio Roberto et aliis.

Seal extant (fragment only) C.R.O. IB/1235

709 c.1240

Charter of Richard son of Adam son of Haldeyn giving to William le Butt' and his heirs, or to whomsoever he will wish to give or assign except to a house of religion, all the land which Walter de Alispath' gave to John his nephew (*nepoti*) with a stone house (*domo Lapideo*) and all appurtenances pertaining to the aforesaid land in length and in width as the land purports; to be held of the grantor and his heirs freely [etc.] by rendering annually 2s. of silver at four terms of the year, namely 6d. at each of thc feasts of the Nativity of St. John the Baptist, St. Michael, St. Andrew and St. Mary in March for all secular service [etc.]. Clause for warranty. William gave 10s. of silver in recognition. Sealing clause. Witnesses: Osbert the clerk then reeve (*p(re)po(s)ito*), Richard Burgeis, Robert de Feug(er)s, Thomas Oky then reeve of the Prior's half (*p(re)po(s)ito ex parte Prioris*), Richard de Fonte, John son of Simon, William de Salowe, Anketill son of Rose (*Rosie*), Roger Spirie, Thomas son of William de Heytele, Ralf le Sergant and others.

Seal missing C.R.O. IA/EC12/11
Endorsed: Carta Ricardi fil' Ade de Aula.

710 Late 1240s–early 1250s

Charter of Richard son of Richard de Wygorn' burgess of Coventry (*Burgensis de Coventr'*) giving to Gilbert de Segrave the service and annual rent of 5s. from Henry Wodemo(n), the service of John de Hulle and 12d. from the same, the service of Nicholas Warin and 2s. from the same, the service of Walter the Goldsmith (*aurifabri*) and Hawise de Senudeford and 12d. from the same, the service of Hugh Coc and 4s. from the same and 2 hens at Christmas, the service of Thomas le Forber and 13d. from the same, the service of Margery de Cropehulle and 13d. from the same, the service of Master Richard the Vintner (*vinitarii*) and 4s. from the same, the service of William the Locksmith (*locarii*) and 4s. from the same, the service of Walter le Taneor' and 2s. from the same, the service of William Herbert and 12d. from the same and 4 hens at Christmas and the work (*opera*) of 2 men for 1 day in Autumn, the service of John Symont and 12d. *per annum*, the service of Robert Groudraf and 12d. from the same, the service of William de Monte and 12d. from the same, and the service of Walter de Coventr' and 12d. from the same, to be taken in each year at four terms of the year namely at the feasts of St. Michael, St. Andrew, St. Mary in March and St. John the Baptist, and all things which can accrue from the aforesaid tenants by reason of the tenements which they formerly held of the grantor in Coventry and henceforth will hold of the aforesaid Gilbert de Segrave, his heirs or assigns, without any reservation by the grantor or his heirs. Moreover he has granted to Gilbert a solar and a stone cellar together with the outside chamber of the same solar (*unum solarium et celarium de Petra simul cum forinseca Camera ejusdem solarii*) concerning which solar an action was brought in the royal court between the grantor and Stephen son of Matthew, and a shop joined (*sopam junctam*) to the same solar which the grantor bought from the aforesaid Stephen and 2s. 2d. from 2 shops (*sopis*) sited between the shops of William de Aula and the shops of Nicholas Warin; to be held to him, his heirs or assigns, of the grantor and his heirs freely [etc.] by rendering annually to William Fundu 12d. at the aforesaid terms, 5d. to Anketinus (*Anque'tinlo*) de Wikewan' and 8d. to Henry de Brinkelawe for all services [etc.]. Clause for warranty. In return for this demise and grant Gilbert de Seg(r)ave has acquitted the grantor of 70s. towards Moses son of Leo (*mossi filium leonis*) Jew of Warwick (*Warewyk*) and 25 marks against Hake of Worcester (*Wygorn'*). Sealing clause. Witnesses: Anketill de Wikewan', Payn Pake, Robert de Cornley, John Beyher, Philip de Winchecumb, Richard de Fonte, Robert le Feug', Nicholas Waryn, John Symon', William Toly, Reginald the Red (*Rufo*), Richard de Henley and others.

Seal extant G.H. 278

Gilbert de Segrave died in October 1254 (*G.E.C.* vol. vii, p. 603).

711 Late 1250s–early 1260s

Remise and quitclaim by William Funduyt, for himself and his heirs, to Nicholas de Segrave and his heirs of 12d. rent with appurtenances which he used to receive from the same Nicholas for a messuage which Henry Wodeman held of Richard de Wygornia and Eda Scatheloc sister of the same Henry afterwards held of the said Nicholas de Segrave in Coventry with all appurtenances, so that the same Nicholas and his heirs should be quit of the aforesaid rent and of all services pertaining to the grantor or his heirs by reason of the aforesaid tenement. Clause for warranty. Nicholas gave 8s. of silver beforehand. Sealing clause. Witnesses: Thomas le Ireys, William de Wauere, Robert de Werdoun, knights, Viellus (*Wyello*) de Folkeshull', Richard Schapeleyn, Richard Erneys, Ranulph de Stivechale and many others.

Seal missing G.H. 287

Nicholas succeeded his father at the age of 16 in December 1254. He had seisin of his lands in April 1258. He was to be knighted by the king in the summer of 1263 (*G.E.C.* vol. VII, p. 603). William de Waver received a grant of free warren in 1257. He died in 1271 (*V.C.H. Warwicks.* vi, p. 177).

712 19 June 1302

Charter of John de Seg(r)ave granting to William his tailor (*cissori meo*) and Margery his wife 11s. annual rent of assize with appurtenances which he used to take from the tenement once of Geoffrey de Styvichale in Coventry; to be held to them for their life or to the survivor of the grantor and his heirs freely [etc.] by the service of 12d. of silver annually to be rendered at the four terms of the year customary for rent of assize in the vill of Coventry for all service save forinsec. Clause for warranty. Clause for reversion. Sealing clause [bipartite]. Witnesses: Robert de Stok', Adam des Okes, Symon Erneys of Sowe, Robert Jabet of the same, Roger Dayesie of Coventry, Adam Russel of the same, John de Langeleye of the same and others. Caludon (*Kalouedon'*), Tuesday after the feast of St. Botulph the Abbot 30 Edward I.

Seal missing G.H. 315

713 Late 1260s–early 1270s

Gift and quitclaim by Adam son of Richard Haldeyn of Coventry for himself, his heirs and assigns, to Henry de Coventr' baker (*pistor'*) of all right and claim in 8d. annual rent to be taken at the four terms of the year fixed in the vill of Coventry from a certain curtilage lying between the land William le Sergant holds on the one hand next to the royal highway (*viam regiam*) and the land which John Tole bought from Alexander de Ruton' on the other; to be held to him, his heirs and assigns freely [etc.] without any secular service, exaction or demand pertaining to the grantor, his heirs or assigns. Henry called Baker (*dictus pistor*) gave ½ mark of sterling beforehand. Sealing clause. Witnesses: Martin Colebront, Adam his son, John [Tole][1], William le Sergant, Thomas Oky, Peter Frewyne, Henry le Sergant, Richard Gilebert, Walter le Arler and others.

Seal missing P.R.O. A 6424

[1] The reading is uncertain.

714 1291

Grant by Prior Thomas and the convent of Coventry as far as they are able (*quantum in nobis est*) to William de Copstone of Coventry and Juliana his wife that they may freely give and assign to Geoffrey the chaplain and all others succeeding him celebrating divine service in their church of Coventry at the altar of St. Edward the King for the souls of Lady Eleanor (*Alianore*) queen of England and of the said William de Copston and Juliana his wife and their parents and the benefactors of the same, 100s. from their fee in the vill of Coventry, saving to the grantors and their church the services due and accustomed and saving also their right of presenting suitable chaplains of the diocese to the said rent and of bestowing the said rent on them. Sealing clause (*sigillum capituli nostri*).

Seal missing P.R.O. C2982

A Mortmain licence for the above alienation was issued on May 28 1291 (*C.P.R. 1281–1292*, p. 429).

715 5 December 1301

Acknowledgement by Walter de Newerk' of Coventry and Isabella his wife that they are bound to Thomas de G(r)antham of Coventry in 44s. sterling for many goods sold to them (*pro pl(ur)ibus m(er)cimoniis nobis venditis*), 4s. to be paid to the same Thomas or his certain attorney bearing this letter at Coventry on Sunday before Christmas 30 Edward I, and on Sunday after the Purification of the blessed Mary following in the year aforesaid 6d. and thus from Sunday to Sunday in each week 6d. without any default or contradiction until the aforesaid debt is fully paid. Should the said Walter and Isabella his wife default in payment of the said debt on any of the aforesaid days, wholly or partly, the bailiffs of the lord prior of Coventry will be allowed to distrain them through all their goods wheresoever found both in their chamber and their house (*in camera nostra quam in domo*) and to retain these until they have satisfied the aforesaid Thomas or his attorney as aforesaid, and nevertheless they bind themselves in 40s. in aid of the Holy Land (*ad subsidiu(m) terre*) for breaching or breaking this agreement. Sealing clause. Witnesses: Elias de Lynne, Hugh le Hosier and others. Coventry, Tuesday before the feast of St. Nicholas in the year aforesaid.

Seal missing W.R.O. DR 429/9

WHITEMORE, AND PARTS NEAR*

*For other references to Whitemore see 28a, 525, 620, 622, 757, 760 and *Langley Cartulary* Nos. 179 (*Alwardsica*) and 386, 451 (*Blakemore*). Also see above pp. 1–2.

Bodleian MS. Top. Warwicks. C.8 contains on pp. 97–100 a series of transcripts, without witnesses and, in places, of doubtful accuracy, said to be taken from a cartulary roll in the possession of William Reader. Bearing the title *Carte & munimenta diversarum parcellarum terre & bosci in parco de Wytemore* they comprise, in addition to copies of Nos. 724–26, 728 (below), the following: a charter of Geoffrey de Langley dated baldly 1274 conveying to the prior and convent 2 fields (*campos*) called *Mayre Feldes*, 3 parcels of moor which he bought from Richard called (*dicto*) Brunhalli together with a parcel of the moor called *Blakemore* and a parcel of land in *Scottesfeld* together with the 2s. rent from Simon Sewale of Coundon (*Cundelme*) from the land with which Geoffrey enfeoffed him in Whitemore (*Whitemore'*); a charter of William Scote granting to Prior William and the monks, for the souls of his father and grandfather, his entire land of *Aylewarddessiche que vocat' Scottesfeld* and all his lands, rents and tenements within and without Coventry in frankalmoin; 2 grants from Roger Lokard, one to Peter son of Gilbert de Blockele quitclaiming any right in the land conveyed in No. 725 (below), the other remising all right *in tercia parte Curie de Whytemore Gardini & grave versus occidentem more & pasture de Whitemore & Grave que vocat' Brademore* which fell to him by hereditary right; a grant by Richard called (*dictus*) Brunhally of Coventry with the assent of his wife Alice granting land in Blakemore field (*in campo de Blakemore*) with an adjacent moor to Prior William and the monks, and a final concord at Warwick dated 8 July 1262 whereby Brunus Hally [*sic*] and Alice his wife acknowledged the right of Prior William and the monks in the entire land they held in Whitemore and Blakemore, viz. a messuage and 4 acres of land; a quitclaim by Richard de Wroxhall to Prior William and the monks of all right in the land called *Scottesfeld* and in the land in Coundon (*Cundelme*) which William Petit once held which lands he possessed by gift of Prior William; a gift and quitclaim by Alice widow of Brun Hally daughter of Anketell Lokard of the chief messuage (*in capitali mansio*) and entire land of Whitemore once her father's and which accrued to her by the death of Richard Lokard her brother; a charter of Vitalis and John sons of Edward de Holbroke granting to Prior William and the monks an acre of land which they held of the prior and convent by the service of 8d. per annum *de assarto bosco de Coventr' que jacet inter terram que Elias de Asscheweye tenuit ex una parte & boscum dicti Prioris ex altera*, with permission to approve from all the wastes and assarts around Coventry (*circa Coventr'*) without hindrance or contradiction by them or their heirs; a release by Alice widow of John de Chilton of Coventry to Prior Henry and the convent of all right in name of dower in the tenement called *Beaufizland* next to the land of Roger Lokard; the grant by Peter son of Gilbert de Blocley to Prior Henry and the convent of a messuage and his land outside the vill of Coventry which he had by the gift of John son of Robert de Chilton; the mortmain licence of 1296 by which Peter son of Gilbert de Blockeley conveyed 4 acres of land in Coventry and Radford next to Coventry (*Radford juxta Coventr'*); and a quitclaim by Robert called (*dictus*) Anketill de Ratesced [*sic*] to the prior and monks of all right in the entire land with moors, meadows and other appurtenances in *Whitemor'* which accrued to him through Cecily his late wife and of which Richard Locard her brother died seised.

716 c.1240s

Charter of Robert de Busservile giving to John de Hwitele[1] and his heirs or to whomsoever he will wish to give or assign, his meadow which is called *Enedemedwe* which lies between the Earl's wood (*boscum comitis*) and the land Nicholas Hornwod held, except to a house of religion, with all appurtenances in length and in width just as the meadow purports; to be held of the grantor and his heirs freely [etc.] by rendering annually 1d. of silver at Easter for all service [etc.]. Clause for warranty. John gave 3½ marks of silver. Sealing clause. Witnesses: Thomas de Stoke, Henry son of Herbert, William de Burmi(n)gha(m), Robert de Feug(er)s, William de Paillinton', John Alewy, Jordan de Franketon', Roger the Weaver (*textore*), Richard de Bukerwill' and others.

Seal extant C.R.O. IA/C12

[1] hWitele

717 Late 1240s–early 1250s

Remise and quitclaim by Robert called Anketill (*dictus Anketill'*) de Radeford, for himself and his heirs, to God, the church of the blessed Mary and the prior and monks of Coventry of all right and claim in the entire land with moors, meadows and all other appurtenances in Whitemore (*In Whythemor'*), which accrued to him through Cecily once his wife whereof Richard Locard brother of the same Cecily died invested and seised (*decessit vestitus et seisitus*). The prior and convent gave 30s. of silver beforehand. Sealing clause. Witnesses: Anketill de Wykewan', Richard de Fonte, John son of Symon the Baker (*pistor'*), Robert de Feuger', Nicholas Waryn, Peter Martyn, Ranulf de Frankethon', Henry de Radeford, William his brother, Robert Beufys, Geoffrey de Craft', Thomas the Porter (*Janitor'*) and others.

Seal extant C.R.O. 2/10

718 1250s

Lease by William Scot to Prior William and the convent of Coventry of his entire land of *Aylwardesich* to cultivate by share-cropping as long as he lives, so that they should take an entire moiety of corn and hay issuing from the land together with a moiety of all his rents in Coventry and elsewhere and he the other moiety. Moreover, he has granted the entire moiety of the land and rent in free alms for the salvation of his soul and those of Robert Scot his grandfather and Ralf his father, saving his chief messuage until they provide an equivalent.

Sciant presentes et futuri quod ego Willelmus Scot tradidi et concessi et hoc presenti scripto confirmavi Domino Willelmo Priori Covintr' et ejusdem loci conventui et eorum successoribus ac ecclesie sue de Covintr' totam terram meam de Aylwardesich' ad gwaniandum ad medietatem quoad vixero, ita quod dicti prior et conventus totam medietatem fructuu(m) tam garbaru(m) quam feni de dicta terra p(ro)venientiu(m) una cum medietate omnium reddituu(m) meorum in Covi(n)tr' et alibi quocumque jure ad me sp(e)ctancium in tota vita mea plenarie p(er)cipiant et ego aliam medietatem p(er)cipiam. Volo etiam et concedo quod tota medietas tam terraru(m) et prati quam reddituu(m) omnium predictorum cum omnibus suis pertinenciis dictis priori et conventui et eorum successoribus ac eorum ecclesie de Covintr' in liberam puram et perpetuam elemosinam inperpetuum remaneat sine aliqua contradictione seu i(n)pedimento mei vel heredum meorum pro salute anime mee et Roberti Scot avi mei et Radulfi patris mei salvo tamen michi et heredibus meis capitali manso quousque michi vel heredibus meis per eosdem priorem et conventum ad valorem tante terre in loco co(m)petentiori fuerit p(ro)visu(m) ad comodum nostrum; habend(a) et tenend(a) omnia predicta dictis priori et conventui et eorum successoribus ac eorum ecclesie de Covi(n)tr' de me et heredibus meis sicut predictum est adeo libere et quiete sicut aliqua elemosina liberius haberi poterit vel teneri. Et ego Willelmus predictus et heredes mei omnia predicta predictis priori et conventui et successoribus eorundem ac ecclesie sue de Covi(n)tr' in forma predicta contra omnes et homines et feminas warantizabimus aquietabimus et defendemus inperpetuum. Et ut hec omnia predicta rata et inconcussa futuris temporibus permaneant presenti scripto sigillum meum apposui. Hiis testibus Vital(e) de Folkeshull' Thom(a) de Karesleg' Magistro Johanne de Billesleg' Hugone de Stok' Anketello de Wykewan' Pagano Pake Rogero clerico Ricardo de Fonte Ricardo de Bruges Johanne Sym' Willelmo la Chnave Brunno Halling' Roberto Anketell' Henr(ico) de Radeford' Willelmo fratre ejus.

Seal extant C.R.O. 1A/C22
Endorsed: Carta Willelmi Scot de Terra de Aywarddes Sych' Juxta Swytemor
Carta Will(elm)i Scot no(n) de pleno feffam(en)to.

719 c.29 September 1259

Agreement made at Michaelmas A.D. 1259 whereby Emma widow of Robert Beufys, in her free power, has leased to Richard son of William de Walesgrave certain land beneath the Earl's wood (*subtus boscu(m) Comitis*) which the father of the said Emma had given in free marriage (*liberum maritagium*) together with an adjacent meadow with all their appurtenances; the said land with the meadow aforesaid extending in length between the street (*vicu(m)*) called *Hornewodeswey* and the land of Matthew le Bolt(er)e, to be held to him, his heirs or assigns, or to whomsoever he will wish to give, sell, bequeath or assign, from Michaelmas of the year aforesaid for a term of 6 years, *ita quod dicta Emma et sui assignati t(er)ciam garbam bladi crescentis super dictam terram annuatim et duodecim denarios ad quatuor anni terminos pro prato predicto percipient pro omni exactione et demanda. Et dictus Ricardus dictam terram sumptibus propriis omnimodis faciet gwaniare, ita quod dicta Emma fimum quantum pot(er)it faciet collig(er)e ad dictam terram cariandum sumptibus predicti Ricardi. Et dicta Emma dictam terram ulli hominu(m)*[1] *nec alicui viventi dictam terram seu pratum vendere pot(er)it nec dare vel assignare infra predictum terminum sine assensu et bona voluntate Ricardi predicti*. Clause for warranty. *Et dictus Ricardus de propriis hayis clausturam capiet sine contradictione aliqua*. Mutual sealing clause [chirograph]. Witnesses: John Sym', William Leuwyne, Robert de Chilthon', Robert de Huchinton' clerk, Alan Odard of Radford (*Radeford*), Nicholas de Teinthon', Henry Beufys, Thomas his brother, William de Burmi(n)gh(am), Matthew le Boltere and others.

Indented
Seal missing W.R.O. DR 429/6

[1] sic

720 2 February 1260

Agreement made on the feast of the Purification of the blessed Mary 1260 whereby Emma Beufiz and Henry her son have leased and granted to Richard de Welhsgrave, his heirs or assigns, a certain furlong in the field of Whitemore (*cultura(m) in camp' de Wytemor'*) with appurtenances lying between the land of Matthew le Bolt(er) on the one hand and Hornwood Lane (*Hornwodelone*) on the other for a term of 10 years; to be held to him, his heirs or assigns, wheresoever he will wish to assign in sickness and in health of the grantors freely [etc.] by rendering annually 9½d. at four terms of the year according to the usage of Coventry for all secular service [etc.]. *Et si forte contingat quod predicta Emma vel Henricus vel heredes sui plen(ar)ie non adquieta(n)t predictum feud(um) versus dominos feodi licitu(m) sit predicto Ricardo et heredibus suis vel suis assignatis adquietare predictum feud(um) usque ad predictum terminum sine contradictione Emme et Henrici de firma predicta.* Richard gave 10s. of silver beforehand. *Hanc q(u)i(dem) convencionem fideliter et sine dolo obs(er)vand(am) ut(r)ique in manu alterius affidaverunt. Et si ita contingat quod predicta Emma vel Henricus predictam terram vendere velint vel alienar[e] infra dictum terminum quod nulli venda(n)t vero aliena(n)t nec invadiant nisi predicto Ricardo vel heredibus suis, obligantes se in quadraginta solidos sterlingor(um) datur(os) fabrice ecclesie de Westm' si con(tr)aieri(n)t umquam in vita sua istam convencionem unde predictus Ricardus habeat jactura(m) vel g(r)avam(en).* Warranty and sealing clauses. Witnesses: William Leuwin, Robert de Chilton', Henry Baker (*pistor'*) then bailiff, William de Alisley, Alexander de Ruiton', John son of Simon, Nicholas de Bulkinton', Roger de Wytemor', Peter Frewin, William Frewin, Henry the Serjeant (*s(er)viente*), Thomas the clerk and others.

2 seals missing W.R.O. 471

721 Late 1260s

Demise and quitclaim by Henry son of Robert Beaufiz, for himself and his heirs, to Robert de Chilton' of Coventry of all right and claim in the entire land with all appurtenances which Robert the grantor's father held of Earl Ranulph of Chester and afterwards of the lord prior of Coventry (*de Ranulpho Comite Cestr' et postea de domino priore Coventr'*) beneath the wood next to Hornwood's Lane (*subtus boscum juxta Hornwodeslane*) with a messuage (*manso*) and with a garden (*gardino*) and all other appurtenances; to be held to him, his heirs or whatsoever assigns, freely [etc.] without any charge or reservation by the grantor or his heirs, with exclusion clause, by rendering annually to the lords of the fee as the perpetual attorneys of the grantor and his heirs 2s. 2d. of silver at the four terms of the year usual in the vill of Coventry for all secular service. Should the grantor or his heirs reclaim against this quitclaim or anyone in their name or through them reclaim against it or begin to reclaim (*Reclamare Incep(er)it*), he binds himself and his heirs to the said Robert, his heirs or whatsoever assigns, in 60s. sterling in name of debt to be paid without any contradiction, which the said Robert gave to the grantor for this demise and entire quitclaim beforehand. Sealing clause. Witnesses: William Lewin then bailiff, Henry Baker (*pistore*), Robert de Clother', Martin Colbrond, John Ingeram, John le Blund, William de Wilmeleyton' clerk and others.

Seal missing C.R.O. IA/C13/40
Endorsed: Quietaclam' henr' fil' Rob(ert)i Beufiz facta Rob(ert)o de Chilton' de terra que d(icitu)r Beaufiz.
Radeford.

C.R.O. 2/1c is a quitclaim by Henry son of Robert Beaufiz, in identical terms and with the same witnesses, to Robert de Chilton' of Coventry and Matilda his wife.

722 1270s

Charter of Matthew le Boltere of Coventry giving to Robert de Chiltone a certain part of his land in the field of Whitemore (*in camp' de Wytemor*) with a certain part of the adjacent moor in the same place lying towards the wood (*Boscum*) with the ditch (*fossat'*) and other appurtenances to the said tenement, namely that which lies between the land of the aforesaid Matthew towards the east (*versus partem orientalem*) on the one hand and the land Roger Locard once held on the other towards the south (*versus partem australem*) in exchange for the land (*In eschambio illius terre*) which Henry Herbert once held in Bishop St. (*in vico Ep(iscop)i*) lying (*adjacente(m)*) between the land John le Bel once held and the land Richard Gilbert once held according to the metes and bounds made there; to be held to him, his heirs or assigns, freely [etc.] with all liberties and free customs pertaining by rendering annually 6d. of silver at the four terms of the year usual and fixed in the vill of Coventry for all service [etc.]. Warranty and sealing clauses. Witnesses: Henry Baker (*Pistore*) then bailiff, Martin Colbront, Walter Bacun, Hugh le Hoser, William Tholy, Geoffrey Bretun, John Thole, Robert de Lundris, John le Orfeure and others.

Seal extant C.R.O. 2/1b

Endorsed: It(e)m alia carta Math(e)i le Bolt(er)e duplicata facta Roberto de Chilton' de terra juxta Blakemor'.

723 1270s

Charter of Matthew le Boltere of Coventry giving to Robert de Chilton' and Matilda his wife a certain part of his land in the field of Whitemore (*in camp' de Wetemor'*) on the same terms and with the same witnesses as 722. Robert and Matilda gave 8s. of silver.

Seal missing C.R.O. 2/85

724 1270s

Charter of Robert de Chilton' of Coventry giving to John his son, for his service, a certain part of his land outside the vill of Coventry which he had by the gift of Henry son of Robert Beufic beneath the wood (*sub bosco*) of the lord prior of Coventry with the meadow, assart (*acsarto*) and all other appurtenances which extends in length along the watercourse (*per ductu(m) aque*) which leads towards the wood up to *Blakemore* and in length from the aforesaid watercourse (*a predicto ductu*) up to the wood of the lord prior of Coventry, and a certain part of the grantor's land which he had by the gift of Matthew le Bolter in the fields of Whitemore (*in campis de Witemor*) with appurtenances which lies between the land the same Matthew held on the one hand and the land Roger Locard held on the other in length and in width as is manifest, and a certain part of the moor of Whitemore (*de mora de Witemor*) towards the aforesaid wood of the lord prior with appurtenances which extends from the aforesaid land up to the aforesaid wood in length and in width as is manifest; to be held to him, his heirs or whatsoever assigns, of the grantor and his heirs freely [etc.] by rendering annually to the lords of the fee the service due and accustomed, namely 2s. 2d. to the lord prior of Coventry at the four fixed terms of the year and to the grantor and his heirs a clove-gillyflower at Easter for all secular service [etc.]. Warranty and sealing clauses. Witnesses: Thomas de Keresley, Henry Baker (*Pistore*) of Coventry, John de Lodelowe, John Tole, Geoffrey de Bretoun, John de Wyteley, William Witte, Nicholas de Condolme, Richard Bonnte, Robert son of Hugh and others.

Seal extant C.R.O. IA/C13/14

Endorsed: Carta Roberti de Chilton' de Co. facta Johanni fil' suo de terra de Beufiz que est in Radeford.

725 c.1290–1296

Charter of John son of Robert de Chiltone of Coventry giving to Peter son of Gilbert de Blockeleye a message and a certain part of his land outside the vill of Coventry which the grantor had by the gift and grant of Robert de Chiltone his father, which land lies beneath the wood (*sub bosco*) of the prior of Coventry and which the aforesaid

Robert had by the gift and grant of Henry son of Robert Beufiz with the meadow, assart (*assarto*) and other appurtenances together with a certain part of the land which the aforesaid Robert had by the gift and grant of Matthew le Boltere in the fields next to Whitemore (*in campis juxta Wytemor'*) according to the metes and bounds made there, and a certain part of the moor of Whitemore (*mora de Wytemor'*) towards the aforesaid wood of the prior of Coventry with appurtenances which extends from the aforesaid land up to the aforesaid wood; to be held to him and his assigns, of the grantor and his heirs freely [etc.] without any reservation by the grantor or his heirs by rendering annually to the lords of the fee the services due and accustomed. Warranty and sealing clauses. Witnesses: Henry Baker (*pistore*) then bailiff of Coventry, Robert his son, William le Parker coroner, Walter de Cuyly, John Tole junior, John Pyhod, Roger Lokard, John son of Hugh de Coundulme, Robert Chatel, Thomas Bodyn, Roger the clerk and others.

Seal extant C.R.O. IA/Misc.I/I
Endorsed: Carta Johannis de Chilton' de terra beufiz facta Pet(r)o de Blockel'.

C.R.O. 2/1a is another copy of this.
The date is probably close to 1296 (see below 726).

726 c.1290–1297

Confirmation (*ratifico et inperpetuum confirmo*) by John son of Robert de Chiltone of Coventry of the gift by Peter son of Gilbert de Blockeleye to Brother Henry prior of Coventry and the convent of the same of the messuage and certain parcels (*p(ar)ticulas*) of land and meadow outside the vill of Coventry which he had by the gift and grant of John son of Robert de Chiltone, as is fully contained in his charter of enfeoffment; with warranty. Sealing clause. Witnesses: Henry Baker (*pistor'*) then bailiff of Coventry, William Parkar' then coroner, Robert de Stok', Walter Cuyly, John Tole senior, Anketill de Colleshul, John Tole junior, John Pyhod, John son of Hugh de Coundulme, Roger Lokard, Robert Chatel, Thomas Bodyn and others.

Seal extant C.R.O. 2/123

Licence in mortmain for the above (described as 4 acres of land in Coventry and Radford next to Coventry) was issued on 14 May 1296 (*C.P.R. 1292–1301* p. 187; *Coventry Priory Register* fos. 90v–91v where the text of Peter's charter is given).

727 c.29 September 1294

Lease and grant for a term by Susan (*Sussanna*) widow of William Hornewod' to the lord prior of Coventry of a certain part of her land towards Whitemore (*Wytemor*) which lies between the land of the said prior on the one hand and the land once of Robert de Chiltone on the other in width and extends in length from the running water up to the land of Roger Locart; to be held with appurtenances freely [etc.] from Michaelmas 22 Edward I for a term of 6 years by rendering annually to the chief lords of that fee 9½d. at the four terms of the year usual in Coventry for all service. Clause for warranty. Sealing clause, for 12s. of silver which the said prior gave beforehand. Witnesses: Henry Baker (*Pistore*) of Coventry, Thomas le Moubray of the same, John Tole of the same, Roger Locart, Roger de Wytemor servant (*s(er)vienti*), Anketell de Colsul, John son of Hugh de Cundulme and others.

Seal missing C.R.O. IB/22EI/13
Endorsed: Radeford.

728 1313–1320

Charter of Ro(bert de Leycest)r'[1] full brother (*frat(er) g(er)man(us)*) of Brother Henry prior of Coventry giving to the church of the blessed Mary of Coventry, Prior Henry and the convent and their successors in free, pure and perpetual alms the chief messuage (*capit(al)e mesuagiu(m)*) with all lands, woods, meadows, pastures and all other appurtenances which were once of Roger Lokard in Whitemore (*Witemore*[2] *juxta Coventr'*) together with the reversion of all the lands and tenements which the same Roger granted (*alienavit*) to Juliana his daughter and to Alice de Birchemor' his wife for the term of their lives, and also the reversion of all the lands and tenements which fell to the said Alice in name of dower, all and each of which he had by the gift and enfeoffment of Thomas son and heir of the said Roger; to be held freely [etc.] of the chief lords of the fee by the services due and accustomed. Warranty and sealing clauses. Witnesses: [John d]e[3] Clifton then bailiff of Coventry, Roger de Pacwode then coroner, Roger Daieseghe, William de H[ ][4]ockley, William de Whiteley, Simon Pakeman and many others.

Seal extant C.R.O. 1A/Misc. II 37

Endorsed: Carta Roberti de Leyc' de ten' quondam Rogeri Locard.

[1] Lost, supplied from endorsement.

[2] *Witemor'* is written in a different hand over an erasure.

[3] Lost.

[4] The end of the last name and the beginning of this are lost.

729 4 February 1294

Charter of Bela and Isabella daughters of William Edwy giving to Henry Baker (*Pistor'*) of Coventry 5 selions of arable land in Shukmore (*in t(er)itorio quod vocat(ur) Soggomor*) lying between the land once of Robert de le Clocher on the one hand and the land of Robert Herberd on the other in length and in width as is manifest according to the metes and bounds made there; to be held with appurtenances to him, his heirs and assigns, of them and their heirs freely [etc.] by rendering annually the service due and accustomed to the chief lords of that fee. Clause for warranty. Henry gave 4s. of silver beforehand. Witnesses: Robert de Stok', Robert de Chilton', Willelmo le Parkere then coroner, Thomas Moubrei, John Pihot, Robert Herberd, John de Teinton' and John Tole. Coventry, Thursday after the Purification of the blessed Mary 22 Edward I.

2 seals extant Q.C. 2323

Endorsed: Ca(m)po Suggemor for heton' quod Sewele de bulkinton tenet

730 1301–1305

Charter of Robert Herbert of Coventry giving to John de Halys and Margaret his wife 4 selions with adjacent headlands (*foreris*) and all other appurtenances in the field next to Shukmore (*in campo juxta Suggemor*) lying between the grantor's land on the one hand and the land of Henry Baker (*pistoris*) on the other in width and which extends in length from the royal highway (*a Regali via*) up to the land of Robert de Redeware in Shukmore (*Suggemor*) according to the metes and bounds made there; to be held to them, their heirs or assigns, of the chief lords of that fee freely [etc.] by rendering annually 7½d. at the four terms of the year usual in Coventry for all secular services [etc.]. Clause for warranty. John and Margaret gave 10 marks beforehand. Sealing clause. Witnesses: Robert son of Henry Baker (*pistor'*) then bailiff of Coventry, John Lewyn then coroner of the same, Alexander de Stonlee,

Robert Kelle, Henry Oky, Robert de Chilton', John Pyhod, Robert de Redewar', Alexander son of Thomas le Moubray and many others.

Seal extant W.R.O. 366

731 19 September 1305

Charter of Robert Herbert of Coventry giving to John de Hales of Coventry and Margaret his wife the entire part of his arable land in Shukmore (*Soggemor*) with headlands (*cheveciis*) and all other appurtenances which lies in width between the land which the same John and Margaret once had by his gift on the one hand and the land of the lord prior and convent of Coventry on the other, and which extends from the royal highway (*a Regia via*) which leads towards the house of Roger Lokard up to the land of Robert de Redeware as the land purports according to the metes and bounds made there; to be held to them, their heirs or assigns, freely [etc.] of the chief lords of that fee by the services owed and by right accustomed, by rendering annually to those same lords 7½d. at the four terms of the year usual in Coventry for all secular services [etc.]. Clause for warranty. John and Margaret gave 6 marks beforehand. Sealing clause. Witnesses: Robert son of Henry Baker (*pistoris*) then bailiff of Coventry, John Lewyn then coroner of the same, Robert Kelle, John Pyhod, Henry Oky, Richard de Daleby, Robert son of Peter de Chilton', Alexander le Vyneter, Alexander son of Thomas de Moubray clerk and many others. Coventry, Sunday after the Exaltation of the Holy Cross 33 Edward I.

Seal missing W.R.O. 367

Endorsed: Evidens of a Clos and a pastur lyes nygh lokyers lane.

FIELDS AND CROFTS*

*For the Poddycroft see also 42, 63, 76, 386, 411 and *Langley Cartulary* No. 272.

732 1280s

Charter of Thomas de Stapelton' and Anabilia his wife giving to Master Guy de Tyllebrok' their land of Poddycroft (*de Podycroft*) and all the other lands, tenements, rents and services in Coventry which they had by the gift of Henry de Rodynton' father[1] of the aforesaid Anabilia; to be held to him, his heirs or assigns, freely and quietly by rendering annually to the grantors and their heirs a clove-gillyflower at Easter, and to the chief lords the service due and accustomed for all secular services, suits, customs and demands. Clause for warranty. Guy gave £20 beforehand. Sealing clause. Witnesses: The venerable father Sir Thomas prior of Coventry, Master Walter rector of the church of Mancetter (*Manecestre*), Peter le Breton', Robert de Chilton', Henry Baker (*Pistore*), Peter Baron', Thomas Celet, William Celet clerk and others.

[1] The document reads *p(at)ris mei.*

This and the following 2 charters are taken from a detached membrane of a charter roll which survives in C.R.O. (Ecclesiastical Records Box No. I). It is preceded by the latter part of a charter (see below) which is undoubtedly a grant of the above property to Henry de Rodinton and Alice his wife, belonging to the late 1250s. Since the bottom part of the membrane is blank it seems to represent the last of the roll.

(. . . . *pertinent'*). Should Alice survive the said Henry she will hold the said land with appurtenances as long as she lives entirely, peacefully and quietly without contradiction by the heirs of the aforesaid Henry or of her heirs, so that if the heirs of the aforesaid Henry and Alice issuing freely from the said Alice should die or in any way fail the heirs of the aforesaid Henry will hold the entire land with all appurtenances well [etc.] by hereditary right. In return for this gift, grant and quitclaim Henry and Alice gave 100s. sterling in recognition beforehand. Witnesses: Richard de Buk(er)vile, John Simon then bailiffs (*ballivis*) of Coventry, John Beer, Philip de Wynchecombe, Richard de Fonte, Anketinus de Wykewane, Pagan Pake, Walter the White (*Blundo*), William de Paylington', William de Allesleye, John Ingeram, William Lewyne, Thomas le Gras, Peter Martin, Nicholas Farthwyne, Henry de Stanford and others.

733 1280s

Charter of Thomas de Stapelton' giving to Master Guy de Tyllebrok' his entire land of Poddycroft (*de Podycroft*) and all other lands, tenements, rents and services in Coventry which he had in marriage with Anabel' his wife; to be held to him, his heirs or assigns, freely and quietly by rendering annually to the grantor and his heirs a clove-gillyflower at Easter and to the chief lords the service due and accustomed for all secular services, suits, customs and demands. Clause for warranty. Guy gave £20 beforehand. Sealing clause. Witnesses: The venerable father Sir Thomas prior of Coventry, Master Walter rector of the church of Mancetter (*Manecestre*), Peter le Breton', Robert de Chilton', Henry Baker (*Pistore*), Peter Baron', Thomas Celet, William Celet clerk and others.

734 1280s

Charter of Guy de Tyllebrok' giving to Henry de Alestote and Alice his wife daughter of Nicholas de Haleford' the grantor's brother, his entire land in Coventry which he had by the gift of Thomas de Stapelton, and Anabilia his wife namely in the Poddycroft and near Wood Mill (*in Podycroft et prope Wodemulne*) with appurtenances together with 12d. annual rent from Robert de Chilton' and his heirs, 14d. annual rent from William le P(ar)kere and his heirs, 2d. annual rent from Master Richard de Bannebury and his heirs, and 5s. annual rent from Simon Pat and his heirs from the lands and tenements which they held of the grantor in Coventry; the aforesaid land with rents, escheats and all appurtenances to be held to them and the heirs issuing from Alice's body of [the grantor] and his heirs freely and quietly, by rendering annually ½d. at Easter and to the lords of that fee the service due and accustomed for all secular service [etc.]. Clause for reversion after the deaths of Alice and Henry her husband should Alice die without heir of her body to Robert brother of the said Alice and his heirs. Warranty and sealing clauses. Witnesses: Alexander the Vintner (*vinetar'*), Robert de Stok', Henry Baker (*Pistore*), Walter Bakun, Thomas Selet, Peter Baron', William Selet clerk and others.

735 c.29 September 1294

Agreement whereby Henry de Allescote and Alice his wife have leased, granted and demised at farm to Richard de la Muyre and John de Langeleye merchants in Coventry their entire land in Poddycroft (*Podycroft*) with a certain part of the land which they had in Shockersfield (*Scocherescroft*) of the gift of Master Guy de Tylebroc; to be held with all appurtenances to them, their heirs or assigns, well [etc.] from the feast of St. Michael A.D. 1294 22 Edward I for a term of 12 years, by rendering annually to the aforesaid Henry and Alice and their heirs 1 mark of silver at the four terms of the year usual in the vill of Coventry and to the lords of the fee as the attorneys of the aforesaid Henry and Alice 3d. of silver at the same four terms for all secular services [etc.]. Clause for warranty. Richard and John gave ½ mark of silver beforehand. Mutual sealing clause [chirograph]. Witnesses: Henry Baker (*pistore*) then bailiff of Coventry, Henry Ballard, Adam Russel, William G(r)antpe, Henry the Painter (*pictore*), Robert de Wynchecu(m)be, Roger the clerk and others.

Indented
Seal missing C.R.O.IB/22EI/12

736 23 August 1297

Agreement whereby Henry de Wyrcestr' burgess of Leicester (*Burgens de leycestr'*) has granted and demised to John de Langeleye and Richard de la Mur' of Coventry merchants the entire arable land which he had of the inheritance (*de hereditar'*) of

Petronilla his wife in the fields (*camp'*) of Coventry namely in the Poddycroft (*In Podicroft*) and in Shockersfield (*in le schocheresfeld*) as is fully manifest according to the metes and bounds there; to be held with all appurtenances to them, their heirs or assigns, of the aforesaid Henry as long as he shall live freely [etc.] by rendering annually 2s. 8d. of silver at the feast of St. Michael the Archangel for all secular services and demands. Clause for warranty. Mutual sealing clause. Witnesses: Henry Baker (*Pistore*) then bailiff in Coventry, William le Parker then coroner, Matthew de Ruyton', John le Teu, Adam Russel, Reginald Ballard and others. Coventry, Friday the vigil of St. Bartholemew the Apostle 25 Edward I.

Indented
Seal missing C.R.O. IB/25 EI/10

737 c.25 March 1304

Charter of Alice widow of Henry de Alscote, in her pure widowhood, giving to John de Langeleye and Henry de la Muyre of Coventry merchants her entire land with an adjacent meadow and all other appurtenances which she had in Coventry in the fields called Poddycroft and Shockersfield (*in campis qui vocantur Podycroft et Schocheresfeld*), and 5s. annual rent with appurtenances which Symon Pat used to render to her annually for a tenement which he held of her in Coventry, 14d. annual rent with appurtenances which William le Parker' used to render to her annually for a tenement which he held of her in the same vill, and 2d. annual rent with appurtenances which Master Richard de Burton' used to render to her annually for a tenement which he held of her in the same vill; to be held to them, their heirs or assigns, of the grantor and her heirs freely [etc.] by rendering to the grantor, her heirs or assigns, for 12 years from the feast of the blessed Mary in March 32 Edward I a rose at the feast of the Nativity of St. John the Baptist and to the lords of the fee as her attorney during the aforesaid time 3d. of silver at the four terms of the year usual in Coventry for all services and demands, and after the end of the 12 years £20 sterling at the aforesaid terms for all services and demands. Clause for warranty. Mutual sealing clause [chirograph]. Witnesses: Peter Barun, William de Schepeye, Robert de Rydewar', William de Bury, Richard le Merc(er), Alexander le Schereman, Richard de St. James and others. Coventry, Wednesday the morrow of St. Matthew the Apostle in the year aforesaid.

Seal missing C.R.O. IB/32 EI/12

738 13 June 1297

Charter of Henry Brayn of Coventry giving to Robert son of Henry Baker (*pistoris*) a part of his arable land outside the vill of Coventry, namely that which is called Shockersfield (*le Schocheresfeld'*) and which lies between the land of Margery widow of Walter de Bannebur' on the one hand and the land of Alexander le Vinet(er) on the other in width and extends in length from the road (*via*) which leads towards Coundon (*Cundulm'*) up to the land of Richard le Porser' as is fully manifest according to the metes and bounds made there; to be held with all appurtenances to him, his heirs or assigns, of the chief lords of that fee freely [etc.] by rendering annually to those same chief lords the services due and by right accustomed for all secular services and demands. Clause for warranty. Robert gave 100s. sterling beforehand. Sealing clause. Witnesses: Henry Baker (*pistore*) then bailiff, William le P(ar)ker' then coroner, John Pyhod, Thomas le Moubray, Matthew de Ruyton', William Mauncel and others. Coventry, Thursday after the feast of St. Barnabas the Apostle 25 Edward I.

Seal missing G.H. 309

739 16 June 1297

Gift and quitclaim by Robert son of Henry Baker (*pistoris*) of Coventry, for himself and his heirs, to the aforesaid Henry his father of all right and claim in a third part of the field (*campi*) which is called Shockersfield (*le Schocheresfeld'*) outside the vill of Coventry which third part lies between the land of Margery widow of Walter de Bannebur' on the one hand and the grantor's land on the other in width and extends in length from the royal highway (*a regia via*) which leads towards Coundon (*Cundulm'*) up to the land of Richard le Bourser as is fully manifest according to the metes and bounds made there. Moreover, he has given and quitclaimed to the aforesaid Henry his father all right and claim in seven selions of arable land in St. Nicholas Field (*In Seynt Nycolasfeld'*) in Coventry which lie between the land once of Robert de Chylton' on the one hand and the grantor's land on the other in width and extends in length from the royal highway (*a regia via*) which leads towards Hazelwood (*Hazelwode*) up to the land of Margery widow of Walter de Bannebur' as is fully manifest according to the metes and bounds made there; the aforesaid third part of the field with all appurtenances and the aforesaid seven selions with appurtenances and adjacent headlands (*foreriis*) to be held to him, his heirs or assigns, with free entrance and exit, of the chief lords of that fee freely [etc.] by rendering annually to those same chief lords the services due and by right accustomed for all secular services [etc.]. Exclusion clause. Henry gave 40s. sterling beforehand. Sealing clause. Witnesses: William le P(ar)kere then coroner, John le Cu, Thomas le Moubray, John Pyhod, Richard Tyllay and others. Coventry, Sunday the vigil of St. Botulf 25 Edward I.

Seal extant G.H. 310

740 16 June 1297

Gift and quitclaim by Robert son of Henry Baker (*pistor'*) of Coventry, for himself and his heirs, to Master Richard de Aula, his heirs or assigns, of all right and claim in a third part of the field (*campi*) which is called Shockersfield (*le scocheresfeld'*) outside the vill of Coventry, which third part lies between the land of William de Nayllestone on the one hand and the land of Alexander le Vineter on the other in width and extends in length from the royal highway (*a regia via*) which leads towards Coundon (*Cundulm'*) up to the land of Richard le Bourcer as is fully manifest according to the metes and bounds made there. Moreover, he has given and quitclaimed to Master Richard, his heirs or assigns, all right and claim in seven selions of arable land with appurtenances which lie in the field nearer to the cemetery of St. Nicholas in Coventry on the northern side (*in propinquiori campo simit(er)io sancti Nicholai in Coventr' ex parte boriali*) between the land of Henry Baker (*pistoris*) on the one hand and the land of William de Nayleston' on the other in width and extends in length from the road (*via*) which leads towards Hazelwood (*Hazelwode*) up to the land of Margery widow of Walter de Bannebur' as is fully manifest according to the metes and bounds made there; the third part of the field and the seven selions of land with adjacent headlands (*foreris*) and all appurtenances to be held to Master Richard, his heirs or assigns, of the chief lords of that fee freely [etc.] by rendering annually to those same lords the services due and accustomed for all secular services and demands. Exclusion clause. Master Richard gave 40s. sterling beforehand. Sealing clause. Witnesses: Henry Baker (*pistore*) then bailiff, William de Nayleston' then coroner, John Pyhod, Thomas le Moubray, Matthew de Ruyton', and others. Coventry, Sunday the vigil of St. Botulf 25 Edward I.

Seal extant C.R.O. IB/25 EI/9b

741 1280s

Charter of Geoffrey de Langeleye knight giving to Henry Baker (*pistori*) of Coventry and Agnes his wife for 9 marks of silver which they gave beforehand 9 acres of land in the field (*campo*) of Stivichall beneath Coventry Park (*stivechale sub parco de Coventr'*), namely the entire land which he had *sup(er) dilhul* with the entire meadow and the entire moor adjacent to the said land and with the liberties and easements in all places belonging to the said land. Moreover, he has given to them all the rents which he had in the vill of Keresley (*Kerisle*) from all his tenements with the homages, escheats, heriots, and all his rights in whatsoever way issuing from the aforesaid rents, namely from William de Norc(r)oft and his heirs from the lands and tenements which he held of him in Keresley (*Kerisle*) 3s. of silver annually at the four terms of the year usual in the vill of Coventry, and from the heirs of Hugh *at þe berne* from the lands and tenements which he held of him in the aforesaid vill 2s. of silver annually at the same four terms, and from Thomas *sup(er) le hul* and his heirs from the lands and tenements which he held of him in the aforesaid vill 3s. of silver annually at the same terms. Moreover, he has given to them 14d. annual rent which he used to receive from the said Henry at the same terms from the land which was once of William Payn in Earl St. (*in vico Comit'*) in Coventry together with 1lb. cumin rent which he used to receive from the master of the Hospital (*Ospital'*) of St. John of Coventry; to be held to them, their heirs or assigns, of him and his heirs freely [etc.] by rendering annually for the entire rent in Keresley (*Kerisle*) to Thomas lord of Keresley (*Kerisle*), his heirs or assigns, 1lb. of cumin at Christmas and to the grantor, his heirs or assigns, a pair of white gloves at Easter worth ½d. of silver for all secular services [etc.]. Warranty and sealing clauses. Witnesses: Robert de Stokys, Adam des Hokys, Robert de Chilton', Ralf de Witele, Adam Myle of the same, John de Barue of Stivichall (*stivechale*), Ranulph son of Hugh of the same, Walter Bacun then (*tunc temporis*) coroner of Coventry, Thomas de Moubray of the same, John Tole of the same, Walter son of Thomas de Kerisle, Richard Beuse, William de Norc(r)oft junior of the same and others.

Seal extant Q.C. 2381

742 28 September 1297

Charter of Henry Brayn of Coventry giving to Master Richard de Bourton' in Coventry doctor (*medico*) his entire pasture which is called Wood Mill Hay (*le Wodemulneheye*) with free entrance and exit just as the grantor used to have and with all other appurtenances; to be held to him, his heirs or assigns, to whomsoever he will wish to give, bequeath or assign, in sickness and in health well [etc.] of the chief lords of that fee by the service of 12d. of silver to be paid to those same lords annually at four terms of the year usual in Coventry for all secular services [etc.]. Clause for warranty. Richard gave £10 sterling beforehand. Sealing clause. Witnesses: Henry Baker (*Pistore*) then bailiff of Coventry, William called (*dicto*) Park(er) then coroner, Thomas le Moubray, Anketill de Coleshul, Matthew de Ruyton', William de Copston', Richard de St. James, John le Vineter, Roger the clerk and others. Coventry, Saturday before the feast of St. Michael 25 Edward I.

Seal missing C.R.O. IB/25EI/7
Endorsed: Sac(r)ista.

743 10 November 1305

Letter of John de Hastings, lord of Abergavenny, acknowledging his grant at the request of Robert de Stokes to Prior Henry de Leicester and the convent of Coventry that they may freely enter his fee of Coventry by the enfeoffment by Peter de Blockley and his heirs of a piece of meadow and pasture called Wood Mill Hay, providing they seek the agreement of the king.

A tous iceus qe ceste presente lettres verrount ou orrount Johan de Hastynges seyngnur' de Bergeveny saluz en nostre seyngur'. Sachez moy a la requeste Robert de Stok' pur moy e pur mes heyrs avoir graunte a frere Henry de Leycestr' prior de Coventr' e a covent de mesme le leu e a lur successours issi qe il quergent le gree le roy qe fraunchement puyssent e de ma bone volunte en mon fee de Coventr' entier par le feffement Pieres de Blockele e ces heirs de une place de pree e de pasture qe leiu apele Wodemulneheye; a avoir e tenir[1] al avauntdit prior e ces successours et nomement al profit del sekersteyn e de la sekersteynrye e de ceus qe serrount gardeins del overayngne de meisme la eglise fraunchement quietement bien e en pees e touz jours, issint qe moy ne mes heyrs vers le avauntdit prior ne ces successours par le statut de morte mein deforenavaunt riens puyssoums clamir ou demander' salve a moy e mes heyrs les services e les custumes dewes e acustumez del avauntdit tenement. En tesmoynaunce de quele chose a ceste lettre patente ay mys mon sceel. Yceus tesmoyngnes William Ryvel, William le Bretoun, Robert de Herle, Robert de Stok', Robert Jabet, Robert le Pestur, Alisaundre de Staunleye e plusours altres. Done a Coventr' la veyle de seint Martin le an du regne nostr' seyngnur le roy Edward filz le roy Henr' trente terce.

Seal extant C.R.O. IB/33EI/12

[1] e tenir repeated.

744 25 March 1307

Charter of Peter de Blockele clerk giving in pure and perpetual alms to Brother Henry the prior and the convent of the church of the blessed Mary of Coventry and especially to the sacrist (*precipue sacriste*) of the same church a third part of Wood Mill Hay (*Wodemulneheye*) as it lies in meadow and moor (*secundum quod jacet in prato et mora*) together with 12d. annual rent once of the prioress of Henwood (*Hynewode*) to be taken from the aforesaid tenement. Moreover, he has given to them his entire part in the meadow of Wyken (*Wykene*) which lies between the land of the lord of Wyken (*Wykene*) and the land once of Yvo de Wykene as is fully manifest. Moreover, he has given to them 12d. annual rent with appurtenances to be taken from a certain virgate of land which Henry called (*dictus*) Blaunche held in the territory (*in territorio*) of Coventry towards Coundon (*Cundulme*), all and each of which he had by the gift of Master Richard de Banebury called (*dicti*) de Aula of Coventry; to be held with all rights, profits, appurtenances and liberties freely [etc.] by making to the chief lords of that fee the services due and by right accustomed. Warranty and sealing clauses. Witnesses: Robert de Herle, Robert de Stoke, Thomas Boydyn of Stretton', Robert Baker (*Pistor'*) of Coventry, Alexander de Stonleye, William Grauntpe, Robert de Chylton' and others. Coventry, the feast of the Annunciation of the blessed Virgin Mary 35 Edward I.

Seal extant C.R.O. IB/35 EI/9

According to the *Priory Register* this land was acquired under the licence granted 6 April 1305 (fos. 96r–v; *C.P.R. 1301–7* p. 334).

745 c.1280

Charter of Avicia the prioress and the convent of Henwood (*Hinewod*) giving to Richard de Burton' and Petronilla his wife, daughter of John de Aula, for 1 mark of silver which they gave beforehand, 12d. annual rent which they had by the gift and grant of Richard the Vintner (*winitarii*) from a certain tenement in the territory (*t(er)itorio*) of Coventry which is called *Albristescroft*; to be held to them, their heirs or assigns, freely [etc.] in fee and inheritance without any charge or reservation by them or their successors. Exclusion and sealing clauses. Witnesses: Robert de Chilton' then bailiff in Coventry, Henry Baker (*Pistor'*) of the same, Walter Bakun of the same, Peter (*Petron'*) Barun of the same, Hugh Bretun of the same, Adam Colbrunt of the same, John Minot of the same, John le Butt(er)e of the same, Richard de Kid(er)mu(n)ster chaplain, maker (*confector'*) of this deed, and others.

Seal missing C.R.O. 1A/C13/22

746 18 December 1297

Grant, remise and quitclaim by Robert son of Henry called Baker (*dicti Pistoris*) of Coventry, for himself and his heirs, to Master Richard de Bourton' in Coventry a third part of the land which was of Henry Brayn in *Albrydescroft* outside Coventry which he had by the gift of the same Henry, and a third part of the mill-pond where there was once a mill called Wood Mill (*terciam partem stangni ubi fuit quondam molendinu(m) quod vocabatur le Wodemulne*) with its appurtenances namely pastures and hedges (*pasturarum et hayarum*) with free entrance and exit; to be held to him, his heirs or assigns, well [etc.] of the lords of that fee by the services due and accustomed without any reservation by him or his heirs. Master Richard gave 40s. sterling beforehand. Sealing clause. Witnesses: Robert de Stoke, William le Parker then coroner in Coventry, Thomas le Moubray, John Thole, John Pyhod, Nicholas Crumpe, William de Copston', Matthew de Ruyton', Roger the clerk and others. Coventry, Wednesday before the feast of St. Thomas the Apostle 25 Edward I.

Seal extant C.R.O. 1B/25E1/6

747 c. 1286

Charter of Adam son of Henry Oliver of Shuckburgh (*Schukeberg'*) for the salvation of his soul and those of his ancestors and successors giving in free, pure and perpetual alms to God, the church of the blessed Mary, Prior Thomas and the monks of Coventry [his][1] croft in Coventry with appurtenances which is called *Spitelcroft* between the land of Robert de Allesleye and the highway (*viam regiam*) and which extends towards the park (*versus parcum*); to be held to them and their successors and the aforesaid church as freely as any alms can be held. Warranty and sealing clauses. Witnesses: Robert de Stok', Simon Erneys, Henry Baker (*pistore*), Robert de Chilton', William de Copstone, Thomas de Barsham, Thomas Selet, Richer de Weston and others.

Seal missing C.R.O. IA/Misc.II/34

Endorsed: cam(er)a P(r)ior'.

[1] nostrum

This croft was acquired under licence in mortmain granted 10 February 1286 (*C.P.R. 1281–92* p. 219; *Coventry Priory Register* fos. 86v–87r).

748 5 September 1296

Agreement whereby Brother Henry prior of the church of Coventry has leased and granted to John de Langeleye of Coventry and Alice his wife a furlong (*culturam*) of land which is called Spitelcroft (*spitele croft*) in Coventry, which furlong Richard de Asseby previously held of the aforesaid prior; to be held with appurtenances to them for their entire life of the aforesaid prior and his successors and the aforesaid church freely and peacefully by the service of 10s. of silver to be paid annually as long as either of them shall live at two terms of the year, namely 5s. at the feast of St. Michael the Archangel and 5s. at Easter for all service. *Et quod in decessu alterius eorum Johannis et Alicie scilicet qui diucius vixerit executores sui omnia blada super dictam terram die obitus ipsius seminata si que fuerint sine alicujus contradiccione capiant et asportent salvo tamen prefato priori et successoribus suis tota redditu predicto, ita videlicet quod post decessum predictorum Johannis et Alicie et post vesturam ultimi anni sicut predictum est asportatam tota dicta terra cum pertinenciis prefato priori et successoribus suis et ecclesie sue predicte quiete et integre sine alicujus contradiccione revertatur.* Mutual sealing clause [chirograph]. Witnesses: Robert de Stok', William de Schulton', Adam Russel, Richard de Mure, Richard de Weston' and others. Coventry, Wednesday before the feast of the Nativity of the blessed Mary 24 Edward I.

Indented
2 seals extant C.R.O. 1B/24EI/7
Endorsed: Scriptum Joh' de langel' de Coventr' de Spitelecroft ad camera Prior'. reversio.

749 c.29 September 1298

Lease, grant and demise at farm by Thomas de Coxham of Coventry to William de Cestria tailor in Coventry (*in Coventr' sutori*) his entire part of the sheaves of corn (*garbar'*) which the grantor ought to receive annually from the land which William de Copston' and Roger de Coundulme in Coventry hold of the grantor for a term of years, to be gathered from part of the field in the territory of Coventry towards Coundon (*ad col(ig)enda(m) ad ca(m)pi parte(m) in t(er)ritorio de Coventr' versus Coundulme*), and five selions of the grantor's land in the aforesaid territory lying between the land William de Copston' holds of the grantor on the one hand and the land of Robert Faccon on the other, and the reversion of the grantor's meadow which Robert de Rothewelle holds of the grantor for a term of years namely after Robert's term, which meadow lies next to Deadmanswell (*juxta Dodemaneswelle*) between the land of Robert Faccon on the one hand and the land of Roger de Coundulme on the other; to be held to him, his heirs or whatsoever assigns, of the grantor and his heirs, well [etc.] from Michaelmas 26 Edward I for a term of four years, by rendering annually to the grantor, his heirs or assigns, 20d. of silver at the four terms of the year usual in the vill of Coventry for all secular services [etc.]. Clause for warranty. Pre-emption clause should the grantor wish to sell or demise for a further term. William gave a certain sum of money beforehand. Sealing clause. Witnesses: Anketill de Coleshul then bailiff of Coventry, Robert in le Huyrne, Eadward le Barkere, William Loteman, John Reymund, William le Wallere, Geoffrey his brother and others.

Seal missing C.R.O. IB/26EI/9

750 17 September 1289

Agreement whereby Hugh de Vienne clerk and Sir Geoffrey de Langeleye knight have leased and granted at farm to Robert de Chilton', John de Langeleye, Richard le Brochere and William le Parkere of Coventry their mills of Shortley (*Shorteleya*), to be held to them and their assigns, from the feast of St. Michael 17 Edward I for a term of 20 years together with a moor called *lorchard* and a plot (*placea*) called *le hamme*, a plot called *Ludelaweshamme* and another plot called *Eyte*, and with free entrance and exit and other appurtenances, by rendering annually 5 marks sterling at two terms of the year, namely 1 moiety at Easter and the other at Michaelmas the first payment being at Easter 18 Edward I. The grantees ought to repair and maintain the aforesaid mills competently at their own cost until the end of the term, and they will be allowed to fish in the waters at will and to repair the mill-ponds of the said mills from the adjacent land whensoever it is necessary. Clause for warranty during the term for the aforesaid farm, to the payment of which the lessees have bound themselves, their heirs and executors, and all their goods wheresoever found, movable and immovable, and those of their heirs. Clause for distraint. Mutual sealing clause [chirograph]. Canterbury (*Cantuar'*), Saturday before the feast of St. Matthew the Apostle 17 Edward I.

Indented
2 seals extant, 2 missing C.R.O. IB/17EI/1

See *Langley Cartulary* No. 187 for an agreement between the four grantees whereby Robert de Chilton and William le Parkere should hold New Mill and the other two Bisseley Mill for the said term.

751 1 November 1290

Charter of Hugh de Vienne clerk, with the assent of Sir Geoffrey de Langele knight, giving to John de Langele and Richard de Mora, merchants of Coventry, the entire mill which he had in the manor of Shortley (*Shortele*) which is called Bisseley Mill (*Busselemulle*); to be held with the mill-ponds, fisheries and all other easements belonging to the said mill in whatsoever way together with an acre of land lying between the said mill and the little grove (*p(ar)va(m) gravam*) on the western side of the aforesaid water which extends to the royal highway (*super viam regia(m)*) which leads towards Coventry and together with easement of the adjacent land for repairing the mill-ponds of the said mill when necessary, to them, their heirs or assigns, of the grantor for his entire life and after his death of Sir Geoffrey de Langel, his heirs or assigns, freely [etc.] in fee and inheritance, by rendering to the grantor for his entire life and after his death to the said Sir Geoffrey, his heirs or assigns, 4 marks of silver at the four usual terms, and similarly by rendering annually for the grantor and the said Sir Geoffrey, his heirs or assigns, 10s. sterling rent of assize to the abbot of Combe (*Comb'*) for all things, saving to the grantor for his entire life and to the said Sir Geoffrey, his heirs or assigns, after the grantor's death multure of every kind of corn when they are present in the aforesaid manor (*multura cuj(us)l(ibet) bladi cum presentes nos esse contigerit in manerio predicto*). Sealing clause. Witnesses: Sirs William de Grandissono, Walter de Helion, William de Cugho knights, Walter de Bathonia, Nicholas de Eton', Henry le Pestour of Coventry, Nicholas de Warrewik, John de Ditton' and others. London, the feast of All Saints 18 Edward I.

Seal extant C.R.O. IB/18EI/4

752

Inspeximus of the above by Geoffrey de Langele knight for which John de Langele and Richard de Mora gave 20s. sterling beforehand. The feast of St. Andrew the Apostle 19 Edward I [30 November 1290]. Witnesses: Sirs William de Grandissono, Lawrence de St. Maur, Fulk de Lucy knights, Henry le Pestour of Coventry, Robert de Stok', Adam Russel and others.

Seal extant C.R.O. IB/19 EI/1

753 11 June 1301

Charter of Eadmund de Langelee, lord of Shortley (*Schortelee juxta Coventr'*), giving to John de Langelee merchant of Coventry (*de Coventr' mercatori*) four portions (*porciones*) of land and a grove which is called Little Grove (*Litlegrove*) lying in the vill of

Coventry, of which one portion contains 34 selions and lies in a certain furlong (*cultura*) which is called New Mill Croft (*Neumulne Croft*) between the land John de Ridewar' holds of the grantor on both sides in width and extends from the royal highway (*a Regali via*) leading towards Coventry up to the running water which is called Sherbourne (*schireburne*) in length, another portion contains 16 selions and lies in Bisseley Furlong (*Bischeleeforlong*) between the land of the aforesaid John de Ridewar' on the one hand and the land of Richard de la Muyre on the other in width and extends from the aforesaid road (*via*) up to Bisseley Mill (*molendinum de Bischelee*) in length, the third portion contains 6 selions and lies in a certain furlong (*cultura*) towards Coventry between the land of Richard de St. James on the one hand and the land of the aforesaid John de Ridewar' on the other in width and extends from the aforesaid road (*via*) up to the meadow which is called Altegeder Meadow (*le Altegedermedewe*) in length, the fourth portion lies in the furlong against Altergeder Mill (*in cultura contra le Altegedermulne*) between the road (*viam*) leading towards the same mill on the one hand and the land of the aforesaid John de Ridewar' on the other in width and extends from the aforesaid road up to Altegeder Mill (*le altegedermulne*) in length and contains four selions, and the aforesaid grove lies next to the aforesaid water which is called Sherbourne (*Schireburne*) between Bisseley Mill and New Mill (*molendinum de Bischelee et le Neuwemulne*) in length and in width as is fully manifest according to the metes and bounds made there; to be held with the hedges, ditches, meadows and pastures adjacent to the same land [and] grove with all appurtenances, profits and easements to him, his heirs or assigns, freely [etc.] of the chief lords of that fee by the services due and by right accustomed. Clause for warranty. Sealing clause. Witnesses: Robert de Stoke, John Loeuwyn then coroner of Coventry, Peter Barun, Thomas Ballard, Thomas de Lilleburne, Robert de Ridewar', Richard de la Muyre, Ralf le Hunte, Geoffrey le Chaluner and many others. Coventry, Sunday the feast of St. Barnabas 29 Edward I.

Seal extant C.R.O. Wyley/8
Endorsed: de grava juxta Coventr' ad capella(m) sancte Anne

Wyley/9 is another copy of the same grant.

754 c.1300

Charter of Eadmund de Langelee knight, lord of Shortley (*Schorteleye*), giving to John de Langele merchant in Coventry (*in Coventr' mercatori*) a moiety of all his land outside Coventry on the western side of the water called Sherbourne (*Schyreburne*) with the meadow, herbage (*herbagio*) and all other easements pertaining to the same land and his entire grove on that side of the aforesaid water which is called Little Grove (*litlegrove*) with herbage and all appurtenances and easements, of which land one piece (*pecia*) lies against Altegeder Mill (*contra altegedermulne*) between the land of Peter Barun on the one hand and the road (*viam*) leading from Coventry towards Altegeder Mill (*Altegedermulne*) on the other, another piece lies beyond the road (*ultra viam*) leading from Coventry towards the mill which is called Bisseley Mill (*Bisschelemulne*) between the land of the aforesaid Peter on the one hand and the land of Richard de St. James on the other, the third piece is called Bisseley Furlong (*Bisschelefurlong*) and lies between the land of the aforesaid Richard on the one hand and the land of John de Rideware on the other, and the fourth piece is called New Mill Croft (*le Newemulnecroft*); to be held with all appurtenances and easements belonging in every single place to John, his heirs or whatsoever assigns, of the grantor and his heirs well [etc.] by making annually to the chief lords the services due and by right accustomed. Clause for warranty. John gave 24 marks sterling beforehand. Sealing clause. Witnesses: Robert de Stoke, Philip le Ireys of the same,

Adam des Okes of Whitley (*Wytele*), Geoffrey son of Ralf of the same, Adam Russel of Coventry, Nicholas Crumpe, Peter Barun, John de Rideware, William G(r)antpe, William de Toucestr', Richard de la Muyre, Geoffrey le Chaloner, Roger the clerk and others.

Seal extant C.R.O. Wyley/10

Around Michaelmas 1300 Sir Edmund de Langley leased a quarter of his land on the west side of the River Sherbourne to John de Rydeware (*Langley Cartulary* No. 233). The two documents are unlikely to be very distant in date.

755 11 January 1290

Grant and sale by Richard de Facham of Coventry to John his son of all his goods, movable and immovable, in the entire arable land with appurtenances and in the entire grange (*Grangia*) with an adjacent curtilage and appurtenances, which land and grange with the curtilage and all appurtenances the aforesaid John had by the grantor's gift and enfeoffment in Coventry and Radford (*Radeford juxta Coventr'*) as is contained (*inferit(ur)*) more fully and clearly in the grantor's charter of enfeoffment to the same John. Exclusion and sealing clauses. Coventry, Wednesday after the feast of the Epiphany 18 Edward I.

Seal extant C.R.O. 1B/18 EI/3

756 Late 1280s

Charter of Richard son of Philip the Crossbowman (*Balistarii*) of Coventry and Agnes his wife, daughter and heiress of Hugh le Breton, with one assent, giving and quitclaiming to Master Richard de Philu(n)gley the entire rent and service which Andrew de Coundulme used to render to them from a certain furlong (*cultura*) outside Coventry in the territory of Coundon (*Coundulme*) which is called *Wychewrihte croft* and which lies between the land John son of Adam the clerk held on the one hand and the land Richard de Cokkisham held on the other namely 10d. at the 4 terms of the year fixed in Coventry and the service of 1 man working for 1 day in autumn; to be held to him, his heirs or assigns, of the chief lord, his heirs or assigns, freely [etc.] with all right and claim therein as in demesne, arrears (*arerag'*), escheats and all other rights and customs without any reservation by the grantors and their heirs. Master Richard gave a sum of money beforehand which they have fully received (*quam conficemus nos recepisse plenarie*). Warranty and sealing clauses. Witnesses: Robert de Cilton then bailiff of the foreign (*ballivo forinseco*) of the lord prior of Coventry, Henry called Baker (*dicto pistore*) then bailiff of Coventry, John Tole of the same, Geoffrey son of John of the same, Nicholas Blaber of Coundon (*Coundulme*), Roger Gobiil of Whoberley (*Wabirley*), Thomas Blake of the same and many others.

2 seals extant G.H. 254

THE ACQUISITIONS OF ROBERT DE STOKE

757 c.1260–1262

Charter of Sir Roger Dayvile knight giving to Sir Thomas de Ardern knight and Lady Roesia his wife for 73 marks sterling his entire tenement with appurtenances in the vills and territory of Stoke, Biggin, Harnall, Exhall, Whitemore and Coventry.

Sciant presentes et futuri quod ego dominus Rogerus Dayvile miles dedi concessi et hac presenti carta mea confirmavi domino Thome de Ardena militi et domine Royse uxori sue pro homagio et servicio suo et pro sexaginta et tresdecim marcis legalium sterlingorum quas dictus dominus Thomas michi donavit premanibus totum tenementum meum cum omnibus pertin(enciis) quod habui in villis et t(er)ritor(iis) de Stok' Bugging Harnale Eccleshale Wytemor et Coventr' una cum toto jure meo et clam(io) quod in tenementis dictarum villarum et dictorum t(er)ritorior(um) tam vilenagiis quam aliis habui vel aliquo modo habere potui utpote in homagiis serviciis redditibus excaettis wardis releviis et omnibus aliis juribus et consuetudinibus que michi vel heredibus meis aliquo casu seu jur(e) tam de dote quam aliis tenementis predictis accidere poterunt inperpetuum; tenend(um) et habend(um) de me et heredibus meis dictis domino Thom(e) et domine Royse uxori sue et eorum heredibus aut cuicumque et quandocumque dictum tenementum cum omnibus pertin(entiis) integris conju(n)ctim aut divisim dare vendere legare vel aliquo modo assignare voluerint tam in egritudine quam in sanitate libere quiete pacifice honorifice et jur(e) hereditar(io) inperpetuum reddendo inde annuatim michi et heredibus meis dicti dominus Thom(as) et domina Roysa uxor ejus et eorum heredes vel assignati quicumque sex denarios argenti ad Pascha pro omnibus secularibus serviciis exactionibus consuetudinibus sect(is) cur(ie) wardis releviis et omnimodis aliis juribus et demandis ad me vel heredes meos pertinentibus salvo nobis tantu(m)modo redditu sex denar(iorum) antedicto. Et ego predictus dominus Rogerus et heredes mei dictis dominis Thome et domine Royse et eorum heredibus vel assignatis quibuscumque omnia predicta tenementa prout plenius predictum est cum omnibus pertinentiis contra omnes gentes warantizabimus acquietabimus et defendemus imperpetuum. Et ut hec mea donacio et concessio perpetue firmitatis robur optineat eam presenti scripto et sigilli mei impressione roboravi. Hiis testibus domino Thoma le Ireys milite domino Radulpho Basset de Drayton domino Roberto de Pinkeny Henrico de Bromleya Johanne de Herci Thoma de Bubbinhul Roberto atte Heth Johanne de Wint(er)ton' Ricardo de Whitsont Ran(ulfo) de Stivech' Henrico clerico de Ruton' Willelmo clerico de eadem Hugone le Bretun istius scripti confectore et aliis.

Seal missing C.R.O. 1A/C13/43

These rents were conveyed by Sir Thomas de Ardern of Hanwell to Sir Thomas de Ardern of Ratley as part of an exchange of lands in July 1262 (*F.F. Warwicks.* No. 841). In 1261 (and again in 1262) Sir Roger d'Eyvile is found entering into Jewish bonds and it seems certain that the above alienation was made at this time to help pay his creditors (*C.A.D.* vol. iii, D25, D28).

758 1280s

Charter of Sir Thomas de Ardern, lord of Ratley, giving to Master Guy de Tilebrook his entire rent in Stoke, Radford, Coundon and Coventry. In return Guy gave a messuage and 52 acres of land with meadow and appurtenances in Radford near Warwick and £30 of silver.

Sciant presentes et futuri quod ego Thomas de Ardern' miles dominus de Rottel' dedi concessi et hac presenti carta mea confirmavi Magistro Gydoni de Tyllebrok pro homagio et servicio suo totum redditum meum quem habui et habere potui in Stoke Radeford Cundolm' et in Coventr' cum homagiis serviciis wardis eschaett(is) sectis nativis eorum sequelis et catallis et omnibus libertatibus et pertinenciis suis; habend(um) et tenend(um) predicto Gydoni et heredibus suis de me et de heredibus meis libere et quiete reddendo inde annuatim michi et heredibus meis idem Gydo et heredes sui unum denar(ium) ad Pasch' et capitali domino de Cheylesmor unum par calcariu(m) deaurator(um) vel sex denar(ios) pro omnibus secularibus serviciis auxiliis sectis consuetudinibus et demandis que exigi possint seu pot(er)unt. Et ego predictus Thomas et heredes mei warantizabimus quietabimus et defendemus predicto Gydoni et heredibus suis imperpetuum totum predictum redditum cum homagiis serviciis wardis eschaett(is) sectis nativis et omnibus libertatibus et pertinenciis contra omnes mortales pro predictis serviciis. Pro hac autem donacione mea et carte confirmacione dedit michi predictus Gydo unum mesuag(ium) quinquaginta duas acras terre cum prato et omnibus pertinenciis in Radeford juxta Warr' et triginta libras argenti. Et ut hec mea donacio perpetuo rata et stabilis permaneat hoc presens scriptum sigilli mei impressione signavi. Hiis testibus dominis Nichol(ao) de Seg(r)ave Ada de Napton' Galfr(ido) de Langele et Ricardo de Loges militibus Petro le Bretun Alexandro Vinetar' Roberto de Chilton' Roberto de Stok' Thom(a) de Wiltesyre Ada ate Okes et aliis.

Seal extant C.R.O. 1A/C39

Sir Thomas de Ardern of Ratley was still holding these rents in the Hundred Rolls of 1279 (*V.C.H. Coventry* p. 97).

759 c.1290

Charter of Guy de Tyllebrok giving to Robert de Stok', for his homage and service, all the rents and services which he had within and without the vill of Coventry by the gift of Sir Thomas de Ardern' with the homages, reliefs, escheats and all other appurtenances entirely, just as the grantor formerly held them except for the homage and service of Thomas de Wylteschyre and his heirs for a messuage and ½ virgate of land in Stoke (*Stok'*); to be held to him, his heirs or whatsoever assigns, of the grantor and his heirs freely and quietly by rendering annually 1d. at Easter, and to the chief lords the service due and accustomed for all secular service [etc.]. Clause for warranty. Robert gave £60 of silver. Sealing clause. Witnesses: Sir Nicholas de Segrave, Sir Geoffrey de Longel', Sir Hugh de Brannteston', Peter le Bretoun, Robert de Chylton', Ralf Cuyly, Simon Erneys, Adam Milon', William Selet clerk and others.

Seal extant C.R.O. 1A/Misc.II/35

760 25 July 1292

Remise and quitclaim by Roysia widow of Sir Thomas de Ardern' of Hanwell (*Hanewell'*), for herself and her heirs, to Robert de Stokes of all right and claim in all lands and tenements, rents and all other appurtenances which Sir Roger Dayvile knight once (*aliquando*) held in Stoke, Biggin, Harnall, Exhall, Radford, Whitemore and Coventry (*Stoke Bugginge harnale Eccleshale Radeford Wytemor et Coventr'*) and which Sir Thomas de Ardern' of Ratley (*Rottel*) had by the gift of Thomas de Ardern' of Hanwell (*Hanewell'*) her husband in the same vills; to be held to him, his heirs or assigns, with exclusion clause. Sealing clause. Witnesses: Hugh de Brandeston', John de Lodbrok, William de Charnel, knights, and Ralph de Ardern' lord of Peddimore (*Pedimor*), Peter Bretu(n), William Bretun, John de Upton, Alexander de Ky'befeld, Jurdan de Suneworth' clerk and others. Hanwell (*Hanewell'*), Friday the feast of St. James 20 Edward I.

Seal missing C.R.O. IB/20 EI/2

761 c.1303–c.1307

Charter of John son of William le Masun of Tilebrook (*Tylebrok'*) giving to Robert de Stok' and his heirs ½d. annual rent with appurtenances to be taken from Alexander son of Alexander le Vyneter of Coventry and William son of Robert de Lodelowe and their heirs from the entire tenement which they held of Master Guy de Tylebrok' in Stoke (*Stok'*) namely from the croft once of John de Lodelowe. Moreover, he has granted the same Robert and his heirs a rent of 2 capons (*alatiliu(m)*) to be taken annually from William de Walton' and his heirs, ½d. rent to be taken annually from Henry in le Hurne from a tenement in Spon St. (*in vico de Sponne*), ½d. rent with appurtenances to be taken annually from the tenement of John de Catysby and Alexander le Shermon which was once of William de Stivichale, 2d. rent with appurtenances to be taken annually from the tenement of William Colle next to the church of St. Michael, Coventry which was once of Master Guy de Tylebrok', 2d. rent with appurtenances to be taken annually from the tenement which John de Norton' held in Lodelawe's Lane (*Lodelowelone*), 2d. rent with appurtenances to be taken annually from the tenement of Bartholemew de Bourton' in Lodelawe's Lane (*Lodelowelone*) which was once of Master Richard de Aula in Coventry. Moreover, he has granted, remised and quitclaimed for himself and his heirs, to Robert and his heirs, all right and claim in 1d. annual rent with appurtenances which Master Guy de Tylebrok' used to receive from the same Robert for the tenements which he held of him in Stoke, Coventry, Radford and Exhall (*Stok' Coventr' Radeford et Eccleshale*); all the aforesaid rents and services with appurtenances to be held to the same Robert and his heirs freely [etc.] from the lords of that fee by the services due and accustomed. Exclusion, warranty and sealing clauses. Witnesses: Robert called Baker (*dicto Pistore*), Brother John master of the hospital of St. John, Robert de Chilton', Alexander de Stonleye, Sir Henry vicar of the church of Holy Trinity, John de Halys, Nicholas le Deyster', Master Robert de Kenylleworth', Richard de Wyken' clerk and others.

Seal extant Fuller II/16/10

A broadly similar grant (C.R.O. 2/51) with witnesses headed by Master Robert de Aula and excluding Master Robert de Kenilworth is no longer in the Coventry collection. See above p. 64.

762 22 or 29 Mary 1299[1]

Grant by Joan widow of John Corbyn of Stoke (*Stok'*), for herself and her heirs, to Robert de Stok' and Joan his wife of the entire rent and services of all her tenants in Coventry which the aforesaid Robert and Joan formerly had from her for a term of years as is manifest by a certain indented deed between them, excepting only the rent and services once of Hugh le Taylour; to be held to them for their life freely [etc.]. Moreover, she has granted to Robert and Joan, for herself and her heirs, all the liberties, profits and easements with all appurtenances which she had or was in anyway able to have in Coventry after the death of Philip de Barbedaveryl her ancestor in pannages, tolls and all issues (*ut in pannagiis tolnetis et aliis provenientibus*), by the aforesaid Robert and Joan making annually to her for their entire life a garland of roses (*unam capella(m) Rosear'*) at the feast of St. John the Baptist for all service and demand. Clause for warranty. Reversion clause. Sealing clause. Witnesses: Robert Baker (*pistore*) of Coventry (*Covyntr'*), Anketill de Coleshulle then bailiff of Coventry (*Covyntr'*), Johanne de Langeleye, Richard de la Mure, Matthew de Ruytone, William de Arnyngworth, Adam Russel and others. Coventry, Friday after the feast of St. Germanus 27 Edward I.

Indented
Seal extant C.R.O. IB/27 EI/7

[1] Since this document appears to precede No. 763, St. Germanus must have celebrated in Coventry on 21 or 28 May (see *Handbook of Dates* ed. C. R. Cheney, Royal Hist. Soc. 1961, p. 52).

763 26 July 1299

Remise, release and quitclaim by Joan de Corbin of Stoke (*Stok'*), in her widowhood and lawful power, for herself and her heirs to Robert de Stok', Joan his wife and the heirs of the same Robert, of her entire rent and service of all her tenants in the vill of Coventry together with the toll and pannage which she used to receive from the same with all appurtenances. Moreover, she has granted, remised and quitclaimed her right and claim in 4 selions lying in the field of Bokervill next to Stoke (*in ca(m)po de bokervul' juxta Stok'*) and in a marlpit (*uno marlerio*) below *Condr'eyam* in the same place next to *le holdeallewey* of which 2 selions lie next to the land of the aforesaid Robert and extend up to *le holdehallewey* and 2 selions lie in the same furlong (*cultura*) between the land the same Robert held on the one hand and the land John de Langeleye held on the other and extend up to *le Holdehallewey*, namely those William le Taylour held with headlands (*cheviciis*) and all other appurtenances; to be held freely [etc.], with exclusion clause. Sealing clause. Witnesses: William Haubrey in Stoke (*Stok'*), Philip le Hyrreys of the same, John de Longeleya in Coventry, William de Arnigwrþe of the same, Robert de Wilnal', Adam le Bond' in Stoke (*Stok'*), John Payn and others. Given in the chapel of Stoke (*Stok'*), Sunday before the feast of St. Margaret the Virgin 27 Edward I.

Seal extant C.R.O. IB/27 EI/1

764 6 October 1303

Charter of John son and heir of John de Bromleye, in his pure and lawful age, giving to Henry Bagod merchant of Coventry and Katherine (*Katerine*) his wife all the rent and services which he had by hereditary right after the death of John his father in the vills of Coventry, Harnall, Henley, Foleshill and Exhall (*Coventr' Harn[hale Henley*

Folkeshull et][1] *Eccleshale*) in the county of Warwick (*Warrewyk'*), namely 10s. rent with appurtenances in Coventr' which the prior and convent of the same vill used to render annually to him for the tenement which they held of him in the same vill namely for the mill which is called Earl's Mill (*le Erlesmulne*), 45s. rent with appurtenances in the same vill which Alexander le Vyneter used to render to him annually for a tenement which he held of him in the same vill namely for the mill called Altegeder Mill (*Altegidermulne*), 3s. 8d. rent in Foleshill (*Folkeshul*) which Thomas le Wolf used to render to him annually for the lands and tenements which he held of him in the same vill with the homage and service of the same Thomas and his heirs, 6s. 2d. rent with appurtenances in the same vill which Thomas de Holebrok' used to render to him annually for the land and tenements which he held of him in the same vill with the homage and service of the same Thomas and his heirs, 3s. rent with appurtenances in the same vill which Richard Fox used to render annually to him for the lands and tenements which he held of him in the same vill with the homage and service of the aforesaid Richard and his heirs, 10s. 6d. rent with appurtenances in the same vill which Robert atte Heth used to render annually to him for the lands and tenements which he held of him in the same vill with the homage and service of the same Robert and his heirs, 18d. annual rent with appurtenances in the same vill which William le Botiler used to render annually to him for the lands and tenements which he held of him in the same vill with the homage and service of the same William and his heirs, 10s. 2d. with appurtenances in Exhall (*Eccleshale*) which Roger atte Rudyng used to render annually to him for the lands and tenements which he held of him in the same vill with the homage and service of Roger and his heirs, 3s. 2d. rent with appurtenances in Henley (*Henleye*) which William de Toucestr' used to render to him annually for the lands and tenements which he held of him in the same vill with the homage and service of the aforesaid William and his heirs, 17d. rent with appurtenances in the same vill which William de Arthingwurthe used to render to him annually for the lands and tenements which he held of him in the same vill with the homage and service of the same William and his heirs, 18d. rent with appurtenances in Harnall (*Harnhale*) which the aforesaid William de Toucestr' used to render annually to him for the lands and tenements which he held of him in the same vill with the homage and service of the same William and his heirs, 14d. rent with appurtenances in the same vill which Geoffrey le Chaloner used to render annually to him for the lands and tenements which he held of him in the same vill with the homage and service of the same Geoffrey and his heirs, 15d. rent with appurtenances in the same vill which Richard Huttyng used to render to him annually for the lands and tenements which he held of him in the same vill with the homage and service of the same Richard and his heirs, 9d. rent with appurtenances in the same vill which Hugh the Smith (*faber*) used to render annually to him for the lands and tenements which he held of him in the same vill with the homage and service of the same Hugh and his heirs, 3s. rent with appurtenances in the same vill which John de Teynton' used to render to him annually for the lands and tenements which he held of him in the same vill with the homage and service of the same John and his heirs, 12d. rent with appurtenances in the same vill which Emma daughter of Roger atte ȝhate used to render to him annually for the lands and tenements which she held of him in the same vill with the homage and service of the same Emma and her heirs, and 2d. rent with appurtenances in the same vill which Richard le Buttere used to render to him annually for the lands and tenements which he held of him in the same vill with the homage and service of the same Richard and his heirs, along with the reversion of all the rent and services which Sibil his mother held in the name of dower from the aforesaid lands and tenements through the death of the aforesaid John his father, when it accrues; all the aforesaid rents with the wardships, marriages, escheats, heriots, reliefs and all other services and free customs issuing therefrom to be held to the aforesaid Henry and Katherine, their heirs or assigns, of the chief lords of that fee freely [etc.] by making annually to those same lords the services due and by right accustomed, namely the 20th part of the service of one [knight][2] for all services [etc.]. Clause for warranty. Henry gave £36 sterling beforehand. Sealing clause. Witnesses: Adam des Okes of Whitley (*Whyteleye*), Geoffrey de Whyteleye, Robert Bandewyne, Robert Baker (*pistore*) of Coventry, Peter Barun, Thomas Ballard, Roger Dayese, John Dobedy and others. Coventry, Sunday after the feast of St. Michael 31 Edward I.

Seal extant C.R.O. IB/31EI/1

The document is badly faded in places but is largely recoverable by ultra violet light.

[1] The original has been written over here.

[2] Ultra violet failed to reveal this, but the reading seems probable.

765

28 April 1303

Agreement whereby William de Berkeleye and Sibil his wife have bound themselves (*concesserunt se teneri*) to make full seisin to Robert de Stoke of a third part of all the lands and tenements with rents, wardships, reliefs, escheats and with profits and all kinds of appurtenances, which fell to the same Sibil in name of dower through the death of John de Bromle her late husband in Coventry, Foleshill, Exhall and Keresley (*Coventr Folkeshul Eccleshale et Keresle*) before the feast of Holy Trinity 31 Edward I [2 June 1303]; to be held to the same Robert and Joan his wife and to Robert's heirs for the entire life of the same Sibil freely [etc.], by rendering (*faciend'*) to William and Sibil or to their certain attorney bearing letters of acquittance for 3 years beginning at Michaelmas 31 Edward I [1303] a clove-gillyflower at Easter, and after the 3 years for Sibil's entire life 32s. annually by the hand of Robert and Joan at Stoke at 2 terms of the year, namely 16s. at the quinzaine of the Annunciation of the blessed Mary and 16s. at the quinzaine of Michaelmas. *Et si contingat dictum Robertum vel Johannam uxorem ejus vel heredes ipsius Roberti de predicta firma ad aliquem diem defic(isse) tunc attornatus predictorum Willelmi et Sibille litteras acquietancie deferens apud Stoke su(m)ptibus dicti Roberti et Johanne et heredum ipsius Roberti morabu(n)t*[1] *quousque eidem plenarie de firma fuerit satisfactum. Et predictus Robertus de Stoke concessit pro se et heredibus suis quod si predictus Willelmus et Sibilla predictam convencionem teneant infra tempus prenominatum quod quoddam scriptum obligatorium decem libr(arum) quod idem Robertus penes se habeat per predictum Willelmum et Sibillam eidem Willelmo et Sibille sine difficultate aliqua liberetur. Concessit et predictus Robertus quod si aliq(uo)d ten(ementum) de eisdem ten(ementis) per eschaetam felonie toto tempore dicte Sibille dicto Roberto eveniat quod proficuum inde perveniens eidem Willelmo et Sibille tota vita ipsius Sibille moratur.* Mutual sealing clause. Stoke, Sunday after the feast of St. Mark the Evangelist in the year aforesaid.

Indented

Seal extant C.R.O. 1B/31EI/11

[1] sic

766

Shortly before June 1309

Charter of Henry Bagot merchant of Coventry (*mercator Coventr'*) and Katerina his wife giving to Robert de Stoke and his heirs 48s. 3d. rent with appurtenances in the vills and hamlets (*hamelettis*) of Foleshill, Exhall, Henley and Harnall (*Folkeshul'*

Eccleshale Henleye et Harnhale), namely 3s. 8d. rent with appurtenances which Thomas le Wolf used to render annually to them for the lands and tenements which he held of them in Foleshill (*Folkeshul'*) and Exhall (*Eccleshale*) with the homage and service of the same Thomas and his heirs, 6s. 2d. rent with appurtenances in the same vills which William de Holebrok used to render annually to them for the land and ten(ements) which he held of them in the same vills with the homage and service of the same William and his heirs, 3s. rent with appurtenances in Foleshill (*Folkeshul*) which Richard le Fox used to render annually to them for the lands and ten(ements) which he held of them in the same vill with the homage and service of the same Richard and his heirs, 10s. 6d. rent with appurtenances in the same vill which Robert atte Heth used to render annually to them for the lands and ten(ements) which he held of them in the same vill with the homage and service of the same Robert and his heirs, 18d. rent with appurtenances in the same vill which William le Botiler used to render annually to them for the lands and ten(ements) which he held of them in the same vill with the homage and service of the same William and his heirs, 10s. 2d. rent with appurtenances in Exhall (*Eccleshale*) which Roger atte Ruding used to render annually to them for the lands and ten(ements) which he held in the same vill with the homages and services of the same Roger and his heirs, 3s. 2d. rent with appurtenances in Henley (*Henle juxta Wykne*) which William le Schepperde used to render annually to them for the lands and ten(ements) which he held of them in Henley (*in eadem Henle*) with the homage and service of the same William and his heirs, 17d. rent with appurtenances in Henley (*Henle*) which William de Arthingworth used to render annually to them for the lands and ten(ements) which he held of them in the same vill with the homage and service of the heirs of the said William, 18d. rent with appurtenances in Harnall (*Harnhale*) which William de Toucestr' used to render annually to them for the lands and ten(ements) which he held of them in the same vill with the homage and service of the heirs of the said William, 14d. rent with appurtenances in the same vill which Geoffrey le Chalouner used to render annually to them for the lands and ten(ements) which he held of them in the same vill with the homage and service of the same Geoffrey and his heirs, 15d. rent with appurtenances in the same vill which Richard Hutting used to render annually to them for the lands and tenements which he held of them in the same vill with the homage and service of the same Richard and his heirs, 9d. rent with appurtenances in the same vill which Hugh the Smith (*Faber*) used to render annually to them for the lands and ten(ements) which he held of them in the same vill with the homage and service of the same Hugh and his heirs, 3s. rent with appurtenances in the same vill which John de Teynton' used to render annually to them for the lands and ten(ements) which he held of them in the same vill with the homage and service of the heirs of the said John, 12d. rent with appurtenances in the same vill which Emma daughter of Roger atte ȝhate used to render annually for the lands and tenements which he held of them in the same vill with the homage and service of the same Emma and her heirs; to be held with the wards, marriages, escheats, heriots, reliefs and all other services and free customs issuing to him, his heirs or assigns, of the chief lords of that fee freely [etc.] by the services due and accustomed. Warranty and sealing clauses. Witnesses: Adam des Okes, Thomas Boydyn, William de Schulton', Robert Jabet, Alexander de Crulefe[l]d, Robert Baudewyne, John de Schuckeboru, Robert de Wilnhale, Robert le Pestour of Coventry, Alexander de Stonle of the same, Peter Barou(n) of the same, John de Langele of the same, Hugh de Meryton' of the same, Henry de Barsham of the same, Robert de Chilton' of the same and others.

2 seals extant C.R.O. IA/Misc.II/43

The charter was strengthened by final concord dated 8 June 1307 (*F.F. Warwicks.* No. 1285).

767

Deeds (abstracts) relating to Coventry from Combe Cartulary.

Two cartularies of the Cistercian abbey of Combe were known to Dugdale in the 17th century. Both, unfortunately, were involved in the Cottonian fire of 1731. Whereas Vitellius D18 was virtually destroyed, however, Vitellius A1, although badly damaged, survived and has been effectively restored. The major section dealing with the Combe interest in Coventry (restored folios 152r–158r and 160r–161r) appears to have survived largely intact. The present folios 156/157, it should be noted, have been restored in the wrong order so that the beginnings and ends of two of the items have been separated. Although the folio numbering no longer quite corresponds, this section remains broadly as it was known to Dugdale.

Dugdale, in fact, collated the two Combe cartularies and briefly listed their contents (Bodleian Library MS. 6502 or Dugdale 12). Although he omits some items extant in the Coventry section of A1 his list does not contain any additional ones. The only gifts in Coventry not listed there are two referred to in a list of lands and rents providing alms for the shoes of the poor (Dugdale, p. 142 citing Vitellius A1 fo. 102r). Here, in addition to the gifts from William Crude and Vincent son of Swanus, there is land from William the Scabbard-maker (*waginatoris*) and 4s. 4d. rent from William de Leicestr', both in Park St. (*in vico parci*). These items aside it would appear that little, if any, Coventry evidence has been lost. Vitellius A1 was compiled in 1255 (fo. 142r). Some of the gifts in the Coventry section belong to the 1230s and 1240s. Most are of the time of Ranulf III. In short we have a reasonably complete picture of the Coventry property acquired by Combe abbey during the late 12th and early 13th centuries.

The Coventry section of Vitellius A1 is in the main hand of the cartulary and entries are separated by red rubric. Unfortunately they are abstracts only, and not entirely standardized in form. All witness lists are omitted. They have been entered in a rather haphazard order. I have endeavoured to convey the maximum detail given in each entry, as far as possible in conformity with the method of calendaring adopted above. The rubric has been omitted. The order of abstracts has been modified somewhat to bring together items relating to the same or connected property. The present folio is indicated at the foot of each item. Dates can usually be assigned, but without the witnesses they must remain, for the most part, fairly wide.

There is one further item of interest. On fo. 32r of Vitellius A1 there is a licence by Ranulf, earl of Chester, for the monks of Combe to acquire land and rents in Coventry. It is in a different hand but one which appears elsewhere in the cartulary. The transcript appears to be slightly corrupt and the folio is damaged, with words lost particularly along the right. It was partially transcribed by Dugdale (MS. 12 p. 158) who omitted the final clause altogether. The licence may well be genuine and, if so, was issued before 1217 when Ranulf became earl of Lincoln, and most probably considerably earlier.

767.1

Licence by Ranulf III, earl of Chester, for the monks of Combe to acquire land and rents in Coventry and elsewhere in his lands.

Scian[t] omnes ad quos presentes littere pervenerint quod ego Ran(ulfus) Comes Cestr' licent(iam) sp(eci)ale(m) et ge(nera)le(m) dedi et concessi [monachis de Cumba][1,2] quod ipsi sine contradictione mei h(eredum) vel succ(essorum) meor(um) licite valea(n)t terras et redd(itus) in Cove(n)tr' et in omni terra potestat(is) mee sibi ap[propriare et in perpetuum][1,2] pacifice[3] possidere, pro quibus terris sic sibi apropriatis[3] et in posterum apropriand(is)[3] ac in perpet(uum) paciff(ice)[3] possidend(is) renuntio pro me h(eredibus) et [successoribus meis][1,2] cur(ie) sect(am) hom(agium) scut(agium) equor(um) toln(etum) et omne servicium seculare. Quare volo et precipio omnibus hominibus et ball(iv)is meis quod [monachos[2] predictos][1] et eorum servientes in nullo de predictis serviciis moleste(n)t vel g(r)ave(n)t seu fieri p(er)mitta(n)t sed eosdem et eorum omnia catalla ac [tenementa][1] protestant[3] manuteneant et defendant. fo. 32r.

[1] There is some loss on the right hand side.

[2] Words supplied from Dugdale's transcript.

[3] sic

[4] sic for *protegant*?

.2 c.1215–c.1225

Charter of Nicholas son of Nicholas of Coventry giving to God, the blessed Mary and the monks of Combe 10s. rent due from himself and his heirs according to the chirograph made in the royal court, to be received by the hands of the said monks in Bisseley Mill (*in molendino de Bussel'*) from whoever holds (*a quocumque homine teneat*) the said mill, so that the monks may be allowed to distrain (*facere districtionem*) for the same rent at fixed terms, namely 2s. 6d. at each of the feasts of St. Mary in March, St. John the Baptist, St. Botulf, St. Michael and St. Andrew[1] *tam in dicto molendino quam in tenente dictum molendinum propria auctoritate*, saving to the grantor and his heirs the entire residue of the said mill except the 10s. afore-written. Warranty. fo. 152r.

[1] 5 terms named.

.3

Final concord made in the royal court at Northampton (*Norhamt'*) Tuesday after the feast of St. John the Baptist 1 Richard I [26 June 1190] before B[enedict] abbot of Peterborough (*Burgi*), Geoffrey fitz Peter and others, between the monks of Combe and Nicholas son of Liulf of Coventry concerning 2½ virgates of land with appurtenances in Withybrook (*Wythibroc*) which Symon brother of the aforesaid Nicholas gave them for his soul, whereof there was a plea between them in the royal court, whereby the aforesaid land remains to the aforesaid Nicholas and his heirs quit from the monks and Nicholas in return has assigned to them 10s. every year in Bisseley Mill (*in molendino de Bussele*) to be rendered at 4 terms namely Michaelmas, St. Andrew, St. John the Baptist and St. Mary in March. Warranty. If Nicholas wishes to give an exchange to the same value he may do so, and this also he will warrant. fo. 152r.

.4 Late 12th century

Charter of Roger son of Liulf of Coventry giving to God, the blessed Mary and the monks of Combe 7 messuages in Coventry [with] the common appurtenances, liberties and customs pertaining to the same messuages and the grantor's body at his death (*corpus meum ad obitum meum*), namely those messuages which he deraigned against Nicholas his brother before the royal justices at Leicester (*leicestr'*) and which Yvo, Miles (*Milo*), Godric, William Wymon, William [nephew of] Sericus (Serichi)[1], the priest of Ansty (*presbiter de Anesti*) and Geoffrey Sumvelin hold, free from all service by rendering annually to the grantor and his heirs 1lb. cumin at Christmas and saving the pannage of pigs pertaining to the aforesaid messuages. fo. 152v.

[1] See below Nos. .5 and .10.

.5

Final concord made in the royal court at Leicester (*Lecest[r]ia(m)*)[1] Saturday after the feast of the apostles Symon and Jude 35 Henry II* before Geoffrey bishop of Ely [*G. eliensi*] and his fellows, between Roger son of Liulf of Coventry and Nicholas his brother concerning 15 messuages and a chamber (*camera*) with appurtenances and 15 selions and ½ acre of land in Coventry, whereof there was a plea between them in the royal court, whereby the aforesaid Roger and his heirs will hold 7 of the aforesaid 15 messuages of the aforesaid Nicholas and his heirs, namely those which Yvo, Miles (*Milo*), Godric, William son of Woman, William the nephew of Sericus (*nepos serici*), the priest (*Presb(ite)r*) and Geoffrey Sum Welin held, with the aforesaid ½ acre and other common appurtenances, by rendering annually to Nicholas and his heirs 1lb. cumin at Christmas saving, however, pannage of the aforesaid messuages which remains to Nicholas and his heirs. In return Roger has quitclaimed all right in 8 of the aforesaid 15 messuages and the aforesaid chamber and their appurtenances, and in the 15 selions, from himself and his heirs to the aforenamed Nicholas and his heirs. fo. 152v.

[1] damaged

*5 November 1189? Either the day or the regnal year is in error. Geoffrey was indeed in eyre in 1189 in Leicestershire and Warwickshire (R. W. Eyton, *Court, Household and Itinerary of King Henry II*, p. 298). However, not only was 6 July the last day of the king's reign but Geoffrey of Ely himself died on 21 August 1180 (*Handbook of British Chronology*, p. 223). It is possible that the year is 1179 when Geoffrey was in eyre in the same counties. He was certainly at Coventry on July 30. However, he and his fellows are said to have accounted on 27 August. Nonetheless their accounts do not appear on the Pipe Rolls until Michaelmas 1180 (*Eyton*, pp. 226, 229).

.6 c.1230s

Charter of Nicholas son of Nicholas of Coventry giving to God, the blessed Mary and the monks of Combe in free, pure and perpetual alms 4s. rent in the vill of Coventry, namely the rent which William de Lond' at one time (*aliquando*) used to render from the land he held of the grantor in Earl St. (*in vico Comitis*) which lies between the land Roger Hacun held and the land which was of Ralf Croleboys, to be rendered at 4 terms of the year [namely] 12d. at each of the feasts of St. Mary in March, St. John the Baptist, Michaelmas and St. Andrew. Moreover he has granted and confirmed to them the 4d. rent which William Crude gave in Bayley Lane for the shoes of the poor (*in viculo qui vocatur le Bayli ad soculares paup(eru)m*), and 4d. rent in Park St. (*in vico parci*) from the land Ralf de Norwych held; to be held of the grantor and his heirs quit from all service. Moreover, the monks will be allowed to enter the grantor's fee for the aforesaid rents and to distrain at will. Clause for warranty. fo. 153r.

.7 Early 13th century

Sale and quitclaim by Richard son of William Wommenesun, entirely and without any reservation by himself and his heirs, to God, the abbot and monks of Combe of the entire land in Earl St. at Gosford (*in vico comitis apud Gosseford*) with all appurtenances which he held of them, namely the entire land which lies between the land Walter the grantor's son held of Nicholas son of Liulf and the land the same Walter held of[1] Walter the earl's steward (*Senescallo Comitis*). Clause for warranty. fo. 162r.

[1] *de ex*

.8 c.1230

Grant and quitclaim by Walter son of Richard Wunmonesun' of Coventry to God, the blessed Mary and the monks of Combe of the entire land which the aforesaid Richard his father sold and quitclaimed to them in the vill of Coventry, without any hindrance and contradiction by the grantor or his heirs just as the charter which his father made to them thereon witnesses. Clause for warranty. fo. 162r.

.9 c.1230s

Remise and quitclaim by Ralf Croleboys, from himself and his heirs, to the abbot and convent of Combe of a hen which Richard son of Wymman used to render to him at one time (*aliquando*) from the land which lies near to the head of his court (*propinquior capiti curie sue*). Clause for warranty. fo. 157v.

.10 Early 13th century

Sale and quitclaim by William kinsman of Serith (*cognatus serithii*) entirely and without any reservation by him or his heirs to God, the abbot and monks of Combe of the entire land with all appurtenances in Park St. (*in vico parci*) which he held of them, and the entire land which lies between the land Christian the Smith (*faber*) held and the land Nicholas Colle held, for 2 marks of silver which the abbot and monks gave to him. Clause for warranty. fo. 154v.

.11 Late 12th century

Gift and confirmation by Gilbert (*Gilleb(er)tus*) son of Picot to Robert Calvin his esquire (*calvino armig(er)o meo*) for his service of the land which Edward le Noreis held of the grantor in the vill of Coventry; to be held to him and his heirs of the grantor and his heirs by hereditary right, free and quit from all service and charge pertaining to the grantor or his heirs, for 2 separate pairs of Coventry gloves (*cirotecar' de Covintr'*) to be rendered annually. fo. 153v. and repeated fo. 156v.

.12 Late 12th–early 13th century

Charter of Robert Cauvin giving to God, the blessed Mary and the monks of Combe in pure and perpetual alms 5 messuages in the vill of Coventry with all appurtenances, liberties and customs pertaining to them, namely the 2 messuages which John le Loker held and 1 messuage which Hugh le Loker held in Upper Park St. (*in superiori vico del parc*) which Gilbert (*Gileb(ert)us*) Picot gave to the grantor for his homage, and 2 messuages in Park St. against the White Cellar (*in vico del parc contra album cellar'*) which the grantor held of William Gerebot for 2d. to be rendered annually to him and his heirs; all these to be held etc. Clause for warranty. fo. 153v.

.13 Late 12th–early 13th century

Charter of William Picot granting and confirming to God, the blessed Mary and the monks of Combe in pure and perpetual alms the entire gift (*donationem*) which Robert Calvin gave to them from the grantor's fee in Coventry with all appurtenances and liberties, namely the 2 messuages which John le Loker held and the messuage which Hugh le Loker held in Upper Park St. (*in sup(er)iori vico del park*); to be held freely etc. Clause for warranty. fo. 154r.

.14 Late 12th–early 13th century

Grant and quitclaim by Agnes widow of John le Loker, in her free widowhood and power, of all right in the messuage which Hugh le Loker held of the aforesaid John her husband in Park St. (*parcstret*) to her son Peter or to whomsoever he will wish to assign it. fo. 155v.

.15 Late 12th–early 13th century

Charter of Peter son of John le Loker giving to God, the blessed Mary and the monks of Combe 12d. rent in the vill of Coventry from the messuage in Park St. (*parcstret*) which Hugh le Loker held of the aforesaid John, the grantor's father, and all right therein without reservation by him or his heirs. Whereas the monks previously had 12d. by the gift of Robert Cauvin, henceforth they will have 2s. at 4 terms of the year, namely 6d. at each of the feasts of St. Michael, St. Andrew, St. Mary in March and St. John the Baptist. fo. 157v.

.16 Early 13th century

Remise and quitclaim by Alexander son of Hugh le Loker, from himself and his heirs, to the abbot and convent of Combe of all right in the land which he held of them in the vill of Coventry in Park St. (*In vico parci*), namely that which lies between the land Anketill held and the land John le Loker held. Clause for warranty. fo. 158v.

.17 Early 13th century

Charter of Richard le Loker and Emma his wife giving to God, the blessed Mary and the monks of Combe in free, pure and perpetual alms 28d. rent to be held at the 4 terms of the year fixed in the vill, namely 2s. from the land which lies between the land Roger the Carter (*caretarius*) held and the land Hugh le Loker held and 4d. from the land William Brond held of the grantors. The grantors have assigned this rent for the light of lamps on saints' days (*? ad lumen lampadaru(m) In festis sanctorum*). Clause for warranty. fo. 158r.

.18 1230s–early 1240s

Charter of William Crude son of Geoffrey Crude of Coventry giving to God, the blessed Mary and the monks of Combe in free, pure and perpetual alms his entire land which fell to him by hereditary right, namely the land which lies between the land Nicholas the Carter (*caretarius*) held and Bayley Lane (*viam Balii*) in length as the land purports. Moreover, he has granted to them all right and claim therein with all appurtenances within and without the vill. Clause for warranty. fo. 155r.

.19 c.1215–c.1225

Charter[1] of Nicholas son of N[icholas] son of Liulf granting to William Crude and his heirs the land in Earl St. (*in vico comitis*) which he held of Nicholas the grantor's father, namely that which lies between the land Nicholas the Carter (*caretarius*) held and Bayley Lane (*viam Balii*) in length and width as the land purports; to be held of the grantor and his heirs freely and quietly etc. by rendering 12d. at 4 terms of the year for all service and all demands. Clause for warranty. fo. 155r.

[1] above No. 176.

.20 c.1220s

Charter of William Crude with the assent of Edith his wife giving to God, the blessed Mary and the monks of Combe 12d. rent in the vill of Coventry from the land which William the Weaver (*textor*) held of the grantor in the Bailey (*in Balliva*), in free, pure and perpetual alms. fo. 156r.

.21 c.1240s

Acknowledgement by Osbert Duredent, clerk of Coventry, that he, his heirs or assigns, are bound to pay to the house of Combe 12d. for ever from a certain messuage which William Crude gave to him and his heirs in the vill of Coventry, namely that which lies in Earl St. (*in vico comitis*) between the land John the White weaver (*albus textor*) held and the land Nicholas the Wheelwright (*rotarius*) held, to be rendered at 4 terms of the year. fo. 156r.

.22 1220s–early 1230s

Charter of William Crude giving to Geoffrey his son the land with appurtenances which he held in Coventry towards the church of St. Michael[1] (*versus ecclesiam sancti Michaelis*) which lies in width between the land Nicholas the Carter (*caretarius*) held and Bayley Lane (*viculum qui vocatur le Baille*) and which lies in[2] length between the land Roger le Fowere held and the highway (*publicam stratam*); to be held for his service with a solar and stone cellar by the side of his court (*et solario et Cellario lapideo ex parte curie*) freely and quietly with appurtenances, to him and his heirs of the grantor and his heirs by the service of 12d. of silver at 4 terms [according to] the use of the vill and 1 pair of gloves worth ½d. at Easter for all service [and] demand pertaining. Clause for warranty. fos. 157v./156r.

[1] after *Nich'* deleted

[2] *inter*

.23 c.1230s

Charter of Manselmus son of Ernis (*h(er)nicii*) granting to Geoffrey son of William Crude and his heirs the charter and gift (*donationem*) which the aforesaid W[illiam] the grantor's uncle (*avunculus*) made to him of a certain land with appurtenances towards the church of St. Michael (*versus ecclesiam sancti Michaelis*). fo. 156r.

.24 1232–1243

Gift and quitclaim by William son of Geoffrey Crude from himself and his heirs to God, the blessed Mary and the monks of Combe of a messuage with all appurtenances in the vill of Coventry which is in the Earl of Arundel's street (*in vico comitis de Arundel*). Clause for warranty. fo. 156r.

.25 c.1230s

Charter of Geoffrey Crude giving to God, the blessed Mary and the monks of Combe 3s. rent in the vill of Coventry from the land which Jori le Brochere held of the grantor in Earl St. (*in vico comitis*), namely from the same tenement from which the same monks have 5s. annually from the grantor and his heirs by the gift of Richard son of Adam de Sponna, to be received annually from the grantor's hand and from the hands of his heirs according to the accustomed terms in the vill of Coventry. Clause for warranty. fo. 156r.

.26 c.1230s

Charter of Richard son of Adam de Sponna giving to God, the blessed Mary and the monks of Combe 5s. rent in the vill of Coventry from the land which lies between the land William le Brocher held and the land Richard le Levict[1] held, which Geoffrey Crude used to render annually to the grantor from 3 messuages in Earl St. (? *in vico Co . . .*)[2]. Moreover [he has granted] to them 12d. in the same street which Hugh son of Roger de Kyrkebi used to render to be received at 4 terms of the year, namely 15d. at each of the feasts of the Annunciation of the blessed Mary, the Nativity of St. John the Baptist, St. Michael and St. Andrew; to be held in pure and perpetual alms saving 8d. annually to Richard son of William de Wilenhale and his heirs at the aforesaid terms. Warranty. fos. 156v./158r.

[1] damaged, reading uncertain

[2] lost

.27 Before 1224

Charter of Swanus son of Adam of Coventry giving to God, the blessed Mary and the monks of Combe in pure and perpetual alms in Coventry 16d. rent from [the land] which John the Mason (*cem(ent)arius*)[1] held of the grantor, to be rendered to them at 4 terms [namely] 4d. at each of the feasts of St. Mary in March, St. John the Baptist, St. Michael and St. Andrew. Clause for warranty. fo. 153v.

[1] damaged, reading uncertain

.28 Before 1232

Charter of Humphrey de Folkeshull' giving to God, the blessed Mary and the monks of Combe in pure and perpetual alms 2 messuages in the vill of Coventry with all appurtenances, namely those which Godwin Copere held of the grantor by the rent of 15d. and 2 coifs (*coifaru(m)*); to be held of the grantor and his heirs freely etc. excepting 2d. which the grantor ought to render annually to the earl of Chester (*cest(r)ie*) for the same land which the aforesaid monks [will pay] to the grantor and his heirs and they will pay to the earl at 4 terms, namely ½d. at Christmas and at each of the feasts of St. Mary in March, St. John the Baptist and St. Michael. Clause for warranty. fo. 154r.

.29

Before 1232

Charter of Humphrey de Folkeshull' with the assent and wish of John his son and heir giving and quitclaiming to God, the blessed Mary and the monks of Combe a messuage in the vill of Coventry which Godwyn Cop(er)e held by the rent of 8d.; to be held of him and his heirs in pure and perpetual alms freely [and] quit from all service. *Et pro hac concessione prefati mon(achi) concesserunt mihi et meis ut participes simus omnium bonorum et elemosinarum que fiunt in domo sua.* fo. 154v.

.30

Salutation by John son of Godwin de la Wycka to Hugh bishop of Coventry* and gift to God, the blessed Mary and the monks of Combe of 12d. annually in Coventry, namely those which Godfrey son of Quenisde owes to the grantor and his heirs every year at 4 terms of the year for the land he holds of him in Coventry in fee and inheritance, namely 3d. at each of the feasts of St. Michael, St. Andrew, St. Mary in March and St. John the Baptist. fo. 154v.

*Hugh de Nonant, 1185–1198 (*Handbook of British Chronology*, p. 233)

.31

Notification by Roger the Cantor (*Cantarius*) of Coventry and Wymarch his wife entirely renouncing the plaints (*renunciavimus omnino querele*) between themselves and the abbot and monks of Combe concerning a certain messuage which Ralf de Brinkel', father of the grantor's wife, had given them and which Rouce held of the aforesaid Ralf, *et hoc ide(m) sub inrenuando*[1] *confirmavimus coram testibus.* fo. 154v.

[1] sic

.32

1230s

Charter of Alice widow of Walter de Alespathe giving to the monks of Combe 4d. rent from her and her heirs for ever, namely that which fell to her (*me contingebat*) from the land Richard de Bucherville held in Park St. (*in vico parci*), with quitclaim. fo. 155r.

.33

c.1230

Charter of Walter de Alespathe giving to God, the blessed Mary and the monks of Combe 12d. rent in the vill of Coventry from the land in Upper Park St. (*in sup(er)iori parkstrete*) which Richard de Buscherville held of him and which lies between the land William de Sallowe held and the earl's ditch (*fossatum comitis*), at 4 terms of the year [namely] 3d. at each of the feasts of St. Mary in March, St. John the Baptist, St. Michael and St. Andrew. Clause for warranty. *Quem redditum assignavi ad ceram cereor(um)*[1] *duorum qui debent accendi in dicta ecclesia in festis ad cotidianam missam beate Marie.* fo. 157r.

[1] after *trium*, deleted

.34

Early–mid 13th century

Sale and quitclaim by Geoffrey the Merchant (*m(er)cat(or)*) with the counsel and wish of Alice his wife, entirely and without reservation by the grantor and his heirs, to John Meruin and his heirs of 2s. rent in Park St. (*in vico parci*) from the land which is between the land John Meruin held and the land Richard the Smith (*fab'*) held; to be held of the abbot of Combe as freely and quietly as the grantor held and by the same service of 12d. Clause for warranty. fo. 155v.

.35 Early–mid 13th century

Charter of John Merwin giving to God, the blessed Mary and the monks of C(ombe) in free, pure and perpetual alms 12d. in Park St. (*in vico parci*) from the land between the land John the Butcher (*carnifex*) held and the land Richard the Smith (*faber*) held. Clause for warranty. fo. 158v.

.36 Early 13th century

Charter of Juliana daughter of Richard le Combere in her widowhood and free power giving to God, the blessed Mary and the monks of Combe in free, pure and perpetual alms 12d. rent in the vill of Coventry which Tolimeus used to render from a messuage in Park St. (*parkstrete*) against the White Cellar (*contra album celariu(m)*), of which Tholi[1] should pay (*debeat*) 10d. to them. fo. 157v.

[1] sic

.37 Early–mid 13th century

Charter of Robert de Pus' giving to God, the blessed Mary and the monks of Combe in pure and perpetual alms 2s. rent in the vill of Coventry which Tole used to render annually to the grantor from the land in Park St. (*parcstret*) from which the monks previously received 12d. annually. Clause for warranty. fo. 158r.

.38 Early 13th century

Charter of Juliana widow of Hugh de Willenh' *le vilor*, in her widowhood and free power, giving to Tholi the Shoemaker (*sutori*) and his heirs the entire land in Park St. (*in vico parci*) which lies between the land Ralf Fridai held and the land Richard le Combere held in length and in width as the land purports. fo. 160r.

.39

Grant and quitclaim by Roesia daughter of Humphrey de Covintr', from herself and her heirs, to the abbot and convent of Combe of the entire land in Park St. (*in vico parci*) which lies next to the land[1] which was of Richard [. . . which][2] fell to her by hereditary right; with exclusion clause. Clause for warranty. fo. 158v.

[1] *jacet inter terram juxta*, with *inter terram* enclosed by oblique strokes

[2] damage and loss here

.40

Charter of Jordan le Teler and Emma his wife giving to God, the blessed Mary and the monks of Combe in pure and perpetual alms 12d. rent in the vill of Coventry from the land Edith widow of Brun le M(er)cer held of the grantors, at 4 terms of the year. Clause for warranty. fo. 155v.

.41

Charter of John son of Emma granting to God, the blessed Mary and the monks of Combe in pure and perpetual alms 12d. rent in the vill of Coventry which they have of the gift of Emma the grantor's mother from the land which Edith widow of Brun le M(er)cer held, without any reservation by the grantor or his heirs. fo. 156v.

.42 c.1240s

Charter of William Brun of Coventry giving to God, the blessed Mary and the monks of Combe in pure and perpetual alms 12d. rent in the vill of Coventry from the land in Gosford St. (*in vico de Gosford*) which lies between the land of Alice widow of Simon le Paumer on the one hand and the land of Roger Bocher[1] on the other; to be taken every year at 2 terms, [namely] 6d. at Michaelmas and 6d. at Easter. Clause for warranty. fo. 155v.

[1] sic

.43 c.1240s

Charter of William Pie of Coventry giving to God, the blessed Mary and the monks of Combe in free, pure and perpetual alms 4s. rent in the vill of Coventry from the land which is called *Rodiche*, which lies between the White Cellar and the bar (*inter album cellar' et Barram*). Of the 4s. the grantor has assigned 2s. to the cellarer's office (*officiu(m) Cellar'*), 12d. to the fabric of the church (*fabricam ecclesie*), and 12d. to the monastic allowance (*Conventui ad pitanciam*); to be held of the grantor and his heirs freely and quietly at 4 terms of the year. Clause for warranty. fo. 155r.

.44 Before 1232

Charter of Vincent son of Swanus le Parker giving to God, the blessed Mary and the monks of Combe in free, pure and perpetual alms 3s. 2d. in Earl St. (*in vico Comitis*) from the land which William held of him peacefully in the vill of Coventry [and] which lies between the land Richard le Fullere held and the land Roger son of Hugh le Harpur held in length and width as the land purports, at 4 terms of the year, [namely] 9½d. at each of the feasts of St. Michael, St. Andrew, St. Mary in March and St. John the Baptist. Clause for warranty. fos. 155v./157r.

.45 c.1240s

Charter of Robert Hauwne of Coventry giving to God, the blessed Mary and the monks of Combe in pure and perpetual alms 3s. 8d. rent in the vill of Coventry from the land which the aforesaid Hauwne his father held of them. Whereas formerly they had 16d., 2 hens, 1 cock and 2 men for 1 day in Autumn, henceforth they will have *pro*[1] *hiis omnibus* 5s. annually from the grantor and his heirs for all services and demands pertaining to the grantor or his heirs, namely 15d. at each of the feasts of St. John the Baptist, St. Michael, St. Andrew and St. Mary in March. Clause for warranty. fo. 157r.

[1] after *de*, deleted

.46

Final concord made in the royal court at Westminster on the morrow of the Invention of the Holy Cross I John [4 May 1200] before G[eoffrey] fitz Peter and his fellows, between William de Verdun and Emma his wife, plaintiffs, and William abbot of Combe defendant, through Brother Nigel in his place *ad lucrandum vel perdendum*, concerning 10s. 4d. rent with appurtenances in Coventry whereof a recognition of mort d'ancestor was summoned between them in the aforesaid court, whereby the abbot acknowledges the entire rent with appurtenances to be the right of the aforesaid William and Emma and in return they have granted it to the aforesaid abbot and his successors, to be held of them and their heirs by the service of 1lb. cumin to be rendered at Christmas for all service pertaining to them and their heirs.

After this item there follows a notification by Richard the Glover (*Wantarius*) and Wymarch his wife that they have renounced [their claim], which is presumably connected in some way with the above since there is no separating rubric. fo. 156v.

.47 1230s–1240s

Charter of Roger son of William Hacun giving to God, the blessed Mary and the monks of Combe 18d. rent in the vill of Coventry from the land which Ysaac the clerk held of the grantor in Gosford St. (*in vico de Gosford*) at 4 terms of the year. Moreover, he has granted to them 4d. rent which Henry de Sowe used to render annually to the grantor on St. Botulf's day from a certain meadow in the meadows of Wyken (*Wyche*) bought from Master Fulk de Ullneya for candles (*ad opus cereor'*). Clause for warranty. fo. 158r.

.48

Charter of Henry son of Henry de Cestr' giving to God, the blessed Mary and the monks of Combe in pure and perpetual alms 10d. rent in the vill of Coventry at the 4 terms of the same vill. Clause for warranty. fo. 158r.

.49 c.1220s

Charter of Robert de Covintr' son of Agnes de Retham giving to God, the blessed Mary and the monks of Combe in pure and perpetual alms 12d. in the vill of Coventry from the land Yvo the Skinner (*pelliparius*) held. Whereas they previously had 2s. henceforth they will have 3s. from the grantor and his heirs at the 4 terms of the year fixed in the vill. Clause for warranty. fo. 158v.

For this property see *Langley Cartulary* Nos. 270, 272, 273.

.50 Before 1224

Charter of Theobald de Newent' giving to Swanus son of Adam and his heirs the land in Earl St. (*in vico Comitis*) which is between the land Matthew the Glover (*Cirothecator*) held and the land William Pave held in length and in width as the land purports, by rendering to the grantor and his heirs 10d.[1] of silver at 4 terms of the year. Clause for warranty. fo. 158v.

[1] *meis* is deleted followed by *et decim d.*

.51 c.1240s

Charter of Richard son of Roger the Gardener (*Gardinar'*) giving to Robert de Cornleia and his heirs 6d. annual rent which the heirs of John de Aula used to render to the grantor from the tenement of William de Aula which lies between the land of the said Roger on the one hand and the land of the lord bishop of Coventry on the other according to the metes and bounds made there. Clause for warranty. fo. 160v.

.52 c.1240s

Gift and quitclaim by Robert de Cornleya from himself, his heirs or assigns, to God, the blessed Mary and the monks of Combe in perpetual alms of 6d. rent in the vill of Coventry from the messuage which the grantor once held at fee farm (*ad feodi firmam*) of Richard son of Roger for a clove-gillyflower annually for all secular service; to be held to them well and in peace, by rendering the clove-gillyflower to Roger, his heirs or assigns, at Easter for all service and demand. fo. 160v.

.53 1230s–1240s

Charter of Jordan son of Stephen son of Herbert giving to God, the church of the blessed Mary and the monks of Combe 16d. rent in the vill of Coventry from the land in Earl St. (*in vico Comitis*) which lies between the land Roger the Carpenter (? *Carpieiarius*) held and the land Hugh le Loker held to be received at the 4 terms of the year fixed in the vill. Clause for warranty. fo. 160v.

.54 After 1236

Charter of Robert de Feugeres giving to God, the blessed Mary and the monks of Combe 8s. rent in the vill of Coventry, namely 6s. from the land Thomas the Goldsmith (*aurifaber*) held at Broadgate (*ad latam portam*) and 2s. from the land Adam le Vinitar' held next to the same land, to be received at the 4 terms of the year fixed in the vill, 6d. at the feast of St. Andrew from Adam the Vintner (*Vinitario*) and 18d. from Thomas the Goldsmith (*aurifabro*) and thus at every term. The grantor has assigned this rent for holding the anniversary mass (*ad faciend' anni(ver)sariu(m)*) of Adam the Miller (*molendinarii*) of Newham and Robert de Feogeres the grantor's father. Clause for warranty. fo. 160v.

.55

Final concord made in the royal court at Coventry the quinzaine of Trinity 20 Henry III [8 June 1236] before Robert de Lexinton' and his fellows, between Robert de Feogeres, plaintiff, and Adam le Vineter and Matilda his wife whom Alice de Witemore has called to warrant and who have so warranted, concerning 10s. rent with appurtenances whereof a recognition of the grand assize was summoned between them in the same court, whereby Adam and Matilda have acknowledged the entire rent with appurtenances to be the right of the same Robert and in return he has granted it to them to be held to them and the heirs of Matilda, of Robert and his heirs, by rendering annually 2s. at the 4 terms fixed in the vill and by rendering (*faciendo*) to the chief lords of the fee that which pertains to the aforesaid rent, for all service. fo. 161r.

.56

Final concord made in the royal court at Coventry the quinzaine of Trinity 20 Henry III [8 June 1236] before Robert de Lexint' and his fellows, between Adam le Vineter and Matilda his wife, plaintiffs, and Robert de Feogeres, defendant, concerning 6s. rent with appurtenances in Coventry whereof a recognition of the grand assize was summoned between them in the same court, whereby the aforesaid Adam and Matilda have acknowledged and quitclaimed all right which they had in the entire rent with appurtenances from themselves and the heirs of Matilda to the aforesaid Robert and his heirs. fo. 161r.

.57

Charter of Bertram (*Bertramius*) son of Robert Bert(r)an giving to God, the church of the blessed Mary and the monks of Combe 4s. rent in the vill of Coventry from the land in Earl St. (*in vico Comitis*) which lies between the land Robert the Dyer (*tinctor*) held and the land Symon the Scribe (*Scriptor*) held, to be received at the 4 terms of the year fixed in the vill. The grantor has assigned a moiety of the rent for holding the anniversary mass (*ad faciend' anni(ver)sariu(m)*) of Geoffrey de Brand' and Margery his wife on the day of St. Giles (*Egidii*) and the other moiety for holding the anniversary mass (*ad faciend' anni(ver)sariu(m)*) of William de Wav(er)e and Richard[1] the grantor's father and Albreda (*albrede*) on the day of St. James the Apostle. fo. 161r.

[1] sic

.58 Before 1224

Charter of Richard son of Ernis (*Hernesii*) of Coventry giving to God, the abbey of St. Mary and the monks of Combe to be held of him and his heirs in pure and perpetual alms a quarry (*quarariam*), namely the old one of Harnall (*vet(er)em de Harnale*) which the same monks previously dug (*prius fod(er)ant*) and a part of the croft which Gilbert held, for the construction of their church and other buildings. Moreover, he has demised to them the house (*dom'*) which the aforesaid G[ilbert]held which was once Alan's and as much land as G[ilbert] held for 6d.; to be held of the grantor and his heirs free from all service for 6d. annually at 2 terms, 3d. at Michaelmas and 3d. at the feast of St. Mary in March. fo. 153r.

.59 Before 1224

Charter of Richard son of Ernis giving to God, the blessed Mary and the monks of Combe a certain messuage in the vill of Coventry with appurtenances which Gilbert the Butcher (*macecarius*) once (*olim*) held and which is between the land Richard the Quarryman (*quararius*) held and the land Robert Scot held; to be held of the grantor and his heirs freely for making a quarry (*quarariam*) or for other uses as they may wish, by rendering annually 6d. at 2 terms for all services pertaining to the grantor and his heirs, as in the former charter. fo. 153r.

.60 Early 13th century

Charter of William Hacun giving to God, the blessed Mary and the monks of Combe in pure and perpetual alms 2 selions on one side of their quarry of Harnall and 1 headland selion on the other as marked by fixed bounds for making a quarry or otherwise (*duos selliones ex una parte quararii sui de harnale et unum sellionem capitalem ex alia prout certis metis designatum est ad quarariu(m) vel aliud quid faciend(um)*). Clause for warranty. fo. 153v.

.61 Early 13th century

Charter of Robert son of Thured granting and confirming to the monks of Combe at perpetual farm the entire land which is between the messuage[1] of the grantor's mother and the messuage of Henry son of (. . . nulfi)[2] and which extends from the lower corner of his mother's court up to the royal highway (*ab inferiori angulo curie matris mee usque ad viam regiam*); to be held of the grantor and his heirs freely and quietly for cutting a quarry or otherwise (*ad quararium effodiend(um) sive ad aliud quid faciendam*)[3] by rendering 8d. annually for all service, 4d. at the feast of the blessed Mary in March and 4d. at the feast of St. Nicholas. Clause for warranty. fo. 154r.

[1] preceded by *terram* and followed by *meum*, both deleted

[2] lost through damage

[3] sic

.62 Mid 13th century

Charter of Pagan Pake of Coventry giving to God, the blessed Mary and the monks of Combe in pure and perpetual alms 17 selions of his furlong at Harnall (*seliones de Cultura mea de harnale que se extendunt in longitudine ab angulo curtilagii in orientali parte quod Geva que fuit uxor Willelmi Beleteste tenuit descendendo secundum novas divisas usque ad Culturam quam richidio*[1] *tenuit Et in latitudine se extendunt a terra mea usque ad altam viam ducentem a quareria mon(achorum) usque ad Boscum comitis*). Clause for warranty. fo. 160r.

[1] sic

.63 Mid 13th century

Charter of Pagan Pake giving to God, the blessed Mary and the monks of Combe a messuage in Harnall (*harhale*) with all appurtenances, namely that next to the Combe land as ditched (*juxta terram de Cumba sicut fossatum est*); to be held of the grantor and his heirs by rendering annually to them 12d. at the 4 terms of the year accustomed in Coventry. Clause for warranty. fo. 160r.

.64 Mid 13th century

Charter of Pagan Pake son of Robert giving to God, the blessed Mary and the monks of Combe in pure and perpetual alms 6d. rent from the land which he previously held of them in the vill of Coventry. Whereas previously he used to render 4 hens to them annually at Christmas, henceforth they will have 6d. from him and his heirs at the 4 fixed terms of the vill. Clause for warranty. fo. 160r.

.65 1208–c.1221

Charter of Walter son of Terry (*terrici*) of Coventry giving to God, the blessed Mary and the monks of Combe in pure and perpetual alms an acre of meadow in the meadows of Sowe, namely that which he had by the gift of William the Marshal (*maresc'*) and afterwards by the charter of William's son; to be held to them without any reservation. Clause for warranty. fo. 153v.

THE COVENTRY HUNDRED ROLLS

768
Professor R. H. Hilton discovered the Coventry Hundred Rolls among the manuscripts of the Leigh Collection deposited in the Shakespeare Birthplace Trust at Stratford on Avon.[1] The document is a neat, careful copy in a fourteenth-century hand of the return made to the royal commission on 31st January 1280. The original, or indeed any official copy, has apparently been lost. The manuscript almost certainly belonged to the Benedictine priory of Coventry since it includes not only the survey of the city, but also the 1279–80 survey of some of the priory's Warwickshire manors.[2] This latter section of the manuscript is similar to, though not quite identical with, the corresponding sections of the survey of the hundreds of Kineton and Stoneleigh to be found among the miscellaneous books of the Exchequer in the Public Record Office.[3]

By the second half of the sixteenth century the manuscript was in the possession of the Leigh family of Stoneleigh Abbey when it was consulted and annotated by Arthur Gregory of Stivichall.[4] Presumably by the Leighs, it was bound into a volume measuring 19 cm × 35 cm, along with the Tripartite Indenture of 1355 – another vital document in the history of Coventry's development – the Taxation of Pope Nicholas of 1291 for the diocese of Coventry and Lichfield, the prophesy of Merlin, a chronicle of English kings to 1387, and other minor pieces.[5]

It has been generally recognized that it is a document of major importance for the early history of Coventry, though there is some debate as to the significance of its evidence.[6] Coventry is certainly shown to be a major urban settlement far larger than the county town of Warwick.[7] There are nearly 900 properties listed held by about 420 individuals. Obviously the number of dwellings and residents in the city would far exceed these totals, but a population calculation is extremely hazardous. There was a great deal of short term sub-letting of property of which the Hundred Rolls takes no notice, and it is difficult to translate the terminology of the document – burgages, cottages, messuages, crofts, curtilages, etc. – into even an approximate number of dwellings. Nevertheless the attempt must be made.

1 Shakespeare Birthplace Trust, Stoneleigh Manuscripts DR 18/31/3 fols. 100–114.

2 Wasperton, Packwood, Honington with Broad Moor, Prior's Hardwick, Prior's Marston, Walsgrave on Sowe, Wyken, Ufton, Offchurch, Whitley, Cubbington, Stivichall, Willenhall, Horwell, Waverley, Coundon, Binley, Ernsford, Radford, Stoke, Biggin, Harnall – fols 114v–132v. This section has not been printed here and must await a complete edition of the Warwickshire Hundred Rolls in preparation by the present editor of this survey for the Dugdale Society.

3 P.R.O. E. 164/15.

4 R. Bearman, *The Gregorys of Stivichall in the Sixteenth Century*, Coventry and Warwickshire History Pamphlets No. 8, (Coventry, 1972), pp. 33–34.

5 Fols. 100–100v and the Tripartite Indenture, fols. 68v–72v. have been printed by Professor R. H. C. Davis as an appendix to *The Early History of Coventry*, Dugdale Society Occasional Papers No. 24. (Oxford, 1976), pp. 21–30.

6 For divergent views on the constitutional and economic significance of the Coventry Hundred Rolls see Miss J. Lancaster & D. K. Bolton in *V.C.H. Coventry*, pp. 152, 208; P. R. Coss, 'Coventry Before Incorporation – A Re-interpretation', *Midland History* Vol. II No. 3, 1974, pp. 143, 147; R. H. C. Davis, *op. cit.*, p. 6; A. & E. Gooder, 'Coventry before 1355: Unity or Division? The Importance of the Earl's Half', *Midland History*, Vol. VI, 1981, p. 13; R. H. Hilton, *A Medieval Society: The West Midlands at the End of the Thirteenth Century*, 2nd. ed., (Cambridge, 1983), pp. 185, 189.

7 Cf. The Hundred Rolls survey of Warwick in P.R.O. E.164/15 fols. 1–6v.

The method used is based on Roger Mols' study of the demographic history of European cities from the fourteenth to the eighteenth century. After an extensive review of the evidence European wide Mols concluded that coefficients of 4 and 5 could give rough approximations of the populations of cities from listings of householders or dwellings. Before the seventeenth century he thought the factor of 5 would produce a result closer to reality, but for cities which have a larger proportion of small households – single persons, couples without children – than rural communities 4.5 was likely to be more accurate. On the other hand Mols showed how in urban communities listing of households and numbers of families by no means exactly corresponded: normally in cities which were in some degree flourishing the number of families exceeded the number of households or dwellings. In some cases, perhaps as much as 10% or more, there was more than one family under one roof. Therefore the population estimation must be increased accordingly. Mols was aware that there were many variables which could affect the factors – of time, of region, of social custom, of quarter, rich or poor, within the city. To apply his method to a time before his field of study is also perhaps risky, but since the thirteenth century was an era of population increase and growth of cities, the result is more likely to be on the side of caution rather than exaggeration. The method has already been applied to convert the 1148 survey of Winchester to population figures.[8]

If only burgages, cottages and messuages represent dwellings and allowing the number of families to be 9–10 per cent in excess of the number of houses, the population of Coventry in 1280 was in the region of 3,500 (taking the average family size as 4.5). If the total number of properties is nearer to the number of dwellings, then the population figure rises to about 4,400. It is possible, however, to judge from the Winchester evidence, that the number of houses exceeded the entries in the urban survey by 40–50 per cent. In this case the population could be as high as 5,600.

In 1280 Coventry may not yet have been among the first rank of medieval English towns: in 1334 it is ranked twelfth equal with Salisbury in wealth.[9] In 1280 it may have been only slightly larger than Cambridge, ranked twenty-first in 1334.[10] Using surnames as evidence of recent immigration into Coventry about 27 per cent of those recorded in the Hundred Rolls are found to be of the place name type, which is not exceptional.[11] However, Coventry's drawing power was in a significant number of cases well beyond the immediate locality, and this indicates that it was already a regional centre. This would be expected of a town situated at the crossing of routes of national importance.[12]

The number and distribution of properties between the two halves of Coventry and the manor of Cheylesmore is shown in the following table:[13]

[8] Roger Mols, *Introduction à la Démographie des Villes d'Europe du XIVe au XVIIIe siècle, Vol. II, Les Résultats*, Louvain 1955, pp. 104, 105, 128, 129, 130, 136–40, 147, 164; M. Biddle (ed.), *Winchester in the Early Middle Ages: An edition and discussion of the Winton Domesday*, Winchester Studies I (Oxford, 1976), pp. 440–441.

[9] H. C. Darby (ed.), *A New Historical Geography of England*, (Cambridge, 1973) p. 184.

[10] For Cambridge see *Rotuli Hundredorum Vol. II* Record Commission 1818, pp. 356–401, and F. W. Maitland's analysis in *Township and Borough*, Cambridge 1898, pp. 100–101. See also M. D. Lobel, *Historic Towns – Cambridge*, The Historic Towns Trust, p. 9.

[11] R. H. Hilton, *op. cit.*, p. 184.

[12] F. M. Stenton, 'The Roads of the Gough Map' in E. J. S. Parsons, *The Map of Great Britain circa 1360 known as The Gough Map – An Introduction to the Facsimile*, (Oxford, 1958), p. 18.

[13] My figures differ slightly from those of Miss J. Lancaster (*V.C.H. Coventry*, p. 152) and A. & E. Gooder, *loc. cit.* This is because of ambiguities in and different interpretations of the manuscript. It is sometimes difficult to know whether the same or a different piece of property is referred to, and double counting can easily take place. Doubtless I have been guilty of it. Dr. & Mrs. Gooder see the Prior's Half as having more room for development because the division of and building on burgage plots had gone further in the Earl's Half.

PROPERTY	CHEYLESMORE	PRIOR'S HALF	EARL'S HALF	TOTAL
BURGAGES		165	116	281
COTTAGES		96	238	334
MESSUAGES	16	37	47	100
CROFTS		5	22	27
CURTILAGES	3	47	65	115

In addition the following types of property appear:
mills (9, one in Cheylesmore, 8 in the Earl's Half)
ovens (7, one in Cheylesmore, 4 in the Prior's Half, 2 in the Earl's Half)
stalls (4, all in the Prior's Half)
shops (3 in the Prior's Half)
houses (3 in the Prior's Half)
gardens (2 in the Prior's Half)
a solar and a cellar (in Cheylesmore)
selions (46, all in the Prior's Half)
butts (6 in the Prior's Half)
parts of land (2 holdings so described – one in each half)
part of a meadow (Earl's Half)
acres (one acre rented for 2s. 2d.; 2 acres for 4s., both holdings in the Earl's Half)
A number of properties are described as tenements, but these sometimes include burgages, cottages, curtilages, etc., and they have been counted under their respective headings. Twenty tenements *tout court* are mentioned: eighteen of them are held by or leased from Henry Baker (*Pestur*). The above list does not include Geoffrey de Langley's estate of a messuage, two carucates and a grove at Shortley, though the cottages and water mills which are part of the estate are included in the above totals.

The fact of more burgages in the Prior's Half together with the location of the market and other commercial centres there suggests that at this time this was on the whole the economically more developed part of the town.[14] So too does the residence there, when it can be determined in the survey, of some of the wealthy citizens. The rents for burgages and messuages can be much higher in the Prior's Half than in the Earl's Half. A burgage can render up to 17s. 8d. in the Prior's Half and up to 10s. in the Earl's; the highest rent for a messuage is 13s. in the Prior's Half and 5s. in the Earl's. Only in rents for cottage property does the Earl's Half match the Prior's: up to 8s. in both parts. Generally, however, the recorded rents are much lower than these examples. The most frequently recurring rent for a burgage plot is 12d., that for messuages rather higher than this, and for cottages about the same. The assumption is that the highest rents indicate the true or potential value of property in the city; many rents recorded in the Hundred Rolls are either the tenurial rent (the original rent of the plot) or a quit rent (merely nominal – the property in effect having been sold).[15]

[14] Also argued by D. K. Bolton in *V.C.H. Coventry*, p. 208.

[15] F. M. Powicke, 'Observations on the English Freeholder in the Thirteenth Century', in *Wirtschaft und Kultur: Festschrift zum 70 Geburtstag von Alfons Dopsch*, Baden bei Wien, (Leipzig, 1938), p. 387; R. H. Hilton, 'Some Problems of Urban Real Property in the Middle Ages' in C. H. Feinstein, *Socialism, Capitalism and Economic Growth: Essays Presented to Maurice Dobb*, (Cambridge, 1967), pp. 329, 331, 334.

The rent roll of the lord of Coventry, the prior of the Benedictine monastery, was greater in the Prior's Half than in the Earl's, though not by very much: £13-10-1d as against £11-19-9½d., though the former would rise by another £1-13-0d. on the death of Alexander of Coventry who had received concessions of rent from the prior for his service. In all, including the rents of Spon chapel and its lands and of messuages in Cheylesmore manor, in 1279–80 the prior's income in Coventry should have been £27-1-8½d. in addition to the profits of fairs, markets and courts.[16] The prior in turn was obliged to render £106-13-4d. per annum to the heirs of Roger de Montalt for the Earl's Half, so his recorded rent income is unlikely to represent the real value of his lordship of Coventry to him.

The Earl's Half is more populous than the Prior's Half: it has over twice as many cottages and it has more space for development in the greater number of crofts and curtilages, normally undeveloped land. Some light labour services are still charged on some plots in the Earl's Half, another indication that much of this area has a more rural and suburban character.[17] But this might well be the area of rapid growth: some 60 individuals have place name surnames indicating recent immigration in the Earl's Half as against 36 in the Prior's.

There is no great concentration of property into a few hands. There are 173 holders of burgage property: the vast majority are holders of a single whole burgage (with perhaps a little more property of a different nature); a few (26) hold parts of burgages or hold in joint tenure. There are 94 holders of burgage land in the Prior's Half and 60 in the Earl's Half. Nineteen individuals have burgage property in both halves. Nineteen individuals (but not the same nineteen – there is an overlap of ten) also hold five or more burgages.[18] Two of these are from the feudal landowning class, but among the others are found the men who dominate the political life of the city.[19] Property was not necessarily the source of their prosperity, however: in some cases their outgoings exceeded their income in rents, and in others the balance was only slightly on the credit side, at least as recorded in the Hundred Rolls.[20] Nonetheless the rent rolls of some of them are very long indeed. Nine of them have extensive interests in both halves of the city, but only four on the evidence of the Hundred Rolls have property outside Coventry.[21]

[16] The prior had outgoings in rent of 14s. 1d. in the Prior's Half, and there are ambiguities in the manuscript which may mean that the given figures ought to be reduced by up to 2s. 2d. For Alexander of Coventry see fol. 104.

[17] The existence of labour services in an English borough at this date is very late; cf. S. Reynolds, *An Introduction to the History of English Medieval Towns*, (Oxford, 1977), p. 100.

[18] The totals of burgage holders given are of those who hold property directly as recorded in the manuscript. A further fifteen individuals or heirs of individuals (ten in the Prior's Half, five in the Earl's Half) have interests in burgage plots by way of rent but do not apparently occupy any burgage property; R. H. Hilton, in Feinstein, *op. cit.*, p. 334. Professor Hilton's figures and mine are very close.

[19] See above pp. xxxviii–ix. Geoffrey de Langley and John de Warwick – the former certainly, the latter most probably – are the aristocratic landowners. For Langley see P. R. Coss, *The Langley Family and its Cartulary – A study in late medieval 'Gentry'*, Dugdale Society, Occasional Papers No. 22, (Oxford, 1974), pp. 4, 5.

[20] For example Henry Baker's outgoings in 'rent' exceeded his income by almost 20s.; Robert Chilton's surplus of income from rent over outgoings was only 3s. 7½d. On the other hand Walter Bacon's income was twice that of his expenditure (26s. 5½d. against 13s. 5d.); Peter Baron's 39s. in excess of his outgoings (excluding the rent of 40s. which Peter son of Peter Baron paid for a mill); and Master Richard de Burton and Petronilla his wife had a surplus of 85s. 3½d. (139s. 8½d. against 54s. 5d.).

[21] Holding property in both halves were Walter Bacon, Peter Baron, Master Richard de Burton and his wife Petronilla, Robert de Chilton, Richard Forwyn, Robert Herberd, Robert de Lodlowe, Henry Baker and John Tole. Bacon, Chilton and Baker had land at Radford and Richard Forwyn property on the Stoneleigh estate (P.R.O. E.164/15 fols. 56v, 57, 19v).

The evidence of surnames suggest that no one craft or trade dominates Coventry. This is typical of English towns at this time and indicates the importance of local trade rather than specialized long distant trade.[22] The age of the wool merchant appears to be yet to come. If any occupation is prominent it is that of the victuallers, and this is characteristic of towns in their early phase of expansion both in England and on the continent.[23] In the Hundred Rolls there are signs that the economy of Coventry is quickening, but the evidence does not justify reading the eminence reached by the city in the fourteenth century back into the thirteenth.

[22] S. Reynolds, *op. cit.*, p. 59.

[23] S. Reynolds, *loc. cit.*; F. R. H. Du Boulay: *Documents Illustrative of Medieval Kentish Society*, Kent Records Vol XVIII, Kent Archaeological Society, 1964, p. 176; Georges Duby, *Rural Economy and Country Life in the Medieval West*, (London, 1962), p. 129.

Leigh MS fol 100

Inquisitio facta die Mercurii proxima ante festum purificationis beate Marie anno regni regis Edwardi filii Regis Henrici octavo coram dominis Henrico de Notyng(ham) Henrico de Sheld(on) militibus et Johanne de Arundel clerico inquisitoribus ipsius Regis Edwardi per xii juratos subscriptos videlicet Walterum Bacoun Thomam de Moubray Johannem Tole Thomam de Fackynham Johannem de Filongleye Willelmum Ottyng' Rogerum le Peschur Ricardum le Fermaylur' Richerum de Weston Ricardum le Bourseir' Ricardum de Esseby Robertum le Mouner' et Adam atte Grene.[1] Qui dicunt per sacramentum suum quod in villa de Coventr' est quidam prioratus nigrorum monachorum in quo est quedam ecclesia cathedralis. Et quod Prior et conventus habent electionem episcopi una cum capitulo Lich' et idem Prior et conventus habent semper primam vocem electionis.

Feoda ii militum.[2]

Dicunt etiam quod idem Prior est dominus ville de Coventr' cujus medietatem cum tota baronia tenet de Rege in capite per servicium feodi duorum militum in exercitu. Et habet ibidem mercatum per diem Veneris et ea que ad mercatum pertinent. Habet etiam ibidem unam feriam semel in anno durantem per viii dies. Et habet warennam in dominicis suis. Et habet coronatorem in eadem villa. Dicunt etiam quod tenet ipsam medietatem ville predicte adeo libere a tempore Sancti Edwardi Regis et Confessoris sicut Leofricus Comes eam tenuit liberius de eodem Sancto Edwardo. Dicunt etiam quod idem Prior et homines sui quieti sunt de murdris et habet furcas collistrigium tribichettum assisam panis et cervisie. Et habet feodalitatem burgensium suorum et duos adventus per annum ad curiam suam. Dicunt etiam quod de ista medietate ville predicte et de libertatibus predictis idem Prior habet cartas Regis Henrici [patris][3] Regis Edwardi qui nunc est et quorumdam aliorum regum Anglie predecessorum suorum.

Pars comitis.[4]

Dicunt etiam quod idem Prior tenet aliam medietatem ville predicte que dicitur pars Comitis cum forinseco bosco in quo tota villa[ta] clamat habere communam pasture ad omnimoda averia sua cum cum[sic] aliis communibus pasture in boscis Abbatis de Stanle de heredibus Rogeri de Monte Alto per servicium c librarum et x marcarum per annum secundum quod in finali concordia inter dictum Rogerum et Ceciliam uxorem ejus et dictos Priorem et conventum plenius continetur. Et iidem heredes tenent eam de domino Rege quo servicio ignorant quia est de scuto Cestr'. Idem Prior [habet][5] in eadem parte ville predicte semel in anno unam feriam durantem per vi dies circa festum Sancte Trinitatis. Et ipsam feriam habet adeo liberam sicut dicti heredes aut eorum antecessores a tempore quo non exstat memoria eam tenuerunt. Idem Prior habet in eadem parte furcas collistrigium tribuchettum assisam panis et cervisie et omnia alia que ad libertatem pertinent. Habet etiam feodalitatem in eadem parte omnium burgensium suorum et duos adventus ad curiam per annum.

[fol 100 b] Idem Prior habet alias liberas curias in tota villata per rationabiles summonitiones[6] faciendum videlicet per viii dies. Et de istis curiis habent burgenses ejusdem ville curias suas liberorum tenentium suorum. Idem Prior habet totam villam liberam ab omni tolneto excepto tolneto equorum de quo burgenses ejusdem ville omnino sunt quieti. Et etiam iidem burgenses habent tolnetum equorum de tenentibus suis in burgagiis suis residentibus. Idem Prior habent in eadem villa tria molendina cum stagnis eorundem et cum duobus vivariis in dominico. Harnale.[7]

1 In fact 13 jurors are named
2 In margin
3 Interlined
4 In margin
5 Omitted in the MS.
6 *suu'* in MS.
7 written in margin

Idem Prior habet in Arnale juxta Coventr' in dominico nomine burgagii i carucatam terre cum grangia domibus et aliis pertinentiis suis.
Dicunt etiam quod quidam Comes Cestr' Hugo Scathelok nomine habuit quemdam de familia sua Willelmum de Anneye nomine militem leprosum cujus occasione et pro salute anime ipsius Comitis et antecessorum suorum dedit in puram et perpetuam elemosinam ad sustentacionem leprosorum villate Coventr' capellam de Sponna cum situ ejusdem et cum medietate unius carucate terre cum pertinentiis. Alii etiam de villa et de patria de quorum nominibus ignoratur dederunt ad sustentacionem dictorum leprosorum terras et redditus sub certa forma quam formam nesciunt et per cartas quarum formas ignorant. In predictis autem situ et loco Sponne solebat antiquitus esse quidam capellanus ad minus celebrans diatim pro (vivis et defunctis).[1] Et solebant ibi esse fratres et sorores una cum leprosis pro omnibus suis benefactoribus deum orantes et deprecantes. Et ipsi fratres et sorores habebant omnes terras liberas et quietas ab omni consuetudine. Et habebant pannagium et tolnetum et curias suas de liberis tenentibus suis. Hanc autem capellam et terras et redditus cum pertinentiis suis appropriant sibi dicti Prior et conventus Coventr' per cartam Rogeri de Monte Alto et dicunt quod capellam terras et redditus cum pertinentiis tenet quidam capellanus Johannes nomine de dictis Priore et conventu pro ii marcis per annum ad firmam. Dicunt etiam quod in villa predicta est quedam domus fratrum minorum qui tenent ecclesiam suam cum loco suo ex concessione Ranulphi quondam Comitis Cestr' et tenent ad voluntatem heredum ipsius Comitis.
Dicunt etiam quod heredes Rogeri de Monto Alto tenent in eadem villa unum mansum quod dicitur Cheilesmor'[2] cum parco et unum molendinum aquaticum cum i vivario et uno stagno incluso in dominico de domino Rege quo servicio ignoratur.
Dicunt etiam quod dicti heredes habent in eadem villa xx liberos tenentes de quibus:
Nicholaus Jory tenet i curtilagium de eisdem heredibus pro iiii d.
Heredes Petri Martyn tenent i messuagium de Priore de Coventr' pro x d.
Johannes le Vynter' tenet i messuagium ibidem de Johanne Hastyng' pro ii s per annum.
Ricardus le Brocher' tenet i messuagium ibidem de predicto Priore pro vi d per annum.
Walterus le Tixtor tenet i messuagium ibidem de predicto Priore pro iii s per annum.
Rogerus Haberdas tenet i messuagium de heredibus Rogeri de Monte Alto pro ii s per annum.
Margeria Pake tenet i furnum de eisdem heredibus pro iiii s viii d per annum.
Willelmus Lalle tenet i curtilagium de eisdem heredibus pro iiii d per annum.
Henricus le Bourser' tenet i messuagium de eisdem heredibus pro vi d per annum.
Ricardus le Gardener' tenet i messuagium de eisdem heredibus pro xviii d per annum.
Willelmus le Hose tenet i messuagium de eisdem heredibus pro xii d per annum.

[fol 101]

Magister Radulphus de Bannebury tenet i messuagium de eisdem heredibus pro iiii d per annum.
Richardus Beyvile tenet i messuagium de eisdem heredibus pro ii s per annum.
Hugo Breton tenet predictum messuagium de predicto Ricardo pro iii s per annum.
Ricardus le Dubber' tenet i messuagium de eisdem heredibus pro xii d per annum.
Willelmus Scot tenet i messuagium de eisdem heredibus pro ii s et Priori de Coventr' x d de eodem.
Henricus de Rodynton tenet ii messuagia de eisdem heredibus pro ii s.
Heredes Gilberti de Grymesby tenet i curtilagium de eisdem heredibus pro xii d.
Willelmus Brid tenet i messuagium de eisdem heredibus pro xii d.

[1] underlined in MS.
[2] *Cheilesmore* in margin in later hand.

Henricus Oky et Agnes uxor ejus tenent i messuagium de eisdem heredibus pro vi d.

Thomas de Fackenham tenet i celerium et i solarium de eisdem heredibus pro iii s. Et omnes isti supradicti tenent per cartas de dictis heredibus et iidem heredes de domino Rege quo servicio ignoratur.

Pars Prioris.

Jurati dicunt per sacramentum suum quod Magister Ricardus de Burton et Petronilla uxor ejus tenent ex parte Prioris i burgagium de ipso Priore pro xii d et ipse Prior de Rege reddendo similiter pro eodem burgagio heredibus Johannis de Olney per annum iiii s. Et ipsi heredes tenent de Willelmo Harcourt. Et idem Willelmus Harcourt tenet de ipso Priore et Prior de Rege ut supra. Sunt etiam in predicto burgagio vii cotarii videlicet:

Johannes le Clerk qui tenet inde i cotagium de predictis Ricardo et Petronilla pro iii s.

Rogerus de Tocsale tenet secundum cotagium de eisdem Ricardo et Petronilla pro xii d.

Gilbertus le Fourner' tenet tertium cotagium de eisdem Ricardo et Petronilla pro viii s et faciendo sectam ad quemdam furnum eorundum.

Rogerus le Peschur tenet quartum cotagium de eisdem pro iiii s vi d.

Matilda Pavy tenet quintum cotagium de eisdem pro ii s ii d.

Heredes Johannis de Wykewane tenent sextum cotagium de eisdem pro ii s.

Henricus Anketilby de Wykewane tenet septimum cotagium de eisdem pro xii d.

Iidem Ricardus et Petronilla habent in eodem burgagio in dominico quoddam furnum commune. Et iidem Ricardus et Petronilla tenent[1] aliud burgagium apud Gosford de predicto Priore pro ii s et Prior de Rege in quo habent ii cotarios qui tenent per cartam videlicet:

Robertus de Lodlowe qui tenet unum cotagium de eisdem pro iii s. Et Robertus Huthered qui tenet aliud de eisdem pro iii s.

Robertus filius Johannis Orfeuer tenet unum burgagium de eisdem Ricardo et Petronilla per cartam pro v s. Et ipsi Ricardus et Petronilla de Priore pro vi d et Prior de Rege.

Walterus de Bannebury et Alicia la Blond tenent de dictis Ricardo et Petronilla unum croftum pro xvi d. Et iidem Ricardus et Petronilla[2] de Priore pro eodem servicio et Prior de Rege.

[fol 101 b] Matilda filia Petri Martyn tenet quinque burgagia de Priore pro xxiii d et Prior de Rege de quibus tenet unum in dominico de Priore pro vi d.

Prior et conventus tenent de dicta Matilda secundum burgagium pro ii s et dicta Matilda de Priore pro iii d. Et Prior de Rege.

Thomas le Moubray tenet tertium burgagium pro ii s de dicta Matilda. Et ipsa Matilda de Priore pro iii d. Et Prior de Rege.

Galfridus de Whiteleye tenet quartum burgagium de dicta Matilda pro iii s. Et ipsa de Priore pro iii d. Et Prior de Rege.

Predicta Matilda tenet quoddam croftum nomine quinti burgagii de Priore pro viii d et Prior de Rege.

Johannes Coterell tenet unum burgagium de Priore pro vi d et Prior de Rege.

Johannes filius Walteri le Orfeuer tenet unum burgagium de Priore pro xii d et Prior de Rege. Et de eodem burgagio Johannes Sampson tenet unum messuagium per cartam de dicto Johanne pro xv d.

Thomas Alutar' tenet unum burgagium de Priore pro xii d et Prior de Rege in quo habet duos liberos tenentes qui tenent per cartam de ipso Thoma videlicet:

Robertus de Chilton qui tenet i messuagium de eodem pro vi d.

Walterus de Banbur' tenet aliud messuagium pro vi d et uno pari cirotecarum pretii unius oboli vel obolo.

[1] *tenet* in MS.

[2] *R et P* in MS.

Hugo Breton tenet i burgagium de Priore pro vi d et Prior de Rege et de eodem burgagio idem Hugo tenet i messuagium de heredibus Ranulphi de Frankton pro iiii d et iidem heredes tenuerunt quondam de Henrico Derlyng per idem servicium et iidem tenuerunt de Priore pro vi d. Et de eodem burgagio Henricus Marie tenet medietatem unius curtilagii pro i d. Et Johannes Hors tenet aliam medietatem ejusdem curtilagii pro i clavo gariofili.[1] Et sic tenet dictus Hugo totum burgagium de Priore per servicium predictorum vi d. Et Prior de Rege.
Robertus Herberd tenet iiii burgagia cum ii croftis de Priore pro vii s ii d et Prior de Rege de quibus idem Robertus tenet i burgagium cum ii croftis in dominico suo et habet unum liberum tenentem qui tenet per cartam de eo pro xii d videlicet Jena de Gosford in dicto burgagio. Robertus de Chilton tenet unum cotagium de ipso de ipsis burgagiis pro viii d et Robertus Herberd de Priore et Prior de Rege.
Ricardus Tayllour tenet i cotagium de dictis burgagiis de Henrico le Pestur pro vi s et Walterus de Banbur' tenet aliud cotagium de eodem Henrico pro v s vi d et idem Henricus tenet de predicto Roberto Herberd pro vii s viii d et idem Henricus tenet v seliones terre de eodem Roberto pro xviii d et idem Robertus de Priore et Prior de Rege.
Willelmus de Copston tenet unum cotagium de dictis burgagiis pro xii d et aliud cotagium de Ricardo Fordwyn pro xii d et Ricardus de predicto Roberto et Robertus de Priore et Prior de Rege.
Idem Robertus tenet unum cotagium de dictis burgagiis in dominico suo de Priore et Prior tenet de Rege.

[fol 102]

Johannes Tole tenet unum croftum de predicto Roberto per cartam pro xx d et Robertus de Priore et Prior de Rege.
Johannes filius Nicholai de Teynton tenet ix seliones terre de predicto Roberto pro uno clavo gariofili et idem Robertus de Priore et Prior de Rege.
Henricus le Pestur tenet ix seliones terre de dictis burgagiis de dicto Roberto pro ii s et i pari cerotecarum pretii ob. et idem Robertus tenet de Priore et Prior de Rege.
Heredes Hugonis Ketelberne tenent i burgagium cum pertinentiis de Priore pro ii s ix d et Prior tenet de Rege.
Rogerus le Peschur' tenet unum cotagium per cartam de dictis heredibus pro xii d et iidem heredes tenent de Priore et Prior de Rege.
Magister Hospitalis Sancti Johannis tenet duo cotagia per cartam de dictis heredibus pro vid et heredes tenent de Priore et Prior de Rege.
Willelmus de Copston tenet unum burgagium per legem Anglie de Priore pro i d ob. et Prior tenet de Rege.
Isabella la Seler' tenet ii burgagia de Priore pro xviii d et Prior de Rege.
Ricardus de Hull tenet i cotagium de dicta Isabella pro xx d per cartam.
Walterus Bacon tenet i cotagium de dicta Isabella per cartam pro ii s.
Johannes filius Rogeri le Mouner tenet i cotagium de eadem Isabella pro xii d.
Robertus le Butter' et Isolda uxor ejus tenent i burgagium de Priore pro xviii d et Prior de Rege in quo sunt vii cotagia de quibus habent iiii in dominico et Johannes Tixtor tenet quintum[2] cotagium de predictis Roberto et Isolda per cartam pro vi d.
Magister Hospitalis Sancti Johannis Coventr' tenet sextum cotagium de eisdem per cartam pro i ob.
Johannes filius Rogeri le Mouner tenet vii^{um} de eisdem per cartam pro ob.
Ricardus Durant tenet i burgagium de Priore pro xii d et Prior de Rege in quo sunt quattuor cotagia de quibus unum tenet in dominico et alia tria tenet Robertus de

[1] The form *gariofilum* has been used throughout the transcription: the MS sometimes has the form *gariophilum*.

[2] *quinque* in MS.

Doggelone per cartam de dicto Ricardo pro xii d et medietate i libre cimini et pari[1] cerotecarum pretii ob.
Johannes Tole tenet i burgagium de Priore pro viii d et Prior de Rege.
Idem Johannes tenet aliud burgagium de Priore apud Harnale pro xx d et uno gallo et i gallina et Prior tenet de Rege.
Johannes de Filongleye tenet i burgagium de Priore pro xvi d et Prior de Rege.
Robertus de Doglone tenet i burgagium de Priore pro xii d et Prior de Rege.
Robertus de Lodelawe tenet v burgagia de Priore videlicet tria pro iii s et i cum quadam quarera pro iiii s et quintum pro xii d et Prior tenet de Rege.
Idem Robertus tenet i burgagium in quo manet de eodem Priore pro vi d et Prior tenet de Rege.
Willelmus le Orfeuer' tenet unum burgagium de Priore pro xii d et Prior de Rege.
Robertus a la Fontayne tenet ii burgagia de Priore pro ii s et Prior de Rege.
Heredes Hugonis le Hosier' tenent tria cotagia de Roberto de Lodelawe per cartam pro i d et Priori inde iiii d.
Rogerus le Pechur' tenet i burgagium de Priore pro xii d et Prior de Rege.
[fol 102 b] Henricus Marie tenet duo curtilagia nomine i burgagii de Priore pro xii d et Prior de Rege.
Alanus le Boucher' tenet i burgagium de Priore pro xviii d et Prior de Rege.
Walterus Hoslok tenet i burgagium de predicto Alano per cartam pro ii s.
Thomas de Fackenham tenet i burgagium de Priore pro ii d et Prior de Rege.
Johannes Wele tenet i burgagium de predicto Thoma per cartam pro ii d.
Henricus Knave tenet tria burgagia de Priore pro ii s et Prior de Rege.
Item[2] Henricus tenet ii crofta nomine unius burgagii de predicto Priore pro xii d.
Johannes le Feuer tenet i burgagium de Priore pro vi d et Prior de Rege.
Idem Johannes habet tres liberos tenentes videlicet Reginaldus le Pestur qui tenet unum curtilagium de eodem pro iiii d per cartam.
Ricardus Asser tenet aliud curtilagium de eodem Johanne pro ii d per cartam.
Johanna filia Walteri le Coupere tenet unum curtilagium de eodem per cartam pro ii d.
Willelmus de Shulton tenet i burgagium de Priore pro xii d et Prior de Rege.
Johannes Pyhod tenet i burgagium de Priore pro iii d et Prior de Rege.
Adam Russell tenet i burgagium de eodem Johanne pro iii d et i clavo gariofili.
Ricardus Midnyht tenet i burgagium de Priore pro xii d et Prior de Rege et reddit Hugoni Tregros pro eodem i par cirotecarum pretii ob.
Johannes Scot tenet i burgagium de Priore pro xiii d et Prior de Rege.
Petrus Baron tenet tria burgagia de Priore pro xii d et Prior de Rege.
Prior et conventus tenent duo cotagia de ipso Petro pro vii s vi d et ii caponibus per cartam
Johannes Ingilram tenet i cotagium de predicto Petro per cartam pro ii s vi d.
Robertus de Chilton tenet i burgagium de predicto Petro per cartam pro iii s.
Predicti Prior et conventus tenent de eodem Petro aliud cotagium per cartam pro xix d.
Fratres et Sorores Hospitalis Sancti Johannis Coventr' tenent duo cotagia per cartam de predicto Petro pro xviii d et aliud pro xii d.
Rogerus le Chaumberleyn et Rogerus le Neve tenent i burgagium de Priore pro xxii d et Prior de Rege et tenent secundum legem Anglie.
Magister Robertus de Leic' tenet ii burgagia de Priore pro viii d et i furnum pro x s et Prior tenet de Rege.
Johannes filius Henrici de Radeford tenet i burgagium de Priore pro xiii d et reddit Roberto Wambe ob. pro eodem burgagio.
Martinus Colebrond tenet viii seliones terre cum pertinentiis de predicto Johanne pro vi d.

[1] *paris* in MS.
[2] sic

Willelmus le Prude tenet vi buttas terre de eodem Johanne pro ii d.
Nicholaus de Condelm' tenet duo cotagia cum pertinentiis de eodem Johanne pro uno ob. et Johannes tenet de Priore et Prior de Rege.
Silvester le Parmenter' tenet i burgagium de Priore pro xxviii d et Prior de Rege.
Walterus Osloc tenet i cotagium de predicto Silvestre per cartam pro xviii d et Willelmus Sparc percipit de ipso Waltero de uno messuagio xviii d et reddit inde Priori xv d. Percipit etiam idem Willelmus de Johanne de Cornle de alio messuagio i par cirotecarum pretii ob. et tenet illud de Priore et Prior de Rege.
Vitalis de Wilenhale tenet unum burgagium cum pertinentiis de Priore pro iiii s et Prior de Rege.

[fol 103]
Hawis que fuit[1] uxor Mathei le Bolter' tenet i cotagium de dicto Vitale pro ii s iiii d.
Magister Hospitalis Sancti Johannis tenet i cotagium de eodem Vitale pro xviii d.
Rogerus le Fulur tenet i curtilagium de eodem Vitale pro xii d.
Willelmus de Monte tenet quandam partem unius curtilagii de eodem Vitale pro vi d.
Alicia Ingelram tenet i curtilagium de eodem Vitale pro xii d.
Agnes Dandy tenet de eodem Vitale i curtilagium pro xii d et Vitalis tenet de Priore et Prior de Rege.
Henricus del Parlur tenet i burgagium de Priore pro xviii d et Prior de Rege.
Isabella filia ejusdem Henrici tenet i burgagium de Priore pro iiii d et Prior de Rege.
Alexander le Moubray tenet duo burgagia de Priore pro xii d et Prior de Rege.
Johannes Ingelram tenet i curtilagium per cartam de ipso Alexandro pro xxx d.
Hugo le Feure tenet i cotagium per cartam de eodem Alexandro pro vi d et idem Alexander tenet tria cotagia in dominico suo reddendo inde per annum et pro alio burgagio predicto Priori xii d et Prior tenet de Rege.
Idem Alexander tenet i cotagium de Priore pro xii d et aliud de eodem pro iiii d et Prior tenet de Rege.
Johannes filius Ade le Clerk tenet quandam partem unius curtilagii de predicto Alexandro pro iiii d.
Willelmus le Proude tenet i cotagium de eodem Alexandro pro xii d et idem Alexander reddit inde per annum Henrico le Pestour ob.
Robertus Bondy tenet unum curtilagium de predicto Alexandro pro xvi d et idem Alexander tenet illud de Thoma Moubray pro viii d et Thomas de Priore et Prior de Rege.
Idem Alexander recipit de i messuagio quod fuit Johannis Ingelram i par cerotecarum pretii ob. et pro alio messuagio precipit de heredibus Ricardi de Fonte i denarium.
Walterus Textor tenet i burgagium de Priore pro iii s et Prior de Rege.
Hugo Page tenet i burgagium de Priore pro xii d et Prior de Rege.
Heredes Jordani Dandi tenet i curtilagium de Priore pro vii s iiii d et Prior de Rege.
Nicholaus de Wykewane tenet i burgagium de Priore pro iii d et Prior de Rege.
Gregorius Sutor tenet iii partes unius burgagii de Nicholao de Segrave pro xii s ii d et idem Gregorius tenet quartam partem illius burgagii de Petro Baron pro v s vi d et idem Petrus reddit inde prefato Nicholao per annum xiii d et idem Nicholaus tenet de Priore et Prior de Rege.
Heredes Johannis Ingelram tenet i burgagium de Priore pro xviii d et Prior de Rege.
Walterus le Taccher' tenet i cotagium de Johanne Tole per cartam pro vi d et idem Johannes reddit inde heredibus Nicholai Forwyn unum clavum gariofili et iidem heredes tenet de Priore et Prior de Rege.

[1] *Hawis que fuit* was also in a cartouche at the bottom of fol 102 b.

Robertus Sibely tenet i curtilagium de Johanne Tole pro xi d et idem Johannes de Blissota de Radeford pro i clavo gariofili.
Cristianus Fulky tenet i cotagium de dicto Johanne pro xi d et Johannes Tole tenet de Johanne Fulky pro i clavo gariofili.
Thomas Seled tenet ii burgagia de Priore pro ii s et Prior de Rege.
[fol 103 b] Idem Thomas tenet duo cotagia de Priore pro xviii d et dat heredibus Rogeri le Mouner inde ii paria cirotecarum pretii i d.
Idem Thomas tenet i cotagium de heredibus Willelmi le Redeknave pro i clavo gariofili.
Walterus Bacon tenet xiiii burgagia de quibus tenet unum in dominico de Priore pro vi d.
Heredes Walteri Pyhod tenent de predicto Waltero secundum burgagium pro xviii d et ii clavis gariofili et idem Walterus tenet illud de Priore pro xviii d.
Idem Walterus tenet tertium de Priore pro xii d.
Idem Walterus tenet unum curtilagium nomine quarti burgagii de Priore pro iii d.
Idem Walterus tenet i croftum nomine quinti burgagii de Priore pro i clavo gariofili.
Idem Walterus tenet sextum de Priore pro vi d.
Heredes Roberti de Eton tenent i messuagium de heredibus Nicholai Forthwyn pro vi s et heredes tenent de dicto Waltero pro iiii s.
Henricus Dybun tenet septimum burgagium de predicto Waltero per cartam pro ii s vi d.
Johannes Tole tenet i messuagium et i curtilagium de dicto burgagio de dicto Waltero per cartam pro ii d et i clavo gariofili et idem Walterus tenet totum burgagium de Priore pro ii d.
Idem Walterus tenet viii^{m} burgagium de Priore pro i clavo gariofili.
Thomas le Moubray tenet per cartam ix^{m} burgagium de predicto Waltero pro vi d et i pari cirotecarum pretii ob.
Walterus Durant tenet x^{m} burgagium per cartam de predicto Waltero pro vi d.
Henricus Oky tenet xi^{m} burgagium de Roberto de Waure pro iiii s et idem Robertus tenet illud per cartam de predicto Waltero Bacon pro xxv d.
Heredes Vincentii Kempe tenent xii^{m} burgagium per cartam de predicto Waltero pro xii d.
Willelmus Hawene tenet xiii^{m} burgagium per cartam de eodem Waltero pro iii s.
Willelmus de Pinnele tenet xiiii^{m} burgagium per cartam de eodem Waltero pro xx d et idem Walterus tenet viii curtilagia pertinentia ad vi ulteria burgagia de quibus tenet duo curtilagia in dominico.
Henricus le Knave tenet tertium curtilagium per cartam de eodem Waltero pro xii d.
Ricardus de Harnal tenet quartum curtilagium per cartam de predicto Waltero pro iii d.
Ricardus Midnyht tenet quintum curtilagium per cartam de eodem Waltero pro vi d.
Nicholaus le Mayden tenet sextum curtilagium per cartam de eodem Waltero pro vi d.
Alicia de Fonte tenet vii^{m} curtilagium de eodem Waltero pro ii d.
Ricardus le Tannur tenet viii^{m} curtilagium de eodem Waltero pro xii d.
Idem Walterus tenet ultimum burgagium cum pertinentiis de Priore pro vi d et Prior de Rege.
Heredes Willelmi Wylace tenent i burgagium de Priore pro xii d et Prior de Rege.
Johannes le Chapeleyn tenet tria burgagia de Priore pro iiii s et Prior de Rege.
Agnes filia Roberti de London tenet unum burgagium de Priore pro vi d et Prior de Rege.
Eadem Agnes tenet quandam partem terre per cartam de Isabella filia Jordani le Seler pro i clavo gariofili et Isabella de Priore et Prior de Rege.
Felicia la Salter' tenet i burgagium de Priore pro iiii d et Prior de Rege.

[fol 104]
Matilda de Whiteleye et Mariota soror ejus tenent i burgagium de Priore pro xx d et Prior de Rege.
Heredes Ricardi a la Fontayne tenent iii burgagia in dominico de Priore pro iiii s et Prior de Rege.
Thomas de Fackenham tenet i burgagium cum pertinentiis de predictis heredibus pro ii s et uno clavo gariofili et heredes tenent de Priore pro vi d.
Robertus de Fonte tenet i messuagium de dictis heredibus per cartam pro xvi d et heredes de Priore pro iiii d.
Iidem heredes tenent tria stallagia de Priore pro xv d et dimidia petra ceparum et iidem heredes precipiunt de tenemento quod fuit Willelmi de Allesleye xvi s et heredes reddunt inde Johanni de Warr' xii d.
Johannes le Blound tenet unum burgagium de Priore pro iiii d et Prior de Rege.
Idem Johannes tenet i curtilagium de Priore pro iiii d et de eodem curtilagio precipit Hugo le Breton vi d et v clavos gariofili.
Johannes le Mouner tenet in dominico quinque burgagia de Priore pro iiii s ii d et dimidia libra piperis et Prior de Rege.
Martinus Colebrond tenet duo burgagia unum in quo manet de quo sunt tria cotagia de quibus Adam filius Willelmi le Taillour tenet i cotagium de predicto Martino pro ix d per cartam.
Heredes Willelmi Frewyn et Magister Hospitalis Sancti Johannis Coventr' tenent aliud cotagium per cartam de predicto Martino pro xii d et predictus Martinus de Priore et Prior de Rege.
Henricus le Pestur tenet i cotagium de Henrico Oky pro i clavo gariofili et idem Henricus tenet de predicto Martino et Martinus de Priore pro ii s viii d.
Johannes Tole tenet i burgagium per cartam de predicto Martino pro xvi d et Martinus de Priore pro xvi d et Prior de Rege.
Gerardus de Alspath tenet i burgagium de Priore pro iiii d unde Johannes de Maxstok tenet medietatem pro iiii s.
Ricardus filius Henrici le Pestour tenet i burgagium de Priore pro iiii d et Prior de Rege.
Heredes Hugonis le Hosier tenent i burgagium de Priore pro xvi d et Prior de Rege.
Iidem heredes tenent medietatem alterius burgagii de Priore pro xii d.
Alexander de Coventr' tenet in Coventr' i burgagium de Priore pro xii d.
Idem Alexander tenet tria messuagia et i furnum cum pertinentiis de Priore sine redditu sed post mortem ipsius Alexandris heredes sui reddent Priori per annum xx s.
Idem Alexander tenet i messuagium in quo manet de Priore pro viii d.
Idem Alexander tenet aliud messuagium de Priore pro xii d.
Idem Alexander tenet aliud messuagium de Johanne le Blound pro xii d et unum curtilagium de eodem pro i clavo gariofili.
[fol 104 b] Idem Alexander tenet duo messuagia de Johanne de Warr' pro v s et ii gardinia de Roberto de Chilton pro ii clavis gariofili.
Item[1] Alexander tenet xii denarios redditus ex dimissione dicti Prioris ad vitam suam tamen et xvi denarios redditus in vico de Sponne et x solidos et viii denarios redditus in vico de Gosford ex dimissione Prioris ad vitam suam.
Idem Alexander tenet iiii messuagia et i furnum ex dimissione ipsius Prioris ad vitam ipsius Alexandris et Isabelle uxoris ejus pro suo servicio.
Idem Alexander tenet i curtilagium de Waltero Bacon pro i clavo gariofili et Walterus de Priore et Prior de Rege.
Ricardus Forthwyn tenet v burgagia cum pertinentiis de Priore de quibus Johannes de Condulme tenet unum burgagium per cartam.
Henricus le Pestour' tenet i burgagium per cartam de Johanne de Condelme pro ii s.

[1] sic

Walterus le Coupere tenet i burgagium per cartam de dicto Johanne pro xii d.
Ricardus Midnyth tenet i burgagium per cartam de dicto Johanne pro xx d.
Predictus Johannes de Condelme tenet iiii cotagia de predicto Ricardo pro vi d per cartam.
Nicholaus Jory tenet i cotagium de predicto Johanne pro xii d per cartam.
Radulphus de Buggyng tenet i cotagium de predicto Johanne per cartam pro x d.
Ricardus le Noreys tenet i cotagium de dicto Johanne per cartam pro x d et Johannes de Priore et Prior de Rege.
Galfridus de Langele tenet i burgagium in quo sunt tria cotagia et vi curtilagia cum pertinentiis de quibus Hugo le Feure tenet i curtilagium per cartam de eodem Galfrido pro x d.
Heredes Johannis Ingelram tenent i curtilagium per cartam de eodem Galfrido pro viii d.
Walterus Bacon tenet i cotagium et ii curtilagia per cartam de eodem pro xviii d.
Ricardus Gilberd tenet i curtilagium per cartam de eodem Galfrido pro xviii d.
Johannes le Bel tenet i cotagium de eodem pro xx d per cartam.
Johannes Minot tenet unum cotagium per cartam de eodem pro iii s.
Henricus de Hynkel' tenet i curtilagium de eodem per cartam pro xx d.
Sacrista Prioratus Coventr' tenet cotagium de eodem per cartam pro v s.
Magister Hospitalis Sancti Johannis Coventr' tenet unum gardinium de eodem per cartam pro i libra cimini et dictus Galfridus tenet de Priore pro vi s iiii d et Prior de Rege.
Johannes de Warr' tenet totum tenementum suum in Coventr' de Priore pro xv s ii d et Prior de Rege.
Unde Walterus Donart tenet i burgagium de dicto Johanne per cartam pro iiii s.
Heredes Willelmi Toly tenet i burgagium de eodem Johanne pro iiii s per cartam.
Robertus de Lich' tenet i burgagium de dicto Johanne pro vi s per cartam.
Alicia de Ponte tenet i burgagium de eodem Johanne per cartam pro ii s.
Willelmus Pake tenet i burgagium de eodem per cartam pro iiii s.
Henricus de Sartrino tenet i burgagium de eodem per cartam pro ii s.
Galfridus le Pestour' tenet quandam partem i burgagii de dicto Johanne per cartam pro iiii s.
Heredes Willelmi le Serjaunt tenent quandam partem unius burgagii de eodem per cartam pro xx d.
Martinus le Pestour' tenet quandam partem unius burgagii per cartam de dicto Johanne pro xx d.

[fol 105]

Johannes de Maxstok tenet quandam partem unius burgagii per cartam de dicto Johanne pro xx d.
Andreas de Stretton tenet quandam partem unius burgagii per cartam de dicto Johanne pro xii d.
Alexander le Vineter' tenet i burgagium de dicto Johanne per cartam pro v s.
Heredes Hugonis le Feure tenet i burgagium de dicto Johanne pro xii d.
Raginaldus[1] le Pestour' tenet i messuagium per cartam de dicto Johanne pro v s et idem Johannes de heredibus Henrici de Hastyng pro vi d.
Johannes Pihod tenet i cotagium per cartam de dicto Johanne pro xii d.
Johannes de Filongl' tenet i cotagium per cartam de dicto Johanne pro xii d.
Johannes Tole tenet i cotagium per cartam de dicto Johanne pro iiii s.
Johannes le Mason tenet i cotagium per cartam de dicto Johanne pro i clavo gariofili.
Magister Hospitalis Sancti Johannis Coventr' tenet i cotagium per cartam de dicto Johanne pro ii s.
Robertus de Doggelone tenet i cotagium per cartam de dicto Johanne pro xii d.

[1] sic

Heredes Thome le Portere tenent i cotagium per cartam de dicto Johanne pro xii d.
Heredes Walteri le Whyte tenent i cotagium per cartam de dicto Johanne pro ii s.
Robertus le Chapeleyne tenet i cotagium per cartam de dicto Johanne pro xii d.
Thomas le Moubray tenet i curtilagium per cartam de dicto Johanne pro xii d.
Robertus filius Johannis le Orfeure tenet i burgagium in dominico de Priore pro vi d.
Idem Robertus tenet i messuagium de dicto Priore pro xii s et Prior de Rege.
Johannes de Corleye tenet i messuagium de Willelmo Uttyng per cartam pro iii s et Willelmus tenet de heredibus Roberti de Recham per cartam pro i pari cirotecarum et heredes de Priore et Prior de Rege.
Johannes de Franckevill tenet ii messuagia de Priore pro ii s et Prior de Rege.
Johannes le Bel capellanus tenet i burgagium cum pertinentiis de Priore pro ii s ii d et Prior de Rege.
Margeria Pake tenet quandam partem unius burgagii in dominico de Priore pro xxv d et Prior de Rege.
Henricus le Pestour' tenet i cotagium de dicta Margeria per cartam pro i clavo gariofili.
Idem Henricus tenet quandam partem unius messuagii de dicta Margeria per cartam pro i clavo gariofili.
Galfridus de Whiteleie tenet quandam partem unius messuagii de dicta Margeria per cartam pro iiii d et Margeria de Priore et Prior de Rege.
Eadem Margeria et Johannes filius Ade le Clerk tenent i burgagium in dominico de Priore pro ii s vi d et Prior de Rege.
Johannes de Ebriton tenet unum burgagium in capite de Priore pro xii d et Willelmus de Copston tenet illud de heredibus Nicholai Forthwyne pro v s et iidem heredes de predicto Johanne pro xii d per cartam et Johannes de Priore pro xii d et Prior de Rege.
Willelmus de Copston tenet per legem Anglie unum burgagium de Priore pro i d ob. et heredes Willelmi Toly tenent illud de dicto Willelmo per cartam pro iiii d et Willelmus tenet de Priore et Prior de Rege.
Idem Willemus tenet aliud burgagium de quo Robertus Reymund tenet i cotagium de predicto Willelmo per cartam pro vi d et Willelmus tenet de Priore per servicium unius floris rose et Prior de Rege.
Johannes Lewyn tenet v burgagia in dominico de Priore et dat pro primo in quo manet eidem Priori iiii s et pro secundo reddit eidem Priori iiii s et pro tertio iii d.
[fol 105 b] Idem Johannes tenet unum cotagium de heredibus Nicholai Warin pro i clavo gariofili et recipit de Roberto Hereberd pro quodam crofto xv d.
Adam Colebrond tenet unum cotagium de predicto Johanne per cartam pro xviii d.
Robertus de Asseby tenet unum cotagium de predicto Johanne pro xii d per cartam.
Ricardus de Harnale tenet i cotagium per cartam de predicto Johanne pro xii d.
Predictus Johannes reddit Priori pro alio cotagio iiii d et pro alio ii s et Prior tenet de Rege.
Johannes le Forest(er) tenet unum cotagium de predicto Johanne per cartam pro iiii s et Johannes tenet de Priore et Prior de Rege.
Walterus Durant tenet unum cotagium de predicto Johanne per cartam pro xviii d.
Predictus Johannes Lewyn tenet xv seliones terre de Johanne Scot pro iii d.
Idem Johannes tenet i croftum de Priore pro ii s viii d et Prior de Rege.
Heredes Ricardi de Pacwod tenent i burgagium in dominico de Priore pro x d et Prior de Rege.
Alicia filia Johannis Minot tenet i burgagium de Priore pro iiii d ob. et Prior de Rege.
Hugo Pope tenet i burgagium de Priore pro viii d et Prior de Rege.
Heredes Johannis le Furn(er) tenet i burgagium de Priore pro iii d et Prior de Rege.
Reginaldus de la Fermery tenet i burgagium de Priore pro xii d et Prior de Rege.
Willelmus Waldgyve tenet i burgagium et Johannes le Tixtor tenet illud de dicto

Willelmo per cartam pro iiii s et Willelmus tenet de Priore pro ii s et Prior de Rege.
Adam le Carpent(er) tenet i burgagium de Priore pro ii s et Prior de Rege.
Henricus de Gildentr' tenet i burgagium de Priore pro ii s et Prior de Rege.
Willelmus le Lepper tenet i burgagium de Priore pro ii s viii d et Prior de Rege.
Willelmus le Lokier tenet i burgagium de Priore pro vi d et Prior de Rege.
Heredes Ranulphi de Frankton tenent vi burgagia de Priore de quibus Johannes Tole tenet primum burgagium cum quadam parte terre de eisdem heredibus pro xvi s et iidem heredes tenent illud burgagium de Priore et Prior de Rege.
Willelmus Illory tenet i burgagium de eisdem heredibus pro ii s et heredes de Priore pro vi d et Prior de Rege.
Isabella filia Thome Blacwyn tenet i burgagium de eisdem heredibus pro v s vi d ob. et heredes de Priore pro x d et Prior de Rege.
Johannes filius Galfridi le Feure Henricus filius Stephani et Johannes filius Ricardi tenent i burgagium de eisdem heredibus pro ii s ix d et heredes de Priore et Prior de Rege.
Petrus le[1] Cotesbech et Mariota uxor ejus tenent i burgagium in dominico de Priore pro vi d et Prior de Rege.
Iidem Petrus et Mariota tenent in dominico quoddam curtilagium de heredibus Willelmi le Torno(ur) pro i clavo gariofili.
Matilda filia Ricardi tenet i burgagium cum pertinentiis de Priore pro viii d et Prior de Rege et Henricus de Hynkel' tenet idem burgagium de dicta Matilda per cartam pro v s et predicta Matilda de Priore et Prior de Rege.

[fol 106]
Thomas Moubray tenet iiii burgagia in dominico et tria cotagia que tenentur de ipso et tenet primum burgagium de Priore pro iiii s et aliud de eodem pro iiii d et aliud de eodem pro ii s et tenet i curtilagium de eodem pro iiii d et Prior de Rege.
Johannes filius Henrici de Radeford tenet i cotagium de predicto Thoma per cartam pro x d.
Alexander de Moubray tenet ii cotagia de dicto Thoma pro xiiii d.
Predictus Thomas tenet i cotagium de ipso Priore pro xx d et est de feodo Johanni Herberd.
Idem Thomas et Thomas Marie et Nicholaus de Allespath tenent per legem Anglie in dominico i croftum de Priore pro xviii d et Prior de Rege.
Thomas Marie tenet ii burgagia de Priore pro ii s et Prior de Rege.
Robertus de Ludlawe tenet i burgagium de predicto Thoma pro ii s.
Nicholaus de Allespath tenet tria burgagia in dominico de Priore pro v s iiii d et Prior de Rege.
Idem Nicholaus habet ii cotagia in dictis burgagiis de quibus Johannes Franceis tenet i de dicto Nicholao pro xx d per cartam et Walterus Oslok tenet aliud de eodem Nicholao pro xvi d per cartam.
Robertus de Hynkel' et Thomas de Moubray tenent i burgagium cum pertinentiis de Priore pro xxviii d.
Thomas le Moubray recipit de quodam stallagio in le Bochery quod Prior de Coventr' tenet in dominico pro viii d[2].
Ranulphus de Condelm' tenet i cotagium de Priore pro iiii s et Prior de Rege.
Simon de Stonle tenet i messuagium de Priore pro vi s vi d et reddendo inde Magistro Johanni de Billesle xii d et Prior tenet de Rege.
Henricus le Pestour' tenet i messuagium de Priore pro v s et Prior de Rege.
Idem Henricus tenet i burgagium de Priore pro xii d et aliud burgagium de eodem pro iiii d ob. et aliud burgagium de eodem pro vi d et i messuagium de eodem pro

[1] sic
[2] Entry is obviously incomplete

xiii s et tenet quoddam tenementum de eodem pro iii d et ii curtilagia de eodem pro iii s.

Idem Henricus tenet quoddam tenementum de eodem pro vi d et tenet aliud tenementum de Margeria Pake pro i clavo gariofili et Margeria tenet de Priore et Prior de Rege.

Idem Henricus tenet quoddam tenementum ibidem de heredibus Nicholai Forthwyn pro ii s et heredes de Priore et Prior de Rege.

Idem Henricus tenet quoddam tenementum ibidem de heredibus Magistri Ricardi le Vineter' pro i clavo gariofili et heredes de Priore et Prior de Rege.

Idem Henricus tenet quoddam tenementum de Ranulpho de Frankton pro xi s iiii d et Ranulphus de Priore et Prior de Rege.

Idem Henricus tenet quoddam tenementum de heredibus Alexandri de Ruyton pro i clavo gariofili et iidem heredes de Martino Colebrond pro i clavo gariofili et Martinus de Priore et Prior de Rege.

Alanus le Keu tenet quoddam tenementum de eodem Henrico pro xii d et Henricus de Priore pro vi d et Prior de Rege.

Willelmus le Carpenter tenet quoddam tenementum de predicto Henrico pro ii s et Henricus de Priore pro xii d et Prior de Rege.

Heredes Ricardi de Fonte tenent quoddam tenementum de predicto Henrico pro ii s et Henricus de Priore pro vi d et Prior de Rege.

Willelmus de Bannebur' tenet quoddam tenementum de predicto Henrico pro v s vi d.

Ricardus le Taillo(ur)[1] tenet aliud tenementum de eodem Henrico pro vi s.

[fol 106 b] Henricus le Taillo(ur)[2] tenet i cotagium de predicto Henrico Pistor' pro ii s vi d et idem Henricus tenet totum illud tenementum de Roberto Herberd pro vii s ix d et Robertus de Priore et Prior de Rege.

Predictus Henricus precipit de quadam domo que fuit Willelmi Frewyne iiii d per annum.

Rogerus le Fuller' tenet quoddam tenementum de predicto Henrico pro iii s et Henricus de Roberto de Doglane pro i clavo gariofili et Robertus de Magistro Hospitalis Sancti Johannis Coventr' et Magister de Priore et Prior de Rege.

Nicholaus Allespath et Thomas Marie tenent quoddam tenementum de predicto Henrico pro xii d.

Ricardus Attegrene tenet quoddam tenementum de predicto Henrico pro uno pari cirotecarum.

Alexander de Moubraye tenet quoddam tenementum de dicto Henrico pro i pari cirotecarum.

Idem Henricus tenet quoddam tenementum de Ricardo Pikedepere pro i rosa et Ricardus de Priore et Prior de Rege.

Willelmus filius Ranulphi de Radeford tenet i messuagium cum pertinentiis de predicto Henrico pro ii s.

Adam Colebrond tenet unum curtilagium de predicto Henrico pro i clavo gariofili et idem Henricus de Priore et Prior de Rege.

Willelmus Hawen tenet i burgagium in dominico de Priore pro iii s vi d et Prior de Rege.

Idem Willelmus tenet i messuagium de Waltero Bacon pro iii s et Walterus de Priore et Prior de Rege.

Idem Walterus tenet i tenementum de dicto Willelmo pro ii s et idem Willelmus tenet unum burgagium de Priore pro xii d et Prior de Rege.

1 *Taillo'* in MS. Is this entry and the previous one of William de Bannebur' a repetition of the entry on fol 101 b? The rents of these tenements are the same as those of the cottages held by Walter and Richard there, and likewise Henry Pistor holds them both of Robert Herberd.

2 As n. 1.

Johanna filia Johannis de la Haye recipit per annum de domo Alani le Boch(er)[1] ii s et de domo Petri Mons iii s et de messuagio Thome Marie ii s.

Johannes de la Hay precipit de quodam tenemento ad portam cimiterii quod est de Sa[2] xi s vi d per annum.

Robertus de Chilton[3] tenet in capite de Priore unum burgagium in quo manet pro xxii d et Prior de Rege.

Idem Robertus tenet i furnum de eodem Priore in Westgard pro xii d et Prior de Rege.

Idem Robertus tenet i messuagium de Roberto Herberd pro vi d et Robertus de Priore et Prior de Rege.

Heredes Simonis de Daventr' tenent de dicto Roberto i cotagium pro ii s et Robertus de Priore et Prior de Rege.

Matilda le Lou tenet i messuagium de dicto Roberto pro i clavo gariofili et Robertus de Priore et Prior de Rege.

Alexander le Vineter' tenet de dicto Roberto ii curtilagia pro ii clavis gariofili et Robertus de Priore et Prior de Rege.

Predictus Robertus tenet de Johanne le Marshall i messuagium pro iii d et Johannes de Priore et Prior de Rege.

Magister Hospitalis Sancti Johannis de Coventr' tenet de dicto Roberto ii curtilagia pro i d ob.

Walterus Bacon tenet tria curtilagia de dicto Roberto pro viii d.

Idem Robertus tenet de feodo Rogeri de Lodelawe vii curtilagia reddendo inde per annum Priori i clavum gariofili et Prior de Rege.

Ricardus le Dubber' tenet i cotagium de Willelmo Rinuld per cartam pro vi d et i pari cirotecarum pretii ob. et idem Willelmus tenet de Nicholao Dale et Nicholaus de Priore et Prior de Rege.

[fol 107]

Predictus Robertus de Chilton tenet iii shoppas in capite de Priore pro i clavo gariofili et Prior de Rege.

Thomas de Stapleton precipit de heredibus Nicholai Forthwyne pro uno cotagio xvi d et de heredibus Willelmi de Staynton pro i messuagio vii s et de Simone Pat pro i messuagio v s et de Rogero le Pesthour pro i messuagio vii s et idem Thomas tenet i messuagium de Magistro Hospitalis Sancti Johannis de Coventr' pro ii s.

Willelmus Rynuld tenet i cotagium de Priore per cartam pro xii d et Prior de Rege.

Galfridus le Bretun tenet i cotagium de Hugone Bretun pro ii s.

Walterus Bacon tenet i curtilagium de Priore pro xii d.

Pars Comitis

Alanus le Peschur tenet i burgagium in dominico de Priore pro x d et Prior de heredibus Roberti de Monte Alto et heredes de Rege quo servicio nescitur.

Henricus Dobedy tenet i burgagium de Priore pro vi d et Prior de predictis heredibus et heredes de Rege.

Ricardus Beyvill' tenet tria burgagia de Priore pro vi s vi d et Prior [etc].[4]

Idem Ricardus tenet i burgagium de Priore pro xviii d et Ricardus de Esseby tenet illud de eodem Ricardo pro ii s.

Nicholaus de Wykewane tenet ii burgagia de Priore pro xv d et Prior [etc].

Ricardus le Tixtor tenet i burgagium de predicto Nicholao pro v d et Nicholaus de Priore pro iii d.

Thomas de Caumpedene tenet aliud burgagium de predicto Nicholao pro xii d et Nicholaus de Priore pro xii d.

1 *Boch'* in MS.

2 for *Sacrista*?

3 *Tenura in capite* written in margin in later hand.

4 [Etc]. indicates that an entry ends with *Prior de heredibus Roberti de Monte Alto et heredes de Rege* or *Prior de predictis heredibus et heredes de Rege.*

Johannes le Chapeleyne tenet i burgagium de Priore pro xii d et Prior [etc].
Idem Johannes tenet i cotagium reddendo inde altari Beate Marie in Prioratu Coventr' viii d et Gilberto de Longedon i clavum gariofili
Johannes Aylmer' tenet i burgagium in quo manet et sunt ibi tria cotagia de quibus Osbertus Aguler' tenet i cotagium per cartam de dicto Johanne pro ii s.
Nicholaus Osbern tenet aliud cotagium per cartam de dicto Johanne pro iis ii d.
Robertus de Coteswold tenet tertium cotagium de dicto Johanne pro i d et idem Johannes tenet totum burgagium de Priore pro vi d et Prior [etc].
Johannes de Gloucestre tenet v burgagia cum pertinentiis de Priore in dominico pro xii s viii d et inveniet i hominem in autumpno et pro ii gallinis ad natale domini et habet ibi quinque cotagia de quibus:
Galfridus filius Johannis tenet i cotagium per cartam de predicto Johanne pro ii d.
Richerus de Weston tenet secundum cotagium de dicto Johanne per cartam pro xii d.
[fol 107 b] Henricus de Lilleborne tenet tertium cotagium de dicto Johanne per cartam pro iii s.
Martinus le Lokywer' tenet quartum cotagium de dicto Johanne per cartam pro xi d.
Westmayns[1] tenet quintum cotagium de dicto Johanne per cartam pro xii d et Johannes de Priore et Prior [etc].
Rogerus de Hales tenet i burgagium de Priore pro xviii d et Prior [etc].
Willelmus de Neweton tenet i burgagium in dominico de Priore de quo Stephanus le Tixtor tenet per cartam unum cotagium de eodem Willelmo pro ob. et uno clavo gariofili et Priori i d.
Henricus Dobedy tenet aliud cotagium per cartam de predicto Willelmo pro viii d et idem Willelmus tenet totum burgagium de Priore pro xii d et Prior [etc].
Willelmus de Pinele tenet tertiam partem unius burgagii et Petrus Baron tenet illam partem de ipso per cartam pro ii s et Willelmus tenet de Priore pro iiii d et Prior [etc].
Willelmus Uttyng' tenet ii messuagia per cartam de Priore pro iiii s vi d et Prior ut supra.
Idem Willelmus tenet i cotagium de heredibus Ricardi de Wigorn' pro ob. et heredes de Prior [etc].
Emma Gamel tenet i cotagium de predicto Willelmo pro xii d et Willelmus de Rogero le Clerk et Rogerus de Priore et Prior [etc].
Matillda de Balleshal et Walterus filius [ejus][2] tenent i burgagium in dominico de Priore pro xii d et Prior [etc].
Walterus Bacon tenet tria burgagia de quibus tenet unum in dominico.
Robertus in le Hurne tenet i burgagium de Willelmo Waldgyve pro vi d et Willelmus tenet illud de predicto Waltero pro i d ob. per cartam et Walterus tenet illa burgagia de Priore pro vi d.
Ricardus Forthwyne tenet i burgagium de predicto Waltero per cartam pro vi d et Walterus de Priore pro iiii d et Prior [etc].
Willelmus Sleth tenet i messuagium de predicto Waltero pro vi d per cartam et Walterus de Priore pro eodem redditu et Prior ut supra.
Heredes Johannis le Orfeure tenent vi cotagia de predicto Waltero pro ii s et Walterus de Priore et Prior ut supra.
Agnes filia Willelmi le Roc tenet ii burgagia in dominico de Priore pro iiii s x d.
Robertus in le Hurne tenet i cotagium de dicta Agnete per cartam pro xvi d.
Ingelwridus[3] tenet aliud cotagium de dicta Agnete per cartam pro iiii d et Agnes tenet de Priore et Prior ut supra.

[1] sic
[2] Omitted from MS.
[3] sic

Robertus de Lodelawe tenet iii burgagia de Priore pro xviii d de quibus Adam a la Grene tenet primum de ipso Roberto per cartam pro xxi d.

Magister Ricardus de Burton tenet secundum burgagium de dicto Roberto per cartam pro i pari cirotecarum pretii ob.

Hugo de Oxon' tenet tertium burgagium de predicto Roberto pro xii d et i pari cirotecarum

[fol 108]

pretii ob. et iii gallinis per cartam et idem Robertus tenet de Priore pro xii d et iii gall(inis) ad natale domini.

Idem Robertus tenet tria cotagia de quibus Thomas filius Johannis de Lodelawe tenet duo de dicto Roberto per cartam pro ii s et i pari cirotecarum pretii i d et idem Robertus tenet de Priore pro ii s.

Robertus en le Hurne tenet tertium cotagium de dicto Roberto pro i flore rose et Robertus de Priore et Prior etc.

Alexander le Riche tenet i burgagium de Priore pro xii d et Prior de heredibus ut supra.

Willelmus Rinuld tenet medietatem unius burgagii per cartam de dicto Alexandro pro ix d.

Robertus Reymond tenet i burgagium de Priore pro xii d et Prior ut supra.

Beatrix filia Ade de Kideministr' tenet i messuagium per cartam de Priore pro xii d et Prior etc.

Johannes de Bosco tenet i burgagium de Priore pro xiiii d et habet ix cotagia unde Thomas Simond tenet i cotagium per cartam de ipso Johanne pro xii d.

Hugo Wyne et Henricus le Feure tenent secundum cotagium de ipso Johanne per cartam pro x d.

Thomas de Burbache tenet tertium cotagium per cartam de eodem Johanne pro xii d.

Walterus Helwys tenet quartum cotagium per cartam de predicto Johanne pro xiii d.

Willelmus Scot tenet quintum cotagium per cartam de predicto Johanne pro vi d.

Nicholaus Pake tenet sextum cotagium per cartam de ipso Johanne pro iiii d.

Radulphus le Taillour tenet septimum cotagium per cartam de ipso Johanne pro v d.

Isabella que fuit uxor Henrici Oisel tenet viii^{m} cotagium per cartam de ipso Johanne pro xii d.

Alicia de Stoke tenet nonum cotagium per cartam de ipso Johanne pro ii d.

Galfridus de Langeleye[1] tenet in dominico unum messuagium ii carucatas terre duo molendina aquatica viii cotagia cum quadam grava et aliis pertinentiis suis in Shorteleye juxta Coventr' de Priore de Coventr' per servicium lvii s iiii d et unius libre piperis et Prior [etc]. quo servicio nescitur.

Idem Galfridus habet cotarios qui tenent[2] de se in Coventr' cotagia subscripta:

[1] On the right hand side beginning with this entry there is a long marginal note in a sixteenth century hand. It reads: 'this Langley auncestor to Ferrers of Tomworth was lorde of Wykyn and these mylnes the said Ferrers hath at this day and they lye under the Charter house specified also in Coventrie charter'. The note continues opposite Richard le Brocher's entry and down to the bottom of the folio as follows: 'Note that the lordship of Wyken and the said premisses be of the fee of Roger de Monte Alto who was Lorde of Chilesmore as here and after is wryten but note that Stichall was never under this fee, but under the fee of the bishop who held of the Kinge always, and therefore hit apperith that Ferrers land in Stichall is of the fee of Stychall and not of the fee of Chilesmore or parcell of the manor of Wycken, for to this day hit never paid chief to Chilesmore, but to the bishop frome the begynnge. And the same chief which you must read in the note of Stichall hereafter ensuinge, is paid to this day.' It was written by Arthur Gregory – see R. Bearman: *The Gregorys of Stivichall in the Sixteenth Century*, p. 33.

[2] *tenet* in MS.

Johannes de Glovern' tenet i cotagium per cartam de ipso Galfrido pro xii d.
Ricardus le Brocher' tenet i cotagium de dicto Galfrido per cartam pro xii d.
Henricus Oysel tenet i cotagium de dicto Galfrido per cartam xii d.
Walterus Hecke tenet unum cotagium de dicto Galfrido per cartam pro iii s.
Ricardus Burgeys tenet i cotagium de dicto Galfrido per cartam pro xii d.
Alexander Brockeston tenet i cotagium de dicto Galfrido per cartam pro viii s.
Richerus de Weston tenet i cotagium per cartam de ipso Galfrido pro i d.
Ricardus filius Richeri tenet i cotagium de ipso Galfrido per cartam pro xviii d.
Walterus Helewys tenet i cotagium per cartam de ipso Galfrido pro ii s viii d et pro **[fol 108 b]** iiii hominibus in autumpno per i diem et iiii gallinis[1] per annum.
Henricus de Denecastr' tenet i cotagium de predicto Galfrido pro xxi d.
Heredes de Johannes de Ponte Fracto tenent i cotagium per cartam de ipso Galfrido pro vi d.
Nicholaus de Allespath tenet i cotagium de eodem Galfrido per cartam pro viii d.
Henricus le Pestur' tenet i cotagium per cartam de ipso Galfrido pro xiiii d.
Robertus de Allesle tenet i cotagium per cartam de ipso Galfrido pro xvi d.
Willelmus de Eggesfeld tenet i cotagium per cartam de ipso Galfrido pro iii s.
Thomas de Barham tenet duo cotagia per cartam de ipso Galfrido pro ii s.
Rogerus le Burser' tenet unum cotagium de predicto Galfrido per cartam pro viii d et Priori de Kenilworth iiii s pro eodem.
Thomas de Fackenham tenet iii cotagia per cartam de predicto Galfrido pro xiii s et Abbati de Stonle xii d pro eodem.
Walterus de Wynchelese tenet i cotagium de predicto Galfrido per cartam pro viii s et pro i gallina et uno homine in autumpno.
Alicia de Norf' tenet unum cotagium per cartam de dicto Galfrido pro una gallina et ad inveniendum eidem Galfrido unum hominem in autumpno per unum diem.
Willelmus Crompe tenet unum cotagium per cartam de predicto Galfrido pro iiii s ii d et una gallina et inveniet unum hominem in autumpno per diem[2]
Johannes Scot tenet i cotagium de predicto Galfrido per cartam pro ii s vi d et una gallina et inveniet i hominem in autumpno per i diem.
Adam Russel tenet i cotagium de predicto Galfrido per cartam pro ii s vi d et uno gallo et inveniet i hominem in autumpno per i diem.
Benedictus le Floute(r)[3] tenet i cotagium de predicto Galfrido per cartam pro xii d.
Galfridus Tixtor tenet i cotagium per cartam de predicto Galfrido pro xviii d.
Ricardus de Esseby tenet ii cotagia per cartam de ipso Galfrido pro iiii s x d.
Wymark la Botene(r)[4] tenet i cotagium per cartam de predicto Galfrido pro x d.
Rogerus de Knychton tenet i cotagium per cartam de ipso Galfrido pro x d.
Thomas de Stapelton tenet i cotagium per cartam de predicto Galfrido pro ii s.
Robertus le Moun(er) tenet x cotagia per cartam de predicto Galfrido pro v s x d.
Ricardus de Newerk tenet i cotagium per cartam de predicto Galfrido pro ii s.
Galfridus le Lef tenet ii cotagia cum pertinentiis per cartam de predicto Galfrido pro vi s vi d.
Willelmus de Whitele tenet i cotagium per cartam de dicto Galfrido pro ii s.
Petrus Baron tenet ii cotagia per cartam de predicto Galfrido pro iiii s vi d.
Walterus le Comber' tenet i cotagium per cartam de predicto Galfrido pro iii s viii d.
Heredes Roberti le Mouner tenent i cotagium per cartam de predicto Galfrido pro ii s.

[1] The abbreviation *gall'* has been extended in the feminine, unless the masculine is specifically indicated.

[2] sic

[3] *Floute'* in MS.

[4] *la Botene'* in MS.

[fol 109]
Heredes Johanni de Lodelawe tenent i cotagium per cartam de ipso Galfrido pro viii d.
Galfridus filius Johannis tenet i cotagium per cartam de predicto Galfrido pro xx d
Willelmus le Bousetur' tenet i cotagium de Galfrido de Langley per cartam pro viii d et i gallina et i homine in autumpno per i diem.
Hugo le Bousetur' tenet i cotagium de eodem Galfrido per cartam pro viii d.
Christiana de Hampton tenet i cotagium de dicto Galfrido per cartam pro ii s.
Gilbertus Corewen' tenet i cotagium de eodem Galfrido per cartam pro xii d.
Adam le Feure tenet i cotagium de eodem Galfrido per cartam pro xii d.
Margeria de Rem tenet i cotagium de eodem Galfrido per cartam pro xii d.
Johannes le Breus tenet i cotagium de eodem Galfrido per cartam pro xx d et ii gallinis et ii hominibus in autumpno per i diem.
Robertus le Romonger' tenet i cotagium de predicto Galfrido per cartam pro ii s viii d et ii gallinis et ii hominibus in autumpno per i diem.
Robertus de Codeswold tenet i cotagium de predicto Galfrido per cartam pro xii d et duabus gallinis et ii hominibus in autumpno per i diem.
Heredes Willelmi Somer' tenent ii cotagia per cartam de dicto Galfrido pro viii d et ii gallinis et ii hominibus in autumpno per i diem.
Robertus Kyng tenet i cotagium de eodem Galfrido pro viii d et i gallina et i homine in autumpno per i diem per cartam.
Robertus Hereberd tenet iiii burgagia de Priore de Coventr' pro xx d et Prior [etc]. de quibus Henricus le Pestour' tenet i burgagium de dicto Roberto per cartam pro vi d et Robertus de Priore pro v d.
Thomas filius Henrici le Seler' tenet i burgagium de predicto Roberto per cartam pro iiii gallinis et Robertus de Priore pro i d.
Predictus Robertus tenet i burgagium in dominico suo de Priore pro v d.
Johannes de Frankevill tenet i cotagium de predicto Roberto per cartam pro vi d.
Alicia de Cestr' tenet i cotagium de predicto Roberto[1] et ii gallinis per cartam et Robertus de Priore pro toto burgagio v d et Prior [etc].
Johannes Tole tenet i burgagium de predicto Roberto per cartam pro xviii d et idem Robertus de Priore pro iiii d et Prior [etc].
Magister Ricardus de Burton et Petronilla uxor ejus tenent iiii burgagia et quoddam molendinum aquaticum de Priore pro xxxiiii s vi d et Prior [etc]. In quibus burgagiis dicti Ricardus et Petronilla habent xxviii cotarios et xviii alios tenentes curtilagia qui omnes tenent per cartam videlicet Robertus le Mouner tenet ii cotagia de eisdem pro v s.
[fol 109 b] Adam filius Milonis tenet i cotagium de eisdem Ricardo et Petronilla pro xx d.
Galfridus le Lef tenet ii cotagia de eisdem pro iiii s ii d.
Johannes le Butter' tenet i cotagium de eisdem Ricardo et Petronilla pro iii s.
Richerus de Weston tenet i cotagium et ii curtilagia de eisdem pro iii s.
Johannes de Mildesby tenet i curtilagium de eisdem pro vi d.
Johannes le Loker' tenet i curtilagium de eisdem pro vi d.
Benedictus le Flouter tenet i curtilagium de eisdem pro viii d.
Rogerus filius Rogeri le Clerk tenet i cotagium de eisdem pro iiii s.
Willelmus le Colle tenet i cotagium de eisdem pro ii s et ii hominibus in autumpno per i diem et ii gallinis ad natale domini.
Heredes Nicholai de Bokervill tenent i curtilagium de eisdem Ricardo et Petronilla pro x d.
Nicholaus Maiden tenet i cotagium de eisdem Ricardo et Petronilla pro v d.
Dulcia la Webbe tenet i curtilagium de eisdem pro v d.
Robertus le Quarreur tenet i curtilagium de eisdem pro v d.

[1] An omission in the MS; probably *pro* and the money rent should precede *et ii gallinis.*

Radulphus Morcok tenet i curtilagium de eisdem pro xiii d ob.
Ricardus Wale tenet i curtilagium de eisdem pro xvi d.
Thomas Tilor tenet i curtilagium de eisdem pro xviii d.
Heredes Roberti de Norff' tenent i curtilagium de eisdem pro xii d.
Robertus a la Barre tenet i curtilagium de eisdem pro xii d.
Thomas Hally tenet i cotagium de eisdem pro iii s et ii hominibus in autumpno per i diem et iii gallinis ad natale domini.
Rogerus le Peynto(ur)[1] tenet i cotagium de eisdem pro xvi d.
Johannes le Somenur' tenet i cotagium de eisdem pro xii d et i pari cirotecarum pretii ob.
Thomas de Stapelton tenet i burgagium et ii cotagia de eisdem pro ix s.
Willelmus Scot tenet i curtilagium de eisdem pro xii d.
Nicholaus de Wykewan' tenet iii cotagia de eisdem pro iiii s.
Henricus le Cartsadeler tenet i cotagium de eisdem pro iiii s.
Thomas Haldayn tenet iii cotagia de eisdem pro v s.
Johannes de Glouc' tenet i cotagium de eisdem pro ii s.
Thomas de Pollesworth et Alicia uxor ejus tenent ii cotagia de eisdem pro vii s ii d.
Johannes Dobbedy tenet i cotagium de eisdem pro xii d.
Robertus le Orfeur' tenet i cotagium de eisdem pro xviii d et i libra piperis.
Heredes Walteri le Orfeure tenent i curtilagium de eisdem pro vi d.
Predicti Ricardus et Petronilla tenent in dominico suo ii cotagia.
Adam Hert tenet i cotagium de eisdem pro xlii d.

[fol 110]
Ricardus Wake tenet i cotagium de predictis Ricardo et Petronilla pro ii s.
Heredes Willelmi Athelm' tenent i cotagium de eisdem pro ii s et iiii gallinis ad natale domini et iiii hominibus in autumpno per i diem.
Margeria Grenecurtel tenet i cotagium de predictis Ricardo et Petronilla pro ii s.
Rogerus le Neve tenet i cotagium de eisdem pro ii s.
Iidem Ricardus et Petronilla tenent medietatem unius carucate terre in iii croftis ut in i libero burgagio de antedictis burgagiis et tenent dicta crofta pro i pari calcarium de auro reddendo Priori de Coventr' ad festum Sancti Johannis Baptiste et tenent tertium croftum de heredibus Milonis Barbedaveril pro i d et i pari cirotecarum ad Pascham et iidem heredes tenent de Priore per idem servicium et Prior [etc]. quo servicio nescitur.
Iidem Ricardus et Petronilla tenent iii cotagia de heredibus Nicholai Lytholf de Sponna pro iiii d et ipsi heredes de Priore per idem servicium et Prior ut supra.
Iidem Ricardus et Petronilla habent iii cotarios scilicet Walterum de Langleye qui tenet i cotagium de eisdem pro xiiii d et Ricardum le Bourser' qui tenet aliud cotagium de eisdem pro ii s et iii hominibus in autumpno per i diem et ii gallinis ad natale domini.
Johannes Watburle tenet i cotagium de eisdem per idem servicium.
Iidem Ricardus et Petronilla tenent quoddam molendinum aquaticum in dominico de heredibus Lytholfi de Sponna per cartam pro vi d et ipsi heredes de Priore per idem servicium et Prior ut supra.
Simon del Aumerye tenet quoddam cotagium de predictis Ricardo et Petronilla pro vii s et ipsi de heredibus Anketill de Wykewan' pro[2] i pari cirotecarum pretii ob.
Petrus Baron tenet xiiii burgagia de Priore pro v s vi d de quibus tenet capitale burgagium suum cum pertinentiis in dominico.
Secundum burgagium continet viii cotagia de quibus Willelmus Crompe tenet vi cotagia de dicto Petro per cartam pro xiiii d.
Ricardus de Esseby tenet vii^m^ cotagium de predicto Petro per cartam pro vi d.

1 *Peynto'* in MS.
2 *Per* in MS

Ricardus le Boche(r)[1] tenet viii^{m} cotagium de predicto Petro pro ii d per cartam.
Robertus de Ichynton tenet tertium burgagium de predicto Petro pro xii d.
Willelmus Uttyng tenet partem quarti burgagii de predicto Petro per cartam pro xviii d et idem Petrus tenet aliam partem illius burgagii in dominico suo.
Nicholaus Pake tenet quintum burgagium de dicto Petro per cartam pro xii d et ii hominibus in autumpno per i diem et iiii gallinis ad natale domini.
Walterus le Butter' tenet vi^{m} burgagium per cartam de predicto Petro pro xii d et ii hominibus in autumpno per i diem et ii gallinis.
Elyas de Lond' et heredes Nicholai Drake tenent vii^{m} burgagium per cartam de predicto Petro pro xviii d et iiii hominibus in autumpno per i diem et vi gallinis ad natale domini.
Matheus Cat tenet viii^{m} burgagium per cartam de predicto Petro pro xii d et i homine
[fol 110 b] in autumpno per i diem et ii gallinis ad natale [domini].[2]
Thomas Simond et Willelmus Bernard tenent ix^{m} burgagium per cartam de predicto Petro pro iii s et i homine in autumpno per i diem et ii gallinis ad natale domini.
Ricardus Forthwyn et Magister Ricardus de Burton et Petronilla uxor ejus tenent x^{m} burgagium de predicto Petro pro xii d et i pari cirotecarum pretii ob.
Thomas Haldayn tenet xi^{m} burgagium de dicto Petro pro ii s x d et ii gallinis ad natale [domini].[3]
Magister Guydo tenet xii$^{(m)}$ cotagium de Priore de Coventr'[4] pro x s.
Willelmus Loteman et Alexander le Vinet(er)[5] et Willelmus Rinuld tenent xiii$^{(m)}$ burgagium de predicto Petro pro iii s vi d videlicet Willelmus Loteman xii d Alexander le Vineter xx d et Willelmus Rinuld x d et i pari cirotecarum pretii ob.
Simon le Vleur' tenet xiiii^{m} burgagium de dicto Petro pro xvi d et sic tenent omnes de dicto Petro per predictum servicium et idem Petrus tenet de Priore et Prior etc.
Hugo le Dispenser' habet quinque liberos tenentes de quibus Robertus le Mouner tenet i messuagium de ipso Hugone pro xii d.
Robertus le Taillour tenet aliud messuagium de ipso Hugone pro xii d.
Henricus de Lilleburn tenet tertium messuagium de eodem Hugone pro xii d.
Galfridus le Leef tenet ii messuagia de eodem Hugone pro ii s.
Robertus Box tenet i messuagium de eodem Hugone pro xii d et idem Hugo tenet de Priore faciendo sibi duos adventus ad curiam suam tantum per annum.
Simon Scathelok tenet i messuagium de Abbate de Stonle pro ii s et Abbas tenet illud in liberam elemosinam.
Idem Simon tenet i curtilagium de eodem Abbate pro xii d et Abbas tenet in liberam elemosinam.
Idem Simon tenet ii curtilagia de Priore pro i d et Prior [etc].
Willelmus Sparc tenet iiii burgagia de Priore pro iiii s vi d et Prior de heredibus ut supra de quibus idem Willelmus tenet i burgagium in dominico in quo sunt iiii cotagia.
Willelmus Hod tenet inde unum cotagium de dicto Willelmo Sparc per cartam pro iiii d.
Heredes Henrici Wodemon tenent i cotagium de eodem Willelmo pro ii s.
Willelmus Bret tenet i cotagium de eodem Willelmo pro iiii s.
Robertus le Peschour' tenet i burgagium de dicto Willelmo pro vi d.
Rogerus a la Porte et Ricardus le Bunde tenent i croftum de dicto Willelmo nomine partis i burgagii pro ii d.
Magister Hospitalis Sancti Johannis Coventr' tenet aliud croftum de dicto burgagio pro viii d.

1 *Boche'* in MS.
2 Omitted in MS.
3 Omitted in MS.
4 Probably an error for *burgagium de dicto Petro*
5 *Vinet'* in MS.

Heredes Johannis de la Sale tenent i burgagium de dicto Willelmo pro xii d in quo sunt ii cotagia i molendinum aquaticum et i furnum et ii crofta cum pertinentiis unde Prior de Coventr' tenet dictum molendinum reddendo inde per annum predicto Willelmo Sparc x d.

Robertus de Lodelawe et Thomas Haldayn tenent dictum furnum de Priore pro vi d.

[fol 111]

Heredes Petri Martin tenent dicta duo cotagia de Priore pro vi d.

Iidem heredes tenent dicta ii crofta de heredibus Willelmi de la Sale et ipsi de heredibus Johannis de la Sale et ipsi de heredibus Roberti de Recham.

Johannes de Fraunkevill tenet i messuagium de Gena de Gosseford per cartam pro iii s et eadem Gena de Roberto Herberd et idem Robertus de Priore et Prior [etc].

Felicia filia Henrici Ballard tenet i messuagium per cartam de Priore pro ii s et Prior ut supra.

Henricus Ballard tenet i messuagium per cartam de Priore pro xii d et Prior de heredibus ut supra.

Willelmus Scot tenet i messuagium per cartam de Priore pro x d et Prior [etc].

Nicholas Pake[1] tenet in capite de Priore de Coventr' duo burgagia in dominico pro ix d et Prior [etc]. quo servicio nescitur.

Galfridus le Lefe tenet i cotagium de predicto Nicholao per cartam pro xviii d.

Rogerus de Camera tenet i curtilagium de predicto Nicholao per cartam pro ii s.

Henricus Ballard tenet i croftum de predicto Nicholao per cartam pro vi d et uno pari cirotecarum pretii i d et unum denarium.[2]

Galfridus filius Johannis tenet unam partem prati de dicto Nicholao per cartam pro x d et uno homine in autumpno per unum diem.

Willelmus de Soudley tenet quartam partem terre de dicto Nicholao per cartam pro x d et uno homine in autumpno per unum diem.

Johannes de Madley tenet quoddam curtilagium per cartam de dicto Nicholao pro i pari cirotecarum pretii ob. vel ob.

Willelmus de Copston tenet unum curtilagium de Priore per cartam pro iii d et Prior [etc]

Matilda filia Petri Martin tenet iii burgagia de quibus Willelmus le Loker tenet i burgagium de predicta Matilda pro xii d et i homine in autumpno[3] et Matilda de Priore pro iii d.

Nicholaus de Neubold tenet secundum burgagium de predicta Matilda per cartam pro x d et Matilda de Priore pro viii d.

Henricus le Tixto(ur)[4] et Editha uxor ejus tenent tertium burgagium de dicta Matilda per cartam pro iiii s et ipsa Matilda de Priore pro i d et Prior [etc].

Predicta Matilda tenet vi s et ii d[5] redditus de heredibus Thome de Wilenhal pro viii d et heredes de Priore et Prior etc.

Robertus Box tenet ii cotagia de dictis burgagiis per cartam pro x d de predicta Matilda et ipsa de Priore per predictum servicium.

Gilbertus Corewen tenet i cotagium de Priore pro ii s et Prior etc.

Vincentius le Orfeur' tenet ii burgagia de quibus ipse tenet unum in dominico suo de Priore pro vii d.

Stephanus de Hales tenet i cotagium de predicto Vincentio pro xii d.

Heredes Petri Martin tenent secundum burgagium de dicto Vincentio per cartam pro vi d et ipse Vincentius de Priore pro vi d et Prior [etc].

Juliana de Chircheyard tenet i burgagium de Priore pro iii d et Prior de heredibus ut supra.

1 *Tenura in capite* written in margin here.
2 sic
3 *per i diem omitted?*
4 *Tixto'* in MS.
5 *solidos* and *denarios* written in full here.

[fol 111 b] Simon de Shepey tenet unam partem unius burgagii de predicta Juliana per cartam pro iiii d.
Nicholaus Jory tenet aliam partem illius burgagii de predicta Juliana per cartam pro iiii d.
Johannes le Floutr' tenet i burgagium de Priore pro xii d et Prior [etc].
Petrus filius Petri Baron tenet unum molendinum aquaticum cum pertinentiis de Alexandro de Glasele Galfrido de Chatereston et Alexandro de Pilkenton attornatis Comitis Cestr' pro xl s et Comes de Willelmo de Andeby quo servicio nescitur.
Johannes Sleth tenet i burgagium per legem Anglie de Priore pro ii d et Prior [etc].
Willelmus Walgive tenet i burgagium de Priore pro xii d et Prior ut supra et uno homine in autumpno per unum diem et ii gallinis ad natale domini.
Walterus de Kildesby tenet tertium partem unius burgagii de predicto Willelmo pro iiii s.
Alexander Bocston tenet i messuagium de predicto Willelmo pro iii s.
Hugo Mayl tenet i cotagium de eodem Willelmo pro ii s et ipse de heredibus Johannis Vincent pro i clavo gariofili.
Lucia la Buttere tenet i burgagium de Priore pro vii d et Prior [etc].
Matilda filia Petri Martin tenet i burgagium de predictis heredibus pro x d et ipsi de Rege.
Walterus de Stok tenet i burgagium de predicta Matilda pro iiii s et Thomas filius Henrici tenet illud de dicto Waltero per idem servicium.
Robertus Reymud tenet i burgagium de Galfrido Breton per cartam pro xii d et Galfridus de Priore pro xii d et Prior de predictis heredibus.
Thomas Seled tenet i burgagium de Thoma Haldayn per cartam pro viii d et heredibus Willelmi Seled uno clavo gariofili.
Agnes de Bussherviil [domina] de Anesty tenet ii crofta ix cotagia et iii curtilagia de dono Ranulpho quondam Comite Cestr' ad albam candelam ardendam in stabulo suo.
Johannes le Vinetere tenet inde i croftum de ipsa Agnete per cartam pro iii s vi d.
Margeria Pake tenet aliud croftum de eadem Agnete per cartam pro iii s vi d.
Aluredus le Ceynturer tenet i cotagium de ipsa Agnete per cartam pro ii s.
Adam de Bannebur' tenet i cotagium de eadem Agnete per cartam pro xii d.
Magister Hospitalis Sancti Johannis Coventr' tenet i cotagium de predicta Agnete per cartam pro ii s.
Aug' Godescob tenet i cotagium per cartam de predicta Agnete pro xx d.
Willelmus de Pynnele tenet i cotagium per cartam de predicta Agnete pro xviii d.
Ricardus le Fermailer tenet i cotagium per cartam de predicta Agnete pro vi d.
Heredes Radulphi Morcok tenet i cotagium per cartam de predicta Agnete pro iii d.
Alicia Haldayn tenet i cotagium de dicta Agnete per cartam pro ix d.
Johannes Anketil tenet i curtilagium de eadem Agnete per cartam pro xvii d.
Margeria la Bakester tenet unum curtilagium de predicta Agnete per cartam pro viii d.

[fol 112]
Ricardus le Purser' tenet iiii burgagia in dominico de Priore pro xxxiiii s viii d et Prior [etc]. et idem Ricardus inveniet dicto Priori unum hominem in autumpno per unum diem et dabit ii gallinas ad natale domini eidem Priori.
Idem Ricardus tenet i messuagium per cartam de Willelmo de Neumastr' pro ii d et Willelmus de Priore per idem servicium et Prior ut supra.
Idem Ricardus tenet aliud burgagium cum pertinentiis per cartam de Ada Haldayn pro vi d ob. et Adam de Priore et Prior etc.
Idem Ricardus tenet i messuagium de Rogero Anketil per cartam pro iiii s et ipse de Priore et Prior ut supra.

Heredes Ricardi Cade tenent i messuagium de predicto Ricardo pro ii d ob.
Heredes Ricardi Bocston tenent i messuagium de predicto Ricardo pro vii d ob.
Willelmus le Palmere tenet i messuagium de ipso Ricardo pro vi d.
Galfridus filius Johannis tenet i messuagium de eodem Ricardo pro i clavo gariofili.
Heredes Willelmi le Whitewright tenent de dicto Ricardo i messuagium pro ob.
Heredes Simonis Bocston tenent i messuagium de dicto Ricardo pro ob. et i clavo gariofili.
Johannes de Henle tenet i burgagium de Priore pro ii d et Prior ut supra.
Heredes Willelmi de la Sale tenent de Magistro Ricardo[1] et Petronilla uxore ejus unum curtilagium per cartam et iidem Ricardus et Petronilla tenent de Abbate de Coumbe pro vi d.
Iidem heredes tenent de dictis Ricardo et Petronilla duo cotagia et iidem Ricardus et Petronilla tenent illa de heredibus Magistri Milonis pro i pari cirotecarum pretii ob.
Predicti heredes tenent quinque cotagia de predictis Ricardo et Petronilla per cartam et iidem Ricardus et Petronilla tenent illa de heredibus Roberti de Recham pro xii d.
Iidem heredes tenent ii cotagia de dictis Ricardo et Petronilla per cartam et iidem Ricardus et Petronilla tenent illa de heredibus Ricardi de Wigorn' pro i libra cimini vel ii d.
Iidem heredes tenent iiii crofta de dictis Ricardo et Petronilla et iidem Ricardus et Petronilla tenent illa de Abbate de Stonle pro xii d et Abbas de heredibus domine de Asthull pro iiii d.
Iidem heredes tenent unum molendinum aquaticum de dictis Ricardo et Petronilla et iidem Ricardus et Petronilla de heredibus Henrici de Hastyng pro xii d.
Iidem heredes tenent i croftum per cartam de dictis Ricardo et Petronilla et iidem Ricardus et Petronilla tenent illud cum pertinentiis de Priore pro ii s vi d et ipsi heredes Willelmi de la Sale tenent totum tenementum predictum de predictis Ricardo et Petronilla pro viii s et ipsi de Priore et Prior ut supra.
Adam Haldeyn tenet ii burgagia de Priore pro ii s vi d.
Robertus de Lodelawe tenet i burgagium de predicto Ada pro i pari cirotecarum pretii i d.
Johannes le Bocmonger tenet unam partem unius burgagii de dicto Ada per cartam pro xii d.
Adam le White tenet aliam partem unius burgagii de dicto Ada pro vi d et ipse de Priore et Prior [etc].
[fol 112 b] Richerus de Weston tenet i cotagium de Magistro Radulpho de Bannebur' pro i clavo gariofili Ricardo de Stretton.
Thomas Haldayn tenet i burgagium de Priore pro ii s et Rogerus de Burthyngber' tenet illud de dicto Thoma pro iiii s et idem Thomas tenet illud de Priore pro ii s.
Thomas Seled tenet i messuagium per cartam de dicto Thoma pro viii d et idem Thomas de Priore et Prior [etc].
Hugo Page tenet iiii messuagia et partem unius messuagii cum pertinentiis de domina de Burthon pro iiii s de quibus:
Martin le Lockier tenet i messuagium de dicto Hugone per cartam pro viii d.
Robertus de Lich' tenet i messuagium de dicto Hugone pro iiii d et i clavo gariofili.
Blissota Benet tenet ii cotagia per cartam de dicto Hugone pro xii d et i clavo gariofili.
Ricardus le Keu tenet i messuagium de predicto Hugone per cartam pro iiii d.
Henricus de Lilleburn tenet quandam partem unius messuagii per cartam de dicto Hugone pro i d.

[1] Presumably *de Burton*

Robertus le Mouner tenet i croftum de dicto Hugone per cartam pro vi d et i pari cirotecarum pretii i d et idem Hugo tenet totum tenementum predictum de Galfrido de Shirford per cartam pro iii s et idem Galfridus de Comite Lincoln' quo servicio nescitur.
Adam atte Grene tenet i messuagium de Roberto de Meisy pro v s et Robertus tenet de Waltero de Langl' quo servicio nescitur.
Ricardus Forthwyn tenet iii burgagia vii cotagia et vi curtilagia de quibus Gilbertus de Longdon tenet i burgagium per cartam de dicto Ricardo pro iiii s.
Thomas Aldith tenet i burgagium per cartam de dicto Ricardo pro iiii s et Hugoni Breton xii d pro eodem.
Robertus Faucon tenet i burgagium per cartam de ipso Ricardo pro xx d.
Willelmus Waldgyve tenet i cotagium de dicto Ricardo per cartam pro x d.
Ricardus de Coxham tenet i cotagium de dicto Ricardo per cartam pro xvi d.
Johannes de Condolme tenet i cotagium de dicto Ricardo per cartam pro iiii d.
Johannes de Billesl' tenet i cotagium de dicto Ricardo per cartam pro xxviii d.
Templarii de Baleshal' tenent i cotagium de dicto Ricardo per cartam pro xxviii d ob.
Johannes Pyhod tenet i cotagium de eodem Ricardo per cartam pro vi d.
Simon le Bocmonger tenet i curtilagium per cartam de dicto Ricardo pro xii d.
Robertus Reymund tenet ii curtilagia de dicto Ricardo per cartam pro xii d.
Heredes Roberti Hamund tenent i curtilagium per cartam de dicto Ricardo pro viii d.
Walterus Bacon tenet i curtilagium de dicto Ricardo per cartam pro vi d.
Ricardus de Colleshull tenet partem unius curtilagii de dicto Ricardo per cartam pro iii d.
Andreas le Merser et Agnes uxor ejus tenent aliam partem unius curtilagii de dicto Ricardo per cartam pro iii d.
Thomas Marie tenet i cotagium de dicto Ricardo per cartam pro vi d.
Walterus Helewys tenet i cotagium de dicto Ricardo per cartam pro ii s.

[fol 113]
Thomas Barsam tenet i cotagium de dicto Ricardo per cartam pro ii s.
Henricus le Pestur' tenet quandam partem unius curtilagii de dicto Ricardo per cartam pro i clavo gariofili.
Willelmus de Waleshal tenet i cotagium de dicto Ricardo per cartam pro vi d et idem Ricardus tenet totum tenementum predictum de Priore pro xviii d et Prior [etc].
Heredes Simonis le Bocmonger tenent i burgagium de Roberto de Chilton pro xii d et Robertus de Priore et Prior [etc]. in quo burgagio predicti Simonis heredes habent ii tenementa videlicet:
Walterus filius Willelmi tenet quandam partem unius burgagii de dictis heredibus pro xii d.
Magister Hospitalis Sancti Johannis Coventr' tenet aliam partem unius burgagii de dictis heredibus per cartam pro vi d.
Juliana de Cannel' tenet i messuagium per cartam de Johanne de Glouc' pro i clavo gariofili et ipse Johannes de Priore et Prior [etc].
Willelmus de Whatburl' tenet i messuagium de predicta Juliana per cartam pro xii d.
Stephanus de Halys tenet i cotagium de Priore per cartam pro ii s et reddit Magistro Johanni de Billesley iiii d de eodem.
Willelmus Siward tenet i cotagium de Priore per cartam pro xii d et Prior ut supra.
Robertus de Meleburn tenet i croftum de heredibus Nigelli le Dispenser pro iiii d et Johannes le Somenour tenet illud per cartam de predicto Roberto pro iii s.
Robertus Faucun tenet i croftum de predicto Roberto per cartam pro iiii s.
Ricardus le Bourser tenet i croftum de predicto Roberto per cartam pro iiii s.

Galfridus le Lanton[1] tenet i cotagium de predicto Roberto per cartam pro ii s.
Nicholaus Pynne tenet i burgagium de Priore pro ii d.
Willelmus Uttyng tenet i cotagium de predicto Nicholao per cartam pro i pari cirotecarum pretii ob. et Nicholaus tenet de Priore et Prior etc.
Gilbertus le White tenet i cotagium de Johanne le Ferro(ur)[2] per cartam pro xii d et uno clavo gariofili Johanni le Loriner[3] pro eodem.
Willelmus Sweytecok tenet i burgagium cum ii cotagiis in dominico de Priore pro vii d ob. et Prior [etc].
Nicholaus Chubbok tenet i messuagium de heredibus Walteri le Wyte per cartam pro viii d et ipsi de Priore et Prior [etc].
Robertus de Chilton[4] tenet in capite de Priore unum burgagium pro iiii d et Prior [etc].
Idem Robertus tenet i cotagium de heredibus Anketill de Wykwane pro iiii d et heredes de Priore et Prior [etc].
Henricus de Donecastr' tenet i messuagium de predicto Roberto pro i d et Robertus de Galfrido de Langl' et ipse Galfridus de Priore et Prior [etc].
Johannes de Bosco tenet i messuagium de dicto Roberto per cartam pro vi d et ipse Robertus de Priore et Prior [etc].
Hugo Shail tenet [de][5] eodem Roberto tria cotagia per cartam pro ii s ii d et ipse de Priore ut supra.
[fol 113 b] Thomas Haldayn tenet i curtilagium de dicto Roberto pro xii d et ii gallinis et i gallo et Robertus de Priore ut supra.
Robertus de Cannel' tenet i cotagium de dicto Roberto pro xii d et Robertus de Priore ut supra.
Ivo le Tannur tenet i cotagium de dicto Roberto per cartam pro xii d.
Idem Robertus de Chilton tenet xxi curtilagia et ii cotagia de Priore pro vi d et Prior [etc].
Idem Robertus tenet de Priore iiii curtilagia et ii cotagia et i burgagium pro vi d et Prior ut supra.
Idem Robertus tenet i curtilagium de Priore pro vi d.
Idem Robertus tenet ii cotagia et i curtilagium de Priore pro i clavo gariofili et Prior [etc].
Idem Robertus tenet i burgagium de Priore pro i flore rose de quo burgagio Rogerus Corwen solvit eidem Roberto ii s.
Ricardus le Bourser' tenet i cotagium de predicto Roberto pro ii s.
Henricus le Pestur' tenet i burgagium de Priore pro vi d et Prior [etc].
Idem Henricus tenet i messuagium de heredibus Rogeri de Monte Alto pro xviii d et ipsi de Rege.
Idem Henricus tenet i messuagium de Vincentio le Orfeur' pro i d et Vincentius de Priore et Prior [etc].
Heredes[6] tenent i messuagium de predicto Henrico pro xii d et Henricus de Priore pro vi d et Prior [etc].
Willelmus de Waleshal tenet i messuagium de predicto Henrico pro vi s vi d et idem Henricus de heredibus Nicholai Fortwyn pro i clavo gariofili et ipsi de Priore et Prior [etc].
Hugo Breton tenet i burgagium de Priore pro vi d et Prior [etc].
Heredes Thome Pavy tenent inde i cotagium de predicto Hugone pro vi d et i clavo gariofili.

[1] or *Lauton*
[2] *Ferro'* in MS.
[3] *Lorin'* in MS.
[4] *Tenura in capite* in margin in later hand.
[5] Omitted in MS.
[6] *Her'* in MS.

Alicia la Blunde tenet de eodem burgagio i curtilagium de eodem Hugone pro viii d ob.
Simon de Kildesby et Agnes uxor ejus tenent i messuagium de Priore pro ii s x d et medietatem unius libre cimini et i pari cirotecarum pretii ob. et Prior [etc].
Willelmus filius Thome Seled tenet i curtilagium de Johanne filio Ade pro i pari cirotecarum pretii ob. et Johannes de Priore et Prior ut supra.
Johannes Burgeis tenet i burgagium de Priore pro ii d et Prior [etc].
Willelmus filius Philipi le Feure tenet i messuagium de Henrico de Lilleburn pro xxvi d et idem Henricus tenet de Nicholao Jory pro i pari cirotecarum pretii ob.
Magister Robertus de Leyc' tenet i messuagium de Waltero de Bannebur' pro xii d et Priori Sancti Sepulcri Warr' xii d pro eodem.
Idem Robertus tenet aliud messuagium de eodem Waltero pro ii s et idem Walterus de Ricardo de la Sale et Ricardus de Priore et Prior ut supra.
Idem Robertus tenet medietatem unius burgagii de Priore pro ii s et Prior ut supra.
Rogerus le Peschur' tenet i cotagium de Magistro Radulpho de Banbur' pro ii s.
Thomas le Prechur' tenet i cotagium de Thoma de Kersle pro i d.

[fol 114]

Willelmus filius Richeri tenet i cotagium de heredibus Johannis Hab(er)dasher pro xii d et uno pari cirotecarum pretii unius denarii.
Robertus de Wynchecomb tenet i cotagium cum pertinentiis de Roberto de Meleburn pro viii s et Robertus de Ricardo de la Sale pro xiiii d.
Willelmus Rynuld tenet i cotagium de Priore per cartam pro ii s vi d et Prior ut supra.
Thomas de Fakenham tenet i cotagium de Waltero Helewys per cartam pro iiii d et Walterus de Johanne le Whytewright et Johannes de Priore et Prior ut supra.
Walterus le Butter tenet de predicto Thoma i messuagium per cartam pro ii s.
Magister Guydo tenet iiii cotagia de Priore pro iiii s et Prior [etc].
Robertus de Cannel' tenet i burgagium de Priore pro ii s iiii d et ii gallinis et uno homine in autumpno per i diem.
Idem Robertus tenet iii messuagia de Priore pro xv d et iii gallinis et i homine in autumpno per i diem et dimidium.
Idem Robertus tenet per legem Anglie i messuagium cum quinque cotagia de Priore pro ii s et iiii gallinis et ii hominibus in autumpno per i diem et Henrico Rachel ii s et Prior [etc].
Hugo le Breton tenet i curtilagium de heredibus Johannis de la Sale pro xvi d.
Robertus Faukun tenet i cotagium de Priore pro i pari cirotecarum pretii ob. et Prior ut supra.
Simon Keng tenet i cotagium de heredibus Ricardi Shirewith pro ii s et heredes de Priore et Prior [etc].
Heredes Johannis le Fletcher habent in dominico i messuagium ibidem et iii crofta et vi cotarios tenentes per cartam quorum primus est
Agnes Abeveton tenet i cotagium de eisdem pro ii s.
Isolda Danvers tenet i cotagium de eisdem pro ii s viii d.
Alexander Aboveton tenet i cotagium de eisdem pro ii s vi d.
Galfridus le Aguler' tenet i cotagium de eisdem pro xx d.
Johannes de Alspath tenet i cotagium de eisdem pro xii d.
Rogerus Werkwot tenet i cotagium de eisdem pro xii d.
Ricardus le Bourser' tenet de eisdem i acram terre cum pertinentiis pro ii s ii d.
Ricardus de Burton et Petronilla uxor ejus tenent i croftum de eisdem pro ii s.
Johanna de Herdborugh tenet de eisdem i croftum pro iiii d.
Ricardus de Burton tenet de eisdem i molendinum pro xii d.
Johannes de Glouc' tenet de eisdem ii acras terre cum pertinentiis pro iiii s et ipsi heredes tenent de Priore pro vi s ii d et Prior [etc].

INDEX OF PERSONS AND PLACES

References in Roman numerals are to the introduction; references in Arabic numbers are to the documents unless otherwise specified.
Place names are given in their modern form wherever possible. Minor places are in Warwickshire unless otherwise stated. As the deeds are arranged according to streets, the latter are indexed only as they occur in the introduction and in the Hundred Rolls. Only the more unusual renderings of names have been cross referenced.

Abbathia, Ralf de, 674
Abbetot, Henry de, 438
Abbot,
—John, 192, 632
—John *alias* John called (*another*), 127, 254–5, 405, 544, 552, 562, 576–7, 599, 625, 628, 630–1, 634, 637–8; *see also* John son of Roger the Miller
—Reginald, of Sowe, 38.12
Abbot's Lane, Coventry, xxxv
Abboth, Ralf, 441
Abel, Roger, 561
Abingdon (Abyndon'), Berks.,
—Robert de, *le Tippere*, 634
——Juliana his wife, 634
Aboveton (Abeveton'),
—Agnes, 768(p. 394)
—Alexander, 768(p. 394)
Adam, Master, 12
—Adam son of, 555
—John son of, 768(p. 394)
—Peter son of Adam, of Northampton *or* Peter son of Adam de Norhant', 9
—Richard son of, 426
—Robert son of, 705
——Gilbert and Henry his brothers, 705
—Swanus son of *see* Swanus the Parker
Agnes,
—Richard son of, 381, 419
——Hugh son of Richard son of, 451–3
Aguler (Aguler'),
—Geoffrey le, 768(p. 394)
—Hugh le, 246
—Osbert, 768(p. 383)
Aidelintu(n), Master Ralf de, 615
Ailm(er) (Alymer', Aylem(er), Aylm(er)),
—John, clerk, 394–5
—John (*?same*), 768(p. 383)
—William, 393, 399
—William son of, 435
Ailrich, Basilia daughter of, 29
Ailwardesich (*Alwardsica*, Aylewarddessiche, Aylwardesich) next to Blakemore, 7, 718; pp. 1–2, 10
Ailwin, Godfrey son of, 605
'Aishaga', nr. Coventry, 408
Aki, Richard son of, 527, 553
Alan, 767.58
—John son of, 273, 535, 564, 570; *see also* John Aleyn
—Nicholas son of, steward of the earl of Chester, xxn; p. 31
Albinus, canon of Derby, 12
Albreda, 767.57
'Albrydescroft' ('Albristescroft'), outside Coventry, 745–6
Alcester (Alencest(r)ia), Robert abbot of, 2
Aldith, Thomas, 768(p. 392)
Aldithel' *see* Audley
Alestote *see* Allescote
Alewy (Alewi), John, 529, 716
Alexander, William son of, 84, 177
Aleyn (Alen, Alein),
—Henry, 571
——heirs of, 568
—John, 536–7, 569, 571; *see also* John son of Alan
—Robert, 691
Alfled, Walter, 62, 260, 264
Aller (Allere, Hallere),
—Hugh *alias* Hugh le, 266, 269
—Jurdan le, 149
—Ralf *alias* Ralf le *alias* Ralph le, 315–16, 339
——Matilda his wife, 315–16
——Nicholas his son, 323, 339
—Richard le, 163–4
Allescote (Alestote, Alscote),
—Henry de, 734–5
——Alice his wife, daughter of Nicholas de Haleford, 734–5
——Alice his widow, 737
———Robert her brother, 734
Allesley (Alesle, Alesleye, Aleyleye, Alisley, Allesle, *Alleslea*, Allesleg', *Allesleya*, Allesleye, Allisley, Allysleg'), xxvn.
—cemetery of, 12
—Adam de, 423
—Robert de, 288–9, 297, 321, 325, 747, 768 (p. 385)
—Roger de, clerk, 110, 117, 155, 220, 224, 307, 365, 499, 575–6, 599, 670
—Thurston de, 517
——Agnes his wife, 517
—Walter de, 39.10
—William de, 136, 237, 280, 283, 525–6, 560, 593, 616, 621, 650, 680–2, 684, 720, 732, 768(p. 377)
—William de, shoemaker, 702–3
——Matilda his wife, 702–3
Almer,
—Hugh le, 275
—Philip le, 275
Alspath (Alespaþe, Alespath, Alespathe, Alispath, Allespache, Allespad, Allespath, Allespathe, Allispath, Allispath', Allyspath', Alspade, Alspath, Alspathe, Alspaye, Alysph', Alysspad') now Meriden,
—chapel of, 5n,12
—church of, xxiv
—land at, 5n.

Alspath (*cont.*)
—family of, xxxviii
—Gerard de, xxxviii; 209, 472, 490, 650–51, 768 (p. 377)
——bailiff, xxviii; 99, 218, 303, 315–16, 361, 397, 473, 489
—Gerard de (*another*), 411
—Hugh de, 43, 48, 63, 426, 530, 532
—Hugh son of Roger de (*?same*); 35.7, 35.16; Richard his brother, 25.11
—Ivo de, 5, 12
—John de, 39.9
—John de (*?another*), 768(p. 394)
—Master John de, 89, 708; his servant *see* Thomas de Haitel
—Nicholas de, 218, 220, 251, 323, 335, 337, 339, 768(pp. 380–1, 385)
——Henry his son, 251
—Robert de, 85–6
—Roger de, 708
—Walter de, 43, 87–8, 530, 532, 709, 767.33
——Alice his widow, 767.32
——John his nephew, 709
Altegeder Meadow (le Altegedermedewe), 753
Altegeder Mill/Mills (*altegedera mulna*, Altegedere Mulne, Altegedermuilnys, Altegedermulne(s), Alteghedermulne, altegideremulnes, Altegidermulne, altogedere mulne), xxxiv; 261, 304–5, 346–50, 352–4, 657, 753–4, 764
Alwardsica see Ailwardesich
Alwine, William, 535
Alymer' *see* Ailm(er)
Alysph', Alysspad' *see* Alspath
Amtera, Jewess of Coventry, xxxii
Amund *see* Hamond
Amundeville (Emundevill'), Sir Richard de, knight, 525
Andeby, William de, 768(p. 390)
Anglio, Anglulo, Angulo, Robert in *see* Robert in the Hurne
Anketell (Anketil, Anketill, Ansketell, Ansketill, Haschat'), 767.16
—Agnes daughter of, 35.5
—Ivo *alias* Yvo son of, 2, 3, 8
—Hugh son of, 8
—John, 196, 768(p. 390)
—Robert, 718; *see also* Robert called Anketill de Radford
—Roger, 768(p. 390)
Anketilby, Henry, of Wykewane, 768 (p. 372)
Anneye, William de, leprous knight, 768 (p. 371)
Ansley (Anesleye), William de, 36.13
Ansty (Anesti, Anesty), 22a
—cemetery of, 12
—chapel of, xxiv; 2, 5, 12, 13; p. 6n.
—lady of, xli; *see also* Agnes de Busherville
—priest of, 767.4, 767.5
—Philip de, 155
Apirdas *see* Haberdasher
Arblaster, Philip le, 74
Arden (Ardarn', Ardern, Erderne),
—Henry son of Siward, 2
—John de, 21
—Ralph de, lord of Peddimore, 760
—Thomas de, of Hanwell, 757, 760; p. 31
——Roesia *alias* Roysia his wife, 757
——Roesia *alias* Roysia his widow, 760
—Thomas de, knight, lord of Ratley, 757n–60
—William de, 16–19
Arler, Walter le, 713
Arnale *see* Harnall
Arrabi, Ralf de, 557
Arraz, Hugh de, xli; 380, 555; his wife *see* Alice daughter of Geoffrey the Goldsmith
Arthingworth (Arhyngworth', Arnigwrþe, Arningeworthe, Arningworth, Arningworthe, Arnyngworth, Arnynworth', Arthingworthe, Arthingwurthe, Arthinworth', Arthyngworthe, Arþingworþe, Artingwrthe),
—Ingeram de, draper, xxxvii; 322
——Margery his wife, 322; *see also* Margery widow of Robert de Lodelawe
—Simon de *alias* Symon de, 322, 334
—William de, 155, 298, 307–9, 317–18, 320, 322, 326–7, 330–1, 333–4, 344, 762–4; p. 32
—William de (*?another*), 34; p. 32
Arundel,
—earl of, xxiv
——street of the, xxx
—John de, clerk, 768 (p. 370)
—Peter de, clerk, 168
Ascellis (Ascens), Philip des, sheriff of Warwick, p. 31
Asewey (Asscheweye, Assewey, Aswey),
—Elias de, p. 326
—Richard de, 28d; p. 31
——Richard son of Richard de, 28e
Ashby (Ascheby, Asscheby, Assebi, Asseby, Assheby, Essceby, Esscheby, Esseby, Exeby, Hessebi),
—Alexander de, chaplain, 155, 253, 370
——Christine his stepmother, 253
——Richard de, his father, 253
—Richard de (*?same*), 103, 112, 118, 137–8, 141–3, 145, 147–8, 170, 194, 196, 199, 201–3, 207–15, 218–19, 230, 232–3, 242–4, 301, 304, 355, 369, 388–9, 398, 597, 748, 768(pp. 370, 382, 385, 387)
—Robert de, 579, 620, 768(p. 379)
——senior, 500
———Margery called la Leche, his wife, 500
—William de, 37.2
Ashow (Ashesoue, Assehoue, *Assesho*, *Assesso*, *Assigho*, *Asso*),
—Vincent de *alias* Wincent de, 451–3, 455, 469
—Vincent son of Roger de, 419
Asser,
—Robert, 616
—Richard, 768 (p. 374)
Assfeld, Walter de, 205
'Assheley', (unidentified), 39.6
Assulf', Robert son of, 705
Asthill (Asthul, Asthull', Esthull), 22a, 206; p. 9
—chapel there, p. 9
—heirs of the lady of, 768(p. 391)
Astley (Astleye, Estel', Estleg', *Estleya*, Estleye), 17, 18
—Alan de, 657
—John de, 588
—Richard de, 161
—Richard son of Robert de (*?same*), 365
—Thomas de, 554
Athelm', William, heirs of, 768(p. 387)
Atherstone, near Nuneaton, xvi
Atte'beh, William, of Foleshill, 329

Attebarre *see* Barre
Attecastelgate, Herman, xxxiin.
Attegrene *see* Grene
Attleborough (Atlberg', Atleberge, Atlebur', *Atleburgo*, Atteleborwe, Attleberge, *Attleborgo*),
—Geoffrey de, 42, 418, 421, 436–7, 439
——Robert his brother, 42
—Geoffrey de (*?another*), 490, 494
—John de, 124
—John son of John de, 132
—Ralf de, 664
Aubenay (Aubeney), John de, 39.5
Aubrey, William, 155, 157
Audley (Aldithel', Audelegh, Audethel, Audethel'), p. 29
—family of, xxxviii
—Henry de, 21, 346; p. 10
—James de, 22a
Aula,
—Adam de, 39.3
——family of, xxxviii
—Avicia de, 58
—Ernard de, 429
—John de, 181, 412–14
——heirs of *alias* heirs of John de la Sale, 767.51, 768 (pp. 389, 394)
—Matilda de, 547
——William her brother, 545–7
—Richard de, 29, 40–1, 43, 60–1, 63, 85, 87–8, 175–7, 262, 347, 349, 408–11, 420, 426–7, 524, 528–33, 553–4, 604, 660–3, 671, 676, 708
——bailiff, xix, xxxviii; 35.1
——Robert his clerk, xix; 420
—Master Richard de *alias* Master Richard called de *alias* Master Richard de Banbury *alias* Master Richard de Burton *alias* Richard de la Sale, xxxviii; 27, 58, 74–6, 112, 124, 162, 169, 240, 307, 344, 362–3, 365, 694, 737, 740, 742, 744–6, 761, 768 (pp. 368n, 372, 384, 386–8, 391, 394); p. 31
——Petronilla his wife, daughter of John de Aula, xxxviii; 76, 169, 307, 361–3, 365, 443, 745, 768 (pp. 368n, 372, 386–8, 391, 394)
—Master Robert de, 761n.
—Roger de, 10
——Richard his brother, 10
—William de, 7, 9, 10, 13, 14, 19
—William son of Roger de (*?same*), 8
—William de (*another*), 181, 710, 767.51
——Elyanora his widow, 454
——heirs of *alias* heirs of William de la Sale, 768 (pp. 389, 391)
—William de (*another*), 58, 250
Aumerye, Simon del, 768(p. 387)
Axholme (Axeholm, Axiholem, Haxholm), Lincs., Henry de, 139–40, 194, 210, 398

Bacon (Bacoun, Bacun, Bakon, Bakun),
—Walter, 49–50, 137, 144, 210, 214, 221, 230, 233, 287, 304, 364, 545–48, 562, 568, 575–6, 593–4, 599, 611, 616, 622–4, 632, 647, 665–8, 670, 683–4, 690, 722, 734, 745, 768 (pp. 368n., 370, 373, 376–8, 381–3, 392)
——coroner, xxviii–ix, xxxviii; 38.2, 113, 141, 212, 305, 596–7, 657, 741
——Joan his wife, 546
——Agnes his daughter, 142–3, 212–13
——Peter his father, 583, 589, 611
—William, 553
—William (*another*), clerk, 230, 658
Baginton (Bakinton', Bathekintone, Bathkynt'), 497
—Richard de, 92
—Thomas servant of the parson of, 167–8
Bagog', Roger, 174
Bagot (Bagod),
—Henry, merchant, 33n., 354, 372, 764, 766
——Katherine *alias* Katerina his wife, 354, 764, 766
——John, his brother, 354
——William, his brother, 354
——Felicia, his sister, 354
Baker (Bacster, Bakere, Bakester, Baxtere, *fornator*, Forner, Fourner' *furnarius*, Furner, Furnere, *f(ur)nerius*, Pesthur, Pestour, Pestour', Pestur, *Pistor*),
—Alice la, daughter of Margery la, 364
—Asketill, the, 708
—Bodinus le, 38.5
—Geoffrey le, 477, 768(p. 378)
——Agnes his wife, 477; Geoffrey her son, 477
—Gilbert le, 768(p. 372)
—Henry *alias* Henry le, 134–5, 179
—Henry *alias* Henry son of Henry called *alias* Henry le *alias* Henry de Coventry (*another*), xxvn, xxvi, xxviii, xxxv, xxxviii–ix, xlii; 26, 37.1, 46, 49–51, 67, 70, 105–6, 112, 117, 137, 142–4, 147, 154, 195, 198, 204, 206, 208, 210–11, 213–19, 220–3, 228–9, 230, 239, 287, 294, 301, 304, 308, 352–3, 360–3, 396, 430–1, 459, 525–6, 542, 551, 560–1, 568, 575, 593–4, 596–7, 614–19, 621–3, 625, 630–1, 633, 647, 653, 656, 666–70, 683–5, 687–8, 690, 694–5, 713, 721, 724, 727, 729–30, 732–4, 739, 745, 747, 751–2, 768 (pp. 367–8n, 373, 375, 377, 379–81, 385–6, 392–3)
——bailiff, xxvi, xxviii, xxix, xxxviii, xlii; 52–4, 56–7, 73–5, 82, 97, 104, 107–11, 113, 115–16, 118–25, 145, 150–3, 158, 169–71, 193, 196, 224–7, 231–7, 240, 242–4, 246, 248, 284, 296, 298, 305, 307, 309, 314, 317–18, 320–2, 324–6, 328–30, 343–4, 355–6, 358–60, 365, 367–9, 377–8, 385, 387, 390, 393, 399–401, 424–5, 446, 448–50, 457, 479–80, 482–5, 488, 497, 499–502, 504, 506–8, 510–12, 544–50, 552, 573–4, 576–7, 598–9, 624, 626–8, 632, 634–5, 643–4, 651–2, 658, 674–5, 686, 689, 691–2, 698–9, 720, 722, 725–6, 735–6, 738, 740, 742, 756
——Agnes his wife, 51, 144, 215–16, 218, 230, 307, 575, 616, 741
——Richard his son, 768(p. 377)
——Robert, his son *alias* Robert called *alias* Robert called the son of, 55, 57, 59, 72, 127, 132, 156, 166, 245, 252, 333, 375, 392, 506, 519–20, 523, 563, 620, 636, 692, 695–6, 700, 704, 725, 738–40, 743–4, 746, 761–2, 764, 766
———bailiff, xxix; 39.10, 69, 71, 79–80, 129–30, 131, 133, 256–8, 323, 341, 374, 391, 404–6, 463, 492–3, 498, 505, 517–18, 521–2, 580, 630–1, 645, 701, 703, 730–1
——William his son *see* Master William de Coventry
——Emma his daughter, 576
—John, heirs of, 768(p. 379)
—Margery la, 768(p. 390)

Baker (*cont.*)
—Martin the, 651, 674, 768(p. 378)
—Osbert the, 62, 600
—Ralf the *alias* Ralph the, 38.5, 46, 650, 666, 675, 683, 687–8
——Geoffrey his brother, 38.5
—Reginald the, 221, 768(pp. 374, 378)
—Rose le, 224
—Sephare son of Ralf the, 134
—Simon le *alias* Simon the, 35.1, 556, 678
——John le *alias* John the, his son, 89, 91–2, 192, 198, 556, 717
——William his son, 605, 706
—Thomas le, 648
—Vincent le *alias* Vincent the, 38.5, 651
—William le, 595, 689
——Alice his daughter, 363
Baldwin (Bandewyne, Baudewyne),
—Ralf son of, 531–3
—Robert, 764, 766
Ballard,
—Henry, 98, 100, 102, 104, 106, 152, 155, 162–3, 203, 211–12, 222, 224, 232–4, 239–40, 247, 309, 342, 377, 485, 597, 685, 735, 768(p. 389)
——Thomas *alias* Thomas called, merchant, his son, 33n, 71, 81, 131, 133, 166, 254, 256, 341, 370, 404, 753, 764
——Felicia his daughter, 768(p. 389)
——Agnes his wife and Alice their daughter, 240
——Agnes his widow, 71, 404
—Reginald, merchant, 104, 114–16, 162, 240–1, 256, 377, 736
——Felicia his wife, 240, 377
—Richard, 327
Balle,
—John, 503
—Nigel, 45–6
Balsall (Baleshal, Balisall', Balleshal),
—Hugh son of Gilbert de, 37.19
—Matilda de, 768(p. 383)
——Walter her son, 768(p. 383)
—Templars of, 768(p. 392)
Banastre,
—Robert, 2, 4, 5
—Thurstan *alias* Turstan, 12
Banbury (Banebury, Bannebery, Banneburi, Bannebury),
—Adam de, 768(p. 390)
—Geoffrey de, 33
—Ralf de *alias* Master Ralph de, 360, 448–9, 768(pp. 371, 391, 394)
—Master Richard de *see* Master Richard de Aula
—Simon de, 47
——Petronilla his widow, 545
—Thomas de, 642, 679
—Walter de, 112, 594, 670, 768(pp. 372–3, 394)
——Margery his wife, 112
——Margery his widow, xxxv; 51, 57, 692–6, 700, 738–40
——Henry his son, 221
—Walter de, butcher (*?same*), 373
—William de, 768(p. 381)
Bangeleys,
—Nicholas, 562
—Richard, 562
Bankewelle, Sir John de, 226
Banne, Walter *alias* Walter called, 549, 686, 690
Barbe d'Avril (*Barba Ap(r)ilis*, Barbe daveryl, Barbe de Averel, Barbe de Averil, Barbeap(r)il', Barbedaveril, Barbedaverul, Barbedaveryl, Barbidaver(i)l, Barbut Averel),
—family of, xxxviii
—fee of, 156
—John, 95
—Miles, 16–19, 29, 83, 174, 524, 705
——heirs of, 768(p. 387)
——Philip his son *alias* Philip, 42, 84, 261, 286, 347, 524
—Philip *alias* Philip de (*another*), 147, 155, 293, 762
——heirs of, 82
——his descendant *see* Joan widow of John Corbin
—Ralph *alias* Ralph the chaplain, 9 and n; p. 6
—William, chaplain, the father of Ralph, p. 6
—William *alias* William the clerk, son of Ralph, 3, 9 and n; p. 6
Barberie (Barbareio), Normandy, monks of, 21
Baret,
—Robert, 192
—William, 126
Barker, Barkere *see* Tanner
Barnet wood (Bernet, Berryt), nr. Coventry, 20a and b
Baron (Baron', Baroun, Barun, Baru(n)e),
—family of, xxxviii
—Peter (*several*), xxvii; 26–7, 37.19, 39.1, 59, 71–2, 95, 98, 100, 102, 105, 107, 111–14, 129–30, 132–3, 137–8, 146–8, 159, 163, 165–7, 172, 192–3, 228–9, 236–7, 239, 241, 249, 252, 256, 286, 304–5, 328, 331–2, 334–6, 339, 341, 353–5, 358, 360, 370, 373, 387–9, 392, 396, 404, 430, 491, 509, 525, 542, 597, 657, 685, 693–4, 732–4, 737, 745, 753–4, 764, 766, 768 (pp. 368n, 374–5, 383, 385, 387–8); *see also* Peter the Welshman
——bailiff, xxviii; 139–40, 204, 206, 270, 295, 443–4, 471
——Peter son of Peter, 345, 768(pp. 368n, 390)
Barraclough, Professor G., pp. 6n., 9n.
Barre (Attebarre, Bare, *Barra*, *Barram*),
—Beatrice de la, 588
—Nicholas a la *alias* Nicholas de la *alias* Nicholas de le *alias* Nicholas de *alias* Nicholas ad, clerk, 93, 147, 152, 167, 184, 193–5, 199, 279–81, 283, 286–7, 470, 525
——bailiff, xxvi; 66, 68, 168, 543
—Robert a la *alias* Robert de la, 149, 768 (p. 387)
—William ad, 571
——Christina his wife, 149
Barrow (Baru, Barue, Barwe, Berwe),
—John de, of Stivichall, 741
—Robert de, 8; p. 8n.
—Walter de la, 205
—William de, 177
——Philip his brother, 177
Barsham (Baresham, Barham, Barsam, Barssam),
—Henry de, 33, 145, 155–6, 166, 243–4, 247, 251–2, 333, 335–6, 339, 359, 372, 643, 766
—Philip de, 33
—Thomas *alias* Thomas de, 94, 107, 139–44, 147, 151, 168, 194, 201–2, 208–13, 215, 217–20, 223, 230, 234, 313, 319, 355, 747, 768(pp. 385, 392)

Basingwerk (Basyngwerk), Flint,
—abbot of, 25
——and convent of, 24
Basset,
—John, 239
—Sir Ralph, of Drayton, 757
—Robert, 2
Bassinges, Peter son of Peter de, 684
Bate, William, 480
Bateman, Edward son of, 36.8
Bath (*Bathonia*), Walter de, 751
Bathekintone, Bathkynt' *see* Baginton
Baudewyne *see* Baldwin
Baxtere *see* Baker
Bayley Lane, xxxii–iii, xxxvii
Bayn, John, 219
Bealca(m)po, Roger de, 8
Bearded (*cu(m)barba*), Wymarca widow of Robert the, 278
Bear-ward (*ursarius*), Roger the, xxxvi; 60–1
Beaufey, R(alf) de, 39.8
Beaufiz (Beufic, Beufiz, Beufys),
—Robert, 7, 717, 721; p. 1
——Emma his widow, 719–20
——Henry their son, 719–21, 724–5
———Thomas his brother, 179
Bec, monks of, xvi
—Anselm, abbot of, xvi
Beeches (Beches) the, in Foleshill, 28d and e; p. 31
—Gilbert del, p. 31
—Richard del, p. 31
—Roger de, p. 31
Beer (Beyer, Beyher, Beyr, Byher),
—John *alias* John le, xxv, xxvi; 36.1, 36.11, 48, 65, 90, 184, 186, 189, 192, 272, 274, 279, 281, 350, 428, 710, 732
—John (*another*), 122
Beket, Henry, 42, 529
Bekke, Richard atte, 372
Bekoc, John, 95
Bektot, John, 483
Bel,
—Amicia le, 559
—John le *alias* Sir John le, chaplain, 424, 629, 722, 768(pp. 378–9)
Beleteste,
—Geva widow of William, 767.62
—John, 188
Belgrave (Belegrave), Ralf de, 314, 320, 338
Benet, Blissota, 768(p. 391)
Berch', Walter le, 306
Bereford, William de, [justice], 33n.
Berengar (Bereng'), Joel, 15
Berewik', Cecily daughter of Robert de, 37.18
Beri *see* Bury
Berkeley (Berkeleye),
—William de, 765
——Sibil his wife, previously wife of John de Bromle, 765
Berkswell (Berchswell, Berkeleswelle, Berkeswell, Berkeswelle, Berkiswelle, Berkyswelle),
—Robert de, 35.2
—Gilbert de (*two*), 451–3, 466, 469, 476, 482, 484, 497
—Luke son of Stephen de, 434–5
Bern (Bren), William, 43, 48
Bernagges, Geoffrey de, 310
Bernard,
—Robert son of, 11
—William, 103, 111, 768(p. 388)
—Thomas, 109, 121–3
Berne, Hugh at þe, 741
Bernet, Bernyt *see* Barnet
Bert(r)an, Bertram son of Robert, 767.57
Berwe *see* Barrow
Betun, William, 33
Beufic, Beufiz, Beufys *see* Beaufiz
Beumeis, Richard de, 9
Beuse, Richard, 741
Beyer, Beyher, Beyr *see* Beer
Beyvile, Beyvill' *see* d'Eyvill
Biggin (Bugging, Bugginge, Bugginton, Buggyng), in Stoke, 757, 760; pp. 31, 365n.
—hamlet (*villula*) of, 28g
—Geoffrey de, 37.4
—Ralph de, 768(p. 378)
Bigot, Roger le, 11
Bilifort, Henry de, 65
Billesley (Billesle, Billesleg'), Master John de, 718, 768(pp. 380, 392)
Bineld, John de, 480
Binley (*Bileneya*, *Billeneia*, *Bilnea*, *Bilneia*, Bilney, *Bilneya*, Bilneye, Bylne, Bylneye), p. 365n.
—chapel of, 2, 5, 12–13; p. 6n.
—Geoffrey de, 47
—John son of Robert de, 263
—Robert de (*another*), 290–2
——William his son, 291, 315
———Felicia his wife, 315
———Richard his brother, 315
—Thomas de, smith, 297
—William de (*another*), 191
Birchmoor (Birchemore),
—Alice de *see* Alice wife of Roger Locard
—Robert de, 36.12
Birdingbury (Burþigburi, Burthigbur', Burthyngber', Burthyngbury),
—Roger de, xxii; 113–14, 768(p. 391)
—Roger de, baker (*?same*), 100
Birmingham (Burmicham, Burmig', Burmingeha(m), Burmingham),
—Richard de, 707
—Walter de, 458, 461
—Sir William de, knight, 22a, 23
—William de, 610, 621, 716, 719
——Bela his wife, 621
Bishop (Bischop, Biscop, Bisscop, Bissop, Bussop, Byscop),
—Adam, 532
—John, 511
—Ralf, 531
—Ralf *alias* Ralph (*another*), 270, 276, 284–5, 290, 302, 307, 312–13, 315–17, 319, 321, 325, 624
—Vincent, 490, 494
——Thomas his son, 399
—William son of John, 516
Bishop's bar, Coventry, xxxiv; 36.12, 617–18, 624, 626–7, 631
Bishop Street, Coventry, xxvi, xxx, xxxv–vi
Bishopston (Bissepesdon), Walter de, 407
Bisseley (Bissel, *Bisseleia*), xxxi; 7–9, 13; p. 9
—intended chapel of, 2, 5, 12; p. 6n.
—Furlong (Bischeleaforlong), 753–4

Bissley (*cont.*)
—Mill (Busselemulne, *molendinum* de Bussele), xxxi; 8–9, 751, 753–4, 767.2, 767.3
Blaber, Nicholas, of Coundon, 756
Blabestere,
—William called, 324
——Agnes his wife, 324
Black (*Niger*),
—Gerard the, 41, 62
——Alice his daughter, 63
—Odo the, 10
—Richard the, 426, 429, 529
—William the, 408–9
Blacwine (Blacwyn, Blagwin, Blakwyn),
—Isabella daughter of Thomas, 768(p. 380)
—John *alias* John son of (*?two*), 36.17, 42, 440, 465, 538, 632, 649, 662–4, 672–3
Blake, Thomas, of Whoberley, 756
'Blakemore', Coventry, 724
Blanche (Blaunche),
—Roger, 42
—Henry called, 744
Blandiman (Blandimer), William, 556, 558
Blauncheval,
—William del, of Stoke, 154
——Isabella his wife, 154
Blessede, Richard le, 613
Blockley (Blockele, Blockeley, Blockeleye, Blocley),
—Peter de, clerk *alias* Peter son of Gilbert de, 725–6, 743–4; p. 326
Blod, William, 89
Blokerwill', Blokevile, Blokeville *see* Bokerville
Blond, Blound *see* White
Bluet, Thomas, 407
Blukevill' *see* Bokerville
Blund, Blunde, Blunt *see* White
Blythe, Symon, of Elvaston, 364
Bocchi (Bochi, Bochy), Hugh, 108–10, 120–3, 128, 361; his daughter *see* Matilda Tynel
Bochart, Beterica, widow of William, 706; her father *see* Henry Steinolf
Bocher *see* Butcher
Bockesberd (Buckesb't, Buckisb(er)t, Bukkesbert), John, 134, 274, 347, 349
Bocmonger (Bocmongere, Bogmonger', Buchemongere, Buckmong(er)e, Bucmang(er), Bucmong(er), Bucmongere),
—John le, 279, 282, 384, 542
—John le (*?anoiher*), 768(p. 391)
—John le (*another*), 255
——Alice his daughter, 254–5
—Simon le *alias* Symon le, 183, 190, 680
——heirs of, 768(p. 392)
—Simon le (*another*), 544, 768(p. 392)
——heirs of, 544
Bocston *see* Buxton
Bodyn *see* Boydin
du Bois, family of, xli
Bokelere, Simon le, xxxvi; 166
Bokerville (Blokerwill', Blokevile, Blokeville, Blukevill', Bocurvile, Bokervile, Bokervill, Bokerville, bokervul', Bokervyle, Bokerwile, Bokevile, Bokirvil, Bokirvil', Boskervill, Boskorvill, Boukeville, Buk(er)vile, Bukervill, Bukerwill'), the field of, next to Stoke, 763
—Nicholas de *alias* Nicholas le, 93, 97, 103, 113, 196
——John son of Nicholas de, 106–7
——Basilia daughter of Nicholas de, 108–9
———John son & heir of Basilia de, 109
——heirs of, 768(p. 386)
—Richard de *alias* Richard le, xxvi, xxxix; 24, 30a, 35.11, 35.16, 47, 89, 92–3, 106–7, 179, 181, 186, 190, 193, 197–9, 287–9, 350, 383–5, 430, 708, 716
——bailiff, xxv–vi; 45, 94, 185, 279, 454–5, 464, 590, 732
——heirs of, 482
—Viel de *alias* Vielis le, 97–8
Bokkeby, William de, 236
Bolter (Boltere),
—Matthew le, 719–20, 722–3, 724–5
——Hawis his widow, 768(p. 375)
Bonde (Bondy),
—Adam le, 156–7, 763
—John, 130–1
—Matilda widow of William, daughter of Thomas the Goldsmith, 502
—Robert, 307, 313–14, 317, 321, 768(p. 375)
Bonnte, Richard, 724
Bony *see* Boni le Mercer
Borbache, Borbage *see* Burbache
Borc(er) *see* Purse-maker
Boreford, Richard de, clerk, 162, 367
Borser *see* Purse-maker
Bosco, John de, 768(pp. 384, 393)
Bosevile,
—Richard le, of Bourton on Dunsmore, 319
——Edith his wife, 319
Boskervill, Boskorvill *see* Bokerville
Botiler *see* Butler
Botoner (Botener, Botonere, Botuner),
—Edelina la, 122
—Geoffrey le, 226
—John le, 226
—Wymark la, 768(p. 385)
Botulfston (Botelston, Botildston', Botuluestan),
—Richard, 174
—Richard de (*another*), 42, 394, 439
Boucer *see* Purse-maker
Boucher, Boucher' *see* Butcher
Boudon',
—Roger de, 299, 310, 326
——Symon his son, 327
———Matilda his sister, 327
Boukeville *see* Bokerville
Bouldere,
—Richard le, 225
——Maria his wife, 225; her father *see* Ranulph de Stivichale
Bourser *see* Purse-maker
Bourtone *see* Burton
Bousetur',
—Hugh le, 768(p. 386)
—William le, 768(p. 386)
Bowstring-maker (Bouhestring(er)e, Bowestrengmakere),
—Henry le, 297
——Matilda his wife, 297–8
Box,
—Robert, 148, 158, 768(pp. 388–9)
—Roger, merchant, 33n, 230, 246, 251, 255, 358–9, 405
——Alice his wife, 405
—Walter, 33n, 249

Boydin (Bodyn, Boyden, Boydin, Boydyn),
—Thomas, of Stretton, 725–6, 744, 766
—William, of Stretton, 296–8
Bracebridge (Bracebrug'), Ralph de, 22a
Brand',
—Geoffrey de, 767.57
——Margery his wife, 767.57
Brandestone (Brandeston', Brannteston', Branteston', Braundestone, Braundiston', Brau(n)ston', Brauntestone),
—Sir Henry de, chaplain, 105
—Sir Hugh de, knight, 759–60
—William de, merchant, 33n, 164, 166, 241, 256, 338, 354, 373, 375, 523
Bras, Matilda widow of John, 155
Brauncestre, Thomas de, 226
Brayn, Henry, 249–50, 353, 620, 738, 742, 746
Brecon, Wales, p. 8n.
Bren *see* Bern
Brenetur (Brenetour),
—Bate le, 310
—Gilbert le, xxxvi; 307
Breton (Bret, Breton', Bretoun, Brett, Bretun, Bretun', *Brito*, Brut'),
—Sir John le, warden of city of London, 226
—Geoffrey *alias* Geoffrey le *alias* Geoffrey de, 37.1, 66, 138, 287, 361, 465, 595, 616, 648–52, 674, 681–2, 684, 722, 724, 768(pp. 382, 390)
—Martin le *alias* Martin son of, 10, 14
—Peter *alias* Peter le, 26–7, 732–3, 758–60
——bailiff, 152
—Robert, 531–2, 538, 604, 607, 663
——Bertram his son, 604, 607, 663
—Bertram (*?same*), 182, 195, 647–9, 664
——Hugh *alias* Hugh le, son of, clerk, xxvii; 37.1, 82, 111–12, 137–9, 185, 191, 201, 218, 231, 294, 352, 423, 431, 454–6, 458, 464, 526, 542, 574, 590, 592, 599, 613, 632, 647, 652–3, 655, 675, 684, 687–8, 745, 757, 768(pp. 371, 373, 377, 382, 391, 392–4)
———Agnes his daughter & heiress, 756
—Walter le, of Wolfhamcote and Wyken, 10 and n.
—William, 768(p. 388)
—William *alias* William le (*another*), 743, 760
—Ywein son of, 175
Brewer (*Braciator*), John the, 516
Brewys (Breus), John *alias* John le, 500, 768(p. 386)
Brid,
—Richard, 95, 298, 314, 317, 321, 328
—William, 332, 768(p. 371)
Brightwalton, William de, Prior *see* St. Mary's, Prior of
Brinklow (*Brinchalauo*, *Brincolao*, *Brinkelawa*, Brinkelawe, Brinkelowe), 38.1
—Henry de, 710
—John de, 39.3, 110
—Liulf de *alias* Liulf of Coventry *alias* Lidulf of Coventry, xxxi; 8, 9, 10n; p. 9
——family of, xxxi, xxxviii; p. 9
—Ralf de, 767.31
—William de, 524, 553, 660
——his sons William & John, 524, 660
Broadgate, Coventry, xxxii–iii, xxxvi–vii
—excavations at, xvn, xxxiii, xxxvin
Brockeston, Alexander, 768(p. 385)
Brodric, William son of William son of, 677–8
Brok', Nicholas juxta, 36.12
Broker, Richard le, 91
Bromley (Bromlee, *Bromleya*, Bromleye),
—Henry de, 352, 757
—John de, 764
——once the husband of Sibil de Berkeley, 765
——John his son, 354, 764
—William de, 349
Bromwich (Bromewich, Bromwych'),
—William de, of Bentley, 315–16
——Matilda his wife, 315–16
Brond (Bronn, Bront', Brot', Brun),
—William, 44, 268, 273–4, 767.17, 767.42
——Christine his wife, 44
Brooch-maker (Brochar, Brochare, Brocher, Brochere, *Brocherus*, *firmacularius*, Fermailer, Fermaylur', Fermeilur, Fermiler, Fermiler', *Firmaclar'*, Formailer),
—?, 568
—Adam le, 33n.
—Alan, 260
—John the, 263, 295
—Jori le, 767.25
—Ralph le, 313, 321
—Richard *alias* Richard le *alias* Richard called le *alias* Richard the, xxxvi–vii; 76, 93, 106–7, 139–40, 148, 168, 196–9, 201, 203–4, 207–10, 214–19, 222–4, 241, 284, 288–9, 291–3, 300–1, 342, 353, 355, 385, 387, 398, 574, 685, 750, 768(pp. 370, 371, 385, 390)
——Guy his son, xxxvii; 226, 301, 356–7; his guardian *see* Richard de la Muyre
——Henry his son, 358–9
——Alice his daughter, 222
——Margery his daughter, 223
——Sarah his daughter, 337
———John her son, 358–9
—Richard le, junior, 211
—Richard le (*?another*), 160, 241
—Richard le, son of Jordan le, 462–3
——Edith Hod his wife, 463
—Roger le, 33
—Walter *alias* Walter le *alias* Walter the, 174, 259, 262–3
—William le, 767.26
Brouneta (of Cheylesmore Lane), 64
Brown (Broun),
—Thomas, 95, 162
—William, of Coleshill, 503
Bruggewrithe *see* Bridgewright
Bruges (Brugges),
—Geoffrey de, 35.7
—Richard de, xxxix, xli–ii; 35.1, 36.16, 37.23, 87, 360, 533, 663, 666, 718
——bailiff, 37.22
—Lady Rose de, 615
Brumerton, Ranulph de, of Ashow, 73
Brun,
—John son of, 229
——Alice his wife, 229; her father *see* Alexander de Gloucester
—John (*another*), 38.13
—William, of Foleshill, 285
—*See also* Brond
Brut' *see* Breton
Bubbenhall (Bubbenhull', Bubbenul, Bubbinhul),
—church or chapel of, 12; p. 6n.
—Roger de, 260

Bubbenhall (*cont.*)
—Thomas de, 757
Buchemongere *see* Bocmonger
Buckesb't, Buckisb(er)t *see* Bockesberd
Buckmong(er)e, Bucmang(er), Bucmong(er), Bucmongere *see* Bocmonger
Bucstan, Bucston *see* Buxton
Budbrooke, 705n.
Bugging, Bugginge, Bugginton, Buggyng *see* Biggin
Bugstan *see* Buxton
Bukechum', Sir John de, knight, 23
Buk(er)vile, Bukervill, Bukerwill' *see* Bokerville
Bukkesbert *see* Bockesberd
Bukston *see* Buxton
'Bulketoniscroft', Radford, 616
Bulkington (Bulkinton', Bulkynton'), 20, 631
—Nicholas de, 720
Bulli, Walter, 553, 606
Bunde, Richard le, 768(p. 388)
Burbache (Borbache, Borbage, Burbathe, Burebathe, Burebe'g),
—Alfred de *alias* Awerad de, 323, 339
—Thomas de, 319, 768(p. 384)
—William de, 267, 273
—William de, merchant, 33, 129
Burcer *see* Purse-maker
Burforde, Robert de, 58n.
Burgess (Burgeis, *Burgens*, *Burgensis*, Burgeys),
—John, 768(p. 394)
—Henry *alias* Henry the, 429, 442, 464, 466, 469
—Richard *alias* Richard le *alias* Richard the, xxiii; 30a & b, 35.1, 36.1, 36.11, 40–4, 63–5, 90, 92, 134–5, 263, 350–1, 412–14, 428, 439–40, 451–2, 529–33, 540, 557, 559, 609, 639, 709
—Richard (*another*), 52, 295, 768(p. 385)
—Richard (*?same*) of Willenhall, 56
——Emma his widow, 56
Burgo herychon', Ralf de, 294
Burgoygne, Roger, 39.6
Burmicham, Burmig', Burmingeha(m), Burmingham *see* Birmingham
Bursar, Burser, Bursere *see* Purse-maker
Burþigburi, Burthigbur', Burthyngber', Burthyngbury *see* Birdingbury
Burtoft, Martin son of Walter de, 235
Burton (Bourtone, Burshon, Burton'),
—Bartholemew de, 761
—Hugh de, 299, 322
—Humphrey, 31n; pp. 2n., 32n.
—lady of, 768(p. 391)
—Master Richard de *see* Master Richard de Aula
—Roger de, 39.4
Burville (*Burvilla*), William de, 8
Bury (Beri),
—William de *alias* William called de, merchant, 33n, 128, 226–7, 256, 737
——Alice, Edith and Agnes, his daughters, 256
Busherville (Bucherville, Buscherevill', Buscherville, Busservile, Busservill', Bussherville),
—family of, xxxviii
—Agnes de, lady of Ansty, 768(p. 390)
—Henry de, 346n, 528
—Ralf de, 5
—Richard de, 767.32, 767.33
—Robert de, 2
—Robert de (*another*), 454, 716
—Roger de, 15, 346; p. 31
Bussop *see* Bishop
Butcher (Bocher, Boucher, Boucher', Bucher, *carnifex*, *macecarius*, *mascecrarius*),
—Alan le *alias* Alan the, 626–7, 768(pp. 374, 382)
—Gilbert the, xxxv; 553, 767.58, 767.59
—Hugh the, xxxv; 553
—John the, 43, 535, 767.35
—Nicholas son of William the, 606
—Richard le, 768(p. 388)
—Roger, 767.42
—William le *alias* William the, 91, 540
Butler (Botiler, *Pincerna*),
—Richard, 3
—William *alias* William le, 22a; p. 31
Butterer (But, But(er)e, *buttarius*, Butter, Buttere, Buttor'),
—John le, 98, 100, 102, 105, 108, 110, 116, 118–20, 123, 353, 745, 768(p. 386)
—John le, minor, (*?same*), 118
—John son of William, 439
—Lucia la, 768(p. 390)
—Osbert le, 98–9, 102, 105–8, 110, 116, 118, 120
—Ralf le, 184
—Richard le, 153, 158, 161, 304, 764
——Hawysia his wife, 161
——John & Sibil his parents, 764
—Robert le, 768(p. 373)
——Isolde his wife, 768(p. 373)
—Walter le, 206, 360
——Geoffrey his brother, 360
—Walter le (*another*), xxxvii; 270, 297–8, 329, 768(pp. 388, 394)
—William *alias* William le, 35.1, 87–9, 96, 177–8, 180, 708–9
—William le (*another*), 329
Buxton (Bocstan, Bucstan, Bucston, Bugstan, Bukston, Buston),
—Alexander, 263
—Alexander (*another*), 295, 768(p. 390)
—Benedict, 263, 439
—Henry son of Reginald, 421
—Herbert, 420, 531–2
——William his son, 419
——Alice his daughter, 420
—Hugh, 419
—Matilda, 381
—Richard, heirs of, 768(p. 391)
—Robert, 434, 442, 466
—Robert (*?same*), 497
—Roger, 419, 436, 439
—Simon, heirs of, 768(p. 391)
—William, 410, 421, 427, 437
—William (*?same*), 499
—William son of William (*?same*), 440
Byher *see* Beer
Bykenour, Alexander de, bailiff of Gloucester, 205
Byle, Nicholas, 38.13
Bylne, Bylneye *see* Binley
Byscop *see* Bishop

Cade,
—Richard, heirs of, 768(p. 391)
—Roger, 508
Caldecote (Caldicote),
—Alice de, 38.13
—William de, 551

Calke, Derbys.,
—priory of, 8n.
—canons of, 9n.
Calle, the boy, 35.11
Caludon (Caloudon, Calwdone, Kaleudon, Kaleudon', Kalouedon'), 22a, 407n, 712; pp. 9, 29
—lords of, p. 64
—Reginald son of Thomas de, 500
Calvin (Cauvin), Robert, 86, 767.11, 767.12, 767.13, 767.15
Cam(er)a, William de, 65; *see also* Chamberlain
Campion, Campyon *see* Champion
Camville (*Camvilla*),
—family of, xxxviii
—Richard de, 1
—Roger de, 13, 15, 16, 554
Canley (Canel, Canele, Canelee, Canle, Cannel, Cannele, Cannelegh, Cannelet', Canneley, Canneleye, Kanel', Kannele, Kanneley, *Kanneleya*, Kanneleye),
—Alexander son of Wyht of, 469
—Gilbert de, 469
—Hugh de, 423, 456, 469, 472–3
——Alice his widow, 476
—Juliana de, 768(p. 392)
—Nicholas de, clerk, 217, 385, 666
—Robert de, 419, 438
—Robert de, tanner, (*another*), xxxv; 394–6, 424–5, 445, 458–60, 469, 471–90, 497, 499–501, 512, 519, 768(pp. 393–4)
——Clarice his wife, 485
——John his son, 487
——Agnes his daughter, 488
——Alice his daughter, 486
—Robert son of Alexander of (*?same*), 470
—Roger the, clerk, 485
—Master Thomas de, 562
——Richard his brother, 562
—William de, 36.16, 47, 422, 431, 434–5, 441–2, 447, 451–4, 459, 466–7, 469–79
Cannebet, William de, 483
Canterbury,
—Robert monk of, 12
—Theobald archbishop of, xviii
Cantor (*Cantarius*),
—Roger the, 767.31
——Wymarch his wife, 767.31; her father *see* Ralf de Brinklow
Cantub', Hugh de, 446
Capeles, William de, 26
Carbuner, Richard le, xxxvi; 264
Carpenter (carentar', *Carpentar'*, *Carp(u)ntarius*, Carpunter),
—Adam le, 768(p. 380)
—Henry the, 582, 588, 603
—Henry the (*another*), 326, 329, 334, 341
——Emma his wife, 329
—Hugh the, 455, 464
—Jordan son of William the, 582–3
—Nicholas the, 260, 264
—Peter le *alias* Peter de Yelvertoft, 503, 505
—Richard the, 183
—Robert the, 197
—Roger the (*?Carpieiarius*), 767.53
—Thomas le, 91
—William le *alias* William the, 95, 768(p. 381)
Carter (*Carectarius*, *Caretarius*, Careter, *Carettarius*, *Cartarius*, Cart(er)e, *Karetarius*),
—David the, 410
—Eadmund the, 277
—Edith widow of William the, 180
—Haldanus, 553
—Hawise daughter of William le, 464
—Herbert the, 134–5, 178
—John the, of Asthill, 39.5
—Matthew the, 84
—Nicholas the, 176, 767.18, 767.19
—Philip son of Sym(on) le, 265, 268
—Ralph the, 310
—Reginald le, 568
—Robert the, 419
—Roger the, 767.17
Cartsaddler (Carsadeler, Cartesadeler, Cartsadelere),
—Alice le, 74
—Henry *alias* Henry le, 37.22, 45–6, 48, 67–8, 190, 385, 502, 595, 613, 623, 702–3, 768(p. 387)
Cat, Matthew, 105, 111, 768(p. 388)
Catesby (Catisby, Cattesby, Catusbi, Catysby, Kateby, Katesb', Katisby),
—nuns of, 438
—family of, p. 64
—John de, 52, 56, 71n, 73, 761
—Reginald de, xli; 193, 197, 286, 290–2
——Symon de, his son, 276, 292, 319
—William de, 458
Cath' (Cath), Hugh, 41, 83
Catone, William de, *Cappemakyere*, 503
Caumpedene, Thomas de, 768(p. 382)
Caus *see* Kaus
Causey (Caucey, Cauci, Caucy, Cause),
—Felicia, 517–19; her son *see* Thomas de Duston'
—Nicholas *alias* Nicholas de *alias* Nicholas le, 42, 418, 464, 529
—Richard, 422
Cauvin *see* Calvin
Cay *see* Kay
Ceinturer *see* Girdler
Celar', Celer *see* Saddler
Celet, Celeth *see* Scelet
Celir *see* Saddler
Cellarar (*Celarius*),
—Thomas the, 659
——Margery his wife, 659
Cemetery (*Cimiterio*, *Cimiterium*, *Cymiterio*),
—Giliana daughter of Richard ad, of Willenhall, 235
—Matthew de, 42, 558
Cempe *see* Kempe
Cesar, Henry, 529
Cetelber' *see* Ketelbern
Ceve, John son of, 543
Ceynturer *see* Girdler
Chadshunt, xixn.
Chail *see* Shayl
Chaloner (Chalonere, Chaloumer, Chalouner, Chaluner, Chalunner, Schalonyr),
—Geoffrey le, 33, 69, 79, 104, 125, 132, 153, 161–3, 232–3, 240, 247, 333, 344, 370, 373, 375, 377, 404, 492, 753–4, 764, 766
——Alice his wife, 375
—Simon le *alias* Symon le, 270, 285, 299, 302, 306–7, 312, 317

Chaloner (*cont.*)
—Thomas le, 326–7
Chamberlain (*Camerarius*, Chamberleyn, Chambleyn, Chamburleyn, Chaumberleyn, Chaumburleyn, Chaunberleyn),
—Bertram the, 9, 14; his wife, the daughter of William Fleming of Great Meols, 9n.
—Roger the, 12
—Roger the (*?same*), 174
—Roger le *alias* Roger the *alias* Roger de Camera (*another*), xxvii, xxxix, xl; 49, 113, 193, 195, 206, 228–9, 276, 286, 290–2, 296, 343, 385, 387–9, 430, 473, 502, 768(pp. 374, 379)
Champion (Campion, Campyon, Champiun),
—Adam le, 496
—John, 498
—Thomas *alias* Thomas le, 424
Chandler (Chaundeler),
—Robert le, 59
——Beatrice his wife, 59
Chaplain (*Capellanus*, Chapeleyn, Chapeleyne),
—Geoffrey the, son of Geoffrey the Baker, 480
—Geoffrey the (*?same*), 714
—Gilbert the, 346
—John the, of Spon, 768(p. 371)
—John le (*?same*), 768(pp. 376, 383)
—Luke the 'treasurer of the lord king', 35.15
—Ralf the *alias* Ralph, 3, 8–9; *see also* Ralph Barbe d'Averil
——William his son, 9; *see also* William Barbe d'Averil
—Ranulf the, 594
—Robert le, 768(p. 379)
—Roger the, 8
—William the, son of Richer de Weston, 252
—William the, son of Roger le Waffrer, 440; his niece *see* Matilda daughter of Elias le Waffrer
—William the, son of William the Weaver, 200
Charnel, William de, knight, 760
Chatel, Robert, 725–6
Chatereston, Geoffrey de, attorney of the earl of Chester, 768(p. 390)
Chaucumbe, Hugh de, 481, 516
Chaworth (Chaurc'), Patrick de, 11
Cheshire, xv
Chester (Cestre, *Cestria*), xv–vi; 16n.
—abbey of, xvi; 2n.
—monks of, xvi
—bishop of, 14, 37.19; p. 3
—clergy of the diocese of, p. 3
—earl(s) of, xvi–viii, xix–xxiv, xxviii–xxxii, xxxviii, xli; 43, 65, 286, 414, 534, 767.28; pp. 1–2, 7, 9n, 64–5
——fee of, xviii, xxiin; 2, 5–6, 12–13
—Hugh I, earl of, xvi
—Hugh II, earl of, xxii, xxxi–ii, xxxviii; 3–10, 13–14, 768(p. 371); pp. 1–10, 64–5; his minority, pp. 4, 7, 9
——Bertrada his wife, p. 10
——Matilda countess of, his mother, 4, 8n, 9; p. 9
——Richard his brother, 6; p. 4
——Richard his uncle, son of Robert, earl of Gloucester, 6
——Geoffrey his homager, p. 10
——Sewal his man, 5; *see also* Turald
——William his clerk, 10
—Ranulf I, earl of, xvi; 11; pp. 6–7
—Ranulf II, earl of, xvii, xix, xxxi; 1–6, 8–9, 11–13, 16–17; pp. 2–4, 6–9; arrest of, p. 8
——Roger his chaplain, 2
——William his priest, 2
—Ranulf III, earl of, xix–xxi, xxiv, xxix, xxxi–ii, xxxviii; 11, 13, 15–20, 407n., 528n–9n, 721, 767.1, 768(pp. 371, 390); pp. 1–10, p. 31, 352; his divorce, 14n, 15n, 16n; his minority, pp. 4–5, 7
——and earl of Lincoln, 16n, 21, 28e, 346n; p. 352
——duke of Brittany and earl of Richmond, 14
——Constance of Brittany, his wife, 14n, 15n, 16n.
——Jocius his chaplain, 21
——Ralf his chaplain *see* St. Michael's, chaplain of
——Simon his clerk, xxn.
——Thomas his clerk, 16–18
——Walter his steward, 767.7
—men of, 22a
—Alice de, 362, 768(p. 386)
—Henry son of Henry de, 767.48
—Nicholas de, 542
—Thomas de, of Northampton, 38.11
—William de, 395
——'Aldith' Wry his wife, 395
—William de, tailor, 749
Chesterfield (Cesterfeld, Cestrefeld), Alan *alias* Alan de, 568, 571
Cheylesmore (Cheilesmor', *Cheilesmora*, Cheylesmor), xxiv–v; 44, 418, 768(p. 371)
—lord of, 27, 758
—tenants of, p. 30
—manor of, 768(pp. 366–8, 371)
—manor house, xxiv, xxxii; 22a; p. 30
—park, xxiv, xxxii, xxxiv; 4, 22a, 133, 152, 160, 169–73, 741, 747, 768(p. 371); p. 30
——mill, 768(p. 371); p. 30
Cheylesmore Lane *alias* Greyfriars' Lane, xxii, xxxii–iv, xxxvi
—bar in, xxxiv
Child, Simon, baker, 646; his wife *see* Alice de Wedon'
Chilton (Chilterne, Chilthon', *Chiltona*, Chiltone, Chiltoun', Chiltrene, Chiltron', Chiltun, Chiltun', Chiltyrne, *Chyltona*, Cilton', Schyltren'),
—family of, xxxviii
—Robert de, xxvn, xxvi, xxviii–ix, xli–ii; 26, 46, 50–1, 66, 74, 97, 99, 105, 107, 112–13, 116–17, 137, 142–4, 147, 152, 169, 194–6, 198, 201, 204, 206–10, 213–20, 224, 226–7, 230–1, 233–5, 237, 239–40, 283–4, 287, 294, 296, 300, 305, 311, 313, 315–16, 318, 320, 343, 352–4, 356, 361, 365, 369, 385, 387–9, 396, 399, 401, 424–5, 430–1, 457–9, 464, 470, 472–3, 477, 482, 484–5, 487–9, 499, 502, 504, 542–4, 546–9, 560, 562–3, 568, 574–6, 589, 592–3, 595, 598, 611–12, 616–18, 620–4, 626, 633, 651–2, 654, 658–9, 665, 670, 674–5, 682–3, 689, 690–1, 704, 719–23, 724–5, 727, 729–30, 732–4, 739, 741, 744, 747, 750, 758–9, 761, 768(pp. 368n, 372–4, 377, 381, 392–3)
——bailiff, xxvi, xxviii, xxxviii; 49, 98, 100–3, 106, 141, 148, 193, 202–3, 211–12, 221–3, 228–9, 297, 301, 304, 310, 312, 319, 342, 360, 364, 376, 386, 394–5, 398, 445, 474–6, 478, 496, 561, 572, 594, 596–7, 632, 647, 653, 655–7, 685, 687–8, 745, 756

——Matilda, his wife, 683, 721n, 723
——John de, his son, 514–15, 523, 695–6, 700, 724–6; p. 326
———Alice his widow, p. 326
——Peter de, his son, 106, 149, 311, 431
———Robert son of Peter de, 157, 493, 701, 731, 766
Chinch, Geoffrey, 531
Chnave *see* Knave
Chore, Ranulf, 46
Chorewenne, Choruenne, Chorvenne *see* Corwenne
Chowhe (Chouhe, Chouwe),
—Richard, 221, 231, 634
——Isabella and Joan his daughters, 617
Christine, of Park Street, 83
Chubbok, Nicholas, 768(p. 393)
Chumbe *see* Combe
Churchyard (Chirchyard), Juliana de, 768(pp. 389–90)
Chyltona, Cilton' *see* Chilton
Clav(er)e, Robert le, 581
Clavill', William de, Treasurer of Chester, 13
Claybroc (Cleybroc, Cleybrok),
—John de, weaver, 511, 548, 599
——Emma, his wife, 511
—Stephen de, weaver, 185, 465
—Roger de, 296, 474
Clement,
—Robert, 33
—William, clerk, 23–4
Clerk (Clerc, *clericus*),
—Adam the, 14
—Adam the (*?same*), 176, 533
—Adam the (*another*), 200, 387, 393, 447, 472–3, 476, 526, 536, 567, 640, 680
——John his son, 210–11, 616, 685, 756, 768(pp. 375, 379); *see also* John the Vintner
——heirs of, 281
—Adam the (*another*), 501
—Alan the, 35.7, 600–2, 605, 611
—Anketell the, 96, 99, 213, 230, 304, 361–3, 399, 459, 596, 624, 651, 653–4, 690
—David the, 266
—Geoffrey the, 542
—Guy the, 430
—Henry the, 300, 567
—Henry the, son of Robert in the Hurne, 74
——Alice his sister, 74; her husband *see* Stephen the Marshal
—Henry the, of 'Roxhalle', 38.5
—Henry the, of Ryton, 757
—Hugh the, 45, 192, 287, 429, 465, 479–80, 486, 572, 589, 591, 594–5, 611, 614–15, 623–4, 642, 665–6
—John le, 768(p. 372)
—John the, 3
—John the (*another*), 10
—John the (*another*), 64, 273
—John the (*another*), 628
—John the, of the monastery, 56
—John the son of the, 264
—Lanfram the, 3
—Laurence the, 485
—Nicholas the, 277
—Liulf son of Robert the, 89
—Nicholas the, 277
—Nicholas le, of Exhall, 17
—Osbert the *see* Osbert Durdent
—Peter the, 355, 424–5
—Ralph the, son of Richard Omnibon, 454
—Richard the, 422, 461
—Richard le, of Smercote, 36.12
—Richard the, son of William the Palmer, 273
—Robert the, 457, 542
—Robert the (*?another*), 125, 667
—Robert the, of Coundon, 442, 452, 466
—Robert the, bailiff of Gloucester, 205
—Robert son of William le, of Coundon, 495
——Edith his wife, 495
—Roger the, 182, 184, 191–2, 275, 278, 280–1, 283
—Roger le *alias* Roger the (*another*), 51, 53, 56, 58, 72, 78, 115–16, 118, 120–1, 144–6, 150–1, 154, 158–9, 165, 172–3, 214, 227, 232, 234, 236, 239, 243, 247, 251–3, 298, 314, 317, 319, 321–2, 324–5, 327–8, 332, 344, 358, 370, 373, 378, 401, 482, 484, 497, 509–10, 512–13, 516, 549, 552, 577, 626, 636–8, 646, 659, 686, 689, 694, 718, 725–6, 735, 742, 746, 754, 768(p. 383)
—Roger son of Roger le (*?same*), 768(p. 386)
—Thomas the, 50, 193, 543, 546–7, 612, 650, 674, 720
—Thomas the (*another*), 340, 448–50, 625, 697
—Thurstan the, 6
—Walter the, 207, 299
—William the, 7
—William the (*another*), 37.8
—William the (*another*), 223, 301, 309, 500
—William the, of Ryton, 757
—William son of Richard the, 35.7
—Ysaac the, 767.47
Clifton, [John de], bailiff, 728
Cline (Clyne), *unidentified*, Sir Roger, rector of the church of, 560–1
Clinton,
—Roger de, bishop of Coventry, xviin, xviii; 12; p. 4
—Osbert de, 705
Clother (Clocher, *Clocherio*, Clother'), Robert de *alias* Robert de le, clerk, 141–3, 212–13, 215, 221, 431, 622, 721, 729
Cnave *see* Knave
Codiscoph *see* Godescop
Codiswold *see* Cotswold
Codu(m) *see* Coundon
Coggeshall (Cockishal', Coggeshale, Coxale),
—Reginald de, 47
—Thomas de, 163–4
Coittyng, Martin, 33
Cokere, Richard le, 38.13
Cokkisham *see* Cuxham
Cokum, John, 687
Colbrand (Colborn', Colbraund, Colbrond, Colbrond', Colbront, Colebrant, Colebraund, Colebron, Colebrond),
—family of, xxxviii
—Adam kinsman of, 539
—Martin, xxiii, xxxix; 36.11, 36.14, 548, 566, 570, 587–8, 593, 609, 611–12, 614–16, 622, 624, 642, 648–50, 679–80, 684, 713, 721–2, 768(pp. 374, 377, 381); bailiff, xxv; 269
——his heirs, 768(p. 381)
——Adam his son, 138, 218, 574, 616, 647, 713, 745, 768(pp. 379, 381)
—Richard, 603

Colbrand (*cont.*)
—Richard, clerk, (*another*), 127, 254–5, 257–8, 495, 505–6, 580, 631, 645, 703
Colchester, Essex, p. 7
Coleshill (Coleshill', Coleshul, Coleshull, Coleshulle, Colesul, Colishul, Colishull, Colishull', Colleshul, Colleshull, Colleshull', Collishul, Collushull', Colshull', Colsul, Colsulle, Colushulle),
—Alexander de, 257, 578, 580–1, 631
—Anget(inus) de *alias* Angketinus de *alias* Ancketetell de *alias* Anketell de *alias* Anketill de *alias* Anketinus de *alias* Anketull de *alias* Anketynus de, clerk, 26, 39.1, 57, 138, 142, 162, 215–16, 231, 233, 311, 340–1, 364, 367–9, 374, 506–7, 519, 580, 625, 638, 645
——bailiff, xxix; 72, 76, 114, 126–7, 146, 160–1, 172–3, 251, 371, 373, 509, 514, 578–9, 629, 636–7, 646, 693–5, 697, 749, 762
——coroner, xxix; 258, 631
——John son of Anketinus de, 374
—Richard de, chaplain, 235, 248, 548, 768(p. 392)
——Nicholas his father, 548
—Roger de, 382
—Symon de, 53–4
—William de, 383, 591
——Richard his son, 547
Coleville (Colevyl),
—family of, 563n.
—William de, knight, 563
Colle (Cole),
—John, 117, 365
—Nicholas, 84, 767.10
—William *alias* William le, 103–4, 123, 761, 768(p. 386)
—William, baker, 125
—William, goldsmith, 124
Colyer (Coliar'), Adam le, 277, 385
Combe (Chumbe, Coombe, *Cumba*),
—abbey and monks of, xli; 87–8, 105, 204, 262, 300–1, 767 *passim*; pp. 3n, 85
—abbot of, 202, 205, 751, 768(p. 391)
—William abbot of, 767.46
—brother Nigel of, 767.46
Comber (Combere, Cumber, Cumbere),
—John le, 207, 689
—Richard le, 767.38
——Juliana his daughter, 767.38
—Richard le (*another*), 393–5, 489
——Luveday his widow, 393; her father *see* Robert the Locksmith
—Robert le, 267
—Robert le (*another*), 107, 249–50, 491
——Basilia his wife, 107
—Thomas le, 33
—Walter le, 100, 768(p. 385)
Co(m)br(ai), Alured de, 4
Condelm, Condenere, Condolm, Condolme, Condonere, Condulme, Conedonere, Conedou(er)e *see* Coundon
Cook (Coc, *Cocus*, Cok, Cok', *coquus*),
—Alexander, 434
—Alexander son of Alexander (*?same*), 279
—Eva, 399
—Geoffrey the, 40
—Hugh, 710
—John the, 669, 697
—Nicholas the, 49
—Philip the, 688
——Matilda his wife, 688
—Ralf, 308
—Richard son of the, 582
——James his son-in-law, 582
—Richard the, 52, 56
—Robert the, 42
—Master Robert the (*another*), 127, 636, 638, 696, 700, 704
—Robert the, of Kenilworth, 669
—Robert, chaplain, son of Simon called, of Berkswell, 562
—William the, of Caludon, 162
Cook Street, Coventry, xxx, xxxvi
Cooper (Copere, Coppere, Couper, Coupere, *cuppar'*, Cuppere, *cuvarius*, Cuver),
—Alan le, 587
—Godwin *alias* Godwyn, 767.28, 767.29
—Guy, xxxvi; 601
—Herbert, xxxvi; 600–2, 605–6
—Richard le, 113
——Milicenda his widow, 114; her husband *see* William de Ecclessale
—Walter le, 613
——Joan his daughter, 768(p. 374)
—Walter le (*another*), 575, 617–20, 625–7, 768(p. 378)
—William, 602
Coppinc,
—Batemo(n), 542
—Richard, 587
Copping (Copping'),
—Alice widow of William, 652
—Richard *alias* Richard son of Robert, 606–8, 623, 679
——Alice his wife, 606
——heirs of, 623
Copston (Copestone, Copstone, Copuston'),
—Sir Geoffrey le, chaplain, 514–15
—Hugh de, merchant, 391, 402, 405
—William de, draper, xl; 53–4, 74–5, 160, 240, 365, 378, 390–1, 400–3, 512, 514–15, 521, 552, 628–9, 714, 742, 746–7, 749, 768(pp. 373, 379, 389); his former servant *see* Hugh de Shilton
——Juliana his wife, 365, 714
Corbin (Corbyn),
—John, of Stoke, 154–5
——Joan his wife, 155
——Joan his widow *alias* Joan de Corbin, 762–3
Cordwainer (Cordewan(er), Cordiwaner, *Cordubanarius*),
—Robert *alias* Robert le, 64–5, 76, 182, 280, 283
—William the, xxxv; 555, 662
Corley (Corle, Corlegh, *Corleya*, Corleye, Cornel', Cornil', Cornle, Cornlegh', *Cornleia*, Cornley, *Cornleya*, Cornleye, Cornlye),
—church or chapel of, xxiv; 12
—John de, 37.8
—John de (*another*), 446, 599, 615, 633–4, 768(pp. 375, 379)
——Giliana his wife, 633
——William his son, 634–5
—N. de, 18
—Richard de, 599
—Roger de, xxiii; 554–5, 582, 641, 707
——Robert de, his son, 65, 92, 182, 273, 275, 278,

535, 541, 545, 559, 565, 567, 569–70, 584–6, 632, 639, 664, 710, 767.51, 767.52
——bailiff, xxii, xxiii; 36.1, 36.11
Cornishman (*Cornubiens'*), John the, 205
Corwenne (Chorewenne, Choruenne, Chorvenne, Corevan, Corewan, Corewen, Corewenne, Corewune, Coruwenne, Corvenne, Corwen, Curuwenne, Curwenne, Korewenn'),
—Geoffrey, 449
—John, 493, 498, 503, 516, 520
—Richard, 516
——Alice his wife, 516
—Roger, 467, 520, 768(p. 393)
——Gilbert, his brother, 424–5, 431, 443–5, 447–50, 483, 486, 497, 499, 500–1, 504, 508, 511, 768(pp. 386, 389)
Cosin (Cosyn, Cusin),
—Adam, 556–8, 584–6, 621
—Alice, 699; her daughter *see* Isabella daughter of Jordan le Saddler
Coterel (Coterell),
—Sir Benedict, chaplain, 406
—John, 383, 652, 654–6, 666, 675, 768(p. 372)
Cotesbech,
—Peter de *alias* Peter le, clerk, 231, 647, 768(p. 380)
——Mariota his wife, 768(p. 380)
Cotiler *see* Cutler
Cotswold (Codiswold, Cotiswold), Robert de, 477, 501, 768(pp. 383, 386)
Coundon (Codu(m), Condelm, Condenere, Condolm, Condolme, Condonere, Condulme, Conedonere, Conedou(er)e, Coundelme, Coundulme, Cundealm', Cundelme, Cundeum', Cundolm, Cundolm', Cundoner', Cundore, Cundouere, Cundulm, Cundulme, Cu(n)dulne, Kundellum'), xxv, xxxiv; 7, 42, 250, 738–40, 744, 749, 756, 758; pp. 326, 365n.
—chapel of, xxiv
—Andrew de, 648
—Andrew de (*another*), 499, 506, 523, 698, 756
—Godfrey de, 678
—John de, 155, 393–5, 458, 461, 474–5, 478, 489, 549, 703, 768(pp. 377–8, 392)
—John son of Hugh de (*?same*), 725–7
—Nicholas de, 724, 768(p. 375)
—Ranulf de *alias* Ranulph de (*?two*), 231, 430, 492, 768(p. 380)
—Richard *alias* Richard de, 51, 57, 367, 494, 686, 692–4, 699
—Robert de, 385, 418, 422–3, 439, 451, 456, 464, 490, 542–3
—Roger de, 402, 521, 702, 749
—Walter de, 681
—Warin de, 529
Couureyour, Richard le, 404
Coventry (*Coventreia*, Coventreie, Coventreye, Covi(n)tre, Covi(n)treu', Covyntr', *Cowentria*, Cowintr', Kovintre), xx
—*bivium* of, 607
—'Earl's half' of, xviin, xix, xxi, xxv–vii, xxxii, xxxiv, xxxvi; 387, 597; pp. 366–8
—manor of, 22a and b, 25; p. 30
—'Prior's half' of, xviin, xix, xxi, xxiii, xxv–vi, xxviii, xxxi, xxxvii; 546–7, 597, 644–5; pp. 2, 366–8
—*quadrivium* of, 708
—suburb of, xxx, xxxiv; 608; *see also* St. Nicholas, church of, area around
—territory (*territorium*) of, xxvi, xxxiv
—abbot, prior of *see* abbot, prior of St. Mary's
—Adam son of Andrew de, clerk, 564
——Juliana his daughter, 705
—Alexander de, xxxix
—Alexander de (*another*), 768(pp. 368, 377)
——Isabella his wife, 768(p. 377)
—Angtell de *alias* Anketell de, clerk, 560, 563
—Benedict de, Jew of Northampton, xxxiii
—Edmund, archdeacon of, 5–7
—Ernis de, 10
—Felice daughter of Godfrey de, burgess of Gloucester, 205
—Henry de *see* Henry Baker
—Henry de, clerk, 494
—Ingenulf de *alias* Eugenulf de, 10, 705
—Jordan de, xli
—Margery de, 37.15
—Nicholas de, chaplain, 318; his brother *see* Geoffrey de Nassington
—R. de, clerk, *see* St. Michael, chapel/church of
—Richard de, 454
—Robert de, xxvii
—Robert de (*another*), son of Agnes de Rethem, 767.49
—Roesia daughter of Humphrey de, 767.39
—Swyft de, 2, 3
—Thomas son of William de, xxvii
—Walter de *see* Walter son of Terry
——Sir Walter de, his grandson, 22a, 34, 382, 454, 710; pp. 31–2
—Master William de, son of Henry Baker, 619
Craft (Craft'), Geoffrey de, 22a, 717
Cras *see* Gras
Crispin, William, 639
Croc (Crok),
—John de, 33n.
—Robert, 401
—William de, 33
Crompe (Crumpe, Crumppe),
—William, 139–40, 149, 168, 194, 201–4, 207–9, 211, 217–18, 224, 242, 245, 656, 768(pp. 385, 387)
——Dyonisia his wife, 201, 245
——Nicholas his son, 39.3, 55, 72, 146, 164–5, 244–5, 247, 249, 251–2, 336, 358–9, 367, 370, 373, 392, 491, 519, 746, 754
——Alice his daughter, 203
Crophill (Cropehulle, Crophull'), Margery daughter of Ralf de, 50, 710
Cross (Cros, Crosse, *Crucem*),
—John ad *alias* John ate *alias* John atte, 127, 378, 448–50, 491, 516, 669, 694–7, 700–1
——Matilda his wife, 448–50
——Agnes their daughter, 449–50
—Ralph ad, 659
Crossbowman (*Balistarius*),
—Philip the, xxxvi; 52, 73
——Agnes his wife *see* Agnes daughter of Hugh le Breton
——Richard his son, 756
Croulebois (Croleboys, Crouleboys), Ralf, 134, 181, 767.6, 767.9

Crow Lane (Croulone, Crowelane, Crowelone),
—Osbert de, 74, 448–50
—Robert, 496
Crow Mill (Croumolne, Crowemulne, Crowmulne, Crwemuln'), 409, 443–4, 481, 500
—meadow (Cruowemulneham), 446
Crowe, William le, 33
Crude,
—William, 35.1, 63, 85–6, 90, 175–6, 180, 259, 261–2, 347, 349, 379, 411, 528, 531–33, , 767.6, 767.19, 767.20, 767.21, 767.22; p. 352
——Edith his wife, 767.20
——Geoffrey his son, 86, 90, 134–5, 180, 347, 349, 767.22, 767.23, 767.25, 767.26
———William his son, 767.18, 767.24
Crulefeld (Crulfeld, Cruylefeld),
—Alexander de, 177, 429
—Alexander de (*another*), 154, 766
Cu *see* Keu
Cubbington, p. 365n.
Cugho, Sir William de, knight, 751
Cumba see Combe
Cumber, Cumbere *see* Comber
Cuppere *see* Cooper
Curli (Cuill(i), Cuyly),
—Hugh de, 1
—John de, 705
—Ralf, 759
—Robert de, 705
—Walter *alias* Walter de, 725–6
Curly (*crispus*), Robert the, 60–1
Curuwenne, Curwenne *see* Corwenne
Cusin *see* Cosin
Custeresse, Mabel la, 427
Cutler (Cotiler, *cultellarius, cutellar', cutillarius*),
—Alexander the, 271
—Liulf the, xxxvi; 84–6
—Thomas le, xxxvi; 194
—William le, 156
Cuver *see* Cooper
Cuxham (Cokkisham, Coxham),
—Richard de, 756, 768(p. 392)
—Thomas de, 749
Cysun (Cysing), Henry, 87–8

Daivill' *see* d'Eyvill
Dale,
—Richard, 38.13
—Robert, 180, 183–4, 192, 194
——Nicholas his son, 656, 768(p. 382)
Daleby,
—Richard de, butcher, 630, 731
——Felicia his wife, 630
Dandy (Dandi),
—Agnes, 768(p. 375)
—heirs of Jordan, 768(p. 375)
Danecastr' *see* Doncaster
Danet,
—Robert son of Ralph Danet of Leicester, 162
——Agnes his wife, 162n.
Danvers, Isolda, 768(p. 394)
Darley, Derbys., Augustinian canons of, xxiiin.
Davenport, Richard de, 6n.
Daventry (Daventre),
—Symon de, 557–8
——his heirs, 768(p. 382)
—Warin de, 707
David, Geoffrey son of, 380, 440
Davill *see* d'Eyvill
Davis, Professor R.H.C., xv, xviii–ix, xxvii; pp. 8–9n.
Dayseye (Daieseghe, Daieseie, Dayese, Dayesegh, Dayesegh', Dayeseie, Dayeseye, Dayesheye, Dayesie, Dayiseye, Dayishee, Daysie, Daysye, Dayuseye),
—Roger, clerk, 69, 79–81, 130–3, 155, 157, 164, 245, 248–9, 368, 507, 669, 695, 712, 728, 764
——bailiff, xxix; 58, 159, 165, 241, 254, 327, 331–2, 335–6, 338–40, 370, 402–3, 462, 495, 516, 520, 581
——Joan his daughter, 133
Dayvile, Dayvill *see* d'Eyvill
Deacon (*Diaconus*),
—Walter the, son of Henry de Fonte, 556
——Richard his brother *see* Richard de Fonte
—William the, 97
Dead Lane, Coventry, xxxiv, xxxvi
Deadmanswell (Dodemaneswelle, Dodemoneswelle), 749
Deivill' *see* d'Eyvill
Dene (Deyne), John de, 39.6
Denecastel, Denecastell', Denecastr, Denecast(r)e, *Denecastro see* Doncaster
Denestapel *see* Dunstable
Derby (*Derbeya*, Dereby, Derbi),
—Nicholas de, 82, 155, 378, 686–7, 690
—Osbert de, 410
—Robert de, 434–5, 437, 466
—Robert de (*another*), 33, 497
Derlyng, Henry, 768(p. 373)
Despenser (Despencere, *dispensarius, Dispensator*, Dispenser, Dispenser'),
—family of, xxxviii
—Elias, xxxii; 42, 411–12n; p. 31
——Alice his wife, 411; *see also* Alice daughter of Richard de Smithford
——Alice his widow, 412–13
——Nigel his son, 28h, 414–16
———heirs of, 471, 768(p. 392)
—Geoffrey, 3
—Hugh, p. 31
——Hugh his son, 22a
—Hugh le (*another*), 768(p. 392)
—Roger le, 522
—Thomas, 15–19
Deyestere, Deyster, Deystere *see* Dyer
Deyvallo, Deyvile, Deyville *see* d'Eyvill
Dick, Alice daughter of Richard dil, 383
Differ, William le, 68
Dile, Robert, 42
Ditton', John de, 751
Dobber, Dobbere *see* Dubber
Dobedy (Dobbedy, Dobedi, Dodeby),
—Henry, 38.1, 74, 106, 138, 185, 200, 231, 386, 394–5, 591–2, 653–5, 684, 768(pp. 382–3)
—Sir Henry (*?same*), 656
—John, 80, 113, 115, 119, 225, 235, 365, 377–8, 768(p. 387)
——Amicia his widow, 77, 80; her first husband *see* John the Goldsmith
——John son of John, clerk, 55, 69, 77–81, 126, 130, 164, 166, 241, 256, 331, 402, 405, 515, 519, 764
—Richard, 515, 628

Doctor (*medicus*),
—Marior' the, 385
—Simon the *alias* Symon the (*two*), 410, 418–19, 423, 426–7, 429, 434–5, 437, 439, 441–2, 452, 465, 573
——Simon son of Simon *alias* Symon son of Symon, 417, 441
Dodemaneswelle, Dodemoneswelle *see* Deadmanswell
Dog Lane (Doggelan', Doggelone, Doglone),
—Godfrey de, 606
—Robert de, 768(pp. 373–4, 378–9, 381)
Dol (Brittany), 5n., 9n.
Dolfyn,
—John, 519
——Isolda his wife, 519
Donart, Walter, 768(p. 378)
Doncaster (Danecastr', Denecastel, Denecastell', Denecastr, Denecast(r)e, *Denecastro*, Donecastr'),
—Henry de, 39.10, 138, 246, 768(pp. 385, 393)
—Robert de, 47, 136, 182, 220, 272, 274, 279–83
——Alice his daughter, widow of Warin le M(er)cer, 295
Donchirche, Donechirche *see* Dunchurch
Doville, Alexander, 22a
Dowel, Thomas, 36.2
Drake,
—Nicholas, 324; his daughter *see* Agnes wife of William called Blabestere
——heirs of, 768(p. 388)
Draper,
—Himg(r)ammus le, 326
—Richard le, of Corley, 598
Dras, Simon, 302
Draycote (Draicote),
—Alice de, 39.3
——William her son, 39.3
—John de, 614
——Susan his wife, formerly the wife of Adam Edolf, 614
—Richard de, girdler, 33, 246
Drayton, Staffs., 407n.
Drivere, Henry le, 35.2
Dru (Dreu, Driu, Dryu),
—Agnes, 581
—H., 556
——John his son, 556
—Henry, 545–7, 572, 589, 609, 680
Dry Marston (Drie Merston'), Ralf of, 38.7
Dubber (Dobber, Dobbere, Dubbere),
—Geoffrey le, xxxvii; 405–6, 634
—Richard le, 231, 240, 390, 393, 397, 400–1, 487, 550, 652–6, 768(pp. 371, 382)
—Robert le, 397
Dueston, Henry de, burgess of Bristol, 353
Dugdale, Sir William, xvin., xxiiin., xxx; 407n; pp. 9, 352
Dun, John, 340
Dunchurch, (Donchirche, Donechirche, Dunchurche), Geoffrey de, merchant, 119, 122, 126, 129, 173
Dunham (Donham, Dunholm),
—Ralf de, 267, 273, 275
—William de, 264, 286
Dunhamlyde, Walter de, 37.11
Dunsmore (*Dunnesmora*, Dun(n)esmore), 35.14
—a grove on, with chapel, 12
Dunstable (Denestapel, Donestapel, Donestaple, Donnestapel, Dunestaple, Dunnestable, Dunstapel, Dunstaple),
—John de, 536–7, 569, 571
—John de (*?another*), 226, 575
—Richard de, 361
——*le Hodere* (*?same*), 172
—Robert de, 125, 667–8
——Margaret his wife, 667–8; her sister *see* Mariota de F(r)anketon'
Dunte, William, the miller, 38.10
Durant (Dourant),
—Richard *alias* Richard son of, 588, 609
—Richard (*?same*), 768(p. 373)
—Walter, 574, 616, 768(pp. 376, 379)
—William son of, 527
Durdent (Duredent),
—Osbert *alias* Osbert the clerk, 30a and b, 35.1, 36.1, 36.9, 36.11, 63–5, 135, 178–82, 272–3, 275, 350–1, 415, 417, 441, 540, 557, 559, 639–40, 767.21
——bailiff or reeve, xxii–iii; 42, 134, 428, 439–40, 709
—Roger, knight, 4n.
—Thomas, 66
—Walter, bishop of Coventry, formerly prior of Christ Church, Canterbury, xvi, xviii–ixn; 4 and n; p. 5n.
——his court, xvi
Duston (Dustone),
—Richard de, 512
—Thomas de, 517–18; his mother *see* Felicia Causey
Dybun, Henry, 768(p. 376)
Dyer (Deyestere, Deyster, Deystere, *tinator*, *Tinctor*, *tintor*, *tynctor*),
—Ailmer the *alias* Aylemer the, 42, 418, 421, 437, 439, 441; p. 66
—Henry the, of Worcester, 534
——Petronilla his wife, 534
—Hugh the, 412–14
—John the, 591, 687–8
—Mancel the *alias* Mansellus the, 420–1, 426, 436–7
——Ralf son of, 418
——Beatrice daughter of, 437
—Michael the, 534, 641
——Henry his son, 535–6
—Nicholas le *alias* Nicholas the, 257, 374, 517, 579, 625, 637–8, 645, 697, 704, 761
—Osbert the, xxxv; 379, 381, 411
—Ralf the, 662
—Robert the, 767.57
—Roger the, 184, 382, 415–17, 540
—Thomas the, 641, 661–2, 671, 707
—Thomas the (*another*), 454, 541, 611

Earl Street, Coventry, xxix, xxx–iii, xxxvi–vii, xxxix, xl
—bar in, xxxiv
Earl's ditch, xxxiii; 767.33; *see also* Coventry castle ditch (Index II)
—garden, 28b, 251, 375n.
—meadow, 259
—park, xxxii; *see also* Cheylesmore Park
—wood, around Coventry, 716, 719, 767.62; *see also* Barnet wood, Hazelwood

Earl's Mill (le Erlesmulne, *molendinum* de Erlesmuln'), xx; 27, 764; p. 10
—Lane, xxxiii–iv, xxxvi–vii
Ebriton, John de, 768(p. 379)
Edgefield (Egefeld, Egesfeld, Egesfend, Egesfeud, Egesford, Eggesfeld, Eggisfeld, Eggisfeld', Eggysfeld', Egisfeild, Egisfeld, Egisfeld'),
—Peter de, 150–2, 162, 211, 227, 233–4, 242, 355–6, 502; his widow *see* Beatrice Haldeyn
—William de, merchant, 107, 139–40, 147, 196, 199, 204, 208, 210, 218–19, 284, 353, 768 (p. 385)
——Alice his wife, 199
Edmund, prince of England, xxvii
Edolf,
—Adam, 614
——Walter son of Adam, 614–15
Edred, Henry son of, 606, 641, 660, 662; p. 66
Edric, Peter son of Henry son of, 677
Edward, of Spon Street, 479
Edward the Confessor, king of England, xvi, xviii; 768(p. 370)
Edward I, king of England, reign of, 768(p. 370)
Edwy, Bela and Isabella daughters of William, 729
Eins, Simon, 501
Eisel, William, 334
Eleanor (*Alianora*), queen of England, 714
Elias,
—the Reeve, 36.12
—Henry son of, 436
—William son of, 407
Ely, Geoffrey, bishop of, 767.5
Emundevill' *see* Amundeville
Enedem(er)e, stream, 7
Enese, Walter del *see* Walter de Norton
Enginur, Philip le, xxxvi; 70
England (Engeland), Robert called de, of Sheldon, merchant, 503
Erderne *see* Arden
Erdington (Erdi(n)tone), Thomas de, 705
Eriscote (Erescote),
—John de, 251
—William de, 334, 341
——Edith his wife, 334, 341
Ernis (Erneis, Erneys, Ernis', Ernys), 478
——Walter his son, 478
—Manselmus son of, 767.23
—Richard son of, 527, 553, 556, 601–3, 607, 767.58; p. 66
——Richard son of Richard *alias* Richard, xx; xxvi; 24, 30a and b, 47, 194–5, 198, 352, 430, 642, 711; bailff, 385
—Robert nephew of *alias* kinsman of, 600–2
——Richard his son, 601–2
—Simon, 27, 747, 759
—Symon, of Sowe (*?same*), 712
Ernsford, p. 365n.
Especer, Espicer *see* Spicer
Essceby, Esscheby, Esseby *see* Ashby
Essex, John de, 39.6
Estel' *see* Astley
Esthull *see* Asthill
Estleg', *Estleya*, Estleye *see* Astley
Eton (*Etona*),
—Gilbert de, 156, 333
—Nicholas de, 751
—Robert de, 68, 674–5
——Yseult his wife, 674–5
——Felice his daughter, 675
——heirs of, 768(p. 376)
Eugenius III, pope, xixn; p. 5n.
Everard, Nicholas son of, 553
Evesham,
—Thomas de, 33n, 153, 161
——Emma his wife, 153
Exeby *see* Ashby
Exhall (Eccleshale, Ecclessale, Ekeleshal), xxv; 22a, 757, 760–1, 764–6
—church or chapel of, xxiv; 2, 5, 12, 13, 18; p. 6n.
—woodland and waste in, 17; p. 2
—Morin de, 2
—William de, 114; his wife *see* Milicenda widow of Richard le Cooper
Eyton, Henry de, 242, 324
Eyton-on-Dee, Denbeigh., xvin.
d'Eyvill (Beyvile, Beyvill', Daivill', Davill, Dayvile, Dayvill, Deivill', *Deyvallo*, Deyvile, Deyville),
—Richard *alias* Richard de, 388, 768(pp. 371, 382)
—Robert de, 42
—Sir Roger, knight, 757, 760; p. 31
—Walter *alias* Walter de, steward of Ranulf III, earl of Chester, xxn, xxxviii; 20a, 28g, 528–9; pp. 10, 31
—Walter (*another*), 22a; p. 31
—William, 28b
—Sir William de, knight, 26

Faber *see* Smith
Facham,
—Richard, 755
——John his son, 755
Fakenham (Facha(m), Fackenham, Fackinham, Fackynham, Fakanham, Fakenham, Fakinham, Fakunham, Fakynham, Frakenham, Phabena(m)),
—Thomas *alias* Thomas de, merchant, xxxviii–ix; 49, 70, 93–4, 107, 137–41, 143, 168–9, 194, 198–9, 204, 208, 210–12, 214–19, 222–3, 283, 286–93, 311, 353, 362, 385, 398, 472, 547, 560–1, 563, 568, 574, 651, 657–8, 665, 768(pp. 370, 372, 374, 377, 385, 394); p. 66
——Margery his wife, 568
——Alice his widow, 214
Falcon (Faccon, Fackon, Facon, Fakkon, Falkon, Faucon, Faukun),
—Robert, 55, 57, 59, 72, 402, 491, 493, 495, 502, 514, 550–1, 749, 768(pp. 392, 394)
Falconer (*Austricarius*), Hugh the, 4
Falke,
—William, 347
——Peter his son, 278, 350–1
———Hugh his kinsman, 350
Fanigwrye, William de, 329
Fann(er)e, William le, 38.6
Farrier (*ferrarius*), Ingelard the *see* Ingelard
Faucon, Faukun *see* Falcon
Fennes, William de, 75
F(er)agu, Roger, 205
Feribihinde(m), Roger, 363
Fermailer, Fermeilur *see* Brooch-maker
Fermery, Reginald de la, 768(p. 379)
Fermiler, Fermiler' *see* Brooch-maker
Ferrour, Feuer, Feu(er)e *see* Smith

Feugers (Felgeris, Felg(er)s, Feng(er)s, Feogeres, Feuegers, Feug(er)es, Feug(er)s, Fug(ers)),
—Robert de *alias* Robert le, xxv, xxxviii, xlii; 35.1, 36.11, 179, 421, 428, 440, 538–9, 541, 545–7, 557, 559, 565–7, 569–70, 583–8, 609–10, 639, 641–2, 664, 677–9, 709–10, 716–17, 767.54, 767.55, 767.56; p. 66
——reeve, 681
——his wife, xlii; 36.11
——Hawise his widow, 589
——Robert his father, 660, 767.54
Feure, Fever, Fevre *see* Smith
Fillongley (Fillongeleye, Fillu(n)geley, Fillungeleye, Filongley, Filongleye, Fylongeleye, Fylu(n)gleye, Philu(n)gley),
—John de, 46, 215, 324, 562, 657, 768(pp. 370, 374, 378)
—Ralf de, 182
—Master Richard de, 375, 756
Filour, William, 290
Fing (Fing'), William, 677–8
Finham,
—Richard de, 94
—Thomas de, 419
Firmaclar', Firma(i)ler *see* Brooch-maker
Fishmonger (Fissher, Fyshere, Fysscher, Pechur', Peschour, Peschour', Peschur, Peschur', Pesthour, *Piscator*),
—Adam the, 105
—Alan the, 96, 101, 103, 110, 112, 310, 768(p. 382)
—Robert the, 151, 154, 768(pp. 388, 394)
—Robert le (*?same*), 33, 39.9, 131
—Roger le *alias* Roger the, 38.1, 70, 361–2, 597, 651, 657, 689, 768(pp. 370, 372–4, 382, 394)
——Agnes his daughter, 509
Fletchamstead (Flechamstud, Flicamestude, Flicha(m)cestude, Flichamestude, Fl(i)chamstude),
—David de, 432–3
——Alice his wife, 432
——Alice his daughter, 433–4
——Alice his sister, 432–3
—John de, 432–3
—John son of Osbert de (*?same*), 419; his uncle *see* Richard son of Peter
—Jordan de, 417
—Jurdan de (*another*), 424
—Mathias de, 432–3
Fletcher (Fleccar', Fleccher, Flecchere, Flecher, Flecher', Flechewer'),
—John *alias* John le, 136, 428–9, 434–5, 441–2, 451–4, 466, 469, 523
——Alice his wife, 428
——heirs of, 768(p. 394)
—Robert le, 39.3
—Robert son and heir of Fiel le, 629; *see also* Robert Fyel
Flouter (Fleuter, Floutar', Floutere, Floutr'),
—Benedict *alias* Benedict le, 82, 147, 186, 191, 194, 201–2, 768(pp. 385–6)
—John le, 49, 207, 232, 237, 768(p. 390)
——Alice his wife, 207
——William le, his son, girdler, xxxvi; 33, 146, 704
Foleshill (Folchesal', Folkesh, Folkeshul, Folkeshull, *Folkeshulla*, Folkesille, Folkesshul, Folkishull', Folkyshul, Folkyshul'), xxv; 22a, 764–6; p. 31
—chapel of, xxiv; 2, 5, 12, 13; p. 6n.
—family of, xxxviii, xli; p. 32
—Gilbert de, 34; p. 32
—Humphrey de, 767.28, 767.29
—Matilda de, 38.4
—Siward de, 2
—Viellus de, 2
—Viellus de (*another*), 176, 346–7, 349, 408–9, 528–9; p. 31
—Viellus de *alias* Vitalis de (*another*), 22a, 24, 47, 454, 711, 718
—William, 661
—William de (*another*), 183, 269, 382, 591
Foliot, Gilbert, bishop of London, p. 6
Folour *see* Fuller
Fonte (Fontayne),
—family of, xxxviii
—David de, 35.13, 35.16, 556, 559, 582, 584, 586, 603–4, 663, 676, 706–7
——Margery his sister, 559
—Richard a la *alias* Richard de *alias* Richard son of Henry de, xxv, xxxvii-viii; 24, 30a and b, 36.1, 36.11, 44, 382, 536, 541, 556–60, 565–7, 569–71, 583–90, 610–11, 639, 648–9, 664, 679–81, 709–10, , 717–18, 732
——reeve, xxii; 609
——Alice his widow *alias* Alice ad *alias* Alice de, 549, 562, 768(p. 376)
——John his son, 560–1, 563
———Richard his brother, 556, 560
———Walter his brother *see* Walter the Deacon
——heirs of, 568, 574, 768(pp. 375, 377, 381)
—Robert a la *alias* Robert de, 560, 563, 768(pp. 374, 377)
—Samson de *alias* Sampson de, 536, 564, 570
Forber *see* Furber
Forcer, Walter, 527
Fordwin (Farthwyne, Ferthwin', Fordewyn', Forduin, Fordwayn, Fordwine, Fordwyn, Forhtwyne, Forthewyne, Forþidwine, Forthwine, Forthwyn, Forthwyne, Fortwin, Fortwine, Fortwyn, Fortwyne, Forwine, Forwyn, Phortwine),
—family of, xxxviii
—Hugh, 418
—Nicholas, 63, 530, 533
—Nicholas *alias* Nicholas son of William (*?another*), 36.1, 36.11, 42, 44, 50, 64–5, 91, 181–4, 263, 272, 350, 384, 470, 535, 538, 595, 616, 623, 642, 672–5, 732
——Joan his wife, 595
——Richard his son, 117, 595
——heirs of, 768(pp. 375–7, 379, 381–2, 393)
—John, xxxix; 43, 91, 134–5, 181, 272, 530, 559
——heirs of, 622
—Richard *alias* Richard son of, 10, 13, 28f, 524, 527; p. 1
——William his son, 7, 10, 29, 85, 175–6, 262, 380, 411, 524, 534, 600, 603, 671; p. 1
—Richard (*another*), 689, 768(pp. 368n, 373, 377, 383, 388, 392)
—Richard (*?another*), 58, 104, 125, 162, 371, 710
—Richard of Hill (*?same*), Margery, Juliana and Edith his daughters, 702–3
—Thomas, 223, 293
Fore, Richard, 385
Forester (*forestar'*), John le *alias* John the, 221, 768(p. 379)

Formailer *see* Brooch-maker
Forner *see* Baker
Foro, Nicholas de, 3
Forsham, William de, 310
Forthewyne, Forþidwine, Forthwine, Forthwyn, Forthwyne, Fortwin, Fortwine, Fortwyn, Fortwyne, Forwine, Forwyn *see* Fordwin
Fossur, William le, of Stretton, Oxon., 37.12
Fowere, Roger le, 767.22
Fox, Richard *alias* Richard le, 764, 766
Frakenham *see* Fakenham
Franceis, Franceys *see* Frenchman
Franciscans, of Coventry, xxiv, xxxii; 22a, 26n, 35.17, 768(p. 371)
Frankevile (Franckevill, Fraunkevill), John de, clerk, 52, 768(pp. 379, 386, 389)
Frankton (Frangketon, Franketon, *Franketona*, Frankethon', Franketun, Franketun'),
—family of, xxxviii
—Jordan de, 716
—William de, xxxviii, xli; 554, 604, 606, 641, 647, 660–2, 707; Ranulph his son, 663
—Ranulf de *alias* Ranulph de (*?same*), 36.1, 36.11, 138, 423, 614–15, 642, 647, 649, 664–6, 717
——Mariota his daughter, 667–8; her sister *see* Margaret de Dunstable
——Petronilla his daughter, 669; her husband *see* Roger le T(r)anour
——his father, 664
——Alice his sister, 647; her husband *see* Bertram Bretun
——heirs of, 670, 768(pp. 373, 380)
—Ranulph (*?another*), 768 (p. 381)
Fredesham *see* Frodsham
Frembald *alias* Frumbald, 10
Frenchman (*franciscus*, Franceis, Franceys, Fraunceis, Fraunceys),
—Gilbert *alias* Gilbert the, 437, 441
—John, 768(p. 380)
—Robert *alias* Robert called *le Parmunter*, 79–81, 494, 518, 686, 692–6, 698–700, 702–3
——Nichola his wife, 693–6, 698–700
—William, 39.7
——Alice his wife, 39.7
Fressi(n)g, Henry, 477
Fretherich, Geoffrey, 42, 533
Frewin (Frewyn, Frewyne),
—Peter, 615, 648, 713, 720
—William, 648, 720, 768(p. 381)
——heirs of, 768(p. 377)
Fridai, Ralf, 767.38
Frodsham (Fredesham, Frodesham, Frodisham, Frodissam, Froþesham), Roger de, 45–6, 421, 664, 672–3
Frokeby, Bartholemew, 37.6
Fuckeram, Richard, 23
Fugelere (Fugheler'), Thomas le, 35.12, 35.16
Fug(ers) *see* Feugers
Fulky,
—Christian, 768(p. 376)
—John, 768(p. 376)
Fuller (Foleur, Fuelere, Fullere, Fulur),
—Edwin the, xxxv; 379
—Ralf le, 419
—Richard le, 767.44
—Roger le, 768(pp. 375, 381)
—William le, 609
Fundu (Funduyt), William, 710–11
Furber (Forber), Thomas le, 44, 710
Furbisher (*Furbar'*), John the, 50
Furner, Furnere *see* Baker
Fyel, Robert, son of Fyel de Coventry, 628; *see also* Robert son and heir of Fiel le Fletcher
Fygon, Hugh, 312
Fyshere, Fysscher *see* Fishmonger

Galeway, William *alias* William called *alias* William de, clerk, 74, 216, 257, 367, 506–7, 645, 698–9
Gamel (Gamil, Gamul),
—Emma, 768(p. 383)
—John, 275
—Robert, 325
—William, 127, 130–1, 133, 257–8, 509
——Alice his wife, 258
Gangerel, Milisent, 576
Ganter *see* Glover
Gardener (Gardener', *Gardinarius*, Gardiner),
—Richard le, 219, 281, 351, 768(p. 371)
——William his son *alias* William le, 137–40, 228–9, 236, 239
———Roesia *alias* Roeysia his wife, 236
—Roger *alias* Roger le, 28b, 35.3, 35.16, 63, 176, 180, 349, 639–40; p. 31
——Alice his widow, 639; p. 31
——Thurstan his father-in-law, 28b
'Gardinerescroft', in Coventry, 636–8
Gascony, xxvn.
Gaunter *see* Glover
Gayton (Gayton'), Philip de, 39.4
Geddeng', Ranulph de, 11
Geliner (Geler, Hennemonger), Thomas *alias* Thomas le, 87–8, 167–8, 171
Geoffrey, 529
—William son of, 36.2
—Felice daughter of, 36.2
Gerard, Master Richard son of *see* Richard son of Gerard the Vintner
Gerebold (Gerebode, Gerebote),
—Geoffrey, 174
—Miles, 22a
—William, 767.12
Ghyldesboru, Robert de, clerk, 401
Gifford, Robert, 38.7
Gilbert (Gilberd, Gilebert), 767.58
—Richard son of, 588
—Richard (*?another*), 549, 713, 722, 768(p. 378)
Gildenetre (Gildentr', Goldentre, Guldentre, Guldinetr', Guldintre),
—Henry de, 264–5, 268, 271
——Henry his son, clerk, 265, 267–8, 270, 768(p. 380)
——heirs of, 284
—Henry de (*either father or son*), 266, 269, 275–7, 302, 318
Girdler (Ceinturer, Ceynturer, Gurdelere, Seynturer, *zonarius*),
—Alfred le *alias* Alured le *alias* Alured the, xxxvi; 246, 358–9, 768(p. 390)
—Elias le *alias* Elias the, xxxvi; 158
—Henry le, 37.14
——Cecily his wife, 37.14
—Matilda widow of Thomas the, 465
—Roger le, 37.5

—Walter le, 33
—Wymarkia daughter of Geoffrey the, 68
Gladewinus, William son of, 263
Glanvill (Glanvill'), Ranulph de, 11
Glaswright (Glasenwryth, Glasewrytthe, Glaswrihte), William le, xxxvi–vii; 162, 165–6
Glazeley (Glasele), Alexander de, attorney of the earl of Chester, 768(p. 390)
Gloucester (Gloucestre, *Glovernia*),
—bailiffs of, 205; *see also* Robert the Clerk *and* Alexander de Bykenour
—Serjeant of *see* William de Hupton'
—family of, xxxviii
—Alexander de, xxv, xlii; 37.1, 37.23, 48, 93, 136, 184–90, 197, 211–13, 228–9, 278–9, 281–3, 383–4, 454, 464, 542, 590, 650; p. 66
——bailiff, xxv–vi, xxxix; 47, 456, 465, 469–70
——John his son, xxxix; 197
——Agnes his daughter, xxxix; 228; her husband *see* Thomas son of Martin the Locksmith
——Alice his daughter, xxxix; 229; her husband *see* John son of Brun
—John de, chaplain, 490, 768(pp. 383, 385, 387, 392, 394)
—Robert de, 39.9
—Thomas de, 33
Glover (*Cerotecar'*, *Cirothecator*, *cirotecar'*, Ganter, Gaunter, G(l)overe, Gouere, Govere, *Wantarius*, Want(er)),
—John le *alias* John the, 39.1, 58–9, 75, 77–81, 125, 127, 248–50, 254–5, 371, 491, 562, 579, 598, 633–4, 636–8, 646, 697, 703; p. 30
—Matthew the, 767.50
—Philip, 671
—Richard *alias* Richard the, 174, 767.46n.
——Wymarch his wife, 767.46n.
—William the, 44
—William the (*another*), 483
Gobiil *see* Gopil
Godescop (Codiscoph, Godescob, Godescop', Godescoup, Godeskoup, Godiscoup),
—Augustine *alias* Angustinus *alias* Anq(us)tinus, 94–5, 98, 101–3, 111, 167, 768(p. 390)
—Christine, 124
—John, 526
Godeslime,
—William, 150
——Ella his wife, 150
Godiva,
—Countess, xv
—lands of, xv–vi
Godiva Street, Coventry, excavations in, xxxiii
Godmo(n),
—John, 631
—Walter, of Keresley, 596
Godric (Godric'), 767.4, 767.5
—Adam son of, 3
—William *alias* William son of, xli; 661
Goldentre *see* Gildenetre
Goldsmith (*Aurifaber*, Golsmith, Orfeuer, Orfeu(er)e, Orfeur, Orfeure),
—Alexander the, 29
—Geoffrey the, xxxviii, xli; 16, 40–1, 60–2, 174, 380, 534; p. 66
——Alice his daughter, 380; her husband *see* Hugh de Arraz
—John le *alias* John the, 45, 167, 192, 525–6, 621, 665, 675, 682–3, 722
——Robert, his son, 768(pp. 372, 379, 387)
——heirs of, 768(p. 383)
—John the (*?two others*), 58, 77, 80, 82, 125, 365, 371, 646, 668
——Alice his wife, 125, 365
——Amicia his widow *see* Amicia widow of John Dobedy
——Emma his daughter, 125
—Richard the, 35.5, 43, 87, 177, 528, 603, 663
—Robert the, 62
—Thomas the, xxxvii; 41, 44, 48, 190, 767.54; his daughter *see* Matilda Bonde
—Vincent the, 200, 384, 386, 654, 768(pp. 389, 393)
—Walter the, 415–16, 672–3, 710
——John son of Walter the, 82, 768(p. 372)
———Isabella his sister, 82
——heirs of, 768(p. 387)
—William le *alias* William the, 625, 659, 768(p. 374)
Good Knight (*bonus miles*), Richard, 267
Gooder, Dr. A., 31n.
Gopil (Gobiil, Gopile, Gopyl, Gupil, Gupill'),
—Henry, 493, 520
——Christine his wife, 520
—Roger, 96
—Roger of Whoberley (*?same*), 522
——Beatrice his wife, 522
—William *alias* William le, 408, 426, 438
—William (*another*), 38.12
—Vincent son of, 409
Gorsi, Robert, 180
Goser,
—William le, 36.16
——Ralf his son, 36.16
Gosford (Goseford', Gosseford), Coventry, xxx–i, xxxvi–vii; 7, 768(p. 372)
—bridge(s), 283, 286, 293, 305, 307–8, 325, 327, 330, 340, 382, 385, 657
—Green, xxxiv; 343–5
—Gena de *alias* Jena de, 768(pp. 373, 389)
Gosford Street, Coventry, xxxiii, xxxvi, xln; 768(p. 377); pp. 64–5
—Far Gosford Street, xxxiv
Gouere *see* Glover
Gourneys, Roger, 64
Govere *see* Glover
Grandson (*Grandissono*), William de, knight, 751–2
Grantham,
—Ranulf de, 271
—Thomas de, soap-maker, xxxvi; 132, 172–3, 715
Grantpe (Grampe, Granntpe, G(r)antpee, Graumpe, Graundpe, Graunpe, Grauntpe),
—Geoffrey, 354
—Laurence, 33
—Robert, 76, 143, 233, 305, 314, 322, 324, 326, 328, 331–2, 343–4, 355, 398
——William his son, 233
——Alice his daughter, 233
—Simon, 33
—William *alias* William senior (*major*), xlii; 33, 52, 76, 115, 128, 146, 150, 158–66, 170–1, 173, 237, 243–4, 247, 256, 323, 332, 336, 340, 345, 354, 356, 358–9, 369–70, 375, 377, 492, 523, 643–4, 735, 744, 754

Grantpe (*cont.*)
—William junior (*minor*), 247, 338
Gras (Cras),
—Sir Hugh le, chaplain, 234, 377
—Thomas le, 682, 732
Graunger, Henry le, 245
Green (Attegrene, *Grena*, *Grenam*, Grene, Lagrene),
—Adam de *alias* Adam de la, 381, 410, 412–14, 421, 426, 428–9, 432–4, 437, 441, 466
——Richard his son, 427
—Adam *alias* Adam a la *alias* Adam ad *alias* Adam at *alias* Adam ate *alias* Adam atte *alias* Adam de la (*another*), 221, 431, 443–4, 461, 467–8, 496, 768(pp. 370, 384, 392)
——Roger his son *alias* Roger ad *alias* Roger atte *alias* Roger del, 498, 508, 514, 516, 643
———Agnes his sister, 643; her husband *see* Hugh de Merington
—Guy del, 33
—Richard, 768(p. 381)
Greenfield, Lincs., priory of, 8n.
Gregory IX, pope, p. 5
Gregory, Arthur, 768(pp. 365, 384n.); pp. 9n–10, 365
Grencurtel (Grenecurtel, Grenec(ur)til),
—Margery, 768(p. 387)
—Richard, 529, 533
Grendon (Grendon'),
—Robert de, 22a
—William de, 299
Gresley (*Greseleia*), Derbys., 2n.
—William de, 2
—William de (*another*), 183
Greyfriars' Lane *see* Cheylesmore Lane
Greygos,
—Robert, of Walsall, 392
——Alice his sister, 392
Grimsby (Gri(m)misbi, Grimmisby, Grymesby),
—Gilbert de, 687–8
——heirs of, 768(p. 371)
—Robert de, 386
Grom,
—John le, 95
—William, 36.19
Groudraf, Robert, 710
Grucoc, Matilda daughter of Richard, 91
Grundel (Grimdel, Gryndel),
—Henry, 120–2, 131
—Thomas, 99, 110
Grym(er), Walter, 460
Gubiun, Richard, 438, 640
Guldentre, Guldinetr', Guldintre *see* Gildenetre
Gundreas (Gundred', *Gundrias*),
—Matthew son of, 60–2, 85–6, 174, 195, 380, 671; p. 66
——Margery his widow, 90
———John her son, 90
Gurney, Walter le, 101
Gustard, Robert, 30b
Guterich, Robert, 533
Guy, Master *see* Guy de Tilbrook
Gymere, Walter, 500
Gynur (Gynor),
—Philip le, 71
——Margery his widow, 71n.
——Stephen his son, 71
ȝhate, Emma daughter of Roger atte, 764, 766
Haberdasher (Apirdas, Haberdas, Habertachs, Habertas, Hapertachs, Hapirtas),
—John, 37.1, 278–81, 283
—John the younger (*?same*), 282
——heirs of, 768(p. 394)
——Roger son of John *alias* Roger, 219–20, 294, 768(p. 371)
Hacon (Hacoun, Hacun, Hakun),
—William, 259–60, 262, 264, 271, 346, 767.60; p. 1
——Roger his son, 263, 274–5, 767.6, 767.47; p. 1
Hadolf, Adam, 587
Hagemund, Richard, 41
Hagene (Hagne), William, 534, 539
Hager, Thomas, 39.6
Hairun (Heirun),
—family of, of Church Lawford, p. 6
—Richard, 3; p. 6
—Roger, 12
Haitel, Thomas de, servant of John de Alspath, 708
Hakenham, Sir Thomas de, 656
Haldane (Haldain, *Haldanus*, Haldayn, Haldein, Halden, Haldeyn, Hayldeyn), 430
—Little (*parvus*) Haldeyn, 616
—family of, xxxviii
—Adam son of, 381, 410; p. 66; *see also* Adam de Spon
——Richard son of Adam *alias* Richard, 48, 410, 428, 709
———Adam son of Richard *alias* Adam, 206, 287–9, 504–6, 713, 768(pp. 390–1)
————Juliana his widow, 504
—Bateman *alias* Batteman, 36.16, 36.18
——Christine, his daughter, 196
———Alice de Willenhall, her mother, 196
—Beatrice, widow of Peter de Edgefield, 145
—Thomas, 37.1, 45, 48, 67, 93, 384–5, 470, 613
——Alice his widow, 49, 768(p. 390)
——Thomas his son, 49, 54, 56, 184, 190, 310, 342–3, 353, 385, 400, 472–3, 502, 768(pp. 387–91, 393)
———Alice his wife, 310, 342–3, 353, 385, 473, 502; her uncle *see* John de Lodelawe
—William, 404
Hales (Halis, Halles, Halys),
—Henry de, dyer, 39.6, 58, 578, 667
—John de, dyer, 127, 257, 552, 562, 578–9, 619, 636–8, 645, 667–8, 697, 730–1, 761
——Margaret his wife, 552, 636–8, 730–1
—Regin(ald) de, 37.10
—Roger de, 200, 397, 592, 653–4, 684, 768(p. 383)
—Stephen de, dyer, 38.1, 231, 389, 394–5, 397, 399, 401, 512, 653–6, 768(pp. 389, 392)
—William de, 618
——Agnes his wife, 618
Haleward (Halleward),
—Durantus, 36.16
—William, 169
Halford (Haleforde), Peter de, 378
Hallere *see* Aller
Halling' (Hally),
—Brunus *alias* Richard called Brunhalli, 718; p. 326
—Alice his wife/widow, p. 326; *see also* Alice daughter of Anketill Locard
Hally,
—John, 37.3

—Thomas, 768(p. 387)
Halstead, Robert, pp. 9–10
Halyday, Jurdan, 541
Hamo/Hamond (Hamun, Hamund, Hamund', Haumond, Haumu(n)d, Haum(un)t), 85, 262, 408, 641, 660; his brothers *see* Leofwin and Herbert
—Hamo (*another*), 33n.
—Hawysia and Alice, daughters of Richard, 46
—Robert son of *alias* Robert, 36.1, 36.11, 37.1, 538, 541, 559, 648–9, 664, 682
——heirs of, 768(p. 392)
Hampton (*Hamtona*),
—Christine, 768(p. 386)
—Geoffrey de, 539
—Robert de, 381
——Eduia his daughter, 436
—William de, 588
Hamslape (Hamselape), Henry de, 655–6
Hanaper (Hanapper),
—John le, 310, 330
——Ysabella his wife, 310
Handsacre (Hondesacre), Robert de, steward *alias* Sir Robert de, knight, 22a, 23
Hanwell (Hanewell'), Oxon., 760
Hapertachs, Hapirtas *see* Haberdasher
Harborough (Herdborough, Herdeberg'),
—Benedict de, 36.3
—Joan de, 768(p. 394)
Harbury (Herburi), John de, 571
Harcourt, William, 768(p. 372)
Hardekin, 530
—Margery his daughter, 530
Harlaund,
—Richard, of Wasberton, 49
——Felicia his wife, 49
Harlewin (Harlewin', Harlewyn, Herlewin), Alexander *alias* Alexander son of, 177, 410, 412–14, 421, 426
Harris, Mary Dormer, p. 64
Harnall (Arnale, Harenhal', harhole, Harnal, Harnale, Harnhal, Harnhale, Harnhelle, Harunhale), xxxiv; 631, 636–40, 757, 760, 764, 766, 767.62, 767.63, 768(pp. 365n, 370–1, 374)
—highway through, 7
—quarry at, xxxvii; 767.58, 767.60
—Ailwardus de, 260
—Sir Benedict de, chaplain, 253
—Sir Henry de, perpetual vicar of the church of Holy Trinity, 127, 761
—Richard de, weaver, 394–5, 768(pp. 376, 379)
——Inga Wry his wife, 394–5
Harnwis, Alice, 437
Harper (Harp(er)e, Harpour, Harpur, Harpuris),
—Henry le, 94
—Richard le, 94, 226
—Roger le, 194
—Roger son of Hugh le, 767.44
—William, 42, 64
Harston (Harestan'), Leics., 20b
Hartshill (Hardredes hull', Hardredeshull'),
—family of, xxxviii
—Hugh de, 3
—William de, 13, 15, 17, 18, 554; p. 31
Harunhale *see* Harnall
Haschat' *see* Anketell
Hastings (Hastinges, Hastyng, Hastynges),
—Henry de, 22a
—Henry de (*another*), heirs of, 768(pp. 378, 391)
—John, 768(p. 371)
—John de, lord of Abergavenny *alias* Sir John de, knight, xxvn; 26, 743
—Robert de, 439
Haubrey, William, in Stoke, 763
Haumond, Haumu(n)d, Haum(un)t *see Hamo*/Hamond
Haustin', Roger, 186
Hawene (Haune, Hauwne, Hawen), 767.45
——Robert his son, 279, 282, 351, 767.45
—Adam, 575–6, 632
——heirs of, 94
—William, 221, 535, 537, 683, 768(pp. 376, 381)
Hawthorn (Hauþorn, Hawethorn, Haweþornh, Haweþornth, Haweyorn),
—William *alias* William de, 200, 609
—William de (*another*), 578–80
Haxholm *see* Axholme
Hay (Haye),
—Adam del, clerk, 200
—John de la, 768(p. 381)
——Joan (*?his daughter*) daughter of John de la, 768(p. 381)
Hay Lane, Coventry, xxxvii
Hazelwood (Haselwode), 7
—highway leading to, 628, 739–40
Hecham, William de, bailiff, xx; 706
Hecke, Walter, 768(p. 385)
Hede, Henry, 564
H(e)dewyt, Isabel daughter of Felicea de, 506
Hegham *see* Higham
Helewis (Helewys, Helwys, Herewis, Holewis),
—Walter, 270, 286, 290, 292, 295–6, 303, 768(pp. 384–5, 392, 394)
——heirs of, 324
—William son of, 176, 261, 271, 661
Helion, Walter de, knight, 751
Henley (Henel', Henle, Henlegh', Henleye), 764, 766
—John de, 768(p. 391)
—Randulph de, 178
—Ranulph de, 208
—Richard de, xxxix, xlii; 36.15, 37.23, 134–5, 710
——Roger his son, 43
——William his son, 423
—Robert de, 192
—Thomas de, 192, 382–3, 682; his wife *see* Petronilla daughter of Thomas de Souley
Henley Mill (*molendinum* de henl'), 43
Hennemonger *see* Geliner
Henry I, king of England, xvn–in.
Henry II, king of England, xvi, xix, xxvii, xxix; 11; pp. 4, 8–9
—charter of, xvi, xl
Henry III, king of England, 11n, 768(p. 370); p. 29
Henry, Thomas son of, 768(p. 390)
Hepel', Robert de, 594
Hentetu, Christine daughter of William, 35.8
Henwood (Hinewod, Hynewode),
—prioress of, 744
—Avicia the prioress and convent of, 745
Herbert (Herberd, Hereberd, Herebert) *see* Herbert son of Jordan; his brothers *see* Hamo and Leofwin
—family of, xxxviii

Herbert (*cont.*)
—Henry son of *alias* Henry, 440, 570, 639, 679, 716, 722
—John, 597, 768(p. 380)
—Roger son of, 524, 553
——Margery his widow, 588, 623, 679
——Richard his son, 181, 440, 532, 541, 557, 568
—Stephen son of, 20a, 60, 346, 524, 527, 660, 662, 671, 676
——his wife, 671
——Matilda his widow, 663, 673
——Jordan his son, 672, 767.53
———Robert his son, 46, 51, 424, 549, 636–8, 659, 729–31, 768(pp. 368n, 373, 379, 381–2, 386, 389)
————Margery his daughter, 637
—William son of, 417–18, 421, 434–5, 437, 441–2, 451–2, 710
——Margery his widow, 455
——William their son, 455–6
Herci, John de, 757
Hereward, 86
—Robert his son, 86
——Hugh his son, 86
Herewis *see* Helewis
Herle, Robert de, 743–4
Herlewin *see* Harlewin
Hermon, Simon le, 274
Herre, Adam, 176, 261
Hersomdich (hursimisdich, Hyrsumdich), Coventry, xxxiii; 66, 185, 279
Hert, Adam, 393, 399, 543–4, 768(p. 387)
Hervy, John, of Allesley, 39.6
Hessebi *see* Ashby
Heth, Robert atte, 757, 764, 766
Heyforde, John de, 164
Heyr,
—Alice le, 302
——Geoffrey her son, 302
Heytele, Thomas son of William de, 709
Hibern' see Ireland
Hichemon, Gilbert, 334
Hidcote (*Hedcota*), 12
Higham (Hegham, Heiham, Heyam, Heyham, Hyam),
—Gilbert de, 33, 249, 446, 448–50, 481, 497, 500, 504, 516–17, 519
—Ramitte de *alias* Ramette de, 649–50
—Robert de, 33
—William de, 382
——Agnes his daughter, 666
Hildelay, Geoffrey, 36.10
Hill (Hul, Hulle), xxi, xxx, xxxiv–v; 525–8, 531–4, 541, 568
—bars towards, xxxiv
—Cross (hullecros), xxxiv; 577
—Field (Hullefeld), 549
—Meadow (Hullemedewe), 28a, 549
—Alexander *alias* Alexander de, 412–14, 416
—John de, 710
—Philip super, 531–2
—Richard de *alias* Richard de Hill Mill, 278, 537, 567
—Richard de (*another*), 768(p. 373)
—Thomas sup(er) le, 741
—Walter de, 454
—William de la, 633–4
Hill Mill (Hulmulne, *molend(inum) de Hulla*), xxxv, xxxix; 7, 28a, 28c, 524–6, 533n, 537–9, 545–8, 552, 575–6, 617–18, 630; p. 1
—pond of, 526, 543
—meadow of, 28c, 525–6, 548
Hill Street, Coventry, xxxiii
Hilton, Professor R.H., p. 365
Hinckley (Hinkel, Hinkele, Hynkele, Hynkeleie),
—Henry de, 669–70, 691, 694, 704, 768(pp. 378, 380)
—Sir Robert de, chaplain, 287, 574, 768(p. 380)
Hingram' *see* Ingram
Hobwyl, William, 299
Hod,
—Alice, 659
—Edith *see* Edith wife of Richard son of Jordan the Brooch-maker
—John, 181, 199, 540
—John (*?another*), 659
—William, 148, 154, 221, 232, 768(p. 388)
Hodart, Alan, 525
Hoden, Gerard, 706
Hodere, Richard le, 170
Hoki *see* Oky
Hokys *see* Okes
Holbrook (Holbroke, Holebrok, Holebrok'),
—Thomas de, 764
—Vitalis and John, sons of Edward de, p. 326
—William de, 766
Holdeburt', Henry, 534
Holdehallewey (*le holdeallewey*), in Stoke, 763
Holeburn', Henry, 539
Holeweye, John, 117, 365
Holewis *see* Helewis
Holland (Holand, Hoy land', Hoyland),
—Simon de *alias* Symon de, 265–6, 270, 284
——Alice his wife, 284
Holoneye *see* Olney
Holt, John de, 563
Holy Land, 522, 715; p. 29
Holy Trinity, Coventry, church or chapel of, xvii, xxiin, xxiv, xxx; 12, 376, 633; p. 64
—altar of blessed Mary of, 127
—chapel of Holy Cross in cemetery of, 12
—dependant chapels of, xxiv
—vicar of *see* Sir Henry de Harnall
Honington (Honitone), p. 365n.
—Thomas de, 500
Honorius III, pope, p. 5
Honslap, Richard de, 653–4
Hore,
—Geoffrey le, 35.14, 35.16
—William le, 33
Horwell (Horewell), p. 365n.
—Thomas de, 429
Hornwood (Hornewod', Hornwod),
—Nicholas, 716
—Susan widow of William, 727
—Hornwood's Lane (Hornewodeswey, Hornwodelone), 719–21
Hors,
—John, 768(p. 373)
—Richard, 217
—Rosa, 140–2
Horsel, Henry, 284
Horsham, William de, 306, 312
Horsepurs', William, 426
Hose, William le, 397–8, 768(p. 371)

Hoser (Hosier, Hosiere, Hosyere),
—Henry le, 33n.
—Hugh le, clerk, 218, 361, 593–4, 647, 722
——bailiff, 299
——coroner, xxviii; 38.2
——heirs of, 768(pp. 374, 377)
—Hugh le (*another*), 33n, 129, 172–3, 715
Hoslok (Osloc, Oslok), Walter, 768(pp. 374–5, 380)
Hotting *see* Utting
Houloneye *see* Olney
Houtred, Houtret, Houtreyd, Howtred *see* Uttred
Hoy land', Hoyland *see* Holland
Hoysel *see* Oysel
Huchinton' (Huehinton'),
—Robert de, clerk, 719
—William de, 537, 649
Hucstere, Mabel le, 37.4
Hugh,
—Ranulph son of, 741
—Robert son of, 724
—William son of, 705
—William son of (*another*), 264
Huldeshut, Alexander, 37.3
Humphrey (*Hu(m)fredus*, *Umfredus*, Umfrei, *Umfrid'*, Unfrey),
—John son of *alias* John, 541, 564, 677
—William son of *alias* William, 524, 527, 534, 555, 604–5, 607, 641, 660–3, 676, 707
——reeve, xx
——John son of William, 524, 555, 604, 641, 660–1, 663, 707; reeve, xx; 557
——William his son, 660
Hundeslane (Hundelan', *Hundelona*, Hundelone),
—Richard de, 35.7, 60, 176, 346, 379, 381, 408–9, 411, 671
——Richard his son, 35.7, 35.16
Hunte,
—Ralf le, xl; 33n, 145–6, 153, 158–9, 162, 165–6, 171, 212, 242, 247, 345, 354, 370, 372, 375, 643, 753
—Robert le, 138
Huntsman (*venator*),
—Ralph the, 141, 143
—Serlo the, 3
Hupton', William de, serjeant of Gloucester, 205
Hurne (*Anglio, Anglulo, Angulo*, Huyrne, Hyrne),
—John in le, 633
—Robert del *alias* Robert en le *alias* Robert in *alias* Robert in le *alias* Robert in the, tanner, xxxv; 38.1, 394–6, 401, 445–6, 448, 462, 479, 482, 484–8, 490–3, 495, 500, 510, 512–13, 521, 550–1, 646, 749, 768(pp. 383–4)
——Agnes his wife, 492
——Henry his son, clerk, 74, 249–50, 493, 495, 761
——Thomas his son, clerk, 493, 517
——Alice his daughter, 74, 491; her husband *see* Stephen the Marshal
——Bela his daughter, 394–5
Hurst,
—Bateman de, 36.12
—Michael de, 179, 412–14
Huthered *see* Uttred
Hutting, Huttink, Huttyng, Huttyng' *see* Utting
Huuere, Richard le, 84
Hwitele *see* Whitley
Hybernia see Ireland
Hylwene, Robert, 278
Hyrenol, Richard, 454
Hyreys, Hyrreys *see* Ireys
Hyrne *see* Hurne

Idelestr, John de, 33n.
Illory, William, 768(p. 380)
Ilpus, William, 35.7
Indgrace, John de, 226
Ingelard (*Ingelardus*, Ingillard, Yngelard) *alias* Ingelard the Farrier, 601–3, 605–7, 677, 706
Ingelwridus, 768(p. 383)
Ingram (Hingram', Ingelram, Ingeram, Ingilram, Yngeram),
—Alice, 768(p. 375)
—John, 195, 424, 546, 590, 611, 616, 621, 649–50, 682, 721, 732
——Ranulph his son, 621
——heirs of, 768(pp. 375, 378)
—John (*another*), 424, 629, 768(pp. 374–5)
—Peter, 36.10
Innocent II, pope, xviii–ixn.
Ireland (*Hibern', Hybernia*, Irlond, Yrland),
—Walter de, cooper, xxxvi; 617–18, 626
—William *alias* William de, 610, 613
Ireys (Hyreys, Hyrreys, Yreis, Yreys, Yrreys),
—Matthew le, 36.13
——Alina his widow, 36.13
———Matilda and Margery her sisters, 36.13
—Geoffrey le, 27
—Philip le, of Stoke, 754, 763
—Sir Thomas le, knight, lord of Ansty, 22a, 65, 711, 757
Isabella, queen of England, pp. 2, 3, 9n, 29–30
—her ministers, p. 2
—her steward, p. 3n.
Itchington (Ichenton', Ichynton, Ikynton'), xixn, xxxix; 197
—Robert de, clerk, 610
—Robert de (*?same*), 768(p. 388)
Ivo, constable of Coventry, pp. 6, 8
Ivo (Yvo) (*another*), 767.4, 767.5

Jabet, Robert, of Sowe, 712, 743, 766
Jacob, Thomas, of Clifton, 39.10
Jeaffreson, J.C., pp. 63–4
John, king of England, 15n.
John,
—Eustace fitz, constable of Chester, xxxiin; 4, 10n; p. 5
—Geoffrey son of, 396, 424–5, 431, 445–50, 457–8, 460, 467–8, 471–2, 477–9, 481–4, 486–7, 491, 497, 499–501, 504, 506–8, 511, 513, 516, 520, 756, 768(pp. 383, 386, 389, 391)
——heirs of, 522
—Walter son of, 555
Joia, John, 174
Joilin', Simon, 30 a and b
Jordan,
—Herbert son of, 175, 408, 411, 538, 553, 582, 603, 660
——Peter his son, 538, 584
——Amilia his daughter, 585
—Leofwin son of *see* Leofwin/Lewin
——Hamo his brother *see* Hamo/Hamond
—Peter son of, 586
Jordan Well, xxxiii

Jory (Jori, Yori),
—Christine daughter of Agnes, 326
—Colin, 268
—Nicholas son of, 265
—Nicholas (*another*), 217, 282, 295, 299, 768(pp. 371, 378, 390, 394)

Kaleudon, Kaleudon', Kalouedon' *see* Caludon
Kalle, Robert, 658
Kancia, Kant *see* Kent
Kanel, Kannele, Kanneley, *Kanneleya*, Kanneleye *see* Canley
Karesleg' *see* Keresley
Kateby, Katesb', Katisby *see* Catesby
Kaus (Caus),
—Ranulf de, 187–8
——bailiff, xxvi; 37.17
Kay (Cay),
—Geoffrey, 37.7
—Richard, 449–50, 497–8, 504, 508, 514, 516, 520, 522
Kelle (Kell),
—Robert, 114, 127, 228–9, 508–9, 579–80, 619–20, 629–31, 633–8, 668, 693, 697, 730–1
—William, 546, 562, 573, 576, 657–8
—William son of William *alias* William (*?another*), 577–80
Kembestere,
—Avicia le, 510
——Susan her daughter, 510
Kempe (Cempe),
—Osbert, 180–1, 199
——Petronilla his widow, 179, 195
—Thomas, 577
—Vincent, 576
——heirs of, 768(p. 376)
—Vincent son of Reginald (*?same*), 541
—Ysabel, 521
Kendal (Kendale),
—John de, saddler, 424, 496–8
——Isabel his wife, 496
——Adam his son, 498
Kenilworth (Kenelworth, Kenelwrthe, Keneyleworth', Kenilleworth', Kenillewrthe, Kenylleworth', Kenylworth), xxvii; 38.1
—prior of, 206, 768(p. 385)
—brother William the prior and convent of, 208
—Nicholas de, 202
—Master Robert de, 761
—William de, 300, 302–3
Kenisbur' *see* Kingsbury
Kent (*Kancia*, Kant, Keint), Peter de, 29, 379, 408–9, 524, 660, 671, 676
Kereby *see* Kirby
Keresley (*Kareslea*, Karesleg', Keresl, Keresle, *Keresleia*, Kerisle, Kersle), xvin, xxv; 13, 17–18, 22a, 741, 765
—intended chapel of; 2, 5, 12; p. 6n.
—woodland and waste in, 17; p. 2
—Thomas de *alias* Thomas lord of, 718, 724, 741, 768(p. 394)
——Walter his son, 741
Keswick (Kesewich, Kesewych'), Roger de, 201–2
Ketel,
—Walter called, 45
——Hawisia his wife, 45; *see also* Hawisia daughter of Richard Hamond
Ketelbern (Cetelber', Ketelberne),
—?, 530
—Hugh, 44, 50, 64–6, 595, 623, 672–3
——heirs of, 768(p. 373)
—Walter, 40–1
Keu (Cu, Kiu),
—Alan le, 768(p. 381)
—John le, 118, 378, 686, 693, 696, 701, 739
——Matilda his wife, 118
—Ralf le, 72
—Master Robert le, 523, 631, 694
——Alice his wife, 523, 631
——John their son, 523
—William le, of Basingwerk, Hospitaller, 39.3
—Richard, 538
—Richard le (*another*), 768(p. 391)
—Symon, 74
Keules, William de, 38.3
Kidderminster (Ked(er)minst(er), Kid(er)-minst(er), Kid(er)mu(n)ster, Kidermu(n)str', Kyderminst(er), Kydremunester),
—Adam de, 55–6, 459–61
——Emma his wife, 455, 459–61
——Beatrice their daughter, 457–61, 768(p. 384)
——Henry called of, her half-brother *alias* Henry son of Thomas the Weaver, 457–8, 460
—Richard de, chaplain, 462–3, 745
Kidelomp (Kidelump, Kydelomb), John, 203, 242
Kildisby (Kildesby, Kildisbi, Kyldesby, Kyldisby),
—Simon de *alias* Symon de, 394–5, 768(p. 394)
——Agnes his wife, 768(p. 394)
—Walter de, tanner, 457, 476, 479, 481, 490, 513, 521, 768(p. 390)
——Agnes his daughter, 513
Kille, William, 622
Kineton (Kinton'), Walter de, 407
King (Keng, King', Kyng),
—Alexander le, 458, 509, 697
—Richard *alias* Richard called, 231, 449, 477, 491, 496–8, 504–6, 508, 516, 522
—Robert, 768(p. 386)
—Simon *alias* Simon le *alias* Symon *alias* Symon called *alias* Symon le, 443–7, 467–8, 477–8, 496, 499, 500, 574, 698, 768(p. 394)
Kingsbury (Kenisbur', Kinesbur', Kynesbur', Kynisbur), 22a
—Adam de, 260
——Gilbert son of Adam de (*?his son*), 283
Kingsland (Kyngeslond), Simon de, 523
Kirby (Kereby, Kirkebi, Kirkeby, Kyrkebi, Kyrkeby),
—Philip de, chaplain, 119
—Roger de, 259, 261, 263, 346
——Hugh his son, 767.26
Knarri, Reginald, 30b
Knave (Chnave, Cnave),
—Henry *alias* Henry le, 51, 230, 575–6, 596, 599, 626, 768(pp. 374, 376)
—John le, 541
—John le (*another*), 630
—William la *alias* William le, 538, 541, 566, 583–6, 609, 706, 718
Knighton (Knyghton), Roger de, 768(p. 385)
Knit, Alexander *alias* Alexander le, 459–60
Koker, Richard le, 543
Kolt, Ralf le, 30b
Korewenn' *see* Corwenne

Kroun, Robert, 95
Kundellum' *see* Coundon
Ky'befeld, Alexander de, 760
Kydelomb *see* Kidelomp
Kyme, Philip de, custodian, p. 7
Kynardeby, William de, tailor, 37.13
Kynesbur', Kynisbur *see* Kingsbury
Kynewoldesham, Henry de, 517
Kynne, Walter, 20
Kyrkebi, Kyrkeby *see* Kirby

Labanc (Labanck, Labbanc, Labounc), Richard, 37.2, 42, 382, 421, 434–5, 664
Lacy (Laci),
—Henry de, earl of Lincoln, 39.3
—Roger [de], constable of Chester, 15
Ladbroke (Lodbrok),
—Sir Henry de, 438
——John his father, 438n.
—John de, knight, 760
Lagrene *see* Grene
Lalle,
—John, 282
—Walter, 259
—William, 768(p. 371)
Lambert, 10
Lange't, Walter de, 280, 283
Langedon' *see* Longdon
Langley (Langel, Langele, Langelee, Langeley, *Langeleya*, Langeleye, Langleye, Longeley, *Longeleya*, Longeleye, Longgele),
—family of, xli
—Lady Alice de, 237, 331, 344
—Sir Edmund de, lord of Shortley, 128, 163–4, 335–7, 753–4
—Sir Geoffrey de, knight, xxvn; 22a, 47, 118, 120, 187–9, 204, 281; p. 326
——heirs of, 212–13
—Sir Geoffrey de, knight (*another*), 121, 149, 236–9, 511, 741, 750–2, 758–9, 768(pp. 367–8n., 378, 384–6, 393)
—Sir John de, lord of Pinley, xxii; 241, 304, 307, 332–3, 335–6, 402
——his court of Coventry, xxii; 241, 332, 402
—John de, merchant, xlii; 33, 71–2, 76, 104, 108–9, 115–16, 120–1, 124, 128–31, 144, 151–2, 160, 162–4, 214, 225–7, 237, 239–41, 246, 249, 256, 309, 327, 330–1, 336, 343–5, 356–9, 369–71, 373, 377, 404, 485, 491, 509, 644, 712, 735–7, 748, 750–4, 762–3, 766
——Alice his wife, 748
——Felicia his wife, 237
—Walter de, xxvn; 22a, 768(pp. 387, 392)
Lanton, Geoffrey le, 768(p. 392)
Latoner (Latouner),
—Adam le, xxxvi; 158–9
—Henry le, 371–3
—William le, 33
Laweles, Adam, 38.3
Laxton, Thomas de, 503
Leamington (Lemynton'), Henry de, 71
Leche,
—Margery called La *see* Margery wife of Robert de Ashby
—Margery daughter of Alice la (*another*), 500
Lechisfeld' *see* Lichfield
Ledbetter (Ledbeter, Ledbetere),
—Henry le, 510
——Mabel his wife, 510
—Richard *alias* Richard le, 442–5
Lef (Leef, Leef', Lef', Luf, Luff),
—Geoffrey *alias* Geoffrey le, xxxvii; 33, 103–4, 108–9, 124–5, 148–9, 151, 156–60, 169–71, 304, 325, 353, 355, 768(pp. 385–6, 388–9)
—William la, 242
Lefwin, Lefwin' see Leofwin/Lewin
Leicester (Leicestre, Leircest', Leycestre), xxx, xxxii, xl; 767.4, 767.5
—Henry de, Prior *see* St. Mary's, Prior of
——Robert de, his brother, 728
—Ralph de *see* St. Michael's, vicar of
—Richard de, 33, 232
——Beatrice his wife, 232
—Master Robert *alias* Master Robert de, 112, 651, 768(pp. 374, 394)
—Simon de *alias* Symon de, 381, 410, 419–20, 427, 432–3, 440, 531–2, 556, 558, 707
—William de, p. 352
Lennis, Richard de, 174
Lent', Master Geoffrey de, 12
Leo, son of Moses, Jew of Warwick, 710
Leofric,
—family of, xv
—earl, xvi, xviii; 768(p. 370); his wife *see* Countess Godiva
Leofwin/Lewin (Lefwin, Lefwin', Leofwine, Leofwyne, Leuewin, Leuin, Leuine, Leuwin, Leuwine, *Leuwinus*, Leuwyn, Leuwyne, Leuyn, Lewine, Lewyn, Lewyne, Loeuwyn, Louwyne), 85, 175, 262, 411, 524, 555, 660–1, 671; p. 66; his brothers *see Hamo*/Hamond and Herbert; his father *see* Jordan
——Richard his son, 30a and b, 43, 91, 181, 272, 538, 541, 559, 584–6, 639, 672–3
—family of, xxxviii
—Alexander, 294
—John, 79, 81, 157, 493, 507, 646, 693–4, 697, 702, 768(p. 379)
——coroner, xxix; 39.7, 72, 127–8, 146, 161–2, 173, 241, 251–2, 254–5, 331–2, 334, 374, 402–3, 462–3, 495, 505, 509, 520–2, 580–1, 636–7, 645–6, 659, 695–6, 700–1, 730–1, 753
—William, xxvi, xxxix; 36.14, 47, 50, 67, 283, 542, 570, 592–3, 611–12, 614–16, 649–50, 664, 682, 719–20, 732
——bailiff, xxv–vi; 37.1, 360, 422, 590, 594, 613, 632, 721
Leoras, Thomas, 649
Leper (Lepere, Lepper),
—Richard le, 310
—William le, 310, 768(p. 380)
Leteman *see* Loteman
Lethe,
—Isolde le, 499
——Alice her daughter, 499
Levict, Richard le, 767.26
Lewis, Mrs. J. C. Lancaster, xvi, xln.
Lexington (Lexinton'), Robert de, 35.17, 767.55, 767.56
Leyre, John de, 504
Lichfield (Lechisfeld', Lichefeld, Lichesfeld, Lychesfeld), xvn, xxx
—canons of, xviin, xviii
—chapter of, xviii, xxiii; 768(p. 370); pp. 5–6n.

Lichfield (*cont.*)
—church of St. Chad of, 14
—church of the blessed Mary of, 228–9, 691
—minster of, 691
—Master Richard the Treasurer of, 13
—Hugh de, 33
—John de, clerk, 305
—Nicholas de, 531–2
——Reginald his son, 532
—Robert de, 302, 768(pp. 378, 391)
Lichfield & Coventry (Lych' et Coventre), bishop of *see* Index II *under* CLERICS
Lifwi, Stephen son of, 527
Lilbourne (Lilleborne, Lillebourne, Lilleburn, Lilleburne, Lylleborn', Lylleburn'),
—Henry *alias* Henry de, merchant, 93, 99, 106–8, 217, 284, 291–2, 295–8, 300–3, 305, 307–8, 311, 313–17, 319–22, 325, 328–9, 338, 342–4, 401, 768(pp. 383, 388, 391, 394)
——Thomas his son *alias* Thomas de, 39.1, 133, 245, 323, 333–4, 338, 753
Limesey (Lymeseye),
—Robert de, bishop of Chester, xv–vi, xxx
—Simon de, 426
Limgel', Simon, serjeant, 35.14
Lincoln (Lincoln'), p. 8
—church of, 2n.
—citizens of, p. 7
—earl of, 768(p. 392); *see also* Henry de Lacy; William de Roumare
—William de, 175
Lincolnshire, p. 32
Lindsey (Lyndeseye), John de, 33
Linlithgow (Linlyscu), 39.6
Linot, Thomas, of Brackley, 383
Linpulator, Alexander, brother of the hospital of St. Leonard, 420
Little Grove (Litlegrove), Coventry, 753–4
Little Park Street, Coventry, xxxii, xxxiv, xxxvi–vii
—bar in, xxxiv
Liuet,
—Walter, 68
—William, 41, 380, 529
Liulf (Lithulph, Liulph, Lythulf) *see* Liulf de Brinklow
—Nicholas fitz, 7, 10, 14, 16, 29, 174, 176, 524, 767.3, 767.4, 767.5, 767.7, 767.19
——Nicholas his son *see* Nicholas de Withybrook
——Roger his brother, 767.4, 767.5
——his brothers, 7
——Simon his nephew, 524
—Nicholas (*?another*), 192, 237
—Nicholas, of Spon, heirs of, 768(p. 387)
Livet, Roger, 6 and n.
Lloyd, Dr. Simon, p. 30n.
Locard (Locart, Lokard),
—Anketill, 7, 10, 535n; p. 1; his widow *see* Alice de Whitemore
——Alice daughter of Anketill, 573; *see also* Alice wife/widow of Brunus Halling'
—Asket' (*?Anketill*), 9; p. 1
—Richard, 717; p. 326
——Cecily his sister, 717; her husband *see* Robert called Anketill de Radford
—Roger, 722, 724
—Roger (*?another*), 725–8, 731; p. 326
——Alice de Birchemor', his wife, 728
——Thomas his son, 728
——Juliana his daughter, 728
Locksmith (*locarius*, *Loccarius*, Lockier, Loker, Loker', Lokkere, Lokywer'),
—Adam the, 260, 264, 271
——Alexander his brother, 260, 271
—Alexander son of Hugh le, 767.16
—Brunus the, 260, 264, 271
——Alice his wife, 271
—Hugh *alias* Hugh le, 87–8, 767.12, 767.13, 767.14, 767.15, 767.17, 767.53
—Ivo the, 271
—John le, 767.12, 767.13, 767.14, 767.15, 767.16
——Agnes his widow, 767.14
——Peter their son, 767.14, 767.15
——Agnes his daughter, 87; her husband *see* Stephen de St. Edmund
—John le *alias* John the (*another*), 195, 266, 547, 768(p. 386)
—Jordan the, 260
—Margery le, widow, 96
—Martin the, 263, 268, 454
——Thomas his son, 228, 265–8, 441
———Agnes his wife, 228; her father *see* Alexander de Gloucester
—Martin le (*another*), 328, 768(pp. 383, 391)
—Richard le, 767.17
——Emma his wife, 767.17
—Robert the, 436, 554
—Robert the (*another*), 393; his daughter *see* Luveday widow of Richard le Comber
—Robert le, of Lawford, 37.7
—William son of Hugh the, 259, 271
——Alice his sister, 259
—William the (*another*), 710
—William le (*another*), 768(pp. 380, 389)
Lodbrok *see* Ladbrook
Lodelowe (Lodeloue, Lodelouue, Lodelowe, Lodlawe, Lodlowe, Loudeloue, Luddelowe, Ludelawe, Ludelowe, Ludlawe),
—family of, xxxviii
—Hugh de, 534, 539, 555, 603
——Margaret his daughter, 539
—John de, xxxvii–viii, xli; 95, 97, 137, 195–8, 201, 206, 283–4, 342–3, 360, 376, 385, 431, 496, 665–6, 683, 724, 761
——bailiff, xxviii; 46, 138, 207–8, 210, 217, 219, 276, 300, 302, 387, 447, 457–8, 468
——Thomas his son, 768(p. 384)
——Alice his niece, 385
——heirs of, 768(p. 386)
—Robert called de *alias* Robert de, 304–7, 310–14, 318–22, 325, 342, 376, 490, 494, 768(pp. 368n, 372, 374, 380, 384, 389, 391)
——Margery his wife, 305, 311
——Margery his widow, 155, 308–9, 314, 322, 345, 494
——William his son, 761
—Roger de, 538
—Roger de (*another*), 768(p. 382)
—Thomas de, 248
—William de, 534
Loeuwyn *see* Leofwin/Lewin
Loges,
—Hugh de, 22a
—Richard de, knight, 39.2, 758; his servant *see* Hugh le Sker

Loker, Lokkere, Lokywer *see* Locksmith
London (*Londona*, *Londoniis*, Londr', Loundres, *Lundoniens'*, Lundris), xxx, xl–i; p. 7
—Ansketill of *alias* Haschat' de, 2, 8; his sons *see under* Anketell
—Elyas de, 768(p. 388)
—Ernaldus de, 539
—Robert *alias* Robert de, 361, 546, 616, 621, 651, 665–6, 674–5, 682–3, 698, 701, 722
——Agnes his daughter, 768(p. 376)
—Robert de (*another*), chaplain, 133
—William de, 263, 265–6, 268, 274–5, 767.6
Long (Longe, *Longus*, Lungh),
—Guy, 412–14
—Henry, 278
—John le, 33
—Roger, 36.12
—Thomas *alias* Thomas le, 265, 268, 273, 287
Longdon (Langedon', Longedon'),
—Gilbert de, 207, 239, 768(pp. 383, 392)
——Alice his daughter, 126
Longeley, *Longeleya*, Longeleye, Longgele *see* Langley
Lonton *see* Lunton
Lorimer (*Loremarius*, *Lorimarius*, Loriner, Lorymer),
—Hugh the, 190
—John le, 768(p. 393)
——heirs of John le and Margery his wife, 378
—Richard son of Richard the, 61–2, 524
——Agnes his aunt, 61, 524
——his heirs, 525
—Richard heir of Richard the, 28c, 526
—Walter the, 29, 85
Losewit (Losewyt, Losewyth),
—Simon *alias* Symon, 579, 630, 634
—William, 579
Loteman (Leteman, Lotemon, Luteman, Lutemon, Lutteman),
—Richard, 422–3, 443–4, 447, 455–6, 459, 469, 471, 474–5, 496
—Walter, 424–5, 481
—William, 249, 364, 394–5, 446, 462, 473, 476–7, 479–80, 482, 484–8, 490–1, 494, 497, 499, 501, 510–13, 521, 550–1, 749, 768(p. 388)
Lou, Matilda le, 768(p. 382)
Loueas, of Little Park Street, 92
Louecot, Henry, 283
Loughborough (Luhteburg'), Leics., 22a
Louwyne *see* Leofwin/Lewin
Love *see* Luve
Lovel, Richard, 33
Lovigny (Lovini), Joel, 15 and n.
Lucius II, pope, xviii
Lucy (Luci),
—Sir Fulk de, knight, 752
—Richard de, 11
Ludborough (Ludboreu), John de, 59
Ludelawe, Ludelowe, Ludlawe *see* Lodelawe
Ludet', Hugh de, 381
Luesham, Thomas de, 165
Luf, Luff *see* Lef
Lungemore, John son of Henry, 36.7
Lungh *see* Long
Lunton (Lonton, Lontoun, Lunton', Luntoun), Geoffrey, 97, 100, 196, 206–7, 228–9, 353, 376
Luteman, Lutemon, Lutteman *see* Loteman
Luterel, Sir Robert, knight, 560, 563
Luton', Richard de, 500
Luttelwrite (Luttelewrite), Robert le, 228–9
Lutterworth (Lutrewurth), Peter de, 35.7
Luve (Love), Nicholas *alias* Nicholas son of, 412–14, 432–3, 466
Luvetot,
—Richard de, 9
—Roger, 10
Lyhtfot (Lythfot), Alan, 153, 309, 369
Lymburg, William de, 155
Lyndon', William de, 563
Lynne, Elias de, 715
Lythulf *see* Liulf

Macsot, Macstoke *see* Maxstoke
Madley, John de, 768(p. 389)
Maggus (*?mag̃go*), Robert, 424
Maiden (Mayden, Maydin),
—Nicholas *alias* Nicholas le, 94, 101–5, 108–9, 120–3, 574, 768(pp. 376, 386)
—William le, 94, 568
Mainwaring (Maisnill' Warin', Meisnilwarin, Meynilwar'),
—Ralf *alias* Ralf de, justiciar of Chester, 7, 13, 15, 16n.
—Ranulf de *see* St. Michael's, chaplain of
Makestoke *see* Maxstoke
Malbank (Malbanc, Maubanch'), William, 4, 5 and n.
Malemote, John de, 32
Malfillastre (Malfylastr'), Roger, 6 and n.
Malmesbury, William de, xv
Maminot, Walkelin, 2
Mancetter (Manecestre), Master Walter rector of the church of, 732–3
Manliv(er), Richard de, 33
Mansel (Mancel, Mansel', Maunceil, Mauncel, Maunscel, Maunsel, Maunsel'), 419; *see also* Mancel the Dyer
—Nicholas, dyer, 691
——Margery his wife, 691
—Robert son of, 451
—Robert (*?same*), 387–90, 397, 422, 424, 458–60, 464, 470, 474–5, 653
——Petronilla his wife, 464
——William his son, 51, 78, 126, 391–2, 424, 457–8, 463, 473, 479, 481, 486, 518, 521, 646, 695, 697, 702–3, 738
—Robert (*?another*), 74, 512, 517, 519
—William (*another*), sheriff of Warwick, 37.11
Marbatin, Walter, 221
Marie (Marye),
—Henry, 768(pp. 373–4)
—Thomas, 218, 230, 251, 284, 300, 302, 309, 315–16, 358, 549, 768(pp. 380–2, 392)
——Edith his wife, 230
Marlborough (*Merleberga*), Wilts., 11 and n.
Marmion (Marmiun),
—Robert II, pp. 8–9
—Robert III, xviii; 1; pp. 8–9
—R[obert] (III *or* IV), 21
Marshal (Marchal, Marchall', Marechal, Marescal, *marescallus*, Mareschal, Marichal, *marscallus*, Marshall),
—?, 49
—Godfrey son of Walter the, of Warwick, 451–3

Marshal (*cont.*)
—Henry the, 87–8
—Henry le *alias* Henry the (*another*), 46, 53–4
——Matilda his wife, 53
——Robert his son, 54–5
———Henry his brother, 55
—John le *alias* John the, 70, 386, 622, 768(p. 382)
——Stephen his son, 377
—John the, of Daventry, 190
—Maria daughter of Richard le, 399
—Nicholas le, of Coventry, xxxvii; 701
—Petronilla widow of John the, 36.17
—Richard le, 628
—Robert the, p. 10
—Stephen le *alias* Stephen the, 53–5, 59, 71, 73–5, 400, 402–3, 405–6, 448, 450, 491, 502, 696, 698; his wife *see* Alice sister of Henry the Clerk
—Walter the, 36.17, 452, 681
—W. the (*?same*), 182
—Walter le (*another*), 38.5
—William the, steward of the earl of Chester, xxn, xxxviii; 15, 528, 767.65; pp. 5n, 9–10; his niece *see* Leticia de Sutton'
——William his son, 767.65
Marston (M(er)sten', Merstone, Meryston),
—Richard de, 249–50, 491
—Thomas de, baker, 171, 173
Martin (Martin', Martyn),
—family of, xxxviii
—Hugh son of, xx; 16, 40n, 41, 60–3, 85, 175–6, 379–80, 408, 524, 529–30, 533, 553–4, 600, 604, 662, 671, 676
——Alice his wife, 40
——Alice his widow and Petronilla her daughter, 43
——Peter *alias* Peter son of, 36.1, 36.11, 37.1, 42, 50, 64–5, 90, 183–4, 588, 593, 642, 672–3, 717, 732
———Avicia his daughter, 66
———Matilda his daughter, 66, 768(pp. 372, 389–90)
———heirs of, 768(pp. 371, 389)
——Robert son of, 43, 588
—Peter son of, 639
—Thomas son of, 267, 269
Mary, Roger son of, 707
Marye *see* Marie
Mason (*cementarius*, *cemetar'*, Masun),
—John the, 767.27
—John le (*another*), 768(p. 378)
—John son of William le, of Tilebrook, 761
—Richard the, 277, 285
—Richard le (*?another*), 353
—Thomas the, xxxv; 601–2, 706
——Thomas his son, 440
—William the, 260, 264–6
Mastlingbeter',
—Beatrice widow of Richard le, 303
——Maria her daughter, 303
——Alice her sister, 303
———Margery her daughter, 303
Matilda,
—Robert son of, 29
——Annes (*sic*) his wife, 29
Matthew, Stephen son of, 710
Maubanch' *see* Malbank
Mauclerc, William, 418, 422, 456, 464
Maunceil, Mauncel, Maunscel, Maunsel, Maunsel' *see* Mansel
Maxstoke (Macscot, Macstoke, Makestoke, Maxstok, Maxthoke),
—Hugh de, 649
—John de, xxxviii; 51, 367, 651–2, 665, 670, 686, 768(pp. 377–8)
——Agnes his widow, 57, 692
—John de, baker, 123
——Alice his wife, 123
—Robert de, 681
—Roger, 648
Mayl, Hugh, 768(p. 390)
Meau *see* Meu
Meisnilwarin *see* Mainwaring
Meisy, Robert de, 768(p. 392)
Meleburn (Meleburn'),
—Robert de, 177
—Robert de (*another*), 768(pp. 392–4)
Melton, Robert de, merchant, 371
Mercer (*mercenarius*, *mercerus*, Merser),
—Andrew le, 147, 768(p. 392); *see also* Andrew the Merchant
——Agnes his wife, 768(p. 392)
—Bogo le *alias* Boni le *alias* Boni the *alias* Bony *alias* Bony the, 139, 147, 149, 201, 210
—Godfrey le *alias* Godfrey the, 186, 189, 204–5, 279, 281, 454; *see also* Godfrey the Merchant
——William his son, 101–2
—Edith widow of Brun le, 767.40, 767.41
—John *alias* John the, 263, 527, 553, 676
—Peter, 271
—Ralf, 271
—Reginald le *alias* Reginald the, 181, 281; *see also* Reginald the Merchant
——Dyonisia his daughter, 245
—Richard le, 33n, 55, 59, 69, 73, 79, 131, 402, 405–6, 737
—Warin le, 134, 136, 279, 288–9, 294; p. 66; his widow *see* Alice daughter of Robert de Doncaster. *See also* Warin the Merchant
Merchant (*mercator*),
—Amfrey the *alias* Amfridus of Park St., *alias* Amfridus the *alias* Aunfridus the, xxxvii; 84, 90, 261, 347, 349
——Reginald *and* Simon *alias* Symon, his sons, xxxvii; 90, 347, 349
—Andrew the, 191; *see also* Andrew le Mercer
—Geoffrey the, 767.34,
——Alice his wife, 767.34
—Godfrey the, 136, 282; *see also* Godfrey le Mercer
—Henry the, of Titchmarsh *alias* Henry de Titchmarsh, 280
—Hugh the, 437
—Reginald the, 134–5, 186, 278, 350–1; *see also* Reginald le Mercer
—Richard the, 186
—Robert the, of Welham, 280
—Warin the, 186; *see also* Warin le Mercer
—William the, 186, 278
Merington (Merington', Merintone, Meriton', Merynton', Meryton, Meryton'),
—family of, xl, xlii
—Henry de, merchant, 33, 39.1, 166
—Hugh de, merchant, xl, xlii, 33, 146, 156, 165–6, 245, 372, 643, 766; his wife *see* Agnes sister of Roger Green

—Peter de, 33, 159
—Walter de, 33, 166
Merewin (Merewin', M(eru)enne, Meruin, Merwin, Merwine, Merwyne),
—Alice, wife of William Parser, 93
—John, 259, 261, 265, 267–8, 346–7, 349–50, 767.34, 767.35
Meryston *see* Marston
Metingham,
—William de, merchant, 69
——Matilda his wife, 69
Meu (Meau),
—Nicholas, 43
—Richard, 40–1, 60, 62–3, 380, 529–30
——Richard *alias* Richard son of Richard at, 36.16, 42, 45, 543
Meuland, Roger, bishop of Coventry and Lichfield, xxivn; 112; p. 6
Meynilwar' *see* Mainwaring
Michael, Henry son of, 537
Middleton (Middelton', Myddelton'), Henry de, 33, 255
Midniht (Midneit, Midneith, Midnit, Midnith, Midnut, Midnyht, Midnyth, Mydnyht, Mynnyht),
—Richard *alias* Richard de, 574–5, 617–18, 620, 626–7, 630, 633, 670, 768(pp. 374, 376, 378); p. 65
—William, 84, 527, 660–2, 676
Milcote (Melcote, Mulcote, Muschote),
—Henry de, girdler, xxxvi; 203, 242
—Richard de, 38.13
Mildenhale,
—John de, merchant, 33, 132, 171, 241, 256
——Agnes his wife, 132
—William de, 33
Mildesby, John de, 768(p. 386)
Miles,
—of Gosford, 767.4, 767.5
—Master, of Gosford, (*another*), 265, 274, 277, 283, 293
——heirs of, 768(p. 391)
—Adam son of, 768(p. 386); *see also* Adam Myle
Miller (*molendinarius*, Molener, Mouner, Mouner', Muner),
—Adam the, 410
—Adam the, of Newham (*?another*), 767.54
—Henry le *alias* Henry the (*two*), 91–2, 94, 102
—Henry son of Richard le, 38.9
——Alice his wife, 38.9
—John le *alias* John the, 362–4, 768(p. 377)
—Nicholas the, 632
—Osbert the *alias* Osbert son of Jordan *alias* Osbert son of Jurdan the, 434–5, 441–4, 447, 454–5, 464–5, 545
——Osbert his son, 447
—Ralf the *alias* Ralph the (*two*), 84, 90, 178, 180, 261, 272, 348–9, 382, 540, 588, 632
—Reginald the, 35.9
—Reginald the (*another*), 648
—Richard the, 298, 324
—Robert the, 90
——heirs of, 768(p. 385)
—Robert le *alias* Robert called the *alias* Robert the (*another*), xxxvii; 38.1, 49, 147–9, 151, 167–9, 199, 218, 246, 281, 293, 304, 325, 768(pp. 370, 385–6, 388, 392)
—Roger the, 604
——heirs of, 768(p. 376)
—Roger the (*another*), 50, 546, 589–90, 592, 598, 622, 624, 632, 684
—Roger son of William le (*?same*), 589–91
—Roger son of Robert the, 118, 152
——John his son *alias* John called Abbot, his son, 644–5, 768(p. 373)
———Richard his son, 645
—Simon the, 572
—Walter the *alias* Walter called le Glover, 39.9
—William son of Godric the, 660
—William the, 285, 566, 582–3, 600
——Matilda his wife, 582
——Richard his son, 583, 612
———Alice his wife, 612
Mine, Thomas de la, 185
Minot (Miniot, Minoth, Mynot),
—John, 33, 97, 206, 362–3, 365, 574, 628, 686, 745, 768(p. 378)
——John his son, 57–8n, 367–8, 373, 692
——Alice his daughter, 768(p. 379)
Minut, Richard, 221
Mire *see* Muyre
Mirourer (Myrourer),
—Clement le, xxxvi; 145–6, 242–5
——Agnes his wife, 243–4
———Alice her mother, 244
—Ralf le, xxxvi; 137
Missi (Missin'), Hervi de, 6 and n.
Mohaut *see* Montalt
Molener *see* Miller
Molle,
—Richard, 527, 534, 555
—Vincent, 536, 567
Mols, Roger, p. 366
Monkeshous, John de le, 46
Monks Kirby, priory of, 5n.
Mons, Peter, 768(p. 381)
Montalt (Mohaut, *monte alto*, Mouhaut),
—Sir Ralf de, 27
—Robert de (d. *circa* 1210), steward [of Chester], 15 and n.
—Robert de (d. 1275), 25n; p. 30
——heirs of, 212–13, 222–3, 768(p. 382 and n.)
—Robert de (d. 1329), 133, 406; his park *see* Cheylesmore park
—Sir Roger de (d. 1260), steward of the earl of Chester, xxi–iin, xxiv, xxix, xxxin, xxxii; 22–26, 768(pp. 370–1, 384n.); pp. 29–30
——Cecily his wife, xxiv; 22 a & b, 26, 768(p. 370); p. 30
——Cecily his widow, 25
——his heirs, 220, 768(pp. 368, 370–2, 393)
—Roger de (d. 1296), steward of Chester, 26–7
Monte, William de, 710, 768(p. 375)
Montpedlers,
—William de, 174
——Ralf his brother, 174
Morcok (Morcoc, Morkoc),
—Ralf, 167–8, 768(p. 387)
——heirs of, 768(p. 390)
More (Mor, *Mora*),
—David de, 277
—Henry de la *alias* Henry de le, 303, 358
—Ranulf de, 259–60, 264, 271
—Roger de, 306

Morin, Syward, 36.12
Mortimer, Roger, 57
Mos (*Mosso*),
—John el *alias* John in, 558, 584–6
—J. (*?same*), 556
Mouner, Muner *see* Miller
Mowbray (Mobray, Mobrey, Moubrai, Moubrai', Moubray, Moubrei, Moubrey, Mowbraye, Mowbrei, Mowbrey, Mubrai, Mubray, Mubrey, Mumbrai),
—family of, xxxviii
—Alexander *alias* Alexander de *alias* Alexander le, 574, 657, 768(pp. 375, 380–1)
—Richard *alias* Richard de *alias* Richard le, 531–2, 539, 564, 606–8, 677–8, 707
——Matthew his son *alias* Matthew *alias* Matthew de *alias* Matthew le, 536, 569, 571, 592, 612, 682
———bailiff, xxv; 613
——Richard his son, 606–7, 707
—Richard le junior (*?same*), 565
—Thomas *alias* Thomas de *alias* Thomas le, 26, 38.1, 46, 51, 57, 70, 76, 117, 141–2, 144, 213–16, 227, 230–1, 324, 362–5, 368, 390, 400, 500, 506, 510–11, 548–9, 552, 560–2, 572–3, 575–7, 596–9, 617–20, 625–7, 629, 633, 635, 643, 657–8, 670, 686, 689–92, 727, 729, 738–42, 746, 768(pp. 370, 372, 375–6, 379–80)
——Adam his son, 581
——Alexander his son *alias* Alexander de *alias* Alexander le, clerk, 81, 258, 374, 493, 520, 631, 704, 730–1
Mower (Mowere),
—Henry le, 56, 248, 403, 502
——Agnes his wife, 403
Moys (Moys'), Richard son of, of Fletchamstead, 416–17
Much Park Street, Coventry, xxx, xxxiii–iv, xxxvi–vii
—bar in, xxxiv
—excavations in, xxxiv, xxxvi
Munsell', Henry, 10
Muschamp, Geoffrey, bishop of Coventry, p. 5
Muschote *see* Milcote
Mustard (Musterd, Muttard),
—Robert, 601–2
—Robert (*?same*), 610
Muyre (Mire, *Mora*, Mure, Muyr', Myre),
—Margery le, 499
—Richard ad *alias* Richard ate *alias* Richard called de *alias* Richard de la *alias* Richard de le *alias* Richard del *alias* Richard dela, xlii; 72–3, 104, 108–9, 114–19, 120–1, 124, 128, 162–3, 212, 214, 222–4, 225–7, 236–40, 249, 256, 305, 309, 331, 343–5, 356–9, 371, 373, 377, 494, 644, 735–6, 748, 751–4, 762; his ward *see* Guy son of Richard the Brooch-maker
——Alice his wife, 222, 225–6, 344, 357
——Henry atte *alias* Henry de la, his heir, xl, xlii; 33, 737
Myle (Milon'), Adam, of Whitley, 96, 741, 759
Mynnyht *see* Midniht

Nailstone (Nayleston', Naylleston', Nayllestone), William de *see* William the Parker
Napton', Sir Adam de, knight, 758
Nassington (Nassinton, Nassinton'),
—Geoffrey de, clerk, 270, 276, 318
——his brother *see* Nicholas de Coventry, chaplain
Natter (Nater, Nat(er)e, Natt(er)e), William *alias* William le, 265–6, 269, 275, 277
Nerbone (Nerbun, N(er)bune),
—Aubrey de, 705
—Stephen de, 705
—William de, 705
Neue (Neve),
—Hugh le, 529, 533
—Roger *alias* Roger le, 221, 393, 399, 467–8, 520, 552, 619, 627, 768(pp. 374, 387)
——Alice his widow, 627
——Stephen their son, 627
Neulest(er), John son of Claricia la, 167–8
Neumastr', William de, 768(p. 390)
Neville (Neuvill, *Nova Villa*),
—Hugh de, 13
—Thomas de, 22a
New Mill (le Neuwemulne), Coventry, 753
—Croft (Neumulne Croft), 753–4
Newark (Newerc, Newerk, Newerk'),
—Master Clement de, 554
—Richard de, 768(p. 385)
—Walter de, 715
——Isabella his wife, 715
Newbiggin (*Nova Bughinear'*, *Nova Bughinega*), Matilda de, 87–8
Newbold (Neubold), Nicholas de, 768(p. 389)
Newcastle (Novecast', *Novo Castro*),
—Robert de, 278
—Thomas de, clerk, 427
Newent', Theobald de, 767.50
Newlands,
—close at, xxxix
—park at, p. 3
Newnham (Neunham, Newenham),
—Ida widow of William de, 75
—Robert de, merchant, 332, 334
Newton (Neuton', Neweton), William de, 185, 768(p. 383)
Nicholas,
—John son of, 38.1, 511, 599, 625, 635, 693
—Nicholas son of *see* Nicholas de Withybrook
Nigel *alias* Nigel of Coventry, 2, 8–9
—Nicholas son of, 439
—Nigel son of, 380
—William son of, 8
Noel,
—Adam, 13
—Thomas, 13
Nonant, Hugh de, bishop of Coventry, xviin, xxi, xxiii, xxx; 13, 14n, 767.30; pp. 5, 7
Norc(r)oft,
—William de, 741
—William de, junior, 741
Norfolk (Norff', Norfouk, Nortfoilk, Nortfolc, Northfolch, *Northfolchia*, Northfolk),
—Alice de, 768(p. 385)
—Godfrey de, 204
—Richard de, 36.16
—Robert de, 136, 186, 201–2, 217, 233
——heirs of, 768(p. 387)
—William de, 38.13
Normandy, 14n, 15n, 16n; pp. 9, 31
Normaund, Henry, 403

Norris (Noreis, Nores, Noreys, Norreis, Norreys, Northerene, Northerenne, Northerne, Northrene, Northurne),
—Edward le, 767.11
—Henry le, 136, 212–13, 217, 280–1, 283, 454
——Margery his daughter, 136, 217
—Richard le, draper, xxxvi; 297–8, 304, 306–8, 310–14, 316–25, 328–30, 338, 342, 344–5, 657, 768(p. 378)
——Margaret his wife, 319; her former husband *see* Symon de Catesby
——Margaret his widow, 323
——John his son, 323
—Robert, 534
—William le, 538–9
Northampton (Norhamton', Norhant'), 37.2, 767.3; pp. 7–8
—Alice de, 39.3
—Peter son of Adam de, *or* Peter son of Adam, of Northampton, 9
Northfeld, Thomas de, 33, 162, 241
Northfolch, *Northfolchia*, Northfolk *see* Norfolk
Norton (Norton'),
—John de, 33, 761
—Richard de, *le Tippere*, 635
—Walter de *alias* Walter del Enese of, 415–16
Norwich (Norych), Ralf de, 767.6
Notte, Henry le, 588, 594
Nottingham (Notingeh(am), Notyng(ham)),
—Henry de, knight, 768(p. 370)
—Robert de, clerk, 35.5
Nova Bughincar', Nova Bughincga see Newbiggin
Nova Villa see Neville
Novecast', *Novo Castro see* Newcastle

Odard, Alan, of Radford, 719
Odein (Odeyn),
—Gerard *alias* Gerard son of, 600–2, 605
—Gerard (*?another*), 610
—Roger son of Robert, 262
Odo,
—Hugh son of, 408, 671, 676
—Richard son of, 85
——Matilda widow of Henry son of Richard son of, 565
—Robert son-in-law (*gener*) of, 29, 85–6
Offchurch (Offechirche), p. 365n.
—William de, 574
——Agnes his wife, 574
Oil-seller (Oiler, *olearius*, Oyler),
—Michael le *alias* Michael Oliatte, 183–4
—Osbert le *alias* Osbert the, xxxv; 564–5, 570
——Agnes his wife, 570
——Alan their son, 570
Okam, William de, 632
Okes (Hokys, Okis), Adam ate *alias* Adam des, of Whitley, 31n, 96, 712, 741, 754, 758, 764, 766; p. 30
Okov(er)e,
—Robert de, 697
——Alice his wife, 697
——Joan his daughter, 697
———Hugh de, her uncle, 697
Oky (Hoki, Oki),
—Ranulph, 576
—Richard *alias* Richard son of, 603, 606–7, 706
——Richard his son, 606–8, 677–9
——Thomas his son, 608, 677, 706
—Thomas (*another*), 567, 588, 609–10, 612–13, 623–4, 640, 642, 678–9, 713
——reeve, 709
——his wives *see* Edith daughter of Roger the Smith *and* Rose daughter of Alexander de Ryton
——Henry his son, butcher, xxxv; 39.1, 145, 255, 577–9, 581, 630, 636–8, 644, 657–8, 693–4, 730–1, 768(pp. 372, 376–7)
———Agnes his wife, 145, 768(p. 372)
—William, 39.9, 403
——Petronilla his wife, 403
Oldman, William, 33
Oldnall (Oldenhal), Robert de, 419
Oliatte, Michael *see* Oil-seller
Oliver (Olyver),
—Adam son of, 27n.
—Adam son of Henry, of Shuckburgh, 747
Olney (Holoneye, Houloneye, *Olneya, Ullneya*), 22a; p. 10
—Master Fulk de, 767.47
—John, miller, 124, 371
—heirs of John de, 768(p. 372)
—William de, 22a
Omnibon, Richard, of Banbury, 454
One-eyed (*monoculus*), Henry son of Robert the, 35.13, 35.16
Orfeu(er)e, Orfeur, Orfeure *see* Goldsmith
Ormerod, G., p. 10
Orreby (Horrebi, Oreby, Orrebi),
—Sir Fulk de, knight, 22a, 23
—Philip de, justiciar of Chester, 15–19, 21; p. 31
Osbern, Nicholas, 768(p. 383)
Osbert,
—Geoffrey son of, p. 10
—Lambert son of, corveiser, 381
—Thomas son of, 191
Oselot, Alice daughter of Robert, 36.5
Osloc, Oslok *see* Hoslok
Otting, Ottyng *see* Utting
'Ouenotesforde' ('Ovenetfforde'), Coventry, 51, 631
Outred *see* Uttred
Ouving (Ouvingh), Warin, 584–6, 588
Oxendona, Henry de, 10
Oxford (Oxenford', Oxneford', *Oxonia*), Hugh de, 98–103, 108–10, 113, 117–24, 126, 225, 228–9, 236, 376, 691, 768(p. 384)
Oyler *see* Oil-seller
Oysel (Hoysel, Oisel),
—Henry, 107, 300, 768(p. 385)
—Isabella widow of Henry, 768(p. 384)
—Richard, 646, 691
——Alice his wife, 691
—William, 328–9, 341

Packington (Pakint(on), Pakynton'),
—Matilda de, 246
—Richard de, 615
Packwood (Pacwod, *Pacw(od)a*, Pacwode, Pakewode, Pakwode), p. 365n.
—wood & church at, 12
—heirs of Richard de, 768(p. 379)
—Roger de, clerk, 39.1, 340, 390, 487–8, 493, 518, 700
——coroner, 728
—William de, tailor, 39.9

Pagan, Robert son of, 261
Page,
—Alexander, 301
—Geoffrey, 42, 584–6
—Hugh, 298, 300, 302–3, 307–8, 314–22, 324–5, 328, 344, 768(pp. 375, 391–2)
Paie, Hugh, 334
Pailton (Pailingtune, Pailint(on), Paillinton', Palintone, Palynton', Paylington, Paylint(on), Paylinton'),
—Henry de, 69, 75–8, 80, 494
—Robert de, 539, 564
——Lady Rose his widow, 569
—William de, 273, 434–5, 539, 541, 649, 663–4, 672–3, 680–2, 716, 732
Painter (Peyntour, Peyntur, *pictor*),
—Athelard the, 44
——Margery his wife, 44
—Geoffrey the, 90
—Geoffrey the (*another*), 235
—Henry the, 610
—Henry le *alias* Henry the (*another*), 121, 235, 248, 376, 547, 735
—John the, 90
——William his son, 44
———Christine his wife, 44
———John his son, 68–9; his wife *see* Wymarkia daughter of Geoffrey the Girdler
—Roger le, 768(p. 387)
—Walter son of Atherard the, 68
Pake,
—family of, xxxviii
—Henry, 341, 354
—Nicholas, 313, 315–16, 320–1, 768(pp. 384, 388, 389)
—Pagan *alias* Pagan son of Robert *alias* Payn, xxvvi; 36.1, 36.11, 37.1, 45, 67, 93, 139, 184–8, 190, 193–5, 197, 199–200, 202, 204, 206, 210, 217, 265, 267, 269–70, 273–4, 276, 279, 281–3, 285–6, 290–3, 295–6, 315–16, 323, 329, 332, 350–1, 382, 384, 400, 430, 454, 469, 525–6, 542, 675, 710, 718, 732, 767.62, 767.63, 767.64
——Margery, his widow, 685–6, 768(pp. 371, 379, 381, 390)
———William her son, 323, 331, 339, 685, 768(p. 378)
——heirs of, 284, 290
—Roger, 84, 259, 262–3
—Sir William, chaplain, 133, 334, 401
Pakeman, Simon, 728
Palmer (*Palmarius*, Palmere, *Palm(er)us*, Paumer, Paumer', Phalmer'),
—Geoffrey *alias* Geoffrey the, 420, 432–3, 436
—John le, 39.9
—Thomas the, 288–9
——Richard his son, 282
—William *alias* William le *alias* William the, 35.1, 274, 440, 534, 538–9, 564–5, 567–8
——Alexander his brother, 440
——Richard his son *see* Richard the Clerk
——William, his son, 273–4, 393–6, 399, 423, 443–5, 467–8, 472, 489–90, 537, 566, 569, 768(p. 391)
——Hawise his daughter, 496
—William le (*father or son*), 535, 559
Pane, Henry, 33n.
Panes, Walter de, 36.14
Paniel, Sir John, knight, 26
Pape *see* Pope
Parber,
—Michael le *see* Michael le Parker
—William le, 37.8
Parcher, P(ar)chur *see* Parker
Parchment-maker (Parcam', parchamen', P(ar)chemenar, Parcheminer, P(er)cbemin(er), *p(er)gamenarius*),
—John *alias* John le *alias* John the, 382, 558, 583–4, 586, 588, 608–9
—Ralf the, 603
—Reginald the, 582
——John his brother, 582
—Roger le, 462
—William le, 609
Paris (P(ar)is', Parys),
—Matthew, xxiiin–iv; pp. 29–30
—Peter de, xxxvii; 237, 367–9
—Robert de, 24, 708
Park ditch, Coventry, 170–1, 173, 223
Parker (Parber, *parcarius*, Parcher, P(ar)chur, *parkarius*, Parkere, Parser),
—Gilbert the, 532
—John le, 38.6
—Michael le *alias* Michael the, 387, 390, 654
—Peter le, 36.16
—Swanus the, 28f, 40, 60, 62, 83, 176, 261, 346, 380, 408, 419, 528, 641, 671, 767.27, 767.50; p. 66
——Richard his son, 94
——Vincent le *alias* Vincent the, his son, 40–1, 419, 532, 641, 767.44; pp. 66, 352
———heirs of, 427
—Walter le, 377
—William the, 89, 91
—William *alias* William called *alias* William le *alias* William the *alias* William de Nailstone, 33, 38.1, 114, 155, 237, 240, 309, 326, 329, 356, 377, 502, 506, 544, 551, 617–18, 667–8, 734, 737, 750
——coroner, xxviii, xxix, xlii; 52–4, 56–7, 73, 75–6, 104, 109, 121–5, 145, 152–4, 158, 160, 171, 225–7, 242–4, 246, 248–9, 298, 308, 330, 343–5, 358–9, 368–9, 390, 400–1, 448–9, 491, 507–8, 510–13, 550, 552, 577, 619–20, 626–9, 635, 643–4, 692, 698–9, 725–6, 729, 736, 738–40, 742, 746
Parlour (Parlur),
—Henry de *alias* Henry del, 38.1, 70, 113, 231, 235, 365, 573–4, 768(p. 375)
——Mary his wife, 573
——Isabella his daughter, 768(p. 375)
—Simon del, 200
—William de *alias* William del *alias* William le, 319, 376, 424, 486, 544, 574, 699
Parmenter, Silvester le, 768(p. 375)
Parser,
—William, of Leicester, 93; his wife *see* Alice Merewin
—William, coroner *see* William Parker
Pasteymaker (Pasteymekere), Simon le, 55, 78
Patrick (Pat(r)ic, *Patricus*), William, 4, 9
Patte (Pat, Path, Pathe),
—Geoffrey, 541
—John, 256, 579, 625
——Alice his wife *see* Alice daughter of William de Bury
—Simon *alias* Symon, 574, 734, 737, 768(p. 382)

—William, 257–8, 271, 448–50, 488, 578–81, 625
Pattishall, Hugh de, bishop of Coventry and Lichfield, xxiii; p. 5
Paucus, Walter, 469
Pauline's Lane, now Cow Lane, Coventry, xxxiv
Paumer, Paumer' *see* Palmer
Paunthon', John de, clerk, 340
Pavy (Pave, Pavey),
—Matilda, 768(p. 372)
—Thomas, 206, 361–5
——his heirs, 768(p. 393)
—William, 767.50
Paylington', Paylint(on), Paylinton' *see* Pailton
Payn (Pain),
—the bishop's chamberlain, 10
—John called, priest, 218
—Sir John, chaplain, 155, 157
—John, clerk, 152, 196, 230, 284, 329, 763
—Walter son of, 36.11
—William, 136, 168, 217, 279–81, 283, 288–9, 430, 741
Paysable (Paisable, Peissable), William, 94–5, 99, 101–3, 105, 110–11
Peche,
—Richard, bishop of Coventry, 12; p. 4
—Robert, bishop of Coventry, xvi
Pechur' *see* Fishmonger
Peleter (Pelter, Poleter, Putter(er)), William le, merchant, xl; 37.21, 47, 67, 110, 187–8, 191, 195, 207, 277, 283, 385
Pembyl, Ralph, 299, 326
Penifader (Penivader),
—Geoffrey, 534–7
——Alice his daughter, 537
'Penymor', Coventry, 631
Pepin, Mary, 554
Périgord, Arnold of, xlin.
Persy, Ralf, of Repton, 39.6
Peschour, Peschur, Pesthour *see* Fishmonger
Pesthur, Pestour, Pestur *see* Baker
Peter,
—Geoffrey fitz, 767.3, 767.46
—Richard son of, 419; his nephew *see* John son of Osbert de Fletchamstead
——Roger his son, 420–1, 434, 440, 451
—Roger son of, 418, 422, 437, 439, 441, 453, 455–6, 464, 469, 479
——Roger his son, 423–4, 470
———Christine his daughter, 424–5
——his heirs, 396
Peterborough, Benedict abbot of, 767.3
Petit, William, p. 326
Petronella (of Little Park Street, Coventry), 91
Peyntour, Peyntur *see* Painter
Phabena(m) *see* Fakenham
Phalmer' *see* Palmer
Philu(n)gley *see* Fillongley
Phispot, Symon del, 190; his son John *see* John the Weaver
Phiton', Richard, 21
Phortwine *see* Fordwin
Picot (Picott, Pigot, Pigott),
—family of, xxxviii
—Gilbert *alias* Gilbert son of, 3, 7, 10, 14, 767.11, 767.12; p. 6
——Robert his son, 10
—Walter, 42, 530
—William, 15, 767.13; his daughter, 528n.
Pihod (piehod, Pihot, Piod, Pyehod, Pyhod, Pyhot, Pyod, Pyot),
—Agnes, 560, 562–3
—John, 76, 127, 142, 213, 215, 221, 254–5, 258, 505, 509, 523, 549, 552, 575–9, 581, 596, 598–9, 617–18, 620, 624–5, 629–31, 633–8, 644–5, 657, 685, 697, 725–6, 729–31, 738–40, 746, 768(pp. 374, 378, 392)
—Master Nicholas, xxxiin.
—Richard, 36.16, 587
——Richard his son, 36.16
——Walter, his son, 526, 587, 594, 615, 648
———his heirs, 768(p. 376)
Pilkenton, Alexander de, attorney of the earl of Chester, 768(p. 390)
Pimme (Pymme),
—Robert, 267, 286, 410
—Roger, 300–1, 315–16
—Simon *alias* Symon, 259, 264
——Alice his wife, 259; her brother *see* William son of Hugh the Locksmith
Pinkeny, Sir Robert de, 757
Pinley (Pinel, *Pinelea*, Pinnele, Pinneleg', *Pinneleia*, Pinnelet, Pynel, Pynnele, *Pynneleia*), 13; p. 32
—intended chapel of, 2, 5, 12; p. 6n.
—Henry de, 441
—Matilda de, 169, 353
—Reginald de, 290–2
—Robert de, 174
—William de *alias* William le, 34, 187–9
——William his son, 575, 768(pp. 376, 383, 390)
Pipere, William son of William le, of Brackley, 37.9
Pit',
—Henry, 278
—William, 278
Plout(er)e, William le, 241
Plumber (*Plumbarius*),
—Henry the, 521
—Richard the, 501
—Robert the, 436, 672–3
Pluminer (Plomin(er)), Richard le, 443–4
Poddycroft (podicroft, Podycroft, Pudicroft), xxxiv, xlii; 42, 63, 162, 411, 732–7
—ditch (*fossa* de podicroft, *magnum fossatum* de Podycroft), xxxiii; 76, 386
Polesworth (Polesworthe, Poleswrthe, Pollesworth, Pollesworthe, Pollisworth'),
—abbess of, 49
—nuns of, xxiv; 21, 22a, 407n.
—Alan de, 689
—Henry de, 402
—Thomas de, merchant, 72, 249, 252, 768(p. 387)
——Alice his wife, 768(p. 387)
Poleter *see* Peleter
Poleyn, Bertram, 589
Pollsing, Adam, 625
Poluut(er), John le, 306
Ponte, Alice de, 768(p. 378)
Pontefract (*Ponte Fracto*, Pontefracte, *Pontefracto*, Pountfreit),
—John de, steward of the prior of Coventry, xxvi; 189, 286, 311, 430, 621
——William his son, 328
——his heirs, 768(p. 385)
Ponter, John le, 299

Pope (Pape),
—Henry, 82, 595
—Hugh, 270, 275–6, 285, 768(p. 379)
——Juliana his wife, 276
—John, 308, 328, 341
——Beatrice his wife, 328
—Robert, 92, 192
Porser' *see* Purse-maker
Porstein, Robert, 446
Porte, Roger a la, 768(p. 388)
Porter (*Janitor'*),
—Thomas the, 717
——his heirs, 768(p. 379)
Portman, John, 635
Portsmouth (Pottesmuth, Pottismud), Hants., xvi, xvii,
—Robert, 259
—Vincent, 272
Potter (*Potarius*, Poter, Potter'),
—Robert, 1
—William le, 332, 338
Potton', Robert de, 563
Pouere, John le, 22a
Poulton, abbey of, Ches., 16n.
Poumfreit, William le, 389
Pountfreit *see* Pontefract
Powick (Poywyk), Sir Richard, dean of, 23
Preacher (P(re)chour, Prechur, *predicator*),
—Ailwin the, 427
—Henry le *alias* Henry the, 458–61
—Thomas le, 506, 768(p. 394)
Preaus, John de, 16
Preest, John, 631
Prest,
—Alexander, 94
—William, 93
Preston (P(re)stone), Gilbert de, royal justice, 22a, 137
Prett, William, 92
Priest, (*p(re)sbit(er)*),
—Sir H. the, 556
—Ralf the, of Wyken, 277
Prior's Hardwick, p. 365n.
Prior's Marston, p. 365n.
Proud (Proude, Prude),
—Hugh, 182
—William le, 424, 768(p. 375)
Pucelle,
—Gerard, bishop of Coventry, 12; pp. 3–6
——Robert, Ivo and Roger his men (*clientes*), 12
Pulter(er) *see* Peleter
Purse-maker (Borc(er), Boucer, Bourser, Bourser', Bourseir, Burcer, Bursar, *Bursarius*, Burser, Bursere, Porser', Purc(er), Purser, Pursere),
—Adam *alias* Adam le, 43, 62
—Alexander the, 410, 427–8, 437, 441, 466
—Henry le *alias* Henry the, 74, 443–4, 768(p. 371)
—Hugh le *alias* Hugh the, 417, 434–5, 442, 451, 470
——Agnes his wife, 478
——Agnes his widow, 474–5
——Adam their son, 475
—John le, of Beverley, 330
—Reginald le, 467
—Richard called *alias* Richard le *alias* Richard the, xxxvii; 37.3, 73, 396, 424–5, 431, 443–4, 458–61, 468, 470–2, 477–8, 483, 499, 504, 507–8, 544, 738–40, 768(pp. 370, 387, 390–4)
——Alice his wife, 431
——Emma his daughter, 644
—Roger le, merchant, xxxvi; 39.8, 94, 168, 208–9, 233, 244, 768(p. 385)
——Alice his wife, 168, 208
——Alice his widow, 243–4
——Thomas his son, 244
Pus', Robert de, 767.37
Pychard, William, of Newton, 233
Pye (Pie),
—William, 134–5, 280, 350–1, 767.43
——Henry his son, xxxvii; 136, 281, 351; p. 66
Pyhot *see* Pihod
Pykedepere (Pikedepere), Richard, 51, 768(p. 381)
'Pykedeperefeld', Coventry, 631
Pynel *see* Pinley
Pynne, Nicholas, 768(p. 393)
Pynnele, *Pynneleia see* Pinley
Pyod, Pyot *see* Pihod

Qhitloue *see* Whytloue
Quarryman (*quararius*, Quareur, Quarreur),
—Richard the, 767.59
—Robert le, 768(p. 386)
——Mary his widow, 123
Quenisde, Godfrey son of, 767.30
Querdeliun, Adam, 40–1
Qwytloue *see* Whytloue

Rachel, Henry, of Fletchamstead, 479, 768(p. 394)
Radford (Radeford, Radeforde, Radefort, Redeford), xxviii, xxxiv; 28a, 42, 525, 529n, 548–9, 605, 609, 616, 627, 670, 726n, 755, 758, 760–1; pp. 326, 365n, 368n.
—field towards, 155
—Mill (*molendinum* de Radeford), xxxix; 7, 28a, 524–5; p. 1
—fish pond of, 525
—Blissota de, 768(p. 376)
—Henry de, 717–18
——William his brother, 717–18
—John son of Henry de, 768(pp. 374–5, 380)
—Matilda daughter of John de, 381
—Ralf de, 529
——Edith his daughter, 529n.
—Robert called Anketill de, 717; p. 326
——Cecily his wife, 717; p. 326; her brother *see* Richard Locard
—William son of Ranulph de, 768(p. 381)
Rafwine *see* Rauwin
Ralf,
—Alexander son of, 539
—Geoffrey son of, of Whitley, 754
—Nicholas son of, 680
—Ralf son of, 35.16
—William son of, 1
Rape(n)don' *see* Repton
Rappoc, Reginald, 649–50
Rase, Thomas de, 407n; his wife *see* Matilda daughter of Liulf de Spon
Rasur, Jordan, 9
Rasurer, Ralf le, 169
Rauwin (Rafwine, Rawin', Reuen),
—Richard, 380
—Richard son of (*?same*), 381, 419

Reader, William, pp. 31, 326
Recham (Retham, *Rogeha*),
—Margery de, 430
——heirs of, 221
—Robert de, 36.1, 36.11, 60, 64, 177–8, 350, 412–14, 531–2
——heirs of, 525, 768(pp. 379, 389, 391)
——Robert and Richard his heirs, 28c, 526
—Robert son of Agnes de *see* Robert de Coventry
Red (Rede, Rous, *Ruffus*, *Rufus*, Rus, *Russus*),
—Adam the, baker, 672–3
—Alexander the, 35.7
——heirs of, 42
—Hugh the, 271
—Ralf the *alias* Ralph the, of Pinley, 198
—Reginald the, 48, 66, 68, 190, 384, 587, 681, 710
—Richard son of Alexander le, 64
—Thomas le *alias* Thomas the, 276, 284, 313, 320–1, 328, 403
—William, xviin.
Red ditch (le Rede dych', le Rededich, Rodiche, *rubea fovea*, *rubeum fossatum*, *ruffa fovea*), Coventry, xxxiii–iv; 128, 149, 165–6, 219–20, 255, 294, 535–7, 767.43
Redeclerc, Richard le, heirs of, 105
Redeford *see* Radford
Redeknave (Redecnave),
—Adam, 603
—Hawise widow of Adam le, 590–2
—William son of Robert le, 589–92, 611–12
——his heirs, 768(p. 376)
Redeware, Redwale *see* Rydeware
Redwy, William, 588
Redza(m)i, William de, 1
Reeve (*prepositus*), William the, xx; 538; *see also* William son of Simon
Reginald, William son of, 445
Rem, Margery de, 768(p. 386)
Repton (Rape(n)don', *Rependona*, Rependun', Repingdon', Repyndon'), Derb.,
—church of, 8n, 9n.
—William de, 7, 35.14, 41, 43, 63, 85, 87–8, 262, 346, 411, 524, 528, 671; p. 1
Restuychim, Sir John, knight, 24
Retham *see* Recham
Reuen *see* Rauwin
Reymund (Remount, Remund, Reymond, Reymud, Reymu(n)te),
—Gilbert, 446
—John, 482, 484, 501, 510, 513, 749
—Robert, 424, 443–5, 471, 474–5, 496, 500, 768(pp. 379, 384, 390, 392)
Reynald, Richard son of William, of Lawford, 124
Rhuddlan (Ruelent), William de, 5–6, 9
Richard I, king of England, reign of, p. 5
Richard II, king of England, reign of, p. 32
Richard,
—John son of, 178
—John son of (*another*), 768(p. 380)
—Matilda daughter of, 768(p. 380)
—Samson son of, 557–8, 584–6
—Symon son of, 417, 557
—Thomas son of, 252
—William son of, 6, 10
—William son of (*another*), 433, 454
Riche,
—Alexander le, 768(p. 384)
—Symon le, 500
Richer,
—Richard son of *see* Richard son of Richer de Weston
—William son of *see* William son of Richer de Weston
Ridding (Ruding, Rudyng, Ruydyng),
—I. del, 18
—Roger atte, 764, 766
Ridewale, Rideware, Ridiware *see* Rydeware
Riggeley, Geoffrey de, 39.2
Riley, H. T., p. 63
Rimild (Rimilt, Rymild, Rinuld, Rynuld), 529
—Robert, 424
—William, 394–5, 447, 471, 474–5, 489, 654, 768(pp. 382, 384, 388, 394)
——Christine his widow, 598–9, 655
Rivaux, Peter des, treasurer of England, xviin.
Rivel (Ryvel),
—John, 195, 388–9
——Sarah his widow, 235
—William, 743
Rivers (*Ripariis*), John de, 407
Robert, 529
—Anketill son of *alias* Anketyl' son of, 177–9, 412–17, 540, 708
—Guy son of, 22a
—Peter son of, 36.6
——Thomas his brother, 36.6
—Richard son of, pp. 9–10
Roc *see* Roke
Rodinton (Rodington', Rodynton, Rodynton', Rodyton'),
—Henry de, 162, 190, 197, 457–8, 463, 732, 768(p. 371)
——Alice his wife, 732
——Anabilia his daughter *see* Anabilia wife of Thomas de Stapleton
Roger, Master, 12
—Matthew son of, xx; 35.1, 41, 524, 527, 553, 556, 582, 604, 660–2, 671, 676
—Richard son of, 35.7
—Simon son of, 381, 421
——Simon his son, 421
Roke (Roc, Rok, Rooc, Rouk),
—William *alias* William le, 422, 424, 431, 443–4, 447, 467–8, 489
——Agnes his daughter, 768(p. 383); *see also* Agnes wife of Robert son of Richard le Teler
Rokeby *see* Rugby
Rome, xviii; 708
Ropere,
—John le, 37.10
——Emma his wife, 37.10
Rose (*Roysia*, Roys),
—Anketill son of *alias* Anketinus son of, 65, 90, 192, 709
——John his son, 95
Rothwell (Rothewell, Rothewelle),
—Richard de, 36.4
—Richard de (*another*), 33
—Robert de, 693, 696, 700, 749
Rouce, 767.31
Rouk *see* Roke
Roumare, William de, earl of Lincoln, p. 8n.

Roumonger (Romonger, Romonger', Roumongere, Rowmonger, Rumangur, Rumong(er)),
—Gilbert le, 471
—Humphrey le, 36.9, 451
—Reginald le, 443–5
—Robert le, 768(p. 386)
Rous *see* Red
Routon' *see* Ryton
Royewelle, Richard de, 486
Roysia, Roys *see* Rose
Ruaut (Rouaat, Ruald), Peter, 13, 15; p. 31
Ruding *see* Ridding
Rudmarleg', Adam de, 438
Rudyng *see* Ridding
Rugby (Rokeby),
—family of, p. 32
—Joan de, 129
—Henry de, 554
—Henry de (*another*), 34
—William de, 332
Rus *see* Red
Russel (Ruscel, Russell),
—Adam, merchant, xxxvii, xlii; 33, 38.1, 39.1, 52, 72, 98, 106, 108, 117, 119, 133, 139–42, 143–6, 150–2, 154, 158–60, 163, 165, 172–3, 203–5, 209–10, 212–16, 220, 222–4, 227, 232, 234, 237, 242–4, 247, 251, 253, 301, 308–9, 323, 327, 330–2, 341–5, 354–6, 358–9, 370–3, 377, 398, 523, 597, 643, 685, 712, 735–6, 748, 752, 754, 762, 768(pp. 374, 385)
——Alice his wife, 215–16
——Henry his son, 354
——William his son, 370
—Alexander, clerk, 63
—Hugh, 37.17
—John, 33n.
—Roger, 205
—Simon *alias* Symon, 119, 160, 227, 240, 243–4, 356, 368–9, 371
——Agnes his wife, 369
Ruthon', *Rutona*, Rutone, Rutun, *Rutuna see* Ryton
Ruydyng *see* Ridding
Rydeware (Redeware, Redwale, Ridewale, Rideware, Ridiware, Rydewale),
—John de, xlii; 33n, 73, 128, 145, 158–9, 163, 166, 223–6, 237, 240, 243, 251–2, 309, 323, 327, 331, 343, 345, 356, 369, 494, 753–4
——Peter his son, 245
—Robert de, 33, 130–2, 164, 224, 241, 245, 253, 256, 730–1, 737, 753
Rynuld *see* Rimild
Rypun, Henry, 37.16
Ryton (Routon', Ruiton', Ruthon', *Rutona*, Rutone, Rutun, *Rutuna*, Ruyton, Ruytone, Rwyton'),
—[on Dunsmore], church of, 12; p. 6n.
—[?] de, 572
——Robert his son, 572
—Adam de, saddler, 494
—Alexander de, xxxix; 37.20, 273, 287, 535–6, 545–7, 564–71, 573, 609, 616, 621–2, 632, 713, 720
——Rose his daughter, 567; her husband *see* Thomas Oky
——heirs of, 768(p. 381)
—Bate de, 249
—Gilbert de, 555
—Matthew de, saddler, xxxvii; 39.5, 51–4, 56, 59, 70, 72–4, 76–8, 118, 126, 128, 162, 235, 250, 371, 400, 402, 508–9, 514–15, 629, 687–8, 695, 702, 736, 738, 740, 742, 746, 762
——Margery his wife, 52
——John his son, 39.5
—Roger de, 522
—Simon de, 33

Sach, Hugh, 399
Saddler (Celar', Celer, Celir, *cellar'*, Sadelere, Sceler, Seler, Seler', *sellarius*, Seller),
—Adam le, 33
—Alan le, 64
—Eadward the, 40
—Geoffrey the, 44
——Alice his daughter, 44
———Walter the, her late husband, 44
—Henry le *alias* Henry the, 44–6, 48, 68, 384–6, 613, 622
——Margery his wife, 613
——Richard his son, 46
——Thomas his son, 768(p. 386)
——Edith his daughter, 623
—Hugh le *alias* Hugh the, 44, 64
—Jordan le *alias* Jurdan le *alias* Jurdan the, 53–4, 424, 502, 629, 698
——Isabella *alias* Ysabella his daughter, 699, 768(pp. 373, 376); her mother *see* Alice Cosin
—Robert the, 40, 62
—Robert le (*another*), 68
—Thomas le, 33, 627
—William the, 44
Sage, William le, 35.12, 35.16
St. Albans, abbey of, xxiii
St. Botulf, Richard de, 261, 393
St. Edmund,
—Stephen de, 88
—William de, 407
St. James, Richard de, 52–6, 73, 75, 80, 392, 400, 402–3, 405–6, 494, 507, 509, 513–15, 523, 646, 737, 742, 753–4
St. John the Baptist, chapel or church of, Coventry, xxiv; 12, 37.12, 37.13
—its hospital, xxiv; 12, 20a and b, 35.4, 35.17, 309, 311, 424, 568, 616, 621, 636–8, 643, 645–6
——Master of, 309, 402, 574, 667–8, 741, 768(pp. 373, 375, 377–8, 381–2, 388, 390, 392); p. 7
———Brother John, Master of, 761
——Brothers of, 22a, 574, 613
———and Sisters of, 645, 667–8, 768(p. 374)
————Petronilla, sister of, 621
St. John, Henry of, clerk, 664
St. Leonard's hospital, Coventry *see* Spon
St. Mark,
—Nicholas de, 549
——Alice his wife, 549
St. Mary, abbey/priory of, Coventry, xv–xxi, xxiii–v, xxvii, xxx, xxxin., xli; 2, 3, 5–7, 12–14, 16–19, 22–7, 28 *passim*, 30a and b, 32, 110, 120, 147, 283, 286, 365, 375, 430–1, 482, 492, 508, 512, 517, 523–6, 558–9, 581, 593, 597, 636–40, 646, 667–8, 691, 706, 714, 717–18, 726, 728, 731, 743–4, 747–8, 764, 768(pp. 365, 370); pp. 1–8, 29–32, 63, 326
—expulsion of monks of, 14n.
—Abbot Leofwine of, xvn–vin.

—Prior of, xv, xviii–xxxi, xxxviii, xl; 8, 13, 25, 33, 35.2, 35.4, 71, 102, 112, 195–6, 221–3, 268–9, 287, 306, 310, 327, 505, 541, 557, 573–4, 598, 604–5, 613, 625, 642, 686, 698, 707, 721, 724, 727, 768(*passim*); pp. 1–2, 5, 9, 29–32
——Geoffrey of, xxiii; 375n.
——Henry de Leicester of, xxv; 375, 492, 523, 726, 728, 743–4, 748; p. 3, 326; his brother *see* Robert de Leicester
——Lawrence of, xvi, xviii–ix, xxiii, xxx; 2, 5; pp. 3–6
———his men, Simon and John, 5
——Moses of, p. 5
——Roger of, xxiii–iv; 30b
——Thomas of, 26–7, 33n., 597, 714, 732–3, 747
——William de Brightwalton of, xxiv, xxix; 22a and b, 23–5, 33n, 286, 430, 593, 718; pp. 29–30, 326
—chapter of, xviii
——chapel of the Blessed Mary of, 683, 696; *see also* Index II, ECCLESIASTICAL matters
—monks' cemetery, 375n.
——chapel of St. Mary in, 12
St. Maur, Lawrence de, knight, 752
St. Medard,
—Geoffrey de, knight, 560
——Geoffrey his son, 560n.
——Nicholas his grandson, 560–3
———Alice his wife, 560–3
—Geoffrey (*?another*), 560n.
St. Michael, chapel/church of, Coventry, xvii–xix, xxiin–xxiv, xxx, xxxii; 2, 5–6, 12–14, 22a, 36.19, 37.11, 39.7, 47, 58, 187, 360–5, 368, 371, 761, 767.22, 767.23; pp. 3, 5–6, 9, 31, 186
—incumbent of,
——Ralf the earl's chaplain, 14; p. 5
——R. de Coventry, clerk, (*?same*), p. 5
——Ranulf de Mainwaring, p. 5
—vicar of, 429; pp. 5–6
——Ralph de Leicester, p. 6
——Sir Richard de Sallowe, 525; p. 6
——Master Guy de Tilbrook, 27, 112, 376, 387, 396, 480, 490, 732–5, 758–9, 761, 768(pp. 388, 394)
——Sir Walter, 74
—appurtenant chapel(s) of, xix, xxiin–iv, xxxi; 2, 5, 12–13, 22a; pp. 3, 5, 6
—cemetery of, 7, 373–4; p. 186
St. Nicholas, chapel/church of, Coventry, xxx, xxxiv–v; 12, 424, 587–8, 600–2, 604, 606–8, 610–16, 621–2, 626–8
—area around, xxx, xxxv, xxxvii
—cemetery of, 620, 740
—quarry towards, xxi
St. Nicholas Field (Seynt Nycolasfeld'), Coventry, 739
St. Nicholas Street, Coventry, bars of, xxxiv
St. Sepulchre, Warwick, prior of, 39.5, 768(p. 394)
St. Werburgh *see* Chester, abbey of
St. Yvo *alias* St. Yvan, Richard de, 182, 282, 288–9, 353
Sakerston', Roger de, 430
Salisbury, Wilts., p. 366
Sallowe (Sallauue, Sallawe, Salowe),
—Richard de *see* St. Michael's, vicar of
—William de, 44, 86–91, 709, 767.33
——Margery his daughter, 92
———William her brother, 92
—William de (*?same*), 36.9
Salmon-fisher (*Salmonarius*), Nicholas the, 524
Salop',
—Master Robert de, 13
—William de, 38.8
Salter (Saltere),
—Felicia la, 768(p. 376)
—Robert le, xxxv; 564–5, 568
—William le, 38.13
——Dulcea his wife, 38.13
Sampson (Sampsum, Sampsun, Samson, Sannsum, Saumsun, Saunsum), 565
—Henry, 622
——Isabella his sister, 622
———Alice her daughter, 622
—John, 70, 73, 75, 77–80, 82, 127, 378, 670, 686–8, 690, 692, 697, 701, 768(p. 372)
——Agnes his wife, 79
Sarah (of Coventry), 35.6
Sarcerin,
—Alexander de la, 36.6
—William de la, 36.6
Sartrin (Saretin, *Sartrino*),
—Henry de *alias* Henry de le, 465, 652, 768(p. 378)
—Roger, 206
Sauenn', William, 9
Saundon', Walter de, 205
Scabbard-maker (*vaginator*), William son of Geoffrey the, xxxvi; 84
Scail *see* Shayl
Scanus, Roger the man of, 91
Scarie, Roger, 37.16
Scathelok (Scatheloc, Schathelok, Schathelot, Skatheloc, Skathelok),
—Eda, 711
—Edith, 234
—Hugh (*recte* Kevelioc) *see* Hugh II, earl of Chester
—Simon *alias* Symon, 76, 386, 768(p. 388)
—Symon (*another*), 37.23, 38.5
——Thomas his brother, 37.23, 38.5
———Isabella his widow, 38.5
—Stephen, 386, 412–14, 416
—William, 454
Scauerib (Sauerib),
—Henry, 583
—Richard, 182, 611, 615
Scayl *see* Shayl
Sceler *see* Saddler
Scelet (Celet, Celeth, Seled, Selet, Seleth),
—Robert, 65
—Thomas, clerk, xxxv; 66–7, 82, 221, 430, 548, 592–3, 616, 626, 633, 647, 657, 665, 675, 683–4, 687–9, 732–4, 747, 768(pp. 376, 390–1)
——William his son, 768(p. 394)
—Master William, clerk, 27, 392, 396, 403, 552, 732–4, 759
—William (*another*), heirs of, 768(p. 390)
Scepeie, Scepeye *see* Shepey
Schalonyr *see* Chaloner
Schapeleyn, Richard, 711
Schauelok', Alan, 704
Schenton' (Scheinton', Seinton', Stheinton),
—Reginald de, 411
—William de, 363
——Nicholas de, his son, 361, 363
Schereman, Alexander le, 402, 737

Schore (Shore), Richard, 393, 399, 496, 542–3
Schorlaston', Henry de, 521
Schort, Walter son of Robert, 501
Schulfton', Schulton' *see* Shilton
Schyltren' *see* Chilton
Scot (Schot, Scote, *scoticus*, Scott),
—Edith, 42
—John, 151, 203, 209, 768(pp. 374, 379, 385)
——Margery his wife, 151
—Nicholas, 36.3
—Robert *alias* Robert the, 7, 718, 767.59; pp. 1, 10, 326
——Ralf his son, 718; p. 326
———William his son, 718; p. 326
—Robert (*another*), 610
—William, 148, 201, 204, 219, 768(pp. 371, 384, 387, 389)
Scotland, 39.6
Scribe (*Scriptor*),
—Adam the, 40, 86
—Ralf the, 174
—Richard the, 200
—Symon the, 767.57
Sefare (Sephare), Juliana *alias* Giliana, 531–2; her sister *see* Matilda daughter of John de Wittenas
Segrave,
—family of, xxxviii, xli
—Sir Gilbert de, xli; 22a, 710; his heirs, 525
—John de, knight, 72, 339, 712
——William his tailor, 712
———Margery his wife, 712
—Sir Nicholas de, knight *alias* Nicholas lord of, xxii, xxxix; 70, 152, 195, 197, 711, 758–9, 768(p. 375)
—Stephen de, 21, 407
Segrim (Segrun),
—William, 44, 65, 182, 272, 535
——Jurdan his son, 182
———Edith his stepmother, 182
Seinton' *see* Schenton'
Seled *see* Scelet
Seler, Seler' *see* Saddler
Seliman, Matthew, 35.3, 35.16
Seller *see* Saddler
Senudeford, Hawise de, 710
Seret (Seiet, *Sericus*, Serith),
—Elufwinus, 527, 676
—William nephew of, 767.4, 767.5, 767.10
Serjeant (Sergant, Serjant, Serjaunt, S(er)jaunt', *serviens*),
—Henry le *alias* Henry the, 713, 720
—Nicholas le, heirs of, 465
—Ralf *alias* Ralf le *alias* Ralf the, 90–1, 180, 709
—Richard the, 566, 584–6
—William le *alias* William the, 33, 566, 609, 615, 713
——heirs of, 768(p. 378)
Sewale, Simon, p. 326
Seynturer *see* Girdler
Sharp, Thomas, pp. 10n, 31
Shayl (Chail, Scail, Scayl, Schail, Schayl, Shail, Shal),
—Hugh, 393–7, 474–5, 489, 496, 521, 542–3, 550, 768(p. 393)
——Richard his son, 551
——Emma his daughter, 550–1
—Richard, 42, 540
Shaynston', Richard de, 39.9
Sheld(on), Henry de, knight, 768(p. 370)
Shepey (Scepeie, Scepeye, Schepeie, Schepey, Schepeye, Seeppey, *Sepeya*, Sepeye, Shepeye),
—family of, xxvii, xl
—Hugh de, 33
—Laurence de *alias* Lawrence de, 33, 39.1, 255, 323, 335, 338
—Nicholas de, 33n, 162
—Robert de, 161, 220, 226, 246, 330; pp. 30–1
—Simon de *alias* Symon de, 295–7, 319–20, 768(p. 390)
—William de, merchant, 69, 129–32, 164, 166, 241, 254, 256, 323, 335, 338, 340, 373, 392, 404, 737
Shepherd (Schepperde, Shephird),
—Roger le, 39.2
—William le, 766
Sherbourne (schireburne), river, xv, xxxi; 753–4
Sheriff,
—Ralf the, 6 and n.
—Ranulf the, 8
Shermon, Alexander le, 761
Shilton (Schulfton', Schulton', Sulfton, *Sulftona*, Sulton'),
—chapel of, xxiv; 2, 5, 12, 13; p. 6n.
—cemetery of, 12
—Henry son of Ralf de, p. 31
—Hugh de, draper, 400, 628–9
—Symon de, 578–9
—William de, 748, 766, 768(p. 374)
Shirewith *see* Skirewith
Shirford (Sireford, Syreford),
—Geoffrey de, 30a and b
—Geoffrey de (*?same*), 768(p. 391)
Shirlok, Roger, 36.12
Shockersfield (Schocheresfeld, Schocheresfeld', Scocherescroft, scocheresfeld'), xxxiv, xlii; 162, 735–40
Shoemaker (*sutor*),
—Gregory the, 768(p. 375)
—John the, 39.8
—Tholi the *alias* Tole *alias* Tolimeus, 767.36, 767.37, 767.38
—Vincent de, 418
Shortley (Shorteleye, *Shortleya*, Sortel'), xxii; 128, 239n, 768(pp. 367, 384)
—manor of, xxxi, xxxiv; 751
—Mills, xlii; 750
Shothewell', William de, 39.4
Shuckborough (Schuckeboru), John de, 766
Shukmore (Soggemor, Soggomor, Suggomor), 729–31
Shustoke (Schustok, Schustok'), Adam de, saddler, 69, 77–8, 402
Sibely (Sybely),
—Robert, 768(p. 376)
—Roger, 701
Sigan, Hugh, 310
Silksewer (Selcsowere, Selkesower', Sulcsouere, Sulcsouher, Sulcsouher', Sulcsowher'),
—William le, xxxvi; 98, 100–2, 108, 113, 115, 118–20, 222, 225, 376
——Margery his wife, 100–2
Simon/Simond (Simund, Simu(n)t, Symon, Symond, Symont, Symound, Symund, Symund'), 266
—Henry, 588

—John *alias* John son of, xxiii; 24, 36.1, 36.11, 37.1, 182, 266, 285, 360, 537, 541, 548, 557–8, 564–7, 569–70, 583–8, 590, 592–3, 608–10, 612, 639, 650, 679–82, 709–10, 718–20
——bailiff or reeve, xxiii, xxv; 269, 283, 572, 589, 594, 611, 614–15, 648–9, 732
—Jordan son of, 432–3
—Simon son of, 36.7
—Thomas, 105, 111, 146, 150, 159, 165, 170, 288–9, 324–5, 768(pp. 384, 388)
——Avicia his wife, 111, 289
—William son of, 604, 608, 678
——bailiff, xix–xxi; 35.1
Sireford *see* Shirford
Siward (Syward),
—Richard *alias* Richard son of Richard *alias* Richard son of Richard son of, 176, 259, 272
—William, 768(p. 392)
Skatheloc, Skathelok *see* Scathelok
Sker, Hugh le, servant of Richard de Loges, 39.2
Skinner (*Pelliparius*),
—Elias the, xxxv; 556
—Henry the, 605
—Walter the, 676
—Walter the (*another*), 454
—Yvo the, 767.49
Skirewith (Schyrewhit, Sckyrewyt, Scyrewit, Shirewith, Skyrewit),
—Robert, 410
——Richard his son, 410, 418, 434–5, 451
———heirs of, 423, 768(p. 394)
Slepere, Robert le, 692, 695–6
Sleper's Lane (Slepuslone), 698
Slepus, William, 524
Sley (Sleth, Sleyth),
—John, 227, 328, 338, 768(p. 390)
—William *alias* William called, 100, 111, 187–8, 191, 193, 228–9, 768(p. 383)
——John his son, xxxvii; 193
Smercote (Smerscote), 17, 18
Smith (*Faber*, Ferrour, Feuer, Feu(er)e, Feure),
—Adam *alias* Adam le *alias* Adam the, 69, 445, 450, 500, 516, 768(p. 386)
—Christian the, 84, 261, 767.10
—Geoffrey the, 521
——John the *alias* John son of, 521, 768(p. 380)
—Gunnilda daughter of Guy the, 546
—Henry le, 768(p. 384)
—Hugh le, 768(p. 375, 378)
—Hugh le, heirs of, 768(p. 378)
—Hugh the (*another*), 764, 766
—John le *alias* John the, 768(pp. 374, 393)
—John the, of Weddington, 424, 473
—Matthew the, 587, 600–2, 606–7, 642, 661, 677–8
—Michael the, 606, 706
—Michael the (*?same*), 613, 642
—Nicholas the, 481–5
——Alice his wife, 482–4
——William their son, 482, 484
—Philip the, xxxvi; 147, 295
——William the, his son, xxxvi; 151, 169, 295, 304, 328, 699, 768(p. 394)
—Richard the, 767.34, 767.35
—Richard the (*another*), 38.11
—Robert the, 527
——Roger the, his son, 606–8, 676–9, 706
———Henry his son, 623, 679
———Matthew his son, 564–5, 679
———Edith his daughter, 678–9; her husband *see* Thomas Oky
—Robert the (*another*), 170, 172
—Roger the, of Witacre, 472
—Walter the, 380
—William the, of Frankton, 676
Smithford (Smerhesforde, Smeþeford, Smethesforde, Smiteford, Smitesford, Smithesford', Smithisford, Smyþeforde, Smytheford, Smytheforde, Smythesforde), xxx, xxxv; 7, 40, 384, 406, 482
—bar, 385, 393–6, 454, 493
—bridge, 401
—Mill, 399
—stream, 382, 399, 404
—Street, xxxvii
—family of, xxxviii
—Nicholas de, 174, 381, 408–9, 427, 535
——Ralf his brother, 381
—Richard de, 10
——Alice his daughter, p. 31; her husband *see* Elias Despenser
Soap-maker (*savenator*, Sopere),
—Amicia widow of Reginald le, 37.3
—Hawise & Mariota, daughters of Geoffrey the, xxxvi; 134–5
——Segilia daughter of Hawise, 135
Soggemor, Soggomor *see* Shukmore
Soleby (Solebi), William de, 535–7
Solers, William de, 9
Solihull (Solihul, Solihull'),
—Ranulph de, tanner, 581
——Alice his wife, daughter of Adam de Chetwode, 581
—Thomas de, baker, 58
Somer (Somer'),
—William, 434–5, 437, 455–7, 465
——William his son, 511
——heirs of, 768(p. 386)
Sortel' *see* Shortley
Sot, Simon son of Geoffrey, 36.9
Soudley, William de, 768(p. 389)
Souley (Souleye, Southleye, Suleg'),
—Thomas de, 36.1, 36.11, 682
——Petronilla his daughter, 382; her husband *see* Thomas de Henley
Southam, xixn.
—church of, p. 6n.
—Master Richard de, 697
Sowe (*Souua*, *Sowa*), now Walsgrave-on-Sowe, xx; 22a, 30b; p. 365n.
—chapel of, xxiv; p. 6n.
—meadows of, 767.65
—Hamond de *alias* Hadmu(n)d de, 315–16
—Henry de, 28d; p. 31
—Henry de (*?same*), 767.47
—Henry de, tailor, 306, 322, 325, 344–5
—Hugh de, 47
—Reginald de, 30b
—Robert de, 627
—Simon de, 554
—Simon de (*another*), 284
—William de, 552
Sower, Henry le, 55
Spalding (Spaldinge, Spaldinges), Lincs.,
—Gilbert de, 527, 607

Spalding (*cont.*)
——Richard his son, 607
—Margery de, 36.16
—Nicholas de, 36.16
—William de, 538
Spark (Sparc, Spart), William, 221, 232, 768(pp. 375, 388–9)
Sparrow (Sparewe, Sparwe),
—Henry, 208
—Margery, 309
Spicer (Especer, Espicer, Specer, Spic(er)e, Spycer),
—John le, 454, 588
—Richard le, 39.1, 59, 77–81, 156, 406, 518, 703
——Alice his wife, 79–81
Spille, Nicholas, 593, 615
Spirie, Roger, 350, 709
Spitelcroft, Coventry, xxxiv; 747–8
Spon (*Spanna*, Spanne, Spaune, *Sponna*, Spo(n)ne), xxx, xxxi, xxxiv, xxxvii; 23, 25, 375, 427–8, 492
—bridge, xxxvii; 428, 504, 508
—church/chapel of, xxiv, xxxi, xxxiin; 2, 5, 12, 13, 23, 25, 38.8, 768(pp. 368, 371); p. 6n.
——hospital/leper house of, (St. Leonard's), xxiv, xxxi, xxxiin; 22a, 443–4, 768(p. 371)
—croft called Cristescroft in, 430
—Dead Lane in, 430
—field, 206, 523
—ford, 482
—garden called Scatherscroft in, 430
—manor of, xxxin
—moor at, 514–15
—Street, xxxi–ii, xxxv; 768(p. 377); pp. 64–5
—watercourse called Syreford in, 469
—Adam de, 529; *see also* Adam son of Haldane
——Richard his son, 767.26
—Liulf de *alias* Lytholf de, xxxi, xxxviii; 10n., 83, 407n–9; pp. 31, 65; his heirs, 768(p. 387)
——Amiria, his wife, xxxi; 407n.
——William his son, 409, 603; p. 65
———Alice his daughter, 426
——Matilda his daughter, 407; her husband *see* Thomas de Rase
Sponsa, William de, 661
Sponsere, Nigel le, 466
Sportot, Richard, 501
Stafford,
—Ranulph de, 689, 699
——Matilda his wife, 689
—Thomas de, preacher, 507
Stamford, Lincs., p. 8
Stanford (Stannford', Staunford),
—Henry de, 281, 682, 732
—Hugh de, 294
—John de, 59
Stanleg, Stanlet, Stanley, Stannley *see* Stoneleigh
Stantilon (Stantilun),
—John, glove-maker, 115–16, 228–9
——Margery his wife, 228–9
Stapleton (Stapelton'),
—Simon de, 525
—Thomas de, 732–4, 768(pp. 382, 385, 387)
——Anabel' *alias* Anabilia his wife, 732–4; her father *see* Henry de Rodinton
Starie, Roger, 681
Staunleye *see* Stoneleigh
Stavensby, Alexander de, bishop of Cov., p. 3
Staynton, William de, heirs of, 768(p. 382)
Steinolf, Henry, 706
Stemprer,
—Roger, 300
——Hawise his daughter, 300–1
Stephen, king of England, xvii–ixn, xxxii–iii; pp. 4, 8
Stephen,
—Bertram son of, 705
—Henry son of, 768(p. 380)
Sternulf, 604
Steward (*Dapifer*, *Senescaldus*),
—Ralf the, 12
—Robert the, 4
Stirthup, Roger, 37.5
Stivichall (Stevechehale, *Stivechala*, Stivechale, Stiveschale, Stivichale, Stivinghale, Styvech', Styveschale, Styvichale), 4, 705n, 768(p. 384n); pp. 10, 365n.
—chapel of, xxiv; 2, 5, 12, 13; p. 6n.
—field of, 741
—Mill, 4
—lords of, p. 64
—Geoffrey de, 712
—Hugh de, 226, 500
—John de, *le buttere*, 110
——Matilda his wife, 110
—Jolinus de, 544
—Nicholas de, glover, 634–5
—Ranulf de *alias* Ranulph de *alias* Ranulph called of, xxxii–iii; 67, 352, 542–3, 711, 757
——Alice his daughter, 226
——Maria his daughter *see* Maria wife of Richard le Bouldere
—Reginald de, 83
—Robert de, 528
—Roger de, 42, 350
—William de, 94, 105, 127, 130–1, 761
——Matilda his wife, 94
Stodley, William de, 38.1
Stoke (Stoc, *Stoca*, *Stocha*, Stockes, Stok, Stokes, Stokys), xxn; 7, 22a, 305, 529n, 757–61, 763, 765; pp. 31, 365n.
—chapel of, xxiv; 2, 5, 12, 13, 763; p. 6n.
—field of, 343
—Agnes daughter of Claricia, of Allesley, 507
—Andrew de, 640
—Herbert, 177, 412–14
—Hugh de, 24, 189, 718
—John, 36.16
—Matilda, 199
—Peter de, 46
—Richard de, 33
—Robert de, 8
—Robert de (*another*), 22a, 90, 182, 528
——Alice his daughter, 387–91, 768(p. 384)
—Robert de (*another*), 26–7, 112, 128, 144, 154–7, 214, 225, 227, 231, 309, 311, 368, 391–2, 619, 704, 712, 726, 729, 734, 741, 743–4, 746–8, 752–4, 758–63, 765–6; pp. 10, 31
——Montalt bailiff, p. 30
——steward of prior of Coventry, xxix; 162, 617–18
——Joan his wife, 154–5, 309, 762–3, 765
——his family, pp. 63–4
—Roger de, 89
—Thomas de, 382, 716
—Thomas de (*another*), 33

—Walter de, 768(p. 390)
Stoke (*?another*), Lamfram priest of, p. 6
Stone, Robert de, xl; 33n, 131, 252–5, 392, 405
Stone-cutter (*Incisor*), Ralf the, xxxvi; 40, 86
Stoneleigh (Stanle, Stanleg', Stanlet, Stanley, Stannley, Staunleye, Stonle, Stonlee, Stonleie, Stonley, Stonleye), 38.1; p. 368n.
—abbey of St. Mary of, 177–9, 412–17, 540; pp. 64, 365
——fee of, 409
—abbot of, 768(pp. 370, 385, 388, 391)
——Richard & monks of, 199, 386
—William, dean of, bishop's proctor, 37.8, 37.19
—Alexander de, 69, 79, 81, 258, 375, 518, 523, 563, 580, 631, 700, 704, 730, 743–4, 761, 766
——coroner, xxix; 257, 406, 492, 498, 517, 703
——Eleanor his wife, 563
—John de, 179, 415–16
——Simon his son, 416
—Simon de (*?another*), 768(p. 380)
Stoyle (Stoile, Stoule), William *alias* William le, 265–8, 270, 273–6, 286, 291–2, 454
Stretton (*St(re)tona*, Stretone, Stretton'),
—Andrew de, 768(p. 378)
—John de, 39.9
—Richard de, 99, 198, 768(p. 391)
—William de, 39.9
Stude, grove, on Dunsmore, with chapel, 12
Suggomor *see* Shukmore
Sulcsouere, Sulcsouher, Sulcsouher', Sulcsowher' *see* Silksewer
Suleg' *see* Souley
Sulfton, *Sulftona*, Sulton' *see* Shilton
Summoner (Somenur', *Su(m)monitor*), John le *alias* John the, 353, 768(pp. 387, 392)
Sumvelin (Sum Welin), Geoffrey, 767.4, 767.5
Suneworth', Jurdan de, clerk, 760
Su(n)nulf (Sunnul'),
—William son of, 705
—William son of (*?same*), 9
——Richard his son, 9
Surdi,
—Ywein, 62
——Matilda his widow, 62
Surebacstere, Robert, 671
Sutton (Sutton'), Leticia daughter of Richard de, 528; her uncle *see* William the Marshal
Swancroft (Swanecroft), in Coventry, 30a
Swaynesmon (Swanismon), Richard son of Roger, 167–8
Sweteman, John son of Walter, the comber, 108–9
Sweyn, Henry, 294
Sweytecok, William, 768(p. 393)
Swyn, William, 200
Syreford *see* Shirford
Sysiston', Henry de, 352

Taborrer, Craddock le, 39.2
Taccher', Walter le, 768(p. 375)
Tackley (Takkel), Oxon., 22a
Tailor (*Cissor*, *scissor*, Taillour, Taillur, *talliator*, Tayllour, Tayllur, Taylour, Taylur),
—Adam son of William le, 768(p. 377)
—Avicia le, 690
—Henry le *alias* Henry the, 317, 690, 768(p. 381)
—Hugh le *alias* Hugh the, 115–16, 121, 124, 126, 128, 133, 245, 762
——Matilda his wife, 116
—Hugh le (*?same*), 39.9
—Ralf the, 83
—Ralph le *alias* Ralph the (*another*), 297, 768(p. 384)
—Richard *alias* Richard le *alias* Richard the, 51, 367, 768(pp. 373, 381)
—Robert le, 768(p. 388)
—William le, 36.16
—William le *alias* William the (*another*), 155, 667, 763
Tait, James, xvi; p. 8
Tamworth, now in Staffs., xxx; 407n.
Tanner (Barker, Barkere, *tanator*, Taneor', *Tannator*, Tannur, Tanour, Tanur, tanur', *thanator*),
—Agnes daughter of Haylward the, 452
—Alan the, 527, 534, 555, 707
—Andrew the, 570
—Eadward le *alias* Eadward the *alias* Edward le *alias* Edward the, 74, 364, 424, 462–3, 482, 484, 487–8, 501, 510, 513, 521, 646, 749
—Glademon the, 411
—Ivo le, 35.3
—Ivo le (*another*), 768(p. 393)
—John le, 257, 405
—Robert le *alias* Robert the (*possibly* Robert in the Hurne), 424–5, 457–8, 472–3, 476, 478, 489, 501
—Richard le, 768(p. 376)
—Simon son of Roger the, 420
——Richard his brother, 420
—Symon the, 424
—Thomas le, 418
——Richard the *alias* Richard his son, 451–3, 535–6, 539, 569
—Thomas the (*another*), 374
—Walter le, 710
—Walter the (*?another*), 397, 471
—Walter son of Henry le, 540
Tawyer (*Alutar'*), Thomas, 768(p. 372)
Teler,
—John le, 588
—Jordan le, 767.40
——Emma his wife, 767.40, 767.41
———John her son, 767.41
—Robert son of Richard le, 512
——Agnes his wife, 512; *see also* Agnes daughter of William le Roke
Tenby, Wales, p. 8n.
Tenterer, Sir John le, 105
Terry (*Tericus*, Terri, *terricus*, *Therricus*),
—Walter *alias* Walter son of *alias* Walter de Coventry, xxn, xxvii, xxxii, xxxviii; 21, 28d, e and f, 346, 528n–9n, 767.65; pp. 31–2
——steward of the earl of Chester, 16–19; p. 32
——Benedict his son, p. 31
——Richard de Coventry, knight, his son, p. 31
———Walter his son *see* Sir Walter de Coventry
Tersi, Robert, 44
Teu, Tewe *see* Tuwe
Teynton (Teinthon', Teinton', Teynton'),
—Nicholas de, 719
——John de, his son, farrier, 51, 626, 631, 729, 764, 766, 768(p. 373)
———William his son and heir, 631
————Robert his brother, 631

Thedwus,
—William brother of, 175
——Geoffrey his son, 175; his half brother *see* Thomas son of Richard de Thurlaston
———Dusa his wife, 175
Theyhere, John le, 228–9
Thoki *see* Toki
Thole (Tole),
—John *alias* John senior, 51, 53, 57, 82, 141, 144, 212, 214, 216, 230, 235, 240, 287, 330, 361–2, 365, 367, 376, 378, 449, 502, 511, 548–9, 552, 560, 562–3, 575–7, 595–8, 617–19, 625, 627, 633, 635, 643, 651, 657–8, 665–8, 670, 675, 683–4, 686–9, 691–2, 698, 704, 713, 722, 724, 726–7, 729, 741, 746, 756, 768(pp. 368n, 370, 373–8, 380, 386)
——John his son *alias* John junior, 54, 226, 511, 725–6
—Reginald son of, 263
Tholi, Tholy *see* Toly
Thomas,
—Master, 12
—Walter son of, 35.8
Thotenhale *see* Totenhale
Thoucestr' *see* Towcester
Throstlewell (Throstlewell'), in Coventry, xxxvii; 562
Thured,
—Nicholas *alias* Nicholas son of, 601–3, 605
—Robert son of, 604, 767.61
Thurlaston (Therlauiston', Thorlawiston, Thurlaston', Thurlauestu(n), Thurlauston', Turlausto(n), Turlaweston'),
—John de, tanner, 488, 513
—Symon de, son of Henry Walt(er), 386
—Thomas son of Richard de, 175; his half brother *see* Geoffrey son of William brother of Thedwus
—William de, 37.1, 45, 184, 190, 384
Tilbrook (Tilebrook, Tillebrok', Tylebroc, Tylebrok', Tyllebrok, Tyllebrok'), Master Guy de *see* St. Michael, vicar of
Tile (Tele, Tyle),
—Matthew, 189, 277, 283
—William, 330
Tilor, Thomas, 768(p. 387)
Tinctor, tintor' see Dyer
Tipper (Tippere, Typpere),
—Richard le, 257–8, 580
——Emma his wife, 580
—Robert le, 635
—Walter le, 63, 67
Titchmarsh (Tichemers), Henry de *see* Henry the Merchant
Tochard, Hugh, 319
Tocsale, Roger de, 768(p. 372)
Todenham,
—Richard de, merchant, 253
——Alice his wife, 253
Toki (Thoki, Toky),
—Vincent, 536, 564, 566, 569–71
—William, 534, 607
——Richard his son, 569, 571
——Richard his brother, 606–7, 677–8
Tole *see* Thole
Toly (Tholi, Tholy, Toli),
—William *alias* William son of, 37.1, 182, 273, 287, 536–7, 539, 541, 545–6, 559, 564–6, 568–71, 573, 609, 616, 621–2, 632, 680, 682, 710, 722
——heirs of, 768(pp. 378–9)
Torel, Thomas, 615
Toser,
—William le, 36.16
——Ralf his son, 36.16
Totenhale (Thotenhale, Totehale, Totenhal, Totushale),
—John de, 36.16
——Ralf de *alias* Ralph de, his son, 97–100, 108, 119; his mother *see* Christine daughter of Thomas de Willenhall
Totyng, Hamo, xl
Towcester (Thoucestr', Toucestre, Touchestr', Touecestr', Touestr'), William *alias* William de, 162, 227, 237, 313, 323, 327–8, 330–2, 334, 336, 339–40, 343–5, 367–9, 754, 764, 766
Town Ditch (*fossatum ville*, le To(u)ndich), Coventry, xxxiii–iv; 147, 217, 237, 333, 335–6, 392, 616
Tranter (T(r)anet(er), T(r)auant(er), Trauenter, T(r)uant(er)), Adam le, 37.1, 45, 50, 82, 294, 384, 387, 464, 470, 568, 623
Tranur (T(r)ann(ur), T(r)anour),
—Roger le, of Canley, 669
—William, 606
Tredegold, Isabella, 701
Tregros, Hugh, 768(p. 374)
Trentham, Staffs., John, prior of, 6
Trot, Walter, 680
Truggere (T(ur)uggere), John son of Stephen le, 546–7
Trussell', William, 22a
Turald *alias* Thorol', 5 and n., 9
Turner (*tornator*, Torneur, Tornour),
—Ralf le, 10
—Ralf le (*another*), 217
——Margery his wife, 217
——Margery his widow, 216, 355
—William the, 600
—William le (*?another*), 642
——heirs of, 768(p. 380)
Turvill (Torvill'),
—Hamo de, 21
—William de, 17
Tuschet (Thuschet),
—Robert, heirs of, 22a
—Simon, 15
Tyllay, Richard, 739
Tylun, Henry, 407
Tynel,
—Walter son of Walter, 120–2
——Matilda his wife, 120–1; her father *see* Hugh Bocchi
Tuwe (Teu, Tewe, Twe),
—family, xl, xlii
—John le, 736
—Ralf de, xl; 33, 71, 128, 133, 166
—Roger de, 33, 71

Ufton, xixn; p. 365n.
Ullneya *see* Olney
Umfredus, Umfrei, *Umfrid' see* Humphrey
Undermayst(er), Robert, 573
Unfrey *see* Humphrey

Upton, John de, 760
Urban III, pope, p. 5n.
Usher (*hostiariu(us)*), William the, 644
Utting (Hotting, Hutting, Huttink, Huttyng, Huttyng', Otting, Ottyng, Ottyng', Uttyng, Uttyng'),
—Richard, 131, 133, 156, 246, 253, 294, 764, 766
—William, 150; William his father, 150
—William (*father or son*), 137–8, 194, 198, 218–19, 224, 234, 288–94, 296, 397–8, 768(pp. 370, 379, 383, 387, 393)
Uttred (Houtred, Houtret, Houtreyd, Howtred, Huthered, Outred, Uthret, Utred),
—Robert, 307, 309, 317, 321–2, 324, 328–9, 768(p. 372)
—Walter, 269, 274, 277, 285

Vache, Stephen, 134–5, 187–8
Vado, Matthew de, 605
Varevic *see* Warwick
Vele *see* Wele
Verdun (Verdoun, Werdoun),
—Robert de, knight, 711
—Thomas de, 4
—William de, 10, 14, 767.46
——Emma his wife, 767.46
Vernon (Vernon', Vernoun, Vernun),
—Warin de, 2
—Warin de (*another*), 15
—William de, justiciar of Chester, 21
Vickewan' *see* Wikewane
Vide [*?for vicecomes*], Ralf *see* Ralf the Sheriff
Vienne (Viena, Vienna), Hugh de, clerk, 237, 239, 750–1
Vincent, xx; 14, 29, 60–2, 175, 379, 408, 524, 528, 533, 540, 554, 660–2, 671, 676
——Vincent son of, 175
——Nicholas nephew of *alias* Nicholas, 175, 421, 532, 540, 672
—Vincent (*?another*), 537
—John, 427, 537
——John son of, 542
—John (*father or son*), 657
——heirs of, 768(p. 390)
Vinchcombe *see* Winchcombe
Vintner (*vinetarius*, Vinetar, Vineter, Vineter', *Vinitarius*, *Vinitor*, *vintarius*, Vint(er), Vyneter, Vyneter', *vynitar'*, Vynter, Vynter', *Winitarius*, Winiter, Wyneter'),
—Adam le *alias* Adam the, 35.1, 35.5, 43, 87–8, 177, 382, 411–14, 417–18, 421, 434, 439, 531–2, 536–7, 540, 603, 767.54, 767.55, 767.56
——Matilda his wife, 767.55, 767.56
———heirs of, 537
—Alexander called *alias* Alexander le *alias* Alexander the, xxii, xxviii, xxxv; 26, 49, 70, 113, 115–16, 119, 137, 141–3, 211–16, 220, 227, 230, 233, 304–5, 329, 343, 377, 388–9, 499, 574, 576, 597–8, 656–8, 685, 690, 734, 738, 740, 758, 764, 768(pp. 378, 382, 388)
——Isabella his wife, 137
——Alexander his son, 114, 305, 354, 493, 580, 731, 761
—Alexander son of Adam the, 140, 596
—Anketell the *alias* Anketinus the, 35.11, 35.16; *see also* Anketell de Wikewane
——Robert his brother, 35.11
—David the, 555, 663, 676
—Gerard the *alias* Garard the, xx, xxxviii–ix; 7, 9, 10, 13, 524, 553, 660, 671, 676; p. 1
——family of, xxxviii–ix
——Gerard his son, xxxviii; 61, 379, 524, 530, 553, 660, 671; p. 1
———Master Richard the *alias* Master Richard called the, his son, xxxv; 28a, 43, 179, 181, 379, 382, 415–17, 427–8, 525, 684–5, 708, 710, 745; his niece *see* Margery Pake
————heirs of, 768(p. 381)
——Robert the, his son, 42, 60, 63, 85, 175, 262, 349, 411, 528–30, 533, 604, 662
—Herbert the, 527
—John le, 158, 552, 652, 685–6, 689, 742, 768(pp. 371, 390)
——John his son, 33
—John son of Adam le, 595
—John the (*another*), 685; *see also* John son of Adam the Clerk
—William le, xxxix
Vleur, Simon le, 768(p. 388)

Wadburleia see Whoberley
Wade, Thomas, 418, 436, 440
Waffre, William de, 32n.
Waffrer, Matilda daughter of Elias le, 440; her uncle *see* William the Chaplain
Wake (Wac),
—Hugh, 1
—Richard, 768(p. 387)
Waldgyve (Waldyeve, Walgive),
—John, 521
——Gerard his father, 521
—William, 768(pp. 379–80, 383, 390, 392)
Waldri(n)g, Ralf, 527, 676
Waldthave, William, 470
Wale,
—Matilda 170
—Richard, 768(p. 386)
Waleis, Wales *see* Welshman
Walerand, Robert, 32n.
Waleys *see* Welshman
Walker, William le, 39.1
Waller (Wallar', Wallere),
—William *alias* William le, 33, 156, 249, 406, 446, 449–50, 462–3, 480, 486, 488, 491–3, 495, 503, 510, 513, 516–21, 646, 749
——Geoffrey *alias* Geoffrey le, his brother, 33, 249, 406, 449–50, 462, 495, 498, 516–17, 519, 520–1, 749
Walsall (Waleshal, Walleshale, Walyshale),
—Richard de, merchant, 156, 391–2
——Juliana his wife, 392
——Alan de, his brother, 392
——William de, his brother, 392
——Margery his sister, 392
—William de (*another*), 768(p. 392–3)
Walsgrave (Walesgrave, Welhsgrave), Richard de *alias* Richard son of William de, 594, 719–20
Walsse, William le, 148
Walter, 296
—Matilda wife of, 434–5
—Ranulph son of John, of Stivichall, 504–5
—Stephen son of, 421
Walton (Waleton, Walton', Wauton'),
—John, 438

Walton (*cont.*)
——Elizabeth his widow, 438
—Richard de, 605
—Richard de (*another*), 187
——Richard his son, 188
—Richard de (*father or son*), 189, 192
—Richard de (*another*), 257–8
—Robert, 35.17
—Master Simon de, 438
—William de, 761
Wambe, Robert, 768(p. 374)
Wandelard, Henry, 201
Want(er) *see* Glover
Warenne (*Warenum*, *Warrena*), William de, 16, 18
Warin (Waryn),
—Nicholas *alias* Nicholas son of, xxxix; 36.15, 92, 639, 664–5, 710, 717
——Joan his daughter, 665
——heirs of, 768(p. 379)
—William, 588
Warude, Gilbert le, 707
Warwick (Varevic, Warewic, Warewich, Warewik, Warewik', Warewyc, Warewyke, Warrewik, Warrewyke, Warwic, Warwyc'), 33n., 39.2, 39.4, 39.6, 39.8, 39.10, 137–8; pp. 326, 365
—earl of, 22a
—justices in eyre at, 138
—sheriff of, xxxvi, xxxix; 22a, 32; *see also* Philip de Ascellis, Philip de Gayton, John de Dene
——Gilbert, sheriff's clerk, 32
—John de *alias* John son of Simon de, chaplain, 486, 572, 574, 768(pp. 368n, 377–9)
—Nicholas de, 751
—Reginald de, 531
—Richard de, 259, 524, 527, 553, 555–6, 582, 605, 660–1
——Sampson *alias* Samson *alias* Sanson, his son, 555–6, 582, 605
—Robert de, 261, 264
—Simon de, 419, 432–3, 442–3
——Ralf his son, 432–3
—William de, 268
Warwickshire, 22a, 705
Wasperton, p. 365n.
Wastett, William, 10
Watburle, *Watburlea*, *Watburleia* *see* Whoberley
Waterwey, Simon de, 400
Watford (Watford'), William de, 200, 397, 653–4
Wattell', Adam son of Godwine de, 37.15
Waure (Wauere, Wav(er)e),
—Richard de, 554
—Robert de, 768(p. 376)
—William de, 554, 767.54
—William de (*another*), knight, 711
Wauton' *see* Walton
Waverley, p. 365n.
Waydur (Waydour'), Thomas *alias* Thomas le, servant of Drugo Malerbe, 512, 518–19
Weaver (*textor*, *Tixtor*, Tixto(ur), Webbe),
—Adam the, 610
—Adam le (*another*), 487
—Agnes daughter of Peter the, 421
——Elena her sister, 421
—Dulcia la, 768(p. 386)
—Geoffrey the, 768(p. 385)
—Gilbert the, 180
—Hamo the, xxxvii; 191, 195, 248
—Henry le, 768(p. 389)
——Edith his wife, 768(p. 389)
—John le, of Grove, 190; his father *see* Symon del Phispot
—John le *alias* John the, 624, 768(pp. 373, 379)
—Ralf the, 175, 262, 411
—Richard le *alias* Richard the (*?one man*), 138, 184, 200, 390, 397, 768(p. 382)
—Richard son of William the, 590
—Robert the (*several*), 83, 200, 436
—Roger the (*?one man*), 30a, 587, 607–8, 611, 621, 642, 677–9, 716
—Roger the (*?another*), 36.17
—Stephen le *alias* Stephen the, 231, 768(p. 383)
—Stephen son of Richard le, 522
——Agnes his wife, 522
—Thomas the, 418
——Emma his wife, 418
—Thomas the (*another*), 614
—Thomas le (*another*), 374
—Walter the, 29
—Walter le *alias* Walter the (*another*, *?one man*), 622, 627, 768(pp. 371, 375)
—William the, 767.20
—William the (*another*), 591–2
——Sarra his wife, 591–2
—William the (*another*), 591–2
—William the (*?another*), 183, 185, 383, 386
—William the, son of Geoffrey de Burebathe, 465
Weccheharm (Wet'hewe), Adam, 39.6
Wed', Richard le, 442
Weddinton, John de, 479
Wedone (Wedon),
—John de, brewer, 58, 104, 117, 123–5, 132, 362–5, 371, 378, 646
——Beatrice his wife, 646
——Alice his daughter, 646
Wekewane *see* Wikewane
Wele (Vele, Wiele),
—Adam, 605
—John, 768(p. 374)
—Nicholas, 534, 571, 678
—Richard, 601–2
Welhsgrave *see* Walsgrave
Well Street, Coventry, xxxv, xxxvii–viii
—excavations in, xxxv
—Upper Well Street, Coventry, excavations in, xxxiii
Welshman (*valenc'*, Waleis, *Walenc'*, *Walensis*, Wales, Waleys),
—Geoffrey the, 90
—Peter the, 63, 262, 347, 436, 531
—Peter *alias* Peter le *alias* Peter the *alias* Peter the, called Barun, 66, 93, 191, 195, 198–9, 201, 207, 210, 217–18, 278, 383–4, 431, 465, 666, 683–4
——Peter his son, 431
Wem, wood of, Staffs., 37.10
Wemme, Adam de, 250
Wenga (*Wengha*), Richard de, 186, 278, 351
Werdoun *see* Verdun
Werkwod (Werkwot), Roger, 523, 768(p. 394)
Werrow, Adam le, 112
Weseham, Bishop Roger de, xxiv; p. 6
West Orchard (Westgard, Le Westgardyn), xxi, xxx, xxxvii–viii; 406, 768 (p. 382)
Westmayns, of Coventry, 768(p. 383)
Westminster, 767.46

Weston (*Westona*, Westone, Westun, Westun'),
—Gilbert de, 21
—Master Nicholas de, 21
—Richer de *alias* Rycher de, 106, 136, 141, 143–4, 147, 150–1, 170–1, 194, 197, 199, 204, 209, 211–16, 218–20, 223, 234, 246, 279, 284, 288–92, 301, 305, 313, 355, 401, 747, 768(pp. 370, 383, 385–6, 391)
——Richard de, his son, 171–3, 768(p. 385)
———Alice his wife, 171
———Thomas his son, 252
——William de, his son, 695–6, 768(p. 394); *see also* William the Chaplain
—Richard de, senior, 173
—Richard de (*either* Richard de, senior *or* Richard son of Richer), xxxiv, xxxvii; 38.1, 52, 108, 113–14, 118, 142, 144, 152, 157, 159, 170, 213–15, 224–7, 230, 232, 234, 237, 239–40, 242–3, 253, 255, 293, 341, 344, 377, 748
—William de (*another*), 648–9
Wetemor, Wetemor' *see* Whitemore
Wetherhog, Richard, 248
Wetot, John, 305
Whatburl' *see* Whoberley
Wheelright (*Rotarius*, Whelwruyte),
—Adam the, 511
—Henry le, 397
——Felicia his wife, 397
—Nicholas the, 194, 767.21
—Robert the, 380–1
—Robert the (*another*), 152
White (*Albus*, Blond, Blound, Blund, Blunde, *Blundus*, Blunt, Whyte, Wyhte, Wyte),
—? le, 564
—Adam le, 111, 209, 768(p. 391)
—Adam son of Walter le (*?another*), 325
—Adam le, of Northampton, 9
—Alice la *alias* Alice le, 249, 768(pp. 372, 394); her son and heir *see* Henry Brayn
—Gilbert called le *alias* Gilbert le, 378, 768(p. 393); his nephew *see* John atte Cross
—John le *alias* John the, 546, 579, 583, 590, 592–3, 611, 623, 644, 721, 768(p. 377)
—John the, clerk, 439, 535, 679
—John the, weaver, 767.21
——Christine his daughter, 67
—Petronilla la, 155, 236
—Robert the, 346, 641
—Sir Thomas, p. 63
—Walter the, 259, 381, 419
—Walter le *alias* Walter the (*another*), xxv; 67, 186–8, 190, 279, 281–2, 360, 384, 456, 470, 542, 732
bailiff or reeve, xxv–vi; 37.17, 48, 184, 191–2, 423
——Adam his son, 325
——heirs of, 768(pp. 379, 393)
—William le, 189
—William the, smith, 553
—William the, weaver, 184, 200, 393
White Cellar (*album celarium*, Wyteceler), tenement in Coventry, xxxiv, xxxvi-vii; 134–6, 143–6, 178, 210–13, 280–1, 767.12, 767.36, 767.43; p. 85
Whitemore (Wetemor, Wetemor', Whythemor', Witemor, *Witemora*, Wytemor, Wytemor'), xxv–vi; 28a, 525, 717, 720, 722–5, 727–8, 757, 760; p. 2
—highway towards, 620, 622
—Alice de, widow of Anketill Locard, 534, 767.55
—Hugh son of John de, 600
—Roger de, 720
—Roger de, servant, 727
Whitewright *see* Wychewrite
Whitley (Hwitele, Whitele, Whiteleie, Whiteleye, Whytele, *Whyteleya*, Whyteleye, Witele, *Witelea*, *Witeleia*, Witeley, Wytelay, Wytele, Wyteleye), 13, 22a; p. 365n.
—intended chapel of, 2, 5, 12; p. 6n.
—Adam son of Henry de, 36.16
—Benjamin de, 174
——Alice his wife, 174
—Geoffrey de, 686, 764, 768(pp. 372, 379)
—Christine widow of Haldanus de, 36.16
—John de, 36.18, 561, 716, 724
——Matilda his widow, 561, 768(p. 377)
———Mariota her sister, 768(p. 377)
—John de, merchant, 160, 659, 693–4
——Margery his wife, 160
—Ralf de, 96, 352, 741
—Richard son of Henry de, 96
—Robert de, 36.18
—William de, 181
—William de (*another*), 96, 149, 169–70, 223, 768(p. 385)
—William de (*?another*), 172–3, 728
Whitmore Park, xxv; pp. 2–3
Whitsont, Richard de, 757
Whoberley (*Wadburleia*, Watburle, *Watburlea*, *Watburleia*, Whatburl'), 13
—intended chapel of, 2, 5, 12; p. 6n.
—John, 768(p. 387)
—William de, 410
—William de (*another*), 768(p. 392)
Whytloue (Qhitloue, Qwytloue), Robert, 38.6
Wic, Wick *see* Wyken
Wico (*Wycho*),
—Henry de, 129
—Nicholas de, 441
Wicumba, Elfred de, 379
Widibrok' *see* Withybrook
Wigginton (Wygynton'), Robert de, 33
Wihithawe, Henry de, 42
Wike, Wikene *see* Wyken
Wikewane (Vickewan', Wekewane, Wickewan', Wigewan, Wigewan', Wikewin', Wyckewane, Wygewan', Wykewan, Wykewane),
—family of, xxxvii
—Anketell de *alias* Anketill de *alias* Anketyl' de *alias* Anketinus de, xxv, xxxix; 30 a and b, 36.14, 37.20, 37.21, 178, 183, 187–9, 280, 283, 360, 382, 412–14, 429, 435, 567, 593, 639, 664, 708, 710, 717–18, 732; reeve, 588
—*see also* Anketell the Vintner
——heirs of, 768(pp. 387, 393)
—John de, 58n, 112, 430, 547, 684
——Ida his wife, 684
——Ida his widow, 58
——heirs of, 768(p. 372)
—Nicholas de, 374, 768(pp. 375, 382, 387)
—Robert de, xxxix; 36.14
—Roger de, 83
—William de, of London, xxxix; 35.11, 35.16
——Robert his boy, 35.11

Wilace (Wilas, Wylace, Wylas), 591
—William, 383, 386, 545
——heirs of, 768(p. 376)
Wilhar, William, 596
Willenhall (Wilenhal, *Wilenhala*, Wilenhale, Wilinhale, Willenhale, Wilnale, Wilnehal', Wilnhale, Wylenhale, Wylnehale, Wylnhale), p. 365n.
—chapel of, xxiv; 12
—Christine de, 103
—Christine daughter of Alice de (*?same*), 98
—Geoffrey de (*brother of* Thomas de *and* William de), xxxviii; 43, 60–1, 175, 411, 530, 538, 582, 588, 600–2, 604, 606, 641, 661–3, 671, 677–8, 706–7
——David de, his son, 588, 615, 681
———his heirs, 621
——Edith his daughter, 682
—Geoffrey de (*?another*), 187–9, 352
—Juliana widow of Hugh de, *le vilor*, 767.38
—Richard de, 223
—Thomas de (*brother of* Geoffrey de *and* William de), 60, 62, 85–90, 97, 180, 708
——Christine his daughter, 97; her son *see* Ralf de Totenhale
——his heirs, 768(p. 389)
—Vitalis de, 768(p. 375)
——Robert de, his son, 154, 157, 625, 763, 766
—Walter de, 603
—William de (*brother of* Geoffrey de *and* Thomas de), xxxix; 29, 30 a and b, 36.15, 42–3, 60–1, 85, 87, 90, 175, 178, 180, 228–9, 386, 411–16, 427, 437, 440, 528, 530, 554, 556–7, 604, 640, 661–4, 671, 680–1, 707
——Richard his son, 767.26
William I, king of England, xviii
William II (Rufus), king of England, xvi–viin.
William,
—Hugh son of, 705
—Simon son of, 1
—Walter son of, 768(p. 392)
Wiltshire (Wiltesire, Wiltesyre, Wylteschyre), Thomas de, 97, 758–9
Wimon *see* Wymon/Wymonson
Winchcombe (Vinchcombe, Winchecombe, Winchecu(m)be, Wychecumbe, Wynchcomb, Wynchecombe, Wynchecumbe),
—Philip de, 47, 70, 187–8, 385, 426–31, 435, 438, 451–4, 466, 469, 525–6, 557, 640, 710, 732
——Alice his wife, 430
——Christine his widow, 431
—Robert de, 235, 735, 768(p. 394)
Winchelsea (Winchelse, Wynchelese, Wynchelze), Sussex,
—bailiffs of, xli
—Walter de, 139–40, 168, 210, 768(p. 385)
Winchester (Wincestr'), p. 366
—John de, 704
Wine (Wyne),
—Hugh, 148, 768(p. 384)
—Walter, 84
Winiter *see* Vintner
Wint(er)king (Wint(er)keng), Richard *alias* Richard son of Thomas, 48, 185
Wint(er)ton', John de, 757
Winton (Wynton'), John de, 39.1
Winwick (Wynewik, Wynewyk), Richard de, chaplain, 167–8
Wirth (Wiþ, Wrþ, Wyþ),
—Nicholas de *alias* Nicholas de le, 442–4
——Adam his son, 445
Withington (Wytinton'),
—Henry de, merchant, 151, 243–4
——Agnes his wife, 151
Withir (Wythir, Wythir'), Robert, 195, 382–3
Withybrook (Widibrok', Withibroc, Wythibroc, Wyþibroc, Wythybroc), 767.3
—Emma de, 299, 326
—Sir Nicholas de *alias* Nicholas son of Nicholas *alias* Nicholas son of Nicholas fitz Liulf, 134–5, 176, 181, 272, 347, 349, 351, 528, 540, 640, 767.2, 767.6, 767.19; p. 66
——his heirs, 42
—Reginald de, 92, 435, 583, 609, 681
Witte, William, 724
Wittenas, Matilda daughter of John de, 531; her sister *see* Juliana Sefare
Wodeman (Wodemo(n)),
—Henry, 710–11; his sister *see* Eda Scathelok
——heirs of, 768(p. 388)
Woderoue, Walter, 576
Wodeward (Wodewarde),
—Richard son of Aleyn le, of Stivichall, 39.5
—Thomas le, 577
Wole,
—Hugh son of Nicholas, 569
—Richard, 527
Wolf,
—Agnes le, 38.4
—Thomas le, 764, 766
Wolston (Wollericheston', Wolricheston', Wolritheston'),
—William de, 39.9
—William de (*?same*), 33
Wolvey (Wlveye), Geoffrey de, 330
Woman, Wommenesun *see* Wymon/Wymonson
Wood Mill (Wodemulne), 508, 734, 746
Wood Mill Hay (le Wodemulneheye), Coventry, 742–4
Worcester (*Wigornia*, *Wygornia*, Wyrcestr', Wyrecestr'),
—bishop of, 39.5, 205
——his official, 205
—Hake of, Jew, 710
—Henry de, burgess of Leicester, 736
——Petronilla his wife, 736
—Richard de, xix, xxxiii; 14, 29, 40–1, 60–2, 83, 85–6, 174–6, 259, 261–2, 379–80, 408, 411, 524, 528, 533, 671
——Richard de, his son, xli; 430, 710–11
———his heirs, 195, 768(pp. 383, 389)
——Stephen his son, 40, 61, 174, 261, 408, 671
——Matthew his brother, 29, 175
——his family, xxxviii, xli
—Walter de *alias* Walter called de, 200, 652
—William de, 8
Wormleighton (Wilmeleyton'), William de, clerk, 721
Wroxall (Wroxhall, Wroxhalle),
—Nicholas de, 38.10
—Richard de, p. 326
Wrþ *see* Wirth
Wry,
—Aldith' *see* Aldith' wife of William de Chester
—Christine, 38.8

—Gilbert, 393, 543
——Inga his wife, 393; *see also* Inga Wry wife of Richard de Harnall
Wunman, Wunmonesun' *see* Wymon/Wymonson
Wurkemon, Geoffrey le, 149
Wyche, Adam le, 255
Wychecumbe *see* Winchcombe
Wychewrite (Wchewritte, Whitewright, Wychewrihte, Wychewritte),
—croft, in Coundon, 756
—John le, 768(p. 394)
—William le *alias* William son of Jordan le, 466–8
——Muriel his wife, 468
——Nicholas his son, 466, 468
——heirs of, 768(p. 391)
Wygewan *see* Wikewane
Wyhtlakesforde, Margery daughter of Robert de, of Ashow, 73
Wyken (Wic, *Wica, Wicha*, Wick, Wike, Wikene, Wyche, *Wycka*, Wyke, Wykene), 22a
—chapel of, xxiv; 2, 5, 12–13; p. 365n.
—cemetery of, 12
—manor of, 768(p. 384n.)
—meadow(s) of, 744, 767.47
—lord of, 744
—Elias de, 174
—John son of Godwin de la, 767.30
—Ranulph de *alias* Ranulph de la, 111, 222, 225, 227, 236
——Agnes his widow, 227
—Richard de, clerk, 761
—Yvo de, 744
Wylenhale, Wylnehale, Wylnhale *see* Willenhall
Wymon/Wymonson (Wimon, Woman, Wommenesun, Wunman, Wunmonesun', Wyma(n), Wymaneson', Wymman),
—William *alias* William son of, 767.4, 767.5
——Richard son of William *alias* Richard *alias* Richard son of Wymon, 767.7, 767.9, 261, 263–4, 346–8
———Walter son of Richard, 767.7, 767.8, 262–4, 347
Wymondham (Wymundh(am)), Master Thomas de, Treasurer [of the Exchequer], 32
Wymplestere, Hawise de, 635
Wymund, Emma widow of William, 126, 508–9, 578–9
Wyneter' *see* Vintner
Wynewik, Wynewyk *see* Winwick
Wynt(er), William, 199
Wysmo(n), John, 155
Wyssendene, Isabella widow of Master Robert de, 130
Wyþ *see* Wirth
Wythe Webbe, Walter le, 403
Wytinton' *see* Withington
Wyttauere, Thurstan le, 495

Yelvertoft, Peter de *see* Peter le Carpenter
Yhicher, Cecily widow of Jordan le, 412–14
Yngelard *see* Ingelard
Yngeram *see* Ingram
Yori *see* Jory
York, xl
Young, Walter the, 587
Yreis, Yreys, Yrreys *see* Ireys
Yrland *see* Ireland
Yvo *see* Ivo

INDEX OF SUBJECTS

Abjuration of the realm, 35.13, 35.14, 36.19, 37.6, 37.8, 37.9, 37.11, 37.12, 37.13, 37.15, 37.18, 38.3, 38.8, 39.7
Access, 207
—free entrance and exit, 191, 428, 529, 616, 651, 739, 746, 750
—easement, 687–8
AGRARIAN matters:
—ditching, xxvn.
—dung, 719
—marlpit, 763
—wagons for hay and ploughs, 428
ANIMALS:
—bull-baiting, 31
—cows, 36.16; *see also* pasture
—dogs, 31
—horse, 37.17
—oxen, 36.16, 234
—piggery, xxvn; *see also* Pannage
Arbitration, xxiv; 57, 231, 429, 691; p. 6
Assizes and recognitions:
—grand assize, 767.55, 767.56; p. 6
—mort d'ancestor, 767.46
—novel disseisin, 529n.

Banleuca, xxiv
Banquet (*convivium*), xlii; 36.11
BARS and gates:
—bars, xxiii–iv; 36.12, 66, 110, 152, 385, 393–6, 424, 454, 493, 527, 560, 563, 566, 588, 607, 609, 614–17, 624, 626–7, 630–1, 767.43
—abbey gate, 42
—Bishop St. gate, 588n.
—castle gates,
——broadgate of, xxxii; 7
——south gate of [?], xxxiin; 4n.
—cemetery gate, p. 381
—park gate, xxxiv; 104, 109, 125
Bounds, 17, 18; p. 3
—boundary between fees of prior of Coventry and earl of Chester, xxi–xxii; 7; pp. 1–2
—parish bounds, xxii
—metes and bounds, *passim*
BUILDINGS:
—xxxvii; 53, 57, 72, 74–5, 100, 119, 121, 129–30, 150–1, 184, 195–6, 198–9, 204, 215, 217–19, 227, 231, 234, 236, 239, 242–3, 251–2, 284, 290, 296, 298, 315, 322, 327–8, 330, 332, 334, 344, 356, 361, 370–1, 377, 383, 387, 389, 396, 400, 424–5, 430, 457–8, 461–3, 469, 476, 482, 484, 493, 495, 506, 508–9, 511, 513, 574, 577, 635, 643, 646, 655, 675, 686, 693–700
—new buildings, xxxiv–v
—alehouses, xxxvii; 165
—bakehouses or ovens, xxxvi; 28f, 31, 72, 430, 588, 596, 670, 691, 698, 768(pp. 367, 374, 377, 382, 389)
——castle bakehouse, xx, xxxii; p. 31
——common oven, 768(p. 372)
——suit to, 768(p. 372)
—barns, 42, 191, 646
—bridges, xxxvii–viii; 286, 293, 305, 307–8, 325, 327, 330, 340, 382, 385, 401, 428, 504, 508, 657–8
—cellars, 710; *see also* White Cellar; solar
——inner cellar, 210
——stone cellar, xli; 767.22
—chambers, 710, 715, 767.5
——new chamber, 218
—churches, 37.6, 37.8, 37.9, 37.10, 37.12, 37.13, 37.15, 37.18, 38.3; pp. 5, 186
——cathedral church, Coventry, 768(p. 370)
——fabric of, 35.17, 228–9, 691, 720, 767.43
——monastic church of Combe, construction of, 767.58
——tower of St. Michael's, xxxii
—cottages, 57, 77, 126, 130–1, 370, 768 *passim*
—conventual buildings, p. 7
—courts and courtyards, 36.2, 767.9, 767.22, 767.61
—dovecotes, 430–1, 646
—houses, xxix, xxxiv, xxxvii–ix; 8, 33, 37.5, 37.10, 38.8, 47, 78, 110, 114, 120, 122, 136, 143, 149, 167–8, 187–8, 197, 207, 209, 212–13, 215–16, 220–3, 231, 233, 235, 271, 278–9, 282, 288–9, 291, 301, 307, 311, 313–14, 342, 353, 362–5, 376, 383, 385, 403, 430, 446, 449, 459, 461, 468, 473, 480, 499, 507, 513, 522, 560, 563–4, 578–9, 580–1, 590–2, 594, 599, 600, 617–19, 626, 634, 641–2, 653–4, 667–8, 691, 697–9, 701, 705, 715, 731, 767.58, 768(pp. 366–7, 371, 382)
——chief houses, 48
——great house, 664
——stone houses, xxxvii; 360, 560, 563, 632, 709
———tiled stone house, xxxviii; 651
—halls, xxxviii; 99, 112, 192, 206, 560, 563
——bishop's hall, 375
——hall with cellar and solar, 58n.
——stone hall, xxxv, xxxvii; 684
—inns,
——Crane Inn, 588n.
—leper house *see* Spon
—manor house, xxiv, xxxii; 22a; *see also* chief messuages
—monastery, Coventry, 365, 581, 646; p. 8
—selds, xxxv; 33, 40, 51, 55, 115–16, 144, 206, 232, 236, 241, 247, 372, 524, 644, 661–2, 677–8, 684–5
—shops, xxix, xxxi, xxxv, xxxvii, xl–xli; 42, 146, 193, 245, 257–9, 386, 660, 701, 710, 768(pp. 367, 382)
——cutler's shop, 193
—solars, xli; 115–16, 210, 212–13, 370, 710, 767.22
——solar and cellar, 768(p. 367)
—stalls, xxix, xxxi, xxxv, xxxvii, xxxix, xl; 33n, 385, 680, 768(pp. 367, 377, 380)
——temporary stall, xxxvii
—roofs, 710
—spouts and gutters, 231, 700

Candles, xli; 525, 767.47, 768(p. 390)
—wax, 524, 633, 767.33
—lamps on saints' days, 767.17

CASTLES:
—Coventry, xxx, xxxii–iii; 7, 11, 15; pp. 7–8, 186
——castle bailey, xxxii *see also* ditches, gates
——constable of *see* OFFICIALS
——siege of *see* REBELLIONS
—of Ranulf II, earl of Chester, p. 8
Cemeteries *see* Holy Trinity, St. Michael, St. Mary priory of, St. Nicholas; Allesley, Ansty, Shilton, Wyken
Chantries, xl; p. 63
CHURCHES and chapels; xviin, xviii, xxx, xxxvii; *see also* Holy Trinity, St. John the Baptist, St. Mary priory of (chapel of), St. Michael, St. Nicholas; Alspath, Ansty, Asthill, Binley, Bisseley, Bubbenhall, Corley, Coundon, Dunsmore, Exhall, Foleshill, Keresley, Lichfield, Packwood, Pinley, Repton, Ryton, Shilton, Southam, Sowe, Spon, Stivichall, Stoke, Whitley, Whoberley, Willenhall, Wyken; *see also* BUILDINGS
CLERICS:
—archbishop of Canterbury, xviii
—archdeacon of Coventry, 5–7, 12, 14, 228–9; p. 3
——his official, 45, 228–9, 302, 429, 591, 613, 691
—bishops of Chester, Coventry, Coventry and Lichfield, xv, xvii, xix, xxiii, xxx; 4, 12–13, 21, 22a, 767.30, 767.51; pp. 3–6; *see also* Roger de Clinton, Walter Durdent, Robert de Limesey, Roger Meuland, Geoffrey Muschamp, Hugh de Nonant, Hugh de Pattishall, Richard Peche, Robert Peche, Gerard Pucelle, Alexander de Stavensby, Roger de Weseham
——chamberlain of, 10
——proctor of, 37.8, 37.19
—bishop of Ely, 767.5
—bishop of Worcester, 39.5, 205; his official, 205
—canons, xvi–viii, xxiii; p. 5
—chaplains, xxxi; 2, 14, 21, 35.15, 105, 119, 133, 155, 167, 234, 253, 318, 334, 370, 377, 401, 406, 462, 490, 514, 548, 562, 574, 629, 714, 745, 768(pp. 371, 379); pp. 5, 6, 9
—clerks, xix, xxn, xxvii; 10, 16, 23–4, 32, 35.5, 36.7, 37.8, 37.17, 37.19, 39.5, 52, 56, 63–4, 66, 74, 79, 89, 93–4, 96, 99, 117, 126–7, 133, 138, 142, 162, 168, 184, 195–6, 199, 200, 210–11, 216, 220–1, 224, 229, 237–9, 241, 248–9, 255, 257–8, 269, 305, 307, 331, 340, 367–8, 385, 390, 394–5, 401–2, 420, 423, 427, 439, 455, 458, 464, 470, 485, 487–8, 493–5, 499, 505, 507, 535, 552, 560, 575, 580, 590, 593, 599, 610, 613, 631–2, 645, 647, 658, 664–5, 670, 679, 683, 695–6, 698, 703, 719, 721, 731–4, 750–1, 759, 760–1, 768(p. 370); pp. 4–5; *see also* Index I under surname
—deans, 23, 37.8, 45, 414, 591, 613, 691
—pittancer, 525
—precentor, 429
—priest, 2, 12, 218, 277, 287, 556, 767.4, 767.5; p. 6
—rector, 560–1, 732–3
—sacrist, 299, 326, 525, 743–4, 768(p. 378)
—vicars *see* Sir Henry de Harnall; St. Michael, church of
—clergy of the diocese of Coventry, pp. 3–5
COMMONS:
428, 631
—common way, 384
—prior's appropriation of, xxv, xxvii; pp. 3, 32
—rights of common, xxv; 25, 375, 428 *see also* pasture
—royal commission to assign, xxv
COMMODITIES:
—ale, 31
——brewing, xxxvii; *see also* assize of bread and ale; VESSELS and utensils
—barley, 31
—bread, 31, 675
—cider, xx
—cloth, xxxix–xl; 33
—corn, xxxix; 197, 692–4, 696, 718–19, 748–9
—fish, 31, 683
——salmon, 31
—flesh, 31
—furs, xl
—girdles, xl; 33
—hay, 687, 718
—iron, 669–70
—mercery, xl
—oil, xxxix
—sendal, silk, xl; 33
—spices, xln.
—wheat, 31
—wine, xxxix, xli
—woad, xlin; 36.10
COURTS:
xxii, xli; 28h, 45, 113, 241, 332, 402, 454, 592, 670, 768(pp. 370–1)
—town courts, xix–xxiii, xxvi–xxix; 768(p. 370)
——pie-powder court, xxix
——portmoot, xix, xx, xxvii–viii; 11, 15; pp. 7–8
—bishop's courts, xvi, xxi
—earl's courts, xx; 29
—prior's courts, xvii, xx–xxi, xxviii, xxxi; 22a, 30b, 768(p. 370); p. 30
—Montalt courts, xxiv, xxix; 22a; p. 30
——court for their military tenants, p. 30
—court leets and leet jurisdiction, xxi, xxiv; p. 3
—hundred court, p. 30
—county court, 35.15, 36.6, 36.12, 36.17, 37.3, 38.5, 705
—royal court, xvi; 23, 39.3, 57, 240, 710, 767.2, 767.3, 767.4, 767.5, 767.46, 767.55, 767.56
—Court of Augmentations, pp. 63–4
—quittance from shire and hundred, xxi
—safeguarding of courts, p. 30
—seignorial rights, xvi; 8; p. 9
—sokemoot, xix
—suits of court, xxii; 28h, 30b, 35.15, 45, 70, 72, 93, 95, 97, 115–16, 149, 199, 202, 204, 206, 210, 237, 241, 281, 289, 332, 373, 387, 402, 446, 469, 542, 592, 649, 684, 732–3, 757–8, 767.1, 768(pp. 370, 388)
CRIME and criminal matters:
—appeals, 35.7, 35.8, 36.6, 36.12, 36.16, 37.3, 37.23, 38.5
—approver, 37.2
—armed force or gang, xxix; 32
—assaults, 32, 36.12, 36.17, 37.4
—crimes, xlii–iii
——crime imputed from hatred, 36.13
—forger, xxvi; 37.11
——false money, 37.11
—homicides, xxii; 35–9 *passim*
——accidental death, 35.5, 35.6, 36.2, 36.4, 36.5, 36.8, 36.10, 36.11

CRIME and criminal matters: (*cont.*)
——self-defence, 39.2
——murder, 36.9, 37.2
——slayer of men, xlii; 35.12
—hue and cry, 22a, 35.2, 35.3
—indictments, 36.16, 38.13
—malefactors, evildoers, 22a, 35.9, 37.10
—outlawry, 35–9 *passim*
——waiving, 38.4, 38.13
—pardon, 39.2, 39.3, 39.6
—prisons, xxi; 35.14, 36.19, 37.11, 38.11, 39.2, 39.4, 39.6, 39.8
——imprisonment or custody, xxvi; 32, 36.19, 37.11, 37.17, 37.23
—purgation, 39.5
—theft,
——thieves, xlii; 35.11, 37 *passim*, 38.11
——burglars, xlii; 35.15
———burglary, 37.23, 38.8
——larceny, 35.13, 35.14, 36.16, 36.19, 37.7, 37.9, 37.12, 37.13, 37.18, 38.13
——robbery, 36.12, 37.23
—weapons,
——axes, 37.8, 38.3, 38.10
——firewood, 37.5
——knives, 35.2, 35.3, 36.7, 36.11
——scythe, 38.4
——sticks, 36.3, 37.16, 38.5, 38.7, 38.12
——sword, 38.9

Distraint, 22a
—aid in, 22a
—clause for, 22a, 55, 57, 75, 127, 145, 148, 178, 205, 240, 282, 392, 405, 417, 431, 632, 649, 715, 750, 767.2, 767.6
—freedom from, xxvii
DOCUMENTS:
—bonds and obligations, 145, 179, 431, 613, 715, 765, 767.21
—charters, *passim*
——Charter of Incorporation, p. 2
——royal charters, grants and confirmations, xvi, xviii–xxi, xxix, xli; 11, 24n, 32, 346n; pp. 1–5, 7–8
———royal Inspeximus, 28; pp. 29, 31–2
——charters of the earls of Chester, xviii–ix, xx-xxi, xxviii–xxxii, xli; 1–10, 13–21; pp. 1–10
——custody of charters, 253; pp. 3, 5
——forged charters, xvi–xix; pp. 1–7
——surrender of charters, 118, 139–40, 184, 554
—chirographs, 22a, 23, 57, 115–16, 126, 231–2, 247, 313, 356, 363, 428–9, 543, 549, 594, 651, 687, 719, 735, 737, 748, 750, 767.2
—chronicles, xv; 560n; pp. 29–30, 365
—Dictum of Kenilworth, xxvii
—eyre rolls, xix, xxii–xxiii, xxv–vi, xxviii–ix, xlii; 35–9; p. 65
—final concords, xxiv, xxv; 26, 766n, 767.3, 767.5, 767.46, 767.55, 767.56, 768(p. 370); pp. 29–30, 326
—grants of protection, xxvii
—inquisition post mortem, p. 30
—letters, 7, 22b, 25, 39.5, 286, 460; pp. 29–30
——of attorney, 136, 336, 357, 559
—licence, 25, 27; pp. 30, 326
——of the earls of Chester, xxxi; 17, 767.1; pp. 2–3, 9–10, 352
——royal licence, 26n.
———Mortmain licence, 27n, 714n, 726n, 745n, 747n; pp. 2, 326
—Magna Carta of Cheshire, 528n.
—Montalt grants to the priory, xxii–xxvii; 22–7; pp. 1, 29–32
—Petition to the Royal Council, p. 2
—Pipe Rolls, xix; 767.5n.
—pleas,
——record of, 33
——pleas of the Crown, 35–9; p. 7
—Priory Register, 744n; pp. 1, 3, 29
—Prophecy of Merlin, p. 365
—quitclaim, remise, *passim*
—renunciations, 767.31, 767.46
—restitutions, 2; pp. 4–6
—schedule, 32n.
—*sedula*, 67
—Statute of Mortmain, 27, 743; p. 2
—surveys,
——Domesday, xv
——Hundred Rolls, xxiv, xxxi, xxxix, xli–ii; 768
——Winchester, 1148, p. 366
—Taxation of Pope Nicholas, p. 365
—Tripartite Indenture, pp. 2, 365
—waste rental, xxv; p. 3
—writs, royal, xl; 33, 36.11, 57, 137–8, 429
——and rolls, 32
——doctored writ of William I, xviii
——register of writs, 31n.
—year book, 33n.
See also leases
Dower, 56, 57, 62, 77, 80, 182, 214, 253, 276, 314, 317, 322, 345, 412, 431, 434, 452, 494, 504, 561, 565, 590, 592, 614, 639, 673, 728, 757, 764–5; p. 326
——plea of, 179

ECCLESIASTICAL matters:
—absolution, 4
—advowson, 22a, 23
—alms, xxxin; 525, 767.6; p. 352
——grants in, 3–5, 13–14, 16–19, 21, 23–4, 26, 28b, 28d, 28e, 28f, 30a, 127, 177–8, 412, 414, 430, 438, 525, 633, 683, 718, 728, 744, 747, 767 *passim*, 768(p. 371) p. 326
—altars,
——of the blessed Mary, 525, 768(p. 383)
——of St. Edward the King (priory church), 714
——high altar (priory church), 13, 680; p. 5
——of St. Katherine, 28d, 28e
—anathema, 14
—anniversary masses, 525, 767.54, 767.57
—appropriation, xxiii–iv, xxxi; 768(p. 371); p. 6
—benefit of clergy, 37.8, 37.19, 39.5
—bishopric of Coventry, xviiin.
—burial and burial rights, 6, 12, 767.4
—crusade, xxiv; pp. 29–30
—ecclesiastical elections, xviii, xxiii; 24n.
—ecclesiastical sanctions, xxxix; 22a, 45, 205, 228–9, 302, 414, 429, 591, 613, 691
—faith, interposition of, 62
——pledge of, 253, 276, 720
—freedom from episcopal control, xviii, xix; p. 4
—malediction, 3, 16, 19; p. 2
—monastic allowance, 767.43
—monastic offices,

——cellarer's office, 767.43
——guest house, 525
——infirmary, 328, 525, 615
——sacristry, 525, 743
—parishes, xxiin; 2, 5
——parochial rights, 2, 12, 13; pp. 3–4
—redemption, 4
—sanctuary, 35.13, 35.14, 36.19, 37.6, 37.8, 37.9, 37.11, 37.12, 37.13, 37.15, 37.18, 38.3, 38.8, 39.7
—spiritual benefits, 767.29
—tithes, xviin; 12–14, 525; pp. 3–5, 9
——extra-parochial tithes, 14
—vicarages, xxivn.
—visitations (bishop's), 375n.
Exchanges (of property), 17–19, 30a and b, 112, 230, 311, 342, 642, 718, 722, 757n, 767.3
Exchequer, 11n.

Fealties, 28h, 768(p. 370)
Fisheries, fishing rights, 4, 347, 349–50, 353–4, 750–1
Fishponds, 4, 22a, 28a, 354, 446, 524–5, 657–8, 768(pp. 370–1)
—evildoers in, 35.12
—provision for sick from, 525
Gilds, p. 63
Gild merchant, xxvii, xlii; 32
Grange, 755, 768(p. 371)

HEDGES, fences and ditches:
—hedges, 19, 343, 354, 418, 631, 719, 746, 753
—fences, 231, 354, 564
—hurdles, 687
—palisade (*palacium*), 705
—ditches, 7, 343, 354, 631, 722, 753, 767.63
——town ditch (including *Hersomdich*, Poddycroft Ditch, Red Ditch), xxxiii–iv; 66, 76, 128, 147, 149, 165–6, 185, 217, 219–20, 237, 255, 279, 294, 333, 335–6, 386, 392, 535–7, 616
——castle ditch, xxxii–iii; 223, 226
——earl's ditch, xxxiii; 767.33
——park ditch, xxxiv; 170–1, 173
——land called Rodiche, 767.43
Homages, 22a, 24, 438, 741, 757–9, 767.1
——homager, of the earl of Chester, p. 10

INDUSTRIAL matters:
—cobbler's workshop, xxxvin.
—cutler's shop, xxxvii
—forges, xxxv; 55, 557, 676
—fulling mill, xxxv
—horner's workshop, xxxv
—kilns, xxxvii; 356, 522, 606, 679[?], 687–8, 701; for ovens *see also* BUILDINGS
—quarries, xxi, xxxv, xxxvii; 541, 604, 615, 767.58–767.62, 768(p. 374)
—tannery, xxxvin.
—tenter-yards, xxxv; 538, 540
—workshops and yards behind, xxxvii
—industrial organization, xxxvi–vii
See also VESSELS and utensils
Inquisitions, 36.11, 39.2
——inquisition post mortem, p. 30

JEWS:
xxxiii; 49, 208, 210, 384, 497, 651, 688, 710
——Coventry Jewry, xxxii–iii
——Jewish bonds, 757n.
——debts to, xxxiii, xli; 710
JURIDICAL matters:
—assize of bread and ale, xxi; 31, 33, 768(p. 370)
—assize of cloth, xxxix, xl; 35.10, 36.15, 37.21
—assize of wine, xxxix, xli; 35.11, 35.16, 36.14, 37.20
—cucking stools, xxi; 31, 768(p. 370)
—frankpledge, tithings, 35–8 *passim*; p. 1
——view of frankpledge, xxi, xxiii; 19, 28g; pp. 2–3, 31
—gibbet, gallows, 7, 768(p. 370)
—juries, xix, xxii–iii, xxv, xxviii; 33, 35.1, 36–9 *passim*, 529n, 768(p. 370); p. 65
——electors of, xxii
—pillories, stocks, xxi; 31, 33, 37.17, 768(p. 370)
—tumbrel, 33

LAND:
—*terra, tenementum, passim*
—approvement and assarting, xx, xxv, xxxi; 20a and b, 34, 724–5; pp. 1, 7, 9–10, 326
—arable land, 25, 162, 262, 304, 534, 560, 563, 631, 731, 736, 738–9, 755
—built-up land, xxxv; 46, 683
—carucates, 768(pp. 367, 371, 384, 387)
—closes, xxix; 7; pp. 30–1
—crofts, xxxiv, xxxix, xlii; 30a, 42, 60–1, 63, 162, 259, 283, 306, 385, 411, 430–1, 523–4, 605, 616, 636–8, 642, 732–7, 745–8, 753–4, 756, 761, 767.58, 768 *passim*
—curtilages, xxxiv; 42, 44, 53, 67, 69, 76–7, 82, 92, 95, 99, 104, 108–9, 114, 120, 122–3, 125, 128, 152, 160, 169, 170–3, 185, 191, 209, 223, 228, 236, 254, 260, 266, 302–3, 311, 355, 358–9, 372–3, 387, 403, 430–1, 443–4, 446, 448, 467–8, 473, 481–2, 489, 495, 503–4, 510–12, 516–17, 519, 521–2, 544–7, 550–2, 568, 581, 602, 622, 625, 630, 632, 648, 658, 670, 695, 701, 713, 755, 767.62, 768 *passim*
—fields, xxxi, xxxiv, xlii; 155, 162, 206, 331, 343, 429–31, 523, 533n, 549, 640, 722–5, 729–31, 735–41, 749, 763
—furlongs, 287, 306, 523, 528, 616, 631, 720, 748, 753, 756, 763, 767.62
—gardens, 28b, 106, 163, 217–18, 251, 261, 375n, 430–1, 466, 508, 520, 523–4, 546, 574, 589, 602, 636, 638, 721, 768(pp. 367, 377–8)
—groves, 12, 18, 28g, 36.3, 751, 753–4, 768(pp. 367, 384)
—meadows, 19, 25, 27, 28a, 28c, 28g, 162, 206, 259, 261, 273, 286, 304–5, 315–16, 323, 328–9, 332, 334, 343, 347, 349–50, 353–4, 430–1, 443, 446, 505, 523, 525–6, 548–9, 560, 563, 631, 646, 716–17, 719, 724–6, 728, 737, 741, 743–4, 749, 753–4, 758, 767.47, 767.65, 768(pp. 367, 389); pp. 10, 326
—moors, xxxix; 19, 27, 28a, 28g, 286, 353, 408, 514–15, 524–5, 559, 579, 631, 717, 722, 724–5, 741, 744, 750; p. 326
—orchard, p. 31
—parcels, plots, pieces of land, 40, 68, 72, 74, 78, 90, 112, 118, 124, 149, 165, 209, 227, 252, 305, 375, 430, 474–5, 480, 502, 505, 523, 578–80, 629, 634, 667, 687, 694, 726, 753; pp. 326, 367
——acres, 17–19, 20a and b, 529n, 726n, 741, 751, 758, 767.5; pp. 31, 326

LAND: (*cont.*)
——butts, 768(pp. 367, 375)
——headlands, 523, 730–1, 739–40, 763, 767.60
——selions, 260, 269, 277, 331, 430–1, 523, 548, 631, 729–30, 739–40, 749, 752, 763, 767.5, 767.60, 767.62, 768(pp. 367, 373–4, 379)
—pasture, common pasture, xxvii, xxxi; 19, 25, 28g, 34, 176, 343, 347, 349–50, 354, 428–9, 631, 728, 742–3, 746, 753, 768(p. 370); p. 32
——herbage, 754
—toft, 426
—virgates, 30b, 744, 759, 767.3; p. 10
—wastes, xxv, xxvii; 17–19, 25, 30b, 375, 492; pp. 2–3, 30, 32, 326
——waste-ground, 385
—woodland, xv, xxv, xxxi; 3, 7, 12, 14n, 17–19, 20a and b, 22a, 25, 37.10, 372, 408, 716, 719, 721–2, 724–5, 728, 767.62, 768(p. 370); pp. 2–3, 9, 30, 32, 326
——access to, for specified purposes, xx; 3, 16–18, 22a, 30b; pp. 2, 6, 7
——enclosure of, pp. 2, 10
Laws and customs,
—of Coventry, 11, 15, 22a
—of Lincoln, 11, 15, 33; pp. 7–8
LAYMEN (status, trades and professions):
—alderman, of London, 226
—bakers, xxxvi; 31, 100, 104, 123, 125, 173, 672–3, 713
—*blobestator*, 31
—brewer, 124
——alewife (*braciatrix*), 31
—burgesses of Coventry (*named*), xxxiii, xli; 197, 292, 470, 490, 666, 683, 710
—burgesses of Coventry (*unnamed*), xix–xxiv, xxvii–viii, xli–ii; 11, 15, 33, 286, 768(p. 370); pp. 7, 9
——aids from, xx, xxiii, xxvii; 534
——association of, xxvii
——burgess or borough community, xviii, xxi
——fellow burgesses, xxvii; 34; p. 32
——burgesses,
———of Bristol, 353
———of Gloucester, 205
———of Leicester, 736
———of Lincoln, 15
—butchers, xxxv; 31, 373, 579
——*bocmongers*, xxxv
—butterer, 110
—capmaker, 503
—carpenters, xxxv–vi; 503
—carters, xxvi
—combers, xxxv; 108–9
—cooks, xxxvi
—coopers, xxxvi–vii; 626
—cottars, 768 *passim*
—craftsmen, xxxvi, xl
——master craftsmen, xxxvi
—drapers, xxxvi, xl; 35.16, 36.2, 307, 313, 316, 322, 344, 400, 514; p. 32
—dyers, xxxv–vi; 31, 57, 397, 636–8, 691
—earls *see* Leofric; Arundel, Chester, Lincoln, Warwick
——countesses *see* Godiva; Chester
—esquire, 767.11
—farriers, xxxv; 626
—free tenants, 768 *passim*
—girdlers, xxxvi–vii, xl; 146, 242, 246
—glovers, xxxix; 39.9, 634–5
—goldsmiths, xxxvi, xl
—groom, xlii; 36.11
—hood-maker (*le Hodere*), 172
—knights (*named*), 4n, 22a, 23–4, 26, 72, 149, 163–4, 197, 236–8, 241, 332, 335–6, 402, 525, 560, 563, 711, 741, 750–2, 754, 757–8, 760, 768(pp. 370–1); p. 31
—knights (*unnamed*), xxiin, xxiv
——leprous knight, 768(p. 371)
—lawyer, 31n.
—locksmiths, xxxvi–vii
—masons, xxxvi
—mercers, xxxvi, xl; 33n.
—merchants, xxvii, xxxi, xxxvi–viii, xl, xlii; 11, 15, 31, 69, 72, 119, 144, 151, 160, 163, 234, 237, 334, 336, 354, 356–7, 371, 375, 377, 405, 503, 735–7; pp. 7, 32
——merchants 'of' or 'in' Coventry, xli; 93–4, 128–9, 132, 162, 164, 166, 195, 199, 214, 225, 227, 239, 241, 253, 256, 308, 333, 335, 337–8, 344–5, 392, 402, 404, 568, 642, 751, 753–4, 764, 766
——corn merchant, xxxix
——wool merchants, xxxix, xl; p. 369
——foreign merchants,
———of Amiens, xl
———Flemish, xli
———Florentine, xxxix
———Italians, xl
———Picards, xlin.
——merchant oligarchs, xl
—military tenants, xxiv; 22a; pp. 30–1
—millers, xxxvi; 124, 371
—mirrorers, xxxvii
—parchment-makers, xxxvi
—preacher, 507
—provisioners, victuallers, xl; p. 369
—rentiers, xxviii, xxxv, xl
—saddlers, xxxvi–vii, xl; 52, 78, 494, 497
—serfs and their offspring (*sequela*), 28d, 28e, 28g, 758; p. 31
—shoemakers, cordwainers, 381, 703
—smiths, xxxv; 297, 553
—soapmakers, xxxvi; 172
—tailors, xxxvi; 37.13, 39.9, 344, 749
—tanners, xxxv–vi; 74, 394–6, 490, 493, 512–13, 581
—tipper (*le tippere*), 634–5
—turners, xxxv
—unfree tenants, p. 31
—vintners, xxxix–xl; 36.2
—weavers, xxxv–vi; 67, 184–5, 393–4, 511, 767.21
—wheelwrights, xxv
See also Index I under particular surnames

Mainpast, 35.2, 36.16
Maintenance, repairs and improvements; 58, 99, 115–16, 126, 161, 197, 232, 236, 251, 273, 294, 311–12, 342, 356, 372, 403, 462, 484, 495, 522, 564, 566, 581, 589, 594, 667, 701–3, 750
Manors, xv, xvii, xix, xxxi, xxxiv, xxxix; 14n, 22a and b, 25, 705n, 751, 768(pp. 365–6, 384n); p. 30
MARKETS, fairs and trading regulations:
—market, xxix, xxx–xxxi, xl, xlii; 31, 33; pp. 1–2
——site of, xxx–xxxi; 7

—market-area, xxxv, xxxvii, xxxix, xli
—*le Bochery*, 768(p. 380)
—cattle market, xxx
—corn market, xxxv; 695 *see also* COMMODITIES
—fish market, xxx
—timber market, xxx
—cross in market-place, xxxv; 684, 687–8
—market stalls,
——regulation of, 31
——profit from allocation of, 33
—trading and provisioning regulations, xxi; 31; *see also* assize of bread and ale
—market and trading offences, xxi; 31
—fairs, xxi, xxiii; 33, 768(pp. 368, 370)
—wool staple, xl
Marriage, xlii; 44, 68, 73–4, 82, 222–3, 240, 259, 303, 380, 393, 420, 437, 440, 491, 500, 524, 560, 567, 642, 646, 678, 719, 733, 764, 766
—*maritagium*, 240, 412
Measurements, 40–1, 72, 120, 252, 266, 358, 474, 505, 581–4, 663, 679, 694
—perch of 25 feet, 18; p. 2
Messuages, *passim*
—chief messuages, xxxv, xxxvii; 51, 55, 58n, 75, 98, 154, 248, 252, 257–8, 356, 370, 372, 405, 508, 560, 563, 687–8, 693, 695–6, 718, 728, 768(p. 371); pp. 30, 326
—stone messuage, 182
MILLS:
xx, xxxi, xxxiv–v, xxxix, xlii; 4, 7–9, 27, 28a, 28c, 43, 261, 304, 346–50, 352–4, 399, 409, 443–4, 481, 500, 508, 524–6, 533n, 537–9, 545–8, 552, 575–6, 617–18, 630, 657, 734, 746, 750–1, 753–4, 764, 767.2, 767.3, 768(pp. 367, 370–1, 384, 386, 389, 391); pp. 1, 10, 30
—mill bays, 304–5
—mill pond, 27, 28a, 28c, 347, 349, 353, 524–6, 543, 746, 750–1
—mill stones, xxxiv; 160
—mill wheel, 35.5
—easements belonging to, 751
—multure, 751

OFFICIALS:
—bailiffs (*named*), xx, xxv–xxix, xxxviii–ix; 35.1, 37.1, 37.17, 37.22, 38.1, 42, 45–9, 52–4, 56–8, 66, 68–9, 71–2, 73–6, 79–80, 82, 97–104, 106–111, 113–16, 118–27, 129–31, 133, 138–41, 145–6, 148, 150–3, 158–61, 165, 168–73, 184–5, 192–3, 196, 202–8, 210–12, 217–19, 221–2, 224–9, 231–37, 240–4, 246, 248, 251, 254, 256–8, 269–70, 276, 279, 283–4, 295–305, 307, 309–10, 312, 314–32, 335–6, 338–44, 355–6, 358–61, 364–5, 367–71, 373–4, 376–8, 385–7, 390–1, 393–5, 397–406, 422–5, 443–50, 454–8, 462–5, 468–71, 473–6, 478, 480, 482–5, 488–9, 492–3, 495–502, 504–12, 514–18, 520–2, 543–50, 552, 561, 572–4, 576–7, 579–81, 589–90, 594, 596–9, 613, 624, 626–31, 634–7, 643–7, 651–3, 655–8, 674–5, 685–9, 691–5, 697–9, 701, 703, 706, 720–2, 725–6, 728, 730–2, 735–6, 738, 740, 742, 745, 749, 756, 762; p. 7
—bailiffs (*unnamed*), xx, xxii, xxviii–ix, xli; 3, 15–17, 21, 22a, 37.11, 528n, 529n, 613, 715, 767.11; pp. 30, 65
——chief bailiff, xxii; 36.11
——coordinating bailiffs, xxiii, xxv–vi
——under-bailiff, xxiii
——misdemeanours of bailiffs, xxvi; 36.11, 37.17, 37.23
——staff of bailiffs, xxvi
—bailiffs, of Gloucester, 205
——of Winchelsea, xli
—chancellor, of the earl of Chester, 16n.
—constable, of Chester *see* Eustace fitz John, Roger de Lacy
——of Coventry, 11, 15; p. 7; *see also* Ivo
—coroners (*named*), xxviii–ix, xxxviii; 35.16, 38.2, 39.7, 52–4, 56–7, 72–3, 75–6, 104, 109, 113, 121–5, 127–8, 141, 145–6, 152–4, 158, 160–2, 171, 173, 212, 225–7, 241–4, 246, 248–9, 251–2, 254–5, 257–8, 298, 305, 308, 330–2, 334, 338, 343–5, 358–9, 368–9, 374, 390, 400–3, 406, 448–9, 462–3, 491–2, 495, 498, 505, 507–13, 517, 520–2, 550, 552, 577, 580–1, 596–7, 619–20, 626–31, 635–7, 643–5, 657, 659, 692, 695–6, 698–701, 703, 725–6, 728–31, 736, 738–42, 746, 753
—coroners (*unnamed*), xxvii–ix; 32, 35.4, 35.12, 36.2, 36.19, 37.8, 37.11, 37.13, 37.16, 37.18, 38.3, 38.8, 39.10, 768(p. 370)
——coroners' rolls, 38.5, 39.7
—custodian of the estates during the minority of Ranulf III, earl of Chester, pp. 4, 7
—foresters, xxxviii; 3, 16, 17, 22a; pp. 6, 10
—justices,
——royal, 33
———in eyre, 22a, 32, 35.5, 36.11, 137–8, 407n, 767.3, 767.4, 767.5, 767.46, 767.55
———of goal delivery, 39.2, 39.8, 39.10
———of oyer and terminer, 39.10; p. 3n.
—*justicia*, of Coventry, xx; 11, 15; p. 7
—justiciar of Chester *see* Ralph Mainwaring, Philip de Orreby, William de Vernon
—ministers, xlii
——of the earls of Chester, xix–xxii, xxxviii; 7, 14; pp. 1, 3, 10
——of Holy Church, 7
——of the prior of Coventry, xx–xxi, xxvn, xxvii–viii, xxxviii
——of queen Isabella, p. 2
——ministerial families, xxxviii
—parkers, xxxviii; 4
—reeves (*named*), xx, xxii–iii, xxv; 35.14, 48, 134, 191, 428, 439–40, 538, 557, 588, 609–11, 614–15, 648–9, 681, 709
—reeves (*unnamed*), xxii
——reeves' deputies, xxiii
——reeve's serjeant, 35.14
—secretariat, of the earls of Chester, xxxviii; 9n; p. 6
—serjeants,
——of Gloucester, 205
——royal serjeants, xxvii; 35.4, 35.14
—sheriffs, xxvii, xxx, xxxix; 32, 33, 35.16, 36.3, 36.4, 36.5, 36.8, 36.9, 36.16, 37.2, 37.3, 37.4, 37.5, 37.8, 37.11, 37.14, 37.16, 38.3, 38.5, 38.9, 39.3, 39.4, 39.5, 39.6, 39.9; p. 31. *See also* Index I *under* Warwick, *and under surname.*
——under-sheriffs, 346n, 407n.
——sheriff's court, p. 31
——sheriff's tourn, xxi
—steward *see* Robert de Handsacre
——of Chester *see* Montalt

OFFICIALS: (*cont.*)
——of the earls of Chester, xx; *see also* Nicholas son of Alan, Walter d'Eyvile, William the Marshal, Walter son of Terry
——of the prior *see* John de Pontefract, Robert de Stoke
——of Queen Isabella, p. 3n.
—treasurer,
——of England *see* Peter des Rivaux, Thomas de Wymondham
——Luke, 'the king's treasurer', 35.15
——of Chester, 13
——of Lichfield, 13
—warden,
——of the assize of bread and ale, 31
——of the city of London, 226
——of the fabric of the church of Coventry, 35.17
——of the altar of the blessed Mary, 525
——of the window of the blessed Mary, Holy Trinity Church, 633

Pannage, xxii; 4, 9, 24, 28h, 113, 155, 762–3, 767.4, 767.5, 768(p. 371); p. 9
Parks, xxiv–v, xxxii, xxxiv; 4, 22a, 133, 152, 160, 169–73, 747, 768(p. 371); pp. 2–3, 30
—park close, p. 30; *see also under* BARS and gates; HEDGES, fences and ditches
PAYMENTS, profits and fines:
—aids, xx, xxiii–iv; 387, 534, 758
——aid for Holy Land, 522, 715
—amercements of the eyre, 35.16
—credit, xxxix; 22a
—damages, 155, 231, 429, 477
—debts, xxiv, xxvii, xxxiii, xxxix, xli; 200, 284, 710, 715; p. 31
—to Crown, 10n.
——bankruptcy, xxxix
—deodands, 35.17
—from allocation of market stalls, 33
—hospitality, 24
—limiting of fines, xxiin; 11, 15, 185, 262, 289, 437, 453, 649; p. 7
—maintenance of grantor, 44
—perquisites and profits of courts, pp. 30, 368
—quittance of murder-fine, 768(p. 370)
—recognition, payments in,
——money, *passim*
———bezants, 86, 347, 604
———talent, 40
——cape of bluet, 469
——green cloak, 706
——pair of leather boots, 671
——pair of leather boots and ribbon, 175
——peacock-blue cape with rabbit-fur hood, 606
——tunic, 458
——white horse, 283
——wimple, 29
—reliefs and heriots, 10n, 22a, 24, 28h, 438, 741, 757, 759, 764–6
—scutage, 767.1
—tallages, 387
—tolls, xxii; 28h, 113, 762–3, 768(p. 371)
——toll of horses, 155, 176, 767.1, 768(p. 370)
See also Pannage; assize of bread and ale
PERSONS acting for others:
—arbitrators, xxiv; p. 6; *see also* Arbitration
—attorneys, 22a, 33, 45, 75, 82, 93, 110–11, 136, 144, 194, 197–8, 201, 204, 212, 217, 220, 224, 253, 276, 279, 281, 283, 292, 294, 301, 307, 328, 350–1, 354, 396, 423, 443, 453, 471, 482, 523, 545, 547, 552, 564, 574, 592, 612, 615, 654, 675, 681, 686, 703, 715, 721, 765, 767.46, 768(p. 389)
—executors, 748
—guardian, xxxvii; 356
—messenger, 35.15
—pledges, xxiii; 35.7, 35.16, 36.9, 36.11, 36.12, 36.17, 36.18, 38.5
POPES and papal matters:
—pope, xviii; *see also* Eugenius III, Gregory IX, Honorius III, Innocent II, Lucius II, Urban III
——appeals to, p. 5
—papal approval, xv
——confirmation, xviii, xxiii
——*Curia*, xxiii
——indult, p. 6
Population of Coventry, xlii; pp. 366–8
Pre-emption, 126, 197, 232, 302, 403, 431, 564, 591, 667, 720, 749
Property accumulation, xxxviii–ix, xlii; p. 368

REBELLIONS and civil wars:
—civil war of Stephen's reign, xvii, xxxi–iii; 5n, 12; pp. 6, 8–9
—rebellion,
——of Hugh II, earl of Chester, 5n, 6n, 9n, 10n.
——of 1088, xvi
—rebels and Montfortian sympathisers, xxvii
—siege,
——of Coventry's castle, p. 8
——of Kenilworth, xxvii
—admission to the king's peace, xl
—king's enemies, xix
RELIGIOUS houses and their heads:
—xli; 30b, 135, 208, 210, 384, 397, 426, 479, 651, 664, 681, 688, 709, 716
—monasteries and their heads *see* Alcester, Barberie (Normandy), Basingwerk, Bec, Calke, Chester, Combe, Darley, Greenfield, Kenilworth, Monks Kirby, Peterborough, Poulton, St. Albans, St. Mary's Coventry, St. Sepulchre Warwick, Stoneleigh, Trentham
—nunneries and their heads *see* Catesby, Henwood, Polesworth
—hospitals and their heads *see* St. John the Baptist, Spon (St. Leonard's)
—friary *see* Franciscans, of Coventry
—Templars *see* Balsall, Templars of
RENTS:
passim
—arrears of, 401, 705, 756, 765
—clause for acquittance of rent to chief lords, 23, 280, 414, 484, 641, 720
—clause for re-entry for arrears or non-payment of, 126, 415, 596, 651; *see also* Distraint
—clause retaining rent in case of future alienation by grantee, 405
ROADS:
xxx, xxxii; 17–18, 20a and b, 257–8, 343, 353–4, 508, 591, 620, 634, 646, 679, 738, 740, 754
—le portweye, 306
—le holdeallewey, 763
—lanes, 47, 178, 234, 257–8, 382, 469, 535–6, 578–80, 663

—highway, xxxiv; 7, 41, 113, 191, 333, 410, 500, 506, 616, 622, 747, 767.22
——royal, 42, 53, 59, 69, 78–9, 106, 110, 118, 126, 132–3, 151, 160, 163, 166, 171, 196, 223, 226–7, 232, 237, 241, 243–4, 246, 307–8, 323, 327, 329, 331, 335–6, 341, 344, 392, 399, 400, 402, 404–6, 443–4, 449, 467–8, 482, 491, 493, 518, 520, 543, 548–9, 575, 596, 621, 626–8, 631, 637, 643–5, 651, 667–8, 670, 683, 692, 694, 701, 713, 730–1, 739–40, 751, 753, 767.61, 767.62
—streets,
——bishop's great, xxx
——high, 47, 178, 234, 257–8, 382, 469, 535–6, 578–80, 663; p. 118
——of the earl of Arundel, xxx
——prior's, 663
——pattern of, xxx
—pavement; 36.10
See also Index I for individual streets
Royal commissions, xxv, xxvii, xxix; 39; pp. 32, 365

SERVICES:
—forinsec service, 410
—knight's service, 768(p. 370)
—of a candle burning in earl of Chester's stable, xli; 768(p. 390)
—of men in autumn, 84, 105, 111, 121, 134–5, 195, 204, 273, 290, 315, 351, 385, 410, 420, 424, 434–35, 451, 453, 482, 500, 511, 592, 710, 756, 767.45, 768(pp. 383, 385–90, 394)
—villein-services, 28g, 757
Ship, shipping, xl–xli
STRANGERS:
—31, 37.7, 37.10, 37.15, 38.3
—travellers, 31
—unknown evildoers, 37.10
—unknown men, xlii; 35.4, 35.15
—vagabonds, xlii; 38.6, 38.7, 38.8, 38.13
—vagrants, xlii; 36.16, 37.11, 37.12, 37.13

Table and trestles, xxxvii; 356n.
TENURE and tenurial matters:
—barony, xvi; 768(p. 370)
—burgages, burgage tenure, xvii, xxxi, xxxiv, xxxviii–ix; 8–11, 15, 22a, 524, 768 *passim*; pp. 7, 9, 31
—coparceners, 256
—courtesy (law) of England, 245, 627, 768(pp. 373–4, 379–80, 390, 394)
—escheats, xii; 19, 22a, 24, 28h, 438, 741, 757–9, 764–6
——escheat for felony, 765
——king's year and waste, 36.9
—free land, xx
—lease (or demise for a term), xlii; 57, 92, 94, 99, 115–16, 126, 155, 197, 232, 235, 247, 250, 273, 294, 302, 311–13, 336, 356, 372, 375, 390, 403, 461, 467, 484, 492, 499, 522, 543–4, 549, 562, 564, 589, 591, 594, 667, 687, 701–2, 718–20, 727, 735–7, 748–50
—life-grants, 58, 75, 251, 523, 581
—livery of inheritance, 4n, 5n.
—minority, 4n, 5n, 8n, 9n, 560n; pp. 4, 5, 7, 9
—remainder, 68, 74, 82, 125, 303, 354, 365, 392, 532
—reversion, 59, 73–4, 82, 96, 120, 133, 161, 222–3, 235–6, 240, 247, 251, 292, 354, 359, 365, 375, 382, 392, 431, 463, 467, 484, 486, 492, 495, 504, 523, 543, 550–1, 560, 581, 590, 643, 646, 687, 697, 712, 728, 734, 748–9, 764
—seisin, 137n, 337, 357, 711, 717, 765
—share-cropping, 718
—soke, xvi, xix; pp. 2, 9
—villeinage, 529n.
——villein land, xx
—wardships, 21n, 24, 757–8, 764–6
Testimony, 2, 11, 13
TREES:
17, 231
—apple tree, 495
—ash tree, 648
—plum tree, 501
—thorn-bush, 426
—stump, 18
—clause forbidding cutting, 523

VESSELS and utensils:
234, 364, 485, 659
—vessels (*named*) used in brewing, xxxvii; 356, 701
—bronze jar, 36.8
—cauldron, 36.5

Wardrobe, 32n.
Warranty, 489
Warren, 22a, 711n, 768(p. 370)
WATER and waterways:
—ford, 482
—pond, 37.19; *see also* Fishponds; MILLS
—river, xv, xxxi; 293, 753–4
—stream, 7, 18, 404
—well, xxxviii; 560, 562–3, 578–80
—easement of water, 401
—fall of water, 231, 700
—waters, watercourse, running water, 7, 19, 28g, 286, 304–5, 308, 328, 341, 350, 353–4, 399, 408, 410, 443–4, 469, 473, 481–2, 498, 500, 506, 509, 522, 533, 542–3, 552, 554, 575, 581, 604, 631, 641, 724, 740, 750, 754
—regulation of the common water, 31

RECORDS OF THE SOCIAL AND ECONOMIC HISTORY OF ENGLAND AND WALES

VOLUMES I–IX

I. Survey of the Honour of Denbigh 1334. Edited by SIR P. VINOGRADOFF and F. MORGAN. 1914.

II. The Register of St. Augustine's Abbey, Canterbury, commonly called the Black Book. Edited by G. J. TURNER and H. E. SALTER. Part I. 1915.

III. The Black Book. Part 2. 1924.

IV. i. A Terrier of Fleet, Lincolnshire. Edited by N. NEILSON.
ii. An 11th-Century Inquisition of St. Augustine's, Canterbury. Edited by A. BALLARD. 1920.

V. Documents illustrative of the Social and Economic History of the Danelaw. Edited by SIR F. M. STENTON. 1920.

VI. The Account Book of a Kentish Estate 1616–1704. Edited by E. C. LODGE. 1927.

VII. The Cartulary and Terrier of the Priory of Bilsington, Kent. Edited by N. NEILSON. 1928.

VIII. Feudal Documents from the Abbey of Bury St. Edmunds. Edited by D. C. DOUGLAS. 1932.

IX. Records of the Templars in England in the Twelfth Century: the Inquest of 1185 with Illustrative Charters and Documents. Edited by B. A. LEES. 1935.

A reprint edition of volumes I–IX is available from: Kraus–Thomson Organization Limited, Route 100, Millwood, New York 10546, U.S.A.

RECORDS OF SOCIAL AND ECONOMIC HISTORY NEW SERIES

I. Charters of the Honour of Mowbray 1107–1191. Edited by D. E. GREENWAY. 1972.

II. The Lay Subsidy of 1334. Edited by R. E. GLASSCOCK. 1975.

III. The Diary of Ralph Josselin. 1616–1683. Edited by ALAN MACFARLANE. 1976.

IV. Warwickshire Grazier and London Skinner 1532–1555. The account book of Peter Temple and Thomas Heritage. By N. W. ALCOCK. 1981.

V. Charters and Custumals of the Abbey of Holy Trinity Caen. Edited by MARJORIE CHIBNALL. 1982.

VI. The Cartulary of the Knights of St. John of Jerusalem in England. Secunda Camera: Essex. Edited by MICHAEL GERVERS. 1982.

VII. The Correspondence of Sir John Lowther of Whitehaven 1693–1698, A Provincial Community in Wartime. Edited by D. R. HAINSWORTH. 1983.

VIII. The Farming and Memorandum Books of Henry Best. Edited by DONALD WOODWARD. 1984.

IX. The Making of King's Lynn, A Documentary Survey. Edited by DOROTHY M. OWEN. 1984.

X. The Compton Census of 1676. A Critical Edition. By ANNE WHITEMAN. 1986.

XI. The Early Records of Medieval Coventry. Edited by PETER R. COSS. 1986